Charlie Calvert's
Delphi™ 4

Charlie Calvert

Unleashed

Charlie Calvert's Delphi™ 4 Unleashed

Copyright © 1999 by Sams Publishing

International Standard Book Number: 0-672-31285-9

Library of Congress Catalog Card Number: 98-84929

Printed in the United States of America

First Printing: November, 1998

01 00 99 98   4   3   2   1

Trademarks

All terms mentioned in this book that are known to be trademarks or service marks have been appropriately capitalized. Sams Publishing cannot attest to the accuracy of this information. Use of a term in this book should not be regarded as affecting the validity of any trademark or service mark.

Delphi is a trademark of Inprise Corporation.

Warning and Disclaimer

EXECUTIVE EDITOR
Brian Gill

ACQUISITIONS EDITOR
Ron Gallagher

DEVELOPMENT EDITOR
Scott Warner

TECHNICAL EDITORS
Chaim Krause
Anders Ohlsson
David Powell

MANAGING EDITOR
Jodi Jensen

PROJECT EDITOR
Dana Rhodes Lesh

COPY EDITOR
Chuck Hutchinson

INDEXER
Bruce Clingaman

PROOFREADER
Eddie Lushbaugh

SOFTWARE DEVELOPMENT SPECIALIST
Dan Scherf

TEAM COORDINATOR
Carol Ackerman

INTERIOR DESIGNER
Gary Adair

COVER DESIGNER
Aren Howell

LAYOUT TECHNICIAN
Susan Geiselman

Overview

Contents

About the Authors

Charlie Calvert is a bestselling author and well-respected programming guru. He is the author of *Charlie Calvert's C++Builder 3 Unleashed*, *Delphi 2 Unleashed*, and *Sams Teach Yourself Windows 95 Programming in 21 Days*. His day job is at Inprise International, where he works as a manager in Developer Relations.

Contributing Authors

Bob Swart (a.k.a. Dr. Bob, www.drbob42.com) is a professional knowledge engineer technical consultant using Delphi, JBuilder, and C++Builder for Bolesian (www.bolesian.com), a freelance technical author for *The Delphi Magazine* and the "UK-BUG" newsletter, and a coauthor of *The Revolutionary Guide to Delphi 2*.

In his spare time, Bob likes to watch videotapes of *Star Trek Voyager* and *Deep Space Nine* with Erik Mark Pascal, his 4.5-year-old son, and Natasha Louise Delphine, his 2-year-old daughter.

Jeff Cottingham is a developer support engineer at Borland International. Jeff lives in Rio Del Mar, California, which is located in mid–Santa Cruz County where the red-woods meet the surf. He spends way too much time coding but still finds time to fly his kites on the beach and spend time with his wife. He fondly remembers using a card reader and punch cards in the good old days. Jeff can be reached at saruan@cruzio.com.

Technical Editors

Chaim Krause is a senior developer support engineer at Inprise Corporation, where he works primarily with Delphi. Chaim himself has authored several Delphi-related articles and book chapters.

Anders Ohlsson is a certified client/server developer and works as a consulting engineer at Inprise Corporation, and he has been working with Inprise/Borland products since 1986. Anders lives in Scotts Valley, California, with his wonderful wife, Elena, who shares many of his interests, such as skiing, snow boarding, hiking, and inline skating.

David Powell is a certified Delphi 4 trainer and works as a consulting engineer at Inprise Corporation. He has been using Pascal since Turbo Pascal 3. He was coauthor for the book *Special Edition Using Delphi 3*.

Dedication

I would like to dedicate this book to all the people who have helped me become a writer either by being my teacher or my editor. Some of the many names deserving particular mention are Mr. Camp from Landon school, Mr. Muldoon from Severn, Doug Riddels from The Alliance, Thad Curtz at Evergreen, Frank DeVaul at The Morton Journal, *David Intersimone at Borland, and Chris Denny, Angelique Brittingham, Mary Interstrodt, Dean Miller, Brian Gill, Scott Warner, and Stacey Hiquet at Sams. I appreciate the patience and good will all these people have shown me over the years.*

Acknowledgments

As always, I would like to thank the technical people at Borland/Inprise who aided me in the development of this book. The key people who helped me over and over include Alain Tadros, David Intersimone, Joe Bentley, Steve Teixeira, Nimish Vora, Jim Tierney, Roland Bouchereau, Ryder Rishel, George Cross, John Thomas, and last but not least, the indefatigable Jason Sprenger. Without these people, there would be no book, and I owe them a tremendous debt of gratitude.

Others who helped on many occasions include David Marancik, Karen Giles, Amber Lee Hein, Allen Bauer, Chuck Jazdzewski, Chloe Redon, the wondrous and multitalented Xavier Pacheco, Bruneau Babet, and my wonderful agent, Alex Hoyt, who came to my aid when I needed help. Alex played a key role in making this book possible, and I value his knowledge and insight.

There are a three others to whom I owe even more, if that is possible. I'm speaking now of the excellent tech editors for this book, Chaim Krause, Anders Ohlsson, and David Powell. These three people double-checked my work, helped clean up the code, and took most of the screen shots. Their talent, warmth, continual good humor, and enthusiasm helped improve this book in many different ways.

I also want to thank Jeff Cottingham and Bob Swart, who each contributed a chapter to this book. Jeff is an enthusiastic and talented graphics programmer, with strong skills and an admirable willingness to share his knowledge with others. Over the years, Bob Swart has been one of the most dedicated of all Delphi promoters and technical experts. Everyone in the Delphi community owes him a note of thanks for his tireless support for this great compiler. Both of these writers do excellent work, and I am proud and grateful to have their contributions within the covers of this book.

Finally, I want to thank the people at Sams, many of whom I will never even get a chance to meet. Brian Gill, whom I have met, was my contact at the company, and his patience and dedication brought this book to you. When crises developed, Brian came through for all of us who wanted to see this book get published. On many occasions, Brian proved himself to be not only a good editor, but also a friend to the Delphi community. Scott Warner, Ron Gallagher, and especially Chuck Hutchinson aided tremendously in improving the often faulty structure of my chapters, as well as my grammar and prose style. I also want to thank Nan Boresson at Inprise, who helped as a liaison to Sams and as a constant source of support and good advice.

Tell Us What You Think!

As the reader of this book, *you* are our most important critic and commentator. We value your opinion and want to know what we're doing right, what we could do better, what areas you'd like to see us publish in, and any other words of wisdom you're willing to pass our way.

As the executive editor for the Programming and Borland Press team at Macmillan Computer Publishing, I welcome your comments. You can fax, email, or write me directly to let me know what you did or didn't like about this book—as well as what we can do to make our books stronger.

Please note that I cannot help you with technical problems related to the topic of this book, and that due to the high volume of mail I receive, I might not be able to reply to every message.

When you write, please be sure to include this book's title and author as well as your name and phone or fax number. I will carefully review your comments and share them with the author and editors who worked on the book.

Fax: 317-817-7070

Email: prog@mcp.com

Mail: Brian Gill
          Executive Editor
          Programming and Borland Press team
          Macmillan Computer Publishing
          201 West 103rd Street
          Indianapolis, IN 46290 USA

Getting Started

IN THIS PART

Program Design Basics

CHAPTER 1

Welcome to *Charlie Calvert's Delphi 4 Unleashed*. This book is about programming in Object Pascal, the world's greatest programming language. The setting for this incarnation of the Pascal language is Delphi, the world's greatest programming tool.

Those who are new to the Delphi world may be surprised to learn that I actually mean the words I wrote in the preceding paragraph. Of course, I also love C++ and Java, and I'm drawn to other tools such as Eiffel and Smalltalk. But Delphi occupies a unique position in the programming world, and I am proud to say that I have been an unabashed fan of the product since the days when the first half-formed prototypes began to trickle out onto the Borland network from the desks of R&D engineers.

Other tools are admirable, intriguing, even at times wonderful. Delphi, however, has been the best compiler on the market from the day it was first shipped.

I doubt that this book lives up to its subject matter, but I will try to make it as entertaining, lively, and informative as possible. The text covers intermediate and advanced programming topics, including discussions of the following:

- COM and distributed computing
- Database programming
- General programming issues
- Graphics and DirectX programming

As always, my goal is to talk about these subjects in clear, easy-to-understand language that makes difficult topics accessible. Whenever possible, I try to use a friendly, conversational tone so that you will feel comfortable and at ease while exploring a wide range of technical subjects.

This chapter features introductory material describing the subject matter of this book. I also talk briefly about designing applications. These latter, more theoretical portions of the chapter focus on the proper use of object-oriented technologies.

In Chapter 2, "IDE and VCL Enhancements," I get down to cases and begin exploring technical issues. If you are eager to begin programming right away, then you can read the section "Notes on the Text of This Book" near the end of this chapter and then move on to Chapter 2. You can always come back later when you feel less rushed. At that point, you can relax and take the time to explore the more theoretical issues discussed in this chapter.

The Structure of This Book

This book is meant to be read. It is not meant to be used as a reference. Delphi comes equipped with an excellent online reference featuring context-sensitive help. Another sort of reference takes the form of the new and rather fabulous capability to hold down the Ctrl key in the Delphi editor, place your mouse cursor under any variable, and click the left button to be taken directly to that variable's declaration. Such techniques make it possible to create a world-class reference vastly superior to anything I can create in the pages of this book.

So, this book is not a reference. It is also not a tutorial, though occasionally I will use short tutorial-like sections to help you walk through the steps of a wizard or of some relatively mundane but essential algorithm. However, by and large, I don't like tutorials because they are almost impossible to read without pulling your hair out from boredom and frustration. One of my favorite products, a graphics program called TrueSpace, comes with a large set of tutorials in lieu of documentation. These tutorials made the product all but unusable for me, and I might never have gotten anywhere with the tool had Peter Plantec not finally written his book on the subject, *Caligari TrueSpace2 Bible*.

Besides being incredibly boring, tutorials are also awkward and confining to use. The reader must be sitting at a computer to benefit from them because they are innately hands on. The reader also has to continually move back and forth between the text of the tutorial and the program on the computer screen. The end result is that the reader is continually losing his or her place in each medium, making it difficult to stay focused for much longer than 15 or 20 painful minutes at a time.

Rejecting both the tutorial and the reference models for the creation of this book, I instead fell back on a more narrative style that is meant to be read quietly while sitting in a comfortable chair, lying on a bed, soaking in a bath or hot tub, or even while catching rays at the beach. I obviously don't expect you to read the entire book through from cover to cover because that is not the approach technical people, including myself, take to this kind of documentation. Instead, I wrote this book so that you can read it one chapter at a time or one portion of a chapter at a time.

> **NOTE**
>
> I can usually program happily for five or six hours in a row. On good days, I'm also happy writing for an equal period of time. But I get tired of working sometimes. On those occasions, I will grab a copy of a book or article by Steve Teixeira, Xavier Pacheco, Marco Cantu, Matt Peitrek, Michael Abrash, Jeff Duntemann, Brian Hook, Jeffrey Richter, or one of my other favorite technical authors. Then I simply read a single chapter that looks like it contains important or interesting information. When I am done, I might not look at that book again for several months, or perhaps I will pick it up again the next time I take a break.
>
> *continues*

> Sometimes I will find a section of a book that holds my attention or that I truly want to understand. In such cases, I will read three or four chapters in a row over a period of several days. Rarely, however, do I read an entire technical book from beginning to end. The task is too daunting, especially when books are as long as 1,000 or more pages.
>
> Reading a good book for an hour or so tends to recharge my batteries. When I am done, I am ready to go on programming or writing. Reading a reference book or tutorial for an hour or two usually drains me. I find it harder to read the book than I do to write code or write text. That means the book will never get read, and it only collects dust on my shelf.

After you have read one of the chapters in this book, then you will find it possible to use it as a reference. Without reading the chapters first, you will probably find them frustrating to use as a simple reference of the type found in the online help. Instead, I recommend taking this book to some quiet place and reading a chapter through from the beginning, going back to the computer and playing with the sample programs, and finally creating your own programs based on the things you have learned.

In our society, people are continually trying to please everyone in order to reach the widest possible audience and to avoid the horrible risk of earning someone's righteous wrath. The problem with this approach is that it often leads to products that offer a little bit to everyone but not much of anything to any one person. Products of this type taste like processed cheese and have the consistency of yogurt.

My fondest hope for this book is that it will delight, or at least prove comfortably satisfying, to the vast majority of readers. However, I know that some will find my style verbose and occasionally repetitious, and others will wish I were more rigorously logical in the arrangement of my material. My answer to these justified complaints is that this book is meant to be read. If I try to please everyone, I'll end up pleasing no one. So, I offer a sincere apology to those who wish I had written a different type of book.

If you arrange material in a strictly logical fashion, then very difficult concepts would be placed immediately adjacent to simple concepts. You never build from the simple to the complex, but rather follow a different order that makes it easy to use the book as a reference but nearly impossible to read more than a few pages through in one sitting without using toothpicks to prop open the old eyes.

This book takes a conceptual view of the material under discussion. I want to show you how something works and why it works that way. After you understand the theory behind the technology, I believe that you can always figure out how things work. For instance, in one section of this book, I explain how and when to use something called a *type library*.

If I were creating a reference, I would just give you a list of when to use type libraries and when not to use them. However, I don't take that approach. Instead, I explain what a type library is, why it exists, and how it helps with core tasks such as marshaling data. After you understand all these things, you don't need a list of when to use a type library and when not to use one. All you have to do is use the theoretical knowledge I have given you, and you can figure out when a type library is needed and when it is not needed. Actually, you shouldn't even have to think about the answer, as it should be obvious to you after you have the theoretical knowledge.

So, yes, I know some readers are going to pick up this book looking for the list of times when to use a type library and when not to use a type library. Instead, they are going to find an explanation of what a type library is, what it does, and how to use it. I recognize that my technique is not going to please everyone, but I believe it will prove satisfying to the largest number of readers.

> **NOTE**
>
> Readers who are desperate to get past the theoretical portions of my chapter will find that I usually start a chapter with from two to six pages of introduction, overview, and theory. After that, I illustrate my points with specific examples. This means you can almost always skip ahead a few pages to find code listings and demos illustrating the points I make in the more prosaic opening passages of a chapter.

A book that works with concepts rather than bare facts will not be divided up into many tiny subsections that last no more than three or four paragraphs at most. I appreciate it when authors break down their material into little sections like that, but I almost always find such books difficult to read. (They are, in fact, much easier to write than the kind of book I create.) The problem with dividing text into little subsections is that it is difficult to develop a theme under such a rigorous regime and then let that theme unfold over several pages. For a book to be read with any degree of enjoyment, it needs to have a sense of continuity, a sense of logical development, a sense of movement from point A to point B in a fluid and comprehensible manner. I prefer this technique to simply dissecting a subject and preserving its constituent pieces in embalming fluid.

Of course, I did not set out to create a style designed to please a large number of readers. Instead, I write books that are as close as possible to the type of technical work that I myself like to read. In particular, I write books that are meant to be understood. I am not here to prove that I am the best programmer in the world, nor that I am smarter than person X, nor that I can give you the most detailed or complete analysis of a particular subject. Instead, I want to show you how to write code and to explain the technologies involved in simple, clear language that is easy and enjoyable to read. I want to create a book that I would enjoy reading on my programming or writing breaks. Most of all, I want to create a book that will teach you something useful you can use in your day-to-day experience as a programmer.

The Sample Programs

After reading the preceding section, you probably realize that I place a great deal of emphasis on writing. That's only appropriate because this is a book. It is, however, a book about programming. As a result, I include a great deal of code. You should take the time to run these programs and to see how they relate to the material I discuss in the pages of this book. As I said earlier, the best way to use this book is through a combination of reading the text and running the programs.

The programs that I have created can be pillaged for your own uses to whatever degree you want, as long as you don't simply recycle them as training materials without first asking for my permission. Teachers in accredited schools and colleges can, of course, use this material as they want, as long as their students buy copies of the book. Programmers can reuse the code anywhere they want to whatever degree they want, as long as they are not simply taking one of my programs and reselling it with few or no modifications.

By all means, use the code I write in your own programs. I don't mind if you lift entire units or forms from my code, as long as you are not basing an entire program solely on what you find on this book's CD.

If you read a chapter in this book and then run the code from that chapter, you should then have all the knowledge you need to begin doing serious work in a particular subject. Creating the programs for a chapter usually takes me as long, or nearly as long, as creating the chapter itself. Spend time with the code, study it, and use it in your own programs. The words in the pages of this book are only part of the story; the rest is on the CD that comes with this book.

Creating Well-Designed Programs

In the next few sections, I will talk about creating programs that work. You will not find this passage particularly technical, unlike the subject matter of the remaining chapters of this book. However, this text is important in that it lays out a series of themes that will be referenced again and again.

Let me be specific about the three things that are important to every programmer:

- Creating a good design for your program before you write it. While writing the program, you should iteratively refine that design so that it incorporates the things you learned from your own experience and from the experience of your testers.
- Understanding the basics of OOP, particularly encapsulation, interface design, and information hiding.
- Knowing how to write and use components.

In abbreviated form, the list of important items is design, OOP, and components. I will cover each of these subjects over the next few pages.

Design Issues: Writing Simple Code

This book's theme is based on a quote from George Sand that I keep pinned above my desk: "Simplicity is the most difficult thing to secure in this world; it is the last limit of experience, and the last effort of genius."

Every book needs to have a main theme, and the theme for this book may seem to contradict its intended audience. I say the book is for intermediate to advanced programmers, but my theme is, "Do everything you can to keep your programs as simple as possible."

It has often been said that programming is not so much a science as an art. If programming is an art, then we must find the aesthetic principles on which it is based. To my mind, the core principle is that of simplicity. Beauty can be achieved in several different ways. One of the ways that I like the most is to follow the path of simplicity.

Almost every single step you take in the programming world is simple. Programming is, at bottom, a very simple profession. It appears difficult because it involves layering many very simple processes one on top of the other. Two simple things are a bit more complex than one simple thing. Twenty simple things are noticeably more complex than one simple thing. Ten thousand simple things placed together in one heap will seem complex to all but a handful of people.

In a typical program, hundreds of thousands of individual pieces come together to form a whole. Even a simple Delphi form consists, when you look at it deeply enough, of thousands of complicated pieces. Your goal as a programmer is to harmonize all these different pieces—to make them work together.

I believe that all Delphi programs should strive to follow the path of simplicity. Furthermore, I believe that the act of programming ought to be simple. This book is about finding ways to make it easy for you to create powerful programs. I strive to be modest in my goals, sparing in my use of resources, and spare and stark in my choice of aesthetics. I strive to create programs that are simple to use and easy to understand.

I want my programs to be easy both for users and for other programmers to understand. The architecture of a good application ought to have the same simple structure as its menu system. The Parthenon is beautiful to look at but easy to understand. That is one of the reasons it is still standing after so many years and why it is so universally admired. The architecture of the Parthenon is based on simple architectural principles, and I believe that Delphi programs should be based on the same model.

This book is not about staying up till four in the morning hacking the deepest parts of your code. It is about getting work done on time in a simple, easy manner. (Well, okay, I occasionally still enjoy staying up until four hacking the deepest parts of my code, but I like doing so in a simple manner.) This book may occasionally focus on digging down to the deepest and darkest parts of the machine, but I always promote doing so in a way that is simple, natural, and powerful. The goal is to achieve success gracefully and easily.

Programming is not just a technical process, it is also a state of mind. Good programmers behave in a sensible fashion. They write code the same way they live, and they live the same way they write code. If you live simply and easily, then you will write code simply and easily.

The design phase occurs when you can discover the little kinks that can make a simple project more complicated than it might at first appear. For instance, initially I might not have considered the need for reports, for saving state, for creating certain kinds of graphs.

I can often design something in 15 minutes or an hour, but executing it takes me an entire day or even several days. The trap to avoid is spending several days coding something that is fundamentally flawed. If 15 or 20 minutes of careful consideration can save me two days of coding, then taking the time is well worthwhile.

Following a Spiral to the Top

Sometimes I can't proceed with a design process without writing some test code. In such cases, I try a few experiments to test the validity of my theories. When I begin to see the shape of an algorithm, I often stop and finalize the design. Then I might write more code and once again study the design of the project.

The process ends up being iterative. Write some code, step back and look for objects, and then step back and work on design issues. Then write more code; then come back and work on design.

The process should ultimately end up being like a spiral. You start at the bottom with a broad cycle and work in successively smaller cycles that iterate between coding and design. Each revolution should be smaller than the last until you finally reach the top. At the peak, the cycle should narrow down to a fine point that defines the correct implementation for your program.

Good OOP Versus Bad OOP

I have made it abundantly clear that the goal I wish to achieve is simplicity. I want my programs to be easy to use and to be based on a clear, simple architecture. The question, then, is how to achieve simplicity of design. For me, the answer is OOP, but I believe that you have to be very careful about the way this powerful technology is used.

OOP is a double-edged sword. The basic idea behind it is very valuable. However, many OOP programs are classic examples of how not to write code.

Consider the following two lines of code:

```
printf("Foo");
WriteLn('Foo');
```

Both of these statements exhibit all the features of good code. Even a nonprogrammer can understand what they do, and everyone in the programming world understands how they work and why they work that way.

Consider the following declaration:

```
TBird = class(TObject)
private
  FName: string;
  FWeight: Integer;
  FColor: TColor;
public
  procedure Fly;
  procedure Walk;
end;
```

Everything about a declaration of this type is elegant and worthy of reverence. It is simple, clean, easy to understand, and very powerful. It ties up a set of specific features into one abstract whole that can be easily manipulated.

To understand how to work with objects, you must understand encapsulation, and you must understand inheritance, and it is best if you understand polymorphism. But the most important thing you can learn is how to structure your objects properly.

The main task of an object-oriented programmer is to discover objects. When I sit down to write code, my main goal is to find the objects in my project and surface them. If I can find the objects in a project, then I can usually complete the program in a robust manner in a short order. If I can't find the objects in a program, then I usually end up writing a lot of code that is unreliable and that needs to be rewritten.

Sometimes finding the objects in a program is easy. For instance, in Delphi, it was obvious that there needed to be objects that would wrap the basic Windows components such as TEdit and TButton. Less obvious were some of the core VCL classes such as TApplication, TControl, TWinControl, TDataSet, and TPersistent.

Sometimes when you discover an object, its existence seems obvious. The need for its existence is completely beyond debate. For instance, TApplication and TDataSet strike me as inevitable objects that were simply waiting to be discovered. This does not mean that understanding that TApplication and TDataSet had to exist was easy. But after they were discovered, they had the ring of inevitability.

Beware the Wily Event Handler

Nothing can lead an OOP programmer down the path to destruction more quickly than the indiscriminate use of event handlers. The quest to discover objects is frustrated at every turn by the ease with which Delphi allows you to fold code into the main form by using event handlers.

In most cases, keeping complex, low-level code out of the file where your form is defined is a good idea. Complex, low-level code belongs in separate objects, not inside your main form.

The implementation of your form is a good place to keep user interface code. If you find yourself writing a lot of complex logic inside one of these PAS files, then chances are good that you are sitting on top of an object that needs to be identified and moved into its own module.

For instance, I was recently working on a form that had a lot of complex logic regarding the reading of strings from several different resources. The code read the strings from the resources, stored them in lists, and then displayed the lists to the user. After looking at my program for a while, I came to the conclusion that the code for reading the resources and converting them into lists was really part of a separate object that had nothing to do with main form. So, I removed it from the form, stuck it in its own module, and then called it with code that looked like this:

```
ResourceObject := TResourceObject.Create;
ComboBox1.Items := ResourceObject.GetItemList;
ResourceObject.Free;
```

These few lines have no complicated logic in them at all. They are trouble free. All the tricky code in `ResourceObject` gets called from the constructor or `GetItemList` method. (The exact nature of the code is not important to the current case; you just need to know that it had 40 or 50 lines of string parsing and list creation inside it.) The goal here is to use the `TResourceObject` to *encapsulate* that complexity in a separate object so that my form code stayed clean and easy to use.

Once again, my point is not that writing tricky code is wrong, but that you should encapsulate that tricky code inside an object. That way, you can call it with little risk of making a careless error.

Another good reason to structure your programs this way is to promote reuse. If I wrapped up my code for reading and parsing the resources inside a single form, then two problems would arise:

- That form would also likely contain logic involving other processes specific to the current program. I would have no way of isolating the code that had to do with resources but would instead mix it in with a lot of other code needed to run the form.

- Even if I decided I could reuse the code, the only good way to reuse it would be to copy the entire form into the new project. In fact, the act of copying the form into the new project is not in itself flawed because that form would then encapsulate the logic in a convenient package. The trouble would come, however, if I needed to tweak the code in the form. In such a case, something like the following scenario would almost certainly occur: I might tweak the code in the form in such a way that it would make the form unusable in the first project. In such a case, I would need to have two copies of the code: one in the new project and one in the old. If I made fixes to one copy of the code, then I would have to go back and make fixes to the same code in its other incarnation. As you well know, almost no one can be counted on to actually fix a single bug in two places, so trouble would soon arise. Conversely, I might decide to keep one copy of the code in both projects, but I would never dare customize if for use in either program on the grounds that it might compromise the other partner in the deal. As a result, I would feel artificially constrained not to fix minor interface problems for which I could easily see a remedy.

In short, encapsulating certain kinds of code inside a form is often not a good idea. Instead, you should keep the code in a separate, easy-to-access object. Then you can write interface code that accesses that object from any form that you might create. In the form, you would have interface code. In the object, you would have low-level code.

Doing things this way might force you to write a few extra lines of code one time, but it would be likely to save you a great deal of time later when you had to customize interfaces or perform basic maintenance on the object. It also makes it easier to reuse your code.

Feeling Too Lazy to Comb the Kinks out of a Program

Sometimes the act of discovering objects is iterative. For instance, I might be working on a form for a while and find that things are finally starting to work correctly. When I was new to programming, I used to think that meant I was nearly finished with the form. But now I tend to comb through the form looking for objects that need to be discovered and given their own scope.

At this point, laziness often leads me astray. Leaving an object buried inside another chunk of code is often simpler—at first. Only later does this laziness catch up with me and cause me trouble.

When I have a portion of a form working correctly, the correct thing to do is often to take the code from that portion of the program out of the form and place it in its own object. This operation takes work at the time I do it, but it saves me work later on. Then I can go back and work on the form some more. Over time, I will once again have to come through the form looking for hidden objects.

Recently, I was performing a lot of relatively complex calculations on an array. After a time, I discovered that the array really needed to be in a separate object so that I could write code that looked like this:

```
GridArray := TGridArray.Create;
AResult := GridArray.PerformCalculations(Data1, Data2, Data3);
GridArray.Free;
```

Now a portion of the work that was embedded in my form was encapsulated inside the TGridArray object.

When I first performed this operation, it seemed like a lot of painful work that wasn't yielding many results. Later, however, I found that I needed to create a series of TDailyTotal objects in my main form, each of which needed to perform calculations on the array. Because I had the right architecture, all I needed to do was pass the GridArray object to my TDailyTotal objects and have them call the PerformCalculations method with their own sets of data. In short, the architecture for my program fell in place with little or no effort on my part.

Had I not created the `TDailyTotal` and the `TGridArray` objects, I would have had a hard time writing code that was easy to maintain and understand. I would have had three or four methods in my main form that performed calculations on an array and three or four more methods that created a daily total. At one point, the daily total method would call the grid methods. But how I could designate that one set of methods belonged to one task and one to the other task? How could I define the relationship between the two sets of methods? There are no good answers to these questions because the architecture of my program demanded the presence of the `TDailyTotal` and `TGridArray` objects. They were inevitable objects just as `TApplication` and `TDataSet` are inevitable parts of the VCL architecture.

When I found the `TDailyTotal` and `TGridArray` objects, my program came together simply and easily, and I'm sure I will understand its architecture almost immediately if I have to return to the program months or years from now. Without these objects, sorting through the spaghetti code that wound back and forth through my form might take me hours or even days.

The key point here is that I must iteratively comb through my code looking for objects. When I discover them, I have to overcome inertia and force myself to separate them out of the form or module I'm creating. At the time, it seems like a waste of effort, but in the long haul, it is usually worth the effort many times over.

Avoid Cross Linking Objects by Hiding Data

Good OOP programmers never allow objects to share private data. They always design objects that stand on their own, and that allow others to use their data only through designated interfaces.

These rules are important for two reasons:

- They help to promote reuse. If you have two or more objects bound tightly together through their data, then reusing one of the objects in a separate project is difficult. The objects are bound to one another, and you cannot easily separate them.

- A primary goal of object-oriented programming is to encapsulate tasks in a single object. One of the main reasons for doing so is that it limits the scope of the problems that can arise. If you build a discreet object with no reliance on other objects, then the domain of possible problems for that object is restricted. The moment you let two objects bind their data together in an intimate manner, then you are immediately widening the scope of your potential problems from one object to two objects. Your problem domain has doubled in size, thereby making maintenance at least twice as hard.

A strict adherence to the principle of encapsulation can do a tremendous amount toward helping you to create small, simple programs. Breaking encapsulation by sharing data indiscriminately between objects can add unneeded complexity to your programs and destroy the purity of your architecture.

For instance, if I tied the TDailyTotal object and the TGridArray object from the preceding section together by sharing their data, then I could not easily reuse the TGridArray object. For instance, if I had found the need to build a TMonthlyTotal object, then I would want to pass it the TGridArray object so that it could be reused. But if TGridArray were bound to the data of the TDailyTotal object, then reuse might be difficult. In fact, I might be forced to rewrite the TGridArray object so that it could be reused. In the process I might end up with both TDailyGridArray and TMonthlyGridArray objects. This arrangement, although probably effective, would nonetheless likely herald the creation of a redundant and overly complex architecture.

Short Methods

In the interest of keeping things simple, I like to create short methods. Not all methods need be short, but most of them should be short. In particular, I think about four out of five methods that I write should be short, where I define short as being 25 lines or fewer.

Just as it is important to see that the Form1 object of a program can contain multiple objects, so is it important to see that a single method can contain multiple methods that need to be broken out. I try to discover the methods buried in my code, just as I seek to find the objects buried in my code.

The most obvious sign that a method is too large appears when it contains chunks of logic that need to be called from two different methods. For instance, I have often written code that extracts the path to my application's root directory. Sometimes I need to reuse this logic in several different places in my program. Rewriting this logic inside each method that requires the information makes no sense. Instead, the simplest course of action is to separate the logic out of these methods and encapsulate it inside a single method that can be called from various different sources. This means that each method used to contain this logic grows smaller because it can now delegate the task to another method.

For instance, I might have two methods that look like this:

```
procedure TForm1.MethodOne;
var
  Path: string;
begin
  Path := ExtractFilePath(ParamStr(0));
  if Path[Length(Result)] <> '\' then
```

```
    Path := Path + '\';
  ... // Code omitted here that manipulates the path...
end;

procedure TForm1.MethodTwo;
var
  path: string;
begin
  result := ExtractFilePath(ParamStr(0));
  if Result[Length(Result)] <> '\' then
    Result := Result + '\';
  ... // Code omitted here that manipulates the path...
end;
```

Both of these methods have redundant code that needs to be separated out into a single method that looks like this:

```
function TForm1.GetStartDir: string;
begin
  Result := ExtractFilePath(ParamStr(0));
  if Result[Length(Result)] <> '\' then
    Result := Result + '\';
end;
```

I ultimately moved this whole method into a unit that contains a set of utility routines that are reused by multiple programs.

If you put a little thought into the process, you usually can discover methods such as GetStartDir easily. However, this is just the tip of the iceberg. Creating short methods that are easy to understand and easy to debug is generally a useful idea. Long methods, though sometimes necessary or sensible, can be the source of innumerable bugs.

Naming Variables, Methods, and Procedures

I find it best to give variables, methods, and procedures clear, easy-to-understand names. Using abbreviations and generic, nondescriptive names can be a source of trouble.

In the short examples found in this book, you will often find that I give objects generic names such as TMyGrid or TMyEdit. However, in complex programs, I try to come up with descriptive names for objects. For instance, TMyGrid might become TDailyEarningsGrid or TMilesTraveledGrid. Typing out these longer names takes a little extra work, but it tends to save me trouble in the long run.

Delphi is smart enough to use short tokens in place of these long names. You will not waste space in your final executable just because you give an object a descriptive name.

Delphi programmers tend to support certain naming conventions. For instance, private data in an object usually has the letter *F* added as a prefix, as in FWidth or FHeight. This letter designates the variable as a private field of an object. Types that you declare in a program should have the letter *T*, for type, added as a prefix. For instance, key Delphi objects have names like `TObject`, `TComponent`, and `TEdit`. Some older types such as `Integers` and `Words` were declared before this convention was established, but most types created within the last 5 to 10 years follow this convention, and I follow it in all the programs used in this book.

Avoiding Feature Creep

The process of continually changing the spec to accommodate new ideas is called *feature creep*. This particular malady has probably been the single biggest source of trouble in my own programming projects. If I try to design and code at the same time, I get tempted to follow each new idea as it arises. Working this way can lead to a process in which projects never seem to come to a finish. One more thing always has to be done, and old code continually has to be rewritten to conform to the new paradigm.

Having a clean design for a project is much better. Then, if I come up with a new idea in mid-project, or if someone involved in the project comes up with the idea, I can discard it on the grounds that it doesn't fit into the current design. "That's great," I might say. "I like it. Let's get it into a notebook as a feature for the next version of the product!"

The middle of a project is not the right time to adopt new programming techniques or to change the design of a product. Its proper place is in between projects or during the design phase.

Creating Components

Perhaps the single most powerful technique I know for creating robust programs is developing components. A component has the following virtues:

- By its very nature, each component I create must stand alone, independent of any other object. This way, I can easily test my object and reuse it.
- Each component I create must be manipulated through the Object Inspector. This restriction forces me to create a simple, easy-to-use interface for an object.
- Components help me to design programs by allowing me to quickly put together demos that test the strength of my ideas.

Using Third-Party Tools

I am at last at the end of this section on designing programs. As a footnote to this subject, I am going to spend a few paragraphs recommending books and products that I believe can help you create better programs. My main purpose here is to promote the idea of using third-party products. If I mention particular names, I do so only because I want to give you a place to start your search for useful tools.

If you are a serious Delphi programmer, you should spend a considerable amount of time exploring third-party libraries. In particular, when you can find companies such as TurboPower Software or Raize Software that sell libraries of components, objects, and routines that ship with source, then you would do well to explore these tools.

Consider, for instance, these excerpts from the SysTools2 User's manual:

Chapter 5: Date/Time Routines

Chapter 6: High-precision Floating Point Math

Chapter 7: Real Business Finance/Statistics

Chapter 8: Operating Systems and Low Level Data Manipulation

Chapter 9: System Components

- `TStShellAbout`
- `TStTrayIcon`
- `TStShortcut`
- `TStVersionInfo`
- And So On

Chapter 10: Bar Codes

Chapter 11: CRC Routines

Chapter 12: Internet Data Conversion Kit (Mime)

Chapter 13: Container Classes

- `TstDQue`
- `TStLMatrix`
- `TStDictionary`
- `TStHashTable`
- `StTree` Unit: Balanced Binary Search Tree
- And So On

Chapter 14: Sort Engine

Chapter 15: Registry and Ini Files

Chapter 16: Astronomical Routines

I'm not going to discuss the significance of this listing but instead leave it up to you to pursue it and judge it on its own merits. TurboPower makes eight different products, and this is just a brief excerpt from the manual to one of those eight products. Can any serious Delphi programmer afford not to dig into resources of this type? How about the fact that versions of all these routines are available not only for Delphi, but also for C++?

Evaluation copies of all of TurboPower's tools are available on the Web site at www.turbopower.com. Classic TurboPower tools such as Orpheus, SysTools, and Async Professional have powered innumerable successful Delphi programs. If you have the desire to expand your knowledge of Delphi, then one resource you should definitely know about is TurboPower Software.

TurboPower, however, is just the tip of the iceberg. The Internet tools from HRef Software (www.href.com) are not one bit less miraculous. You can use these tools to develop powerful commercial Web sites, and you can find whole libraries of routines that every developer should explore.

I always stand in awe of the fine-tuned precision of Ray Konopka's components from www.raize.com. Ray is a perfectionist, and every single one of his components is a little jewel that elegantly fulfills its task in life. Woll2Woll Software is yet another company that consistently earns top honors from Delphi developers. You should check out the powerful InfoPower grid at www.woll2woll.com.

Other companies that build valuable tools include Apiary, Dart, Distinct, Eagle Software, Attachmate, Logic Works, Luxent Software, Rational Software, Software Science, Sylvan Faust, Eagle Research, Regatta, NuMega, Nevrona, Starbase, Ryle Design, MicroEdge, Premia, American Cybernetics, Skyline Tools, Ted Gruber Software, Opaque Software, Blue Sky Software, Pegasus Imaging, Bill White Software, InstallShield, SAGE Inc, 20/20 Software, Ensemble, Cayenne, and many, many more.

I mention these companies not because I want to promote their products above others that I don't mention, but because I want to make you a better Delphi programmer. These tools are incredibly powerful, and if you leverage them, your code will be the better for it. No Delphi programmer ever has to look at the resources of C++ programmers and think that it would be nice to get at some of those goodies. The Delphi world is rife with more resources than any one programmer could ever use, and it is madness not to take advantage of it. For more information, go to http://www.inprise.com/Delphi/deltools.htm. There, you will find a relatively complete list of tool vendors, including links to their home pages.

Of course, in all this discussion, I haven't even mentioned all the free resources available on the Net or the magazines that you can buy. One place to start is www.informant.com, the home of the excellent *Delphi Informant* magazine, where you can pick up hundreds of free components.

Another invaluable source of free components is the excellent *Delphi Magazine* site at `http://www.itecuk.com/delmag/index.htm`. The *Delphi Magazine* is very fine, if somewhat pricey, resource. Like the *Delphi Informant*, this magazine sells CDs packed with past articles and components. The CD is a relatively inexpensive gold mine and well worth the price of admission.

I have listed many other resources on my Web site at the following URL: `http://users.aol.com/charliecal`. Among the links I list there are `http://www.doit.com/delphi/home.html` and `http://www.drbob42.com/`, which is maintained by Bob Swart, one of the coauthors of this book.

All Delphi developers should have certain books on their desks. For advanced programmers, these books include the following:

> *Delphi 4 Developer's Guide* by Steve Teixeira and Xavier Pacheco, Sams Publishing
>
> *Developing Custom Delphi Components*, by Ray Konopka, The Coriolis Group
>
> *The Tomes of Delphi 3: Win32 Core API*, John Ayres, WordWare Publishing

Other important books are the following:

> *Delphi Developers Handbook*, by Marco Cantu, Sybex Press
>
> *Delphi Database Development*, John Kaster, M&T
>
> *Delphi Database Developers Guide*, Ken Henderson, Sams Publishing

Finally, I want to remind you to visit `www.turbopower.com` and to also check my home page at `http://users.aol.com/charliecal` or `http://members.aol.com/charliecal` for news and updates to this book. Setting a day or so aside a month to just explore Delphi resources is a worthwhile endeavor.

Notes on the Text of This Book

In most of the remainder of this chapter, I will add a few general notes about the text of this book. These comments about the general framework of my text apply not to any one particular chapter, but to the book as a whole.

The `Unleash` and `Merc40` Packages

A number of the programs on the CD that comes with this book use one of two custom packages that I have created for this text. One package is called `Unleash`, and it contains a number of small components that you might find useful or that I use to explain how components and packages are put together. The other package is called `Merc40`, and it contains graphics components for using the gaming section. You will find two sets of graphics components: one in the `Merc40` package and one in the `Merc40DX` package. Both components have identical names and identical interfaces. The difference between them is that the latter package supports a powerful graphics interface called DirectDraw.

You should probably install both packages immediately after finishing this chapter, if not sooner. To install the packages, first run the standard installation program on the CD that comes with this book. Then start Delphi, and select Component, Install Packages. Browse across your hard drive until you find the `Units` directory created by the installation program on the CD that comes with this book. Add the `Merc40.bpl` and `Unleash.bpl` packages to Delphi.

Making sure that the `Units` directory is on your Library Path would probably also be a good idea. Choose Tools, Environment Options, Library and then set the path there to point to the `Units` directory.

Neither of the tasks described in this section are particularly difficult. I can usually install a new package in about 30 seconds, and setting a path is also fairly simple. However, if you don't perform both of these tasks, you will find it difficult or impossible to run some of the programs on the CD that comes with this book. Save yourself some time and perform this simple operation now, while it is still fresh in your mind.

The `CodeBox` Unit

A unit called `CodeBox.pas` gets called on fairly frequently in this book. This unit contains many utility routines and objects that I use not just in one program, but in multiple programs. It plays much the same role in this book as the `SysUtils.pas` unit plays in Delphi programming as a whole.

If you did a default installation of the code from the CD that accompanies this book, then you can reach the file by choosing Project, Options, Directories/Conditionals and then clicking the button to the right of the Search Path option. Now type in `..\..\..\Units`, and click the Add and OK buttons. (The actual path I have quoted here [`..\..\..\Units`] might be somewhat different on your system. If you are confused by the dots in my path statement, then you can probably just hard-code the full path into the dialog. For instance, on my system, the full path would be `c:\SrcPas\Units`. I cannot tell you the path as it will appear on your system because that decision is made by the people who create the install for the CD that accompanies this book.)

Setting Up a Network

Many of the programs in this book are network based. At work, I can tap into the very sophisticated Inprise network. However, most of the testing I did for this book was carried out at home. My home network consists of a couple run-of-the-mill PCs (one for me and one for my wife) and an NT-based laptop that I use at work and usually carry home with me in the evenings. For a long while I had a 486 as part of this network, but that machine has now been retired.

When talking to developers, I have sometimes mentioned my home network and found that it generated a certain amount of interest. Although many people already have home networks, others asked, "Hey, how did you do that?" The answer is that overall it is not very difficult.

You can learn a lot about networks just by buying a couple $20 network cards and hooking up two machines in your home. If you have a little extra cash, then you might want to spend up to $100 on a network card, which is what I usually do. But for years I had good luck with a simple $20 no-name card.

Windows 95/98 and Windows NT machines come with built-in peer-to-peer and TCP/IP networks. Setting them up is simple. The peer-to-peer network requires almost no configuration. For help with TCP/IP, see the document called "Setting Up TCP/IP" on the CD that comes with this book. This document is excerpted from Chapter 19, "WinINet and FTP." In particular, I quote from the Chapter 19 sections "Making Sure That FTP Is Working on Your System" and "Some Notes on Installing TCP/IP."

Overall, I can't emphasize enough the value of having a home network to play with and test your code on. I think Margie is only vaguely aware that I have networked her computer to mine, but I actually end up using both machines quite often for testing. Don't tell anyone I said this, but the less technical (yet perhaps wiser and more worthy) members of your household don't really need to know every time you send a few packets of data back and forth between their machines and yours! Of course, the other great benefit of a home network is that it can allow you to engage in some fairly serious network gaming!

The Borland/Inprise Name Change

As readers of this book no doubt know, Borland recently changed its name to Inprise. However, Delphi 4 ships under the name *Borland Delphi*, and the brand name is still associated with the company. As a result, I will tend to refer to the company as *Borland* throughout most of this book, though I may occasionally use *Inprise* or even *Borland/Inprise*.

I think it's only fair that you, the reader, should know that I have been working for Borland since March 2, 1992. This is an unusually long time for anyone to work for any one company in this industry. I have a rather strong loyalty to the company after all these years, much of it based on my admiration for the company's Object Pascal, Java, and C++ compilers.

I want to make it clear, however, that my primary loyalty is to the field of computer science. I like working at Borland because its products contribute to computer science and to the sum total of knowledge that we have about computers. I get paid for doing what I love, which is a great thing, and I am grateful to Borland for providing me with a good job.

Borland does not, however, own my mind, and this book is written under a contract between Sams and me, not between Borland and me. Therefore, I will generally say what I believe to be true, and not necessarily what I think is best for Borland. Still, you as the reader need to be conscious of how long I have worked for this company and to be aware that no one can remain entirely objective after such a long tenure.

Commenting My Code

Readers who have seen my other books might be surprised to find that I have had a change of heart about documenting my code. I first started doing this when I found I could use Ctrl+Shift+C to jump back and forth between a method declaration and its implementation. This feature made it possible for me to skip over my comments with little effort, so they no longer got in my way.

After using comments for a while, however, I began to find them extremely helpful, perhaps in part because I no longer remember things as well as I did when I was younger. But there is a potentially more significant reason. We are now facing a time in computing where one of the primary difficulties is managing the complexity of our systems. We all write huge amounts of code, dealing with very large APIs. To manage this degree of complexity, I have to use every tool at my disposal, and writing extensive comments seems to help.

At any rate, you will find that I comment my code fairly heavily now, though I still can't bring myself to mix code and comments. My comments are nearly all placed before a method, or at the top of a unit. I still find it annoying to come across comments in the middle of a class declaration or method implementation.

One further note on this matter: I found that the default italic font for comments was annoying. So, I tend to turn the italics off by choosing Tools, Environment Options, Colors, Text Attribute. For some reason, it is easier on my eyes if I just have the comments appear in a different color, without the italics. I realize that this use of color versus italics is subjective, but it makes a significant difference to me.

A Note to the Reader

As a programmer, the future of our society rests partially in your hands. You have the ability to decide what shape parts of our society will take, and in particular, you have the power to influence the young, who are enamored of computers. Only cowardice or lack of foresight would allow you to trade that power away for the dubious blessings bestowed on you by people who neither comprehend the nature of your own talents nor the importance of the technology that you have mastered.

When you program, think about your wife or husband; think about your children; think about your neighbors, the members of your church, synagogue, or sangha. When you program, think about the poor people in your town, think about the talented children in your schools, think about that beautiful man or woman you passed in the street. Think about your pets, about animals that live in the forest, trees that grow on mountainsides, and the stars that you see in pictures returned from the Hubble telescope. Think about a beautiful painting you saw in a museum, about a piece of music that moved you, or a book that touched your heart. Programmers are part of a larger world to which they owe allegiance. Study that world and strive to serve it.

Whether you live in Washington, D.C., or Bangkok, Thailand, your society is under attack by small-minded people who value money or power more than their own family or the members of their community. They live off the effluvia sparked by seesawing exchanges of power the same way normal people live off love, laughter, and the wonder of the natural world. Don't fall prey to their folly. Practice your profession for the sake of those you love and for the good of others. In the long run, your only heritage will be the one you create with your own hands. Make sure it is worthy of you and that you are worthy of it.

Summary

I believe that programming is among the most fascinating of all human endeavors. I think we all are wonderfully privileged to be alive at a time when it is possible to pursue this discipline. For those of us with an inward and studious turn of mind, it is hard to imagine any more worthy subject of intellectual pursuit.

When I first started working with computers, back in the mid-1980s, I found them to be magical machines. My study of them was motivated as much by the mystery of their operation as by my desire to truly understand them. The first computers I played with seemed inexplicable to me, and I have to confess that I was drawn strongly to the sense of wonder they invoked in my perhaps too credulous soul.

Over time, I came to understand computers all too well, and I lost my sense of wonder. I now know the answers to the questions that used to mystify me. Yet strangely enough, in recent months I've found myself coming around full cycle, back to the point where I am intrigued by the fundamental mystery of computers. At the heart of these machines is the ability to carefully and precisely control the flow of electrons whirling through silicon. But what is electricity? What is an electron? Scientists aren't even sure whether electrons are solid particles or simply tiny flows of raw energy in a constant state of flux.

If there were true magicians walking the world today, would their art really be any more mysterious than our ability to manipulate words, sounds, pictures, and mathematical expressions with a computer? They say that any technology that is sufficiently advanced appears magical to the user. What is miraculous about computers is that they allow us to manipulate the formless particles such as electrons and light that lie near the outer edges of our understanding of the world. It is as if we can take the formless raw energy out of which the universe is made and tap into that wellspring of incomprehensible intelligence.

Computers are logic machines, and science is a rigorous discipline that leaves little room for sentiment or superstition. Yet science itself is wonderful, particularly on its subtlest, most rarified levels. Quantum physics, chaos theory, and computer science have turned out to be as miraculous and mysterious as the superstitions that science has displaced.

This book is about computer science. As such, it should invoke not just the smell of dusty schoolrooms and powdered chalk. It should also conjure up a sense of mystery and wonder. At least it does that in my mind, and I hope that you will share that sense of wonder when you travel with me on this exploration of Delphi programming and the Object Pascal language.

CHAPTER 2

IDE and VCL Enhancements

In this chapter, you will learn about the new features added to the Delphi IDE and to the Object Pascal language itself. This chapter is not particularly difficult, but it does contain information that all users of Delphi 4 should understand. As a rule, this book will not contain material that is quite this fundamental. However, I have included this material here because I know that people familiar with Delphi will buy this book rather than a beginning book, and yet they will still need a quick reference about the new features in the product. So, in this one case, I have included material that might normally go into a beginning-level programming book.

This chapter describes the following topics:

- Dockable toolbars
- Docking VCL windows
- Action lists
- Dynamic arrays
- Function overloading
- Default parameters

Dockable Toolbars

The main window is now filled with dockable toolbars. Everything in the window can be moved, including the toolbars, the Component Palette, and the menu. The primary means of controlling these windows is by using the mouse or by choosing View, Toolbars from the menu.

Five major elements can be pulled off the main window. A sixth element, the main menu, can be moved, but cannot be entirely undocked from the main window. Here's a listing of what appears by default in each of these windows:

- The main menu—File, Edit, Search, View, Project, Run, Component, Database, Tools, Workgroups, Help
- The View toolbar—View Units, View Forms, Toggle Unit/Form, and New Form
- The Debug toolbar—Run, Pause, Trace Into, Step Over
- The Standard toolbar—New, Open, Save, Save All, Open Project, Add to Project, Remove from Project
- The Custom toolbar—A Help button
- The Component Palette—The Visual Component Library (VCL) and ActiveX components

The process of manipulating these windows is trivial and intuitive, so I won't dwell on the subject for long. However, I will give a brief discussion of working with the Standard toolbar, so you can see how the process works. If you are confused as to which is the Standard toolbar, choose View, Toolbar to identify each toolbar.

A small thumb, or *move handle*, appears on the far left of the Standard toolbar; you can click and drag it with the mouse. The move handle appears as two small vertical lines. If you pull out the toolbar, you can resize it by pulling on its edges just as you would any other window. Simply hold the mouse cursor over the edge of the toolbar, and wait for it to change shape. After the system is ready, you can resize the toolbar so that it is arranged either horizontally or vertically.

The same general process can be applied to all the toolbars. Spend a few minutes working with this system so you can get the feel of how it works.

Now pull out the Custom toolbar so that it is floating freely. Right-click on the body of the window, not on the caption bar, and choose Customize. You will now be able to add new icons to the toolbar by dragging and dropping them from the Commands page of the Customize dialog.

The position you place a toolbar in and the icons you add to the Custom toolbar will be preserved between sessions. This means you can add all kinds of new tools to the IDE, and place them somewhere handy, such as in the open space above the Component Palette.

Working with Tool Windows

Tool windows are a set of programming tools, each of which can be docked inside the editor. They are different from toolbars, which cannot be docked anywhere but the main window. Furthermore, toolbars just provide menu options or speed buttons and don't offer the kind of in-depth tools found in tool windows.

The primary window of this kind is the Code Explorer, which will be explained in more depth in the next section. By default, you will find the Code Explorer nestled along the left side of the editor. The Object Inspector can also be docked inside the editor, along with the following debug windows:

- Breakpoints
- CallStack
- Watches
- Threads

- Modules
- CPU
- EventLog

Docking a window in the editor is an intuitive process, but I will explain it briefly so you can get a sense of how the process works.

Choose View, Debug Windows and then choose to view the Watch window. Grab the window by its caption by left-clicking and dragging with the mouse. Move the window around near the bottom of the editor. If you get the window in the right place, a rectangular outline will appear across the bottom of the editor. Your window can be docked in the approximate location drawn by the outline. Simply let go of the left mouse button to complete the operation. The final result is shown in Figure 2.1.

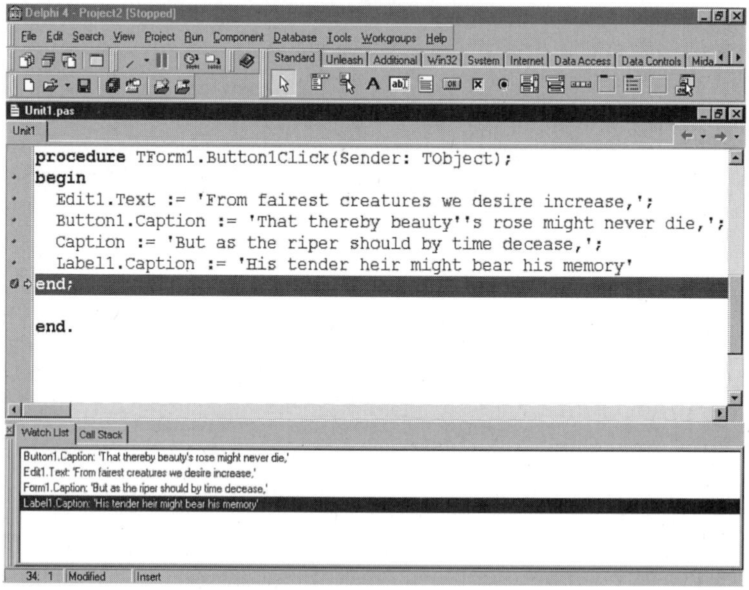

FIGURE 2.1

Docking the Watch window at the bottom of the editor.

At this point, the Watch window will have a move handle on its left-hand side. To undock the window, simply click and drag on this handle.

You can try docking the window on the right side of the editor, or above the Code Explorer on the left side of the window. When you move the window over the Code Explorer, you will see several different outlines drawn showing the different ways you can dock the window. For instance, you can dock the window directly over the Code Explorer, as if it were the second story in a two-story building, or you can dock it beside the Code Explorer, as if there were two tall buildings standing next to each other, like the World Trade Center in New York City.

Any of these windows can be docked together into tabbed tool windows, as shown in Figure 2.2. You can have multiple tabbed tool windows if you want. For instance, you can create one tabbed tool window that contains the Breakpoint and Watch windows, and another that contains the Object Inspector and Explorer. You can dock tabbed tool windows inside the editor if you want, using the same process described when docking a single window.

FIGURE 2.2

Two floating tabbed tool windows and two additional windows docked at the bottom of the editor.

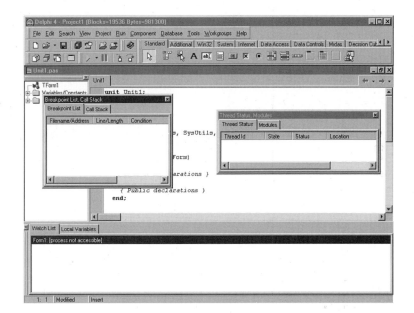

At first, you may struggle to get the windows arranged as you want. In other words, you may want to create tabbed windows and end up with them stacked, or vice versa. To create a tabbed window, drag one window over the other, and wait till the black outline that is drawn becomes a square in the middle of the window on which you are going to dock. When that square is right in the middle, let go, and you will end up with tabbed windows.

Overall, this intuitive process is perhaps best learned by experimentation. Take your time working with the process and discovering how it works. For instance, try arranging the Code Explorer and Project Manager on the left, and the Object Inspector on the right, as shown in Figure 2.3.

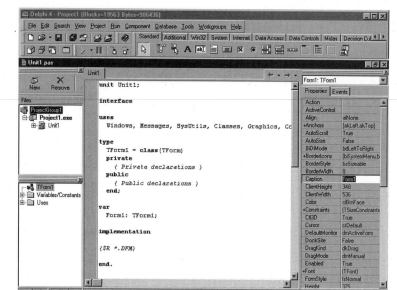

You cannot save the position of the tool windows from one session inside the IDE to another. This means you will often have to begin your work on a project by arranging the windows as you like. For instance, I often start a session by placing the Project Manager above the Code Explorer on the left side of the editor.

Working with the Code Explorer

The Code Explorer is designed to help you navigate through your code and to manipulate the elements found in your units. In particular, you can use this tool to get an overview of the objects, methods, and variables declared and used in any one unit.

In this section of the chapter, I will show you how to use the Code Explorer and how to use various hotkeys that can help you navigate through your code. Again, this section is designed to do nothing more than give you an overview of a very simple subject that you should be able to master with a few moments of experimentation, and with the help of a few hints and tips.

To get started, type code into a class declaration, and notice that it shows up automatically in the Code Explorer. For instance, if you create a new procedure in your form, you can turn to the Code Explorer and see the declaration there, as shown in Figure 2.4.

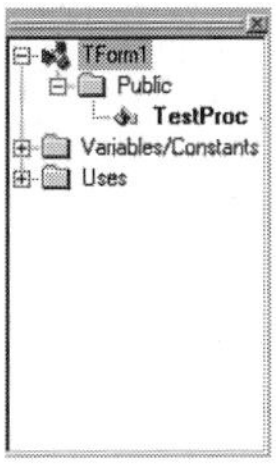

FIGURE 2.4

*The declaration
for a procedure as
shown in the Code
Explorer.*

The opposite is also true. If you right-click on the private or public nodes found under the Form1 section in the Code Explorer, you will be able to declare a new method or procedure. Be sure you type the complete syntax, including parameters, parentheses, and a final semicolon.

If you declare a method in an object and then place the cursor over it, you can create the outline for its implementation by pressing Ctrl+Shift+C. For instance, start a new project. Go to the public section of the class declaration and declare a simple procedure named Foo:

```
TForm1 = class(TForm)
private
  { Private declarations }
public
  { Public declarations }
  procedure Foo;
end;
```

Now put your cursor anywhere on the line where your new procedure is declared, and press Ctrl+Shift+C. The following code will be automatically inserted into your unit:

```
procedure TForm1.Foo;
begin

end;
```

To move from the declaration for a method to the implementation, or vice versa, simply press Ctrl+Shift+Up arrow or Ctrl+Shift+Down arrow.

To automatically implement a property, simply type the core of its declaration:

```
TForm1 = class(TForm)
private
  { Private declarations }
public
  { Public declarations }
  procedure Foo;
  property MyProp: Integer;
end;
```

Now if you place the cursor over the property called MyProp, and press Ctrl+Shift+C, the following code related to this property is generated:

```
procedure TForm1.SetMyProp(const Value: Integer);
begin
  FMyProp := Value;
end;
```

Listing 2.1 shows the complete program generated by this example.

LISTING 2.1 A SAMPLE METHOD AND PROPERTY AUTO-GENERATED BY PRESSING CTRL+SHIFT+C IN DELPHI

```
unit Unit1;

interface

uses
  Windows, Messages, SysUtils, Classes, Graphics, Controls, Forms,
Dialogs;

type
  TForm1 = class(TForm)
  private
    FMyProp: Integer;
    procedure SetMyProp(const Value: Integer);
    { Private declarations }
  public
    { Public declarations }
    procedure Foo;
    property MyProp: Integer read FMyProp write SetMyProp;
  end;

var
  Form1: TForm1;

implementation

{$R *.DFM}

{ TForm1 }

procedure TForm1.Foo;
begin

end;

procedure TForm1.SetMyProp(const Value: Integer);
begin
  FMyProp := Value;
end;

end.
```

The read and write parts, as a well as the setter method, for your property, were auto-generated. This technology is called *Class Completion.*

Conversely, you can type the implementation for a method, place the cursor over the header for your method, and its declaration will be automatically generated. If you declare multiple methods or multiple implementations, pressing Ctrl+Shift+C will auto-matically complete the code for all the proper declarations or implementations in your object.

> **NOTE**
>
> If you declare your methods in the Code Explorer and allow Delphi to automati-cally insert the real declarations and implementations, then your code should, by default, appear in alphabetical order. If you do anything to violate this order, all future methods will simply be inserted in the order in which you declare them. In other words, the IDE won't be able to insert methods in alphabetical order if the existing methods are not in alphabetical order.

When you choose Tools, Environment Options from the menu, you see a page called the Explorer, as shown in Figure 2.5. You can use this page to change various default set-tings for the Explorer. Because this is an intermediate-to advanced-level book, I will leave it up to you to explore this page and discover what can be done with it.

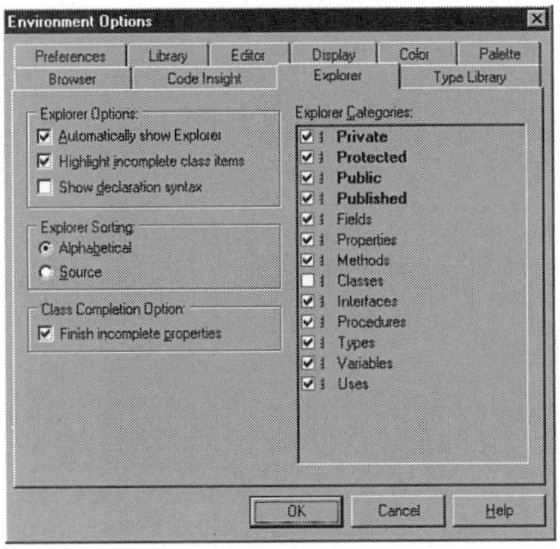

2

IDE AND VCL
ENHANCEMENTS

FIGURE 2.5

Choose Tools, Environment Options to see this configuration page.

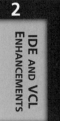

Clearly, the Code Explorer and the related subject of Class Completion are two of the most important new features in Delphi 4. Within days of the first time I saw Class Completion, it changed the way I wrote code, and going back to using Delphi 3 became very difficult for me.

New Tools Found in Delphi 4

In the next few sections, I will discuss some of the new programmer's tools found in Delphi 4. The topics covered include the Project Manager, Modules view, Event Viewer, advanced debugging tools, and a few other new features.

I could dedicate an entire chapter to each of these topics. However, I want to keep the focus of this book primarily on writing code. As a result, these subjects will be covered briefly, giving you enough of an introduction to be sure you are aware of the key new tools and know something of what they can do for you. For more information, see the online help, Delphi documentation, or a third-party booked designed to cover the IDE in depth.

Working with the Project Manager and Debugger

The Project Manager is another very important tool in Delphi 4. Like the Code Explorer, this tool has changed the way I write code. The main purpose of the Project Manager is to allow you to work easily with large projects that contain

- More than one executable
- An executable and one or more DLLs
- Any other combination of DLLs and executables

I find the Project Manager to be easiest to use when I dock it above the Code Explorer in the editor window, as shown in Figure 2.6. In this configuration, I can usually reach all the tools I need with simple motions of the mouse. If I need to start working with a form, I can just press F12 to reach it, and I can press F11 to get at the Object Inspector.

The Project Manager allows you to add new or existing executables or DLLs to your project. If you go to the File menu and choose New Application, your current set of projects will be closed, and a single application will be started. But if you work from inside the Project Manager, you can work on two or more applications or DLLs at the same time.

FIGURE 2.6

*The Project
Manager, with two
executables in it,
docked above the
Code Explorer.*

To add a new application or DLL to a project, I find it simplest to right-click on the root
node at the top of the Project Manager. I am then presented with the option of creating a
new project or inserting an existing project. If I choose to create a new application, a
modified version of the Object Repository will be opened. From the repository I can
choose to create an executable, DLL, ActiveX control, MTS project, and so on.

When you are using the Project Manager, you can reach most of the options available to
you by right-clicking with the mouse or by opening the Project menu. You can also
browse through the tree view control in the Code Explorer, right-clicking when necessary, to see the various options. I will not waste precious space in this book by explaining each menu item in turn. Instead, I will leave it up to you to explore the control, and
remind you that you can always press F1 to get context-sensitive help on options that are
not readily comprehensible to you.

Some issues about the Project Manager are not entirely intuitive, however. For instance,
it is not always obvious which process is currently selected or how to switch from using
one process to another.

If you add two executables to the Project Manager, notice that one project is highlighted
in bold. The bold print means that a particular project is currently active. To confirm this
fact, open the Project menu, where you will see that you can compile either all programs
and DLLs, or the currently selected program or DLL. The actual name of the currently
selected project will be spelled out in the menu. For instance, if project Foo is currently
selected, the menu will give you the option to compile either all projects or project Foo
alone.

To select another project, simply double-click on it. Alternatively, click once on the project you want to use and then click on the Activate icon that is highlighted in green at the
top of the Project Manager. If no icon is highlighted in green, the currently selected project is already active.

On Windows NT, you run and debug two executables at one time from a single instance
of the IDE. To get started, perform the following steps:

1. Use the project manager to open two executables inside the IDE.

2. Use the Project menu to build all projects.

3. Run the currently selected program.

4. On Windows NT, you can then run the second project by activating it and clicking the Run button.

If you change any code in either project, you will need to stop running both projects and recompile them both before you can again run them at the same time.

When running multiple executables from the IDE, you can set breakpoints anywhere you want, in as many projects as you want. You will automatically be taken to the appropriate place at the appropriate time, regardless of how many applications or DLLs you have loaded.

Note, in particular, that you now can simultaneously debug both the client and server side of a multitier application. For instance, if you set the breakpoint in a client program on the method that calls into a server program, and you set a breakpoint in the server where it is called by the client, you can step automatically from one local copy of the program to the next by using the debugger. This process will not work if you do not set breakpoints in both programs. In other words, you aren't really stepping from one program to the next; rather, you are merely jumping from one breakpoint to the next.

Debugging DLLs

To debug a DLL, you should first compile both the DLL and the executable that runs it. Activate the DLL and choose Run, Parameters from the menu. Enter the name of the host application that will call into your DLL, and set a breakpoint in your DLL code. Now run the DLL. Normally, an attempt to run a DLL will generate an error. However, in this case, Delphi will first start the host application and then take you to the breakpoint you set in your DLL the moment your code is called.

Later in the book, I will explain how you can debug a remote application—that is, how you can run the Delphi IDE on one machine, while stepping through the code of an executable running on a second machine.

Now that we are entering the age of distributed applications, a tool such as the Project Manager is almost essential. I find myself using it all the time, and I don't feel the product would be complete without it. Of course, if you aren't building multitier applications, or you aren't creating applications that use DLLs, then you might not find this feature particularly appealing. But if you are stepping into the world of complex projects, you will find the Project Manager one of the most important new tools in Delphi 4.

Working with the Modules View

Two other features in Delphi 4 can aid in the process of debugging an application. One is called the Module window, and the second is the Event Log. You can reach both at runtime by selecting View, Debug Windows from the menu.

The Modules view, when accessed at runtime, gives you a list of the modules loaded by your application. This list will include your current executable or DLL, plus all the Windows DLLs accessed by your program. For instance, every program you load will also load KERNEL32.dll and will probably also load GDI32.dll and USER32.dll.

If you double-click on your project in the main Modules view window, the symbols from your project will be displayed on the right side of the Modules view, as shown in Figure 2.7. If you scroll down to the bottom of the list, you should see symbols from the code in your application, such as Form1. If you double-click on that symbol, you should be taken to the appropriate line of code in your application.

2

IDE AND VCL
ENHANCEMENTS

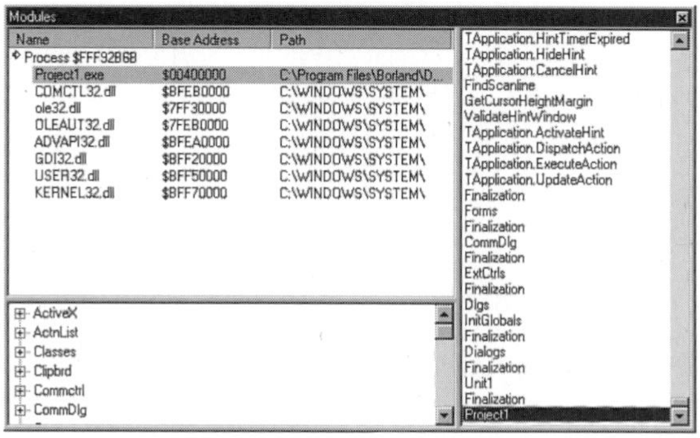

FIGURE 2.7

The Modules view can list the symbols in your project.

If, at any time, you pick a symbol that is not available in any source module, the CPU view will be loaded into memory, and you can see the assembly level source for the code associated with that symbol. If debug information is available for the assembly level code, you can see that information, and if no debug symbols are available, then you will see raw machine code. You are able to view this raw machine code even for modules such as USER32.dll, for which you probably do not have source.

The modules in your currently selected application should also be visible in a tree view control located at the bottom of the Modules view. You can select one of these nodes and browse through the code in your application.

The Module window is probably not the kind of tool most developers will use regularly, but knowing that it is there in case you have a need for it is useful.

Working with the Event Log Windows

The Event Log allows you to track events that occur to your application at runtime. For instance, you will be able to track when modules such as GDI32.dll get loaded into memory, and you can also track standard Windows messages or OutputDebugStrings.

To customize the Event Log, you can right-click on it, or you can choose Tools, Event Log, Debugger Options, Event Log. Nothing shows up in the Event Log at design time, and the information you see at runtime may not be complete. Often, you cannot track everything that has happened in the event log until after a program has run.

To trace a Windows message in the Event Log, you must turn on the option to receive messages before you launch your program. When you run your program, you might get some messages that look something like this:

```
Module Load: SHLWAPI.dll. No Debug Info.
  Base Address: $BFB50000. Process ID: $FFFC20D3.
Module Load: WININET.dll. No Debug Info.
  Base Address: $70200000. Process ID: $FFFC20D3.
Message sent: hwnd=$00000C1C WM_NCCREATE
  wParam $00000000 lParam $0067F9FE
  Process ID: $FFFC20D3.Message sent: hwnd=$00000C1C WM_NCCALCSIZE
  wParam $00000000 lParam $0067FA1E Process ID: $FFFC20D3.
Message sent: hwnd=$00000C1C WM_CREATE
  wParam $00000000 lParam $0067F9FE Process ID: $FFFC20D3.
Message sent: hwnd=$00000C1C WM_SIZE
  wParam $00000000 lParam $00000000 Process ID: $FFFC20D3.
Message sent: hwnd=$00000C1C WM_MOVE
  wParam $00000000 lParam $01960203 Process ID: $FFFC20D3.
```

The first two messages show some Windows DLLs that got loaded when your application launched. Note that no debug information is available for these modules.

The first five messages received by the program were WM_NCCREATE, WM_NCCALCSIZE, WM_CREATE, WM_SIZE, and WM_MOVE. As you would expect, each message was accompanied by three parameters called hwnd, wParam, and lParam. The values of these parameters are passed to the Event Viewer.

TIP

I have found that it is best not to leave the option to trace Windows messages on after you have used it. In fact, I definitely advise you to turn off this option as soon as you are done with it. If you don't, the IDE may become bogged down by all the messages you receive and may appear to be hung.

To track a debug string, you can add the following code to your application:

```
procedure TForm1.Button1Click(Sender: TObject);
begin
  OutputDebugString('Sam Goo Meanie');
end;
```

When this method is called, it will add a message to the Event Log. This method is actually a very reasonable way to debug an application, and I often use it in lieu of some of the fancier debug options available through the powerful Delphi 4 debugger.

The CPU View

The CPU view is available to you at runtime when you choose View, Debug Windows. The CPU view allows you to trace into the assembly language code behind the Object Pascal that you write. You can see the machine code being executed, the current value of the registers, and the code that is being pushed on the stack. Figure 2.8 shows what the CPU view looks like at runtime.

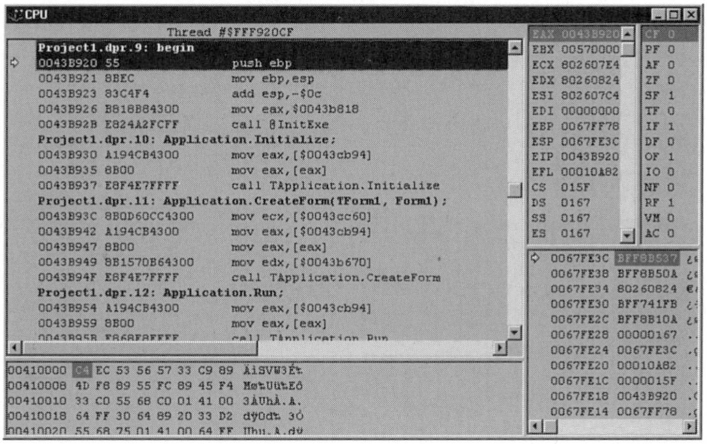

FIGURE 2.8

The CPU view as it appears when stepping through the code that initializes a Delphi application.

At the bottom of the CPU view is a window you can right-click on to browse a particular symbol. If you choose this option, you will be taken to the raw bytes stored in memory. This view is very different from looking at a symbol in the Watch window, but it can often be exactly what you need, particularly when you are working with pointers to memory.

ASSEMBLER AND OTHER PROGRAMMING LANGUAGES

Pascal programmers do not look at assembly code nearly as often as C programmers do. The primary reason for this is simply that C was designed to be a high-level assembly code, and good C programmers can generally guess what kind of machine code is generated when they use a particular function.

Neither C++ nor Pascal is designed to be as close to the metal as C. As a result, looking at a few lines of Object Pascal and guessing what the assembly language code behind it might look like can be hard.

Furthermore, today's advanced compilers are so smart that few people try to second guess them by writing their own handcrafted assembly code. The simple truth is that most people will have a hard time writing assembly code that is anywhere near as efficient as the code produced by standard Object Pascal statements.

Given this situation, you might wonder why the CPU view is included with Delphi 4. I believe most people will use it to help them debug complex problems involving pointers or the stack. Sometimes you end up with an access violation that appears to arise out of nowhere with no apparent cause. By stepping through the assembly code surrounding it, sometimes you can see exactly why you are having trouble. Of course, this feature is obviously advanced, and many programmers will have no need for it.

Some New Features in the Debugger

The CPU view is an advanced feature meant primarily for experienced and intelligent programmers. A more useful tool for the average programmer is the powerful inspect option found in the debugger.

To learn how to inspect a variable in a Delphi program, first start a new application. Drop a button on it and click on the button to create a method. Fill in the method as follows:

```
procedure TForm1.Button1Click(Sender: TObject);
begin
  ShowMessage('Hi ho for the wind and the rain!');
end;
```

Place a breakpoint on this line of code, and run the program. Click on the button so you can view the breakpoint.

Scroll up in the unit to the place where Form1 is declared:

```
var
  Form1: TForm1;
```

Place your cursor on the word `Form1` and double-click to select it. Now right-click on the word and choose Debug, Inspect from the menu. A window like the one shown in Figure 2.9 should appear.

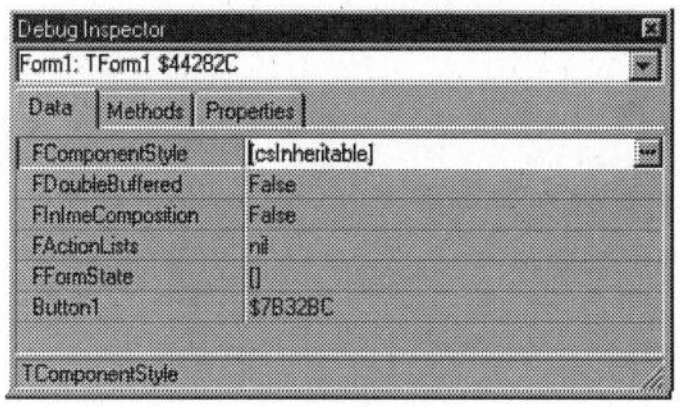

FIGURE 2.9

The Debug Inspector as it appears when you are browsing `Form1`.

Notice that the Debug Inspector has a few tabbed pages in it. You can use them to view the data, methods, and properties in your objects. Some of the fields of your object may be editable at runtime. For instance, you can sometimes use the Debug Inspector to change the value of a variable in your program at runtime. To do so, inspect `Form1` in a running project. Turn to the data page, and click on the icon at the right side of the editor for the `FDoubleBuffered`. You will now be able to change this value from `True` to `False`.

For some objects in the Debug Inspector, you can double-click to open a second window that will let you browse the field you have selected. For instance, `Form1` will have an object called `Button1` in it, and you can double-click this symbol to pop up a window that will let you browse the `Button1` object.

TIP

Sometimes you might want to inspect or watch a variable that the IDE will claim is currently unavailable due to an optimization. To get around this problem, close your program, choose Project, Options, Compiler, and then turn off optimizations. Now rebuild your project, and run it again. This time, you should be able to browse any of the symbols in your program. You will probably want to once again turn on optimizations before you release your program to the public.

You should take as much time as possible to learn about the debugger. For instance, you should learn how to set conditional breakpoints from the Breakpoint window by choosing View, Debug Windows. It's true that the best way to write clean applications is to design them correctly. However, sometimes even the best programmers have to rely on the debugger, and learning about everything it can do for you is well worth your time.

> **NOTE**
>
> Debugger options are now controlled from a dialog you can reach by choosing Tools, Debugger Options. At the very bottom of the General page for this dialog is an option that allows you to turn the integrated debugger on and off. The other pages of this dialog are also worth exploring, but again I will save room for less intuitive subjects by leaving it to you to pursue this course of action with the aid of the online help.

The Code Browser and Tooltip Symbol Insight

If you hold down the Ctrl key and place your mouse cursor under a symbol in your program, the symbol will be highlighted in blue, as if it were a hyperlink. If you left-click on the highlighted symbol, you will be taken to its declaration. If you have the source to the VCL, you can use these feature to jump immediately to the declaration of TForm in the Forms.pas unit.

A related feature called Tooltip Symbol Insight enables you to see where a variable is declared in a small pop-up window. For instance, if you pass the mouse under the word TForm in the declaration for the main form in your program, you will see that it is declared in Forms.pas on line 590.

Class Completion and the Code Browser are my two favorite new IDE features in Delphi 4. I find myself using both continuously, and I would be hard pressed to switch to an IDE that didn't support these great tools.

Docking Windows

It's time now to move away from new features in the IDE and start looking at some of the new features you can add to your own programs. Perhaps the most obvious enhancement in Delphi 4 is the capability to dock windows in a form or on top of another control.

Docking windows is easy to implement. Here is how to convert a standard form, panel, or TControlBar into a place where other windows can be docked:

- Set its DockSite property to True.
- If you are working with a control such as panel or the new TControlBar component from the Additional page, then you can hide it on the side of a form until such time as a user wants to dock something on it. To do so, set the control's AutoSize property to True. Now, when the user drags a component to the side of your form,

your panel or control bar will suddenly appear as a place to dock a homeless control. To the user, this action will feel like he or she is just docking the control on the side of the form; the user need never know that the component has come to rest on a panel or control bar.

Two simple steps to make a control dockable are as follows:

1. Set its DragKind property to dkDock.
2. Set its DragMode property to dmAutomatic.

Docking Controls Within Forms

A simple docking example is demonstrated on the CD that accompanies this book in the program called SimpleDock. This program has two panels on either side of the main form, each with its DockSite property set to True. At the bottom of the form is a TControlBar, with its AutoSize property set to True. By default, the DockSite property of a TControlBar is set to True. In the middle of the form are six TShape controls, each with its DragKind and DragMode properties set up for docking, and each assigned a bright color. The main form also has its DockSite property set to True.

If you run the program, you can drag the TShape objects onto the panels, the control bar, or back onto the main form. Experiment with this process, learning all the different possibilities and combinations of controls, as shown in Figure 2.10.

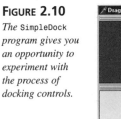

FIGURE 2.10

The SimpleDock *program gives you an opportunity to experiment with the process of docking controls.*

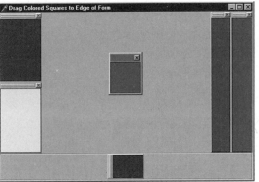

The UseDockManager property is associated with some controls, such as TPanel. When this property is set to True, it causes controls dropped on a panel to conform to the shape of the panel or the existing room available in a panel. For instance, if you drop a TShape object on a panel in the SimpleDock program, the dock manager will automatically make the control fill up the available space on the panel. If you drop a second control on the panel, it will fill up one half the space, and the first control will have the other half of the available space. To see this process in action, toggle the UseDockManager property on for one panel in the SimpleDock program, and turn it off on the other panel. Now drag components onto both panels. Figure 2.11 shows how this process looks at runtime.

FIGURE 2.11

The panel on the right has its UseDockManager *property set to* True; *the one on the left has this property set to* False.

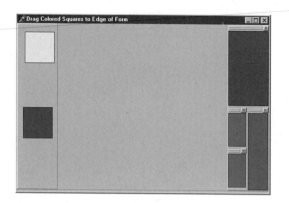

Docking Forms Within Forms

A more advanced example of what you can do with dockable windows is shown in the DockableForm program from the CD that accompanies this book. This program has a main form with some TGauge controls decorating its top third, and a page control inserted into the bottom two-thirds of the form. The DockSite property of the TPageControl is set to True.

The program also has two additional forms in it, each with the dkKind and dkMode properties set to make them dockable. At runtime, you can launch all three forms and dock the second two inside the page control found on the first form. The result is shown in Figure 2.12, and the code for the program is shown in Listing 2.2.

FIGURE 2.12

The DockableForm *program with forms two and three embedded in the program's main form.*

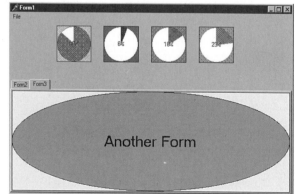

LISTING 2.2   THE DockableForm PROGRAM SHOWING HOW TO DOCK TWO FORMS INTO A
TABBED PAGE CONTROL

```pascal
//////////////////////////////////////
//    Name: Main.pas
// Project: DockableForm
//  Author: Copyright  1998 by Charlie Calvert
//
unit Main;

interface

uses
  Windows, Messages, SysUtils,
  Classes, Graphics, Controls,
  Forms, Dialogs, StdCtrls,
  StdActns, ActnList, Menus,
  ComCtrls, ToolWin, ExtCtrls,
  Gauges;

const
  MAX = 3;

type
  TMyGauge = class(TGauge)
  private
    FGauge: TGauge;
    FTimer: TTimer;
  public
    constructor Create(AOwner: TComponent); override;
    destructor Destroy; override;
    procedure Timer1Timer(Sender: TObject);
  end;

  TForm1 = class(TForm)
    PageControl1: TPageControl;
    MainMenu1: TMainMenu;
    File1: TMenuItem;
    ShowForms1: TMenuItem;
    N1: TMenuItem;
    Exit1: TMenuItem;
    procedure Exit1Click(Sender: TObject);
    procedure ShowForms1Click(Sender: TObject);
    procedure FormCreate(Sender: TObject);
    procedure FormDestroy(Sender: TObject);
  private
    { Private declarations }
    FGauge: array [0..MAX] of TMyGauge;
  public
    { Public declarations }
```

continues

LISTING 2.2   CONTINUED

```pascal
  end;

var
  Form1: TForm1;

implementation

uses
  DockWindow1, DockWindow2;

{$R *.DFM}

procedure TForm1.FormCreate(Sender: TObject);
var
  i: Integer;
begin
  Randomize;
  for i := 0 to MAX do begin
    FGauge[i] := TMyGauge.Create(Self);
    FGauge[i].Parent := Self;
    FGauge[i].Visible := True;
    FGauge[i].Left := (Width div 6) * (i + 1);
    FGauge[i].Top := 8;
    FGauge[i].Color := RGB(Random(255), Random(255), Random(255));
    FGauge[i].ForeColor := RGB(Random(255), Random(255), Random(255));
  end;
  PageControl1.Top := FGauge[0].Height + 5;
  PageControl1.Align := alBottom;
end;

procedure TForm1.FormDestroy(Sender: TObject);
var
  i: Integer;
begin
  for i := 0 to MAX do
    FGauge[i].Free;
end;

procedure TForm1.Exit1Click(Sender: TObject);
begin
  Close;
end;

procedure TForm1.ShowForms1Click(Sender: TObject);
begin
  Form2.Show;
  Form3.Show;
end;
```

```
{ TMyGauge }

constructor TMyGauge.Create(AOwner: TComponent);
begin
  inherited Create(AOwner);
  FTimer := TTimer.Create(Self);
  FTimer.OnTimer := Timer1Timer;
  FTimer.Interval := 10;
  Width := 75;
  Height := 75;
  Kind := gkPie;
end;

destructor TMyGauge.Destroy;
begin
  FTimer.Enabled := False;
  FTimer.Free;
  inherited Destroy;
end;

procedure TMyGauge.Timer1Timer(Sender: TObject);
var
  i: Integer;
begin
  Progress := Progress + 1;
  if Progress >= 100 then begin
    Progress := 0;
    for i := 0 to MAX do begin
      Color := RGB(Random(255), Random(255), Random(255));
      ForeColor := RGB(Random(255), Random(255), Random(255));
    end;
  end;
end;

end.
```

When you launch this program, you will see a series of animated gauge controls across the top and an empty page control on the bottom. Use the main menu to bring up the other two forms available in the project. Drag each of them in turn over the page control, and dock them. When you are done, you can page between the two secondary forms.

This program also sports a descendant of TGauge that is designed to automatically change colors and to automatically animate itself. In most cases, you would want to save a control like this to the Component Palette, but I have not done that in this case so as to spare you the trouble of having to install the component just to run this rather mindless example.

I hope that by now you have a feeling for what you can do with dockable windows. You might want to experiment further by creating panels that contain multiple controls, and by dragging and dropping these panels onto control bars or onto other panels and forms.

Action Lists

The TActionList object appears on the Standard page of the Component Palette. This object provides a single place in your application from which a set of one or more methods can be managed.

Using an Action List

Consider a simple application that can display a bitmap in a TImage control. Three actions occur inside this application:

- You can open a file and display it.
- You can decide whether an image is stretched.
- You can close the application.

On the CD that accompanies this book, you will find a program called SimpleAction. This sample program implements the actions just listed.

To get started creating this application, drop a TActionList object on your main form. Add three actions to this list by clicking on the icon in the upper-left corner of the ActionList dialog. This icon has the hint New Action associated with it. If you don't want to use the mouse, you can create a new action by pressing the Insert key.

The default action you create can change depending on the value you choose from the Standard Actions dialog. To reach this dialog, double-click on the TAction component. By doing so, you bring up a dialog named after your form and your TAction component. On the top of the dialog is an icon with a black arrow next to it. Select this arrow, and you will see a menu with two choices on it. The first choice is New Action, and the second reads New Standard Action. Select this latter option to bring up the Standard Actions dialog. The shortcut for getting to this dialog is Ctrl+Insert.

After you have the Standard Actions dialog available, you will see a list of possible actions. For now, select the first item in the list, which should be called TAction. Later in this section, I will discuss standard actions such as TEditCut and TEditPaste.

By default, the actions you have created should be called Action1, Action2, and Action3. If you accidentally created other actions with other names, you can delete them by selecting the second of the two icons at the top of the TAction component editor. Rename these actions so they have Name and Captions properties as shown in Table 2.1.

TABLE 2.1 THE ACTIONS FOR THE SimpleAction PROGRAM

Name	Caption
ExitApp	Exit
LoadFile	Open
StretchPicture	Stretch Picture

Go to the events page for the actions, and assign an event to each page. For instance, the event associated with the ExitApp action should look like this:

```
procedure TForm1.ExitAppExecute(Sender: TObject);
begin
  Close;
end;
```

Here are the events associated with the LoadFile and StretchPicture actions:

```
procedure TForm1.LoadFileExecute(Sender: TObject);
begin
  if OpenDialog1.Execute then
    Image1.Picture.LoadFromFile(OpenDialog1.FileName);
end;

procedure TForm1.StretchPictureExecute(Sender: TObject);
begin
  Image1.Stretch := not Image1.Stretch;
end;
```

If you'd like, you can also drop down a TImageList control from the Win32 page, and associate it with the TActionList control. Add a few pictures to the image list. You might find the images you want to use in the following directory:

```
c:\Program Files\Common Files\Borland Shared\Images\Buttons
```

Of course, the details of how this path will depend on the options you chose when installing Delphi 4.

Now associate each action you created with one of the images in the ImageList. You can do so by changing the value found in the Object Inspector for the ImageIndex property associated with each action. If you set the ImageIndex to 0, you will get the first image in your image list; if you set it to 1, you will get the second image; and so on.

At this stage, you have created an application with a set of actions in it. Each of these actions is associated with an action found inside your TActionList component. In a sense, your application is complete. The only thing missing is a way to allow the user to call each of these actions.

2

IDE AND VCL
ENHANCEMENTS

To finish the application, drop a TMenu control on the main form. Add new menu items to the TMenu control. Instead of filling in the caption and other values for each menu item, simply associate the menu item with a particular action from the TActionList. In particular, create a new menu item called Options that will appear on the top of your program. Beneath this menu item, add three more menu items.

As you select each item, don't give it a caption or an event; instead, associate the Action property of the TMenuItem with one of the custom actions you created. When you do so, you will find that the Caption and OnClick event for the menu item will be set automatically to the Caption and OnExecute properties from the action you selected. Furthermore, if you link the TImageList with the menu via the Images property, the icon you associated with the action will also appear on your menu at runtime. (To do this, select the TMenu control you dropped on the form. Find its Images property, drop down the list associated with it, and select the TImageList control you dropped on the form. If you need clarification on this process, study the SimpleAction program on the CD that accompanies this book.)

Add additional controls such as a TToolBar or a TButton to the application. Now you can associate each button on the TToolBar with a different action, and its properties and caption will be filled in automatically.

In Listing 2.3, you will find the source for the SimpleAction program. The program is also shown in Figure 2.13, and the full source for the application is available on the CD that accompanies this book.

FIGURE 2.13

The SimpleAction program at design time.

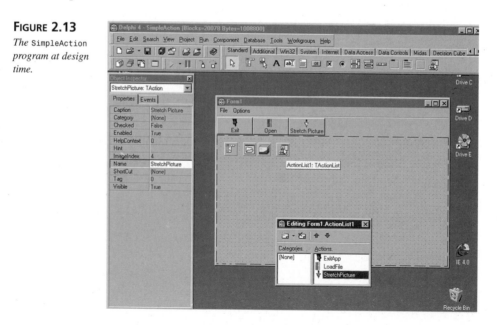

LISTING 2.3 THE SimpleAction PROGRAM SHOWING HOW TO WORK WITH ACTION LISTS

```pascal
//////////////////////////////////////
//    File: Main.pas
// Project: SimpleAction
//   Author: Copyright  1998 by Charlie Calvert
//
unit Main;

interface

uses
  Windows, Messages, SysUtils,
  Classes, Graphics, Controls,
  Forms, Dialogs, ActnList,
  ExtCtrls, Menus, ImgList, ComCtrls, ToolWin;

type
  TForm1 = class(TForm)
    ActionList1: TActionList;
    ExitApp: TAction;
    LoadFile: TAction;
    StretchPicture: TAction;
    Image1: TImage;
    OpenDialog1: TOpenDialog;
    MainMenu1: TMainMenu;
    File1: TMenuItem;
    LoadFile1: TMenuItem;
    N1: TMenuItem;
    Exit1: TMenuItem;
    Options1: TMenuItem;
    StretchPicture1: TMenuItem;
    ToolBar1: TToolBar;
    ToolButton1: TToolButton;
    ToolButton2: TToolButton;
    ToolButton3: TToolButton;
    ImageList1: TImageList;
    procedure ExitAppExecute(Sender: TObject);
    procedure LoadFileExecute(Sender: TObject);
    procedure StretchPictureExecute(Sender: TObject);
  private
    { Private declarations }
  public
    { Public declarations }
  end;

var
  Form1: TForm1;

implementation
```

2

IDE AND VCL
ENHANCEMENTS

continues

LISTING 2.3 CONTINUED

```
{$R *.DFM}

procedure TForm1.ExitAppExecute(Sender: TObject);
begin
  Close;
end;

procedure TForm1.LoadFileExecute(Sender: TObject);
begin
  if OpenDialog1.Execute then
    Image1.Picture.LoadFromFile(OpenDialog1.FileName);
end;

procedure TForm1.StretchPictureExecute(Sender: TObject);
begin
  Image1.Stretch := not Image1.Stretch;
end;

end.
```

You can use this program's menu or toolbar to select a picture and display it either stretched or at its normal resolution.

Using Standard Actions

Standard actions are predefined actions designed to add certain features to your program automatically. To see how they work, take a look at the StandardAction program on the CD that accompanies this book.

The StandardAction program has three menu items and three toolbar buttons labeled Copy, Cut, and Paste. Each of these items will perform the expected actions when selected.

Two edit controls reside on the main form of the application. At runtime, select these controls and highlight some text. Now click one or more of the toolbar buttons to see how you can copy, cut, and paste the text in these controls.

You can easily create the StandardAction program. First, drop a TMenu, TToolbar, TimageList, and TActionList control on the main form of a new application. If you bring up the Standard Action dialog, you will find three choices called TEditCut, TEditPaste, and TEditCopy. Highlight all three of them and click the OK button. Now add some images to the TImageList and associate the image list with the TActionList, the TMenu, and the TToolbar. Add three buttons to the toolbar, associating each with a different action. Create three parallel items in the menu for the program. You can now compile and run your code, and you should find that it behaves exactly like the StandardAction program.

ActionLists were added to Delphi because the developers of the product found that they needed them. They allow you to centralize certain commands in a single location, even if the interface for that command is spread out across one or more forms. When you are in maintenance mode on your application, you can simply click on your TActionList component, and you will have one single, centralized reference for all the commands your users can select. It will help you create programs that have an orderly interface, with easy-to-understand icons, hotkeys, and labels.

Function Overloading

Function overloading was added to Delphi in part to lay the groundwork for better inter-operability among Delphi, C++Builder, and JBuilder. For instance, in C++, constructors for a particular class all have the same name and are distinguished solely by their parameters. By adding function overloading to Delphi, the developers were better able to support this type of C++ syntax.

Function overloading allows you to have two functions with the same name but different sets of parameters:

```
function Foo(i: Integer): string; overload;
function Foo(S: string): string; overload;
```

The compiler can distinguish between these methods because they take different parameters. This capability can help make your code more easily maintainable and more elegant.

- Function overloading makes code easier to maintain—Suppose you have a method that takes a single parameter of type Integer. Over time, it may become clear that you can improve the functionality of your object by designing the method to take both an integer and a string. For instance, you may want to support distributed computing by letting the user pass in an integer and the IP address of a machine. If you changed the signature of your function in Delphi 3, then you would break everyone's code, which is definitely bad. Alternatively, you can add a second function, which can end up cluttering your code. With function overloading, you can add new overloaded functions that increase the power of the object for new users, or simply extend the reach of existing functions. In either case, your code would still support your old users.

- Function overloading helps you write simple, easy-to-read code—You might have a need to call a function with different parameters. For instance, you might sometimes call it with a string and at other times with an integer. Or sometimes you might call it with a float and sometimes with an integer. You could ask the user to support that by always converting a parameter to a single type, say a string. But then the developer would have to write lots of code that parsed that string, to see what kind of variable was being passed in. Or you could have a series of functions with different names, such as `MyFunctionInt`, `MyFunctionString`, and `MyFunctionFloat`. Obviously, none of these solutions is ideal. The best way to handle the situation is to use function overloading. Then you can have one function name but have different functions called depending on the type of parameter passed in.

Listing 2.4 provides a simple example of a class, called `TMyObject`, that supports function overloading. This program can be found in the directory called `FunctionOverload` on the CD that accompanies this book.

LISTING 2.4   A SIMPLE DELPHI CLASS THAT SUPPORTS FUNCTION OVERLOADING

```
/////////////////////////////////////////
//    File: Main
// Project: FunctionOverload
// Copyright  1998 by Charlie Calvert
//
unit Main;

interface

uses
  Windows, Messages, SysUtils,
  Classes, Graphics, Controls,
  Forms, Dialogs, StdCtrls;

type
  TMyObject = class(TObject)
    function Foo(i: Integer): string; overload;
    function Foo(S: string): string; overload;
  end;

  TForm1 = class(TForm)
    Button1: TButton;
    ListBox1: TListBox;
    procedure Button1Click(Sender: TObject);
  private
    { Private declarations }
  public
```

```
    { Public declarations }
  end;

var
  Form1: TForm1;

implementation

{$R *.DFM}

{ TMyObject }

function TMyObject.Foo(i: Integer): string;
begin
  Result := 'IntFoo says: ' + IntToStr(i);
end;

function TMyObject.Foo(S: string): string;
begin
  Result := 'StringFoo says: ' + S;
end;

procedure TForm1.Button1Click(Sender: TObject);
var
  MyObject: TMyObject;
  S: string;
begin
  MyObject := TMyObject.Create;

  S := MyObject.Foo('Sam');
  ListBox1.Items.Add(S);

  S := MyObject.Foo(1);
  ListBox1.Items.Add(S);

  MyObject.Free;
end;

end.
```

This program sports a simple window with one button and one list box in it. If you click the button, two messages pop up in the list box:

```
StringFoo says: Sam
IntFoo says: 1
```

The key piece of code in this example is the declaration for the TMyObject class:

```
  TMyObject = class(TObject)
    function Foo(i: Integer): string; overload;
    function Foo(S: string): string; overload;
  end;
```

As you can see, this class has two methods called Foo. In the old world of Delphi 3, having these two methods would have been an impossibility. The compiler would have complained when you declared two methods with the same name. However, in Delphi 4, this use is legal, as long as the signature of each method is unique, and as long as you use the overload keyword to distinguish the methods you are overloading.

Method Overloading and Inheritance

Method overloading works as you would expect up and down the hierarchy of a set of related methods. In other words, if you declare a method with the keyword overload in an ancestor class, you will not obscure the method if you declare an overloaded method with the same name in a later class. This principle is shown in the OverloadClass program from the CD that accompanies this book, and is shown in Listing 2.5.

LISTING 2.5 THE OverloadClass PROGRAM SHOWING HOW OVERLOADED METHODS WORK IN AN OBJECT HIERARCHY

```
unit Main;

interface

uses
  Windows, Messages, SysUtils,
  Classes, Graphics, Controls,
  Forms, Dialogs, StdCtrls;

type
  TMyObject = class(TObject)
  private
    FName: string;
  public
    procedure InitObject(AName: string); overload;
  end;

  TAnimal = class(TMyObject)
  private
    FType: string;
  public
    procedure InitObject(AName: string; AType: string); overload;
  end;

  TForm1 = class(TForm)
    Button1: TButton;
    procedure Button1Click(Sender: TObject);
  private
    { Private declarations }
  public
```

```
    { Public declarations }
  end;

var
  Form1: TForm1;

implementation

{$R *.DFM}

procedure TMyObject.InitObject(AName: string);
begin
  FName := AName;
  ShowMessage('TMyObject called');
end;

procedure TAnimal.InitObject(AName: string; AType: string);
begin
  FName := AName;
  FType := AType;
  ShowMessage('TAnimal called');
end;

procedure TForm1.Button1Click(Sender: TObject);
var
  A: TAnimal;
begin
  A := TAnimal.Create;
  A.InitObject('Object');
  A.InitObject('Harry', 'Horse');
end;

end.
```

This program shows overloaded methods across an object hierarchy. Consider the following class declarations:

```
TMyObject = class(TObject)
private
  FName: string;
public
  procedure InitObject(AName: string); overload;
end;

TAnimal = class(TMyObject)
private
  FType: string;
public
  procedure InitObject(AName: string; AType: string); overload;
end;
```

In this example, `InitObject` is an overloaded method. If the keyword `overload` were not present, the second instance of `InitObject` would simply obscure the first instance. Because the code does use `overload`, you are free to call either method from a single instance of `TAnimal`, depending on your needs:

```
procedure TForm1.Button1Click(Sender: TObject);
var
  A: TAnimal;
begin
  A := TAnimal.Create;
  A.InitObject('Object');
  A.InitObject('Harry', 'Horse');
end;
```

This example first calls the instance of `InitObject` in `TMyObject` and then calls the same method as it is implemented in `TAnimal`.

Pitfalls to Avoid When Using Method Overloading

Method overloading is usually reasonably straightforward, but you need to watch for a few issues. I will cover these delicate situations in this section, and the following section, "Default Parameters."

If you declare a virtual method, you need to use the `reintroduce` keyword if you overload it in a descendant object. An example is shown in Listing 2.6 and is found in the project called `ReintroduceMethod` on the CD that accompanies this book.

LISTING 2.6   ReintroduceMethod

```
////////////////////////////////////////
//    File: Main
// Project: ReintroduceMethod
// Copyright  1998 by Charlie Calvert
//
unit Main;

interface

uses
  Windows, Messages, SysUtils,
  Classes, Graphics, Controls,
  Forms, Dialogs, StdCtrls,
  ExtCtrls;

type

  TMyObject = class(TObject)
    procedure DoSomething(I: Integer); virtual;
```

```pascal
  end;

  TAnimal = class(TMyObject)
    procedure DoSomething(S: string); reintroduce; overload;
  end;

  TForm1 = class(TForm)
    Button1: TButton;
    Edit1: TEdit;
    Edit2: TEdit;
    Label1: TLabel;
    Label2: TLabel;
    Bevel1: TBevel;
    Bevel2: TBevel;
    Bevel3: TBevel;
    procedure Button1Click(Sender: TObject);
  private
    { Private declarations }
  public
    { Public declarations }
  end;

var
  Form1: TForm1;

implementation

{$R *.DFM}

procedure TForm1.Button1Click(Sender: TObject);
var
  Animal: TAnimal;
begin
  Animal := TAnimal.Create;
  Animal.DoSomething('Cat');   // calls TAnimal.DoSomething
  Animal.DoSomething(7);         // calls TMyObject.DoSomething
end;

{ TMyObject }

procedure TMyObject.DoSomething(I: Integer);
begin
  Form1.Edit1.Text := IntToStr(i);
end;

{ TAnimal }

procedure TAnimal.DoSomething(S: string);
begin
  Form1.Edit2.Text := S;
end;

end.
```

If you run this program, it presents you with a single button that you can click in order to fill in the two edit controls shown on the main form.

The key section of code in this program is the declaration for the first two of the three objects used by the program:

```
TMyObject = class(TObject)
  procedure DoSomething(I: Integer); virtual;
end;

TAnimal = class(TMyObject)
  procedure DoSomething(S: string); reintroduce; overload;
end;
```

Note that the code shown here uses `reintroduce` to declare the second instance of the `DoSomething` method. This code is a bit awkward to use, but you need to understand it if you want to take full advantage of the method overloading in Delphi.

A second tricky aspect of using method overloading involves a simple rule that states that you cannot overload a method in the published section of an object. Consider the following declarations:

```
TMyObject = class(TObject)
public
  procedure DoSomething(I: Integer); overload; virtual;
published
  procedure Foo; overload;
end;

TAnimal = class(TMyObject)
public
  procedure DoSomething(S: string); reintroduce; overload;
published
  procedure Foo(i: Integer); overload;
end;
```

What you see here is entirely legal. However, the following declaration for `TAnimal` is illegal:

```
TAnimal = class(TMyObject)
public
  procedure DoSomething(S: string); reintroduce; overload;
published
  procedure Foo(i: Integer); overload;
  procedure Foo(S: string); overload;
end;
```

The problem here is simply that you cannot overload `Foo` twice in the published section of the same object. You can do so multiple times across the hierarchy of an object but not in the published section of the same object. This rule is necessary because of the way RTTI information is implemented in Object Pascal.

There is one last gotcha when you are working with method overloading. This last problem has to do with potentially ambiguous calls to an overloaded method. I can best demonstrate this very important issue after first introducing the topic of default parameters.

Default Parameters

Default parameters allow you to assign default values to parameters passed to a function. Consider the following code fragment:

```
procedure TForm1.Sam(A: Integer = 3);
begin
  ShowMessage(IntToStr(A));
end;

procedure TForm1.Button1Click(Sender: TObject);
begin
  Sam;
end;
```

In this example, the method called Sam takes a single parameter of type Integer. By default, this parameter will be set to the value 3. This means that Sam will pop up a message box showing the value 3 if you call the method like this:

```
Sam;
```

However, the function will pop up the value 1 if you call the method like this:

```
Sam(1);
```

This is not really the same thing as allowing functions to have a variable number of parameters passed to them. Procedure Sam always takes one parameter; but sometimes the parameter is assigned a default value.

Object Pascal is fairly strict about what you can do with variable parameter lists. For instance, consider the following example:

```
procedure Sam(A: Integer = 3); overload;
procedure Sam(A: Integer = 3; S: string = 'Sam'); overload;
```

This example introduces an ambiguity because it is unclear what will happen if you make the following call:

```
Sam;
```

This call could legally be resolved to either function, which means it is profoundly ambiguous. As a result, the compiler will not let you make the call. Making the declarations is legal; the trouble comes when you try to call them.

Dynamic Arrays

Long-term Pascal programmers are usually familiar with the various tricks used to allocate an arbitrary number of bytes for an array at runtime. These tricks are a time-honored tradition, but one that has usually been left to intermediate and advanced programmers.

Delphi 4 introduces a simple solution to the whole problem of allocating memory for an array at runtime or even changing the length of an array at runtime. This feature is called *dynamic arrays*. You need to know four key pieces of syntax to use this feature:

- How to declare a dynamic array
- How to allocate additional memory for an existing array
- How to assign one array to another array
- How to determine the size of an existing array

Here is the syntax for declaring and allocating memory for a dynamic array:

```
var
  A: array of Integer;
begin
  SetLength(A, 10);
end;
```

Variable A is declared to be an `array of Integer`. After the declaration, it has no elements assigned to it. To grow the array so that it can hold 10 elements, you use the `SetLength` procedure.

You can use the `Copy` procedure to resize an array at runtime:

```
Copy(A, 0, 200);
```

This code fragment reallocates A so that it now holds 200 elements.

If two arrays are of the same type, you can assign one to another:

```
type
  TMyArray = array of Integer;
Var
  A: TMyArray;
  B: TMyArray;
  Len: Integer;
Begin
  SetLength(A, 10);
  B := A;
  B[9] := 2;
  Len := High(B);
  Edit1.Text := IntToStr(Low(B));
  Edit2.Text := IntToStr(High(B));
end;
```

During the assignment, any memory that might be associated with B is automatically disposed, and then A is copied into it.

You can determine the size an array by using the High and Low functions. In the code fragment shown before the preceding paragraph, Edit1.Text would get the value 0 (zero), and Edit2.Text would get the value 9. This result occurs because dynamic arrays are assigned zero-based numbering schemes. Therefore, a dynamic array of 10 elements would always range from 0 to 9. To get the number of elements in an array, use the Length function.

For whatever it is worth, I would have to say that dynamic arrays strike me as the perfect addition to the Object Pascal language. They provide an excellent service without causing any confusion, and their implementation is, in my opinion, flawless.

I provide a short sample program in Listing 2.7 illustrating how easy dynamic arrays are to use. It is found in the program called DynArray on the CD that accompanies this book.

LISTING 2.7 THE DYNAMIC ARRAY PROGRAM SHOWING HOW TO ALLOCATE ARRAYS ON-THE-FLY

```
unit Main;

interface

uses
  Windows, Messages, SysUtils,
  Classes, Graphics, Controls,
  Forms, Dialogs, StdCtrls;

type
  TMyArray = Array of Integer;

  TForm1 = class(TForm)
    Button1: TButton;
    ListBox1: TListBox;
    procedure Button1Click(Sender: TObject);
  private
    procedure ShowArray(A: TMyArray);
    { Private declarations }
  public
    { Public declarations }
  end;

var
  Form1: TForm1;

implementation
```

continues

LISTING 2.7 CONTINUED

```
{$R *.DFM}

function GetArray(NumElements: Integer): TMyArray;
var
  A: TMyArray;
  i: Integer;
begin
  SetLength(A, NumElements);
  for i := 0 to NumElements - 1 do
    A[i] := Sqr(i);

  Result := A;
end;

procedure TForm1.ShowArray(A: TMyArray);
var
  i: Integer;
begin
  for i := 0 to High(A) do
    ListBox1.Items.Add(IntToStr(A[i]));
end;

procedure TForm1.Button1Click(Sender: TObject);
var
  B: TMyArray;
begin
  B := GetArray(10);
  ShowArray(B);
end;

end.
```

If you run the DynArray program, it does nothing more than put the numbers 0 and 9 in two edit controls and show a series of numbers in a list box. Hardly a stunning accomplishment. Nevertheless, the program has some interesting features.

The DynArray program shows how to work with arrays when you know very little about their size and shape at compile time. For instance, in this program I create a method that allocates memory for an array of arbitrary size:

```
function GetArray(NumElements: Integer): TMyArray;
var
  A: TMyArray;
  i: Integer;
begin
  SetLength(A, NumElements);
  for i := 0 to NumElements - 1 do
```

```
   A[i] := Sqr(i);

 Result := A;
end;
```

This method knows only that it needs to work with an array of integers. The code uses
`SetLength` to create an array of the size you specify. After creating the array, I fill in its
elements with the square of the current value of i.

At runtime, you can create an array that is 10 elements long, or you can create one that is
10,000 elements long. It's up to you. (This statement is actually literally true; both the
list box control and the range of an integer are large enough to support passing in the
value 10,000 to the `GetArray` function.) In the example on the CD that accompanies this
book, I pass in `10` to the `GetArray` function:

```
B := GetArray(10);
```

You will probably want to play with this number some, though, and pass in larger values.

The following method shows how to work with an array of some arbitrary length:

```
procedure TForm1.ShowArray(A: TMyArray);
var
  i: Integer;
begin
  for i := 0 to High(A) do
    ListBox1.Items.Add(IntToStr(A[i]));
end;
```

The `ShowArray` method uses the `High` function to determine the range of the array. In this
case, it is certain that the low value in the range is zero because this is a dynamic array.
You might, however, improve the routine's robustness by having it use the `Low` function
to determine the starting point of the array:

```
for i := Low(A) to High(A) do
  ListBox1.Items.Add(IntToStr(A[i]));
```

As I stated earlier, using this feature is very simple. However, it is a valuable piece of
syntax and something that almost all Delphi programmers will use at one time or
another.

The `implements` Keyword

A new keyword called `implements` allows you to combine the merits of interface with
the virtues of aggregation. This fairly technical subject may not be of interest to all
Delphi programmers.

In the past, Delphi programmers were forced to use a syntax closely resembling multiple inheritance when they wanted to implement an interface. This approach was convenient under certain circumstances, but it could also cause confusion. Consider the following declaration:

```
TMyClass = class(TInterfacedObject, IFoo, IBar, IGoo)
```

This class declaration begins an object that will implement the `IFoo`, `IBar`, and `IGoo` interfaces by declaring and implementing all their methods inside a single object. This process can be confusing because telling which methods of `TMyClass` implement which method declaration in your interfaces is hard.

Aggregation is the technology Delphi programmers use to get the benefits of multiple inheritance without the drawbacks of multiple inheritance. Now you can use aggregation to create a new declaration for `TMyClass` that is much easier to understand and implement:

```
TMyClass = class(TObject)
private
  FFoo: TFoo;
  FBar: TBar;
  FGoo: TGoo;
published
  property Foo: TFoo read FFoo implements IFoo;
  property Bar: TBar read FBar implements IBar;
  property Goo: TGoo read FGoo implements IGoo;
end;
```

This syntax allows you to implement the `IFoo`, `IBar`, and `IGoo` interfaces in their own separate objects called `TFoo`, `TBar`, and `TGoo`. To me, this is a much cleaner solution to the problem of implementing multiple interfaces in a single object.

Listing 2.8 shows how this technology works in practice. The program shown in this listing can be found in the directory called `ImplementInterface` on the CD that accompanies this book. Contrary to my usual practice, the code I use here is very close to an example provided in the Delphi online help.

LISTING 2.8   USING A PROPERTY TO IMPLEMENT AN INTERFACE THROUGH DELEGATION

```
program ImplementInteface;

type
  IMyInterface = interface
    procedure P1;
    procedure P2;
  end;

  TMyImplClass = class
    procedure P1;
```

```
      procedure P2;
   end;

   TMyClass = class(TInterfacedObject, IMyInterface)
     FMyImplClass: TMyImplClass;
     property MyImplClass: TMyImplClass read FMyImplClass implements
IMyInterface;
   end;

procedure TMyImplClass.P1;
begin
  WriteLn('P1');
end;

procedure TMyImplClass.P2;
begin
  WriteLn('P2');
end;

var
  MyClass: TMyClass;
  MyInterface: IMyInterface;
begin
  MyClass := TMyClass.Create;
  MyClass.FMyImplClass := TMyImplClass.Create;
  MyInterface := MyClass;
  MyInterface.P1;          // calls TMyImplClass.P1;
  MyInterface.P2;          // calls TMyImplClass.P2;
  ReadLn;
end.
```

This program is a console application, so when you run it, a DOS box is opened, and you see the output produced by the program as if you were time traveling back into the 1980s.

The key part of the program is the declaration for the classes and interfaces:

```
IMyInterface = interface
  procedure P1;
  procedure P2;
end;

TMyImplClass = class
  procedure P1;
  procedure P2;
end;

TMyClass = class(TInterfacedObject, IMyInterface)
  FMyImplClass: TMyImplClass;
  property MyImplClass: TMyImplClass read FMyImplClass implements
IMyInterface;
end;
```

The code shown here declares a class called `TmyImplClass`, which can be used to implement `IMyInterface`. This implementation is then added to `TMyClass` via aggregation. Notice that the declaration for the `MyImplClass` property explicitly states that `MyImplClass` implements `IMyInterface`.

The example shown here should give you some idea of what you can do with the `implements` keyword. COM programmers will find that this syntax presents additional uses, but the code I have shown here should give you some sense of how the word is used and of what you can do with it. The key point of this section is that the `implements` keyword allows you to use aggregation instead of a form of pseudo multiple inheritance when implementing an interface.

Summary

Delphi 4 provides many new IDE features and several important extensions to the Object Pascal language. In this chapter, you learned about the following:

- Dockable toolbars
- Dockable windows
- The Project Manager
- The Code Explorer
- Dynamic arrays
- Method overloading
- The new `implements` keyword

CHAPTER 3

Polymorphism

Please refer to the CD-ROM for the entire chapter.

This chapter covers the fundamental, but often misunderstood, subject of polymorphism. If you use object-oriented programming (OOP) but skip polymorphism, you miss out on a key tool that yields robust, flexible architectures.

You don't need to understand polymorphism or much about objects to program in Delphi. However, if you want to be an expert Delphi programmer and want to create components, you should master this material.

In this chapter, I take you through several fairly simple programs designed to illustrate key aspects of polymorphism. By the time you're done, you should understand why the simple ability to assign a child object to a parent object is one of the most important features of the entire Object Pascal language.

CHAPTER 4

Exception Handling

Please refer to the CD-ROM for the entire chapter.

In this chapter, you learn how to add error handling to your programs. You do so almost fentirely through a mechanism called *exceptions*.

In particular, the following subjects are covered:

- Exception-handling theory
- Basic exception classes
- `try..except` blocks
- Raising and reraising exceptions
- Creating your own exception classes
- Saving error strings in resources and retrieving them with `LoadString`
- Internationalizing your program with string tables
- Using the `try..finally` blocks to ensure that code is executed even after an exception occurs
- Overriding the default exception handler

To a large degree, Delphi and the VCL allow you to write programs that almost entirely ignore the subject of error checking. This is possible because exceptions are built into most classes and standalone routines and will be raised automatically whenever something goes wrong. Furthermore, your entire program is automatically wrapped inside a `try..except` block. Professional programmers, however, will want to go beyond even this level of safety and add additional error checking to their code, or else change the default error handling performed by Delphi. Also, your programs might need to raise their own errors, so you will need to add and raise new exception classes.

Delphi does a great job of automatically surfacing exceptions in your Object Pascal code. As far as Delphi programmers are concerned, most exceptions seem to occur automatically without your having to do anything.

In general, the subject of exceptions is not a complicated one. If you are new to this subject, you may have to play with the technology for a bit to get the hang of it, but overall, it is not a difficult subject. Furthermore, I believe exceptions are the correct model for reporting errors in any application. Don't listen to people who complain about some aspect of exceptions. This tool is the right one. And because exceptions play such a big role in all VCL programs, you should have a good understanding of this topic.

## CHAPTER 5

Threads

Please refer to the CD-ROM for the entire chapter.

This chapter is about advanced Windows 95/98 and Windows NT programming. It is a gateway to the upper echelons of Windows programming and introduces you to some of the most powerful capabilities of Win32.

In particular, this chapter covers the following:

- The basics of the Win32 architecture
- Processes
- Threads
- Critical sections
- Mutexes
- The VCL TThread object
- Thread priorities
- Open queries inside a thread
- VCL thread-safe objects

All these advanced subjects are entirely Windows 95/98 and Windows NT specific. The programs included in this chapter will not run under Windows 3.1 no matter how you dice or slice them.

My goal is to isolate some of the most important aspects of advanced Windows programming and introduce you to them in clear language so you can use them in your applications. I present five different programs in this chapter, each designed to show off a key feature related to threads and multitasking.

I have used the word *advanced* in this overview several times, but you will find that most of the code in this chapter is easy to use. I have sought to show you simple ways to get at some of the most powerful features in the Windows operating system. I would need another 500 or 600 pages to cover these subjects in depth, but the material you find here will get you started with these invaluable technologies. In fact, you will find plenty of information in this lengthy chapter to enable you to incorporate threading into your own programs.

I want to thank Jeff Cottingham, who added valuable sections to this chapter on using databases and threads and on executing graphics code in threads. All the sections of this chapter that apply to those subjects were written by him.

Creating Components

IN THIS PART

Creating Components: Part I

CHAPTER 6

This chapter and the next cover building components. Components are one of the most important developments in contemporary programming, and no environment on the market makes them easier or more efficient to use or create than Delphi.

You'll build three types of components in this chapter:

- Descendants that change default settings in existing components
- Descendants that add features to existing components
- Compound components made up of several different components

This chapter presents material on learning how to build visual components, and the next chapter explores how to build several generally useful components and how to convert them into ActiveX controls. You will also see some nonvisual components in the next chapter. Nonvisual components descend directly from TComponent and appear on the form only at design time.

More specifically, the components built in this chapter fall into two categories:

- The first group is a set of TEdit, TLabel, and TPanel descendants that show how to change default colors, captions, and fonts.
- Compound components that consist of multiple inherited or aggregated components make up the second category. This section of the chapter covers building components that consist of several different child components; that is, it shows how to group components together to form new components. The specific example included with this book shows a panel that comes with two radio buttons.

As a bonus, I throw in a truly useful component that combines a label and an edit control that work together as a single unit. This component, presented at the end of the chapter, is used in several other places throughout this book. In the next chapter, I'll develop other useful controls such a nonvisual component that knows how to iterate through subdirectories. You can use it to build programs that search for files, delete all files with a certain extension, and so on.

Components are one of the most important topics in Delphi programming. If you don't understand and use components, you are missing out on one of Delphi's best features. This chapter is designed to get you up and running and to go further by teaching you a few of the nontrivial subtleties involved in this topic. In the next chapter, you will take the subject further by looking at several advanced components.

Component Theory

Delphi components have three outstanding strengths:

- They are native components, built in Delphi's language. This means that you can write, debug, and test your components from inside standard Delphi programs. In short, learning to dig in and really write your own Delphi component is much easier than trying to understand and write your own ActiveX controls. Wizards can make creating an ActiveX control fairly easy, but actually understanding the technology is extremely difficult.

- Delphi components are fully object-oriented, which means you can easily change or enhance existing components by creating descendant objects.

- They are small, fast, and light, and can be linked directly into your executables. ActiveX controls, on the other hand, tend to be bulky and slow, and they cannot be linked directly into your program but must be distributed separately.

Few people would claim that VBXs weren't groundbreaking, that ActiveX controls aren't going to be very important, or that COM is not an enormously promising architecture. However, Delphi components are relatively easy to create and come in light, easy-to-use packages. You can create Delphi components that do nearly anything, from serial communications to database links to multimedia. This capability gives Delphi a big advantage over other visual tools that force you to move to C++ or else use very abstract, highly generalized tools if you want to build components.

> **NOTE**
>
> Most publicly available components cost in the range of $50 to $150, though many good ones are given away for free. Some of these tools encapsulate functionality that might cost tens of thousands of dollars to produce in-house. For instance, a good communication library might take a year to build. However, if a company can sell this tool in volume, it can afford to charge $100 or $200 for the same product. That's a real bargain. And most of these tools are easy to use. Building components is a great way for relatively small third-party companies to make money, and buying components is a great way to save time on big projects. These groundbreaking tools are changing everything about the way programs are constructed.

Delphi components are flexible tools easily built by anyone who knows OOP and the Delphi language. In this book and its CD, you'll find explanations detailing all the prerequisite knowledge component builders need, from a description of Delphi itself, through a description of its language, and on to an overview of its implementation of OOP. From this foundation, you can easily begin building your own components.

Creating Descendants of an Existing Component

In this section, you will see how to create a series of custom TEdit, TPanel, and TLabel controls. The changes made to the standard TEdit and TLabel components involve tweaking their colors, as well as their fonts' colors, names, sizes, and styles. The goal is to show how to create a suite of custom controls that you can place on the Component Palette and use for special effects, or to define the look and feel of a certain set of applications belonging to a particular department or company.

Creating a Simple Component

When tackling a new subject, starting with one simple example is best; then you can move on to one with a larger number of objects. In Listing 6.1, you find the code for a first version of a unit that will hold the descendants of TEdit, TPanel, and TLabel controls. Scan through it and check out its basic structure, and then I will briefly discuss how to use the component editor to put it together. Listing 6.2 shows a sample program designed to test your new component.

LISTING 6.1   A SIMPLE COMPONENT DESCENDING FROM TEdit

```
//////////////////////////////////////
// Purpose: First example of how to create a component
// Project: Unleash.dpk
// Copyright  1998 by Charlie Calvert
//
unit UnleashedControlsA;

interface

uses
  SysUtils, WinTypes, WinProcs,
  Messages, Classes, Graphics,
  Controls, Forms, Dialogs,
  StdCtrls;

type
```

```
TCCSmallEditA = class(TEdit)
private
  { Private declarations }
protected
  { Protected declarations }
public
  { Public declarations }
  constructor Create(AOwner: TComponent); override;
published
  { Published declarations }
end;

procedure Register;

implementation

constructor TCCSmallEditA.Create(AOwner: TComponent);
begin
  inherited Create(AOwner);
  Color := clBlue;
  Font.Color := clYellow;
  Font.Name := 'Times New Roman';
  Font.Size := 12;
  Font.Style := [fsBold];
end;

procedure Register;
begin
  RegisterComponents('Unleash', [TCCSmallEditA]);
end;

end.
```

LISTING 6.2 THE MAIN FORM FOR THE TestEds1 PROGRAM SERVES AS A TEST BED FOR THE UNLEASH1 UNIT

```
//////////////////////////////////////
// Purpose: Test TCCSmallEditA control
// Project: TestUnleashedA.dpr
// Copyright  1998 by Charlie Calvert
//
unit Main;

interface

uses
  Windows, Messages, SysUtils,
  Classes, Graphics, Controls,
  Forms, Dialogs, StdCtrls;
```

continues

LISTING 6.2   CONTINUED

```
type
  TForm1 = class(TForm)
    RunTestBtn: TButton;
    procedure RunTestBtnClick(Sender: TObject);
    procedure FormResize(Sender: TObject);
  end;

var
  Form1: TForm1;

implementation

uses
  UnleashedControlsA;

{$R *.DFM}

procedure TForm1.RunTestBtnClick(Sender: TObject);
var
  MyEdit: TCCSmallEditA;
begin
  MyEdit := TCCSmallEditA.Create(Self);
  MyEdit.Parent := Self;
  MyEdit.Show;
end;

{-------------------------------------------------------------------
  This code can now be replaced by the new Delphi4 Anchors
  property.
-------------------------------------------------------------------}
procedure TForm1.FormResize(Sender: TObject);
var
  CaptionHeight: Integer;
begin
  CaptionHeight := GetSystemMetrics(SM_CYCaption);
  RunTestBtn.Left := 5;
  RunTestBtn.Top := Height - (RunTestBtn.Height + CaptionHeight + 10);
end;

end.
```

You can easily create this unit, test it, and compile it as a component that's merged in with the rest of the tools on the Component Palette. To get started, choose File, New and select Component from the first page of the Object Repository. Doing so causes the dialog shown in Figure 6.1 to appear.

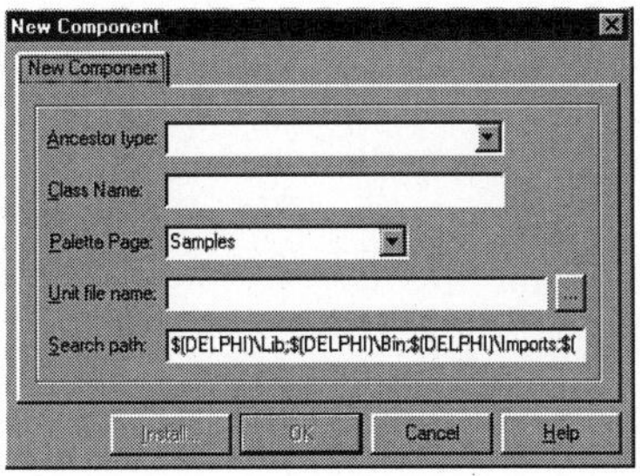

FIGURE 6.1

The dialog used by the Component Wizard.

The Component Wizard is a simple code generator of the type that any reader of this book who has made it this far should be able to write in an hour or two. All it does is ask you for the name of the component you want to create and to then select its parent from a drop-down list. After you have defined the type of component you want to create, you can select the page in the Component Palette where you want it to reside. To follow along with my first example, you should fill in the blanks with the following information:

```
Ancestor type: TEdit
Class Name: TCCSmallEdit
Palette Page: Unleash
```

For your efforts, the Component Wizard churns out the code in Listing 6.3, in which everything is boilerplate except for the first line of the class declaration, the global var declaration, and the parameters passed to the RegisterComponents method.

LISTING 6.3   THE STANDARD BOILERPLATE OUTPUT OF THE COMPONENT WIZARD

```
unit Unit2;

interface

uses
  SysUtils, WinTypes, WinProcs,
  Messages, Classes, Graphics,
  Controls, Forms, Dialogs,
  StdCtrls;

type
  TCCSmallEdit = class(TEdit)
  private
    { Private declarations }
  protected
    { Protected declarations }
  public
    { Public declarations }
```

continues

LISTING 6.3   CONTINUED

```
published
  { Published declarations }
end;

procedure Register;

implementation

procedure Register;
begin
  RegisterComponents('Unleash', [TCCSmallEdit]);
end;

end.
```

The Component Wizard starts by giving you a `uses` clause designed to cover most of the bases you are likely to touch in a standard component:

```
uses
  SysUtils, WinTypes, WinProcs,
  Messages, Classes, Graphics,
  Controls, Forms, Dialogs,
  StdCtrls;
```

The next step is to provide a basic class declaration, in which the name and parent are filled in with the choices you specified in the Component Wizard dialog. All this business about the scoping directives is just for your convenience, and you can delete any portion of it that you don't think you'll need.

```
type
  TCCSmallEdit = class(TEdit)
  private
    { Private declarations }
  protected
    { Protected declarations }
  public
    { Public declarations }
  published
    { Published declarations }
  end;
```

Two-Way Tools

Borland calls Delphi a *two-way tool*. Two-way tools allow you to edit code either visually or manually. In other words, you can make changes to your source either in a visual tool or in a text editor.

This capability is important because it means that nothing is hidden from you—no secret bits of information stored where you can't find it. If you want to change the name of your component, you can just use the text editor. No secret cookies are stored behind the scenes.

This concept is true of all facets of Delphi programming. All you need to compile the programs is the source code. Even the DFM files that define the forms can be saved and edited as source if you simply right-click on them.

A lot of functionality for an object is defined in the classes from which they descend. For instance, the TCCSmallEdit control derives a lot of capability from the TEdit control. However, the source for the TEdit controls ships with most versions of Delphi or can be purchased from Borland.

You won't find any big secrets here. With the exception of a few units that contain proprietary technology, all the source to the VCL is available, and it is all written in Object Pascal. For instance, all the source for Delphi's component technology is freely available.

The few units that don't ship with Delphi are generally obscure bits of the Client/Server version, such as some low-level CORBA technology or the Decision Cube code. Not too many people really want to see that code, and it wouldn't do them much good if they could see it.

By and large, all the code that you want to see is available. The code Inprise hides is either not yet ready to see the light of day, or else it is aimed at a small number of programmers who are prepared to pay large sums of money for it. The general-purpose code in the Standard and Pro versions of the product is, to my knowledge, all freely available.

Registering a Component

Before you can place a component on the Component Palette, you must first register it with the system:

```
procedure Register;
begin
  RegisterComponents('Unleash', [TCCSmallEdit]);
end;
```

Registering a class makes it known to the Delphi Component Palette when the unit is compiled into the Delphi component library. The Register procedure has no impact on programs compiled with this unit. Unless your program calls the Register procedure (which it should *never* do), the code for the Register procedure will never even appear in your executable.

After using the Component Wizard, you should save the project. Proceed as you normally would by creating a directory for the project and saving `Main.pas` and `TestUnleashedA.dpr` inside it. The new unit that you created, however, should not be saved into the same directory but should be placed in the `Units` directory where `CodeBox.pas` is stored. This code is now going to come into play as part of Delphi itself, and as such, you want a single path that leads to all related files of this type. If you have all your components in different subdirectories, you will end up with a source path that is long and unwieldy.

However, I'm getting a bit ahead of myself, as I don't want you to place this component on the Component Palette quite yet. Instead, just add the units to your main form's `uses` clause. It's best not to open the Project Manager and make this class a part of your project. If you add the class to your project, the path to it becomes hard-coded into your DPR file, which may cause problems later.

Changing the Default Behavior of a Component

The goal of this project is to give a component of type `TEdit` a new set of default behaviors so that it starts out with certain colors and certain fonts. To do so, you need to override the `Create` method and change the fonts inside it. To declare the method, write the following in your class declaration:

```
TCCSmallEdit = class(TEdit)
public
  constructor Create(AOwner: TComponent); override;
end;
```

Notice that in the preceding declaration I have removed the `private`, `published`, and `protected` directives created by the Component Wizard. This is neither here nor there, and I do it just to keep the amount of code you need to look at as small as possible.

The `Create` method for `TCCSmallEdit` is declared as `public`. If you think about the process of creating a component dynamically, you will see in a moment that the `Create` method has to be `public`. This is one method that must be exposed.

`Create` is passed a single parameter of type `TComponent`, which is a base class that encapsulates the minimum functionality needed to be an owner of another component. In particular, whatever form you place a component on usually will be the owner of that component. However, the owner does not have to be a form. For instance, it could be a `TPanel`. In fact, any control in the VCL has the built-in capability to act properly as the owner of another control. Finally, use the `override` directive to specify that this is a virtual method that you want to redefine.

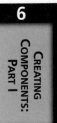

The implementation of the `Create` method is simple:

```
constructor TCCSmallEdit.Create(AOwner: TComponent);
begin
  inherited Create(AOwner);
  Color := clBlue;
  Font.Color := clYellow;
  Font.Name := 'Times New Roman';
  Font.Size := 12;
  Font.Style := [fsBold];
end;
```

The code first calls `Create`, passing in the variable `AOwner`. As I stated previously, the owner of a component will often, though not always, be the form on which the component is to be displayed. In other words, the user will drop the component onto a form, and that form will become the owner of the component. In such a case, `AOwner` is a variable that points to the form. The VCL uses it to initialize the `Owner` property, which is one of the fields of all components.

The owner of a control is responsible for destroying the control. This process takes place when the owner itself is being destroyed. If you dispose of a control yourself, be sure to set it to `nil`, or else you will risk raising an exception when the control's owner tries to destroy it. Most of the time, however, you do not need to worry about destroying the control; you can just let the owner take over that job.

The next step is to define the color and font that you want to use, with `Font.Style` defined as follows:

```
TFontStyle = (fsBold, fsItalic, fsUnderline, fsStrikeOut);
TFontStyles = set of TFontStyle;
```

If you want to add the underline and bold style to the text in the edit control, write the following:

```
Font.Style := [fsBold, fsUnderline];
```

If you want to then add the italic style at runtime, write

```
Font.Style := Font.Style + [fsItalic];
```

in which the plus symbol (+) is used as a set operator for unions.

At this stage, the code is ready to go on the Component Palette. However, most of the time when you write components, you should test them first to see whether they work.

Creating and Testing a Component Dynamically

To test the new class, drop a button on the program's main form and create an `OnClick` handler:

```
procedure TForm1.Button1Click(Sender: TObject);
var
  MyEdit: TCCSmallEdit;
begin
  MyEdit := TCCSmallEdit.Create(Self);
  MyEdit.Parent := Self;
  MyEdit.Show;
end;
```

This code creates the component and shows it on the main form. Self, of course, is the way that TForm1 refers to itself from inside one of its own methods. The owner of the new component is Form1, which will be responsible for disposing of the component when finished with it. As I mentioned earlier, this process happens automatically. You never need to worry about disposing of a visible component shown on a form.

The parent of the component is also Form1. The Parent variable is used by Windows when it is trying to decide how to display the form on the screen. If you place a panel on a form and drop a button on the panel, the owner of that button is the form, but the parent is the panel. Ownership determines when and how the component is deallocated, and parental relationships determine where and how the component is displayed. Ownership is fundamentally a Delphi issue, whereas parental relationships are primarily a concern of Windows.

I want to emphasize that this process of creating a control dynamically is useful primarily when you are testing your controls. In particular, it helps prevent you from adding a buggy, access-violation-creating component to the Component Palette. If you put a really unstable component on the Component Palette, you can destabilize the whole Delphi environment. In the next section, I will show you how to place a component on the Component Palette so that it acts like a normal control of the kind that ships with Delphi.

Packages: Placing a Component on the Component Palette

After you run the program and test the component, the next step is to put it on the Component Palette. This process involves working with something called a package. In the next section, I will describe packages and then tell you the simple steps required to build your own packages.

What Is a Package?

In Delphi 1 and 2, all the components that were displayed on the Component Palette were kept in one large library called COMBLIB.DCL or CMPLIB32.DCL. This system has been abandoned in favor of a more flexible but also more complex system called *packages*.

A package is a special kind of DLL that can contain one or more components, objects, or functions. Its primary benefit is to allow you to wrap up components in a library and share them with multiple programs. Packages emerged out of the Object Pascal team's desire to create a good way to store objects in a DLL. During development, they began to take on a larger and more complex role.

A package has a .bpl extension. As a rule, you should place packages in a directory that is on your path, such as the Windows/System or Winnt/System32 directory. Packages can reduce the size of the average Delphi program from 400 to 500KB to under 25KB. Of course, all that missing weight has to go somewhere, and at least one core VCL package is over a megabyte in size. However, that file can be used by multiple executables. As result, the sum total of your files is smaller than if you used normal executables.

Delphi gives you the choice to use packages or to build normal executables. By default, you create normal executables. You can choose Project, Options, Packages to decide whether you want to include packages with any particular executable. As a rule, you should always choose to build your projects with packages because doing so saves disk space. However, packages are somewhat more difficult to work with and to distribute than simple executables. As a result, you might choose not to use them under certain circumstances, particularly if you are new to Delphi.

If you want to place a component on the Component Palette, you must create a package. All the Delphi components shown on the Component Palette are stored in packages. The components stored on the Component Palette can be linked directly into your programs. Just because the Component Palette uses packages, that doesn't mean your executable has to use them. In particular, notice the DCU files in the Delphi LIB directory. These DCU files contain components that can be linked directly into your program.

The most important package is called VCL40.BPL. You can't do much with Delphi without using that package because it contains all the core components. Most of the other packages are optional. In particular, if you are not doing database programming, then you might select Components, Install Components from the Delphi menu and remove the database and quick report components. The IDE loads more quickly and has a smaller footprint without them installed.

> **NOTE**
>
> You can rebuild most of the components used by the IDE, but Delphi is designed so that you cannot rebuild VCL40.BPL. One or two key files that are needed to compile it are not available to you, primarily because Borland does not want you to be able to recompile VCL40. All Delphi programs rely on this file, so letting programmers create their own versions of it is simply not an option. Doing so would risk potentially destabilizing all the Delphi programs on a particular system. In such a case, Borland would likely take the blame, even though it did not create the problem.
>
> None of the missing files from VCL40 have any significant functionality in them. This means you could create your own instance of some package that looks and acts almost exactly like VCL40, but you must give it another name. You do not have the right to create a file called VCL40.BPL. However, if you want to rebuild the key parts of the VCL for your own purposes, you can do so by creating a package that is very similar to VCL40, as long as it does not have the same name.

You can create packages that contain discreet sets of functionality. For instance, if you create a suite of multimedia components, putting them in their own package would make sense. Clever programmers can create small packages that contain only the components used by their program. Furthermore, you can update a particular program's behavior simply by creating a new version of one of your packages.

You can browse the contents of existing installed Delphi packages. To do so, choose Components, Install Packages from the Delphi menu. Select the Components button when a package you are interested in is highlighted. A list of the components in that package will be displayed in a dialog. Obviously, you can also use the Install Packages menu selection to add or remove existing packages from Delphi. You can also temporarily disable a particular package by removing the check from the box at the left of the package name.

I should mention one final benefit of using packages at least briefly. If you are working over the Internet, you can supply your customers with a few key VCL packages, such as VCL40.BPL. If you then build your programs or ActiveForms with packages, they will be very small and can be sent over the Internet in just a few seconds.

Creating Packages

You can create a package by choosing Components, Install Components and then selecting the Into New Component page. Now you can browse across your hard drive for the UnleashedControlsA.pas file and allow Delphi to build the package for you automatically in the background. However, I am going to recommend that you use a second, somewhat more complex technique because it allows you to have better control over the process of creating a package.

To get started with this second technique, choose File, New, Package from the Delphi menu. This action will bring up the Package Editor and create a new file called Package1.dpk, shown in Listing 6.4 and Figure 6.2. Save this package with the name Unleash.dpk in the Units directory. (If you don't want to overwrite the version of Unleash.dpk that I supply, then call the package Unleash1.dpk or some other name of your choosing.) To view the source of the package, right-click on the word Contains in the Package Editor and choose View Source from the menu.

FIGURE 6.2

The Delphi Package Editor with one file called UnleashedControl-sA.pas *added to it.*

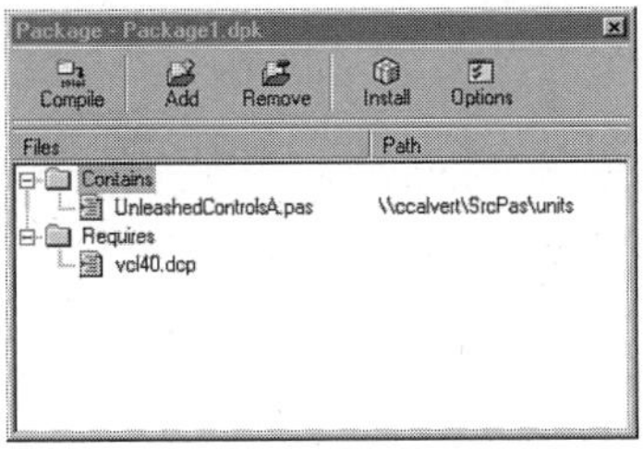

To add a unit to the package, you can manually edit the uses clause yourself, or else you can click on the Add button at the top of the Package Editor. If you click on the Add button, you will be prompted to browse for the files you want to include in the package. You should also choose Tools, Environment Options, Library and make sure the Units directory where UnleashedControlsA.pas is stored has been added to your Library Path.

LISTING 6.4 A SIMPLE DELPHI PACKAGE CONTAINING THE TCCSmallEditA COMPONENT IN THE UNIT CALLED UnleashedControlsA.pas

```
package Package1;

{$R *.RES}
{$ALIGN ON}
{$ASSERTIONS ON}
{$BOOLEVAL OFF}
{$DEBUGINFO ON}
{$EXTENDEDSYNTAX ON}
```

continues

LISTING 6.4   CONTINUED

```
{$IMPORTEDDATA ON}
{$IOCHECKS ON}
{$LOCALSYMBOLS ON}
{$LONGSTRINGS ON}
{$OPENSTRINGS ON}
{$OPTIMIZATION ON}
{$OVERFLOWCHECKS OFF}
{$RANGECHECKS OFF}
{$REFERENCEINFO ON}
{$SAFEDIVIDE OFF}
{$STACKFRAMES OFF}
{$TYPEDADDRESS OFF}
{$VARSTRINGCHECKS ON}
{$WRITEABLECONST ON}
{$MINENUMSIZE 1}
{$IMAGEBASE $00400000}
{$IMPLICITBUILD OFF}

requires
  vcl40;

contains
  UnleashedControlsA in 'UnleashedControlsA.pas';

end.
```

After you have created a package and added the units that contain your components to it, then you can simply click the Compile and Install buttons at the top of the Package Editor to install your component on the Component Palette.

In Chapter 7 in the section "Creating Icons for Components," I will explain how to make the DCR files that contain the bitmaps displayed in the Component Palette. For now, all you need to know is that a DCR file is a special kind of resource and that you can add these DCR files directly to a package file or to a unit that contains your component source. The following example shows a package with several DCR files added at the top:

```
package Unleash;

{$R *.RES}
{$R 'Fileiter.dcr'}
{$R 'Gradient.dcr'}
{$R 'Ftp1.dcr'}
```

You can add as many units and packages to a DPK file as you want. When you want to edit an existing DPK file, just choose File, Open and browse for files with a `.dpk` extension.

You can keep the Package Editor open at the same time as you have another project open. If the `UnleashedControlsA.pas` file is linked into your current project, any changes you make to the control will be reflected in your project the first time you compile your project. However, these changes will not make it into the component you use at design time until you rebuild the package that contains the component. For instance, if you add a new published property to a component, you can use it in the code of your program right away, but it won't show up in The Object Inspector until you rebuild the package that contains it.

Some packages use other packages. For instance, the `TCCSmallEdit` control descends from the `TEdit` control, which is stored in `VCL40.BPL`. This means that the `Unleash.dpk` file requires that `VCL40.BPL` be used so that it will know how to use `TEdit` controls. Because of this dependency, a `requires` clause appears in your package:

```
requires
  vcl40,
  inet40,
  VCLX40;
```

In wrapping up this subject, let me just add that many programmers are confused by packages when they first see them. I suggest doing whatever you can to alleviate this situation. Build your own packages, experiment with packages, spend as much time in the Package Editor as you possibly can. Packages are a powerful tool, but you can't use them unless you understand them. I've explained how they work in the preceding pages, but to really understand them, you have to get your hands dirty creating your own packages. My suggestion is that you start doing so immediately and dedicate some significant periods of time to becoming familiar with this whole process.

NOTE

Delphi 2 and the 16-bit version of Delphi handle components quite differently than do Delphi 4 and Delphi 3. In particular, they don't support packages. In this note, I include a brief description of working with the old 16-bit code or Delphi 2 to install a component.

To get started, select Components, Install, and click the Add button. Browse through the directories until you find the UNLEASH1 unit, click OK, and then close the Install Components dialog by clicking OK. At this point, a project called CMPLIB32.DPR is compiled. This project creates a huge DLL called CMPLIB32.DCL, which contains all the components in the Component Palette, all the component and Property Editors associated with those components, the form designer part of the IDE, the experts, and other support modules.

continues

After CMPLIB32.DCL finishes recompiling, you can start a new project, turn to the newly created Unleash page, and drop your new component onto a form. It will have a blue background, default to Times New Roman, and have its font style set to bold and its font color to yellow. Notice that all the properties of TEdit have been inherited by TCCSmallEdit. That's OOP in action.

You can save the CMPLIB32.DPR file used during compilation of CMPLIB32.DCL to disk if you choose Tools, Project, Library, Options, Save Library Source Code. After choosing this option and recompiling CMPLIB32.DCL, you can go to the \DELPHI\BIN directory and view your copy of CMPLIB32.DPR.

After you have created a component and installed it, you can create a new program and drop your component on its main form. If you do so, you will find that you have created your own component that works exactly like the components that come preinstalled with Delphi. In the rest of this chapter, I will dig further into the subject of components, explaining exactly how you can access all their most important features.

Extending the `Unleash` Unit

The next step is to expand the Unleash package so that it contains more controls. The goal is to give you lots of experience with this subject so that you can start to see all the possibilities offered by components, their properties and events, and the various editors that support them.

It's time now to create a second version of the Unleash unit, containing a new edit control, along with two labels and two panels. The additional edits and labels show how quickly you can build on an idea or object when you understand where you're headed. One of the panels shows how you can get rid of the annoying label that always shows up in the middle of a panel, and the other shows how you can create a single component that contains other components. Specifically, it shows how to create a panel that already comes equipped with two radio buttons.

The code for the new version of the UnleashControls unit is shown in Listing 6.5, and its test bed appears in Listing 6.6. If you have two units on your system, both of which contain instances of TCCSmallEdit, you probably should uninstall the first instance before trying to install the new instance. Or, you can do as I have done here, and name one version of the control TCCSmallEditA and the second version TCCSmallEdit. If you don't rename the controls, you may have two files on your system, one called UnleashedControlsA.pas and the second called UnleashedControls.pas. Both might contain an instance of TCCSmallEdit. Under such circumstances, you have to choose Component, Install, Remove to remove the first version of TCCSmallEdit before replacing it with a second version. If you have only one version of TCCSmallEdit, and you just want to update it, you don't need to remove the first instance before installing the updated instance.

In the preceding paragraph, you also can see why I call my control TCCSmallEdit rather than simply TSmallEdit. The problem is that many developers are creating controls, and the chance of a name collision is fairly large. If you append your initials before the name of each control you create, then the chance of a name collision becomes much smaller. This system is not perfect, and it is not guaranteed to work, but it certainly improves the odds of things working out correctly.

> **NOTE**
>
> I work in the Developer Relations group at Borland. As a result, lots of people send me controls that they want Borland to promote. Sometimes these people send me controls that have the same names as existing controls on the Delphi Component Palette. Because I'm often showing the product in front of audiences, I must have a complete version of the original Delphi component set on my system at all times, and I can't remove an existing built-in Delphi component and replace it with a third-party control. If the developers of the third-party controls had followed the simple rule I show here, then it is unlikely that name collisions would have occurred, and I could have better evaluated their products and maybe even shown them to the public.
>
> Admittedly, my case is an extreme situation, but the same problem might arise for these people everywhere they go when they try to show their components. Furthermore, if their control happened to conflict with the name of a popular component from a big shop such as TurboPower, then once again, it might not fit in very well on a large number of systems. The system of prefacing your component name with the initials of a person or company is not ideal, but it is one you should probably employ in your own work.

LISTING 6.5 THE SECOND VERSION OF THE UNLEASHEDCONTROLS UNIT CONTAINS A PANEL THAT COMES EQUIPPED WITH TWO RADIO BUTTONS

```
//////////////////////////////////////
// Purpose: Examples of how to create simple components
// Project: Unleash.dpk
// Copyright  1998 by Charlie Calvert
//
unit UnleashedControls;

{-----------------------------------------------------------------
  This file contains a bunch of very simple minded components. Though
  some of them are useful, the intent of this file is just to provide
  examples used to teach how to build components.

  Since I use a radio button as a subcomponent in one of these
  examples, I must register the TRadioButton component in the
  initialization section for this unit.
-----------------------------------------------------------------}
interface

uses
  SysUtils, WinTypes, WinProcs,
  Messages, Classes, Graphics,
  Controls, Forms, Dialogs,
  StdCtrls, ExtCtrls;

const
  HotKeyF_Alt = $04;

type
  TCCSmallEdit = class(TEdit)
  public
    constructor Create(AOwner: TComponent); override;
  end;

  TCCBigEdit = class(TCCSmallEdit)
  public
    constructor Create(AOwner: TComponent); override;
  end;

  TCCSmallLabel = class(TLabel)
  public
    constructor Create(AOwner: TComponent); override;
  end;

  TCCBigLabel = class(TCCSmallLabel)
  public
```

6

```pascal
    constructor Create(AOwner: TComponent); override;
  end;

  TCCKeyCheckBox = class(TCheckBox)
  protected
    procedure wmGetDlgCode(var Msg: TMessage);
      message wm_GetDlgCode;
  published
    property OnKeyDown;
  end;

  TCCEmptyPanel = class(TPanel)
  public
    constructor Create(AOwner: TComponent); override;
  published
    property OnKeyDown;
  end;

  { This object makes a panel act like a button }
  TCCMousePanel = class(TCCEmptyPanel)
  private
    function XYWithinClient(P: TSmallPoint): Boolean;
  protected
    procedure wmMouseDown(var Msg: TWMMouse);
      message wm_LButtonDown;
    procedure wmMouseUp(var Msg: TWMMouse);
      message wm_LButtonUp;
{    procedure wmKeyDown(var MsgL: TWMKey);
      message wm_KeyDown; }
  public
    constructor Create(AOwner: TComponent); override;
  end;

  TCCLabelPanel = class(TCCEmptyPanel)
  private
    FLabel: TLabel;
    FPanel: TPanel;
    function GetLabelStr: string;
    procedure SetLabelStr(S: string);
  protected
    procedure CMTextChanged(var Message: TMessage);
      message CM_TEXTCHANGED;
  public
    constructor Create(AOwner: TComponent); override;
  published
    property LabelStr: string read GetLabelStr write SetLabelStr;
  end;

  TCCRadio2Panel = class(TCCEmptyPanel)
  private
```

continues

LISTING 6.5   CONTINUED

```
    FRadio1: TRadiobutton;
    FRadio2: TRadioButton;
    function GetRadio1Caption: string;
    function GetRadio2Caption: string;
    procedure SetRadio1Caption(const Value: string);
    procedure SetRadio2Caption(const Value: string);
  protected
    procedure WmSize(var Message: TMessage); message wm_Size;
  public
    constructor Create(AOwner: TComponent); override;
    property Radio1: TRadioButton read FRadio1;
    property Radio2: TRadioButton read FRadio2;
  published
    property Radio1Caption: string
      read GetRadio1Caption write SetRadio1Caption;
    property Radio2Caption: string
      read GetRadio2Caption write SetRadio2Caption;
  end;

procedure Register;

implementation

constructor TCCSmallEdit.Create(AOwner: TComponent);
begin
  inherited Create(AOwner);
  Color := clBlue;
  Font.Color := clYellow;
  Font.Name := 'Times New Roman';
  Font.Size := 12;
  Font.Style := [fsBold];
end;

constructor TCCBigEdit.Create(AOwner: TComponent);
begin
  inherited Create(AOwner);
  Font.Size := 24;
end;

constructor TCCSmallLabel.Create(AOwner: TComponent);
begin
  inherited Create(AOwner);
  Color := clBlue;
  Font.Color := clYellow;
  Font.Name := 'Times New Roman';
  Font.Size := 12;
  Font.Style := [fsBold];
end;
```

Creating Components: Part I

CHAPTER 6

101

6

CREATING
COMPONENTS:
PART I

```pascal
constructor TCCBigLabel.Create(AOwner: TComponent);
begin
  inherited Create(AOwner);
  Font.Size := 24;
end;

procedure TCCKeyCheckBox.wmGetDlgCode(var Msg: TMessage);
begin
  Msg.Result := DLGC_WantArrows;
end;

constructor TCCEmptyPanel.Create(AOwner: TComponent);
begin
  inherited Create(AOwner);
  Caption := ' ';
end;

{ --- TMousePanel --- }

constructor TCCMousePanel.Create(AOwner: TComponent);
begin
  inherited Create(AOwner);
  BevelInner := bvRaised;
  BevelWidth := 2;
end;

{procedure TMousePanel.wmKeyDown(var MsgL: TWMKey);
var
  B: Integer;
begin
  B := SendMessage(Handle, wm_GetHotKey, 0, 0);
  if HiWord(B) = HotKeyF_Alt then
    ShowMessage('hi');
end; }

procedure TCCMousePanel.wmMouseDown(var Msg: TWMMouse);
begin
  BevelInner := bvLowered;
  SetCapture(Handle);
end;

function TCCMousePanel.XYWithinClient(P: TSmallPoint): Boolean;
begin
  Result := (P.X < ClientWidth) and (P.Y < ClientHeight);
end;

procedure TCCMousePanel.wmMouseUp(var Msg: TWMMouse);
var
 AOnClick: TNotifyEvent;
begin
```

continues

LISTING 6.5   CONTINUED

```
  BevelInner := bvRaised;
  ReleaseCapture;
  AOnClick := OnClick;
  if Assigned(AOnClick) then
    if XYWithinClient(Msg.Pos) then
      OnClick(Self);
end;

{ --- TLabelPanel --- }

constructor TCCLabelPanel.Create(AOwner: TComponent);
const
  ATop = 4;
  Aleft = 5;
  ABevelWidth = 2;
begin
  inherited Create(AOwner);

  ParentFont := False;
  BevelInner := bvRaised;
  BevelWidth := ABevelWidth;

  FLabel := TLabel.Create(Self);
  FLabel.Parent := Self;
  FLabel.ParentFont := False;
  FLabel.Left := ALeft;
  FLabel.Top := ATop;
  Flabel.Caption := 'ALabel';
  FLabel.Width := 50;
  FLabel.Show;

  FPanel := TPanel.Create(Self);
  FPanel.Parent := Self;
  FPanel.Top := ATop;
  FPanel.BevelInner := bvRaised;
  FPanel.BevelWidth := ABevelWidth div 2;
  FPanel.Height := Height - (2 * ATop);
  FPanel.Left := FLabel.Width + (FPanel.BevelWidth);
  FPanel.Width := Width - FPanel.Left - (FPanel.BevelWidth * 4);
  Caption := 'FPanel';
  FPanel.ParentFont := False;
  FPanel.Show;
end;

procedure TCCLabelPanel.CMTextChanged(var Message: TMessage);
begin
  inherited;
  FPanel.Caption := Caption;
end;
```

```pascal
function TCCLabelPanel.GetLabelStr: string;
begin
  Result := FLabel.Caption;
end;

procedure TCCLabelPanel.SetLabelStr(S: string);
var
  Extent: TSize;
  DC: HDC;
  P: PChar;
begin
  FLabel.Caption := S;
  DC := GetDC(Handle);
  GetMem(P, Length(S) + 1);
  StrPCopy(P, S);
  GetTextExtentPoint(DC, P, StrLen(P), Extent);
  FPanel.Left := Extent.cx;
  FPanel.Width := Width - FPanel.Left - (BevelWidth * 2);
  ReleaseDC(Handle, DC);
  Font.Color := Color;
  FreeMem(P, Length(S) + 1);
end;

{ --- TCCRadio2Panel ---}

constructor TCCRadio2Panel.Create(AOwner: TComponent);
begin
  inherited Create(AOwner);
  Width := 175;
  Height := 60;

  FRadio1 := TRadioButton.Create(Self);
  FRadio1.Parent := Self;
  FRadio1.Caption := 'Radio1';
  FRadio1.Left := 20;
  FRadio1.Top := 10;
  FRadio1.Show;

  FRadio2 := TRadioButton.Create(Self);
  FRadio2.Parent := Self;
  FRadio2.Caption := 'Radio2';
  FRadio2.Left := 20;
  FRadio2.Top := 32;
  FRadio2.Show;

end;

function TCCRadio2Panel.GetRadio1Caption: string;
begin
  Result := Radio1.Caption;
```

continues

LISTING 6.5   CONTINUED

```
end;

function TCCRadio2Panel.GetRadio2Caption: string;
begin
  Result := Radio2.Caption;
end;

procedure TCCRadio2Panel.SetRadio1Caption(const Value: string);
begin
  Radio1.Caption := Value;
end;

procedure TCCRadio2Panel.SetRadio2Caption(const Value: string);
begin
  Radio2.Caption := Value;
end;

procedure TCCRadio2Panel.WmSize(var Message: TMessage);
begin
  inherited;
  FRadio1.Width := Width - (FRadio1.Left + 10);
  FRadio2.Width := Width - (FRadio2.Left + 10);
end;

procedure Register;
begin
  RegisterComponents('Unleash', [TCCSmallEdit, TCCBigEdit, TCCMousePanel,
    TCCSmallLabel, TCCBigLabel, TCCKeyCheckBox, TCCEmptyPanel,
    TCCRadio2Panel, TCCLabelPanel]);
end;

initialization
  RegisterClasses([TRadioButton]);
end.
```

LISTING 6.6   THE TEST BED FOR THE UnleashedControls UNIT

```
/////////////////////////////////////
// Purpose: Test components from the UnleashedControls unit
// Project: TestUnleashed.dpr
// Copyright  1998 by Charlie Calvert
//
unit Main;

interface

uses
  Windows, Messages, SysUtils,
```

Creating Components: Part I

CHAPTER 6

105

6

CREATING
COMPONENTS:
PART I

```
    Classes, Graphics, Controls,
    Forms, Dialogs, ExtCtrls,
    UnleashedControls, StdCtrls, ComCtrls,
    Menus;

type
  TForm1 = class(TForm)
    PageControl1: TPageControl;
    TabSheet1: TTabSheet;
    TabSheet2: TTabSheet;
    CCRadio2Panel1: TCCRadio2Panel;
    CCEmptyPanel1: TCCEmptyPanel;
    CCSmallLabel1: TCCSmallLabel;
    CCSmallEdit1: TCCSmallEdit;
    CCEmptyPanel2: TCCEmptyPanel;
    CCBigLabel1: TCCBigLabel;
    CCBigEdit1: TCCBigEdit;
    MainMenu1: TMainMenu;
    CreateControlsonTabSheet11: TMenuItem;
    procedure CreateControlsonTabSheet11Click(Sender: TObject);
    procedure CCRadio2Panel1Resize(Sender: TObject);
  private
    { Private declarations }
  public
    { Public declarations }
  end;

var
  Form1: TForm1;

implementation

{$R *.DFM}

{--------------------------------------------------------------------
  This method shows an example of how to test a component before you
  place it on the component palette. This is always a good idea, since
  you may have problems with your component that causes it to generate
  access violations. Since your component becomes part of Delphi
  itself access violations in the component can cause instability
  in the IDE. Hence it is often a good idea to test it like this
  first, before compiling it as a component.
--------------------------------------------------------------------}
procedure TForm1.CreateControlsonTabSheet11Click(Sender: TObject);
var
  MyEdit: TCCBigEdit;
  Radio2Panel: TCCRadio2Panel;
begin
```

continues

LISTING 6.6 CONTINUED

```
  MyEdit := TCCBigEdit.Create(Self);
  MyEdit.Parent := Tabsheet1;
  MyEdit.Text := 'Inheritance!';
  MyEdit.Left := 10;
  MyEdit.Top := 10;
  MyEdit.Width := 200;
  MyEdit.Show;

  Radio2Panel := TCCRadio2Panel.Create(Self);
  Radio2Panel.Parent := TabSheet1;
  Radio2Panel.Left := MyEdit.Left;
  Radio2Panel.Top := MyEdit.Height + MyEdit.Top + 5;
  Radio2Panel.Width := MyEdit.Width;
  Radio2Panel.Radio1Caption := 'Delphi';
  Radio2Panel.Radio2Caption := 'Unleashed';
  Radio2Panel.Radio1.Checked := True;
  Radio2Panel.BevelWidth := 3;
  Radio2Panel.Show;
end;

{ - - - - - - - - - - - - - - - - - - - - - - - - - - - - - - - - - - - - - - - - - - - - - - - - - - - - - - -
  I'm responding to this method just so you can see that OnResize
  events are being handled properly, even with the TCCRadio2Panel
  WM_SIZE handler, shown in UnleashedControls.pas. In particular,
  the progam should beep or bong once when started.
- - - - - - - - - - - - - - - - - - - - - - - - - - - - - - - - - - - - - - - - - - - - - - - - - - - - - - - - -}
procedure TForm1.CCRadio2Panel1Resize(Sender: TObject);
begin
  MessageBeep(0);
end;

end.
```

The TestUnleashed program shown here takes some of the key controls from the new
UnleashedControls.pas unit through their paces. It is very similar to the test bed that
you created for the UnleashedControlsA.pas unit, except that it is a bit more complex.

The TestUnleashed program has a page control on its main form. One page of this control contains a button that will allow you to dynamically create an instance of a component for testing, as explained in the section called "Creating Descendants of an Existing Component." The second page contains actual copies of the controls as they appear when dropped from the Component Palette. As a result, this program will not load properly unless you update the Unleash.dpk file to contain not only UnleashedControlsA.pas, but also UnleashedControls.pas.

The `TCCBigEdit` and `TCCEmptyPanel` Controls

When you've created a component that does something you like, you can easily create children of it. Class `TCCBigEdit` descends from `TCCSmallEdit`:

```
TCCBigEdit = class(TCCSmallEdit)
```

It inherits its font nearly unchanged from `TSmallEdit`, except that it sets `Font.Size` to 24, a nice hefty figure that helps the control live up to its name:

```
constructor TCCBigEdit.Create(AOwner: TComponent);
begin
  inherited Create(AOwner);
  Font.Size := 24;
end;
```

This elegant syntax is a good example of how OOP can save you time and trouble while still allowing you to write clear code.

The label controls shown in this code work in exactly the same way the edit controls do, except that they descend from `TLabel` rather than from `TEdit`. The `TCCEmptyPanel` component rectifies one of the petty issues that sometimes annoys me: Every time you put down a panel, it gets a caption. Most of the time, the first thing you do is delete the caption so you can place other controls on it without creating a mess.

Once again, you can change `TPanel` by overriding its constructor. This time, all you need to do is set the `Caption` property to an empty string:

```
constructor TCCEmptyPanel.Create(AOwner: TComponent);
begin
  inherited Create(AOwner);
  Caption := ' ';
end;
```

All these controls are trivial to create. That is, however, also their great virtue. After you understand what a component is and how to go about creating it, then you can easily start building up whole suites of your own components.

Creating Compound Components

The last new component in this version of the `Unleash` unit enables you to drop down a panel that comes equipped with two radio buttons. This makes a single control out of a set of components that are often combined. You could create other controls that contained three, four, or more radio buttons. Or you could even create a panel that would populate itself with a specific number of radio buttons.

The declaration for this new radio button is still fairly simple but considerably more complex than the declarations you have seen so far:

```
TCCRadio2Panel = class(TCCEmptyPanel)
private
  FRadio1: TRadioButton;
  FRadio2: TRadioButton;
  function GetRadio1Caption: string;
  function GetRadio2Caption: string;
  procedure SetRadio1Caption(const Value: string);
  procedure SetRadio2Caption(const Value: string);
protected
  procedure WmSize(var Message: TMessage); message wm_Size;
public
  constructor Create(AOwner: TComponent); override;
  property Radio1: TRadioButton read FRadio1;
  property Radio2: TRadioButton read FRadio2;
published
  property Radio1Caption: string
    read GetRadio1Caption write SetRadio1Caption;
  property Radio2Caption: string
    read GetRadio2Caption write SetRadio2Caption;
end;
```

I will explain the WmSize handler soon, and then after that, I will talk about the Radio1Caption and Radio2Caption properties. For now, I want to concentrate on the Radio1 and Radio2 properties.

The actual radio buttons themselves are declared as private data, and access to them is given by the Radio1 and Radio2 properties. This is the way that Delphi performs something called *aggregation*, which is an alternative to multiple inheritance. After declaring these two components as private data and exposing them as properties, you have essentially allowed the TPanel object to inherit the functionality of two radio controls. In other words, it now does everything that a panel does, such as having a border and bevel 3D look, plus everything that you can do with two radio buttons. For all intents and purposes, aggregation is the same thing as multiple inheritance, but it is cleaner and much less troublesome.

> **NOTE**
>
> For what it's worth, when I program in C++, I always use aggregation and never use multiple inheritance. That is literally true. As best I can recall, it has been over five years since I have declared a C++ object that used multiple inheritance, and I program in C++ as often as I program in Object Pascal, which is quite a bit.

Creating Components: Part I

CHAPTER 6

109

6

CREATING
COMPONENTS:
PART I

Modifying a property of these radio buttons doesn't require write access to the radio button property, so you don't need to add a Write clause. The following statement performs one read of RP.Radio1 and one write to the Caption property of that radio button:

```
RP.Radio1.Caption := 'hello'
```

You don't want write access to the radio button properties either because that would allow the user to assign them garbage (or nil). It's a different matter to give the user read and write action to the Caption property of the TRadioButton because that does no harm. But if the user assigns nil or garbage to Radio1 itself, then trouble could lie ahead.

The Create method for the Radio2Panel begins by setting the width and height of the panel:

```
constructor TCCRadio2Panel.Create(AOwner: TComponent);
begin
  inherited Create(AOwner);
  Width := 175;
  Height := 60;

  FRadio1 := TRadioButton.Create(Self);
  FRadio1.Parent := Self;
  FRadio1.Caption := 'Radio1';
  FRadio1.Left := 20;
  FRadio1.Top := 10;
  FRadio1.Show;

  FRadio2 := TRadioButton.Create(Self);
  FRadio2.Parent := Self;
  FRadio2.Caption := 'Radio2';
  FRadio2.Left := 20;
  FRadio2.Top := 32;
  FRadio2.Show;
end;
```

The next step is to create the first radio button. Notice that the code passes Self as the owner and sets the parent to the panel itself. The rest of the code in the Create method is too trivial to merit comment.

The control sports a WmSize handler simply because the two RadioControls have captions that can stick out over the end of the control, creating an unsightly mess. By handling WM_SIZE events, I can be sure that these two captions never stick out over the end of the panel:

```
procedure TCCRadio2Panel.WmSize(var Message: TMessage);
begin
  inherited;
```

```
  FRadio1.Width := Width - (FRadio1.Left + 10);
  FRadio2.Width := Width - (FRadio2.Left + 10);
end;
```

The code that controls the widths of the radio buttons is fairly trivial. However, talking for a moment about the whole idea of handling Wm_Size messages might be worthwhile.

The following is the declaration for the WmSize method:

```
procedure WmSize(var Message: TMessage); message wm_Size;
```

This routine will be called every time Windows sends a Wm_Size message to the program. This action will occur when the control is being resized; for instance, it will be called at program startup.

In Delphi programming, this kind of event is usually handled by creating an OnResize handler. However, I don't want to create an OnResize handler for this object because the user of the component may want to create one of his or her own. Delphi events are simply method pointers pointing to a particular method, and they can't point to two methods at the same time. To avoid a conflict, I respond to WM_SIZE messages, which is the same thing the VCL responds to when it sends out its own OnResize events. In particular, the VCL class called TWinControl handles WM_SIZE events. TPanel and thus TCCRadio2Panel both descend from TWinControl. Therefore, I need to call the inherited WM_SIZE handler, or else my control will not work properly. As you can see, the first line of my WM_SIZE handler does call inherited. This means that TWinControl.WmSize is called properly, and therefore the user's OnResize events will also be called.

I'm almost through describing this control, but I need to cover one last tricky issue. At the very end of the unit, the TRadioButton class is registered:

```
RegisterClasses([TRadioButton]);
```

This event would normally occur when you drop a component on a form. However, in this case, a TRadioButton is not necessarily ever dropped explicitly on a form. In particular, it is simply created in the constructor for TCCRadio2Panel and is therefore never officially registered with the system. As a result, the safe thing to do is register the component explicitly, as I do here.

When you're ready to test the TCCRadio2Panel object, you can write the following code in the test-bed program to take it through its paces:

```
procedure TForm1.CreateControlsonTabSheet11Click(Sender: TObject);
var
  MyEdit: TCCBigEdit;
  Radio2Panel: TCCRadio2Panel;
begin
  MyEdit := TCCBigEdit.Create(Self);
```

Creating Components: Part I

CHAPTER 6

111

6

CREATING
COMPONENTS:
PART I

```
MyEdit.Parent := Tabsheet1;
MyEdit.Text := 'Inheritance!';
MyEdit.Left := 10;
MyEdit.Top := 10;
MyEdit.Width := 200;
MyEdit.Show;

Radio2Panel := TCCRadio2Panel.Create(Self);
Radio2Panel.Parent := TabSheet1;
Radio2Panel.Left := MyEdit.Left;
Radio2Panel.Top := MyEdit.Height + MyEdit.Top + 5;
Radio2Panel.Width := MyEdit.Width;
Radio2Panel.Radio1Caption := 'Delphi';
Radio2Panel.Radio2Caption := 'Unleashed';
Radio2Panel.Radio1.Checked := True;
Radio2Panel.BevelWidth := 3;
Radio2Panel.Show;
end;
```

Here, Radio2Panel is declared to be of type TCCRadio2Panel. Note that each of the radio buttons that belong to the panel act exactly as you would expect a normal radio button to act, except that you have to qualify them differently before you access them. Furthermore, I can access the bevel property of TPanel to give my control a fancy 3D look, as shown in Figure 6.3.

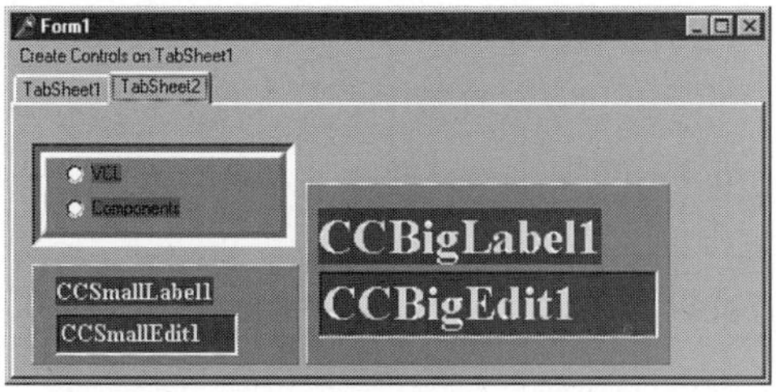

FIGURE 6.3

The TCCRadio2Panel *control can use the bevel and border properties of* TPanel *control to create a fancy 3D look.*

Creating Published Properties of a Component

A published property of a component appears in the published section of the class declaration:

```
TCCRadio2Panel = class(TCCEmptyPanel)
  ... // Code ommitted here
published
  property Radio1Caption: string
    read GetRadio1Caption write SetRadio1Caption;
  property Radio2Caption: string
    read GetRadio2Caption write SetRadio2Caption;
end;
```

These two published properties will now appear in the Object Inspector. That is the purpose of declaring a property as published: It makes the property visible in the Object Inspector. In particular, Delphi adds extra runtime type information to these properties so that the IDE can read that information at design time and expose the values of these properties to the user.

If you want, you can surface Radio1 and Radio2 as published properties of TCCRadio2Panel. However, when you first do so, they will have no Property Editors available because Delphi has no built-in Property Editors for TRadioButtons. To build your own, you can refer to the DSGNINTF.PAS unit that ships with Delphi, as well as the discussion of the Clock component and the Tools API found in the next chapter.

You can use a second, simpler way to work around the lack of a default editor. Specifically, you can create custom properties for each of the properties of an aggregated control that you want to surface. In this case, I create properties for the Radio1Caption and Radio2Caption properties. Both of these properties have read and write clauses designed to give automatic access to the Caption property of the underlying radio button control:

```
function TCCRadio2Panel.GetRadio1Caption: string;
begin
  Result := Radio1.Caption;
end;

procedure TCCRadio2Panel.SetRadio1Caption(const Value: string);
begin
  Radio1.Caption := Value;
end;
```

As you can see, these simple methods just expose the underlying Radio1.Caption property inside the Object Inspector.

> **NOTE**
>
> Remember that when you are declaring properties like this, much of the grunt work can be performed by Delphi. All you need do is declare the properties themselves:
>
> ```
> property Radio1Caption: string read GetRadio1Caption write
> SetRadio1Caption;
> ```
>
> After you've done so, you can press Ctrl+Shift+C, and Delphi will automatically create the declaration and outline for the implementation of the GetRadio1Caption and SetRadio1Caption methods. In this case, you will still have to fill in the single line of each implementation, but the header and begin..end pair for the methods are generated automatically.

I should perhaps add that nothing is wrong with asking the user to write `Radio1.Caption` instead of giving him or her a `Radio1Caption` property. The only reason I am creating this property is simply so that it can be exposed easily in the Object Inspector itself.

A Note on Streaming Properties

Before closing this section, I would like to add some additional notes about how Delphi handles streaming chores. The good news is that, most of the time, you do not have to concern yourself with streaming at all. Delphi handles most streaming chores automatically. In particular, it will automatically stream `published` properties that are simple types. Only under limited circumstances must you explicitly stream the fields of your object.

If a property type is a `TComponent` or descendant, the streaming system assumes it must create an instance of that type when reading it in. If a property type is `TPersistent` but not `TComponent`, the streaming system assumes it is supposed to use the existing instance available through the property and read values into that instance's properties.

As you have already seen, the Object Inspector knows to expand the properties of `TPersistent` but not `TComponent` descendants. This is not done for `TComponent` descendants because `TComponents` are likely to have a lot more properties, which would make navigating the Object Inspector difficult. For that reason, I had to create the `TRadio1Caption` property.

What all this information boils down to is that you don't have to worry about writing custom code to stream the `Radio1Caption` and `Radio2Caption` properties into a DFM file. The system takes care of that chore for you automatically. The only time you would have to start streaming a property would be if you declared it to be of some type, such as a record, that Delphi did not know. In that case, you would have to build your own Property Editor. In general, such cases are very rare, and you can usually assume that Delphi will handle the streaming for you automatically.

Automatic streaming of properties may not be big news to some readers. However, back in the bad old days of DOS and the TurboVision library, everyone had to do his or her own streaming, which proved to be a nontrivial and error-prone process. We all owe a note of thanks to the Delphi team for implementing this feature for us so that we could be spared a great deal of pain and trouble. Delphi would not be the same tool that it is if we had to stream our own properties. In fact, this might have been one of those subtle features that really helped to catapult the tool into the first line of success.

Creating a Truly Useful Component

By this time, you have enough knowledge in your head to start making real components that will be of some genuine use in your own programs. To help you get started, I'll show a TCCLabelEdit component. This control combines a label and an edit control into one component, as shown in Figure 6.4. This control is one I use all the time, as it automates the boring task of placing a label and edit control on a form and laboriously lining them up correctly. The source for the control is shown in Listing 6.7.

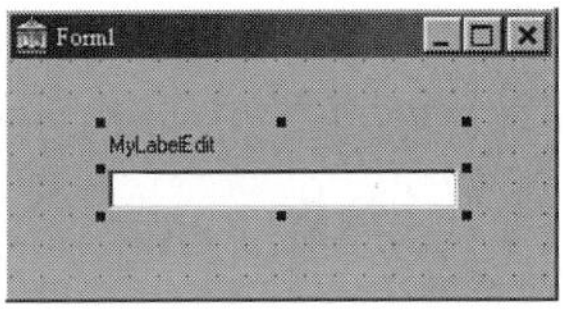

FIGURE 6.4

A TCCLabelEdit component combines a label control and an edit control into one entity.

LISTING 6.7   THE SOURCE FOR THE TCCLabelEdit CONTROL

```
/////////////////////////////////////
// Purpose: An edit control and label control that work as one unit.
// Project: Unleash.dpk
// Copyright  1998 by Charlie Calvert
//
unit LabelEdit;

{-------------------------------------------------------------------
  This is an edit control and a label control that work as one unit.
  This control should be part of the Unleash.dpk file and is stored
  in the Unleash page of the Component Palette.
-------------------------------------------------------------------}

interface

uses
  Windows, Messages, SysUtils,
  Classes, Graphics, Controls,
  Forms, Dialogs, StdCtrls;

type
  TCCLabelEdit = class(TCustomControl)
  private
    FEdit: TEdit;
```

Creating Components: Part I

CHAPTER 6

115

6

CREATING
COMPONENTS:
PART I

```
    FLabel: TLabel;
    function GetEditText: string;
    function GetLabelText: string;
    procedure SetLabelText(const Value: string);
    procedure SetEditText(const Value: string);
  protected
    procedure WmSize(var Message: TMessage); message WM_SIZE;
    procedure CMFontChanged(var Message: TMessage); message
CM_FONTCHANGED;
  public
    constructor Create(AOwner: TComponent); override;
  published
    property EditText: string read GetEditText write SetEditText;
    property Font;
    property LabelText: string read GetLabelText write SetLabelText;

  end;

procedure Register;

implementation

procedure Register;
begin
  RegisterComponents('Unleash', [TCCLabelEdit]);
end;

{ TLabelEdit }

procedure TCCLabelEdit.CMFontChanged(var Message: TMessage);
begin
  inherited;
  FEdit.Top := FLabel.Top + FLabel.Height + 5;
  Height := FEdit.Top + FEdit.Height + 5;
end;

constructor TCCLabelEdit.Create(AOwner: TComponent);
const
  Gap = 5;
begin
  inherited Create(AOwner);
  Width := 200;
  Height := 50;

  FLabel := TLabel.Create(Self);
  FLabel.Parent := Self;
  FLabel.Caption := 'Temp';
  FLabel.Left := Gap;
  FLabel.Top := Gap;
  FLabel.Width := 55;
  FLabel.Height := 15;
```

continues

LISTING 6.7 CONTINUED

```
  FLabel.Visible := True;

  FEdit := TEdit.Create(Self);
  FEdit.Parent := Self;
  FEdit.Left := FLabel.Left;
  FEdit.Top := FLabel.Top + FLabel.Height + Gap;
  FEdit.Width := Width - FEdit.Left - Gap;
  FEdit.Visible := True;
end;

function TCCLabelEdit.GetEditText: string;
begin
  Result := FEdit.Text;
end;

function TCCLabelEdit.GetLabelText: string;
begin
  Result := FLabel.Caption;
end;

procedure TCCLabelEdit.SetEditText(const Value: string);
begin
  FEdit.Text := Value;
end;

procedure TCCLabelEdit.SetLabelText(const Value: string);
begin
  FLabel.Caption := Value;
end;

procedure TCCLabelEdit.WmSize(var Message: TMessage);
begin
  inherited;
  FEdit.Width := Width - (FEdit.Left + 5);
end;

end.
```

This object is a good deal like the Radio2Panel control, only considerably more useful. Consider the following declaration:

```
TCCLabelEdit = class(TCustomControl)
  private
    FEdit: TEdit;
    FLabel: TLabel;
    function GetEditText: string;
    function GetLabelText: string;
    procedure SetLabelText(const Value: string);
    procedure SetEditText(const Value: string);
```

Creating Components: Part I

Chapter 6

117

6

CREATING
COMPONENTS:
PART I

```
protected
    procedure WmSize(var Message: TMessage); message WM_SIZE;
    procedure CMFontChanged(var Message: TMessage); message
CM_FONTCHANGED;
  public
    constructor Create(AOwner: TComponent); override;
  published
    property EditText: string read GetEditText write SetEditText;
    property Font;
    property LabelText: string read GetLabelText write SetLabelText;
  end;
```

You can see that this control aggregates one label and one edit control. It has three properties:

- One for reading and writing the caption of the label.

- One for reading and writing the caption of the edit control.

- One for changing the font of the label and edit control. Notice that I don't have to declare the get and set methods for the Font control because the Font control is inherited from TCustomControl by way of TControl. All I have to do here is surface it as a published property. In TControl, the Font property is declared as protected, which means it will not show up in the Object Inspector. My code here says only that I want the property to be visible to the user in the Object Inspector.

This control is superficially similar to the TCCRadio2Panel. The big difference here is that this control descends from something called TCustomControl rather than from a known control such as TPanel. As such, TCCLabelEdit doesn't inherit the fancy border and bevel technology found in an edit control. On the other hand, it doesn't carry the baggage associated with a TPanel control with it either. Not that a TPanel control is all that bulky, but it has properties that this control doesn't need, such as a bevel and border, so why include them?

All TCCLabelEdit really directly inherits is the ability to be a visual component that can have width and height and can be stored on the Component Palette. This is exactly what you need in this case, whereas TPanel would be overkill.

You can descend from several different base classes such as TCustomControl if you want to create a control that has only generic component-based technology, without having any specific functionality such as you find in a TEdit or a TPanel. I descended TCCSmallEdit from TEdit because I wanted to inherit the capabilities of an edit control, and I inherited to TCCRadioPanel from TPanel because I wanted to inherit the bevel and border capabilities of TPanel. I inherited TCCLabelEdit from TCustomControl because all I really wanted was a control that had width and height and that could be placed on the Component Palette.

> **NOTE**
>
> As I imply in the preceding paragraphs, there is actually a bit more to the story of TCustomControl than I cover in this chapter. However, I want to cover the nitty-gritty aspects of this subject in the next chapter, where I will have more room to maneuver and when your mind is fresh and ready for a new topic. For now, all you really need to know is that you can create a component by descending from TCustomControl, and in the next chapter, I will explain the details of this rather involved subject.
>
> I should add, however, that descending from TCustomControl gives a component very little overhead compared to what you find when you create an ActiveX control. Even the best ActiveX controls tend to be a bit bulky, whereas TCustomControl is really a very lightweight ancestor.

The following is the constructor for this control:

```
constructor TCCLabelEdit.Create(AOwner: TComponent);
const
  Gap = 5;
begin
  inherited Create(AOwner);
  Width := 200;
  Height := 50;

  FLabel := TLabel.Create(Self);
  FLabel.Parent := Self;
  FLabel.Caption := 'Temp';
  FLabel.Left := Gap;
  FLabel.Top := Gap;
  FLabel.Width := 55;
  FLabel.Height := 15;
  FLabel.Visible := True;

  FEdit := TEdit.Create(Self);
  FEdit.Parent := Self;
  FEdit.Left := FLabel.Left;
  FEdit.Top := FLabel.Top + FLabel.Height + Gap;
  FEdit.Width := Width - FEdit.Left - Gap;
  FEdit.Visible := True;
end;
```

As you can see, this method creates both a label and an edit control, assigns them a width and height and some default text values, and then makes them visible. In this case, I make the controls visible by setting the Visible property to True, which is much the same as calling their Show method. Notice that I do not hard-code in the values for the edit control but rather let it be defined by values assigned to the label control.

Creating Components: Part I

CHAPTER 6

119

6

CREATING
COMPONENTS:
PART I

Like the `TCCRadio2Panel`, this control responds to `WM_SIZE` messages:

```
procedure TCCLabelEdit.WmSize(var Message: TMessage);
begin
  FEdit.Width := Width - (FEdit.Left + 5);
end;
```

The effect of this code is to ensure that the edit control is always more or less the same width as the underlying `TCustomControl`. That way, when the user resizes the entire component, the edit control will follow suit in a logical and well-behaved manner.

Somewhat more complex is the behavior that occurs when you change the font of the control. The font of the `TCustomControl` is automatically transferred to the edit and label controls because they have `TCustomControl` as an owner. In particular, they all respond to a VCL message called `CM_FONTCHANGED` that gets propagated by the owner up the tree to the children. Suppose `TControl` gets the message. It will then pass the message to its child, `TWinControl`, which will in turn pass it to `TCustomControl`, and so on up the line.

When the font inside these controls is changed, they might no longer be arranged correctly on the form. For that reason, I want my descendant of `TCustomControl` to respond to these messages and make the appropriate changes to the appearance of the control:

```
procedure TCCLabelEdit.CMFontChanged(var Message: TMessage);
begin
  inherited;
  FEdit.Top := FLabel.Top + FLabel.Height + 5;
  Height := FEdit.Top + FEdit.Height + 5;
end;
```

In particular, notice that I adjust the location of the edit control and the bottom of the entire control so that they can accommodate the new font size. This code works if the font is being made either larger or smaller.

The `TCCLabelEdit` control is one that I find incredibly useful. Something in my constitution does not enjoy messing around with forms and ensuring that all their controls are the right height and width. At any rate, sometimes I find that kind of thing very boring and frustrating. This simple control eliminates a good deal of the petty work required in such situations, and it ensures that each edit and label pair will be lined up exactly right, to the pixel.

Summary

In this chapter, you learned about building components. Specifically, you learned

- How to create components that change an ancestor's default settings. For instance, you created `TEdit` descendants with new default colors and fonts.

- How to create compound components that consist of multiple inherited or aggregated components.

- How to create packages and how to install components.

- How to create your own published properties.

- How to respond to Windows and VCL messages.

You cannot deny that the basics of component development in Delphi are quite simple. However, some readers might be thinking that I performed a few tricks in this chapter that required a bit of background understanding of how the VCL is put together, such as knowing about the CM_FONTCHANGED message. Even a little knowledge of Windows API basics came in handy here, particularly when you encountered something like a WM_SIZE message.

In fact, component development can get to be a little tricky at times; the more you know about the VCL and about the Windows API, the better you will be at it. However, you can pull quite a few tricks without having deep knowledge. Furthermore, component development is a field that you can expand into after you start to find the basics of Delphi development a bit too easy.

Creating
Components:
Part II

CHAPTER 7

This chapter continues the exploration of VCL components. Tools and technologies covered in this chapter include the following:

- Creating several clock components that can be dropped on a form and stopped and started at will.
- Creating nonvisual controls. In particular, you will see how to create a control that iterates through the directories on your hard drive.
- Creating custom event handlers for your controls.
- Creating tools built on top of abstract component base classes such as TWinControl, TCustomControl, TComponent, and TGraphicControl. You descend from these classes if you want to build your own components from the bottom up.

Besides core component creation issues, this chapter also covers two related topics:

Property editors are used to edit the properties of components. The classic examples are the common dialogs that pop up when you edit the Color or Font properties that belong to most visible components. The drop-down lists and string editing capabilities found in the Object Inspector are also property editors.

Component editors are associated not with a single property, but with an entire component. An example is the Fields Editor used with TTable and TQuery components.

The property editors and component editors are related to a broader topic called the *Tools API*. The Tools API consists of a series of interfaces to the Delphi IDE. They allow you to build experts, interfaces to version control systems, and similar utilities. The API for property editors, component editors, and the Tools API are defined in files with names that end in INTF. INTF stands for Interface. For instance, the TPropertyEditor class is found in DSGNINTF.PAS.

Other subjects covered in this chapter include the following:

- Creating components that contain entire Delphi forms that can be popped up at runtime.
- Working with component templates to create quick and dirty compound components
- Creating ActiveX controls

This chapter is one of the key places where you can learn to take the basic tools found in every copy of Delphi and use them to build powerful systems. Delphi is a fabulous resource waiting for people to come along and unlock its secrets. This chapter contains some of the keys you need to fully utilize all the capabilities of this wonderful tool.

Building Components from Scratch

Except for the last example, the preceding chapter focused on creating descendants of existing components. Now it's time to explore the subject of creating entirely new components.

A new component can descend from four abstract classes. The term *abstract* can have a specific technical meaning, but here I am using it to refer to any object that exists only so that you can create descendants of it. In short, the following four objects have built-in functionality that all components need to access, but you would rarely want to instantiate an instance of any of them:

- TWinControl and TCustomControl are base classes that can be used to produce a standard Windows control such as a TEdit. Descendants of these two classes exist inside their own window, can receive input focus, and have a standard Windows handle. TListBox, TTabbedNoteBook, TNoteBook, and TPanel are all examples of this type of control. Most components of this type actually descend from TCustomControl, which is in turn a descendant of TWinControl. The distinction between the two classes is that TCustomControl has a Paint method, and TWinControl does not. If you want to draw the display of your new component, you should inherit from TCustomControl. If the object already knows how to draw itself, inherit from TWinControl.

- TGraphicControl is for components that don't need to receive input focus, don't need to contain other components, and don't need a handle. These controls draw themselves directly on their parent's surface, thereby saving Windows resources. Not having a window handle eliminates a lot of Windows management overhead, and that translates into faster display updates. In short, TGraphicControls exist inside their parent's window rather than having their own window like a TWinControl descendant. They use their parent's handle and their parent's device context. They still have Handle and Canvas fields that you can access, but they actually belong to their parent. TLabel and TShape objects are examples of this type of component.

- TComponent enables you to create nonvisual components. If you want to make a tool such as the TTable, TQuery, TOpenDialog, or TTimer devices, this is the place to start. These components reside on the Component Palette, but they perform internal functions that you access through code rather than appear to the user at runtime. The TCCFileIterater component shown later in this chapter is an example of this type of control. A tool such as TOpenDialog is also technically a nonvisual control. It can pop up a dialog, but the component itself remains invisible. You will see an example of how to create this kind of control when you see the TCCPickDirDlg example later in this chapter.

You can follow these two rules when trying to decide where to create a `TWinControl` or `TGraphicControl` descendant:

- Create a `TWinControl` or `TCustomControl` descendant whenever the user needs to directly interact with a visible control.
- If the user doesn't need to interact with a visible component, create a `TGraphicControl` descendant.

To get a handle on the issues involved here, you should place a `TShape` or `TLabel` control on a form and run the program. Clicking or attempting to type on these controls produces no noticeable result. These components don't ever receive the focus. Now place a `TEdit` control on the form. It responds to mouse clicks, gets the focus, and you can type in it. `TEdit` controls are descendants of `TWinControl`, and `TShape` is a descendant of `TGraphicControl`.

> **NOTE**
>
> I should add one caveat to the rules about `TGraphicControl` explained previously. In one limited sense, the user can interact with `TGraphicControls`. For instance, they do receive mouse messages, and you can set the mouse cursor when the mouse flies over them. They just can't receive keyboard-input focus. If an object can't receive focus, it usually seems inert to the user.

If you can't decide whether you want to descend from `TWinControl` or `TCustomControl`, go with `TCustomControl`. It has a real `Paint` method and some other functionality that is useful when you're creating a component of your own. If you want to wrap an existing Windows control inside a VCL object, you should start with `TWinControl`.

Most Delphi components that descend from `TWinControl` create intermediate custom objects. `TEdit`'s hierarchy looks like this:

```
TWinControl
TCustomEdit
TEdit
```

`TListBox`'s hierarchy looks like this:

```
TWinControl
TCustomListBox
TListBox
```

Each has an intermediate `TCustomXXX` control.

The difference between TCustomEdit and TEdit is that TCustomEdit does not publish any of its properties, whereas TEdit does publish its properties. TCustomEdit gives you a chance to create your own TEdit control with just the properties you want to see in the Object Inspector.

Following are the declarations for TGraphicControl and TCustomControl as they appear in CONTROLS.PAS or CONTROLS.INT:

```
TGraphicControl = class(TControl)
private
  FCanvas: TCanvas;
  procedure WMPaint(var Message: TWMPaint); message WM_PAINT;
protected
  procedure Paint; virtual;
  property Canvas: TCanvas read FCanvas;
public
  constructor Create(AOwner: TComponent); override;
  destructor Destroy; override;
end;

TCustomControl = class(TWinControl)
private
  FCanvas: TCanvas;
  procedure WMPaint(var Message: TWMPaint); message WM_PAINT;
protected
  procedure Paint; virtual;
  procedure PaintWindow(DC: HDC); override;
  property Canvas: TCanvas read FCanvas;
public
  constructor Create(AOwner: TComponent); override;
  destructor Destroy; override;
end;
```

These objects are fairly simple. They do little more than add painting capabilities to their parent controls. If you went back one step further in the hierarchy to TControl or TWinControl, you would see huge objects. For instance, the declaration for TWinControl is nearly 200 lines long (not the implementation, mind you, just the type declaration).

Component builders usually should work directly with the VCL source rather than use the online help or the docs. For simple jobs, you can easily create your own components without the source. For big projects, you have to get the source code. The INT files that ship with all versions of Delphi in the Docs directory are very helpful, but you'll find no replacement for the source.

The Clock Component

It's now time to build a relatively sophisticated component from the ground up. The controls from the Clock unit (shown in Figure 7.1) are little clocks that you can pop onto a form and activate and deactivate at will. You can start the clock running and then tell it to stop by changing the value of a Boolean property called Running.

FIGURE 7.1

The TestClockComponent *sample program shows off the various kinds of clocks made in the chapter.*

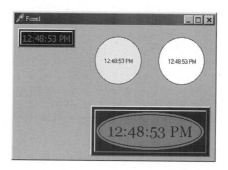

When you're constructing class TCCClock (pronounced *Tee See See Clock*), the first thing you need to decide is whether the clock is going to descend from TWinControl or TGraphicControl. If you've built a clock in Windows before, you know that one of the best ways to drive it is with a Windows timer. Timers require the presence of a Handle so that they can be stopped and started; furthermore, they send their WM_TIMER messages to the window that owns them. Because a TGraphicControl descendant isn't a real window, it will not automatically get the messages. As a result, TGraphicControl is not an ideal choice for this type of object.

The objections to using TGraphicControl raised in the preceding paragraph aren't insurmountable. However, I find no point in expending effort that isn't strictly necessary, so I have opted for the simplest design possible and descended the class from TCustomControl. I chose TCustomControl rather than TWinControl because I needed a Paint method in which I could draw the clock.

> **NOTE**
>
> The decision to use Windows API calls to create a timer rather than using a TTimer object was simply born out of a desire to save memory.

You will see that the code, shown in Listings 7.1 through Listing 7.3, also contains a special property editor, as well as a simple component editor. Neither of these tools is inherently difficult to build. Listing 7.4 contains a test bed program that takes the components through their paces.

LISTING 7.1 THE CODE FOR THE Clock COMPONENT SHOULD BE KEPT IN THE Units SUBDIRECTORY WHERE YOU STORE CodeBox AND OTHER UTILITY UNITS

```
unit Clock;

{ Program copyright  1995..1998 by Charles Calvert }
{ Project Name: Unleashed.dpk }

interface

uses
  SysUtils, WinTypes, WinProcs,
  Messages, Classes, Graphics,
  Controls, Forms, StdCtrls,
  DsgnIntf, Dialogs;

type
  TCCClock = class(TCustomControl)
  private
    FTimer: Integer;
    FRunning: Boolean;
    procedure SetRunning(Run: Boolean);
  protected
    procedure Paint; override;
    procedure WMTimer(var Message: TMessage); message WM_TIMER;
    procedure WMDestroy(var Message: TMessage); message wm_Destroy;
  public
    constructor Create(AOwner: TComponent); override;
  published
    property Running: Boolean read FRunning write SetRunning;
  end;

  TCCColorClock = class(TCCClock)
  private
    FFaceColor: TColor;
  protected
    procedure Paint; override;
    procedure SetFaceColor(NewColor: TColor); virtual;
  public
    constructor Create(AOwner: TComponent); override;
  published
    property Color;
    property FaceColor: TColor read FFaceColor write SetFaceColor;
  end;
```

continues

LISTING 7.1 CONTINUED

```pascal
  TCCClockStyle = (csEllipse, csRectangle);

  TCCFancyClock = class(TCCColorClock)
  private
    FClockStyle: TCCClockStyle;
    FBevelWidth: Integer;
    FBorderWidth: Integer;
    procedure DrawBorder;
    procedure SetBevelWidth(const Value: Integer);
    procedure SetBorderWidth(const Value: Integer);
  protected
    procedure wmTimer(var Msg: TMessage); override;
    procedure Paint; override;
  public
    constructor Create(AOwner: TComponent); override;
  published
    property BevelWidth: Integer read FBevelWidth write SetBevelWidth;
    property BorderWidth: Integer read FBorderWidth write SetBorderWidth;
    property ClockStyle: TCCClockStyle read FClockStyle write FClockStyle;
    property Font;
  end;

  TCCClockEdit = class(TComponentEditor)
    procedure Edit; override;
  end;

  TCCColorNameProperty = class(TColorProperty)
  public
    function GetAttributes: TPropertyAttributes; override;
    procedure Edit; override;
  end;


procedure Register;

implementation

uses
  CodeBox, ExtCtrls, ColorPicker1,
  ClockEditor1;

procedure Register;
begin
  RegisterComponents('Unleash', [TCCClock, TCCColorClock, TCCFancyClock]);
  RegisterComponentEditor(TCCFancyClock, TCCClockEdit);
  RegisterPropertyEditor(TypeInfo(TColor),
                TCCClock, 'Color',
                TCCColorNameProperty);
end;
```

```
{------------------------------------------------------------------}
{ TCCClock -------------------------------------------------------}
{------------------------------------------------------------------}
constructor TCCClock.Create(AOwner: TComponent);
begin
  inherited Create(AOwner);
  Width := 100;
  height := 100;
  FTimer := 1;
end;

procedure TCCClock.wmDestroy(var Message: TMessage);
begin
  KillTimer(Handle, FTimer);
  FTimer := 0;
  inherited;
end;

procedure TCCClock.Paint;
begin
  Canvas.Ellipse(0, 0, 100, 100);
end;

procedure TCCClock.SetRunning(Run: Boolean);
begin
  if Run then begin
    SetTimer(Handle, FTimer, 50, nil);
    FRunning := True;
  end else begin
    KillTimer(Handle, FTimer);
    FRunning := False;
  end;
end;

procedure TCCClock.WMTimer(var Message: TMessage);
var
  S: string;
begin
  S := GetTimeString;
  Canvas.TextOut((Width div 2) - (Canvas.TextWidth(S) div 2),
    (Height div 2) - (Canvas.TextHeight(S) div 2), S);
end;


{------------------------------------------------------------------}
{ TCCColorClock --------------------------------------------------}
```

continues

LISTING 7.1   CONTINUED

```
{----------------------------------------------------------------}

constructor TCCColorClock.Create(AOwner: TComponent);
begin
  inherited Create(AOwner);
  FFaceColor := clGreen;
end;


procedure TCCColorClock.Paint;
begin
  Canvas.Brush.Color := FFaceColor;
  inherited Paint;
end;

procedure TCCColorClock.SetFaceColor(NewColor: TColor);
begin
  FFaceColor := NewColor;
  InvalidateRect(Handle, nil, True);
end;

{----------------------------------------------------------------}
{ TFancyCLock ---------------------------------------------------}
{----------------------------------------------------------------}

constructor TCCFancyClock.Create(AOwner: TComponent);
begin
  inherited Create(AOwner);
  FBevelWidth := 1;
  FBorderWidth := 1;
end;

procedure TCCFancyClock.DrawBorder;
var
  R: TRect;
begin
  R := Rect(0, 0, Width, Height);
  Frame3D(Canvas, R, clBtnHighLight, clBtnShadow, FBevelWidth);
  R := Rect(FBorderWidth, FBorderWidth, Width - FBorderWidth,
    Height - FBorderWidth);
  Frame3D(Canvas, R, clBtnHighLight, clBtnShadow, FBevelWidth);
end;

procedure TCCFancyClock.Paint;
var
```

```
    Gap: Integer;
begin
  Canvas.Font.Name := Font.Name;
  Canvas.Font.Size := Font.Size;
  Canvas.Font.Color := Font.Color;
  Canvas.Brush.Color := FFaceColor;
  case FClockStyle of
    csEllipse: begin
      Canvas.Pen.Color := Font.Color;
      Canvas.Pen.Width := FBevelWidth;
      Gap := (FBevelWidth + FBorderWidth);
      Canvas.Ellipse(FBevelWidth + Gap, FBevelWidth + Gap,
        Width - FBevelWidth - Gap, Height - FBevelWidth - Gap);
      Canvas.Ellipse(FBorderWidth + Gap, FBorderWidth + Gap,
        Width - FBorderWidth - Gap, Height - FBorderWidth - Gap);
      DrawBorder;
      end;
    csRectangle: begin
      Canvas.Rectangle(0, 0, Width, Height);
      DrawBorder;
    end;
  end;
end;

procedure TCCFancyClock.SetBevelWidth(const Value: Integer);
begin
  FBevelWidth := Value;
  Invalidate;
end;

procedure TCCFancyClock.SetBorderWidth(const Value: Integer);
begin
  FBorderWidth := Value;
  Invalidate;
end;

procedure TCCFancyClock.wmTimer(var Msg: TMessage);
begin
  inherited;
end;

{-------------------------------------------------------------------------}
{ TCCClockEdit -----------------------------------------------------------}
{-------------------------------------------------------------------------}


procedure TCCClockEdit.Edit;
var
```

continues

LISTING 7.1   CONTINUED

```
  ClockEditor: TCCClockEditor;
begin
  ClockEditor := TCCClockEditor.Create(nil);
  ClockEditor.BackColor := TCCFancyClock(Component).Color;
  ClockEditor.FaceColor := TCCFancyClock(Component).FaceColor;
  ClockEditor.FontColor := TCCFancyClock(Component).Font.Color;
  ClockEditor.ShowModal;
  TCCFancyClock(Component).Color := ClockEditor.BackColor;
  TCCFancyClock(Component).FaceColor := ClockEditor.FaceColor;
  TCCFancyClock(Component).Font.Color := ClockEditor.FontColor;
  ClockEditor.Free;
end;


{-------------------------------------------------------------------}
{ TColorNameProperty -----------------------------------------------}
{-------------------------------------------------------------------}

function TCCColorNameProperty.GetAttributes;
begin
  Result := [paMultiSelect, paValueList, paDialog];
end;

procedure TCCColorNameProperty.Edit;
var
  S: String;
  ColorPicker: TColorPicker;
begin
  S := '';
  ColorPicker := TColorPicker.Create(nil);
  ColorPicker.ShowModal;
  S := ColorToString(ColorPicker.ColorChoice);
  ColorPicker.Free;
  SetValue(S);
end;

end.
```

LISTING 7.2   A PROPERTY EDITOR FOR THE CLOCK UNIT

```
////////////////////////////////////////
// Purpose: Allow the user to pick a color
// Project: Unleash.dpk
// Copyright  1998 by Charlie Calvert
//
unit ColorPicker1;
```

```
interface

uses
  Windows, Messages, SysUtils,
  Classes, Graphics, Controls,
  Forms, Dialogs, StdCtrls,
  Buttons, ExtCtrls, ColorGrd;

type
  TColorPicker = class(TForm)
    ColorGrid1: TColorGrid;
    Bevel1: TBevel;
    BitBtn1: TBitBtn;
    BitBtn2: TBitBtn;
    procedure BitBtn1Click(Sender: TObject);
  private
    FColorChoice: TColor;
    { Private declarations }
  public
    property ColorChoice: TColor read FColorChoice;
  end;

var
  ColorPicker: TColorPicker;

implementation

{$R *.DFM}

procedure TColorPicker.BitBtn1Click(Sender: TObject);
begin
  FColorChoice := ColorGrid1.ForegroundColor;
end;

end.
```

LISTING 7.3 A COMPONENT EDITOR FOR THE CLOCK UNIT

```
//////////////////////////////////////
// Purpose: A component editor for the clock unit
// Project: Unleash.dpk
// Copyright  1998 by Charlie Calvert
//
unit ClockEditor1;

interface

uses
```

continues

LISTING 7.3   CONTINUED

```
  Windows, Messages, SysUtils,
  Classes, Graphics, Controls,
  Forms, Dialogs, ExtCtrls,
  StdCtrls, Buttons;

type
  TCCClockEditor = class(TForm)
    Panel1: TPanel;
    GroupBox1: TGroupBox;
    Backgroundbtn: TButton;
    FaceColorBtn: TButton;
    FontColorBtn: TButton;
    BGShape: TShape;
    FaceShape: TShape;
    FontShape: TShape;
    ColorDialog1: TColorDialog;
    BitBtn1: TBitBtn;
    BitBtn2: TBitBtn;
    procedure BackgroundbtnClick(Sender: TObject);
    procedure FaceColorBtnClick(Sender: TObject);
    procedure FontColorBtnClick(Sender: TObject);
  private
    FBackColor: TColor;
    FFaceColor: TColor;
    FFontColor: TColor;
    procedure SetBackColor(Value: TColor);
    procedure SetFaceColor(Value: TColor);
    procedure SetFontColor(Value: TColor);
  public
    property BackColor: TColor read FBackColor write SetBackColor;
    property FaceColor: TColor read FFaceColor write SetFaceColor;
    property FontColor: TColor read FFontColor write SetFontColor;
    { Public declarations }
  end;

var
  ClockEditor: TCCClockEditor;

implementation

{$R *.DFM}

procedure TCCClockEditor.BackgroundbtnClick(Sender: TObject);
begin
  if ColorDialog1.Execute then
    BackColor := ColorDialog1.Color;
end;

procedure TCCClockEditor.FaceColorBtnClick(Sender: TObject);
```

```
begin
  if ColorDialog1.Execute then
    FaceColor := ColorDialog1.Color;
end;

procedure TCCClockEditor.FontColorBtnClick(Sender: TObject);
begin
  if ColorDialog1.Execute then
    FontColor := ColorDialog1.Color;
end;

procedure TCCClockEditor.SetBackColor(Value: TColor);
begin
  FBackColor := Value;
  BGShape.Brush.Color := Value;
end;

procedure TCCClockEditor.SetFaceColor(Value: TColor);
begin
  FFaceColor := Value;
  FaceShape.Brush.Color := Value;
end;

procedure TCCClockEditor.SetFontColor(Value: TColor);
begin
  FFontColor := Value;
  FontShape.Brush.Color := Value;
end;

end.
```

LISTING 7.4 THE TEST BED FOR THE CLOCK COMPONENT IS STORED IN THE CLOCK3 SUBDIRECTORY

```
/////////////////////////////////////
// Purpose: Test the TCCColorClock component
// Project: ClockTestBed.dpr
// Copyright  1998 by Charlie Calvert
//
unit Main;

interface

uses
  Windows, Messages, SysUtils,
  Classes, Graphics, Controls,
  Forms, Dialogs, StdCtrls,
  Clock;
```

continues

TINUED

LISTING 7.4

```
                   lass(TForm)
    type      tn:  TButton;
        TFor ckBtn: TButton;
             sBtn: TButton;
           rDialog1: TColorDialog;
          ocedure CreateBtnClick(Sender: TObject);
         rocedure RunClockBtnClick(Sender: TObject);
         procedure ColorsBtnClick(Sender: TObject);
       rivate
         FMyClock: TCCColorClock;
       public
         { Public declarations }
       end;

var
  Form1: TForm1;

implementation

{$R *.DFM}

procedure TForm1.CreateBtnClick(Sender: TObject);
begin
  FMyClock := TCCColorClock.Create(Self);
  FMyClock.Parent := Self;
end;

procedure TForm1.RunClockBtnClick(Sender: TObject);
begin
  FMyClock.Running := not FMyClock.Running;
end;

procedure TForm1.ColorsBtnClick(Sender: TObject);
begin
  if ColorDialog1.Execute then
    FMyClock.FaceColor := ColorDialog1.Color;
end;

end.
```

The ClockTestBed program in Listing 7.4 is a small executable designed to check the status of the simplest of the clock components. I created it when I first designed the control to test the feasibility of the project.

To run this program, you should first press the button that creates the clock and makes it visible on the form. The next logical step is to start the clock running; then, if you'd like, you can also change its color. You get an Access Violation if you click on the latter two buttons before pushing the first. The problem is that it is an error to call a method or property of the TCCClock object before the object itself has been created. To prevent this situation from happening, you could enable and disable the second two buttons.

Understanding `TCCClock`

The code for the clock components uses inheritance, virtual methods, and properties. TCCClock has two pieces of private data:

```
FTimer: Integer;
FRunning: Boolean;
```

One is an identifier for the timer, and the other is a Boolean value that specifies whether the clock is running.

Windows timers are managed by two Windows API calls. When you want to start a timer, use SetTimer; when you want to stop a timer, use KillTimer. SetTimer takes four parameters:

- Handle is the HWND of your current window.
- IDEvent is an integer identifier that uniquely identifies the timer inside the window that created it. You can make up this value off the top of your head, although I generally set the IDTimer for the first timer in a window to 1, the second timer to 2, and so on. Because you're going to have only one timer in each instance of a TCCClock window, you can set its IDEvent to 1.
- Elapse is the length of time between calls to the timer, measured in milliseconds.
- TimerFunc is a callback function that is not used in this program. One of the Delphi developers' big goals was to create a Windows product that didn't need to use callbacks, and I see no reason to open that can of worms now if it can be avoided. (If you want to create a callback in Delphi, you will be able to do so, but it's usually not necessary.)

A typical call to SetTimer looks like this:

```
SetTimer(Handle, FTimer, 1000, nil);
```

1000 specifies that the timer is called once every 1000 milliseconds, or once a second. SetTimer returns zero if the call fails. In 32-bit Windows, this is unlikely, but programs should include error checking to inspect this value and put up a MessageBox if the call fails.

KillTimer takes two parameters, the first being the handle of your window and the second being the unique identifier associated with that timer:

```
KillTimer(Handle, FTimer);
```

When you are not using the callback function, timer events are sent to your window by
way of messages:

```
procedure WMTimer(var Message: TMessage);
  message WM_TIMER;
```

This example is a classic Delphi dynamic method. The response to this event is a simple
procedure that calls TextOut and gets the time from a function called GetTimeString in
the CodeBox unit:

```
procedure TCCClock.WMTimer(var Message: TMessage);
var
  S: string;
begin
  S := GetTimeString;
  Canvas.TextOut((Width div 2) - (Canvas.TextWidth(S) div 2),
    (Height div 2) - (Canvas.TextHeight(S) div 2), S);
end;
```

Notice that I use the TextWidth and TextHeight functions from the Graphics unit to calculate the distance the text will extend both horizontally and vertically. My goal is to
ensure that the center of the text string lies as close as possible to the center of the
control.

The calls to SetTimer and KillTimer are managed primarily through a property called
Running:

```
property Running: Boolean read FRunning write SetRunning;
```

The write mechanism, a procedure called SetRunning, is a fairly straightforward tool:

```
procedure TCCClock.SetRunning(Run: Boolean);
begin
  if Run then begin
    SetTimer(Handle, FTimer, 50, nil);
    FRunning := True;
  end else begin
    KillTimer(Handle, FTimer);
    FRunning := False;
  end;
end;
```

If the user sets the Running property to True, this procedure is executed and a call is
made to the SetTimer function. If the user sets Running to False, KillTimer is called
and the clock immediately stops functioning.

The final issue involving the timer concerns a case in which the user closes a form while
the clock is still running. In such a situation, you should call KillTimer before the application exits.

The logical place to call `KillTimer` is the `Destroy` method for the `TCCClock` object. In some versions of Delphi, the window associated with the clock has already been destroyed by the time this call is made, so no valid handle is available for use when you call `KillTimer`. As a result, the control responds to `wm_Destroy` messages to be sure the timer is killed before the `TCCClock` window is closed:

```
procedure TCCClock.wmDestroy(var Message: TMessage);
begin
  KillTimer(Handle, FTimer);
  FTimer := 0;
  inherited;
end;
```

Before leaving this description of the `TCCClock` object, I should briefly mention the `Paint` method:

```
procedure TCCClock.Paint;
begin
  Canvas.Ellipse(0, 0, Width, Height);
end;
```

This procedure is called whenever the circle defining the circumference of the clock needs to be repainted. You never have to check for this circumstance, and you never have to call `Paint` directly. Windows keeps an eye on the `TCCClock` window, and if the window needs to be painted, it sends a `wm_Paint` message. Logic buried deep in the VCL converts the `wm_Paint` message into a call to `Paint`, the same way `TCCClock` translates `WM_TIMER` messages into calls to `TCanvas.TextOut`.

> **NOTE**
>
> Sometimes writing components is easiest if you can get right down to the Windows API level or as near to it as you would like to get. The following code reviews the techniques used to hook directly into the Window procedure:
>
> ```
> procedure TMyObject.WndProc(var M: TMessage);
> begin
>   case M.Msg of
>     WM_TIMER: DoSomething;
>     wm_Paint: PaintSomething;
>   else
>     M.Result := DefWindowProc(Handle, M.Msg, M.wParam, M.lParam);
>   end;
> ```
>
> `WndProc` is typically declared in the private section as follows:
>
> ```
>     procedure WndProc(var Msg: TMessage);
> ```
>
> See the Delphi VCL source for the `TTimer` object for another example of how to use the `WndProc` function.

The `TCCColorClock`

The `TCCColorClock` component, which is a descendant of `TCCClock`, adds color to the control. I made `TCCColorClock` a separate object, rather than just adding color to `TCCClock`, for two different reasons (both of which are related to design):

- You might want to create a descendant of `TCCClock` that doesn't have color, or that implements color differently than `TCCColorClock` does. By creating two objects, one called `TCCClock` and the other called `TCCColorClock`, I enable programmers to have the greatest amount of freedom when creating descendants. This principle has only minimal weight in a simple object such as `TCCClock`, but it can become extremely important when you are developing large and complex hierarchies. In short, be careful of building too much functionality into one object.

- `TCCClock` and `TCCColorClock` also provide another example of inheritance and vividly demonstrate how this technology can be used to your advantage.

`TCCColorClock` declares a private data store called `FFaceColor` that is of type `TColor`. Users can set the `FColor` variable by manipulating the `FaceColor` property:

```
property FaceColor: TColor read FFaceColor write SetFaceColor;
```

`SetFaceColor` is a simple procedure that sets the value of `FFaceColor` and calls the Windows API call `InvalidateRect`:

```
procedure TCCColorClock.SetFaceColor(NewColor: TColor);
begin
  FFaceColor := NewColor;
  InvalidateRect(Handle, nil, True);
end;
```

In this case, you can call either the VCL `Validate` function or `InvalidateRect`. Just to be sure this information makes sense, let me take a paragraph or two to provide a refresher course on `InvalidateRect`. The following is the declaration for the routine:

```
procedure InvalidateRect(Wnd: HWnd; Rect: PRect; Erase: Bool);
```

`InvalidateRect` forces the window specified in the first parameter to completely redraw itself if the second parameter is set to `nil`. If the third parameter is set to `False`, then the background of the redrawn portions of the control is not erased before redrawing. The middle parameter is a pointer to the `TRect` structure that can be used to define the area that you want to redraw. Compare this function with the native Delphi function called `Invalidate`.

Creating Components: Part II

CHAPTER 7

141

Calls to InvalidateRect naturally force calls to the TCCColorClock.Paint method:

```
procedure TCCColorClock.Paint;
begin
  Canvas.Brush.Color := FFaceColor;
  inherited Paint;
end;
```

Paint sets the brush associated with the window's device context to the color specified by the user; then it calls the Paint method defined in TCCClock.

Notice that I also surface the Color property of TControl:

```
property Color;
```

Back in the source for TControl, found in CONTROLS.PAS, you can find the original dec-laration for this property in the protected section of the class declaration. All I'm doing here is surfacing the property in the published section so it appears in the Object Inspector.

The Color property defines the background color of the form, and the face color defines the color of the clock face. If you want the clock face to appear to be drawn directly on the surface of the parent control, then just leave color at its default value or set it to the color of its parent.

Creating a Fancy Clock

The fancy clock takes the color clock and makes it more appealing by giving the user a choice of fonts. The object also adds a border and bevel, and it allows the user to draw the face as either a rectangle or an ellipse:

```
TClockStyle = (csEllipse, csRectangle);
TCCFancyClock = class(TCCColorClock)
private
  FClockStyle: TClockStyle;
  FBevelWidth: Integer;
  FBorderWidth: Integer;
  // Code ommitted here
published
  property BevelWidth: Integer read FBevelWidth write SetBevelWidth;
  property BorderWidth: Integer read FBorderWidth write SetBorderWidth;
  property ClockStyle: TClockStyle read FClockStyle write FClockStyle;
  property Font;
end;
```

All this would seem like a fairly complicated process, but it ends up being fairly simple to do if you just take advantage of the code found in the VCL.

Adding font support, for instance, would seem to be a very complex operation, given the nature of Windows fonts. However, the VCL allows you to give the user complete control over the font by just adding two words to your program:

```
property Font;
```

Adding this code to the `published` section of your object surfaces the `Font` property declared in the object's ancestry. It also automatically brings along the font editor. The font editor appears as part of the Object Inspector, as shown in Figure 7.2.

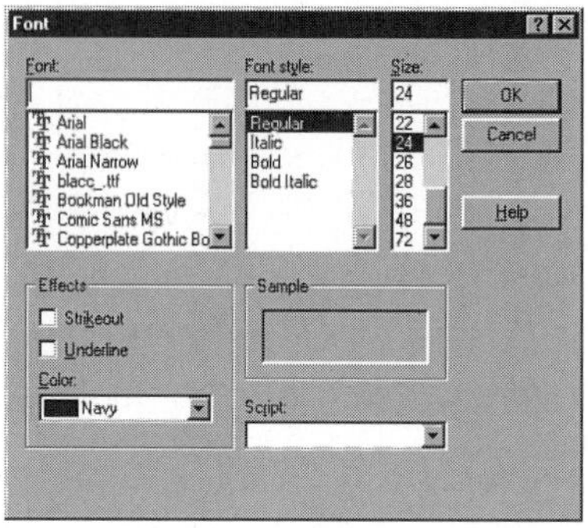

FIGURE 7.2

The property editor for fonts is used by default for all published properties declared to be of type TFont.

Besides the new `TFont` property, the `TCCFancyClock` component gives the user two different looks for the clock, one oval and the other rectangular, as shown earlier in the chapter in Figure 7.1. The `TClockStyle` enumerated type gives the component a way to track the user's choice:

```
TClockStyle = (csEllipse, csRectangle);
```

At this stage, all you need to know is that the user has the choice of either of these options. In just a moment, I will show the new `Paint` method. In the `Paint` method, the implementation of these two options is developed. You might also note that Delphi automatically creates a property editor that gives the user a drop-down list for choosing these new properties, as shown in Figure 7.3.

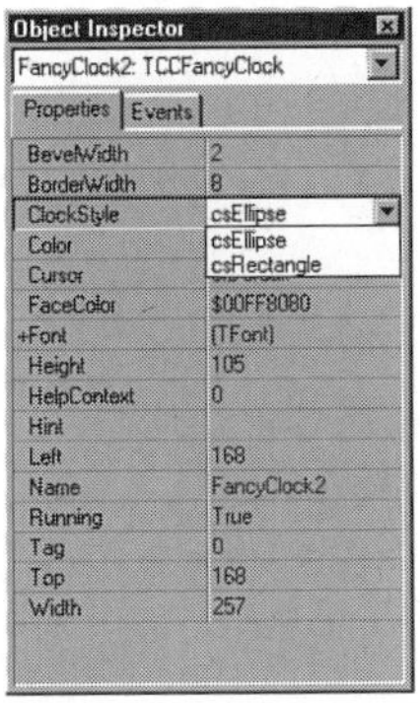

FIGURE 7.3

Delphi automatically creates a drop-down list to act as the property editor for the ClockStyle *property.*

The BevelWidth and BorderWidth are the last two properties added to the TCCFancyClock object. The set and get methods for the BevelWidth and BorderWidth properties look just as you would expect:

```
procedure TCCFancyClock.SetBevelWidth(const Value: Integer);
begin
  FBevelWidth := Value;
  Invalidate;
end;

procedure TCCFancyClock.SetBorderWidth(const Value: Integer);
begin
  FBorderWidth := Value;
  Invalidate;
end;
```

The complicated code appears in the Paint method:

```
procedure TCCFancyClock.Paint;
var
  Gap: Integer;
begin
  Canvas.Font.Name := Font.Name;
  Canvas.Font.Size := Font.Size;
  Canvas.Font.Color := Font.Color;
  Canvas.Brush.Color := FFaceColor;

  case FClockStyle of
    csEllipse: begin
      Canvas.Pen.Color := Font.Color;
      Canvas.Pen.Width := FBevelWidth;
      Gap := (FBevelWidth + FBorderWidth);
      Canvas.Ellipse(FBevelWidth + Gap, FBevelWidth + Gap,
        Width - FBevelWidth - Gap, Height - FBevelWidth - Gap);
      Canvas.Ellipse(FBorderWidth + Gap, FBorderWidth + Gap,
        Width - FBorderWidth - Gap, Height - FBorderWidth - Gap);
```

```
    DrawBorder;
    end;
  csRectangle: begin
    Canvas.Rectangle(0, 0, Width, Height);
    DrawBorder;
    end;

  end;
end;
```

The `Paint` method begins by setting the font of the object's `Canvas` to the font chosen by the user. The next line sets the `FaceColor`, exactly like the code found in the `TCCColorClock` object.

A case statement is then set up to draw either a rectangle or an ellipse, depending on the user's needs:

```
case FClockStyle of
csEllipse: begin
  // DrawEllipse
csRectangle: begin
  // Draw Rectangle
end;
```

The rectangle style does a fairly good job of drawing a bevel and a border that look reasonably professional. The ellipse code was a bit harder to implement, so I ended up fudging things a bit. In particular, I draw two ellipses, one inside the other. This arrangement gives the impression that there is a border, then a space, and then a bevel. I simply create the width of the bevel by changing the width of the pen used to draw the circumference of the ellipse.

Both the rectangle and ellipse styles call the `DrawBorder` method:

```
procedure TCCFancyClock.DrawBorder;
var
  R: TRect;
begin
  R := Rect(0, 0, Width, Height);
  Frame3D(Canvas, R, clBtnHighLight, clBtnShadow, FBevelWidth);
  R := Rect(FBorderWidth, FBorderWidth, Width - FBorderWidth,
    Height - FBorderWidth);
  Frame3D(Canvas, R, clBtnHighLight, clBtnShadow, FBevelWidth);
end;
```

`DrawBorder` lets a routine called `Frame3D` do most of its work. `Frame3D` is a public function from the VCL found in the `ExtCtrls.pas` unit. It is the same routine the Delphi controls use to create 3D effects, and overall it works quite well. In particular, it uses the `InflateRect` Windows API call to create a 3D bevel or border that has the right kind of corners. The lesson to learn here is that the VCL has a lot of good routines hidden away in its back corners. The more you know the VCL, the easier it will be to create your programs.

Overall, TCCClock, TCCColorClock and TCCFancyClock are fairly simple components, interesting primarily because they show you how to go about constructing your own controls from scratch. This kind of exercise lies very much at the heart of Delphi's architecture, and I expect some readers will be spending most of their time engaged almost exclusively in the business of building components.

Creating Icons for Components

The icon associated with a component and placed in the Component Palette is defined in a file with a .dcr extension. If you do not provide this file, Delphi uses the icon associated with the object's parent. If no icon appears anywhere in the component's ancestry, a default icon is used.

> **NOTE**
>
> A DCR file is a Windows resource file with the extension changed from .res to .dcr. The resource file contains a bitmap resource with the same name as your component. For instance, the bitmap resource in a DCR file for a TColor component would have a resource ID of TCOLOR. This resource should be a 28×28 pixel (or smaller) bitmap that can be edited in the Image Editor. All you need to do is place this DCR file in the same directory as your component, and the images defined therein will show up on the Component Palette. Use the Image Editor to explore the DCR files that ship with Delphi. They are stored in the \DELPHI\LIB directory.

Complete the following steps to associate your own bitmaps with a particular component:

1. Open the Image Editor and choose New.
2. In the New Project dialog, choose Component Resource (DCR) and click OK. A dialog called UNTITLED.DCR appears.
3. Choose the New button. A dialog called New Resource appears.
4. Choose Bitmap and click OK. A dialog called New Bitmap Attributes appears.
5. Set Colors to 16 colors because this technology is available on nearly all Windows systems. Set Size in Pixels to 28×28, or some smaller size such as 24×24.

6. Use the zoom feature of the editor to make the bitmap large enough so you can see what you are doing. Now draw a shape or picture of some kind.

7. Close the bitmap edit window and save the file as CLOCK.DCR. Rename the bitmap you have created to TCCCLOCK. (Apparently, you cannot save your file while the bitmap edit window is open. You must close it first.)

If you don't like the Image Editor, you can create a 28×28 bitmap in PBRUSH.EXE or some other bitmap editor and then create an RC file that looks like this:

```
TCCCLOCK BITMAP clock.bmp
```

Save the file as CLOCK.RC. Run the Borland Resource Compiler from the command line:

```
brc -r clock.rc
```

The resulting file will be called CLOCK.RES. Rename that file CLOCK.DCR. An example of the latter method is used for the TCCColorClock component and stored in the UNITS directory along with CODEBOX.PAS and the other utility files.

The Tools API: Property Editors and Component Editors

Just creating a component is often only half the battle. You also should make the component easy to use. One way to do so is to create a well-designed component with an intuitive interface. However, sometimes you need to give the user help by designing custom property editors or component editors. The following sections show you how to proceed.

The Five Main Tools APIs

You can use five main Tools APIs, each accessible through a separate set of routines that ship with Delphi. These APIs enable you to write code that can be linked directly into the Delphi IDE. Specifically, you can link your tools into packages, the same way you link in components. Table 7.1 lists the Tools APIs and the native Delphi source files that define them.

TABLE 7.1 DELPHI TOOLS APIs

Tools API	Description/Files
Experts	Enables you to write your own experts
	EXPINTF.PAS
	VIRTINTF.PAS

Tools API	Description/Files
	`TOOLINTF.PAS` (for enumerating the component pages and components installed, adding modules to the project, and so on)
Version Control	Enables you to write your own Version Control system or to link in a third-party system
	`VCSINTF.PAS`
	`VIRTINTF.PAS`
	`TOOLINTF.PAS` (for opening and closing files in the editor)
Component Editors	Create dialogs associated with a control at design time (for instance, the DataSet Designer is a component editor)
	`DSGNINTF.PAS`
Property Editors	Create editors for use in the Object Inspector
	`DSGNINTF.PAS`
Editor Interfaces	Allows third parties to access the Delphi editor
	`EDITINTF.PAS`
	`FILEINTF.PAS`

The letters *INTF* are an abbreviation for the word *interface*. The Tools API is an interface between your own code and the Delphi developers' code.

Most people will never use the Tools API. However, it will be important to a small minority of developers, and its existence means that everyone can buy or download tools that extend the functionality of the IDE.

Property Editors

The Tools API for creating property editors is perhaps the most commonly used interface into the heart of the IDE. When you first use Delphi and start becoming familiar with the Object Inspector, you are bound to think that it is a static element that never changes. However, you can change the functionality of the Object Inspector by adding new property editors to it.

As mentioned earlier, property editors control what takes place on the right side of the Properties page of the Object Inspector. In particular, when you click on the Color property of a TEdit, you can select a new color from a drop-down list, from a common dialog, or by typing in a new value. In all three cases, you are using a property editor.

If you want to create a new property editor, you should create a descendant of TPropertyEditor, a class declared in DSGNINTF.PAS. The following is the declaration for the property editor associated with the TCCColorClock component:

```
TColorNameProperty = class(TColorProperty)
public
    function GetAttributes: TPropertyAttributes; override;
    procedure Edit; override;
end;
```

The DSGNINTF unit is unusual in that it is very carefully documented by the developer who created it. For instance, here are excerpts from that unit describing the two methods I call in my descendant of TPropertyEditor:

```
Edit
        Called when the '...' button is pressed or the
        property is double-clicked. This can, for example,
        bring up a dialog to allow the editing of the component
        in some more meaningful fashion than by text
        (e.g. the Font property).

GetAttributes
        Returns the information for use in the Object
        Inspector to be able to show the appropriate tools.
        GetAttributes return a set of type TPropertyAttributes.
```

I won't quote further, for fear of sounding like I'm plagiarizing. The point, however, is that these entries were written by the developers, and they extensively document this important interface to the core code inside the heart of the IDE. The following are declarations for Edit and GetAttributes, as well as the other key functions in TPropertyEditor:

```
TPropertyEditor = class
public
  destructor Destroy; override;
  function AllEqual: Boolean; virtual;
  procedure Edit; virtual;
  function GetAttributes: TPropertyAttributes; virtual;
  function GetComponent(Index: Integer): TComponent;
  function GetEditLimit: Integer; virtual;
  function GetName: string; virtual;
  procedure GetProperties(Proc: TGetPropEditProc); virtual;
  function GetPropType: PTypeInfo;
  function GetValue: string; virtual;
  procedure GetValues(Proc: TGetStrProc); virtual;
  procedure Initialize; virtual;
  procedure SetValue(const Value: string); virtual;
  property Designer: TFormDesigner read FDesigner;
  property PrivateDirectory: string read GetPrivateDirectory;
  property PropCount: Integer read FPropCount;
  property Value: string read GetValue write SetValue;
end;
```

Creating Components: Part II

CHAPTER 7

149

7

CREATING
COMPONENTS:
PART II

Once again, all these methods are carefully documented inside DSGNINTF.PAS. You should study that file carefully if you want to learn more about creating complex property editors.

> **NOTE**
>
> I'm not going to step you through the methods of TPropertyEditor one by one. I am quoting the declaration here just to make you conscious of the fact that the source is available. In *Star Wars*, when Obi Wan says "Use the Source, Luke," he is not talking about just any source code, he is referring specifically to the VCL source.

The Edit method of TPropertyEditor is the one you want to override to change the way a property editor actually edits data:

```
procedure TColorNameProperty.Edit;
var
  S: String;
begin
  S := '';
  InputQuery('New Color', 'Enter Color', S);
  SetValue(S);
end;
```

In this case, I am creating a substitute for the TColorDialog that pops up when you click on the ellipsis icon in Object Inspector. I am, of course, replacing the fancy Windows common dialog with a simpler one that asks the user to enter a string such as "clBlue" or "clGreen". The point, however, is that you are learning how to create your own property editors.

In a more complex example, you might open a form that allowed the user to make extensive changes to a property. This is what I do in the TCCColorClock component. In particular, I create a dialog that has a TColorGrid, two bevels, and two BitBtns in it, as shown in Figure 7.4.

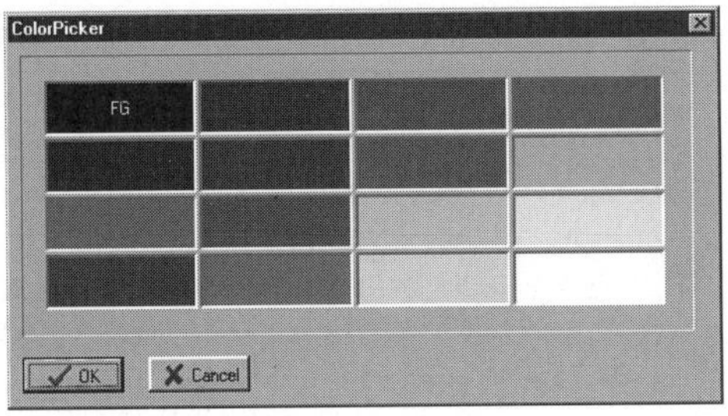

FIGURE 7.4

The property editor for the Color property of the TCCColorClock and its descendants.

This is still probably not as fancy a dialog as the one used by the VCL, but it serves as a good example of how to create your own custom component editors.

The `TColorNameProperty.Edit` method that launches this dialog looks like this:

```
procedure TCCColorNameProperty.Edit;
var
  S: String;
  ColorPicker: TColorPicker;
begin
  S := '';
  ColorPicker := TColorPicker.Create(nil);
  ColorPicker.ShowModal;
  S := ColorToString(ColorPicker.ColorChoice);
  ColorPicker.Free;
  SetValue(S);
end;
```

The code creates an instance of the TColorPicker dialog, shows it to the user, and then makes use of the color the user chose.

`SetValue`, called at the end of this procedure, is another method of `TPropertyEditor`. To create a flexible, polymorphic hierarchy, the `SetValue` method requests that you convert the value you have edited into a string. Therefore, the `SetValue` method for strings, integers, floats, and even `TColor` properties has the same declaration. Underneath, the `SetValue` method must convert the string back into an integer, float, `TColor` object, or what have you. In this particular case, the `ColorToString` and `StringToColor` methods from the `Graphics.pas` VCL unit help to make this task relatively simple.

Using the `GetAttributes` method is a way of defining what types of property editors you want to have associated with `TColorNameProperty`:

```
function TColorNameProperty.GetAttributes;
begin
  Result := [paMultiSelect, paValueList, paDialog];
end;
```

A property editor that has the `paMultiSelect` flag remains active even if the user has selected more than one component of that type. For instance, you can select 10 edit controls and change all their fonts in one step. Delphi enables you to do so because TEdits have their `paMultiSelect` flag set.

The `paValueList` flag dictates that the property editor drops down a list of values from an enumerated or set type when the user clicks the arrow button at the far right of the editor. This functionality is built into Delphi, and you need only set the flag to have it be supported by your property editor.

Finally, paDialog states that the property editor pops up a dialog. Because the Edit function shown earlier uses either an InputQuery or the TColorPicker dialog, I have decided that this flag should be set. Ultimately, the paDialog flag does little more than assure that the ellipsis button appears at the right of the property editor.

> **NOTE**
>
> When you choose both paDialog and paValuelist in a single component, the property editor button always winds up being a combo drop-down list button. In other words, the dialog button is obscured, even though the functionality is still present. See, for instance, the Color property of a TForm or TEdit.

More on Registering Your Component and Component Editors

You must register property editors with the system before compiling them into packages:

```
procedure Register;
begin
  ...
  RegisterPropertyEditor(TypeInfo(TColor),
                TCCClock, 'Color',
                TColorNameProperty);
end;
```

The declaration for RegisterPropertyEditor looks like this:

```
procedure RegisterPropertyEditor(PropertyType: PTypeInfo;
                ComponentClass: TClass;
                const PropertyName: string;
                EditorClass: TPropertyEditorClass);
```

The following describes the various parameters:

- PropertyType—The first parameter passed to this function states the type of data handled by the editor. In this case, it is TColor. Delphi uses this information as the first in a series of checklists that determine which properties should be associated with this editor.

- ComponentClass—The second parameter further qualifies which components will use this editor. In this case, I have narrowed the range down to TCCClock and its descendants. If I had written TComponent instead of TCCClock, or if I had set this parameter to nil, all properties of type TColor would start using that editor. Therefore, you could build a new editor for Fonts or Colors, install it on a customer's system, and it would work with all properties of that type. In other words, you don't have to have created a component to be able to write an editor for it.

- PropertyName—The third parameter limits the scope to properties with the name passed in this string. If the string is empty, the editor is used for all properties that get passed the first two parameters.

- EditorClass—This parameter defines the class of editor associated with the properties defined in the first three parameters.

If you want to find out more about this function, refer to the comments in DSGNINTF.

While I'm at it, I'm going to add a few more words about registering components in general. To add the clock components to the Component Palette, you must first register them:

```
procedure Register;
begin
  RegisterComponents('Unleash', [TCCClock, TCCColorClock, TFancyClock]);
  ...
end;
```

Here, I specify that the TCCClock, TFancyClock, and TCCColorClock objects should be placed in a group called Unleash.

> **NOTE**
>
> The second parameter to RegisterComponents takes an array of type TComponentClass:
>
> ```
> procedure RegisterComponents(const Page: string;
>   ComponentClasses: array of TComponentClass);
> ```
>
> Delphi supports open-arrays, which means that you do not have to declare how many members are going to be included in an array. Instead, you need to declare only the types of members that will go in the array, as shown earlier. Furthermore, when creating these arrays, you can build them on-the-fly rather than having to declare an array variable. To do so, write an open bracket and then enter the members of the array separated by commas. To close the array, write a closing bracket. For more information, look up "Open-Array Construction" in the online help.

Component Editors

After you have seen how to build property editors, you can easily understand component editors. These tools are descendants of TComponentEditor, just as property editors are descendants of TPropertyEditor:

```
TCCClockEditor = class(TComponentEditor)
  procedure Edit; override;
end;
```

The simplest possible `TClock` component would have an editor that pops up a dialog specifying a copyright:

```
procedure TCCClockEditor.Edit;
begin
  MessageDlg('Clock copyright  1995..1998 Charlie Calvert',
             mtInformation, [mbOK],0);
end;
```

This example, of course, is the simplest possible component editor, but it gets you started working with these useful tools.

A more interesting component editor would pop up a custom Delphi form, such as the one shown in Listing 7.3, and found in the file called `ClockEditor1.pas` on the book's CD. This dialog is designed to let you see the colors for the main elements of the control, as shown in Figure 7.5. You could easily improve on this component editor by dropping down a `TTabbedNotebook` and adding mechanisms for setting most of the properties of the control.

FIGURE 7.5

The minimalist component editor for the `TCCColorClock` *component.*

You can access a component editor by double-clicking on a component. This code gets executed when double-clicked:

```
procedure TCCClockEdit.Edit;
var
  ClockEditor: TClockEditor;
begin
  ClockEditor := TClockEditor.Create(nil);
  ClockEditor.BackColor := TCCFancyClock(Component).Color;
  ClockEditor.FaceColor := TCCFancyClock(Component).FaceColor;
  ClockEditor.FontColor := TCCFancyClock(Component).Font.Color;
  ClockEditor.ShowModal;
  TCCFancyClock(Component).Color := ClockEditor.BackColor;
  TCCFancyClock(Component).FaceColor := ClockEditor.FaceColor;
  TCCFancyClock(Component).Font.Color := ClockEditor.FontColor;
  ClockEditor.Free;
end;
```

7

CREATING COMPONENTS: PART II

The code first creates an instance of the object. It then assigns default values to all the fields the user is going to edit. Finally, it shows the dialog and then retrieves the users' input.

The `Register` method for `TCCClockEditor` looks like this:

```
procedure Register;
begin
  ...
  RegisterComponentEditor(TCCClock, TCCClockEditor);
  ...
end;
```

The declaration for this procedure looks like this:

```
procedure RegisterComponentEditor(ComponentClass: TComponentClass;
  ComponentEditor: TComponentEditorClass);
```

The first parameter specifies the class with which the editor is associated, and the second parameter specifies the class of the editor.

In this section, you have had an introduction to property editors and component editors. These examples are important primarily because they help focus your attention on `DSGNINTF.PAS`, which is one of several files that ship with Delphi to define the Tools API. If you want to extend the Delphi IDE, you should get to know all the files with names that end in INTF.

Nonvisual Components

Now you're ready to look at one reusable nonvisual component called `TFileIterator`. It is designed to let you iterate through a directory tree. It is used in two different sample programs. The first is a relatively simple program called `FindAllW`, and the second is a more complex program called `CompDirs`.

Both the `CompDirs` and `FindAllW` programs depend on the `TFileIterator` component. To use this component, you must first load the Unleash package from the CD that accompanies this book, as described in Chapter 1, "Program Design Basics."

The `FindAllW` program allows you to scan your directory looking for files and then view them in an editor. The `CompDirs` program allows you to compare two directory trees to see whether they are identical. If they differ, lists of files and directories are drawn up, and by using those lists, you can sync up the two directories so that they are identical.

Both of these programs use the `TFileIterator` component. As a result, they graphically demonstrate the concept of component reuse. You write the `TFileIterator` component only once, but you can reuse it in multiple programs. The big bonus here is that

`TFileIterator` is a visual component and thereby makes a relatively complex task simple enough that you can perform it by just dropping an object on a form and plugging it into your program.

The `FindAllW` Program

In Listing 7.5 through 7.7, you will find the `FindAllW` program. It can be used to iterate through the subdirectories on a hard drive looking for files with a particular name or file mask. For instance, you could look for `*.pas` or `m*.pas` or `ole2.pas`. It will put all the files that match the mask you pass to it in a list box. You can then double-click any item in the list box, and it will be loaded into WordPad. From there, you can scan through the file, looking for particular entries, or do whatever you want.

`TFileIterator`, like `TTable` and `TQuery`, is a nonvisual component. As such, it does not appear on your form at runtime. It is only visible at design time. The `TFileIterator` component is also important because it shows how to create custom event handlers.

After it has been created, `TFileIterator` can be reused in multiple programs. It makes a relatively complex task simple. You need only drop the object on a form and plug it into your program. The result is that visual tools are used to manipulate aspects of a relatively abstract process such as iterating through directories. It is something of a triumph for OOP and components to be able to produce tools that can take seemingly intangible concepts and make them tangibly present on your form.

LISTING 7.5 THE `FileIter` UNIT ENABLES YOU TO ITERATE THROUGH DIRECTORIES AND HAVE THE NAME OF EACH FILE FOUND PASSED TO `ProcessNameFile`

```
/////////////////////////////////////////////
// Purpose: Work with Alldirs.pas to iterate through directories
// Project: Unleash.dpk
// Copyright  1994..1998 by Charlie Calvert
//
unit Fileiter;

interface

{$H+}

uses
  SysUtils, Windows,
  Messages, Classes, Graphics,
  Controls, Forms, AllDirs;

type
```

continues

LISTING 7.5 CONTINUED

```
  TFileIterator = class(TRunDirs)
  private
    FFileList: TStringList;
    FDirList: TStringList;
    FUseFileList: Boolean;
    FUseDirList: Boolean;
    procedure SetFileList(UseList: Boolean);
    procedure SetDirList(UseList: Boolean);
  protected
    procedure ProcessName(FName: String; SR: TSearchRec); override;
    procedure ProcessDir(Start: String); override;
  public
    destructor Destroy; override;
    property FileList: TStringList read FFileList;
    property DirList: TStringList read FDirList;
  published
    property UseFileList: Boolean read FUseFileList write SetFileList;
    property UseDirList: Boolean read FUseDirList write SetDirList;
    property OnFoundFile;
    property OnProcessDir;
  end;

procedure Register;

implementation

procedure Register;
begin
  RegisterComponents('Unleash', [TFileIterator]);
end;

destructor TFileIterator.Destroy;
begin
  FFileList.Free;
  FDirList.Free;
  inherited Destroy;
end;

procedure TFileIterator.SetFileList(UseList: Boolean);
begin
  FUseFileList := UseList;
  if FUseFileList then
    FFileList := TStringList.Create
  else
    FFileList.Free;
end;

procedure TFileIterator.SetDirList(UseList: Boolean);
begin
```

```
    FUseDirList := UseList;
    if FUseDirList then
      FDirList := TStringList.Create
    else
      FDirList.Free;
end;

procedure TFileIterator.ProcessName(FName: String; SR: TSearchRec);
begin
  inherited ProcessName(FName, SR);
  if FUseFileList then FFileList.Add(FName);
end;

procedure TFileIterator.ProcessDir(Start: string);
begin
  inherited ProcessDir(Start);
  if FUseDirList then FDirList.Add(CurDir);
end;

end.
```

LISTING 7.6 THE AllDirs UNIT CONTAINS THE BRAINS FOR THE FileIter UNIT

```
////////////////////////////////////////
// Purpose: Iterate through a hierarchical list of directories.
// Project: Unleash.dpk
// Copyright  1996..1998 by Charlie Calvert
//
unit AllDirs;

{ Define Debug }

{--------------------------------------------------------------------
  This unit needs to be rewritten using TLists instead of arrays. Right
  now
  you could get in trouble if you tried to compare more than 1000
  directories
  at a time. I have compared up to 300 hundred directories at a time,
  which
  is a big tree, but not as big as they get.
---------------------------------------------------------------------}


interface

{$H+}
```

continues

LISTING 7.6   CONTINUED

```pascal
uses
  Classes, Controls, SysUtils;

type
  DirStr = string;
  PathStr = string;
  NameStr = string;
  ExtStr = string;

  TStack = class;
  TShortStack = class;

  TStackAry = array[1..1000] of PString;
  TStacksAry = array[1..1000] of TShortStack;

  TStack = class(TObject)
    First,
    Last: Word;
    constructor Create;
    procedure InitCount;
    function IsEmpty: Boolean;
    function Count: Integer;
  end;

  TBigStack = class(TStack)
    Stacks: TStacksAry;
    destructor Destroy; override;
    procedure Push(P: TShortStack);
    function Pop: TShortStack;
    function PopValue(var Num: Integer): String;
  end;

  TShortStack = class(TStack)
    StackAry: TStackAry;
    destructor Destroy; override;
    procedure Push(S: String);
    function Pop: String;
    function GetMoreDirs(DirAndWildCard: String): Integer;
    procedure Show;
  end;

  TFoundFileEvent = procedure(FileName: string; SR: TSearchRec) of Object;
  TFoundDirEvent = procedure(DirName: string) of Object;

  TRunDirs = class(TComponent)
  private
    FOnFoundFile: TFoundFileEvent;
    FOnProcessDir: TFoundDirEvent;
    FFileMask: String; //was Str12
    FCurDir: DirStr;
```

```
    FBigStack: TBigStack;
    FShortStack: TShortStack;
  protected
    procedure PushStack;
    procedure ProcessName(FName: String; SR: TSearchRec); virtual;
    procedure ProcessDir(Start: String); virtual;
  public
    constructor Create(Owner: TComponent); override;
    destructor Destroy; override;
    function Run(Start: PathStr; StartingDirectory: String): String;
  published
    property OnFoundFile: TFoundFileEvent
      read FOnFoundFile write FOnFoundFile;
    property OnProcessDir: TFoundDirEvent
      read FOnProcessDir write FOnProcessDir;
    property CurDir: DirStr read FCurDir;
  end;

implementation

{$IfDef Debug}
var
  F: Text;
{$EndIf Debug}

function Shorten(S: string; Cut: Integer): string;
begin
  SetLength(S, Length(S) - Cut);
  Shorten := S;
end;

/////////////////////////////////////
// TStack
/////////////////////////////////////
constructor TStack.Create;
begin
  inherited Create;
  InitCount;
end;

procedure TStack.InitCount;
begin
  First := 1;
  Last := 0;
end;

function TStack.IsEmpty: Boolean;
var
  OutCome: Boolean;
begin
  OutCome := First > Last;
```

continues

LISTING 7.6 CONTINUED

```pascal
  IsEmpty := OutCome
end;

function TStack.Count: Integer;
begin
  Count := Last - First;
end;

{====================================================}

destructor TBigStack.Destroy;
var
  i: Integer;
begin
  for i := First to Last do
    Stacks[i].Destroy;
  inherited Destroy;
end;

procedure TBigStack.Push(P: TShortStack);
begin
  Inc(Last);
  Stacks[Last] := P;
end;

function TBigStack.Pop: TShortStack;
begin
  Result := nil;
end;

function TBigStack.PopValue(var Num: Integer): String;
begin
  Num := 0;
  if IsEmpty then begin
    PopValue := '-1';
    Num := -1;
    Exit;
  end;
  while Stacks[Last].IsEmpty do begin
    Inc(Num);
    Stacks[Last].Destroy;
    Dec(Last);
    if IsEmpty then begin
      PopValue := '-1';
      Num := -1;
      Exit;
    end;
  end;
  if Last = 0 then begin
    PopValue := '-1';
```

```
      Exit;
    end;
    PopValue := Stacks[Last].Pop;
  end;


  {=================================================}

  destructor TShortStack.Destroy;
  var
    i: Integer;
  begin
    if not IsEmpty then
      for i := First to Last  do
        DisposeStr(StackAry[i]);
    inherited Destroy;
  end;

  procedure TShortStack.Show;
  var
    i: Integer;
  begin
    for i := First to Last do begin
      {$IfDef Debug}
      WriteLn(F, StackAry[i]^);
      {$EndIf}
      WriteLn(StackAry[i]^);
    end;
    {$IfDef Debug}
    WriteLn(F, '===============');
    {$EndIf}
  end;

  procedure TShortStack.Push(S: String);
  begin
    if (S <> '.') and (S <> '..') then begin
      Inc(Last);
      StackAry[Last] := NewStr(S);
    end;
  end;

  function TShortStack.Pop: String;
  var
    S: PString;
    Temp: ShortString;
  begin
    S := StackAry[First];
    if S <> nil then begin
      Temp := S^;
      DisposeStr(StackAry[First]);
      Inc(First);
      Pop := Temp;
```

7

CREATING
COMPONENTS:
PART II

continues

LISTING 7.6 CONTINUED

```
    end
  else begin
    WriteLn('Error TShortStack.Pop');
    Halt;
  end;
end;

{ - - - - - - - - - - - - - - - - - - - - - - - - - - - - - - - - - - - - - - - - - - - - - - - - - - - - - - - - - - - - -
  DirAndWildCard contains the name of a new directory and a wildcard:
  c:\*.*

  This routine iterates through the directory looking for all
  sub directories.
  - - - - - - - - - - - - - - - - - - - - - - - - - - - - - - - - - - - - - - - - - - - - - - - - - - - - - - - - - - - - - }
function TShortStack.GetMoreDirs(DirAndWildCard: String): Integer;
var
  SR: SysUtils.TSearchRec;
  Total: Integer;
begin
  Total := 0;
  if FindFirst(DirAndWildCard, faDirectory + faReadOnly, SR) = 0 then
    repeat
      if (SR.Attr and faDirectory = faDirectory) then begin
        Push(SR.Name);
        Inc(Total);
      end;
    until FindNext(SR) <> 0;
  FindClose(SR);
  GetMoreDirs := Total;
end;

{=======================================}

constructor TRunDirs.Create(Owner: TComponent);
begin
  inherited Create(Owner);
  {$IfDef Debug}
  Assign(F, 'DirLists.dat');
  ReWrite(F);
  {$EndIf}
  FShortStack := TShortStack.Create;
  FBigStack := TBigStack.Create;
end;

destructor TRunDirs.Destroy;
begin
  FShortStack.Free;
  FBigStack.Free;
```

```
  {$IfDef Debug}
  Close(F);
  {$EndIf}
  inherited Destroy;
end;

procedure TRunDirs.PushStack;
begin
  FBigStack.Push(FShortStack);
  FShortStack := TShortStack.Create;
end;

procedure SplitDirName(Path: PathStr; var Dir: DirStr; var WName: String);
begin
  Dir := ExtractFilePath(Path);
  WName := ExtractFileName(Path);
end;

function RemoveDir(Start: String; NumDirs: Integer): String;
var
  i, j: Integer;
  CurDir: DirStr;
  FileMask: string;
begin
  SplitDirName(Start, CurDir, FileMask);
  i := Length(CurDir);
  for j := 1 to NumDirs + 1 do begin
    if CurDir[i] = '\' then  begin
      CurDir := Shorten(CurDir, 1);
      Dec(i);
    end;
    while CurDir[i] <> '\' do begin
      CurDir := Shorten(CurDir, 1);
      Dec(i);
    end;
  end;
  RemoveDir := CurDir;
end;

procedure TRunDirs.ProcessName(FName: String; SR: SysUtils.TSearchRec);
begin
  if Assigned(FOnFoundFile) then
    FOnFoundFile(FName, SR);
end;

procedure TRunDirs.ProcessDir(Start: String);
var
  SR: SysUtils.TSearchRec;
  DoClose: Boolean;
begin
  DoClose := False;
```

continues

LISTING 7.6   CONTINUED

```
    if Assigned(FOnProcessDir) then FOnProcessDir(FCurDir);
    if FindFirst(Start, faArchive, SR) = 0 then begin
      DoClose := True;
      repeat
        ProcessName(UpperCase(FCurDir) + SR.Name, SR);
      until FindNext(SR) <> 0;
    end;
    if DoClose then
      FindClose(SR);
end;

function TRunDirs.Run(Start: PathStr; StartingDirectory: string): string;
const
  DirMask = '*.*';
var
  Finished: Boolean;
  NewDir, StartedAt: string;
  NumDirs: Integer;
  OutCome: Integer;
  SaveDir: string;
begin
  GetDir(0, SaveDir);
  try
    ChDir(StartingDirectory);
  except
    raise Exception.Create('Directory does not exist: ' +
      StartingDirectory);
  end;
  Start := ExpandFileName(Start);
  FCurDir := ''; FFileMask := '';
  Finished := False;
  StartedAt := Start;
  SplitDirName(Start, FCurDir, FFileMask);
  Start := FCurDir + DirMask;
  while not Finished do begin
    FCurDir := ExtractFilePath(Start);
    ProcessDir(FCurDir + FFileMask);
    OutCome := FShortStack.GetMoreDirs(Start);
    if OutCome > 2 then begin
      PushStack;
      Start := FCurDir + FBigStack.PopValue(NumDirs) + '\' + DirMask
    end else begin
      NewDir := FBigStack.PopValue(NumDirs);
      FCurDir := RemoveDir(Start, NumDirs);
      Start := FCurDir + NewDir + '\' + DirMask;
      if (Start = StartedAt) or (NewDir = '-1') then Finished := True;
    end;
  end;
  ChDir(SaveDir);
end;

end.
```

LISTING 7.7 THE MAIN FORM FOR THE FindAllW PROGRAM

```
/////////////////////////////////////
// Purpose: Do what dir /s or 4DOS FindAll program does
// Project: FindAllW.dpr
// Copyright  1995..1998 by Charlie Calvert
//
unit Main;

{-----------------------------------------------------------------
  Use this program to iterate through the directories
  on your hard drive and search for files. Enter
  the path where you want to start searching, with
  no backslash at the end, and then enter the mask
  that you want to search with, for instance '*.pas'.
-----------------------------------------------------------------}

interface

uses
  WinTypes, WinProcs, Classes,
  Graphics, Forms, Controls,
  AllDirs, StdCtrls, Fileiter,
  FileCtrl, Dialogs, SysUtils, ExtCtrls;

type
  TForm1 = class(TForm)
    BStartSearch: TButton;
    ListBox1: TListBox;
    MaskEdit: TEdit;
    Label1: TLabel;
    Label2: TLabel;
    FileIterator1: TFileIterator;
    DirectoryListBox1: TDirectoryListBox;
    DriveComboBox1: TDriveComboBox;
    Label3: TLabel;
    Bevel1: TBevel;
    Bevel2: TBevel;
    procedure BStartSearchClick(Sender: TObject);
    procedure ListBox1DblClick(Sender: TObject);
    procedure FileIterator1FoundFile(FileName: string; SR: TSearchRec);
    procedure ListBox1Click(Sender: TObject);
  end;

var
  Form1: TForm1;

implementation

{$R *.DFM}
```

continues

LISTING 7.7   CONTINUED

```
{------------------------------------------------------------------
  Make sure the FILEITERATOR's UseFileList property
  is set to true!
  ----------------------------------------------------------------}
procedure TForm1.BStartSearchClick(Sender: TObject);
var
  RootDirectory, Mask, SaveCaption: String;
begin
  SaveCaption := Label3.Caption;
  FileIterator1.FileList.Clear;
  ListBox1.Clear;

  Mask := MaskEdit.Text;
  RootDirectory := DirectoryListBox1.Directory;

  FileIterator1.Run(Mask, RootDirectory);
  ListBox1.Items := FileIterator1.FileList;
  Label3.Caption := SaveCaption;
end;

procedure TForm1.FileIterator1FoundFile(FileName: string; SR: TSearchRec);
begin
  Label3.Caption := FileName;
  Label3.UpDate;
end;

procedure TForm1.ListBox1Click(Sender: TObject);
var
  S: string;
begin
  S := ListBox1.Items.Strings[ListBox1.ItemIndex];
  Label3.Caption := 'File Name: ' + ExtractFileName(S);
end;

procedure TForm1.ListBox1DblClick(Sender: TObject);
var
  S: string;
begin
  S := 'Write ' + ListBox1.Items.Strings[ListBox1.ItemIndex];
  WinExec(PChar(S), sw_ShowNormal);
end;

end.
```

Earlier I described what this program does. Now I'm going to describe how to use it.

To use `FindAllW`, point it to a subdirectory on your hard disk. Type a file mask in the edit control at the bottom of the form. For instance, you might type in `*.pas`. When you click the button at the bottom of the program, the code iterates through all the directories beneath the one you pointed to and finds all the files that have a `*.pas` extension. It then places these files in a list box, as shown in Figure 7.6. If you double-click one of the files in the list box, it will be loaded into the WordPad program that ships with Windows 95/98 or NT 4 or into the Write program that ships with Windows NT 3.51.

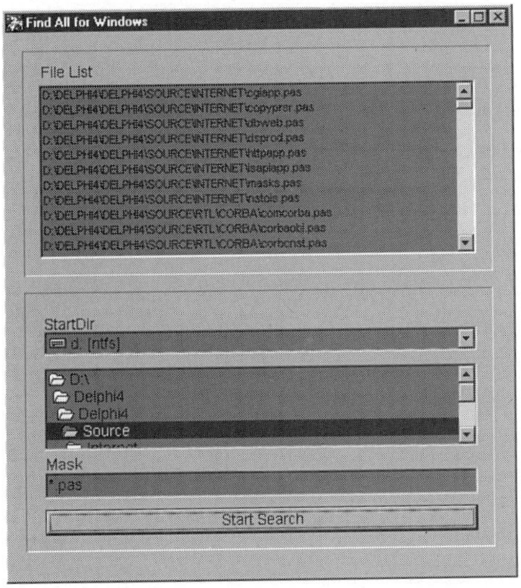

FIGURE 7.6

The `FindAllW` *program allows you to search through multiple directories looking for files with a particular extension.*

Looking at the code listings shown in this chapter is in one sense deceptive. All you, as a programmer, have to write is the code in the last of these three listings, which consists of three short methods. All the code in the `FileIter` and `AllDirs` units is wrapped up in a component that you just drop down on a form. The key point here is that the `FindAllW` program is incredibly easy to write, especially when you consider the functionality inherent in it.

Iterating Through Directories with `TFileIterator`

The `FindAllW` program uses the `TFileIterator` component to iterate through directories. The `TFileIterator` component sends events to your program whenever a new directory or a new file is found. The events include the name of the new directory or file, as well as information about the size and date of the files it finds. You can respond to these events in any way you want. The `FindAllW` program elects not to respond to the event triggered when a directory is found. However, it will respond to the events associated with finding files.

For instance, the `FindAllW` program responds like this when a file with the proper extension is found:

```
procedure TForm1.FileIterator1FoundFile(FileName: string; SR: TSearchRec);
begin
  Label3.Caption := FileName;
  Label3.UpDate;
end;
```

As you can see, the code does nothing more than show the filename to the user. The call to `Update` forces the label to display the file before giving the processor any more clock cycles.

Part of the built-in functionality of the `TFileIterator` component is to maintain lists of the files it finds. To get this functionality, you must set the `UseFileList` property to `True`. When you finish searching all the directories, the list is ready for you to do with as you wish. This list is kept in a `TStringList` object, so you can just assign it to the `Items` property in a list box, as shown in this excerpt from the `BStartSearchClick` method:

```
FileIterator1.Run(Mask, RootDirectory);
ListBox1.Items := FileIterator1.FileList;
```

The first line shown here passes in the file mask that you want to search on. For instance, you might typically pass in `*.pas` in the `Start` parameter. The second parameter, `RunDir`, designates the directory where you want your search to start. By calling `Run`, you start the process. As each file that meets the requirements is found, it is passed to the `FileIterator1FoundFile` event handler and displayed. When the run is finished, you can access the list of files as shown previously.

The following is a more literal example of calling `FileIterator1.Run`:

```
FileIterator1.Run('*.pas', 'c:\Source');
```

In this example, you will find all files that have a `.pas` extension and that reside in the `C:\SOURCE` directory or one of its child directories.

Notice that the `FileIterator1FoundFile` method is an event handler. Component consumers create this handler by clicking once on the `OnFoundFile` event in the Object Inspector Events page for the `TFileIterator`. The `TFileIterator` has events for both finding files and for finding directories. The same is true of the lists it maintains. One is for finding files, the other for finding directories. The `FindAllW` program opts to work only with the files that are found; it does not keep lists of directories that are found. It will, however, iterate over all the directories beneath the one you pass in via the second parameter of the `Run` method.

After the `TFileIterator` component has completed a run, you can view the files that were found in a list box. If you double-click one of these files, it is loaded into the Windows Write or WordPad program:

```
procedure TForm1.ListBox1DblClick(Sender: TObject);
var
  S: string;
begin
  S := 'Write ' + ListBox1.Items.Strings[ListBox1.ItemIndex];
  WinExec(PChar(S), sw_ShowNormal);
end;
```

The `WinExec` procedure launches an executable and then returns control to your program. It takes the name of the file and any parameters you want to pass to it in the first parameter. The second parameter tells `WinExec` how you want the program to start. For instance, `sw_ShowMinimized` would start the program in a minimized state.

> **NOTE**
>
> `WinExec` is a Windows API routine that is officially labeled obsolete. It is, however, still part of this incarnation of WIN32. The official Microsoft function for this purpose, called `CreateProcess`, is a bear to use. The following, however, is a version of `WinExec` called `WinExec2` that uses `CreateProcess`:
>
> ```
> procedure WinExec2(ProgramToStart: string; Params: string; Show:
> Integer);
> var
>   StartupInfo: TStartupInfo;
>   ProcessInfo: TProcessInformation;
> begin
>   if Params[1] <> ' ' then
>     Params := ' ' + Params;
>   FillChar(StartupInfo, SizeOf(TStartupInfo), 0);
>   StartupInfo.cb := SizeOf(TStartupInfo);
>   StartupInfo.dwFlags := STARTF_USESHOWWINDOW;
>   StartupInfo.wShowWindow := Show;
>   if not (CreateProcess(PChar(ProgramToStart), PChar(Params), nil,
>     nil, False, NORMAL_PRIORITY_CLASS, nil, nil,
>     StartupInfo, ProcessInfo)) then
>     RaiseLastWin32Error;
> end;
>
> procedure TForm1.Button1Click(Sender: TObject);
> begin
>   WinExec2('c:\windows\notepad.exe', 'c:\autoexec.bat', SW_SHOWNORMAL);
> end;
> ```
>
> *continues*

The `Button1ClickMethod` shows how you might call the function. I have placed this routine in `CodeBox.pas`.

If you can stand a rather abrupt change of topic, I might add that under the default installation of Windows 95/98, if you go to the Run menu on the taskbar and type in the word `Write` and press Enter, you will end up launching WordPad, not Write. The same results occur if you type `Write` from the command line or if you pass it as a parameter to `WinExec`. I believe that the mechanism employed here involves a small stub program, called `WRITE.EXE`, that ends up launching `WORDPAD.EXE`. At any rate, my point is that I pass in Write to `WinExec` not because I am primarily a Windows NT 3.51 user, but because the program name works in both Windows NT and Windows 95/98.

When Should Objects Become Nonvisual Components?

Whether you should turn a particular object into a component is not always clear. For instance, the `TStringList` object has no related component and cannot be manipulated through visual tools. The question then becomes "Why have I taken the `TFileIterator` object and placed it on the Component Palette?"

As it turns out, the advantages of placing `TFileIterator` on the Component Palette are two-fold:

- You might need to tweak several options before you use this object. In particular, you need to decide whether you want to have the lists of directories and files that you find saved to memory in a `TStringList`. Letting the programmer decide these matters by clicking a property can go a long way toward presenting a clean, easy-to-use interface for an object.

- The `TFileIterator` object has two features that can be accessed through the Events page. Specifically, custom event handlers can be notified every time a new file or directory has been found. However, it can be confusing to construct an event handler manually, particularly if you don't know what parameters will be passed to the functions involved. If you place a component on the Component Palette, the programmer doesn't need to guess about how to handle an event. All it takes is a quick click on the Events page, and the event handler is created for you automatically.

Creating a component also has the enormous advantage of forcing, or at least enticing, programmers to design a simple interface for an object. After I have placed an object on the Component Palette, I always want to ensure that the user can hook it into his or her program in only a few short seconds. I am therefore strongly inclined to create a simple, easy-to-use interface. If I don't place the component on the Component Palette, then I find it easier to attempt to slip by with a complex interface that takes many lines of code for myself and others to utilize. To my mind, good components are not only bug free, but they are also very easy to use.

The `AllDirs` and `FileIter` Units

The program shown in this chapter uses two units called `AllDirs` and `FileIter`. The `AllDirs` unit has built-in stacks and an object called `TRunDirs` that knows how to iterate through subdirectories. Notice that `TRunDirs` is a descendant of `TComponent`. Nonvisual components often descend directly from `TComponent`. By definition, a nonvisual component would never descend from `TCustomControl`, `TGraphicControl`, or `TWinControl`, as they are visual controls.

`FileIter` features a simple descendant of `TRunDirs` called `TFileIterator` that adds list management capabilities. In other words, `TRunDirs` knows how to iterate through subdirectories and how to call the `OnFoundFile` and `OnFoundDir` events. You may, however, want to add list-keeping to the set of skills found in `TRunDirs`. I have therefore added the `TFileIterator` component as a second layer of additional functionality.

This idea of layering your components so that you can create different objects, descending from different parents, under different circumstances, is key to object-oriented design. You don't want to push too much functionality up too high in the object hierarchy, or you will be forced to rewrite the object to get access to a subset of its functionality. For instance, if the Delphi developers had not created a `TBDEDataSet` component but had instead created one component called `TTable`, they would have had to duplicate that same functionality in the `TQuery` component. This duplication is wasteful. The smart thing to do is to build a component called `TDataSet` and end its functionality at the point at which the specific attributes of `TQuery` and `TTable` need to be defined. That way, `TQuery` and `TTable` can both reuse the functionality of `TBDEDataSet` rather than your having to rewrite that same functionality for both objects.

Before closing this section, let me reiterate some key points. The `AllDirs` unit is the brains of this particular operation. It knows how to iterate through directories, how to find all the files in each directory, and how to notify the user when new directories or files are found. The `FileIter` unit adds the capability to store lists of files and directories in `TStringList` objects. You can, of course, write these lists to disk by using the `SaveToFile` command.

Iterating Through Directories

The task of iterating through directories has a simple recursive solution. However, recursion is a slow and time-consuming technique that is also wasteful of stack space. As a result, AllDirs creates its own stacks (that use the heap rather than the stack) and pushes the directories it finds onto them.

> **NOTE**
>
> Delphi has some built-in tools for creating stacks and lists—for instance, the TList and TStringList objects. I avoided these tools at the time I wrote this code because they were not compatible with 16-bit Turbo Pascal code. I should now rewrite the code to use these objects but have not yet gotten around to that chore. On the other hand, the code I have here works.

The following objects are in the AllDirs unit:

- The TStack object is an abstract class that provides some basic functionality for handling all classes of stacks. You'll never have a reason to instantiate an object of this type.

- The TShortStack object handles an array of up to 1000 long strings. It contains all the logic needed for storing and deleting these items. It holds them in an array that takes up only 4000 bytes of memory. That's 4 bytes per long string times 1000 possible long strings, which equals 4000 bytes. This is a huge amount of overkill for this type of program, as it is very unlikely that you will encounter a case in which you have 1000 nested directories.

- The TBigStack object creates stacks of TShortStack objects. One directory's worth of subdirectories can be stored in a TShortStack. However, if a directory has multiple subdirectories that have multiple subdirectories, you need TBigStack.

- The TRunDirs object is built around a series of FindFirst and FindNext calls. It uses these Delphi functions to find the files in a directory. It then pushes the directories it finds onto the TShortStack and TBigStack objects.

To dust off the classic analogy used in these situations, the FIFO (first in, first out) and LIFO (last in, first out) stacks implemented here are like piles of plates in a kitchen cabinet. You can put one plate down and then add another one to it. When you need one of the plates, you take the first one off either the top or the bottom depending on whether it's a FIFO or a LIFO stack. Putting a new plate on the top of a stack is called *pushing* the object onto the stack, and removing a plate is called *popping* the object off the stack.

For more information on stacks, refer to any book on basic programming theory such as *Algorithms in Pascal* by Robert Sedgewick, published by Addison Wesley (ISBN 0-201-510590-6), or *Turbo Pascal 6 Object-Oriented Programming* by Namir Shammas, published by Sams (ISBN 0-672-30221-7).

Using FindFirst, FindNext, and FindClose

This section continues the examination of the stacks created in the AllDirs units. The cores of these stacks are the calls to FindFirst, FindNext, and FindClose that search through directories looking for particular files.

Using FindFirst, FindNext, and FindClose is like typing DIR in a directory at the DOS prompt. FindFirst finds the first file in the directory, and FindNext finds the remaining files. You should call FindClose when you are finished with the process.

These calls enable you to specify a directory and file mask, as if you were issuing a command of the following type at the DOS prompt:

```
Dir c:\aut*.bat
```

This command would, of course, show all files beginning with aut and ending in .bat. This particular command would typically find AUTOEXEC.BAT and perhaps one or two other files.

When you call FindFirst, you pass in three parameters:

```
function FindFirst(
  const Path: string;
  Attr: Word;
  var F: TSearchRec
): Integer;
```

The first parameter contains the path and file mask that specify the files you want to find. For instance, you might pass in 'c:\delphi32\source\vcl*.pas' or 'c:\program files\borland\delphi 2.0' in this parameter. The second parameter lists the type of files you want to see:

faReadOnly	$01	Read-only files
faHidden	$02	Hidden files
faSysFile	$04	System files
faVolumeID	$08	Volume ID files
faDirectory	$10	Directory files
faArchive	$20	Archive files
faAnyFile	$3F	Any file

Most of the time, you should pass in faArchive in this parameter. However, if you want to see directories, pass in faDirectory. The Attribute parameter is not a filter. No matter what flags you use, you will always get all normal files in the directory. Passing

`faDirectory` causes directories to be included in the list of normal files; it does not limit the list to directories. You can OR together several different `faXXX` constants, if you wish. The final parameter is a variable of type `TSearchRec`, which is declared as follows:

```
TSearchRec = record
  Fill: array[1..21] of Byte;
  Attr: Byte;
  Time: Longint;
  Size: Longint;
  Name: string[12];
end;
```

The most important value in `TSearchRec` is the `Name` field, which on success specifies the name of the file found. `FindFirst` returns zero if it finds a file and nonzero if the call fails.

`FindNext` works exactly like `FindFirst`, except that you have to pass in only a variable of type `TSearchRec` because it is assumed that the mask and file attribute are the same. Once again, `FindNext` returns zero if all goes well and a nonzero value if it can't find a file. You should call `FindClose` after completing a `FindFirst`/`FindNext` sequence.

Given this information, you can use this simple way to call `FindFirst`, `FindNext`, and `FindClose`:

```
var
  SR: TSearchRec;
begin
  if FindFirst(Start, faArchive, SR) = 0 then
    repeat
      DoSomething(SR.Name);
    until FindNext(SR) <> 0;
  FindClose(SR);
```

As I said earlier, you can learn more about stacks by studying a book on basic programming data structures. This book, however, is about Delphi, so I'm going to move on to a discussion of creating event handlers.

Creating Your Own Event Handlers

Whenever `TRunDirs` is ready to process a new directory, it passes its name to a method called `ProcessDir`:

```
procedure TRunDirs.ProcessDir(Start: String);
var
  SR: SysUtils.TSearchRec;
  DoClose: Boolean;
begin
  DoClose := False;
```

```
      if Assigned(FOnProcessDir) then FOnProcessDir(FCurDir);
      if FindFirst(Start, faArchive, SR) = 0 then begin
        DoClose := True;
        repeat
          ProcessName(UpperCase(FCurDir) + SR.Name, SR);
        until FindNext(SR) <> 0;
      end;
      if DoClose then
        FindClose(SR);
end;
```

ProcessDir iterates through all the files in a directory and passes each file it finds to the ProcessName method:

```
procedure TRunDirs.ProcessName(FName: String; SR: SysUtils.TSearchRec);
begin
  if Assigned(FOnFoundFile) then
    FOnFoundFile(FName, SR);
end;
```

Both ProcessDir and ProcessName are virtual methods. Therefore, you can create a descendant of TRunDirs, override either of these methods, and respond to them in any way you like.

Creating a descendant of TRunDirs is a simple enough operation, but it's even simpler to respond to event handlers through the delegation model. In other words, you could create a descendant of TRunDirs (or TFileIterator) and then override the ProcessName method. Doing so would give you easy access to each name as it is processed. However, you can achieve the same end in a simpler way. Specifically, you could create an event handler and have that event called each time a file is found.

To create an OnXXX event handler, you must first declare a pointer to a method. The method pointer you are creating will point to the method that will be called if the event takes place. Each particular type of method handler will have a signature. For instance, OnClick events always get passed a parameter called Sender, which is of type TObject.

The Sender/TObject type of routine, called a TNotifyEvent, is declared like this:

```
TNotifyEvent = procedure(Sender: TObject) of object;
```

The preceding is just a declaration for a method pointer. The confusing part is the "of object" statement. If you strip that out, you can easily say what is happening here. The "of object" bit is just a way of telling the compiler that this is a pointer to a method, and not a pointer to function or procedure.

Getting from a TNotifyEvent method pointer declaration to an event like this is easy to see:

```
procedure TForm1.Button1Click(Sender: TObject);
```

A `Button1Click` method is just an instance of a method of type `TNotifyEvent`. All an `OnClick` event does is provide an instance of a method that matches the `OnClick` method pointer stored inside an object.

You can declare the method pointer for the `OnFoundDir` event this way:

```
TFoundDirEvent = procedure(DirName: string) of Object;
```

This pointer references a method that takes a single string as a parameter. Methods of this type will be created when you click the `OnFoundDir` event in the Events page. Exactly this same process occurs when you click an `OnClick` event for a button, except that the signature of the method types is different, and more particularly, this time the signature is defined in the `AllDirs` unit, not in some unit that ships with Delphi.

> **NOTE**
>
> An `OnFoundFile` signature looks like this:
> ```
> TFoundFileEvent = procedure(FileName: string;
>     SR: SysUtils.TSearchRec) of Object;
> ```
> The `OnFoundFile` event is the one that is actually used in the `FindAllW` program, but I am concentrating on the `OnFoundDir` event because it takes only one parameter and is therefore a bit easier to understand.

You declare a variable that can point to an object of this type as follows:

```
FOnProcessDir: TFoundDirEvent;
```

Now the `TRunDirs` object has the tools it needs to use the delegation model. Specifically, it contains an internal variable that can be set equal to a method of the correct type. Whenever a particular event occurs, the `TRunDirs` object can use this variable to call the method delegated to handle the event:

```
if Assigned(FOnProcessDir) then FOnProcessDir(FCurDir);
```

This code is from the body of the `ProcessDir` method. It first checks to see whether `FOnProcessDir` is set to `nil`. If it is not `nil`, that means you have assigned a method to handle this event, and the event is called.

Event handlers are merely properties that consist of pointers to functions rather than to some other kind of data. The following is the declaration for the `OnProcessDir` event:

```
property OnProcessDir: TFoundDirEvent
  read FOnProcessDir
  write FOnProcessDir;
```

You can see that this property is declared to be of type TFoundDirEvent rather than being of some other, more common type such as a string, integer, or set. This property serves as an interface for the FOnProcessDir variable, mentioned earlier. FOnProcessDir is hidden from other objects in the private section:

```
private
  FOnProcessDir: TFoundDirEvent;
```

As you can see, FOnProcessDir is just a method pointer. It's just another four-byte pointer to some variable, except that this variable happens to be a method pointer or, more specifically, an event handler.

Event handlers are attractive because they can be accessed readily from the Object Inspector. Double-click the property editor for an event handler, and the method associated with that event is immediately inserted into your code. In short, event handlers are a modest form of code generator, in which the code that is generated is a declaration for any sort of method you might wish to define.

You now know how to create your own event handlers. This important information can set you free to start really taking advantage of the power of the programming environment in which you work. This is the end of my discussion of the FindAllW program and also the end of my overview of the TFileIterator component. In the next section, I will give an example of reusing the component.

The CompDirs Program

The CompDirs program, found on the CD that comes with this book, can be used to compare the files in two directory trees. If some of the files in one directory tree are newer or missing from the other directory tree, then the files can be copied over to the second tree. When you are done, the two directory trees should be identical.

My discussion of this program is going to be brief. The FindAllW program took the TFileIterator component through a good workout, and this second program's primary purpose is to demonstrate the principle of reuse. In other words, it will show how easily you can reuse a component in more than one program. It is also a generally useful program and one that demonstrates a number of interesting aspects of programming. Listing 7.8 shows the object in the program that tests to see whether any directories are missing from the second directory tree.

LISTING 7.8   THE CompDir1 UNIT CHECKS TO SEE WHETHER THE SECOND DIRECTORY TREE
MATCHES THE FIRST DIRECTORY TREE

```pascal
unit CompDir1;

interface

uses
  Windows, Messages, SysUtils,
  Classes, Graphics, Controls,
  Forms, Dialogs, AllDirs,
  Fileiter, DB, DBTables,
  StdCtrls, Grids, DBGrids,
  ExtCtrls, ComCtrls;

type
  TCompDir = class(TForm)
    FileIterator1: TFileIterator;
    MakeRunBtn: TButton;
    procedure FileIterator1ProcessDir(DirName: string);
    procedure FormCreate(Sender: TObject);
    procedure FormDestroy(Sender: TObject);
  private
    FCapStr: string;
    FDirFile: TextFile;
    FDirList1: TStringList;
    FDirList2: TStringList;
    FDirRun: Integer;
    FDirsFound1: Integer;
    FDirsFound2: Integer;
    FFileName: string;
    procedure EmptyTables;
    procedure PutInFile(NewDir: string; OriginalDir: string);
    procedure RunCompare(Dir1, Dir2: string);
    procedure SetDirList1(const Value: TStringList);
    procedure SetDirlist2(const Value: TStringList);
  public
    procedure MakeRun(Dir1, Dir2: string);
    property BatchFileName: string read FFileName;
    property DirList1: TStringList read FDirList1 write SetDirList1;
    property Dirlist2: TStringList read FDirlist2 write SetDirlist2;
  end;

var
  CompDir: TCompDir;

implementation

uses
  PickDir2, CodeBox, DMod1,
  Globals, DirectorySelection1, Main;
```

```
{$R *.DFM}

function ReplaceStringSpecial(NewStr, ReplaceStr, Data: string): string;
var
  OffSet: Integer;
begin
  OffSet := Pos(ReplaceStr, Data);
  Delete(Data, OffSet, Length(ReplaceStr));
  if Length(Data) = 0 then begin
    Result := '';
    Exit;
  end else if Data[1] <> '\' then
    Data := '\' + Data;
  Insert(NewStr, Data, OffSet);
  Result := Data;
end;

{-----------------------------------------------------------------------}
{-- TCompDir ----------------------------------------------------------}
{-----------------------------------------------------------------------}

procedure TCompDir.EmptyTables;
begin
  FDirList1.Clear;
  FDirList2.Clear;
end;

procedure TCompDir.FormCreate(Sender: TObject);
begin
  FCapStr := Caption + ' -- ';
  FDirList1 := TStringList.Create;
  FDirList2 := TStringList.Create;
end;

procedure TCompDir.FormDestroy(Sender: TObject);
begin
  FDirList1.Free;
  FDirList2.Free;
end;

procedure TCompDir.FileIterator1ProcessDir(DirName: string);
begin
  case FDirRun of
    1: begin
      Inc(FDirsFound1);
      FDirList1.Add(UpperCase(DirName));
```

continues

LISTING 7.8 CONTINUED

```
      Form1.DirNameA.Caption := DirName;
      Form1.DirFoundA.Caption := IntToStr(FDirsFound1);
    end;
    2: begin
      FDirList2.Add(UpperCase(DirName));
      Inc(FDirsFound2);
      Form1.DirNameB.Caption := DirName;
      Form1.DirFoundB.Caption := IntToStr(FDirsFound2);
    end;
  end;
  Form1.Update;
end;

procedure TCompDir.MakeRun(Dir1, Dir2: string);
begin
  Screen.Cursor := crHourGlass;
  FDirsFound1 := 0;
  FDirsFound2 := 0;
  Application.ProcessMessages;
  try
    EmptyTables;
    FDirRun := 1;
    Caption := FCapStr + 'Processing: ' + Dir1;
    FileIterator1.Run('*.*', Dir1);
    FDirRun := 2;
    Caption := FCapStr + 'Processing: ' + Dir2;
    FileIterator1.Run('*.*', Dir2);
    RunCompare(Dir1, Dir2);
  finally
    Screen.Cursor := crDefault;
  end;
end;

procedure TCompDir.PutInFile(NewDir: string; OriginalDir: String);
begin
  AssignFile(FDirFile, FFileName);
  Append(FDirFile);
  WriteLn(FDirFile, 'REM ', OriginalDir, ' ', NewDir);
  WriteLn(FDirFile, 'md "', NewDir, '"');
  CloseFile(FDirFile);
end;

procedure TCompDir.RunCompare(Dir1, Dir2: string);
var
  NewDir, OriginalDir: string;
  i, Index: Integer;
begin
  FFileName := GetMissingDirsName;
  CreateNewFile(FDirFile, FFileName);
```

```
{$IFDEF DEBUG}
FDirList1.SaveToFile('c:\temp\DirList1.txt');
FDirList2.SaveToFile('c:\temp\DirList2.txt');
{$ENDIF}
for i := 0 to FDirList1.Count - 1 do begin
  OriginalDir := FDirList1.Strings[i];
  NewDir := ReplaceStringSpecial(Dir2, Dir1, OriginalDir);
  if FDirList2.IndexOf(NewDir) = -1 then begin
    if Length(NewDir) > 0 then
      PutInFile(NewDir, OriginalDir);
  end;
end;
end;

procedure TCompDir.SetDirList1(const Value: TStringList);
begin
  FDirList1 := Value;
end;

procedure TCompDir.SetDirlist2(const Value: TStringList);
begin
  FDirList2 := Value;
end;

end.
```

This program allows you to compare two directory structures to see whether they differ. The code takes in account not only the current directory, but any subdirectories beneath it. In other words, it is a GUI version of the XCopy command.

The typical usage for the program would be to compare two directory structures to see how the differ. In particular, I had three copies of the code for this book: one on my laptop, one on my home machine, and one on a removable disk.

To maintain the systems, I could copy all the files from one place to another each time I changed machines, or else I could use XCopy to compare the files. Murphy's law dictates that I would eventually end up writing new code on both the laptop and the home machine without first copying all the files from one machine to the other. If I then copied all the files from one machine to the other, I would overwrite new work on one of the machines. The only good way out of the mess was either to use XCopy or a program like this one.

This program has two parts: one for comparing directory structures and one for comparing every file in the two directory structures. The usual operation for the program is to pop up the SelectDirectory dialog and give the users a chance to choose the directories they want to compare, as shown in Figure 7.7. This list of directories is part of a Paradox table that the users can update or edit as they wish.

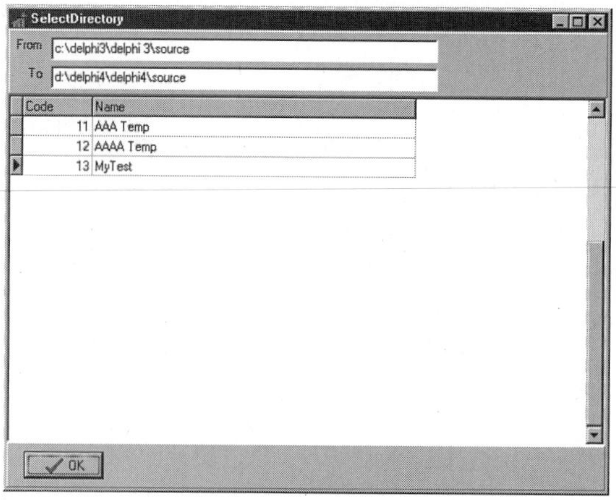

FIGURE 7.7

Selecting directo-
ries in the
SelectDirectory
dialog of the
CompDirs *program.*

After you make the selection, the program iterates through all the directories and files and compares them. When it is done, it creates a text file listing the files that don't match. These text files can be run from the DOS prompt as batch files or processed by the program to let Windows routines copy the files and create the new directories. In other words, you can perform the actual file copy and directory creation from the DOS prompt or from inside the CompDirs program.

The only part of the comparison that matters is the part of the path and filename that appears after the listing of the two directories. For instance, if you choose to compare the directories

```
c:\src\unleash
d:\unleash
```

then the following two files will be considered identical, assuming that they both have the same date:

```
c:\src\unleash\chap33\bitdll\bitdll.dpr
c:\unleash\chap33\bitdll\bitdll.dpr
```

You usually need to compare the directories twice, once from the source to destination and once from destination to source. In the PickDirs dialog, you can use a swap button to swap the two directories easily after you have completed one run. If a run completes and a blank list of files or directories appears, then the two directories' structures should be identical.

This method gets called when a directory is found:

```
procedure TCompDir.FileIterator1ProcessDir(DirName: string);
begin
  case FDirRun of
```

```
    1: begin
       Inc(FDirsFound1);
       FDirList1.Add(UpperCase(DirName));
       Form1.DirNameA.Caption := DirName;
       Form1.DirFoundA.Caption := IntToStr(FDirsFound1);
     end;
    2: begin
       FDirList2.Add(UpperCase(DirName));
       Inc(FDirsFound2);
       Form1.DirNameB.Caption := DirName;
       Form1.DirFoundB.Caption := IntToStr(FDirsFound2);
     end;
  end;
  Form1.Update;
end;
```

This code puts the name of a directory in a `TStringList` called `FDirList1` if the first tree is being processed. If the second directory tree is being processed, then it puts the newly found name in the second string list maintained by the object. (As you can see, I could not use the `TFileIterator` built-in lists in this case, as I had a need not for one list, but for two specially constructed lists.)

After the two lists are created, the following method is called to decide which directories that appear in list one are not present in list two:

```
procedure TCompDir.RunCompare(Dir1, Dir2: string);
var
  NewDir, OriginalDir: string;
  i, Index: Integer;
begin
  FFileName := GetMissingDirsName;
  CreateNewFile(FDirFile, FFileName);
  {$IFDEF DEBUG}
  FDirList1.SaveToFile('c:\temp\DirList1.txt');
  FDirList2.SaveToFile('c:\temp\DirList2.txt');
  {$ENDIF}
  for i := 0 to FDirList1.Count - 1 do begin
    OriginalDir := FDirList1.Strings[i];
    NewDir := ReplaceStringSpecial(Dir2, Dir1, OriginalDir);
    if FDirList2.IndexOf(NewDir) = -1 then begin
      if Length(NewDir) > 0 then
        PutInFile(NewDir, OriginalDir);
    end;
  end;
end;
```

As you can see, I use the `IndexOf` property of the `TStringList` object to check for duplications. If I don't find the directory from the first list in the second list, then I write its name to a special file. When the program finishes its run, this special file will contain the list of directories that need to be created. (This is one of the times when you might consider using one of the binary trees available from third parties such as TurboPower, as it could speed up the search for a string.)

As you can see, the logic in this part of the CompDirs program is pretty straightforward. The reason it is so simple to write is that the TFileIterator component takes all the hard work and encapsulates it inside a reusable component. Other parts of the CompDirs program are more complex, but the code I've shown here is sufficient to give you a sense of how the program works, at least within the context of the subject matter for this chapter.

Some Notes on Component Maintenance

Over the years, I have found problems with the CompDirs program that owed their origin to bugs in the TFileIterator component. When I found one of those bugs or suspected its existence, then I could take TFileIterator out of the CompDirs program and create a simple test bed. For instance, I could just shut down the relatively complex CompDirs program and test the component inside something simple like FindAllW, or a program custom-made to stress the part of the component that I thought might not be working correctly. Inside these custom test beds, I could usually find the problem fairly quickly and fix it. Then I could go back to the CompDirs program and see whether everything was working correctly.

My point in the preceding paragraph is simply that components help you structure programs so that they can be easily maintained. Binding an object into a program so that it can't be easily tested on its own is a terrible mistake. Components not only make it difficult for you to make that kind of mistake, but they also make it particularly easy to test an object in a new environment. In short, components can help you write well-ordered, proper, object-oriented code. They make it easy, or at least easier, for you to maintain your code.

TCCPickDirDlg

In this section, I will show you a nonvisual component that pops up a custom Delphi form. The TOpenDialog and TColorDialog are similar components, except that they are popping up common dialogs, whereas this control pops up a Delphi dialog.

The control used in this example is called a TCCPickDirDlg. It is an extremely simple TComponent descendant that allows the user to select a directory, as shown in Figure 7.8. This task commonly needs to be performed in programs, yet no component that ships with Delphi allows you to select directories. To help you understand the component, let me draw a parallel between it and some controls with which you are familiar:

- `TOpenDialog` lets the user select a file.

- The `TColorDialog` lets the user select a color.

- Now the `TCCPickDirDlg` lets the user select a directory.

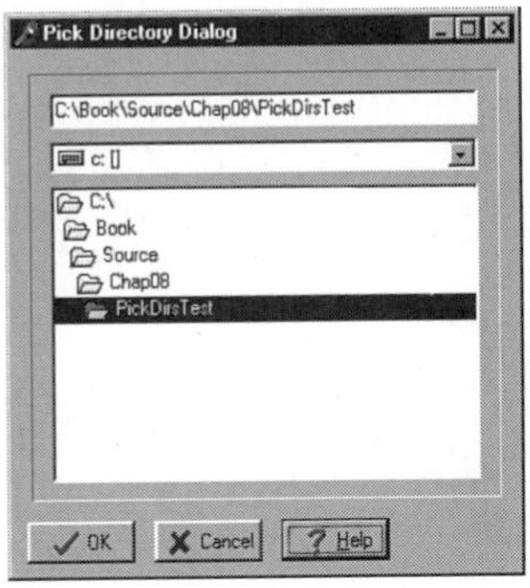

FIGURE 7.8

The `TCCPickDirDlg` *in action.*

7

Beneath the covers, the component does little more than create an instance of a Delphi form, display it to the user, and relay the results of the user's actions in the form. A component like this is not difficult to create, but it is extremely powerful. Essentially, it lets you place all the resources of Delphi on a form and then wrap that form inside a component. Of course, the `TCCPickDirDlg` just uses a paltry sprinkling of Delphi's resources. However, it shows you how to proceed if you want to create more complex components of this type.

The `TCCPickDirDlg` component is shown in Listings 7.9 and 7.10. Listing 7.9 contains the component itself, and Listing 7.10 shows the form that is wrapped inside the component.

LISTING 7.9 THE SIMPLE COMPONENT USED TO PICK DIRECTORIES USES A DELPHI FORM TO HANDLE ITS CORE TASKS

```
unit PickDirDialog;

interface

{------------------------------------------------------------------------
  This is a nonvisual component that launches a form. In doing
  this, you can see one way to create very complex components
  that consist of multiple other components. For more information
  on combining multiple components into one component, see the
  TCCLabelEdit component.
------------------------------------------------------------------------}
```

continues

LISTING 7.9   CONTINUED

```
uses
  Windows, Messages, SysUtils,
  Classes, Graphics, Controls,
  Forms, Dialogs, PickDirectory2;

type
  TCCPickDirDlg = class(TComponent)
  private
    { Private declarations }
    FPickDialog: TPickDirectory;
    function GetDirectory: string;
    procedure SetDirectory(const Value: string);
  protected
    { Protected declarations }
  public
    constructor Create(AOwner: TComponent); override;
    destructor Destroy; override;
    function Execute: Boolean;
  published
    property Directory: string read GetDirectory write SetDirectory;
    { Published declarations }
  end;

procedure Register;

implementation

procedure Register;
begin
  RegisterComponents('Unleash', [TCCPickDirDlg]);
end;

{ TPickDirectory }

constructor TCCPickDirDlg.Create(AOwner: TComponent);
begin
  inherited Create(AOwner);
  FPickDialog := TPickDirectory.Create(AOwner);
end;

destructor TCCPickDirDlg.Destroy;
begin
  // The form owns the dialog, so don't destroy it.
  inherited Destroy;
end;

function TCCPickDirDlg.Execute: Boolean;
begin
  Result := False;
```

```
    if FPickDialog.ShowModal = mrOk then
      Result := True;
end;

function TCCPickDirDlg.GetDirectory: string;
begin
  Result := FPickDialog.Directory;
end;

procedure TCCPickDirDlg.SetDirectory(const Value: string);
begin
  FPickDialog.Directory := Value;
end;

initialization
  RegisterClass(TPickDirectory);
end.
```

LISTING 7.10 THE USER PICKS A DIRECTORY IN THIS DELPHI FORM, AND THE INFORMATION IS RELAYED BACK TO THE TCCPickDirDlg COMPONENT

```
unit PickDirectory2;

interface

uses
  Windows, SysUtils, Classes,
  Graphics, Forms, Controls,
  StdCtrls, Buttons, ExtCtrls,
  FileCtrl;

type
  TPickDirectory = class(TForm)
    HelpBtn: TBitBtn;
    DirectoryListBox1: TDirectoryListBox;
    DriveComboBox1: TDriveComboBox;
    OkBtn: TBitBtn;
    CancelBtn: TBitBtn;
    Bevel1: TBevel;
    Edit1: TEdit;
    procedure HelpBtnClick(Sender: TObject);
    procedure OKBtnClick(Sender: TObject);
    procedure bbSetDirOneClick(Sender: TObject);
    procedure DirectoryListBox1Change(Sender: TObject);
    procedure Edit1KeyDown(Sender: TObject; var Key: Word;
      Shift: TShiftState);
    procedure FormShow(Sender: TObject);
  private
    FDirectory: string;
    procedure SetDirectory(const Value: string);
```

continues

LISTING 7.10   CONTINUED

```
  public
    function EditDirs(Dir1, Dir2: string): Boolean;
    property Directory: string read FDirectory write SetDirectory;
  end;

var
  PickDirectory: TPickDirectory;

implementation

uses
  Dialogs;

{$R *.DFM}

function TPickDirectory.EditDirs(Dir1, Dir2: string): Boolean;
begin
  if ShowModal <> mrOk then
    Result := False
  else begin
    FDirectory := Edit1.Text;
    Result := True;
  end;
end;

procedure TPickDirectory.HelpBtnClick(Sender: TObject);
begin
  Application.HelpContext(HelpContext);
end;

procedure TPickDirectory.OKBtnClick(Sender: TObject);
begin
  FDirectory := Edit1.Text;
  ModalResult := mrOk;
end;

procedure TPickDirectory.bbSetDirOneClick(Sender: TObject);
begin
  FDirectory := UpperCase(DirectoryListBox1.Directory);
  Edit1.Text := FDirectory;
end;

procedure TPickDirectory.DirectoryListBox1Change(Sender: TObject);
begin
  Edit1.Text := DirectoryListBox1.Directory;
end;

procedure TPickDirectory.Edit1KeyDown(Sender: TObject; var Key: Word;
  Shift: TShiftState);
```

```
begin
  if Key = Ord(#13) then
    DirectoryListBox1.Directory := Edit1.Text;
end;

procedure TPickDirectory.FormShow(Sender: TObject);
begin
  Edit1.Text := DirectoryListBox1.Directory;
end;

procedure TPickDirectory.SetDirectory(const Value: string);
begin
  FDirectory := Value;
end;

end.
```

If you want to test this component before placing it on the Component Palette, you can create a simple Delphi project, place a button on its main form, and respond to button clicks as follows:

```
procedure TForm1.Button1Click(Sender: TObject);
begin
  PickDlg := TCCPickDirDlg.Create(Self);
  if PickDlg.Execute then
    ShowMessage(PickDlg.Directory);
  PickDlg.Free;
end;
```

These lines of code first create an instance of `TCCPickDirDlg`. The `Execute` method of the component is called to show the form to the user, as shown in Figure 7.8. After the user has selected a directory, the memory for the component is disposed.

The key methods in the component are the ones that create an instance of the Delphi form, display it to the user, and implicitly destroy it. Here is the routine that creates an instance of the form:

```
constructor TCCPickDirDlg.Create(AOwner: TComponent);
begin
  inherited Create(AOwner);
  FPickDialog := TPickDirectory.Create(AOwner);
end;
```

As you can see, the code does nothing more than call the `Create` method of the Delphi form. It passes in the owner of the control as the owner of the form. This is done so that the control and its form will be automatically destroyed at the proper time.

I include the destructor for this form simply because I accidentally freed the form the first time I wrote the control. Freeing the form was an error because the form's owner will later try to destroy the form, and you don't want to have the same destructor called twice. In particular, doing so will usually raise an access violation. However, I find it easy to forget this fact, so I explicitly include the destructor to remind you not to destroy the form:

```
destructor TCCPickDirDlg.Destroy;
begin
  // The form owns the dialog, so don't destroy it.
  inherited Destroy;
end;
```

Of course, you can destroy the form here if you want, but if you do so, you would need to see that the variable that points to it is set to nil:

```
FPickDialog.Free;
FPickDialog := nil;
```

If you check this variable, then Delphi will know that you destroyed this memory and will not try to do so again. In most cases, there is no advantage to writing code like this. Nevertheless, it's nice to know how to proceed if you need to follow this path.

The only other important method is the one that actually pops up the Delphi form:

```
function TCCPickDirDlg.Execute: Boolean;
begin
  Result := False;
  if FPickDialog.ShowModal = mrOk then
    Result := True;
end;
```

This code essentially does nothing more than call ShowModal on the Delphi form. This Boolean method also takes care to relay back to the user whether the user selected the form's OK or Cancel button.

In designing the Execute method, I intentionally mimicked the behavior of TOpenDialog. I do so because I know developers are familiar with it. One of the rules of good component design is that you should leverage the user's knowledge of existing components whenever possible. In the nineties, everyone is rushed. As a result, people are very impatient, and when they test your component, they want to get it up and running very quickly. If it strikes them as quirky or peculiar, they might unceremoniously throw it out in favor of a component they can more quickly understand. So my suggestion is to make the interface for your component familiar and simple, and to learn about and follow conventions wherever possible. Save your creative impulses for the component's feature set or for your implementation of its functionality.

Finally, I should say a few words about the Delphi form that allows the user to select a directory. This form is a modified version of the TPickDir dialog from the CompDirs program. In this case, however, the user can select only one directory rather than two. The dialog contains a TDirectoryListBox from the Win31 page of the Component Palette, though I might do well to upgrade this control to a TDirectoryOutline component from the samples page. At any rate, the TDirectoryListBox lets the user see a list of directories and to select one particular directory. I also supply a TDriveComboBox for selecting drives.

Most of this dialog is too simple to merit comment in a book of this type, but I will take a brief look at the OkBtnClick method, which is selected by the user after he or she has chosen a directory:

```
procedure TPickDirectory.OKBtnClick(Sender: TObject);
begin
  FDirectory := Edit1.Text;
  ModalResult := mrOk;
end;
```

This simple code sets the internal string variable FDirectory of the form to the name of the directory the user choose. The Edit1 text field gets set each time the user chooses a directory in a TDirectoryListBox control:

```
procedure TPickDirectory.DirectoryListBox1Change(Sender: TObject);
begin
  Edit1.Text := DirectoryListBox1.Directory;
end;
```

The TCCPickDirDlg can then access this value through the Directory property of the form.

All in all, this last example is a very simple one. I have included it only because it demonstrates an important point, namely that you can wrap an entire form up inside a control.

Component Templates

I've already shown you traditional compound components and also components such as TCCPickDirDlg that wrap whole forms and their sub components in a single component. Using component templates is a third way to bring multiple components together and reuse them. Component templates are so simple to use that I will only say a few brief words about them. However, they are important words, as this technology can be very useful under certain circumstances.

To create a component template, drop a button and an edit control on a form. Associate a method with the button that places some text in the edit control:

```
procedure TForm1.SampleBtnClick(Sender: TObject);
begin
```

```
SampleEdit.Text :=
  'The greatest thing in the world is to ' +
  'know how to be one''s own self. - Montaigne'
end;
```

Now select both of the controls on the form with the mouse and choose Component, Create Component Template from the Delphi menu. You will be asked to give your creation a name and an optional icon. Click on the OK button to finish the operation.

At this stage, a new page called `Templates`, by default, will be added to the Component Palette. This page is usually placed way over on the far right, where you need to scroll over to see it. On this page will be the new component that you just created. This component will be a combination of the button and edit control that you created. Even the source code you wrote will remain associated with this control and will be re-created exactly as you wrote it in your form if you reuse the component. To see this action, create a new project and drop your new component template on it, just as you would any other control.

The great advantage of component templates is their ease of use. The disadvantage is that they don't effectively support basic OOP principles such as encapsulation, inheritance, or polymorphism. For instance, the code you write ends up in the form you drop the component on rather than tucked away in a separate object. This placement is not necessarily a bad thing, but it violates the principle of encapsulation. It is also difficult to share components created in this manner with other developers. Nevertheless, this technology is powerful and easy to use.

ActiveX Controls

To wind up this long chapter, I'm going to say a few brief words about creating ActiveX controls. On this topic one could choose to write a few hundred words or a few hundred thousand words. In my case, I'm going to opt to write only a few hundred words.

Creating ActiveX controls in Delphi is trivial in the extreme. To give the devil its due, I have to confess that this great ease of use is in part the product of the Borland marketing department. The people in marketing got their heart set on creating "one-step" ActiveX controls. They wanted to write that on the box very badly, and they just never let up on the development team until they got what they wanted. Good for them: one-step ActiveX controls are a great feature!

I'm going to convert the `TCCLabelEdit` control into an ActiveX control and use it inside Word 97. To get started, choose File, Close All, and close any active projects open in Delphi. Select File, New, ActiveX, ActiveX Control from the Delphi menu. You will be presented with the ActiveX Control Wizard shown in Figure 7.9.

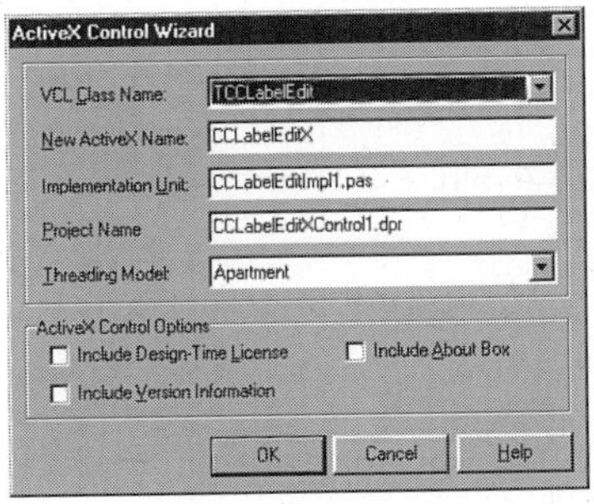

FIGURE 7.9

*The ActiveX
Control Wizard
allows you to
convert the
TCCLabelEdit
component into an
ActiveX compo-
nent in one step.*

At the top of the wizard, choose the TCCLabelEdit control as the VCL class on which
you want to base your control. A default name, implementation unit, and project unit will
be filled in for you automatically. In this case, you can just stick with these default
names, as shown in Figure 7.9. You should stick with the default threading model unless
A) you are absolutely sure you know why you want to pick a different threading model
and B) you are crazy enough to pursue a subject that can easily get you in real trouble.

You can also add Design Time Licensing, Version Information, and an About box to your
control. To add these items, merely select the appropriate check boxes. In the sample
control found in the Chap07 directory on this book's CD, you will find that I selected all
these options. Therefore, a file called CCLabelEditXControl1.lic was generated. It is
the license file for the ActiveX control, and it must be present, or the control will not
work properly.

You can now build your control and test it inside Delphi. To compile the project, choose
Project, Build. To register the control, choose Run, Register ActiveX Server.

To install the control in the Delphi environment, choose Component, Import ActiveX
control. The Import ActiveX control dialog will appear. Near the top of the list box in the
dialog will be the CCLabelEditXControl1 control. Choose to use this control by clicking
the Install button.

You will be given the option of choosing which package ought to contain this control.
You could put it in the Unleash package if you want, or you can browse to the Delphi
4\Lib directory and put it in dclusr40.dpk. DclUsr40 is a generic package meant for
"the user" to store his or components. You will also be given a chance to decide which
page of the Component Palette you want the control to use. In this case, you can just take
the default ActiveX page.

When you are finished, a new component will appear on the ActiveX page in the
Component Palette. Start a new project and drop this component on it, just as you would
any other control.

Your control can also be used in other programs such as Word, Excel, Microsoft Visual C++, or even Visual Basic—perish the thought!

To use the control in Word 97, open Word and start a new document. To duplicate the work I have done in the `Chap08\LabelEditActiveX` directory, save the document as `LabelEditWordEdit.doc`.

Choose Tools, Macro, Visual Basic Editor from the Word 97 menu. Make sure to select View, Project Explorer from the Visual Basic menu. Find `Project(LabelEditWordTest)` in the Project Explorer. Right-click on it and select Insert, User Form. A form and Control Toolbox will appear. Right-click on the Toolbox, and choose the Additional Controls option. You then see a dialog that will allow you to select the `CCLabelEditX` control. Put a check mark in front of the control, as shown in Figure 7.10.

FIGURE 7.10

The Word Visual Basic editor displaying the Project Manager, a form with the `CCLableEditX` *on it, the toolbox, and the Additional Controls dialog.*

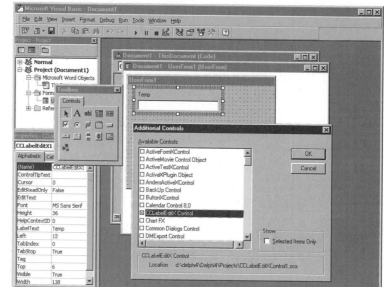

After selecting the OK button, the label edit control will appear on the Toolbox, and you can place it on the VB form. Use the control exactly as you would in Delphi. Choose View, Properties to bring up the VB equivalent of the Object Inspector. Use this tool to set the properties of your control or even to handle events associated with your control.

Choose File, Close and Return to Microsoft Word. In Word, choose View, Toolbars, Control Toolbox to bring up a Toolbox similar to the one in VB. Select a button control and drop it on your document. Double-click on the button to create a VB event handler.

Edit the handler so that it looks like this:

```
Private Sub CommandButton1_Click()
  UserForm1.Show
End Sub
```

You can now close VB. Select the icon at the top left of the Control Toolbox that will let you switch in and out of Design mode. You should test your work, so elect to exit Design mode. If necessary, choose View, Page Layout so you can see your button. You can now click on the button, and the form will appear with the label edit control on it, as shown in Figure 7.11.

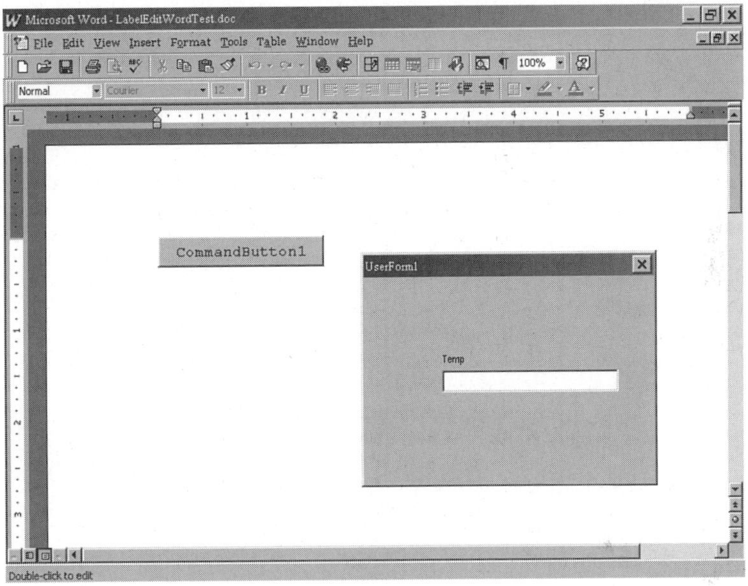

FIGURE 7.11

A Word document with a button on it. After you select the button, a dialog that contains a Delphi ActiveX control appears.

The ability to create tools in Delphi and use them in Word, VB, or even in IE greatly expands the power of our computers. I like Linux a great deal, and I like the Mac, but my gosh, the things you can do inside Windows! COM-based technology such as ActiveX controls, automation, and DCOM is simply extraordinary. It is becoming increasingly trivial for developers to program nearly every aspect of the operating system and the key tools supported by the operating system. As we gain finer and finer control over Windows, we will have the ability to create powerful interactive systems that can freely utilize the best features of the available tools on the system. I will add to my discussion of this kind of interactivity in future portions of this book. See Chapter 15, "Creating COM Automation Servers and Clients," Chapter 16, "Using Delphi to Automate Word and Excel," Chapter 17, "Interfaces and Internet Explorer," and Chapter 20, "DCOM."

As I mentioned at the beginning of this section, I am taking the minimalist approach to Delphi ActiveX development. However, for most users, this is exactly the approach you should take:

- Create your control in Delphi.
- Use the wizard to convert it into an ActiveX control.
- Import the control into your tool of choice.

To go much further, you would have to spend weeks, if not months, digging into the details of ActiveX. That is not one of my intentions in this book, so I will take the matter no further. However, you shouldn't have to go any further. The information I presented here is all you should ever need to know to fully leverage Delphi ActiveX creation. Build the functionality into your VCL control, then just export it for use in other environments.

Summary

In this chapter, you had a chance to broaden your knowledge of Delphi component creation. In particular, you saw

- Which controls to descend from if you want to create a control from scratch.
- How to add functionality not available in an ancestor object. For instance, the TCCColorClock object does things that TCCClock does not.
- How to build up controls from scratch so that they can add new functionality to the programming environment. For instance, the TCCClock component brings something entirely new to Delphi programming that does not exist in any other component that ships with the product.
- Details about the Tools API and specifically about the art of making property editors and component editors.
- How to create nonvisual controls.
- How to create nonvisual controls that contain an entire Delphi form that can be displayed at runtime.
- How to create a component template.
- How to create an ActiveX control in Delphi.

In many ways, I wish I could explore this topic in even more depth, but a book like this has only so much room for even the most interesting subjects. If you want to move on from here, I suggest that you read Ray Konopka's excellent book *Developing Custom Delphi Components*, published by The Coriolis Group. You should also peruse the invaluable classic Delphi tome known as the *Delphi 4 Developer's Guide*, written by Delphi gods Xavier Pacheco and Steve Teixeira, and published by our very own Sams Publishing.

Database Programming

PART

III

IN THIS PART

Fields and Database Tools

Please refer to the CD-ROM for the entire chapter.

CHAPTER 8

IN THIS CHAPTER

This chapter covers a set of visual tools you can use to simplify database development. The major areas of concentration are as follows:

- Relational databases
- The Fields Editor
- `TField` descendant objects
- Calculated fields
- The `TDBGrid` component
- Lookup fields
- The Database Explorer
- The Database Desktop
- Query by Example (QBE)
- Multirecord objects—`TDBCtrlGrid`

Using Delphi's visual and programmatic tools to manage relational databases is the theme binding these subjects together. Delphi has become a very sophisticated database tool, so getting a feeling for the breadth of the tools available to client/server developers takes time. One of the goals of this chapter is to give you some sense of the key components used when designing database applications.

One of the most frequently mentioned tools in this chapter is the Fields Editor. By using the Fields Editor, you can create objects that you can use to influence the manner and types of data that appear in visual controls such as `TDBEdit` and `TDBGrid`. For instance, you can use the objects made in the Fields Editor to format data so that it appears as currency or as a floating-point number with a defined precision. These same changes can be accomplished through the Data Dictionary in the Database Explorer, or through the Database Desktop. These latter tools, however, have a global impact on the field's potential values, whereas the changes made in the Object Inspector affect only the current application.

The `Columns` property of the `TDBGrid` control can be used to change the appearance of a grid so that its columns are arranged in a new order or are hidden. You can also use the `Columns` property to change the color of columns in a grid, or to insert drop-down combo boxes into a grid.

The lessons you learn in this chapter demonstrate techniques used by most programmers when they present database tables to their users. Much of the material involves manipulating visual tools, but the basic subject matter is fairly technical and assumes an understanding of the Delphi environment and language.

Flat-File Real-World Databases

Please refer to the CD-ROM for the entire chapter.

CHAPTER 9

This chapter is the first of a "two-part series" on constructing real-world databases. The goal is to move from the largely theoretical information you received in the preceding chapter into a few examples of how to make programs that someone could actually use for a practical purpose in the real world.

In several sections of this chapter, I go into considerable depth about design-related issues. One of the burdens of this chapter isn't merely to show how database code works, but to talk about how to create programs that have some viable use in the real world. Design-related issues are among the most important challenges that programmers face. Learning how to program is much easier than learning how to create programs that work.

Here is quick look at the terrain covered in this chapter:

- Sorting data.
- Filtering data.
- Searching for data.
- Dynamically moving a table in and out of a read-only state.
- Forcing the user to select a field's value from a list of valid responses.
- Allowing the user to choose the colors of a form at runtime.
- Saving information to the Registry. In particular, you see how to use the Registry to replace an INI file and how to save and restore information to and from the Registry at program startup.
- Using events that occur in a TDataModule inside the main form of your program. That is, the chapter shows how to respond to events specific to one form from inside a second form. Or, more generally, it shows how to handle events manually rather than let Delphi set up the event handler for you.

You should also be sure to read the readme files on the CD that accompanies this book for information about the alias used in the ADDRESS2 program and in other programs in this book. If you have trouble getting any of these programs running, check my Web site (http://users.aol.com/charliecal) for possible updates. The key to getting the program up and running is to create a standard Paradox alias called D4UNLEASHED and point it to the directory where you have placed Address.db, Cats.db, and related files. These tables are stored by default in the Data directory on the CD that accompanies this book, and you should copy them onto your hard drive before you try to use them. As always, the best way to install the files is to use the installation program that comes with the CD. You can also copy the files over directly, but if you do, you should be sure they are not marked as read only. You can remove the read-only attribute from a file using the Windows Explorer.

CHAPTER 10

Relational Databases

Now you can take a look at a real relational database in action. The preceding chapters have really been nothing but a long prelude to this chapter, where all the pieces finally come together.

This chapter features another address book program, but this time it will be based on a relational database. This second database will allow you to add multiple addresses, phone numbers, and email addresses to each name in the address book.

Subjects covered in this chapter include the following:

- Creating the tables for a relational database
- Creating cascading deletes
- Iterating through the controls on a form or a data module and performing certain actions on selected components at runtime (For instance, the code shows how to iterate through all the tables on a TDataModule to make sure that they are all posted.)
- Working with the TPageControl and TTabSheet objects
- Working with TTreeView, TImageList, and TTreeNode
- Retrieving error strings from a resource
- Using the TSession object

After you look at the address book program, I start a second program called kdAddExplore. This program looks and feels a lot like a miniature version of the Database Explorer. You can use this program to explore the structure of the five tables used in the address book program found in the first half of this chapter.

The main purpose of the kdAddExplore program is to let you see some of the functionality of the global TSession object that is automatically available in all Delphi database applications. The Session object is created automatically when you call Application.Initialize at the startup of a database program. This call is found in the program source generated for you by Delphi. To view the program source, choose View, Program Source from the main Delphi menu.

Don't forget to check the readme file on the CD that comes with this book for additional information about the aliases used in this book. In particular, the programs in this chapter use an alias called D4UNLEASHED, which points to the Data directory on the CD that accompanies this book. Remember that you must copy the data off the CD before you use it, and you must be sure the files are not marked as ReadOnly.

Chapter 8, "Fields and Database Tools," covers some of the theory behind relational databases. This chapter is about using that theory in practice. Unless you already understand relational databases, you should probably read Chapter 8 before reading this chapter. Furthermore, you will probably find a considerable difference between the theory of relational databases and what they start to look like in practice. In particular, the order of complexity increases almost geometrically as you add tables to a relational database. This chapter will introduce you to some of the principles you must master before you can create order out of that complexity.

Data in the Real World

The code in this chapter addresses the kinds of problems you find in real-world situations. In particular, I focus on the conflict between the rigid, inflexible nature of simple tables and the fluid, kaleidoscope-like nature of information in the real world.

When most people first try to build database programs, they tend to create one simple table, like the one shown in the ADDRESS2 program from the preceding chapter. The limitations of that kind of system might well emerge on the first day of use. For example, you might start transferring handwritten addresses into the database. Problems arise when you encounter entries in which one person has multiple phone numbers or multiple addresses. One person having three or more email addresses is not at all unusual. The ADDRESS2 program does not have a good solution for that kind of problem.

In professional settings, this problem can be multiplied many times. For example, I need to track all the Borland offices in the world. This task involves tracking addresses in Germany, England, France, Australia, Hong Kong, Japan, and various other locations throughout the world. I need numerous address entries under the name of a single company.

My job puts me in contact with a number of software vendors (ISVs) that use or create Borland tools. Many of these people maintain offices both at home and at their business. Some of them frequent certain sites, and others have complex relationships with their companies that I can track in single table database only via freehand notes.

As you can see, information in the real world is messy and complex. The ADDRESS2 program is simple and straightforward. Many people can make do with simple tools, but others need to have a more sophisticated system.

The kdAdd program found in this chapter is an attempt to resolve the kinds of problems you find in real-world situations. In the form you see it here, it is not quite as polished as the ADDRESS2 program. It is, however, much more sophisticated and much more powerful. With some work, it could easily form the basis for a professional-level database.

Examining the Relational Address Program

The kdAdd program uses five tables called kdNames, kdAdds, kdPhone, kdMemo, and kdEmail. The kdNames table is the master table that "owns" the other four tables. The other tables are detail tables. (As I stated in an earlier chapter, this relationship is reflexive, but in this program, the kdNames table is always in charge.)

When the program first appears, it looks like the image shown in Figure 10.1. As you can see, the program uses a TPageControl with five pages, one for each of the tables. The kdAdds and kdPhone tables are also shown on the first page so that the user can see them easily. If you want to delete items from either an address or phone number, you should turn to the respective pages for those items.

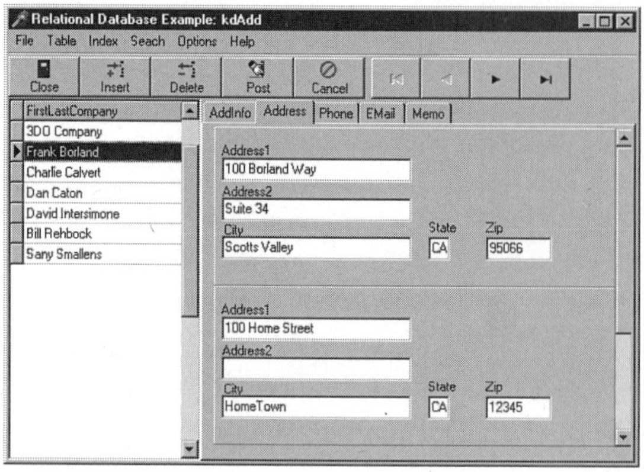

FIGURE 10.1

The main screen for the kdAdd program.

The data for the program is kept in the Data directory on the CD that comes with this book. You should create a Standard Paradox alias called D4UNLEASHED that points to a copy of this directory that resides on your hard drive. Refer to the readme file on the CD that comes with this book if you need additional information about setting up the alias. The fields for the tables in the database are shown in Table 10.1 through Table 10.5.

TABLE 10.1 THE STRUCTURE FOR THE kdName TABLE

Table Name	Type	Size	Primary Index
NameCode	+		*
FirstName	A	30	
LastName	A	30	
Company	A	30	

TABLE 10.2   THE STRUCTURE FOR THE kdAdds TABLE

Table Name	Type	Size	Primary Index
AddCode	+		*
Address1	A	30	
Address2	A	30	
City	A	30	
State	A	3	
Zip	A	10	
NameCode	I		

TABLE 10.3   THE STRUCTURE FOR THE kdPhone TABLE

Table Name	Type	Size	Primary Index
PhoneCode	+		*
Description	A	15	
Number	A	25	
Ext	A	5	
NameCode	I		

TABLE 10.4   THE STRUCTURE FOR THE kdEmail TABLE

Table Name	Type	Size	Primary Index
EMailCode	+		*
Address	A	50	
Description	A	65	
Service	A	25	
NameCode	I		

TABLE 10.5   THE STRUCTURE FOR THE kdMemo TABLE

Table Name	Type	Size	Primary Index
MemoCode	+		*
Description	A	25	
MemoData	M	15	
NameCode	I		

Four constraints are placed on the table in the form of foreign keys called `NameCode`. They are placed in each of the program's tables except for the master table. These constraints are shown in Figure 10.2.

FIGURE 10.2

By opening the Referential Constraints section of kdNames *in DBX, you can see the foreign keys used by the database.*

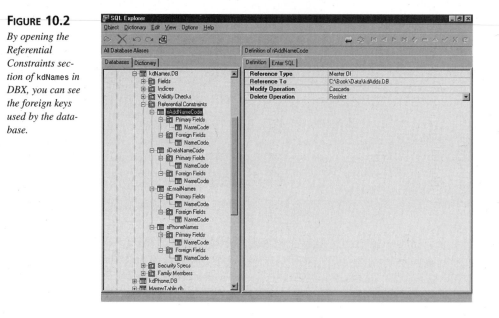

When you're viewing this information in the Database Explorer (DBX), you should highlight the name of each constraint and then look at the definition page to read the `Reference Type` and `Reference To` fields. As you can see from Figure 10.2, these fields show which table the constraint references. The view shown here is of the `kdNames` table, and it is the master table in these relationships. The `riAddNameCode` constraint references the `kdAdds` table.

Table 10.6 shows another way to think about the referential integrity in this database.

TABLE 10.6   THE KEYS IN THE DATABASE SHOWN IN TABLE FORMAT

Table	Primary Key	Foreign Key
kdName	NameCode	
kdAdd	AddCode	NameCode references kdName.NameCode
kdPhone	PhoneCode	NameCode references kdName.NameCode
kdEmail	EMailCode	NameCode references kdName.NameCode
kdMemo	MemoCode	NameCode references kdName.NameCode

As you can see, `kdAdd`, `kdPhone`, `kdEmail`, and `kdMemo` all have a single foreign key called `NameCode` that references the `NameCode` primary key in `kdNames`. The number in the foreign keys therefore must be a number found in the primary key of the `kdNames` table. Furthermore, you cannot delete a row from the `kdNames` table unless all its related fields in the other tables have been deleted first. You also cannot change the value in the `NameCode` field of `kdNames` if it will leave records in the other tables "stranded."

> **NOTE**
>
> If you are new to referential integrity, take the time to play with the database and test these constraints. Referential integrity exists to prevent the user from accidentally deleting needed data and from accidentally entering erroneous data. During the course of this chapter, you should test the restraints on this database so you can see how it establishes rules that help both the programmer and the user maintain a valid set of data.

The referential integrity relationships you see here represent the classic simplest case for constructing a real relational database. Most databases in the real world have more tables and more foreign keys. However, this one has all the elements of a real relational database, and the complexity level is sufficient for programmers who are new to this kind of programming.

Several secondary indices are used in this program, as shown in Table 10.7 through Table 10.11. Most of these indices are the result of the foreign keys on the `NameCode` fields of `kdAdds`, `kdPhone`, `kdEmail`, and `kdMemo`. However, indices are also set up on the `Company`, `FirstName`, and `LastName` fields of the `kdNames` table. Note that `idxLastName` consists of both the last name and first name of each entry in the `kdNames` table. This convention is helpful when sorting lists wherein you have more than one entry with a particular last name. For instance, if you have two people with the last name of Jones, creating a key on the last and first names will ensure that Able Jones is listed before Betty Jones. If you further study the tables shown here, you will see that the `kdPhone` and `kdMemo` tables also have indices on their description fields.

TABLE 10.7   THE INDICES ON THE `kdNames` TABLE

Table	Index Fields
idxCompany	Company
idxFirstName	FirstName
idxLastName	LastName, FirstName

10

RELATIONAL DATABASES

TABLE 10.8 THE INDEX ON THE kdAdds TABLE

Table	Index Fields
NameCode	NameCode

TABLE 10.9 THE INDICES ON THE kdPhone TABLE

Index	Index Fields
idxDescription	Description
NameCode	NameCode

TABLE 10.10 THE INDEX ON THE kdEmail TABLE

Index	Index Fields
NameCode	NameCode

TABLE 10.11 THE INDEX ON THE kdMemo TABLE

Index	Index Fields
NameCode	NameCode
idxDescription	Description

You now know all the core facts about the kdAdd program. After you have laid out the tables as shown here, all the really heavy work in constructing the program is completed. You still have considerable work to do in creating a front end for the program, but the core work for the project is done after you have created the tables and defined the ways in which they interrelate.

The Code for kdAdd

The code for the kdAdd program is shown in Listings 10.1 through 10.5. Notice the custom RC file and the include file for the project. These two tiny files store error strings. In later versions of the program, these files will become larger as more error strings are added to the code. For this release, all I have done is stub out these files so that they can easily be expanded later.

LISTING 10.1   THE MAIN FORM FOR THE kdAdd PROGRAM

```
////////////////////////////////////
//     File: Main.pas
// Project: KdAdd
// Copyright (c) 1998 by Charlie Calvert
//
unit Main;

interface

uses
  Windows, Messages, SysUtils,
  Classes, Graphics, Controls,
  Forms, Dialogs, ImgList,
  Menus, ExtCtrls, DBCtrls,
  ComCtrls, ToolWin, StdCtrls,
  DBCGrids, Mask, Grids,
  DBGrids;

type
  TForm1 = class(TForm)
    FirstLastGrid: TDBGrid;
    PageControl1: TPageControl;
    AddInfo1: TTabSheet;
    Label15: TLabel;
    Label16: TLabel;
    Label17: TLabel;
    DBEdit13: TDBEdit;
    DBEdit14: TDBEdit;
    DBEdit15: TDBEdit;
    DBCtrlGrid4: TDBCtrlGrid;
    Bevel1: TBevel;
    Bevel4: TBevel;
    Bevel3: TBevel;
    DBText1: TDBText;
    DBEdit17: TDBText;
    DBEdit18: TDBText;
    DBEdit19: TDBText;
    DBEdit20: TDBText;
    Bevel2: TBevel;
    PhoneCtrlGrid: TDBCtrlGrid;
    Bevel7: TBevel;
    Bevel6: TBevel;
    A: TBevel;
    Bevel5: TBevel;
    DBEdit8: TDBText;
    DBEdit7: TDBText;
    DBEdit16: TDBText;
    Label6: TLabel;
```

continues

LISTING 10.1 CONTINUED

```
DBCtrlGrid2: TDBCtrlGrid;
Label1: TLabel;
Label2: TLabel;
Label3: TLabel;
Label4: TLabel;
Label5: TLabel;
DBEdit1: TDBEdit;
DBEdit2: TDBEdit;
City: TDBEdit;
DBEdit4: TDBEdit;
Zip: TDBEdit;
tsPhone: TTabSheet;
DBCtrlGrid5: TDBCtrlGrid;
Label23: TLabel;
Label24: TLabel;
Label25: TLabel;
DBEdit21: TDBEdit;
DBEdit22: TDBEdit;
DBEdit23: TDBEdit;
tsEMail: TTabSheet;
DBCtrlGrid3: TDBCtrlGrid;
Label12: TLabel;
Label13: TLabel;
Label14: TLabel;
DBEdit10: TDBEdit;
DBEdit11: TDBEdit;
DBEdit12: TDBEdit;
tsMemo: TTabSheet;
DBGrid2: TDBGrid;
DBMemo1: TDBMemo;
ToolBar1: TToolBar;
CloseBtn: TToolButton;
InsertBtn2: TToolButton;
DeleteBtn2: TToolButton;
PostBtn2: TToolButton;
CancelBtn2: TToolButton;
ToolButton1: TToolButton;
DBNavigator1: TDBNavigator;
MainMenu1: TMainMenu;
File1: TMenuItem;
Exit1: TMenuItem;
Table1: TMenuItem;
Insert1: TMenuItem;
Post1: TMenuItem;
Delete1: TMenuItem;
Cancel1: TMenuItem;
Index1: TMenuItem;
Last1: TMenuItem;
First1: TMenuItem;
```

```
    Company1: TMenuItem;
    Seach1: TMenuItem;
    Last2: TMenuItem;
    First2: TMenuItem;
    Company2: TMenuItem;
    Options1: TMenuItem;
    Help1: TMenuItem;
    Contents1: TMenuItem;
    N1: TMenuItem;
    About1: TMenuItem;
    ImageList1: TImageList;
    procedure FormCreate(Sender: TObject);
    procedure InsertBtn2Click(Sender: TObject);
    procedure DeleteBtn2Click(Sender: TObject);
    procedure PostBtn2Click(Sender: TObject);
    procedure CancelBtn2Click(Sender: TObject);
    procedure IndexClick(Sender: TObject);
    procedure SearchClick(Sender: TObject);
    procedure PageControl1Change(Sender: TObject);
    procedure Exit1Click(Sender: TObject);
    procedure DBText1Click(Sender: TObject);
  private
    procedure SetupIndex(Sender: TObject);
  public
    { Public declarations }
  end;

var
  Form1: TForm1;

implementation

uses
  DMod1, Globals;

{$R *.DFM}

{$R KDERRS.RES}

procedure TForm1.FormCreate(Sender: TObject);
begin
  PageControl1.ActivePage := AddInfo1;
end;

procedure TForm1.InsertBtn2Click(Sender: TObject);
begin
  case (PageControl1.ActivePage).Tag of
    1: DMod.NamesTable.Insert;
    2: DMod.AddressTable.Insert;
    3: DMod.PhoneTable.Insert;
```

continues

10

RELATIONAL
DATABASES

LISTING 10.1   CONTINUED

```pascal
   4: DMod.EMailTable.Insert;
   5: DMod.MemoTable.Insert;
  end;
end;

procedure TForm1.DeleteBtn2Click(Sender: TObject);
const
  Btns:TMsgDlgButtons = [mbYes, mbNo];
var
  S, Msg: string;

begin
  Msg := 'Are you sure you want to delete %s?';

  case PageControl1.ActivePage.Tag of
    1: begin
      Msg :=  Format(Msg, [DMod.NamesTableFirstLastCompany.AsString]);
      if (MessageDlg(Msg, mtInformation, Btns, 0) = ID_YES) then
        DMod.CascadingDelete;
    end;

    2: begin
      Msg :=  Format(Msg, [DMod.Address]);
      if (MessageDlg(Msg, mtInformation, Btns, 0) = ID_YES) then
        DMod.AddressTable.Delete;
    end;

    3: begin
      Msg :=  Format(Msg, [DMod.Phone]);
      if (MessageDlg(Msg, mtInformation, Btns, 0) = ID_YES) then
        DMod.PhoneTable.Delete;
    end;

    4: begin
      Msg := Format(Msg, [DMod.EMail]);
      if (MessageDlg(Msg, mtInformation, Btns, 0) = ID_YES) then
        DMod.EMailTable.Delete;
    end;

    5: begin
      Msg := Format(Msg, [DMod.MemoTableDescription.AsString]);
      if (MessageDlg(Msg, mtInformation, Btns, 0) = ID_YES) then
        DMod.MemoTable.Delete;
    end;

  else
    ShowMessage(GetError(1, S));
  end;
end;
```

```
procedure TForm1.PostBtn2Click(Sender: TObject);
begin
  DMod.PostAll;
end;

procedure TForm1.CancelBtn2Click(Sender: TObject);
var
  S: string;
begin
  case PageControl1.ActivePage.Tag of
    1: DMod.NamesTable.Cancel;
    2: DMod.AddressTable.Cancel;
    3: DMod.PhoneTable.Cancel;
    4: DMod.EMailTable.Cancel;
    5: DMod.MemoTable.Cancel;
  else
    ShowMessage(GetError(1, S));
  end;
end;

procedure TForm1.SetupIndex(Sender: TObject);
begin
  case TComponent(Sender).Tag of
    100: DMod.NamesTable.IndexName := 'idxLastName';
    101: DMod.NamesTable.IndexName := 'idxFirstName';
    102: DMod.NamesTable.IndexName := 'idxCompany';
    103: DMod.NamesTable.IndexName := '';
  end;
end;

procedure TForm1.IndexClick(Sender: TObject);
begin
  SetupIndex(Sender);
  DMod.NamesTable.FindNearest(['AAAA']);
end;

procedure TForm1.SearchClick(Sender: TObject);
var
  S, IndexName: string;
begin
  S := '';
  if (InputQuery('Search for Name', 'Enter Name: ', S)) then begin
    IndexName := DMod.NamesTable.IndexName;
    SetupIndex(Sender);
    DMod.NamesTable.FindNearest([S]);
    DMod.NamesTable.IndexName := IndexName;
  end;
end;
```

continues

10

RELATIONAL
DATABASES

LISTING 10.1   CONTINUED

```pascal
procedure TForm1.PageControl1Change(Sender: TObject);
begin
  DMod.PostAll;
  case PageControl1.ActivePage.Tag of
    1: DBNavigator1.DataSource := DMod.dsNames;
    2: DBNavigator1.DataSource := DMod.dsAddress;
    3: DBNavigator1.DataSource := DMod.dsPhone;
    4: DBNavigator1.DataSource := DMod.dsEmail;
    5: DBNavigator1.DataSource := DMod.dsMemo;
  end;
end;

procedure TForm1.Exit1Click(Sender: TObject);
begin
  Close;
end;

procedure TForm1.DBText1Click(Sender: TObject);
begin
  PageControl1.ActivePage := tsAddress;
end;

end.
```

LISTING 10.2   THE DATA MODULE FOR THE kdAdd PROGRAM

```pascal
////////////////////////////////////
//    File: DMod1.pas
// Project: KdAdd
// Copyright (c) 1998 by Charlie Calvert
//
unit DMod1;

interface

uses
  Windows, Messages, SysUtils,
  Classes, Graphics, Controls,
  Forms, Dialogs, DBTables,
  Db;

type
  TDMod = class(TDataModule)
    NamesTable: TTable;
    NamesTableNameCode: TAutoIncField;
    NamesTableFirstName: TStringField;
    NamesTableLastName: TStringField;
    NamesTableCompany: TStringField;
```

```
    NamesTableFirstLastCompany: TStringField;
    dsNames: TDataSource;
    AddressTable: TTable;
    AddressTableAddCode: TAutoIncField;
    AddressTableAddress1: TStringField;
    AddressTableAddress2: TStringField;
    AddressTableCity: TStringField;
    AddressTableState: TStringField;
    AddressTableZip: TStringField;
    AddressTableNameCode: TIntegerField;
    PhoneTable: TTable;
    PhoneTablePhoneCode: TAutoIncField;
    PhoneTableDescription: TStringField;
    PhoneTableNumber: TStringField;
    PhoneTableExt: TStringField;
    PhoneTableNameCode: TIntegerField;
    MemoTable: TTable;
    MemoTableMemoCode: TAutoIncField;
    MemoTableDescription: TStringField;
    MemoTableMemoData: TMemoField;
    MemoTableNameCode: TIntegerField;
    dsAddress: TDataSource;
    dsPhone: TDataSource;
    dsMemo: TDataSource;
    EMailTable: TTable;
    EMailTableEMailCode: TAutoIncField;
    EMailTableAddress: TStringField;
    EMailTableDescription: TStringField;
    EMailTableService: TStringField;
    EMailTableNameCode: TIntegerField;
    dsEmail: TDataSource;
    EMailDeleteQuery: TQuery;
    MemoDeleteQuery: TQuery;
    PhoneDeleteQuery: TQuery;
    AddressDeleteQuery: TQuery;
    NamesDeleteQuery: TQuery;
    procedure DModCreate(Sender: TObject);
    procedure NamesTableCalcFields(DataSet: TDataSet);
    function GetAddress: string;
    function GetEMail: string;
    function GetPhone: string;
  public
    procedure CascadingDelete;
    procedure DoPost(Data: TDataSet);
    procedure PostAll;
  published
    property Address: string read GetAddress;
    property Phone: string read GetPhone;
    property EMail: string read GetEMail;
  end;
```

continues

10

RELATIONAL
DATABASES

LISTING 10.2   CONTINUED

```pascal
var
  DMod: TDMod;

implementation

{$R *.DFM}

procedure TDMod.DModCreate(Sender: TObject);
begin
  NamesTable.Open;
  AddressTable.Open;
  PhoneTable.Open;
  MemoTable.Open;
  EMailTable.Open;
end;

procedure TDMod.NamesTableCalcFields(DataSet: TDataSet);
var
  Temp: string;
begin
  Temp := NamesTableFirstName.Value + ' ' + NamesTableLastName.Value;
  if (Temp = '') then
    NamesTableFirstLastCompany.Value := NamesTableCompany.Value
  else
    NamesTableFirstLastCompany.Value := Temp;
end;

procedure TDMod.DoPost(Data: TDataSet);
begin
  if ((Data.State = dsInsert) or (Data.State = dsEdit)) then
    Data.Post;
end;

procedure TDMod.PostAll;
var
  i: Integer;
begin
  for i := 0 to ComponentCount - 1 do
    if Components[i] is TTable then
      DoPost(TDataSet(Components[i]));
end;

procedure TDMod.CascadingDelete;
begin
  EMailDeleteQuery.ParamByName('NameCode').AsInteger :=
    EMailTableNameCode.Value;
  EMailDeleteQuery.ExecSQL;

  MemoDeleteQuery.ParamByName('NameCode').AsInteger :=
    MemoTableNameCode.Value;
```

```
  MemoDeleteQuery.ExecSQL;

  PhoneDeleteQuery.ParamByName('NameCode').AsInteger :=
    PhoneTableNameCode.Value;
  PhoneDeleteQuery.ExecSQL;

  AddressDeleteQuery.ParamByName('NameCode').AsInteger :=
    AddressTableNameCode.Value;
  AddressDeleteQuery.ExecSQL;

  NamesDeleteQuery.ParamByName('NameCode').AsInteger :=
    NamesTableNameCode.Value;
  NamesDeleteQuery.ExecSQL;

  NamesTable.Refresh;
end;

function TDMod.GetAddress: string;
begin
  Result := DMod.AddressTableAddress1.AsString + CR +
    DMod.AddressTableAddress2.AsString + CR +
    DMod.AddressTableCity.AsString + CR +
    DMod.AddressTableState.AsString + CR +
    DMod.AddressTableZip.AsString;
end;

function TDMod.GetPhone: string;
begin
  Result := DMod.PhoneTableDescription.AsString + CR +
    DMod.PhoneTableNumber.AsString + CR +
    DMod.PhoneTableExt.AsString;
end;

function TDMod.GetEMail: string;
begin
  Result := DMod.EMailTableAddress.AsString + CR +
    DMod.EMailTableDescription.AsString + CR +
    DMod.EMailTableService.AsString;
end;

end.
```

LISTING 10.3   THE MAIN MODULE FOR THE Globals UNIT

```
unit Globals;

interface

function GetError(ErrNo: Integer; var S: string): string;
```

continues

LISTING 10.3   CONTINUED

```
implementation

uses
  Windows;

const
  ERR_STRING_SIZE = 255;

function GetError(ErrNo: Integer; var S: string): string;
begin
  SetLength(S, ERR_STRING_SIZE);
  LoadString(HInstance, 1, PChar(S), ERR_STRING_SIZE);
  Result := S;
end;

end.
```

LISTING 10.4   THE CUSTOM RC FILE FOR THE PROJECT (THIS IS A STUB TO BE FILLED OUT LATER.)

```
#include "kderrs.inc"
STRINGTABLE
{
  KDERR_CASESTATEMENT, "Command fell through case statement"
}
```

LISTING 10.5   THE INCLUDE FILE FOR THE PROJECT HAS ONLY ONE ENTRY (THIS IS A STUB TO BE FILLED OUT LATER.)

```
#define KDERR_CASESTATEMENT 1
```

The pages in the TPageControl are hidden from view in Figure 10.1. In Figure 10.3 through Figure 10.6, you can see the remaining TTabSheet objects.

Using the kdAdd Program

The kdAdd program has the minimal functionality needed to support the user's needs. For example, you can perform Insert, Post, Delete, and Cancel operations on all the tables. Access to these features is provided through both the menus and a toolbar. You can also set the index to the Company, First, or Last fields of the kdNames table. Finally, you can search on either the Company, First, or Last fields.

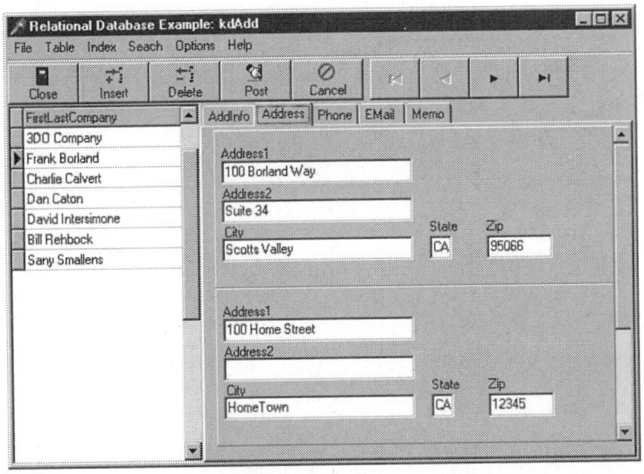

FIGURE 10.3

The tab sheet for the Address *table.*

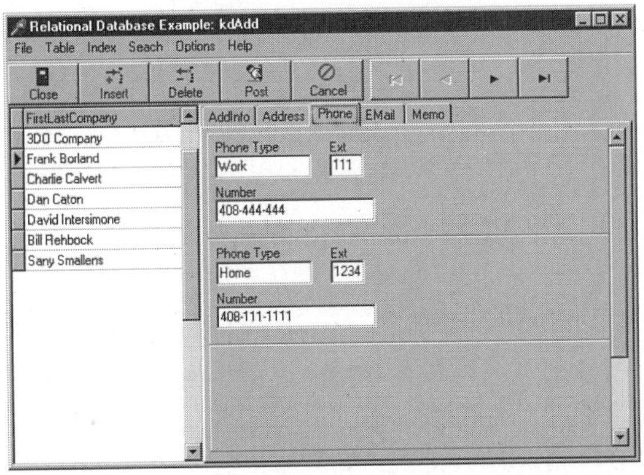

FIGURE 10.4

The tab sheet for the Phone *table.*

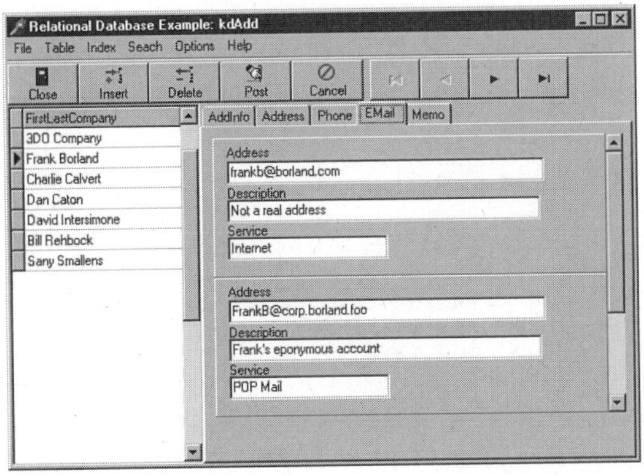

FIGURE 10.5

The tab sheet for the Email *table.*

10

RELATIONAL DATABASES

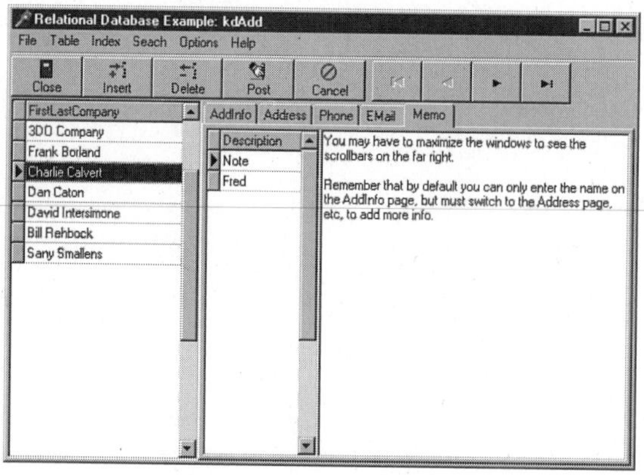

FIGURE 10.6

*The tab sheet for
the* Memos *table.*

Setting Up the Index for kdAdd

The code that controls the index for the program forms one of the hubs around which the
kdAdd program revolves. This code is called from several different places in the program.
The obvious place to start studying it, however, is in the response method for the menu
items that let the user change the index:

```
procedure TForm1.SetupIndex(Sender: TObject);
begin
  case TComponent(Sender).Tag of
    100: DMod.NamesTable.IndexName := 'idxLastName';
    101: DMod.NamesTable.IndexName := 'idxFirstName';
    102: DMod.NamesTable.IndexName := 'idxCompany';
    103: DMod.NamesTable.IndexName := '';
  end;
end;

procedure TForm1.IndexClick(Sender: TObject);
begin
  SetupIndex(Sender);
  DMod.NamesTable.FindNearest(['AAAA']);
end;
```

The code has three menu choices for changing the index. The first lets the user set the
index to the last name; the second, to the first name; and the third, to the company name.
All three menu items are attached to the IndexClick method shown here.

IndexClick calls SetupIndex to do the real work. You use the tag property of the
TMenuItem that is clicked to decide which index to choose:

```
case TComponent(Sender).Tag of
```

Depending on the current value of the `Tag` field, you can choose which index to use.

This system is flexible enough to allow you to call the `SetupIndex` method with just one parameter:

```
SetupIndex(Sender);
```

`SetupIndex` then casts the `Sender` object so that it can get access to the `Tag` field.

After the index has been set up properly, you can search for the first relevant record in the database:

```
DMod.NamesTable.FindNearest(['AAAA']);
```

The goal of this line is to skip over all the records that contain blanks in the field on which you're searching. For example, if you switch to the company index, you might find 20, 100, or even 5,000 records in the table that have no information in the `Company` field. To skip over these records, you can search for the first row that begins with the letter *A*.

Searching for Records

The `kdAdd` program also uses the `SetupIndex` method when it conducts searches. As I stated previously, you can use three possible menu items to start a search. The first searches on last names; the second, on first names; and the third, on a company name. I have assigned the same values to the `Tag` fields of these `TMenuItems` that I did to the `Tag` fields of the `TMenuItems` concerned with switching indices. That way, I can set up the index properly with a simple call to `SetupIndex`:

```
procedure TForm1.SearchClick(Sender: TObject);
var
  S, IndexName: string;
begin
  S := '';
  if (InputQuery('Search for Name', 'Enter Name: ', S)) then begin
    IndexName := DMod.NamesTable.IndexName;
    SetupIndex(Sender);
    DMod.NamesTable.FindNearest([S]);
    DMod.NamesTable.IndexName := IndexName;
  end;
end;
```

As you can see, the code also saves the current index so that the current state of the index can be restored after the search.

The big point to notice here is how easily you can take care of these chores by using the VCL. Delphi makes database programming easy, even when you're working with a fairly complex program.

Inserting Data and Canceling Operations

Because this database has five tables, you have to devise a technique for specifying the name of the table on which you want to perform an insertion, deletion, or post. I use the TPageControl to handle these chores. In particular, I assume that if the user is looking at the Address page, then he or she wants to perform an action on the kdAdds table, and if the user is looking at the first page, then he or she wants to perform an operation on the kdNames table, and so on:

```
procedure TForm1.InsertBtn2Click(Sender: TObject);
begin
  case (PageControl1.ActivePage).Tag of
    1: DMod.NamesTable.Insert;
    2: DMod.AddressTable.Insert;
    3: DMod.PhoneTable.Insert;
    4: DMod.EMailTable.Insert;
    5: DMod.MemoTable.Insert;
  end;
end;
```

As you can see, I have set the Tag field for each of the pages to a unique value so that I can easily determine the current page:

```
case (PageControl1.ActivePage).Tag of
```

If the user accidentally makes a wrong decision, he or she can undo the most recent operation on the currently selected table by clicking Cancel:

```
procedure TForm1.CancelBtn2Click(Sender: TObject);
var
  S: string;
begin
  case PageControl1.ActivePage.Tag of
    1: DMod.NamesTable.Cancel;
    2: DMod.AddressTable.Cancel;
    3: DMod.PhoneTable.Cancel;
    4: DMod.EMailTable.Cancel;
    5: DMod.MemoTable.Cancel;
  else
    ShowMessage(GetError(1, S));
  end;
end;
```

This system is easy to implement, but it can be a bit confusing to the user when he or she is looking at the first page, which holds information about not only the kdNames table, but also the kdAdds and kdPhone tables. The issue here is that the database itself won't be much fun if you have to flip pages to get even the most basic information about a name. To remedy this problem, I put the Name, Address, and Phone information on the first page but don't let the user edit it. If the user wants to edit a phone number or address, he or she has to turn to the appropriate page.

The design of the program helps the user by putting each table on a separate page. That way, the user can rely on the page metaphor when thinking about the underlying structure of the database. Providing metaphors for the user is a useful way to simplify the operation of an application.

NOTE

As you may recall, when I first talked about the ADDRESS2 program, I said that for many users, a simple flat-file database is best. When I said that, I was thinking particularly about the kinds of problems currently under discussion. Using a relational database takes a certain amount of conceptual ability that some users may not have the patience to master. The actual ideas involved are simple, but many users are still so overwhelmed by the very idea of computers that they can't clear their heads sufficiently to grasp concepts that would be easy for them to assimilate in some other field with which they are more familiar.

It may sound as though I am being overly polite in this note, but I'm trying to state the facts as I see them. Many intelligent people's minds really do become inexplicably opaque when it comes to thinking about computers. This problem will disappear as more and more children grow up using these machines, but for now programmers have to think seriously every time they add any level of complexity to their programs. Programmers will understand relational databases, and so will the small subset of users targeted by a program of this type; but it is important to understand that at this point in history, many users will find relational databases perhaps too difficult to understand.

Large numbers of computer users are simply baffled by features such as Windows Explorer. It's not at all unusual for computer users to have no idea how to create a directory or copy a file. Something as complex as a SQL prompt would just elicit a faint chuckle of resignation from them. They wouldn't even try to master it. When I give these examples, in some cases I'm talking about friends or family who earned more than 700 in one or more board scores, who graduated from Ivy League schools with honors, who wrote books on history or politics that sold in the hundreds of thousands. These people aren't idiots, not by a long shot, but they don't understand computers at all. If you want to appeal to this audience, you need to keep your programs very simple.

Please understand that I am not saying that you, the reader, don't understand this subject. It's the typical user that I am concerned with in this note. Readers of this book are not typical users!

10

RELATIONAL
DATABASES

Deleting Data: A First Look at the Program's Data Module

Deleting data is the last topic to be covered before moving over to examination of the TDataModule for the application. In fact, you will find that this subject touches on matters that are specific to the program's data module, so it serves as a good segue into new territory.

The main form uses this method to delete data:

```
procedure TForm1.DeleteBtn2Click(Sender: TObject);
const
  Btns:TMsgDlgButtons = [mbYes, mbNo];
var
  S, Msg: string;

begin
  Msg := 'Are you sure you want to delete %s?';

  case PageControl1.ActivePage.Tag of
    1: begin
      Msg := Format(Msg, [DMod.NamesTableFirstLastCompany.AsString]);
      if (MessageDlg(Msg, mtInformation, Btns, 0) = ID_YES) then
        DMod.CascadingDelete;
    end;

    2: begin
      Msg := Format(Msg, [DMod.Address]);
      if (MessageDlg(Msg, mtInformation, Btns, 0) = ID_YES) then
        DMod.AddressTable.Delete;
    end;

    3: begin
      Msg := Format(Msg, [DMod.Phone]);
      if (MessageDlg(Msg, mtInformation, Btns, 0) = ID_YES) then
        DMod.PhoneTable.Delete;
    end;

    4: begin
      Msg := Format(Msg, [DMod.EMail]);
      if (MessageDlg(Msg, mtInformation, Btns, 0) = ID_YES) then
        DMod.EMailTable.Delete;
    end;

    5: begin
      Msg := Format(Msg, [DMod.MemoTableDescription.AsString]);
      if (MessageDlg(Msg, mtInformation, Btns, 0) = ID_YES) then
        DMod.MemoTable.Delete;
    end;
```

```
    else
      ShowMessage(GetError(1, S));
    end;
end;
```

As you can see, this code uses the `Tag` field of the `TTabSheet` to determine which table is focused.

The code then pops up a message box asking the user if he or she is sure about continuing with the deletion. In some cases, you can easily give the user an intelligent prompt about the contents of the current field:

```
Msg := Format(Msg, [DMod.NamesTableFirstLastCompany.AsString]);
```

In this case, the string garnered from one of the fields of the `NamesTable` provides all the information the user needs. In fact, the `FirstLast` field of the database is a calculated field. This calculated field consists of combined information from the `First`, `Last`, and `Company` fields of the `kdNames`. This combined information uniquely identifies a record so the user can feel secure when deleting it:

```
procedure TDMod.NamesTableCalcFields(DataSet: TDataSet);
var
  Temp: string;
begin
  Temp := NamesTableFirstName.Value + ' ' + NamesTableLastName.Value;
  if (Temp = '') then
    NamesTableFirstLastCompany.Value := NamesTableCompany.Value
  else
    NamesTableFirstLastCompany.Value := Temp;
end;
```

As you can see, this code combines the first and last names into a single string. If the string is not empty, it is shown to the user as if it were a standard field of the database. If the current record has no information in either the first or last field, then the program assumes that the record must contain only company information:

```
NamesTableFirstLastCompany.Value := NamesTableCompany.Value
```

The end result of this system is to show the user records that contain either someone's first or last name or else just a company name. This way, you can ask the database to perform double duty as both a way of tracking company names and as a means of tracking the names of people.

This calculated field can be used not only to help with deletions, but also as an index appearing on the extreme left of the main form, as shown in Figure 10.1. The user will never edit this field directly but will use it as a guide to all the nearby records in the database. This kind of index is useful if you're searching for a particular name. For example,

I use the database to track the members of my family. As a result, it has lots of Calverts in it. I can use the Last Name search to find the section where the Calverts are stored and then use the index to move back and forth between members of the family.

You actually have no guarantee that the string generated by this calculated field will be unique. The program is designed to make sure the NameCode in the kdNames table is unique, but nothing in the program prevents you from entering two identical names, addresses, phone numbers, and so on.

If the user wants to delete an address, you once again need to provide information from several different fields to identify a record uniquely, as you can see in Figure 10.7.

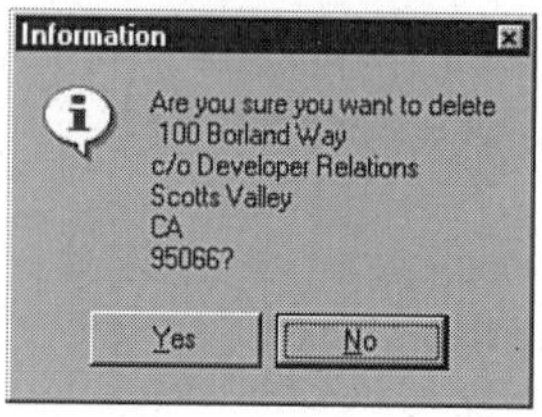

FIGURE 10.7

A prompt that uniquely identifies the address shown in particular row.

This time, I found it more convenient simply to add to the data module a method that would return a string uniquely identifying a record:

```
function TDMod.GetAddress: string;
begin
  Result := DMod.AddressTableAddress1.AsString + CR +
    DMod.AddressTableAddress2.AsString + CR +
    DMod.AddressTableCity.AsString + CR +
    DMod.AddressTableState.AsString + CR +
    DMod.AddressTableZip.AsString;
end;
```

I thought the most sensible approach was to add a read-only property to the data module to aid in retrieving this information:

```
property Address: string read GetAddress;
```

You can access this property by writing code that looks like this:

```
var
  S: string;
begin
  S := DMod.Address;
```

In this particular case, it is arguable that a property doesn't do much for you other than cover the remote contingency that you might change the parameters of the GetAddress method. On the other hand, the property doesn't cost you anything either because the compiler will obviously map any calls to the Address property directly to the

`GetAddress` method. In other words, this programming is very cautious because it is unlikely that the `GetAddress` method will ever change its spots. However, being conservative when writing code is almost always best, as long as you're not doing serious damage to the performance of your program.

It has taken me a long time just to show you the various techniques I employ to prompt the user for the name of the record he or she is about to delete. However, after this process is taken care of, just one line is required to delete the record:

```
DMod.EMailTable.Delete;
```

I won't bother discussing any of the means for deleting from the other tables in this program, as they follow the same pattern already established. The key point to grasp is that you have to show several fields to the user to identify a record uniquely. Furthermore, placing the burden of generating these strings on the program's data module is probably best. The reason for doing so is simply that the generation of these strings is dependent on the structure of the tables underlying the program. Isolating all code dependent on these structures inside one object is best so that you won't have to hunt all over your program to find code that might need to be modified because of a change in the program's database.

The Data Module: Cascading Deletes

You have already seen that the data module contains special properties that retrieve strings uniquely identifying certain records. You have also seen the calculated field that generates a string "uniquely" identifying records from the `kdNames` table. You have yet to explore methods that aid in posting and deleting records.

The issue here is simply that the database contains a number of tables. If the user wants to delete a name from the database, then he or she is really asking to not just delete the name, but also the addresses, phone numbers, and other information associated with that name. This process is known as a *cascading delete*.

Delphi provides support for cascading deletes via the referential integrity dialog found in the Database Desktop. You can see this option in Figure 10.8.

Many databases do not support cascading deletes, so you can implement it on the client side with just a few lines of code:

```
procedure TDMod.CascadingDelete;
begin
  EMailDeleteQuery.ParamByName('NameCode').AsInteger :=
    EMailTableNameCode.Value;
  EMailDeleteQuery.ExecSQL;
```

```
MemoDeleteQuery.ParamByName('NameCode').AsInteger :=
  MemoTableNameCode.Value;
MemoDeleteQuery.ExecSQL;

PhoneDeleteQuery.ParamByName('NameCode').AsInteger :=
  PhoneTableNameCode.Value;
PhoneDeleteQuery.ExecSQL;

AddressDeleteQuery.ParamByName('NameCode').AsInteger :=
  AddressTableNameCode.Value;
AddressDeleteQuery.ExecSQL;

NamesDeleteQuery.ParamByName('NameCode').AsInteger :=
  NamesTableNameCode.Value;
NamesDeleteQuery.ExecSQL;

NamesTable.Refresh;
end;
```

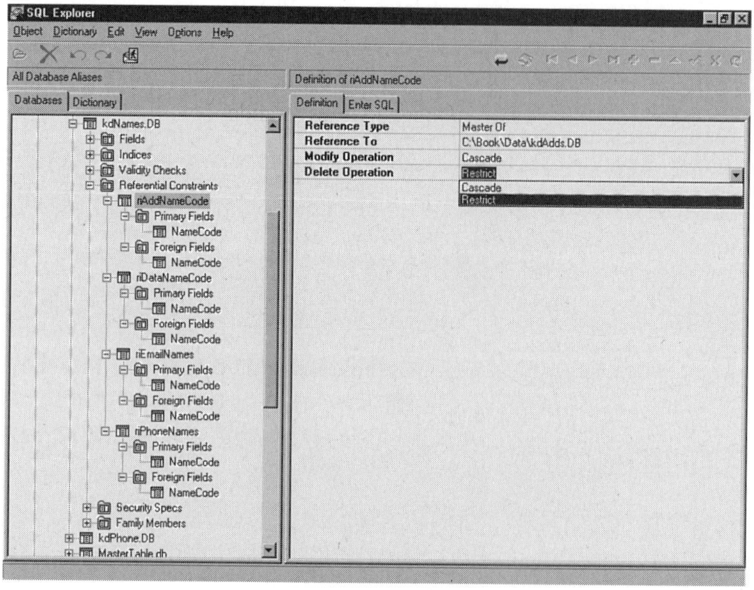

FIGURE 10.8

Choose Cascade or Restrict to get support for cascading deletes in databases that support this feature.

This code looks a bit complicated, in part because some of the lines are long and need to be wrapped. Underneath, however, its structure is very simple. I simply walk down the list of tables in the database, accessing the kdNames table last. I have created an SQL statement for each table that will delete all the records in the table that have a particular

NameCode. For example, I use these SQL statements for deleting records in the kdNames or kdAdds tables:

```
Delete from kdNames where NameCode = :NameCode
Delete from KDAdds where NameCode = :NameCode
```

As I said, this technology is very simple, and the act of implementing cascading deletes in your application is trivial. The key to the whole process is recognizing that it's simplest to delegate the responsibility for deletions to the program's data module. Then you can create a simple method in the data module to handle the logic of the operation, and after about five minutes work, you have a method that can be called from anywhere in your application with a single line of code. (You should, however, take more than five minutes to test your code against sample data to make sure that it is working properly.) Furthermore, you will find that many databases automatically support cascading deletes.

The Data Module: Mass Posts

The opposite problem from deleting records occurs when you have to post the data in your program. In these cases, you need to make sure that all the data in all the tables is posted. You wouldn't want to post just the data in the kdNames table and then leave updates to the kdAdds or kdPhones tables stranded.

The methods that handle posting the data look like this:

```
procedure TDMod.DoPost(Data: TDataSet);
begin
  if ((Data.State = dsInsert) or (Data.State = dsEdit)) then
    Data.Post;
end;

procedure TDMod.PostAll;
var
  i: Integer;
begin
  for i := 0 to ComponentCount - 1 do
    if Components[i] is TTable then
      DoPost(TDataSet(Components[i]));
end;
```

This code iterates through all the components on the program's data module looking for TTable objects. When the code finds one, it passes the object to a method called DoPost that calls the Post method for the table. The code in DoPost first checks to make sure the table is in dsInsert or dsEdit mode, as it is an error to call post on a table that is in dsBrowse or some other mode in which a post can't occur. You can alternatively check the Boolean value of TTable.Modified to find out the status of a record.

Notice that I use the ComponentCount property of TDataModule to determine how many components I need to check. I then use the is operator to check whether I can safely assume the current component is a TTable.

Putting Error Strings in String Resources

The other subject worth touching on briefly in regard to this program involves the matter of using string resources to handle error strings. The program has a small string resource that contains only one string:

```
#include "kderrs.inc"
STRINGTABLE
{
  KDERR_CASESTATEMENT, "Command fell through case statement"
}
```

In a program used in the real world, you would probably want to generate many more error strings.

You can use the following method to retrieve error strings from the program's resource:

```
function GetError(ErrNo: Integer; var S: string): string;
begin
  SetLength(S, ERR_STRING_SIZE);
  LoadString(HInstance, 1, PChar(S), ERR_STRING_SIZE);
  Result := S;
end;
```

This code calls the Windows API routine called LoadString to do the actual grunt work. Several built-in VCL routines also provide this same functionality. Notice that an include file defines the KDERR_CASESTATEMENT constant:

```
#define KDERR_CASESTATEMENT 1
```

If you want more information about this error-handling code, you can refer to the discussion of string resources at the end of Chapter 4, "Exception Handling."

The About Box

For the sake of completeness, I will wrap up the examination of this program by showing you the About box for the program, shown in Figure 10.9. You can generate About boxes automatically in Delphi by choosing File, New, turning to the Forms page of the Object Repository, and choosing About Box, as shown in Figure 10.10. I choose to Copy the code rather than to Inherit or Use it, as you can see in the bottom left of Figure 10.10. Proceeding this way is usually the best and simplest method unless you're sure you have mastered the technology involved with form inheritance.

FIGURE 10.9

The About box for the kdAdd program.

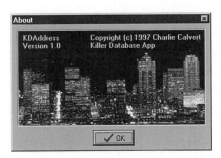

FIGURE 10.10

Creating an About box from the Object Repository.

After you add the sample About box to your program, you can modify it so that it is attractive, or at least informative. I'll let you decide how to decorate the dialogs you want to use.

You've now come to the end of the discussion of the kdAdd program. The rest of the chapter consists of a discussion of two utilities associated with this program. One will transfer data from the ADDRESS2 program to the kdAdd program, and the second will show how to use the TSession object to explore the structure of the tables used in the kdAdd program. The next section begins an explanation of the TSession object and TTreeView object.

Using the **kdAddExplore** Program

The kdAddExplore program uses the TSession object to explore the tables used in the kdAdd program. The TSession object is often overlooked by VCL programmers because its operation is usually handled behind the scenes without need for intervention. However, if you want to explore the structure of a database at runtime, this object is the one to use. In fact, this object might have been more usefully called the TDataExplorer object rather than TSession.

10

**RELATIONAL
DATABASES**

> **NOTE**
>
> TSession is created automatically by an application on startup. If you're working inside a DLL or in a console mode application, then no default TApplication object exists to start up a session. As a result, you might have to create your own TSession object or call the Initialize method of a TApplication object. Otherwise, you cannot use databases inside your program.

Before you read the technical part of this section, spending a few moments running the kdAddExplore program found on the CD might be helpful. This program demonstrates techniques of examining the structure of an existing database.

> **NOTE**
>
> The kdAddExplore program bears a close resemblance to a cut-down version of the Database Explorer (DBX). Nothing about this similarity is coincidental. However, I have never seen the source to DBX nor discussed its structure with its author. My intention here is not to create a substitute for the DBX, but only to provide a simple means of showing you how to explore database objects at run-time.
>
> You can use this kind of information to provide utilities for your users or merely to extend your own knowledge of the BDE and VCL. The code also provides an example of how to use the TTreeView object.

Throughout the rest of this chapter, I will use a global TSession object created automatically whenever you include database code in your programs. However, you also can drop down a TSession component on your forms if you want to look at a visual object. I do not use it here because it would bring no additional functionality to my program. However, you might want to view the TSession component at least and take a look at its password-related properties.

Working with **TSession**

TSession is used to manage all the database connections within a session. It is a global object that wraps up not only TTable and TQuery, but also TDatabase. A single TSession object might manage many tables, queries, and databases.

The TSession object has two sets of methods. The first has to do with managing a session. The methods encompassing this set of functionality are shown in Table 10.12.

TABLE 10.12 THE SESSION MANAGEMENT ROUTINES FROM THE TSession OBJECT

Routine	Description
Close	Closes all databases
CloseDatabase	Closes a particular database
Open	Opens the session: Active = True;
OpenDatabase	Opens a specific database
AddPassword	Creates a password for the session
RemovePassword	Deletes a password
RemoveAllPasswords	Clears the password list
DropConnections	Closes all currently inactive databases and datasets

The second set of routines found in TSession includes the methods that are of interest in the current context of this book. These routines are shown in Table 10.13.

TABLE 10.13 ROUTINES FOR QUERYING A SESSION REGARDING THE AVAILABLE DATABASES, TABLES, DRIVERS, AND STORED PROCEDURES

Routine	Description
GetAliasNames	Gets the list of BDE aliases for a database
GetAliasParams	Gets the list of parameters for a BDE alias
GetAliasDriverName	Gets the BDE driver for an alias of a database
GetDatabaseNames	Gets a list of BDE aliases and TDatabase objects
GetDriverNames	Gets the names of installed BDE drivers
GetDriverParams	Gets parameters for a BDE driver
GetTableNames	Gets tables associated with a database
GetStoredProcNames	Gets stored procedures for a database

Routines such as GetDatabaseNames and GetTableNames can retrieve a list of all the available databases and tables on the current system. You can see this data on display inside the kdAddExplore program. For example, all the databases in my system at the time of this writing are visible in the main screen of the kdAddExplore program, as shown in Figure 10.11.

FIGURE 10.11

The kdAddExplore program displays all the available databases on my system.

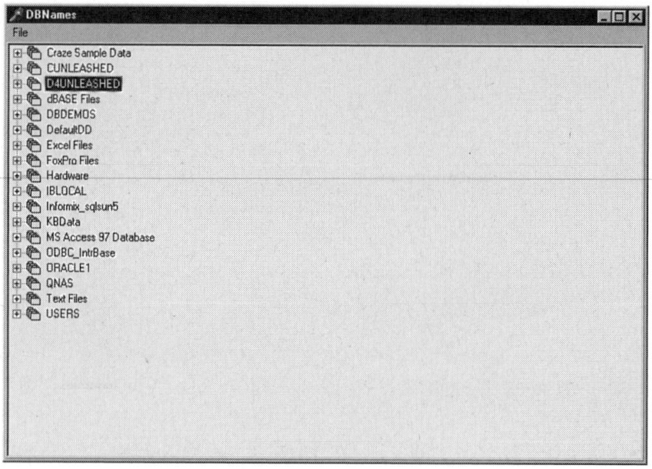

You can open the nodes of kdAddExplore program to see a list of all the tables in a particular database, as shown in Figure 10.12. You can then drill down even further to the names of the fields and indices in a particular table. Finally, you can even see the names of the fields involved in a particular index, as shown in Figure 10.13.

FIGURE 10.12

The tables in the D4UNLEASHED database that holds most of the data used in this book.

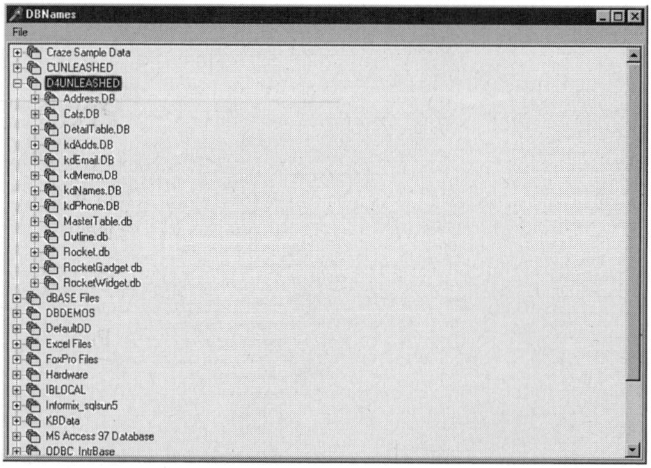

Another set of TSession functionality tapped into by the kdAddExplore program involves looking at the alias found on a system. You can drill down in this dialog to see the parameters passed to a particular alias, as shown in Figure 10.14.

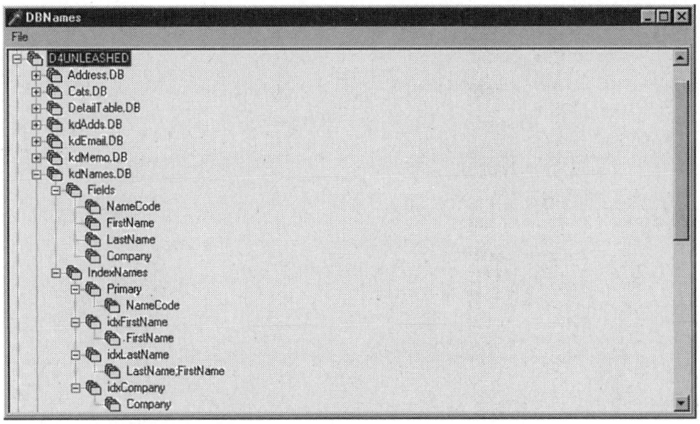

FIGURE 10.13

The fields and indices on the kdNames table. Notice that you can drill down to see the fields in each index.

FIGURE 10.14

The kdAddExplore program shows all the aliases on the system. The open branch is from an InterBase database.

The Code for the `kdAddExplore` Program

Most of the complexity in the `kdAddExplore` program comes from manipulating the `TTreeView` object. The code for querying the `TSession` object is fairly straightforward in most cases; the `TTreeView` makes the code a bit tricky in places. The source for this program is shown in Listing 10.6 through Listing 10.8.

LISTING 10.6 THE MAIN MODULE FOR THE kdAddExplore PROGRAM

```
///////////////////////////////////////
//    File: Main.pas
// Project: KdAddExplore
// Copyright (c) 1998 by Charlie Calvert
//
unit Main;

interface

uses
```

continues

LISTING 10.6 CONTINUED

```pascal
  Windows, Messages, SysUtils,
  Classes, Graphics, Controls,
  Forms, Dialogs, Menus,
  ImgList, ComCtrls, ExtCtrls,
  DBTables;

type
  TDBNames = class(TForm)
    Panel1: TPanel;
    TView: TTreeView;
    ImageList1: TImageList;
    MainMenu1: TMainMenu;
    File1: TMenuItem;
    AliasView1: TMenuItem;
    N1: TMenuItem;
    Exit1: TMenuItem;
    procedure TViewExpanding(Sender: TObject; Node: TTreeNode;
      var AllowExpansion: Boolean);
    procedure Exit1Click(Sender: TObject);
    procedure AliasView1Click(Sender: TObject);
    procedure FormShow(Sender: TObject);
  private
    procedure AddTables(Node: TTreeNode);
    procedure DeleteTemp(Node: TTreeNode);
    procedure FindFields(Node: TTreeNode; Table: TTable);
    procedure FindFieldsAndIndices(Node: TTreeNode);
    procedure FindIndices(Node: TTreeNode; Table: TTable);
    { Private declarations }
  public
    { Public declarations }
  end;

var
  DBNames: TDBNames;

implementation

uses
  DMod1, DB, AliasView1;

{$R *.DFM}

procedure TDBNames.FormShow(Sender: TObject);
var
  i: Integer;
  S: AnsiString;
  DBNamesList: TStringList;
  Node: TTreeNode;
begin
```

```
  DBNamesList := TStringList.Create;
  ImageList1.ResourceLoad(rtBitmap, 'FolderShut', clPurple);

  Session.GetDatabaseNames(DBNamesList);
  for i := 0 to DBNamesList.Count -1 do begin
    S := DBNamesList.Strings[i];
    Node := TView.Items.Add(TView.Selected, S);
    TView.Items.AddChild(Node, 'TEMP');
  end;
  DBNamesList.Free;
end;

{**********************************************************************
 .DeleteTemp

 .Delete child if it's one of the 'TEMP' placeholders.
 **********************************************************************}
procedure TDBNames.DeleteTemp(Node: TTreeNode);
var
  TempNode: TTreeNode;
begin
  if (Node.Count = 1) then begin
    TempNode := Node.getFirstChild;
    if (TempNode.Text = 'TEMP') then
      TempNode.Delete;
  end;
end;

{**********************************************************************
 .AddTables

 .Delete child if it's one of the 'TEMP' placeholders.
  Add all tables belonging to the database as children.

  When calling GetTableNames, third parameter is set to
  true, which means the extension of the table is also
  retrieved. Without the extension, there can be trouble
  exploring dBase files.
 **********************************************************************}
procedure TDBNames.AddTables(Node: TTreeNode);
var
  j: Integer;
  S: string;
  TempNode, ChildNode: TTreeNode;
  List: TStringList;
begin
  S := Node.Text;
  List := TStringList.Create;
```

continues

10

**RELATIONAL
DATABASES**

LISTING 10.6   CONTINUED

```
  DeleteTemp(Node);

  Session.GetTableNames(S, '*.*', True, False, List);
  for j := 0 to List.Count - 1 do begin
    TempNode := TView.Items.AddChild(Node, List.Strings[j]);
    ChildNode := TView.Items.AddChild(TempNode, 'Fields');
    TView.Items.AddChild(ChildNode, 'TEMP');
    ChildNode := TView.Items.AddChild(TempNode, 'IndexNames');
    TView.Items.AddChild(ChildNode, 'TEMP');
  end;
  List.Free;
end;

procedure TDBNames.FindFields(Node: TTreeNode; Table: TTable);
var
  i: Integer;
begin
  for i := 0 to Table.FieldCount - 1 do
    TView.Items.AddChild(Node, Table.Fields[i].FieldName);
end;

{
  FindIndices

  One way to get a list of the names of the Indices on a table
  is through the GetIndexNames function:

    TStringList *List = new TStringList;
    Table.GetIndexNames(List);

  However, here I need a bit more information, so I used the
  IndexDefs property instead. However, I still seem to need
  to call GetIndexNames to prime the pump.
}
procedure TDBNames.FindIndices(Node: TTreeNode; Table: TTable);
var
  i: Integer;
  List: TStringList;
  ChildNode: TTreeNode ;
  S: string;
  IndexDefs: TIndexDefs;
begin
  List := TStringList.Create;
  Table.GetIndexNames(List);
  IndexDefs := Table.IndexDefs;
  for i := 0 to IndexDefs.Count - 1 do begin
    S := IndexDefs.Items[i].Name;
    if (Length(S) = 0) then
      S := 'Primary';
```

```
    ChildNode := TView.Items.AddChild(Node, S);
    S := IndexDefs.Items[i].Fields;
    TView.Items.AddChild(ChildNode, S);
  end;

  List.Free;
end;

procedure TDBNames.FindFieldsAndIndices(Node: TTreeNode);
var
  Table: TTable;
begin
  Table := TTable.Create(Self);

  Table.DatabaseName := Node.Parent.Parent.Text;
  Table.TableName := Node.Parent.Text;
  Table.Open;

  DeleteTemp(Node);

  if (Node.Count < 1) then
    case (Node.Index) of
      0: FindFields(Node, Table);
      1: FindIndices(Node, Table);
    end;

  Table.Free;
end;

procedure TDBNames.TViewExpanding(Sender: TObject; Node: TTreeNode;
  var AllowExpansion: Boolean);
begin
  case (Node.Level) of
    0: if (Node.Count <= 1) then AddTables(Node);
    2: FindFieldsAndIndices(Node);
  end;
end;

procedure TDBNames.Exit1Click(Sender: TObject);
begin
  Close;
end;

procedure TDBNames.AliasView1Click(Sender: TObject);
begin
  AliasForm.Show;
end;


end.
```

LISTING 10.7 THE Aliasview UNIT ALLOWS YOU TO VIEW ALIASES AVAILABLE ON YOUR SYSTEM

```
/////////////////////////////////////
//     File: AliasView1.pas
// Project: KdAddExplore
// Copyright (c) 1998 by Charlie Calvert
//
unit AliasView1;

interface

uses
  Windows, Messages, SysUtils,
  Classes, Graphics, Controls,
  Forms, Dialogs, StdCtrls, DBTables;

type
  TAliasForm = class(TForm)
    ListBox1: TListBox;
    Memo1: TMemo;
    procedure ListBox1Click(Sender: TObject);
    procedure FormShow(Sender: TObject);
  private
    { Private declarations }
  public
    { Public declarations }
  end;

var
  AliasForm: TAliasForm;

implementation

uses DMod1;

{$R *.DFM}

procedure TAliasForm.ListBox1Click(Sender: TObject);
var
  S: string;
begin
  S := ListBox1.Items.Strings[ListBox1.ItemIndex];
  Session.GetAliasParams(S, Memo1.Lines);
end;

procedure TAliasForm.FormShow(Sender: TObject);
begin
  Session.GetAliasNames(ListBox1.Items);
end;

end.
```

LISTING 10.8 THE DATA MODULE FOR THE MAIN PROGRAM CONTAINS A TDatabase OBJECT BUT NO CUSTOM CODE

```
unit DMod1;

interface

uses
  Windows, Messages, SysUtils,
  Classes, Graphics, Controls,
  Forms, Dialogs, DBTables;

type
  TDMod = class(TDataModule)
    Database1: TDatabase;
  private
    { Private declarations }
  public
    { Public declarations }
  end;

var
  DMod: TDMod;

implementation

{$R *.DFM}

end.
```

Using a TTreeView to Display the Databases on a System

When the kdAddExplore program is launched, it first iterates through the available databases on the system and displays to the user in a TTreeView:

```
procedure TDBNames.FormShow(Sender: TObject);
var
  i: Integer;
  S: AnsiString;
  DBNamesList: TStringList;
  Node: TTreeNode;
begin
  DBNamesList := TStringList.Create;
  Session.GetDatabaseNames(DBNamesList);

  for i := 0 to DBNamesList.Count -1 do begin
    S := DBNamesList.Strings[i];
    Node := TView.Items.Add(TView.Selected, S);
```

```
    TView.Items.AddChild(Node, 'TEMP');
  end;
  DBNamesList.Free;
end;
```

This code needs to have an icon that it can use to spruce up the nodes of the `TTreeView`. It stores that bitmap, called `FldrShut.bmp`, in an `ImageList` component. `FldrShut.bmp` is one of the files that ships in the `Images` subdirectory beneath the Borland `Shared` directory that is created when you install Delphi or C++Builder.

Because only one image appears in this image list, it will automatically be associated with all the nodes of the `TTreeView` object. In this particular case, that is a satisfactory solution to the problem of how to give some visual interest to the object.

After it sets up the icon, the program retrieves the list of available aliases from the `TSession` object and stores them inside a `TStringList`:

```
DBNamesList := TStringList.Create;
Session.GetDatabaseNames(DBNamesList);
```

After you have the list of items, you can easily store each one inside a `TTreeNode` object that can be hung on the `TTreeView` for display to the user:

```
for i := 0 to DBNamesList.Count -1 do begin
  S := DBNamesList.Strings[i];
  Node := TView.Items.Add(TView.Selected, S);
  TView.Items.AddChild(Node, 'TEMP');
end;
```

Clearly, the `TTreeNode` object is the key to working with `TTreeViews`. This object represents an individual node on a `TTreeView`. It encapsulates a bitmap and a caption, and can be identified by a unique index number.

Notice that I call two methods of the `Items` property of the `TTreeView` object, which in this program is called `TView`; it is not a type, but an abbreviation for `TreeView`. The first call adds the name of the database as a node. The next call adds a child to that database node containing a string consisting of the word `"Temp"`. The `"Temp"` node is never shown to the user but exists only to force the `TTreeView` to display a plus sign indicating to the user that the node can be expanded further. When it comes time to expand the node, I delete the word `Temp` and substitute a word that actually displays the name of one of the tables in the database.

The use of the `"Temp"` node may seem like a nasty kluge at first. However, doing things this way is easier than forcing the user to sit still while I open all the databases, including those that might need a password, and find all the tables inside them. When you think of things from this perspective, adding a temporary node to each item in the tree suddenly seems very logical. If the user wants to expand a particular node, then you can retrieve detailed information about that particular database. This approach is much better than trying to retrieve information about every table on the system in one long, time-consuming process.

Expanding the Nodes of the `TTreeView`

The program must respond appropriately when the user clicks on a node of the `TTreeView` object. In particular, if the user is first opening a particular database node, the code needs to retrieve the list of tables in that database and display them to the user. If the user clicks one of the tables, a list of fields and indices must be retrieved, and so on.

An `OnExpanding` event gets called automatically when the user wants to open a node. The following is how the `kdAddExplore` program responds to this event:

```
procedure TDBNames.TViewExpanding(Sender: TObject; Node: TTreeNode;
  var AllowExpansion: Boolean);
begin
  case (Node.Level) of
    0: if (Node.Count <= 1) then AddTables(Node);
    2: FindFieldsAndIndices(Node);
  end;
end;
```

As you can see, the program calls a method named `AddTables` if the user is working at the first level of the tree, and it calls a method called `FindFieldsAndIndices` if the user is working at the second level of the tree. The level the user is currently exploring appears in the `Level` field of the `TTreeNode` passed to the `OnExpanding` event handler.

Before calling `AddTables`, I check to see if more than one child node already appears on this particular node of the `TTreeView`. If more than one node exists, I assume that the database has already been explored and that the node can be opened without any further querying of the system. If only one node exists, I assume that this is the `"Temp"` node created in the program's `OnShow` event, and I call `AddTables` so that the node can be updated.

Adding a List of Available Tables to the `TTreeView`

The following code is called when it's time to explore the tables on the system:

```
procedure TDBNames.DeleteTemp(Node: TTreeNode);
var
  TempNode: TTreeNode;
begin
```

```
  if (Node.Count = 1) then begin
    TempNode := Node.getFirstChild;
    if (TempNode.Text = 'TEMP') then
      TempNode.Delete;
  end;
end;

procedure TDBNames.AddTables(Node: TTreeNode);
var
  j: Integer;
  S: string;
  TempNode, ChildNode: TTreeNode;
  List: TStringList;
begin
  S := Node.Text;
  List := TStringList.Create;

  DeleteTemp(Node);

  Session.GetTableNames(S, '*.*', True, False, List);
  for j := 0 to List.Count - 1 do begin
    TempNode := TView.Items.AddChild(Node, List.Strings[j]);
    ChildNode := TView.Items.AddChild(TempNode, 'Fields');
    TView.Items.AddChild(ChildNode, 'TEMP');
    ChildNode := TView.Items.AddChild(TempNode, 'IndexNames');
    TView.Items.AddChild(ChildNode, 'TEMP');
  end;
  List.Free;
end;
```

The first method shown here, called `DeleteTemp`, is used to delete the `"Temp"` nodes created in the `OnShow` event. The code checks to make sure the string is actually set to `"Temp"` just to be sure that I haven't stumbled across a database that has only one table in it. The program would, of course, behave badly if it encountered a database with a single table called `"Temp"` in it!

The next step is for the program to retrieve the list of tables in a database from the `Session` object:

```
Session.GetTableNames(S, '*.*', True, False, List);
```

The code uses the string name from the node passed to the `OnExpanded` event to query `TSession` for the proper set of tables. You can look up `GetTableNames` in the online help for detailed explanation of this call, but most readers should be able to figure out what is going on from this declaration:

```
procedure GetTableNames(const DatabaseName,
  Pattern: string; Extensions, SystemTables: Boolean; List: TStrings);
```

Set `Extensions` to `True` if you want to retrieve the extension for a dBASE or Paradox table. Also set `Extensions` to `True` if you want to retrieve system tables for SQL databases such as InterBase.

The program is at last ready to add the tables to the `TTreeView`:

```
TempNode := TView.Items.AddChild(Node, List.Strings[j]);
ChildNode := TView.Items.AddChild(TempNode, 'Fields');
TView.Items.AddChild(ChildNode, 'TEMP');
ChildNode := TView.Items.AddChild(TempNode, 'IndexNames');
TView.Items.AddChild(ChildNode, 'TEMP');
```

This code first adds a table name to the `TTreeView`:

```
TempNode := TView.Items.AddChild(Node, List.Strings[j]);
```

It then adds two child nodes labeled `Fields` and `IndexNames` to the table name. Once again, I resort to the trick of placing a `"Temp"` node under these two fields to indicate to the user that the nodes can be expanded further. However, I do not actually expand the nodes at this time because the user may not ever want to see the data in question.

Finding Out About Indices and Fields

To find out about indices and fields, I abandon the `TSession` object and instead create a `TTable` object because this object can give me the information I need:

```
procedure TDBNames.FindFieldsAndIndices(Node: TTreeNode);
var
  Table: TTable;
begin
  Table := TTable.Create(Self);

  Table.DatabaseName := Node.Parent.Parent.Text;
  Table.TableName := Node.Parent.Text;
  Table.Open;

  DeleteTemp(Node);

  if (Node.Count < 1) then
    case (Node.Index) of
      0: FindFields(Node, Table);
      1: FindIndices(Node, Table);
    end;

  Table.Free;
end;
```

The program first queries TTreeView to retrieve the name of the database the user wants to explore and the name of the particular table under examination:

```
Table.DatabaseName := Node.Parent.Parent.Text;
Table.TableName := Node.Parent.Text;
```

The table is then opened, and the "Temp" node associated with it is deleted:

```
Table.Open;
DeleteTemp(Node);
```

I hung the nodes with the labels Fields and IndexNames in a particular order, so I can use the Index field of the current Node to know when to retrieve information on fields and when to retrieve information on indices:

```
if (Node.Count < 1) then
case (Node.Index) of
  0: FindFields(Node, Table);
  1: FindIndices(Node, Table);
end;
```

The FindFields method is very simple, in large part because it is a leaf node on the tree and does not need to be expanded further:

```
procedure TDBNames.FindFields(Node: TTreeNode; Table: TTable);
var
  i: Integer;
begin
  for i := 0 to Table.FieldCount - 1 do
    TView.Items.AddChild(Node, Table.Fields[i].FieldName);
end;
```

I have to do a little coaxing to get the system to give up information on indices:

```
procedure TDBNames.FindIndices(Node: TTreeNode; Table: TTable);
var
  i: Integer;
  List: TStringList;
  ChildNode: TTreeNode ;
  S: string;
  IndexDefs: TIndexDefs;
begin
  List := TStringList.Create;
  Table.GetIndexNames(List);
  IndexDefs := Table.IndexDefs;
  for i := 0 to IndexDefs.Count - 1 do begin
    S := IndexDefs.Items[i].Name;
    if (Length(S) = 0) then
      S := 'Primary';
    ChildNode := TView.Items.AddChild(Node, S);
```

```
    S := IndexDefs.Items[i].Fields;
    TView.Items.AddChild(ChildNode, S);
  end;

  List.Free;
end;
```

I first get the list of index names from the TTable object and then retrieve the relevant TIndexDefs object. This object contains information on a particular index. I iterated through the Items in the IndexDefs and display the information to the user.

You might think that I would need to have a second loop inside the first loop to handle a case in which an index consists of more than one field. However, a second loop is not necessary because the list is sent to me in the form of a single string, with each index delimited by a semicolon. For example, the primary index of the Items table from DBDEMOS consists of two fields. This information is displayed by TIndexDefs as follows:

```
OrderNo;ItemNo
```

Displaying Aliases and Alias Parameters

After all the work involved with displaying information about databases, tables, indices, and fields, you will find that querying the system about aliases is relatively trivial. One of the main reasons this process is so much simpler is that I use list boxes rather than a TTreeView to display information. TTreeViews are great for the user, but not much fun for the programmer.

The following is the custom code from the unit that displays alias to the user. All the other code in the unit is generated by the system.

```
procedure TAliasForm.ListBox1Click(Sender: TObject);
var
  S: string;
begin
  S := ListBox1.Items.Strings[ListBox1.ItemIndex];
  Session.GetAliasParams(S, Memo1.Lines);
end;

procedure TAliasForm.FormShow(Sender: TObject);
begin
  Session.GetAliasNames(ListBox1.Items);
end;
```

The program opts to display this information in a separate form rather than overlay it on top of the information about databases. This form has two list boxes in it. The first list box holds the various aliases available on the system, and the second list box holds the parameters for the currently selected alias.

When the form is first shown, I call the `GetAliasNames` method of the global `Session` object and then pass it the `TStrings`–based property of `TListBox`. That's all I need to do to show the user the aliases.

If the user selects a particular item in the first list box, then the `ListBox1Click` event handler is called. This code initializes a string to the name of the currently selected alias:

```
S := ListBox1.Items.Strings[ListBox1.ItemIndex];
```

Then it queries the `Session` object for the list of parameters associated with that object:

```
Session.GetAliasParams(S, Memo1.Lines);
```

As you can see, this second list is displayed in the second list box, as shown in Figure 10.14.

Summary

In this chapter, you looked at relational databases. The core material was divided into two sections. The first section looked at a simple relational database program consisting of five interrelated tables. You saw how these tables are tied together and how to add, delete, insert, and edit records in these tables. Also included is a relatively lengthy discussion of the indices and keys in the table and of why they were created. Other subjects included searching and storing strings in a string table.

The second half of the chapter was dedicated to an examination of the global `TSession` object that is created automatically whenever you use the BDE database tools in your program. You can use this object to query the system about aliases, databases, and tables. You also saw how to query a `TTable` object about its fields and indices.

Other information included in this chapter related mostly to using standard Delphi components such as `TTreeView`. You saw that the powerful `TTreeView` object allows you to display information in a way that the user can easily comprehend. Several portions of the chapter focused on the `TTreeNode` object used to fill in the nodes of a `TTreeView`. In particular, you saw how to add child nodes to a `TTreeView`.

Working with the Local InterBase Server

Delphi ships with the Local InterBase Server, which is sometimes simply called LIBS. This tool provides all the capabilities of the full InterBase server, but it runs on a local machine. You do not need to be connected to a network to be able to run the Local InterBase Server.

The client software you get with Delphi will talk to either LIBS or the standard version of the InterBase server. From your point of view as a programmer, you will find no difference between talking to LIBS and talking to an InterBase server across a network. The only way to tell which server you're connected to is by examining the path in your current alias. In short, LIBS is the perfect tool for learning or practicing real client/server database programming even if you're not connected to a LAN.

The goal of this chapter is to provide you with a useful introduction to LIBS and also a brief overview of transactions. In particular, you will learn how to do the following:

- Connect to local InterBase tables
- Connect without having to specify a password
- Create databases
- Work with TDatabase objects
- Create tables
- Commit and roll back transactions in both local and InterBase tables
- Maintain the data you have created
- Work with cached updates
- Create many-to-many relationships
- Grant rights on a table
- Back up a database

Everything you read about the local InterBase in this chapter applies equally to the full-server version of InterBase. As a result, this chapter will also be of interest to people who use InterBase on a network.

If you work with another database such as Oracle, you might still be interested in the material found in this chapter.

Getting Started with InterBase

In particular, this chapter shows how you can use a local system to create a database that is fully compatible with the network version of InterBase. To convert a LIBS database to a real client/server application on a network, you just have to copy your database onto another machine:

```
copy MyDatabase.gdb p:\remote\nt\drive
```

You just copy the one file onto the network. No other steps are necessary, other than changing the path in your alias. Of course, you will also need a real copy of the InterBase server.

Note that the Client/Server version of Delphi ships with five licenses for the full InterBase server. The real InterBase server runs on most platforms, including Windows 95/98, Windows NT, and a wide range of UNIX platforms.

Many readers of this book will come from the world of "big iron," where the only kinds of databases that exist are servers such as Oracle, Sybase, InterBase, AS400, or DB2. Other readers come from the world of PCs, where tools such as dBASE, Paradox, Access, or FoxPro are considered to be the standard database tools. Overemphasizing the huge gap that exists between these two worlds is almost impossible.

Readers who are familiar with "big iron" and large network-based servers are likely to find the Local InterBase Server very familiar. Readers who come from the world of PCs are likely to find InterBase very strange indeed, especially at first.

InterBase is meant to handle huge numbers of records, which are stored on servers. It does not come equipped with many of the amenities of a tool such as dBASE or Paradox. In fact, InterBase supplies users with only the most minimal interface and instead expects you to create programs with a client-side tool such as Delphi. However, you will find that InterBase is not a particularly difficult challenge after you get some of the basics under your belt.

Databases and the Job Market

You probably work inside a corporation or at a small company. However, if you are a student or someone who wants to enter the computer programming world, you should pay special attention to the material in this and other chapters on InterBase.

Perhaps 80 percent of the applications built in America today use databases in one form or another. Indeed, most of these applications revolve around, and are focused on, manipulating databases. Furthermore, client/server databases such as InterBase, Oracle, or MS SQL Server form the core of this application development.

If you want to enter the programming world, getting a good knowledge of databases is one of the best ways to get started. Right now, there is virtually an endless need for good database programmers.

One note of caution should perhaps be added here. I happen to enjoy database programming. However, it is not the most romantic end of the computer business. If you're primarily interested in systems programming or game programming, then you should hold out for jobs in those fields rather than focus your career in an area of only minor interest to you.

Databases, however, offer the greatest opportunity for employment. In particular, client/server database programmers are almost always in demand. Because LIBS ships with your copy of Delphi, you have a great chance to learn the ins and outs of this lucrative field.

Setting Up the Local InterBase

Owners of Delphi 4 Professional and Client/Server will have LIBS installed automatically when they install Delphi. Client/Server users will also get a five-user license to a full-blown network-based version of the product. In most cases, InterBase will run smoothly without any need for you to worry about setup. However, you should take several key steps to ensure that all is as it should be.

If you own the Client/Server version of Delphi, turn to the online help by searching in the index for the following key: InterBase: installing. There you will learn that the Client/Server version of Delphi comes with a five-user license for InterBase Server, and both the Professional and Client/Server versions of Delphi come with the Local InterBase Server. As a result, if you have the Client/Server version of Delphi, take a few moments to install the full network-based version of InterBase server, and use that instead of LIBS. As I stated elsewhere in this chapter, you will find no difference in the way LIBS works and the way the full InterBase server works; one just has more power than the other.

When you install the true version of the InterBase server, you will find a file called IBKey in the IB5 directory on the CD-ROM. This file contains the certificate information needed to get past the copyright screens you encounter during the installation. To install the InterBase server, you must go to the CD-ROM and explicitly install it. It won't be loaded automatically for you when you install Delphi.

After you install the full InterBase server and client, it probably won't be configured correctly until you enter all the keys to activate it. To do so, choose Start, Programs, InterBase, InterBase License Registration. After the License Registration application loads, enter all the keys you need, as defined in IBKey.txt from the CD-ROM.

Here is an example of what one of the keys looks like:

```
Certificate ID:  XX-XX-DEC-XXXXX
Certificate Key:  XX-X-X-X
```

The simplest way to enter these keys is to cut and paste between the list on the CD and the InterBase License Registration program. After you are finished, you will probably have entered five sets of keys.

Getting everything set up properly is very important. InterBase does not always give you sensible error messages when you don't have the keys installed properly. Instead, you might get an error message that leads you to look in some completely different area to fix the problem. You simply must have the product registered properly before you try to use it; otherwise, the product's behavior is completely undefined.

You can drive yourself mad by having the product partially registered. For example, you might be able to get data from the product, update records, and so on, and think all is fine. Then you try to change some metadata. If the product is not registered to support this feature, your attempts will fail and the error messages you get back might not even hint at the fact that the product is not correctly registered. They might point you off in some other direction altogether. Follow my suggestion: The simplest thing is to fully register the product right from the start and then run simple tests to ensure that it is working.

After you register the product, find out if LIBS or the real InterBase server is running. By default, it will load into memory every time you boot up the system. If you're running Windows 95, Windows 98, or NT 4, you should see the InterBase Guardian as a little splash of green on the system tray to the right of the toolbar. On Windows NT 3.51, an icon appears at the bottom of your screen. Whatever shape it takes on your system, just click this green object, and you will see a report on the Local InterBase Server configuration.

The InterBase Guardian is actually a helper program designed to keep the server running. If, for some reason, your server is blown out of the water, then the Guardian will start it up again automatically. The Guardian will do nothing if you intentionally shut down the server. On NT, both the Guardian and the server are listed in the Services applet in the Control Panel. You can read more about the Guardian in the Operations Guide for InterBase.

You must know where your copy of LIBS is installed. Most likely, it is in the `..\PROGRAM FILES\INTERBASE CORP\INTERBASE` subdirectory on the boot drive of your computer. Alternatively, it could be in the `..\PROGRAM FILES\BORLAND\INTRBASE` subdirectory, which is where this file was put in previous versions of Delphi. For example, my copy of the local InterBase is in `C:\PROGRAM FILES\INTERBASE CORP\INTERBASE`. To find out for sure, right-click the InterBase icon on your taskbar and choose Properties, or if you started InterBase as a service, examine the properties of your InterBase icons on the Windows Start menu.

To find this same information in the Registry, run `REGEDIT.EXE` and open `HKEY_LOCAL_MACHINE/SOFTWARE/INTERBASE CORP/INTERBASE`. Several nodes report on the location of your server and other related information. (On Windows NT 3.51 machines, the program is called `REGEDIT32.EXE`.)

In the `INTERBASE` subdirectory, you will find a copy of a file called `INTERBAS.MSG`. You should also be able to locate a copy of `GDS32.DLL` somewhere on your system, most likely in the `..\WINDOWS\SYSTEM` subdirectory or the `WINNT\SYSTEM32` subdirectory, but possibly in either your `BDE` or `INTRBASE` subdirectory.

A common problem occurs when InterBase users end up with more than one copy of `GDS32.DLL`. If you work with the networked version of InterBase, you probably already have a copy of the InterBase Client on your system. If this is the case, you should make sure that you don't have two sets of the file `GDS32.DLL` on your path. On my system, I use the copy of `GDS32.DLL` that comes with the InterBase server, instead of the one for LIBS. These tools communicate with both LIBS and the full networked version of InterBase. This setup works fine for me. However, the point is not which version you use, but only that you know which version is on your path and that you have only one version on your system at a time.

Borland almost always puts the version number of a product as the time at which the files were modified. InterBase is on version 5 at the time I write. Therefore, your version of `GDS32.DLL` should be made at 5:00 a.m. or later, and should have a date of 12-01-97 or later. Make sure you are not running on older version of `GDS32.DLL` that might have gotten copied over the new version installed by Delphi.

> **NOTE**
>
> InterBase once was a Borland product. The creators of this product have since split off into a wholly owned subsidiary of Borland called the InterBase Corporation. When this split happened, the developers and staff of InterBase began to enjoy a certain degree of autonomy.

To find out which version of InterBase you are currently using, run the InterBase Communications Diagnostics Tool that ships with Delphi.

Use the Browse button to find the `EMPLOYEE.GDB` file, which is probably located in the `..PROGRAM FILES\INTERBASE CORP\INTERBASE\EXAMPLES` subdirectory. Enter `SYSDBA`, all uppercase, as the username, and `masterkey` as the password, all lowercase. (This example assumes that you have not changed the password from its default value.) You should get the following readout, or something like it:

```
Path Name      := C:\WINDOWS\SYSTEM\gds32.dll
    Size           := 321536 Bytes
    File Time      := 05:00:00
    File Date      := 12/01/1997
    Version        := 5.0.0.627
    This module has passed the version check.

    Attempting to attach to c:\program files\
    ➥interbase corp\interbase\examples\employee.gdb
            Attaching    ...Passed!
            Detaching    ...Passed!

    InterBase versions for this connection:
    InterBase/x86/Windows NT (access method), version "WI-V5.0.0.627"
    on disk structure version 9.0

    InterBase Communication Test Passed
```

The key piece of information you're getting here is the location and version number of
GDS32.DLL.

Here is how part of this output would look if you are connecting to the previous version
of the server:

```
InterBase versions for this connection:
InterBase/x86/Windows NT (access method), version "WI-V4.2.1.328"
on disk structure version 8.0
```

This report comes from InterBase version 4.2, not from 5. If possible, you should make
sure that your system is upgraded to version 5. Of course, you might have a later version
of the product on your system. The point here is that you should be able to find a version
number and be able to read it.

> **NOTE**
>
> If you want to connect to the full server version of InterBase, you will find that
> the procedure I have just outlined works fine, except that you must have a net-
> work protocol such as TCP/IP loaded first. This task is usually handled
> automatically by either Windows 95/98 or Windows NT. Setting up an InterBase
> connection is usually a fairly straightforward process when compared to setting
> up other servers.

The most obvious thing that can go wrong with an InterBase connection is simply that it
is not being started automatically when you start Windows. If you are having trouble, try
simply pointing the Explorer to the `InterBase/bin` subdirectory and clicking the

IBServer.exe icon. The trouble could be that all is set up correctly, but for some reason the server is not currently running on your machine.

Setting Up an InterBase Alias

In the preceding section, you learned how to run a diagnostic tool to be sure that you are connected to InterBase. This section deals with the issue of making sure that the BDE is able to connect to InterBase through the native SQL Links driver. In other words, the previous section deals with making sure that InterBase was running correctly on your machine; this section deals with making sure Delphi is connected to InterBase. You should also check the readme file on the CD-ROM that accompanies this book for general information about setting up aliases for the programs.

After you have InterBase set up, take a few minutes to make sure the connection to the BDE is working correctly. In particular, make sure an alias points to one of the sample tables that ships with LIBS. For example, after a normal full installation of Delphi, you should have an alias called IBLOCAL that points to the EMPLOYEE.GDB file.

Next, you'll learn how to set up an alias identical to the IBLOCAL alias, except you can give it a different name. To begin, open the SQL Explorer and turn to the Databases page. (The SQL Explorer once was called the Database Explorer in previous versions of the product.) Select the first node in the tree, the one that's called Databases. Choose Object, New, and then select InterBase as the Database Driver Name in the New Database Alias page dialog box. Click OK.

Name the new alias TESTGDB, or give it whatever name you prefer. The ServerName property for this alias should be set to

```
C:\Program Files\InterBase Corp\InterBase\Examples\employee.gdb
```

You can adjust the drive letter and path to reflect the way you have set up the files on your machine.

> **NOTE**
>
> When you are running against a server on a remote machine, you should reference that server in your server name:
>
> ```
> Spider:/Program File\InterBase Corp\InterBase\Examples\Employee.gdb
> ```

Instead of trying to type this information directly, use the Browse button to search across your hard drive with the File Open dialog box. To get to this dialog box, look for the ellipsis (…) button on the far right of the editor control that lets you type in the server name.

Set the username to SYSDBA, and the default password you will use is masterkey. (If someone has changed the password on your system, use the new password. You can change the default password in the InterBase Server Manager, as described later in this chapter in the section "Security and the InterBase Server Manager.") All the other settings in the Database Explorer can have their default values, as shown in Figure 11.1. After you have everything set up correctly, choose Object, Apply.

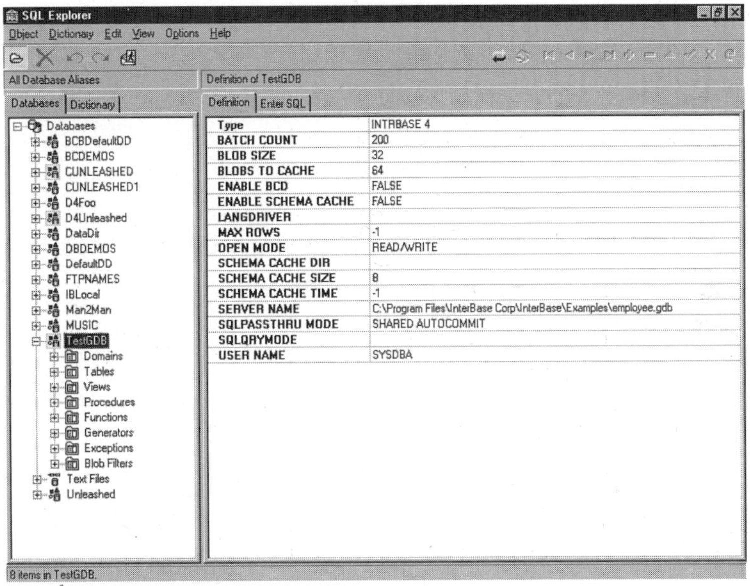

FIGURE 11.1

A sample InterBase alias as it appears in the Database Explorer.

After you have set up and saved your alias, you can connect to the TESTGDB alias exactly as you would with any other set of data. From inside the Explorer, just click the plus symbol before the TESTGDB node. A dialog box will pop up prompting you for a password. Make sure that the username is set to SYSDBA and then enter masterkey as the password. Everything else will then be the same as when you're working with a Paradox table, except that you will find many new features such as stored procedures and triggers. Most of these new features are described in this chapter and the next.

To connect to the database from Delphi, first drop a table onto a form, and set its DatabaseName property to TESTGDB. When you try to drop down the list of TableNames, you will be prompted for a password. Enter masterkey at this point, all in lowercase. Now drop down the list again and select a table. After taking these steps, you can set the

`Active` property for `Table1` to `True`. If this call succeeds, everything is set up correctly, and you can begin using the InterBase to create Delphi database programs. If you can't set `Active` to `True`, go over the steps outlined previously, and see whether you can correct the problem.

> **NOTE**
>
> I usually use `SYSDBA` and `masterkey` as the username and password combination for the InterBase databases in this book. However, I sometimes work with `USER1` and `USER1` instead, simply because typing `USER1` is easier than typing `masterkey`. One way to change the sign-on criteria for InterBase is via the InterBase Server Manager. The Server Manager is discussed later in this chapter in the section "Security and the Server Manager."

In the preceding two sections, you learned the basic facts about using LIBS. The next step is to learn how to create your own databases and tables.

Creating Databases

Unlike local Paradox or dBASE files, InterBase tables are not stored in separate files located within a directory. Instead, InterBase tables are stored in one large file called a database. Therefore, you must first go out and create a database, and then you can create a series of tables inside this larger database.

> **NOTE**
>
> The single-file system is, in my opinion, vastly superior to having a series of separate files. I'm sure you've noticed what happens after you have placed a few indexes on a typical Paradox table. The end result is that your table is associated with six or seven other files, some of which must be present or you can't get at your data. These files have names like `Address.XG0` and `Address.XG1`. A big Paradox database might consist of a hundred or more files, all of which must be backed up, moved from place to place, and maintained. Life is much simpler when your whole database is stored in a single file!

The simplest way to create a database is with a third-party CASE tool such as SDesigner or Cadet. However, these tools do not ship with Delphi, so you must instead choose from the Database Desktop, Delphi itself, or the WISQL program that ships with the Local

InterBase Server. Without a CASE tool, I find that my weapon of choice is WISQL, though this decision is certainly debatable. You can open this program by choosing Start, Programs, InterBase, InterBase Windows ISQL.

Using WISQL

WISQL stands for Windows Interactive Standard Query Language, or simply the Interactive SQL tool. WISQL is fundamentally a tool for entering SQL statements, with a few other simple features thrown in for good measure. One advantage of relying on WISQL is that it enables you to work directly in the mother tongue of databases, which is SQL. I find that defining databases directly in SQL helps me understand their structure, though of course there is little reason for resorting to these measures if you have a copy of SDesigner or ERWin available. (Cadet is a much less expensive tool that might still be available as shareware when you read this chapter.)

Also remember that WISQL bypasses the BDE altogether. You can therefore use it to test your connections to InterBase even if you are not sure whether you have the BDE set up correctly. For example, if you're having trouble connecting to InterBase and you're not sure where the problem lies, start by trying to connect with WISQL. If that works, but you can't connect from inside Delphi, the problem might lie not with your InterBase setup, but with the way you have deployed the BDE.

After you start WISQL, choose File, Create Database. A dialog box like the one shown in Figure 11.2 appears. Set the Location Info to Local Engine because you are, in fact, working with Local InterBase. (Actually, I can't think of any reason why you must use Local InterBase rather than the full server version when you're working through these examples. However, I will reference LIBS throughout this chapter because it is the tool of choice for most readers.)

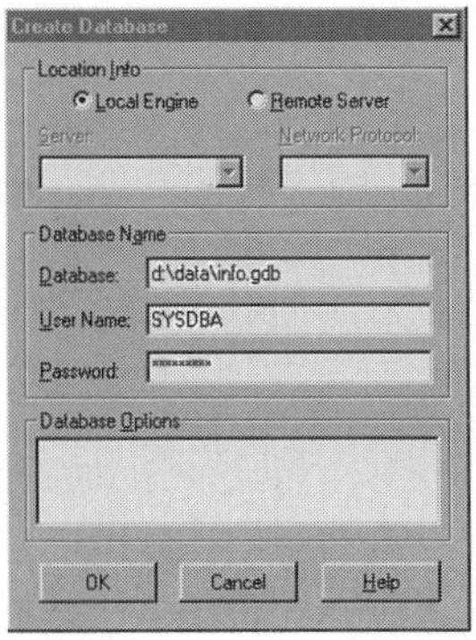

FIGURE 11.2

The dialog box used to create databases inside WISQL.

In the Database field, enter the name of the database you want to create. If it is to be located inside a particular directory, include that directory in the database name. For practice, create a database called INFO.GDB that is located in a subdirectory called DATA. If it does not already exist on your system, first go to DOS or the Windows Explorer and create the DATA subdirectory. After you set up the subdirectory, enter the following in the Database field, where you can replace D with the appropriate drive on your system:

```
D:\DATA\INFO.GDB
```

> **NOTE**
>
> The extension .gdb is traditional, though not mandatory. However, I suggest always using this extension so that you can recognize your databases instantly when you see them. Accidentally deleting even a recently backed up database can be a tragedy.

You can set the username to anything you want, although the traditional entry is SYSDBA and the traditional password is masterkey. When you first start out with InterBase, sticking with this username and password combination is probably best. Even if you assign new passwords to your database, the SYSDBA/masterkey combination will still work unless you explicitly remove it using the InterBase Server Manager (IBMGR.EXE). Of course, when you have sensitive data to protect, you want to be more careful about how you set up your password.

After you enter a username and password, you can create the database by clicking OK. If all goes well, you are then placed back inside WISQL. At this stage, you can either quit WISQL or add a table to your database. If something goes wrong, an error message will appear. Click the Details button to try to track down the problem.

Creating a Table

Assuming all goes well, you can run the following SQL statement inside WISQL if you want to create a very simple table with two fields:

```
CREATE TABLE TEST1 (FIRST VARCHAR(20), LAST INTEGER);
```

Enter this line in the SQL Statement field at the top of WISQL, and then click Run (the Run button has a lightning bolt on it). You can also select Query, Execute from the menu or press Ctrl+Enter to run the query. If all goes smoothly, your statement will be echoed in the ISQL output window without being accompanied by an error dialog box. The lack of an error dialog box signals that the table has been created successfully.

Working with the Local InterBase Server

CHAPTER 11

263

11

WORKING WITH
THE LOCAL
INTERBASE SERVER

The preceding CREATE TABLE command creates a table with two fields. The first is a character field that contains 20 characters, and the second is an integer field. After you create a database and table, choose File, Commit Work. This command causes WISQL to actually carry out the commands you have issued. Then choose File, Disconnect from Database.

The table-creation code shown here is used to describe or create a table in terms that WISQL understands. In fact, you can use this same code inside a TQuery object in a Delphi program. Throughout most of this chapter and the next, I work with WISQL rather than with the DBD. In describing how to perform these actions in WISQL, I do not mean to imply that you can't use the Database Desktop to create or alter InterBase tables. In fact, the 32-bit version of DBD provides pretty good support for InterBase tables. Still, I have found WISQL to be considerably more powerful than I suspected when I first started using it. Once again, I should add that neither of these tools is as easy to use as a good CASE tool.

In this section, you learned the basic steps required to use InterBase to create a database and table. The steps involved are not particularly complicated, although they can take a bit of getting used to if you're new to the world of SQL.

Exploring a Database with WISQL

WISQL provides several tools that can help you explore a database and its contents. In the preceding section, you created a database with a single table. In this section, you will learn how to connect to the database and table from inside WISQL. You also will see how to examine the main features of the entities you have created.

To connect to INFO.GDB, choose File, Connect to Database, which brings up the dialog box shown in Figure 11.3. Enter the drive and the database as e:\data\info.gdb, where e: represents the appropriate drive on your machine. Enter the user as SYSDBA and the password as masterkey. If all goes well, you should be able to connect to the database by clicking OK. Once again, success is signaled by the lack of an error message.

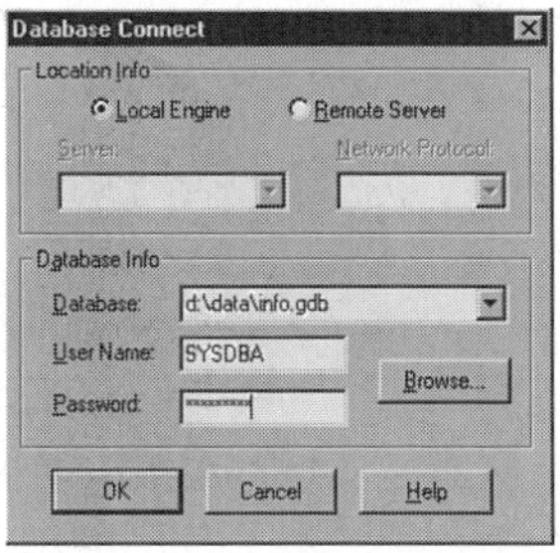

FIGURE 11.3

Connecting to the INFO.GDB database using WISQL.

Choose Metadata, Show, and select Database from the options, as shown in Figure 11.4. After you click OK, the information displayed in the ISQL output window should look something like this:

```
SHOW DB
Database: c:\data\info.gdb
        Owner: SYSDBA
PAGE_SIZE 1024
Number of DB pages allocated := 210
Sweep interval := 20000
```

FIGURE 11.4

Preparing to view information on the INFO.GDB *database.*

To see the tables available in a database, choose Metadata, Show, and select Table from the list of options. You can leave the edit control labeled Object Name blank. If you fill it in with a table name, you will get detailed information on a specific table; in this case, though, you want general information on all tables. Click OK and view the information, which should look like the following in the ISQL output window:

```
SHOW TABLES
      TEST1
```

Browsing through the View Information dialog from the Metadata, Show menu choice, you can see that InterBase supports triggers, stored procedures, views, and a host of other advanced server features.

By choosing Metadata, Extract Database, you can find out more detailed information about the database and its tables. For example, if you choose Extract, SQL Metadata for a Database, you get output similar to the following:

```
/* Extract Database e:\data\info.gdb */
CREATE DATABASE "e:\data\info.gdb" PAGE_SIZE 1024
;
/* Table: TEST1, Owner: SYSDBA */
CREATE TABLE TEST1 (FIRST VARCHAR(20),
        LAST INTEGER);
/* Grant permissions for this database */
```

If you choose Metadata, Extract Table, you get the following output:

```
/* Extract Table TEST1 */
/* Table: TEST1, Owner: SYSDBA */
CREATE TABLE TEST1 (FIRST VARCHAR(20),
        LAST INTEGER);
```

Working with the Local InterBase Server

CHAPTER 11

265

11

WORKING WITH
THE LOCAL
INTERBASE SERVER

Note that WISQL often asks whether you want to save the output from a command to a text file, and the File menu gives you some further options for saving information to files. You can take advantage of these options when necessary, but 90 percent of the time I pass them by with barely a nod. (Some CASE tools use the output from your choosing Metadata, Extract Database to reverse-engineer a database. If your CASE tool asks you for a script file, you can produce one this way.)

> **NOTE**
>
> The WISQL program accepts most SQL statements. For example, you can per-form `Insert`, `Select`, `Update`, and `Delete` statements from inside WISQL. Just enter the statement you want to perform in the SQL Statement area, and then click Run.
>
> Earlier versions of WISQL also came equipped with a handy online reference to SQL. If you had questions about how to format an `Alter`, `Drop`, `Insert`, `Create Index`, or other SQL statement, you could look it up in the help for WISQL. (A book I have found useful for checking SQL syntax is called *The Practical SQL Handbook*, by Bowman, Emerson, and Darnovsky, Addison Wesley, ISBN 0-201-62623-3.)

After reading the previous sections, you should have a fair understanding of how WISQL works and how you can use it to manage a database. The information provided in this chapter is simply an introduction to a complex and very sophisticated topic. However, you now know enough to begin using the Local InterBase. This accomplishment is not insignificant. Tools such as InterBase, Oracle, and Sybase lie at the heart of the client/server activity that is currently so volatile and lucrative. If you become proficient at talking to servers such as InterBase, you might find yourself at an important turning point in your career.

Transactions

Now you can break out of the abstract theory rut and start writing some code that actual-ly does something. In this section, you will look at transactions, followed by a discussion of cached updates and many-to-many relationships. In the next chapter, you will see another "real-world" database when you look at a sample program that tracks the albums, tapes, and CDs in a music collection.

The TRANSACT program, found on the CD-ROM that accompanies this book, gives a brief introduction to transactions. To use transactions, you must have a TDataBase component on your form. Transactions work not only with real servers such as Sybase, Informix, InterBase, or the Local InterBase, but also with the 32-bit BDE drivers for Paradox or dBASE files. In other words, transactions can be part of most of the database work you will do with Delphi. Using transactions is, however, a technique most frequently associated with client/server databases.

Creating the TRANSACT Program

To begin, drop a TDatabase component on a TDataModule. Name the TDataModule DMod, and save it in a file called DMod1, per the usual standards employed in this book. Set the AliasName property of the TDataBase object to a valid alias such as IBLOCAL. Create your own string, such as TransactionDemo, to fill in the DatabaseName property of the TDatabase object. In other words, when you're using a TDatabase component, you make up the DatabaseName rather than pick it from a list of available aliases.

Drop a TQuery object on the data module and hook it up to the EMPLOYEE.GDB file that ships with Delphi. In particular, set the DatabaseName property of the TQuery object to TransactionDemo, not to IBLOCAL. In other words, set the DatabaseName property to the string you made up when filling in the DatabaseName property of the TDatabase component. You will find that TransactionDemo, or whatever string you chose, has been added to the list of aliases you can view from the Query1.DatabaseName Property Editor. Now rename Query1 to EmployeeQuery and attach a TDataSource object called EmployeeSource to it. Set the EmployeeQuery.SQL property to the following string:

```
select * from employee
```

Then set the Active property to True and set RequestLive to True.

Add a TTable object to the project, hook it up to the SALARY_HISTORY table, and call it SalaryHistoryTable. Attach a data source called SalaryHistorySource to it. Relate the SalaryHistoryTable to the EmployQuery table via the EMP_NO fields of both tables. In particular, you should set the MasterSource property for the SalaryHistoryTable to EmployeeSource. Then click the MasterFields property of the TTable object, and relate the EMP_NO fields of both tables. This way, you can establish a one-to-many relationship between the EmployeeQuery and the SalaryHistoryTable.

After you're connected to the database, you can add two grids to your main form so that you can view the data. Hook up one grid to one table via a TDataSource component and the second grid to the second table via a TDataSource component. Remember that you should choose File, Use Unit to link the TDataModule to the main form.

On the surface of the main form, add four buttons and give them the following captions:

```
Begin Transaction
Rollback
Commit
Refresh
```

The code associated with these buttons should look like this:

```pascal
procedure TForm1.BeginTransactionClick(Sender: TObject);
begin
   DMod.TransDemo.StartTransaction;
end;

procedure TForm1.RollbackClick(Sender: TObject);
begin
  DMod.TransDemo.Rollback;
  RefreshClick(nil);
end;

procedure TForm1.CommitClick(Sender: TObject);
begin
  DMod.TransDemo.Commit;
end;

{ Because of the indexing, we can't call Refresh explicitly }
procedure TForm1.RefreshClick(Sender: TObject);
var
  Bookmark: TBookmark;
begin
  Bookmark := DMod.EmployeeQuery.GetBookmark;
  DMod.EmployeeQuery.Close;
  DMod.EmployeeQuery.Open;
  DMod.EmployeeQuery.GotoBookmark(Bookmark);
  DMod.EmployeeQuery.FreeBookmark(Bookmark);
end;
```

Using the TRANSACT Program

At this point, run the program, click Start Transaction, and edit a record of the
SalaryHistoryTable. When you do so, be sure to fill in all the fields of the table except
for the first and last, which are called EMP_NO and NEW_SALARY. Be sure not to touch
either of those fields because they will be filled in for you automatically. In particular,
you might enter the following values:

```
CHANGE_DATE: 12/12/12
UPDATER_ID: admin2
OLD_SALARY: 105900
PERCENT_CHANGE:
```

These values are not randomly chosen. For example, you must enter admin2, or some other valid UPDATER_ID, in the UPDATER_ID field. You can, of course, enter whatever values you want for the date, old salary, and percent change fields. Still, you must be careful when working with the Employee tables. This database has referential integrity with a vengeance.

After entering the preceding values, you can post the record by moving off it. When you do, the NEW_SALARY field will be filled in automatically by something called a *trigger*. Go ahead and experiment with these tables if you want. For example, you might leave some of the fields blank or enter invalid data in the UPDATER_ID field, just to see how complex the rules that govern this database are. This data is locked up tighter than Fort Knox, and you can't change it unless you are very careful about what you're doing. (It's worth noting, however, that the developers of this database probably never planned to have anyone use these two tables exactly as I do here. Defining rules that limit how you work with a database is easy, but finding ways to break them is easier still. For all of its rigor, database programming is still not an exact science.)

If you started your session by clicking the Start Transaction button, you can now click RollBack and then Refresh. You will find that all your work is undone, as if none of the editing occurred. If you edit three or four records and then click Commit, you will find that your work is preserved.

> **NOTE**
>
> Although you are safe in this particular case, in some instances like this you can't call Refresh directly because the table you're using is not uniquely indexed. In lieu of this call, you can close the table and then reopen it. You could use bookmarks to preserve your location in the table during this operation, or if you're working with a relatively small dataset you can just let the user fend for himself or herself.

Note that when you run the TRANSACT program included on the CD-ROM, you don't have to specify a password because the LoginPrompt property of the TDatabase object is set to False, and the Params property contains the following string:

```
password:=masterkey
```

Understanding Transactions

Now that you have seen transactions in action, you probably want a brief explanation of what they are all about. Here are some reasons to use transactions:

- *To ensure the integrity of your data.* Sometimes you must perform a transaction that affects several different interrelated tables. In these cases, altering two tables and then finding the session is interrupted for some reason before you can alter the next two tables might not be a good idea. For example, you might find that a data entry clerk posts data to two records, but the system crashes before he can finish updating two more records in a different table. As a result, the data in your database might be out of sync. To avoid this situation, you can start a transaction, edit all the rows and tables that must be edited, and then commit the work in one swift movement. This way, an error is far less likely to occur because of a system crash or power failure.

- *To handle concurrency issues in which two or more people are accessing the same data at the same time.* You can use a transactions feature called `TransIsolation` levels to fine-tune exactly how and when updates are made. This way, you can decide how you will react if another user is updating records exactly on or near the record you're currently editing.

Now that you have read something about the theory behind transactions, you might want to think for a moment about the `TransIsolation` property of the `TDatabase` object, which affects the way transactions are handled. Here are some quotes from the very important online help entry called "Transaction Isolation Levels":

- `tiDirtyRead`—Permits reading of uncommitted changes made to the database by other simultaneous transactions. Uncommitted changes are not permanent and can be rolled back (undone) at any time. At this level a transaction is least isolated from the effects of other transactions.

- `tiReadCommitted`—Permits reading of committed (permanent) changes made to the database by other simultaneous transactions. This is the default `TransIsolation` property value.

- `tiRepeatableRead`—Permits a single, one-time reading of the database. The transaction can't see any subsequent changes made by other simultaneous transactions. This isolation level guarantees that after a transaction reads a record, its view of that record does not change unless it makes a modification to the record itself. At this level, a transaction is most isolated from other transactions.

Usually, you can simply leave this field set to `tiReadCommitted`. However, you need to understand that you have several options regarding how the data in your database is affected by a transaction. The whole subject of how one user of a database might alter records in a table while they are being used by another user is quite complicated, and it poses several paradoxes for which no simple solution exists. The preceding `TransIsolation` levels enable you to choose your poison when dealing with this nasty subject.

You must consider other issues when you're working with transactions, but I have tried to cover some of the most important here. In general, I find that transactions are extremely easy to use. However, they become more complex when you consider the delicate subject of concurrency problems, which are frequently addressed through setting the TransIsolation levels of your transactions.

Cached Updates

Cached updates are like the transactions just described, except that they enable you to edit a series of records without causing any network traffic. When you are ready to commit your work, cached updates enable you to do so on a record-by-record basis, where any records that violate system integrity can be repaired or rolled back on a case-by-case basis.

> **NOTE**
>
> Some users have reported remarkable increases in performance on some operations when they use cached updates.

The key feature of cached updates is that they let you work with data without allowing any network traffic to occur until you are ready for it to begin. A relatively complex mechanism also enables you to keep track of the status of each record on a field-by-field basis. In particular, when cached updates are turned on, you can query your records one at a time and ask them whether they have been updated. Furthermore, if they have been updated, you can ask the current value of each field in the updated record, and you can also retrieve the old, or original, value of the field.

You can do three things with the records in a dataset after the CachedUpdates property for the dataset has been set to True:

- You can call ApplyUpdates on the dataset, which means that you will try to commit all the other records updated since CachedUpdates was set to True or since the last attempt to update the records. This is analogous to committing a transaction.

- You can call CancelUpdates, which means that all the updates made so far will be canceled. This is analogous to rolling back a transaction.

- You can call RevertRecord, which will roll back the current record but no other records in the dataset.

An excellent sample program in the `Delphi4\Examples\CachedUP` subdirectory shows how to use cached updates. This program is a bit complex in its particulars, however, and can therefore be hard to understand. So, instead of trying to go it one better, I will create a sample program that takes the basic elements of cached updates and presents them in the simplest possible terms.

The `CachedUpdates` program, shown in Figure 11.5, has one form. On the form is a copy of the Orders table. Recall that the Orders table is related to both the Customer table and the Items table. As a result, changing either the `OrderNo` or `CustNo` fields without violating system integrity in one way or another is difficult. When working with this program, you should change these fields to values like 1 or 2, which will almost surely be invalid. You can then watch what happens when you try to commit the records you have changed.

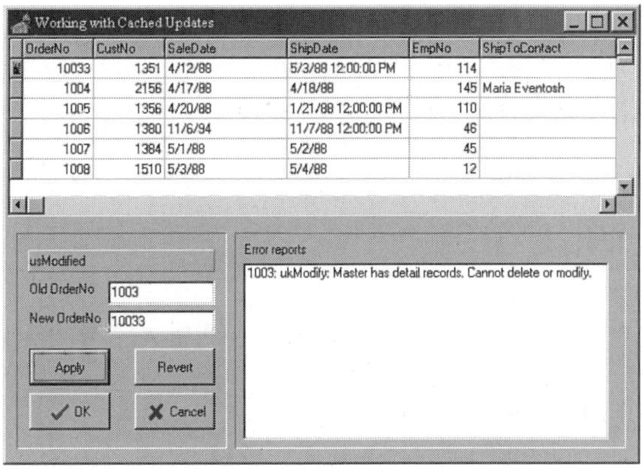

FIGURE 11.5

The `CachedUpdates` *program.*

The code for the `CachedUpdates` program is shown in Listing 11.1. Go ahead and get this program up and running, and then come back for a discussion of how it works. When you're implementing the code shown here, the key point to remember is that none of it will work unless the `CachedUpdates` property of the `OrdersTable` is set to `True`.

LISTING 11.1 THE FORM FOR THE `CachedUpdates` PROGRAM

```
/////////////////////////////////////
//    File: Main.pas
// Project: CacheUp
// Copyright (c) 1998 by Charlie Calvert
//
unit main;
```

continues

LISTING 11.1 CONTINUED

```
{ Copyright 1996 by Charlie Calvert

  Working with cached updates.

  The simplest way to see the program in action is
  to change the OrderNo of several records to small
  integer values such as 1, 2, or 3. Then press
  apply to see the errors this generates. The errors
  occur because these small integer values violate
  database integrity. To revert back to the old
  values press cancel. To change one value back at
  a time, first select the value, then press Revert. }

interface

uses
  Windows, Messages, SysUtils,
  Classes, Graphics, Controls,
  Forms, Dialogs, DB,
  Grids, DBGrids, DBTables,
  StdCtrls, Buttons, TypInfo,
  ExtCtrls;

type
  TForm1 = class(TForm)
    Table1: TTable;
    DBGrid1: TDBGrid;
    DataSource1: TDataSource;
    bApply: TBitBtn;
    bRevert: TBitBtn;
    BitBtn1: TBitBtn;
    Panel1: TPanel;
    Edit1: TEdit;
    Edit2: TEdit;
    Label1: TLabel;
    Label2: TLabel;
    ListBox1: TListBox;
    BitBtn2: TBitBtn;
    Label3: TLabel;
    Bevel1: TBevel;
    Bevel2: TBevel;
    procedure bApplyClick(Sender: TObject);
    procedure bRevertClick(Sender: TObject);
    procedure Table1UpdateError(DataSet: TDataSet; E: EDatabaseError;
      UpdateKind: TUpdateKind; var UpdateAction: TUpdateAction);
    procedure BitBtn1Click(Sender: TObject);
    procedure DataSource1DataChange(Sender: TObject; Field: TField);
    procedure BitBtn2Click(Sender: TObject);
  end;
```

Working with the Local InterBase Server

CHAPTER 11

273

11

WORKING WITH
THE LOCAL
INTERBASE SERVER

```
var
  Form1: TForm1;

implementation

{$R *.DFM}

procedure TForm1.bApplyClick(Sender: TObject);
begin
  Table1.ApplyUpdates;
end;

procedure TForm1.bRevertClick(Sender: TObject);
begin
  Table1.RevertRecord;
end;

procedure TForm1.Table1UpdateError(DataSet: TDataSet; E: EDatabaseError;
  UpdateKind: TUpdateKind; var UpdateAction: TUpdateAction);
var
  S1, S2: string;
begin
  S1 := GetEnumName(TypeInfo(TUpdateKind), Ord(UpdateKind)) + ': ' +
      ➥E.Message;
  S2 := DataSet.Fields[0].OldValue;
  S2 := S2  + ': ' + S1;
  ListBox1.Items.Add(S2);
  UpdateAction := uaSkip;
end;

procedure TForm1.BitBtn1Click(Sender: TObject);
begin
  Table1.CancelUpdates;
end;

procedure TForm1.DataSource1DataChange(Sender: TObject; Field: TField);
begin
  Panel1.Caption := GetEnumName(TypeInfo(TUpdateStatus),
                    ➥Ord(Table1.UpdateStatus));
  if Table1.UpDateStatus = usModified then begin
    Edit1.Text := Table1.Fields[0].OldValue;
    Edit2.Text := Table1.Fields[0].NewValue;
  end else begin
    Edit1.Text := 'Unmodified';
    Edit2.Text := 'Unmodified';
  end;
end;
```

continues

LISTING 11.1   CONTINUED

```
procedure TForm1.BitBtn2Click(Sender: TObject);
begin
  Close;
end;

end.
```

The first thing to notice about the CachedUpdates program is that it tracks which records have been modified. For example, change the OrderNo field of the first two records to the values 1 and 2. If you now select one of these records, you will see that the small panel in the lower-left corner of the screen gets set to Modified. This means that the update status for this field has been set to modified.

Here is the TUpdateStatus type:

```
TUpdateStatus = (usUnmodified, usModified, usInserted, usDeleted);
```

Any particular record in a database is going to be set to one of these values.

Here is the code that sets the value in the TPanel object:

```
procedure TForm1.DataSource1DataChange(Sender: TObject; Field: TField);
begin
  Panel1.Caption := GetEnumName(TypeInfo(TUpdateStatus),
                     ➥Ord(Table1.UpdateStatus));
  if Table1.UpDateStatus = usModified then begin
    Edit1.Text := Table1.Fields[0].OldValue;
    Edit2.Text := Table1.Fields[0].NewValue;
  end else begin
    Edit1.Text := 'Unmodified';
    Edit2.Text := 'Unmodified';
  end;
end;
```

The relevant line in this case is the second in the body of the function. In particular, notice that it reports on the value of OrdersTable.UpdateStatus. This value will change to reflect the update status of the currently selected record.

At the same time the CachedUpdates program reports that a record has been modified, it also reports on the old and new value of the OrderNo field for that record. In particular, if you change the first record's OrderNo field to 1, it will report that the old value for the field was 1003 and the new value is 1. (This assumes that you have the original data as it shipped with Delphi. Remember that if you end up ruining one of these tables performing these kinds of experiments, you can always copy the table over again from the CD. If you copy them directly using the Windows Explorer, remember that they will probably have the Read Only flag turned on. You can use the Windows Explorer to remove these flags.)

Working with the Local InterBase Server

CHAPTER 11

275

11

WORKING WITH
THE LOCAL
INTERBASE SERVER

The following code reports on the old and new value of the OrderNo field:

```
Edit1.Text := Table1.Fields[0].OldValue;
Edit2.Text := Table1.Fields[0].NewValue;
```

As you can see, this information is easy enough to come by; you just have to know where to look.

If you enter the values 1 and 2 into the OrderNo fields for the first two records, you will encounter errors when you try to commit the data. In particular, if you try to apply the data, the built-in referential integrity will complain that you cannot link the Orders and Items table on the new OrderNo you have created. As a result, committing the records is not possible. The code then rolls back the erroneous records to their original state.

When you are viewing these kinds of errors, choose Tools, Environment Options, Debugger and then turn off Integrated Debugging. Or, if you want, you can keep debugging on but let the User Program handle Delphi exceptions and Object Pascal exceptions. You can tell Delphi to let the User Program handle the exception by selecting Tools, Environment Options, Debugger and looking for the User Program option in the Exceptions section of the dialog box toward the bottom of the page. You first select either OBJECT PASCAL Exceptions or Delphi Exceptions in the list box and then select the User Program radio button. The issue here is that you want the exception to occur, but you don't want to be taken to the line in your program where the exception surfaced. You don't need to view the actual source code because these exceptions are not the result of errors in your code. In fact, these exceptions are of the kind you want and must produce and which appear to the user in an orderly fashion via the program's list box.

> **NOTE**
>
> Referential integrity is a means of enforcing the rules in a database. Some tables must obey rules, and the BDE won't let users enter invalid data that violates these rules.

Here is the code that reports on the errors in the OrderNo field and rolls back the data to its original state:

```
procedure TForm1.Table1UpdateError(DataSet: TDataSet; E: EDatabaseError;
  UpdateKind: TUpdateKind; var UpdateAction: TUpdateAction);
var
  S1, S2: string;
begin
  S1 := GetEnumName(TypeInfo(TUpdateKind), Ord(UpdateKind)) +
➥': ' +  E.Message;
  S2 := DataSet.Fields[0].OldValue;
```

```
    S2 := S2  + ': ' + S1;
    ListBox1.Items.Add(S2);
    UpdateAction := uaSkip;
end;
```

This particular routine is an event handler for the OnUpdateError event for the Table1 object. To create the routine, click once on the Table1 object, select its Events page in the Object Inspector, and then double-click the OnUpdateError entry.

The OrdersTableUpdateError method will be called only if an error occurs in attempting to update records. It will be called at the time the error is detected and before Delphi tries to commit the next record.

OrdersTableUpdateError gets passed four parameters. The most important is the last, which is a var parameter. You can set this parameter to one of the following values:

```
TUpdateAction = (uaFail, uaAbort, uaSkip, uaRetry, uaApplied);
```

If you set the UpdateAction variable to uaAbort, the entire attempt to commit the updated data will be aborted. None of your changes will take place, and you will return to edit mode as if you had never attempted to commit the data. The changes you have made so far will not be undone, but neither will they be committed. You are aborting the attempt to commit the data, but you are not rolling it back to its previous state.

If you choose uaSkip, the data for the whole table will still be committed, but the record that is currently in error will be left alone. That is, it will be left at the invalid value assigned to it by the user.

If you set UpdateAction to uaRetry, that means you have attempted to update the information in the current record and that you want to retry committing it. The record you should update is the current record in the dataset passed as the first parameter to OrdersTableUpdateError.

In the OrdersTableUpdateError method, I always choose uaSkip as the value to assign to UpdateAction. Of course, you could pop up a dialog box and show the user the old value and the new value of the current record. The user would then have a chance to retry committing the data. Once again, you retrieve the data containing the current "problem child" record from the dataset passed in the first parameter of OrdersTableUpdateError. I show an example of accessing this data when I retrieve the old value of the OrderNo field for the record:

```
S2 := DataSet.Fields[0].OldValue;
S2 := S2  + ': ' + S1;
ListBox1.Items.Add(S2);
```

The OldValue field is declared as a Variant in the source code to DB.PAS, which is the place where the TDataSet declaration is located:

Working with the Local InterBase Server

CHAPTER 11

277

11

WORKING WITH
THE LOCAL
INTERBASE SERVER

```
function GetOldValue: Variant;
property OldValue: Variant read GetOldValue;
```

Two other values are passed to the TableUpdateError method. The first is an exception reporting on the current error, and the second is a variable of type TUpdateKind:

```
TUpdateKind = (ukModify, ukInsert, ukDelete);
```

The variable of type TUpdateKind just tells you how the current record was changed. Was it updated, inserted, or deleted? The exception information is passed to you primarily so that you can get at the message associated with the current error:

```
E.Message;
```

If you handle the function by setting UpdateAction to a particular value, say uaSkip, then Delphi will not pop up a dialog box reporting the error to the user. Instead, it assumes that you are handling the error explicitly, and it leaves it up to you to report the error or not as you see fit. In this case, I just dump the error into the program's list box, along with some other information.

At this point, you should go back and run the Cache program that ships with Delphi. It covers all the same ground covered in the preceding few pages, but it does so in a slightly different form. In particular, it shows how to pop up a dialog box so that you can handle each OnUpdateError event in an intelligent and sensible manner.

In general, cached updates give you a great deal of power you can tap into when updating the data in a dataset. If necessary, go back and play with the CachedUpdates program until it starts to make sense to you. This subject isn't prohibitively difficult, but absorbing the basic principles involved takes some thought.

Many-to-Many Relationships

To save space in this book, this section has been placed on the CD. You will find this section and the accompanying code on the CD that accompanies this book in the Chap11 directory.

Security and the InterBase Server Manager

Before beginning the discussion of the Music program, covering a few basic issues regarding security might be a good idea. I included enough information so far to make any Delphi programmer dangerous, so I might as well also equip you with some of the tools you need to defend your work against prying eyes. If you have the skill to create programs that others can use, then you must know how to manage those clients.

When you are working with passwords, making a distinction between user security for an entire server and access rights for a particular table is important. If you open the InterBase Server Manager, log on, and select Tasks, User Security, you will find menu options that let you create new users for the system. By default, these users have access to very little. All you do is let them in the front door. You haven't yet given them a pass to visit any particular rooms in the house. As this discussion matures, I'll discuss how to grant particular rights to a user after he or she has been admitted into the "building."

If you are interested in setting up real security for your database, the first thing you should do is change the SYSDBA password. To change the password, sign on to the InterBase Server Manager as SYSDBA using the password masterkey. Select Tasks and then User Security from the menu. Select the username SYSDBA, and choose Modify User. Now enter a new password. After you do this much, the system is truly under your control. No one else can get at your data unless you decide that user should have the right to do so. Even then, you can severely proscribe that user's activities with a remarkable degree of detail. (If you are a control freak, this is paradise!)

After you establish your sovereignty, the next step is to go out and recruit the peons who will inhabit your domain. After you find a new user, select Tasks, User Security and choose Add User. Then give him or her a password. The person who creates users is the one who signs on as SYSDBA. SYSDBA has all power, which is the reason that changing the SYSDBA password is important if you are really serious about security.

If you create a new user, this newcomer has no rights on the system by default. To give a user rights, you must use the SQL grant command, which is discussed in the next section.

Defining Access Rights to a Table

After you create a user in the InterBase Server Manager, you grant him or her rights to access a table. To do so, open WISQL or the SQL Explorer and connect to the database you want to work with. To grant rights, you can enter SQL statements into SQL and then execute them by pressing Ctrl+Enter. The actual statements you can use are discussed over the course of the next few paragraphs.

SQL databases give you extraordinary control over exactly how much access a user can have to a table. For example, you can give a user only the right to query one or more tables in your database:

```
grant select on Test1 to user1
```

Conversely, you may, if you want, give a user complete control over a table, including the right to grant other people access to the table:

```
grant all on album to Sue with grant option
```

Working with the Local InterBase Server

CHAPTER 11

279

11

WORKING WITH
THE LOCAL
INTERBASE SERVER

The `with grant option` clause shown here specifies that Sue not only has her way with the Album table, but also can give access to the table to others.

You can give a user six distinct types of privileges:

- `all`—Has select, delete, insert, update, and execute privileges
- `select`—Can view a table or portion of a table
- `delete`—Can delete from a table or view
- `insert`—Can add data to a table or view
- `update`—Can edit a table or view
- `execute`—Can execute a stored procedure

Using these keys to the kingdom, you can quickly start handing out passes to particular rooms in the palace. For example, you can write

```
grant insert on Test1 to Sue
grant delete on Test1 to Mary with grant option
grant select on Test1 to Tom, Mary, Sue, User1
grant select, insert, delete, update on Test1 to Mary
grant delete, insert, update, references on country to public
➥with grant option;
```

The last statement in this list comes from the `Employee.gdb` example that ships with Delphi. Notice that it grants rights to the public, which means all users have absurdly liberal rights on the table.

The opposite of the `grant` command is `revoke`. `Revoke` removes privileges given with `grant`. Here is an example of using `revoke`:

```
revoke select on Test1 from Sue
```

This brief overview of the Server Manager and some related issues involving the `grant` command should give you a sense of how to limit access to your database. None of this material is particularly difficult, but SQL databases can be frustrating if you don't know how to control them.

Backing Up Tables with the Server Manager

Another important feature of the InterBase Server Manager is backing up tables. This task can be especially important if you must move a table from Windows 95/98 or Windows NT to UNIX. The highly compressed backup format for InterBase tables is completely version independent, so you can back up an NT table and then restore it on a UNIX system.

To get started backing up a database, sign on to the InterBase Server Manager. To sign on, all you must do is specify the `masterkey` password; everything else is automatic when signing on to the local version of InterBase. Of course, if you changed the SYSDBA password from masterkey to something else, then you must use the new password you created.

Go to the Tasks menu and select Backup. Enter the path to the local database you want to back up. For example, you might type c:\data\info.gdb in the edit control labeled Database Path. This means you want to back up the database called info.gdb.

Enter the name of the backup table you want to create in the Backup File or Device field. For example, you might type c:\data\info.gbk. Use the GDB extension for live tables and GBK for backed-up tables. These are just conventions, but they are good ones.

Select Transportable Format from the Options group box, and set any other flags you want to use. Click OK and then be prepared for a short delay while InterBase contemplates certain knotty passages from the works of the philosopher Immanuel Kant. If all goes well, the results of your work might look something like this:

```
Backup started on Tue Dec 24 15:26:42 1996...
gbak: gbak version WI-V4.1.0.194
gbak:     Version(s) for database "e:\data\info.gdb"
    InterBase/x86/Windows NT (access method), version "WI-V4.2.1.328"
    on disk structure version 8.0
Request completed on Tue Dec 24 15:26:45 1996
```

You can now close the InterBase Server Manager and copy your backed-up file to a floppy disk, zip drive, or other storage medium. Remember, the great thing about these files is that they are small, highly compressed, and can be moved from one operating system to another.

> **NOTE**
>
> InterBase runs on a wide variety of UNIX platforms.

Summary

This chapter gave you a basic introduction to the Local InterBase and to several related subjects. In particular, you learned how to create and open InterBase databases, how to set up aliases, and how to perform fundamental database tasks such as transactions.

I should stress that InterBase is a very complex and powerful product, and what you read in this chapter should serve as little more than a brief introduction that will whet your appetite. In the next chapter, you will look at stored procedures, triggers, InterBase calls, and a few other tricks that should help you grasp the extent of the power in both the local and server-based versions of InterBase.

Delphi protects you from the details of how a server handles basic database chores. However, Delphi also enables you to tap into the power associated with a particular server. This was one of the most delicate balances that the developers had to consider when they created Delphi: How can you make a database tool as generic as possible, without cutting off a programmer's access to the special capabilities of a particular server? The same type of question drove the developers' successful quest to make Delphi's language as simple and elegant as possible without cutting off access to the full power of the Windows API.

Now you can forage on to the next chapter. By this time, we are deep into the subject of databases. In fact, the stage is now set to open a view onto the most powerful tools in a database programmer's arsenal. After you master the stored procedures, generators, and triggers shown in the next chapter, you will be entering into the world of real client/ server programming as it is done on the professional level. These tools drive the big databases used by corporations, governments, and educational institutions around the world.

CHAPTER 12

InterBase Programming

In this chapter, you get a look at a fairly entertaining relational database and accompanying program called Music that tracks a CD and record collection. The program shows a good deal about working with relational databases in general and about working with InterBase in particular. The text and code are designed to advance your knowledge of SQL, database design, and client/server programming.

Important subjects covered in this chapter include

- Relational database design.
- Referential integrity.
- Stored procedures and the TStoredProc components.
- Triggers.
- Generators.
- Domains.
- Using SQL to extract facts from a database. How many of this type of item do I have? How can I write a stored procedure that retrieves information from several tables at once while still answering a real-world question about the amount of a particular kind of data?
- Placing forms on a TabControl. The kdAdd program had a huge number of fields in the main form for the application. In this chapter, you will see how to create separate forms for each page in a tabbed notebook. Each page exists inside its own discrete object, which helps you create well-organized, robust applications.
- Storing multiple types of data in a database and displaying it in a flexible manner. This database contains a table with information on books and another table with information on records. The TabControl technique described in the preceding bullet point allows you to seamlessly integrate different types of data in what appears to the user as one form. From the user's point of view, it appears that the program morphs to accommodate the type of data currently being displayed.
- Using SQL to alter a table.

The burden of the argument for this chapter is again carried by a sample database application. This one is designed to track household items such as books, CDs, or records. However, you can easily expand it to hold many different types of data. The core strength of this program is its flexible, extensible design.

By the time you finish this chapter, you should have a pretty good feel for how to tap into the power of InterBase. This chapter is not meant to appeal only to InterBase developers, however. It also contains many general comments about working with relational databases in general and SQL databases in particular. In other words, this chapter is about real client/server database programming.

Admittedly, database programming is not a particularly sexy subject. But it does have its joys, and I hope that some of them will become apparent while you are reading this chapter. The Music program digs far enough down into the guts of database design to let you have a little bit of fun. It's actually fairly interesting to see just how far you can go with a few tables and a couple of lines of SQL. By the time you are done, you should get the sense that you can ask this database just about anything about your record collection, and it will come back with all kinds of interesting bits of information.

About the Music Program

One of the interesting features of the Music database is the way it uses stored procedures to report on the information in the database. For instance, it lets you store CDs, tapes, and records and rate them according to four different, extensible criteria:

- What type of music is it? Classical? Jazz? Rock? Do you have categories of your own you want to add?
- How loud is the music? Is it peaceful, moderate, or raucous? You can add other categories if you want.
- How good is the music? On a scale of 1 to 10, how do you rate it?
- Finally, what medium is it on? CD? Tape? Record? DVD?

You can easily expand most of these lists to create as many categories as you want. Furthermore, you can query the database to ask questions such as

- How many records do I have?
- How many different artists are listed here?
- How many albums do I have that I rated in a certain range? For instance, which records did I rate as a complete 10? Which ones did I rate as only a 1 or 2?
- Which albums did I rate as loud?
- What albums are listed under the categories called Jazz or Folk?

The Music program uses several advanced database features of Borland Delphi. For instance, you will find examples of data modules, lookups, filters, and searching a database with `FindFirst` and `FindNearest`. This program uses many other standard database techniques, such as calculated fields and working with ranges. You will also find numerous examples of how to use stored procedures and also an example of how to search on records in the detail table of a master-detail relationship.

A complete copy of the Music database is available on the CD that accompanies this book. Throughout the first half of this chapter, I talk about the incremental steps involved in creating this database, but if you feel the need to see the complete database at any time, you can retrieve it from the CD in the file called `Music.ddl` in the `Data` directory.

To set up the alias for the database, choose Database, Explore to bring up the SQL Explorer, which is called the Database Explorer in some versions of Delphi. From the menu in the SQL Explorer, choose Object, New. Select INTRBASE as the type of alias you want to create. Set the User Name property to SYSDBA and the Server Name property so that it points to the place on your hard drive where you have installed the `MUSIC.GDB` file that comes on the CD that accompanies this book. Choose Object, Apply to save your work. Figure 12.1 shows how the alias should look when you are done.

FIGURE 12.1

The alias for MUSIC.GDB *as it appears in the Database Explorer.*

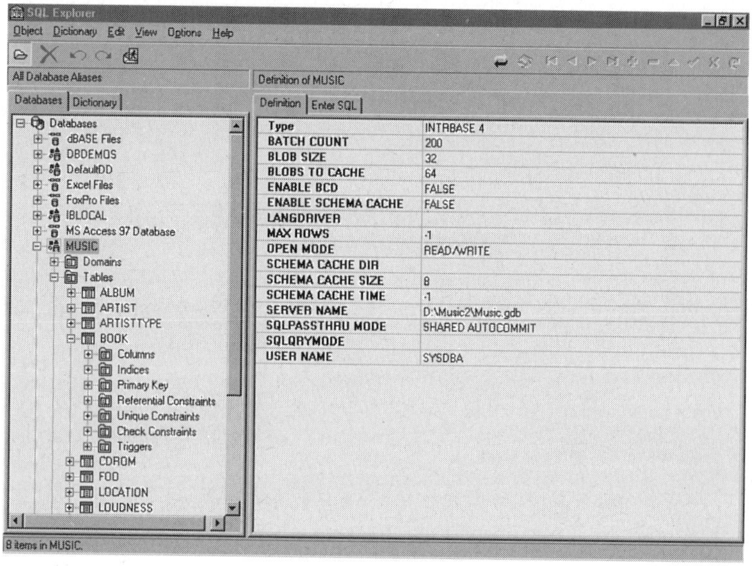

Music is a fairly complex program, but it gives you lots of hints on how to use a SQL database to your advantage. If you are having trouble with it, check my Web sites for tips or hints on using the program (`http://www.borland.com/techvoyage` or `http://users.aol.com/charliecal`).

Overall, this chapter aims at taking the discussion of databases to a new level. After you read the text, you will be prepared to write professional-level client/server applications. All the information in this chapter applies to common professional database tasks such as creating an inventory system or even a point of sales application.

Designing the Music Program

It's now time to begin work on the Music program. This program enables you to keep track of CDs, records, tapes, and books. The main goal of the program is to enable you to enter the name of an artist (a musician or a writer) and add one or more titles associated with that artist.

> **NOTE**
>
> The main table of the Music program is called Artist for historical reasons. The database was originally intended to hold only CDs, records, and tapes. I expanded the program's scope later when I suddenly saw the way clear to add the Books table to the project.

The Music program uses eight tables, but three of them, called `Artist`, `Book`, and `Album`, dominate the application. The `Artist` table is the master table, and the `Book` and `Album` tables are detail tables.

Besides the three main tables, several lookup tables are used to store the various lists of possible categories to which the albums and books can belong. Lookups are described in Chapter 8, "Fields and Database Tools," and Chapter 9, "Flat-File Real-World Databases." In this case, a lookup can allow you to convert a simple integer value into a string, by "looking up" the string associated with an integer. For instance, a record can be of type Jazz, Rock, Folk, Blues, and so on, and a book can be of type Fiction, Computer, Mystery, Science Fiction, Reference, and so on. These words are stored in lookup tables, while only a simple integer value is stored in the main table. This feature saves room in your database by allowing you to store a simple integer such as 1 or 2 in your main table and the string associated with that integer in a lookup table. Therefore, you store the string value only in one row rather than having to store it over and over again in multiple rows. You can store information used by both the `Album` and `Book` tables in one lookup table. You can then use a filter and the range of the table's primary key to distinguish between the different groups of information. You will read more about this technique later in the chapter.

Even with this relatively simple structure, however, you still have enough tables to provide some food for thought. In particular, how are these tables related, and how can you put constraints on them so that it's difficult for the user to accidentally break a dependency? For instance, if six albums are associated with an artist, a user should not be able to delete the artist without first deleting or reassigning the albums. How about generating the IDs for each artist and each album? This is not Paradox, so you won't find an autoincrement field. This means that you must create generators and employ some means of accessing the generators.

Clearly, there are enough questions to keep someone busy for an hour or two. The next few pages of this chapter provide answers for most of the questions I've been asking. In particular, you'll find that to resolve many of these issues, you need to generate a specific database schema.

Creating the Database Schema

To get started with your database schema, it's probably best to start your work at the top with the Artist table:

```
/* Table: ARTIST, Owner: SYSDBA */
CREATE TABLE ARTIST (CODE CODE_DOM NOT NULL,
        LAST VARCHAR(30),
        FIRST VARCHAR(30),
        BORN DATE,
        DIED DATE,
        BIRTHPLACE VARCHAR(35),
        COMMENT BLOB SUB_TYPE TEXT SEGMENT SIZE 80,
        ARTISTTYPE INTEGER NOT NULL,
        PRIMARY KEY (CODE));
```

The definition for this table assumes the presence of a domain called CODE_DOM. You can create a domain in WISQL with the following code:

```
CREATE DOMAIN CODE_DOM AS INTEGER;
```

This code states that CODE_DOM is a domain of type Integer.

A *domain* is an alias for a type that is used more than once in the program. For instance, the Code field used in the Album table is referenced in the Album table in the GroupCode field:

```
CREATE TABLE ALBUM (CODE CODE_DOM NOT NULL,
        ALBUM VARCHAR(25) NOT NULL,
        TYPES SMALLINT,
        LOUDNESS SMALLINT,
        MEDIUM SMALLINT,
        RATING SMALLINT,
        GROUPCODE CODE_DOM NOT NULL,
        PRIMARY KEY (CODE));
```

The GroupCode field in the Album table is a foreign key. It references the group, or artist, associated with this particular album. For instance, if Bob Dylan's code is 57, and the name of the current album is *Blonde on Blonde*, the GroupCode field for the current record in the Album table is set to 57. This number ties the album *Blonde on Blonde* to the artist Bob Dylan.

Creating a domain called CODE_DOM allows you to easily assign the same type to the Code field in the Artist table and the GroupCode field in the Album table. It's not earth shattering in importance, but it can be helpful.

Altering Tables: To Null or Not to Null

Notice that the Code field is declared as Not Null. This means that the user cannot leave this field blank, and any attempt to do so will raise an exception. This rule is implemented by the server and is enforced regardless of which front end you use to access the data. By definition, all primary keys must be declared Not Null.

The ArtistType field in the Artist table is declared as Not Null. All artists must be distinguished by type; that is, they have to be labeled as either Authors or Musicians. If they don't fit into one of these two categories, then they are never seen by the user because I set up a filter on this field, excluding all but the one type that the user currently wants to see. In short, the table is filtered to show either only musicians or only authors. If an entry in the Artist table does not fit into one of these two categories, then it is never seen by the user. As a result, I declare this field as Not Null and then use a lookup table to give the user only two choices when filling it in. This way, I am sure that no records are lost.

Deciding which fields should get the value Not Null is one of the more difficult chores in creating a database. This is one of those decisions that I almost never get right in design mode. Instead, I am forced to go back and massage my data after creating a first draft of the data definition.

To change a table using WISQL, you must use a SQL command called Alter Table:

```
ALTER TABLE MYTABLE
   ADD NAME VARCHAR(25),
   DROP NAMES
```

This code adds a field called NAME to a table and drops a field called NAMES. You don't have to add and drop fields at the same time; for instance, you can write

```
ALTER TABLE MYTABLE
   ADD NAME VARCHAR(25)
```

You can also write

```
ALTER TABLE MYTABLE
   DROP NAMES
```

Because you often alter the structure of an existing table, make sure you run many tests on your program before entrusting a large amount of data to your tables.

> **CAUTION**
>
> You should take extreme care whenever you alter a table. I suggest backing up the entire GDB file by copying it to a safe location. Alternatively, the InterBase Server Manger also provides a means for backing up tables.

In InterBase, you cannot alter a field that is part of a unique index, primary key, or foreign key, nor can you drop a unique index, primary key, or foreign key. You can, however, drop a standard index:

```
drop index myindex
```

Renaming a Field in an Existing Table

When you start altering tables, you soon need to transfer the values from one field to a new field. To show how to proceed, I will create a simple table that can serve as a scratch pad. All the work shown here was done with the WISQL32 utility that ships with InterBase in the BIN directory. I always keep WISQL on the Tools menu of my copy of Delphi.

Consider the following SQL statements:

```
create table foo (sam Integer not null, Name VarChar(30),
➡primary key (Sam));
insert into foo (Sam, Name) values (1, "Fred");
insert into foo (Sam, Name) values (2, "Sam");
insert into foo (Sam, Name) values (3, "Joe");
```

The four lines shown here create a table called Foo and place some simple values in it. WISQL lets you use the Previous and Next commands so you can easily alter the insert command without retyping it each time.

After creating the table, I can easily test the data:

```
select * from foo
        SAM NAME
========== ==============================
          1 Fred
          2 Sam
          3 Joe
```

Suppose that I now decide I want to change the Name field to be Not Null and somewhat longer. How do I proceed?

The first step is to create a new field with all the traits in it that I want:

```
alter table foo
  add AName Varchar(50) Not Null;
```

Now the table has a field called AName that is longer than the Name field and declared Not Null.

To copy the data from the Name field to AName, issue the following command in WISQL:

```
update foo
  set Aname = Name;
```

Here is how things stand at this point:

```
select * from Foo;
        SAM NAME                                ANAME
=========== ============================= =========
          1 Fred                          Fred
          2 Sam                           Sam
          3 Joe                           Joe
```

Now you can simply delete the Name column:

```
alter table foo
  drop name;
```

Your efforts yield a table with the traits you sought:

```
select * from foo;
        SAM ANAME
=========== ================================================
          1 Fred
          2 Sam
          3 Joe
```

If necessary, you can then repeat the process to copy AName to a field called Name, or else you can just keep the new name for your table.

This whole technique is a bit laborious. However, if you play with SQL for a while, all this work starts to become second nature. For instance, I can copy the AName field back to a new field called name in well under a minute just by rapidly typing the following:

```
alter table foo add Name varchar(50) not null;
update Foo
  set Name = AName;
alter table foo drop Aname;
```

Note the user of semicolons to separate the three statements I enter here. You can execute them all at once or one at a time, depending on your needs or taste.

After you learn SQL, and assuming you can type well, you can usually invoke WISQL, enter the commands, and get out faster than you can load the weighty Database Desktop application. Certainly by the time I open Database Desktop, open the Restructure window, and start making changes, I've usually spent more time than it takes to do the whole procedure in WISQL. Another nice thing about WISQL is that it has a small footprint and can be left in memory without slowing down the system.

Creating Blob Fields

You can use blob fields to store bitmapped images, sounds, video segments, and text. InterBase has full support for blob fields.

After the discussion of `Code` field and the related `Null` versus `Not Null` issues, the other fields in the `Artist` table are pretty straightforward:

```
CREATE TABLE ARTIST (CODE CODE_DOM NOT NULL,
        LAST VARCHAR(30),
        FIRST VARCHAR(30),
        BORN DATE,
        DIED DATE,
        BIRTHPLACE VARCHAR(35),
        COMMENT BLOB SUB_TYPE TEXT SEGMENT SIZE 80,
        ARTISTTYPE INTEGER NOT NULL,
        PRIMARY KEY (CODE));
```

The code for creating a blob field is a bit tricky, but fortunately, you can just block copy this code any time you need to create a text blob in InterBase. If you create a blob field as shown previously, then you can use it with the `TDBMemo` data-aware control that ships with Delphi.

Delphi offers two objects for working with blobs: `TBlobField` and `TBlobStream`. `TBlobField` has methods called `LoadFromFile`, `SaveToFile`, `LoadFromStream`, and `SaveToStream`. Use these methods to read and write blob data in and out of a database. You can also usually cut and paste data directly into a `TDBMemo` or `TDBImage` control by copying it to the Clipboard. Then paste it into the control by pressing Ctrl+V. To copy an image from a blob field to the Clipboard, press Ctrl+C or Ctrl+X. Alternatively, you can use the built-in `CopyToClipBoard` feature of both `TDBMemo` or `TDBImage`.

Primary Keys and Foreign Keys

You were introduced to primary and foreign keys in Chapter 8. It's now time to put that theory into practice.

The final line in the definition for the `Artist` table defines the primary key:

```
PRIMARY KEY (CODE));
```

This line states that the primary key is the `Code` field. It's important that `Code` is a keyed field because it is referenced by a foreign key in the `Album` table. Furthermore, you want to be sure that no two rows have the same code in it, and the primary key syntax enforces this rule. Remember that all primary keys must be Not Null by definition.

Here, once again in slightly different form, is the definition for the Album table:

```
CREATE TABLE ALBUM (CODE CODE_DOM NOT NULL,
        ALBUM VARCHAR(25) NOT NULL,
        TYPES SMALLINT,
        LOUDNESS SMALLINT,
        MEDIUM SMALLINT,
        RATING SMALLINT,
        GROUPCODE CODE_DOM NOT NULL,
        PRIMARY KEY (CODE),
        FOREIGN KEY (TYPES) REFERENCES TYPES(CODE),
        FOREIGN KEY (LOUDNESS) REFERENCES LOUDNESS(CODE),
        FOREIGN KEY (MEDIUM) REFERENCES MEDIUM(CODE),
        FOREIGN KEY (GROUPCODE) REFERENCES ARTIST(CODE)
        );
```

As you can see, I modified the table to include foreign keys. These keys use the References syntax to show the dependencies that this table has on the fields of other tables.

The Code field contains a unique number for each new album entered by the user. A character field designates the name of the album or book, and the GroupCode field relates each record to the Artist table.

Notice that the GroupCode field is a foreign key referencing the Code field of the Artist table. A foreign key provides *referential integrity,* through the use of the References syntax. The foreign key asserts that

- Every GroupCode entry must have a corresponding Code field in the Artist table.
- You can't delete an Artist record if you have a corresponding record in the Album table with a GroupCode the same as the Code field of the record you want to delete.

These rules are enforced by the server, and they are implemented regardless of what front end attempts to alter the table. Delphi will surface any violation of these rules.

You rarely should make a foreign key unique because the whole point of this exercise is to relate multiple albums with one artist.

To see referential integrity in action, run the Music program and try to delete one of the artist records that has an album associated with it. For instance, try to delete Bob Dylan, Miles Davis, or Philip Glass. Your efforts are stymied because albums are associated with all these artists. In particular, you get a lovely message that reads something like the following:

12

INTERBASE PROGRAMMING

```
General SQL Error: Violates FOREIGN KEY constraint
"INTEG_19" on table "Album"
```

You might as well savor this one because it is as close to poetry as you can get in the SQL database world.

Referential integrity is enforced automatically in Delphi and the Database Desktop. To see how it works, go into the Database Desktop, enter a new album, and try to give it a GroupCode that does not have a corresponding entry in the Code field of the Artist table. The Database Desktop doesn't let you do it. (Note that other fields in this table have foreign keys, so you have to give valid values all the way around, or you aren't able to enter a record. You can, however, leave the other fields blank if you want.)

The Types, Loudness, Medium, and Rating fields are all integers. Types, Loudness, and Medium are all foreign keys that reference one of three small tables called, logically enough, Types, Loudness, and Medium:

```
/* Table: LOUDNESS, Owner: SYSDBA */
CREATE TABLE LOUDNESS (LOUDNESS VARCHAR(15) NOT NULL,
        CODE INTEGER NOT NULL,
        PRIMARY KEY (CODE));
/* Table: MEDIUM, Owner: SYSDBA */
CREATE TABLE MEDIUM (MEDIUM VARCHAR(15) NOT NULL,
        CODE INTEGER NOT NULL,
        PRIMARY KEY (CODE));
/* Table: TYPES, Owner: SYSDBA */
CREATE TABLE TYPES (TYPES VARCHAR(15) NOT NULL,
        CODE INTEGER NOT NULL,
        PRIMARY KEY (CODE));
```

The structure of these tables ought to be intuitively obvious. The Types table, for instance, is designed to hold the following records:

```
select * from types
TYPES                 CODE
=============== ===========
JAZZ                     1
ROCK                     2
CLASSICAL                3
NEW AGE                  4
FOLK                     5
BLUES                    6
COMPUTER              1000
FICTION              1001
SCIFI                1002
MYSTERY              1003
REFERENCE            1004
```

What you have here are six categories for albums and five categories for books. I separate the two types of categories by a large range so that you can add a virtually unlimited number of additional categories of either kind. If you want to work with more than 999 different types of music, then you have needs that cannot be met by this database in its current form.

Astute readers will probably notice that I designed the relationship between the Types field of the Album table and the Types table itself so that you can easily perform lookups on the Types table when necessary. You will hear more about this topic later in the chapter in the section "Working with Data in the Music Program," or you can refer to the discussion of lookup fields in Chapter 8.

Here is the definition for the Book table, which plays the same role in this program as the Album table:

```
CREATE TABLE BOOK (CODE CODE_DOM NOT NULL,
        ALBUM VARCHAR(25) NOT NULL,
        TYPES SMALLINT,
        MEDIUM SMALLINT,
        RATING SMALLINT,
        COMMENT BLOB SUB_TYPE TEXT SEGMENT SIZE 80,
        GROUPCODE CODE_DOM NOT NULL,
        PRIMARY KEY (CODE),
        Foreign key(GroupCode) references Artist(Code),
        Foreign key(Types) references Types(Code),
        Foreign key(Medium) references Medium(Code)
   );
```

Note that the two tables differ in several particulars. The interesting thing about the Music program is that it can handle both kinds of tables seamlessly. To the user, the forms involved with displaying this data just seem to morph as needed to accommodate the data.

Creating Indices on the Music Table

By now, you have seen most of the data definition for MUSIC.GDB. However, I want to discuss a few more details before moving on to take a look at the interface for the program.

The indices on the Music database provide fast access and automatic sorting of the data. If any of your searches takes too long, one of the best ways to address the problem is through enhancing your indices.

You need to see the difference between the primary and foreign keys that create referential integrity and add constraints to a table and the ordinary indices, which speed up access to a particular record. A primary key is a type of super index. It gives you everything an index gives you and then a little more. When you create a primary key or foreign key in InterBase (or in Paradox), a unique index is automatically created on that key.

One simple way to view indices is to open the Database Explorer and examine the indices listed under the `Album` or `Artist` table. The `Artist` table, for instance, has two indices. One is called `Artist_LastFirst_Ndx`, and I will describe it later in this section. The other index has the strange name `RDB$PRIMARY1`. This index was created when the code field was designated as a primary key. The name has that sibilant poetic ring to it that is so typical of automatically generated computer identifiers

---

NOTE

You can add a primary or foreign key after a table is created, as long as doing so does not violate any other database rules. You should make sure that the tables involved are not in use by another program when you make these kinds of modifications.

Here is an example of adding a primary key:

```
ALTER TABLE FOO ADD PRIMARY KEY (Sam);
```

Here is an example of adding a foreign key:

```
ALTER TABLE FOO ADD FOREIGN KEY (Foreigner) REFERENCES Book(CODE);
```

The foreign key example shown here assumes that you added an `Integer` field called `Foreigner` to the `Foo` table.

Besides the primary keys and foreign keys, the following indices are also defined on the `Artist` and `Album` table:

```
CREATE INDEX GROUPALBUM_IDX ON ALBUM(GROUPCODE, ALBUM);
CREATE INDEX ARTIST_LASTFIRST_NDX ON ARTIST(LAST, FIRST);
```

If you want to create a new index in WISQL, you can do so with the SQL `Create Index` command, as shown in the preceding code. The command takes the name of the index, the name of the table on which the index is enforced, and finally, in parentheses, the names of the fields in the index. For more information on this and other commands, see the *InterBase 5 Server Language Reference*. Also helpful are third-party books such as the *Practical SQL Handbook* (ISBN: 0-201-62623-3).

I created these two indices for different reasons. The `Artist_LastFirst_Ndx` is meant primarily to speed up searches and sorts in the `Artist` table.

The GroupAlbum_Idx is created for a more specific reason. I need to create a new index that both relates the Album table to the Artist table and also makes sure that the Album table is sorted correctly. The GroupAlbum_Idx serves this purpose. (I had a little trouble getting the GroupAlbum_Idx to work properly at first, but things cleared up when I closed the Album table and then reopened it.)

Generators, Triggers, and Stored Procedures

The next few sections of this chapter deal with triggers and generators. You will read a good deal about automatically generating values for primary keys and a little about the relative merits of triggers and generators.

Three generators provide unique numbers to use in the Code fields of the Artist, Book, and Album tables. Generators provide almost the same functionality in InterBase tables that autoincrement fields provide in Paradox tables. That is, they provide numbers to use in the keyed fields that bind tables together.

Autoincrement fields are filled in automatically at runtime. Generators, however, are not directly tied to any field. They merely generate random numbers in sequence, where the first number generated might be one, the second two, and so on. You can tell a generator to start generating numbers at a particular starting value, where the first number might be x, the next x + 1, and so on.

Here is how you create a generator in WISQL and set it to a particular value:

```
CREATE GENERATOR MUSIC_GEN;
SET GENERATOR MUSIC_GEN TO 300;
```

As a result of this code, the first number generated is 300, the next is 301, and so on.

I will now show how to write a trigger. The Music program uses triggers on the Artist table but not on the Album table. The reason for splitting things up this way is explained in this section and in the upcoming section of this chapter called "Don't Use Triggers on Active Indices."

Here is how you write a trigger that automatically puts a generated value into the Code field of the Artist table whenever an Insert occurs:

```
CREATE TRIGGER SETMUSICGEN FOR ARTIST
BEFORE INSERT AS
BEGIN
  NEW.CODE = GEN_ID(MUSIC_GEN, 1);
END
```

This code is stored and run on the server side. It's not Delphi code. You enter it into WISQL exactly as shown. You never need to call this procedure explicitly. The whole point of triggers is that they run automatically when certain events occur. This one is designed to run right before an `Insert` occurs. In other words, the way to call this procedure from Delphi is to perform an `Insert`.

The code states that you want to create a trigger called `SetMusicGen` to run on the `Artist` table. The generator is called before an `insert` operation:

```
BEFORE INSERT AS
```

The actual body of the code is simple:

```
NEW.CODE = GEN_ID(MUSIC_GEN, 1);
```

The `NEW` statement says that you are going to define the new value for the `CODE` field of the record that is about to be inserted into a table. In this case, you reference the new value for the `CODE` field of the `Artist` table.

`GEN_ID`, which is a function built into InterBase, produces an integer value. It takes a generator as its first parameter and a step value as its second parameter. The step value increases or decreases the value produced by the generator. For instance, the preceding code increments the value by 1, which parallels the behavior of an autoincrement variable in Paradox.

Don't Use Triggers on Active Indices

You can get a generator to fill in a field automatically with the trigger shown in the preceding section. Unfortunately, Delphi does not provide particularly good support for triggers on indexed or keyed fields.

One reason this weakness exists is that each server generates a different kind of trigger. The developers of the VCL didn't want to run around finding out how to handle triggers for 10 different kinds of servers and neither did the developers of the BDE.

In this case I need to be very explicit to make sure you are following my logic. It would be better if Delphi had good support for triggers on keyed fields. However, it does not. In the next two sections after this one, I will show you a workaround for this unfortunate weakness in Delphi.

Some third-party solutions to this problem include a good one called the `IBEventAlerter`, which works with InterBase. This solution ships with Delphi but is found on the samples page. Its presence on the samples page means it lives in a never-never land between the high-quality code made by the VCL team and the sample code, written by me and many others like me, that appears in the Examples directory of a standard Delphi installation.

In the example under discussion, Delphi's poor support for triggers is not crucial because the table is not sorted on the Code field, but on the Last and First fields. If it were sorted on the Code field, this trigger might cause Delphi to lose track of the current record after the insert operation. Delphi would not know that the Code value was inserted because it would not know that the trigger fired. As a result, the current record might be lost—not permanently lost, but removed from Delphi's field of sight. In other words, the index would cause the record to be moved to a particular place in the dataset, but Delphi would not know how to follow it.

> **NOTE**
>
> Here is another example of how to create a trigger using WISQL:
>
> ```
> CREATE TRIGGER SET_COMPANY_UPPER FOR COMPANY
> ACTIVE BEFORE INSERT POSITION 1
> AS
> BEGIN
>   NEW.COMPANY_UPPER = UPPER(NEW.COMPANY);
> END
> ```
>
> This code is called just before an insert operation on a table from another database called Company. This table contains a string field also called Company and a second field called Company_Upper. The second field is meant to mirror the Company field but with all its characters in uppercase. This second field takes up a lot of space, but it allows you to conduct searches and sorts on the Company field without taking into account character case. The goal of the trigger shown previously is to take the new value for the Company field and convert it into an uppercase version of the string for use in the Company_Upper field. The Upper macro shown here is built into InterBase.
>
> Notice the line that states when this trigger is fired
>
> ```
> ACTIVE BEFORE INSERT POSITION 1
> ```
>
> Delphi does not need to know that the Set_Company_Upper trigger occurred because the table is not sorted on the Company_Upper field.

If you find yourself in a situation in which you can't use a trigger, you don't have any great need for alarm. The absence of trigger support is not a big concern under most circumstances. Instead of using a trigger, you can use a stored procedure to retrieve the next number from a generator. The next two sections show how to proceed.

12

INTERBASE PROGRAMMING

Working with Stored Procedures

In this section, you will see a discussion of the stored procedures used by the Music program to enforce or support referential integrity. These simple stored procedures use a generator to fill in the value of a primary key. In other words, they solve the problem that triggers could not solve. Near the end of the chapter, in the section "Asking the Database a Question: An Abbreviated SQL Primer," I discuss a series of more complicated stored procedures used to query the data in the database.

A *stored procedure* is simply a routine that is stored on the server side rather than listed in your source code. Like the language for writing triggers, there is a unique language for writing stored procedures that has nothing to do with Object Pascal or SQL. In fact, you need to keep in mind that no particular relationship exists between Delphi and InterBase. They are made by two different teams, using two different languages, with two different goals in mind.

One key difference between Delphi code and InterBase code is that the language of stored procedures is completely platform independent. If you want to move your database back and forth between Windows and UNIX, then you might find it helpful to create many stored procedures that handle the majority of work for your databases. Then you can write very thin clients that simply ask the stored procedures to do all the work.

Stored procedures are not difficult to create. Here, for instance, is a stored procedure that returns the next number generated by the Music_Gen generator:

```
CREATE PROCEDURE GETMUSICGEN
RETURNS (NUM INTEGER)
AS
  BEGIN  NUM = GEN_ID(MUSIC_GEN, 1);
END
```

The first line tells WISQL that you are going to create a procedure called GetMusicGen. The next line states that it is going to return a value called Num, which is an integer. The AS statement tells InterBase that you are now ready to define the body of the procedure. The procedure itself appears between a BEGIN..END pair and consists of a call to the GEN_ID function, which returns the next number from the MUSIC_GEN generator. When it retrieves the number, it asks InterBase to increment its value by one. You can increment by a larger number if you want.

Stored procedures are handled on the Delphi end with either a TStoredProc component or by returning an answer set by way of a SQL statement. Here are some rules to guide you when deciding how to handle a stored procedure:

- In general, if the stored procedure returns several rows of data, you access it by way of a SQL statement in a TQuery component. The SQL statement to use in such a case is `Select * from GetAlbumGen`, where `GetAlbumGen` is the name of the procedure that returns one or more rows of data.

- If the stored procedure returns only a single item of data, you can call it with a `TStoredProc` component. Examples of both methods for calling stored procedures from Delphi appear in the next section, in the form of excerpts from the Music program.

Stored Procedures from Delphi's End

The `Album` and `Book` tables of the Music program use stored procedures to fill in their primary index. Because both procedures are identical, I describe only the one for the `Album` table.

To get started, you need to be sure the stored procedure is set up on the server side. Here is the code you should enter into WISQL to create the procedure:

```
CREATE PROCEDURE GETALBUMGEN RETURNS (NUM INTEGER)
AS
BEGIN
  NUM = GEN_ID(ALBUM_GEN, 1);
END
```

As you can see, this simple stored procedure does nothing more than return a single value.

If you are having trouble setting up the procedure, the entire data definition for the database is supplied on disk. If you want to create this database from scratch, you can run this entire statement through WISQL from the File menu. Otherwise, you can create the database and pass the statements through one at a time. A third use for the code is simply to give you one place to look when you need a reference for `MUSIC.GDB`. If you already have a copy of the database, you can create the output shown here; to do so, select Extract, SQL Data from Database from the WISQL menu.

NOTE

You can start a new project, create a data module, and drop a `TDatabase` object on it. Connect it to the Music database that ships on the CD that accompanies this book. After you connect the `TDatabase` object to `MUSIC.GDB`, you can drop down the `TStoredProc` and start working with it, as described in the rest of this section.

Setting up the alias for the database is described in depth in the `readme` file from the CD. In general, just follow the rules for creating aliases laid out in the preceding chapter. This time, though, create an alias called `Music`, and point it to the `MUSIC.GDB` file.

To get started using a TStoredProc, drop it onto the Album page or onto a data module. Set the StoredProcName alias to the GetAlbumGen stored procedure.

After selecting the procedure to use with the TStoredProc, you can pop up the Params field to see the parameters passed to or returned by the function. In this case, only one parameter is returned as the result of the function.

Whenever the user inserts a record into the Album table, the following procedure is called by the AfterInsert event of the TTable object:

```
procedure TDMod.AlbumTableAfterInsert(DataSet: TDataSet);
begin
  AlbumTableCODE.Value := 0;
  AlbumTableGROUPCODE.Value := 0;
end;
```

It doesn't matter what value you assign to the CODE and GROUPCODE fields. Just make sure they aren't set to Not Null. The correct value is filled in later by the BeforePost event of the AlbumTable object:

```
procedure TDMod.AlbumTableBeforePost(DataSet: TDataSet);
begin
  if (AlbumSource.State = dsInsert) then begin
    GetAlbumGen.Prepare;
    GetAlbumGen.ExecProc;
    AlbumTableCODE.AsInteger := GetAlbumGen.ParamByName('Num').AsInteger;
    AlbumTable.FieldByName('GroupCode').AsInteger :=
    ➥ArtistTableCODE.AsInteger;
end;
end;
```

This code first executes the stored procedure and then snags its return value from the Params field of the TStoredProc. The Params field for stored procedures works the same way as the Params field for TQuery objects. Calling Prepare can help to optimize your code.

The rest of the object for updating the table occurs in the AlbumForm where the user does his or her work:

```
procedure TAlbumForm.sbInsertClick(Sender: TObject);
var
  S: string;
begin
  S := '';
  if not InputQuery('Insert New Album Dialog',
  ➥'Enter album name', S) then Exit;
  DMod.AlbumTable.Insert;
  DMod.AlbumTable.FieldByName('Album').AsString := S;
  DMod.AlbumTable.FieldByName('Types').AsString := '';
```

```
    DMod.AlbumTable.FieldByName('Loudness').AsString := '';
    DMod.AlbumTable.FieldByName('Medium').AsString := '';
    DMod.PostAll;
    lcbType.SetFocus;
end;
```

This code just makes sure that all the fields not handled by the stored procedure are filled in properly by the values the user entered. The call to Post in this procedure will cause AlbumTableBeforePost to execute.

Near the end of this chapter, I return to the subject of stored procedures when I discuss techniques for querying the data in a database in the section "Asking the Database a Question: An Abbreviated SQL Primer."

Following is the code for generating both the trigger and the stored procedure described previously. You should never include both the trigger and the stored procedure in the same database. You have to choose between the two techniques:

```
CREATE GENERATOR IMAGECODE;
CREATE PROCEDURE GETIMAGECODE RETURNS (NUM INTEGER)
AS
  BEGIN  NUM = GEN_ID(IMAGECODE, 1);
END

CREATE TRIGGER GENERATE_IMAGECODE FOR IMAGES
ACTIVE BEFORE INSERT POSITION 0
AS BEGIN
  New.Code = Gen_ID(ImageCode, 1);
END
```

Server-Side Rules Versus Client-Side Rules

In many people's minds, the holy grail of contemporary client/server development is to place as many rules as possible on the server side of the equation. This means that no matter how the user accesses the data, and no matter how many front ends are written to access the data, the basic rules of the database are enforced.

To avoid enforcing rules on the client side, you must create referential integrity on the server side using foreign keys or whatever tools are at your disposal. Furthermore, you should use triggers whenever possible to enforce additional rules. For instance, some people view it as an error to insert the Code field of the Album table using a stored procedure rather than a trigger; however, you might have no choice about how to proceed in some circumstances.

Even using triggers and referential integrity is not enough for many hard-core adherents of the server-side philosophy. This book, however, is written about a client-side tool, so I generally promote just placing the referential integrity on the server side and then maybe adding a few more triggers or stored procedures where necessary.

I find that many database chores are easier to perform on the Delphi side. Delphi is a powerful language with powerful debuggers to back it up. Most servers have neither a powerful language nor a powerful debugger. As a result, I feel defining certain kinds of database logic in Object Pascal is often wisest, as long as doing so does not exact a huge penalty in terms of performance. Obviously, if you need to fetch a lot of rows and then process them, doing that on the server side where the data itself is stored is best.

The emergence of Distributed OLE, CORBA, and other tools that support Remote Procedure Calls (RPC) is rapidly changing how databases are constructed. PC-based developers can now use Distributed COM or CORBA to place Object Pascal–based rules on middle tier servers. I can therefore use Delphi to enforce a bunch of rules and then encapsulate those rules in an object that resides on the same machine as the InterBase server, or on a middle tier machine. This puts all my database logic on servers where they can be called from multiple clients. The goal is to provide a few entry points for my front-end program to call. That way, I keep the logic off the front end but still get to use a real language to define my business logic.

You will find out more regarding distributed architectures in Chapter 15, "Creating COM Automation Servers and Clients," and Chapter 20, "DCOM."

An Overview of the Interface for the Music Program

The interface for MUSIC.DPR presents the user with a main screen with three pages imbedded inside it. One page (shown in Figure 12.2) is meant only for performing searches. It gives you a view of both the Artist table and either the Book table or the Album table. You can't alter the Artist table from this screen, but you can change the Album or Book table.

> **NOTE**
>
> I use the following code to prevent the user from using the Insert key to insert a record into either of the grids on the Index page:

```
void __fastcall TIndexForm::ArtistGridKeyPress(TObject *Sender,
   char &Key)
{
   if ((Key == VK_INSERT) || (Key == VK_DELETE))
      Key = 0;
}
```

This code disarms Insert and Delete keystrokes. Users never know the method is called but find that they can't use the Insert or Delete keys. The code is called in response to OnKeyDown events.

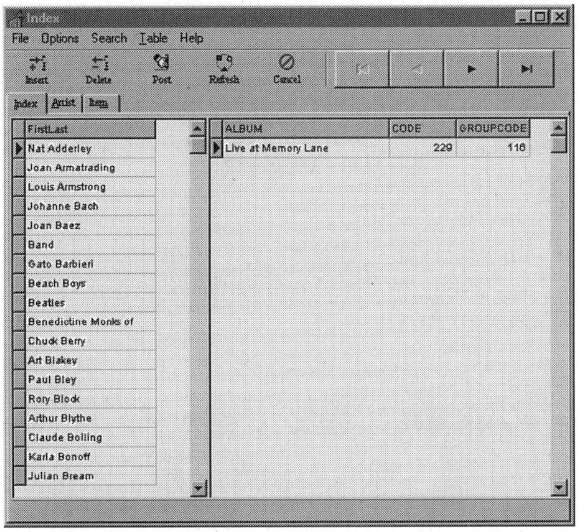

FIGURE 12.2

The Index *page from* MUSIC.DPR *enables you to view artists and their related productions.*

The second page in the Music program allows you to see one record from the Artist table, as shown in Figure 12.3. Users can use the Index page to browse or search through the data, as shown in Figure 12.2.

If users want to look at a particular record, they can switch to the Artist, Album, or Book pages. Figures 12.4 and 12.5 show the latter two of these three pages.

The Book or Album page is always the third page in the program. There is no fourth page. If the current record is an album, then the Album form is shown; if it is a book, then the Book form is shown.

Working with Child Forms

Delphi provides a number of paged dialogs or notebooks that you can use to present data to the user. In this particular program, I use the TTabControl tool in conjunction with a series of forms. My primary concern is allowing the programmer to place each major object in a separate unit rather than force the combination of various different sets of functionality into one paged notebook. In other words, the `Album` page is a separate object, not a part of the `TNotebook` object.

FIGURE 12.3

The `Artist` page from the Music program.

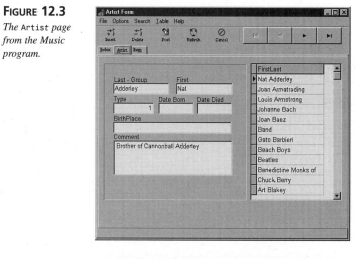

FIGURE 12.4

The `Album` page from the Music program.

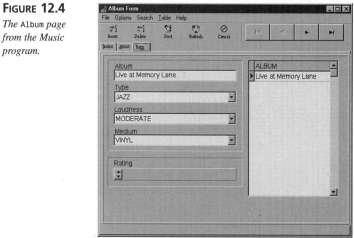

The Music program has five major forms in it. The first supports the frame for the entire program, and the rest support the `Index`, `Artist`, `Album`, and `Book` pages. The next few paragraphs describe how to make a form become a child of a second form, which is what is really happening inside the Music program.

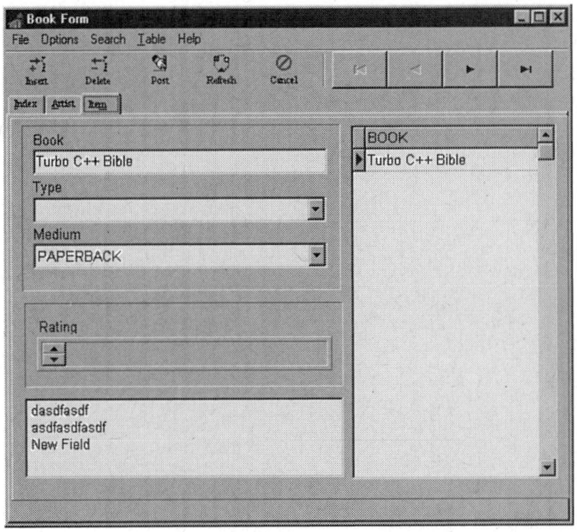

FIGURE 12.5

The Book *page from the Music program.*

You need to convert the standard Delphi pop-up form to a child form that has Form1 as its parent. Here is how to proceed:

```
//////////////////////////////////////////
//     File: ChildForm1
// Project: Music
// Copyright (c) 1998 by Charlie Calvert and Pat Ritchey
//
unit ChildForm1;

interface

uses
  Windows, Messages, SysUtils,
  Classes, Graphics, Controls,
  Forms, Dialogs;

type
  TChildForm = class(TForm)
  private
    procedure Loaded; override;
    procedure CreateParams(var Params: TCreateParams); override;
  public
  end;

var
  ChildForm: TChildForm;

implementation

{$R *.DFM}
```

```
procedure TChildForm.Loaded;
begin
   inherited Loaded;
   Visible := false;
   Position := poDefault;
   BorderIcons := [];
   BorderStyle := bsNone;
   HandleNeeded;
   SetBounds(0,0,Width,Height);
end;

procedure TChildForm.CreateParams(var Params: TCreateParams);
begin
   inherited CreateParams(Params);
   Params.WndParent := (Owner as TForm).Handle;
   Params.Style := WS_CHILD or WS_CLIPSIBLINGS;
   Params.X := 0;
   Params.Y := 0;
end;

end.
```

The logic for the code shown here was based on work done by Pat Ritchey.

In the Music program, all the main forms descend from the ChildForm shown previously. As a result, they inherit the capability to live as a child form pasted on top of another form:

```
TAlbumForm = class(TChildForm)
   Panel1: TPanel;class TAlbumForm : public TChildForm
```

When using this technique, you want the parent form to explicitly create the child forms. To do so, do not autocreate the forms; instead, choose Project, Options, Forms and move the forms from the Auto-Create list box into the Available Forms list box. Then you can create the forms as needed inside Form1 with code that looks like this:

```
procedure TForm1.FormCreate(Sender: TObject);
var
   i: Integer;
begin
   IndexForm := TIndexForm.Create(Self);
   AlbumForm := TAlbumForm.Create(Self);
   ArtistForm := TArtistForm.Create(Self);
   BookForm := TBookForm.Create(Self);
   ChildForms[0] := IndexForm;
   ChildForms[1] := ArtistForm;
   ChildForms[2] := AlbumForm;
   ChildForms[3] := BookForm;
   for i := 0 to MaxForms do
     ChildForms[i].Show;
end;
```

I describe this process in more depth later in this chapter in the section that examines the
FormCreate event for the main module.

To make sure the form adheres to the dimensions of its parent, you can respond to
OnResize events:

```
procedure TForm1.FormResize(Sender: TObject);
var
  i: Integer;
  R: TRect;
begin
  R := TabControl1.DisplayRect;
  R.top := R.Top + ToolBar1.Height;
  R.bottom := R.Bottom - ToolBar1.Height;

  for i := 0 to MAXFORMS do
    MoveWindow(ChildForms[i].Handle, R.left, R.top,
    ➥R.right, R.bottom, True);
end;
```

This code uses the TabControl1.DisplayRect function call to get the size of the window
to draw in, excluding the location where the tabs reside. It then resizes the child form so
that it fits in this space.

The Code for the Music Program

Now that you understand the basic structure of the Music program, the next step is to
take a look at the code and analyze any sections that need explanation. The code is too
long to present in total. It is, of course, available in full on the CD that accompanies this
book. The most important methods from the program are quoted in the body of the text
itself.

Using the Music Program

When you study the Music program, note how you can make the tables in a relational
database work together seamlessly toward a particular end. Because this program uses
InterBase, you can use it in a rigorous multiuser environment without fear that it would
collapse under the load. For instance, there is no reason why this program, as is, cannot
handle two or three hundred simultaneous users.

Suppressing the Password: The TDatabase Object

The TDatabase object on the main form has its AliasName property set to the Music
alias. This alias was defined in the Database Explorer (refer to Figure 12.1), and it points
to the tables that make up the music database.

The `DatabaseName` property of the `TDatabase` object is set to the string `MusicData`, which is the alias all the other `TTable`, `TStoredProc`, and `TQuery` objects in the program are attached to. Remember: Only the `TDatabase` object attaches directly to the `Music` alias. This way, you can point the entire program to a second database by changing only one variable: the `AliasName` property. This feature can be handy if you need to experiment without touching your primary data.

The `Params` property for the `TDatabase` object contains the following information:

```
USER NAME=SYSDBA
PASSWORD=masterkey
```

The `LoginPrompt` property is then set to `False`, which enables you to launch the program without entering a password. This is pretty much a necessity during development, and it's a useful trait in a program such as this that probably has little fear of hostile attacks on its data.

The `FormCreate` Event

As you learned earlier, the constructor for the main form has to create the child windows that hold all the main controls used in the program:

```
procedure TForm1.FormCreate(Sender: TObject);
var
  i: Integer;
begin
  IndexForm := TIndexForm.Create(Self);
  AlbumForm := TAlbumForm.Create(Self);
  ArtistForm := TArtistForm.Create(Self);
  BookForm := TBookForm.Create(Self);
  ChildForms[0] := IndexForm;
  ChildForms[1] := ArtistForm;
  ChildForms[2] := AlbumForm;
  ChildForms[3] := BookForm;
  for i := 0 to MaxForms do
    ChildForms[i].Show;
end;
```

The first four lines of the routine create the forms. The next four lines assign them to an array of `TForm` objects. You can then use this array to iterate through all the main forms for the program, as shown in the last two lines of the routine, and in the `OnResize` response method shown previously.

As you can see, an ordinal value of `0` gives you immediate access to the `Index` form if you write code that looks like this:

```
ChildForms[0] := IndexForm;
```

One of the most important methods in the program is the `TabControl1Change` event handler:

```
procedure TForm1.TabControl1Change(Sender: TObject);
begin
  DMod.PostAll;
  case (TabControl1.TabIndex) of
    0: begin
      ChildForms[TabControl1.TabIndex].BringToFront;
      Caption := 'Index';
      DBNavigator1.DataSource := DMod.ArtistSource;
      DMod.TypesTable.Filtered := False;
    end;

    1: begin
      ChildForms[TabControl1.TabIndex].BringToFront;
      Caption := 'Artist Form';
      DBNavigator1.DataSource := DMod.ArtistSource;
      InsertBtn.OnClick := ArtistForm.sbInsertClick;
      Insert1.OnClick := ArtistForm.sbInsertClick;
      DeleteBtn.OnClick := ArtistForm.sbDeleteClick;
      PostBtn.OnClick := ArtistForm.PostBtnClick;
      CancelBtn.OnClick := ArtistForm.CancelBtnClick;
    end;

    2: if (DMod.ArtistTable.FieldByName('ArtistType').AsInteger = 1)
      ➡then begin
        ChildForms[2].BringToFront;
        Caption := 'Album Form';
        DBNavigator1.DataSource := DMod.AlbumSource;
        InsertBtn.OnClick := AlbumForm.sbInsertClick;
        Insert1.OnClick := AlbumForm.sbInsertClick;
        DeleteBtn.OnClick := AlbumForm.sbDeleteClick;
        CancelBtn.OnClick := AlbumForm.CancelBtnClick;
        PostBtn.OnClick := AlbumForm.PostBtnClick;
        DMod.TypesTable.Filtered := False;
        DMod.MaxTypes := 999;
        DMod.MinTypes := 0;
        DMod.TypesTable.Filtered := True;
      end else begin
        ChildForms[3].BringToFront;
        Caption := 'Book Form';
        DBNavigator1.DataSource := DMod.BookSource;
        InsertBtn.OnClick := BookForm.sbInsertClick;
        Insert1.OnClick := InsertBtn.OnClick;

        DeleteBtn.OnClick := BookForm.sbDeleteClick;
        CancelBtn.OnClick := BookForm.CancelBtnClick;
        PostBtn.OnClick := BookForm.PostBtnClick;
        DMod.TypesTable.Filtered := False;
        DMod.MaxTypes := 1999;
```

```
        DMod.MinTypes := 1000;
        DMod.TypesTable.Filtered := True;
        BookForm.TypesCombo.Update;
    end;
  end;
end;
```

The primary burden of this code is to move the appropriate form to the front when requested by the user:

```
ChildForms[2].BringToFront;
```

This code brings the AlbumForm to the front. To the user, this looks as though a hit on the TabControl caused the "page to be turned" inside the control. Of course, what really happens is that you simply push one form down in the Z order and bring another to the top. In short, you create your own page control out of separate forms. The beauty of this arrangement is that it ensures that each page of the TabControl exists as a separate object in its own module. This arrangement is much better than the system used in the kdAdd program.

Another key chore of the TabControlOnChange handler is to set the OnClick event for the buttons at the top of the form so that they reflect what happens inside the current page. For instance, if the BookForm is selected, then a click on the Post button ought to call the Post method of the Book table, not the Album or Artist table. To ensure that all works correctly, this method simply sets the OnClick method to the appropriate routine whenever the TabControl is moved:

```
InsertBtn.OnClick := AlbumForm.sbInsertClick;
DeleteBtn.OnClick := AlbumForm.sbDeleteClick;
CancelBtn.OnClick := AlbumForm.CancelBtnClick;
PostBtn.OnClick := AlbumForm.PostBtnClick;
```

In this case, the methods associated with the InsertBtn and so on are the methods from the AlbumForm. This technique helps you to see how dynamic the delegation model can be if you need to push the envelope a bit.

I mentioned earlier that the Types table holds a series of types that can apply to either musical or written works. For instance, the table might look like this:

```
TYPES              CODE
================ ===========
JAZZ                   1
ROCK                   2
CLASSICAL              3
NEW AGE                4
FOLK                   5
BLUES                  6
COMPUTER            1000
```

```
FICTION              1001
SCIFI          .     1002
MYSTERY              1003
REFERENCE            1004
```

When the application is in Music mode, the first half of the table is used; otherwise, the second half of the table is used. Here is code from the `TabControlOnChange` event that ensures that the proper part of the code is operative when the program is in Book mode:

```
DMod.TypesTable.Filtered := False;
DMod.MaxTypes := 1999;
DMod.MinTypes := 1000;
DMod.TypesTable.Filtered := True;
```

The following lines are executed when the user switches the program into Music mode:

```
DMod.TypesTable.Filtered := False;
DMod.MaxTypes := 999;
DMod.MinTypes := 0;
DMod.TypesTable.Filtered := True;
```

After you look at the code, you should not be surprised to learn that the `Types` table has an `OnFilterRecord` event handler:

```
procedure TDMod.TypesTableFilterRecord(DataSet: TDataSet;
  var Accept: Boolean);
begin
  Accept := (DMod.TypesTable['Code'] >= MinTypes) and
      (DMod.TypesTable['Code'] <= MaxTypes);
end;
```

After this method is defined, all you have to do is set the `TypesTable filtered` property to `true`, and only the selected half of the `Types` table is visible. By the time the `Album` or `Book` form gets at this table, it appears that it contains only value pertinent to the relevant form.

Of course, I defined a property so that the code in the main form never directly touches the privates of the `TDataModule` object:

```
property MaxTypes: Integer read FMaxTypes write FMaxTypes;
property MinTypes: Integer read FMinTypes write FMinTypes;
```

`FMinTypes` and `FMaxTypes` are private data for the program.

The following code from the main module of the program gets executed whenever the user switches between Music and Book mode:

```
procedure TForm1.FilterOptionsClick(Sender: TObject);
begin
  DMod.ArtistTable.Filtered := False;
  case TFilterIndex(TComponent(Sender).Tag) of
    fiAlbumFilter: begin
```

```
    IndexForm.BookGrid.Align := alNone;
    IndexForm.BookGrid.Visible := False;
    DMod.FilterType := Ord(fiAlbumFilter);
    IndexForm.AlbumGrid.Align := alClient;
    IndexForm.AlbumGrid.Visible := True;
  end;

  fiBookFilter: begin
    IndexForm.AlbumGrid.Align := alNone;
    IndexForm.AlbumGrid.Visible := False;
    DMod.FilterType := Ord(fiBookFilter);
    IndexForm.BookGrid.Align := alClient;
    IndexForm.BookGrid.Visible := True;
  end;
  end;
  DMod.ArtistTable.Filtered := True;
end;
```

The purpose of this code is to properly set up the two grids on the Index page. When the program is in Music mode, you want the right-hand grid on the Music page to show the Music table, and when you are in Book mode, you want it to show the Book table. I could have simply switched the DataSource for one form as needed, but that does not take care of the issue of defining the fields to be shown in the grid. Rather than try to create the columns on-the-fly, I decided instead to use the code shown here.

Working with Data in the Music Program

So far, most of the code you have analyzed from the Music program has been centered on the program's interface. Now it is time to move away from Object Pascal–centered issues, and see something of code used to display and handle data. Subjects covered in this section include using lookups, using ranges, and asking the database a question.

The data for this program is quite complex. You can see this fact most easily by looking at the data module for the program, shown in Figure 12.6.

Lookups

This program uses a large number of lookups. All of them are defined on the TDataModule itself, although some are used in the grids on the Index form, others on the Book and Album pages, and some in both locations. In particular, when you enter a new album, you use lookups to specify whether the album is Loud, Medium, or Peaceful, and you use lookups to specify whether it is in a particular category such as Jazz, Folk, Rock, and so on.

FIGURE 12.6

The data for the Music program is fairly complex, as you can see from glancing at the `TDataModule` *object found in* `DMod1.cpp`.

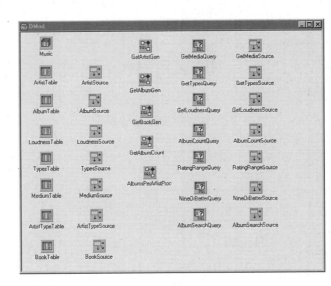

The primary purpose of the lookups is to ensure that the user always chooses from prese-lected lists of values and does not start typing in his or her own values on-the-fly. For instance, you want the user to choose a type from the Types table and not make up new types at random.

Because these lookups are so readily available, the user rarely has to type anything into a control. Instead, he or she can quickly select options from a lookup list. It is not current-ly available, but it is a nice gesture to the user to provide a means of editing the lookup tables, as shown in the Address program from Chapter 9.

Asking the Database a Question: An Abbreviated SQL Primer

By this time, you know most of what you need to know to construct a reasonably power-ful database. This feeling is good, and knowing that you can get this kind of control over an important domain of information is nice.

Nevertheless, despite this sense of accomplishment, you may still have a nagging feeling that something is missing. After all, work is required to construct the database and to enter data into it, so where is the fun part? Where is the part that makes you say, in the cultured words of that dubious soul from Redmond, "Hey, that's cool!"

After you have a database up and running, the way to get joy from it is to ask it ques-tions. At first, you might just want to ask simple questions. For instance, you might remember the beginning of the name of an album, but you can't remember the whole thing.

Suppose that you remember that an album name begins with the letter *L*. If you bring up WISQL, you can ask the following question:

```
select Album from album where album like "L%"
ALBUM
==========================
Letter From Home
La Mer
Life
Landing on Water
Live at the BBC
Longing in their Hearts
Live at the Royal Festival
Love Deluxe
Live at Memory Lane
Lookout Farm
Living
Lives in the Balance
Lawyers in Love
```

As you can see, the results returned from this question are names of the albums and books that start with the letter *L*.

This capability is fairly useful, but you really want to know not only the name of the album, but also the artist behind the album. You could, of course, ask the following question:

```
select Album, GroupCode from album where album like "L%"
ALBUM                       GROUPCODE
========================== ===========
Letter From Home                11
La Mer                          50
Life                             9
Landing on Water                 9
Live at the BBC                 13
Longing in their Hearts         28
Live at the Royal Festiva       92
Love Deluxe                     61
Live at Memory Lane            116
Lookout Farm                   130
Living                         161
Lives in the Balance           142
Lawyers in Love                142
```

This question gives you the name of an album plus the `GroupCode` associated with the album. Then, all you have to do is run one more query to get the answer you need:

```
select First,Last from Artist where Code = 11
FIRST                          LAST
============================== ==============================
Pat                            Metheny
```

Of course, not having to ask this question in two stages would be nice. Instead, you might want to ask the following question, which performs a join between the Album and Artist tables:

```
select Artist.Last, Album.Album
   from  Album, Artist
where artist.code = album.groupcode and
Album.Album like "L%"
order by Artist.last
LAST                           ALBUM
============================== ==========================
Adderley                       Live at Memory Lane
Beatles                        Live at the BBC
Browne                         Lawyers in Love
Browne                         Lives in the Balance
Collins                        Living
Debussy                        La Mer
Liebman                        Lookout Farm
McLaughlin                     Live at the Royal Festiva
Metheny                        Letter From Home
Raitt                          Longing in their Hearts
Sade                           Love Deluxe
Young                          Landing on Water
Young                          Life
```

Now you are starting to get somewhere. This information is fairly valuable to you. When composing the preceding query, you should be careful to include where clauses that both specify the letters you want to search on and the relationship between the Artist and Album tables:

```
where artist.code = album.groupcode
```

If you don't qualify the question in this way, you end up getting a much larger result set than you want. In particular, you indicate that the query shouldn't link the resulting albums to all the names in the Artist table but just link them to the names of the artists that have the same code as the groupcode of a particular album.

Now that you have seen this much, most people also want to get information about the rating for the album, as well as its type. One way to ask that question looks like this:

```
select Artist.Last, Album.Album, Album.Rating, Album.Types
   from  Album, Artist
   where artist.code = album.groupcode and
      Album.Album like "L%"
   order by Artist.last
```

```
LAST                             ALBUM                      RATING  TYPES
==============================   ========================   ======  ======
Adderley                         Live at Memory Lane        <null>       1
Beatles                          Live at the BBC                 6       2
Browne                           Lawyers in Love                 6       2
Browne                           Lives in the Balance            6       2
Collins                          Living                          6       5
Debussy                          La Mer                          7       3
Liebman                          Lookout Farm                    6       1
McLaughlin                       Live at the Royal Festiva  <null>       1
Metheny                          Letter From Home                9       1
Raitt                            Longing in their Hearts    <null>  <null>
Sade                             Love Deluxe                     8       1
Young                            Landing on Water                7       2
Young                            Life                            7       2
```

When you're reviewing this data, you may find it hard not to feel that something is missing from the types field. After all, what does the number 1 mean? What type is that?

Once again, you can get the question answered by going to the well a second time and querying the Types table. However, you should not be surprised to learn that a second solution is possible:

```
select Artist.Last, Album.Album, Album.Rating, Types.Types
   from  Album, Artist, Types
where artist.code = album.groupcode and
Album.Album like "L%" and
Types.Code = Album.Types
order by Artist.last
LAST                             ALBUM                      RATING  TYPES
==============================   ========================   ======  =========
Adderley                         Live at Memory Lane        <null>  JAZZ
Beatles                          Live at the BBC                 6  ROCK
Browne                           Lawyers in Love                 6  ROCK
Browne                           Lives in the Balance            6  ROCK
Collins                          Living                          6  FOLK
Debussy                          La Mer                          7  CLASSICAL
Liebman                          Lookout Farm                    6  JAZZ
McLaughlin                       Live at the Royal Festiva  <null>  JAZZ
Metheny                          Letter From Home                9  JAZZ
Sade                             Love Deluxe                     8  JAZZ
Young                            Landing on Water                7  ROCK
Young                            Life                            7  ROCK
```

Here you broadened the question by specifying that you want to bring in the Types table:

```
from  Album, Artist, Types
```

Include one of its fields in the result set:

```
select Artist.Last, Album.Album, Album.Rating, Types.Types
```

Link the `Album` table and `Types` table on the primary and foreign keys of the two tables:

```
where ... Types.Code = Album.Types
```

You get all the things you need; the only problem is that you can't ask the user to open up WISQL—of all applications!—just to get the answer to a simple question.

You can take a number of courses at this point, but one of the best is to simply wrap your query in a stored procedure:

```
CREATE PROCEDURE ALBUMSEARCH (ANALBUMNAME VARCHAR(75))
RETURNS (ARTISTNAME VARCHAR(30),
ALBUMNAME VARCHAR(30),
RATINGVALUE VARCHAR(30),
TYPENAME VARCHAR(30),
MEDIUMNAME VARCHAR(30))
AS
begin
  for
    select Artist.Last, Album.Album, Album.Rating,
    ➥Types.Types, Medium.Medium
    from Album, Artist, Types, Medium
    where artist.code = album.groupcode
      and Album.Album like :AnAlbumName
      and Types.Code = Album.Types and  Medium.Code = Album.Medium
    order by Artist.Last
    into :ArtistName, :AlbumName, :RatingValue, :TypeName, :MediumName
  do  suspend;
end
```

You can break this procedure down into several sections to make some sense of it. First, notice the header:

```
CREATE PROCEDURE ALBUMSEARCH (ANALBUMNAME VARCHAR(75))
```

This header says that you are creating a stored procedure named `AlbumSearch` that takes a string as a parameter. You supply the name of the album you want to search in this string.

The next part of the procedure declares what is returned to the user:

```
RETURNS (ARTISTNAME VARCHAR(30),
ALBUMNAME VARCHAR(30),
RATINGVALUE VARCHAR(30),
TYPENAME VARCHAR(30),
MEDIUMNAME VARCHAR(30))
```

These rows set up what you want returned from the procedure. At the very bottom of the procedure, you state these names again, saying that you want the query to be returned in these variables:

```
into :ArtistName, :AlbumName, :RatingValue, :TypeName, :MediumName
```

The query itself sits in between a `begin..end` pair, which nests around a `for...do` statement:

```
as
begin  for      // Query goes here
  do   suspend;
end
```

If you forget to wrap your query in this faintly ridiculous-looking syntactical sugar, then InterBase complains about a singleton query not being able to return multiple rows.

Now that you have your stored procedure all set up, the next thing to do is call it from Delphi. The syntax for doing so could not be simpler:

```
select * from AlbumSearch(:SearchValue);
```

This simple SQL statement should reside inside the SQL property of a Delphi `TQuery` component. You can then call this procedure with code that looks like this:

```
procedure TDMod.AlbumSearcher(SearchValue: string);
begin
  AlbumSearchQuery.Close;
  AlbumSearchQuery.ParamByName('SearchValue').Value := SearchValue;
  AlbumSearchQuery.Open;
end;
```

That's all there is to it. Now you can hook up a `TDataSource` to the `TQuery` and a `TDBGrid` to the `TDataSource`, and after calling the `AlbumSearch` function, you see the results of your query inside a Delphi application.

You can access a number of interesting stored procedures in this manner from the menus of the Delphi program. Some of the most interesting ones involve asking about the ratings you assign to albums. For instance, you can ask to see all the albums that have a rating between five and seven or a rating higher than nine. This is set of queries is so important that I review them in the last section of this chapter, "Viewing a Range of Data."

Stored Procedures That Do Not Return Datasets

In the preceding section, you saw how to ask a question that returns a dataset. A different kind of stored procedure asks how to return a particular value such as a single number or string. For instance, you might want to ask the answer man how many albums are in the database:

```
select Count(*) from album;
     COUNT
```

```
===========
        290
```

To create a stored procedure that returns this kind of information, you should write

```
CREATE PROCEDURE ALBUMCOUNT
RETURNS (NUM INTEGER)
AS
begin
  for
    select Count(*) from Album
    into :Num
  do    exit;
end
```

This procedure doesn't take any parameters:

```
CREATE PROCEDURE ALBUMCOUNT
```

It does, however, return a value:

```
RETURNS (NUM INTEGER)
```

Because you ask for a single answer and not a series of rows, you can use `exit` instead of `suspend`:

```
 for    // Query goes here
 do     exit;
```

After you compose the query, you can use a stored procedure on the Delphi end to get data from it. To set up the stored procedure, all you have to do is drag it off the Component Palette, set its `DataBaseName` to the `Music` alias, and drop down the list from its `StoredProcName` property so you can choose the appropriate stored procedure.

The following code shows how to call the stored procedure from Delphi:

```
function TDMod.GetTotalAlbumCount: Integer;
begin
  GetAlbumCount.Prepare;
  GetAlbumCount.ExecProc;
  Result := GetAlbumCount.ParamByName('Num').AsInteger;
end;
```

This method returns an integer, which you can display to the user in any manner you think appropriate.

Viewing a Range of Data

Two interesting stored procedures allow you to ask questions such as What albums have a particular rating? What albums have a rating of nine or better? The following is the first of the two routines:

```
CREATE PROCEDURE NINEORBETTER
RETURNS (LAST VARCHAR(30),
ALBUM VARCHAR(30),
RATING INTEGER)
AS
begin
  for
    select Artist.Last, Album.Album, Album.Rating
    from Album, Artist
    where Album.GroupCode = Artist.Code
      and Album.Rating >= 9
    Order By Album.Rating Desc
    into :Last, :Album, :Rating
  do suspend;
end
```

The query at the heart of this procedure asks to see albums that have a rating larger than or equal to nine. To properly qualify the query, the code also asks to see only the entries from the Artist table that are associated with the albums that make it into the result set. The last line of the query asks to order the result set on the album.rating field with the highest ratings first.

The stored procedure shown here lets you ask for data from the table that falls into a particular range:

```
CREATE PROCEDURE RATINGRANGE (LOWRATING INTEGER,
HIGHRATING INTEGER)
RETURNS (LAST VARCHAR(30),
ALBUM VARCHAR(30),
RATING INTEGER)
AS
begin
  for
    select Artist.Last, Album.Album, Album.Rating
    from Album, Artist  where Album.GroupCode = Artist.Code
      and  Album.Rating >= :LowRating
      and  Album.Rating <= :HighRating
    Order By Album.Rating Desc
    into :Last, :Album, :Rating
  do      suspend;
end
```

This procedure is very much like the previous one, but it takes parameters that allow you to specify the range you want to see, and it uses those parameters to customize the result set to your needs:

```
Album.Rating >= :LowRating and Album.Rating <= :HighRating
```

I've shown you several examples of stored procedures so that you might understand how much power exists in a simple query. To me, the most interesting thing about database programming is the ability to ask questions of the data you have collected. The key to that process is to write a query and then place it in a stored procedure so you can call it from your applications. You can also place the query directly in a TQuery component, but then the query takes longer to execute, and you have the bother of managing it on the client side. Everything is easier if you just leave the query on the server where it belongs. But either solution is reasonable in most cases.

Summary

I didn't mention a few lines of code in the Music program, but I reviewed most of the application in this chapter. This program contains code commonly used when constructing a relational database with Delphi. The particular example shown is not robust enough to use in a professional setting, but it gives you a good feeling for how to proceed if you want to construct such an application.

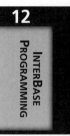

In particular, you got a good look at the techniques used to create a powerful database with referential integrity. You also saw how to use generators, triggers, and stored procedures and how to perform filters and lookups on relational data. In general, this chapter sums up the core information necessary for you to produce a professional database program. If you understand all this material, you are not yet necessarily an expert, but you are ready to start building relational databases in a professional setting.

COM

PART

IV

Interfaces and the Basics of COM

CHAPTER 13

This chapter is about COM and the way it is implemented in Delphi. The material in this chapter is vital to your understanding of much of the material presented in the rest of this book. By the time you are done with this chapter, you should understand the basic facts about how Delphi's implementation of COM is put together. You should also learn a good deal about interfaces and should see how they can be used in your programs even if you are not particularly interested in COM. However, I should stress that this chapter is primarily theoretical in nature, and is designed to give you the background necessary to understand the other chapters on COM that are included in this book.

I am assuming that readers of this chapter have very little understanding of COM. This approach should be great for one set of readers but a bit frustrating for people who know COM well and are trying to find out how Delphi implements a technology they already understand. I ask this second class of readers to have patience while reading the chapter. I know what it is you need to find out, and I will give you all the information you want; it's just not likely that you will find me presenting the relevant materials quite as quickly, or exactly in the same order, as you might prefer.

Understanding COM Interfaces

Few things in all programming are as large and as vast as COM. It is quite possible that COM is the single largest programming effort ever undertaken in the world of PC programming.

Despite its size and its sophistication, the first thing to understand about COM is that its architecture is not universally applauded. In fact, it's arguable that Microsoft could have come up with a better way to implement the lowest levels of COM, and in the future Microsoft may indeed improve its structure. Nevertheless, right now COM is what it is, and you and I both must come to terms with the very nature of the beast. Furthermore, the system undeniably works, and indeed it works well.

Delphi does everything possible to make COM easy to use. In fact, it's arguable that Delphi has come along and essentially rewritten COM as it should have been done originally. Indeed, some of the plans that Microsoft has developed for improving COM look a lot like the implementation of COM found in Delphi.

The foundation for Delphi's implementation of COM is interfaces. Interfaces are easy to understand and easy to use. As a result, COM in Delphi has an admirable simplicity to it. Good programmers make complicated technologies seem simple, and that is exactly what Delphi has done in this case.

What Is COM?

COM stands for the Component Object Model. The theoretical purposes of COM are twofold:

- It provides a means for defining a specification for creating a set of nonlanguage–specific standard objects.
- It provides a means of allowing you to implement objects that can be called between different processes, even if those processes are running on separate machines (DCOM).

In the nontheoretical world of day-to-day practice, COM is most well known for bringing programmers the capability to do four things:

- Write code that can be used by multiple programming languages
- Create ActiveX controls
- Control other programs via OLE automation
- Talk to objects or programs on other machines (DCOM)

When you take all these traits together, you end up with a very powerful solution to a wide range of problems. The solution is so powerful that Microsoft will increasingly be using COM as the primary interface into Windows.

COM and Windows

In the future, we will come to think of Windows as a set of COM interfaces that we can call when we need services. Even at this time, many services are already COM based. For instance, the Windows Explorer is accessed primarily through COM. If you want to change features on the taskbar, you use COM. If you want to program some other feature of the basic Windows UI, then you use a set of COM interfaces called the Shell API.

With Microsoft's rollout of Windows 98 and Windows NT 5, you will find that the entire operating system is starting to revolve around COM. For instance, Word and Excel can be completely automated via COM. The same is true of the Internet Information Server, Internet Explorer, and many of the new features such as the Active Directory, the successors to DAO, the Microsoft Transaction Server (MTS), the Microsoft Message Queue, and innumerable other features.

Plug-and-Play Applications

At least in theory, there is no reason why programmers can't make their programs out of a series of COM servers. These child programs could be plugged in to a main program as needed. For instance, a debugger could be a standalone applet that is thoroughly integrated into an IDE via COM. It would sit unnoticed on the hard drive until the programmer needed it, and then it would pop up on demand, immediately integrating itself with the compiler. If you wanted to use another vendor's debugger, it too could support the same basic COM interfaces and therefore seamlessly plug itself into the current program.

Word and Excel currently support applets of this type. For instance, Paint and the Equation editor can both be seamlessly integrated into Word as needed.

This kind of integration is often implemented through something called *in-place activation*. You can explore this technology by opening Word and choosing Insert, Object, Bitmap Image. This menu command should make a copy of Paint integrate into your version of Word as if they were one application. Of course, there is no reason why another third-party application might not take the place of Paint on your system. In short, you can, at least theoretically, delete Paint from your system and use another third-party's tool in its place. This second tool could also integrate itself into Word.

Programs such as Word and Paint follow the generic rules for integrating applications published in the OLE specification. This type of process falls under the general category of *object linking and embedding*, from which the acronym *OLE* is derived.

C++Builder and Delphi, on the other hand, allow you to integrate DLLs into the IDE by extending a non-OLE–based set of routines. In both the VCL Expert API and OLE automation, the key is to learn a particular API and then use it to integrate your tools into a second program.

> ### NOTE
>
> The Expert API is much easier to use than OLE. On the other hand, it is not quite as powerful. The VCL Expert API allows you to integrate code only with Delphi and C++Builder, and it is designed primarily to support only DLLs. At this time, it supports only the creation of wizards and does not allow you to integrate a new debugger or new editor with the environment. The code you write to create wizards must be in either C++ or Object Pascal.
>
> OLE automation, on the other hand, is a broader specification that enables you to integrate your code with any compliant OLE client program. You can write your OLE code in whatever language you choose, as long as that language supports the basic needs of COM.

Technology that allows you to integrate one application into another is very flashy. However, I do not believe that it is the most powerful part of COM.

The core of COM, to my mind, is not ActiveX controls, not in-place activation, but the relatively simple art of automation. The idea that you can use one program to control another program means that you can begin to view the entire system as nothing more than a suite of services that you can access as needed.

If you are writing a Delphi program and need powerful word processing or spreadsheet functionality, one way to get it is to automate Word or Excel with COM. Let the user use these tools to develop or view documents. These same tools can be used to print or mail documents. In short, you can ask the VCL to do what it does best, which is work with databases, access system resources, or construct complex interfaces. If you need a spreadsheet, then use COM as a conduit that allows you to call on Excel services. If you need a Word processor, then you use COM to call on Word.

As systems become more distributed, COM steps in and allows you to reach out across the network to access services. Custom objects on the network might know how to access a particular database or how to run a particular query against your company's financial records. In a true distributed architecture, you would never have to open an Oracle database or write a complex query. Those chores would be handled by remote objects. Your job would be to simply call on the object to provide the service and then display the results to the user.

In the future, we may increasingly come to view our operating systems and the network as nothing more than a series of services that appear in the form of automated COM objects. Some developers will be creating these services, and others will be calling them. But behind them all will be COM automation and the very closely related field of Distributed COM.

Problems with COM

I have spent a few paragraphs praising COM, but pointing out a few of its flaws is also worthwhile. The biggest problem with COM is that it is Windows-centric. As you will learn in the section called "COM on UNIX," there is a port of COM to UNIX. However, it is currently a new and untried technology. Certainly, most experts view Microsoft's primary goal as being the development of COM on the Windows platform with the intent of keeping its users locked into that operating system.

Another problem with COM is the fact that a plug-in or distributed architecture can be prone to bugs. These bugs often surface because of a lack of true compatibility between the different pieces of a program or integrated system.

If you integrated a program with Word via in-place activation, and that program were buggy or misused the OLE specification, then you could crash both Word and Windows.

13

INTERFACES AND THE BASICS OF COM

A crash can happen because of careless programming or a failure on Microsoft's part to clearly define the OLE specification. Another set of problems would arise if some portion of Microsoft's specification for OLE proved to be fundamentally flawed, which is not an unthinkable scenario.

Furthermore, software vendors in the current age are notably lacking in the sense of cooperation needed to pull something like this off gracefully. For instance, it would be typical of today's software vendors to add custom interfaces that only they knew about or that they failed to document properly. As a result, third parties would always be struggling to keep up with a standard setter who did not have their best interests at heart.

CONSEQUENCES OF STANDARDS-BASED PROGRAMMING

In the software business, much is decided during the first few months or years after a technology is developed. The people who get in first establish themselves as the standard and make most of the money. Unless you have some huge leverage (such as owning the operating system or controlling large sums of R&D and marketing capital), breaking into an established market is very hard.

As a result, a clever strategy for a standard maker to develop is to introduce a new standard but to fail to thoroughly document it. Then the developer of the standard can come out with the first generation of tools for the new technology, facing a marketplace in which essentially no competition exists. After establishing the standard, the developer can begin to publicize or firm up an API. The trick, of course, is to always thoroughly document the version of the API that is one generation behind the current standard. That way, the developer of the standard always stays one step in front of those who are attempting to support it.

If the standard maker ever fears that someone else is actually gaining preeminence in a particular field, then the trick is to redefine the standard in such a way that it breaks that third party's code. The developer can play this game in various ways, but the most powerful is to control the operating system itself. Then the developer can deal the competition serious blows by intentionally breaking their tools or by not revealing the latest changes in the operating system until the competition won't have time to catch up.

If you have been watching the industry for a while, you can see these situations coming from miles away. For instance, Sun is currently attempting to make Java a standard. If that language remains in the hands of Sun, then everyone using Java will have to dance to Sun's tune. The only way out of this trap is to wrestle the standards out of the hands of individual companies and into the hands of independent entities that do not directly profit from their work. The problem with that scenario, of course, is that independent committees often do sloppy work or fail to implement reasonable guidelines.

Despite the potential pitfalls, the idea of creating suites of relatively small standalone tools that work well together is very intriguing. COM can indeed help programmers achieve this goal.

COM on UNIX

In the preceding section, I mentioned that COM is now being ported to UNIX. The company that has done most of the work in this field is called Software AG, which you can find on the Web at `http://www.sagus.com/`.

Software AG has already released the first commercial version of DCOM for UNIX. Apparently in the grip of an uncontrollable poetic frenzy, the people at Software AG decided to call their tool EntireX/DCOM. (Holy marketing mania, Batman! Have these people entireXly lost their minds?) A version for Sun Microsystems' Solaris and OS/390 is available, as well as a version for Digital UNIX and Linux. The company says that additional releases, including one for IBM mainframes, will be coming down the pike in the next few months.

A recent news release reads as follows: "In an unprecedented truce between Microsoft and the CORBA object standard camps, Iona Technologies has licensed Microsoft's ActiveX core technologies, and will deliver next month OrbixComet, a product that will bridge the competing protocols." This technology has special bridges to Delphi and VB. For more information, go to `http://www.iona.com`.

COM+ and the Future of COM

In this section, I'm going to say a few words about the direction COM will likely move over the next few years. In several places, I will reference specific technologies that will be explained immediately after this section, when I begin an examination of the technical side of COM.

Microsoft has decided to make major changes to COM. In truth, facets of the whole COM creation and object management scheme are perhaps less than optimal. Microsoft therefore plans to create something called COM+, which is an ongoing process that will take several years to complete.

One of the goals of COM+ is to promote the creation of type-rich objects that can be explored at runtime just like a VCL class. COM+ will replace the ATL and any other scheme designed to automatically handle reference counting and object creation. In fact, the whole complex of calls surrounding IUnknown and IClassFactory will be eliminated or, rather, handled for you automatically. As a result, COM+ will eliminate the programmer's need to focus on reference counting, IUnknown, IClassFactory, type libraries and many other core COM-based technical schemes, most of which are discussed in the remainder of this chapter or in the next. Code that uses the old technologies should still be compatible with COM+, but new development will be done using COM+ itself.

Perhaps I should point out that Inprise has gone a long way toward bringing you COM+ today, before anyone has even seen the final spec for this technology. In particular, Delphi can automatically handle reference counting, the creation of type libraries, and the chore of working with IUnknown and IClassFactory. Some of these tasks are automated with help from the ATL, others with Inprise's native tools. All of them mirror the types of developments you can expect to see from COM+.

For more information on COM+, go to the Microsoft Web site and look for articles written by Mary Kirtland. You can find her articles by going to http://www.microsoft.com/com. The very useful COMSPEC is also available at the same site.

An Introduction to Interfaces

Now that you understand something of what COM is all about, its time to see how to it is implemented both inside the operating system and in your Delphi code. Interfaces are very much at the heart of this subject. When you thoroughly understand interfaces, you should be able to use COM and Delphi to perform powerful feats that will greatly expand the reach of your programs.

Delphi programmers can think of an interface as nothing more than a set of virtual abstract public methods for manipulating an object. If you took a standard VCL object, stripped away the protected and private sections, and then declared all the remaining methods as virtual abstract, you would have something very much like an interface.

The big difference between the public interface to a VCL object and a COM interface is that the COM interface has no implementation. Its methods are virtually abstract. An interface simply defines a set of public methods for accessing an object, but it says nothing about the actual implementation of that object. In this sense, an interface is a great deal like a virtual abstract public interface to a standard VCL object.

The best way to fully understand this subject matter is just to jump right in and see some code. Delphi makes both COM and interfaces very easy to implement, so I'm going to show you how things work before I explain why they work that way, or even why they exist at all. After you see how easily you can create valid COM interfaces, then I'll come back and explain what COM is and what you can do with it.

The New Interface Type

As of Delphi 3, a new type called an interface was introduced into Object Pascal. Here is what an interface looks like:

```
IMyObject = interface
  Procedure MyProcedure;
end;
```

This simple interface has one method called MyProcedure. To declare the object, I first stated the name of the object and then wrote an equals sign and the new interface keyword. Finally, I declared a simple interface with one method and wrote the keyword end to wrap things up.

If I wanted, I could have stated in parentheses the name of an interface from which this interface will descend:

```
IMyObject = interface(IUnknown)
  Procedure MyProcedure;
end;
```

For now, you don't have to understand anything about IUnknown other than it is another interface. An interface cannot descend from a class; it must descend from either nothing or from another interface.

Now, it so happens that the two declarations I have shown you here are actually identical, just as the following two class declarations are identical:

```
TMyObject = class
end;
```

```
TMyObject = class(TObject)
end;
```

These two declarations are identical because all Delphi classes descend by default from a class called TObject. Therefore, even if you don't say that TMyObject descends from another class, it still descends from TObject. It's just a fact of life in Delphi, and it is so for several good reasons. However, this is not the place to describe those reasons.

Just as all Delphi classes must descend either directly or indirectly from TObject, so must all Delphi interfaces descend either directly or indirectly from IUnknown. I am not, however, going to explain IUnknown to you yet, as I don't want to clutter up your mind with that subject until a bit later.

An Interface Is Not a Class!

Interfaces look a lot like classes, but they are not classes. For instance, interfaces have no data. There are no fields, no instance data, in an interface. The following declaration is entirely illegal:

```
IMyObject = interface(IUnknown)
  FMyData: Integer;  // This is illegal!
  Procedure MyProcedure;
end;
```

This declaration is no good because you cannot declare any data inside an interface. That's completely against the rules.

Furthermore, all members of interfaces are public by default. In fact, you can't add any scoping directives at all to an interface. For instance, the following declaration is entirely illegal:

```
IMyObject = interface(IUnknown)
Private  // This scoping directive is illegal!
  Procedure MyProcedure;
end;
```

This declaration is no good because you can't use scoping directives such as private, public, protected, or published in an interface declaration. All methods are declared public by default, and that's all there is to it.

You Can't Directly Implement an Interface

You never implement an interface by itself. Instead, you make it part of a class. Using interfaces is a way of creating a specification for an object, not a way of declaring an object. For instance, the following unit will not compile:

```
unit Unit2;

interface
type
  IMyObject = interface(IUnknown)
    procedure MyProcedure;
  end;

implementation

procedure IMyObject.MyProcedure;
begin
  ShowMessage('Hi from MyObject');
end;

end.
```

The problem here is that I am attempting to declare an implementation of the IMyObject.MyProcedure method. You can't directly implement any of the methods of an interface. Instead, you use a class to implement an interface.

Using a Class to Implement an Interface

In this section, I'm going to show you a very simple program called SimpleInterface, which shows how to declare an interface, implement it, and then call it. The program is found on the CD that comes with this book, and the code for the program is shown in Listings 13.1 and 13.2.

LISTING 13.1 A SIMPLE UNIT THAT DECLARES AN INTERFACE AND IMPLEMENTS IT

```
///////////////////////////////////
// Purpose: Declare and implement a simple interface
// Project: SimpleInterface.dpr
// Copyright (c) 1998 by Charlie Calvert
//
unit SimpleObject;

interface

type
  IMyInterface = interface
    function GetName: string;
  end;

  TMyClass = class(TInterfacedObject, IMyInterface)
    function GetName: string;
  end;

implementation

function TMyClass.GetName: string;
begin
  Result := 'MyInterface';
end;

end.
```

LISTING 13.2 THE MAIN FORM FOR A DELPHI APPLICATION THAT USES AN INTERFACE AND ITS IMPLEMENTATION

```
///////////////////////////////////
// Purpose: Use an interface declared in SimpleObject.pas
// Project: SimpleInterface
// Copyright (c) 1998 by Charlie Calvert
//
unit Main;

interface

uses
  Windows, Messages, SysUtils,
  Classes, Graphics, Controls,
  Forms, Dialogs, StdCtrls;
```

continues

13

INTERFACES AND
THE BASICS OF
COM

LISTING 13.2 CONTINUED

```pascal
type
  TForm1 = class(TForm)
    UseInterface2Btn: TButton;
    UseObjectBtn: TButton;
    UseInterface1Btn: TButton;
    procedure UseInterface2BtnClick(Sender: TObject);
    procedure UseObjectBtnClick(Sender: TObject);
    procedure UseInterface1BtnClick(Sender: TObject);
  end;

var
  Form1: TForm1;

implementation

uses
  SimpleObject;

{$R *.DFM}

{----------------------------------------------------------------
  Just call the method of an object
----------------------------------------------------------------}
procedure TForm1.UseObjectBtnClick(Sender: TObject);
var
  MyClass: TMyClass;
begin
  MyClass := TMyClass.Create;
  ShowMessage(MyClass.GetName);
  MyClass.Free;
end;

{----------------------------------------------------------------
  Retrieve an interface, and call one of its methods
----------------------------------------------------------------}
procedure TForm1.UseInterface1BtnClick(Sender: TObject);
var
  MyInterface: IMyInterface;
  MyClass: TMyClass;
begin
  MyClass := TMyClass.Create;
  MyInterface := MyClass;
  ShowMessage(MyInterface.GetName);
end;

{----------------------------------------------------------------
  Retrieve an interface, and call one of its methods
----------------------------------------------------------------}
```

```
procedure TForm1.UseInterface2BtnClick(Sender: TObject);
var
  MyInterface: IMyInterface;
begin
  MyInterface := TMyClass.Create;
  ShowMessage(MyInterface.GetName);
end;

end.
```

When you run this program, you see a form with three buttons on it, as shown in Figure 13.1. If you click the buttons on the form, various methods of the interface or the object that implements it are called.

FIGURE 13.1

The form to the SimpleInterface *program.*

The following is the declaration for the interface used in this program and for the class used to implement the interface:

```
IMyInterface = interface
  function GetName: string;
end;

TMyClass = class(TInterfacedObject, IMyInterface)
  function GetName: string;
end;
```

The simple interface shown here declares a single method called GetName. This method is implemented in TMyClass as follows:

```
function TMyClass.GetName: string;
begin
  Result := 'MyInterface';
end;
```

As you can see, nothing at all is unusual about the implementation for this method. It could not possibly be simpler. It's just a normal implementation of a very simple method.

So what ties TMyClass.GetName to IMyInterface.GetName? What is the relationship between these two syntactical entities?

To understand what is happening here, you need to take a careful look at the declaration for TMyClass:

```
TMyClass = class(TInterfacedObject, IMyInterface)
```

This line of code says that `TMyClass` descends from another class called `TInterfacedObject`, and it implements an interface called `IMyInterface`.

> **NOTE**
>
> You need to understand that `TMyClass` does not support true multiple inheritance. It looks a lot like it supports multiple inheritance, and in a sense, it does support multiple inheritance, but it's not that true, hard-core, multiple inheritance that you get in C++.
>
> True multiple inheritance occurs when one class descends from at least two other classes. `TMyClass` descends from one class and one interface. This difference is actually more than a semantic quibble because an interface is fundamentally different from a class in that it cannot implement any methods.
>
> You cannot have two implementations of the same method of an interface in the same inheritance tree. I will discuss this topic more fully when I examine the program `MultipleInterface` later in this chapter.

So `TMyClass` descends from one standard Delphi class called `TInterfacedObject` and one interface called `IMyInterface`. It declares a single method called `GetName` that implements the `GetName` method declared in `IMyInterface`. The thing that ties `TMyClass.GetName` to `IMyInterface.GetName` is the simple fact that the two methods have the same name. (There is slightly more to this story, but again I will ask you to wait for a full explanation until you see the `MultipleInheritance` program.)

You are probably wondering about `TInterfacedObject` and where it comes from. `TInterfacedObject` is a special class that does certain things to make it possible for the class from which it descends to automatically and easily implement an interface. In particular, `TInterfacedObject` implements the methods of `IUnknown`, just as `TMyClass` implements the single method of `IMyInterface`.

If you wanted, you could implement the methods of `IUnknown` in `TMyClass`. In other words, you could write something like the following:

```
TMyClass = class(TObject, IMyInterface);
```

But in this case `TMyClass` would have to implement not only `GetName`, but also the methods declared in `IUnknown`. As I'm sure you can tell, I'm *still* not going to tell you about `IUnknown`.

If you want, you can think about this situation in a slightly different way. If you want to create a form to use in your own program, then you descend from `TForm`:

```
TForm1 = class(TForm)
```

In the same way, if you want to implement an interface, just descend from `TInterfacedObject`:

```
TMyClass = class(TInterfacedObject, IMyInterface)
```

Calling the Methods of an Interface

The main form for the `SimpleInterface` program contains three buttons. The first button allows you to call the sole method of `TMyClass`. The second two buttons show you two different ways to call a method of `IMyInterface`. Over the next few paragraphs, I will explain all these methods.

This method does nothing more than create an instance of `TMyClass` and call its method:

```
procedure TForm1.UseObjectBtnClick(Sender: TObject);
var
  MyClass: TMyClass;
begin
  MyClass := TMyClass.Create;
  ShowMessage(MyClass.GetName);
  MyClass.Free;
end;
```

This example is as simple a piece of code as you can write in Delphi, so I won't bother explaining it to you. I just want to give you a base point to start from, so you can see what is different when you start working with an interface:

```
procedure TForm1.UseInterface1BtnClick(Sender: TObject);
var
  MyInterface: IMyInterface;
  MyClass: TMyClass;
begin
  MyClass := TMyClass.Create;
  MyInterface := MyClass;
  ShowMessage(MyInterface.GetName);
end;
```

In this example, you first create an instance of `TMyClass`:

```
MyClass := TMyClass.Create;
```

Then you retrieve the interface from that class:

```
MyInterface := MyClass;
```

This line of code is very important. It allows you to create a reference to an interface through a simple assignment statement.

> **NOTE**
>
> People who understand COM probably have some pretty pressing questions by this time, so I will take a moment to answer one of them. In particular, those who understand COM are probably wondering whether a real COM object is being created here. The answer is an emphatic yes. In particular, the following call is legal and will succeed:
>
> ```
> MyInterface.QueryInterface(IUnknown, Unknown);
> ```
>
> Or, if you want to be more purely correct, you can add ActiveX to your uses clause and write
>
> ```
> var
>    Hr: HResult;
>   Unknown: IUnknown;
> begin
>   hr := MyInterface.QueryInterface(IUnknown, Unknown);
>     if SUCCEEDED(hr) then
>       Unknown._AddRef;
> ```
>
> If you are used to seeing this kind of code in C, then you probably still have some questions, but I'm going to ask you to be patient, as I will explain all this in good time.

After you have retrieved an instance of IMyInterface from an object, then you can call the method of IMyInterface:

```
ShowMessage(MyInterface.GetName);
```

As you know, this is really the same thing as calling TMyClass.GetName. In fact, you are literally calling TMyClass.GetName. In other words, UseObjectClick and UseInterface1BtnClick end up doing pretty much the same thing. The only difference is that one uses an interface and the other doesn't. Or to state the matter somewhat differently, one is just a plain Delphi object, and the other is a valid COM interface. In just a few moments, I'll start explaining what a COM object really is, and then you will see why all this is being done. For now, however, I ask that you just keep taking all this information on faith and concentrate on becoming comfortable with the basic syntax of using a COM object.

The following is the second method that retrieves the interface from TMyClass and calls the IMyInterface.GetName method:

```
procedure TForm1.UseInterface2BtnClick(Sender: TObject);
var
  MyInterface: IMyInterface;
begin
  MyInterface := TMyClass.Create;
  ShowMessage(MyInterface.GetName);
end;
```

Destroying Interfaces

The watchful readers of this book will have noticed that I do nothing to destroy the interfaces that I create. As it happens, this is the correct thing to do. An interface does not need to be destroyed, as Delphi will do so automatically.

To understand what is happening here, the first thing you want to do is see for yourself that what I am saying is really true. To understand what is happening, you need only make one small modification to the SimpleObject.pas file. In particular, you just need to add a destructor, as shown in Listing 13.3.

LISTING 13.3 A SECOND VERSION OF THE SimpleObject.pas FILE WITH AN EXPLICIT DESTRUCTOR FOR TMyClass

```
/////////////////////////////////////////
// Purpose: Declare and implement a simple interface
// Project: SimpleInterface.dpr
// Copyright (c) 1998 by Charlie Calvert
//
unit SimpleObject;

interface

type
  IMyInterface = interface
    function GetName: string;
  end;

  TMyClass = class(TInterfacedObject, IMyInterface)
    function GetName: string;
    destructor Destroy; override;
  end;

implementation

uses
  Dialogs;

destructor TMyClass.Destroy;
begin
```

continues

LISTING 13.3   CONTINUED

```
  ShowMessage('Destroy');
  inherited Destroy;
end;

function TMyClass.GetName: string;
begin
  Result := 'MyInterface';
end;

end.
```

Because I call ShowMessage in the destructor of this object, you have a simple way to tell whether the object is being freed.

If you call the first method on the main form, the destructor gets called for an obvious reason:

```
procedure TForm1.UseObjectBtnClick(Sender: TObject);
var
  MyClass: TMyClass;
begin
  MyClass := TMyClass.Create;
  ShowMessage(MyClass.GetName);
  MyClass.Free;
end;
```

Here I explicitly call MyClass.Free, and so it's obvious that the destructor is going to be called. Now take a look at the second example:

```
procedure TForm1.UseInterface1BtnClick(Sender: TObject);
var
  MyInterface: IMyInterface;
  MyClass: TMyClass;
begin
  MyClass := TMyClass.Create;
  MyInterface := MyClass;
  ShowMessage(MyInterface.GetName);
end;
```

If you run this example, you will see that the destructor gets called in this case too. But why? Why should the destructor be called in this second case when there obviously is no explicit call to free or destroy?

Well, the answer is simply that behind the scenes, Delphi is keeping track of this object, and Delphi will free it the moment it goes out of scope. These objects work exactly the same way that local objects work in C++, or the way Variants and strings work in Delphi; as soon as they go out of scope, their destructors will be called automatically.

All this is good and well, but what if you want to explicitly destroy an object? Intelligent readers not already in the know are likely to make one of two guesses as to how an interface should be destroyed:

- Programmers with a strong Delphi background would assume that you could call the Free method on these objects.

- Programmers with a COM background would assume that you could call Release on these objects.

Though both are intelligent, reasonable guesses, it so happens that either approach will end up generating an access violation. The correct way to destroy these objects is to set them equal to nil:

```
MyInterface := nil;
```

If you make this call, the COM method called Release will be automatically called, as will the destructor for TMyClass. I find this behavior to be extremely surprising, and it is therefore a fact I need to make explicit note of and keep in mind at all times.

To test this behavior, try conducting a few experiments. For instance, try the following method:

```
procedure TForm1.UseInterface1BtnClick(Sender: TObject);
var
  MyInterface: IMyInterface;
  MyClass: TMyClass;
begin
  MyClass := TMyClass.Create;
  MyInterface := MyClass;
  ShowMessage(MyInterface.GetName);
  MyInterface := nil;
  ShowMessage('Foo');
end;
```

Or try things this way:

```
procedure TForm1.UseInterface1BtnClick(Sender: TObject);
var
  MyInterface: IMyInterface;
  MyClass: TMyClass;
begin
  MyClass := TMyClass.Create;
  MyInterface := MyClass;
  ShowMessage(MyInterface.GetName);
  MyClass := nil;
  ShowMessage('Foo');
end;
```

Again, you might find the results of this little experiment surprising. For instance, in the first case, the program first pops up the name of the object, then says that the destructor is being called, and then shows the message 'Foo'. In the second case, however, the object name is popped up, then the message Foo is displayed, and then the destructor for the object is called. In other words, you can free TMyClass by setting MyInterface equal to nil, but you cannot free TMyClass by setting MyClass equal to nil. In the one case, you are causing things to happen behind the scenes, whereas in the second case, you are merely setting a pointer variable equal to nil.

An important point to grasp here is that an interface has no separate life to live apart from the object that implements it. The interface is just an abstraction. It's just an idea. The only thing that gets created is TMyClass. IMyInterface is just an abstraction of some subset of functionality of TMyClass and TInterfacedObject.

The Theory Behind Interfaces

By this time, you know enough about interfaces to understand something of what they look like in practice. The next step is to start to see why this piece of syntax exists.

It turns out that you use interfaces for several reasons. The first and most obvious reason is that they provide an implementation for COM objects inside Object Pascal. A second reason is that they provide a simple way to create standards or specifications. If you define an interface, then you or others can implement it according to a predefined and easily understood standard. The TStrings and TStream classes play roles similar to this in the VCL, in that they are abstract classes that are used primarily as a way to define the behavior to be exhibited by a whole series of other classes such as TFileStream and TStringList.

Suppose you want to create a specification for creating objects that deliver a specific set of functionality. For instance, you might want to define a set of objects that allow people to create certain geometrical shapes. Your goal is to allow multiple vendors to create their own shapes but to define a common API that all vendors would use. That way, you could write one set of code for displaying shapes but create different results by plugging in different vendors' objects. For instance, you might write code for manipulating a spherical shape, but when you used Vendor A's implementation of the sphere shape, you would get a sphere with polka dots, and if you used Vendor B's implementation, then you would get a sphere with a hippie tie-dye pattern on it. Or perhaps one vendor's sphere would have fewer facets than another vendor's sphere, thus making it more purely round.

To make your objects have this kind of plug-and-play functionality, each vendor would have to conform to a predefined specification for defining geometric shapes. To start defining that specification, you might create a simple interface that defines points in space:

```
IPoint = Interface(IUnknown)
  procedure SetPoints(X, Y: Integer);
  procedure Draw;
end;
```

This declaration says nothing at all about the actual implementation of class IPoint. It just represents a specification for the class. Any one particular vendor might choose to implement it as follows:

```
TPoint = class(TInterfacedObject, IPoint)
private
  XPos: Integer;
  YPos: Integer;
public
  procedure SetPoints(X, Y: Integer);
  procedure Draw; virtual;
end;
```

But this implementation is really beside the point. What matters here is that a specification has been laid out, and all the vendors who want to participate have to follow that specification. They can develop their own implementations to suit their own needs; it's the specification that can't change.

As you will see, the COM specification is about more important things than merely defining points in space. In particular, the core set of COM objects, such as IUnknown or IClassFactory, defines a way for a variety of different vendors, working in a variety of different languages, to create instances of COM objects. Other classes define a specification for creating ActiveX controls, another set for implementing in-place activation, and yet a third set for streaming data to disk.

In a short while, I will start explaining some of these features of COM to you. For now, however, I want to spend just a little more time thinking about raw interfaces and what they can do for you as a Delphi programmer.

Reasons for Using Interfaces

Besides the explanations given in the preceding section, I can think of a third reason for creating an interface. Interfaces provide an excellent way to define the behavior of a set of object-oriented classes. Typical examples of this type of behavior are the ActiveX classes and Windows Shell Extensions. These simple classes have a very shallow hierarchy.

In fact, you might argue that interfaces provide a better way to define a set of objects than the technologies provided by traditional OOP. This fact was not at all clear to me when I first started using interfaces, but the more I have played with this technology, the more I have come to see how valuable it can be.

To understand what I am driving at, coming up with a concrete example might be helpful. Suppose you want to create a set of objects that will be used to communicate with a piece of hardware that will be used to control some fanciful object such as an automated kite. The object you create might look something like this:

```
TKite = class(TObject)
  Procedure Launch;
  Procedure Land;
  Procedure LetOutString;
  Procedure ReelInString;
  Procedure Swoop(Direction: TDirection);
  Procedure UntangleString;
  Procedure FreeStringFromTelephoneWire;
end;
```

The company you are working for might create a whole line of automated kites, and the implementation for each of these methods would differ depending on the kind of kite you create. Interfaces provide a simple mechanism for defining the way each of these kite objects should look, without saying anything about their implementation.

For instance, you could recast the class shown previously as an interface:

```
IKite = interface(IUnknown)
  Procedure Land;
  Procedure LetOutString;
  Procedure ReelInString;
  Procedure Swoop(Direction: TDirection);
  Procedure UntangleString;
  Procedure FreeStringFromTelephoneWire;
end;
```

This simple declaration is more powerful than it might seem. It serves as a specification for the kite object. You can give these few lines to several teams of programmers and tell them to create objects that implement this interface. When they are through, you will have a series of entirely compatible objects guaranteed to behave in a similar manner. In other words, an interface can be a simple means of documenting and designing shallow hierarchies of objects. At the same time, these interfaces provide a built-in means of enforcing a clearly defined and especially lucid design standard.

To help emphasize this point, let me show you what some of these implementations might look like. For instance, the kite teams might end up implementing the following classes:

```
TBatKite = class(TInterfacedObject, IKite);
  Procedure Land;
```

```
  Procedure LetOutString;
  // Code omitted here to avoid repetition
end;

TChineseKite = class(TInterfacedObject, IKite)
  Procedure Land;
  Procedure LetOutString;
  // Other methods of IKite interface defined here…
end;
```

These two objects will behave in the same way. After you have taught someone to work with one of these kites, he or she will know how to work with them all because they all support the same interface. The adoption of interfaces by the kite team can make a lot of programming and design issues quite simple. (Now, if only we could figure out a way to get the bugs out of that darn `FreeStringFromTelephoneWire` method...)

Of course, as shown here, this technology does not provide much in the way of reuse. In some cases, you might just forgo the reuse of code and say that the benefits of interfaces are sufficient for the particular situation at hand. Or, if you desire, you can create an intermediate class that implements some of the functionality of the interface and leaves it up to each individual class to implement the rest.

You must understand, however, that some people like the fact that interfaces don't tend to promote deep hierarchies. Consider what happens when you are in hierarchy several levels deep and you want to implement a particular virtual method. To be reminded of the complications that can ensue, consider the following hierarchy:

```
TKite = class;
TChineseKite = class(Kite);
TVultureKite = class(TChineseKite);
TTwoStringedVultureKite = class(TVultureKite);
```

Suppose a virtual method called `Launch` is implemented in each of these objects. If you are creating or maintaining the `TTwoStringedVultureKite` class, then you might have to decide whether you want to call the ancestor class's version of `Launch` from your implementation of the `Launch` method. Well, perhaps you should. On the other hand, maybe you should skip the implementation of `Launch` in `TVultureKite` and go directly to the one in `TChineseKite`. Hmm. Maybe. Truth is, when you get right down to it, knowing for sure what the best course of action might be a bit hard. You will have to study quite a bit of source code and maybe do some guesswork or experimentation before you can make a decision.

The difficult decisions outlined in the preceding paragraph do not exhaust the list of ambiguous situations that OOP commonly creates. For instance, what if you are a programmer called in to maintain an existing implementation of the code, and you see that

TTwoStringedVultureKite.Launch calls TVultureKite.Launch, but you missed the fact that TVultureKite.Launch skips calling TChineseKite.Launch and instead calls TKite.Launch? What are the potential ramifications of that particular oversight? Well, once again, it's a bit hard to say without doing a considerable amount of guesswork and experimentation.

The more you ponder the difficulties inherent in the scenarios described in the preceding paragraph, the better it sounds to implement simple interface/object pairs that go only one level deep. Sure, you can't reuse the code as easily as you can reuse traditional OOP code, but the code you do write will be easy to understand and easy to maintain. If you are working in C++, you will also know that you don't have to worry about true multiple inheritance throwing even more monkey wrenches into the works.

My point here is not that interfaces and shallow inheritance are necessarily better than traditional OOP, but only that the issue is more open to debate than it might seem at first glance. Keeping code as simple and clean as possible is a very worthwhile goal, and one that might be worth pursuing even at the cost of losing certain fun-to-use features. Certainly, it's hard to argue with the fact that you can teach most programmers how to take advantage of interfaces in just a few days, whereas it usually takes years for a programmer to fully grasp all the nuances of traditional OOP programming.

Before closing this section, let me just remind you that interfaces can be used as a way of defining a standard for very deep hierarchies. That's not a misuse of interfaces, nor is it uncommon practice. I'm merely pointing out that on some occasions you might find it useful to use a very shallow hierarchy of the kind found so often in Windows API classes such as IDirectDraw or ICopyHook. Interfaces may provide an enticing alternative to standard OOP-based programming practices.

Maintaining or Updating an Interface

I need to make one other important point about interfaces and the way they are used in most programming environments. As a rule, you should never attempt to update or improve an interface. After you have created it and released it to the public, then that is the final draft, and it should never be changed.

If you want to make changes to an interface, then you usually create a new version of the interface and release it under a new name:

```
IKite2 = class(TObject)
  Procedure Launch;
  Procedure Land;
  Procedure LetOutString(NumInches: Integer);
  Procedure ReelInString(NumInches: Integer);
```

```
  Procedure Swoop(Direction: TDirection);
  Procedure UntangleString;
  Procedure FreeStringFromTelephoneWire;
  Function GetWindStatus: TDirection;
end;
```

This new interface is identical to the original `IKite` interface, except for the fact that it supports a new function called `GetWindStatus`. Furthermore, the `LetOutString` and `ReelInString` methods now take parameters.

If a developer wants to access the new features in `IKite2`, he or she can use that interface. But your object should also still support the `IKite` interface so that you do not break old code. In other words, you should consider creating one object server that supports at least two interfaces, one called `IKite` and the other called `IKite2`.

Poking holes in the theory behind this kind of system is easy, but the truth is that it works fairly well in practice. For instance, both `IKite` and `IKite2` can use the same implementation of most of their methods. Only the new or changed methods have to be reimplemented to support the new interface. So the system is not as wasteful as it might appear at first glance. Furthermore, the technique described here is a standard and easy-to-understand means of version control. You should note that standard OOP has no established convention for versioning classes. But here is a ready-made system that is so simple that it will always work and always prove robust.

So yes, I agree that interfaces have certain obvious limitations, but finding cases in which interfaces collapse under the weight of their own infrastructure is hard. Standard OOP, on the other hand, seems to have an answer to every question but no good way to put a lid on what can sometimes become a spiraling, geometrically increasing level of complexity.

Despite all the virtues of OOP, a large and very significant number of programmers have stuck with straight C programming simply because it provides such an admirable economy of design. Interfaces might provide a way for these "old-fashioned" programmers to start realizing some of the benefits of OOP without having to become mired in the complexities inherent in concepts such as polymorphism, virtual inheritance, and multiple inheritance.

Programming is difficult because of the complexity inherent in many of the real-world problems that need to be solved. Maybe it's best to not try to solve those complex problems with complex tools that are hard to manage. Maybe the best tools are the simplest tools that provide good flexibility and fast performance. After all, interfaces usually create code that is much faster than standard OOP. What slows OOP programs down is deep, complex hierarchies. By their very nature, interfaces tend to discourage the creation of deep hierarchies, thereby promoting relatively simple programs that have good performance characteristics. I could, of course, argue the case from the opposite side, but I'm playing devil's advocate here and saying a few words in favor of a system that is not promoted as frequently or loudly as standard OOP. Yet I do so not entirely as an academic exercise, but at least in part because I genuinely admire the system.

Creating and Using COM Interfaces

It's at last time to start digging into the specifics of creating a COM interface. In the next few pages, I will show you most of what you need to see how Delphi implements the core low-level functionality of a COM interface. Note, however, that I deal with IUnknown and reference counting in this chapter and begin talking about class factories in the next chapter.

Understanding GUIDs

Very briefly, a GUID is a 128-bit number that is guaranteed to be "statistically unique"—whatever that means. The basic assumption is that only one instance of each GUID occurs in the entire world. To achieve this result, Windows combines a unique number found on your network card with other information such as the current date to generate a number that is "guaranteed" to be unique. The algorithm for creating this number was created by the Open Software Foundation.

To create your own GUIDs, you should first initialize COM by calling the Windows API function CoInitialize. Then you can call CoCreateGuid to retrieve an instance of your unique GUID:

```
CoInitialize(nil);
CoCreateGuid(FGUID);
```

In 32-bit Windows, passing in anything but nil to CoInitialize is an error. CoCreateGuid takes a variable of type TGUID as an out parameter.

GUIDs are sometimes called IIDs, sometimes UUIDs, sometimes CLSIDs, and are referenced in Delphi by the TGUID type that is defined as follows in System.pas:

```
PGUID = ^TGUID;
TGUID = record
  D1: LongWord;
  D2: Word;
  D3: Word;
  D4: array[0..7] of Byte;
end;
```

Add all those fields together, and you will come up with 16 bytes.

On the CD that accompanies this book, you will find a program called `GuidGen` that shows how to create GUIDs. This program will also do several other things for you, such as convert a GUID into a Pascal record, a C record, or register a GUID for you in the Registry. The registration option will either register the GUID for you directly or else prepare a text file that you can use to register your objects. The following declaration for the class does all the work in the program:

```
TMakeGuid = class
private
  FClassInfo: TClassInfo;
  FGuid: TGuid;
  FClassName: string;
  function GUIDToString: string;
protected
public
  constructor Create(AClassName: string); virtual;
  function CreateClassInfo(FileName, ProgID, Description: string;
    UpdateReg: Boolean): TClassInfo;
  destructor Destroy; override;
  function GUIDToNewPascalRecord: string;
  function GUIDToOldPascalRecord: string;
  function GUIDToCStruct: string;
  function CreateRegFile: string;
  procedure UpdateRegistry(DoRegister: Boolean);
  function StringGUIDToPascalRecord(S: string): string;
  property GUID: TGUID read FGuid;
  property GuidAsString: string read GuidToString;
end;
```

`TMakeGuid` is declared and implemented in `CodeBox.pas`, from the `Units` directory on the CD that comes with this book.

All About the Registry and GUIDs

As far as COM objects are concerned, the Registry is a simple database that has one primary task: It associates a numerical value with each of the COM objects available on the system. This definition of the Registry is not complete, but it's what you need to know about it for now.

To work with the Registry, open `REGEDIT.EXE`. You will see something that looks like Figure 13.2.

Open the tree called `HKEY_CLASSES_ROOT`. Scroll down the list of entries until you come to one called `CLSID`. Open the `CLSID` tree and scroll down the entries, as shown in Figure 13.3.

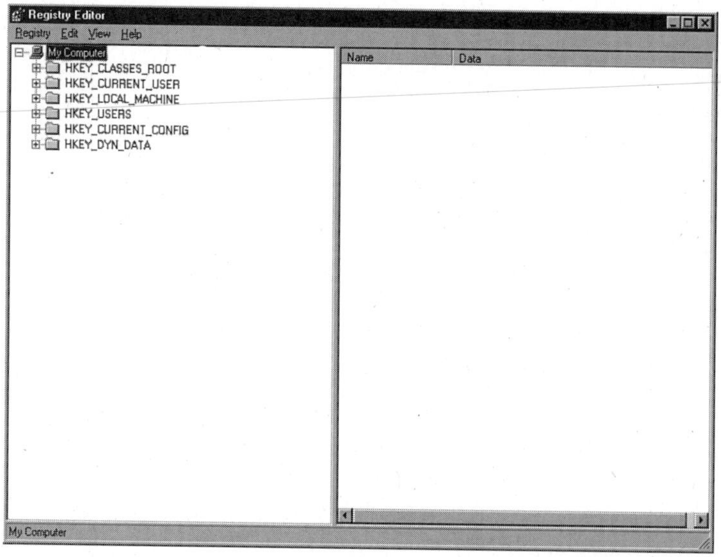

FIGURE 13.2

The Registry Editor displays this screen when it first opens.

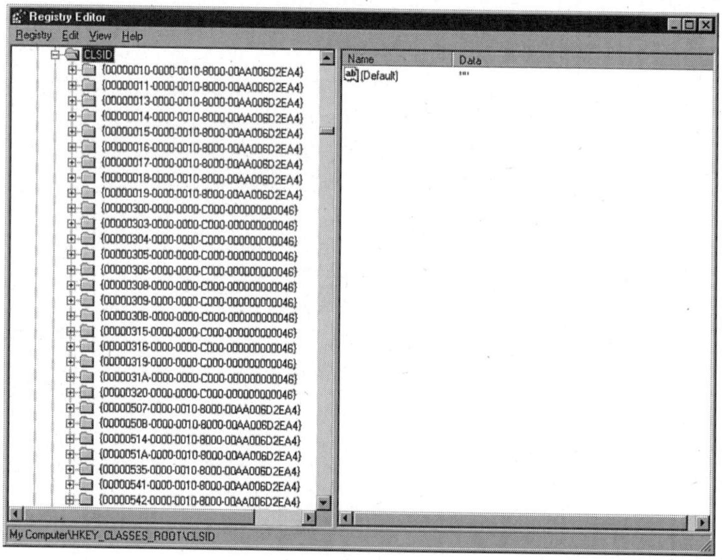

FIGURE 13.3

The CLSID section of HKEY_CLASSES_ROOT in the RegEdit program. The CLSIDs are on the left; the associated program, class, or file type is on the right.

You might notice that, as you scroll down the list, various familiar names appear on the right side of the RegEdit screen. For instance, the CLSID {0003000C-0000-0000-C000-000000000046} is associated with the Package program. Scroll down even further in HKEY_CLASSES_ROOT, and you come to an entry on the left side that reads Package. If you open the tree for the Package entry, as shown in Figure 13.4, you see a CLSID entry identical to the one you found earlier.

FIGURE 13.4

The Package entry in REGEDIT.EXE *has leaves called* CLSID, protocol, server, *and* verb.

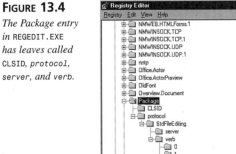

The point here is that you can find the CLSID of the Package program by looking it up by name in the Registry. Conversely, if you have the CLSID of an object, you can find out its name. Figure 13.4 suggests that other important pieces of information are also stored in RegEdit and associated with the Package program, but for now all you need to know is that it's a place to store CLSIDs.

If you want to insert an entry or set of entries in the Registry, you can often let Delphi perform the task for you automatically. You can also call certain VCL functions certain Windows API functions or the CreateRegKey function from the CodeBox unit. Alternatively, you can register a GUID by preparing text like the WIN32.REG file shown in Listing 13.4. Consider the following entry in that file:

```
HKEY_CLASSES_ROOT\MyObject\CLSID =
  {C9B0B160-1308-11cf-AB35-0000C07EBA2B}
```

I have divided this entry into two lines because of space considerations. You, however, should type it as a single line. The code shown here tells the Registry to create an entry called MyObject\CLSID in the Registry and to associate a particular CLSID with that entry.

LISTING 13.4 THE REGISTRATION FILE FOR A FILE CALLED SIMPOBJ.DLL

```
REGEDIT
HKEY_CLASSES_ROOT\MyObject1.0 = MyObject Test 1
HKEY_CLASSES_ROOT\MyObject1.0\CLSID =
```

continues

13

INTERFACES AND THE BASICS OF COM

LISTING 13.4   CONTINUED

```
{C9B0B160-1308-11cf-AB35-0000C07EBA2B}
HKEY_CLASSES_ROOT\MyObject = MyObject Test 1
HKEY_CLASSES_ROOT\MyObject\CurVer = MyObject1.0
HKEY_CLASSES_ROOT\MyObject\CLSID =
  {C9B0B160-1308-11cf-AB35-0000C07EBA2B}

HKEY_CLASSES_ROOT\CLSID\{C9B0B160-1308-11cf-AB35-0000C07EBA2B} =
  MyObject Test 1
HKEY_CLASSES_ROOT\CLSID\
  {C9B0B160-1308-11cf-AB35-0000C07EBA2B}\ProgID = MyObject1.0
HKEY_CLASSES_ROOT\CLSID\
  {C9B0B160-1308-11cf-AB35-0000C07EBA2B}\VersionIndependentProgID =
  MyObject
HKEY_CLASSES_ROOT\CLSID\{C9B0B160-1308-11cf-AB35-0000C07EBA2B}\
➥InProcServer32 = c:\src\unleash\chap30\simpdll\simpobj.dll
HKEY_CLASSES_ROOT\CLSID\{C9B0B160-1308-11cf-AB35-0000C07EBA2B}\
➥NotInsertable
```

In order to print this file in the book, I have had to break lines at some unusual locations. As a result, you might want to reference the source on the CD that accompanies this book.

Besides associating a CLSID with a name and a name with a CLSID, the Registry also associates a CLSID with a path to an executable or DLL:

```
HKEY_CLASSES_ROOT\
  CLSID\
    {C9B0B160-1308-11cf-AB35-0000C07EBA2B}\InProcServer32 =
      c:\src\unleash\chap30\simpdll\simpobj.dll
```

Given an entry like this in the Registry database, you can easily see how you can give the COM services a CLSID and then have COM in turn load a DLL or executable that is associated with the CLSID. The fact that you can easily create an error condition by specifying the wrong path in your REG file should also be obvious. If you are having trouble with one of the programs in this chapter, look carefully at the REG file and make sure that it points to the file you want to launch. You should also make sure this information is listed correctly in the Registry itself.

For now, I am not going to spend any more time discussing the Registry, though the subject will come up again frequently in the remaining chapters of this book. The key point to remember is that the Registry is just a database. This database serves a wide range of purposes, but one of the most important is that it associates CLSIDs with the names of programs and with other associated bits of information, such as version numbers and the location at which binaries are stored. In the next chapter, I will give explicit examples of how Delphi registers an object for you automatically.

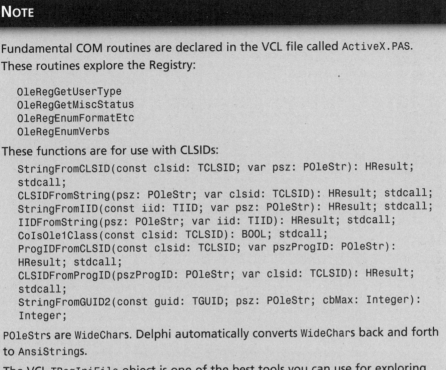

13

INTERFACES AND
THE BASICS OF
COM

Understanding `IUnknown`

`IUnknown` is the base class from which all COM classes must derive. Any interface that does not implement `IUnknown` is not a true COM interface. Because all Interface implementations in Delphi must support `IUnknown`, then it follows that Delphi interfaces always support `IUnknown`.

Consider the following simple interface that you worked with earlier in the chapter:

```
IMyInterface = interface
  function GetName: string;
end;
```

This object has a single method that returns a string. Assuming you have an instance of an object implementing this interface, then you can call this method off it:

```
var
  MyInterface: IMyInterface;
  S: string;
Begin
  MyInterface := TMyClass.Create;
  S := MyInterface.GetName;
end;
```

This example shows how to exercise the entire functionality of the interface.

At any rate, it *appears* to exercise the entire functionality of the object. But just as all Delphi classes descend from TObject, whether you will or no, so do all Delphi interfaces descend from IUnknown. As a result, the full declaration for this object looks like this:

```
IUnknown = interface
  ['{00000000-0000-0000-C000-000000000046}']
  function QueryInterface(const IID: TGUID; out Obj): HResult; stdcall;
  function _AddRef: Integer; stdcall;
  function _Release: Integer; stdcall;
end;

IMyInterface = interface(IUnknown)
  function GetName: string;
end;
```

Furthermore, the following code is entirely legal:

```
var
  MyInterface: IMyInterface;
  S: string;
Begin
  MyInterface := TMyClass.Create;
  S := MyInterface.GetName;
  MyInterface._AddRef;
  MyInterface._Release;
end;
```

What is going on here?

IUnknown is the mechanism that COM uses to do reference counting on its objects. The issue is really quite simple. A COM object can have more than one client. As a result, you should not destroy an object simply because one client has let go of the object. Instead, you should let go only when the entire object is destroyed. To understand exactly how this process works, you need to see the whole operation in action. Listings 13.5 and 13.6 show you how to proceed.

LISTING 13.5 A SIMPLE COM OBJECT THAT IMPLEMENTS IUnknown

```delphi
///////////////////////////////////////
// Purpose: Show how to implement IUnknown
// Project: UserUnknown1.dpr
// Copyright (c) 1998 by Charlie Calvert
//
unit UserUnknown1;

{-------------------------------------------------------------------
  TUserUnknown plays the same role in this program that
  TInterfacedObject plays in a standard Delphi application.
-------------------------------------------------------------------}
interface

type
  TNotifyEvent = procedure (Sender: TObject) of object;

  TUserUnknown = class(TObject, IUnknown)
  protected
    FRefCount: Integer;
    function QueryInterface(const IID: TGUID; out Obj): HResult; stdcall;
    function _AddRef: Integer; stdcall;
    function _Release: Integer; stdcall;
  public
    property RefCount: Integer read FRefCount;
  end;

  IName = interface(IUnknown)
    ['{87494220-1B29-11D2-9CE8-006008928EEF}']
    function GetName: string;
  end;

  INumber = interface(IUnknown)
    ['{87494222-1B29-11D2-9CE8-006008928EEF}']
    function GetNumber: integer;
  end;

  TMyClass = class(TUserUnknown, IName, INumber)
  private
    FOnDestroy: TNotifyEvent;
  public
    constructor Create;
    destructor Destroy; override;
    function GetName: string;
    function GetNumber: Integer;
    property OnDestroy: TNotifyEvent read FOnDestroy write FOnDestroy;
  end;

implementation
```

continues

13

INTERFACES AND
THE BASICS OF
COM

LISTING 13.5   CONTINUED

```
uses
  Windows, Dialogs;

{ TUserUnknown }

function TUserUnknown.QueryInterface(const IID: TGUID; out Obj): HResult;
const
  E_NOINTERFACE = $80004002;
begin
  if GetInterface(IID, Obj) then
    Result := 0
  else
    Result := E_NOINTERFACE;
end;

function TUserUnknown._AddRef: Integer;
begin
  Inc(FRefCount);
  Result := FRefCount;
end;

function TUserUnknown._Release: Integer;
begin
  Dec(FRefCount);
  Result := FRefCount;
  if Result = 0 then
    Destroy;
end;

{ TMyClass }

constructor TMyClass.Create;
begin
  inherited Create;
  MessageBeep(0);
end;

destructor TMyClass.Destroy;
begin
  if Assigned(FOnDestroy) then
    FOnDestroy(Self);
  inherited Destroy;
end;

function TMyClass.GetName: string;
begin
  Result := 'IName';
end;
```

```
function TMyClass.GetNumber: Integer;
begin
  Result := 42;
end;

end.
```

LISTING 13.6   A CLIENT FOR THE TUserUnknown COM OBJECT

```
unit Main;

interface

{------------------------------------------------------------------
  When using this program you must create TMyClass before you can
  retrieve an interface. If you release both interfaces, then you
  need to create MyClass again before you can retrieve a new
  interface.
------------------------------------------------------------------}
uses
  Windows, Messages, SysUtils,
  Classes, Graphics, Controls,
  Forms, Dialogs, StdCtrls,
  UserUnknown1, LabelEdit, ExtCtrls;

type
  TForm1 = class(TForm)
    CreateMyClassBtn: TButton;
    NameCreateBtn: TButton;
    NumberCreateBtn: TButton;
    NameReleaseBtn: TButton;
    NumberReleaseBtn: TButton;
    UpdateRefCountBtn: TButton;
    GroupBox1: TGroupBox;
    LabelEdit1: TLabelEdit;
    LabelEdit2: TLabelEdit;
    GroupBox2: TGroupBox;
    GroupBox3: TGroupBox;
    Bevel1: TBevel;
    procedure NameCreateBtnClick(Sender: TObject);
    procedure NumberCreateBtnClick(Sender: TObject);
    procedure UpdateRefCountBtnClick(Sender: TObject);
    procedure NameReleaseBtnClick(Sender: TObject);
    procedure CreateMyClassBtnClick(Sender: TObject);
    procedure NumberReleaseBtnClick(Sender: TObject);
  private
    FMyClass: TMyClass;
    FName: IName;
    FNumber: INumber;
```

13

INTERFACES AND
THE BASICS OF
COM

continues

LISTING 13.6   CONTINUED

```pascal
    procedure EnableButtons(Value: Boolean);
    procedure MyClassDestroyed(Sender: TObject);
  end;

var
  Form1: TForm1;

implementation


{$R *.DFM}

procedure TForm1.CreateMyClassBtnClick(Sender: TObject);
begin
  CreateMyClassBtn.Enabled := False;
  FMyClass := TMyClass.Create;
  UpdateRefCountBtnClick(nil);
  EnableButtons(True);
  FMyClass.OnDestroy := MyClassDestroyed;
end;

procedure TForm1.NameCreateBtnClick(Sender: TObject);
begin
  if FMyClass <> nil then
    FName := FMyClass;
  UpdateRefCountBtnClick(nil);
end;

procedure TForm1.EnableButtons(Value: Boolean);
begin
  NameCreateBtn.Enabled := Value;
  NumberCreateBtn.Enabled := Value;
  NameReleaseBtn.Enabled := Value;
  NumberReleaseBtn.Enabled := Value;
end;

procedure TForm1.MyClassDestroyed(Sender: TObject);
begin
  EnableButtons(False);
  CreateMyClassBtn.Enabled := True;
end;

procedure TForm1.NameReleaseBtnClick(Sender: TObject);
begin
  FName := nil;
  UpdateRefCountBtnClick(nil);
end;

procedure TForm1.NumberCreateBtnClick(Sender: TObject);
```

```
begin
  if FMyClass <> nil  then
    FNumber := FMyClass;
  UpdateRefCountBtnClick(nil);
end;

procedure TForm1.NumberReleaseBtnClick(Sender: TObject);
begin
  FNumber := nil;
  UpdateRefCountBtnClick(nil);
end;

{---------------------------------------------------------------
  This method shows a quick and dirty way to determine the refcount on
  any existing object. Just call _AddRef, check the return value,
  subtract one from it, then call _Release.
---------------------------------------------------------------}
procedure TForm1.UpdateRefCountBtnClick(Sender: TObject);
begin
  if FName <> nil then begin
    LabelEdit1.EditText := IntToStr(FName._AddRef - 1);
    FName._Release;
  end else
    LabelEdit1.EditText := '0';

  if FNumber <> nil then begin
    LabelEdit2.EditText := IntToStr(FNumber._AddRef - 1);
    FNumber._Release;
  end else
    LabelEdit2.EditText := '0';
end;

end.
```

This example, called UnknownByUser, allows you to create and destroy two interfaces. As you work with each interface, you can see the reference count on your server. If you pay close attention, you can even see exactly when the constructor and destructor for the server object gets called. The interface for the program is shown in Figure 13.5.

The whole purpose of the UnknownByUser program is to give you a chance to measure the life of two interfaces and to see how they are destroyed and created. Furthermore, you can see how reference counting works. I can think of no real-world application of this program other than as a teaching mechanism in this book.

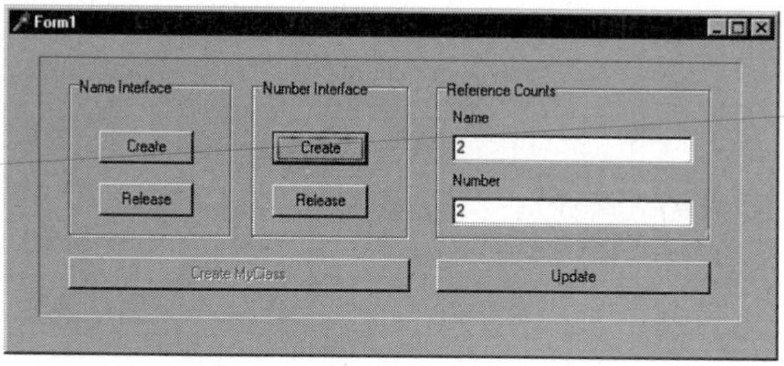

FIGURE 13.5

The
UnknownByUser
*program lets you
spy on the refer-
ence count of your
object.*

Implementing IUnknown

The most interesting thing about this program is that it shows how you can implement
IUnknown yourself. I want to stress that I do not recommend using it in your own programs. Just use TInterfacedObject or one of its descendants. But if you really want to
understand how IUnknown works, and you definitely should want to understand it, then
here is how to proceed.

The following declaration for the class takes the role usually allocated to
TInterfacedObject:

```
TUserUnknown = class(TObject, IUnknown)
protected
  FRefCount: Integer;
  function QueryInterface(const IID: TGUID; out Obj): HResult; stdcall;
  function _AddRef: Integer; stdcall;
  function _Release: Integer; stdcall;
public
  property RefCount: Integer read FRefCount;
end;
```

I want to stress that this object looks very much like TInterfacedObject. The declarations are not identical, but they are very similar. This similarity is hardly a coincidence
because the role of this object is very specialized.

The _AddRef method looks like this:

```
function TUserUnknown._AddRef: Integer;
begin
  Inc(FRefCount);
  Result := FRefCount;
end;
```

As you can see, this method does nothing more than increment the reference count on
the object. Each time an instance of the interfaces supported by a descendant of this class

is called, the _AddRef will be called automatically by Delphi. In other words, it is not the consumer of the interface that calls _AddRef, but the descendant of TUserUnknown.

The implementation for _Release is as follows:

```
function TUserUnknown._Release: Integer;
begin
  Dec(FRefCount);
  Result := FRefCount;
  if Result = 0 then
    Destroy;
end;
```

This method will be called whenever you assign nil to one of the interfaces you are working with:

```
MyInterface := nil;
```

You must understand that you would not normally call _Release yourself. Leave it up to Delphi to call _Release after you assign your interface to nil or after you let it go out of scope. (In this program, I will show you a case in which I feel it is okay to call _Release, but as you will see, that is a very special case.)

The final IUnknown method implemented by TUserUnknown is called QueryInterface:

```
function TUserUnknown.QueryInterface(const IID: TGUID; out Obj): HResult;
const
  E_NOINTERFACE = $80004002;
begin
  if GetInterface(IID, Obj) then
    Result := 0
  else
    Result := E_NOINTERFACE;
end;
```

In this case, I called a method of TObject called GetInterface. It will perform all the grunt work necessary in QueryInterface for you. If you didn't want to let Delphi handle the call automatically, then you could just return Self yourself:

```
Obj := Pointer(Self);
```

This approach would work, but it is not nearly as elegant as letting GetInterface set up a more economical version of your interface. In particular, GetInterface uses black magic to return a small VMT that contains only the methods in the interface that you request, while just typecasting Self as a pointer returns a pointer to all the methods in your object. Both techniques work, but one is obviously more economical. I'm not going to explore this subject further at this time because Delphi makes it very unlikely that you will ever have to implement `QueryInterface` yourself. I will talk about calling `QueryInterface` in the next chapter and also in the "Calling `CoCreateInstance`" section of Chapter 15, "Creating COM Automation Servers and Clients."

Now that you see how to implement `IUnknown`, you can probably better understand what is happening in the class that implements an interface:

```
IName = interface(IUnknown)
  ['{87494220-1B29-11D2-9CE8-006008928EEF}']
  function GetName: string;
end;

INumber = interface(IUnknown)
  ['{87494222-1B29-11D2-9CE8-006008928EEF}']
  function GetNumber: integer;
end;

TMyClass = class(TUserUnknown, IName, INumber)
private
  FOnDestroy: TNotifyEvent;
public
  constructor Create;
  destructor Destroy; override;
  function GetName: string;
  function GetNumber: Integer;
  property OnDestroy: TNotifyEvent read FOnDestroy write FOnDestroy;
end;
```

As you can see, `TMyClass` inherits the capability of `TUserUnknown`. It thereby automatically knows how to implement `IUnknown`. In fact, `TMyClass` implements three different interfaces: `IUnknown`, `IName`, and `INumber`.

Delphi will allow you to implement as many interfaces in one class as you desire. In this case, `TMyClass` implicitly implements `IUnknown` by inheriting the implementation from `TUserUnknown`, and it explicitly implements `IName` and `INumber`. Certain complications can arise if both interfaces declare a method with the same name. That subject will be covered later in the chapter in the section called "Method Resolution Clauses."

For now, all you really need to understand is that all implementations of Delphi interfaces need to include an implementation of `IUnknown`. Usually, you get that functionality by descending from `TInterfacedObject`. In this case, I have shown you what goes on in `TInterfacedObject` by creating a simulacrum of it in the `TUserUnknown` object. The program called `UnknownByVCL` on the CD that accompanies this book will show you exactly how `TInterfacedObject` is declared and allow you to easily step through the relevant code. I will not, however, discuss the `UnknownByVCL` program further in this book.

Assigning GUIDs to an Interface

You have no doubt noticed that the interfaces in this program have GUIDs associated with them:

```
IName = interface(IUnknown)
  ['{87494220-1B29-11D2-9CE8-006008928EEF}']
  function GetName: string;
end;

INumber = interface(IUNknown)
  ['{87494222-1B29-11D2-9CE8-006008928EEF}']
  function GetNumber: integer;
end;
```

This syntax allows you to easily and organically associate a GUID with a particular interface. To generate the GUIDs, I just ran the GuidGen program discussed earlier in this chapter. The GuidGen program is found in the Chap13 directory on the CD that comes with this book. In Delphi 3 and Delphi 4, you can also automatically generate a GUID by pressing Shift+Ctrl+G.

The great advantage of the syntax shown here is that it allows you to simply state a class name whenever you need to use a GUID in your programs. For instance, you now know that you have to pass a GUID in the first parameter when you call QueryInterface. To do so, you can simply write

```
var
  Unknown: IUnknown;
  Name: IName;
begin
  FName.QueryInterface(IUnknown, Unknown);
  FName.QueryInterface(IName, Name);
```

In other words, you can just state the type of a class whenever a GUID is required. This is possible simply because Delphi allows you to declare GUIDs as the first field in an interface declaration.

A Whole Lot of Magic Going On

In standard COM programming, you have to be very careful about when you call AddRef and when you call Release. Furthermore, you always have to call QueryInterface if you want to retrieve an instance of an interface.

A quick look at the UnknownByUser program shows that you really never have to call any of these methods inside a Delphi COM program. The reason for this is that the Delphi team wanted you to be able to forget about all this nonsense and simply create and destroy interfaces in more or less the same manner that you would create and release a

13

INTERFACES AND
THE BASICS OF
COM

standard object. The only significant difference is that when you work with Delphi inter-faces, you don't even have to bother destroying the object, as it will normally be destroyed for you automatically. In other words, Delphi interface programming is designed to be even simpler than standard Delphi object-based programming.

The last sentence of the preceding paragraph would probably come as a shock to many COM programmers. Low-level COM programming is notoriously difficult and tricky, and it usually is the source of innumerable hard-to-find bugs in standard COM. The sub-ject is so tricky because Microsoft is really asking you to perform a task that is usually performed by the compiler. In particular, Microsoft is asking the programmer to create and manage interfaces. In C++ and Delphi programming, objects are managed by the compiler; you need only fool with constructors, destructors, and the occasional new or delete operator. Standard COM programming, however, is different.

Delphi COM programming takes care of most of these details for you. You don't have to implement IUnknown; you can just inherit from TInterfacedObject. You don't have to call _AddRef or _Release; Delphi will make these calls for you.

Of course, sometimes you might want control over the lifetime of a COM object rather than letting Delphi release (and thereby often dispose) the object for you automatically. As I explained earlier, you can call _Release on an interface by setting it equal to nil:

```
FName := nil;
```

In one case in this program, I do call _Release explicitly:

```
procedure TForm1.UpdateRefCountBtnClick(Sender: TObject);
begin
  if FName <> nil then begin
    LabelEdit1.EditText := IntToStr(FName._AddRef - 1);
    FName._Release;
  end else
    LabelEdit1.EditText := '0';

  if FNumber <> nil then begin
    LabelEdit2.EditText := IntToStr(FNumber._AddRef - 1);
    FNumber._Release;
  end else
    LabelEdit2.EditText := '0';
end;
```

In this code, I want to show you the reference count on your object. In particular, I want to show that when you retrieve one interface, say FName, the reference count on your object is set to 1. If you then retrieve the FNumber interface, the count on the object goes up to 2. If you then set either interface equal to nil, the reference count goes down to 1, and if you set them both to nil, the reference count goes to zero, and MyClass is automatically destroyed:

```
function TUserUnknown._Release: Integer;
begin
  Dec(FRefCount);
  Result := FRefCount;
  if Result = 0 then
    Destroy;
end;
```

I'm showing you the `_Release` method again so you can be sure to notice the point at which `TMyClass` will be destroyed.

My point here is simply that the technique shown in `UpdateRefCountBtnClick` is an illustration of one common debugging mechanism used by COM programmers. Sooner or later, you are going to wonder exactly what the reference count might be on a particular interface. If that object is a Delphi interface, then you can probably access the public `RefCount` property of that object. (Both `TUserUnknown` and `TInterfacedObject` support this property.) However, if the object is made by another compiler, it may not be quite so easy to get the reference count, in which case you can use the technique shown here. The `UpdateRefCountBtnClick` method should also be interesting to you on general pedagogical grounds because it helps illustrate exactly how `_Release` works.

At this stage, you might think that creating and destroying COM objects in Delphi is almost preternaturally simple. However, you will find in the next chapter that some complications can arise when you are retrieving interfaces from objects created in non-Delphi programs. Those problems have solutions, but I want to put off discussing them until you have finished reading about the basic facts of Delphi interfaces and COM objects.

Notes of the **UnknownByUser** Program

The `UnknownByUser` program has one sly little trick that it pulls to keep the main form aware of the moment when the object that owns `IName` and `INumber` is destroyed. In particular, notice that I declare a method pointer called `OnDestroy` in the `TMyClass` definition:

```
TMyClass = class(TUserUnknown, IName, INumber)
private
  FOnDestroy: TNotifyEvent;
public
  constructor Create;
  destructor Destroy; override;
  function GetName: string;
  function GetNumber: Integer;
  property OnDestroy: TNotifyEvent read FOnDestroy write FOnDestroy;
end;
```

This pointer has absolutely nothing to do with either COM or with interfaces. I am simply employing a simple technique that allows me to tell the main form when the destructor for TMyClass gets called:

```
destructor TMyClass.Destroy;
begin
  if Assigned(FOnDestroy) then
    FOnDestroy(Self);
  inherited Destroy;
end;
```

As you can see, TMyClass.Destroy calls FOnDestroy if it is not equal to nil. Back in the main form, the FOnDestroy pointer is set equal to a method of TForm1:

```
procedure TForm1.CreateMyClassBtnClick(Sender: TObject);
begin
  CreateMyClassBtn.Enabled := False;
  FMyClass := TMyClass.Create;
  UpdateRefCountBtnClick(nil);
  EnableButtons(True);
  FMyClass.OnDestroy := MyClassDestroyed;
end;

procedure TForm1.MyClassDestroyed(Sender: TObject);
begin
  EnableButtons(False);
  CreateMyClassBtn.Enabled := True;
end;
```

The last line of the CreateMyClassBtnClick method assigns the FOnDestroy pointer of TMyClass to the TForm1.MyClassDestroyed method. When TMyClass.Destroy gets called, TForm1.MyClassDestroyed is called in turn. In response to this event, the UnknownByUser program disables all the buttons that can be used to manipulate IName and INumber, and it enables the button that can be used to create an instance of TMyClass:

```
procedure TForm1.EnableButtons(Value: Boolean);
begin
  NameCreateBtn.Enabled := Value;
  NumberCreateBtn.Enabled := Value;
  NameReleaseBtn.Enabled := Value;
  NumberReleaseBtn.Enabled := Value;
end;
```

The reason for this maneuver ought to be fairly obvious. In particular, you should not try to retrieve an instance of IName unless you have a valid instance of TMyClass. Pressing the CreateMyClassBtn will produce a valid instance of TMyClass and put the buttons in a state in which you can't create an instance of TMyClass but can retrieve or release IName and INumber. After you have released both IName and INumber, then TMyClass will automatically be destroyed, thereby completing the circle with another call to `MyClassDestroyed`.

By this time, you should begin to see how COM interfaces are implemented in Delphi. There is more to this story, but I am not going to pursue the tale any further at this point. Instead, I'm going to let the subject slide for a bit and wind up the chapter with a look at a few fancy and rather complicated facts about Delphi interfaces. Then in the next chapter, I will come back and show you how to take all this raw material, start adding in some class factories, and begin learning about the wide world of COM programming on the open desktop.

Advanced Interface Issues

In the last few pages of this chapter, I am going to show you some of the fine points of working with interfaces. In particular, I'm going to show why interfaces can never lead down that dark alley traveled by multiple inheritance. Interfaces make Delphi look like it is supporting multiple inheritance, and indeed it is supporting a kind of multiple inheritance. It is not, however, that dark ugly multiple inheritance that can keep you up three nights running hovered over the debugger. In this section of the chapter, I'll show you exactly why you won't end up in that kind of trouble.

Another subject covered in these last pages of the chapter is method resolution clauses. These little critters, mentioned earlier in the chapter, involve the case in which one class attempts to implement interfaces that have methods that sport the same name.

Finally, I'm going to cover the new `Implements` keyword, which allows you to use aggregation when implementing an interface. Aggregation can help you write clean code because it gives you a way to implement each interface in its own object yet create one object that packages the whole business together in one neat bundle for the user.

Multiple Interfaces in My Past

The `MultipleInterface` program from the CD that accompanies this book shows you how to handle deep interface hierarchies and how to use method resolution clauses. The code for the program is shown in Listings 13.7 and 13.8.

LISTING 13.7 ComplexObject.pas ILLUSTRATES SOME OF THE FINE POINTS OF INTERFACE PROGRAMMING

```
//////////////////////////////////////
// Purpose: Declare and implement a simple interface
// Project: SimpleInterface.dpr
```

continues

LISTING 13.7   CONTINUED

```
//
unit ComplexObject;

interface

type
  IMyInterface = interface
    function GetName: string;
  end;

  TMyClass = class(TInterfacedObject, IMyInterface)
    function GetName: string;
  end;

{-------------------------------------------------------------------
  IMyInterface appears twice in this class's hierarchy, but
  only TMyComplexClass.GetName will be called. There are not
  two implementations of GetName in the hierarchy of this class,
  thus it is not true multiple inheritance.
-------------------------------------------------------------------}
  TMyComplexClass = class(TMyClass, IMyInterface)
    function GetName: string;
  end;

  IMyOtherInterface = interface
    function GetName: string;
  end;

{-------------------------------------------------------------------
  Show how to use a method resolution clause
-------------------------------------------------------------------}
  TMyMultipleInterface = class(TInterfacedObject,
    IMyInterface, IMyOtherInterface)
    function IMyOtherInterface.GetName = MyOtherInterfaceGetName;
    function GetName: string;
    function MyOtherInterfaceGetName: string;
  end;

implementation

function TMyClass.GetName: string;
begin
  Result := 'TMyClass.MyInterface';
end;

{ TMyComplexClass }

function TMyComplexClass.GetName: string;
begin
  Result := 'TMyComplexClass.GetName';
```

```
end;

{ TMyMultipleInterface }

function TMyMultipleInterface.GetName: string;
begin
  Result := 'IMyInterface';
end;

function TMyMultipleInterface.MyOtherInterfaceGetName: string;
begin
  Result := 'IMyOtherInterface';
end;

end.
```

LISTING 13.8 THE MAIN FORM FOR THE MultipleInterface PROGRAM

```
//////////////////////////////////////
// Purpose: Use an interface declared in SimpleObject.pas
// Project: SimpleInterface
// Copyright (c) 1998 by Charlie Calvert
//
unit Main;

interface

uses
  Windows, Messages, SysUtils,
  Classes, Graphics, Controls,
  Forms, Dialogs, StdCtrls;

type
  TForm1 = class(TForm)
    SimpleInterfaceBtn: TButton;
    ComplexInterface1Btn: TButton;
    MultipleClassBtn: TButton;
    procedure SimpleInterfaceBtnClick(Sender: TObject);
    procedure ComplexInterface1BtnClick(Sender: TObject);
    procedure MultipleClassBtnClick(Sender: TObject);
  end;

var
  Form1: TForm1;

implementation

uses
  ComplexObject;
```

continues

13

INTERFACES AND THE BASICS OF COM

LISTING 13.8   CONTINUED

```
{$R *.DFM}

{- - - - - - - - - - - - - - - - - - - - - - - - - - - - - - - - - - - - - - - - - - - - - - -
  Retrieve an interface, and call one of its methods. This is the
  simple example meant to set off the complex example shown in
  ComplexInterface1BtnClick.
- - - - - - - - - - - - - - - - - - - - - - - - - - - - - - - - - - - - - - - - - - - - - - -}
procedure TForm1.SimpleInterfaceBtnClick(Sender: TObject);
var
  MyInterface: IMyInterface;
begin
  MyInterface := TMyClass.Create;
  ShowMessage(MyInterface.GetName);
end;


{- - - - - - - - - - - - - - - - - - - - - - - - - - - - - - - - - - - - - - - - - - - - - - -
  Create an instance of the Complex class and call its
  GetName method. This shows that we are not working
  with true multiple inheritance. When you create
  TMyComplexClass, you get the Complex version of the
  GetName method, and the original version is
  obliterated. Look at ComplexObject.pas to see what
  is happening. This is why you don't have to worry about
  multiple inheritance tripping you up in Delphi.
- - - - - - - - - - - - - - - - - - - - - - - - - - - - - - - - - - - - - - - - - - - - - - -}
procedure TForm1.ComplexInterface1BtnClick(Sender: TObject);
var
  MyInterface: IMyInterface;
begin
  MyInterface := TMyComplexClass.Create;
  ShowMessage(MyInterface.GetName);
end;



{- - - - - - - - - - - - - - - - - - - - - - - - - - - - - - - - - - - - - - - - - - - - - - -
  This routine shows how to work with method resolution
  clauses.
- - - - - - - - - - - - - - - - - - - - - - - - - - - - - - - - - - - - - - - - - - - - - - -}
procedure TForm1.MultipleClassBtnClick(Sender: TObject);
var
  MultipleInterface: TMyMultipleInterface;
begin
  MultipleInterface := TMyMultipleInterface.Create;
  ShowMessage(MultipleInterface.GetName + #13 +
    MultipleInterface.MyOtherInterfaceGetName);
end;

end.
```

This program has a very simple interface with three buttons on it, as shown in Figure 13.6. Clicking any of the buttons on the form allows the user to exercise the interface supplied in the ComplexObject.pas unit. This program also has no real-world application outside of teaching someone how interfaces work.

FIGURE 13.6

The simple main form for the TMultipleInterface *program.*

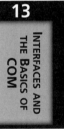

TMyComplexClass gets its name because it has two instances of IMyInterface in its inheritance tree:

```
IMyInterface = interface
  function GetName: string;
end;

TMyClass = class(TInterfacedObject, IMyInterface)
  function GetName: string;
end;

TMyComplexClass = class(TMyClass, IMyInterface)
  function GetName: string;
end;
```

In particular, notice that TMyClass implements IMyInterface, and so does TMyComplexClass. Because TMyComplexClass inherits from TMyClass, this makes it appear that TMyComplexClass has two implementations of GetName in it. Though not an exact duplicate of the truly troublesome situations, nonetheless, this kind of situation can lead to sleepless nights over the debugger in standard C++ multiple inheritance programming.

In this program, TMyComplexClass knows nothing about the TMyClass implementation of the GetName method. When Delphi finds two implementations of the same class in a hierarchy, only the most recent one is kept, and any inherited instances are discarded. As such, things are kept very clean and simple. You always know which instance of a particular method is going to execute.

You should also note that the Delphi form of inheritance is kept simple because you can inherit from multiple interfaces, but from only one class. This means that you can't have two implementations of a single interface coming at you from two different directions, as it were. Any implementations of an interface can only come up a single line of inheritance, and if more than one implementation of an interface appears in that line of inheritance, then it is only the most recent one that is active.

13

INTERFACES AND THE BASICS OF COM

Method Resolution Clauses

The TMyMultipleInterface implements two interfaces, and both of these interfaces have methods with the same name:

```
IMyInterface = interface
  function GetName: string;
end;

IMyOtherInterface = interface
  function GetName: string;
end;

TMyMultipleInterface = class(TInterfacedObject,
  IMyInterface, IMyOtherInterface)
  function IMyOtherInterface.GetName = MyOtherInterfaceGetName;
  function GetName: string;
  function MyOtherInterfaceGetName: string;
end;
```

This particular case may look a lot like the programming problem discussed in the preceding section, but it is fundamentally different. In this case, you don't have two implementations of the GetName method. Instead, you have a problem because two interfaces have declared a method with the same name.

To handle this problem, you can declare a method resolution clause that assigns the implementation of a particular interface method declaration to a method of your current class that sports a slightly different name:

```
function IMyOtherInterface.GetName = MyOtherInterfaceGetName;
```

Here the IMyOtherInterface.GetName method will be implemented by a method called MyOtherInterfaceGetName. If you look at the declaration for TMyMultipleInterface, you will see that the IMyInterface.GetName method is handled by TMyMultipleInterface.GetName.

All in all, digesting this matter is pretty simple. Nothing is complicated about method resolution clauses other than simply remembering that they exist. You may not get hit by the problem shown here right away, but sooner or later you are going to stumble across it. If you can just remember that this is the solution, then you will have it made.

> **NOTE**
>
> For some reason, I have a terrible time remembering the exact syntax for method resolution clauses. But I have managed to keep the name of the technology tucked away in my brain. Fortunately, in this case, the online help can

come to your rescue. Just plug the phrase `method resolution clause` into the Index page of the online help, and you will be taken to an example of the syntax.

The `Implements` Directive

The last technique I want to show you in this chapter involves a new keyword called `Implements`. Delphi R&D guru and fellow Sams author Steve Teixeira first told me about this addition to the language, and I have to admit that when he told me about it, I didn't pay it much mind.

At the time, I was going out to show the Delphi 4 beta to some close partners, and I said to Steve, "Okay, the new language features are function overloading, dynamic arrays, default parameters, and the new `Integer` types. I've got everything, right?"

Steve shook his head and said, "Don't forget the `Implements` keyword!"

"The `Implements` keyword? What's that?"

Steve then said something or another about COM and aggregation and a bunch of stuff that eluded my grasp like bats flitting over a candlelit cocktail party on someone's suburban patio. Despite the lucidity of his explanation, I just wasn't in the mood to focus, and I left only half understanding what he said, his thoughts fluttering about dimly just beyond the reach of my fingers.

A few exhausting days later, I was several thousand miles from home trying to explain the `Implements` keyword to a bunch of developers and making a general hash of it. After I was done, international Delphi author and Wunderkind Dick Lantim came up to me and said (I'm paraphrasing quite roughly): "Look, Charlie, this thing isn't that complicated. The great advantage of the `Implements` directive is that it lets you implement an object in its own class. Then you can use aggregation to fold that class into your current object rather than trying to do things through that crazy multiple inheritance–like technology."

Finally, a shaft of light penetrated into the dim recesses of the fog-enshrouded foliage of my brain, and I at last saw the biggest and most obvious benefit of this technology. I tell you all this just because it is the end of another long chapter, and I want to try to get you focused on one last problem. This one seems a bit tricky at first, but after you concentrate on it, you'll find that it's not really so bad. Just take a look at Listing 13.9.

13

INTERFACES AND
THE BASICS OF
COM

LISTING 13.9 THE PropObject.pas FILE SHOWS HOW TO USE THE Implements
DIRECTIVE

```
////////////////////////////////////////
// Purpose: Declare and implement a simple interface
// Project: PropertyImplement.dpr
// Copyright (c) 1998 by Charlie Calvert
//
unit PropObject;

interface

type
  IMyPropInterface = interface
    function GetName: string;
  end;

  TMyPropInterface = class
    function GetName: string;
  end;

  TMyClass = class(TInterfacedObject, IMyPropInterface)
  private
    FMyPropInterface: TMyPropInterface;
  public
    constructor Create;
    property MyPropInterface: TMyPropInterface
      read FMyPropInterface
      write FMyPropInterface
      implements IMyPropInterface;
  end;

implementation

function TMyPropInterface.GetName: string;
begin
  Result := 'MyPropInterface';
end;

{ TMyClass }

constructor TMyClass.Create;
begin
  inherited Create;
  MyPropInterface := TMyPropInterface.Create;
end;

end.
```

This program has the same front end as the `SimpleInterface` program that I showed you at the beginning of this chapter. As a result, I'm not going to bother talking about what the program looks like or how it behaves. All it does is call the `TMyPropInterface.GetName` method through a standard Delphi class and through an interface.

What's important about this program is that it uses a class called `TMyPropInterface` to implement `IMyPropInterface`. Then `TMyClass` declares a single property called `MyPropInterface` that provides access to `TMyPropInterface`, and hence to any and all implemented methods of `IMyPropInterface`. In this case, `IMyPropInterface` supports only the methods of `IUnknown` plus our old friend `GetName`, but obviously greater benefits would be derived if `IMyPropInterface` were more complex.

Note that I create an instance of `TMyPropInterface` in the class's constructor. Furthermore, note that `TMyPropInterface` does not have to support any of the syntax normally associated with interfaces:

```
TMyPropInterface = class
  function GetName: string;
end;
```

Just from looking at this declaration you would not know that this class could implement an interface. But by using the `Implements` keyword and the syntax shown in this example, you find that it can.

On the client side, you can write code that looks like this:

```
procedure TForm1.UseInterface1BtnClick(Sender: TObject);
var
  MyInterface: IMyPropInterface;
  MyClass: TMyClass;
begin
  MyClass := TMyClass.Create;
  MyInterface := MyClass;
  ShowMessage(MyInterface.GetName);
end;
```

This code is no different from the standard code you would write for any of the interface implementations shown earlier.

The difference between this example and the examples shown earlier in the chapter is that you do not have to fold in the implementation of `IMyPropInterface` into the `TMyClass` implementation. Instead, you can implement the methods in their own class, which leads to much cleaner, much easier-to-read code.

Other benefits of this technology include the fact that you can assign an implementation of an interface to a class at runtime:

```
MyClass := TMyClass.Create;
MyClass.MyPropInterface := TMyPropInterface.Create;
MyInterface := MyClass;
ShowMessage(MyInterface.GetName);
```

Using this syntax, you could assign any one of a number of different implementations to the property, depending on your needs. For instance, if you were implementing some kind of online service, you could create a flexible object that would use a modem or TCP/IP depending on the implementation you assigned to one of its properties. In other words, one implementation would have methods that used TCP/IP, whereas another might have methods that used a modem-based transport.

You can declare a property of this type to be either a class or an interface. I've already shown you how to work with a property that uses a class. If you want to use an interface, then you would first create the class that hosts the interface and then assign it to the property you created just as you assign `MyInterface` to `MyClass` in the example shown here. The point is that it doesn't matter how a particular property supports an interface; all that matters is that the property does support that interface.

You could rewrite the current example as follows to support the idea of declaring property directly as an interface:

```
type
  IMyPropInterface = interface
    function GetName: string;
  end;

  TMyPropInterface = class(TInterfacedObject, IMyPropInterface)
    function GetName: string;
  end;

  TMyClass = class(TInterfacedObject, IMyPropInterface)
  private
    FMyPropInterface: IMyPropInterface;
  public
    constructor Create;
    property MyPropInterface: IMyPropInterface
      read FMyPropInterface
      write FMyPropInterface
      implements IMyPropInterface;
  end;
```

Here you can see that `MyPropInterface` is declared to be not of type `TMyPropInterface`, but of type `IMyPropInterface`. Meanwhile, I have changed the declaration of `TMyPropInterface` so that it fully implements `IMyPropInterface`. This allows me to write code that looks like this on the client side:

```
procedure TForm1.UseInterface1BtnClick(Sender: TObject);
var
  MyInterface: IMyPropInterface;
  MyClass: TMyClass;
begin
  MyClass := TMyClass.Create;
  MyClass.MyPropInterface := TMyPropInterface.Create;
  MyInterface := MyClass;
  ShowMessage(MyInterface.GetName);
end;
```

I like the syntax shown in this latter example because it forces me to make explicit the relationship between TMyPropInterface and IMyPropInterface:

```
TMyPropInterface = class(TInterfacedObject, IMyPropInterface)
  function GetName: string;
end;
```

Unlike the earlier example in which TMyPropInterface could be used to implement IMyPropInterface without once mentioning the interface, this example makes explicit the tie between the two declarations. To my way of thinking, this example is a cleaner, better documented way to write code.

Virtual Method Tables

I have gone through a rather long description of COM and interfaces without ever once mentioning VTables. VTables play a key role in the implementation of interface technology, so I will say a few general words about them before closing this chapter.

A virtual method table is sometimes called a VTable, and C programmers occasionally abbreviate it as vtbl. A VTable is what you get when you declare an object entirely from virtual methods. In short, if you declare an object with all or some of its methods declared as virtual or virtual abstract, then you have created a virtual method table. A slightly different take on the subject would define a virtual method table as just a record whose members are all method pointers.

Earlier in this chapter, you learned that an interface was similar to an object declared as a set of public virtual abstract methods. As a matter of fact, it just so happens that an interface is laid out exactly like a virtual abstract class declared in Object Pascal or the Microsoft or Borland versions of C++. (By *exactly*, I mean an absolute one-to-one correspondence exists between the elements of each construct. In a computer's memory, they look identical.)

You can use a virtual abstract class to define a COM object in Object Pascal. The compiler will generate code to access the methods of this class directly, as if it were a standard Object Pascal class. You can then call the methods of a COM object directly from

Object Pascal or C++. These methods are called according to the order in which they are declared, and not according to the names of the actual methods involved.

> **NOTE**
>
> You may be wondering how you can call the methods of an object defined as virtual abstract. The trick is to first define the virtual abstract interface in Object Pascal either in a virtual abstract class declaration or in an interface. Then you make a COM call and retrieve a pointer to the implementation of this class that resides in a COM object.
>
> The next step is to set a pointer to your interface or abstract class equal to a pointer to its COM-based implementation. At this stage, calls to the virtual abstract methods will succeed. The trick works because the VTable describing the COM implementation exactly matches the VTable describing the interface or virtual abstract declaration in your Object Pascal code. By simply assigning your interface declaration to a COM-based implementation, you trick the compiler into making fast calls into your object.
>
> A COM object implemented in a separate process, or on a separate machine, is never actually present in your client program. Instead, a proxy for that object is available, and when you call this proxy's methods, it is the job of COM or DCOM to use either local procedure calls or remote procedure calls to span the gap between the two processes. You will hear more on this subject in the next few chapters.

Summary

In this chapter, you learned about the basics of COM and interfaces. You saw how to implement one or more classes in a single interface and how to access those implementations from a client. You also learned about method resolution clauses, the new `Implements` directive, and several other fine points of interface programming.

This chapter also discussed COM in general terms, describing some of the benefits that can be derived from this technology. A number of those benefits involve some pretty fancy concepts such as ActiveX controls and DCOM, where the latter technology allows you to call an object's methods remotely from another machine and get function results or parameters sent back to you over the network. It seems like a long leap from the topics discussed in this chapter to something such as an ActiveX control or to DCOM. However, I believe you will find that many of the most complicated subjects involved with this technology are already in your ken. In fact, before the next chapter is half over, you will start to see how you can put this stuff to use in your own programs.

I should perhaps add that you probably could have gotten up to speed on ActiveX controls and perhaps even DCOM without understanding all the material in this chapter. However, having this knowledge under your belt will enable you to get a much deeper and much more useful understanding of all Delphi's COM-related technologies. Having a good base to build on is often the key to creating a robust infrastructure. After reading this chapter, you should be ready to set forth on a productive career as a COM programmer.

13

INTERFACES AND THE BASICS OF COM

CHAPTER 14

TComObject, TTypedComObject, and Type Libraries

IN THIS CHAPTER

This chapter takes the primarily theoretical material covered in the preceding chapter and shows how you can apply it to creating COM objects that you can use in your programs. In particular, this chapter covers the following:

- Using the `TComObject` class to place COM objects in DLLs
- Using type libraries to document the structure of an object

It might also be helpful if I tell you what isn't covered in this chapter. This chapter does not cover either automation or the `IDispatch` interface. Those subjects are covered in Chapter 15, "Creating COM Automation Servers and Clients." Type libraries are also revisited in more depth in that chapter.

Sample Programs

This chapter contains three sample programs:

- `SystemInfo`—This example features a simple DLL that contains a COM object that can be used to query a system about some of its basic capabilities.
- `VarArray`—This example shows how to use `Variant` arrays.
- `TypedSystemInfo`—This program shows how to create a COM object that contains a type library. The client program attaches to a DLL containing the COM object and then retrieves the COM object and calls its methods. The program also retrieves information about the methods in the COM object and about the parameters passed to the methods. It even finds the help file for the object. The point of this example is to show how you can find out everything you need to know about a COM object, as long as the creator took the minimal steps necessary to document it in a type library.

TComObject

`TComObject` is the class you should descend from if you want to create a simple object for use in your current or other Delphi applications, or for use in C++ applications. As a rule, `TComObject` classes reside in a DLL. They can also exist inside your own program. `TComObject` direct descendants cannot, however, easily go inside one application and be called from a second application. In other words, they are not OLE automation classes.

Taking just another moment to consider what you can and cannot do with `TComObject` direct descendants might be worthwhile. If you want to control another executable or create objects that can be used from a second executable, you want to descend from `TAutoObject`, not from `TComObject`. `TComObject` is no good for cross-program communication because it has no support for marshaling inside it. However, if you want to create your own implementation of IMarshal, you can use this class in programs that practice interprocess communication.

TComObject insists that its consumers know about interfaces. Therefore, languages that don't really understand objects, such as VB, aren't going to have much use for TComObject and its direct descendants. VB and VBA want automatable objects that support IDispatch. Among Borland's tools, only Object Pascal and C++ are smart enough to understand TComObject. I believe that among Microsoft's tools, only C++ would be smart enough to understand it.

Despite its limited range of uses, TComObject provides an excellent means of creating objects, placing them in DLLs, and sharing them between Delphi and C++ programs. In particular, COM objects have the ability to register themselves. As a result, you can register each DLL and each object in each DLL in one central place. This capability puts an end to the nonsense about wondering whether a DLL is on your current path or of wondering whether you have more than one copy of a DLL on your path or on your system. If you are using a registered COM DLL, only one possible DLL can respond to your calls. Furthermore, you have a simple and easy way of knowing where it resides.

TComObject has a descendant called TTypedComObject that supports a type library. You can use a type library to fully describe the methods in a class in such a way that the descriptions can be easily read by a variety of programs and by other objects.

The combined capabilities of TComObject and TTypedComObject give you the means to know exactly where your DLL is located. You can access the DLL even if it is not on the path, and you can query the DLL to find out about all its interfaces, its methods, and even the number, names, and types of its parameters. Furthermore, if a help file is associated with the object, it can be retrieved automatically. You can even retrieve brief comments about each method or interface supported by an object.

The machines I'm using these days have between 4 and 8GB of disk space, and between 128 and 196MB of RAM. They are nice but not top-of-the-line machines. Today's high-end machines become tomorrow's low-end machines. In a world full of 8GB hard drives, there is plenty of room to store information about the objects we are using.

By documenting objects in type libraries and the Registry, programmers provide a means to track resources, to avoid duplication, and to discover new resources available on a system. TComObject and TTypedComObject may appear to be fairly humble at first, but if you look at them for a while, you will see that they are actually very powerful tools that can improve our ability to create robust systems.

A final reason for using TComObject is that it can support licensing. Licensing provides a means of placing a DLL on a system and yet providing access to only a limited set of users. This issue will be very important for certain types of developers, but I will not explore it in this book. You can refer to the Microsoft MSDN for additional information on this subject.

Putting Commonly Used Interfaces in a DLL

One of the most useful things you can do with COM is create DLLs that contain objects that can be reused by multiple applications. In this section, I will create a simple COM DLL and use it from Delphi.

Unlike the COM objects you saw in the preceding chapter, this object descends not from TInterfacedObject, but from TComObject. The primary difference between the two is that TComObject supports a class factory, so it can be stored in a DLL that will be located and launched automatically. The source for the program is shown in Listings 14.1 through 14.3.

LISTING 14.1   THE Globals UNIT DECLARES INFORMATION USEFUL TO BOTH THE DLL AND THE EXECUTABLE THAT USES IT

```
//////////////////////////////////////////
// Purpose: Declare an interface
// Project: SystemInfo.dpr
// Copyright (c) 1998 by Charlie Calvert
//
unit Globals;

{-------------------------------------------------------------------
  This file is designed to be linked into either a DLL or the executable
  that uses the DLL. It declares any information that will be useful
  to both entities.
-------------------------------------------------------------------}

interface

uses
  ActiveX;


const
  Class_SystemHelp: TGUID = '{9C2E0720-1C96-11D2-9CE8-006008928EEF}';
  IID_ISystemInfo: TGUID = '{137BFDC0-1C9A-11D2-9CE8-006008928EEF}';

type
  TDriveInfoRec = record
    SectorsPerCluster, BytesPerSector: Cardinal;
    NumberOfFreeClusters, TotalNumberOfClusters: Cardinal;
    TotalFree, FreeAvailable, TotalSpace: LargeInt;
```

```
  end;

  ISystemInfo = interface
    ['{137BFDC0-1C9A-11D2-9CE8-006008928EEF}']
    function ComputerName: WideString; safecall;
    procedure DriveInfo(out TotalCount: Integer;
      out DriveInfo: Variant);
    function GetName: WideString; safecall;
  end;

implementation

end.
```

LISTING 14.2   THE `ISystemInfo` INTERFACE PROVIDES SERVICES FOR PROGRAMS THAT
WANT TO CHECK ON THE STATUS OF A MACHINE

```
/////////////////////////////////////////
// Purpose: COM Object in a DLL
// Project: SystemInfo
// Copyright (c) 1998 by Charlie Calvert
//
unit SystemHelp1;

interface

{-------------------------------------------------------------------
  A simple program designed to be stored in a DLL and accessed from
  an executable. This interface does not support either type libraries
  or automation; it's just meant to be used inside a DLL.
-------------------------------------------------------------------}

uses
  Windows, ActiveX, ComObj,
  Globals;

type
  TSystemHelp = class(TComObject, ISystemInfo)
  protected
    function ComputerName: WideString; safecall;
    procedure DriveInfo(out TotalCount: Integer;
      out DriveInfo: Variant);
    function GetName: WideString; safecall;
  end;

implementation

uses
  ComServ, SysUtils;
```

LISTING 14.2 CONTINUED

```
function TSystemHelp.ComputerName: WideString;
var
  Len: DWord;
  S: PChar;
begin
  Len := MAX_COMPUTERNAME_LENGTH + 1;
  GetMem(S, Len);
  if GetComputerName(S, Len) then
    Result := S
  else
    raise Exception.Create('Could not get computer name.');
  FreeMem(S, Len);
end;

procedure TSystemHelp.DriveInfo(out TotalCount: Integer;
  out DriveInfo: Variant);
const
  Size = 28 * 5;   // 26 letters plus 2 extra times plenty of room
                   // for letters
var
  DriveStrings, TempDriveStrings: PChar;
  DriveType: string;
  SectorsPerCluster, BytesPerSector: Cardinal;
  NumberOfFreeClusters, TotalNumberOfClusters: Cardinal;
  FreeAvailable, TotalSpace: LargeInt;
  TotalFree: LargeInt;
  DriveInfoRec: TDriveInfoRec;
  ADrive: Variant;
  TempVar: Variant;
  TempPtr: Pointer;
begin
  TotalCount := 0;
  DriveInfo := VarArrayCreate([0, 28], VarVariant);
  GetMem(DriveStrings, Size);
  GetLogicalDriveStrings(Size, DriveStrings);
  TempDriveStrings := DriveStrings;

  while StrLen(TempDriveStrings) <> 0 do begin
    ADrive := VarArrayCreate([0, 3], VarVariant);
    case GetDriveType(TempDriveStrings) of
      DRIVE_UNKNOWN: DriveType := 'Unknown';
      DRIVE_NO_ROOT_DIR: DriveType := 'Not a root drive';
      DRIVE_REMOVABLE: DriveType := 'Removable';
      DRIVE_FIXED: DriveType := 'Hard Drive';
      DRIVE_REMOTE: DriveType := 'Network';
      DRIVE_CDROM: DriveType := 'CDROM';
      DRIVE_RAMDISK: DriveType := 'RAMDisk';
    else
      DriveType := 'Error';
```

```
    end;

    ADrive[0] := AnsiString(TempDriveStrings);
    ADrive[1] := DriveType;

    GetDiskFreeSpace(TempDriveStrings, SectorsPerCluster, BytesPerSector,
      NumberOfFreeClusters, TotalNumberOfClusters);

    DriveInfoRec.SectorsPerCluster := SectorsPerCluster;
    DriveInfoRec.BytesPerSector := BytesPerSector;
    DriveInfoRec.NumberOfFreeClusters := NumberOfFreeClusters;
    DriveInfoRec.TotalNumberOfClusters := TotalNumberOfClusters;

    GetDiskFreeSpaceEx(TempDriveStrings, FreeAvailable,
      TotalSpace, @TotalFree);
    DriveInfoRec.FreeAvailable := FreeAvailable;
    DriveInfoRec.TotalSpace := TotalSpace;
    DriveInfoRec.TotalFree := TotalFree;

    TempVar := VarArrayCreate([0, SizeOf(TDriveInfoRec)], VarByte);
    TempPtr := VarArrayLock(TempVar);
    Move(DriveInfoRec, TempPtr^, SizeOf(TDriveInfoRec));
    VarArrayUnlock(TempVar);
    ADrive[2] := TempVar;

    DriveInfo[TotalCount] := ADrive;
    Inc(TempDriveStrings, StrLen(TempDriveStrings) + 1);
    Inc(TotalCount);
  end;
  FreeMem(DriveStrings, Size);
end;

function TSystemHelp.GetName: WideString;
begin
  Result := 'TSystemHelp';
end;

initialization
TComObjectFactory.Create(
    ComServer,
    TSystemHelp,
    Class_SystemHelp,
    'SystemHelp',
    'Get information about a computer',
    ciMultiInstance,
    tmSingle);
end.
```

LISTING 14.3   THE MAIN FORM FOR THE CLIENT PROGRAM THAT USES THE SystemInfo INTERFACE

```
/////////////////////////////////////
// Purpose: Use the SystemInfo interface
// Project: SystemClient.dpr
// Copyright (c) 1998 by Charlie Calvert
//
unit MainClient;

{--------------------------------------------------------------
  This is the client program that uses the ISystemInfo interface
  declared in Global.pas. The interface reports on system status.

  The purpose of this program is to show how to access a COM object
  that is stored in a DLL.

  This program uses TCCLabelEdit component from the Unleash package
  on the CD that comes with this book. You have to install that
  package or this program will not run. (If you really can't find
  the package, the component is nothing more than an Edit control
  and Label control tied together.)
--------------------------------------------------------------}
interface

uses
  Windows, Messages, SysUtils,
  Classes, Graphics, Controls,
  Forms, Dialogs, StdCtrls,
  LabelEdit, ExtCtrls, Globals;

type
  TForm1 = class(TForm)
    ConnectBtn: TButton;
    Bevel1: TBevel;
    CCLabelEdit1: TCCLabelEdit;
    CCLabelEdit2: TCCLabelEdit;
    Memo1: TMemo;
    procedure ConnectBtnClick(Sender: TObject);
  private
    FSystemHelp: ISystemInfo;
    procedure ReportOnDriveStatus;
  end;

var
  Form1: TForm1;

implementation

{$R *.DFM}
```

```
uses
  ActiveX, ComObj;


procedure TForm1.ConnectBtnClick(Sender: TObject);
begin
  OleCheck(CoCreateInstance(Class_SystemHelp, nil, CLSCTX_ALL,
    ISystemInfo, FSystemHelp));
  CCLabelEDit1.EditText := FSystemHelp.GetName;
  CCLabelEdit2.EditText := FSystemHelp.ComputerName;
  ReportOnDriveStatus;
end;


procedure TForm1.ReportOnDriveStatus;
const
  Size = 28 * 5;  // 26 letters plus A and B times plenty of room
                  // for letters
var
  TotalCount, i: Integer;
  ADrive, DriveInfo: Variant;
  DriveInfoRec: TDriveInfoRec;
  TempVar: Variant;
  TempPtr: Pointer;
begin
  if FSystemHelp = nil then
    Exit
  else
    FSystemHelp.DriveInfo(TotalCount, DriveInfo);


  Memo1.Clear;

  for i := 0 to TotalCount - 1 do begin

    ADrive := DriveInfo[i];
    Memo1.Lines.Add('[' + ADrive[0] + '] ' + ADrive[1]);

    TempVar := ADrive[2];
    TempPtr := VarArrayLock(TempVar);
    Move(TempPtr^, DriveInfoRec, SizeOf(TDriveInfoRec));

    with Memo1.Lines, DriveInfoRec do begin
      Memo1.Lines.Add('Sectors Per Cluster: ' +
        IntToStr(SectorsPerCluster));
      Memo1.Lines.Add('Bytes Per Sector: ' + IntToStr(BytesPerSector));
      Memo1.Lines.Add('Number of Free Clusters: ' +
        IntToStr(NumberOfFreeClusters));
      Memo1.Lines.Add('Total Number of Clusters: ' +
        IntToStr(TotalNumberOfClusters));
```

continues

14

COM CLASSES AND
TYPED LIBRARIES

LISTING 14.3   CONTINUED

```
      Memo1.Lines.Add('Free Available: ' + IntToStr(FreeAvailable));
      Memo1.Lines.Add('Total Space: ' + IntToStr(TotalSpace));
      Memo1.Lines.Add('Total Free: ' + IntToStr(TotalFree));
      Memo1.Lines.Add('');
    end;

  end;
end;

end.
```

When you run this program you see a form with a single button on it, as shown in Figure 14.1. If you click on the button, a COM object will be loaded into memory. The object reports on the status of the system, such as the name of the current machine, and the status of the drives on the machine.

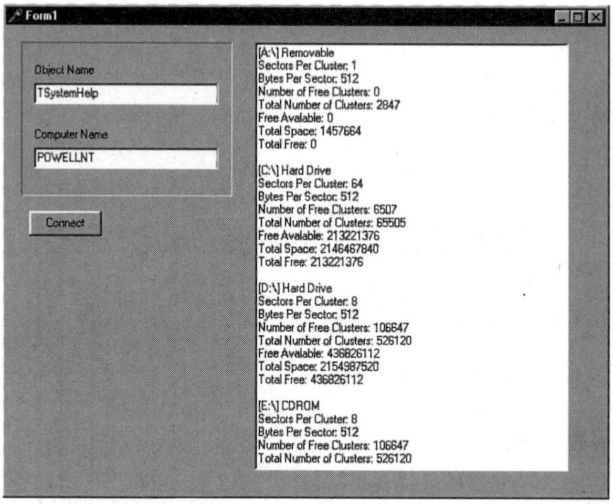

FIGURE 14.1

The main form for the SystemClient *program lets you talk to a COM object stored in a DLL.*

To create this program, you should close any current projects and then choose File, New, Active X, ActiveX Library. Next, you can create your COM object. Choose File, New, Active X, COM Object from the Delphi menu. The COM Object Wizard will be loaded. Type in the class name, which in this case is SystemHelp. Leave the instancing and threading models at their default values, pausing only long enough to note that COM provides support for multiple simultaneous clients. The implemented interface field in the wizard should be set to ISystemInfo. Do not create a type library, but you should enter a short description of your object because this latter bit of information will help document your work. Now click OK to close the wizard.

The result of your efforts should be a simple COM object defined as follows:

```
unit Unit1;

interface

uses
  Windows, ActiveX, ComObj;

type
  TSystemHelp = class(TComObject, ISystemInfo)
  protected
    {Declare ISystemInfo methods here}
  end;

const
  Class_SystemHelp: TGUID = '{1CCF3B00-1E91-11D2-9CE8-006008928EEF}';

implementation

uses ComServ;

initialization
  TComObjectFactory.Create(ComServer, TSystemHelp, Class_SystemHelp,
    'SystemHelp', 'This comment...', ciMultiInstance, tmSingle);
end.
```

The most important part of this simple unit is the last four lines. Here the TComObjectFactory is created automatically when the DLL is loaded into memory. The object factory is an internal Delphi object that implements the IClassFactory interface. This interface must exist if you want to call an object that resides in a DLL.

In the preceding chapter, I very carefully stepped you through the methods of IUnknown. Doing any COM programming without understanding IUnknown is difficult. IClassFactory is a different matter altogether. On very few or even no occasion should you, as a Delphi programmer, need to consider this object. However, theoretical knowledge is often valuable, particularly when you are debugging a complex problem. As a result, I will discuss IClassFactory briefly in the section "IClassFactory."

The point here is not to understand how TComObjectFactory works. Simply note that it is the implementation of the object used to automatically launch your DLL and pass an interface back to a client program.

The call to TComObjectFactory.Create is declared for you automatically, but you might want to think about it for just one moment:

```
TComObjectFactory.Create(
  ComServer,            // A Delphi class for managing your object
  TSystemHelp,          // The implementation of your interface
```

14

COM CLASSES AND
TYPED LIBRARIES

```
Class_SystemHelp,     // The CoClass GUID, or Class ID
'SystemHelp',         // The class name
'This comment...',    // A description of the class
ciMultiInstance,      // Instancing
tmSingle);            // Threading
```

The following is a more in-depth description of the fields:

- The ComServer object is declared in ComServ.pas, and it provides a simple means for managing your object. It knows the name of your object, the name of its help file, the name of its type library, how many clients are talking to the object, and so on.

- The second parameter is the name of the object you are creating.

- The third parameter is the Class ID of the object you are creating. (The GUID is associated with your CoClass.)

- The fourth parameter is the class name.

- The fifth parameter is a description of your object.

- The sixth parameter handles instancing. You can create an object that is internal to an existing executable, which is not what we are doing here. The other choices specify whether your object can be accessed by only one or by multiple clients. If you choose single instancing, only one client can talk to your object at a time. After that connection is made, your object is not available to other clients. This enumerated type declares the constants for this field:

  ```
  type TClassInstancing = (ciInternal, ciSingleInstance,
  ciMultiInstance);
  ```

- The seventh parameter allows you to specify a threading model. The Single threading model means you have no support for threading. The Apartment threading model means each object you create will have its own thread, but any global data in your DLL is not protected. With this model, you should use mutexes or critical sections to protect your global data. The Free threading model and the Both model are more or less a free-for-all, and you shouldn't use them unless you know a lot about computers, know that you know it, and are prepared to suffer just so you can prove that you know it. The following are your choices for the threading model:

  ```
  type TThreadingModel = (tmSingle, tmApartment, tmFree, tmBoth);
  ```

Threading is really a very complex issue, so I am going to discuss it in more depth in Chapter 20, "DCOM." For now, you can play it safe by choosing tmSingle, or live a bit dangerously if you feel certain that you can either create interfaces that do not access any global data or that protect the data when you do access it. The best way to protect the data is with a mutex or critical section.

TComObjectFactory.Create is designed to let you forget about the mechanisms used to create a COM object. It really isn't any of our business how an object gets created. That's low-level stuff that should be handled by the compiler, and there is no reason why you or I should have to think about it. So if you don't feel comfortable thinking about TComObjectFactory, then just forget about it. The creators of the VCL went to a lot of effort to give you that luxury.

Besides automatically creating a class factory, the COM Object Wizard also produces a declaration for your implementation:

```
TSystemHelp = class(TComObject, ISystemInfo)
protected
  {Declare ISystemInfo methods here}
end;
```

This simple class descends from TComObject, which means that it has a built-in capability to work with a class factory. It is also prepared to implement ISystemInfo, but Delphi does nothing to help you declare or define this interface. As you can see, you are expected to declare the implementation of your interface in the protected section.

Another bit of code auto-generated by the wizard is your class ID:

```
const
  Class_SystemHelp: TGUID = '{1CCF3B00-1E91-11D2-9CE8-006008928EEF}';
```

The Class ID uniquely identifies your object. Assuming that you have a valid network card on your system, the number generated here is guaranteed to be unique. You can generate GUIDs forever and never duplicate this same number--or at least so the theory goes. COM won't let you register two objects that have the same Prog ID on the same system. However, you can register two objects with the same name on two different systems, which can become a problem when you are using DCOM or ActiveX controls in a browser. The GUID declared here, however, is guaranteed to be unique, so you won't have to worry about naming conflicts on a network or even on the Internet.

Finally, you might want to glance at your uses clause:

```
uses
  Windows, ActiveX, ComObj;
```

ActiveX is the unit in which most basic COM type declarations are made. A few core COM interfaces such as IUnknown and IDispatch are declared in System.pas. However, the vast majority of standard COM interfaces and constants are declared in ActiveX.pas. It plays the same role in COM that Windows.pas plays in Windows API programming.

TComObject, TTypedComObject, TAutoObject and their respective class factories are declared in ComObj.pas. In other words, ComObj.pas is the unit in which all the key classes that make VCL COM programming possible are declared.

IClassFactory

IClassFactory is the helper class that creates instances of COM interfaces for export from a DLL or executable. Both IUnknown and IClassFactory are implemented for you automatically by the VCL, so you will not usually have to worry about them when working with Delphi. Nevertheless, having an understanding of such matters is often helpful, particularly when you are chasing bugs.

The following is the declaration for the simple IClassFactory interface:

```
IClassFactory = interface(IUnknown)
  ['{00000001-0000-0000-C000-000000000046}']
  function CreateInstance(const unkOuter: IUnknown; const iid: TIID;
    out obj): HResult; stdcall;
  function LockServer(fLock: BOOL): HResult; stdcall;
end;
```

IClassFactory inherits AddRef, Release, and QueryInterface from IUnknown. It contains two method declarations, the most important of which is called CreateInstance. This method is called when an instance of an interface implementation needs to be created. You will very rarely have to implement this method in Delphi because the VCL does it for you.

If you just can't stand the idea of having the VCL handle this aspect of your code, nothing is preventing you from handling this code on your own. For more information, you can read the chapter called "COM Object Basics," from *Delphi 2 Unleashed*. Or you can read the excellent book called *Inside COM*, written by Dale Rogerson and published by the Microsoft Press. This latter volume is one of the better technical books I've ever read.

If you are familiar with COM and want to learn more about the details of TComObjectFactory, you can look in the ComObj unit, where you will find the implementation for IClassFactory.CreateInstance. In Delphi's implementation, this function ends up resolving into a call to CreateInstanceLic. This latter method handles licensing issues, thereby allowing you to decide who can and can't use your object. You might want to step through this code at times if you are having trouble connecting to one of your objects.

The ISystemInfo Interface

Now, you're ready to create the interface for ISystemInfo. This declaration contains three methods:

```
ISystemInfo = interface
  ['{137BFDC0-1C9A-11D2-9CE8-006008928EEF}']
  function ComputerName: WideString; safecall;
  procedure DriveInfo(out TotalCount: Integer;
```

```
  out DriveInfo: Variant);
  function GetName: WideString; safecall;
end;
```

The GetName and ComputerName methods are just trivial routines that return a string. For instance, the ComputerName method calls a Windows API function named GetComputerName to return the name of your current computer, as you declared it during the Windows installation process:

```
function TSystemHelp.ComputerName: WideString;
var
  Len: DWord;
  S: PChar;
begin
  Len := MAX_COMPUTERNAME_LENGTH + 1;
  GetMem(S, Len);
  if GetComputerName(S, Len) then
    Result := S
  else
    raise Exception.Create('Could not get computer name.');
  FreeMem(S, Len);
end;
```

The second parameter of GetComputerName asks for the length of the buffer you are passing in, so I declare that string to be MAX_COMPUTERNAME_LENGTH + 1. I then assign the return result to a WideString, which means that Delphi will take over allocating and deallocating memory for the string.

The final method in the interface, called DriveInfo, is a special case placed in this program to show you some important things about standard COM parameters. This subject is actually rather complex, so I'm going to put it on hold for a few minutes. My plan is to first show you how to register the DLL and then how to create a client that connects to this DLL and calls its methods. After getting those relatively straightforward matters out of the way, I will come back and tackle the subject of Variant arrays.

Registering a DLL

Describing how to register a COM DLL with the system takes just a moment. The simplest way to proceed is to allow Delphi to register an object by choosing Run, Register ActiveX server. Another simple technique is to go to the DOS prompt and type one of the following lines:

```
RegSvr32 SystemInfo.dll
TRegSvr SystemInfo.dll
```

RegSvr32 comes with Windows, and TRegSvr comes with Delphi.

14

COM CLASSES AND
TYPED LIBRARIES

Any of the techniques described here will register the server with the system, placing entries in the Registry. If you run RegEdit.exe, you can see the entries you created under the listing SystemInfo.SystemHelp. This process was described in more depth in the preceding chapter.

You need to understand that all either RegSvr32 or TRegSvr does is call entries in your COM object that will cause it to automatically register itself with the system. In other words, the code that registers the object is in SystemInfo.dll, not in RegSvr32 or TRegSvr. Later in this chapter, you will see that you can also register a DLL from the Type Library Editor used to create a type library.

Accessing a COM Object Stored in a DLL from an Executable

When working with the client program for the System Information example, I use a file called Global.pas that contains the declarations for the interface. This file contains the interface declaration, as well as the necessary class IDs and GUIDs.

> **NOTE**
>
> Before I could compile the client program, I needed to choose View, Project Options, Directory/Conditionals to change the Search Path so my client could find Global.pas. In particular, I entered the string ..\Server so that my client could find Global.pas in the Server directory.

To access a COM object stored in a DLL, use CoCreateInstance:

```
procedure TForm1.ConnectBtnClick(Sender: TObject);
begin
  OleCheck(CoCreateInstance(Class_SystemHelp, nil, CLSCTX_ALL,
    ISystemInfo, FSystemHelp));
  CCLabelEDit1.EditText := FSystemHelp.GetName;
  CCLabelEdit2.EditText := FSystemHelp.ComputerName;
  ReportOnDriveStatus;
end;
```

In this example, I do the following:

- I pass in the Class ID in the first parameter. This key makes it possible for Windows to locate the binary file that contains your object and to launch it if necessary.

- I always set the second parameter to nil, as it is used for an advanced feature called aggregation, which is not relevant to the current discussion.

- I set the third parameter to one of the following values:

CLSCTX_INPROC_SERVER	The object is in a DLL.
CLSCTX_LOCAL_SERVER	The object is in an executable, such as an automation server.
CLSCTX_ALL	The object is in either an automation server or an executable.

- The fourth parameter, ISystemInfo, specifies the interface on the server that I want to access.

- The last parameter, FSystemHelp, contains a pointer to the value that I want to retrieve. That is, when the call is over, it should contain an initialized variable pointing to my interface.

Later in the chapter, I will show you a means to get at an interface using some built-in Delphi routines. But for now, calling CoCreateInstance is really quite simple. For more information on CoCreateInsance, see the numerous references to it in the next chapter, as well as the section "Calling CoCreateInstance" at the end of the next chapter. All in all, I find CoCreateInstance to be one of those fundamental OLE functions that I simply have to know how to use, just as developers more or less have to know how to use the MessageBox function. CoCreateInstance has plenty of wrappers, but ultimately it's best to just know the function well and to use it whenever necessary.

NOTE

I usually wrap calls to CoCreateInstance and other OLE functions in a routine called OleCheck from the ComObj unit. OLE functions usually return a variable called an HResult, which is declared to be of type LongWord. This variable usually contains either zero on success, or some negative value specifying a standard error value declared in ActiveX.pas. If HResult is not set to zero, then OleCheck will attempt to convert the numeric HResult value into a human readable string. It will then raise an exception and display the string for your perusal.

If you don't want to use OleCheck, you can use the functions SUCCEEDED or FAILED to check the result of your call, as in this example:

```
var
  hr: HResult;
begin
  hr := MyOleFunc;
  if SUCCEEDED(hr) then ...
```

continues

> There are various forms of madness in this world, but undoubtedly one of the most egregious is to call an OLE function and not check its return value. Doing so is akin to trying to cross the desert without water or trying to climb Mount Everest without a pair of well-tested boots. Certainly, people have tried to do things like this, but the results usually aren't pretty. My suggestion for beginners is just to wrap all your calls in the OleCheck routine.

After you have called CoCreateInstance, you are ready to start calling the methods on your interface:

```
CCLabelEDit1.EditText := FSystemHelp.GetName;
CCLabelEdit2.EditText := FSystemHelp.ComputerName;
```

I can't say much about these two lines of code other than that they use the TCCLabelEdit component from the Unleash package that ships in the Units directory on the CD that comes with this book. I describe using the Unleash package in section "The Unleash and Merc40 Packages" in Chapter 1, "Program Design Basics."

Marshaling Data Across Program Boundaries

It's finally time to focus on the DriveInfo method from the ISystemInfo interface. This method is used to report on the drives available on a system. For instance, it gives this report on my C: drive:

```
[c:\] Hard Drive
Sectors Per Cluster: 64
Bytes Per Sector: 512
Number of Free Clusters: 18823
Total Number of Clusters: 65385
Free Available: 616800256
Total Space: 2142560256
Total Free: 616800256
```

I'm not going to spend much time on the Windows API functions that enable you to retrieve all this arcane data. Instead, I will describe how to retrieve this data in a form compatible with all types of COM programming.

When you are working with a DLL, the functions you create are inside the address space of the calling program. Windows therefore doesn't need to marshal any data for you. However, astute readers will no doubt have considered the possibility that this interface could be stored in a remote COM object on a second machine. In that location, it could be used to report on the status of a machine that is located somewhere on your network.

To perform that task, Windows is going to have to marshal some data for you, or else you are going to have to implement IMarshal yourself. Because you don't want to have to marshal your own data, the best thing to do is store the elements of your data in some COM-compliant manner, which in this case means using Variants. The salient point in this paragraph is that Variants are a type Windows will automatically marshal between program boundaries, or even between machine boundaries.

I use the following structure to store information when reporting on the status of a hard drive:

```
TDriveInfoRec = record
  SectorsPerCluster, BytesPerSector: Cardinal;
  NumberOfFreeClusters, TotalNumberOfClusters: Cardinal;
  TotalFree, FreeAvailable, TotalSpace: LargeInt;
end;
```

Clearly, this type cannot be automated. Fortunately, there is a way to move types like this back and forth between machines. To understand that technology, you need to understand Variant arrays, a subject I cover in the section "Variant Arrays."

Marshaling Data

Explaining what marshaling is and why it is necessary might be worthwhile. COM needs to marshal data between programs on the same or different machines because the variables are declared in different address spaces. For instance, the variables in program A may be loaded at some address, say $A00E4000. The problem with this address is that it is in virtual memory, not real memory. If you pass the address to a second program, it will not be able to access the variable at that address because it has a different virtual view of the memory on the machine. Or, to state the matter somewhat differently, it cannot normally access the memory located in another program's address space.

The use of virtual memory means that Windows has to go behind the scenes and move data back and forth between programs using special low-level calls. When it does this, it can automatically move certain types back and forth between programs for you. Other types are invalid and cannot be used, unless you explicitly support them via the IMarshal interface. Delphi structures and arrays, for instance, are not allowed types.

If you look up "marshaling data" in the Delphi online help and then click on the link to Valid Types, you will be able to see a complete list of types you can use in a type library. The following types can be marshaled for you automatically even in an automation program: SmallInt, Integer, Single, Double, Currency, TDateTime, WideString, IDispatch, SCODE, WordBool, OleVariant, IUnknown, and Byte. These latter types are the ones you should use if you want to create automation-compatible programs.

14

COM CLASSES AND TYPED LIBRARIES

Variant Arrays

Delphi enables you to create Variant arrays, which are the Delphi version of the safe arrays used in OLE automation. Variant arrays (and safe arrays) are costly in terms of memory and CPU cycles, so you would not normally use them except in automation code, or in special cases in which they provide obvious benefits over standard arrays. For instance, the database code makes some use of Variant arrays.

The most important calls for manipulating Variant arrays are VarArrayCreate and VarArrayOf. In particular, these functions are both used to create Variant arrays.

The declaration for VarArrayCreate looks like this:

```
function VarArrayCreate(const Bounds: array of Integer;
  VarType: Integer): Variant;
```

The Bounds parameter defines the dimensions of the array. The VarType parameter defines the type of variable stored in the array. A one-dimensional array of Variants would be allocated like this:

```
MyVariant := VarArrayCreate([0, 5], varVariant);
```

This array has six elements in it, where each element is a Variant. You can assign a Variant array to one or more of the elements in this array. That way, you can have arrays within arrays within arrays, if you so desire.

If you know the type of each element to be used in an array, you can set the VarType parameter to that type. For instance, if you knew you were going to be working with integers, you could write

```
MyVariant := VarArrayCreate([0, 5], varInteger);
```

You cannot use varString in the second parameter; instead, use varOleStr. Remember that an array of Variant takes up 16 bytes for each member of the array, whereas other types might take up less space.

Arrays of Variant can be resized with the VarArrayRedim function:

```
procedure VarArrayRedim(var A: Variant; HighBound: Integer);
```

The variable to be resized is passed in the first parameter, and the number of elements to be contained in the resized array is held in the second parameter.

A two-dimensional array would be declared like this:

```
MyVariant := VarArrayCreate([0, 5, 0, 5], varVariant);
```

This array has two dimensions, each with six elements. To access a member of this array, you would write code that looks like this:

```
procedure TForm1.GridClick(Sender: TObject);
var
  MyVariant: Variant;
begin
  MyVariant := VarArrayCreate([0, 5, 0, 5], varVariant);
  MyVariant[0, 1] := 42;
  Form1.Caption := MyVariant[0, 1];
end;
```

Notice that the array performs type conversions for you, as it is an array of Variants and not, for instance, an array of integer.

You can use the VarArrayOf routine to quickly construct a one-dimensional Variant array:

```
function VarArrayOf(const Values: array of Variant): Variant;
```

The function internally calls VarArrayCreate, passing an array of Variant in the first parameter and varVariant in the second parameter. Here is a typical call to VarArrayOf:

```
V := VarArrayOf([1, 2, 3, 'Total', 5]);
```

The following code fragment shows how to use the VarArrayOf function:

```
procedure TForm1.ShowInfo(V: Variant);
begin
  Caption := V[3];
end;

procedure TForm1.Button1Click(Sender: TObject);
var
  V: Variant;
begin
  V := VarArrayOf([1, 2, 3, 'Total', 5]);
  ShowInfo(V);
end;
```

This code prints the word "Total" in the caption of Form1.

The ShowInfo method demonstrates how to work with a Variant array passed as a parameter. Notice that you don't have to do anything special to access a Variant as an array. The type travels with the variable.

If you tried to pass a Variant with a VType of varInteger to this function, Delphi would raise an exception when you tried to treat the Variant as an array. In short, the Variant must have a VType of VarArray or the call to ShowInfo will fail. You can use the VarType function to check the current setting for the VType of a Variant, or you can call VarIsArray, which returns a Boolean value.

You can use the VarArrayHighBound, VarArrayLowBound, and VarArrayDimCount functions to find out about the number of dimensions in your array and about the bounds of each dimension. The following function creates a pop-up message box showing the number of dimensions in a Variant array, as well as the high and low values for each dimension:

```
procedure TForm1.ShowInfo(V: Variant);
var
  Count, HighBound, LowBound, i: Integer;
  S: string;
begin
  Count := VarArrayDimCount(V);
  S := #13 + 'DimCount: ' + IntToStr(Count) + #13;
  for i := 1 to Count do begin
    HighBound := VarArrayHighBound(V, i);
    LowBound := VarArrayLowBound(V, i);
    S := S + 'HighBound: ' + IntToStr(HighBound) + #13;
    S := S + 'LowBound: ' + IntToStr(LowBound) + #13;
  end;
  ShowMessage(S);
end;
```

This routine starts by getting the number of dimensions in the array. It then iterates through each dimension, retrieving its high and low values. If you created an array with the call

```
MyVariant := VarArrayCreate([0, 5, 1, 3], varVariant);
```

the ShowInfo function would produce the following output if passed MyVariant:

```
DimCount: 2
HighBound: 5
LowBound: 0
HighBound: 3
LowBound: 1
```

ShowInfo would raise an exception if you passed in a Variant that would cause VarIsArray to return False.

A certain amount of overhead is involved in working with Variant arrays. If you want to process the arrays quickly, you can use two functions called VarArrayLock and VarArrayUnlock. The first of these routines returns a pointer to the data stored in an array. In particular, VarArrayLock takes a Variant array and returns a standard Pascal array. For this routine to work, the array must be explicitly declared with one of the standard types, such as Integer, Bool, string, Byte, or Float. The type used in the Variant array and the type used in the Pascal array must be identical.

Consider this example of using VarArrayLock and VarArrayUnlock:

```
const
  HighVal = 12;

function GetArray: Variant;
var
  V: Variant;
  i, j: Integer;
begin
  V := VarArrayCreate([0, HighVal, 0, HighVal], varInteger);
  for i := 0 to HighVal do
    for j := 0 to HighVal do
      V[j, i] := i * j;
  Result := V;
end;

procedure TForm1.LockedArray1Click(Sender: TObject);
type
  TData = array[0..HighVal, 0..HighVal] of Integer;
var
  i, j: Integer;
  V: Variant;
  Data: ^TData;
begin
  V := GetArray;
  Data := VarArrayLock(V);
  for i := 0 to HighVal do
    for j := 0 to HighVal do
      Grid.Cells[i, j] := IntToStr(Data^[i, j]);
  VarArrayUnLock(V);
end;
```

Notice that this code first locks down the array and then accesses it as a pointer to a standard array. Finally, it releases the array when the operation is finished. You must remember to call VarArrayUnlock when you are finished working with the data from the array:

```
Data := VarArrayLock(V);
for i := 0 to HighVal do
  for j := 0 to HighVal do
    Grid.Cells[i, j] := IntToStr(Data^[i, j]);
VarArrayUnLock(V);
```

Remember that the point of using VarArrayLock and VarArrayUnlock is that it speeds access to the array. The actual code you write is more complex and verbose, but the performance is faster.

One of the most useful reasons for using a Variant array is to transfer binary data to and from a server. If you have a binary file, say a WAV file or AVI file, you can pass it back and forth between your program and an OLE server using Variant arrays. Such a situation would present an ideal time for using VarArrayLock and VarArrayUnlock. You would, of course, use VarByte as the second parameter to VarArrayCreate when you were creating the array. That is, you would be working with an array of Byte, and accessing it directly by locking down the array before moving data in and out of the structure. Such arrays are not subject to translation while being marshaled across boundaries.

Listing 14.4 contains a single sample program that encapsulates most of the ideas that you have seen in this section on Variant arrays. The program from which this code is excerpted is called VarArray.

LISTING 14.4   THE VarArray PROGRAM SHOWS HOW TO USE Variant ARRAYS

```
unit Main;

{ Copyright (c) 1996..1998 by Charlie Calvert

  This program provides very simple examples
  of using Variant Arrays. Variant Arrays are
  Delphi's version of the Safe Arrays used in
  standard OLE programming.

  The code shown here provides examples of using
  both one dimensional and two dimensional variant
  arrays }

interface

uses
  Windows, Messages, SysUtils,
  Classes, Graphics, Controls,
  Forms, Dialogs, StdCtrls, Buttons, Grids, ExtCtrls, Menus;

type
  TForm1 = class(TForm)
    Grid: TStringGrid;
    MainMenu1: TMainMenu;
    Options1: TMenuItem;
    OneDimensional1: TMenuItem;
    TwoDimentional1: TMenuItem;
    NormalArray1: TMenuItem;
    LockedArray1: TMenuItem;
    procedure bOneDimClick(Sender: TObject);
    procedure bTwoDimClick(Sender: TObject);
    procedure NormalAryBtnClick(Sender: TObject);
    procedure LockedAryBtnClick(Sender: TObject);
  private
    procedure ShowInfo(V: Variant);
    procedure ClearGrid;
```

```
      end;

var
  Form1: TForm1;

implementation

{$R *.DFM}

procedure TForm1.ClearGrid;
var
  i,j :Integer;
begin
  for j := 0 to Grid.RowCount - 1 do
    for i := 0 to Grid.ColCount - 1 do
      Grid.Cells[i,j] := '';
end;

procedure TForm1.ShowInfo(V: Variant);
var
  Count, HighBound, LowBound, i: Integer;
  S: string;
begin
  Count := VarArrayDimCount(V);
  S := #13 + 'DimCount: ' + IntToStr(Count) + #13;
  for i := 1 to Count do begin
    HighBound := VarArrayHighBound(V, i);
    LowBound := VarArrayLowBound(V, i);
    S := S + 'HighBound: ' + IntToStr(HighBound) + #13;
    S := S + 'LowBound: ' + IntToStr(LowBound) + #13;
  end;
  ShowMessage(S);
end;

{ Simple example showing how to use a one
  dimensional variant array }
procedure TForm1.bOneDimClick(Sender: TObject);
var
  MyVariant: Variant;
  S: string;
  i: Integer;

begin
  MyVariant := VarArrayOf(['Variant Info', 12, 15, 23, 25]);
  ShowInfo(MyVariant);

  ClearGrid;

  S := '';
  MyVariant := VarArrayCreate([0, 5], varVariant);
```

14

COM CLASSES AND
TYPED LIBRARIES

continues

LISTING 14.4 CONTINUED

```
  for i := 0 to 5 do
    MyVariant[i] := i * 2;
  for i := 0 to 5 do
    Grid.Cells[i + 1, 1] := IntToStr(MyVariant[i]);
end;

{ Simple example showing how to use a two
  dimensional variant array }
procedure TForm1.bTwoDimClick(Sender: TObject);
var
  MyVariant: Variant;
  i, j: Integer;
  S: string;
begin
  S := '';

  MyVariant := VarArrayCreate([0, 5, 0, 5], varInteger);

  for i := 0 to 5 do
    for j := 0 to 5 do
      MyVariant[i, j] := i * j;

  ClearGrid;
  for i := 0 to 5 do begin
    for j := 0 to 5 do
      Grid.Cells[i, j] := IntToStr(MyVariant[i, j]);
  end;
end;

function GetArray: Variant;
var
  V: Variant;
  i, j: Integer;
begin
  V := VarArrayCreate([0, 12, 0, 12], varInteger);
  for i := 0 to 12 do
    for j := 0 to 12 do
      V[j, i] := i * j;
  Result := V;
end;

procedure TForm1.NormalAryBtnClick(Sender: TObject);
var
  i, j: Integer;
  V: Variant;
begin
  V := GetArray;
  for i := 0 to VarArrayHighBound(V, 1) do
    for j := 0 to VarArrayHighBound(V, 2) do
```

```
        Grid.Cells[i, j] := V[i, j];
end;

procedure TForm1.LockedAryBtnClick(Sender: TObject);
type
  TData = array[0..12, 0..12] of Integer;
var
  i, j: Integer;
  V: Variant;
  Data: ^TData;
begin
  V := GetArray;
  Data := VarArrayLock(V);
  for i := 0 to 12 do
    for j := 0 to 12 do
      Grid.Cells[i, j] := IntToStr(Data^[i, j]);
  VarArrayUnLock(V);
end;

end.
```

This program has two menu items:

- One enables you to look at the dimensions and bounds of two different Variant arrays. The first array has one dimension, and the second has two.

- The second pop-up menu enables you to display an array in a string grid using two different methods. The first method accesses the array through standard techniques, and the second lets you lock down the data before accessing it.

Remember that Variant arrays are of use only in special circumstances. They are useful tools, especially when making calls to OLE automation objects. However, they are slower and bulkier than standard Delphi arrays and should be used only when necessary.

Marshaling the ISystemInfo Data

Now you can look at the DriveInfo method that wraps data inside a Variant so that it can be passed as an automatable type. Notice in particular the second parameter, which is used to return information about the drives on a machine:

```
procedure TSystemHelp.DriveInfo(out TotalCount: Integer;
  out DriveInfo: Variant);
const
  Size = 26 * 5;  // 26 letters + 2, times plenty of room for letters
var
  DriveStrings, TempDriveStrings: PChar;
  DriveType: string;
  SectorsPerCluster, BytesPerSector: Cardinal;
```

14

COM CLASSES AND
TYPED LIBRARIES

```
      NumberOfFreeClusters, TotalNumberOfClusters: Cardinal;
      FreeAvailable, TotalSpace: LargeInt;
      TotalFree: LargeInt;
      DriveInfoRec: TDriveInfoRec;
      ADrive: Variant;
      TempVar: Variant;
      TempPtr: Pointer;
  begin
    TotalCount := 0;
    DriveInfo := VarArrayCreate([0, 28], VarVariant);
    GetMem(DriveStrings, Size);
    GetLogicalDriveStrings(Size, DriveStrings);
    TempDriveStrings := DriveStrings;

    while StrLen(TempDriveStrings) <> 0 do begin
      ADrive := VarArrayCreate([0, 3], VarVariant);
      case GetDriveType(TempDriveStrings) of
        DRIVE_UNKNOWN: DriveType := 'Unknown';
        DRIVE_NO_ROOT_DIR: DriveType := 'Not a root drive';
        DRIVE_REMOVABLE: DriveType := 'Removable';
        DRIVE_FIXED: DriveType := 'Hard Drive';
        DRIVE_REMOTE: DriveType := 'Network';
        DRIVE_CDROM: DriveType := 'CDROM';
        DRIVE_RAMDISK: DriveType := 'RAMDisk';
      else
        DriveType := 'Error';
      end;

      ADrive[0] := AnsiString(TempDriveStrings);
      ADrive[1] := DriveType;

      GetDiskFreeSpace(TempDriveStrings, SectorsPerCluster, BytesPerSector,
        NumberOfFreeClusters, TotalNumberOfClusters);

      DriveInfoRec.SectorsPerCluster := SectorsPerCluster;
      DriveInfoRec.BytesPerSector := BytesPerSector;
      DriveInfoRec.NumberOfFreeClusters := NumberOfFreeClusters;
      DriveInfoRec.TotalNumberOfClusters := TotalNumberOfClusters;

      GetDiskFreeSpaceEx(TempDriveStrings, FreeAvailable, TotalSpace,
                         ➥@TotalFree);
      DriveInfoRec.FreeAvailable := FreeAvailable;
      DriveInfoRec.TotalSpace := TotalSpace;
      DriveInfoRec.TotalFree := TotalFree;

      TempVar := VarArrayCreate([0, SizeOf(TDriveInfoRec)], VarByte);
      TempPtr := VarArrayLock(TempVar);
      Move(DriveInfoRec, TempPtr^, SizeOf(TDriveInfoRec));
      VarArrayUnlock(TempVar);
      ADrive[2] := TempVar;
```

```
    DriveInfo[TotalCount] := ADrive;
    Inc(TempDriveStrings, StrLen(TempDriveStrings) + 1);
    Inc(TotalCount);
  end;
  FreeMem(DriveStrings, Size);
end;
```

This code starts out by creating an array of Variants 28 members long:

```
DriveInfo := VarArrayCreate([0, 28], VarVariant);
```

This code provides one Variant for each of the possible drives on your system, plus a little extra room for safety's sake.

Variant arrays can be nested, so you can place a Variant array inside a Variant array inside a Variant array, and so on. That is what I do here. Information about each drive that needs to be documented is stored inside a Variant array. Next, look at how I create the second Variant array, which ends up being nested inside the first array:

```
ADrive := VarArrayCreate([0, 3], VarVariant);
```

I use the first element of this array to store the drive name, such as A:\. The second Variant is used to describe its type, such as Fixed or CDROM:

```
ADrive[0] := AnsiString(TempDriveStrings);
ADrive[1] := DriveType;
```

The third Variant, ADrive[2], contains yet another Variant array. This last Variant array contains the record detailing the size of a drive and its current status:

```
TDriveInfoRec = record
  SectorsPerCluster, BytesPerSector: Cardinal;
  NumberOfFreeClusters, TotalNumberOfClusters: Cardinal;
  TotalFree, FreeAvailable, TotalSpace: LargeInt;
end;
```

If you consider this record for a moment, you will note that it has a fixed size. In other words, it has no embedded strings or pointers. This means that we can easily calculate how large it will be.

If you have a structure with a fixed or easy-to-calculate size, then storing it in a Variant array of byte is simple:

```
Var
  ADrive: Variant;
  TempVar: Variant;
  TempPtr: Pointer;
begin
  ... // Code omitted here
  TempVar := VarArrayCreate([0, SizeOf(TDriveInfoRec)], VarByte);
```

14

COM CLASSES AND
TYPED LIBRARIES

```
TempPtr := VarArrayLock(TempVar);
Move(DriveInfoRec, TempPtr^, SizeOf(TDriveInfoRec));
VarArrayUnlock(TempVar);
ADrive[2] := TempVar;
DriveInfo[TotalCount] := ADrive;
... // More code omitted
end;
```

This code first creates a `Variant` array of byte the same size as the `TDriveInfoRec`. It then locks down this array, retrieving a pointer to it. Using the `Move` function, data is stored in the array. Finally, the memory is unlocked, and the array is stored inside the array that is stored inside the array that is returned to the user.

A few paragraphs back I commented on some of the inconveniences inherent in using `Variant` arrays. It's probably also worth pointing out that they are powerful data structures that can solve a wide range of complex problems with considerable ease. I don't recommend using them when you could just as easily use a standard Delphi array. However, if you have a good reason to use one, don't shy away from them, as they are very handy.

NOTE

Let me point out one other feature of this program: It uses pointer arithmetic. You can't use pointer arithmetic on a standard Delphi pointer. You can, however, do so on a string on a typed pointer. That is what I do in this code. First, I use the Windows API called `GetLogicalDriveStrings` to retrieve a pointer to a list of all the drives on the system:

```
Var
  DriveStrings, TempDriveStrings: PChar;
Begin
  ... // Code omitted here.
  GetLogicalDriveStrings(Size, DriveStrings);
  TempDriveStrings := DriveStrings;
  ADrive[0] := AnsiString(TempDriveStrings);
```

So far, things are very straightforward, but trouble is just around the corner. The next drive on the system is stored in the `TempDriveStrings` variable but separated from the first string by a null character. The end of the list of strings is marked by two null characters. To get to that next string, I use pointer math:

```
  Inc(TempDriveStrings, StrLen(TempDriveStrings) + 1);
```

Now `TempDriveStrings` points to the next string in the list. For instance, the string may have first pointed to "A:\", but after calling `Inc`, it might point to "C:\". In memory, the entire string looked something like this: "a:\<null> c:\<null>d:\<null><null>", where I am using <null> to show a null-terminated string and two nulls to mark the end of the string.

When writing this program, I got help with some of the obscure Windows API calls by referencing *The Tomes Of Delphi: Win32 Core API*, from WordWare Publishing. It is a great reference book to use when you want Pascal translations and examples of difficult Windows API calls.

Type Libraries and Querying Objects

The final example in this chapter shows how to add a type library to your DLL that will describe the COM object that it supports. I'm actually going to spread out the discussion of type libraries over two chapters, with the most important material in Chapter 15.

In this chapter, I'm going to focus on just two aspects of type libraries:

- How to use a type library to document an interface.
- How to talk to a type library from a client. In particular, I will show how to retrieve the ITypeInfo interface from a server and how to ask that interface to yield up information about the interfaces, methods, and types supported by the object.

Before going on, I should mention that most developers use type libraries only when creating Automation or ActiveX objects. Only a few developers take advantage of the tools that I will show you in this section. It's not that the tools aren't useful. In fact, I think they are extremely valuable. Nevertheless, you can create and use a TComObject descendant without ever developing a type library. If you don't need the library, then most people won't bother to develop one. However, if you do create one, then you will have a way to document your objects and to allow your objects to be completely self-descriptive at runtime.

> **NOTE**
>
> When reading the information in this chapter, you might want to have an alternative type library viewer besides the one built into Delphi. To retrieve this second viewer, go to the Microsoft Web site and retrieve the latest version of OleView from the following page:
>
> http://www.microsoft.com/oledev/olecom/oleview.htm
>
> OleView is distributed for free. It allows you to view many of the COM objects on your system, and also to open up a type library and browse it. You cannot edit the type library as you can in the Delphi Type Library Editor.

Creating a Type Library

The example shown in this section is found in the directory called `TypedSystemInfo` on the CD that comes with this book. The DLL is identical to the `SystemInfo` object used in the first portion of this chapter, except that it supports a type library. I will introduce type libraries in this chapter and add considerably more details on this subject in the next chapter.

To create the project, begin just as you did in the previous example. Start an ActiveX library, and then add a COM object to it. State that your `CoClass` is called `SystemHelp2`. Rather than leave the type library option unchecked, this time you should check it. Click OK to close the wizard. Save your project under the name `SystemInformation` and save your main form as `MainServerIMPL`.

You now have a project that contains an empty type library. The Type Library Editor, shown in Figure 14.2, should be visible to you the moment you close the editor. If necessary, you can choose to view the editor by selecting View, Type Library from the Delphi menu.

FIGURE 14.2

The Type Library Editor after you have created and saved an empty library.

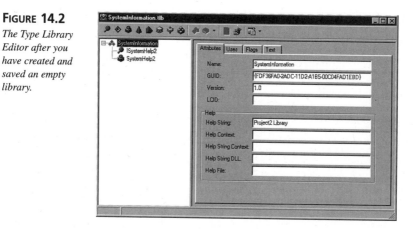

The Type Library Editor has a tree view control on the left side. If you open the nodes in this control, you will see the following hierarchy:

```
SystemInformation:
  ISystemHelp2
  SystemHelp2
```

`SystemInformation` is the name of the type library. In particular, the file on disk where the type library is stored is called `SystemInformation.tlb`. `ISystemHelp2` is the name of your interface. In my program, I renamed this interface to `ISystemInfo`. COM will never confuse this ISystemInfo object with the one in the previous program because each one has a separate GUID associated with it.

The last item in the hierarchy shown by the Type Library Editor is SystemHelp2. This is the name of your CoClass. Each CoClass can support one or more interfaces. To see the interfaces supported by a particular CoClass, first click on the CoClass and then select the Implements tab in the Type Library Editor. (Due to a perhaps unfortunate quirk of the editor's implementation, the Implements tab won't appear until you click on the CoClass itself.) To find the CoClass in the Registry, look under SystemInformation.SystemHelp2. The Prog ID for the first example in this chapter is SystemInfo.SystemHelp. Clearly, each CoClass is differentiated both by its class ID and by its Prog ID.

A toolbar appears at the top of the Type Library Editor. If you don't see the toolbar at first, right-click on the tree view control, and turn on the toolbar feature from the menu. The fifth icon from the right on the toolbar will let you add a method to your interface. To make the icon active, select the interface in the tree view with the left mouse button. Now add three methods to your interface:

```
GetName
GetComputer
DriveInfo
```

When you are done, the Type Library Editor should appear as it does in Figure 14.3.

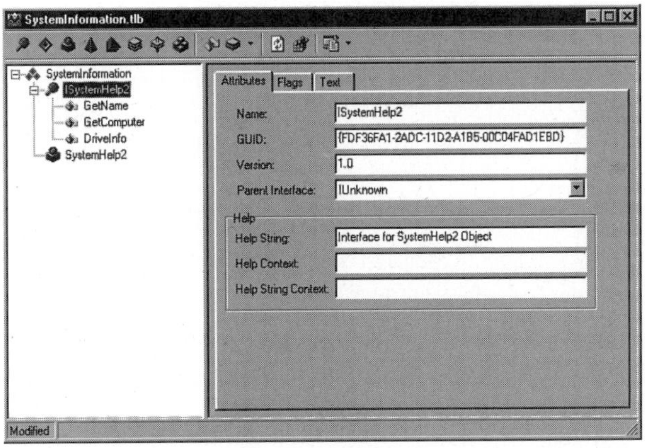

FIGURE 14.3

The Type Library Editor showing three methods on the ISystemInfo *interface.*

If you select the GetName method and turn to the Parameters page, you can specify that this function should have a return type of WideString. Do the same for the GetComputer method. The DriveInfo method should take two parameters: one called TotalCount of type Integer, and the second called DriveInfo of type OleVariant. Both should have a modifier set to out, as shown in Figure 14.4.

FIGURE 14.4

The parameters to the DriveInfo *method as they appear in the Type Library Editor.*

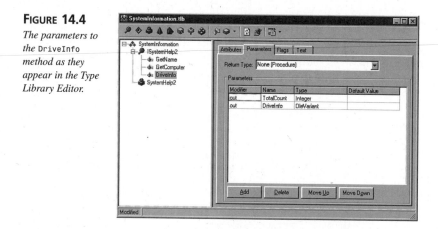

Turn back to the Attributes page in the Type Library Editor and enter a brief help string for each method that you created. Click on the interface itself, and give it a help string. Provide a help string for your CoClass, and then click on the entire Type Library and write the name of a help file, such as SysInfo.hlp. You do not need to add the path to the help file because it will be supplied automatically.

Your type library would be functional without adding the various help strings described in the preceding paragraph. However, this is your chance to document your object so that others can query it and learn about your object dynamically. In particular, the type library you are creating will be linked into your DLL and will travel with it. If you include this kind of information, then you or others can discover exactly what this object is all about.

NOTE

I have included the SysInfo.hlp file on the CD that comes with this book. I will not, however, discuss the generation of that help file in this book other than saying a few short words in this note.

I created the help file in Microsoft Word and saved my work to an RTF file. I then used the HCW.exe utility that ships with Delphi in the Delphi4\Help\Tools directory to convert the RTF document into an HLP file.

The whole process involves doing nothing more than creating a series of cryptic footnotes in the Word document. In particular, if you want to create a hyperlink, enter a word such as GetName with double underlines. Then repeat the word, but remove the double underline attributed from the repetition: GetNameGetName. Set the second copy of GetName to have the hidden attribute. Press Ctrl+Enter to insert a page break after you finished with the GetNameGetName pair. Choose Tools, Options, Nonprinting Characters, All from the Word menu so you can properly view your work.

After the page break type the word GetName again. Right before the word, but after the page break, add two footnotes, both of which contain only the word GetName. To insert the footnote, choose Insert, Footnote from the Word menu, and choose to add a Custom mark. The first footnote should have a $ sign as the Custom mark, and the second should have a # sign as the custom mark. Save your work as `SysInfo.rtf`.

Open `HCW.exe`. Create a new project and add the RTF file to it. Click the Save button and then the Compile button at the bottom of HCW, and you are done. Your completed help file should contain one hyperlink that jumps to the word GetName. For more information, view the `SysInfo.rtf` file and the `SysInfo.hlp` file on the CD that comes with this book. They are stored in a separate directory called `Chap14\HelpFile`.

Now that you have created your type library, you can click the Refresh button on the toolbar at the top of the Type Library Editor. Clicking this button will automatically generate a file called `SystemInformation_TLB.pas`. I will describe this file in some depth in the next chapter. For now, you will use this file only to help you connect to your server from your client program. This is also a good time to register your object by selecting the Register Type Library icon from the toolbar.

The Type Library Editor added three methods to your `MainServerIMPL` file. It should come as no surprise that these methods are called `GetComputer`, `GetName`, and `DriveInfo`:

```
TSystemHelp2 = class(TTypedComObject, ISystemInfo)
protected
  function GetComputer: WideString; stdcall;
  function GetName: WideString; stdcall;
  procedure DriveInfo(out TotalCount: Integer; out DriveInfo:
    OleVariant); stdcall;
end;
```

Fill in the implementations for these methods exactly as you did in the `SystemInfo` example shown earlier in the chapter. When you are done, you should have a file like the one shown in Listing 14.5.

LISTING 14.5 THE IMPLEMENTATION OF DIRECT TTypedComObject DESCENDANT THAT SUPPORTS A TYPE LIBRARY

```
////////////////////////////////////////
// Purpose: COM Object with Type Library
// Project: SystemInformation
// Copyright (c) 1998 by Charlie Calvert
//
unit MainServerIMPL;

{-------------------------------------------------------------------
  This simple implementation of a COM object differs from the one in
  the SystemInfo directory because it descends from TTypedComObject
  rather than from TComObject. TTypedComObject has the ability to
  support a type library, while TComObject does not.

  To understand this file better, view the SystemInformation_TLB
  file, and/or select View, Type Library from the Delphi menu.
-------------------------------------------------------------------}

interface

uses
  Windows, ActiveX, ComObj,
  SystemInfomation_TLB;

type
  TDriveInfoRec = record
    SectorsPerCluster, BytesPerSector: Cardinal;
    NumberOfFreeClusters, TotalNumberOfClusters: Cardinal;
    TotalFree, FreeAvailable, TotalSpace: LargeInt;
  end;

  TSystemHelp2 = class(TTypedComObject, ISystemInfo)
  protected
    function GetComputer: WideString; stdcall;
    function GetName: WideString; stdcall;
    procedure DriveInfo(out TotalCount: Integer; out DriveInfo:
      OleVariant); stdcall;
  end;

implementation

uses
  ComServ, SysUtils;

function TSystemHelp2.GetComputer: WideString;
var
  Len: DWord;
  S: PChar;
begin
```

```
  Len := MAX_COMPUTERNAME_LENGTH + 1;
  GetMem(S, Len);
  if GetComputerName(S, Len) then
    Result := S
  else
    raise Exception.Create('Could not get computer name.');
  FreeMem(S, Len);
end;

function TSystemHelp2.GetName: WideString;
begin
  Result := 'TSystemHelp';
end;

procedure TSystemHelp2.DriveInfo(out TotalCount: Integer;
  out DriveInfo: OleVariant);
const
  Size = 28 * 5;  // 26 letters + 2 extra times plenty of room
                  // for letters
var
  DriveStrings, TempDriveStrings: PChar;
  DriveType: string;
  SectorsPerCluster, BytesPerSector: Cardinal;
  NumberOfFreeClusters, TotalNumberOfClusters: Cardinal;
  FreeAvailable, TotalSpace: LargeInt;
  TotalFree: LargeInt;
  DriveInfoRec: TDriveInfoRec;
  ADrive: Variant;
  TempVar: Variant;
  TempPtr: Pointer;
begin
  TotalCount := 0;
  DriveInfo := VarArrayCreate([0, 28], VarVariant);
  GetMem(DriveStrings, Size);
  GetLogicalDriveStrings(Size, DriveStrings);
  TempDriveStrings := DriveStrings;

  while StrLen(TempDriveStrings) <> 0 do begin
    ADrive := VarArrayCreate([0, 3], VarVariant);
    case GetDriveType(TempDriveStrings) of
      DRIVE_UNKNOWN: DriveType := 'Unknown';
      DRIVE_NO_ROOT_DIR: DriveType := 'Not a root drive';
      DRIVE_REMOVABLE: DriveType := 'Removable';
      DRIVE_FIXED: DriveType := 'Hard Drive';
      DRIVE_REMOTE: DriveType := 'Network';
      DRIVE_CDROM: DriveType := 'CDROM';
      DRIVE_RAMDISK: DriveType := 'RAMDisk';
    else
      DriveType := 'Error';
    end;
```

14

COM CLASSES AND
TYPED LIBRARIES

continues

LISTING 14.5   CONTINUED

```
    ADrive[0] := AnsiString(TempDriveStrings);
    ADrive[1] := DriveType;

    GetDiskFreeSpace(TempDriveStrings, SectorsPerCluster, BytesPerSector,
      NumberOfFreeClusters, TotalNumberOfClusters);

    DriveInfoRec.SectorsPerCluster := SectorsPerCluster;
    DriveInfoRec.BytesPerSector := BytesPerSector;
    DriveInfoRec.NumberOfFreeClusters := NumberOfFreeClusters;
    DriveInfoRec.TotalNumberOfClusters := TotalNumberOfClusters;

    GetDiskFreeSpaceEx(TempDriveStrings, FreeAvailable, TotalSpace,
                       ➥@TotalFree);
    DriveInfoRec.FreeAvailable := FreeAvailable;
    DriveInfoRec.TotalSpace := TotalSpace;
    DriveInfoRec.TotalFree := TotalFree;

    TempVar := VarArrayCreate([0, SizeOf(TDriveInfoRec)], VarByte);
    TempPtr := VarArrayLock(TempVar);
    Move(DriveInfoRec, TempPtr^, SizeOf(TDriveInfoRec));
    VarArrayUnlock(TempVar);
    ADrive[2] := TempVar;

    DriveInfo[TotalCount] := ADrive;
    Inc(TempDriveStrings, StrLen(TempDriveStrings) + 1);
    Inc(TotalCount);
  end;
  FreeMem(DriveStrings, Size);
end;

initialization
  TTypedComObjectFactory.Create(
    ComServer,
    TSystemHelp2,
    Class_SystemHelp2,
    ciMultiInstance,
    tmSingle);
end.
```

When you're viewing this file, you should recognize only a few significant points:

- The SystemInformation_TLB file is automatically included in the uses clause.

- This object descends from TTypedComObject rather than from TComObject. TTypedComObject supports the concept of a type library. In particular, it supports the IProvideClassInfo interface, as described in the next section.

- Each of the method implementations generated by the Type Library Editor is explicitly declared as stdcall. These declarations are necessary when you're working with COM objects. In the next chapter, you will learn about `safecall`, which is an extension of `stdcall`, which automatically supports exception handling.

It is now time to create the client for this program. The client is a very important part of this example because it shows how to retrieve the information from a server's type library and display it to the user.

Creating a Client That Queries a Type Library

The main form for the client program is shown in Listing 14.6. This program is very much like the client program for the `SystemInfo` example, except it supports querying a type library.

LISTING 14.6 THE MAIN FORM FOR THE CLIENT PROGRAM THAT QUERIES THE `SystemInformation` TYPE LIBRARY

```
/////////////////////////////////////////
// Purpose: Query a type library
// Project: SystemInformationClient.dpr
// Copyright (c) 1998 by Charlie Calvert
//
unit MainClient;

{-------------------------------------------------------------------
  Attach to a DLL containing a COM object, retrieve the COM object, talk
  to it, then get information about the methods in the COM object, and
  about the parameters passed to the methods, and even the help file
  for the object. The point of this example is that you can find out
  everything you need to know about the object, so long as the creator
  took the minimal steps necessary to document it in a type library.
  --------------------------------------------------------------------}

interface

uses
  Windows, Messages, SysUtils,
  Classes, Graphics, Controls,
  Forms, Dialogs, StdCtrls,
  SystemInfomation_TLB, ExtCtrls;

type
  TForm1 = class(TForm)
    ListBox1: TListBox;
    Panel1: TPanel;
    ConnectBtn: TButton;
    HelpFileBtn: TButton;
```

continues

14

COM CLASSES AND
TYPED LIBRARIES

LISTING 14.6   CONTINUED

```
    procedure ConnectBtnClick(Sender: TObject);
    procedure HelpFileBtnClick(Sender: TObject);
  private
    FSystemHelp: ISystemInfo;   // The Interface
    FHelpFile: WideString;      // The Interface's Helpfile
    procedure ShowMethods;
  end;

var
  Form1: TForm1;

implementation

uses
  ActiveX, ComObj;

{$R *.DFM}

{-------------------------------------------------------------------------
  A simple generic function that just gets hold of an Interface
  and calls some methods on it. The real action in this example
  is down below in the ShowMethods call.
-------------------------------------------------------------------------}
procedure TForm1.ConnectBtnClick(Sender: TObject);
begin
  FSystemHelp := CoSystemHelp2.Create;
  ListBox1.Items.Add('   Object Name: ' + FSystemHelp.GetName);
  ListBox1.Items.Add('Computer Name: ' + FSystemHelp.GetComputer);
  ListBox1.Items.Add('');
  ShowMethods;
end;

{-------------------------------------------------------------------------
  This function returns at least two TypeInfo interfaces. The first is
  for the coclass, and the second or additional ones are for the
  supported interfaces, such as ISysInfo. (In this case, there will be
  only one.)

  ITypedComObject supports IProvideClassInfo, and it can be used to
  retrieve the ITypeInfo interfaces for a coclass.

  I then call GetRefTypeInfo to get the ITypeInfo for the first and any
  additional interfaces.

  Notice that I have to ReleaseTypeAttr to free the memory for the
  TypeAttr structure.
-------------------------------------------------------------------------}
procedure TForm1.ShowMethods;
var
```

```pascal
    ClassInfo: IProvideClassInfo;
    CoTypeInfo, TypeInfoInterface: ITypeInfo;
    W: PBStrList;
    TypeAttr: PTypeAttr;
    i,j,k, NumInterfaces, NumNames : Integer;
    AWideString: WideString;
begin
    GetMem(W, SizeOf(TBStrList));
    ClassInfo := FSystemHelp as IProvideClassInfo;
    OleCheck(ClassInfo.GetClassInfo(CoTypeInfo));
    OleCheck(CoTypeInfo.GetTypeAttr(TypeAttr));
    ListBox1.Items.Add('GUID: ' + GuidToString(TypeAttr^.GUID));
    OleCheck(CoTypeInfo.GetDocumentation(1, nil, nil, nil, @FHelpFile));
    ListBox1.Items.Add(FHelpFile);
    NumInterfaces := TypeAttr.cImplTypes;
    ListBox1.Items.Add('');
    CoTypeInfo.ReleaseTypeAttr(TypeAttr);

    for k := 1 to NumInterfaces do begin
      OleCheck(CoTypeInfo.GetRefTypeInfo(k, TypeInfoInterface));
      TypeInfoInterface.GetTypeAttr(TypeAttr);
      ListBox1.Items.Add('Methods, Description and Parameters');
      ListBox1.Items.Add('---------------------------------');
      for j := 1 to TypeAttr^.CFuncs do begin
        CoTypeInfo.GetNames(j, W, SizeOf(TBStrList), NumNames);
        for i := 0 to NumNames - 1 do
          if I = 0 then begin
            ListBox1.Items.Add('Method Name: ' + W[i]);
            if SUCCEEDED(CoTypeInfo.GetDocumentation(j, nil,
              @AWideString, nil, nil)) then
                ListBox1.Items.Add('Description: ' + AWideString);
          end else
            ListBox1.Items.Add('Parameter: ' + W[i]);
        ListBox1.Items.Add('');
      end;
      TypeInfoInterface.ReleaseTypeAttr(TypeAttr);
    end;
    FreeMem(W, SizeOf(TBStrList));
    if FHelpFile <> '' then
      HelpFileBtn.Enabled := True;
end;

procedure TForm1.HelpFileBtnClick(Sender: TObject);
begin
  WinExec(PChar('Winhlp32.exe ' + AnsiString(FHelpFile)), sw_ShowNormal);
end;

end.
```

When you run this program, it initializes an instance of your COM object that supports a type library. It then calls the GetName and GetComputer methods just so you can see that the object is working. Finally, it queries the server's type library, displaying a raft of information to the user, as shown in Figure 14.5.

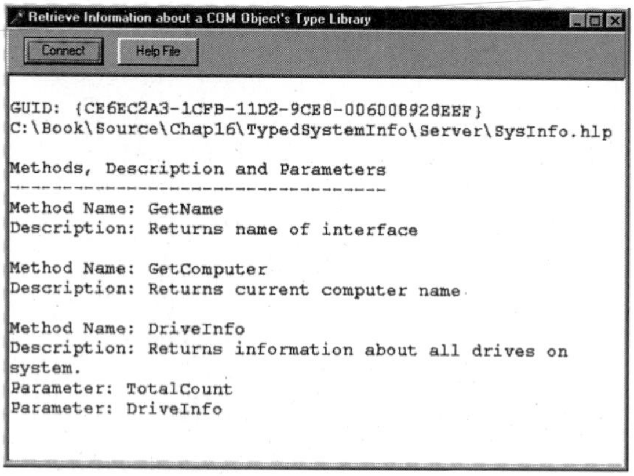

FIGURE 14.5

The memo in the SystemInformation- Client *program displays data supplied by a type library.*

```
Retrieve Information about a COM Object's Type Library          _□×

[ Connect ]   [ Help File ]

GUID: {CE6EC2A3-1CFB-11D2-9CE8-006008928EEF}
C:\Book\Source\Chap16\TypedSystemInfo\Server\SysInfo.hlp

Methods, Description and Parameters
-----------------------------------------
Method Name: GetName
Description: Returns name of interface

Method Name: GetComputer
Description: Returns current computer name

Method Name: DriveInfo
Description: Returns information about all drives on
system.
Parameter: TotalCount
Parameter: DriveInfo
```

The first thing to notice about the SystemInformationClient program is that it has a new technique for creating a COM object instance:

```
procedure TForm1.ConnectBtnClick(Sender: TObject);
begin
  FSystemHelp := CoSystemHelp2.Create;
  ListBox1.Items.Add('  Object Name: ' + FSystemHelp.GetName);
  ListBox1.Items.Add('Computer Name: ' + FSystemHelp.GetComputer);
  ListBox1.Items.Add('');
  ShowMethods;
end;
```

CoSystemHelp2.Create is found in the SystemInformation_TLB.pas file that was automatically generated when you created your client. It is a class method designed explicitly to automatically create an instance of your COM object:

```
class function CoSystemHelp2.Create: ISystemInfo;
begin
  Result := CreateComObject(CLASS_SystemHelp2) as ISystemInfo;
end;
```

As in the Global.pas portion of the previous example, I needed to take some simple steps so my client could find the SystemInformation_TLB.pas file. In particular, note that I saved the server in a directory called server, and the client in a directory called client. In the client, I needed to choose View, Project Options, Directory/Conditionals to change the Search Path so that my client could find the SystemInformation_TLB.pas.

In particular, I entered ..\Server in the Search Path field so that my client could find the XXX_TLB.pas file in the Server directory.

CoSystemHelp2.Create is really a very simple method. In fact, if you trace it through, you will find that it resolves into a simple call to CoCreateInstance. The developers of Delphi just felt that calling CoCreateInstance automatically is easier than your having to fill out its numerous parameters. The declaration for CoSystemHelp2.Create states that this is a class method. Class methods can be called without first initializing an instance of the class to which they belong. In other words, you can directly call CoSystemHelp2.Create without first calling the CoSystemHelp2 constructor.

Retrieving `ITypeInfo`

After you have created an instance of the object, the only thing left to do is retrieve information about the type library from the server:

```
procedure TForm1.ShowMethods;
var
  ClassInfo: IProvideClassInfo;
  CoTypeInfo, TypeInfoInterface: ITypeInfo;
  W: PBStrList;
  TypeAttr: PTypeAttr;
  i,j,k, NumInterfaces, NumNames : Integer;
  AWideString: WideString;
begin
  GetMem(W, SizeOf(TBStrList));
  ClassInfo := FSystemHelp as IProvideClassInfo;
  OleCheck(ClassInfo.GetClassInfo(CoTypeInfo));
  OleCheck(CoTypeInfo.GetTypeAttr(TypeAttr));
  ListBox1.Items.Add('GUID: ' + GuidToString(TypeAttr^.GUID));
  OleCheck(CoTypeInfo.GetDocumentation(1, nil, nil, nil, @FHelpFile));
  ListBox1.Items.Add(FHelpFile);
  NumInterfaces := TypeAttr.cImplTypes;
  ListBox1.Items.Add('');
  CoTypeInfo.ReleaseTypeAttr(TypeAttr);

  for k := 1 to NumInterfaces do begin
    OleCheck(CoTypeInfo.GetRefTypeInfo(k, TypeInfoInterface));
    TypeInfoInterface.GetTypeAttr(TypeAttr);
    ListBox1.Items.Add('Methods, Description and Parameters');
    ListBox1.Items.Add('-----------------------------------');
    for j := 1 to TypeAttr^.CFuncs do begin
      CoTypeInfo.GetNames(j, W, SizeOf(TBStrList), NumNames);
      for i := 0 to NumNames - 1 do
        if I = 0 then begin
          ListBox1.Items.Add('Method Name: ' + W[i]);
          if SUCCEEDED(CoTypeInfo.GetDocumentation(j, nil,
            @AWideString, nil, nil)) then
```

```
              ListBox1.Items.Add('Description: ' + AWideString);
          end else
            ListBox1.Items.Add('Parameter: ' + W[i]);
        ListBox1.Items.Add('');
      end;
      TypeInfoInterface.ReleaseTypeAttr(TypeAttr);
    end;
  FreeMem(W, SizeOf(TBStrList));
  if FHelpFile <> '' then
    HelpFileBtn.Enabled := True;
end;
```

The key call in this object is the one that retrieves the IProvideClassInfo interface from your ISystemHelp2 CoClass:

```
Var
  ClassInfo: IProvideClassInfo;
  CoTypeInfo, TypeInfoInterface: ITypeInfo;
Begin
  // ... Code omitted here
  ClassInfo := FSystemHelp as IProvideClassInfo;
  OleCheck(ClassInfo.GetClassInfo(CoTypeInfo));
```

This code works because your server supports TTypedComObject rather than TComObject. In particular, TTypedComObject supports one new method called GetClassInfo:

```
TTypedComObject = class(TComObject, IProvideClassInfo)
protected
  { IProvideClassInfo }
  function GetClassInfo(out TypeInfo: ITypeInfo): HResult; stdcall;
end;
```

This is the complete declaration for TTypedComObject. All it does is add a single method to TComObject.

GetClassInfo is the only method of the IProvideClassInfo interface:

```
IProvideClassInfo = interface
  ['{B196B283-BAB4-101A-B69C-00AA00341D07}']
  function GetClassInfo(out ti: ITypeInfo): HResult; stdcall;
end;
```

GetClassInfo allows you to retrieve an instance of the ITypeInfo interface. ITypeInfo allows you to query a type library. In particular, it allows you to ask the type library to supply all the methods supported by a particular interface, as well as their parameters and parameter types. Furthermore, you can retrieve any help strings associated with a method, as well as the name and path of the help file for the entire object.

You can use the following to get the Class ID for your CoClass, the name of the CoClass' help file, and the number of interfaces supported by the CoClass:

```
OleCheck(CoTypeInfo.GetTypeAttr(TypeAttr));
ListBox1.Items.Add('GUID: ' + GuidToString(TypeAttr^.GUID));
OleCheck(CoTypeInfo.GetDocumentation(1, nil, nil, nil, @FHelpFile));
ListBox1.Items.Add(FHelpFile);
NumInterfaces := TypeAttr.cImplTypes;
ListBox1.Items.Add('');
CoTypeInfo.ReleaseTypeAttr(TypeAttr);
```

`TypeAttr` is declared to be of type `PTypeAttr`. `TTypeAttr` is declared in `ActiveX.pas`, and is described in detail in the `Ole.hlp` file that ships with Delphi. `Ole.hlp` is installed by default in the `c:\program files\common files\borland shared\mshelp` directory. You can reach it from the Delphi section of the Windows Start menu, but I also like to add it to my Tools menu in the Delphi IDE.

The following is the declaration for `TTypeAttr`:

```
PTypeAttr = ^TTypeAttr;
tagTYPEATTR = record
  guid: TGUID;
  lcid: TLCID;
  dwReserved: Longint;
  memidConstructor: TMemberID;
  memidDestructor: TMemberID;
  lpstrSchema: POleStr;
  cbSizeInstance: Longint;
  typekind: TTypeKind;
  cFuncs: Word;
  cVars: Word;
  cImplTypes: Word;
  cbSizeVft: Word;
  cbAlignment: Word;
  wTypeFlags: Word;
  wMajorVerNum: Word;
  wMinorVerNum: Word;
  tdescAlias: TTypeDesc;
  idldescType: TIDLDesc;
end;
TTypeAttr = tagTYPEATTR;
```

I'm not going to describe all the details of this structure. However, you should notice the `cImplTypes` field, which specifies how many interfaces a `CoClass` supports. If this structure is describing an interface rather than a `CoClass`, then the `cFuncs` and `cVars` fields will say how many functions and variables are associated with an interface.

The `GetDocumentation` call can be used to retrieve information about a `CoClass` or interface. In this case, I want only one of the possible fields that the object can retrieve, so I set all the rest of them to `nil`. You can read more details about this call in `Ole.hlp`.

Notice that when I am through with the `TypeAttr` variable that I call `ITypeInfo.ReleaseTypeAttr` to deallocate the memory associated with the object.

Getting Information on an Interface

After I have queried the CoClass, I can get information about the ISystemInfo interface:

```
OleCheck(CoTypeInfo.GetRefTypeInfo(k, TypeInfoInterface));
```

This call is to the GetRefTypeInfo method of the original ITypeInfo interface retrieved from the server. I am simply asking the original interface, which described the CoClass, for a second ITypeInfo interface. This second ITypeInfo instance describes the ISystemInfo interface. GetRefTypeInfo takes two parameters: the first is the index of the interface I want to retrieve, and the second is a pointer holding the interface that is returned to me by COM.

After I have the interface, I can query it for information about the ISystemInfo interface:

```
TypeInfoInterface.GetTypeAttr(TypeAttr);
for j := 1 to TypeAttr^.CFuncs do begin
  CoTypeInfo.GetNames(j, W, SizeOf(TBStrList), NumNames);
```

The TypeAttr^.CFuncs method, as described earlier, tells me how many functions my interface has. I then call the GetNames method of my CoClass' ITypeInfo interface to retrieve the names and parameters of the functions on the ISystemInfo interface. GetNames takes four parameters:

- The first is the index of the method I want to retrieve.
- The second is a variable of type TBStrList that will hold the list of names.
- The third is the size of the memory allocated for the variable of type TBStrList.
- The last is an out parameter containing the number of names in the TBStrList variable.

If the function I am researching has zero parameters, then NumNames is set to one. If the function takes parameters, then NumNames will be larger than one. On the basis of that simple fact, I can construct the following loop:

```
for i := 0 to NumNames - 1 do
  if i = 0 then begin
    ListBox1.Items.Add('Method Name: ' + W[i]);
    if SUCCEEDED(CoTypeInfo.GetDocumentation(j, nil,
      @AWideString, nil, nil)) then
    ListBox1.Items.Add('Description: ' + AWideString);
  end else
    ListBox1.Items.Add('Parameter: ' + W[i]);
```

This loop lists the name and description of each function on my interface, and it lists the name of each parameter. You won't find a description for a method unless you included it in the type library, as described previously.

This loop uses the GetDocumentation method to retrieve a string describing a particular method. For instance, here is the output for the GetName method:

```
Method Name: GetName
Description: Returns name of interface
```

Here is the output from the DriveInfo method:

```
Method Name: DriveInfo
Description: Returns information about all drives on system.
Parameter: TotalCount
Parameter: DriveInfo
```

My formatting of this data is not very fancy, and I do not do the work necessary to retrieve the types of the individual functions I am querying. Furthermore, rather than just pop up a help file on the ISystemInfo interface as I do in this program, you can dig a little further and pop up the help file open to the function you are currently examining.

The ability to retrieve an ITypeInfo interface from a COM object and query it is really a very impressive bit of technology. Self-describing objects are an enormously powerful feature.

In Delphi, programmers use RTTI to find out about an object. Type libraries are interesting because they let you examine objects made by different compilers and supporting different languages. Using this technology as a base, you can even imagine a time when two objects could come into contact on a network, negotiate a protocol for communication, and begin exchanging information. Right now, Delphi can already use this technology to retrieve the interface for an object written in Object Pascal or in another language. To take advantage of this feature, just choose Project, Import Type Library from the Delphi menu. However, if you explore the distributed programming section of this book, you will see that the idea of having objects floating on a network and communicating with one another is no longer science fiction. These networked-based objects are becoming increasingly intelligent, and the capability for an object to be self-describing is clearly an important, if still nascent, aspect of this technology.

Summary

A number of interesting technologies were discussed in this chapter. One of the highlights was the discussion of Variant arrays. Borland's powerful and very expensive Midas technology is built on top of Variant arrays. In this chapter, you saw how you can easily harness this same powerful technique in your own programs to move complex chunks of data. In Chapter 20 I will show you how to move that same data from one machine to another.

You can use any Delphi type in a DLL that contains COM objects. However, if you want to later move your interface into a DCOM or automation object, then you should choose automation-compatible types, as described in this chapter. Automation-compatible types will be automatically marshaled by the COM subsystem. The discussion of `Variant` arrays shows that there should be no reason to feel too limited by the types available to automation and DCOM programmers. `Variant` arrays are slower than standard Delphi arrays, but they are more flexible.

The most important technology described in this chapter was the simple `TComObject` VCL class. This class allows you to create COM objects that reside in DLLs. A COM object in a DLL can be accessed directly by Delphi using VTables. As a result, you can get very high performance from these objects. At the same time, you can use COM support to control exactly how an object is registered and used on the system. This powerful technology can be harnessed to help control the proliferation of DLLs that litter our hard drives like so much spilled popcorn. In particular, after you register a COM DLL, a simple call to `CoCreateInstance` will retrieve the correct object, and only the correct object, without consumers of the object having to worry about the user not setting up the current path correctly.

In the last few pages of the chapter, you had a chance to look at type libraries and their relationship to a simple COM object. I am going to talk about type libraries in more depth in the next chapter. However, this chapter showed that they provide a simple means of thoroughly describing an object. Type libraries get linked into a DLL and travel with it. A DLL with a type library attached is a DLL that can document and describe itself. This very powerful feature helps you organize and maintain the code on your system. The right kind of COM browser will let you view all the COM objects on your system and will automatically take you to the help files that should, in an ideal world, be associated with each of those objects.

Creating COM Automation Servers and Clients

CHAPTER 15

In this chapter, you will learn about OLE automation; that is, you will learn how to create COM servers and clients. This material is closely related to important topics covered later in the book, such as using MIDAS, using DCOM, and automating Word and Excel.

More particularly, in this chapter, you will learn

- Why OLE automation exists and what it does
- How to create simple clients and servers
- What type libraries are and how to work with them
- How `IDispatch` works
- How dispinterfaces work
- How to work with `OleVariants`, `Variants`, and `Variant` arrays

A great deal of material is presented in this chapter. Most of it is not particularly difficult to understand, but it takes awhile to absorb. If you are new to this subject, I suggest you read this chapter in its entirety. Sometimes I will introduce a topic, tell you enough about it to allow you to get some work done, and then put the topic aside until later. This means you won't know all you need to learn about some topics until you have read the entire chapter.

In general, however, OLE automation is not a particularly difficult subject. You just need to understand a little theory and get acquainted with a few tools, and in no time you will be up and running.

Understanding OLE Automation Clients and Servers

Together, simple COM clients and servers of the type shown in this chapter are, in my opinion, one of the most important developments in contemporary programming. We already have multitasking operating systems that allow us to smoothly and easily run multiple programs at the same time. What COM brings to the picture is the ability to get these programs working together in a single, concerted effort.

Often programmers build large monolithic programs that could easily be broken up into a series of smaller COM objects. These smaller programs are easier to debug, easier to understand, and easier to maintain. Any shared code that needs to be used by all the applications in a project can be placed in DLLs, preferably COM-based DLLs.

Programmers might object to this kind of architecture for one reason or another, but one thing you don't need to worry about is the possibility that the COM subsystem will let you down. OLE automation has always worked for me. I've never asked a local COM server to do something and have it fail to respond or fail to work because of some innate shortcoming in the COM subsystems. OLE automation is very reliable. I regard it as reliable in the same sense I think of a DOS batch file as reliable—it always works.

> **NOTE**
>
> Do not allow yourself to be tempted to use DDE instead of COM. DDE, in my opinion, and in the opinion of many others, was simply a failed first attempt at automation. Its primary value stems from the lessons Microsoft engineers learned in this, their first attempt at interprocess communication. In particular, I think DDE is overly complex and fraught with hard-to-track-down bugs that Microsoft never satisfactorily resolved. It is also a dead-end technology that is no longer evolving. COM, on the other hand, is a clean technology that is continually evolving, and it is the focus of a great deal of effort at Redmond.

Another reason to embrace OLE automation is simply because it's the polite thing to do. I'm reaching the point where I find it very annoying to discover applications that won't let me use their resources via automation. As a programmer, I get frustrated paying money for a product and then finding that I can't script it with OLE automation. Here is this great tool sitting on my system that can perhaps solve all kinds of problems for me, but I always have to use it through a slow, clunky, menu-based interface. Why won't the developers let me take full advantage of their tool?

Viewing this situation from the opposite perspective, many programmers might find new audiences for their tools by providing automation interfaces. Suddenly, their programs might sell not only to end users, but also to programmers who might want to distribute the application widely in order to use its services.

The final vision that OLE automation brings to mind is a version of the distributed programming model discussed later in this book. In this vision, small automation objects are distributed widely across one or more machines and are available on most systems for a variety of purposes. In this world of distributed automation objects, programmers rarely write low-level code. Instead, they simply call the various COM objects and automation services available on a particular system. This distributed computing model may seem far-fetched to some people, but it is becoming more and more of a reality almost daily.

I think wise programmers will begin to think in terms of creating systems of related COM and automation objects. Then they can call on these services from a variety of locations and use them for whatever purpose they see fit. The technology to do so reliably is totally in place; the difficulty is in learning to redesign and rethink our applications so that they fit into this model. Portions of the game presented in Part VII, "Game Programming," will use this technology, so you will get at least one example of how it might work in a real-world situation.

Building a Simple COM Server and Client

In this section, you will see how to create a simple automation server and client. Later in the chapter, after I discuss more about the theory behind COM, I will return to this subject and show how to create more complex automation servers.

This section of the chapter is built around two sample programs: one a client and the other a server. You can find both examples in the directory called SimpleAutoServer on the CD.

Building a Simple Server

To create a new automation object, you should open an existing project that you want to turn into a server or else create a new project. In this particular case, starting with a new project would be best, but in your own work, you should be aware that you may sometimes begin with an existing program that you want to offer as a service to others. When you are ready to go, you should proceed as follows:

1. Select File, New and choose the ActiveX page from the New Items dialog.
2. Click the icon labeled Automation Object.
3. The Automation Object Wizard appears and prompts you for a class name. Type a reasonable name, such as MethodObject. You will be taken immediately to the Type Library Editor.
4. Save your project under the name SimpleAutoMethods, with Unit2 being saved as MethodObjectIMPL.pas, Unit1 being saved as MainServer, and the project source saved as SimpleAutoServer.dpr.

These steps are the only ones necessary to create an automation server. At this point in your project development, you have a main program, an attached module for defining your automation object, and a type library. In short, you have a complete automation server that doesn't yet do anything useful.

I have a fairly simple convention for naming clients and servers. In a classic situation, I will name the file that implements my server XXXIMPL.pas, the main form for the project

`MainServer.pas`, and the server itself `XXXServer.dpr`. The main form of the client is usually called `MainClient`, and the project source will be named `XXXClient.dpr`. I often save the client into a directory called `Client`, and the server into a directory called `Server`.

TIP

If you want to convert a standard application to an automation server, you should leave the body of your application unchanged. Simply add a new file or files to your application, and use it to define objects that wrap the functionality of your main application. In other words, don't try to integrate the automation objects into the source for your application. Instead, simply wrap your main objects inside an automation object.

Adding Methods to Your Server

Take a moment to consider the steps necessary to create a method in the Type Library Editor. This method can be called from a client program, and so it will add real-world functionality to your program. (If you are having trouble reaching the Type Library Editor, chose View, Type Library from the Delphi menu. If this option is grayed out, then you are not working with a valid automation server. Review the steps in the preceding section to fix this problem.)

Here are the steps you take in the Type Library Editor to add a method to your interface:

1. As shown in Figure 15.1, you should select the interface you want to work with. In this case, it is called `IMethodObject`.

FIGURE 15.1

A type library, as it should appear just before you start inserting methods or properties.

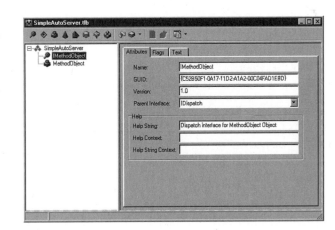

2. Select the Method button from the toolbar at the top of the editor.

3. As shown in Figure 15.2, in the Name field of the Attributes page, type the name of your method. In this case, you should type GetName.

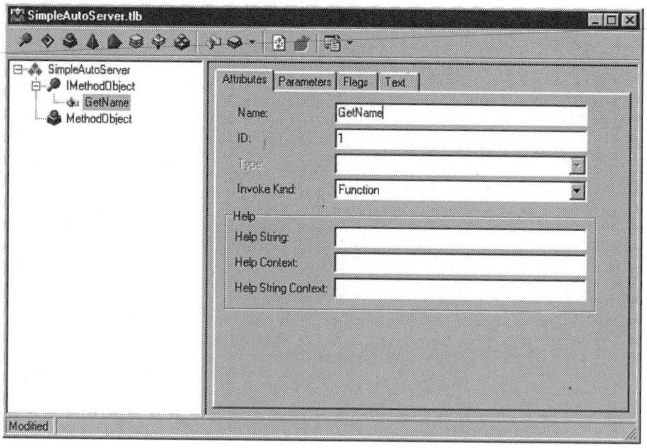

FIGURE 15.2

Giving your method a name.

4. Turn to the Parameters page and state that your function should return a WideString. You can do so by using the drop-down list at the top of this page, as shown in Figure 15.3.

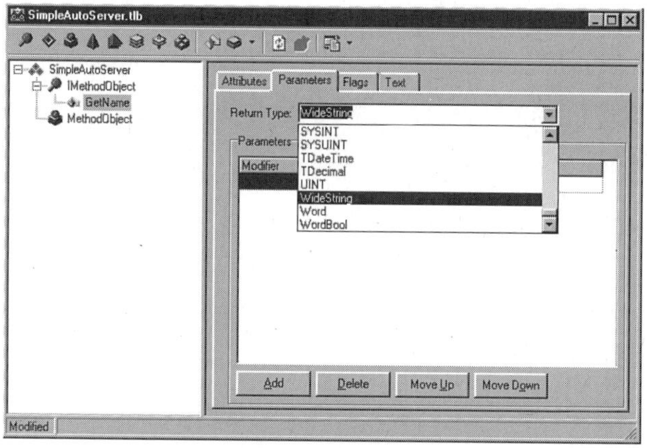

FIGURE 15.3

Turn to the Parameters page and declare that you want to create a function that returns a WideString.

5. If you turn to the Text page, you can check the code generated for your method:

```
function GetName: WideString [dispid $00000001]; safecall;
```

6. Click the Refresh button at the far right of the toolbar at the top of the Type Library Editor. (Saving your project performs an automatic refresh.)

At this stage, you are free to leave the Type Library Editor, as your work there is completed. If you want to return to it at any time, you can select View, Type Library.

Several files were created while you were in the Type Library Editor, as shown in Table 15.1 (the default filenames shown here may be different in your project). Some of these files, particularly the TLB file, may not be fully generated until you click the Refresh button. Furthermore, you may need to go to the View, Units menu item to actually view the file. However, by the time you save and compile the files, you should be able to find them in complete form.

TABLE 15.1 THE FILES CREATED WHEN YOU ARE IN THE TYPE LIBRARY EDITOR

File	Description
`SimpleAutoServer_TLB.pas`	This file contains the declarations for your interfaces and classes. It is designed to allow you to access them easily. You should never edit this file by hand, but you should look at it carefully so you understand what it does. If you want to make changes to the file, select View, Type Library and make changes through the editor. I will explain more about the code in this file later in this chapter.
`MethodObjectIMPL.pas`	Here, you can find the implementation for your interface. In this file, you can add code that makes your object do what you want it to do. Most of the time you can ignore the TLB file and focus your attention primarily on this one. Programmers often save this file with a name that ends in IMPL because it is the place where you *impl*ement your objects.

I discuss the Type Library Editor in much more depth later in this chapter, in the section called "Type Libraries," and in the subsections that immediately follow it.

Viewing the Generated Source Code

In your `MethodObjectIMPL` source code, you should now find the following object declaration:

```
TMethodObject = class(TAutoObject, IMethodObject)
protected
  function GetName: WideString; safecall;
  { Protected declarations }
end;
```

An empty implementation for your object is shown in the CPP file for your custom object:

```
function TMethodObject.GetName: WideString;
begin

end;
```

15

CREATING COM
SERVERS AND
CLIENTS

You should leave the format of this code alone, doing nothing more than adding your implementation:

```
function TMethodObject.GetName: WideString;
begin
  Result := 'TMethodObject: ' + TimeToStr(Now);
end;
```

You will need to add SysUtils to your unit to support the TimeToStr function.

At this point, you can save and compile your application server. Be sure to run it once so that it is registered with the system. To check that you server is registered, open RegEdit.exe, a utility that comes with Windows, and look for your server by its application name in the HKEY_CLASSES_ROOT section. Note that this section begins with a bunch of extensions, all of which begin with a period. You should be looking for a listing that reads SimpleAutoServer.MethodObject.

Adding Properties to Interfaces

This sample program doesn't provide a property, but if you want to create a new one, click on the Property button on the toolbar. On the Attributes page, you can rename the property and give it a type. You can also add parameters to a property or fine-tune its features on the Flags page. However, I will not use either of these options in this book, as they are beyond the scope of the current work. For more information on types that automation objects use, see the "Valid Automation Types" section in this chapter.

You should note that in Delphi you usually access a COM property by calling its get or set method directly. In other words, you don't use the simple direct assignments to a property that you would use in the VCL. The one exception to this rule occurs when you are using a dispinterface (see the "Calling Methods via a Dispinterface" section in this chapter) rather than a dual interface.

Building a Simple Client

Your client program is going to access the automation objects that reside in your server. A description of those objects is stored in both SimpleAutoServer_TLB and in the server's type library. The type library was created automatically when you were in the Type Library Editor. You can recognize this file on disk by its .tlb extension.

On the client side, you can now do one of two things:

- Add SimpleAutoServer_TLB.pas to the uses clause of your client.
- Go to the Delphi menu, and choose Project, Import Type Library. Doing so automatically causes the re-creation of SimpleAutoServer_TLB.pas.

At this stage, I don't want to talk too much about type libraries, as that is a subject I will explore in depth later in this chapter, in a section called "Type Libraries." All you really have to see right now is that as long as you have a binary automation object and its type library, you can automatically generate the header file that will declare the object's types and give you access to the object itself.

Now take a look at `SimpleAutoServer_TLB.pas`, shown in Listing 15.1, and try to understand why it exists and what it can do for you.

LISTING 15.1 `SimpleAutoServer_TLB.pas` CONTAINS THE DECLARATIONS FOR THE OBJECTS IN YOUR SERVER

```
unit SimpleAutoServer_TLB;

// **************************************************************** //
// WARNING                                                         //
// -------                                                         //
// The types declared in this file were generated from data read   //
// from a Type Library. If this type library is explicitly or      //
// indirectly (via another type library referring to this type     //
// library) reimported, or the 'Refresh' command of the Type Library //
// Editor activated while editing the Type Library, the contents of //
// this file will be regenerated and all manual modifications      //
// will be lost.                                                   //
// **************************************************************** //

// PASTLWTR : $Revision:   1.11.1.62  $
// File generated on 6/16/98 9:09:23 PM from Type Library
// described below.

// **************************************************************** //
// Type Lib: D:\SrcPas\Unleash4\Chap15\SimpleAutoMethods\
// SimpleAutoMethods.tlb
// IID\LCID: {EA948DE0-055C-11D2-9CE8-006008928EEF}\0
// Helpfile:
// HelpString: Project1 Library
// Version:    1.0
// **************************************************************** //

interface

uses Windows, ActiveX, Classes, Graphics, OleCtrls, StdVCL;

// **************************************************************** //
// GUIDS declared in the TypeLibrary. Following prefixes are used:  //
//    Type Libraries     : LIBID_xxxx                              //
//    CoClasses          : CLASS_xxxx                              //
//    DISPInterfaces      : DIID_xxxx                              //
```

continues

LISTING 15.1 CONTINUED

```
//    Non-DISP interfaces: IID_xxxx                                    //
// ******************************************************************* //
const
  LIBID_SimpleAutoMethods: TGUID =
  ➥'{EA948DE0-055C-11D2-9CE8-006008928EEF}';
  IID_IMethodObject: TGUID =
  ➥'{EA948DE1-055C-11D2-9CE8-006008928EEF}';
  CLASS_MethodObject: TGUID =
  ➥'{EA948DE3-055C-11D2-9CE8-006008928EEF}';
type

// ******************************************************************* //
// Forward declaration of interfaces defined in Type Library          //
// ******************************************************************* //
  IMethodObject = interface;
  IMethodObjectDisp = dispinterface;

// ******************************************************************* //
// Declaration of CoClasses defined in Type Library                   //
// (NOTE: Here we map each CoClass to its Default Interface)           //
// ******************************************************************* //
  MethodObject = IMethodObject;


// ******************************************************************* //
// Interface: IMethodObject
// Flags:     (4416) Dual OleAutomation Dispatchable
// GUID:      {EA948DE1-055C-11D2-9CE8-006008928EEF}
// ******************************************************************* //
  IMethodObject = interface(IDispatch)
    ['{EA948DE1-055C-11D2-9CE8-006008928EEF}']
    function GetName: WideString; safecall;
  end;

// ******************************************************************* //
// DispIntf:  IMethodObjectDisp
// Flags:     (4416) Dual OleAutomation Dispatchable
// GUID:      {EA948DE1-055C-11D2-9CE8-006008928EEF}
// ******************************************************************* //
  IMethodObjectDisp = dispinterface
    ['{EA948DE1-055C-11D2-9CE8-006008928EEF}']
    function GetName: WideString; dispid 1;
  end;

  CoMethodObject = class
    class function Create: IMethodObject;
    class function CreateRemote(const MachineName: string):
    ➥IMethodObject;
  end;
```

```
implementation

uses ComObj;

class function CoMethodObject.Create: IMethodObject;
begin
  Result := CreateComObject(CLASS_MethodObject) as IMethodObject;
end;

class function CoMethodObject.CreateRemote(
  const MachineName: string): IMethodObject;
begin
  Result := CreateRemoteComObject(MachineName,
    CLASS_MethodObject) as IMethodObject;
end;

end.
```

Here are the major objects declared inside `SimpleAutoServer_TLB` and a definition of each:

```
IMethodObject = interface(IDispatch)
IMethodObjectDisp = dispinterface
CoMethodObject = class
```

- `IMethodObject` (`IDispatch`)—This class implements the `IDispatch` interface, which makes an object callable from languages such as VB that do not support virtual function tables. You can easily use this class inside Delphi by calling its methods off a `Variant`, but doing so entails considerable overhead that you can avoid by using a virtual function table (VTable) as described elsewhere in this chapter. In Delphi, you won't have much use for this rather slow and awkward interface, but it is absolutely necessary to your object. As you will see later in the chapter, there is no such thing as automation without the `IDispatch` interface.

- `IMethodObjectDisp` (`dispinterface`)—This class gives you an easy means of directly calling the methods and properties supported by an `IDispatch` interface, and you will have somewhat better performance. When you use this class, you call the methods of your object via a dual interface; that is, you make calls directly through `IDispatch.Invoke` rather than having to first call `GetIDsOfNames`.

- `CoMethodObject`—Use this class to automatically create instances of your object. Notice that the methods of this object are declared as class methods, so you don't have to allocate an instance of the class on the heap before using these methods to create an instance of your class. `CoMethodObject` exists because the standard means of creating a COM class involves calling a somewhat complicated function named `CoCreateInstance`. The call to this function can be confusing to neophytes and annoying to sophisticates, so `CoMethodObject` can be used to call the function for you automatically. I will, however, show you how to call `CoCreateInstance` at the end of this chapter.

Calling Methods via `TCOMInterface`

You can access the methods of an automation object from a remote program in several different ways. One method allows you to access the methods via `Variants`, and a second lets you get at them via something called a smart interface. A third technology, involving dispinterfaces, is also commonly used. Examples of both of the first two technologies are shown in Listing 15.2.

LISTING 15.2   THE MAIN FORM FROM THE `SimpleAutoClient` PROJECT

```
/////////////////////////////////////////
// Purpose: Call SimpleAutoServer.exe
// Project: SimpleAutoClient
// Copyright (c) 1998 by Charlie Calvert
//
unit MainClient;

interface

uses
   Windows, Messages, SysUtils,
   Classes, Graphics, Controls,
   Forms, Dialogs, StdCtrls,
   ExtCtrls, SimpleAutoServer_TLB, Buttons;

type
   TForm2 = class(TForm)
     CallServerBtn: TButton;
     Edit1: TEdit;
     Bevel1: TBevel;
     CloseServerBtn: TBitBtn;
     procedure CallServerBtnClick(Sender: TObject);
     procedure CloseServerBtnClick(Sender: TObject);
   private
      F: IMethodObject;
   end;

var
   Form2: TForm2;

implementation

uses
   ComObj;
```

```
{$R *.DFM}

procedure TForm2.CallServerBtnClick(Sender: TObject);
begin
  if F = nil then
    F := IMethodObject(CoMethodObject.Create);
  Edit1.Text := F.GetName;
end;

procedure TForm2.CloseServerBtnClick(Sender: TObject);
begin
  if F <> nil then
    F := nil;
end;

end.
```

When you run this program, you will see that the interface contains a single button and an edit control. If you click on the button, the server is called, and the GetName method on the server returns a string that is displayed in the client's edit control. The outcome is shown in Figure 15.4. This application has its FormStyle set to fsStayOnTop. I use this setting to ensure that the server does not cover up the client, thereby hiding the client's interface from you.

FIGURE 15.4

The string retrieved by calling GetName *is visible in the client's edit control.*

Here is a method that uses CoMethodObject to create an instance of your class and then calls its methods:

```
TForm2 = class(TForm)
  ...
```

```
    F: IMethodObject;
    ...
  end;

procedure TForm2.Button1Click(Sender: TObject);
begin
  if F = nil then
    F := CoMethodObject.Create;
  ShowMessage(F.GetName);
end;
```

CoMethodObj.Create is declared in SimpleAutoServer_TLB.pas. If you want to be comfortable with OLE automation in Delphi, you must spend a considerable amount of time with this file that was auto-generated by the Type Library Editor. Furthermore, you must include SimpleAutoServer_TLB in your uses clause. Note that I declare F globally, which means the server will stay in memory until the client closes or until someone sets F to nil.

This code uses the CoMethodObject object to return an instance of your object. If you look beneath the hood, you will see that CoMethodObject just calls CoCreateInstance, as explained in the preceding section of this chapter. CoCreateInstance is the standard Microsoft OLE technology for creating an instance of an object. Here is the declaration for your CoMethodObject proxy:

```
CoMethodObject = class
  class function Create: IMethodObject;
  class function CreateRemote(const MachineName: string): IMethodObject;
end;
```

This declaration provides two methods: one for creating a remote object and one for creating a local object. You can actually use either method to perform either task, but here I use the local routine (see Chapter 20, "DCOM," to learn about creating remote objects):

```
F = CoMethodObject.Create;
```

After you have the object back, you can call its methods directly. In fact, your calls do not go through IDispatch at all, you are actually making a direct call into the object's VMT. However, the call must still be marshaled across the boundary between your client application and the server. This marshaling is handled automatically by Windows, and neither you nor the Delphi developers have to do anything special to make it happen.

When you're examining this call, note the use of the WideString type. The WideString type has two bytes per character, and is therefore compatible with BSTRs, which are BASIC strings used to marshal string data in COM. I will talk more about both marshaling and BSTRs later in this chapter. For now, all you really need to know is that whenever COM requests that you use a BSTR, you can simply use a WideString. Delphi automatically handles conversion between WideStrings and standard Delphi AnsiStrings.

Before closing this section, I should perhaps make a few other points. The first is that you should never close a server manually if it was launched via automation. Instead, simply let the variable that points at it in your client go out of scope, or set it to nil:

```
procedure TForm2.BitBtn1Click(Sender: TObject);
begin
  if F <> nil then
    F := nil;
end;
```

The code shown here will close the server. You can legally launch and close the server as many times as you want during the run of the client. If you want, you can even write code like this:

```
procedure TForm2.Button1Click(Sender: TObject);
var
  F: IMethodObject;
begin
  if F = nil then
    F := CoMethodObject.Create;
  Edit1.Text := F.GetName;
end;
```

This code will hang onto the server just long enough to call GetName. Then, the moment F goes out of scope, the server will disappear.

That is all I really need to say about this simple example. In the next section, I will talk a little about using dispinterfaces.

Calling Methods via a Dispinterface

Ninety-nine percent of the time, you will want to make your calls to a server using standard interfaces as shown in the preceding section. However, some tools, such as Visual Basic, don't have great support for standard interfaces. As a result, Delphi supports dispinterfaces, to magnanimously give a leg up to its less-gifted competitors.

Here is an example of how to get to an object using a dispinterface:

```
procedure TForm2.Button1Click(Sender: TObject);
var
  F: IMethodObjectDisp;
begin
  F := IMethodObjectDisp(CoMethodObject.Create);
  ShowMessage(F.GetName);
end;
```

If you look in the header for the `SimpleAutoServer_TLB` file, you will find the following method of the `IMethodObjDisp` class:

```
function GetName: WideString; dispid 1;
```

This code is generated for you automatically by the Type Library Editor. It will call the method of the object you want to access, using the dispatch identifier of the method. Notice that the dispatch `ID` is hard-coded into the method. The fact that the `dispatch ID` is hard-coded into the code is the reason that it is called a dispinterface. The call to `OleFunction` ultimately resolves into a call to `IDispatch.Invoke`. In short, the hard-coded `dispatch ID` helps circumvent the need for a call to `IDispatch.GetIDsOfNames`, but the call to `OleFunction` ultimately resolves into a call to `IDispatch.Invoke`.

To understand all this information better, you should copy `ComObj.pas` from the Delphi source directory into the current directory, rebuild your program, and then step directly into `ComObj` when you call `GetName`. Try this approach in all three possible ways. That is, step into `GetName` with dispinterface, as shown in this section. If you use this approach, you will be taken into special assembler-based methods that invoke your method off the dispatch interface.

Next, go back to the original version of the `Button1Click` method, and try to step into `GetName`. This time, you won't be able to step into it because you are making the call directly off the VTable.

Finally, rewrite your code to access the method off a `Variant`:

```
procedure TForm2.Button2Click(Sender: TObject);
var
  V: Variant;
begin
  V := CreateOleObject('SimpleAutoMethods.MethodObject');
  ShowMessage(V.GetName);
end;
```

When you call this method, you will have to step through the `GetIDsOfNames` and `Invoke` methods from `ComObj.pas`, showing that you had to make two round trips to the object to call one method. If you are unclear about this `Variant`-based technology, you can explore it in considerable depth in Chapter 16, "Using Delphi to Automate Word and Excel," and in somewhat less depth in the next section of this chapter.

Calling methods in all three ways should help drive home the difference between these technologies. In most cases, you call methods directly off a VTable, as shown in the first example. This technology is preferable because it gives you compile-time type checking and somewhat better performance.

Once again, I want to stress that dispinterfaces are supported primarily for the sake of other languages that don't know how to call methods directly off a VTable. In other words, it's a good thing that Delphi supports dispinterfaces, but most Delphi programmers can pass over this subject.

Calling Methods off a `Variant`

If you don't have access to the requisite headers or to a type library, you can still call the methods of an object off the `IDispatch` interface. If you want, you can call `IDispatch.GetIDsOfNames` and `IDispatch.Invoke` directly. A simpler way to access the same technology is provided by the `Variant` type:

```
procedure TForm2.Button2Click(Sender: TObject);
var
  V: Variant;
begin
  V := CreateOleObject('SimpleAutoServer.MethodObject');
  ShowMessage(V.GetName);
end;
```

In the technology shown here, you can create an instance of an object by calling the VCL routine `CreateOleObject`. Simply pass in the ProgID of the object you want to retrieve, and you will receive in return a `Variant` that wraps an instance of `IDispatch`. The ProgID is a string made up of the name of your server, a period, and the name of your automation object.

If you are unclear as to what the ProgID for your class might be, simply open `RegEdit.exe`. Look in the `HKEY_CLASSES_ROOT` section for the alphabetically arranged listings of all the automation servers on your system. At the start, extensions are listed, each beginning with a period. Obviously, they are listed before the servers, which are listed by name, where the name in question is the name of your server, plus your automation class. So skip over the extensions, and then look for `SimpleAutoServer.MethodObject`. (You can figure out the ProgID for yourself, but if you do get confused, you can always look up the name in the Registry.)

The `Variant` type has a number of tricks up its sleeve. The big one is simply to call `GetIDsOfNames` and `Invoke` for you automatically if you pass in the name of the method you want to call:

```
S := V.GetName;
```

As I explained earlier, you should normally use interfaces instead of `Variant`s. However, `Variant`s do have the major advantage of allowing you to work in the absence of type libraries or interface declarations, or when you're just in too much of a hurry to want to mess with either of those tools. Once again, I will go into this whole subject in great depth in the next chapter.

This is the end of my description of a simple Automation client and server. At this stage, you should begin to have some sense of how automation is put together, but you may still have a number of unanswered questions. To help you better understand how automation works, I'm going to back away from the hands-on material found in this section and talk a little bit more about the theory behind this technology.

IDispatch, Dual Interfaces, and Dispinterfaces

IDispatch is an important interface that plays a big role in OLE automation. This interface is meant primarily for Visual Basic users, though Object Pascal and C++ programmers can also access it. IDispatch is useful to VB programmers because it lets them access COM interfaces without using objects. In particular, VB is not an OOP-based language, so it can't take full advantage of COM. It can, however, use dispinterfaces. IDispatch is a helper class that brings VB into the fold of COM. Many other tools, such as Word and Excel, can also call COM interfaces via IDispatch.

> **NOTE**
>
> IDispatch is typically slower than other interfaces. However, COM interfaces accessed across program or network boundaries are always quite slow compared to calls into your current program or into a DLL. It's arguable that these cross boundary calls are so slow that the additional overhead of IDispatch isn't particularly significant.

You might find IDispatch useful under two circumstances:

- When you want to find a quick and dirty way to get to an automation object. (I personally never underestimate the value of quick-and-dirty programming techniques!)

- When you want to make sure that the objects you create can be used by third-party developers. In particular, you might want your code callable from VB or some other language that does not support true objects.

Delphi uses a technology called dual interfaces that enables a single object to support both IDispatch and a custom interface. Therefore, the objects you create can be accessed via IDispatch from VB or Word, or the same object can be accessed directly from Object Pascal or C++. (When I say you can access the object directly, I mean you can access it the same way you would access standard, non-COM objects via Object Pascal or C++.)

A third technique, called a dispinterface, is also automatically available in Delphi. A dispinterface lives in a world halfway between an `IDispatch` interface and a true Object Pascal object. In particular, `IDispatch` works by allowing you to query an object and ask for a series of numeric tokens that can be used to access the object's functions or parameters. The method used to query the object is called `IDispatch.GetIDsOfNames`.

When you know the tokens to use, you can pass them to the object to invoke its methods. The call used to invoke a method on an object is called `IDispatch.Invoke`.

The problem with `IDispatch` is that you have to make two calls to the object to invoke one method. The first call retrieves the token you want to use, and the second actually invokes the method in question.

The tokens mentioned in the preceding paragraph are called dispatch identifiers or Disp IDs. A dispinterface is an interface that has knowledge of the set of dispatch IDs for an object implemented via `IDispatch`. The client can process this dispinterface and then make calls into an `IDispatch` interface in one single trip. In other words, it already knows the tokens that need to be used, so it does not need to query for them before calling `IDispatch.Invoke`. This knowledge speeds up the process of using an `IDispatch` interface, but the process is still not as fast as calling a method directly via a virtual function table, which is what you can do when using a true interface in Object Pascal or C++. The following section discusses the use of virtual function tables. I am going to continue this discussion of dual interfaces in the next subsection by one of this chapter.

Calling the SimpleAutoServer from Word

Calling your Delphi automation server from Word is extremely simple. To get started, create a new blank document in Microsoft Word. This example uses Word 97 but should also work with earlier versions that support COM.

In the document, enter some text that says "Press button to call Delphi Server." In Word, choose View, Toolbar and pop up the Control Toolbox dialog. Drop a button on your document from the Control Toolbox. You are automatically placed in design mode when you drop buttons. Now double-click on the button, and Visual Basic for Word will come up automatically.

Enter the following method into Visual Basic:

```
Private Sub CommandButton1_Click()
  Dim DelphiObject As Object
```

```
Set DelphiObject = CreateObject("SimpleAutoServer.MethodObject")
ActiveDocument.Paragraphs(1).Range.InsertAfter (DelphiObject.GetName)
End Sub
```

Now save your work. When you click the button on your document, the Delphi server will be called, and the text retrieved from the server will be displayed in your document.

> **NOTE**
>
> If you make a typo entering the ProgID of your server, you will have to wait for the operation to time out. This process can take quite awhile, perhaps several minutes. In the meantime, Word and Visual Basic for Word will not respond at all.

For the sake of clarity, I should perhaps add that a special edition of Visual Basic comes with each copy of Word 97. It is not the standard version of Visual Basic, but it is powerful enough for you to do fairly serious programming inside it, assuming that you are willing to live within the constraints of the BASIC language. Chapter 22, "ActiveForms," discusses this version of Visual Basic in greater detail and shows how to embed an entire Delphi form inside a Microsoft Word or Microsoft Excel document.

You can find an example of the code discussed in this section of the chapter in the Word 97 document named `CallDelphiObjectFromWord.doc` on the CD that accompanies this book. To get to the code stored in the document, load the document into Word, and select Tools, Macro, Visual Basic Editor.

As a final note to this section, I should perhaps add that I am as concerned as anyone I know about the degree to which Microsoft has come to dominate the desktop. Nevertheless, the fact that Word and Excel come with built-in versions of Visual Basic that are automation-aware is an extremely significant fact from the point of view of many developers. This incredibly powerful technology significantly changes the range of things you can easily do with a copy of Delphi.

VTables and Dual Interfaces

By now, you should have some sense of the importance of `IDispatch` and dispinterfaces. However useful they may be for Word, Excel, and Visual Basic developers, though, Delphi programmers still rely primarily on standard interfaces and their VTables. If you are not clear what a VTable is, refer to Chapter 13, "Interfaces and the Basics of COM," for more information.

Obviously, a conflict of interest exists between the needs of Word, Excel, and VB and the needs of Delphi programmers. One group of people likes IDispatch and dispinterfaces, whereas the second group likes straight VTables. The solution to this problem is provided by Delphi with something called a dual interface.

A dual interface is an interface that will let the "easy" languages such as VB or Excel call COM objects via IDispatch. At the same time, Object Pascal and C++ programmers can call the object's methods via a virtual function table.

The same Delphi mechanism that creates dual interfaces will also automatically create a dispinterface, which means that in this one case, you can have your cake and eat it too, and still have something left over for late-night snacks. That is, you can create one object that supports both VB and Object Pascal, while also supporting IDispatch, dispinterfaces, and virtual function tables. I should perhaps add that the most recent versions of VB know how to use dispinterfaces. As a result, VB can call COM objects with a fairly high degree of efficiency. By default, Delphi creates dual interfaces for all your objects. For instance, the SimpleAutoServer has a dual interface.

Dual interfaces are not nearly as complicated as they might sound. They are simply objects that have virtual function tables that include all the methods from IDispatch plus any functions you want to tack on to the end. If you want to call your custom methods, you can simply jump to the point in the VTable where your method pointers are found. It's simply not important to Object Pascal programmers that your interface also supports IDispatch.Invoke and the rest of the IDispatch interface. In particular, IDispatch has four methods that would appear in your object in addition to the three from IUnknown and any that you might declare. Here is the IDispatch interface as it appears in System.pas:

```
IDispatch = interface(IUnknown)
  ['{00020400-0000-0000-C000-000000000046}']
  function GetTypeInfoCount(out Count: Integer): HResult; stdcall;
  function GetTypeInfo(Index, LocaleID: Integer;
    out TypeInfo): HResult; stdcall;
  function GetIDsOfNames(const IID: TGUID; Names: Pointer;
    NameCount, LocaleID: Integer; DispIDs: Pointer): HResult; stdcall;
  function Invoke(DispID: Integer; const IID: TGUID; LocaleID: Integer;
    Flags: Word; var Params; VarResult, ExcepInfo,
    ArgErr: Pointer): HResult; stdcall;
end;
```

In effect, when you create a dual interface in the SimpleAutoServer object, you end up with a declaration that looks like this:

```
IMethodObject = interface(IUnknown)
  function GetTypeInfoCount(out Count: Integer): HResult; stdcall;
```

```
function GetTypeInfo(Index, LocaleID: Integer;
  out TypeInfo): HResult; stdcall;
function GetIDsOfNames(const IID: TGUID; Names: Pointer;
  NameCount, LocaleID: Integer; DispIDs: Pointer): HResult; stdcall;
function Invoke(DispID: Integer; const IID: TGUID; LocaleID: Integer;
  Flags: Word; var Params; VarResult, ExcepInfo,
  ArgErr: Pointer): HResult; stdcall;
function GetName: WideString; safecall;
// Additional methods can be declared here.
end;
```

This object has all the methods of IDispatch in it, plus your method called GetName. Additional methods can be tacked on to the end of this object, just as GetName has already been added to the object.

Having waxed so poetic in my explanation of the virtues of virtual function tables, I'll now turn around and speak a few closing words in defense of IDispatch. The great thing about IDispatch is that it lets you call the methods of an object without having complete knowledge of the object's full structure. In other words, you can call its methods without ever having to see, or declare, its interface. Even though calls of this type take longer than standard Object Pascal method calls, the innate human propensity toward laziness finds a certain attraction in this arrangement. (And, of course, Object Pascal purists throw up their hands in horror at the very thought of such an arrangement!)

Of course, Object Pascal programmers always have ways of overcoming adversity. A binary construct called a type library can contain a copy of the interface for an object. If you talk to this library politely, it will give you a premade copy of the interface for an object. In other words, it will generate the header file for that object automatically.

Delphi has technology that allows you to automatically generate and read type libraries for COM objects. I will discuss this extremely important technology in the next section, "Type Libraries."

Before closing this section, however, I probably ought to say a few words about which technology you should use when building COM objects. There is some virtue in simply creating objects that derive directly from IUnknown—that is, that don't implement IDispatch. However, dual interfaces give you most of the advantages of code that descends directly from IUnknown, and yet classes of this type are still available to other programming languages because they implement IDispatch. IDispatch is a small class and does not add much code to your programs. Therefore, if you are in doubt, always use dual interfaces that implement IDispatch. Advanced programmers will find reasons for taking another approach, but this default is good if you are unsure what to do.

Type Libraries

This section explains what a type library is and how you work with the Delphi Type Library Editor. You got a brief introduction to this material in the section "Building a Simple COM Server and Client." The subject will come up again in several other places in this chapter, notably the section "Getting Two or More Interfaces from One `CoClass`."

The most basic fact you need to know is how to create a type library. The most common way to build such a library is to let one of the wizards do it for you. For instance, if you turn to the ActiveX page in the Object Repository, most of the options you select will result in the creation of a type library. For instance, creating an automation object, as explained earlier in this chapter, causes a type library to be created automatically. To view that library while you are working on your project, choose View, Type library from the Delphi menu.

When you are looking at a type library, as shown in Figure 15.5, you will see a toolbar along the top of the object. At the bottom of the window is a status bar. On the left is the object list pane. On the right are several pages of type information.

FIGURE 15.5

The Type Library Editor with the toolbar, status bar, object list pane, and type information.

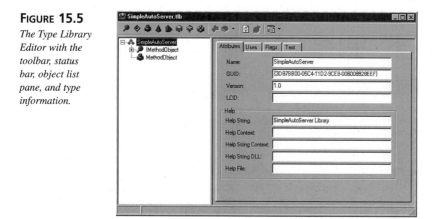

When you want to get help on the type library, you can usually press F1 to bring up the help page called the Type Library Editor. At the bottom of the Type Library Editor page in the help is a link called `type information`. This link leads to a description of the various types found on the toolbar, as shown in Figure 15.6. In fact, this help page is the key to getting the scoop on most of the top-level functions of the Type Library Editor.

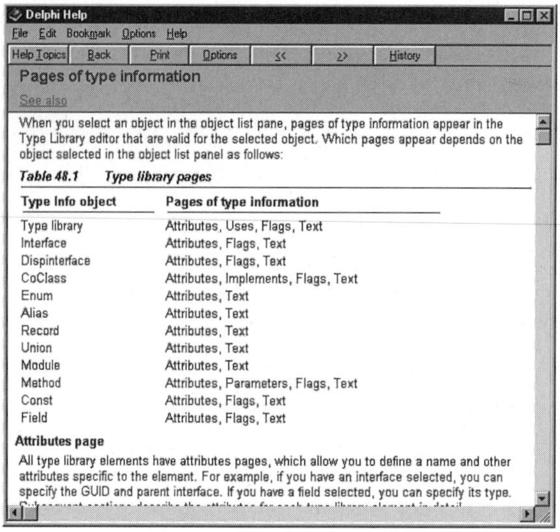

FIGURE 15.6

Is this what you
were looking for?
Here is a key page
that provides help
on the Type
Library Editor.

If you right-click on the Type Library Editor, you can open a small window that will show any errors in the library you are creating. This window is similar to the messages window commonly displayed at the bottom of the IDE.

So much for the bare basics of using type libraries. To go much further, I need to step back for a moment and explain some terminology.

What Is a Type Library?

If the only people who used COM objects were Object Pascal programmers, I could pass around a Delphi interface definition to define the proper way to access an interface. However, COM needs to be available to a wide range of programmers using a diverse set of tools.

Fortunately, the declarations for COM objects can be stored in something called a type library. Type libraries contain code that can be called to describe the structure of a particular object, including its names, methods, the parameters passed to the methods, and some of the types used by the object.

In short, a type library is just a Delphi interface declaration packaged so multiple languages can use it. A type library defines the types found in a particular interface or set of interfaces. If you build an ActiveX control, it should have a type library defining all the interfaces and types supported by that object. Each language—VB, Object Pascal, C++, and so on—can open a type library, read its contents, and generate code or other symbols of use to programmers accessing that object from a particular language or tool.

Besides using a type library for defining dispinterfaces and interfaces, you can use it for defining enumerated types and records. A few other options are also available, but they are used infrequently, so I consider them beyond the scope of this book.

Creating Type Libraries

As is often the case with this sort of thing, the people who created the specification for type libraries did not consider the development of a clean, easy-to-understand, easy-to-use, well-defined graphical user interface as one of their highest priorities. As a result, the science of creating type libraries is a black art.

Before Delphi 3, programmers who created type libraries usually first defined their objects in a language called the Interface Definition Language (IDL). The programmers' newly minted IDL script was then passed to a compiler of some sort—the most common being a Microsoft tool called MIDL. The output from this compiler is a binary type library with TLB extension.

You can also pass a type library to a compiler or other tool. The compiler will then generate a declaration of the objects found in that type library in the current language, such as C++ or Object Pascal. (In Delphi, you can pass a library this way by choosing Project, Import Type Library.)

IDL is an industrywide standard also used to define CORBA objects. As a result, many people have gone to the trouble to learn IDL, and understanding the basics of this language is a valuable asset for most programmers. Therefore, IDL plays a role in Delphi development, but it is not necessarily the primary means of creating a type library. If you select the appropriate button in the Type Library Editor, you can convert your interfaces into raw IDL. You can choose to generate either COM or CORBA IDL, where COM IDL follows Microsoft's standards, and CORBA IDL follows the OMG's standards. For more information on CORBA and the OMG, read Chapter 24, "CORBA."

You can also usually see the IDL you are generating by selecting the Text page in the Type Library Editor. If you are looking at an individual method property, then the Text page will show you a Pascal declaration for that method or property. However, if you are looking at an interface, CoClass, or the entire type library, then the Text page will show you the underlying COM-based IDL.

15

CREATING COM
SERVERS AND
CLIENTS

> **NOTE**
>
> The purpose of IDL is simply to provide a language-neutral way to define an interface. Like a type library, IDL is meant to be usable by a wide range of programmers working in a wide range of languages. The Type Library Editor exists solely so that you do not have to wrestle with the vagaries of the IDL specification.
>
> Given the prevailing climate in the computer industry, it goes without saying that the Interface Definition Language is itself a rather opaque and ill-defined standard. To complicate matters further, a commonly used variation of IDL called ODL is in use, and it too is a somewhat opaque and ill-defined entity. As I mentioned earlier, two different versions of IDL are available: one created by Microsoft and the other by the OMG.
>
> I should add that IDL is not a particularly complicated language. Nevertheless, today's over-worked programmers don't really need to have yet another specification thrown at them. But you don't need to despair, as the Type Library Editor is available to help lighten your load.

By using the Type Library Editor, you can define a COM interface by using an intuitive and easy-to-understand technology. If your goal is to go the other way around, from existing type library to code, a built-in solution also is available. Simply go to the Delphi menu, choose Project, Import Type Library, and select a type library that will be automatically converted into a set of Object Pascal declarations.

Valid Automation Types

You can pass any of the following types back and forth in an automation server. In particular, any of these types will be marshaled for you automatically.

Byte	Currency
Real	Double
Longint	Integer
Single	Smallint
AnsiString	WideString
TDateTime	Variant
OleVariant	WordBool

All interface types

A list of this type is no longer nearly as important as it once was, because now the Type Library Editor shows you what types you can pass to a procedure or function, and what types you can return from a function.

Ignoring Parameters with EmptyParam

The VCL contains a special type called `EmptyParam` that is designed to allow you to ignore parameters that need to be passed into an automation function. When you're working with certain interfaces, particularly from big Microsoft products such as Word or Excel, you will find that some methods expect 10, 20, sometimes even 30 parameters. Trying to find the right types to pass into a method of that description is simply too much busywork. As a result, the `EmptyParam` type was created:

```
MyClass.MyMethod(EmptyParam, EmptyParam, EmptyParam);
```

This type is initialized in `System.pas` as follows:

```
TVarData(EmptyParam).VType := varError;
TVarData(EmptyParam).VError := $80020004; {DISP_E_PARAMNOTFOUND}
```

The `EmptyParam` type does not play a particularly large role in this chapter, but in the next two chapters, `EmptyParam` will prove to be very helpful.

Registration Issues

Before going further, I want to mention a few issues about CLSIDs and the Registry. If you already understand the Registry, you can skip this section.

The Registry is a place where information can be stored. It's a database. GUIDs are statistically unique numbers that can be used by the operating system or a programmer to reference an OLE object. A CLSID is a GUID that references a COM object that contains one or more interfaces. You declare a COM object inside a `CoClass`. For instance, here is the `CoClass` from the `SimpleAutoServer` example shown earlier in this chapter:

```
coclass MethodObject
{
  [default] interface IMethodObject;
};
```

CLSIDs are stored in the Registry. In this case, visiting the actual perpetrator in its native habitat is probably best. In the example explained here, I'm assuming that you have a copy of Word loaded on your system.

To get started, use the Run menu on the Windows taskbar to launch the RegEdit program that ships with Windows NT or Windows 95/98. To start the program, just type `RegEdit` in the Run box and click OK. The program is on your path.

After the program is open, search through `HKEY_CLASSES_ROOT` for the `Word.Basic` entry, as shown in Figure 15.7. (If you don't have Word, you can look instead for one of the following entries: `InternetExplorer.Application`, `Paint.Picture`, or `WordPad.Document.1`.) When you find `Word.Basic`, you can see that it's associated with the following CLSID:

`{000209FE-0000-0000-C000-000000000046}`

FIGURE 15.7

If you run the Windows program Regedit.exe, you can see the registration database entry for Word.Basic *appears under* HKEY_CLASSES_ROOT.

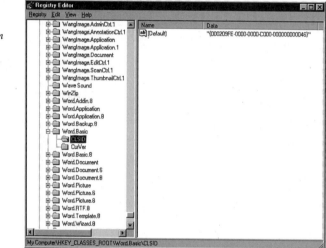

This unique class ID is inserted into the Registry of all machines that contain a valid and properly installed copy of Word for Windows. The only application that uses this ID is Word for Windows. It belongs uniquely to that application.

Now go further up `HKEY_CLASSES_ROOT` and look for the CLSID branch. Open it and search for the CLSID shown previously. When you find it, you can see two entries associated with it: one is called `LocalServer`, or `LocalServer32`, and the other is called `ProgID`. The `ProgID` is set to `Word.Basic`. The `LocalServer32` entry looks something like this:

`C:\WINWORD\WINWORD.EXE /Automation`

If you look at this command, you can begin to grasp how Windows can translate the CLSID passed to `CoCreateInstance` or `CoGetClassObject` into the name of an executable. In particular, Windows looks up the CLSID in the Registry and then uses the

`LocalServer32` entry to find the directory and name of the executable or DLL you want to launch. You are loading the DLL or executable so that you can access the COM objects that reside inside it.

Having these kinds of entries in the registration database does not mean that the applications in question are necessarily automation servers. For example, many applications with `LocalServer` and `ProgID` entries are not automation servers. However, all automation servers do have these two entries. Note, further, that this example is a reference to the automation server in Word, not a reference to Word as a generic application. It references an automation object inside Word, not Word itself. (The automation object is an instance of `IDispatch`. It was not created with the Delphi ActiveX Wizard, but it has all the same attributes. Many, but not all, of the Word interfaces support both dual interfaces and dispinterfaces.)

The same basic scenario outlined here takes place when you call `CoGetClassObject` or `CoCreateInstanceEx` and specify the CLSID of an object on another machine. In particular, Windows contacts the specified machine, asks it to look up the CLSID in the Registry, and then marshals information back and forth between the two machines. You will learn much more about this subject in the next chapter.

CLSIDs are said to be statistically unique. You can create a new CLSID by calling `CoCreateGuid`. The following code shows one way to make this call:

```
CoInitialize(nil);
CoCreateGuid(GUID);
// eventually you should call CoUninitialize;
```

The code shown here begins by calling `CoInitialize`, which is usually unnecessary in Delphi because the RTL will ensure that the call is made for you.

`CoCreateGuid` is the call that retrieves the new CLSID from the system. This ID is guaranteed to be unique as long as you have a network card on your system. Each network card has a unique number on it, and this card number is combined with the date and time and other random bits of information to create a unique number that could only be generated on a machine with your network card at a particular date and time. Rumors that the phase of the moon and current ages of Bill Gates's children are also factored in are probably not true. At any rate, the result is a number that is guaranteed to be statistically unique, within the tolerance levels for your definition of that word given your faith in mathematicians in general and Microsoft-based mathematicians in particular. (Actually, the algorithm used here was developed by the Open Software Foundation.)

The `StringFromCLSID` routine converts a CLSID into a string. Seen in its raw form, a CLSID looks like this:

```
{FC41CC90-C01D-11CF-8CCD-0080C80CF1D2}
```

These numbers can be converted into a record of type `TGUID` that can be used in a Delphi. The `TGUID` type is defined in `System.pas` as follows:

```
PGUID = ^TGUID;
TGUID = record
  D1: LongWord;
  D2: Word;
  D3: Word;
  D4: array[0..7] of Byte;
end;
```

This subject can appear a bit tricky at first, but ultimately it is not really as tough as you might think. The truth is that I found out a lot about GUIDs simply by wandering around in the Registry, poking my nose into this and that. The Registry is a dry and dusty place, but it can develop a certain elusive charm if you come to see it in the right light. Of course, you have to keep this kind of interest to yourself, as nothing is more apt to destroy your popularity at a cocktail party than a reference to a personal hobby that involves exploring the more obscure nodes of the Windows system Registry.

Marshaling Data Automatically

Marshaling is a COM-specific term for the technique used to transfer data or function calls back and forth between two applications that reside in separate processes. For example, if you pass a parameter to a function across application boundaries, you have to be sure that it is treated properly by both applications. If you declare the parameter as an `Integer` in Pascal, that means you're passing a four-byte ordinal value. In C, you might describe that as an `int` or a `long`. But how do you describe it in Visual Basic? How can you find a common language that will define the object once and for all in a wide range of languages? The answers to these questions are expressed in COM by a complex interface called `IMarshal` that is beyond the scope of this chapter. Indeed, `IMarshal` is notorious for being difficult to implement.

Here is how the Microsoft documentation, in a rare moment of clarity, defines `IMarshal`: "'Marshaling' is the process of packaging data into packets for transmission to a different process or machine. 'Unmarshaling' is the process of recovering that data at the receiving end. In any given call, method arguments are marshaled and unmarshaled in one direction, while return values are marshaled and unmarshaled in the other." This is all good and well. Unfortunately, as I stated earlier, the `IMarshal` interface is very hard to implement.

It happens that if you're using a standard COM object, you don't have to implement `IMarshal` because these interfaces will be marshaled for you automatically by the system. In other words, if you're implementing an instance of `IDispatch`, `IUnknown`,

`IClassFactory`, `IOleContainer`, or any other predefined COM class, you don't have to worry about marshaling. Microsoft will take care of this job for you. If you're creating a custom object of your own, you will need to implement `IMarshal` unless you stick with the safe parameter types listed in the section "Valid Automation Types."

You can use techniques involving `Variant` arrays to marshal complex custom types such as records or arrays. Chapter 13 describes this terminology.

Getting Two or More Interfaces from One `CoClass`

In most cases, you will want to store multiple automation interfaces inside a single library. The sample program shown in this section of the chapter will demonstrate how to store these interfaces. In particular, you will see how to export three interfaces from one server, and one of the interfaces you create will be descended from one of the other interfaces.

To get started, create a new program, and save it in to its own directory. Choose File, New and turn to the ActiveX page. Create a new automation object and call it `TwoFaceServer`. At this stage, you have a `CoClass` and one interface with no methods in it. To enrich the object somewhat, give it a single method called `GetNameOne` that takes a pointer to a `BSTR` as a parameter:

```
HRESULT _stdcall GetNameOne([out] BSTR * S );
```

Now create a second interface by choosing the Interface button on the far left of the toolbar at the top of the Type Library Editor. Rename the interface as `IFaceTwo`. Create a single method for this interface called `GetNameTwo`:

```
HRESULT _stdcall GetNameTwo([out] BSTR * S );
```

> **NOTE**
>
> If you have more than one interface in a `CoClass`, then all those methods will be implemented by a single Object Pascal class. In other words, one class that appears in your `XXX_IMPL` file will contain all the methods from the different interfaces in one `coclass`.
>
> If you insert more than one `CoClass` into a single type library, then the second `CoClass` will not automatically get an `XXX_IMPL` file associated with it. Instead, you will have to create the `XXX_IMPL` file by hand.

Now, highlight the CoClass, which may be called TwoFacedObject but can have whatever name you choose. Flip to the Implements page, right-click on the center of the white area, and select Insert Interface from the pop-up menu. You will see a list of available interfaces, one of which is called IFaceTwo. Select this interface. (The Implements page won't show up unless you have first clicked directly on the CoClass.)

To check on how you are doing, continue to highlight the CoClass and turn to the Text page, where you can see the IDL that is being generated (see Listing 15.3). You should see both of your interfaces listed in the CoClass. The code that wraps the type library is shown in Listing 15.4, and other key units in this example are shown in Listings 15.4 and 15.5.

LISTING 15.3 THE IDL FOR THE TwoMoonServer PROGRAM

```
[
  uuid(45DFE240-0601-11D2-9CE8-006008928EEF),
  version(1.0),
  helpstring("TwoMoonServer Library")
]
library TwoMoonServer
{

  importlib("STDOLE2.TLB");
  importlib("STDVCL40.DLL");

  [
    uuid(45DFE241-0601-11D2-9CE8-006008928EEF),
    version(1.0),
    helpstring("Dispatch interface for TwoMoons Object"),
    dual,
    oleautomation
  ]
  interface ITwoMoons: IDispatch
  {
    [id(0x00000001)]
    HRESULT _stdcall GetName([out, retval] BSTR * Value );
  };

  [
    uuid(45DFE243-0601-11D2-9CE8-006008928EEF),
    version(1.0),
    helpstring("TwoMoons Object")
  ]
  coclass TwoMoons
  {
    [default] interface ITwoMoons;
    interface IOtherMoon;
  };
```

```
  [
    uuid(45DFE245-0601-11D2-9CE8-006008928EEF),
    version(1.0),
    dual,
    oleautomation
  ]
   interface IOtherMoon: IDispatch
  {
    [id(0x00000001)]
    HRESULT _stdcall GetName([out, retval] BSTR * Value );
    [propget, id(0x00000002)]
    HRESULT _stdcall DayStatus([out, retval] SunStatus * Value );
    [propput, id(0x00000002)]
    HRESULT _stdcall DayStatus([in] SunStatus Value );
  };

  [
    uuid(45DFE247-0601-11D2-9CE8-006008928EEF),
    version(1.0)
  ]
  typedef enum tagSunStatus
  {
    Day = 0,
    Night = 1
  } SunStatus;

};
```

LISTING 15.4 THE TwoMoonServer_TLB FILE IS CREATED AUTOMATICALLY BY THE TYPE LIBRARY EDITOR

```
unit TwoMoonServer_TLB;

// ***************************************************************** //
// WARNING                                                          //
// -------                                                          //
// The types declared in this file were generated from data read    //
// from a Type Library. If this type library is explicitly or       //
// indirectly (via another type library referring to this type      //
// library) reimported, or the 'Refresh' command of the Type        //
// Library Editor activated while editing the Type Library, the     //
// contents of this file will be regenerated and all                //
// manual modifications will be lost.                               //
// ***************************************************************** //

// PASTLWTR : $Revision:   1.11.1.62  $
// File generated on 6/17/98 4:55:01 PM from Type Library
// described below.
```

continues

15

CREATING COM
SERVERS AND
CLIENTS

LISTING 15.4   CONTINUED

```
// ***************************************************************** //
// Type Lib: D:\SrcPas\Unleash4\Chap15\TwoMoonChild\TwoMoonServer.tlb
// IID\LCID: {45DFE240-0601-11D2-9CE8-006008928EEF}\0
// Helpfile:
// HelpString: TwoMoonServer Library
// Version:    1.0
// ***************************************************************** //

interface

uses Windows, ActiveX, Classes, Graphics, OleCtrls, StdVCL;

// ***************************************************************** //
// GUIDS declared in the TypeLibrary. Following prefixes are used:  //
//   Type Libraries      : LIBID_xxxx                               //
//   CoClasses           : CLASS_xxxx                               //
//   DISPInterfaces      : DIID_xxxx                                //
//   Non-DISP interfaces: IID_xxxx                                  //
// ***************************************************************** //
const
  LIBID_TwoMoonServer: TGUID = '{45DFE240-0601-11D2-9CE8-006008928EEF}';
  IID_ITwoMoons: TGUID = '{45DFE241-0601-11D2-9CE8-006008928EEF}';
  IID_IOtherMoon: TGUID = '{45DFE245-0601-11D2-9CE8-006008928EEF}';
  CLASS_TwoMoons: TGUID = '{45DFE243-0601-11D2-9CE8-006008928EEF}';

// ***************************************************************** //
// Declaration of Enumerations defined in Type Library             //
// ***************************************************************** //
// SunStatus constants
type
  SunStatus = TOleEnum;

const
  Day = $00000000;
  Night = $00000001;

type

// ***************************************************************** //
// Forward declaration of interfaces defined in Type Library       //
// ***************************************************************** //
  ITwoMoons = interface;
  ITwoMoonsDisp = dispinterface;
  IOtherMoon = interface;
  IOtherMoonDisp = dispinterface;

// ***************************************************************** //
// Declaration of CoClasses defined in Type Library                //
```

```
// (NOTE: Here we map each CoClass to its Default Interface)        //
// ***************************************************************** //
  TwoMoons = ITwoMoons;


// ***************************************************************** //
// Interface: ITwoMoons
// Flags:      (4416) Dual OleAutomation Dispatchable
// GUID:       {45DFE241-0601-11D2-9CE8-006008928EEF}
// ***************************************************************** //
  ITwoMoons = interface(IDispatch)
    ['{45DFE241-0601-11D2-9CE8-006008928EEF}']
    function GetName: WideString; safecall;
  end;

// ***************************************************************** //
// DispIntf:   ITwoMoonsDisp
// Flags:      (4416) Dual OleAutomation Dispatchable
// GUID:       {45DFE241-0601-11D2-9CE8-006008928EEF}
// ***************************************************************** //
  ITwoMoonsDisp = dispinterface
    ['{45DFE241-0601-11D2-9CE8-006008928EEF}']
    function GetName: WideString; dispid 1;
  end;

// ***************************************************************** //
// Interface: IOtherMoon
// Flags:      (4416) Dual OleAutomation Dispatchable
// GUID:       {45DFE245-0601-11D2-9CE8-006008928EEF}
// ***************************************************************** //
  IOtherMoon = interface(IDispatch)
    ['{45DFE245-0601-11D2-9CE8-006008928EEF}']
    function GetName: WideString; safecall;
    function Get_DayStatus: SunStatus; safecall;
    procedure Set_DayStatus(Value: SunStatus); safecall;
    property DayStatus: SunStatus read Get_DayStatus write
    ➥Set_DayStatus;
  end;

// ***************************************************************** //
// DispIntf:   IOtherMoonDisp
// Flags:      (4416) Dual OleAutomation Dispatchable
// GUID:       {45DFE245-0601-11D2-9CE8-006008928EEF}
// ***************************************************************** //
  IOtherMoonDisp = dispinterface
    ['{45DFE245-0601-11D2-9CE8-006008928EEF}']
    function GetName: WideString; dispid 1;
    property DayStatus: SunStatus dispid 2;
  end;
```

continues

LISTING 15.4 CONTINUED

```
CoTwoMoons = class
  class function Create: ITwoMoons;
  class function CreateRemote(const MachineName: string): ITwoMoons;
end;

implementation

uses ComObj;

class function CoTwoMoons.Create: ITwoMoons;
begin
  Result := CreateComObject(CLASS_TwoMoons) as ITwoMoons;
end;

class function CoTwoMoons.CreateRemote
➥(const MachineName: string): ITwoMoons;
begin
  Result := CreateRemoteComObject
  ➥(MachineName, CLASS_TwoMoons) as ITwoMoons;
end;

end.
```

LISTING 15.5 THE IMPLEMENTATION FOR THE TWOMOON SERVER

```
/////////////////////////////////////
//     File: TwoMoonIMPL
// Project: TwoMoonServer
// Copyright (c) 1998 by Charlie Calvert
//
unit TwoMoonIMPL;

interface

uses
  ComObj, ActiveX, TwoMoonServer_TLB;

type
  TTwoMoons = class(TAutoObject, ITwoMoons, IOtherMoon)
    FDayStatus: Integer;
  protected
    function GetName: WideString; safecall;
    function IOtherMoon.GetName = OtherMoonGetName;
    function OtherMoonGetName: WideString; safecall;
    function Get_DayStatus: SunStatus; safecall;
    procedure Set_DayStatus(Value: SunStatus); safecall;
    { Protected declarations }
  end;
```

```
implementation

uses ComServ;

function TTwoMoons.GetName: WideString;
begin
  Result := 'ITwoMoons';
end;

function TTwoMoons.OtherMoonGetName: WideString;
begin
  Result := 'IOtherMoon';
end;

function TTwoMoons.Get_DayStatus: SunStatus;
begin
  Result := FDayStatus;
end;

procedure TTwoMoons.Set_DayStatus(Value: SunStatus);
begin
  FDayStatus := Value;
end;

initialization
  TAutoObjectFactory.Create(ComServer, TTwoMoons, Class_TwoMoons,
    ciMultiInstance, tmApartment);
end.
```

The purpose of this program is to show how you can support more than one interface on a single automation object, or more specifically, on a single CoClass. This subject is very important because you will want to create automation servers that support a wide range of capabilities and some very complex class structures. This program shows you how to get started.

When you are looking at an IDL file like this one, a good place to begin is in the CoClass statement:

```
coclass TwoMoons
{
  [default] interface ITwoMoons;
  interface IOtherMoon;
};
```

Here you can see the two interfaces that will be exported from this file.

To find out about these interfaces, you need to go to the TwoFaceServer_TLB file. In it, you will find the IDispatch interface for both objects.

Note, however, that the `Class Creator` returns only the first interface:

```
CoTwoMoons = class
  class function Create: ITwoMoons;
  class function CreateRemote(const MachineName: string): ITwoMoons;
end;
```

This use represents a special problem for the developer, which this section addresses after the main form for the client program, found in Listing 15.6.

One other important point about this IDL file is that I have declared an enumerated type inside it. To declare the type, I pushed the Enumerated Type button at the top of the Type Library Editor. I then clicked the const button at the top of the Type Library Editor once for each of the constants I wanted to be part of the enumerated type. When I was done, I could look in my XXX_TLB.pas file and see the declarations I had created:

```
type
  SunStatus = TOleEnum;

const
  Day = $00000000;
  Night = $00000001;
```

This code shows the enumerated type I am working with in this program. TOleEnum is declared as an Integer, and Day and Night are two numeric constants representing the two pieces of the enumerated type. Delphi provides no simple way to translate these constants into strings, but a hard-to-use low-level COM function called GetDocumentation will perform the task for you.

I have added this enumerated type to this example primarily so you can see how to use it. My goal in this example is to give you a few tips on how to put together a relatively advanced OLE automation server and client.

Before showing you the client, I need to discuss the declaration for TTwoMoons:

```
TTwoMoons = class(TAutoObject, ITwoMoons, IOtherMoon)
  FDayStatus: Integer;
protected
  function GetName: WideString; safecall;
  function IOtherMoon.GetName = OtherMoonGetName;
  function OtherMoonGetName: WideString; safecall;
  function Get_DayStatus: SunStatus; safecall;
  procedure Set_DayStatus(Value: SunStatus); safecall;
  { Protected declarations }
end;
```

This class is used to implement both the ITwoMoons and IOtherMoon interfaces. Because both ITwoMoons and IOtherMoon have a class member called GetName, you need to add a method resolution clause:

```
function IOtherMoon.GetName = OtherMoonGetName;
```

This line of code states that `IOtherMoon.GetName` is implemented by the method called `OtherMoonGetName`:

```
function TTwoMoons.OtherMoonGetName: WideString;
begin
  Result := 'IOtherMoon';
end;
```

Of course, the question now is whether Delphi will be able to sort these two classes when you call them from the client. The answer to that question is yes, but you will have to take a look at the client program in Listing 15.6 to see exactly how it is done.

LISTING 15.6   THE MAIN FORM FOR THE TwoClient PROGRAM

```
/////////////////////////////////////////
//     File: MainClient
// Project: TwoMoonClient
// Copyright (c) 1998 by Charlie Calvert
//
unit MainClient;

interface

uses
  Windows, Messages, SysUtils,
  Classes, Graphics, Controls,
  Forms, Dialogs, TwoMoonServer_TLB,
  StdCtrls, ExtCtrls;

type
  TForm2 = class(TForm)
    ClassCreateBtn: TButton;
    Edit1: TEdit;
    Edit2: TEdit;
    Edit3: TEdit;
    CoCreateBtn: TButton;
    Bevel1: TBevel;
    procedure ClassCreateBtnClick(Sender: TObject);
    procedure CoCreateBtnClick(Sender: TObject);
    procedure FormCreate(Sender: TObject);
  private
    procedure ClearControls;
    function GetStatus(Value: Integer): string;
    { Private declarations }
  public
```

continues

15

CREATING COM
SERVERS AND
CLIENTS

LISTING 15.6   CONTINUED

```pascal
    { Public declarations }
  end;

var
  Form2: TForm2;

implementation

uses
  ActiveX, ComObj;

{$R *.DFM}

procedure TForm2.FormCreate(Sender: TObject);
begin
  ClearControls;
end;

procedure TForm2.ClearControls;
var
  i: Integer;
begin
  for i := 0 to ComponentCount - 1 do
    if Components[i] is TEdit then
      TEdit(Components[i]).Text := '';
end;

procedure TForm2.ClassCreateBtnClick(Sender: TObject);
var
  TwoMoon: ITwoMoons;
  OtherMoon: IOtherMoon;
begin
  TwoMoon := CoTwoMoons.Create;
  Edit1.Text := 'Class Creator: ' +  TwoMoon.GetName;
  OtherMoon := TwoMoon as IOtherMoon;
  Edit2.Text := OtherMoon.GetName;
  OtherMoon.DayStatus := Night;
  Edit3.Text := GetStatus(OtherMoon.DayStatus);
end;

procedure TForm2.CoCreateBtnClick(Sender: TObject);
var
  TwoMoon: ITwoMoons;
  OtherMoon: IOtherMoon;
  hr: HResult;
begin
  ClearControls();
  hr := CoCreateInstance(CLASS_TwoMoons, nil,
    CLSCTX_LOCAL_SERVER, IID_ITwoMoons, TwoMoon);
```

```
  if SUCCEEDED(hr) then begin
    Edit1.Text := 'CoCreateInstance: ' + TwoMoon.GetName;
    TwoMoon.QueryInterface(IOtherMoon, OtherMoon);
    Edit2.Text := OtherMoon.GetName;
    OtherMoon.DayStatus := Day;
    Edit3.Text := GetStatus(OtherMoon.DayStatus);
  end else
    OleCheck(hr);
end;

function TForm2.GetStatus(Value: Integer): string;
begin
  case Value of
    0: Result := 'Day';
    1: Result := 'Night';
  else
    Result := 'Error';
  end;
end;

end.
```

In the `ClassCreateBtnClick` method, I create an instance of `FaceOne` by using a standard Delphi technology:

```
TwoMoon := CoTwoMoons.Create;
Edit1.Text := 'Class Creator: ' +  TwoMoon.GetName;
```

Here everything is more or less as you would expect. I create an instance of the class, call one of its methods, and show the results to the user in an edit control.

When it comes time to get the second interface, I use the `As` operator:

```
OtherMoon := TwoMoon as IOtherMoon;
```

Behind the scenes, this code calls `QueryInterface`. I declare `OtherMoon` exactly as I would declare any other interface:

```
TwoMoon: ITwoMoons;
OtherMoon: IOtherMoon;
```

After you have back the interface to your class, you can call its methods just exactly as you did when you retrieved the reference with a `Class Creator`:

```
Edit2.Text := OtherMoon.GetName;
OtherMoon.DayStatus := Night;
Edit3.Text := GetStatus(OtherMoon.DayStatus);
```

You actually can use low-level COM functions to return the string associated with an enumerated type, but in this case I've written a small helper function that helps make the conversion:

15

CREATING COM
SERVERS AND
CLIENTS

```
function TForm2.GetStatus(Value: Integer): string;
begin
  case Value of
    0: Result := 'Day';
    1: Result := 'Night';
  else
    Result := 'Error';
  end;
end;
```

Calling `CoCreateInstance`

This section explains how to call `CoCreateInstance` directly rather than having Delphi call it for you. The following method shows you how to proceed:

```
procedure TForm2.CoCreateBtnClick(Sender: TObject);
var
  TwoMoon: ITwoMoons;
  OtherMoon: IOtherMoon;
  hr: HResult;
begin
  ClearControls();
  hr := CoCreateInstance(CLASS_TwoMoons, nil,
    CLSCTX_LOCAL_SERVER, IID_ITwoMoons, TwoMoon);
  if SUCCEEDED(hr) then begin
    Edit1.Text := 'CoCreateInstance: ' + TwoMoon.GetName;
    TwoMoon.QueryInterface(IOtherMoon, OtherMoon);
    Edit2.Text := OtherMoon.GetName;
    OtherMoon.DayStatus := Day;
    Edit3.Text := GetStatus(OtherMoon.DayStatus);
  end else
    OleCheck(hr);
end;
```

`CoCreateInstance` takes five parameters:

```
function CoCreateInstance(
  const clsid: TCLSID;     // Class identifier (CLSID) of the object
  unkOuter: IUnknown;      // For use with aggregation, ignore
  dwClsContext: Longint;   // Context for running executable code
  const iid: TIID;         // Reference to the interface you want
  out pv):                 // Pointer to requested interface
HResult; stdcall;
```

Here is a detailed explanation of each parameter:

- `CLSID`—The first parameter is the CLSID for the `CoClass` you created.

- `unkOuter`—The second can always be `nil`, as it is used only by aggregation, which is an advanced technique not relevant to this chapter.

- dwClsContext—The third parameter is a constant designating the kind of server you want to access. The possible values are declared as follows:

```
typedef enum tagCLSCTX
{
    CLSCTX_INPROC_SERVER   = 1,
    CLSCTX_INPROC_HANDLER  = 2,
    CLSCTX_LOCAL_SERVER    = 4
    CLSCTX_REMOTE_SERVER = 16
} CLSCTX;
```

  In this case, of course, you can pass in CLSCTX_LOCAL_SERVER. CLSCTX_INPROC_SERVER is for DLLs loaded into your program's address space, and the other commonly used option is CLSCTX_REMOTE_SERVER. Remote applications will be discussed in the next chapter.

- iid—The fourth parameter is the TGUID of the interface that you want to retrieve.

- pv—The final parameter is a pointer to a pointer to a pointer to the object that you want to retrieve from the COM server.

CoCreateInstance returns an HRESULT, and you can pass it through the SUCCEEDED macro to see whether everything worked out as you had planned. If it did not, then you can call the VCL routine OleCheck, to see what went wrong. OleCheck will not report on all possible OLE errors, but it catches a lot of the big ones. If you want, you can just wrap each of the COM calls inside a call to OleCheck:

```
OleCheck(CoCreateInstance(....));
```

This syntax ensures that any call that fails will be reported to you immediately. If you ever end up doing any serious COM programming, then not checking the value of every single HRESULT returned to your by your program is absolute folly.

After calling CoCreateInstance, I then call QueryInterface to retrieve the second interface:

```
OleCheck(TwoMoon.QueryInterface(IOtherMoon, OtherMoon));
```

QueryInterface is part of IUnknown, so it will be part of all COM objects. After you have a CoClass or some interface from a CoClass, you should always be able to call QueryInterface to retrieve an instance of the CoClass or of some interface on the CoClass. In this case, I call QueryInterface on the TwoMoon interface and ask for a pointer to the OtherMoon interface. This simple call is pretty much guaranteed to work, but I still use OleCheck to check the HResult returned by the function.

The value that is returned from QueryInterface in its second parameter is a pointer to the object you requested. You can use this object exactly as you would had you retrieved the interface via one of the standard Delphi techniques:

15

CREATING COM
SERVERS AND
CLIENTS

```
TwoMoon.QueryInterface(IOtherMoon, OtherMoon);
Edit2.Text := OtherMoon.GetName;
OtherMoon.DayStatus := Day;
Edit3.Text := GetStatus(OtherMoon.DayStatus);
```

Delphi provides code that makes calling these relatively low-level COM functions unnecessary. Nonetheless, knowing about them is a very good idea, as understanding the underlying technology is always best.

Summary

In this chapter, you learned some of the basic facts about OLE automation. As we move into a world based on distributed architectures that consist of suites of applications, COM will become central to our vision of computer programming on the Windows platform.

In particular, this chapter covered creating COM servers and clients, working with type libraries, interfaces and CoClass, and also calling core COM functions such as CoCreateInstance and QueryInterface.

If you are thinking of moving to Java or to CORBA, much of the information presented in this chapter will still be germane. Java is even more applet- and control-centric than Windows. The whole idea of presenting interfaces defined by a language like IDL is central to the very idea of CORBA programming. In short, distributed architectures built on top of COM, or something like COM, are almost certain to be part of any conceivable programming future.

In Chapter 20 you will see how to take the principles learned in this chapter and move them onto the network. You will find that almost everything you learned in this chapter applies to DCOM programming. So gather your wits about you, and prepare to journey into the future of computer programming.

CHAPTER 16

Using Delphi to Automate Word and Excel

IN THIS CHAPTER

The goal of this chapter is to get you up to speed automating Excel and Word from a Delphi application. Most of the text will focus on Excel, but you will find that if you understand Excel automation, you need only a few hints to get started automating Word. If you are primarily interested in Word, I ask you to patiently read through the material on Excel, as almost all of it applies to Word.

You can use Delphi to fully control virtually all the features of Excel and Word. There is very little that you can do from inside Excel or Word that you cannot also automate from outside Excel or Word. In other words, both Excel and Word can be fully controlled from Delphi applications using OLE automation.

For the most part, the act of controlling Excel or Word from a Delphi application is not terribly challenging. Whatever difficulty you experience comes not from Delphi's side of the equation, but from the innate complexity of the Excel and Word object hierarchies. Not that I find the hierarchies unreasonable, but they do encapsulate sufficient complexity to require a significant period of study. In particular, these automation classes give you rather detailed control over all the features of Word and Excel that you can access through those program's menus. Because they are complex applications, the interface to them also needs to be complex. The purpose of this chapter is to unscramble that hierarchy and show its underlying structure.

The subject matter of this chapter is continued in Chapter 17, "Interfaces and Internet Explorer." This chapter shows automating Word and Excel using `Variants` and `IDispatch`, and Chapter 17 shows how to perform similar tasks with dispinterfaces and standard COM interfaces. All these technologies are closely related. However, you will find two significant differences between them:

- Using `Variants` is usually the easiest, the most terse, but also the slowest way to get things done in terms of performance.
- Using COM interfaces is usually the most difficult, the most verbose, but also yields the highest performance.

When writing this chapter, I attempted to explain concepts as clearly as possible. I'm aiming this material primarily at intermediate or experienced programmers, but I hope it is accessible to anyone who has a basic understanding of how to use Delphi, Word, and Excel. Though you should not need a high level of expertise to understand this chapter, I am trying to cover the subject in some depth. Other sources, such as my book *Delphi 2 Unleashed* (Chapter 29, in particular), and the magazine *Delphi Informant* (June 1997), cover some of this same material in a simpler, less in-depth fashion. For many people, a more high-level, abstract view may be more appropriate. But I believe some people also have a need for a more-detailed look at this subject, which is why I have written this chapter.

System Requirements for Automating Office Applications

This chapter assumes the use of Microsoft Office 97. Portions of the chapter would also work with Office 95, but the sections on interfaces, in particular, require that you use Office 97.

To perform automation successfully with Excel or Word, you need a fairly powerful system with lots of RAM. I've been automating Excel for at least four years. When I first started, I considered the technology a bit suspect simply because it was terribly slow. Now, however, machines are powerful enough to take Excel through its paces in a few short moments. In particular, if you have a Pentium 120 class machine or above, and at least 48MB of RAM, this technology works well for many types of projects. Excel or Word will now load quite quickly, and you can open and insert data into them in the blink of an eye. However, if you want to iterate over lots of data inside a Word or Excel document, that process can be a time-consuming when compared to performing similar tasks inside a Delphi database application.

The bottom line here is that if you know Excel can do something well, and you know your target machines are powerful and will have Excel loaded on them, you don't need to search for third-party components to perform spreadsheet-related functions. Instead, you can just automate Excel from inside a Delphi application and get your work done professionally in just a few short hours. The icing on the cake is that you can then use MAPI to mail the results of your work to anyone who has a mail system and the ability to read Excel files. Or, if you want, you can simply print the document using the printing facilities built into Word or Excel. Other options include faxing the document and saving it in HTML format. The point is that the recipient of your work need not actually have a copy of your Delphi application running when viewing the output from your program. Instead, you can just send the recipient the results in an Excel or Word document. Word document viewers can be downloaded for free from Microsoft's Web site at www.microsoft.com.

Getting Started with Delphi and Excel

You can run OLE automation from inside Delphi in two different ways. One involves using interfaces, and the second involves using an OLE class called IDispatch along with a Delphi type called a Variant. Interfaces give you the advantage of type-checking your code on the client side, as well as providing relatively high performance.

Initially, this chapter discusses the somewhat easier-to-understand IDispatch and Variants technology and then moves on to cover interfaces after all the basics are clearly established. Do not worry if you don't yet understand the differences between the two techniques, as this subject will be cleared up over the course of the chapter. At this stage, you just need to be aware that you can use at least two ways to access OLE automation objects from Delphi, and that I am going to start out by showing you one that uses IDispatch and Variants.

Launching Excel

Listing 16.1 shows a bare-bones example of a Delphi application that launches Excel. Just skim over the code for now, as I will spend the rest of this section explaining how it works.

LISTING 16.1 THE MAIN FORM FROM THE Excel1 APPLICATION FOUND WITH THE CODE SAMPLES THAT ACCOMPANY THIS CHAPTER

```
unit Main;

interface

uses
  Windows, Messages, SysUtils,
  Classes, Graphics, Controls,
  Forms, Dialogs, StdCtrls;

type
  TForm1 = class(TForm)
    Button1: TButton;
    procedure Button1Click(Sender: TObject);
    procedure FormDestroy(Sender: TObject);
  private
  public
    V: Variant;
  end;

var
  Form1: TForm1;

Implementation

uses
  ComObj;

{$R *.DFM}

procedure TForm1.Button1Click(Sender: TObject);
```

```
begin
  V := CreateOleObject('Excel.Application');
  V.Visible := True;
end;

procedure TForm1.FormDestroy(Sender: TObject);
begin
  if not VarIsEmpty(V) then
    V.Quit;
end;

end.
```

You can find this example in the program called `Excel1.dpr` on the CD that accompanies this book. The code does nothing more than create an instance of Excel, make it visible, and then close it down when the user exits the Delphi application. The code does not check to make sure the user is not creating multiple instances of the application, but it does close down a single copy of Excel when the user exits.

Using `COMObj`

From Delphi's side, you should always start your automation applications by including `COMObj` in the uses clause. `COMObj` contains routines for retrieving OLE automation objects and for dispatching calls to them. In particular, when using `IDispatch`, you generally call `CreateOleObject` to retrieve an automation object, and behind the scenes, Delphi uses the `COMObj` routines `VarDispInvoke`, `DispatchInvoke`, and `GetIDsOfNames` to call an object. I will give you more information on these routines later. The rest is simply a matter of using a built-in Delphi type called a `Variant` to reference the objects that reside inside Excel.

These simple lines of code launch Excel from inside Delphi:

```
var
  V: Variant;
begin
  V := CreateOleObject('Excel.Application');
  V.Visible := True;
end;
```

The first line of code after the `begin` statement launches Excel. The background behind the call to `CreateOleObject` is relatively complex, so I will explain it in the section "Understanding `CreateOleObject`."

After executing the first line, Excel will come up in the background, entirely offscreen, invisible to the user. This effect may, in fact, be what you want to achieve. However, when you first start programming Excel, and whenever you are debugging your Excel

automation application, you probably want to be able to see what is going on inside Excel. Therefore, I set the `Visible` property of the Excel `Application` object equal to `True`. This setting ensures that you can see what is actually happening on the Excel server. If you have thoroughly debugged your application, you may want to skip this step, but I will include it in all the examples I cover in this chapter.

Understanding Simple Automation of Excel

I haven't told you enough yet to make the code shown in the preceding sections entirely comprehensible. What is the purpose, for instance, of the variable `V`? What does `CreateOleObject` actually do?

As it turns out, the answers to these questions are nontrivial. The variable `V` is a `Variant`, and `CreateOleObject` creates an instance of a COM object called `IDispatch` and returns it to you inside a `Variant`. But saying as much doesn't help if you don't understand COM, `IDispatch`, and `Variants`.

I could take three courses at this point. One would involve an in-depth explanation of COM and OLE, a second would give you only the minimal amount of information needed to keep going, and the third would be to find some middle ground. In this case, I am going to opt for the latter solution and leave it up to you to pursue COM in more depth on your own. I will, however, discuss this subject over the next few paragraphs and come back to it again in the next chapter. If you want even more information, you can look at the following references to get started:

- I have an article on *Delphi and DCOM* on my Web site (`http://users.aol.com/charliecal`) and also cover the subject in Chapter 20 of this book, "DCOM."

- Microsoft has extensive documentation on this subject; you can find it at `http://ww.microsoft.com/com`.

The only thing you really need to know at this stage is that Microsoft has created a special type of object-oriented programming called COM, which allows you to retrieve and call the methods of an object from a number of different languages. The COM object model is different from the one used by native Delphi programmers, so Borland gives you two choices:

- You can follow Microsoft's lead and call the methods of these special objects off a variable type called a `Variant`. This technique is described in this chapter.

- You can follow a more technical approach and use interfaces or dispinterfaces. This latter technique is described in the previous chapter.

Using Delphi to Automate Word and Excel

CHAPTER 16

483

16

USING DELPHI TO
AUTOMATE WORD
AND EXCEL

Comparing Interfaces and `Variants`

One of the key differences between using interfaces and using `Variants` is that interfaces allow you to call COM objects using the much faster dispatching technologies native to Object Pascal. As I will explain later in this chapter, dispinterfaces follow a middle path between the `Variant` technology and the interface technology.

COM is the underlying object model that makes OLE and ActiveX programming possible. At times, I will use OLE and COM as virtual synonyms. ActiveX is yet a third, very closely related technology, but I will not touch on it in this chapter. However, it is no longer incorrect to also use the words *COM* and *ActiveX* as virtual synonyms.

`Variants` get their name because they can provide a wide *variety* of functions, depending on the circumstances. For instance, they can contain a string, an integer, or, in special cases, a COM object. In other words, the type of variable held in a `Variant` *varies* from one occasion to the next. That's why they're called `Variants`. (For more information, look up "Variant Types" in the Delphi online help, or else look at the declarations for the structures used with `Variants` at the top of `System.pas`.)

Understanding `CreateOleObject`

`CreateOleObject` calls a number of internal systemwide OLE functions. The end result of these series of calls is that the function returns a COM object to you containing an interface to the object you want to call. In particular, you get back a `Variant` that is wrapped around a COM object called `IDispatch`. A combination of the built-in `IDispatch` methods and various Delphi technologies covered later in this chapter allows you to call the methods of the object you requested.

With all this information in mind, let's go back and view the two lines of code that retrieve the Excel object:

```
V := CreateOleObject('Excel.Application');
V.Visible := True;
```

The first line of code asks for an object called `Application` that resides inside Excel. `CreateOleObject` retrieves an instance of the object in the form of an `IDispatch` interface encapsulated inside a `Variant` called V. This `Variant` is valuable to you because it allows you to call the methods and properties of the Excel object using a simple syntax. For instance, you can access the `Visible` property of the object by simply writing `V.Visible := True`.

You would be mistaken, however, if you were to assume that the line of code containing the `Visible` property is doing the same thing as a standard Delphi line of code that looks like this:

```
Form1.Visible := True;
```

Admittedly, these two lines look the same and have exactly the same syntax. But internally, something very different is going on. In particular, if you call the `Visible` property of a Delphi form object, the property is changed almost instantly. Calling the `Visible` property of an OLE automation `Variant` sets off a series of internal events that result in a change to the `Visible` property of an object inside Excel, but many steps occur along the way. In particular, several methods of `IDispatch` such as `GetIDsOfNames` and `Invoke` must first be called behind the scenes before the call is complete.

This chapter is not designed to cover the mechanisms used in dispatching a call on a `Variant`-encapsulated COM object, nor do you need to understand how it works to use this technology. The key point to grasp is merely that things aren't quite as simple as they at first appear. Having said all that, I will now show you how to get into this subject a bit deeper if you so desire, and if you have the source to the VCL on your machine.

To get started, copy `COMObj.pas` and `COMObj.inc` from the Delphi `Source\Rtl\Sys` directory to the same directory where `Excel1` is stored. Now rebuild the project so these local copies of `COMObj` are linked into your program. Put a breakpoint on the line `V.Visible := True`, and then run the program. When you get to the breakpoint, press F7 to step into the code. You are taken immediately to the `VarDispInvoke` method found in `COMObj.pas`. From there, you will go to `GetIDsOfNames` and finally to `DispatchInvoke`. Behind the scenes, Delphi is calling the appropriate methods of the `IDispatch` interface to "invoke" your call to Excel.

One of the lessons to be learned from this example is that, at bottom, not such a big difference exists between the interface technology shown in the second part of this chapter and the `Variant`-based technology I am discussing here. For instance, `IDispatch` is an interface, and ultimately this interface must be called for the `Variant`-based technology to work. In fact, `IDispatch` is designed in such a way as to make the `Variant`-based technology even more complex than the standard interface technology described in the next chapter. Only Delphi is able to hide that complexity from you, so you do not need to understand it at all to use `Variants` to call automation objects. (Once again, I need to emphasize that I am not giving a full explanation of this technology in this chapter. If you want to really understand `IDispatch`, you should check out the resources mentioned earlier in this section.)

> **NOTE**
>
> Calling a method off `IDispatch` is usually a two-step process. First, you call `IDispath.GetIDsOfNames` to get an ID or code for the method you call. You pass in the name of the method you want to call, and `GetIDsOfNames` returns some

numerical values that will help you make the call. Then you call `IDispatch.Invoke`, passing in the IDs returned to you by `GetIDsOfNames`. This two-step process allows you to invoke a method off an instance of `IDispatch`. This process is handled automatically for you behind the scenes in `COMObj.pas`.

Variants and Types

One of the biggest consequences of calling the methods of an object off a `Variant` is that Delphi cannot type-check your code at design time. In other words, Delphi does not really know whether the Excel `Application` object has a property called `Visible`. It takes you at your word when you claim this is true. In this case, this approach proves to be the correct thing to do. However, it would also compile the following code without error:

```
V.TransferMoney("From := Bill Gates",
  "To := Charlie Calvert", 100000);
```

This code is certainly intriguing, but the Excel `Application` object unfortunately does not support it. Therefore, a program containing it will compile and load without error, but a call to the `TransferMoney` property at runtime will raise an exception. Both Delphi and Excel are able to handle this exception flawlessly, without destabilizing the system in any way. It is nice, however, if you can type-check at design time rather than having to wait to runtime to see whether all is set up correctly. The interface and dispinterface technologies covered in the second part of this chapter show how to get design-time type-checking of OLE objects.

`IDispatch` and `Variants` are important subjects, but you need not understand them in depth to use this technology. If all is not clear to you yet, you can still continue without fear. If you are hungry for more details, be patient and I will return to this subject in the next chapter, or else you should follow the links shown earlier in this section.

After you create an Excel `Application` object, you need some way to close it down. You can do so by calling its `Quit` method:

```
if not VarIsEmpty(V) then
  V.Quit;
```

This code checks to make sure that the `Variant` V refers to something, and then it attempts to call the `Quit` method of the Excel `Application` object. If V is indeed a valid pointer to such an object, then Excel will close. This code is not perfect in all cases, because V could contain a reference to something other than an Excel `Application` object, thereby allowing `VarIsEmpty` to return `True`, even though the call to `V.Quit` would fail. For instance, I could write

```
V := 10;
```

After making this call, `VarIsEmpty` would return `False`, but the call to `V.Quit` would obviously fail. However, in the `Excel1` application, found in Listing 16.1, `V` usually is either empty or points to a COM object. Therefore, the code is reasonably robust. The key point, at any rate, is that you don't want to fail to `Quit` the `Application` object, or else you can end up cluttering memory with instances of this object. Remember that Excel owns the `Application` object, and it will not necessarily be removed from memory just because you close your Delphi application. In other words, you should definitely call `Application Quit`, or else repeated calls to Excel from a Delphi application will bog down your machine by draining system resources.

Creating Excel Automation Objects

Now that you have been introduced to the topic of automating Excel, the next step is to learn something about what creating an OLE automation object means.

The call to `CreateOleObject` returns a COM object called `IDispatch` housed inside a `Variant`. You can pass a string to `CreateOleObject` specifying the name of the COM object you want to retrieve. In this case, I have retrieved the main Excel Automation object by passing in the string `Excel.Application`. If you are familiar with the Registry, you can find this string there, and can trace that reference to the CLSID associated with the Local Server that returns the object. If you don't know anything about CLSIDs or about Local Servers, don't feel too concerned. The point is simply that `CreateOleObject` returns a COM object of your choice if you pass in the correct string. In particular, it looks up your string in the Registry, finds the CLSID associated with the string, looks up the CLSID, and finds the Local Server associated with that CLSID. The Local Server will be a string pointing to the application that contains the object you want to retrieve. For instance, in this case, on my system, the Local Server string looks like this:

```
C:\Program Files\Microsoft Office\Office\excel.exe /automation
```

This string is copied directly from the `REGEDIT.EXE` application. I found it in `HKEY_CLASSES_ROOT\CLSID`, under the GUID listed next to `Excel.Application`. GUIDs are 64-byte numbers designed to uniquely identify an object.

If you want to trace the details of this operation, and if you have the source to the VCL, you can open `COMObj.pas` and find the implementation of `CreateOleObject`. It consists of a simple call to `CoCreateInstance`. `CoCreateInstance` is a Windows API routine that is part of the OLE specification. Its purpose is to retrieve an object from a binary file such as an executable or DLL.

The strings you pass into `CreateOleObject` are called ProgIDs. As you just saw, all the ProgIDs valid on your system are listed in the Registry under the section `HKEY_CLASSES_ROOT`. (Chapters 13, "Interfaces and the Basics of COM," and 14, "`TComObject`,

TTypedComObject, and Type Libraries," cover this subject in more depth.) The Delphi documentation is not the place to turn to find the ProgIDs you pass in to the various COM servers available on your system. Instead, you should turn to the documentation for the application you want to control. For instance, Excel has extensive COM documentation in an online help file called VBAXL8.HLP that ships with Microsoft Office. (Break down this filename: VBA: Visual Basic for Applications; XL: Excel; 8: Version number.) If you are doing a lot of OLE automation with Excel, you should add this file to Delphi's Tools menu so you can get to it easily. For information on retrieving objects, use the Index feature in the Excel help to look up "OLE programmatic identifiers."

In the Excel online help, you will find that this spreadsheet application has three main objects you can retrieve by using CreateOleObject:

```
CreateOleObject('Excel.Application');
CreateOleObject('Excel.Sheet');
CreateOleObject('Excel.Chart');
```

These strings, and slight variations on these strings, are the only valid parameters to pass to CreateOleObject if you want to talk to Excel via COM. Many more objects are available inside Excel. However, these three are the only ones you can retrieve from outside Excel by using the CreateOleObject function. After you retrieve one of these objects, you can use it as your access to all the other objects in the Excel hierarchy. Getting at these objects is a bit like unwinding a ball of thread. You first need a handle to the ball of thread, which you get by calling CreateOleObject. After you have a handle, you can use it to get to all the different objects inside Excel. Just keep pulling at the thread you get back from CreateOleObject, and all the rest of the objects will come unraveled. This subject is explained in more depth in the next section.

Understanding Excel Automation Objects

If you are an experienced Delphi programmer, you may find OLE objects a bit confusing at first. Like standard Pascal objects, they exist inside a hierarchy, but that hierarchy, at least as it is presented to the public, is not based on inheritance. Instead, the main glue that holds the hierarchy together is the fact that you can access one particular object from another particular object.

For instance, the top member of the Excel hierarchy is called Application. Beneath it is the Workbooks object, and beneath that are the Worksheets and Charts objects:

```
1) Application:
  A) Workbooks
    i) Worksheets
    ii) Charts
```

Accessing Objects Within the Application Object

If you want to get to the Workbooks object, you can access it from the Application object:

```
MyWorkbooks  := Application.Workbooks;
```

If you want to get to the Worksheets object, you can access it from the Workbooks object, and so on. In the code shown here, you would declare MyWorkbooks as a Variant. In all cases, during this first part of this chapter, I am using Variants to access the underlying Excel objects.

If you saw this hierarchy in a Delphi application, you would assume that Workbooks is a descendant of Application, and Worksheets a descendant of Workbooks. That kind of thinking is completely off center when it comes to OLE automation. The standard OOP hierarchy found in C++ and Pascal has nothing to do with OLE automation. Here you find a totally different kind of hierarchy intended only to express which objects can be accessed from another object. As you will see in the second part of this chapter, it may also be true that a valid OOP inheritance-based hierarchy is simultaneously implemented on these objects. However, that hierarchy is not the main one you focus on when using automation, and in fact, I think it is easiest at first to pretend that it does not exist at all.

If you want to talk about all the Worksheets and Charts in a Workbook, you use the Sheets object. When thinking about the Sheets object, you could rewrite the preceding hierarchy as follows:

```
1) Application
  A) Workbooks
    i) Sheets
    ii) Worksheets
    iii) Charts
```

The point is that this hierarchy is meant to denote the order in which you access objects, and as such it has a somewhat more slippery structure than you would find in a typical inheritance hierarchy. In fact, it seems that you can get to most any object from any one point in the hierarchy, so the actual structure of the hierarchy is a little dependent on your current position inside it.

You get to the Workbooks object from Application object. You get to the Sheets, Worksheets, and Charts objects from the Workbooks object:

```
MyCharts := Application.Workbooks[I];
```

Using Delphi to Automate Word and Excel

CHAPTER 16

489

16

USING DELPHI TO
AUTOMATE WORD
AND EXCEL

It would be untrue to say that the Application object is synonymous with the binary file Excel.exe, but it does have some things in common with this executable. For instance, the Application object is the most abstracted, the most generalized way that you have of referring to the set of available Excel automation objects. If you open Excel and have no documents loaded, then you are looking at a visual representation of the Application object. It is not the same thing as the Application object, but it can serve as a metaphor for what the object does. It is analogous to it. It is the highest level container for accessing all the functionality available from Excel. However, it is so generalized that it can't do much that is useful without help from other objects. But you get to those other objects by starting with the Application object. All this is equally true of Excel.exe. If you open Excel.exe with no documents in it, then it has little use on its own, but it is still the gateway you would use to access all these documents.

The Workbooks object contains a collection of Worksheets and Charts. A Worksheet is just a standard page from a spreadsheet, while a Chart is just a graph. The Sheets object contains both Worksheets and Charts, whereas the Worksheets and Charts objects contain only Worksheets or Charts. Your job as an Excel automation programmer is to start learning how to make statements like these. In other words, this kind of logic underlies the Excel hierarchy of objects. As an automation programmer, your job is to figure out how to get to one object from another object and to understand what each object does.

Here is another way to think about what you, as an Excel automation programmer, are really trying to do. Most computer users understand how to use Excel. The automation objects discussed in this chapter allow you to write code that manipulates Excel just as you would manipulate Excel with a mouse. You probably already know how to open a spreadsheet, enter data, perform calculations, and chart data. Your goal as an automation programmer is to find out how to do the same things in code. You just need to know which object refer to which sets of tools inside Excel. Figure that out and figure out how to get to each of these objects given the existence of an Application object, and then you are ready to roll.

Using Automation

The program shown in Listing 16.2 provides a summary of the major points made here. Glance over it once, and then read on to find an explanation of how it works.

LISTING 16.2 THE Excel2 PROGRAM SHOWS HOW THE OBJECTS IN EXCEL ARE ARRANGED HIERARCHICALLY

```
unit Main;

interface

uses
```

continues

LISTING 16.2   CONTINUED

```
  Windows, Messages, SysUtils,
  Classes, Graphics, Controls,
  Forms, Dialogs, StdCtrls;

type
  TForm1 = class(TForm)
    Button1: TButton;
    ListBox1: TListBox;
    procedure Button1Click(Sender: TObject);
    procedure FormDestroy(Sender: TObject);
  private
    XLApplication: Variant;
  public
  end;

var
  Form1: TForm1;

Implementation

uses
  ComObj;

{$R *.DFM}

procedure TForm1.Button1Click(Sender: TObject);
const
{ XlSheetType }
  xlChart = -4109;
  xlDialogSheet = -4116;
  xlExcel4IntlMacroSheet = 4;
  xlExcel4MacroSheet = 3;
  xlWorksheet = -4167;
{ XlWBATemplate }
  xlWBATChart = -4109;
  xlWBATExcel4IntlMacroSheet = 4;
  xlWBATExcel4MacroSheet = 3;
  xlWBATWorksheet = -4167;
var
  i, j: Integer;
  Sheets: Variant;
begin
  XLApplication := CreateOleObject('Excel.Application');
  XLApplication.Visible := True;
  XLApplication.Workbooks.Add;
  XLApplication.Workbooks.Add(xlWBatChart);
  XLApplication.Workbooks.Add(xlWBatWorkSheet);
  XLApplication.Workbooks[2].Sheets.Add(,,1,xlChart);
```

Using Delphi to Automate Word and Excel

CHAPTER 16

491

16

USING DELPHI TO
AUTOMATE WORD
AND EXCEL

```
    XLApplication.Workbooks[3].Sheets.Add(,,1,xlWorkSheet);
    for i := 1 to XLApplication.Workbooks.Count do begin
      ListBox1.Items.Add('Workbook: ' + XLApplication.Workbooks[i].Name);
      for j := 1 to XLApplication.Workbooks[i].Sheets.Count do
        ListBox1.Items.Add('  Sheet: ' +
          XLApplication.Workbooks[i].Sheets[j].Name);
    end;
  end;

  procedure TForm1.FormDestroy(Sender: TObject);
  begin
    if not VarIsEmpty(XLApplication) then begin
      XLApplication.DisplayAlerts := False;  // Discard unsaved files....
      XLApplication.Quit;
    end;
  end;

end.
```

This application starts an instance of Excel and then populates it with three workbooks. One of the workbooks contains a default number of worksheets, a second contains a user-defined number of worksheets, and a third contains some workcharts. The following paragraphs explain how this example works.

Take a moment to study the core of the `Button1Click` method:

```
begin
  XLApplication := CreateOleObject('Excel.Application');
  XLApplication.Visible := True;
  XLApplication.Workbooks.Add;
  XLApplication.Workbooks.Add(xlWBatChart);
  XLApplication.Workbooks.Add(xlWBatWorkSheet);
  XLApplication.Workbooks[2].Sheets.Add(,,1,xlChart);
  XLApplication.Workbooks[3].Sheets.Add(,,1,xlWorkSheet);
  for i := 1 to XLApplication.Workbooks.Count do begin
    ListBox1.Items.Add('Workbook: ' + XLApplication.Workbooks[i].Name);
    for j := 1 to XLApplication.Workbooks[i].Sheets.Count do
      ListBox1.Items.Add('  Sheet: ' +
        XLApplication.Workbooks[i].Sheets[j].Name);
  end;
end;
```

`XLApplication` is a `Variant` that contains an instance of `IDispatch` used for accessing the Excel `Application` object. As you know, `Application` contains a property called `Visible`. If you set it to `True`, Excel will appear on your screen. Once again, this is not the time or place to explore the subject, but COM objects support the notion of properties. These properties are very different internally from Delphi properties, but they behave more or less the same.

Workbooks is a collection object. It contains a collection of workbooks. This pattern is followed over and over in Excel. The Sheets object contains a collection of sheets. The Worksheets object contains a collection of worksheets. The Charts object contains a collection of charts. Inside Word, the Paragraphs object contains a collection of paragraphs. The Words object contains a collection of words. The Tables object contains a collection of tables and so on.

Depending on which automation server you are using, you get to members of a collection through one of four possible syntaxes. Sometimes all syntaxes are available to you, sometimes fewer:

```
MyChart := Charts[1];
MyChart := Charts.Item[1];
MyChart := Charts(1);
MyChart := Charts.Item(1);
```

You need to be conscious of the difference between a collection object and a normal object. For instance, to understand a Worksheets object, you should look up both Worksheets and Worksheet in the Excel help; to understand the Tables object, you should look up both Tables and Table in the Word help.

Workbooks contains a method called Add, which you use to add a workbook to a workbooks collection. COM objects support the idea of variable parameter lists. You therefore can simply skip passing in parameters to a method if you want. In this case, if you call Workbooks.Add with no parameters, you will create a workbook with some predefined number of worksheets in it. The default number is three, but you can change the number from inside Excel if you so desire. When you are working with interfaces rather than Variants, you cannot omit parameters. I will explain in the second part of this chapter how to work with interfaces in situations such as this one, where not passing in a parameter has a special meaning.

If you want to create a new Workbook with exactly one Worksheet in it, then you call Add and pass in the constant xlWBatWorksheet. I declare this constant explicitly inside this program. In the next section, I will tell you how to get a complete list of all the Excel and Word constants.

If you want to create a new workbook with exactly one chart in it, then you call Add and pass in the constant xlWBatChart.

If you then want to add one worksheet to the second workbook you created, you would write the following code:

```
XLApplication.Workbooks[2].Sheets.Add(,,1,xlWorkSheet);
```

Using Delphi to Automate Word and Excel

CHAPTER 16

493

16

USING DELPHI TO
AUTOMATE WORD
AND EXCEL

Here is how to create a new chart:

```
XLApplication.Workbooks[2].Sheets.Add(,,1,xlChart);
```

In this case, the Add method of the Sheets object takes four parameters:

- Before—A Variant containing the sheet before which the new sheet is added
- After—A Variant containing the sheet after which the new sheet is added
- Count—The number of sheets to add, with the value defaulting to one
- Type—One of the following constants:

    xlWorksheet (default type)

    xlChart

    xlExcel4MacroSheet

    xlExcel4IntlMacroSheet

The first two parameters specify the location in the workbook where you want the new chart or worksheet to appear. The third parameter states how many sheets you want to add, and the fourth specifies the type of sheet you want to add. Here is how the method is declared in the Microsoft documentation:

```
expression.Add(Before, After, Count, Type);
```

In the preceding examples using Add, I don't care what order the sheets are inserted, so I just omit the first two parameters by simply placing commas in my code where the parameters would be listed. If I want to state the order, I write something like this:

```
Sheets := Application.Sheets;
Sheets.Add(, Sheets.Item[2], 1, xlChart);
```

In this case, the code still leaves the Before parameter blank, but it references the 2 sheet in the After parameter.

The for loop at the bottom of the sample method iterates through each of the workgroups, finds the names of each of the sheets available in each workbook, and then adds them to list box. In short, the code shows how to retrieve the names of the members of a series of workbooks, while simultaneously showing how to iterate over all their members.

Here is how to reference the number of workbooks in the application:

```
for i := 1 to XLApplication.Workbooks.Count do begin
```

And here is how to count the number of sheets in a Workbook:

```
for j := 1 to XLApplication.Workbooks[i].Sheets.Count do
```

Here is how to find the name of a particular worksheet or chart in `Workbook`:

```
XLApplication.Workbooks[i].Sheets[j].Name;
```

If you spend a little while contemplating the `Button1Click` method, the logic behind the objects in Microsoft Excel should become clear to you. Of course, I have additional matters to cover, such as entering data and creating graphs. But, as you will see, most of that material is relatively straightforward after you understand the way the Excel object hierarchy works.

One important point to make before closing this section is that assigning a specific variable to one of the sub-objects in the hierarchy often helps. For instance, in the previous example, I declared a `Variant` named `Sheets` and set it equal to the `Application.Sheets` object:

```
Sheets := Application.Sheets;
```

To my mind, mentally parsing code that is written this way is sometimes easier than trying to always reference a series of qualified objects such as

```
XLApplication.Workbooks[i].Sheets.Count
```

Obviously, more overhead is involved if you use the technique of storing an object reference in a separate `Variant`. However, the technology used to implement OLE automation on the Excel side is perhaps necessarily not particularly efficient, so you shouldn't balk at using techniques like this if you think they will help you write clear, easy-to-maintain code. When you're trying to optimize your code, remember that trips between your application and Excel are very expensive. If you can limit the number of trips you need to make, you will save clock cycles. But once again, this whole process is innately slow, so fretting over a few lost clock cycles that most users will never even notice is a bit silly.

As always, you should be particularly aware of saving clock cycles when you are inside a loop. A call that takes one second to execute is easy for the user to bear if it occurs once. But put it in a loop, execute it 2,000 times, and the user will hate you. A general rule of thumb is that the user should never have to wait for anything, that everything should happen in real time. If that is not possible, you might be comforted to know that most users will happily wait up to two seconds for you to do most chores. Longer than that, and they get impatient. Two seconds is several eons in computer time, so normally you don't have to fret about optimization issues. The Delphi team already did all the sweating for you. But when automating Excel or Word, you can get in trouble fairly quickly, so you may need to think about optimization in places where you wouldn't worry about it in a normal Delphi application. Remember that Excel automation is called "Visual Basic for Applications." As you will see later, these Excel classes are actually real objects, so clearly this subject doesn't have much to do with Visual Basic, but the mere presence of the word Basic costs you, by default, thousands of clock cycles.

Using Delphi to Automate Word and Excel

CHAPTER 16

495

16

USING DELPHI TO
AUTOMATE WORD
AND EXCEL

Finding the Constants Used in Excel

You can determine all the constants used by Excel by reading its type library. You can read a type library in at least two simple ways:

- You can read the type library with a third-party tool, such as the OleView application that ships with the Microsoft SDK.

- You can ask Delphi to read the library for you and to translate the information stored in the library into Object Pascal. Obviously, this is the preferred technique.

I have included the translations of the Excel and Word type libraries with this chapter on the CD. However, if you want to create your own versions of these libraries, you can select Project, Import Type Library from the Delphi menu, and then select the appropriate type library. A Delphi translation of the type library will be created automatically.

The files you want to import usually have either a .tlb or .exe extension. When working with Office 97, however, you want one with an .olb extension. The file to use with Word is MSWORD8.OLB, and the one to use with Excel is EXCEL8.OLB. On my system, I found these entries in the ...\Microsoft Office\Office directory.

After you import the OLB file, a new file called Excel_TLB.pas will be created in the Delphi4\Imports directory. In this file, you will find declarations for all the constants used by Excel 97.

The Pascal translations of the interfaces to all the objects used in Excel or Word are found in the files created by importing EXCEL8.OLB and MSWORD8.OLB. Throughout this part of the chapter, I will ignore these interfaces and show you how to work directly with Variant objects. However, in the next chapter I will return to this subject and show you how to work with interfaces. At that time, I will present a discussion of the relative merits of working with Variants and interfaces.

Storing and Accessing Data in an Excel Worksheet

Throughout the next few sections, I will be working with a sample program called Excel3. The source for the main form of this program is shown in Listing 16.3. Just take a quick look at the code for now, and then read on to get an explanation of how it works.

LISTING 16.3   THE SOURCE FOR THE MAIN FORM OF THE Excel3 PROGRAM

```
unit Main;

interface

uses
  Windows, Messages, SysUtils,
```

continues

LISTING 16.3   CONTINUED

```delphi
  Classes, Graphics, Controls,
  Forms, Dialogs, StdCtrls;

type
  TForm1 = class(TForm)
    Button1: TButton;
    Button2: TButton;
    procedure Button1Click(Sender: TObject);
    procedure FormDestroy(Sender: TObject);
    procedure Button2Click(Sender: TObject);
  private
    XLApp: Variant;
    procedure InsertData;
    procedure ChangeColumns;
    procedure HandleRange;
  public
  end;

var
  Form1: TForm1;

Implementation

uses
  ComObj, XLConst;

{$R *.DFM}

procedure TForm1.FormDestroy(Sender: TObject);
begin
  if not VarIsEmpty(XLApp) then begin
    XLApp.DisplayAlerts := False;  // Discard unsaved files....
    XLApp.Quit;
  end;
end;

procedure TForm1.Button1Click(Sender: TObject);
begin
  XLApp:= CreateOleObject('Excel.Application');
  XLApp.Visible := True;
  XLApp.Workbooks.Add(xlWBatWorkSheet);
  XLApp.Workbooks[1].WorkSheets[1].Name := 'Delphi Data';
  InsertData;
  HandleRange;
  ChangeColumns;
end;

procedure TForm1.InsertData;
var
```

Using Delphi to Automate Word and Excel

CHAPTER 16

497

16

USING DELPHI TO
AUTOMATE WORD
AND EXCEL

```
  i: Integer;
  Sheet: Variant;
begin
  Sheet := XLApp.Workbooks[1].WorkSheets['Delphi Data'];
  for i := 1 to 10 do
    Sheet.Cells[i, 1] := i;
  Sheet.Cells[i, 1] := '=Sum(A1:A10)';
end;

procedure TForm1.HandleRange;
var
  Range: Variant;
begin
  Range :=
   XLApp.Workbooks[1].WorkSheets['Delphi Data'].Range['C1:F25'];

  Range.Formula := '=RAND()';
  Range.Columns.Interior.ColorIndex := 3;
  Range.Borders.LineStyle := xlContinuous;
end;

procedure TForm1.ChangeColumns;
var
  ColumnRange: Variant;
begin
  ColumnRange := XLApp.Workbooks[1].WorkSheets['Delphi Data'].Columns;
  ColumnRange.Columns[1].ColumnWidth := 5;
  ColumnRange.Columns[1].Font.Bold := True;
  ColumnRange.Columns[1].Font.Color := clBlue;
end;

procedure TForm1.Button2Click(Sender: TObject);
var
  Sheet: Variant;
  Num: Integer;
begin
  Sheet := XLApp.Workbooks[1].WorkSheets['Delphi Data'];
  Num := Sheet.Range['C1:F25'].Columns.Interior.PatternColor;
  ShowMessage(Format('Value: %x', [Num]));
end;

end.
```

As shown here, you can easily insert data in a spreadsheet. In fact, the technique involved is similar to what you would use putting data into a TStringGrid control in Delphi.

To get started, open Excel and create a new spreadsheet:

```
procedure TForm1.Button1Click(Sender: TObject);
```

```
begin
  XLApp:= CreateOleObject('Excel.Application');
  XLApp.Visible := True;
  XLApp.Workbooks.Add(xlWBatWorkSheet);
  XLApp.Workbooks[1].WorkSheets[1].Name := 'Delphi Data';
  InsertData;
  HandleRange;
  ChangeColumns;
end;
```

As you can, see, I create a single workbook with one worksheet in it. The code then names the worksheet `Delphi Data`. The `InsertData`, `HandleRange`, and `ChangeColumns` calls are custom Delphi routines that I will now describe.

To insert data into the spreadsheet, execute the following function:

```
procedure TForm1.InsertData;
var
  i: Integer;
  Sheet: Variant;
begin
  Sheet := XLApp.Workbooks[1].WorkSheets['Delphi Data'];
  for i := 1 to 10 do
    Sheet.Cells[i, 1] := i;
  Sheet.Cells[i, 1] := '=Sum(A1:A10)';
end;
```

The method starts by retrieving a pointer to the worksheet you want to manipulate. As you know, this pointer is an instance of `IDispatch` that is stored inside a `Variant`. You don't need to know anything about how `IDispatch` works to call the methods of this object.

The code inserts 10 integers into the sheet. The `Cells` property works exactly as you would expect, except Excel puts the `Row` first and the `Column` second.

After the numbers are inserted in the worksheet, the final stage is to insert a formula and add the column of numbers. To do so, you simply insert the formula much as you would if you were in Excel itself. In particular, you store the formula in a string and then insert it into the appropriate cell:

```
Sheet.Cells[i, 1] := '=Sum(A1:A10)';
```

Working with `Columns` and `Range` Attributes

Sometimes you might want to perform an operation on a range of data in the spreadsheet. To do so, you use the Excel `Range` object:

```
Sheet.Range['C1:F25'].Formula := '=RAND()';
```

Using Delphi to Automate Word and Excel

CHAPTER 16

499

16

USING DELPHI TO
AUTOMATE WORD
AND EXCEL

This code could be inserted into the bottom of the InsertData method. It fills all the cells between C1 and F25 with random numbers between 0 and 1.

One of the key objects in both Excel and Word is the Range object. It allows you to work with a range of cells or columns at one time. In either Word or Excel, you generally enter or read data by using the Range object. In short, if you want to insert text into a Word document, you will generally use the Range object.

> **NOTE**
>
> With Word, it is also possible to insert data via a considerably simpler method. For instance, the following procedure enters data at the current insertion point into an open document in Microsoft Word:
>
> ```
> procedure TForm1.Button1Click(Sender: TObject);
> var
>   V: Variant;
> begin
>   V := GetActiveOleObject('Word.Basic');
>   V.Insert('Sam');
> end;
> ```
>
> In this case, I have chosen not to open a new version of Word, but instead to call GetActiveOleObject to get a handle to a document in an instance of Word that is already running. This kind of technology is very easy to use and is perfect for some projects. It doesn't, however, have the power of the technology I am showing you in this paper.

To access a Range object in Excel, simply specify the range with which you want to work:

```
Range := Sheet.Range['C1:F25'];
```

In this case, the code defines a range from cell C1 to cell F25. Any operations performed on the returned Range object will affect all the cells in that range.

This simple function shows how to change the values and appearance of a range of cells:

```
procedure TForm1.HandleRange;
var
  Range: Variant;
begin
  Range :=
  XLApp.Workbooks[1].WorkSheets['Delphi Data'].Range['C1:F25'];

  Range.Formula := '=RAND()';
```

```
    Range.Columns.Interior.ColorIndex := 3;
    Range.Borders.LineStyle := xlContinuous;
end;
```

The first line of code in the body of the procedure returns a pointer to the range you want to manipulate. The second line fills all the values in the range C1:F25 with random numbers between 0 and 1, as explained earlier.

The next to last line of code in the body of the procedure changes the color of the entire block of cells to red. You can use the Excel online help to see the values in the ColorIndex, but the first few default values are as follows: black, white, red, green, blue, yellow, purple, cyan. Red is the third item in the list, so setting the ColorIndex to 3 makes the selected range of cells red.

At the same time that you change the color, you also lose your borders. This loss is a peculiarity of Excel, and you can work around it by resetting the LineStyle of the selected cells as shown in the last line of code in the procedure. Once again, when you are working with constants like this, you can find them in the XLCONST.pas or EXCELTLB.pas files included with the sample programs found on the CD that accompanies this book, or you can retrieve them from the type library as explained earlier.

If you are interested, this line of code changes the background of a range:

```
Range.Columns.Interior.Pattern := xlPatternCrissCross;
```

The following function changes the width and font of a column:

```
procedure TForm1.ChangeColumns;
var
  ColumnRange: Variant;
begin
  ColumnRange := XLApp.Workbooks[1].WorkSheets['Delphi Data'].Columns;
  ColumnRange.Columns[1].ColumnWidth := 5;
  ColumnRange.Columns[1].Font.Bold := True;
  ColumnRange.Columns[1].Font.Color := clBlue;
end;
```

As you can see, when you want to work with the columns in a worksheet, you can access them from a Range object. In particular, the Range object contains a collection of columns that you can access using array notation.

To change the width of a column, use the ColumnWidth property, and to change the font, use the Font property. Going into much more detail would be pointless, as this code is easy to write.

Sharing a Chart Between Excel and Word

Creating and working with a chart is just as easy as doing everything else in Excel automation. In the example shown in this section, refer to the program called `Excel4.dpr`. The listing for this program is shown in Listing 16.4. I include the listing here so that you can take a quick glance through it, and then refer back to it during the discussion of its inner workings that follows this listing. In other words, I don't expect you to understand the program completely at a single glance but will instead spend the remainder of this section discussing it in some depth.

LISTING 16.4   THE Excel4 PROGRAM SHOWS HOW TO WORK WITH CHARTS

```
unit Main;
{
  Main.pas
  Copyright (c) 1997..1998 by Charlie Calvert
  Creating data and a chart in Excel and copying both to Word.
}

interface

uses
  Windows, Messages, SysUtils,
  Classes, Graphics, Controls,
  Forms, Dialogs, StdCtrls;

type
  TForm1 = class(TForm)
    Button1: TButton;
    procedure Button1Click(Sender: TObject);
    procedure FormDestroy(Sender: TObject);
  private
    XLApp: Variant;
    WordApp: Variant;
  public
    procedure HandleData;
    procedure ChartData;
    procedure CopyData;
    procedure CopyChartToWord;
    procedure CopyCellsToWord;
    procedure MailDocument;
  end;

var
  Form1: TForm1;
```

continues

LISTING 16.4   CONTINUED

```
Implementation

uses
  ComObj, XLConst, WordConst,
  ActiveX;

{$R *.DFM}

procedure TForm1.Button1Click(Sender: TObject);
begin
  XLApp := CreateOleObject('Excel.Application');
  XLApp.Visible := True;
  XLApp.Workbooks.Add[XLWBatWorksheet];
  XLApp.Workbooks[1].Worksheets[1].Name := 'Delphi Data';
  HandleData;
  ChartData;
  CopyData;
  MailDocument;
end;

procedure TForm1.HandleData;
var
  Sheet: Variant;
  i: Integer;
begin
  Sheet := XLApp.Workbooks[1].Worksheets['Delphi Data'];
  for i := 1 to 10 do
    Sheet.Cells[i, 1] := i;
end;

procedure TForm1.ChartData;
var
  ARange: Variant;
  Sheets: Variant;
begin
  XLApp.Workbooks[1].Sheets.Add(,,1,xlChart);
  Sheets := XLApp.Sheets;
  ARange := Sheets.Item['Delphi Data'].Range['A1:A10'];
  Sheets.Item['Chart1'].SeriesCollection.Item[1].Values := ARange;
  Sheets.Item['Chart1'].ChartType := xl3DPie;
  Sheets.Item['Chart1'].SeriesCollection.Item[1].HasDataLabels := True;
  XLApp.Workbooks[1].Sheets.Add(,,1,xlChart);
  Sheets.Item['Chart2'].SeriesCollection.Item[1].Values := ARange;
  Sheets.Item['Chart2'].SeriesCollection.Add(ARange);
  Sheets.Item['Chart2'].SeriesCollection.NewSeries;
  Sheets.Item['Chart2'].SeriesCollection.Item[3].Values :=
    VarArrayOf([1,2,3,4,5, 6,7,8,9,10]);
  Sheets.Item['Chart2'].ChartType := xl3DColumn;
```

```
end;

procedure TForm1.CopyData;
var
  Sheets: Variant;
begin
  SetFocus;

  Sheets := XLApp.Sheets;
  Sheets.Item['Delphi Data'].Activate;
  Sheets.Item['Delphi Data'].Range['A1:A10'].Select;
  Sheets.Item['Delphi Data'].UsedRange.Copy;
  CopyCellsToWord;
  Sheets.Item['Chart1'].Select;
  XLApp.Selection.Copy;
  CopyChartToWord;
end;

procedure TForm1.CopyChartToWord;
var
  Range: Variant;
  i, NumPars: Integer;
begin
  NumPars := WordApp.Documents.Item(1).Paragraphs.Count;
  Range := WordApp.Documents.Item(1).Range(
    WordApp.Documents.Item(1).Paragraphs.Item(NumPars).Range.Start,
    WordApp.Documents.Item(1).Paragraphs.Item(NumPars).Range.End);
  Range.Text := 'This is graph: ';
  for i := 1 to 3 do WordApp.Documents.Item(1).Paragraphs.Add;
  Range := WordApp.Documents.Item(1).Range(
    WordApp.Documents.Item(1).Paragraphs.Item(NumPars + 1).Range.Start,
    WordApp.Documents.Item(1).Paragraphs.Item(NumPars + 1).Range.End);
  Range.PasteSpecial(,,,,wdPasteOleObject);
end;

procedure TForm1.CopyCellsToWord;
var
  Range: Variant;
  i: Integer;
begin
  WordApp := CreateOleObject('Word.Application');
  WordApp.Visible := True;
  WordApp.Documents.Add;
  Range := WordApp.Documents.Item(1).Range;
  Range.Text := 'This is a column from a spreadsheet: ';
  for i := 1 to 3 do WordApp.Documents.Item(1).Paragraphs.Add;
  Range := WordApp.Documents.Item(1).Range(
      WordApp.Documents.Item(1).Paragraphs.Item(3).Range.Start);
  Range.Paste;
```

continues

LISTING 16.4   CONTINUED

```
   for i := 1 to 3 do WordApp.Documents.Item(1).Paragraphs.Add;
end;

procedure TForm1.FormDestroy(Sender: TObject);
begin
  if not VarIsEmpty(XLApp) then begin
    XLApp.DisplayAlerts := False;  // Discard unsaved files....
    XLApp.Quit;
  end;
  if not VarIsEmpty(WordApp)then begin
    WordApp.Documents.Item(1).Close(wdDoNotSaveChanges);
    WordApp.Quit;
  end;
end;

procedure TForm1.MailDocument;
begin
  WordApp.Documents.Item(1).SaveAs('c:\foo.doc');
  WordApp.Options.SendMailAttach := True;
  WordApp.Documents.Item(1).SendMail;
end;

end.
```

This code opens a copy of Excel, inserts some data into it, and creates two graphs of the data. Then it opens a copy of Word, copies the cells from the worksheet to a new Word document, and then copies one of the charts into the same document. When you are through, you have a Word document containing some spreadsheet cells with Delphi data in them, and below these cells, a graph. You may not see the graph at first when looking at your copy of Word. To find the graph, scroll down the document a bit. By default, a fairly large margin appears at the top of a graph, so you may need to scroll down further than you think. After you create the Word document, you have a chance to mail it via Microsoft Mail.

Creating a Spreadsheet

The Button1Click method drives the entire application:

```
procedure TForm1.Button1Click(Sender: TObject);
begin
  XLApp := CreateOleObject('Excel.Application');
  XLApp.Visible := True;
  XLApp.Workbooks.Add[XLWBatWorksheet];
  XLApp.Workbooks[1].Worksheets[1].Name := 'Delphi Data';
  HandleData;
  ChartData;
```

Using Delphi to Automate Word and Excel

CHAPTER 16

505

16

USING DELPHI TO
AUTOMATE WORD
AND EXCEL

```
  CopyData;
  MailDocument;
end;
```

This method starts by creating an Excel `Application` object, sets the `Visible` property of the object to `True`, and adds a new workbook and stuffs a single worksheet into it. The Delphi application then calls my custom `HandleData` method to insert data into the spreadsheet:

```
procedure TForm1.HandleData;
var
  Sheet: Variant;
  i: Integer;
begin
  Sheet := XLApp.Workbooks[1].Worksheets['Delphi Data'];
  for i := 1 to 10 do
    Sheet.Cells[i, 1] := i;
end;
```

The code found in the `HandleData` method is explained earlier in this chapter, so I won't cover it again.

Creating a Chart

Now that you have a worksheet and some data, the next step is to create a graph. The following procedure from the `Excel4` program should get you started working with charts:

```
procedure TForm1.ChartData;
var
  ARange: Variant;
  Sheets: Variant;
begin
  XLApp.Workbooks[1].Sheets.Add(,,1,xlChart);
  Sheets := XLApp.Sheets;
  ARange := Sheets.Item['Delphi Data'].Range['A1:A10'];
  Sheets.Item['Chart1'].SeriesCollection.Item[1].Values := ARange;
  Sheets.Item['Chart1'].ChartType := xl3DPie;
  Sheets.Item['Chart1'].SeriesCollection.Item[1].HasDataLabels := True;
  XLApp.Workbooks[1].Sheets.Add(,,1,xlChart);
  Sheets.Item['Chart2'].SeriesCollection.Item[1].Values := ARange;
  Sheets.Item['Chart2'].SeriesCollection.Add(ARange);
  Sheets.Item['Chart2'].SeriesCollection.NewSeries;
  Sheets.Item['Chart2'].SeriesCollection.Item[3].Values :=
    VarArrayOf([1,2,3,4,5, 6,7,8,9,10]);
  Sheets.Item['Chart2'].ChartType := xl3DColumn;
end;
```

This function creates two different charts. I've arranged things this way so you can get a look at some of the different techniques needed to create charts.

The code starts by adding a single chart to a Sheets object in a Workbook:

```
XLApp.Workbooks[1].Sheets.Add(,,1,xlChart);
```

As you can see, I just ignore the first two parameters, explicitly state that I want to insert one sheet, and then define its type as xlChart. I described the Add method in more depth earlier in this chapter.

A lot of the trick to working with Excel is to find the right object to work with. The Sheets object provides a simple and convenient way to create a chart, but it is not the only way of doing so. Remember that the Sheets object contains both the Worksheets and Charts objects inside a Workbook, so you can use it to add either worksheets or charts.

You should further understand that I am talking about adding Charts to a Sheets object, which is different from adding ChartObjects to a worksheet. In other words, you can insert a graph into a worksheet, but that operation is different from the one shown here. The key to embedding a chart into a worksheet is the Excel ChartObjects collection, which is not discussed further in this chapter.

After the chart has been created, the code then finds a range of data in the sheet to work on. In this particular example, the range is the same used in the Excel3 application, when I inserted 10 numbers into the A column and then supplied a formula to add them up. In particular, note that I create a Range object and then set the SeriesCollection of a Chart object to this range:

```
ARange := Sheets.Item['Delphi Data'].Range['A1:A10'];
Sheets.Item['Chart1'].SeriesCollection.Item[1].Values := ARange;
```

That is all you need to do to graph a range of data. As I will explain in a moment, you may want to manipulate the chart further, but just doing what I have done here is enough to start charting data.

Using the SeriesCollection Object

Stepping back and looking at the SeriesCollection object to see what it represents may be worthwhile. To get started, you need to understand that a Series is simply a range of data that you want to graph. A SeriesCollection is a collection of ranges of data; that is, it is a collection of Series. For instance, if you have the values 1, 2, 3 in three cells in a spreadsheet, they would represent a range of three numbers that could be placed in a Series. By default, the graph of that Series might look something like this, where each dash represents one unit in the Series 1, 2, 3:

```
-
- -
- - -
```

If you have several `Series` together in one place, you would have a `SeriesCollection`.

To see a `SeriesCollection` on the Excel side, load an Excel chart, right-click on it, select the Source Data item from the menu, and turn to the Series page, as shown in Figure 16.1.

FIGURE 16.1

Showing a Series *inside Excel.*

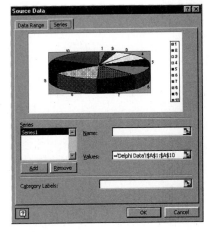

This `Series` is created for the first graph made by the `Excel4` program. As you can see, the `Series` is described with a single cryptic line:

```
='Delphi Data'!$A$1:$A$10
```

If you think about this line for a second, you can see how it corresponds to the code you wrote in Delphi. To help you see the relationship, I will write the following pseudocode designed to highlight the relationship:

```
SeriesCollection.Item[1].Values :=
    Sheets.Item['Delphi Data'].Range[A1:A10];
```

This code will not compile, but it contains the essence of what happens in the two lines of Delphi code that creates the `Series` shown from the `SeriesCollection`. It is similar to the data seen on the Excel side.

When you create a new chart, one `Series` is made for you automatically. By default, it charts whatever value is in cell A1 of a particular worksheet. In this case, I have changed that `Series` to point to a new range of data. In other words, I have changed the "Values" associated with the `Series`. As you will see in one moment, you can add additional `Series` if you so desire.

After you create the chart, the code defines it further by stating its type:

```
Sheets.Item['Chart1'].ChartType := xl3DPie;
```

It then goes on to specify that the chart has a `Series` of data labels:

```
Sheets.Item['Chart1'].SeriesCollection.Item[1].HasDataLabels := True;
```

Now you're ready to look at the second chart created by the `ChartData` method:

```
XLApp.Workbooks[1].Sheets.Add(,,1,xlChart);
Sheets.Item['Chart2'].SeriesCollection.Item[1].Values := ARange;
Sheets.Item['Chart2'].SeriesCollection.Add(ARange);
Sheets.Item['Chart2'].SeriesCollection.NewSeries;
Sheets.Item['Chart2'].SeriesCollection.Item[3].Values :=
  VarArrayOf([1,2,3,4,5,6,7,8,9,10]);
```

This chart graphs a `SeriesCollection` that contains not one, but three `Series`. The first and second `Series` are identical to the `Series` graphed by the first chart, but the third `Series` is slightly different, in that its values come not from an Excel worksheet, but from a range of data directly specified inside Delphi.

Take a moment to consider what is happening here. The first set of data graphed is specified exactly as in the previous example:

```
Sheets.Item['Chart2'].SeriesCollection.Item[1].Values := ARange;
```

Adding a new range specifies the next `Series`:

```
Sheets.Item['Chart2'].SeriesCollection.Add(ARange);
```

Finally, the code creates a new `Series` with no particular data:

```
Sheets.Item['Chart2'].SeriesCollection.NewSeries;
```

The program then creates a `Variant` array containing the values you want to chart in this third `Series`:

```
Sheets.Item['Chart2'].SeriesCollection.Item[3].Values :=
  VarArrayOf([1,2,3,4,5,6,7,8,9,10]);
```

I do not discuss `Variant` arrays here, but the subject is treated in Chapter 20 and Chapter 21, "MIDAS." The `Series` created by this code is shown on the Excel side in Figure 16.2.

In this case, I need not change the type of graph because the default column chart does the job adequately. I could, however, add the following line of code to create a new effect:

```
Sheets.Item['Chart2'].ChartType := xl3DColumn;
```

FIGURE 16.2

A Variant *array created in Delphi as it is depicted inside Excel.*

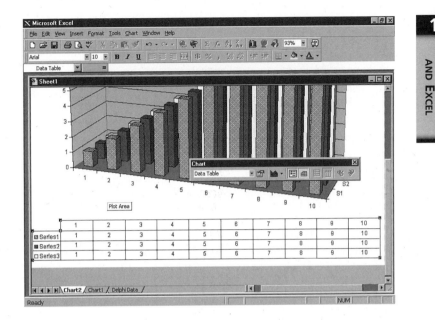

You are at last ready to copy the worksheet and two charts that you have created from Excel into Word. This operation is relatively complex, so I will start a new section in this chapter to discuss it.

Copying Data from Excel to Word

The process of copying data from Excel to Word has two parts. The first part involves copying the data to the Clipboard, and the second part involves pasting the data into the Word document. In other words, you need to have both Excel and Word open to make this process work. Furthermore, the tricky part is not so much copying the data from Excel, but inserting it correctly into Word.

The following procedure copies the data from Excel to the Clipboard. Note that I have created two methods called `CopyCellsToWord` and `CopyChartToWord`. These methods handle the Word side of the process, allowing me to isolate the Excel code in one method:

```
procedure TForm1.CopyData;
var
  Sheets: Variant;
begin
  SetFocus;

  Sheets := XLApp.Sheets;
```

```
Sheets.Item['Delphi Data'].Activate;
Sheets.Item['Delphi Data'].Range['A1:A10'].Select;
Sheets.Item['Delphi Data'].UsedRange.Copy;
CopyCellsToWord;
Sheets.Item['Chart1'].Select;
XLApp.Selection.Copy;
CopyChartToWord;
end;
```

To copy data from a range in a worksheet to the Clipboard, I first retrieve a `Sheets` object and then do the following:

```
Sheets.Item['Delphi Data'].Activate;
Sheets.Item['Delphi Data'].Range['A1:A10'].Select;
Sheets.Item['Delphi Data'].UsedRange.Copy;
```

I first activate the worksheet, then select a range of data in it, and finally copy the data to memory. In this process, I essentially mirror the actions I would take when doing this process manually. In other words, I first "click" on the worksheet I want to use; that is, I activate it. I then select a range of data from it, and finally I "press Ctrl+C" to copy it to the Clipboard. Of course, I'm not really doing these things, but I'm executing in code the steps necessary to duplicate these actions as follows:

1. Call `Activate`—Click on page using the mouse.

2. Call `Select`—Select data using the mouse.

3. Call `Copy`—Press Ctrl+C or pull down the Edit menu and choose Copy.

After the program copies a range of cells to memory, the next step is to copy the cells to Word. In this explanation, however, I will temporarily pass over the act of copying the data to Word, and instead show you how to copy the Chart to memory. Note, however, that you obviously must do these things one at a time because the Clipboard can hold only one object in memory at a time. In short, you can't copy both the worksheet and the chart to two separate places in the Clipboard and then copy them both to Word in one motion. The problem, of course, is that the Clipboard has only one area available in memory.

Here is how to copy a chart to the Clipboard:

```
Sheets.Item['Chart1'].Select;
XLApp.Selection.Copy;
```

This code first selects `Chart1` and then copies it to the Clipboard. Again, I am mirroring the actions I would take were I performing these steps manually. That is, I first select the object and then "press Ctrl+C" to copy it. Once again, I don't explicitly press Ctrl+C, but instead perform the steps in code that duplicate this action.

Using Delphi to Automate Word and Excel

CHAPTER **16**

511

16

USING DELPHI TO
AUTOMATE WORD
AND EXCEL

Automation Inside Word

Next, I will discuss the following procedure, which gets you up and running with automation in Word:

```
procedure TForm1.CopyCellsToWord;
var
  Range: Variant;
  i: Integer;
begin
  WordApp := CreateOleObject('Word.Application');
  WordApp.Visible := True;
  WordApp.Documents.Add;
  Range := WordApp.Documents.Item(1).Range;
  Range.Text := 'This is a column from a spreadsheet: ';
  for i := 1 to 3 do WordApp.Documents.Item(1).Paragraphs.Add;
  Range :=
    WordApp.Documents.Item(1).Range(WordApp.Documents.Item(1).
    Paragraphs.Item(3).Range.Start);
  Range.Paste;
  for i := 1 to 3 do WordApp.Documents.Item(1).Paragraphs.Add;
end;
```

To get started in Word, you just follow more or less the same steps you would in Excel:

```
WordApp := CreateOleObject('Word.Application');
WordApp.Visible := True;
WordApp.Documents.Add;
```

This code creates a Word `Application` object, sets the `Visible` property of the object to `True`, and adds a single document to it.

To add text to the document, you can execute the following code:

```
Range := WordApp.Documents.Item(1).Range;
Range.Text := 'This is a column from a spreadsheet: ';
```

In this case, the code retrieves a `Range` object representing the entire document, which, of course, starts out completely empty. To start to place text in the document, you can use the `Text` property of the range.

You could simply paste the data from Excel directly in your document. However, you want to be able to have some control over the location where the cells are placed. To have this control, you need some whitespace in the document; that is, you need a series of carriage returns through which you can iterate:

```
for i := 1 to 3 do WordApp.Documents.Item(1).Paragraphs.Add;
```

You can now use the `Goto` method of the `Range` or `Document` object to move back and forth across this range of paragraphs. Or, if you want, you can select a new range, and then paste your Excel data into that range. In my experience, this second method is the easiest means of moving through a document. Here is the code for selecting a `Range` covering the third paragraph of a document:

```
Range :=
   WordApp.Documents.Item(1).Range(WordApp.Documents.Item(1).
     Paragraphs.Item(3).Range.Start);
```

Note that this is one single line of code. I wrap it here because I must do so to fit it in a word processing or HTML document. In your code, however, you should type it on one single line. This code states that I want to define a range on the third paragraph of the document. I explicitly state that the range starts at the beginning of the paragraph, but I do not define the end of the range. Later, I will show you how to also specify the end of a range.

I can now paste in the Excel code with a single, easy-to-write line:

```
Range.Paste;
```

After pasting in this range of cells, I find that several new paragraphs have been added to my document. There is no specific way for me to be sure how many because the number of cells I paste in may vary with different versions of my program. So when I get ready to paste in the chart from Excel, I begin by asking how many paragraphs are currently in the document:

```
procedure TForm1.CopyChartToWord;
var
  Range: Variant;
  i, NumPars: Integer;
begin
  NumPars := WordApp.Documents.Item(1).Paragraphs.Count;
  Range := WordApp.Documents.Item(1).Range(
    WordApp.Documents.Item(1).Paragraphs.Item(NumPars).Range.Start,
    WordApp.Documents.Item(1).Paragraphs.Item(NumPars).Range.End);
  Range.Text := 'This is graph: ';
  for i := 1 to 3 do WordApp.Documents.Item(1).Paragraphs.Add;
  Range := WordApp.Documents.Item(1).Range(
    WordApp.Documents.Item(1).Paragraphs.Item(NumPars + 2).Range.Start,
    WordApp.Documents.Item(1).Paragraphs.Item(NumPars + 2).Range.End);
  Range.PasteSpecial(,,,,wdPasteOleObject);
end;
```

I return the paragraph count in the variable `NumPars`. I then create a domain that ranges over the last paragraph of the document. In other words, I count the paragraphs in the document, and then say I want to establish a range on the last paragraph. Once again, this is one way to position yourself in the document:

```
Range := WordApp.Documents.Item(1).Range(
  WordApp.Documents.Item(1).Paragraphs.Item(NumPars).Range.Start,
  WordApp.Documents.Item(1).Paragraphs.Item(NumPars).Range.End);
```

After I locate myself in the proper position, the next step is to enter a single, descriptive line of text, followed by a few additional paragraphs:

```
Range.Text := 'This is graph: ';
for i := 1 to 3 do WordApp.Documents.Item(1).Paragraphs.Add;
```

I then once again position myself on the last paragraph in the document:

```
Range := WordApp.Documents.Item(1).Range(
  WordApp.Documents.Item(1).Paragraphs.Item(NumPars + 1).Range.Start,
  WordApp.Documents.Item(1).Paragraphs.Item(NumPars + 1).Range.End);
```

Notice that when creating this range, I explicitly state that it "ranges" from the beginning of the paragraph to the end. In an earlier example, I filled in the first part of the range but left the second part open. In this case, either method would work, but I show you both so you can see various examples of how the syntax works.

In that same spirit, I use a slightly different technique when pasting in the chart data:

```
Range.PasteSpecial(,,,,wdPasteOleObject);
```

In this case, I call the `PasteSpecial` method and ask to insert an OLE object. This approach ensures that you can edit the document in place by double-clicking on it. The `PasteSpecial` method takes a wide range of parameters, but they are beyond the scope of this discussion. For more details, look up `PasteSpecial` in the Word Visual Basic help. In this particular case, you can just leave all these parameters blank, merely conceding their presence by the simple means of adding one comma for each omitted parameter. Needless to say, default values are inserted by Word for each omitted parameter.

NOTE

Remember that the Word VBA help file is not installed by default, so you may need to run the Word installation and explicitly ask for the file, or else copy it off the CD manually.

Mailing a Document

The `Documents` object also has `Save`, `SaveAs`, and `Open` methods you can use when opening or saving a document. In fact, many methods and properties are associated with most of the objects discussed in this chapter. The only way to get to know them all is to open the Word or Excel help and start browsing through them. This chapter is meant to give you a conceptual overview of how to use Word and Excel automation objects; it is not a complete examination of the subject.

You can save the current Word document as follows:

```
WordApp.Documents.Item(1).SaveAs('c:\foo.doc');
```

The following code allows you to send a mail message:

```
procedure TForm1.MailDocument;
begin
  WordApp.Documents.Item(1).SaveAs('c:\foo.doc');
  WordApp.Options.SendMailAttach := True;
  WordApp.Documents.Item(1).SendMail;
end;
```

If you have a MAPI client set up on your computer, you can send a document to another user directly from Excel. You use the preceding code to do so. This code will automatically open the mail services, allowing you to pick a user and send the document. The document you created will automatically be attached to your message. If you don't have mail set up on your machine, then this code obviously won't work.

Summary

This chapter covers only the basic steps involved with automating Excel and Word from Delphi. This subject is obviously large, and I could say much more about it. However, the information you read here should open up the topic sufficiently to allow you to perform most tasks.

By now, it should be obvious to you that the automation objects in Excel and Word are extremely powerful. Were you creating an actual word processor, you couldn't ask for much more in terms of functionality, but, of course, you would look for a little better performance.

The next chapter covers using interfaces in automation programs. This topic is extremely important, and indeed your education in automating Excel or Word is definitely not complete without an understanding of this subject matter. In the next chapter, I rewrite most of the Excel4 application, giving you a second, somewhat more complicated, but more powerful set of tools. So far, I've shown you code that duplicates more or less what you can do in Visual Basic. The next chapter shows how you can leverage the power of Delphi to take full advantage of automation. I will also show some of the things you can do to automate Internet Explorer.

Internet

IN THIS PART

Interfaces and Internet Explorer

CHAPTER 17

This chapter is about how Delphi can interact with some of the key programs and controls on a typically well-equipped Windows 98 or Windows NT system. While reading the chapter, you will hear a lot about accessing automation objects via interfaces. In a sense, this chapter is a continuation of the preceding chapter, except that this time the focus is on calling objects via custom interfaces rather than calling them via a Variant and IDispatch.

The text begins with a brief overview of COM and interfaces. I already covered COM basics earlier in the book, so I am just going to add a few more comments specific to working with interfaces and automation objects.

After getting the theoretical issues out of the way, I'll show an example from the preceding chapter that is rewritten to use interfaces rather than Variants. After that, I'll show an example of manipulating an ActiveX control via an interface, and finally, I'll divulge the core subject matter of the chapter with several fairly involved examples of using interfaces to manipulate Internet Explorer. As a final bonus, I'll throw in a simple example showing how to use the Wang Image editor control.

The section on the Explorer shows how to use a Web browser as an ActiveX control that can be hosted in a Delphi application. Because IE itself can host ActiveX controls inside a Web page, the chapter can feature some fairly interesting code in which Delphi is seen manipulating both Internet Explorer and a series of controls hosted by the Explorer.

By the end of the chapter, you should have a fairly good sense of how to use interfaces to control objects found on your system or imported to your system. This field of endeavor represents an extremely important aspect of contemporary programming and one that is likely to become increasingly valuable as the body of available COM-based work grows.

Comparing Variants and Interfaces

As you know, when you use a Variant to access an automation class, what is really happening is that Delphi is calling the methods of your objects via an interface called IDispatch.

When using IDispatch to access a method, a programmer either explicitly or implicitly calls GetIDsOfNames, which returns the ID of the method to be called. For instance, if you want to access a method called GetVisible, then you need to find out the ID of that method. To get the ID, you call IDispatch.GetIDsOfNames. After you have the ID, then you call IDispatch.Invoke, passing in the ID. (To see exactly how Delphi calls

Interfaces and Internet Explorer
CHAPTER 17

519

17

INTERFACES AND
INTERNET
EXPLORER

GetIDsOfNames and Invoke, open COMObj.pas. This file is located in the
..\Source\RTL\Sys directory provided with all versions of Delphi that ship with the
source to the RTL.)

When you use Variants, each time you want to call a method, you have to first call
GetIDsOfNames and then call Invoke. That's one trip over to the host application, one
trip back, and a third trip over again to actually invoke the procedure. That's a lot of
overhead to make a simple call. Remember that each trip between applications can be
very lengthy when compared to making a call to a method or function inside your
address space.

A further problem with the Variant method of calling an automation procedure is that
you can't type-check the call at design time. Delphi knows only that it needs to pass
some information over to the server using IDispatch. If it can do that, then it gives your
app a clean bill of health. It has no way of checking whether you are calling a real function or whether you are passing valid parameters.

Interfaces to the Rescue

So now you are familiar with the problem that needs to be solved. The possible solutions
come in two flavors. One is called an *interface*, and the second is called a *dispinterface*.

Let's take a look at one interface and one dispinterface:

```
ISeriesCollection = interface(IDispatch)
    ['{0002086C-0001-0000-C000-000000000046}']
    function Get_Application(out Retval: Application): HResult; stdcall;
    function Get_Creator(out Retval: XlCreator): HResult; stdcall;
    function Get_Parent(out Retval: IDispatch): HResult; stdcall;
    function Add(Source: OleVariant; Rowcol: XlRowCol;
       SeriesLabels, CategoryLabels, Replace: OleVariant;
       out Retval: Series): HResult; stdcall;
    function Get_Count(out Retval: Integer): HResult; stdcall;
    function Extend(Source, Rowcol,
       CategoryLabels: OleVariant): HResult; stdcall;
    function Item(Index: OleVariant; out Retval: Series):
➥HResult; stdcall;
    function _NewEnum(out Retval: IUnknown): HResult; stdcall;
    function Paste(Rowcol: XlRowCol; SeriesLabels, CategoryLabels,
       Replace, NewSeries: OleVariant): HResult; stdcall;
    function NewSeries(out Retval: Series): HResult; stdcall;
  end;

SeriesCollection = dispinterface
    ['{0002086C-0000-0000-C000-000000000046}']
    property Application: Application readonly dispid 148;
    property Creator: XlCreator readonly dispid 149;
```

```
      property Parent: IDispatch readonly dispid 150;
      function Add(Source: OleVariant; Rowcol: XlRowCol;
       SeriesLabels, CategoryLabels, Replace: OleVariant):
       ➡Series; dispid 181;
      property Count: Integer readonly dispid 118;
      procedure Extend(Source, Rowcol, CategoryLabels:
       ➡OleVariant); dispid 227;
      function Item(Index: OleVariant): Series; dispid 170;
      function _NewEnum: IUnknown; dispid -4;
      procedure Paste(Rowcol: XlRowCol; SeriesLabels, CategoryLabels,
          Replace, NewSeries: OleVariant); dispid 211;
      function NewSeries: Series; dispid 1117;
    end;
```

As you can see, these two interfaces to a single valid Excel object are nearly identical. But they do have some differences. In particular, note that SeriesCollection supports properties, whereas ISeriesCollection does not.

The problem at hand, as you know, is that the Variant method of calling a method is slow, and it does not allow for type checking. Creating an interface for a COM object helps to solve both problems. First, it gives the Delphi compiler some way to type-check your code. Here is the interface for an object. The implementation is still over on the Excel side, but at least the compiler now has some way of knowing the structure of the object in question and the parameters that its methods take.

Second, if you look closely at the dispinterface, you will see that each function, procedure or property is followed by something called a Dispatch ID. This is the number that is normally retrieved by a call to GetIDsOfNames. If you have a dispinterface, then you can call IDispatch Invoke directly without having to first call GetIDsOfNames. Dispatch IDs save two of the three trips that have to be made each time you call a procedure or function. Dispinterfaces are a huge improvement over the technology involved in a simple automation call against a Variant.

Chapter 13, "Interfaces and the Basics of COM," ends by discussing how an interface allows you to call the VTable of an object directly. If you use VTables, you have a proxy for the object on the client side. Calling the methods of the object is simply a matter of letting the compiler directly dispatch the call without ever having to call Invoke or without having to marshal information back and forth. In other words, Delphi can call the methods of the object using the same speedy technology it uses when calling a standard Delphi object. The actual call still needs to be marshaled between the client and the server, so it is not nearly as fast a regular object call, but all the overhead associated with IDispatch is gone.

Many COM objects have something called a *dual interface*. A dual interface means that the object supports both IDispatch, and a standard VTable interface. Go back up and look at the declaration of ISeriesCollection. As you can see, it descends directly from IDispatch. In other words, it supports both IDispatch and ISeriesCollection. This means that an application can call its methods using either an interface or a Variant. It has a dual interface! As you have seen in earlier chapters, many of the COM objects you create in Delphi descend from IDispatch and thus support dual interfaces.

Working with Type Libraries

As you know, a type library is a binary file, usually with a .tlb or .olb extension, that contains binary information describing an interface. Quite often, these binary files are appended onto an executable, and sometimes they are kept separate. Wherever a type library is stored, you or the system needs to find it and open it if you want to get to the description of an interface.

Select Project, Import Type Library from the Delphi menu to read a type library and automatically convert the binary information found therein into Object Pascal. For instance, the ISeriesCollection and SeriesCollection interfaces shown previously are from one of these automatically generated files.

Why, you might ask, does Delphi generate an interface for both ISeriesCollection and SeriesCollection? Wouldn't Delphi users always want to use a real interface such as ISeriesCollection rather than a dispinterface? The answer is simply that Delphi creates both interfaces because it can do so. It has enough information to create both interfaces, and so it does create them. In many cases, Delphi only creates dispinterfaces because that is all that Microsoft provides.

This is the end of the section of this chapter dedicated to theoretical issues.

Files Needed in This Chapter

You will need the following programs if you want to run all the examples in this chapter:

- Internet Explorer 4.0 or higher
- Microsoft Word 97 (I'm using Service Release 1)
- Microsoft Excel 97 (I'm using Service Release 1)

If you don't have Word or Excel, you will miss out on part of this chapter, but you can still understand all the main points. My original plan was to write this chapter entirely on Word and Excel, but I decided that I should instead focus on free products that everyone can own, such as Internet Explorer and the controls mentioned in the next few paragraphs of this section.

You need to have the following free controls on your system:

- The TWebBrowser control (comes automatically with IE4). I explain how to import the control in more depth later in the chapter, but if you already understand the mechanisms involved, you can just select Component, Import ActiveX Control from the Delphi menu and import the Microsoft Internet Controls.

- The DirectAnimation control (comes with some copies of IE4). Follow the same general pattern you followed getting the TWebBrowser control but search for the DirectAnimation Library.

- The Wang Image control (comes with all copies of Windows 95 and NT). Import as with DirectAnimation but search on Wang Edit Control. (This control might not ship with all copies of Windows 98 or NT 5.)

- The ActiveMovie control comes with some copies of IE 4 or can be downloaded from www.microsoft.com. Import the Microsoft Active Movie Control just as you have the other controls in this section.

As you import each of these files, notice that new PAS files are installed in your imports directory.

You need to import the following type libraries. By default, they wind up in the Delphi4\Imports directory, which also, by default, should be on your path. You may have to explicitly compile some of these files from the command line using dcc32:

- Excel_TLB.pas: Choose Project, Import Type Library from the Delphi menu and find Excel8.olb in the c:\program files\microsoft office\office directory.

- Word_TLB.pas: Import MSWord8.olb from the same place as the Excel8.olb file.

- Office_tlb: You can find the Microsoft Office entry preregistered in the files you see when you choose Project, Import Type Library from the Delphi menu. Select this file and import its type library.

- VBIDE_TLB.pas: This file is generated automatically when you create Office_TLB.pas.

- MSHTML_TLB.pas: Import this important type library from the MSHTML.dll file in the Windows\System or Winnt\System32 directories.

- ShdDocVw_TLB.pas: This file is generated automatically when you import the WebBrowser control.

- DirectAnimation_TLB.pas: This file is generated automatically when you import the DirectAnimation control.

You will find copies of all the headers mentioned here in the MSTypeLibraryHeaders directory on the CD that comes with this book. However, generating all the headers yourself is a good idea, in part because it helps you get used to the technology involved.

Working with Word and Excel

It's time now to take a look at some programming using interfaces. The following program, shown in Listings 17.1 and 17.2, is a translation of the Excel4 program from the preceding chapter, altered so that it uses interfaces rather than variants. The program is called Excel4I, pronounced *Excel Four Eye*, where the *I* stands for interface.

LISTING 17.1 THE Excel4I PROGRAM GIVES INTERFACES A GOOD WORKOUT

```
//////////////////////////////////////////
// Purpose: Use Word and Excel from Delphi
// Project: Excel4I.dpr
// Copyright (c) 1998 by Charlie Calvert
//
unit Main;

{--------------------------------------------------------------
  Creating data and a chart in Excel and copying both to Word.
  This example is like Excel4, only it uses interfaces instead
  of variants.
--------------------------------------------------------------}
interface

uses
  Windows, Messages, SysUtils,
  Classes, Graphics, Controls,
  Forms, Dialogs, StdCtrls,
  Office_Tlb, Excel_TLB, Word_TLB;

type
  TForm1 = class(TForm)
    RunBtn: TButton;
    SendMailBtn: TButton;
    procedure RunBtnClick(Sender: TObject);
    procedure FormDestroy(Sender: TObject);
    procedure SendMailBtnClick(Sender: TObject);
  private
    XLApp: Excel_TLB.Application_;
    WordApp: Word_TLB.Application_;
  public
    procedure HandleData(WorkSheet: _WorkSheet);
    procedure ChartData(var WorkSheets: Sheets);
    procedure CopyData;
    procedure CopyChartToWord;
    procedure CopyCellsToWord;
  end;

var
```

continues

LISTING 17.1 CONTINUED

```
  Form1: TForm1;

implementation

uses
  ComObj, ActiveX;

{$R *.DFM}

{----------------------------------------------------------------
  In Delphi 4 this function is no longer necessary, but
  I keep it here for Delphi3 programmers who want to see
  how to create a Variant that can be passed as an empty,
  or inert, parameter.
----------------------------------------------------------------}
function CreateEmptyParam: OleVariant;
begin
  TVarData(EmptyParam).VType := VT_ERROR;
  TVarData(EmptyParam).VError := DISP_E_PARAMNOTFOUND;
end;

procedure TForm1.RunBtnClick(Sender: TObject);
var
  WorkSheet: _Worksheet;
  WorkBks: WorkBooks;
  WorkSheets: Sheets;
  Workbk: WorkBook;
begin
  XLApp := Excel_TLB.CoApplication_.Create;
  //CreateOleObject('Excel.Application') as ExcelTlb.Application;
  XLApp.Visible[0] := True;
  WorkBks := XLApp.WorkBooks as WorkBooks;
  Workbks.Add(XLWBatWorksheet, 0);
  WorkBk := WorkBks.Item[1];
  WorkSheets := Workbk.WorkSheets;
  WorkSheet := WorkSheets.Get_Item(1) as _WorkSheet;
  Worksheet.Name := 'Delphi Data';
  HandleData(WorkSheet);
  ChartData(WorkSheets);
  CopyData;
  SendMailBtn.Enabled := True;
end;

procedure TForm1.HandleData(WorkSheet: _WorkSheet);
var
  i: Integer;
begin
  for i := 1 to 10 do
    WorkSheet.Cells.Item[i, 1] := i;
end;
```

```
{------------------------------------------------------------------
   In this method I try to make the following call:
      AChart := WorkSheets.Add(EmptyParam, EmptyParam, 1, xlChart, 0)
        as Chart;
   And I get back this apparently undocumented error: $800A03EC. I can't
   resolve this one, so I create the object off a Variant:

      AChart := XLApp.WorkBooks.Item[1].Sheets.Add(EmptyParam,
        EmptyParam, 1, xlChart, 0) as Chart;

------------------------------------------------------------------}
procedure TForm1.ChartData(var WorkSheets: Sheets);
var
  ARange: Excel_TLB.Range;
  AWorksheet: Worksheet;
  AChart: Chart;
  Index: OleVariant;
  aSeries: Series;
  ASeriesCollection: SeriesCollection;
begin
  AWorkSheet := WorkSheets.Item['Delphi Data'] as Worksheet;
  ARange := AWorksheet.Range['A1', 'A10'];

  AChart := XLApp.WorkBooks.Item[1].Sheets.Add(EmptyParam,
    EmptyParam, 1, xlChart, 0) as Chart;
  Index := 1;
  ASeries := AChart.SeriesCollection(Index, 0) as Series;
  ASeries.Values := ARange;
  AChart.ChartType := xl3DPie;
  ASeries.HasDataLabels := True;

  AChart := XLApp.Workbooks.Item[1].Sheets.Add(NULL,
    NULL,1,xlChart,0) as Chart;
  ASeries := AChart.SeriesCollection(Index, 0) as Series;
  ASeries.Values := ARange;
  ASeriesCollection := AChart.SeriesCollection(EmptyParam,
    0) as SeriesCollection;
  ASeriesCollection.NewSeries;
  Index := 2;
  ASeries := AChart.SeriesCollection(Index, 0) as Series;
  ASeries.Values := ARange;
  ASeriesCollection.NewSeries;
  Index := 3;
  ASeries := AChart.SeriesCollection(Index, 0) as Series;
  ASeries.Values := VarArrayOf([1,2,3,4,5, 6,7,8,9,10]);
  AChart.ChartType := xl3DColumn;
end;
```

17

continues

LISTING 17.1 CONTINUED

```
{------------------------------------------------------------------
  I could not copy the chart to the Clipboard using interfaces. The
  following line works, but it copies the chart to a new location in
  Excel, not to the clipboard:

    AChart.Copy(EmptyParam, EmptyParam, 0);

  So I copied the chart using Variants, as shown here:

    V := AChart.Application_;
    V.Selection.Copy;
------------------------------------------------------------------}
procedure TForm1.CopyData;
var
  ASheets: Sheets;
  AChart: Chart;
  V: Variant;
  AWorksheet: Worksheet;
  ARange: Excel_TLB.Range;
begin
  SetFocus;

  ASheets := XLApp.Sheets as Sheets;

  AWorksheet := ASheets.Item['Delphi Data'] as Worksheet;
  AWorksheet.Activate(0);
  ARange := AWorksheet.Range['A1', 'A10'];
  ARange.Select;
  ARange := AWorksheet.UsedRange[0];
  ARange.Copy(EmptyParam);

  CopyCellsToWord;

  AChart := ASheets.Item['Chart1'] as Chart;
  AChart.Activate(0);
  AChart.Select(EmptyParam, 0);
  V := AChart.Application_;
  V.Selection.Copy;
  CopyChartToWord;
end;

procedure TForm1.CopyChartToWord;
var
  ARange, ParRange: Range;
  StartRange, EndRange: OleVariant;
  NumPars, i: Integer;
  Index: OleVariant;
  DataType: OleVariant;
```

Interfaces and Internet Explorer

CHAPTER 17

527

17

INTERFACES AND
INTERNET
EXPLORER

```
    Docs: Documents;
    Doc: Document;
    Pars: Paragraphs;
    Par: Paragraph;
begin
    Index := 1;
    Docs := WordApp.Documents;
    Doc := Docs.Item(Index);
    Pars := Doc.Paragraphs;
    NumPars := Pars.Count;
    Par := Pars.Item(NumPars);
    ParRange := Par.Range;
    StartRange := ParRange.Start;
    EndRange := ParRange.End_;
    ARange := Doc.Range(StartRange, EndRange) as Range;
    ARange.Text := 'This is a graph of the column: ';

    for i := 1 to 3 do
      Pars.Add(EmptyParam);

    Par := Pars.Item(NumPars + 2);
    ParRange := Par.Range;
    StartRange := ParRange.Start;
    EndRange := ParRange.End_;
    ARange := Doc.Range(StartRange, EndRange);

    DataType := wdPasteOleObject;
    ARange.PasteSpecial(EmptyParam, EmptyParam, EmptyParam, EmptyParam,
      DataType, EmptyParam, EmptyParam);
end;

{ -------------------------------------------------------------------
    In some cases, you may gain performance with interfaces.
    For instance, the following line:
      Pars.Item(3).Range.Start;
    Would probably execute just as fast as:
      Par := Pars.Item(3);
      TempRange := Par.Range;
      AStart := TempRange.Start;
  -----------------------------------------------------------------}
procedure TForm1.CopyCellsToWord;
var
    ARange, TempRange : Range;
    i: Integer;
    AStart, Template, OpenAsTemplate: OleVariant;
    Docs: Documents;
    Doc: Document;
    Pars: Paragraphs;
    Par: Paragraph;
begin
```

continues

LISTING 17.1   CONTINUED

```pascal
  WordApp := CoApplication_.Create;
  WordApp.Visible := True;

  Template := 'Normal';
  OpenAsTemplate := False;

  Docs := WordApp.Documents;
  Doc := Docs.Add(Template, OpenAsTemplate);
  ARange := Doc.Range(EmptyParam, EmptyParam);
  ARange.Text := 'This is a column from a spreadsheet: ';

  Pars := Doc.Paragraphs;
  for i := 1 to 3 do
    Pars.Add(EmptyParam);

  Par := Pars.Item(3);
  TempRange := Par.Range;
  AStart := TempRange.Start;
  ARange := Doc.Range(AStart, EmptyParam);
  ARange.Paste;

  for i := 1 to 3 do
    Pars.Add(EmptyParam);
end;

procedure TForm1.FormDestroy(Sender: TObject);
var
  Index: OleVariant;
  SaveChanges: OleVariant;
  Docs: Documents;
  Doc: Document;
begin
  Index := 1;
  SaveChanges := wdDoNotSaveChanges;
  if not VarIsEmpty(XLApp) then begin
    XLApp.DisplayAlerts[0] := False;  // Discard unsaved files....
    XLApp.Quit;
  end;

  if not VarIsEmpty(WordApp)then begin
    Docs := WordApp.Documents;
    Doc := Docs.Item(Index);
    Doc.Close(SaveChanges, EmptyParam, EmptyParam);
    WordApp.Quit(EmptyParam, EmptyParam, EmptyParam);
  end;
end;

procedure TForm1.SendMailBtnClick(Sender: TObject);
var
```

```
  Index: OleVariant;
  SaveFile: OleVariant;
begin
  SaveFile := 'c:\foo.doc';
  WordApp.Documents.Item(Index).SaveAs(SaveFile, EmptyParam, EmptyParam,
    EmptyParam, EmptyParam, EmptyParam, EmptyParam, EmptyParam,
    EmptyParam, EmptyParam, EmptyParam);
  WordApp.Options.SendMailAttach := True;
  WordApp.Documents.Item(Index).SendMail;
end;

initialization

end.
```

LISTING 17.2 THE PROJECT SOURCE FILE FOR THE Excel1I APPLICATION, SHOWING FILES FROM THE Imports DIRECTORY

```
program Excel4I;

uses
  Forms,
  Main in 'Main.pas' {Form1},
  Excel_TLB in 'Excel_TLB.pas',
  Office_TLB in 'Office_TLB.pas',
  VBIDE_TLB in 'VBIDE_TLB.pas',
  Word_TLB in 'Word_TLB.pas';

{$R *.RES}

begin
  Forms.Application.Initialize;
  Forms.Application.CreateForm(TForm1, Form1);
  Forms.Application.Run;
end.
```

This program does all the same things as the Excel4 program from the preceding chapter. In particular, it opens copies of both Word and Excel and then creates a spreadsheet and some graphs in Excel. Finally, it copies both the spreadsheet data and one of the graphs over to Word and gives you the option of emailing the result across the network.

Excel4I is a straight port of the IDispatch-based Excel4 program to an interface-based program. I simply took routines crafted to use Variants and rewrote them to use interfaces. As a rule, this port was very successful: however, I still used IDispatch in one place because I had trouble making the code work correctly using interfaces.

Using Interfaces with Excel and Word

If you look at the declaration for the Form1 object, you can see that it declares the following variables:

```
XLApp: Excel_TLB.Application_;
WordApp: Word_TLB.Application_;
```

Obviously, I am no longer declaring XLApp and WordApp to be simple Variants. Instead, I am declaring them as instances of the Application object from the Excel_TLB and Word_TLB files generated automatically when I selected Project, Import Type Library and imported EXCEL8.OLB. These files are both huge documents. For instance, Excel_TLB contains over 20,000 lines of code. The vast majority of these files are simply declarations for objects that are implemented inside Excel itself. If you contemplate this situation for a moment, you might begin to get a feeling for the huge scope of the resources available to you as a Delphi programmer sitting on the doorstep of the COM resources available in Word and Excel. Indeed, every corner of either of these two huge applications can be accessed using COM.

> **NOTE**
>
> You will notice that some of the objects in Excel_TLB or Word_TLB have underscores appended to their name. This convention helps you avoid name conflicts with internal Delphi objects. For instance, the VCL Application object plays a big role in many Delphi applications. As a result, the compiler avoids a name clash by appending an underscore to the name assigned to Application objects hosted by Excel and Word and listed in the XXX_TLB files. This simple device makes it easy for you to distinguish the Excel Application object from the VCL Application object. It also makes sure that neither one will accidentally obscure the other inside the scope of a particular Delphi object.

To create an instance of the Excel.Application_ object, the Excel4I program executes the following code:

```
procedure TForm1.RunBtnClick(Sender: TObject);
var
  WorkSheet: _Worksheet;
  WorkBks: WorkBooks;
  ASheets: Sheets;
  Workbk: WorkBook;
begin
  XLApp := Excel_TLB.CoApplication_.Create;
  XLApp.Visible[0] := True;
```

```
    WorkBks := XLApp.WorkBooks as WorkBooks;
    Workbks.Add(XLWBatWorksheet, 0);
    WorkBk := WorkBks.Item[1];
    ASheets := Workbk.WorkSheets;
    WorkSheet := ASheets.Get_Item(1) as _WorkSheet;
    Worksheet.Name := 'Delphi Data';
    HandleData(WorkSheet);
    ChartData(ASheets);
    CopyData;
    SendMailBtn.Enabled := True;
end;
```

You should compare this method to the one from the Excel4 program in the preceding chapter that uses Variants:

```
procedure TForm1.Button1Click(Sender: TObject);
begin
    XLApp := CreateOleObject('Excel.Application');
    XLApp.Visible := True;
    XLApp.Workbooks.Add[XLWBatWorksheet];
    XLApp.Workbooks[1].Worksheets[1].Name := 'Delphi Data';
    HandleData;
    ChartData;
    CopyData;
    SendMailBtn.Enabled := True;
end;
```

If you perform a simple line count, it should be immediately evident that using interfaces is more difficult than using Variants. It is, however, often more efficient, and certainly it gives you a more fine-tuned control over your application.

You can create an instance of the object in these two different ways:

```
XLApp := Excel_TLB.CoApplication_.Create;     // Initialize an interface
XLApp := CreateOleObject('Excel.Application');  // Initialize a Variant
```

In the first case, I am creating an interface; in the second, I create an IDispatch-based Variant.

CoApplication.Create is a method from an object declared automatically when Excel_TLB was created. To view this class, go to the bottom of the Excel_TLB file and look for the following code:

```
    CoApplication = class
      class function Create: Application_;
      class function CreateRemote(const MachineName: string): Application_;
    end;

class function CoApplication.Create: Application_;
begin
```

```
    Result := CreateComObject(Class_Application) as Application_;
end;

class function CoApplication.CreateRemote(
  const MachineName: string): Application_;
begin
  Result := CreateRemoteComObject(MachineName,
    Class_Application) as Application_;
end;
```

As you can see, CoApplication.Create generates an instance of the Application_ class. Here is another way to create an instance of this class:

```
V := CreateOleObject('Excel.Application') as Application;
```

This code returns an instance of IDispatch and then uses the as operator to call a function called QueryInterface that returns the underlying Application_ object. CreateComObject, shown in the excerpts from Excel_TLB, does more or less the same thing, but it starts with a CLSID rather than a ProgID. If you wanted to get even more technical, you could call CoCreateInstance, which would also return an instance of this class. In fact, both CreateComObject and CreateOleObject ultimately end up calling CoCreateInstance.

Regardless of how you create it, you wind up with an instance of the Application object. In most cases, doing so via the predeclared objects such as CoApplication is simplest.

Comparing Variant and Interface Technologies

In the next few paragraphs, I am going to step you through the rest of the Variant and interface code shown in the RunBtnClick and Button1Click methods from the preceding section. I am going to compare the way things are done in each instance. I'm taking this approach because all the documentation for these objects always shows you how to do things using Variants. Knowing how to translate Variant-based code into interface-based code is therefore useful. By showing you the two techniques side by side, I'm hoping I'll give you enough information so that you can learn the general principles behind each technology and can start writing your own code based on the many Visual Basic-centered documents you will find in the Microsoft documentation.

Here are the next two lines in the two routines used to start Excel4 and Excel4I applications:

```
XLApp.Visible[0] := True;   // Uses an interface
XLApp.Visible := True;      // Uses a Variant
```

As you can see, the interface call uses array syntax, whereas the Variant call does not. The following is the declaration for the interface property:

```
property Visible[lcid: Integer]: WordBool read Get_Visible write
➡Set_Visible;
```

An `lcid` is a language ID, specifying whether the current language used by a particular copy of Windows is English, German, Japanese, and so on. You can always pass in 0 for this ID to get the default language. You will find that this parameter needs to be passed to a number of methods found in `Word_TLB` and `Excel_TLB`.

The following are the declarations for the getters and setters for these methods:

```
function Get_Visible(lcid: Integer): WordBool; safecall;
procedure Set_Visible(lcid: Integer; RHS: WordBool); safecall;
```

`lcid` here is the language ID, and `RHS` indicates whether you want to set `Visible` to `True` or to `False`.

You use the following lines to add a worksheet to the default workbook object using an interface:

```
var
  WorkSheet: _Worksheet;
  WorkBks: WorkBooks;
  ASheets: Sheets;
  Workbk: WorkBook;
begin
  WorkBks := XLApp.WorkBooks;
  Workbk := Workbks.Add(XLWBatWorksheet, 0);
  ASheets := Workbk.WorkSheets;
  WorkSheet := ASheets.Get_Item(1) as _WorkSheet;
  Worksheet.Name := 'Delphi Data';
```

You can do the same thing this way by using `Variants`:

```
XLApp.Workbooks.Add[XLWBatWorksheet];
XLApp.Workbooks[1].Worksheets[1].Name := 'Delphi Data';
```

When you're writing the interface code shown here, the goal is to never end up calling one object off another object. For instance, when I write `XLApp.Workbooks.Add` in the `Variant` code, I am asking the Excel application object to retrieve an instance of the `Workbooks` object and call its add method. In other words, there has to be a place where code like this is executed:

```
WorkBks := XLApp.WorkBooks;
Workbks.Add(XLWBatWorksheet, 0);
```

As you can see, the preceding is the same code that I wrote in the interface example. The point is that you end up having to perform the same actions whether you do things with interfaces or with `Variants`, but with `Variants` a lot of the tricky stuff is handled in the background for you. In other words, the `Variant` code is not faster just because it is shorter.

NOTE

The 0 that I have passed in the second parameter on the call to `Workbks.Add` is again an `lcid`. As I mentioned earlier in this section, the `lcid` parameter pops up in a number of places.

The next line of code in the `Variant` version again calls instances of one object off another object:

```
XLApp.Workbooks[1].Worksheets[1].Name := 'Delphi Data';
```

This code is quite easy to write, but somewhere in the background the same kind of thing you see in the interface code has to occur:

```
ASheets := Workbk.WorkSheets;
WorkSheet := ASheets.Get_Item(1) as _WorkSheet;
Worksheet.Name := 'Delphi Data';
```

As you can see, the interface code explicitly goes and retrieves each interface that you need to use and then calls methods off those interfaces.

Because of space considerations, I'm not going to be able to analyze all the code in the `Excel4I` application. However, if you study it, you will find that the same general pattern shown here is continued in multiple settings. You should note in particular places where I retrieve an interface once and then reuse it over and over. In the contrasting `Variant` code, I often end up repeatedly retrieving that same interface. For instance, in the following code from the `ButtonClick` method, I retrieve the `Workbooks` object twice:

```
XLApp.Workbooks.Add[XLWBatWorksheet];
XLApp.Workbooks[1].Worksheets[1].Name := 'Delphi Data';
```

This code looks very efficient, but behind the scenes the following code gets executed twice:

```
WorkBks := XLApp.WorkBooks;
```

In the corresponding interface code, I retrieve the `Workbooks` object once and then hang on to it so that I can use it a second time. This example can help to illustrate how you can increase performance by using interfaces or by intelligent use of `Variants`. The moral here is that the capability to call objects off other objects using dot notation is very slick and easy to use, but it is not always as efficient as digging in and working with interfaces.

Working with IE and TWebBrowser

Microsoft's Internet Explorer versions 3.x and 4.x are based on ActiveX controls. You can import these ActiveX controls into Delphi and use them in your own applications. For instance, if you have IE installed on your system, then you need only choose Components, Import ActiveX Control from the Delphi menu to add the full functionality of the Explorer to the Component Palette and hence to your applications. The act of importing the control is shown in Figure 17.1. After you have placed the control on the Component Palette, you can just drop it into your applications as you would any other component.

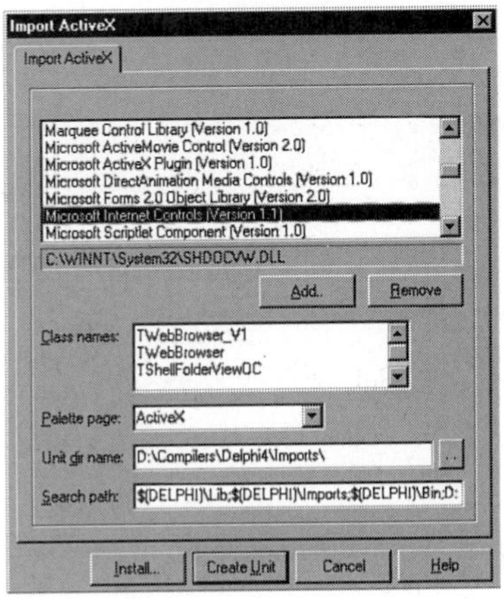

17

INTERFACES AND INTERNET EXPLORER

FIGURE 17.1

When you import the Internet Controls from IE 4.x into Delphi, you find three components called TWebBrowser_V1, TWebBrowser, *and* TShellFolder-ViewOC.

You are free to distribute the Microsoft WebBrowser control as widely as you want, as long as you bring the entirety of Internet Explorer along with you. This decision is driven in part by marketing and in part by the fact that the WebBrowser control relies on a large number of DLLs and other controls that are distributed with IE. Of course, if your target machine already has IE installed, then you need do nothing to run your application. In Windows 98, God and the Justice department willing, you will find copies of IE on each and every properly installed system.

When you drop an instance of the Internet Explorer browser control on one of your forms, you get the complete set of tools that come with IE. You have support for VBScript, JScript, Java, HTML, FTP, VRML, and who knows what else directly inside your application.

You can find out details about the objects in the WebBrowser object by getting hold of the Internet Client SDK from Microsoft. You can find these files at www.microsoft.com, in the MSDN, and in the standard Microsoft CD that contains IE4.

Getting Started: Accessing the Elements in a Web Page

The DocumentObject program from the CD that accompanies this book shows how to use the TWebBrowser (IE) control in a Delphi application. It also shows how to retrieve an interface from the object and use it to explore an HTML file in some depth.

Listing 17.3 shows the main form for the program, and Figure 17.2 shows the browser displaying a famous Web site. This form provides code for accessing the most important features of the TWebBrowser control, such as opening a Web site and browsing through recently displayed files. Listing 17.4 shows a form from the program that is used to report detailed information about the particular HTML file currently displayed in the TWebBrowser control.

FIGURE 17.2

Using the
DocumentObject
*program to
browse to the cen-
trally important*
http://www.elder-
mage.com *site.*

The program allows you to browse to a site of your choice on the Internet and to examine in some depth the HTML file you find there. One of the program's dialogs, shown in Figure 17.3, reports on the date an HTML file was created, the character set it uses, and other detailed bits of information.

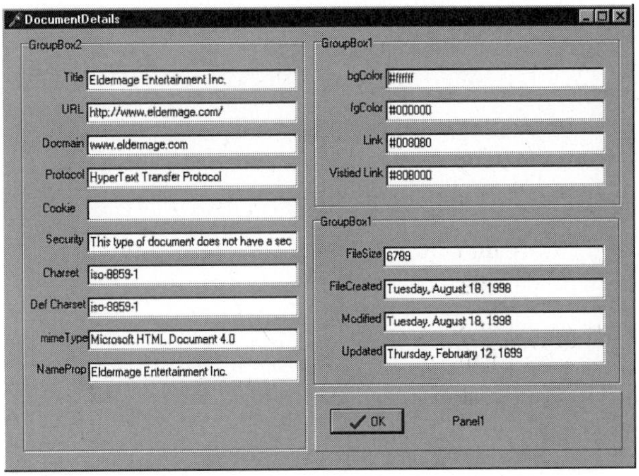

FIGURE 17.3

The DocumentDetails dialog shows some of the information you can retrieve about an HTML file displayed in the TWebBrowser *control.*

LISTING 17.3   THE MAIN FORM FOR THE DocumentDetails PROGRAM

```
unit Main;

interface

uses
  Windows, Messages, SysUtils,
  Classes, Graphics, Controls,
  Forms, Dialogs, OleCtrls,
  SHDocVw_TLB, ExtCtrls, StdCtrls;

type
  TForm1 = class(TForm)
    WebBrowser1: TWebBrowser;
    Panel1: TPanel;
    Edit1: TEdit;
    ConnectBtn: TButton;
    DetailBtn: TButton;
    GoBackBtn: TButton;
    GoForwardBtn: TButton;
    procedure ConnectBtnClick(Sender: TObject);
    procedure DetailBtnClick(Sender: TObject);
    procedure Edit1KeyDown(Sender: TObject; var Key: Word;
      Shift: TShiftState);
    procedure GoBackBtnClick(Sender: TObject);
    procedure GoForwardBtnClick(Sender: TObject);
  private
    { Private declarations }
  public
    { Public declarations }
  end;
```

continues

LISTING 17.3   CONTINUED

```
var
  Form1: TForm1;

implementation

uses
  MSHTML_TLB, DocumentDetails1;

{$R *.DFM}

procedure TForm1.ConnectBtnClick(Sender: TObject);
var
  A, B, C, D: OleVariant;
begin
  WebBrowser1.Navigate(Edit1.Text, A, B, C, D);
end;

procedure TForm1.DetailBtnClick(Sender: TObject);
var
  Doc: IHTMLDocument2;
begin
  Doc := WebBrowser1.Document as IHTMLDocument2;
  DocumentDetails.ShowDoc(Doc);
end;

procedure TForm1.Edit1KeyDown(Sender: TObject; var Key: Word;
  Shift: TShiftState);
begin
  if Key = 13 then
    ConnectBtnClick(nil);
end;

procedure TForm1.GoBackBtnClick(Sender: TObject);
begin
  WebBrowser1.GoBack;
end;

procedure TForm1.GoForwardBtnClick(Sender: TObject);
begin
  WebBrowser1.GoForward;
end;

end.
```

LISTING 17.4 THE `DocumentDetails` UNIT USES THE `HTMLDocument2` OBJECT TO DESCRIBE AN HTML FILE

```pascal
unit DocumentDetails1;

interface

uses
  Windows, Messages, SysUtils,
  Classes, Graphics, Controls,
  Forms, Dialogs, StdCtrls,
  MSHTML_TLB, Buttons, ExtCtrls;

type
  TDocumentDetails = class(TForm)
    GroupBox1: TGroupBox;
    Edit1: TEdit;
    Edit2: TEdit;
    Label1: TLabel;
    Label2: TLabel;
    Edit3: TEdit;
    Edit4: TEdit;
    Label3: TLabel;
    Label4: TLabel;
    GroupBox2: TGroupBox;
    Edit5: TEdit;
    Edit6: TEdit;
    Label5: TLabel;
    Label6: TLabel;
    Edit7: TEdit;
    Edit8: TEdit;
    Label7: TLabel;
    Label8: TLabel;
    Edit9: TEdit;
    Label9: TLabel;
    Label10: TLabel;
    Edit10: TEdit;
    Edit11: TEdit;
    Edit12: TEdit;
    Label11: TLabel;
    Label12: TLabel;
    Edit13: TEdit;
    Label13: TLabel;
    Label14: TLabel;
    Edit14: TEdit;
    GroupBox3: TGroupBox;
    Label15: TLabel;
    Label16: TLabel;
    Label17: TLabel;
    Label18: TLabel;
```

17

INTERFACES AND
INTERNET
EXPLORER

continues

LISTING 17.4   CONTINUED

```
      Edit15: TEdit;
      Edit16: TEdit;
      Edit17: TEdit;
      Edit18: TEdit;
      Panel1: TPanel;
      BitBtn1: TBitBtn;
      procedure BitBtn1Click(Sender: TObject);
    private
      FDoc: IHTMLDocument2;
      procedure ShowColors;
      procedure ShowCoreSettings;
      procedure ShowFileInfo;
    public
      procedure ShowDoc(Doc: IHTMLDocument2);
      { Public declarations }
    end;

var
  DocumentDetails: TDocumentDetails;

implementation

{$R *.DFM}

procedure TDocumentDetails.ShowColors;
begin
  Edit1.Text := FDoc.bgColor;
  Edit2.Text := FDoc.fgColor;
  Edit3.Text := FDoc.LinkColor;
  Edit4.Text := FDoc.VLinkColor;
end;

procedure TDocumentDetails.ShowCoreSettings;
begin
  Edit5.Text := FDoc.Title;
  Edit6.Text := FDoc.URL;
  Edit7.Text := FDoc.Domain;
  Edit8.Text := FDoc.Protocol;
  Edit9.Text := FDoc.Cookie;
  Edit10.Text := FDoc.Security;
  Edit11.Text := FDoc.CharSet;
  Edit12.Text := FDoc.DefaultCharSet;
  Edit13.Text := FDoc.MimeType;
  Edit14.Text := FDoc.NameProp;
end;

procedure TDocumentDetails.ShowFileInfo;
begin
  Edit15.Text := FDoc.FileSize;
```

```
  Edit16.Text := FDoc.FileCreatedDate;
  Edit17.Text := FDoc.FileModifiedDate;
  Edit18.Text := FDoc.FileUpdatedDate;
end;

procedure TDocumentDetails.ShowDoc(Doc: IHTMLDocument2);
begin
  FDoc := Doc;
  Show;
  ShowColors;
  ShowCoreSettings;
  ShowFileInfo
end;

procedure TDocumentDetails.BitBtn1Click(Sender: TObject);
begin
  Close;
end;

end.
```

When you want to connect to a site using the TWebBrowser control, just pass the URL of the site to the Navigate method:

```
procedure TForm1.ConnectBtnClick(Sender: TObject);
var
  A, B, C, D: OleVariant;
begin
  WebBrowser1.Navigate(Edit1.Text, A, B, C, D);
end;
```

The last four parameters passed to Navigate are rarely used and can be filled in with Variants. Variants and OleVariants are always automatically set to the value UnAssigned, so you do not need to initialize them.

If you want to move forward or backward in the files displayed in the browser, then you can call the GoForward or GoBackward methods of TWebBrowser:

```
procedure TForm1.GoBackBtnClick(Sender: TObject);
begin
  WebBrowser1.GoBack;
end;

procedure TForm1.GoForwardBtnClick(Sender: TObject);
begin
  WebBrowser1.GoForward;
end;
```

All this code is fairly prosaic. A somewhat more exotic feature of the TWebBrowser control is its support for many detailed interfaces, just as Excel and Word support many detailed interfaces. These interfaces are found in ShDocVw_TLB.pas and in MSHTML.pas. These two huge, labyrinthine files are key guide books for those willing to embrace some portion of Bill Gate's vision of the future.

> **NOTE**
>
> I hope, though without much confidence, that readers of this chapter will understand that I am promoting COM technology, and not necessarily particular products such as IE or Word. My point in this chapter is not to say, "Hey, look at IE, look at Word, aren't these cool apps?" Instead, I'm trying to say, "Hey, look at this COM technology, isn't it wonderful?"

The obvious place to start exploring the TWebBrowser interfaces is the Document object:

```
procedure TForm1.DetailBtnClick(Sender: TObject);
var
  Doc: IHTMLDocument2;
begin
  Doc := WebBrowser1.Document as IHTMLDocument2;
  DocumentDetails.ShowDoc(Doc);
end;
```

By definition, TWebBrowser.Document is a variant containing an instance of IDispatch. You can use this object directly if you wish. However, you can get better control over the object by getting a real interface rather than just using a Variant. The first line of this method retrieves the IHTMLDocument2 document by calling QueryInterface on the instance of IDispatch wrapped in the Document Variant.

IHTMLDocument2 is found in MSHTML_TLB.pas. As you may recall from the beginning of the chapter, MSHTML is a DLL found in the System or System32 directory. You can import the type library from that DLL by choosing Project, Import Type Library.

After the program has the interface it wants to use, it passes the interface to the TDocumentDetails form where it can be queried at some length. Understanding all the things you can do with a Document object is not really so terribly important. However, the following method should give you some faint clue as to the expansive list of possibilities:

```
procedure TDocumentDetails.ShowCoreSettings;
begin
  Edit5.Text := FDoc.Title;
  Edit6.Text := FDoc.URL;
  Edit7.Text := FDoc.Domain;
  Edit8.Text := FDoc.Protocol;
```

```
    Edit9.Text := FDoc.Cookie;
    Edit10.Text := FDoc.Security;
    Edit11.Text := FDoc.CharSet;
    Edit12.Text := FDoc.DefaultCharSet;
    Edit13.Text := FDoc.MimeType;
    Edit14.Text := FDoc.NameProp;
end;
```

Here, the code accesses various properties of the Document object such as the Title, URL, Domain, and Protocol. This is such a tiny and humble sliver of the options available to you in the TWebBrowser object that it's hardly worth mentioning in comparison to the riches piled up before you. Nevertheless, it should help introduce you to the subject and might serve to pique your interest.

Manipulating HTML in a Browser at Runtime

In IE4 and later, you have virtually complete programmatic control over what is going on inside the TWebBrowser control. In particular, you can access each of the HTML elements in your browser and treat each of them as objects. For instance, you can get hold of a tag, such as a Paragraph tag, and call the methods of the object that represents that tag to change its properties dynamically.

In the ChangeHTML program, you can see how this process works. The program, shown in Figure 17.4 and Listing 17.5, loads a simple HTML file into the TWebBrowser control. It then iterates through all the elements in the HTML file and shows them to you in a combo box. Menu items let you choose options to dynamically change the text in the HTML file or the background color of the file.

LISTING 17.5   THE MAIN FORM OF THE ChangeHTML PROGRAM

```
unit Main;

interface

uses
  Windows, Messages, SysUtils,
  Classes, Graphics, Controls,
  Forms, Dialogs, StdCtrls,
  ExtCtrls, OleCtrls, SHDocVw_TLB,
  MSHTML_TLB, Menus;

type
  TForm1 = class(TForm)
    WebBrowser1: TWebBrowser;
    Panel1: TPanel;
    ViewAllBtn: TButton;
```

continues

LISTING 17.5   CONTINUED

```
  ComboBox1: TComboBox;
  Edit1: TEdit;
  RefreshBtn: TButton;
  OpenDialog1: TOpenDialog;
  MainMenu1: TMainMenu;
  File1: TMenuItem;
  N1: TMenuItem;
  Exit1: TMenuItem;
  Options1: TMenuItem;
  ChangeColor: TMenuItem;
  Open1: TMenuItem;
  ChangeText1: TMenuItem;
  ShowObject1: TMenuItem;
    procedure OpenFileBtnClick(Sender: TObject);
    procedure ViewAllBtnClick(Sender: TObject);
    procedure Edit1KeyDown(Sender: TObject; var Key: Word;
      Shift: TShiftState);
    procedure ComboBox1Click(Sender: TObject);
    procedure RefreshBtnClick(Sender: TObject);
    procedure Exit1Click(Sender: TObject);
    procedure ChangeColorClick(Sender: TObject);
    procedure FormShow(Sender: TObject);
    procedure ChangeText1Click(Sender: TObject);
    procedure ShowObject1Click(Sender: TObject);
    procedure FormCreate(Sender: TObject);
  private
    A, B, C, D: OleVariant;
    FAll: IHTMLElementCollection;
  public
    procedure HandleObject(Item: OleVariant);
  end;

var
  Form1: TForm1;

implementation

uses
  DirectAnimation_TLB, CodeBox;

{$R *.DFM}

procedure TForm1.ChangeColorClick(Sender: TObject);
var
  Doc: OleVariant;
begin
  Doc := WebBrowser1.Document;
  Doc.BGColor := $0000FF;
end;
```

```
procedure TForm1.ChangeText1Click(Sender: TObject);
var
  Item: OleVariant;
  Len, i: Integer;
begin
  if FAll = nil then
    ViewAllBtnClick(nil);
  Len := FAll.Length;
  for i := 0 to Len - 1 do begin
    Item := FAll.Item(i, varEmpty);
    if Item.TagName = 'H1' then
      Item.InnerText := 'New Text is Shown Here';
  end;
end;

procedure TForm1.ComboBox1Click(Sender: TObject);
var
  Item: OleVariant;
begin
  Item := FAll.Item(ComboBox1.ItemIndex, varEmpty);
  if Item.TagName = 'H1' then begin
    ShowMessage(Item.InnerText);
    Item.InnerText := 'New Text is Shown Here';
  end else if Item.TagName = 'OBJECT' then
    HandleObject(Item)
  else
    ShowMessage(Item.ClassName + ' Tag: ' + Item.TagName);
end;

procedure TForm1.Edit1KeyDown(Sender: TObject; var Key: Word;
  Shift: TShiftState);
begin
  if Key = 13 then
    WebBrowser1.Navigate(Edit1.Text, A, B, C, D);
end;

procedure TForm1.Exit1Click(Sender: TObject);
begin
  Close;
end;

procedure TForm1.FormCreate(Sender: TObject);
const
  MCW_EM = DWord($133f);
begin
  Set8087CW(MCW_EM);
end;

procedure TForm1.FormShow(Sender: TObject);
```

continues

LISTING 17.5   CONTINUED

```
begin
  WebBrowser1.Navigate(GetStartDir + Edit1.Text, A, B, C, D);
end;

procedure TForm1.HandleObject(Item: OleVariant);
var
  Disp: IDispatch;
  I: IDAViewerControl;
  M: IDAStatics;
  LS: IDALineStyle;
  fs: OleVariant;
  arc1: IDAImage;
  Arc2, Arc3, Arc4, Arc5, Arc6: IDAImage;
  MyArray: OleVariant;
begin
  if VarType(Item) = varDispatch then
    Disp := IDispatch(TVarData(Item).vDispatch)
  else
    Exit;

  I := Disp as IDAViewerControl;
  m := I.MeterLibrary;

  // Use the default line style, set to red, to draw the arcs
  ls := m.DefaultLineStyle.Color(m.Red);

  // Use the default font style for the labels
  fs := m.DefaultFont;

  // Example 1
  // This is an 180 degree arc that starts at 0 and goes to 180 degrees
  arc1 := m.ArcDegrees(0, 180,
    0.04, 0.04).Draw(ls).Transform(m.Translate2(-0.06, 0.07));
  arc2 := m.ArcDegrees(90, 270,
    0.04, 0.04).Draw(ls).Transform(m.Translate2(0.01, 0.07));
  arc3 := m.ArcDegrees(90, -90,
    0.04, 0.04).Draw(ls).Transform(m.Translate2(0.05, 0.07));
  arc4 := m.ArcDegrees(0, -180,
    0.04, 0.04).Draw(ls).Transform(m.Translate2(-0.06, 0.01));
  arc5 := m.ArcDegrees(0, 360,
    0.04, 0.04).Draw(ls).Transform(m.Translate2(0.01, 0.01));
  arc6 := m.ArcRadiansAnim(m.DANumber(0), m.DANumber(PI * 2),
    m.Mul(m.DANumber(0.04), m.Sin(m.LocalTime)), m.Mul(m.DANumber(0.04),
    m.Sin(m.LocalTime))).Draw(ls).Transform(m.Translate2(0.01, -0.04));


  MyArray := VarArrayCreate([0, 5], VarVariant);
  MyArray[0] := Arc1;
  MyArray[1] := Arc2;
```

```
    MyArray[2] := Arc3;
    MyArray[3] := Arc4;
    MyArray[4] := Arc5;
    MyArray[5] := Arc6;

    I.Image := M.OverLayArray(MyArray);
    I.UpdateInterval := 0.50;
    I.Start;

end;

procedure TForm1.OpenFileBtnClick(Sender: TObject);
begin
  if OpenDialog1.Execute then
    WebBrowser1.Navigate(OpenDialog1.FileName, A, B, C, D);
end;

procedure TForm1.RefreshBtnClick(Sender: TObject);
begin
  WebBrowser1.Refresh;
end;

procedure TForm1.ViewAllBtnClick(Sender: TObject);
var
  Doc: IHTMLDocument2;
  i, Len: Integer;
begin
  Doc := WebBrowser1.Document as IHTMLDocument2;
  FAll := Doc.All;
  Len := FAll.Length;
  for i := 0 to Len - 1 do begin
    A := FAll.Item(i, varEmpty);
    ComboBox1.Items.Add(A.Tagname);
  end;
  ComboBox1.ItemIndex := 0;
end;

procedure TForm1.ShowObject1Click(Sender: TObject);
var
  Item: OleVariant;
  Len, i: Integer;
begin
  if FAll = nil then
    ViewAllBtnClick(nil);
  Len := FAll.Length;
  for i := 0 to Len - 1 do begin
    Item := FAll.Item(i, varEmpty);
    if Item.TagName = 'OBJECT' then
      HandleObject(Item)
```

continues

LISTING 17.5   CONTINUED

```
  end;
end;

end.
```

FIGURE 17.4

The ChangeHTML program lets you dynamically change the text and background color in an HTML file.

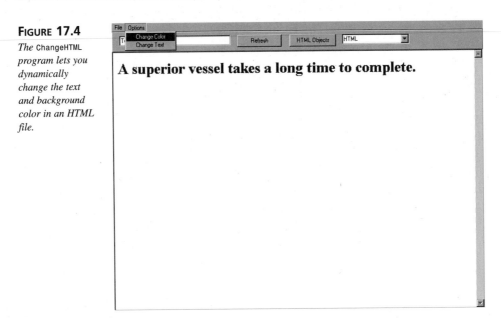

Consider the following bit of HTML:

```
<P>A superior vessel takes a long time to complete.</P>
```

If this code fragment were in an HTML file you were viewing inside your Delphi program, then you could iterate through all the tags in the browser until you found this one tag. Then the TWebBrowser control would allow you to access an object that encapsulates this tag and change the text associated with it:

```
MyParagraph.InnerHtml := 'Look within, thou art the Buddha.'
```

After executing this line of Pascal, the text displayed in the HTML file would change accordingly. This does not mean that the actual HTML file will change, but rather the dynamic image of that file as shown in the browser will change so that the string about the Buddha would be shown to the user.

Here is another way to think about what all this information means. You have no doubt heard about dynamic HTML and the promise that it brings to the Web. Well, the technology I'm describing here allows you to do everything that Dynamic HTML can do, except that instead of relying on VBScript or JavaScript, you can harness your own version of IE to use Object Pascal as the engine behind your Web pages.

The following code shows how to access the HTML elements in a Web page:

```
procedure TForm1.Button2Click(Sender: TObject);
var
  Doc: IHTMLDocument2;
  i, Len: Integer;
begin
  Doc := WebBrowser1.Document as IHTMLDocument2;
  FElements := Doc.All;
  Len := FElements.Length;
  for i := 0 to Len - 1 do begin
    A := FElements.Item(i, varEmpty);
    ComboBox1.Items.Add(A.tagname);
  end;
  ComboBox1.ItemIndex := 0;
end;
```

The first line of code retrieves the Document object from the browser. The Document object is a COM interface belonging to the internal structure of IE4. In other words, using COM, you are able to start calling the methods of objects internal to IE4. This capability does more than just give you dynamic control over the menu in a program. You are actually calling the methods of an object internal to the structure of the program itself!

The next line of code retrieves the All object, which contains all the elements of an HTML file. For instance, the first three elements in the All object represent an HTML tag, a TITLE tag, and a BODY tag. Each of these elements will be wrapped inside a COM object and made available to you to manipulate as you please.

The individual methods of the COM objects for each tag are set forth in the Internet Client SDK, mentioned earlier in this chapter. In this case, the only important element is the tagname property.

A slightly different thing happens in the following method, which singles out one element in the file and changes the text associated with it:

```
procedure TForm1.ChangeText1Click(Sender: TObject);
var
  Item: OleVariant;
  Len, i: Integer;
begin
  if FAll = nil then
    ViewAllBtnClick(nil);
  Len := FAll.Length;
```

```
  for i := 0 to Len - 1 do begin
    Item := FAll.Item(i, varEmpty);
    if Item.TagName = 'H1' then
      Item.InnerText := 'Look within, thou art the Buddha.';
  end;
end;
```

The H1 tag has a property called InnerText that defines the text displayed in the tag. For instance, the following line has the line "That thou mayest seek to know everything" as its InnerText:

```
<H1>That thou mayest seek to know everything</H1>
```

This tag has the words "Seek to know nothing" as its InnerText:

```
<H1>Seek to know nothing.</H1>
```

The point of this example is that you can use interfaces to find the individual elements of an HTML file and change them to suit you own needs. You will find that this technology is not shallow and that you have the power to make an HTML document do just about anything of which it is capable. In short, it lets you enrich the limited powers of an HTML document with the virtually unlimited resources found in the VCL and the Object Pascal language.

Placing an ActiveX Control Within a Browser

This next program is a bit like one of those Russian dolls that you open to find yet another doll. Inside that doll is yet another and so on. In particular, this example shows how to create a Delphi application that hosts a Web browser that hosts an ActiveX control. The ActiveX control is driven by the Object Pascal code that you write in your program.

The Delphi application in this example is called AnimationViewer; it is shown in Figure 17.5. AnimationViewer contains a TWebBrowser component. Inside the Web browser, you can load an HTML file that hosts a DirectAnimation ActiveX control. AnimationViewer then proceeds to use Delphi interfaces to drive the animation control. The end result is a relatively simple Delphi application that rotates a three-dimensional cube or other shape in a window. When you run this program, you may have to scroll the window to see the cube.

The AnimationViewer program can draw a series of curves using the Microsoft DirectAnimation control, or it can use the control to load an X file and rotate the object in your browser. X files have an .x extension and contain geometry defining a shape

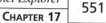

such as a cube, a sailboat, or anything else you can draw with a program such as 3D studio. The DirectX SDK includes programs to import .3DS files to .x files, as discussed in Chapter 28, "More DirectX Technologies." Listing 17.6 contains the main form of the AnimationViewer1 program.

FIGURE 17.5

The AnimationViewer *program features a rotating 3D cube or any other shape you wish to import from an X file.*

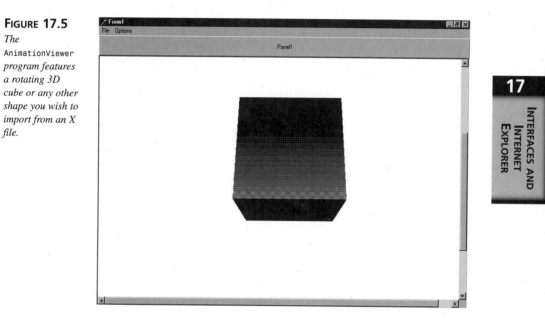

LISTING 17.6   THE MAIN FORM FROM THE AnimationViewer1 PROGRAM

```
unit Main;

{------------------------------------------------------------------
  When you run this program, you may have to scroll the window
  in order to see the cube or certain other shapes that you might
  load that are not particularly large.
  ------------------------------------------------------------------}

interface

uses
  Windows, Messages, SysUtils,
  Classes, Graphics, Controls,
  Forms, Dialogs, Menus,
  ExtCtrls, OleCtrls, SHDocVw_TLB,
  DirectAnimation_TLB, MSHTML_TLB;

type
```

continues

LISTING 17.6 CONTINUED

```pascal
  TForm1 = class(TForm)
    WebBrowser1: TWebBrowser;
    Panel1: TPanel;
    MainMenu1: TMainMenu;
    File1: TMenuItem;
    N1: TMenuItem;
    Exit1: TMenuItem;
    Options1: TMenuItem;
    Cube1: TMenuItem;
    Arcs1: TMenuItem;
    OpenDialog1: TOpenDialog;
    procedure Cube1Click(Sender: TObject);
    procedure FormShow(Sender: TObject);
    procedure Arcs1Click(Sender: TObject);
    procedure FormCreate(Sender: TObject);
  private
    A, B, C, D: OleVariant;
    FViewer: IDAViewerControl;
    function GetViewer: IDaViewerControl;
  public
    { Public declarations }
  end;

var
  Form1: TForm1;

implementation

uses
  CodeBox;

{$R *.DFM}

procedure TForm1.FormShow(Sender: TObject);
var
  FileName: string;
begin
  FileName := GetStartDir + 'TestPage.htm'; // In CodeBox
  WebBrowser1.Navigate(FileName, A, B, C, D);
end;

function TForm1.GetViewer: IDaViewerControl;
var
  Doc: IHTMLDocument2;
  FElements: IHTMLElementCollection;
  HTMLElement: OleVariant;
  Len,i: Integer;
begin
```

```
  Doc := WebBrowser1.Document as IHTMLDocument2;
  // CoHTMLDocument.Create;
  FElements := Doc.All;

  Len := FElements.Length;
  for i := 0 to Len - 1 do begin
    HTMLElement := FElements.Item(i, varEmpty);
    if HTMLElement.tagName = 'OBJECT' then Break;
  end;

  if VarType(HTMLElement) = varDispatch then
    FViewer := IDispatch(HTMLElement) as IDAViewerControl
  else
    FViewer := nil;

  Result := FViewer
end;

procedure TForm1.Cube1Click(Sender: TObject);
const
  RotateSpeed = 50;
var
  Camera: IDACamera;
  DLight, PLight: IDAGeometry;
  FinalGeo, Geo, ACube: IDAGeometry;
  RenderedGeo: IDAImage;
  MeterLib: IDAStatics;
  SRate: IDANumber;
begin
  if not OpenDialog1.Execute then Exit;

  GetViewer;
  MeterLib := FViewer.MeterLibrary;

  // Import the X File. This is a 1-meter cube
  geo :=   MeterLib.ImportGeometry(OpenDialog1.FileName);

  // Add light.
  pLight  := MeterLib.PointLight.Transform(MeterLib.Translate3(0,0,4));
  dLight := MeterLib.DirectionalLight.Transform(
    MeterLib.Rotate3(MeterLib.YVector3, 0.5));

  // Scale
  geo := geo.Transform(MeterLib.Scale3Uniform(0.5));

  // Create and rotate cube
  srate := MeterLib.Mul(MeterLib.LocalTime,
➥MeterLib.DANumber(RotateSpeed));
  ACube := geo.Transform(MeterLib.Compose3(MeterLib.Translate3(0, 0, 2),
    MeterLib.Rotate3Anim(MeterLib.Vector3(1, 0, 0),
    MeterLib.Mul(MeterLib.DANumber(0.04), srate))));
```

continues

LISTING 17.6   CONTINUED

```
  finalgeo := ACube;

  // Add a camera
  Camera := MeterLib.PerspectiveCamera(5.5,
    4.5).Transform(MeterLib.Scale3(30, 30, 1));

  // Combine the lights and Cube
  Finalgeo := MeterLib.UnionGeometry(Finalgeo, pLight);

  // Render and display the image.
  RenderedGeo := Finalgeo.Render(Camera);
  FViewer.Image := MeterLib.Overlay(RenderedGeo,
    MeterLib.SolidColorImage(MeterLib.White));

  // Set the background in case of a non-windowless browser (like IE3).
  FViewer.BackgroundImage := MeterLib.SolidColorImage(MeterLib.Blue);

  // View your work
  FViewer.Start;
end;


procedure TForm1.Arcs1Click(Sender: TObject);
var
  I :IDAViewerControl;
  M: IDAStatics;
  LS: IDALineStyle;
  fs: OleVariant;
  arc1: IDAImage;
  Arc2, Arc3, Arc4, Arc5, Arc6: IDAImage;
  MyArray: OleVariant;

begin
  I := GetViewer;
  m := I.MeterLibrary;

  // Use the default line style, set to red, to draw the arcs
  ls := m.DefaultLineStyle.Color(m.Red);

  // Use the default font style for the labels
  fs := m.DefaultFont;

  // Draw some arcs
  arc1 := m.ArcDegrees(0, 180, 0.04,
    0.04).Draw(ls).Transform(m.Translate2(-0.06, 0.07));
  arc2 := m.ArcDegrees(90, 270,
    0.04, 0.04).Draw(ls).Transform(m.Translate2(0.01, 0.07));
  arc3 := m.ArcDegrees(90, -90,
```

```
    0.04, 0.04).Draw(ls).Transform(m.Translate2(0.05, 0.07));
  arc4 := m.ArcDegrees(0, -180,
    0.04, 0.04).Draw(ls).Transform(m.Translate2(-0.06, 0.01));
  arc5 := m.ArcDegrees(0, 360,
    0.04, 0.04).Draw(ls).Transform(m.Translate2(0.01, 0.01));
  arc6 := m.ArcRadiansAnim(m.DANumber(0),
    m.DANumber(PI * 2), m.Mul(m.DANumber(0.04),
    m.Sin(m.LocalTime)), m.Mul(m.DANumber(0.04),
    m.Sin(m.LocalTime))).Draw(ls).Transform(m.Translate2(0.01, -0.04));

  MyArray := VarArrayCreate([0, 5], VarVariant);
  MyArray[0] := Arc1;
  MyArray[1] := Arc2;
  MyArray[2] := Arc3;
  MyArray[3] := Arc4;
  MyArray[4] := Arc5;
  MyArray[5] := Arc6;

  I.Image := M.OverLayArray(MyArray);
  //  DAViewer.UpdateInterval := 0.50;
  I.Start;
end;

{-----------------------------------------------------------------
  This method sets up Delphi's floating point exception handling to
  conform with Microsoft standards.
  ----------------------------------------------------------------}

procedure TForm1.FormCreate(Sender: TObject);
const
  MCW_EM = DWord($133f);
begin
  Set8087CW(MCW_EM);
end;

end.
```

This program has two menu items: one lets you draw curves on an HTML form; the other lets you rotate a three-dimensional object in the form.

The following is the HTML file displayed in the TWebBrowser object:

```
<HTML>
<HEAD>
<TITLE>DirectAnimation SDK, JScript sample</TITLE>
</HEAD>

<BODY BGCOLOR= WHITE TOPMARGIN=15 LEFTMARGIN=10>
<FONT FACE = "Verdana, Arial, Helvetica" SIZE=2>
```

```
<DIV ID=controlDiv>
<OBJECT ID="DAViewer" class="classviewer"
   STYLE="position:absolute; left:10; top:50;width:800;
   ➥height:900;z-index: -1"
   CLASSID="CLSID:B6FFC24C-7E13-11D0-9B47-00C04FC2F51D">
</OBJECT>
</DIV>

</BODY>
</HTML>
```

The important part of this file is the code called `ControlDiv` in the `DIV` section; it loads the `DirectAnimationViewer` control into the browser. The line that does the real work is the code containing the GUID for the object:

```
CLASSID="CLSID:B6FFC24C-7E13-11D0-9B47-00C04FC2F51D">
```

This line allows the `TWebBrowser` control to retrieve the control and load it into memory. After reading the previous chapters on COM, you should clearly understand why this information is enough to allow the `TWebBrowser` to accomplish its task.

The key method in the program is the one that iterates through the elements in the HTML file, finds the `DirectAnimation` viewer, and makes it available to other portions of the `DirectAnimation` program:

```
function TForm1.GetViewer: IDaViewerControl;
var
  Doc: IHTMLDocument2;
  FElements: IHTMLElementCollection;
  HTMLElement: OleVariant;
  Len,i: Integer;
begin
  Doc := WebBrowser1.Document as IHTMLDocument2;
  // CoHTMLDocument.Create;
  FElements := Doc.All;

  Len := FElements.Length;
  for i := 0 to Len - 1 do begin
    HTMLElement := FElements.Item(i, varEmpty);
    if HTMLElement.tagName = 'OBJECT' then Break;
  end;

  if VarType(HTMLElement) = varDispatch then
    FViewer := IDispatch(HTMLElement) as IDAViewerControl
  else
    FViewer := nil;

  Result := FViewer
end;
```

The first lines of this method should be familiar to you from the preceding section of this chapter. The most interesting code, however, is the line that retrieves the DirectAnimation control from the appropriate element of the All collection:

```
FViewer := IDispatch(HTMLElement) as IDAViewerControl
```

The elements retrieved from the All collection are just Variants containing a standard IDispatch interface. You can therefore query the interface asking whether it supports the IDAViewControl interface, which is part of the DirectAnimation control. In this case, your call should succeed, and you will get an instance of the interface back. (Recall that the Object Pascal as operator ends up calling QueryInterface and, in this case, passes in the GUID for the IDAViewControl interface as its first parameter. The second parameter is an out parameter containing your FViewer control variable.)

After you have tucked the IDAViewControl interface away in the FViewer variable, you can then safely execute the Cube1Click method:

```
procedure TForm1.Cube1Click(Sender: TObject);
const
  RotateSpeed = 50;
var
  Camera: IDACamera;
  DLight, PLight: IDAGeometry;
  FinalGeo, Geo, ACube: IDAGeometry;
  RenderedGeo: IDAImage;
  MeterLib: IDAStatics;
  SRate: IDANumber;
begin
  if not OpenDialog1.Execute then Exit;

  GetViewer;
  MeterLib := FViewer.MeterLibrary;

  // Import the X File. This is a 1-meter cube
  geo :=   MeterLib.ImportGeometry(OpenDialog1.FileName);

  // Add light.
  pLight  := MeterLib.PointLight.Transform(MeterLib.Translate3(0,0,4));
  dLight := MeterLib.DirectionalLight.Transform(
    MeterLib.Rotate3(MeterLib.YVector3, 0.5));

  // Scale
  geo := geo.Transform(MeterLib.Scale3Uniform(0.5));

  // Create and rotate cube
```

```
    srate := MeterLib.Mul(MeterLib.LocalTime,
  ➥MeterLib.DANumber(RotateSpeed));
    ACube := geo.Transform(MeterLib.Compose3(MeterLib.Translate3(0, 0, 2),
      MeterLib.Rotate3Anim(MeterLib.Vector3(1, 0, 0),
      MeterLib.Mul(MeterLib.DANumber(0.04), srate))));

    finalgeo := ACube;

    // Add a camera
    Camera := MeterLib.PerspectiveCamera(5.5,
      4.5).Transform(MeterLib.Scale3(30, 30, 1));

    // Combine the lights and Cube
    Finalgeo := MeterLib.UnionGeometry(Finalgeo, pLight);

    // Render and display the image.
    RenderedGeo := Finalgeo.Render(Camera);
    FViewer.Image := MeterLib.Overlay(RenderedGeo,
      MeterLib.SolidColorImage(MeterLib.White));

    // Set the background in case of a non-windowless browser (like IE3).
    FViewer.BackgroundImage := MeterLib.SolidColorImage(MeterLib.Blue);

    // View your work
    FViewer.Start;
end;
```

This code works with the `FViewer` object to display a three-dimensional scene to the user. Note that all the code shown here works primarily with real interfaces, though I sometimes call an instance of `IDispatch` off one of these interfaces:

```
pLight  := MeterLib.PointLight.Transform(MeterLib.Translate3(0,0,4));
```

Though I would enjoy talking about this code at some length, it is really not germane to the topic at hand. Instead, you need only note that the code you see here is based on one of the standard Microsoft VBScript examples found in the Internet Client SDK. Porting the code over to Delphi was not hard work, and it would have been considerably simpler had I stuck with `Variants` rather than digging up all the interfaces you see here.

This example illustrates several key points:

- You can use ActiveX controls such as `TWebBrowser` in your application.
- You can use HTML, DHTML, and related technology in your Delphi applications.
- You can use large chunks of Visual Basic Automation code in your applications with only minor changes to the original source.
- You can tap into the resources of the operating system, such as its Browser and Automation controls and harness them inside a Delphi program.

Summary

We are entering a time when the rich resources of a computer system are all becoming relatively easily accessible in the form of interfaces and ActiveX controls. In this chapter, you learned how to tap into those resources.

I've shown you many different examples of the types of things you can do with automation objects, ActiveX controls, and interfaces. However, even this plethora of examples might not quite give you a sense of the scope of available objects on a typical Windows 98 or NT system.

If you spend some time seeking them out and browsing the Web in search of additional resources, you will find that your entire computer is fast becoming a cornucopia of useful routines and utilities available through automation, interfaces, and ActiveX controls. I've seen people use some pretty crazy excuses as to why they don't want to tap into this vast wealth of good code. As a rule, I think most of those excuses are just nonsense, and there is no reason why COM objects cannot help us all write richer, more interesting programs. Certainly, I find them useful and expect that they shall play an ever increasing role in Windows programming over the next few years.

CHAPTER 18

The WebBroker: CGI and ISAPI

by Bob Swart (a.k.a. Dr. Bob)

IN THIS CHAPTER

In this chapter, you will learn how to create sophisticated database-driven, HTML-based Web applications that run in any modern browser. The Delphi 4 WebBroker Technology consists of a Web Server Application Wizard and Database Web Application Wizard, together with the `TWebModule`, `TWebDispatcher`, `TWebRequest`, `TWebResponse`, `TPageProducer`, `TDataSetPageProducer`, `TDataSetTableProducer`, and `TQueryTableProducer` components.

The WebBroker Wizards and components are found in the Client/Server suite of Delphi 4 or available as a separate add-on package for Delphi 4 Professional users. For additional information and updates, visit my Web sites at `www.drbob42.com` and `www.bolesian.com`.

Web Modules

In this chapter, you'll find that the terms *WebBroker* and *Web Module* are used to refer to the same thing. Actually, the WebBroker could be seen as a part of the entire Web Module (the Action Dispatcher, to be precise), but for the purpose of this chapter, you can assume both terms refer to the entire collection of wizards, components, and support classes.

The WebBroker technology allows you to build ISAPI/NSAPI, CGI, or WinCGI Web server applications without having to worry about too many low-level details. In fact, to the developer, the development of the Web Module application is virtually the same no matter what kind of Web server application is being developed (you can even change from one type to another during development, as you'll see later). Specifically, the Web Bridge allows developers to use a single API for both Microsoft ISAPI (all versions) and Netscape NSAPI (up to version 3), so you don't have to concern yourself with the differences between these APIs. Moreover, Web server applications are nonvisual applications (that is, they run on the Web server, but the "user interface" is represented by the client using a Web browser), and yet the Web Module wizards and components offer design-time support, compared to writing nonvisual Object Pascal code.

Web Server Application Wizard

You can find the basic Web Server Application Wizard in the Repository. To open it, choose File, New, and the New Items dialog box then appears, as shown in Figure 18.1.

If you start the Web Server Application Wizard, you can specify what kind of Web server application you need: ISAPI/NSAPI (the default choice), CGI, or WinCGI. Figure 18.2 shows the New Web Server Application dialog box.

FIGURE 18.1

The Object Repository: Web Server Application Wizard.

FIGURE 18.2

The Web Server Application Wizard.

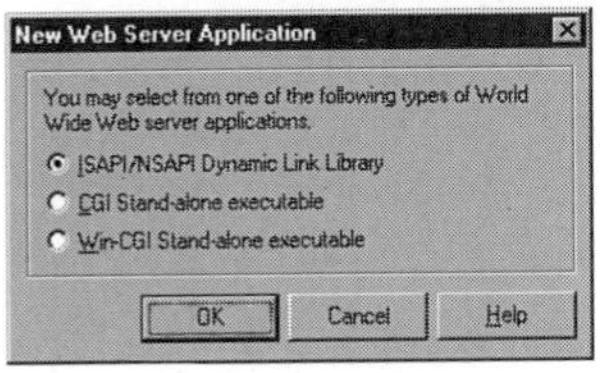

CGI

A Common Gateway Interface (CGI) Web server application is a console application, loaded by the Web server for each request and unloaded directly after completing the request. Client input is received on the standard input, and the resulting output (usually HTML) is sent back to the standard output. The application object is of type `TCGIApplication`.

WinCGI

WinCGI is a Windows-specific implementation of the CGI protocol. Instead of standard input and standard output, an INI file is used to send information back and forth. The application object is again of type `TCGIApplication`; the only programming difference with a standard (console) CGI application is that a WinCGI application is now a GUI application, albeit still a nonvisible one, of course.

The generated source code for a CGI or WinCGI Web Module application is almost identical. The only difference is the fact that a CGI (console) application has the line `{$APPTYPE CONSOLE}}`, as shown here, whereas WinCGI has `{$APPTYPE GUI}`.

```
program Unleashed;
{$APPTYPE CONSOLE} // change to GUI for WinCGI
uses
  HTTPApp,
```

```
CGIApp,
Unit1 in 'Unit1.pas' {WebModule1: TWebModule};

{$R *.RES}

begin
  Application.Initialize;
  Application.CreateForm(TWebModule1, WebModule1);
  Application.Run;
end.
```

You can switch from standard CGI to WinCGI by changing CONSOLE to GUI in the Web Module project file. Because the differences between CGI and WinCGI are minor (compared to the similarities), I'll use the term *CGI* in the remainder of this chapter when, in fact, I'm talking about both CGI and WinCGI.

ISAPI/NSAPI

ISAPI (Microsoft IIS) or NSAPI (Netscape) Web server extension DLLs are just like WinCGI/CGI applications, with the important difference that the DLL stays loaded after the first request. This means that subsequent requests are executed faster (no loading/unloading).

The generated ISAPI/NSAPI DLL source code is very similar to the CGI source code, except for three exported APIs that are used by the Web server to load and run the DLL as a Web server extension DLL, as shown by the following:

```
library Unleashed;
uses
  HTTPApp,
  ISAPIApp,
  Unit1 in 'Unit1.pas' {WebModule1: TWebModule};

{$R *.RES}

exports
  GetExtensionVersion,
  HttpExtensionProc,
  TerminateExtension;

begin
  Application.Initialize;
  Application.CreateForm(TWebModule1, WebModule1);
  Application.Run;
end.
```

Netscape will also support the ISAPI protocol in the future, and because you can use a "translation" DLL to map ISAPI calls to NSAPI (when using an older Netscape Web server), I'll use the term *ISAPI* in the remainder of this chapter when, in fact, I'm talking about both ISAPI and NSAPI.

CGI Versus ISAPI

Personally, I always start to develop an ISAPI Web server extension DLL. Even if you actually want to develop a CGI application, you can start more easily with an ISAPI DLL and change the main project file from ISAPI to CGI after you're done (compare the first two listings of this chapter).

The main disadvantages of the different approaches are the fact that CGI is slower compared to ISAPI (the CGI application needs to be loaded and unloaded for every request), whereas the ISAPI DLL is less robust, as a rogue DLL could potentially crash the entire Web server with it. The latter is a good reason to make sure an ISAPI DLL is 100 percent error proof. So, it's important to test and debug your Web server application before deployment—maybe even more important than with your regular applications.

WebBroker Components

After you make a choice in the New Web Server Application dialog, Delphi generates a new WebBroker project and an empty Web Module unit. Save this new project with the name Unleashed to be used for the entire chapter.

The Web Module is the place to drop the special WebBroker components, such as the PageProducers and TableProducers. You can find the WebBroker components on the Internet tab of the Delphi 4 Component Palette, as shown in Figure 18.3.

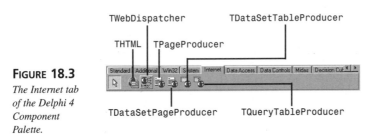

TWebDispatcher   TDataSetTableProducer

THTML   TPageProducer

FIGURE 18.3

The Internet tab of the Delphi 4 Component Palette.

TDataSetPageProducer   TQueryTableProducer

The THTML ActiveX component is not part of the WebBroker components but is used to implement the IntraBob host application with which you can debug Web Module applications from within the Delphi IDE itself. Apart from the components on the Component Palette, you'll also take a closer look at the TWebModule component and the TWebRequest and TWebResponse support classes.

> **NOTE**
>
> The `TWebDispatcher` component seldom needs to be dropped on a Web Module. In fact, this component is already built in the Web Module itself and is merely available to transform an existing Data Module into a Web Module (that is, `TDataModule` + `TWebDispatcher` = `TWebModule`).

TWebModule

The most important property of the Web Module is the Actions property of type `TWebActionItems`. You can start the Action Editor for these `TWebActionItems` in a number of ways. First, you can go to the Object Inspector and click on the ellipsis next to the (`TWebActionItems`) value of the `Action` property. You can also right-click on the Web Module (see Figure 18.4), and select the Action Editor to specify the different requests that the Web Module will respond to.

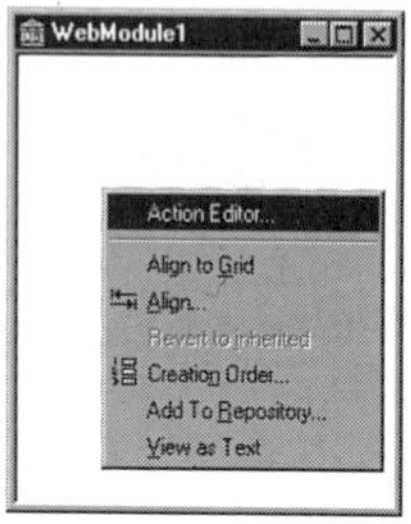

FIGURE 18.4

The Web Module and pop-up menu.

Inside the Action Editor, you can define a number of `WebActionItems`. Each of these items can be distinguished from the others by the `PathInfo` property. This `PathInfo` contains extra information added to the request, right before the `Query` fields. Therefore, a single Web server application can respond to different `WebActionItems`, as you'll see several times in this chapter.

For the examples used in this chapter, you can define nine different `TWebActionItems` to illustrate the different usage and capabilities of the Web Module components. Figure 18.5 shows the Editing dialog box used to select `WebActionItems`.

Note that the first item has no `PathInfo` specified and is the (only) default `WebActionItem`. It's therefore both the `TWebActionItem` that will be selected when no `PathInfo` is given or when no other `PathInfo` matches the given `PathInfo` (for example, when the default action is needed). In this chapter, that's the `TWebActionItem` that will mostly used to demonstrate a certain effect. The other eight `PathInfo` values—`/hello`,

`/alias`, `/table`, `/fields`, `/connect`, `/browse`, `/image`, and `/query`—will be used for bigger examples throughout the chapter.

Figure 18.5

The Action Editor.

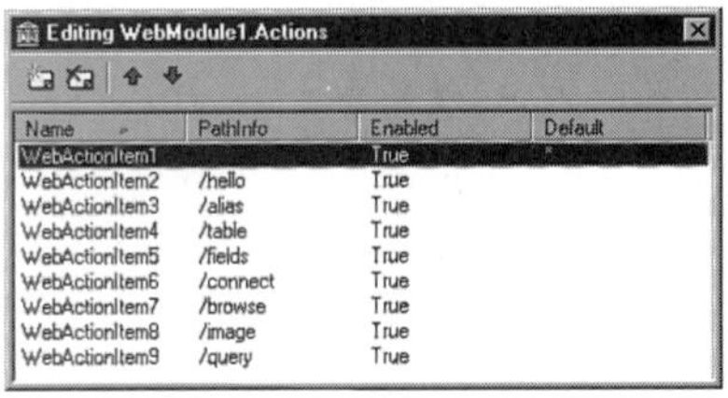

Name	PathInfo	Enabled	Default
WebActionItem1		True	
WebActionItem2	/hello	True	
WebActionItem3	/alias	True	
WebActionItem4	/table	True	
WebActionItem5	/fields	True	
WebActionItem6	/connect	True	
WebActionItem7	/browse	True	
WebActionItem8	/image	True	
WebActionItem9	/query	True	

To write an event handler for the default `TWebActionItem`, select the `WebActionItem1` in the Action Editor (refer to Figure 18.5), go to the Events tab of the Object Inspector, and double-click on the `OnAction` event. This operation will take you to the code editor where you'll see the following code:

```
procedure TWebModule1.WebModule1WebActionItem1Action(Sender: TObject;
  Request: TWebRequest; Response: TWebResponse; var Handled: Boolean);
begin

end;
```

Before you write any event handling code here, you should first learn the internals of the `Request` and `Response` parameters.

TWebResponse

`Response` (of type `TWebResponse`) has a number of properties to specify the generated output. The most important property is `Content`, a string in which you can put any HTML code that should be returned to the client. The following code will produce `"Hello, world!"`, for example:

```
procedure TWebModule1.WebModule1WebActionItem1Action(Sender: TObject;
  Request: TWebRequest; Response: TWebResponse; var Handled: Boolean);
begin
  Response.Content := '<H1>Hello, world!</H1>'
end;
```

Of course, you can assign anything to the `Response.Content` property. Usually, it will be of type `text/html`, which is the default value of the `Response.ContentType` property. In case you want to return anything else, you need to set the `Response.ContentType` to the correct type. Binary output (such as images) cannot be returned directly using the `Response.Content`, in which case you must use the `Response.ContentStream` property instead.

TWebRequest

`Request` (of type `TWebRequest`) contains a number of useful properties and methods that hold the input query. Based on the method used to send the query (`GET` or `POST`), the input data can be found in the `QueryFields` or the `ContentFields`. In code, you can determine this information as follows:

```
procedure TWebModule1.WebModule1WebActionItem1Action(Sender: TObject;
  Request: TWebRequest; Response: TWebResponse; var Handled: Boolean);
begin
  Response.Content := '<H1>Hello, world!</H1>';
  if Request.Method = 'GET' then
    Response.Content := Response.Content + '<B>GET</B>' +
      '<BR>Query: ' + Request.Query
  else
    if Request.Method = 'POST' then
      Response.Content := Response.Content + '<B>POST</B>' +
        '<BR>Content: ' + Request.Content
end;
```

You will find a number of differences between the `GET` and the `POST` protocol; they are important to know. When you're using the `GET` protocol, the query fields are passed on the URL. This operation is fast but limits the amount of data that can be sent (a few kilobytes at most, enough for most cases). A less visible way to pass data is by using the `POST` protocol, in which content fields are passed using standard input/output techniques (or a Windows INI file for WinCGI). This method is slower but is limited only to the amount of free disk space.

> **NOTE**
>
> When using `POST`, you cannot see the data being sent on the URL itself, so there's no way of (accidentally) tampering with it and getting incorrect results.

Usually, I prefer to use the `POST` protocol (clean URLs, no limit on the amount of data, but slightly slower) and use the `GET` protocol only when I have a good reason to.

IntraBob

It's time to test the first Web Module application. But because it's a DLL, you cannot just click the Run button. In fact, you actually need a Web server to test the Web Module application. This means you should deploy the application to your remote Web server or test it with a personal Web server first.

Chapter 28 of the *Delphi 4 Developer's Guide* (Sams Publishing, ISBN 0-672-31284-0) contains clear instructions on how to set up your (Personal) Web server to be able to test and debug ISAPI DLLs or CGI applications. However, for simple cases, you can get a helping hand from IntraBob v3.02, my personal ISAPI Debugger "host" that replaces the (Personal) Web server. Just put a copy of `IntraBob.exe` (available on the CD-ROM or from my Web site at `http://www.drbob42.com`) in the same directory as your ISAPI project source code. Then choose Run, Run Parameters to open the Run Parameters dialog box (see Figure 18.6) and enter the location of IntraBob as the Host Application.

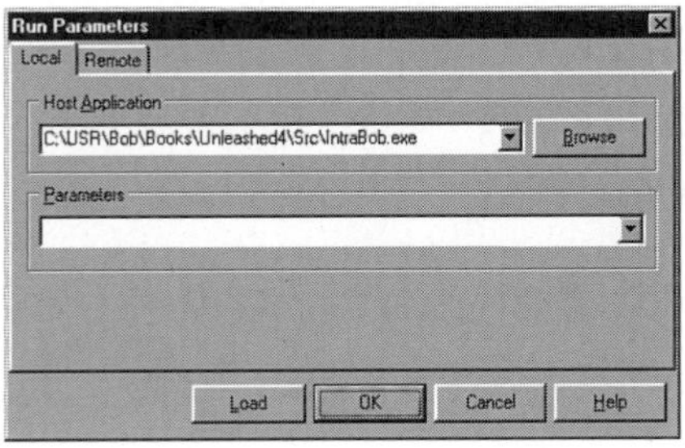

FIGURE 18.6

IntraBob as a Web Module host application.

When you execute the ISAPI DLL, the host application IntraBob (or your Web server) is executed instead. And the best thing is that you can now use the Delphi integrated debugger to set breakpoints in the source code. For example, set a breakpoint at the first line that checks the `Request.Method`, and you'll see that the Delphi IDE will break here as soon as you run the Web Module application.

To actually start the ISAPI DLL, you must write a Web page containing an HTML form that will load the Web Module application. If you uploaded the ISAPI DLL called `Unleashed.dll` to the `cgi-bin` directory on my Web server at `http://www.drbob42.com`, for example, you need an action with value `"http://www.drbob42.com/cgi-bin/Unleashed.dll"`, as seen in the following HTML form code:

```
<HTML>
<BODY>
<H1>WebBroker HTML Form</H1>
<HR>
<FORM ACTION="http://www.drbob42.com/cgi-bin/Unleashed.dll" METHOD=POST>
Name: <INPUT TYPE=EDIT NAME=Name><P>
<INPUT TYPE=SUBMIT>
</FORM>
</BODY>
</HTML>
```

When you load this Web page in IntraBob, you'll see the WebBroker HTML Form Web page, as shown in Figure 18.7. You are now ready to click on the Submit button to load and start your first Web Module application.

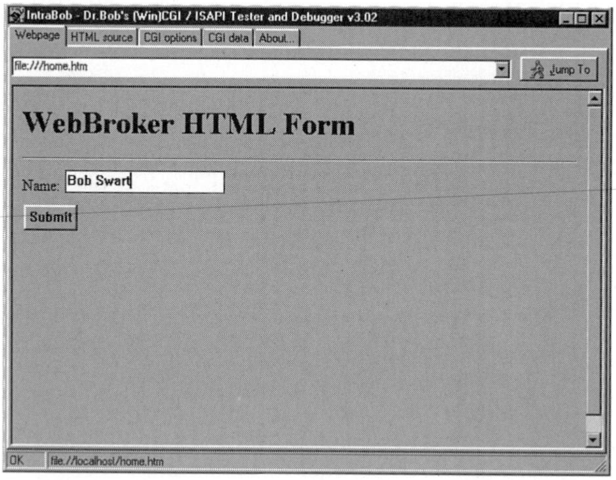

FIGURE 18.7

IntraBob in action.

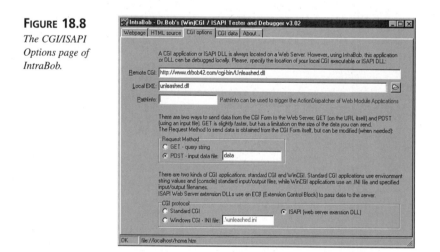

IntraBob parses the HTML form and automatically fills in the CGI Options tab (see Figure 18.8) with the value of the remote CGI (or ISAPI) application, the name of the local executable (or DLL), and the PathInfo, if specified. You can also go to the CGI Options tab and set these options manually (this way, you can easily change the value of PathInfo and fire another WebActionItem).

FIGURE 18.8

The CGI/ISAPI Options page of IntraBob.

Remember the breakpoint you set on the first line that checked the Request.Method value? Well, as soon as you click on the Submit button, the default WebActionItem will be fired, meaning this breakpoint will be triggered, and you end up in the Delphi

Integrated Debugger. Here, you can use Tooltip Expression Evaluation to check the value of `Request.Method` directly, as shown in Figure 18.9.

FIGURE 18.9

The Web Module breakpoint in the Delphi IDE.

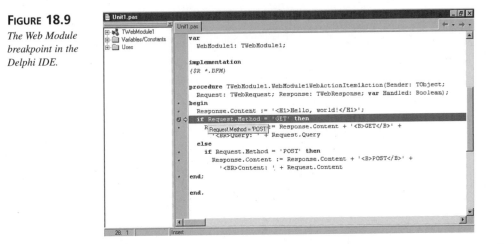

If you press F9, you see the final result in IntraBob, as shown in Figure 18.10.

FIGURE 18.10

IntraBob results.

Voilà, you now have an HTML form "debugger." It will return what (you think) you've specified as input fields. This capability can be quite helpful when a certain `WebActionItem` doesn't seem to work, and you need to check whether it received the input data in good order. Note that spaces are replaced by plus signs, and you'll find all special characters to be replaced by a percent sign followed by the hexadecimal value of the character itself.

> **NOTE**
>
> Another way to see the (not encoded) CGI data is by looking at the CGI Data tab of IntraBob.

TPageProducer

You can put anything in the `Response.Content` string variable, even whole Web pages. Sometimes you might want to return HTML strings based on a template, where only certain fields need to be filled in (with a name and date, or specific fields from a record in a table, for example). In those cases, you should use a `TPageProducer` component. Figure 18.11 shows a `TPageProducer` in a Web Module.

FIGURE 18.11

The Web Module and `PageProducer`.

`TPageProducer` has two properties to specify a predefined content. `HTMLFile` points to an external HTML file. This feature is useful if you want to be able to change your Web page template without having to recompile the application itself. The `HTMLDoc` property, on the other hand, is of type `TStrings` and contains the HTML text (hard-coded in the DFM file).

The predefined content of a `TPageProducer` component can contain any HTML code as well as special # tags. These # tags are "invalid" HTML tags, so they will be ignored by Web browsers but not by the `OnHTMLTag` event of `TPageProducer`. Inside this event, you can change an encountered `TagString` and replace it with `ReplaceText`. For more flexibility, # tags can also contain parameters, right after the name itself (like a parameter `Format=YY/MM/DD` to specify the format to print the date).

As an example, fill the HTMLDoc property with the following content:

```
<H1>TPageProducer</H1>
<HR>
<#Greeting> <#Name>,
<P>
It's now <#Time> and we're playing with the PageProducers...
```

You see three # tags that will fire the OnHTMLTag event of the TPageProducer. To replace each of them with sensible text, see the following code for the OnHTMLTag event:

```
procedure TWebModule1.PageProducer1HTMLTag(Sender: TObject; Tag: TTag;
  const TagString: String; TagParams: TStrings; var ReplaceText: String);
begin
  if TagString = 'Name' then
    ReplaceText := 'Bob' // hardcoded name...
  else
  if TagString = 'Time' then
    ReplaceString := DateTimeToStr(Now)
  else { TagString = 'Greeting' }
    if Time < 0.5 then
      ReplaceText := 'Good Morning'
    else
      if Time > 0.7 then
        ReplaceText := 'Good Evening'
      else
        ReplaceText := 'Good Afternoon'
end;
```

Using a ReplaceText with a fixed value of 'Bob' feels a bit awkward, especially because the HTML form specifically asks the user to enter a name. Can't you just use that value here instead (by using the QueryFields or the ContentFields)? Well, you might want to, of course, but you're inside the OnHTMLTag event of the TPageProducer, and not in the OnAction event where you can directly access the Request object. Fortunately, you *can* access the Request property of the TWebModule, which is always assigned to the Request property of the current Action. The same holds true for the Response property, by the way.

So, accessing this property effectively changes the code for the OnHTMLTag event as follows:

```
procedure TWebModule1.PageProducer1HTMLTag(Sender: TObject; Tag: TTag;
  const TagString: String; TagParams: TStrings; var ReplaceText: String);
begin
  if TagString = 'Name' then
  begin
    if Request.Method = 'POST' then
      ReplaceText := Request.ContentFields.Values['Name']
    else // GET
```

```
        ReplaceText := Request.QueryFields.Values['Name']
    end
    else
    if TagString = 'Time' then
      ReplaceString := DateTimeToStr(Now)
    else { TagString = 'Greeting' }
      if Time < 0.5 then
        ReplaceText := 'Good Morning'
      else
        if Time > 0.7 then
          ReplaceText := 'Good Evening'
        else
          ReplaceText := 'Good Afternoon'
end;
```

This will be the last time that you explicitly check the Request.Method field. From now on, you can assume a POST method at all times (but you can still support GET as well as POST using the technique outlined previously).

Before you can finally test this code, you need to write the code for the "/hello" OnAction event to connect the TPageProducer output to the Response argument:

```
procedure TWebModule1.WebModule1WebActionItem2Action(Sender: TObject;
  Request: TWebRequest; Response: TWebResponse; var Handled: Boolean);
begin
  Response.Content := PageProducer1.Content
end;
```

To activate this specific WebActionItem, you need to be sure to pass the "/hello" PathInfo to the Web Module, either by specifying it in the PathInfo edit box of IntraBob (refer to Figure 18.8) or by including the PathInfo string in the ACTION value:

```
<FORM ACTION="http://www.drbob42.com/cgi-bin/Unleashed.dll/
hello" METHOD=POST>
```

If you load the HTML form in IntraBob and click on the Submit button, you'll get the output shown in Figure 18.12.

TDataSetPageProducer

The TDataSetPageProducer component is derived from the TPageProducer. Instead of just replacing # tags with a regular value, the TDataSetPageProducer has a new DataSet property and will try to match the name of the # tag with a FieldName from the DataSet property. If TDataSetPageProducer finds one, it will replace the # tag with the actual value of that field.

To illustrate the use of this component, drop a TDataSetPageProducer and a TTable component on the Web Module. Rename the TTable component to Master, assign the

DatabaseName to DBDEMOS, assign the TableName to BIOLIFE.DB, and set the Active property of the Master table to True (so you don't have to open the table yourself). Next, connect the DataSet property of the TDataSetPageProducer component to the Master table and put the following lines in the HTMLDoc property:

```
<H1>BIOLIFE Info</H1>
<HR>
<BR><B>Category:</B> <#Category>
<BR><B>Common_Name:</B> <#Common_Name>
<BR><B>Species Name:</B> <#Species Name>
<BR><B>Notes:</B> <#Notes>
```

FIGURE 18.12

Output of TPageProducer.

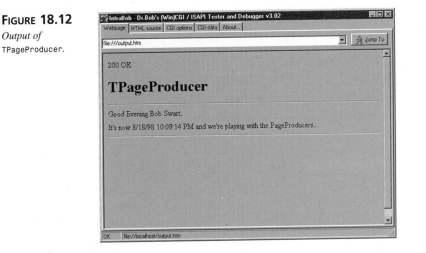

These special HTML # tag codes indicate that you want to see four specific fields from the BIOLIFE table. The TDataSetPageProducer will automatically replace the # tags with the actual values of these fields, so the only code you need to write is for the TWebActionItem event handler. Use the default TWebActionItem again, without a specific PathInfo. Start the Action Editor, click on the first ActionItem, go to the Events tab of the Object Inspector, and double-click on the OnAction event to write the following code (you can remove the existing code from the previous example):

```
procedure TWebModule1.WebModule1WebActionItem1Action(Sender: TObject;
  Request: TWebRequest; Response: TWebResponse; var Handled: Boolean);
begin
  Response.Content := DataSetPageProducer1.Content
end;
```

You also need to change the ACTION= value of the HTML form back to start the default TWebActionItem again as follows:

18

THE WEBBROKER:
CGI AND ISAPI

```
<FORM ACTION="http://www.drbob42.com/cgi-bin/Unleashed.dll" METHOD=POST>
```

The result from running the Web Module with this request is shown in Figure 18.13.

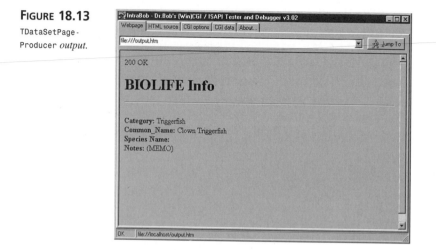

Two things here strike me as being not correct. First, you see (MEMO) instead of the actual contents of this Notes field, and second, you don't get the value of the Species Name field.

You can solve the first problem by making use of the fact that the TDataSetPageProducer is derived from the TPageProducer, so for every # tag the OnHTMLTag event is still fired. Inside this event handler, you can check the value of the ReplaceText argument to see whether it has been set to '(MEMO)', in which case you should change it to the real contents. You can do so by using the AsString method of the field:

```
procedure TWebModule1.DataSetPageProducer1HTMLTag(Sender: TObject;
  Tag: TTag; const TagString: String; TagParams: TStrings;
  var ReplaceText: String);
begin
  if ReplaceText = '(MEMO)' then
    ReplaceText := Master.FieldByName(TagString).AsString
end;
```

The second problem can be explained by the fact that the Species Name field contains a space, and spaces are used as terminators for the # tag names, so the TDataSetPageProducer would have been looking for a field named "Species" instead of the field "Species Name".

You can solve this problem with the same trick: After the TDataSetPageProducer has had a go at replacing the # tags to their field values, the inherited OnHTMLTag event is called, where you can check to see whether a certain ReplaceText is still empty. Now, because you must actually supply the real FieldName but cannot use spaces in the # tag name or its parameters, you must encode the string in a way that you can decode it again to obtain the true FieldName. And the encoded string can consist only of letters, digits, and the underscore character (a true identifier name). The encoding routine is simple: Anything that's not a letter or digit gets encoded by an underscore followed by the hex value of the character that's encoded—like the HTTP % encoding. In fact, when replacing the underscores with percents, you can use the standard HTTPDecode function to get the real FieldName back again.

The resulting functions FieldNameEncode and FieldNameDecode are implemented as follows:

```
function FieldNameEncode(const FieldName: String): String;
var
  i: Integer;

  function Hex(B: Byte): String;
  const
    HexChar: PChar = '0123456789ABCDEF';
  begin
    Hex := '_00';
    Hex[2] := HexChar[B SHR $04];
    Hex[3] := HexChar[B AND $0F]
  end;

begin
  Result := '';
  for i:=1 to Length(FieldName) do
    if FieldName[i] in ['A'..'Z','a'..'z','0'..'9'] then
      Result := Result + FieldName[i]
    else
      Result := Result + Hex(Ord(FieldName[i]))
end {FieldNameEncode};

function FieldNameDecode(const FieldName: String): String;
var
  i: Integer;
begin
  Result := FieldName;
  for i:=1 to Length(Result) do
    if Result[i] = '_' then Result[i] := '%';
  Result := HTTPDecode(Result)
end {FieldNameDecode};
```

`FieldNameEncoding` the field `"Species Name"` yields the following HTML code, which you should use in the original HTML file to get the field value:

```
<BR><B>Species Name:</B> <#Species_20Name>
```

This HTML snippet will fail to find the correct field when used by the `TDataSetPageProducer` component. However, in the `OnHTMLTag` event, you now use `FieldNameDecode` to determine the real `FieldName`:

```
procedure TWebModule1.DataSetPageProducer1HTMLTag(Sender: TObject;
  Tag: TTag; const TagString: String; TagParams: TStrings;
  var ReplaceText: String);
begin
  if ReplaceText = '(MEMO)' then
    ReplaceText := Master.FieldByName(TagString).AsString
  else
    if ReplaceText = '' then
    try
      ReplaceText :=
      ➡Master.FieldByName(FieldNameDecode(TagString)).AsString
    except
      on E: Exception do
        ReplaceText := '(' + E.ClassName + ': ' + E.Message + ')'
    end
end;
```

Using the preceding changes in HTML and source code, the final result is finally as you would like to see it (see Figure 18.14).

FIGURE 18.14

`TDataSetPage-Producer` *output.*

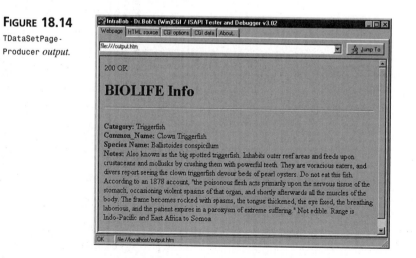

Browsing State

Seeing a single record from a table in a Web browser is fine, but you might like to see the next record as well, and the next, and the last, and back to the first again. In short, you want the ability to browse through the records in the table. To do so, you can use the `TDataSetPageProducer` and code written so far, but extend it just a little bit to support browsing.

The main problem you have to solve when it comes to moving from one record to another is maintaining state information—which record (number) are you currently looking at? HTTP itself is a stateless protocol, so you must find a way to store this information. You can save state information in three different ways: using Fat URLs, cookies, or hidden fields. The following sections discuss each of these methods.

Fat URLs

A common way to retain state information is by adding Form variables with their value to the URL itself. Adding the `RecNo` property of the Master table, for example, this could lead to the following `ACTION` URL:

```
<FORM ACTION="http://www.drbob42.com/cgi-bin/
Unleashed.dll?RecNo=1" METHOD=POST>
```

Note that the general `METHOD` to send Form variables is still `POST`, although the state (`RecNo`) variable is passed using the `GET` protocol. This means you'll see the `RecNo` and its value appear on the URL—something that can be experienced with some search engines on the Web as well.

Personally, I believe that any information sent on the URL is error prone, so I generally try to avoid it (although using the `POST` method to send regular Form fields and the `GET` method to send state fields is actually a nice way to separate the two kinds of fields).

Cookies

Cookies are sent by the server to the browser. When you're using cookies, the initiative is with the Web server, but the client has the ability to deny or disable a cookie. Sometimes, servers even send cookies when you don't ask for them, which can be a reason that some people don't like cookies (like me, for example).

Cookies can be set as part of the `Response`, using the `SetCookieField` method. Like CGI values, a cookie is of the form `"NAME=VALUE"`, so you can put a `"RecNo=value"` in there as follows:

```
var
  Cookies: TStringList;
```

```
begin
  Cookies := TStringList.Create;
  Cookies.Add('RecNo='+IntToStr(Master.RecNo));
  Response.SetCookieField(Cookies,'','',Now+1,False);
  Cookies.Free
```

Note that you use a `TStringList` to set up a list of cookie values. Each list of cookies can have a `Domain` and `Path` associated with it to indicate which URL the cookie should be sent to. You can leave them blank. The fourth parameter specifies the expiration date of the cookie, which is set to `Now+1` day, so next time the user is back, the cookie should have expired. The final argument specifies whether the cookie is used over a secured connection.

Now, assuming the user accepts the cookie, having set the cookie is still only half the work. In a follow-up `OnAction` event, you need to read the value of the cookie to determine how far to step with the Master table to be able to show the next record. In this case, cookies are part of the `Request` class, just like the `ContentFields`, and they can be queried using the `CookieFields` property.

```
begin
  RecNo := StrToInt(Request.CookieFields.Values['RecNo']);
```

Other than that, cookies work just like any CGI content field. Just remember that while a content field is part of your request (and is always up-to-date), a cookie may have been rejected, resulting in a possible older value (which was still on your disk).

Hidden Fields

Using hidden fields is the third, and in my book most flexible, way to maintain state information. To implement hidden fields, you first need to write an HTML form again, specifying the default `WebActionItem` and using four different "submit" buttons (each with a different value as caption). You also need to make sure the current record number is stored in the generated HTML form, and you can do so by embedding a special # tag with the `RecNo` name inside. This tag will be replaced by the current record number of the table:

```
<FORM ACTION="http://www.drbob42.com/cgi-bin/Unleashed.dll" METHOD=POST>
<H1>BIOLIFE Info</H1><HR>
<INPUT TYPE=SUBMIT NAME=SUBMIT VALUE="First">
<INPUT TYPE=SUBMIT NAME=SUBMIT VALUE="Prior">
<INPUT TYPE=SUBMIT NAME=SUBMIT VALUE="Next">
<INPUT TYPE=SUBMIT NAME=SUBMIT VALUE="Last">
<#RecNo>
<BR><B>Category:</B> <#Category>
<BR><B>Common_Name:</B> <#Common_Name>
<BR><B>Species Name:</B> <#Species_20Name>
```

```
<BR><B>Notes:</B> <#Notes>
</FORM>
```

To replace the #RecNo tag with the current record number, you use the HTML syntax for hidden fields, which is as follows:

```
<INPUT TYPE=HIDDEN NAME=RecNo Value=1>
```

This syntax indicates that the hidden field named RecNo has a value of 1. Hidden fields are invisible to the end user, but the names and values are sent back to the Web server and Web Module application as soon as the user hits any of the four Submit buttons. For ergonomic reasons, you can also display the current record number as well as the total number of records in the table:

```
procedure TWebModule1.DataSetPageProducer1HTMLTag(Sender: TObject;
  Tag: TTag; const TagString: String; TagParams: TStrings;
  var ReplaceText: String);
begin
  if TagString = 'RecNo' then
    ReplaceText :=
      '<INPUT TYPE=HIDDEN NAME=RecNo VALUE=' +
        IntToStr(Master.RecNo) + // current record number
      '> ' + IntToStr(Master.RecNo) +'/'+
      ➥IntToStr(Master.RecordCount) + '<P>'
  else
    if ReplaceText = '(MEMO)' then
      ReplaceText := Master.FieldByName(TagString).AsString
    else
      if ReplaceText = '(GRAPHIC)' then
        ReplaceText :=
          '<IMG SRC="Unleashed.dll/image?RecNo=' +
            IntToStr(Master.RecNo) + '" ALT="RecNo=' +.
            IntToStr(Master.RecNo) + '">'
      else
        if ReplaceText = '' then
        try
          ReplaceText :=
            Master.FieldByName(FieldNameDecode(TagString)).AsString
        except
          on E: Exception do
            ReplaceText := '(' + E.ClassName + ': ' + E.Message + ')'
        end
end;
```

Now all you need to do is specify the action the WebActionItem has to perform for each of the Submit buttons. You could have split this up in four different WebActionItems themselves, but then you would have had to use four forms, meaning four copies of the hidden field and any other information necessary (and this situation gets worse, like the next example I will show you in a minute). For now, the WebActionItem event handler just needs to obtain the value of the hidden `RecNo` field and the value of the Submit button (with the specific action to be taken):

```
procedure TWebModule1.WebModule1WebActionItem1Action(Sender: TObject;
  Request: TWebRequest; Response: TWebResponse; var Handled: Boolean);
var
  RecNr: Integer;
  Str: String;
begin
  RecNr := 0;
  Str := Request.ContentFields.Values['RecNo'];
  if Str <> '' then
  try
    RecNr := StrToInt(Str)
  except
  end;
  Str := Request.ContentFields.Values['SUBMIT'];
  if Str = 'First' then RecNr := 1
  else
    if Str = 'Prior' then Dec(RecNr)
    else
      if Str = 'Last' then RecNr :=
        DataSetPageProducer1.DataSet.RecordCount
      else // if Str = 'Next' then { default }
        Inc(RecNr);
  if RecNr > DataSetPageProducer1.DataSet.RecordCount then
    RecNr := DataSetPageProducer1.DataSet.RecordCount;
  if RecNr < 1 then RecNr := 1;
  if RecNr <> DataSetPageProducer1.DataSet.RecNo then
    DataSetPageProducer1.DataSet.MoveBy(RecNr
                              DataSetPageProducer1.DataSet.RecNo);
  Response.Content := DataSetPageProducer1.Content
end;
```

The result is the display you saw in Figure 18.14, but this time with four buttons that enable you to go to the First, Prior, Next, or Last record of the BIOLIFE table, as shown in Figure 18.15.

You'll find one problem when testing the preceding technique with IntraBob: you use the fact that each Submit button can have a special value—the captions of the four buttons in Figure 18.15. However, the THTML component, which is the basis for IntraBob, is not able to "capture" the value of the Submit buttons, so IntraBob can't tell the difference when you click on any of these buttons. For IntraBob, any Submit button triggers the "Next" action, so at least you can test it. For a fully functional test, you need a real (Personal) Web server.

The techniques used here to keep state information and use it to browse through a table can be used in other places as well, of course. Note that while you used the `RecNo` to retain the current record number, you could also pass the current (unique) key values and use them to search for the current record instead (especially when browsing a dynamic table where lots of users are adding new records while you're browsing it).

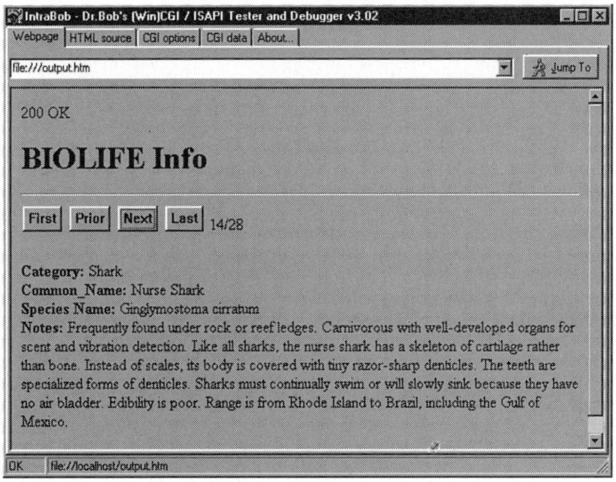

FIGURE 18.15

TDataSetPage-Producer and state information.

Advanced Page Producing

You saw what the individual Page Producers can do. However, the situation gets really interesting when you combine these components and connect the "output" of one to the "input" of another. The example you're going to build at this time is a Table viewer, like the BIOLIFE example you just saw, but this time with the capability to dynamically specify the DatabaseName (alias), TableName, and FieldNames.

Responding to HTTP requests is the purpose of the WebActionItems with the "/alias", "/table", and "/fields" PathInfo. First, select the third ActionItem (with the "/alias" PathInfo) and write the following code in the OnAction event handler. The code calls the Session.GetAliasNames method to obtain a list of known aliases:

```
procedure TWebModule1.WebModule1WebActionItem3Action(Sender: TObject;
  Request: TWebRequest; Response: TWebResponse; var Handled: Boolean);
var
  AliasNames: TStringList;
  i: Integer;
begin
  Response.Content := '<H1>Alias Selection</H1><HR><P>';
  AliasNames := TStringList.Create;
  AliasNames.Sorted := True;
  try
    with Session1 do
```

```
  begin
    Active := True;
    GetAliasNames(AliasNames);
    Active := False
  end;
  Response.Content := Response.Content +
    'Please select a database alias.' +
    '<FORM ACTION="Unleashed.dll/table" METHOD=POST>' +
    'Alias: <SELECT NAME="alias">';
  for i:=0 to Pred(AliasNames.Count) do
    Response.Content := Response.Content +
      '<OPTION VALUE="'+AliasNames[i]+'">'+AliasNames[i];
  Response.Content := Response.Content +
    '</SELECT>' +
    '<P>' +
    '<INPUT TYPE=RESET> <INPUT TYPE=SUBMIT>' +
    '</FORM>';
  finally
    AliasNames.Free
  end
end;
```

Note that the ACTION part of the generated HTML form is just "Unleashed.dll/table". This means that the name of the ISAPI DLL and the PathInfo is specified correctly, but not the exact location on the actual Web server. This example works fine in combination with IntraBob (which is a local ISAPI DLL debugger host), but you need to specify the full ACTION path when deploying and testing using your real (Personal) Web server.

Running this action (remember to set the value of PathInfo to "/alias") will return the output shown in Figure 18.16.

FIGURE 18.16

Alias selection.

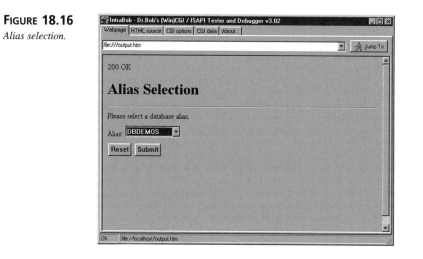

After you've selected an alias, the `"/table"` WebActionItem's OnAction event will be executed when you click on the Submit button.

The next step consists of generating a list of TableNames for the alias that you selected in the previous step. Again, you can do so by using the TSession component, this time by calling the GetTableNames method:

```
procedure TWebModule1.WebModule1WebActionItem4Action(Sender: TObject;
  Request: TWebRequest; Response: TWebResponse; var Handled: Boolean);
var
  TableNames: TStringList;
  i: Integer;
begin
  Response.Content := '<H1>Table Selection</H1><HR><P>';
  TableNames := TStringList.Create;
  TableNames.Sorted := True;
  try
    with Session1 do
    begin
      Active := True;
      Session1.GetTableNames(Request.ContentFields.Values['alias'],
                        '',True,False,TableNames);
      Active := False
    end;
    Response.Content := Response.Content +
      'Please select a database table.' +
      '<FORM ACTION="Unleashed.dll/fields" METHOD=POST>' +
      '<INPUT TYPE=HIDDEN NAME="alias" VALUE="' +
        Request.ContentFields.Values['alias'] + '">' +
      '<TABLE>';
    Response.Content := Response.Content +
      '<TR><TD ALIGN=RIGHT>Master: </TD><TD><SELECT NAME="table">';
    for i:=0 to Pred(TableNames.Count) do
      Response.Content := Response.Content +
        '<OPTION VALUE="'+TableNames[i]+'">'+TableNames[i];
    Response.Content := Response.Content +
      '</SELECT></TD></TR>';
    Response.Content := Response.Content +
      '</TABLE><P>' +
      '<INPUT TYPE=RESET> <INPUT TYPE=SUBMIT>' +
      '</FORM>';
  finally
    TableNames.Free
  end
end;
```

Note that you need to pass the Alias field with the previously selected value to the next Web page as well (so you can use it to combine with the selected TableName). You do so by passing a hidden field with the "alias" name.

Running this `WebActionItem` results in an HTML form with the new `"/fields"` `PathInfo`. Figure 18.17 shows the output inside IntraBob.

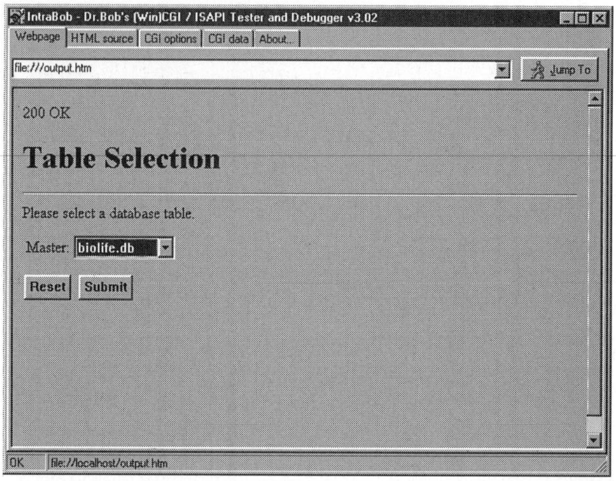

FIGURE 18.17

Table selection.

After you select a `TableName` and click on the Submit button, the `"/fields"` `WebActionItem` is executed, which is implemented as follows:

```
procedure TWebModule1.WebModule1WebActionItem5Action(Sender: TObject;
  Request: TWebRequest; Response: TWebResponse; var Handled: Boolean);
var
  i: Integer;
begin
  Response.Content := '<H1>Table Fields</H1><HR><P>' +
      '<FORM ACTION="Unleashed.dll/browse" METHOD=POST>' +
        '<INPUT TYPE=HIDDEN NAME="alias" VALUE="' +
          Request.ContentFields.Values['alias'] + '">' +
        '<INPUT TYPE=HIDDEN NAME="table" VALUE="' +
          Request.ContentFields.Values['table'] + '">';
  Session1.Active := True;
  with Master do
  begin
    DatabaseName := Request.ContentFields.Values['alias'];
    TableName := Request.ContentFields.Values['table'];
    FieldDefs.Update; { no need to actually Open the Table }
    Response.Content := Response.Content +
      '<TABLE><TR><TD WIDTH=200 BGCOLOR=FFFF00> <B>Table: </B>' +
        TableName + ' </TD>' +
      '<TR><TD BGCOLOR=CCCCCC VALIGN=TOP>';
    for i:=0 to Pred(FieldDefs.Count) do
      Response.Content := Response.Content +
        '<INPUT TYPE="checkbox" CHECKED NAME="M' +
          FieldDefs[i].DisplayName + '" VALUE="on"> ' +
```

```
           FieldDefs[i].DisplayName + '<BR>';
  end;
  Response.Content := Response.Content +
    '</TD></TR></TABLE><P>' +
    '<INPUT TYPE=RESET> <INPUT TYPE=SUBMIT>' +
    '</FORM>'
end;
```

Note that you now need to pass both the `Alias` field and the `Table` field with the previously selected values to the next Web page (so you can use it to combine with the selected `FieldNames`). You do so by passing two hidden fields.

Executing this `OnAction` event finally results in a form with the `"/browse"` `PathInfo`, where you can select the fields from the table you selected in the previous step. Note that the selected `FieldNames` must be encoded and decoded using your previously written `FieldEncode` and `FieldDecode` methods to be sure they can be handled by the `TDataSetPageProducer`. The output can be seen in IntraBob again, as shown in Figure 18.18.

FIGURE 18.18

Specifying table fields.

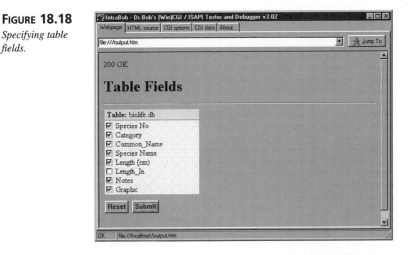

After you select a `TableName` and click on the Submit button, the final `"/browse"` `TWebActionItem` is executed, which is implemented as follows:

```
procedure TWebModule1.WebModule1WebActionItem7Action(Sender: TObject;
  Request: TWebRequest; Response: TWebResponse; var Handled: Boolean);
var
  Str,S: String;
  RecNr,i: Integer;
begin
  Str := '<H1>Table Contents</H1><HR><P>' +
```

```
            '<FORM ACTION="Unleashed.dll/browse" METHOD=POST>' +
            '<INPUT TYPE=HIDDEN NAME="alias" VALUE="' +
            Request.ContentFields.Values['alias'] + '">' +
            '<INPUT TYPE=HIDDEN NAME="table" VALUE="' +
            Request.ContentFields.Values['table'] + '">' +
            '<INPUT TYPE=SUBMIT NAME=SUBMIT VALUE="First"> ' +
            '<INPUT TYPE=SUBMIT NAME=SUBMIT VALUE="Prior"> ' +
            '<INPUT TYPE=SUBMIT NAME=SUBMIT VALUE="Next"> ' +
            '<INPUT TYPE=SUBMIT NAME=SUBMIT VALUE="Last"> ' +
            '<#RecNo>';
    Session1.Active := True;
    with Master do
    try
      DatabaseName := Request.ContentFields.Values['alias'];
      TableName := Request.ContentFields.Values['table'];
      Open;
      for i:=0 to Pred(Fields.Count) do
        if Request.ContentFields.Values['M'+Fields[i].FieldName] =
        ➥'on' then
          Str := Str +
            '<INPUT TYPE=HIDDEN NAME="M' + Fields[i].FieldName +
            ➥'" VALUE="on">';
      // locate correct record
      RecNr := 0;
      S := Request.ContentFields.Values['RecNo'];
      if S <> '' then
      try
        RecNr := StrToInt(S)
      except
      end;
      S := Request.ContentFields.Values['SUBMIT'];
      if S = 'First' then RecNr := 1
      else
        if S = 'Prior' then Dec(RecNr)
        else
          if S = 'Last' then RecNr := Master.RecordCount
          else // if S = 'Next' then { default }
            Inc(RecNr);
      if RecNr > Master.RecordCount then RecNr := Master.RecordCount;
      if RecNr < 1 then RecNr := 1;
      if RecNr <> Master.RecNo then
        Master.MoveBy(RecNr - Master.RecNo);
      // display fields
      Str := Str + '<TABLE CELLSPACING=4>';
      for i:=0 to Pred(Fields.Count) do
        if Request.ContentFields.Values['M'+Fields[i].FieldName] =
        ➥'on' then
          Str := Str + '<TR><TD VALIGN=TOP ALIGN=RIGHT><B>' +
                  Fields[i].FieldName + ':</B> </TD><TD>' +
            '<#' + FieldNameEncode(Fields[i].FieldName) + '></TD></TR>'
          else
```

```
        Str := Str + '-';
    Str := Str + '</TABLE>';
    DataSetPageProducer1.HTMLDoc.Clear;
    DataSetPageProducer1.HTMLDoc.Add(Str);
    Str := DataSetPageProducer1.Content;
  finally
    Close;
    Session1.Active := False;
    Response.Content := Str
  end
end;
```

Note that because you want to browse through the result, you need to keep the value of the Alias, the Table, and all selected FieldNames. They are all passed as hidden fields.

The final output, in which you can browse through the BIOLIFE table, showing all the fields you've selected, is shown in Figure 18.19.

FIGURE 18.19

TDataSetPage-
Producer *brows-ing* BIOLIFE.DB.

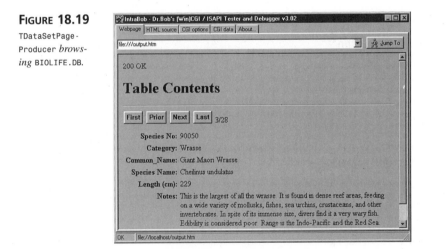

Note that all fields are shown as you want them; even the fields with spaces in their names and the (MEMO) fields are nicely expanded, too. Finally, you can even turn this into a master-detail output, but for that, you need the TDataSetTableProducer compo-nent that hasn't been covered yet.

TDataSetTableProducer

The TDataSetTableProducer also uses a DataSet property, just like the TDataSetPageProducer. This time, however, you get more than one record, and the out-put is formatted in a grid-like table.

Drop a second `TTable` component on the Web Module and call it `Detail` (to prepare for the master-detail relationship you're going to build in a little while). Set the `DatabaseName` (alias) to `DBDEMOS` again, set the `TableName` to `CUSTOMER.DB`, and open the table by setting `Active` to `True`. Now, drop a `TDataSetTableProducer` on the Web Module and set the `DataSet` property to the Detail table. The `TDataSetTableProducer` has a number of properties that are used to control the HTML code being generated. First, you have the `Header` and `Footer` properties, which hold the lines of text that precede and follow the table output. Then you have the `TableAttributes` and `RowAttributes` properties that can be used to define the layout (`Alignment`, `Color`, and so on) of the table itself and the rows. You can experience a more visual approach to specifying what the table should look like by using the `Column` property and especially the `Column` Property Editor. From the Object Inspector, start the `Columns` Property Editor by clicking on the ellipsis next to the `Columns` property (`THTMLTableColumns`) value. This action brings up the `DataSetTableProducer1.Columns` editor, as shown in Figure 18.20.

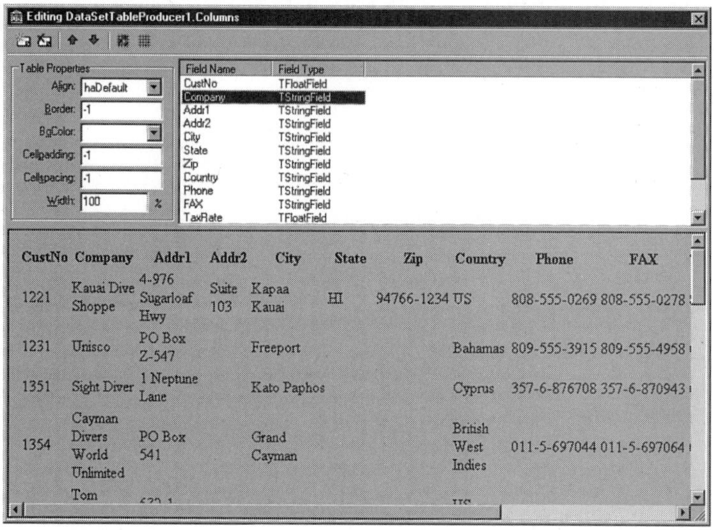

FIGURE 18.20

TableProducer
Columns Editor.

Since you opened the `Detail` table, you immediately see all fields in the Columns editor. Initially, you cannot delete any fields from this view, nor can you move them. This may "feel" like a bug (and probably is), but it can be explained by the fact that you haven't explicitly specified which fields you want to see in the output table. You see all fields at this time because that's the default behavior from the `TTable` component (if you don't specify which fields you want, you get them all). However, to delete fields from the complete list or change the order in which the fields should appear, you need to add a physical list of fields. Right-click on the list of `FieldNames` and pick the Add All Fields option.

You'll see no apparent change right now. However, the default list of all fields suddenly becomes an actual list of all fields, and now you can delete fields or move them around in the list.

You can also set the output table options, such as `Border=1` to get a border, a background color by specifying a value for the `BgColor` property, and so on. To change individual field (= column) settings, you have to select a field and go to the Object Inspector to set the `BgColor`, `Align` (left, center, right), and `VAlign` (top, middle, bottom, baseline) properties. To change the caption of the fields, you can modify the `Title` property (again in the Object Inspector). The `Title` property consists of subproperties such as `Align` (this time for the title only, not the entire column) and `Caption`. Hence, to change the title of the `Addr1` field to `Address`, you only need to change the `Title.Caption` property of the `Addr1` field in the Object Inspector, as shown in Figure 18.21.

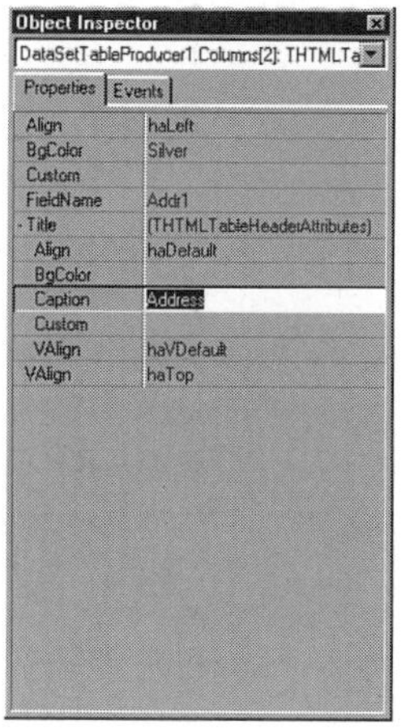

FIGURE 18.21

The Object Inspector.

The latter changes will automatically be reflected back in the Columns editor, so after you play around with these properties, your output preview may look like Figure 18.22.

That concludes the design-time tweaking of the `TDataSetTableProducer` output. Note that you haven't written a single line of code (for the `TDataSetTableProducer` example) yet. Of course, you need to hook it up to a `WebActionItem` `OnAction` event handler, and you can use the default `WebActionItem` again (removing the existing lines of code) as follows:

```
procedure TWebModule1.WebModule1WebActionItem1Action(Sender: TObject;
  Request: TWebRequest; Response: TWebResponse; var Handled: Boolean);
begin
  Response.Content := DataSetTableProducer1.Content
end;
```

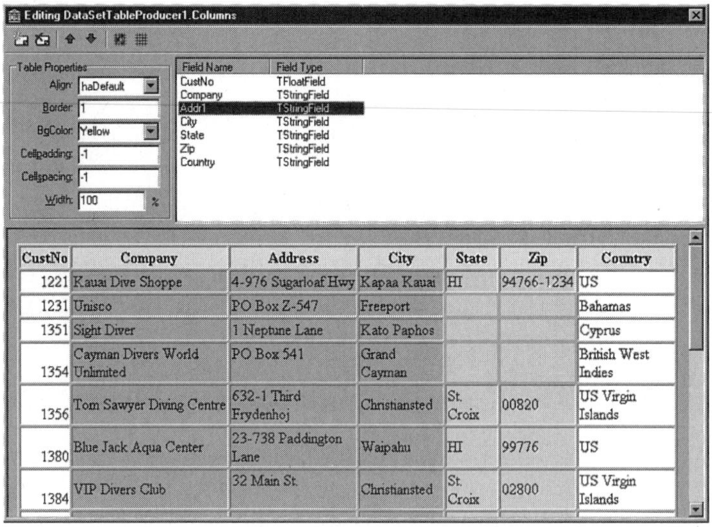

FIGURE 18.22

TableProducer
Columns Editor.

You can tweak and customize the output a little further by using a few more methods. First, you might want to "flag" certain countries with a special color—like the U.S. for which shipping can be done over land instead of by sea or by air. Or you might want to display fields with no contents (like the state and zip code for non-U.S. addresses in a silver color so they don't stand out too much). Both these changes can be done in the OnFormatCell event of the TDataSetTableProducer component. All you need to do is check whether the CellData is empty and then assign Silver to the BgColor, or, if the CellData is 'US' and the CellColumn = 6, you should change the BgColor to Red, for example:

```
procedure TWebModule1.DataSetTableProducer1FormatCell(Sender: TObject;
  CellRow, CellColumn: Integer; var BgColor: THTMLBgColor;
  var Align: THTMLAlign; var VAlign: THTMLVAlign;
  var CustomAttrs, CellData: String);
begin
  if CellData = '' then BgColor := 'Silver'
  else
    if (CellData = 'US') and (CellColumn = 6) then
      BgColor := 'Red'
end;
```

Executing this code produces the output shown in Figure 18.23.

As a last enhancement, you might want to see the orders for a specific customer in a follow-up window. Orders are linked to the CustNo identifier, so you could change that one to a link that would start another Web Module request to (dynamically) generate HTML output with an overview of the orders for the given customer. Put that one on hold for now because you can use the final component (the `TQueryTableProducer`) to assist in solving this request.

FIGURE 18.23

TableProducer
output in
IntraBob.

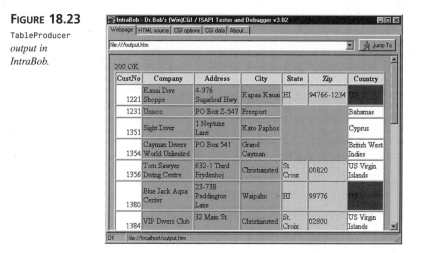

Database Web Application Wizard

Before you continue with the last component from the WebBroker toolset, first quickly check out a wizard related to the `TDataSetTableProducer`. Compared to Delphi 3 C/S, the Database Web Application Wizard, found on the Business tab in the Object Repository, is a new addition to the WebBroker set of components and wizards. However, a long name is not enough to impress me, and if you check out this DB Web Application Wizard in action, you'll find that all it does is allow you to specify a database alias, a table name, some `FieldNames`, and finally a few properties for the `TDataSetTableProducer`. All it generates is a new Web Module Application, with a `TWebModule`, a `TSession` (`AutoSessionName = True`), a `TTable`, a `TDataSetTableProducer`, and that's it. You could have dropped these components and set their properties in the same time it took to fill in the wizard, but maybe the wizard is helpful for developers who're just beginning with the WebBroker technology.

TQueryTableProducer

The `TQueryTableProducer` produces output similar to the `TDataSetTableProducer`. The difference is not based on the fact that you can connect only a `TQuery` component to the `TQueryTableProducer` (after all, you can connect any `TDataSet` or derived component, including `TTable`s and `TQueries` to the `TDataSetTableProducer` already), but the fact that the `TQueryTableProducer` has special support for filling in the parameters of a parameterized `TQuery`.

Drop a `TQueryTableProducer` component and a `TQuery` component on the Web Module. Set the `DatabaseName` (alias) of the `TQuery` component to `DBDEMOS` and write the following code in the `SQL` property:

```
SELECT * FROM ORDERS.DB AS O
WHERE (O.CustNo = :CustNo)
```

This `SQL` query has one parameter. You now need to specify the type of the parameter in the `Parameter` Property Editor of the `TQuery` component. Click on the ellipsis next to the `Params` property in the Object Inspector to edit that value, as shown in Figure 18.24.

FIGURE 18.24

TQuery Params
Editor.

Note that the `Params` Property Editor changed from Delphi 3 to Delphi 4. Select the `CustNo` parameter in the list and go to the Object Inspector to set the `DataType` to `ftInteger`, the `ParamTyp` to `ptInput`, and optionally the `Value` to `0` (or leave it unassigned).

You can open the `TQuery` component (set `Active` to `True`) to check whether you made any typing mistakes. Now, click on the `TQueryTableProducer` and assign the `Query` property to the `TQuery` component. Note that the `TQueryTableProducer` contains the same properties to customize its output as the `TDataSetTableProducer` (see the preceding section). In fact, the `TQueryTableProducer` and `TDataSetTableProducer` are both derived from `TDSTableProducer`, and `TQueryTableProducer` adds only the *Query Parameter Handling* to its special behavior.

The `TQueryTableProducer` works by looking for the parameter name (`CustNo`, in this case) among the `ContentFields` (or `QueryFields`, if we're using the `GET` method) and filling in the value of the field as value for the parameter. In this case, you need a sample HTML startup file defined as follows:

```
<HTML>
<BODY>
<H1>WebBroker HTML Form</H1>
<HR>
<FORM ACTION="http://www.drbob42.com/cgi-bin/Unleashed.dll/
➥query" METHOD=POST>
```

```
CustNo: <INPUT TYPE=EDIT NAME=CustNo>
<P>
<INPUT TYPE=SUBMIT>
</FORM>
</BODY>
</HTML>
```

Note that the name of the input field is CustNo, which is exactly the name of the Query parameter. If you fill in a value, like 1221 (refer to Figure 18.23), then you should get all orders for this particular customer. As long as you set the MaxRows property to a really high value (999 will do fine), you'll probably see all detail records. Note that setting the MaxRows property to a high value (especially for the TDataSetTableProducer) results in more records that are shown, but also bigger and certainly slower output. The latter is not only caused by the fact that the output is simply bigger and has to be transferred over the network, but also by the fact that an HTML table doesn't show itself until the closing </TABLE> tag is reached. This means that for a really big table with 999 rows, you may actually see a blank browser window for a while until suddenly the table is drawn.

To finish this example, you need to write only one line of code in the OnAction event handler for the "/query" WebActionItem:

```
procedure TWebModule1.WebModule1WebActionItem9Action(Sender: TObject;
  Request: TWebRequest; Response: TWebResponse; var Handled: Boolean);
begin
  Response.Content := QueryTableProducer1.Content
end;
```

By running the WebActionItem with the "/query" PathInfo and entering 1221 in the CustNo edit box, you get the result shown in Figure 18.25.

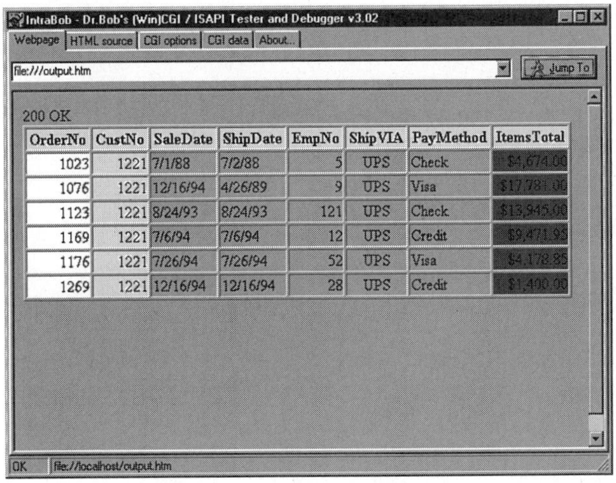

FIGURE 18.25

TQueryTable-Producer *output in IntraBob.*

18

THE WEBBROKER: CGI AND ISAPI

Now, this example just screams to be used together with the previous
`TDataSetTableProducer` on the Customer table. And, in fact, you can do so by extending the `OnFormatCell` event handler from the `TDataSetTableProducer` to generate a
request to the `"/query"` WebActionItem accompanied by a hidden field (with the name
`CustNo`) that holds the value of `CustNo` that you're interested in. Basically, for the first
column (where `CellColumn` has the value 0), you can change the actual `CellData` to a
hyperlink to the `"/query"` WebActionItem with the current `CellData` (for example, the
`CustNo`) as value of a field named `CustNo`, all passed on the URL—thus by using the GET
protocol in a useful way for the very first time this chapter.

Alternatively, you can change each `CustNo` value to a new form with the `"/query"` action
and a hidden field with the `CustNo` name and specific `CustNo` value. Both options are
implemented in the extended `OnFormatCell` event handler code that follows (you can
switch by using the LINK compiler directive):

```
procedure TWebModule1.DataSetTableProducer1FormatCell(Sender: TObject;
  CellRow, CellColumn: Integer; var BgColor: THTMLBgColor;
  var Align: THTMLAlign; var VAlign: THTMLVAlign;
  var CustomAttrs, CellData: String);
begin
  if (CellColumn = 0) and (CellRow > 0) then { first Column - CustNo }
    CellData :=
    {$IFDEF LINK}
      '<A HREF="http://www.drbob42.com/cgi-bin/Unleashed.dll/
      ➥query?CustNo=' + CellData + '>' + CellData + '</A>'
    {$ELSE}
      '<FORM ACTION="Unleashed.dll/query" METHOD=POST>'+
      '<INPUT TYPE=HIDDEN NAME=CustNo VALUE=' + CellData + '>' +
      '<INPUT TYPE=SUBMIT VALUE=' + CellData + '>' +
      '</FORM>'
    {$ENDIF}
  else
    if CellData = '' then BgColor := 'Silver'
    else
      if (CellData = 'US') and (CellColumn = 6) then
        BgColor := 'Red'
end;
```

Because IntraBob can be used only to test and debug ISAPI requests that are started by
an HTML form, you cannot test the hyperlink option (but you can test and deploy that
option using your (Personal) Web server). Instead, you can test the Form option, which
generates the output shown in Figure 18.26 for the `TDataSetTableProducer` on the
Customer table.

It should be clear from Figure 18.26 what will happen as soon as you click on one of
these CustNo buttons. For example, if you click on the 1231 button to see which orders
are placed for this company from the Bahamas (apart from a holiday for me and my family, that is), you get the output shown in Figure 18.27.

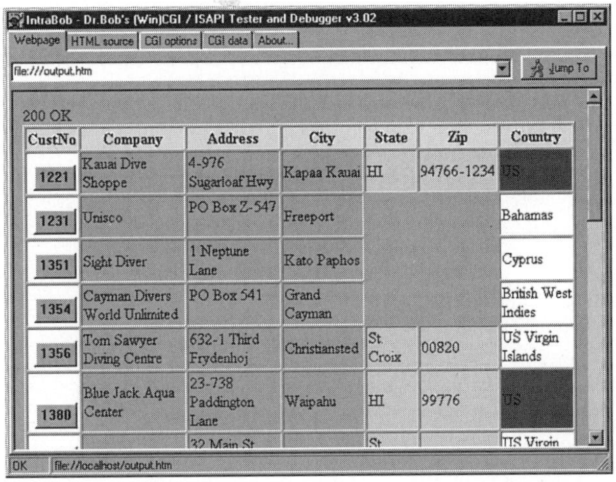

FIGURE 18.26

Master `TableProducer` *output in IntraBob.*

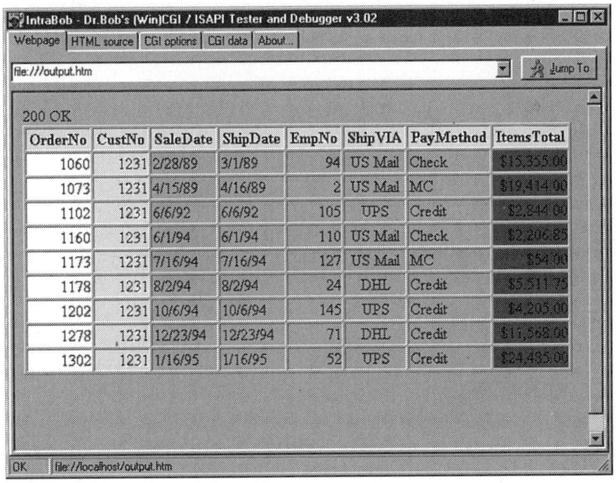

FIGURE 18.27

Detail `QueryTable- Producer` *output in IntraBob.*

If that example doesn't smell like a master-detail overview, I don't know what does. Okay, I know what does: Let's backtrack to the dynamic table browser (refer to Figure 18.19). Wouldn't it be nice to connect this `TDataSetPageProducer` (with the master record) with the output of a `TDataSetTableProducer` (with the detail records), but this time all in one page? Figure 18.28 shows the result.

The final result should be worth the effort: a dynamic master-detail relationship in which you can specify both the master and detail tables, their fields, and the master-detail connection all at runtime. This example provides truly any data, any time, anywhere.

FIGURE 18.28

Master-detail output in IntraBob.

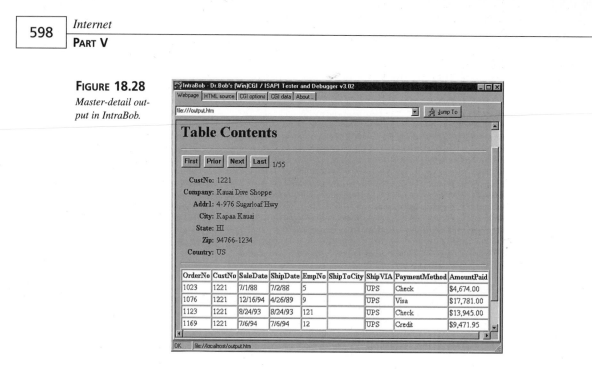

Summary

You've seen it all: Web Modules, `WebActionItems`, Page Producers, and Table Producers for CGI and ISAPI. You've encountered problems and solved them or produced workarounds. And you produced some pretty useful and powerful sample programs along the way.

The chapter covers both CGI and NSAPI/ISAPI-based servers. You've seen that CGI servers are application based, and NSAPI/ISAPI applications are shipped in DLLs. DLLs are loaded into the address space of the Web server and therefore potentially respond more quickly than CGI applications.

You've seen that `WebActionItems` provide a means for you to create intelligent applications that respond to input from a user. By combining the technology found in `WebActionItems` and `PageProducers`, you can create sophisticated database applications that allow users to intelligently edit and explore a complex database. This chapter shows that the WebBroker technology even allows you to properly work with multiple tables that are related through a network of primary and foreign keys.

All in all, I hope to have shown that the Delphi 4 WebBroker technology is a powerful set of tools for Internet server-side application development. I certainly enjoyed writing this chapter, and I will keep pushing Web Modules to the limit in my daily work and on my Web sites at `www.drbob42.com` and `www.bolesian.com`.

WinINet and FTP

CHAPTER 19

In this chapter, you will look at techniques for building FTP clients. Most of the chapter is dedicated to a discussion of WinINet, which is a relatively simple Windows API for creating FTP, Gopher, and HTTP applications. This API is especially appealing because it is built into the operating system, ships with all versions of Windows after Windows NT 4, and enables you to create small, fast applications. If you don't have `WinINet.DLL` on your system, you can download it free from Microsoft's Web site. It works with all 32-bit versions of Windows and ships with Windows NT 4 and Windows 98.

A standard FTP component wrapped around WinINet is the central focus of this chapter. As a result, you will get a chance to take another look at building components. Included in the chapter is some discussion about how to create easy-to-use components.

Another topic I touch on in this chapter is how to use the `TListView` control. This subject comes up in the course of creating an application that can display the files shown in an FTP directory search. I also discuss callbacks, albeit in a manner specific to WinINet. Nevertheless, callbacks are a generally useful programming technique, and the functionality shown in this chapter has general applicability.

> **NOTE**
>
> I've shown earlier versions of the central program in this chapter in previous versions of this book and in *C++Builder 3 Unleashed*. However, the version in this chapter is much improved, adding the capability to track the transfers with a progress bar and the capability to copy and send multiple files at one time.

Understanding WinINet, FTP, and TCP/IP

In the next few sections, I provide general information about WinINet and the services upon which it relies. Most people will want to read the first section called "Required Files." The next two sections on setting up FTP and TCP/IP may not be interesting to experienced Internet users. As soon as this introductory material is covered, I will begin an explanation of the technical aspects of WinINet and its FTP services.

Required Files

Delphi ships with `WinINet.pas` in the `Source\Rtl\Win` directory and `WinINet.dcu` in the `lib` directory. `WinINet.pas` contains manifests, functions, types, and prototypes for the Microsoft Windows Internet Extensions. Therefore, you can now easily add FTP and

HTTP support to your programs. Microsoft's `WinINet.DLL` is freely distributable and is available from Microsoft if it is not already installed in your `Windows/System` or `Winnt/System32` directory. As I stated earlier, Windows NT 4 ships with `WinINet.DLL`, as does Windows 98. `WinINet.DLL` also runs fine on Windows 95.

One of the best places to get help on this subject is in the ActiveX SDK that ships as part of the MSDN and that has frequently been available for downloading from `www.microsoft.com`. Here is how, at the time of this writing, to get the help file for `WinINet.pas`:

```
http://www.microsoft.com/msdn/sdk/inetsdk/help/itt/wininet/wininet.htm
```

Another important link for this type of programming is the following:

```
http://www.microsoft.com/workshop/
```

FTP services rely on TCP/IP, which is built into Windows 98 and Windows NT. In other words, you don't need to add anything to the operating system to have your system act as an FTP client. However, you must have TCP/IP set up correctly on your system. I cover this subject in the next two sections of this chapter.

You can use public FTP server sites to test against, such as `ftp.microsoft.com` or `ftp.inprise.com`. However, you will be better off if you have an FTP server of your own. Windows NT 4 Server comes with the excellent Internet Information Server (IIS), or you can usually download the Personal Web Server from the Microsoft Web site or get it with a copy of FrontPage. Personal Web Server supports FTP and ISAPI, and it runs on Windows 95, Windows 98, or Windows NT. I have heard a few complaints about the Personal Web Server's robustness in commercial settings. These complaints might or might not be well founded, but the usefulness of the tool cannot be denied when you are developing an application. If need be, you can copy your finished files to a more robust server after you complete the development cycle.

Making Sure That FTP Is Working on Your System

FTP stands for the *File Transfer Protocol*, and its sole purpose is to transfer files between computers using TCP/IP services. Programmers sometimes add a bit of humor to this mundane but essential task by insisting that the initials stand for teaching Fido to Phetch. I discuss setting up TCP/IP services in the next section of this chapter.

If you're connected to the Internet, even just over a modem, you should be able to FTP into various sites to see the contents of directories and to transfer files. For example, to connect to the Inprise FTP site, type the following at the command prompt:

```
ftp ftp.inprise.com
```

When the system asks for a username, type anonymous. When it requests a password, type your email address. Figure 19.1 shows a screen shot of a typical old-fashioned, command-line–based FTP session.

FIGURE 19.1

FTP from the command line. This chapter shows how to do the same thing in a Windows program that uses graphical controls.

If you can't FTP into inprise.com, microsoft.com, ftp.download.com, or some site on the Internet, something is wrong with your Windows setup. You should clear up that problem first before tackling the material in this chapter. I provide some help in this regard in the section "Some Notes on Installing TCP/IP."

Figure 19.2 shows the program developed in this chapter, which works from inside Windows. The program, called FTP Pipeline, allows you to use standard Windows controls to make and maintain your connections. FTP Pipeline has provisions for copying multiple files from and to FTP sites, for deleting files and creating directories, and for using the mouse to navigate through directories.

Some Notes on Installing TCP/IP

In this section, I briefly discuss the process of setting up TCP/IP on a Windows 95/98 machine. The process is nearly identical on a Windows NT 4 machine, though the dialogs may have a slightly different name or appearance.

TCP/IP is the protocol of choice when you're working over the Internet. In fact, it is the backbone on which the Internet is built. It ships automatically with 32-bit Windows products. To see whether it is installed on your system, open the Control Panel and launch the Network applet. If you have TCP/IP installed, it will show up on the Configuration page of this applet, as shown in Figure 19.3. (On NT, it's the Protocols page.)

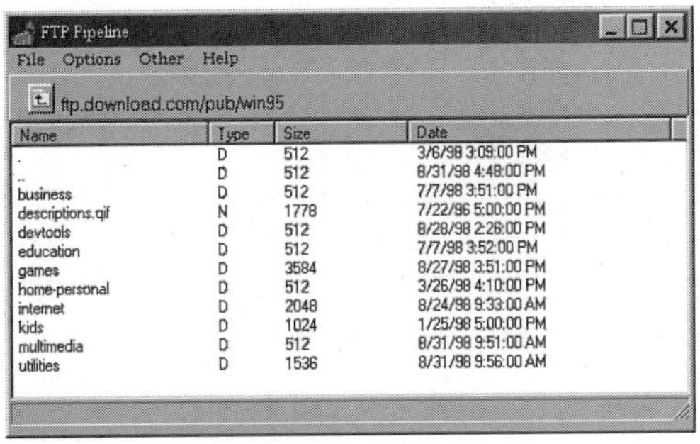

FIGURE 19.2

The main form for the FTP Pipeline program. Here, I'm connected to ftp.download.com *in the* public *directory.*

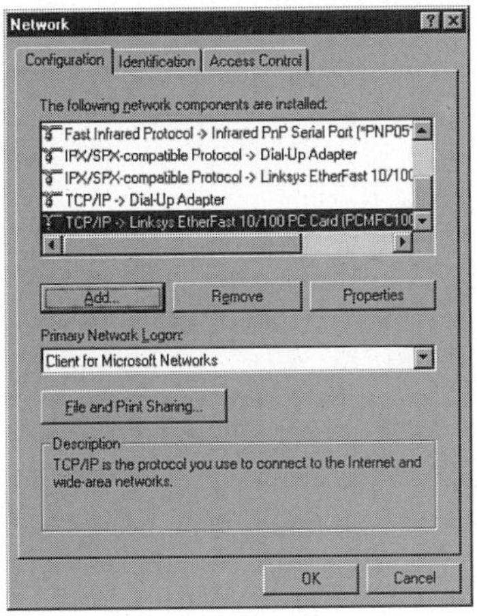

FIGURE 19.3

The TCP/IP information from the Control Panel on Windows 95/98.

If TCP is not installed, you should click the Add button on the Configuration page to bring up the Select Network Component Type dialog. Select Protocol from the list of drivers and again choose the Add button. In the Select Network Protocol dialog, choose Microsoft in the left-hand list box and TCP/IP in the right-hand list box. Windows will then install the necessary software, which may require the use of your Windows Install CD-ROM.

You will probably also have to specify an IP address, subnet mask, gateway, and DNS server. This information can be garnered from your network administrator. If you are working on a small local network with Windows machines that you have set up in your office or home, you can ignore the DNS server and can make up your own IP address, subnet mask, and gateway. For instance, the following numbers would do, as long as you are not connected to the real Internet and are talking only to the machines in your home or office:

```
IP Address: 192.168.0.2
Subnet mask: 255.255.255.0
Gateway: 192.168.0.1
```

The other machines on your network should have the same subnet and gateway, but the IP address should be unique. For instance, the next machine should have an IP address of 192.168.0.3, and then 192.168.0.4, and so on. Remember, don't make up your own numbers if you are connected to the real Internet. The IP address shown here has been set aside for people who do not want to communicate with the Internet. If you have an Internet connection, contact your network administrator or Internet service provider (ISP) for more information. Your network administrator should be completely familiar with this subject because it is as central to network computing as the idea of a method or function is to programming.

To check whether you are connected properly, open a DOS window and try to ping one of the machines in your network. Ping is a built-in application that ships with Windows 95/98 and Windows NT. If you installed TCP/IP as explained previously, ping will be set up on your machine.

To get started, you can try to ping yourself:

```
Ping 192.168.0.2
```

The following is a built-in address for referencing your own machine:

```
Ping 127.0.0.1
```

This number is aliased as `localhost`, so you can also type the following:

```
Ping localhost
```

Or you can try to ping one of the other machines in your network:

```
Ping 192.168.0.3
```

Here is the result of a successful session:

```
c:\4dos>ping 143.186.186.2
Pinging 143.186.186.2 with 32 bytes of data:
Reply from 143.186.186.2: bytes=32 time=55ms TTL=32
Reply from 143.186.186.2: bytes=32 time=1ms TTL=32
Reply from 143.186.186.2: bytes=32 time=1ms TTL=32
Reply from 143.186.186.2: bytes=32 time=1ms TTL=32
c:\4dos>
```

Here is the result of a failed session:

```
c:\4dos>ping 143.186.186.3
Pinging 143.186.186.3 with 32 bytes of data:
Request timed out.
Request timed out.
Request timed out.
Request timed out.
c:\4dos>
```

Failed sessions usually occur because your machine is not configured properly, the server is busy, or the wires connecting you to the network are not set up correctly. (For instance, you might have forgotten to plug into the network.)

If you are attached to the Internet and have a DNS server, you can try to ping one of the big servers on the Net:

```
Ping compuserve.com
```

The following is successful session:

```
c:\>ping compuserve.com
Pinging compuserve.com [149.174.207.12] with 32 bytes of data:
Reply from 149.174.207.12: bytes=32 time=298ms TTL=239
Reply from 149.174.207.12: bytes=32 time=280ms TTL=239
Reply from 149.174.207.12: bytes=32 time=333ms TTL=239
Reply from 149.174.207.12: bytes=32 time=332ms TTL=239
c:\>
```

Pinging `compuserve.com` is the same thing as pinging `149.174.207.12`. In fact, it's the job of the DNS server (the Domain Name Server) to resolve a human-readable name such as `compuserve.com` into an IP address.

If you want to create a human-readable IP address on a local office or home network, you can edit the HOSTS files that ship with Windows 95/98 or Windows NT. Under Windows 95/98, you will find a sample HOSTS file called `Hosts.sam` in your Windows directory. The file looks like this:

```
# Copyright (c) 1994 Microsoft Corp.
#
# This is a sample HOSTS file used by Microsoft TCP/IP for Chicago
#
# This file contains the mappings of IP addresses to host names. Each
# entry should be kept on an individual line. The IP address should
# be placed in the first column followed by the corresponding host name.
# The IP address and the host name should be separated by at least one
# space.
#
# Additionally, comments (such as these) may be inserted on individual
# lines or following the machine name denoted by a '#' symbol.
```

19

WinINet AND FTP

```
#
# For example:
#
#      102.54.94.97      rhino.acme.com      # source server
#       38.25.63.10      x.acme.com          # x client host
127.0.0.1 localhost
```

You can rename this file to HOSTS. with no extension and then add your own list of IP addresses to it:

```
192.168.0.3 MarysPC
192.168.0.4 MikesPC
```

After adding your list, you can ping the other machines with a human-readable name:

```
ping maryspc
```

FTP Using WinINet

Now you're ready to look at the code needed to use the WinINet DLL in an FTP session. This study will not be exhaustive, but it should help to get you up and running. The first fact you must know about this technology is that some of the functions in WinINet.pas return a pointer variable declared to be of type HINTERNET:

```
HINTERNET = Pointer;
```

This pointer acts as a handle to the various Internet services you employ. After retrieving the handle, you will pass it in as the first parameter to many of the other WinINet functions you call throughout the life of a single session.

You must remember to return the handle to the system when you're finished using it, usually by calling the WinINet function InternetCloseHandle:

```
function InternetCloseHandle(hInet: HINTERNET): BOOL; stdcall;
```

Just hearing this much information should tip you off to the fact that you should make use of OOP when using WinINet and should consider creating a component. The tip-off here is the need to perform housekeeping chores with pointers.

I no longer believe in trying to write complex cleanup code on-the-fly. Most of the time I remember to deallocate memory that I have allocated, and I almost always remember to allocate memory before trying to use it. However, computers aren't very considerate about human weaknesses, even infrequent weaknesses. You want to get these things right all the time, and "most of the time" just isn't good enough.

Possible solutions involve using a language such as Java or Visual Basic. These languages generally take allocation chores out of your hands. Of course, you pay a price for using tools of that kind, and it generally involves a severe performance penalty. If you want speed and flexibility, working in a language such as Object Pascal or C++ is always better.

Objects and components are the tools you can use to make Object Pascal safe. If you build an object properly, then it will always take care of chores such as allocating and deallocating memory for you. You get the job done right once, or find someone who has done it right once, and then you can reuse the object over and over without concern for petty housekeeping chores.

In particular, a good practice is to allocate memory in the constructor and deallocate memory in the destructor. I like to vary from this approach only when I allocate and deallocate memory inside the span of a single method.

What causes trouble is allocating memory in one routine other than the constructor and then planning to deallocate it in another routine other than the destructor. The problem isn't so much that you are unlikely to remember to deallocate the memory as that it is very hard to figure out what has gone wrong or even to know that something is wrong if you do make a mistake. On the other hand, if you follow the methodical scheme laid out in the beginning of this chapter, you can double-check your work relatively easily and make sure you got it right.

On occasions when you can't allocate memory in the constructor, try to provide a second routine with an obvious name such as `Initialize` for allocating memory. Then, if at all possible, deallocate the memory in the destructor. The most important goal is to be able to look in one place, the destructor, to make sure all your global pointers are freed.

The key point to absorb is that some developers, myself included, believe that almost any moderately complicated chore that involves allocating and deallocating memory is a strong candidate for wrapping in an object. Even better, put the code in a component; then there is almost no chance you will misuse it.

In the next few pages, you will learn how to create a component that wraps the FTP calls found in WinINet. I will present the WinINet calls to you at the same time I slowly construct the pieces of a component called `TMyFTP`. The listing for the control is too long to include in the book, but you can find it on the CD that accompanies this book in the `Units` directory. All the key methods from the control are quoted in full in the text.

Before explaining the WinINet-specific code in this component, I want to take one moment to glance at the constructor:

```
constructor TCCFtp.Create(AOwner: TComponent);
begin
  inherited Create(AOwner);
```

```
  FCurFiles := TStringList.Create;
  FFileList := TList.Create;
  Instance := Self;
end;
```

The constructor allocates memory for a TStringList and a TList. I then deallocate the
memory in the destructor. These lists will be used to hold the names of the files in the
directories visited by the FTP session. The record stored on the TList looks like this:

```
PFileInfo = ^TFileInfo;
TFileInfo = record
  Attribute: PChar;
  FileName: PChar;
  FileSize: Int64;
  FileTime: TDateTime;
end;
```

The TStringList version of the files in a directory is very easy to use because you can
just assign it to a TListBox.Items field. The list box will then contain a series of strings,
each one showing the names of the files, their sizes, dates, and types.

The TList version is more flexible than the TStringList version because it gives you
separate fields for each of the attributes of a file. You might want to use this kind of
structure if you are working with a TListView or TTreeView component. It is, however,
harder to use than the TStringList version.

The Instance variable shown in the last line of the Create method is used in the callback function that I will explain in the section "Creating a Callback." Callbacks can be
useful when you want the system to report back to you on the progress it is making while
completing a potentially time-consuming process.

NOTE

As you may recall from Chapters 6, "Creating Components: Part I," and 7,
"Creating Components: Part II," I usually preface the names of the components
I create with the letters CC, which are my initials. I do so to help avoid name col-
lisions. Delphi can have only one component with a particular name installed at
any one time. Because a TFTP component may already exist on the Component
Palette, I avoid a potentially annoying name collision by calling my component
TCCFtp.

FTP1.PAS has a dependency on CODEBOX.PAS. Both files are stored in the Units
directory on the CD-ROM that accompanies this book. FTP1.PAS needs the
D4UNLEASHED alias set up in the Database or SQL Explorer. The ReadMe file on the
CD discusses this alias at some length. Basically, it's a Paradox alias pointing to

the `Data` directory of the CD that accompanies this book. As always, you should make sure the source code and data are copied from the CD to your hard drive before trying to compile or run this program.

Using `InternetOpen`

To get a `WinINet` session started, you call `InternetOpen`:

```
function InternetOpen(
  lpszAgent: PChar;        // Name of app opening the session
  dwAccessType: DWORD;     // The access type, usually set to 0
  lpszProxy: PChar;        // For use in specifying a proxy, pass nil
  lpszProxyBypass: PChar;  // For use in specifying a proxy, pass NULL
  dwFlags: DWORD           // You can set up a callback here.
): HINTERNET; stdcall;
```

As shown in my brief comments, the first parameter is the name of the application opening the session. You can pass in any string you want in this parameter. For what it's worth, the Microsoft documentation states, "This name is used as the user agent in the HTTP protocol." The remaining parameters can be set to 0 or `nil`.

The following are some options for use in the `dwAccessType` parameter:

`LOCAL_INTERNET_ACCESS`	Connects only to local Internet sites
`GATEWAY_INTERNET_ACCESS`	Allows connections to any site on the Web
`CERN_PROXY_INTERNET_ACCESS`	Uses a CERN proxy to access the Web

The options appear like this in `WinINet.pas`:

```
{ access types for InternetOpen }
const
  INTERNET_OPEN_TYPE_PRECONFIG              = 0; { Use Registry config.}
  INTERNET_OPEN_TYPE_DIRECT                 = 1; { direct to net        }
  INTERNET_OPEN_TYPE_PROXY                  = 3; { via named proxy      }
  INTERNET_OPEN_TYPE_PRECONFIG_WITH_NO_AUTOPROXY =
➥4; { no java/script/INS }


{ old names for access types }

  PRE_CONFIG_INTERNET_ACCESS   = INTERNET_OPEN_TYPE_PRECONFIG;
  LOCAL_INTERNET_ACCESS        = INTERNET_OPEN_TYPE_DIRECT;
  GATEWAY_INTERNET_ACCESS      = 2;  { Internet via gateway }
  CERN_PROXY_INTERNET_ACCESS   = INTERNET_OPEN_TYPE_PROXY;
```

As you can see, passing in 0 means that you will use information already stored in the Registry.

19

WinINET AND FTP

The next two parameters for `InternetOpen` are involved with setting up a proxy server, a subject I do not cover in this book. The last parameter has only one possible flag:

```
INTERNET_FLAG_ASYNC
```

This chapter is not meant to be an exhaustive reference to WinINet, so I'm going to ask you to refer to the Microsoft documentation for additional information on this function.

The following is an example of a typical call to `InternetOpen`:

```
FINet := InternetOpen('Pipeline', 0, nil, nil, 0);
```

Using InternetConnect

After you open the session, the next step is to connect to the server using `InternetConnect`:

```
function InternetConnect(
  hInet: HINTERNET;                // Handle from InternetOpen
  lpszServerName: PChar;           // Server: e.g., www.borland.com
  nServerPort: INTERNET_PORT;      // Usually 0
  lpszUsername: PChar;             // Usually anonymous
  lpszPassword: PChar;             // Usually your email address
  dwService: DWORD;                // FTP, HTTP, or Gopher?
  dwFlags: DWORD;                  // Usually 0
  dwContext: DWORD                 // User-defined context number
                                   // for a callback
): HINTERNET; stdcall;
```

If you have made it this far in the chapter, you should have no trouble understanding the first five parameters to this function. All you need to do is read my short comments on each field. The main purpose of the first five parameters is to give you a chance to explain what server, password, and username you want to use.

These three self-explanatory and mutually exclusive flags can be passed in the `dwService` parameter:

```
INTERNET_SERVICE_FTP
INTERNET_SERVICE_GOPHER
INTERNET_SERVICE_HTTP
```

The following is the option for the `dwFlags` parameter:

```
INTERNET_CONNECT_FLAG_PASSIVE
```

This option is valid only if you passed `INTERNET_SERVICE_FTP` in the previous parameter. At this time, no other flags are valid for this parameter.

If the session succeeds, `InternetOpen` returns a valid pointer; otherwise, it returns `nil`. Remember that you will have to deallocate the return value later. I do so in the object's destructor.

My use of the `InternetConnect` method provides code that pops up a message explaining exactly what might have gone wrong in case of an error:

```
procedure TCCFtp.Connect(AppName: string);
var
  S: string;
begin
  FContext := ContextNum;
  FINet := InternetOpen(PChar(AppName), 0, nil, nil, 0);
  FftpHandle := InternetConnect(FINet, PChar(FServer), 0,
   PChar(FUserID), PChar(FPassWord),
   Internet_Service_Ftp, 0, FContext);
  if FFtpHandle = nil then begin
    S := 'Connection failed' + CR +
          'Server: ' + FServer + CR +
          'UserID: ' + FUserID + CR +
          'Password: ' + FPassword;
    raise FTPException.Create(S)
  end else begin
    SetUpNewDir;
  end;
end;
```

This function raises an exception in case of an error. As a result, it does not return a value. You don't have to concern yourself with whether the function succeeds because none of the code after the exception is raised will be executed. Your program itself won't end, but you will automatically be popped out of the current process and sent back to the message loop if something goes wrong. The only way to stop that process is to catch the exception. As you learned in Chapter 4, "Exception Handling," it is usually best not to try to handle the exception in a `try..except` block, but instead to let the exception-handling process resolve the problem for you automatically.

Notice that I have created an object called `FTPException`. Here is the entire declaration for the object:

```
FtpException = class(Exception);
```

I create this object only so you can know where the error came from. In other words, you can see that the type of the exception is `FTPException` and know immediately that it must have originated in the `Ftp1.pas` unit.

After the object is complete, you can start a session by simply calling the `Connect` method, passing in the name of your application as a parameter:

```
procedure TForm1.Connect1Click(Sender: TObject);
begin
  CCFTP1.Connect('MyAppName');
end;
```

Getting the Current Directory

After you are connected, you can call GetCurrentDirectory to retrieve the name of the current directory:

```
function TCCFtp.GetCurrentDirectory: string;
var
  Len: DWord;
  S: string;
begin
  Len := 0;
  ftpGetCurrentDirectory(FFTPHandle, PChar(S), Len);
  SetLength(S, Len);
  ftpGetCurrentDirectory(FFTPHandle, PChar(S), Len);
  Result := S;
end;
```

This function is declared as follows:

```
function FtpGetCurrentDirectory(
  hConnect: HINTERNET;               // handle from InternetConnect
  lpszCurrentDirectory: PChar;       // directory returned here
  var lpdwCurrentDirectory: DWORD    // buf size of 2nd parameter
): BOOL; stdcall;                    // True on success
```

Here, I have included my own comments on the value of each field.

If you set the last parameter to zero, WinINet will use this parameter to return the length of the directory string. You can then allocate memory for your string and call the function a second time to retrieve the directory name. This process is shown earlier in the GetCurrentDirectory method. Notice the call to SetLength. Delphi requires that you allocate memory for long strings in situations like this. The issue here is that the string will be assigned a value by the operating system, not inside your Delphi application. As a result, Delphi can't perform its usual surreptitious string allocations.

Finding Files in a Directory: Part I

The following function returns the currently available files in a particular directory:

```
function TCCFtp.FindFiles: TStringList;
var
  FindData: TWin32FindData;
  FindHandle: HInternet;
begin
  FCurFiles.Clear;

  FindHandle := FtpFindFirstFile(FFtphandle, '*.*', FindData, 0, 0);

  if FindHandle <> nil then begin
```

```
      FCurFiles.Add(GetFindDataStr(FindData));
      while InternetFindnextFile(FindHandle, @FindData) do
        FCurFiles.Add(GetFindDataStr(FindData));
      InternetCloseHandle(Findhandle);
      GetCurrentDirectory;
    end;

    Result := FCurFiles;
end;
```

The key WinINet functions to notice here are `FtpFindFirstFile`,
`InternetFindNextFile`, and `InternetCloseHandle`. You use these functions in a manner
similar to that employed when calling the Delphi functions `FindFirst`, `FindNext`, and
`FindClose`. In particular, you use `FtpFindFirstFile` to get the first file in a directory.
You then call `InternetFindNextFile` repeatedly until the function returns `False`. After
you finish the session, call `InternetCloseHandle` to inform the operating system that it
can deallocate the memory associated with this process. Calling `InternetCloseHandle` is
by no means optional, and in fact, forgetting to call it constitutes a fairly serious error.

Unlike the functions and structures mentioned in the preceding few paragraphs,
`TWin32FindData` is not defined in `WinINet.pas`, but instead can be found in
`Windows.pas`:

```
WIN32_FIND_DATAA = record
  dwFileAttributes: DWORD;
  ftCreationTime: TFileTime;
  ftLastAccessTime: TFileTime;
  ftLastWriteTime: TFileTime;
  nFileSizeHigh: DWORD;
  nFileSizeLow: DWORD;
  dwReserved0: DWORD;
  dwReserved1: DWORD;
  cFileName: array[0..MAX_PATH - 1] of AnsiChar;
  cAlternateFileName: array[0..13] of AnsiChar;
end;
```

This structure is designed to hold information about a file, such as its size, date and time
of creation, date and time of last access, and so on. Notes in the WinINet help file state
that not all the date and time fields will necessarily be filled out correctly by WinINet
routines. This is particularly true if you are accessing a UNIX box via FTP. I discuss the
`nFileSizeHigh` and `nFileSizeLow` fields in the next section.

`FindFiles` stores all information in a string list called `FCurFiles`. You can access the
`FCurFiles` list through the `TCCFtp` property called `CurFiles`. In your main program, you
can simply assign it to the items property of a list box. `FCurFiles` is created in the
object's constructor and destroyed in the destructor.

The following function returns a simple string designating what type of file is retrieved by a call to `FtpFindFirstFile` or `InternetFindNextFile`:

```
function GetFindDataStr(FindData: TWin32FindData): string;
var
  S: string;
  Temp: string;
  LocalFileTime: TFileTime;
  DosTime: Integer;
  DateTime: TDateTime;
  FileTimeStr: string;
  FileSize: Int64;
begin
  case FindData.dwFileAttributes of
    FILE_ATTRIBUTE_ARCHIVE: S := 'A';
    FILE_ATTRIBUTE_COMPRESSED: S := 'C';
    FILE_ATTRIBUTE_DIRECTORY: S := 'D';
    FILE_ATTRIBUTE_HIDDEN: S := 'H';
    FILE_ATTRIBUTE_NORMAL: S := 'N';
    FILE_ATTRIBUTE_READONLY: S := 'R';
    FILE_ATTRIBUTE_SYSTEM: S := 'S';
    FILE_ATTRIBUTE_TEMPORARY: S := 'T';
  else
    S := IntToStr(FindData.dwFileAttributes);
  end;
  S := S + GetDots(75);
  Move(FindData.CFilename[0], S[6], StrLen(FindData.CFileName));

  Int64Rec(FileSize).Lo := FindData.nFileSizeLow;
  Int64Rec(FileSize).Hi := FindData.nFileSizeHigh;
  Temp := IntToStr(FileSize);
  Move(Temp[1], S[25], Length(Temp));

  FileTimeToLocalFileTime(FindData.ftLastWriteTime, LocalFileTime);
  FileTimeToDosDateTime(LocalFileTime, LongRec(DosTime).Hi,
    LongRec(DosTime).Lo);
  DateTime := FileDateToDateTime(DosTime);
  FileTimeStr := DateTimeToStr(DateTime);
  Move(FileTimeStr[1], S[45], Length(FileTimeStr));

  Result := S;
end;
```

I use this information to create a simple string I can show to the user explaining the type of file currently under examination. For example, if I find a directory, the string might look like this:

```
D WINDOWS 0 4/01/98 19:38:00
```

If I find a file, the string might look like this:

```
F AUTOEXEC.BAT 706 7/22/98 15:48:00
```

The most difficult part of writing this function was converting the `TWin32FindData` date and time information into something that Delphi can use. To accomplish this feat, I used the Windows API functions `FileTimeToLocalFileTime` and `FileTimeToDosDateTime`.

> **NOTE**
>
> The `GetFindDataStr` routine takes some special steps to handle a case in which a file is larger than 4 billion bytes. I explain this issue in the next section, where I show you a second version of the routine.

Finding Files in a Directory: Part II

Retrieving the information about a directory as a string provides a simple method to get up and running, but it is probably not the right solution for a more professional program. Aiming a little higher, I rewrote the routines shown in the preceding section for those people who have the time to create a more polished program.

As I mentioned earlier, the key step was to store the information not in a single string, but in a record:

```
PFileInfo = ^TFileInfo;
TFileInfo = record
  Attribute: PChar;
  FileName: PChar;
  FileSize: Int64;
  FileTime: TDateTime;
end;
```

I stored these records on a TList object as follows:

```
function TCCFtp.FindFileRecs: TList;
var
  FindData: TWin32FindData;
  FindHandle: HInternet;
begin
  FindHandle := FtpFindFirstFile(FFtphandle, '*.*', FindData, 0, 0);
  EmptyList(FFileList);
  if FindHandle <> nil then begin
    FFileList.Add(GetFindDataRec(FindData));
    while InternetFindnextFile(FindHandle, @FindData) do
      FFileList.Add(GetFindDataRec(FindData));
    InternetCloseHandle(Findhandle);
    GetCurrentDirectory;
  end;
  Result := FFileList;
end;
```

19

WinINet and FTP

This is the same routine as the `FindFile` method in the preceding section, except that this time I store the information in a `PFileInfo` record:

```
function GetFindDataRec(FindData: TWin32FindData): PFileInfo;
var
  S: string;
  LocalFileTime: TFileTime;
  DosTime: Integer;
  FileInfo: PFileInfo;
begin
  GetMem(FileInfo, SizeOf(TFileInfo));
  case FindData.dwFileAttributes of
    FILE_ATTRIBUTE_ARCHIVE: S := 'A';
    FILE_ATTRIBUTE_COMPRESSED: S := 'C';
    FILE_ATTRIBUTE_DIRECTORY: S := 'D';
    FILE_ATTRIBUTE_HIDDEN: S := 'H';
    FILE_ATTRIBUTE_NORMAL: S := 'N';
    FILE_ATTRIBUTE_READONLY: S := 'R';
    FILE_ATTRIBUTE_SYSTEM: S := 'S';
    FILE_ATTRIBUTE_TEMPORARY: S := 'T';
  else
    S := IntToStr(FindData.dwFileAttributes);
  end;

  GetMem(FileInfo.Attribute, Length(S) + 1);
  StrCopy(FileInfo.Attribute, PChar(S));
  GetMem(FileInfo.FileName, StrLen(FindData.CFileName) + 1);
  StrCopy(FileInfo^.FileName, FindData.CFileName);
  Int64Rec(FileInfo^.FileSize).Lo := FindData.nFileSizeLow;
  Int64Rec(FileInfo^.FileSize).Hi := FindData.nFileSizeHigh;

  if FileTimeToLocalFileTime(FindData.ftLastWriteTime, LocalFileTime)
  ➡then
    FileTimeToDosDateTime(LocalFileTime, LongRec(DosTime).Hi,
      LongRec(DosTime).Lo);
  FileInfo^.FileTime := FileDateToDateTime(DosTime);

  Result := FileInfo;
end;
```

Again, you can see that I carefully tucked away key information about the filename, file size, and so on. Notice that the size of the file is stored in two fields: `nFileSizeLow` and `nFileSizeHigh`. Each is declared to be of type `DWORD`, which is in turn defined as a `LongWord`, or an unsigned 32-bit value.

To convert two `LongWords` into a single 64-bit value, I use an `Int64Rec` from the `SysUtils` unit:

```
Int64Rec = packed record
  Lo, Hi: DWORD;
end;
```

I can use this record to typecast the high and low words of an `Int64` to assign them the two halves of the file size as reported in the `TWin32FindData` structure. I assume that Windows returns these values in two `DWORDS` because no such thing as a 64-bit integer value existed when this record was created or because the Microsoft developers were afraid that most compilers could not handle a 64-bit type. At any rate, that restriction has disappeared over the years, and now this code exists only for historical reasons.

Retrieving a File: Part I

You can use the `FtpGetFile` function from `WinINet.pas` to retrieve a file via FTP:

```
BOOL FtpGetFile(
  IN HINTERNET hFtpSession,      // Returned by InternetConnect
  IN LPCTSTR lpszRemoteFile,     // File to get
  IN LPCTSTR lpszNewFile,        // Where to put it on your PC
  IN BOOL fFailIfExists,         // Overwrite existing files?
  IN DWORD dwFlagsAndAttributes, // File attribute-See CreateFile.
  IN DWORD dwFlags,              // Binary or ASCII transfer
  IN DWORD dwContext             // Usually zero
);                               // True on success
```

The following is an example of how to use this call:

```
function TCCFtp.GetFile(FTPFile, NewFile: string): Boolean;
var
  P: Pointer;
begin
  P := InternetSetStatusCallback(FFtpHandle, @MyCallBack);

  if P = Pointer(INTERNET_INVALID_STATUS_CALLBACK) then
    ShowMessage('No callback');

  Result := FtpGetFile(FFTPHandle, PChar(FTPFile), PChar(NewFile),
    False, File_Attribute_Normal, Ftp_Transfer_Type_Binary, ContextNum);

  if Result = False then
    raise Exception.Create('Copy Failed: ' + FtpFile);

  InternetSetStatusCallBack(FFtpHandle, nil);
end;
```

The function takes the handle to your session in the first parameter. The second and third parameters contain the local and remote versions of the name of the file you want to call. The next parameter defines whether you want to automatically overwrite existing copies of the file.

The following are the possible file attributes:

```
FILE_ATTRIBUTE_NORMAL.
FILE_ATTRIBUTE_ARCHIVE
```

19

WiNINET AND
FTP

```
FILE_ATTRIBUTE_COMPRESSED
FILE_ATTRIBUTE_HIDDEN
FILE_ATTRIBUTE_NORMAL
FILE_ATTRIBUTE_OFFLINE
FILE_ATTRIBUTE_READONLY
FILE_ATTRIBUTE_SYSTEM
FILE_ATTRIBUTE_TEMPORARY
```

I retrieved these values by looking up `CreateFile` in the Windows API help file. The `dwFlags` parameter can be set to either `FTP_TRANSFER_TYPE_BINARY` or `FTP_TRANSFER_TYPE_ASCII`.

The `FtpGetFile` method transfers a file for you in one fell swoop, as if it were a bird carrying something in its beak between point A and point B. This process is a bit like going to the DOS prompt and typing

```
Copy a:\FileA.Txt c:\FileA.txt.
```

The copy takes places simply and easily, but you get no feedback on what is happening. Because file transfers can take a long time, I try to give the user some feedback on what is happening by setting up a callback. I will discuss the callback in the next section.

The following is an example of how to call the `GetFile` method:

```
procedure TForm1.GetFile1Click(Sender: TObject);
var
  S: string;
  Item: TListItem;
begin
  Item := ListView1.Selected;
  S := Item.Caption;
  OpenDialog1.FileName := S;
  if OpenDialog1.Execute then
    CCFtp1.GetFile(S, OpenDialog1.FileName);
end;
```

This method retrieves the name of the file to copy from a list view. I will explain how to set up the list view at the end of this chapter, when I discuss the code for the `Pipeline` program. The `GetFile1Click` method gets the name of the file to write from a `TOpenDialog`. It then copies the file using the `TCCFtp1` component and its `GetFile` method.

Creating a Callback

As I'm sure you noticed, the `TCCFtp.GetFile` method begins and ends by setting up a callback. This callback receives notice when the handle for the transfer is created and destroyed, and it receives notices of progress at regular intervals during the actual file transfer.

The first thing you need to do is set up a method that will receive your callback:

```
procedure MyCallBack(Handle: HInternet; Context: DWord;
  Status: DWord; Info: Pointer; StatLen: DWord); stdcall;
var
  S: string;
begin
  case Status of
    INTERNET_STATUS_RESOLVING_NAME: S := 'Resolving';
    INTERNET_STATUS_NAME_RESOLVED: S := 'Resolved';
    INTERNET_STATUS_CONNECTING_TO_SERVER: S := 'Connecting to server';
    INTERNET_STATUS_CONNECTED_TO_SERVER: S:= 'Connected';
    INTERNET_STATUS_SENDING_REQUEST: S := 'Sending Request';
    INTERNET_STATUS_REQUEST_SENT: S := 'Request sent';
    INTERNET_STATUS_RECEIVING_RESPONSE: S := 'Receiving response';
    INTERNET_STATUS_RESPONSE_RECEIVED: S := 'Response received';
    INTERNET_STATUS_CTL_RESPONSE_RECEIVED: S := 'CTL Response received';
    INTERNET_STATUS_PREFETCH: S := 'Prefetch';
    INTERNET_STATUS_CLOSING_CONNECTION: S := 'Closing connection';
    INTERNET_STATUS_CONNECTION_CLOSED: S := 'Connection closed';
    INTERNET_STATUS_HANDLE_CREATED: S := 'Handle created';
    INTERNET_STATUS_HANDLE_CLOSING: S := 'Handle closing';
    INTERNET_STATUS_REQUEST_COMPLETE: S := 'Request complete';
    INTERNET_STATUS_REDIRECT: S := 'Status redirect';
    INTERNET_STATUS_INTERMEDIATE_RESPONSE: S := 'Intermediate response';
    INTERNET_STATUS_STATE_CHANGE: S := 'State change';
  else
    S := 'Unknown status';
  end;
  if Assigned(Instance) then
    if Assigned (Instance.OnStatus) then
      Instance.OnStatus(Instance, Context, S, Info, StatLen);
end;
```

Procedure `MyCallback` is of type `Internet_Status_Callback`, which is declared in `WinINet.pas` simply as a `TFarProc`. I have created the actual declaration for it here, using information from the WinINet help file. I translate the status into a string and then send it all to an event handler.

The declaration for the event handler is as follows:

```
TStatusEvent = procedure(Sender: TObject; Context: DWord;
  Status: string; Info: Pointer; StatLen: DWord) of object;
```

NOTE

Delphi programmers don't always declare a lot of their own events, so let me step you through the process. First, you declare the event method type, as

continues

19

WinINet and FTP

shown in the preceding statements. Then you make the event a property of the object as follows:

```
TCCFtp = class(TComponent)
  private
    ... // Code omitted here
    FOnStatus: TStatusEvent;
    ... // Code omitted here
  published
    property OnStatus: TStatusEvent read FOnStatus write FOnStatus;
end;
```

Now when the user drops a TCCFtp component on a form, he or she can turn to the Events page, double-click on the OnStatus event, and automatically create a method that looks like this:

```
procedure TForm1.CCFtp1Status(Sender: TObject; Context: Cardinal;
  Status: String; Info: Pointer; StatLen: Cardinal);
```

The last three lines of MyCallBack check to see whether the user has assigned a method response handler to the OnStatus event:

```
if Assigned(Instance) then
  if Assigned (Instance.OnStatus) then
    Instance.OnStatus(Instance, Context, S, Info, StatLen);
```

The Assigned method just checks to see whether a variable is nil. The Instance variable shown here is a pointer to the TCCFtp component, and it is created explicitly so that this method can get at the fields of the TCCFtp object. In particular, note that MyCallback is not a method, but just a standard function. I want it to have access to TCCFtp, so I assign the variable Instance to Self during the constructor of TCCFtp, as described earlier in this chapter.

The handler for the OnStatus event is going to be called when the handle for the file transfer is created and at various other times during the file transfer. In particular, it appears to be called after each 4,096 bytes of the file are successfully transferred.

Though I looked rather assiduously, I could not find any specification defining exactly when and how my callback was going to be called. So the best I can do for you here is show you the results that I got.

The following is a method handler for the OnStatus event:

```
procedure TForm1.CCFtp1Status(Sender: TObject; Context: Cardinal;
  Status: String; Info: Pointer; StatLen: Cardinal);
{$IFDEF DEBUG}
var
```

```
  F: TextFile;
  IAR: TInternetAsyncResult;
{$ENDIF}
begin
  {$IFDEF DEBUG}
  AssignFile(F, 'c:\PipeLine.txt');
  try
    Append(F);
  except
    ReWrite(F);
  end;
  if Info <> nil then
    Move(Info^, IAR, SizeOf(TInternetAsyncResult));
  WriteLn(F, 'Context: ', Context, ' Status: ', Status,
    ' Result: ', IAR.dwResult);
  CloseFile(F);
  {$ENDIF}
  StatusBar1.SimpleText := Status;
end;
```

This method writes the current status of the transfer to the program's status bar. Furthermore, if you define DEBUG, then it will create a written record of the transfer that looks something like this:

```
Context: 255 Status: Handle created Result: 13369360
Context: 255 Status: Sending Request Result: 7468436
Context: 255 Status: Request sent Result: 8
Context: 255 Status: Receiving response Result: 0
Context: 255 Status: Response received Result: 20
Context: 255 Status: Sending Request Result: 7468500
Context: 255 Status: Request sent Result: 26
Context: 255 Status: Receiving response Result: 980645236
Context: 255 Status: Response received Result: 30
Context: 255 Status: Sending Request Result: 46729952
Context: 255 Status: Request sent Result: 18
Context: 255 Status: Receiving response Result: 30
Context: 255 Status: Response received Result: 72
Context: 255 Status: Receiving response Result: 5177356
Context: 255 Status: Response received Result: 4096
Context: 255 Status: Receiving response Result: 4096
 ... // 4096 returned until all the file is transferred
Context: 255 Status: Receiving response Result: 4096
Context: 255 Status: Response received Result: 1404
Context: 255 Status: Receiving response Result: 1701978213
Context: 255 Status: Response received Result: 24
Context: 255 Status: Handle closing Result: 13369360
```

I'm afraid I can't really tell you very much about what this record means. Clearly, the most important part begins when the Result field gets set to 4096. Almost certainly, this number is a record of how many bytes are being transferred. In the quotation shown

19

WinINet AND FTP

here, I show this number only three times, but when transferring a large file, this one line may be repeated hundreds of times, presumably once for each 4,096 bytes that are transferred.

Clearly, you could check the size of the file you are going to transfer and then use the information shown here to record the progress of the transfer. However, it turns out that a second technique for transferring files is a little better documented. I will show that technique in the next section.

NOTE

I'm showing you two techniques for transferring files, but I do not mean to imply that I favor one technology over the other. I wish the callbacks for the FtpGetFile function were more clearly documented, but certainly the function is very easy to use, and with a little testing, you could confirm the validity of the technique I describe here for tracking the progress of the file transfer.

The FtpGetFile method ensures that the whole transfer is handled by the system. I hope that this means it is handled in the most reliable manner possible. The technique I show you in the next section is easy to implement but possibly not quite as robust, depending a little on how the boys and girls in Redmond actually implemented FtpGetFile. I have to confess, however, that you could probably feel pretty safe putting your money on the Redmondites in this matter.

After you have set up the callback function, you need to tell the system to call it. To do so, call InternetSetStatusCallback:

```
var
  P: Pointer;
begin
  P := InternetSetStatusCallback(FFtpHandle, @MyCallBack);
  if P = Pointer(INTERNET_INVALID_STATUS_CALLBACK) then
      ShowMessage('No callback');
  // Call FTPGetfile here
  InternetSetStatusCallBack(FFtpHandle, nil);
end;
```

This method passes in the handle to the session and the address of the callback to InternetSetStatusCallback. The callback is then made active. To deactivate it, I pass in the handle to the session and nil.

Setting up the callback for each step you take in the process of working with an FTP session is very important. In other words, you might be inclined to set up the callback during the constructor of the program and to set it back to `nil` in the destructor. However, this approach would cause a series of errors to occur. Rather than trying for one global callback, you need to set up a "new" callback for each step of the FTP session that you undertake. For instance, here I set up the callback for a file transfer. If I wanted to then get the current directory, I would have to set up the callback again. If I didn't, I would risk getting a series of nasty access violations.

The final, key point you need to grasp about callbacks is that they require you to specify the context for your session. In this control, I declare a global constant called `ContextNum` and set it to 255. I pass this number into the initialization of the entire session in the last parameter of `InternetConnect`:

```
FftpHandle := InternetConnect(FINet, PChar(FServer), 0,
    PChar(FUserID), PChar(FPassWord),
    Internet_Service_Ftp, 0, ContextNum);
```

When you call `FtpGetFile`, you need to pass this number in again as the last parameter, or your callback will not be called:

```
Result := FtpGetFile(FFTPHandle, PChar(FTPFile), PChar(NewFile),
  False, File_Attribute_Normal, Ftp_Transfer_Type_Binary, ContextNum);
```

This whole process of setting up and handling a callback is not difficult, but it is a bit involved and takes time to set up correctly. However, taking the time to create callbacks for all the key steps in this process will enable you to create a very professional-looking program that handles FTP file transfers gracefully.

Retrieving a File: Part II

WinINet provides a function called `InternetReadFile` that lets you transfer a file back and forth X number of bytes at a time. It enables you to tell the user exactly how many bytes you have transferred so far and how many more need to be transferred. In other words, it provides a 100 percent reliable means of obtaining the information you need to set up a progress bar. It is slightly more difficult to call than `FtpGetFile`, but it saves you the hassle of having to set up a callback, thereby making the method a bit easier to use than `FtpGetFile`.

The following method shows how to call `InternetReadFile`:

```
function TCCFtp.GetFile2(FTPFile: string; NewFile: string): Boolean;
const
  BufSize = 1000;
var
  FHandle: HInternet;
  Buffer: Pointer;
  NumRead: Cardinal;
```

19

WinINet AND FTP

```
      FileStream: TFileStream;
      TotalSent: Int64;
begin
   TotalSent := 0;
   FileStream := TFileStream.Create(NewFile, fmCreate);
   FHandle := FtpOpenFile(FFTPHandle, PChar(FTPFile), GENERIC_READ,
                          FTP_TRANSFER_TYPE_BINARY, 0);
   GetMem(Buffer, BufSize);
     if FHandle <> nil then begin
     repeat
       InternetReadFile(FHandle, Buffer, Bufsize, NumRead);
       if NumRead > 0 then
         FileStream.Write(Buffer^, NumRead);
       if Assigned(FOnTransfer) then begin
         TotalSent := TotalSent + NumRead;
         FOnTransfer(Self, NumRead, TotalSent);
       end;
     until NumRead < BufSize;
   end else
     ShowMessage('Failed');
   InternetCloseHandle(FHandle);
   FreeMem(Buffer, BufSize);
   FileStream.Free;
   Result := True;
end;
```

A call to `InternetReadFile` begins by first opening the file using `FtpOpenFile`:

```
function FtpOpenFile(
   hConnect: HINTERNET;    // Handle to the ftp session
   lpszFileName: PChar;    // File to open
   dwAccess: DWORD;        // GENERIC_READ or GENERIC_WRITE,
   dwFlags: DWORD;         // FTP_TRANSFER_TYPE_ASCII or
                           // FTP_TRANSFER_TYPE_BINARY
   dwContext: DWORD        // This is the context used for callbacks.
): HINTERNET; stdcall;
```

This method returns a handle to your file transfer session. You need this handle to call `InternetReadFile`. The `FtpOpenFile` method itself is straightforward, providing a means to specify the file you want to transfer, whether you want to read or write it, and whether you want to use ASCII or binary transfer. You can set up a callback if you want to trace the progress of opening the file.

The following is the declaration for `InternetReadFile`, along with my comments on each field:

```
function InternetReadFile(
   hFile: HINTERNET;                  // Handle FtpOpenFile
   lpBuffer: Pointer;                 // Pointer to buffer
   dwNumberOfBytesToRead: DWORD;      // Size of buffer
```

```
     var lpdwNumberOfBytesRead: DWORD      // returns number of bytes read
  ): BOOL; stdcall;                         // Failure or success
```

Again, this method is very straightforward. You just pass in the handle you got from `FtpOpenFile` and then a buffer that can hold a few bytes. Add information on the size of your buffer or on the amount of the buffer that you want to use. Because you normally want to use the whole buffer, this third parameter usually boils down to just being a report on the size of the buffer you created. The fourth parameter tells you how many bytes were actually read.

My implementation of this method works with a standard VCL file stream to write the bytes to disk on the client machine. Look at this paired-down version of the transfer method that focuses on the parts that use the `TFileStream` object:

```
FileStream := TFileStream.Create(NewFile, fmCreate);
repeat
  InternetReadFile(FHandle, Buffer, Bufsize, NumRead);
  if NumRead > 0 then
    FileStream.Write(Buffer^, NumRead);
until NumRead < BufSize;
FileStream.Free;
```

This method is straightforward because all the program needs to do is create the stream, call its `Write` method, and close the stream when done.

Once again, I have created an event handler that a program can subscribe to if it wants to trace the progress of the file transfer:

```
if Assigned(FOnTransfer) then begin
  TotalSent := TotalSent + NumRead;
  FOnTransfer(Self, NumRead, TotalSent);
end;
```

The following is the declaration for the `OnTransfer` method type:

```
TTransferEvent = procedure(Sender: TObject; BytesSent: Integer;
  TotalSent: Int64) of Object;
```

Each time the method is called, the client program is notified of how many bytes were sent in the last transfer and how many bytes have been sent total.

It seems to me rather unlikely that anything would ever go wrong using the techniques outlined in this section. However, as I mentioned earlier, `FtpGetFile` allows the system to handle all the details. All you have to do is set up the callback, do some mind reading to figure out how the callback is called, and then just sit back and wait while the transfer occurs. If you use `InternetReadFile`, you are involved in more of the nitty-gritty; therefore, you have to handle things such as full disks or writes to bad sectors, and so on.

19

WinINet and FTP

Sometimes you will want complete control over a file transfer, so `InternetReadFile` might be your only choice in those cases. In particular, I believe I will have to use `InternetReadFile` when I add the ability to cancel a file transfer to this program.

Sending Files to the Server (Simple Method)

When you're sending files to an NT site, remember that you probably don't have rights in the default FTP directory. Instead, you should change to another directory where your user has rights. You can usually configure what rights a particular user has on a server through the server-side tools provided for administrating user accounts.

This function copies a file to a server:

```
function TCCFtp.SendFile1(FTPFile, NewFile: string): Boolean;
const
  Size:DWord = 3000;
var
  Transfer: Bool;
  Error: DWord;
  S: string;
begin
  Transfer := FtpPutFile(FFTPHandle, PChar(FTPFile), PChar(NewFile),
    Ftp_Transfer_Type_Binary, 0);

  if not Transfer then begin
    Error := GetLastError;
    ShowMessage(Format('Error Number: %d. Hex: %x', [Error, Error]));
    SetLength(S, Size);
    if not InternetGetLastResponseInfo(Error, PChar(S), Size) then begin
      Error := GetLastError;
      ShowMessage(Format('Error Number: %d. Hex: %x', [Error, Error]));
    end;
    ShowMessage(Format('Error Number: %d. Hex: %x Info: %s',
      [Error, Error, S]));
  end else
    ShowMessage('Success');
  Result := Transfer;
end;
```

The core function looks like this:

```
Transfer := FtpPutFile(FFTPHandle, PChar(FTPFile), PChar(NewFile),
  Ftp_Transfer_Type_Binary, 0);
```

`FtpPutFile` takes the following:

- The session handle in the first parameter.
- The file to copy from your hard drive in the second parameter.

- The name the file will have on the server stored in the third parameter.
- Whether to conduct a binary or ASCII transfer in the fourth parameter.
- Information about the context of the transfer. You can usually set this parameter to zero.

The rest of the code in the `SendFile1` function is dedicated to error handling. Call `GetLastError` to retrieve the error code and call `InternetGetLastResponseInfo` to retrieve a human-readable description of the error.

You can set up a callback for this function as described in the analysis of the `FtpGetFile` function. Furthermore, the `TCCFtp` component shows a second method for sending files that uses `InternetReadFile`. However, this second method, called `SendFile2`, is nearly identical to `GetFile2`, so I will not describe it here.

Deleting Files

The act of deleting a file on a server is extremely simple:

```
procedure TCCFtp.DeleteFile(S: string);
begin
  if not FtpDeleteFile(FFtpHandle, PChar(S)) then
    raise FtpException.Create('Could not delete file');
end;
```

`FtpDeleteFile` takes a handle to the current FTP session in the first parameter and a string specifying the file to delete in the second parameter. I find it hard to imagine how the call could be much simpler.

Creating and Removing Directories

WinINet makes the process of creating and deleting directories trivial. One function is used for each task, and each takes the `HINTERNET` for your connection in the first parameter and the name of the directory you want to create or destroy in the second parameter:

```
function FtpCreateDirectory(
  hConnect: HINTERNET; // Handle to session
  lpszDirectory: PChar // Name of directory
): BOOL; stdcall;

function FtpRemoveDirectory(
  hConnect: HINTERNET; // Handle to session
  lpszDirectory: PChar // Name of directory
): BOOL; stdcall;
```

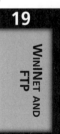

The following two simple functions demonstrate how to use the routines:

```
procedure TCCFtp.CreateDirectory(S: string);
begin
  if not FtpCreateDirectory(FFtpHandle, PChar(S)) then
    raise FtpException.Create('Could not create directory');
end;

procedure TCCFtp.DeleteDirectory(S: string);
begin
  if not FtpRemoveDirectory(FFtpHandle, PChar(S)) then
    raise Exception.Create('Could not remove directory');
end;
```

Assuming the presence of these routines, you can then write a function like the following to provide an interface with which the user can interact:

```
procedure TForm1.DeleteDirectory1Click(Sender: TObject);
var
  S: string;
  ListItem: TListItem;
begin
  ListItem := ListView1.Selected;
  S := ListItem.Caption;
  if InputQuery('Remove Directory', 'Directory Name', S) then begin
    CCFtp1.DeleteDirectory(S);
    MyFtp1NewDir(nil);
  end;
end;
```

This routine first retrieves the name of the directory you want to delete from a list view. The InputQuery function is then used to check with the user to be sure that this action is really what he or she wants to do. If the user replies in the affirmative, then the directory is deleted, and the new state of the directory is shown to the user. I explain the InputQuery routine at the end of this section of the chapter.

Here is a similar function used to create a directory:

```
procedure TForm1.CreateDirectory1Click(Sender: TObject);
var
  S: string;
begin
  S := '';
  if InputQuery('Create Directory', 'Directory Name', S) then begin
    CCFtp1.CreateDirectory(S);
    MyFtp1NewDir(nil);
  end;
end;
```

In this case, the VCL `InputQuery` dialog box is invoked. This function takes a title in the first parameter, a prompt in the second parameter, and the string you want the user to edit in the third parameter. If the user clicks OK in the dialog box, then the directory is created, and the user's view of the directory is refreshed by a call to `MyFtp1NewDir`.

Using the FTP Control in a Program

In the `Units` directory, the book's CD-ROM includes the complete code to the simple program that can set up an FTP session for you that was discussed earlier in the chapter. The program uses the `TCCFtp` component. As is, the control lets you use the Object Inspector to define the `RemoteServer`, `UserID`, and `Password`. The code also automatically returns the contents of the current remote directory in either a `TStringList` or a `TList` object. It enables you to perform file transfers, delete files, create and delete directories, and navigate through directories. You need to add a function to the program to let you enter in the name of a directory so that you can switch to directories that cannot be immediately browsed.

In Listing 19.1, you will find the main form of the program called `FTP Pipeline`. Listing 19.2 contains a dialog used to report the status of the program when transferring a file. Additional dialogs and forms are included with the complete source for the program found in the `Chap19\PipeLine` directory on the CD that comes with this book.

The main screen for the program is shown earlier in this chapter in Figure 19.2. A form in which users can select FTP connections is shown in Figure 19.4, and a form for transferring multiple files is shown in Figure 19.5.

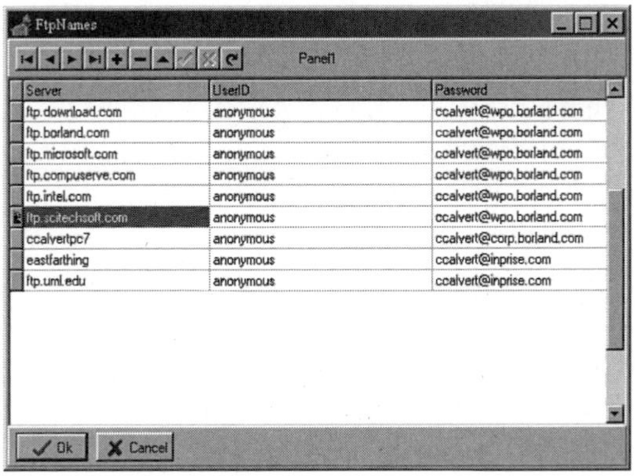

FIGURE 19.4

A form used by the FTP Pipeline program to allow users to select an FTP connection from a table.

FIGURE 19.5

*The File transfer
form downloading
several files from
a remote site.*

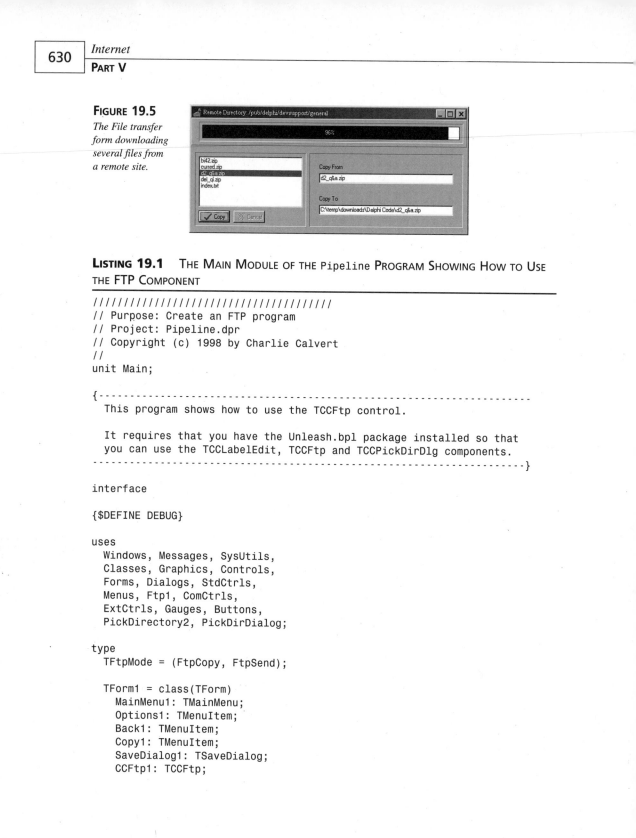

LISTING 19.1   THE MAIN MODULE OF THE Pipeline PROGRAM SHOWING HOW TO USE
THE FTP COMPONENT

```
///////////////////////////////////////////
// Purpose: Create an FTP program
// Project: Pipeline.dpr
// Copyright (c) 1998 by Charlie Calvert
//
unit Main;

{-------------------------------------------------------------
  This program shows how to use the TCCFtp control.

  It requires that you have the Unleash.bpl package installed so that
  you can use the TCCLabelEdit, TCCFtp and TCCPickDirDlg components.
  -------------------------------------------------------------}

interface

{$DEFINE DEBUG}

uses
  Windows, Messages, SysUtils,
  Classes, Graphics, Controls,
  Forms, Dialogs, StdCtrls,
  Menus, Ftp1, ComCtrls,
  ExtCtrls, Gauges, Buttons,
  PickDirectory2, PickDirDialog;

type
  TFtpMode = (FtpCopy, FtpSend);

  TForm1 = class(TForm)
    MainMenu1: TMainMenu;
    Options1: TMenuItem;
    Back1: TMenuItem;
    Copy1: TMenuItem;
    SaveDialog1: TSaveDialog;
    CCFtp1: TCCFtp;
```

```
    Splitter1: TSplitter;
    ListView1: TListView;
    Panel1: TPanel;
    File1: TMenuItem;
    Connect2: TMenuItem;
    N1: TMenuItem;
    Exit1: TMenuItem;
    N2: TMenuItem;
    Send1: TMenuItem;
    SpeedButton1: TSpeedButton;
    OpenDialog1: TOpenDialog;
    CCPickDirDlg1: TCCPickDirDlg;
    N3: TMenuItem;
    Refresh1: TMenuItem;
    StatusBar1: TStatusBar;
    Label1: TLabel;
    N4: TMenuItem;
    DeleteFile1: TMenuItem;
    CreateDirectory1: TMenuItem;
    DeleteDirectory1: TMenuItem;
    Help1: TMenuItem;
    Contents1: TMenuItem;
    N5: TMenuItem;
    About1: TMenuItem;
    MyWebSite1: TMenuItem;
    Other1: TMenuItem;
    GetFile1: TMenuItem;
    procedure About1Click(Sender: TObject);
    procedure Back1Click(Sender: TObject);
    procedure CCFtp1Status(Sender: TObject; Context: Cardinal;
      Status: String; Info: Pointer; StatLen: Cardinal);
    procedure CCFtp1Transfer(Sender: TObject; BytesSent: Integer;
      TotalSent: Int64);
    procedure Connect1Click(Sender: TObject);
    procedure Copy1Click(Sender: TObject);
    procedure CreateDirectory1Click(Sender: TObject);
    procedure DeleteDirectory1Click(Sender: TObject);
    procedure DeleteFile1Click(Sender: TObject);
    procedure FormShow(Sender: TObject);
    procedure GetFile1Click(Sender: TObject);
    procedure ListView1DblClick(Sender: TObject);
    procedure MyFtp1NewDir(Sender: TObject);
    procedure Send1Click(Sender: TObject);
  private
    { Private declarations }
    FTPMode: TFtpMode;
    FFolderBitmap: TBitmap;
    FFileBitmap: TBitmap;
  public
```

19

WinINet AND
FTP

continues

LISTING 19.1   CONTINUED

```
    { Public declarations }
  end;

var
  Form1: TForm1;

implementation

uses
  FtpNames1, CodeBox, ProgressDlg1,
  SendDlg1, AboutBox1, WinINet;

{$R *.DFM}

procedure TForm1.About1Click(Sender: TObject);
begin
  AboutBox.ShowModal;
end;

procedure TForm1.Back1Click(Sender: TObject);
begin
  CCFTP1.BackOneDir;
end;

procedure TForm1.CCFtp1Transfer(Sender: TObject; BytesSent: Integer;
  TotalSent: Int64);
begin
  if FtpMode = ftpCopy then
    ProgressDlg.Gauge1.Progress := TotalSent
  else
    SendDlg.Gauge1.Progress := TotalSent;
  Application.ProcessMessages;
end;

procedure TForm1.CCFtp1Status(Sender: TObject; Context: Cardinal;
  Status: String; Info: Pointer; StatLen: Cardinal);
{$IFDEF DEBUG}
var
  F: TextFile;
  IAR: TInternetAsyncResult;
{$ENDIF}
begin
  {$IFDEF DEBUG}
  AssignFile(F, 'c:\PipeLine.txt');
  try
    Append(F);
  except
    ReWrite(F);
  end;
```

```
  if Info <> nil then
    Move(Info^, IAR, SizeOf(TInternetAsyncResult));
  WriteLn(F, 'Context: ', Context, ' Status: ', Status,
    ' Result: ', IAR.dwResult);
  CloseFile(F);
  {$ENDIF}
  StatusBar1.SimpleText := Status;
end;

procedure TForm1.Connect1Click(Sender: TObject);
begin
  if FtpNames.GetConnectionData then begin
    Application.ProcessMessages;
    Screen.Cursor := crHourGlass;
    CCFtp1.Server := FtpNames.Server;
    CCFtp1.UserID := FtpNames.UserID;
    CCFtp1.Password := FtpNames.Password;
    CCFTP1.Connect('Pipeline');
    Screen.Cursor := crDefault;
  end;
end;

procedure TForm1.Copy1Click(Sender: TObject);
var
  S: string;
  SaveFile: string;
  Item: TListItem;
begin
  if ListView1.Selected = nil then
    ShowMessage('Select a file first')
  else if CCPickDirDlg1.Execute then begin
    FtpMode := FtpCopy;
    ProgressDlg.Run(ListView1, CCPickDirDlg1.Directory, CCFtp1.CurDir);
  end;
end;

procedure TForm1.CreateDirectory1Click(Sender: TObject);
var
  S: string;
begin
  S := '';
  if InputQuery('Create Directory', 'Directory Name', S) then begin
    CCFtp1.CreateDirectory(S);
    MyFtp1NewDir(nil);
  end;
end;

procedure TForm1.DeleteFile1Click(Sender: TObject);
var
```

19

WinINet and FTP

continues

LISTING 19.1 CONTINUED

```
    ListItem: TListItem;
    i: Integer;
begin
  ListItem := ListView1.Selected;
  if MessageBox(Handle, PChar('Delete selected files?'),
    'Delete File Dialog', MB_ICONQuestion or MB_YesNoCancel) =
    ➥IDYes then begin
    CCFtp1.DeleteFile(ListItem.Caption);
    for i := 1 to ListView1.SelCount - 1 do begin
      ListItem := ListView1.GetNextItem(ListItem, sdAll, [IsSelected]);
      CCFtp1.DeleteFile(ListItem.Caption);
    end;
    MyFtp1NewDir(nil);
  end;
end;

procedure TForm1.DeleteDirectory1Click(Sender: TObject);
var
  S: string;
  ListItem: TListItem;
begin
  ListItem := ListView1.Selected;
  S := ListItem.Caption;
  if InputQuery('Remove Directory', 'Directory Name', S) then begin
    CCFtp1.DeleteDirectory(S);
    MyFtp1NewDir(nil);
  end;
end;

procedure TForm1.FormShow(Sender: TObject);
begin
  Label1.Caption := 'Not connected.';
end;

procedure TForm1.GetFile1Click(Sender: TObject);
var
  S: string;
  Item: TListItem;
begin
  Item := ListView1.Selected;
  S := Item.Caption;
  OpenDialog1.FileName := S;
  if OpenDialog1.Execute then
    CCFtp1.GetFile(S, OpenDialog1.FileName);
end;

procedure TForm1.ListView1DblClick(Sender: TObject);
```

```
var
  ListItem: TListItem;
begin
  ListItem := ListView1.Selected;
  CCFTP1.ChangeDirExact(ListItem.Caption);
end;

procedure TForm1.MyFtp1NewDir(Sender: TObject);
var
  L: TList;
  ListItem: TListItem;
  i: Integer;
  FileInfo: PFileInfo;
begin
  L := CCFTP1.FindFileRecs;
  ListView1.Items.Clear;
  for i := 0 to L.Count - 1 do begin
    ListItem := ListView1.Items.Add;
    FileInfo := L.Items[i];
    ListItem.Caption := FileInfo.FileName;
    ListItem.SubItems.Add(FileInfo.Attribute);
    ListItem.SubItems.Add(IntToStr(FileInfo.FileSize));
    ListItem.SubItems.Add(DateTimeToStr(FileInfo.FileTime));
  end;
  Label1.Caption := FtpNames.Server + CCFtp1.CurDir;
end;

{------------------------------------------------------------------
  The Gauge uses a LongInt for the MaxValue field, so I can be
  working with a file that is too large. In that case I need
  to divide by 10, but haven't implemented that feature yet.
------------------------------------------------------------------}
procedure TForm1.Send1Click(Sender: TObject);
var
  Item: TListItem;
  Size: Int64;
  i: Integer;
begin
  if OpenDialog1.Execute then begin
    FtpMode := FtpSend;
    SendDlg.Run(OpenDialog1, CCFtp1.CurDir);
  end;
  MyFtp1NewDir(nil);
end;

end.
```

LISTING 19.2   A DIALOG USED TO HELP SEND FILES TO AN FTP SERVER

```
unit SendDlg1;

interface

uses
  Windows, Messages, SysUtils,
  Classes, Graphics, Controls,
  Forms, Dialogs, StdCtrls,
  LabelEdit, Buttons, Gauges,
  ExtCtrls;

type
  TSendDlg = class(TForm)
    Bevel1: TBevel;
    Bevel2: TBevel;
    Panel1: TPanel;
    Gauge1: TGauge;
    Bevel3: TBevel;
    BitBtn1: TBitBtn;
    CopyBtn: TBitBtn;
    CopyFromEdit: TCCLabelEdit;
    CopyToEdit: TCCLabelEdit;
    ListBox1: TListBox;
    procedure CopyBtnClick(Sender: TObject);
    procedure FormShow(Sender: TObject);
  private
    FCurDir: string;
    FOpenDialog: TOpenDialog;
    procedure SendMultipleFiles;
  public
    procedure Run(OpenDialog: TOpenDialog; CurDir: string);
  end;

var
  SendDlg: TSendDlg;

implementation

uses
  Main, CodeBox;

{$R *.DFM}

procedure TSendDlg.CopyBtnClick(Sender: TObject);
begin
  SendMultipleFiles;
  ShowMessage('Success!');
  Close;
end;
```

```
procedure TSendDlg.Run(OpenDialog: TOpenDialog; CurDir: string);
begin
  FOpenDialog := OpenDialog;
  Caption := 'Remote Directory: ' + CurDir;
  FCurDir := CurDir;
  ShowModal;
end;


procedure TSendDlg.FormShow(Sender: TObject);
var
  i: Integer;
begin
  ListBox1.Clear;
  for i := 0 to FOpenDialog.Files.Count - 1 do
    ListBox1.Items.Add(FOpenDialog.Files.Strings[i]);
end;

procedure TSendDlg.SendMultipleFiles;
var
  i: Integer;
  Size: Int64;
begin
  ListBox1.ItemIndex := 0;
  ListBox1.Update;
  for i := 0 to ListBox1.Items.Count - 1 do begin
    ListBox1.ItemIndex := i;
    Size := BigFileSize(ListBox1.Items.Strings[i]);
    Gauge1.MaxValue := Size; // MaxValue can't handle this big a number
    Gauge1.Progress := 0;
    Gauge1.Update;
    CopyFromEdit.EditText := ListBox1.Items.Strings[i];
    CopyToEdit.EditText :=
      FCurDir + ExtractFileName(ListBox1.Items.Strings[i]);
    Form1.CCFtp1.SendFile2(ExtractFileName(ListBox1.Items.Strings[i]),
      ListBox1.Items.Strings[i]);
  end;
end;

end.
```

19

WinINet AND
FTP

The TCCFtp component is used in the FTP Pipeline program found on the CD-ROM that comes with this book. To use the component, simply drop it on a form and then use the Object Inspector to fill in the Server, UserID, and Password properties. The component itself is part of the Unleash.bpk package that comes with the CD that accompanies this book. To learn more about installing components and packages, read Chapters 6 and 7.

Connecting to the Server

When `Pipeline` calls the `TCCFtp.Connect` function, it does so in a function that looks like this:

```
procedure TForm1.Connect1Click(Sender: TObject);
begin
  if FtpNames.GetConnectionData then begin
    Application.ProcessMessages;
    Screen.Cursor := crHourGlass;
    CCFtp1.Server := FtpNames.Server;
    CCFtp1.UserID := FtpNames.UserID;
    CCFtp1.Password := FtpNames.Password;
    CCFTP1.Connect('Pipeline');
    Screen.Cursor := crDefault;
  end;
end;
```

The `GetConnectionData` function makes sure that the `Server`, `UserID`, and `Password` properties are filled in correctly:

```
function TFtpNames.GetConnectionData: Boolean;
begin
  if (ShowModal() = mrOk) then begin
    FServer := FTPTableServer.Value;
    FUserID := FTPTableUserID.Value;
    FPassword := FTPTablePassword.Value;
    Result := TRUE;
  end else
    Result := False;
end;
```

This function is located in the program's data module. The program stores a list of previously used FTP sessions in a Paradox table. This table ensures that you don't have to retype the user ID, password, and server name for sites that you have already visited.

To improve `Pipeline`, create a second version of this program that uses a `TClientDataSet` instead of a Paradox table. This later system is more easily deployable because it does not tie you to the BDE. `TClientDataSet`, however, ships only with the client/server version of the product.

Notice that the `Connect` function sets the program's icon to an hourglass and calls `Application.ProcessMessages`. The program takes this step to be sure that the screen is properly redrawn before handing control over to the system. Especially if something goes wrong, the system could take a minute or more to return from a call to `InternetConnect`. While you're waiting for the system to either time out or resolve the call, you want the screen to look right, and you want to tell users that all is well and that they should sit tight.

Responding to `OnNewDir` Events

If you respond to the `OnNewDir` event, you can get a directory listing for the current FTP site mirrored in a `ListView` by writing the following lines of code:

```
procedure TForm1.MyFtp1NewDir(Sender: TObject);
var
  L: TList;
  ListItem: TListItem;
  i: Integer;
  FileInfo: PFileInfo;
begin
  L := CCFTP1.FindFileRecs;
  ListView1.Items.Clear;
  for i := 0 to L.Count - 1 do begin
    ListItem := ListView1.Items.Add;
    FileInfo := L.Items[i];
    ListItem.Caption := FileInfo.FileName;
    ListItem.SubItems.Add(FileInfo.Attribute);
    ListItem.SubItems.Add(IntToStr(FileInfo.FileSize));
    ListItem.SubItems.Add(DateTimeToStr(FileInfo.FileTime));
  end;
  Label1.Caption := FtpNames.Server + CCFtp1.CurDir;
end;
```

The `FindFileRecs` method called is explained in the section "Finding Files in a Directory: Part II." The rest of the code in the `MyFtp1NewDir` method just iterates through the files available in a directory and puts them in a list view.

To work with a list view, first drop a `TListView` component on a form. Then use the `Columns` property in the Object Inspector to give the list view four columns called Name, Type, Size, and Date. Finally, set the `ViewStyle` property of the `TListView` to `vsReport`.

To add items to the list in code, call the `Items.Add` method of a `TListView` control to create a new node in the list. Then give the node a caption by writing the following:

```
ListItem := ListView1.Items.Add;
ListItem.Caption := FileInfo.FileName;
```

You can then call the `SubItems.Add` method to fill in additional nodes on the item:

```
ListItem.SubItems.Add(FileInfo.Attribute);
ListItem.SubItems.Add(IntToStr(FileInfo.FileSize));
ListItem.SubItems.Add(DateTimeToStr(FileInfo.FileTime));
```

Changing Directories

After you have displayed a directory of files, the program still must provide a technique for letting the user change directories. One simple method is to respond to double-clicks on a directory name by changing into the selected directory:

```
procedure TForm1.ListView1DblClick(Sender: TObject);
var
  ListItem: TListItem;
begin
  ListItem := ListView1.Selected;
  Screen.Cursor := crHourGlass;
  CCFTP1.ChangeDirExact(ListItem.Caption);
  Screen.Cursor := crDefault;
end;
```

Notice that this code sets the program's cursor to an hourglass so that the user feels comfortable while waiting for the operation to complete.

The following is the code for `ChangeDirExact` from `TCCFtp` component:

```
function TCCFtp.ChangeDirExact(S: string): Boolean;
begin
  if S <> '' then
    FtpSetCurrentDirectory(FFTPHandle, PChar(S));
  Result := True;
  FindFiles;
  SetUpNewDir;
end;
```

This code calls the self-explanatory `FtpSetCurrentDirectory` method and then updates the file list to automatically show the contents of the new directory.

Techniques similar to this are used for creating directories, deleting directories, and for deleting files. However, the code is too trivial to explain in this text.

Tracking a File Transfer

When the user wants to copy or send files, the program provides the opportunity to transfer multiple files at one time. This capability allows you to update or download the contents of an entire directory with a single command.

To allow a user to select multiple files in a `TListView` control, set its `MultiSelect` property to `True`. To do the same thing in a `TOpenDialog`, set the `Options.ofMultiSelect` property to `True`.

I set up a separate dialog for both sending and receiving files. I do this in part to create a clean interface and in part because I can pop it up as a modal dialog, thereby ensuring that the user does not try to do anything else while the transfer is occurring.

The following is the code to set up the `TSendDlg` used to send files:

```
procedure TForm1.Send1Click(Sender: TObject);
var
  Item: TListItem;
```

```
    Size: Int64;
    i: Integer;
begin
  if OpenDialog1.Execute then begin
    FtpMode := FtpSend;
    SendDlg.Run(OpenDialog1, CCFtp1.CurDir);
  end;
  MyFtp1NewDir(nil);
end;
```

As you can see, I have opted to simply pass in the TOpenDialog object itself and leave it up to the SendDlg object to parse the user's selections:

```
procedure TSendDlg.FormShow(Sender: TObject);
var
  i: Integer;
begin
  ListBox1.Clear;
  for i := 0 to FOpenDialog.Files.Count - 1 do
    ListBox1.Items.Add(FOpenDialog.Files.Strings[i]);
end;

procedure TSendDlg.SendMultipleFiles;
var
  i: Integer;
  Size: Int64;
begin
  ListBox1.ItemIndex := 0;
  ListBox1.Update;
  for i := 0 to ListBox1.Items.Count - 1 do begin
    ListBox1.ItemIndex := i;
    Size := BigFileSize(ListBox1.Items.Strings[i]);
    Gauge1.MaxValue := Size; // MaxValue can't handle this big a number
    Gauge1.Progress := 0;
    Gauge1.Update;
    CopyFromEdit.EditText := ListBox1.Items.Strings[i];
    CopyToEdit.EditText :=
      FCurDir + ExtractFileName(ListBox1.Items.Strings[i]);
    Form1.CCFtp1.SendFile2(ExtractFileName(ListBox1.Items.Strings[i]),
      ListBox1.Items.Strings[i]);
  end;
end;
```

In the FormShow method, I iterate over the selected items in the OpenDialog, transferring their names to a list box. I do so just to give the user a second chance to be sure he or she has picked the files correctly. Also, I can point at each of the files in turn in the list box, helping the user to see which file is currently being transferred and how many more files need to be sent. The program could be improved by displaying the size of the files in the list box.

I actually do retrieve the size of each file so that I can accurately gauge the progress of the file transfer. To get information on the size of the file, I can't call the Delphi FileSize routine because it returns a 32-bit integer. Instead, I call a custom function called BigFileSize from the CodeBox unit:

```
function BigFileSize(FileName: string): Int64;
var
  hFile: THandle;
  LoSize, HighSize: DWORD;
begin
  if Length(FileName) = 0 then Exit;

  hFile := CreateFile(PChar(FileName), GENERIC_READ,
             FILE_SHARE_READ, nil, OPEN_EXISTING,
             FILE_FLAG_SEQUENTIAL_SCAN, 0);

  if (hFile = 0) then Exit;

  LoSize := GetFileSize(hFile, @HighSize);
  Int64Rec(Result).Lo := LoSize;
  Int64Rec(Result).Hi := HighSize;
  CloseHandle(hFile);
end;
```

This function calls the Windows API CreateFile routine to open the file. It then uses the Windows API GetFileSize routine to return the size of the file. Finally, the routine closes the file and returns its size with the help of the Int64Rec, as described earlier in the chapter.

The SendDlg object contains a TGauge control from the Samples page of the Component Palette. Using this control is not ideal because its 32-bit integer range won't allow it to handle really large numbers. However, it will do well enough for the purposes of this sample program.

With each iteration of the loop, I set the max value of the gauge to the size of the file and its current position to zero:

```
Size := BigFileSize(ListBox1.Items.Strings[i]);
Gauge1.MaxValue := Size; // MaxValue can't handle this big a number
Gauge1.Progress := 0;
Gauge1.Update;
```

I then inform the user explicitly where the file is being copied from and to:

```
CopyFromEdit.EditText := ListBox1.Items.Strings[i];
CopyToEdit.EditText :=
  FCurDir + ExtractFileName(ListBox1.Items.Strings[i]);
```

Finally, I send the file itself using the `SendFile2` routine from the `TCCFtp1` component:

```
Form1.CCFtp1.SendFile2(ExtractFileName(ListBox1.Items.Strings[i]),
  ListBox1.Items.Strings[i]);
```

While the file is being transferred, status messages are being sent to the main form of the program by the `TCCFtp` component. This process is explained earlier in the chapter in the section "Retrieving a File: Part II." The following routine handles the message after it is sent to the main form:

```
procedure TForm1.CCFtp1Transfer(Sender: TObject; BytesSent: Integer;
  TotalSent: Int64);
begin
  if FtpMode = ftpCopy then
    ProgressDlg.Gauge1.Progress := TotalSent
  else
    SendDlg.Gauge1.Progress := TotalSent;
  Application.ProcessMessages;
end;
```

As you can see, this trivial code first checks to see whether the user is in the `ProgressDlg` for copying files or the `SendDlg` for sending files. It then updates the gauge in the appropriate dialog. Because the range of the gauge has already been set, nothing else needs to be done, and the program only needs to pause to update the screen before exiting the method.

In this section, you have followed the whole process of sending a series of files to a remote server. I'm not going to take you through the same process for copying files from the server because it differs in only minor ways from the process shown here.

Summary

In general, the `Pipeline` program provides a fairly robust means of transferring files to and from a server via FTP. I developed the program because I needed a way to help maintain my AOL Web site. However, I use it for a wide range of purposes. As a rule, this kind of tool is now meant mostly for programmers and IS employees, as the hoi polloi now use Web browsers to initiate FTP transfers.

Someday I would like to create a second chapter or article showing how to use the HTTP services that are also part of WinINet. As you have seen, WinINet is a very elegantly designed interface and extremely easy to use. Taking advantage of its HTTP services by wrapping them in a component would be a useful service for many programming shops.

This chapter focuses mostly on WinINet and FTP. WinINet turns out to be a fairly simple API to use. It provides a great means for creating small, powerful objects that enable you

to access the key features of the Internet. You should visit Microsoft's Web site to download additional information about WinINet. Remember that the DLL that makes this all possible is called, naturally enough, `WinINet.DLL`. Starting with Windows NT 4, it ships with all versions of Windows and is freely available for distribution with your applications. It works fine on Windows 95 and ships with Windows 98.

Distributed
Programming

PART
VI

IN THIS PART

DCOM

CHAPTER 20

This chapter is about distributed computing. I want to show you how to build DCOM applications so that you can call objects that reside on other machines. I also want to show you how to use DCOM to create a lightweight, no-cost technology for distributing your databases across the network,

In Chapter 22, "ActiveForms," I will show how you can convert a Delphi form into a component you can use in a Web browser or in a second application such as VB or Visual C++. In that chapter, I show how active forms can be combined with the Borland MIDAS technology to create Web-based applications that break past what many folks think of as the limitations of HTML-based technology. I will also talk about how to distribute active forms, packages, and DLLs in CAB files.

You will find a number of sample programs in the current chapter. The included code shows you how to do the following:

- Create simple DCOM programs
- Build distributed database applications without using MIDAS
- Share the same set of data between multiple clients accessing a single server

You should look on the CD or my Web site to see whether I have an example of using COM callbacks to set up conversations between a server and client. If nothing is available, Binh Ly, of Brickhouse Systems, `www.brickhouse.com`, had an article on this topic in the *Delphi Informant*. You can download the code from `www.informant.com`.

COM and Distributed Architectures

It is now time to start looking at how DCOM actually performs its magic. I will begin by discussing exactly what the technology does and then describe how to use it on both Windows NT and Windows 95/98.

What Is DCOM?

The true power of COM is revealed when you remove it from the context of a single machine and spawn it on a network. DCOM is possibly the strongest and most mature of the available tools in this field, but it has historically been hampered by the fact that it worked primarily on 32-bit Windows operating systems. There, are however, ports of COM to UNIX, as discussed in the "COM on UNIX" section of Chapter 13, "Interfaces and the Basics of COM."

Distributed COM is important because it allows applications to talk to one another across a network. In particular, it allows you to share objects that reside on two separate machines. This means you can create an object in one application or DLL and then call the methods of that object from an application that resides on a different computer. When you are making these calls, the application server is loaded in the address space of the server machine and does not consume resources on the client. In particular, DCOM maps method calls down to standard RPC calls and then marshals the data passed as parameters between machines.

If you already understand COM, then you will find it trivial to learn about DCOM. DCOM works on the same principles as COM. Through the use of the `DComCnfg.exe` utility, you can convert existing COM objects into DCOM objects with no change to your code. Even without `DComCnfg.exe`, you should not have to change your server at all. Changes to your client involve only adding one or two lines of code.

Running DCOM Servers on Windows 95/98 and Windows NT

The hard part of DCOM is setting up your system correctly. After you get over the setup issues, everything else should be easy.

You can set up DCOM networks in three ways:

- DCOM servers and clients work very well between two Windows NT machines.
- If you are using Windows 98 as the client, then all works well as long as the server is running on an NT machine.
- You also can use a Windows 98 machine as a server, but the results are a bit more problematic, particularly when it comes to the all-important matter of security.

On the Windows NT side, you should install at least Service Pack 3 on a Windows NT 4 Server. Windows NT 5 is in beta as I write this chapter, so I will not comment on its impact on this issue at all. I have used DCOM on Windows 95 and 98, and all of what I am saying in this chapter works fine on both those operating systems.

DCOM is built into Windows 98 and NT, but as it ships, DCOM is not built into Windows 95. As a result, Windows 95 users should download DCOM95 from the site `http://www.microsoft.com/com/dcom95/download-f.htm`.

If you have trouble reaching this site, try removing the `download-f.htm` part of the URL.

> **NOTE**
>
> In this chapter, if I speak directly of Windows 98, what I am saying is also true of Windows 95, unless I explicitly say otherwise.

Your Windows 98 machine should probably be switched from the default Share Level to User Level access. You can do so via the Network applet found in the Control Panel.

User Level sharing requires that an NT Domain Server or some other source of user access lists be available on your network. With user level access, administrators of a server grant each user certain rights. In particular, the user can be granted the right to run one or more DCOM programs. If you give the user rights to run all DCOM programs on your server, then you are in effect giving the user the right to do whatever he or she wants on the server. A clever user who can run any DCOM server on your machine can probably figure out how to give himself or herself the right to do just about anything.

To help configure your server and its DCOM security levels, you can use the DComCnfg.exe application, shown in Figure 20.1. It comes with Windows 98 and Windows NT and is freely available from Microsoft's Web server at the same site as DCOM95. Note that after installing DCOM95 version 1.1, you will find a set of notes on using this tool beneath your Windows/System directory in a subdirectory called DCOM95.

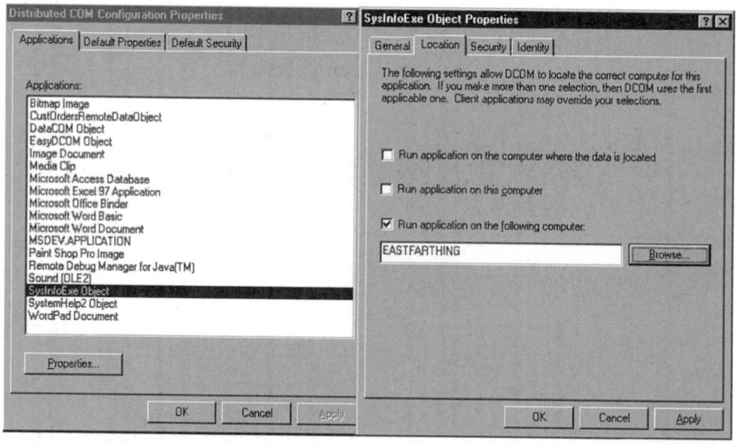

FIGURE 20.1

You can use the DComCnfg.exe utility to make remote servers appear as local servers so that you can call them with CreateOleObject.

NOTE

As I stated earlier, you can connect to a DCOM server on a Windows NT machine without switching to user access, but you will probably lose some security options when taking that route. I have been able to consistently connect to any Windows NT DCOM server, regardless of how the NT and 98 machines are configured, just by signing on to both my Windows 98 client and my Windows NT machine with the same username and password. Under those circumstances, I don't have to make any other changes to either Windows 95/98 or Windows NT, other than ensuring that DCOM is installed on Windows 95. In particular, you don't need a domain set up to run this way.

I hear that you can also avoid user level access by running `Dcomcnfg.exe` on the NT Server and selecting the Default security page and granting access to "Everyone." (I have not been able to run `Dcomcnfg.exe` on a Windows 98 machine if I did not have user level access selected.)

The problem with these kinds of solutions is that they aren't very practical if you care about security. What this all comes down to is that if you don't give a hoot about security, then you can forget about Domain Servers and user level access. If you want to maintain some kind of security, then you need to start reconfiguring your Windows 98 and Windows NT machines so they support Domain Servers. As Microsoft moves us into the age of NT 5, some of this may change, but the need for security will probably become only more pressing.

Here are some points to keep in mind:

- To convert a standard Windows NT 4 Server to a Domain Server requires a complete reinstallation.

- You cannot remotely launch an OLE server that resides on a Windows 98 machine. The process must be in memory before you can call it. This is not true of NT machines, which can automatically launch a server if it is not already in memory.

- On a Windows NT 4 machine, `DComCnfg.exe` is found by default in the `WinNt/System32` directory, whereas on a Windows 98 machine, it is found in the `Windows/System` directory.

- I like Domain Servers, and I have found that user level access on Windows 98 machines is much more powerful and convenient than share level access. However, it took awhile for me to understand how domains were set up. To understand them, you really need to get a book that describes how NT servers work.

Using Windows 98 as a DCOM Server

A Windows 98 box is crippled as a server. I prefer to have an NT machine act as my DCOM server and to let Windows 98 machines act only as clients. However, if you are determined to use a Windows 98 machine as a server, the following article describes in more depth how to set up a Windows 98 machine as a DCOM server:

`http://support.microsoft.com/support/kb/articles/q165/1/01.asp`

If you have trouble reaching this link, then look for Microsoft Article ID: Q165101, titled "HOWTO: Use Win95 as a DCOM Server."

20

DCOM

Additional related information is found at the following URL:

```
http://support.microsoft.com/support/kb/articles/q165/3/00.asp
```

If you have trouble reaching this link, then look for Microsoft Article ID: Q165300, titled "BUG: Remote COM Calls Fail Because RPCSS Is Not Started."

The inestimable Dan Miser has been maintaining a page that focuses on Windows 98 DCOM users:

```
http://www.execpc.com/~dmiser/dcom95.htm
```

Dan is one of the foremost experts in this field, and his many articles on the subject are worth seeking out. He is also one of those sainted individuals who contribute frequently to the Borland newsgroups, and going to the multitier forum at `http://www.inprise.com/newgroups` to get his opinion on various DCOM and distributed computing related questions is worthwhile. Certainly, if you are using DCOM on Windows 98, you should definitely check out Dan's page.

Much of the information regarding Windows 98 DCOM servers in the previously mentioned articles can be rather sketchily summarized as follows:

You may have to manually launch a program called `RPCSS.EXE` on Windows 98 machines that are acting as servers.

Change the following key in the Windows 98 Registry:

```
HKEY_LOCAL_MACHINE\Software\Microsoft\OLE\EnableRemoteConnect
```

When you are done, the value of the key should be set to Y. Failure to set this key results in the following error on the client:

```
Run-time error '429': ActiveX component can't create object
```

Dan Miser also suggests setting the following value in the same part of the Registry:

```
LegacyAuthenticationLevel = 1.
```

If all this information seems a bit confusing, it can be summarized even more succinctly: Microsoft apparently wants you to buy its server product if you want to use DCOM. As a result, any attempts to use Windows 98 machines as servers will prove to be little more than hacks. What the situation will be like under Windows NT 5 is not clear at the time of this writing, but you can check my Web sites (`http://users.aol.com/charliecal`, `http://www.borland.com/techvoyage`) for possible updates on this matter.

You might be a bit overwhelmed at first. The key point to grasp is that DCOM is really nothing more than a new capability added to the already existing COM technology. If you have working COM objects, then upgrading them to work with DCOM is trivial.

It is now time to start developing some DCOM clients and servers. You will find that Delphi makes this subject reasonably simple, so you should be able to master it in a fairly short time.

A Simple DCOM Client and Server

You learned in Chapter 15, "Creating COM Automation Servers and Clients," about the basics of the IDispatch interface. IDispatch is the COM object that makes OLE automation possible from many programming environments. Because of Delphi's support for dual interfaces, using IDispatch is the preferred way to make distributed programs. This section shows how to implement OLE automation that works not only between two applications, but also between two applications that reside on separate machines.

You will find that the server part of the client/server pair shown in the first simple example is just a standard automation server like the one you created in Chapter 15. As a result, my examination of it will be short. However, I'm going to say a few words about its creation, putting particular emphasis on the fact that its methods are declared to be of type safecall. As you will see, safecall plays an important role in Delphi DCOM applications.

Building the Server

To get started creating the server, do the same things you would when creating a simple automation server. A Delphi automation server is no different from a DCOM server. In particular, go to the File menu in Delphi and choose New, ActiveX, Automation Object, as shown in Figure 20.2.

FIGURE 20.2

Selecting the automation object from the Object Repository.

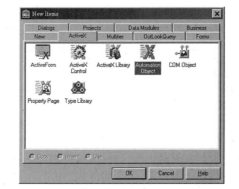

After selecting the Automation Object icon, you are presented with a dialog requesting the name of your server. In this case, you might call it the EasyDCOM. Leave everything else at the default value and then click the OK button.

20

DCOM

You should now save your work. I suggest saving `Unit2` as `MainIMPL.pas` and the main form as `MainServer.pas`. You can save the project itself as `EasyDCOMServer.dpr`.

If the Type Library Editor is not already visible, bring it up by choosing View, Type Library from the Delphi menu. Use the editor to create two methods: one called `GetName` and the other called `Square`. `GetName` returns a `WideString`, and `Square` takes two integers as parameters. The first parameter is called `InX`, and the second is an out parameter called `OutX`.

Understanding `Safecall`

You can view the IDL for your type library by selecting Export to IDL from the far right of the toolbar at the top of the Type Library Editor. If the toolbar is not visible, right-click on the Type Library Editor and select the Toolbar option. The following is the IDL for the two routines you created in the preceding section:

```
interface IEasyDCOM: IDispatch
{
  [id(0x00000001)]
  HRESULT _stdcall GetName([out, retval] BSTR * Value );
  [id(0x00000002)]
  HRESULT _stdcall Square([in] long InX, [out] long * OutX );
};  interface IEasyDCOMObject: IDispatch
```

When you click the Refresh button in the Type Library Editor, the following class is created for you automatically in `MainIMPL.pas`:

```
TEasyDCOM = class(TAutoObject, IEasyDCOM)
protected
  function GetName: WideString; safecall;
  procedure Square(InX: Integer; out OutX: Integer); safecall;
end;
```

Here, you can see the declarations for the two methods you declared in the Type Library Editor. Notice that they are both declared `safecall`. This means that they will each be wrapped inside a `try..except` block and will each surreptitiously return an `HResult`.

Consider the following method:

```
function TEasyDCOM.GetName: WideString;
begin
  Result := 'TEasyDCOM';
end;
```

This routine returns the string "`TEasyDCOM`". If the method were not declared `safecall`, it would look something like this:

```
function TEasyDCOM.GetName(out Name: WideString): HResult;
begin
```

```
  try
    Result := S_OK;
    Name := 'TEasyDCOM';
  except
    Result := E_UNEXPECTED
  end;
end;
```

This code wraps the entire functionality of your method inside a `try..except` block. If something goes wrong, then the exception will be suppressed and returned as an `HResult`. This approach is necessary because it would be a bad thing for an exception to be raised on a remote server. To understand why it is such a bad thing, consider the following somewhat whimsical scenario.

Suppose you are in Denver using the client part of a DCOM application. You pick an option from the program's menu and raise an exception on a server running in San Francisco. This exception caused the creation of a dialog reporting the error. Only this dialog appears not on your machine in Denver, but on the machine in San Francisco! To fix the problem, you would have to get on a plane, fly to San Francisco, click the OK button on the Exception dialog, fly back to Denver, and then continue running your program. To put it mildly, this scenario is less than optimal. As a result, Delphi automatically wraps all your methods in `try..except` blocks and suppresses any exceptions. Delphi will then automatically return the exception to the client and then reraise it. To help make your code easier to write, all this is hidden from you so that you think you are calling a normal function that returns a string. Behind the scenes, however, considerably more is going on.

Marshaling Data Between Machines

The `TEasyDCOMObject` exports two methods that `IDispatch` will automatically marshal for you across application or machine boundaries. Remember, some limits to the marshaling will be done for you by `IDispatch`. Here is a short list of commonly passed types, as discussed in Chapter 15:

Byte	Currency	Real	Double
Longint	Integer	Single	Smallint
AnsiString	WideString	TDateTime	Variant
OleVariant	WordBool	All interface types	

The apparent limitations created by the lack of support from `IDispatch` for custom types can be considerably mitigated by an intelligent use of `Variant` arrays, as described in Chapter 14, "TComObject, TTypedComObject, and Type Libraries)."

20

DCOM

The complete source for a simple `EasyDCOMServer` is shown in Listing 20.1 through Listing 20.3. You also can find the program on the CD-ROM that accompanies this book.

LISTING 20.1   THE IMPLEMENTATION FOR THE EasyDCOMServer

```
unit MainIMPL;

interface

uses
  ComObj, ActiveX, EasyDCOMServer_TLB;

type
  TEasyDCOM = class(TAutoObject, IEasyDCOM)
  protected
    function GetName: WideString; safecall;
    procedure Square(InX: Integer; out OutX: Integer); safecall;
  end;

implementation

uses ComServ;

function TEasyDCOM.GetName: WideString;
begin
  Result := 'TEasyDCOM';
end;

procedure TEasyDCOM.Square(InX: Integer; out OutX: Integer);
begin
  OutX := InX * InX;
end;

initialization
  TAutoObjectFactory.Create(ComServer, TEasyDCOM, Class_EasyDCOM,
    ciMultiInstance, tmApartment);
end.
```

LISTING 20.2   THE TYPE LIBRARY FOR THE EasyDCOMServer

```
unit EasyDCOMServer_TLB;

//******************************************************************** //
// WARNING                                                            //
// -------                                                            //
// The types declared in this file were generated from data read      //
// from a Type Library. If this type library is explicitly or         //
// indirectly (via another type library referring to this type        //
// library) reimported, or the 'Refresh' command of the Type Library  //
```

```
// Editor activated while editing the Type Library,                    //
// the contents of this file will be regenerated and all               //
// manual modifications will be lost.                                  //
//********************************************************************* //

// PASTLWTR : $Revision:   1.11.1.63  $
// File generated on 8/2/98 2:58:55 PM from Type Library
// described below.

//********************************************************************* //
// Type Lib: D:\SrcPas\Unleash4\Chap20\EasyDCOM\Server\
// EasyDCOMServer.tlb
// IID\LCID: {41E564E0-2A18-11D2-9CE8-006008928EEF}\0
// Helpfile:
// HelpString: EasyDCOMServer Library
// Version:    1.0
//********************************************************************* //

interface

uses Windows, ActiveX, Classes, Graphics, OleCtrls, StdVCL;

//********************************************************************* //
// GUIDS declared in the TypeLibrary. Following prefixes are used:     //
//    Type Libraries     : LIBID_xxxx                                  //
//    CoClasses          : CLASS_xxxx                                  //
//    DISPInterfaces     : DIID_xxxx                                   //
//    Non-DISP interfaces: IID_xxxx                                    //
//********************************************************************* //
const
  LIBID_EasyDCOMServer: TGUID = '{41E564E0-2A18-11D2-9CE8-006008928EEF}';
  IID_IEasyDCOM: TGUID = '{41E564E1-2A18-11D2-9CE8-006008928EEF}';
  CLASS_EasyDCOM: TGUID = '{41E564E3-2A18-11D2-9CE8-006008928EEF}';
type

//********************************************************************* //
// Forward declaration of interfaces defined in Type Library           //
//********************************************************************* //
  IEasyDCOM = interface;
  IEasyDCOMDisp = dispinterface;

//********************************************************************* //
// Declaration of CoClasses defined in Type Library                    //
// (NOTE: Here we map each CoClass to its Default Interface)           //
//********************************************************************* //
  EasyDCOM = IEasyDCOM;


//********************************************************************* //
// Interface: IEasyDCOM
```

continues

LISTING 20.2   CONTINUED

```
// Flags:     (4416) Dual OleAutomation Dispatchable
// GUID:      {41E564E1-2A18-11D2-9CE8-006008928EEF}
//******************************************************************** //
  IEasyDCOM = interface(IDispatch)
    ['{41E564E1-2A18-11D2-9CE8-006008928EEF}']
    function GetName: WideString; safecall;
    procedure Square(InX: Integer; out OutX: Integer); safecall;
  end;

//******************************************************************** //
// DispIntf:  IEasyDCOMDisp
// Flags:     (4416) Dual OleAutomation Dispatchable
// GUID:      {41E564E1-2A18-11D2-9CE8-006008928EEF}
//******************************************************************** //
  IEasyDCOMDisp = dispinterface
    ['{41E564E1-2A18-11D2-9CE8-006008928EEF}']
    function GetName: WideString; dispid 1;
    procedure Square(InX: Integer; out OutX: Integer); dispid 2;
  end;

  CoEasyDCOM = class
    class function Create: IEasyDCOM;
    class function CreateRemote(const MachineName: string): IEasyDCOM;
  end;

implementation

uses ComObj;

class function CoEasyDCOM.Create: IEasyDCOM;
begin
  Result := CreateComObject(CLASS_EasyDCOM) as IEasyDCOM;
end;

class function CoEasyDCOM.CreateRemote
➥(const MachineName: string): IEasyDCOM;
begin
  Result := CreateRemoteComObject
  ➥(MachineName, CLASS_EasyDCOM) as IEasyDCOM;
end;

end.
```

LISTING 20.3   THE MAIN FORM FILE FOR THE EasyDCOMServer

```
unit MainServer;

interface
```

```
uses
  Windows, Messages, SysUtils,
  Classes, Graphics, Controls,
  Forms, Dialogs, StdCtrls,
  ExtCtrls;

type
  TForm1 = class(TForm)
    Image1: TImage;
    Label1: TLabel;
  end;

var
  Form1: TForm1;

implementation

{$R *.DFM}

end.
```

This program is meant to be run from a client. As such, it has no controls on it and no public interface other than the OLE object itself. I do, however, give the main form a distinctive look, as shown in Figure 20.3.

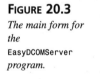

FIGURE 20.3

The main form for the
EasyDCOMServer
program.

Of course, there is no reason why a single program could not simultaneously have an OLE server interface and a set of standard controls. For instance, Word and Excel are OLE servers, but they are also standard applications run through a set of menus and other controls. It is not unusual for the same application to work as a server, a standard application, and as a client. In fact, many programmers will want to extend standard applications so that they also work as servers.

> **NOTE**
>
> After you have created the server, don't forget to register it by running it once. You must register the server, or the client will not be able to access it.
>
> Delphi automation objects will be registered repeatedly, whenever you run the program. If you move the application to a new location, you can register this change with the system by running it once. By doing so, you guarantee that the old information associated with your CLSID will be erased, and new information will be entered automatically. Registering a class ID multiple times does not mean that you will end up with multiple items in the Registry because each registration of a CLSID will overwrite the previous registration. All OLE servers worth their salt provide this service. For instance, Word and Excel update the Registry each time they are run.

Remember that this code will not work unless you first register the IEasyDCOM object with the system by running the server once.

Creating the DCOM Client

You can access the EasyDCOMServer with the EasyDCOMClient program found on the CD-ROM that accompanies this book. EasyDCOMClient will automatically launch the server program and then call its GetName and Square functions. This client program is much like the type of application you write in a standard Delphi automation program. However, I'm going to cover key aspects of its creation, emphasizing the parts of the program used to retrieve an object remotely rather than locally.

If you look at the main form for the program, as shown in Figure 20.4, you can see that it has several buttons. One is for launching the server remotely, and another is for launching it locally. In this chapter, I'm going to make short shrift of the techniques used to call the program locally and will focus instead on remote invocation of the server.

FIGURE 20.4

The main form for the GetDCOM application.

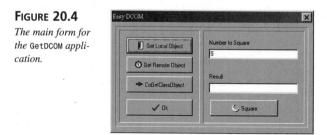

The source for the `EasyDCOMClient` program is shown in Listings 20.4 and 20.5. Note that it makes use of the `EasyDCOMServer_TLB.pas` file from the server. You can do one of three things to bring this file into your program:

- Add the file to your uses clause, thereby linking it into your program directly from the directory where the server resides. To do so, choose Project, Options, turn to the Directories/Conditionals page, and add the `..\Server` directory to your search path.

- Copy the file into your current directory or a local directory on your search path.

- Re-create the file by choosing Project, Import Type Library and importing the TLB file from your server.

LISTING 20.4 THE MAIN FORM FOR THE OLE CLIENT APPLICATION CALLED
`EasyDCOMClient`

```
//////////////////////////////////////////
// Purpose: DCOM Client example
// Project: EasyDCOMClient
// Copyright (c) 1998 by Charlie Calvert
//
unit MainClient;

{-------------------------------------------------------------------
  This program provides three ways to connect to server:
    * Connect locally
    * Connect via the VCL
    * Connect by calling CoGetClassObject
  After you are connected, you can call the Square method on the server.
  -----------------------------------------------------------------}

interface

uses
  Windows, Messages, SysUtils,
  Classes, Graphics, Controls,
  Forms, Dialogs, StdCtrls,
  Buttons, EasyDCOMServer_TLB, ExtCtrls,
  LabelEdit;

type
  TForm2 = class(TForm)
    GetLocalObjectBtn: TBitBtn;
    GetRemoteObjectBtn: TBitBtn;
    SquareBtn: TBitBtn;
    CCLabelEdit1: TCCLabelEdit;
    CCLabelEdit2: TCCLabelEdit;
```

continues

LISTING 20.4   CONTINUED

```
    Bevel1: TBevel;
    CoGetClassBtn: TBitBtn;
    Bevel2: TBevel;
    Bevel3: TBevel;
    OkBtn: TBitBtn;
    procedure GetLocalObjectBtnClick(Sender: TObject);
    procedure GetRemoteObjectBtnClick(Sender: TObject);
    procedure SquareBtnClick(Sender: TObject);
    procedure CoGetClassBtnClick(Sender: TObject);
    procedure OkBtnClick(Sender: TObject);
  private
    { Private declarations }
    FEasyDCOM: IEasyDCOM;
  public
    { Public declarations }
  end;

var
  Form2: TForm2;

implementation

uses
  ActiveX, ComObj; // For IClassFactory in CoGetClassObject call

{$R *.DFM}

procedure TForm2.GetLocalObjectBtnClick(Sender: TObject);
var
  S: WideString;
begin
  FEasyDCOM := CoEasyDCOM.Create();
  S := FEasyDCOM.GetName;
  Caption := ' Connected to: ' + S;
end;

procedure TForm2.GetRemoteObjectBtnClick(Sender: TObject);
var
  ServerName: string;
  S: string;
begin
  if (InputQuery('Enter Server Name', 'Server Name', ServerName))
  ➥then begin
    Screen.Cursor := crHourGlass;
    FEasyDCOM := CoEasyDCOM.CreateRemote(WideString(ServerName));
    Screen.Cursor := crDefault;
    S := FEasyDCOM.GetName;
    Caption := ' Connected to: ' + S;
  end;
```

```
end;

procedure TForm2.SquareBtnClick(Sender: TObject);
var
  Value, Num: Integer;
begin
  try
    Num := StrToInt(CCLabelEdit1.EditText);
    if FEasyDCOM <> nil then begin
      FEasyDCOM.Square(Num, Value);
      CCLabelEdit2.EditText := IntToStr(Value);
    end;
  except
   on E:Exception do
     ShowMessage(E.Message);
  end;
end;

procedure TForm2.CoGetClassBtnClick(Sender: TObject);
var
  hr: HResult;
  ClassFactory: IClassFactory;
  CoServerInfo: TCoServerInfo;
  ServerName: string;
  AServerName: WideString;
begin
  ServerName := '';
  if (InputQuery('Enter Server Name', 'Server Name', ServerName))
  ➥then begin
    ClassFactory := nil;
    FillChar(CoServerInfo, sizeof(CoServerInfo), 0);
    AServerName := ServerName;
    CoServerInfo.pwszName := PWideChar(AServerName);

    hr := CoGetClassObject(CLASS_EasyDCOM, CLSCTX_REMOTE_SERVER,
      @CoServerInfo, IClassFactory, ClassFactory);
    OleCheck(hr);
    if ClassFactory = nil then
      ShowMessage('no classfactory');

    hr := ClassFactory.CreateInstance(nil, IID_IEasyDCOM, FEasyDCOM);
    if Succeeded(hr) then begin
      ClassFactory := nil;
      Caption := ' Connected to: ' + FEasyDCOM.GetName;
    end else
      ShowMessage('No object');
  end;
end;

procedure TForm2.OkBtnClick(Sender: TObject);
```

20

DCOM

continues

LISTING 20.4   CONTINUED

```
begin
  Close;
end;

end.
```

When you run this program, you get the option of three different methods for accessing the server. The first lets you access the object locally, the second lets you use the VCL to access it remotely, and the third lets you use the Windows API to access it remotely.

If you want to create an instance of the object locally, just call the predeclared CoEasyDCOM constructor from the EasyDCOMServer_TLB file:

```
procedure TForm2.GetLocalObjectBtnClick(Sender: TObject);
var
  S: WideString;
begin
  FEasyDCOM := CoEasyDCOM.Create();
  S := FEasyDCOM.GetName;
  Caption := ' Connected to: ' + S;
end;
```

I'm not going to discuss this technology because it was covered in Chapter 15.

NOTE

By using DComCnfg.exe, you can configure your machine so that it will launch a remote program using the same commands that you use to launch a local program. In particular, you can use Dcomcnfg.exe to insert certain symbols in the Registry that will cause Windows to look for a program not on the local machine, but on a remote machine.

To get started, launch DComCnfg.exe. Select the program you want to run. If it does not appear in the list on the Applications page, then run the server once on your current machine so that it is registered. Double-click on the application once you find it on the Applications page. Turn to the Location page, select Run Application on the Following Computer, and enter the name of the computer. Now the program will be launched on that remote computer even if you use the standard COM calls for launching it locally.

The following VCL technology is used for creating the object remotely:

```
procedure TForm2.GetRemoteObjectBtnClick(Sender: TObject);
var
  ServerName: string;
```

```
    S: string;
begin
  if (InputQuery('Enter Server Name', 'Server Name', ServerName))
  ➥then begin
    Screen.Cursor := crHourGlass;
    FEasyDCOM := CoEasyDCOM.CreateRemote(WideString(ServerName));
    Screen.Cursor := crDefault;
    S := FEasyDCOM.GetName;
    Caption := ' Connected to: ' + S;
  end;
end;
```

In this case, you are once again calling one of the class methods from the premade proxy objects in the EasyDCOMServer_TLB file. These classes are very easy to use, but you should step through them at least once to see how they work. I will explain what happens when you call this function in the next two subsections. Note, however, that the CreateRemote function initializes a field of TForm2 called FEasyDCOM, which is of type IEasyDCOM.

CoCreateInstanceEx

When you call CreateRemote, you are mapped to the following function in the ComObj.pas file in the include\vcl directory:

```
const ClassID: TGUID): IUnknown;
const
  LocalFlags =
    CLSCTX_LOCAL_SERVER or CLSCTX_REMOTE_SERVER or CLSCTX_INPROC_SERVER;
  RemoteFlags = CLSCTX_REMOTE_SERVER;
var
  MQI: TMultiQI;
  ServerInfo: TCoServerInfo;
  IID_IUnknown: TGuid;
  Flags, Size: DWORD;
  LocalMachine: array [0..MAX_COMPUTERNAME_LENGTH] of char;
begin
  if @CoCreateInstanceEx = nil then
    raise Exception.Create(SDCOMNotInstalled);
  FillChar(ServerInfo, sizeof(ServerInfo), 0);
  ServerInfo.pwszName := PWideChar(MachineName);
  IID_IUnknown := IUnknown;
  MQI.IID := @IID_IUnknown;
  MQI.itf := nil;
  MQI.hr := 0;
  { If a MachineName is specified check to see if it is the local
    machine. If it isn't, do not allow LocalServers to be used. }
  if Length(MachineName) > 0 then
  begin
    Size := Sizeof(LocalMachine);   // Win95 is hypersensitive to size
```

```
   if GetComputerName(LocalMachine, Size) and
     (AnsiCompareText(LocalMachine, MachineName) = 0) then
    Flags := LocalFlags else
    Flags := RemoteFlags;
  end else
   Flags := LocalFlags;
  OleCheck(CoCreateInstanceEx
  ➥(ClassID, nil, Flags, @ServerInfo, 1, @MQI));
  OleCheck(MQI.HR);
  Result := MQI.itf;
end;
```

CoCreateInstanceEx is a Windows API routine similar to the CoCreateInstance function, discussed at the end of Chapter 15:

```
HRESULT CoCreateInstanceEx(
    const clsid: TCLSID;        //CLSID of the object to be created
    unkOuter: IUnknown;  //If part of an aggregate, controlling IUnknown
    dwClsCtx: LongInt;          //CLSCTX values
    ServerInfo: PCoServerInfo;
        //Machine where object is to be instantiated
    DwCount: LongInt;       //Number of MULTI_QI structures in rgmqResults
    RgmqResults: PMultiQIArray //Array of MULTI_QI structures
    );
```

The last three parameters are the ones that differ from CoCreateInstance. The COSERVERINFO structure looks like this:

```
_COSERVERINFO = record
  dwReserved1: Longint;
  pwszName: LPWSTR;
  pAuthInfo: Pointer;
  dwReserved2: Longint;
end;
TCoServerInfo = _COSERVERINFO;
```

The first field of this record is just a version check field that should contain the size of the TCoServerInfo record. The second parameter contains a Unicode string that has the name of the server or its IP address embedded in it. If you need to declare a variable for this field, then it should be a WideString. The pAuthInfo field has to do with security and will not be covered in this book.

The next parameter in CoCreateInstanceEx is a digit that specifies the number of items in the array that makes up the last parameter. This last parameter consists of an array of MULTI_QI structures:

```
PMultiQI = ^TMultiQI;
tagMULTI_QI = record
  IID: PIID;
  Itf: IUnknown;
```

```
    hr: HResult;
end;
TMultiQI = tagMULTI_QI;
MULTI_QI = TMultiQI;
```

A `MULTI_QI` structure takes the place of the last two parameters to `CoCreateInstance` that have been omitted from `CoCreateInstanceEx`. In particular, they give you a place to declare the `GUID` of the interface you want to retrieve and a pointer that can contain the interface when you retrieve it. The `HResult` field returns a report on any errors that might occur. Needless to say, if `HResult` is set to 0, then you know all went well. You can test `HResult` by passing it to the `SUCCEEDED` macro or the `OleCheck` function from the `ComObj` unit.

If you want to retrieve multiple interfaces in a single call to `CoCreateInstanceEx`, then you just pass in an array filled with multiple `MULTI_QI` structures. This can be useful because each trip between a client and a server can be time consuming, so the ability to retrieve multiple interfaces at one stroke can be a significant optimization in a multitier application. (Apparently, `MULTI_QI` stands for "Multiple `QueryInterfaces`," as in "You can automatically make multiple calls to `QueryInterface` by filling in this structure.")

You don't really have to understand `CoCreateInstanceEx` to create an instance of a remote server. However, if you understand this function then your life will probably be simpler.

CoGetClassObject

Unless you make changes to the Registry either manually or by using `DComCnfg.exe`, you cannot use `CoCreateInstance` to create a remote object. However, an alternative to `CoCreateInstanceEx` for creating remote objects is a call to `CoGetClassObject`. This routine has long been a part of COM, but it has been altered slightly to support DCOM. Here is how the routine was previously declared and the way that it is still declared in the version of `ActiveX.pas` that ships with Delphi 4:

```
function CoGetClassObject(
  const clsid: TCLSID;   // The Class ID of the object you want
  dwClsContext: Longint; // In process, local or remote server?
  pvReserved: Pointer;   // Previously reserved, now used for CoServerInfo
  const iid: TIID;       // Usually IID_IClassFactory
  out pv                 // Where the class factory is returned
): HResult;
```

The function returns an `HResult` variable containing information on the outcome of the call. If the `HResult` is set to zero, then the call succeeded; most other values represent an error in the form of a number. You can retrieve a human readable string describing the error by passing that number to a VCL function called `OleCheck`.

Note that the GUID that you pass in for the second parameter of this function is the class ID for your object, not the IID of the interface that you ultimately want to retrieve. This class ID is declared in your XXX_TLB.pas file. The other GUID that you pass to this function, the one in the fourth parameter, is again not the IID of your interface. Instead, it is almost always IID_IClassFactory. In Object Pascal, you don't pass in IID_IClassFactory directly, but you can access the equivalent value by just passing in IClassFactory. After you get the ClassFactory back, then you can use it to retrieve the interface you are seeking.

CoGetClassObject looks like this now, and it probably should have been declared this way in Delphi 4:

```
STDAPI CoGetClassObject(
    const clsid: TCLSID;          // The ID of the object you want
    dwClsContext: Longint;        // In process, local or remote server?
    ServerInfo: PCoServerInfo;
        //Pointer to machine where object is located
    const iid: TIID;              // Usually IID_IClassFactory
    out pv
);
```

The third parameter to CoGetClassObject was previously reserved. It is now the place where you can pass in the name of the server you want to access in a CoServerInfo structure, as discussed in the preceding section. The server is usually designated with either a human-readable string or a literal IP address, such as 143.186.149.111. You pass in the IP address in the form of a string. That is, don't try to pass a number; just put the IP address in quotation marks as a string.

The call to CoGetClassObject retrieves a ClassFactory. After you have the ClassFactory back from the server, then you can use it to retrieve an instance of the object you want to call. In particular, the IClassFactory interface supports a method called CreateInstance that requests the GUID for the interface that you want to retrieve.

A call to CoGetClassObject looks like this in action:

```
procedure TForm2.CoGetClassBtnClick(Sender: TObject);
var
  hr: HResult;
  ClassFactory: IClassFactory;
  CoServerInfo: TCoServerInfo;
  ServerName: string;
  AServerName: WideString;
begin
  ServerName := '';
  if (InputQuery('Enter Server Name', 'Server Name', ServerName))
  ➥then begin
```

```
    ClassFactory := nil;
    FillChar(CoServerInfo, sizeof(CoServerInfo), 0);
    AServerName := ServerName;
    CoServerInfo.pwszName := PWideChar(AServerName);

    hr := CoGetClassObject(CLASS_EasyDCOM, CLSCTX_REMOTE_SERVER,
      @CoServerInfo, IClassFactory, ClassFactory);
    OleCheck(hr);

    hr := ClassFactory.CreateInstance(nil, IID_IEasyDCOM, FEasyDCOM);
    if Succeeded(hr) then begin
      ClassFactory := nil;
      Caption := ' Connected to: ' + FEasyDCOM.GetName;
    end else
      ShowMessage('No object');
  end;
end;
```

This method first prompts the user for the name of the machine on which the server resides. It then fills in the CoServerInfo structure accordingly and passes it to CoGetClassObject. If the call to CoGetClassObject succeeds, then you can call ClassFactory.CreateInstance to retrieve your object.

NOTE

In this sample method, I show two different ways to check the result of a call to a COM method:

```
hr := CoGetClassObject(CLASS_EasyDCOM, CLSCTX_REMOTE_SERVER,
      @CoServerInfo, IClassFactory, ClassFactory);
OleCheck(hr);

hr := ClassFactory.CreateInstance(nil, IID_IEasyDCOM, FEasyDCOM);
if Succeeded(hr) then begin
```

If you call the VCL OleCheck routine, an exception will be raised if an error occurs. If possible, a string will be shown to the user specifying the nature of the error. If you call Succeeded, no exception will be raised if an error occurs. You can also write the following:

```
OleCheck(CoGetClassObject(CLASS_EasyDCOM, CLSCTX_REMOTE_SERVER,
      @CoServerInfo, IClassFactory, ClassFactory));
```

This third technique may be the best way to handle this situation, but I provide several alternatives just so you can understand your options.

The end result of this process is that you get back the same interface you would get from CoCreateInstanceEx. Clearly, CoCreateInstanceEx is easier to use, so it is the preferred call in most circumstances. However, you might call CoGetClassObject for two reasons:

- You might call CoGetClassObject if you need to retrieve multiple interfaces from the same class. In such a case, you can call CoGetClassObject once and then call CreateInstance repeatedly. This approach is more efficient than calling CoCreateInstance, which is really a wrapper around both calls and would, in effect, cause you to call CoGetClassObject multiple times, when only one call is needed.

- Sometimes when you are debugging an app, you may find CoGetClassObject useful. In particular, CoGetClassObject separates the act of accessing the server from the act of retrieving your interface. In some cases, knowing that you are, in fact, getting to the server by calling CoGetClassObject is helpful, even though you aren't successfully getting the interface you want when you call ClassFactory.CreateInstance. Because of the way CoGetClassObject is structured, it can help you pinpoint this not atypical case.

Using a Remote Object

I've spent a considerable amount of time describing how to create a remote server. Using the server once you have it is trivial:

```
procedure TForm2.SquareBtnClick(Sender: TObject);
var
  Value, Num: Integer;
begin
  try
    Num := StrToInt(CCLabelEdit1.EditText);
    if FEasyDCOM <> nil then begin
      FEasyDCOM.Square(Num, Value);
      CCLabelEdit2.EditText := IntToStr(Value);
    end;
  except
    on E:Exception do
      ShowMessage(E.Message);
  end;
end;
```

I've put some window dressing on the call, but all I'm really doing here is calling the Square method directly off the field of TForm2 called FEasyObject. You don't have to include exception-handling code in your own programs.

At this stage, you should start to have a feeling for how DCOM programs are put together.

Revisiting the `SystemInformation` Program

I want to revisit the `SystemInformation` program first discussed in Chapter 14. The original version of the program supplied a COM DLL that reported basic facts about the system, such as the name of the current machine, the current users, and size, and available space for the drives on a system. My plan in this section is to convert that DLL into an executable and to use it remotely. The source is shown in Listings 20.5 through 20.7.

Until very recently, all DCOM objects had to reside in executables. Since NT 4 Service Pack 3, you can access remote servers that reside in DLLs. However, I will not be showing that feature in this chapter.

LISTING 20.5   THE CORE FUNCTIONALITY FOR THE SERVER IS CONTAINED IN THIS UNIT

```
//////////////////////////////////////
// Purpose: Contains core functionality of server
// Project: SysInfoExeServer.dpr
// Copyright (c) 1998 by Charlie Calvert
//
unit SystemInformation1;

interface

uses
  ActiveX;

type
  TDriveInfoRec = record
    SectorsPerCluster, BytesPerSector: Cardinal;
    NumberOfFreeClusters, TotalNumberOfClusters: Cardinal;
    TotalFree, FreeAvailable, TotalSpace: LargeInt;
  end;

  TSystemInformation = class
    function GetComputer: WideString;
    procedure GetDriveInfo(out TotalCount: Integer;
      out DriveInfo: OleVariant);
  end;


implementation

uses
  Windows, SysUtils;
```

continues

20

DCOM

LISTING 20.5 CONTINUED

```
{ TSystemInformation }

function TSystemInformation.GetComputer: WideString;
var
  Len: DWord;
  S: PChar;
begin
  Len := MAX_COMPUTERNAME_LENGTH + 1;
  GetMem(S, Len);
  if GetComputerName(S, Len) then
    Result := S
  else
    raise Exception.Create('Could not get computer name.');
  FreeMem(S, Len);
end;

procedure TSystemInformation.GetDriveInfo(out TotalCount: Integer;
  out DriveInfo: OleVariant);
const
  Size = 28 * 5;  // 26 letters, plus 2 extra, times plenty of room

var
  DriveStrings, TempDriveStrings: PChar;
  DriveType: string;
  SectorsPerCluster, BytesPerSector: Cardinal;
  NumberOfFreeClusters, TotalNumberOfClusters: Cardinal;
  FreeAvailable, TotalSpace: LargeInt;
  TotalFree: LargeInt;
  DriveInfoRec: TDriveInfoRec;
  ADrive: Variant;
  TempVar: Variant;
  TempPtr: Pointer;

begin
  TotalCount := 0;
  DriveInfo := VarArrayCreate([0, 28], VarVariant);
  GetMem(DriveStrings, Size);
  GetLogicalDriveStrings(Size, DriveStrings);
  TempDriveStrings := DriveStrings;

  // Drives A or B might not be valid or no disk in them
  while (TempDriveStrings = 'A:\') or (TempDriveStrings = 'B:\') do
    Inc(TempDriveStrings, StrLen(TempDriveStrings) + 1);

  while StrLen(TempDriveStrings) <> 0 do begin
    ADrive := VarArrayCreate([0, 3], VarVariant);
    case GetDriveType(TempDriveStrings) of
      DRIVE_UNKNOWN: DriveType := 'Unknown';
      DRIVE_NO_ROOT_DIR: DriveType := 'Not a root drive';
```

```
      DRIVE_REMOVABLE: DriveType := 'Removable';
      DRIVE_FIXED: DriveType := 'Hard Drive';
      DRIVE_REMOTE: DriveType := 'Network';
      DRIVE_CDROM: DriveType := 'CDROM';
      DRIVE_RAMDISK: DriveType := 'RAMDisk';
    else
      DriveType := 'Error';
    end;

    ADrive[0] := AnsiString(TempDriveStrings);
    ADrive[1] := DriveType;

    GetDiskFreeSpace(TempDriveStrings, SectorsPerCluster, BytesPerSector,
      NumberOfFreeClusters, TotalNumberOfClusters);

    DriveInfoRec.SectorsPerCluster := SectorsPerCluster;
    DriveInfoRec.BytesPerSector := BytesPerSector;
    DriveInfoRec.NumberOfFreeClusters := NumberOfFreeClusters;
    DriveInfoRec.TotalNumberOfClusters := TotalNumberOfClusters;

    GetDiskFreeSpaceEx(TempDriveStrings, FreeAvailable,
      TotalSpace, @TotalFree);
    DriveInfoRec.FreeAvailable := FreeAvailable;
    DriveInfoRec.TotalSpace := TotalSpace;
    DriveInfoRec.TotalFree := TotalFree;

    TempVar := VarArrayCreate([0, SizeOf(TDriveInfoRec)], VarByte);
    TempPtr := VarArrayLock(TempVar);
    Move(DriveInfoRec, TempPtr^, SizeOf(TDriveInfoRec));
    VarArrayUnlock(TempVar);
    ADrive[2] := TempVar;

    DriveInfo[TotalCount] := ADrive;
    Inc(TempDriveStrings, StrLen(TempDriveStrings) + 1);
    Inc(TotalCount);
  end;
  FreeMem(DriveStrings, Size);
end;

end.
```

LISTING 20.6   THE IMPLEMENTATION FOR THE DCOM SERVER

```
////////////////////////////////////
// Purpose: Implementation for DCOM Server
// Project: SysInfoExeServer.dpr
// Copyright (c) 1998 by Charlie Calvert
//
unit MainIMPL;
```

continues

20

DCOM

LISTING 20.6 CONTINUED

```pascal
interface

uses
  Windows, ComObj, ActiveX,
  SysUtils, SysInfoExeServer_TLB, SystemInformation1;

type
  TSysInfoExe = class(TAutoObject, ISysInfoExe)
  private
    FSystemInformation: TSystemInformation;
    procedure Initialize;
  protected
    destructor Destroy; override;
    function GetComputer: WideString; safecall;
    function GetName: WideString; safecall;
    procedure GetDriveInfo(out TotalCount: Integer;
      out DriveInfo: OleVariant); safecall;
  end;

implementation

uses ComServ;

destructor TSysInfoExe.Destroy;
begin
  FSystemInformation.Free;
  FSystemInformation := nil;
  inherited Destroy;
end;

function TSysInfoExe.GetComputer: WideString;
begin
  if FSystemInformation = nil then
    Initialize;
  Result := FSystemInformation.GetComputer;
end;

function TSysInfoExe.GetName: WideString;
begin
  Result := Self.ClassName;
end;

procedure TSysInfoExe.GetDriveInfo(out TotalCount: Integer;
  out DriveInfo: OleVariant);
begin
  if FSystemInformation = nil then
    Initialize;
  FSystemInformation.GetDriveInfo(TotalCount, DriveInfo);
```

```
end;

procedure TSysInfoExe.Initialize;
begin
  FSystemInformation := TSystemInformation.Create;
end;

initialization
  TAutoObjectFactory.Create(
    ComServer,
    TSysInfoExe,
    Class_SysInfoExe,
    ciMultiInstance,
    tmApartment);
end.
```

LISTING 20.7   THE MAIN FORM FOR THE CLIENT PROGRAM

```
/////////////////////////////////////
// Purpose: Main form for DCOM client
// Project: SysInfoExeClient.dpr
// Copyright (c) 1998 by Charlie Calvert
//
unit MainClient;

interface

uses
  Windows, Messages, SysUtils,
  Classes, Graphics, Controls,
  Forms, Dialogs, StdCtrls,
  SysInfoExeServer_TLB, Buttons, ExtCtrls,
  Menus, LabelEdit;

type
  TForm2 = class(TForm)
    Memo1: TMemo;
    Panel1: TPanel;
    MainMenu1: TMainMenu;
    Options1: TMenuItem;
    ConnectLocal1: TMenuItem;
    ConnectRemote1: TMenuItem;
    CCLabelEdit1: TCCLabelEdit;
    CCLabelEdit2: TCCLabelEdit;
    procedure ConnectLocalClick(Sender: TObject);
    procedure ConnectRemoteClick(Sender: TObject);
  private
    FSysInfoExe: ISysInfoExe;
    procedure BasicInfo;
```

20

DCOM

continues

LISTING 20.7   CONTINUED

```
    procedure ReportOnDriveStatus;
  end;

var
  Form2: TForm2;

implementation

uses
  ActiveX, ComObj, SystemInformation1;
{$R *.DFM}

procedure TForm2.ConnectLocalClick(Sender: TObject);
begin
  FSysInfoExe := CoSysInfoExe.Create;
  Caption := 'Connected: ' + FSysInfoExe.GetName;
  BasicInfo;
  ReportOnDriveStatus;
end;

procedure TForm2.ConnectRemoteClick(Sender: TObject);
var
  MachineName: string;
begin
  MachineName := '';
  if InputQuery('Enter Machine Name', 'Machine Name', MachineName)
  ➥then begin
    FSysInfoExe := CoSysInfoExe.CreateRemote(MachineName);
    Caption := FSysInfoExe.GetName;
    BasicInfo;
    ReportOnDriveStatus;
  end;
end;

procedure TForm2.BasicInfo;
begin
  CCLabelEdit1.EditText := FSysInfoExe.GetName;
  CCLabelEdit2.EditText := FSysInfoExe.GetComputer;
end;

procedure TForm2.ReportOnDriveStatus;
const
  Size = 28 * 5;
      // 26 letters plus A and B times plenty of room for letters
var
  TotalCount, i: Integer;
  ADrive, DriveInfo: OleVariant;
  DriveInfoRec: TDriveInfoRec;
  TempVar: Variant;
```

```
    TempPtr: Pointer;
begin
  if FSysInfoExe = nil then
    Exit
  else
    FSysInfoExe.GetDriveInfo(TotalCount, DriveInfo);

  Memo1.Clear;

  for i := 0 to TotalCount - 1 do begin

    ADrive := DriveInfo[i];
    Memo1.Lines.Add('[' + ADrive[0] + '] ' + ADrive[1]);

    TempVar := ADrive[2];
    TempPtr := VarArrayLock(TempVar);
    Move(TempPtr^, DriveInfoRec, SizeOf(TDriveInfoRec));

    with Memo1.Lines, DriveInfoRec do begin
      Memo1.Lines.Add('Sectors Per Cluster: ' +
      ➥IntToStr(SectorsPerCluster));
      Memo1.Lines.Add('Bytes Per Sector: ' + IntToStr(BytesPerSector));
      Memo1.Lines.Add('Number of Free Clusters: ' +
        IntToStr(NumberOfFreeClusters));
      Memo1.Lines.Add('Total Number of Clusters: ' +
        IntToStr(TotalNumberOfClusters));

      Memo1.Lines.Add('Free Available: ' + IntToStr(FreeAvailable));
      Memo1.Lines.Add('Total Space: ' + IntToStr(TotalSpace));
      Memo1.Lines.Add('Total Free: ' + IntToStr(TotalFree));
      Memo1.Lines.Add('');
    end;

  end;
end;

end.
```

This program is interesting because it illustrates the fact that a DCOM server is running on the remote machine, not in the address space of the client. When you launch this server, it explores the hard drive and some other aspects of the machine on which it is running. It sends that information back to the client, where it is displayed for the user. Thus, if the client is on machine A, and the server is on machine B, then the client program run on machine A reports on the status of the program on machine B.

The fact that the server runs in a separate address space from the client is important for two reasons:

- The server does not take up address space, clock cycles, or hard drive space on the client, thus leaving the client machine free to handle other chores.

- If the server is much more powerful than the client, the client program can delegate tasks to the server that the client machine cannot handle.

Understanding the Server

This program totally separates the functionality of the server from the implementation of the DCOM object. In the file called `SystemInformation1.pas`, I create an object that looks like this:

```
TSystemInformation = class
  function GetComputer: WideString;
  procedure GetDriveInfo(out TotalCount: Integer;
    out DriveInfo: OleVariant);
end;
```

This object does the same thing as the code in Chapter 14. As a result, I will not bother to discuss it here.

What is important here, however, is the separation of the object implementation from the DCOM server implementation. This is a good way to construct an application because it allows you to easily reuse the core functionality of the program in multiple settings. For instance, you could create a standalone EXE with this functionality, a DLL with this functionality, and, as I have done here, a DCOM server with this same functionality. To do so, you don't have to rewrite or reconstruct the `TSystemInformation` object. It can be used as is in each program, and only the methods for accessing the object need to change. In short, this technology promotes reuse.

To use the `TSystemInformation` object, I simply construct the methods of my DCOM object as wrappers around it:

```
procedure TSysInfoExe.Initialize;
begin
  FSystemInformation := TSystemInformation.Create;
end;

procedure TSysInfoExe.GetDriveInfo(out TotalCount: Integer;
  out DriveInfo: OleVariant);
begin
  if FSystemInformation = nil then
    Initialize;
  FSystemInformation.GetDriveInfo(TotalCount, DriveInfo);
end;
```

The implementation for my distributed interface does nothing more than call the relevant method of `TSystemInformation`.

Lightweight Remote Datasets

In this section, you are going to learn how to build a multitier application without using MIDAS. The MIDAS technology is quite expensive, and the technology shown here comes for free with all versions of Delphi. The code shown here is not as fancy or easy to use as the MIDAS technology, but it is much less expensive, and it will give you the knowledge you need to work intelligently with the MIDAS or Delphi Enterprise technology. Regardless of its shortcomings, this code shows you how to create true distributed database applications.

Believing that you have to pay $5,000 or more to start building distributed database applications is simply ludicrous. What I am showing you here is the VW Beetle of distributed computing, whereas MIDAS and CORBA are much fancier models. Nevertheless, they are all cars. They all get the job done.

The DataCom directory on the CD-ROM that accompanies this book has two programs in it. One is an OLE automation server, and the other is an OLE automation client. I will talk about the server first. It is shown in Listing 20.8 through Listing 20.11. The interface for the server isn't very important from the perspective of this book, but I show it in Figure 20.5. The purpose of the server is to export a dataset to a remote client without using MIDAS.

FIGURE 20.5

The DataCOMServer OLE automation program enables you to view data and test routines that will be exported to other applications.

20

DCOM

LISTING 20.8   THE MAIN FORM FILE FOR THE DataCOMServer APPLICATION

```
///////////////////////////////////////
// Purpose: The main form
// Project: DataCOMServer.dpr
// Copyright (c) 1998 by Charlie Calvert
//
unit MainServer;

interface

uses
  Windows, Messages, SysUtils,
  Classes, Graphics, Controls,
  Forms, Dialogs, Grids,
  DBGrids, StdCtrls, Globals,
  ExtCtrls, DBCtrls, Menus;

type
  TForm1 = class(TForm)
    DBGrid1: TDBGrid;
    Grid: TStringGrid;
    MainMenu1: TMainMenu;
    Options1: TMenuItem;
    FillStringGrid1: TMenuItem;
    Update1: TMenuItem;
    Panel1: TPanel;
    DBNavigator1: TDBNavigator;
    InsertRecord1: TMenuItem;
    procedure FillStrGridClick(Sender: TObject);
    procedure UpdateClick(Sender: TObject);
    procedure UpdateParams(SQLStatement: string);
    procedure InsertRecord1Click(Sender: TObject);
  public
    procedure GetData(out V: OleVariant);
    procedure InsertCustomer(Customer: TCustomer);
    procedure UpdateCustomer(Customer: TCustomer);
    function VariantToCustomer(V: OleVariant): TCustomer;
    function VariantToCustomers(V: OleVariant): TCustomerRecords;
  end;

var
  Form1: TForm1;

implementation

uses
  DMod1, BDE;

{$R *.DFM}
```

```
{-------------------------------------------------------------------
  This method tests GetData, which is the code that creates the
  variant array containing the data set that will be sent to the
  client.
-------------------------------------------------------------------}
procedure TForm1.FillStrGridClick(Sender: TObject);
var
  Customers: TCustomerRecords;
  V: OleVariant;
  P: Pointer;
  i: Integer;
begin
  GetData(V);
  Customers := VariantToCustomers(V);

  Grid.RowCount := Customers.Count;
  for i := 0 to Customers.Count do begin
    Grid.Cells[0, i] := Customers.CustAry[i].CustNo;
    Grid.Cells[1, i] := Customers.CustAry[i].Company;
    Grid.Cells[2, i] := Customers.CustAry[i].Address;
    Grid.Cells[3, i] := Customers.CustAry[i].City;
    Grid.Cells[4, i] := Customers.CustAry[i].State;
    Grid.Cells[5, i] := Customers.CustAry[i].Zip;
  end;
end;


{-------------------------------------------------------------------
  The GetData method creates the variant to be exported from
  the program.
-------------------------------------------------------------------}
procedure TForm1.GetData(out V: OleVariant);
var
  Customers: TCustomerRecords;
  P: Pointer;
begin
  V := VarArrayCreate([0, SizeOf(TCustomerRecords)] , varByte);
  DMod.GetCustAry(Customers);
  P := VarArrayLock(V);
  Move(Customers, P^, SizeOf(TCustomerRecords));
  VarArrayUnlock(V);
end;

procedure TForm1.InsertCustomer(Customer: TCustomer);
begin
  DMod.UpDate2(Customer, True);
  DMod.CustomerTable.Refresh;
end;

procedure TForm1.InsertRecord1Click(Sender: TObject);
```

20

DCOM

continues

LISTING 20.8   CONTINUED

```pascal
const
  Title = 'Insert Record';
var
  Customer: TCustomer;
  CustNo: string;
begin
  CustNo := '';
  if InputQuery(Title, 'Enter New CustNo: ', CustNo) then begin
    Customer.Company := 'Company';
    Customer.Address := 'Address';
    Customer.City := 'City';
    Customer.State := 'State';
    Customer.Zip := 'Zip';
    Customer.CustNo := CustNo;
    InsertCustomer(Customer);
  end;
end;

{---------------------------------------------------------------------
  This routine lets me update the current record.
  I wrote it to have a local method that could test my SQL
  update code (DMod.Update2). It's not a generally useful routine.
  If you want to edit an existing record enter its Company when
  prompted.
---------------------------------------------------------------------}
procedure TForm1.UpdateClick(Sender: TObject);
const
  Title = 'Enter New Company Name';
var
  Customer: TCustomer;
  Company: string;
begin
  Company := DMod.CustomerTableCompany.Value;
  if InputQuery(Title, 'Company: ', Company) then begin
    Customer.CustNo := DMod.CustomerTableCustNo.AsString;
    Customer.Company := Company;
    Customer.Address := DMod.CustomerTableAddr1.Value;
    Customer.City := DMod.CustomerTableCity.Value;
    Customer.State := DMod.CustomerTableState.Value;
    Customer.Zip := DMod.CustomerTableZip.Value;
    UpdateCustomer(Customer);
  end;
end;

procedure TForm1.UpdateCustomer(Customer: TCustomer);
begin
  DMod.UpDate2(Customer, False);
  DMod.CustomerTable.Refresh;
end;
```

```
procedure TForm1.UpdateParams(SQLStatement: string);
begin
  DMod.UpDateSQL(SQLStatement);
end;

{------------------------------------------------------------------
  Returns a TCustomer structure.
  Compare with VariantToCustomers
------------------------------------------------------------------}
function TForm1.VariantToCustomer(V: OleVariant): TCustomer;
var
  P: Pointer;
begin
  P := VarArrayLock(V);
  Move(P^, Result, SizeOf(TCustomer));
  VarArrayUnlock(V);
end;

{------------------------------------------------------------------
  Returns a TCustomerRecords structure.
  Compare with VariantToCustomer
------------------------------------------------------------------}
function TForm1.VariantToCustomers(V: OleVariant): TCustomerRecords;
var
  P: Pointer;
begin
  P := VarArrayLock(V);
  Move(P^, Result, SizeOf(TCustomerRecords));
  VarArrayUnlock(V);
end;

end.
```

LISTING 20.9 THE DATA MODULE FOR THE DataCOMServer APPLICATION

```
//////////////////////////////////////
// Purpose: The DataModule
// Project: DataComServer
// Copyright (c) 1998 by Charlie Calvert
//
unit DMod1;

interface

uses
  Windows, Messages, SysUtils,
  Classes, Graphics, Controls,
  Forms, Dialogs, DB,
```

continues

LISTING 20.9 CONTINUED

```
DBTables, Globals;

type
  TDMod = class(TDataModule)
    CustomerTable: TTable;
    DataSource1: TDataSource;
    CustomerTableCustNo: TFloatField;
    CustomerTableCompany: TStringField;
    CustomerTableAddr1: TStringField;
    CustomerTableAddr2: TStringField;
    CustomerTableCity: TStringField;
    CustomerTableState: TStringField;
    CustomerTableZip: TStringField;
    CustomerTableCountry: TStringField;
    CustomerTablePhone: TStringField;
    CustomerTableFAX: TStringField;
    CustomerTableTaxRate: TFloatField;
    CustomerTableContact: TStringField;
    CustomerTableLastInvoiceDate: TDateTimeField;
    UpdateQuery2: TQuery;
    procedure DModCreate(Sender: TObject);
  public
    procedure GetCustAry(var Customer: TCustomerRecords);
    procedure UpDate2(Customer: TCustomer; Insert: Boolean);
    procedure UpdateSQL(SQLStatement: string);
  end;

var
  DMod: TDMod;

implementation

uses
  BDE, CodeBox;

{$R *.DFM}

procedure TDMod.DModCreate(Sender: TObject);
begin
  CustomerTable.Open;
end;

procedure TDMod.GetCustAry(var Customer: TCustomerRecords);
var
  i: Integer;
  V: Variant;
  Num: Double;
begin
  i := 0;
```

```
    dbiGetRecordCount(CustomerTable.handle, Customer.Count);
    CustomerTable.First;
    DMod.DataSource1.Enabled := False;
    while not CustomerTable.Eof do begin
      Num := CustomerTable['CustNo'];
      Customer.CustAry[i].CustNo := Format('%f', [Num]);
      Customer.CustAry[i].Company := CustomerTableCompany.Value;
      Customer.CustAry[i].Address := CustomerTableAddr1.Value;
      Customer.CustAry[i].City := CustomerTableCity.Value;
      Customer.CustAry[i].State :=
      ➥CustomerTable.FieldByName('State').AsString;
      Customer.CustAry[i].Zip := CustomerTable.FieldByname('zip').AsString;
      Inc(i);
      CustomerTable.Next;
    end;
    DMod.DataSource1.Enabled := True;
end;

procedure TDMod.UpDate2(Customer: TCustomer; Insert: Boolean);
const
  InsertString = 'Insert into "customer.db" ' +
    ' (CustNo, Company, Addr1, City, State, Zip) ' +
    ' Values(%s, "%s", "%s", "%s", "%s", "%s")';

  UpdateString = 'update Customer ' +
    ' set Company="%s", Addr1="%s", City="%s", State="%s", Zip="%s" ' +
    ' where CustNo = %s';

var
  S: string;
begin
  UpdateQuery2.Close;
  UpdateQuery2.SQL.Clear;
  if Insert then
    S := Format(InsertString, [Customer.CustNo, Customer.Company,
      Customer.Address, Customer.City, Customer.State, Customer.Zip])
  else
    S := Format(UpdateString, [Customer.Company, Customer.Address,
      Customer.City, Customer.State, Customer.Zip, Customer.CustNo]);
  UpdateQuery2.SQL.SetText(PChar(S));
  UpdateQuery2.ExecSql;
end;

procedure TDMod.UpdateSQL(SQLStatement: string);
var
  TempList: TStrings;
begin
  TempList := UpdateQuery2.SQL;
  UpdateQuery2.SQL.SetText(PChar(SQLStatement));
  UpdateQuery2.ExecSQL;
```

20

DCOM

continues

LISTING 20.9   CONTINUED

```
  UpdateQuery2.SQL := TempList;
end;


end.
```

LISTING 20.10   THE OLE AUTOMATION OBJECT IMPLEMENTATION IN THE DataCOMServer APPLICATION

```
///////////////////////////////////////
// Purpose: Implementation for OLE Object
// Project: DataCOMServer.dpr
// Copyright (c) 1998 by Charlie Calvert
//
unit MainIMPL;

interface

uses
  ComObj, ActiveX, DataComServer_TLB;

type
  TDataCOM = class(TAutoObject, IDataCOM)
  protected
    function GetData: OleVariant; safecall;
    function GetName: WideString; safecall;
    function UpdateRecord(Data: OleVariant): WordBool; safecall;
  end;

implementation

uses
  ComServ, Globals, MainServer;

function TDataCOM.GetData: OleVariant;
begin
  Form1.GetData(Result);
end;

function TDataCOM.GetName: WideString;
begin
  Result := Self.ClassName;
end;

function TDataCOM.UpdateRecord(Data: OleVariant): WordBool;
var
  P: Pointer;
  C: TCustomer;
```

```
begin
  C := Form1.VariantToCustomer(Data);
  Form1.UpdateCustomer(C);
end;

initialization
  TAutoObjectFactory.Create(ComServer, TDataCOM, Class_DataCOM,
    ciMultiInstance, tmApartment);
end.
```

LISTING 20.11   THE Globals UNIT CONTAINS SOME DECLARATIONS USED BY BOTH THE
DataCOMServer AND THE DataCOMClient APPLICATIONS

```
unit Globals;

interface

uses
  BDE, DB;

type
  TCustomer = record
    CustNo: ShortString;
    Company: ShortString;
    Address: ShortString;
    City: ShortString;
    State: ShortString;
    Zip: ShortString;
  end;

  PCustAry = ^TCustAry;
  TCustAry = array[0..100] of TCustomer;

  PCustomerRecords = ^TCustomerRecords;
  TCustomerRecords = record
    Count: LongInt;
    CustAry: TCustAry;
  end;

implementation

uses
  Sysutils;

end.
```

This program exports selected columns from the Customer table to remote clients. It also allows the clients to edit a particular row of data. The user can therefore both view and edit the data from a database without ever loading any database tools on his or her machine. In short, this program creates a distributed database application complete with middleware and a thin client.

Understanding the `DataCOMServer` Program

`DataCOMServer` is fairly long, but the important sections of code are brief and not particularly difficult to understand. I include the whole program so that you can follow the logic of the entire application at your leisure, but I will focus mostly on a few key elements.

The following is the declaration for the `Automation` class from the `DataCOMServer_TLB` class:

```
IDataCOM = interface(IDispatch)
  ['{41E564F4-2A18-11D2-9CE8-006008928EEF}']
  function GetName: WideString; safecall;
  function UpdateRecord(Data: OleVariant): WordBool; safecall;
  function GetData: OleVariant; safecall;
end;
```

The object itself is created in the Type Library Editor. I'm not going to explain how that process works again, as I've already given numerous examples of how to use it.

The `GetName` function is provided primarily so you can test your connection to the server. The `GetData` function retrieves a `Variant` array that contains select fields from an entire dataset. The code iterates through all the records of the dataset to get the information. The `UpdateRecord` function is used by the client when it wants to update data on the server. For instance, the user might edit one particular record and then send the edits back to the server via this function.

> **NOTE**
>
> The MIDAS technology needs a more flexible solution for passing datasets than the one I show in this program. The issue is that MIDAS needs to deal with a wide variety of datasets, and not just one particular table.
>
> One possible solution to this type of problem would be to send one packet of data describing all the fields in a dataset and their types. Then you could send X additional packets of data, each containing a column of data. If you wanted, you could even wrap the metadata and all the fields inside one long `Variant` array. At the other end, you could unpack the data and display it in a grid. If you used a handmade descendant of the VCL's virtual dataset, then you could even hook up your data to the VCL database controls.

The GetData method looks like this:

```
function TDataCOM.GetData: OleVariant;
begin
  Form1.GetData(Result);
end;
```

As you can see, I delegate the actual implementation of the GetData method to the main form. This practice is common in OLE automation because the automation object is supposed to be a wrapper around the built-in functionality of your server. For instance, ServerData provides access to the Customer table from the DBDEMOS alias. The goal of the automation server is simply to export that functionality to other programs. As a result, it makes sense that the automation object would simply wrap methods already existing in the program.

The TForm1 implementation of GetData looks like this:

```
procedure TForm1.GetData(out V: OleVariant);
var
  Customers: TCustomerRecords;
  P: Pointer;
begin
  V := VarArrayCreate([0, SizeOf(TCustomerRecords)] , varByte);
  DMod.GetCustAry(Customers);
  P := VarArrayLock(V);
  Move(Customers, P^, SizeOf(TCustomerRecords));
  VarArrayUnlock(V);
end;
```

This method calls the GetCustAry routine from the data module to retrieve a custom structure that contains the data from the Customer table. I will explain how that process works in one moment. For now, just concentrate on the fact that the GetData methods convert the custom structure into a Variant array by using VarArrayLock and VarArrayUnlock. This process was described in the section called "Variant Arrays" in Chapter 14.

As declared in the Globals unit, the custom data structure used by this program consists of an array of TCustomer structures:

```
TCustomer = record
  CustNo: ShortString;
  Company: ShortString;
  Address: ShortString;
  City: ShortString;
  State: ShortString;
  Zip: ShortString;
end;

PCustAry = ^TCustAry;
```

```
TCustAry = array[0..100] of TCustomer;
```

The program takes this array and hides it inside a custom structure that defines the number of records in the array:

```
PCustomerRecords = ^TCustomerRecords;
TCustomerRecords = record
  Count: LongInt;
  CustAry: TCustAry;
end;
```

Clearly, you can store this data in more memory-efficient ways, but I wanted to keep this part of the program simple so that you would be able to follow the logic of the program without getting bogged down by a mass of irrelevant pointer manipulation. The important point of this program is how it handles OLE automation; finding the best way to store data in memory is really another subject altogether.

After the data structures are declared, filling them out in the data module for the application is a simple matter:

```
procedure TDMod.GetCustAry(var Customer: TCustomerRecords);
var
  i: Integer;
  V: Variant;
  Num: Double;
begin
  i := 0;
  dbiGetRecordCount(CustomerTable.handle, Customer.Count);
  CustomerTable.First;
  DMod.DataSource1.Enabled := False;
  while not CustomerTable.Eof do begin
    Num := CustomerTable['CustNo'];
    Customer.CustAry[i].CustNo := Format('%f', [Num]);
    Customer.CustAry[i].Company := CustomerTableCompany.Value;
    Customer.CustAry[i].Address := CustomerTableAddr1.Value;
    Customer.CustAry[i].City := CustomerTableCity.Value;
    Customer.CustAry[i].State :=
    ➥CustomerTable.FieldByName('State').AsString;
    Customer.CustAry[i].Zip := CustomerTable.FieldByname('zip').AsString;
    Inc(i);
    CustomerTable.Next;
  end;
  DMod.DataSource1.Enabled := True;
end;
```

This simple code iterates through the entire dataset, using brute force methods to copy the data into the array. Notice that I disable the DataSource for the module so that the program does not waste time updating the visual display for a program that is, after all, usually running on a remote server.

The data module also provides a method for updating the dataset when the user sends back a record with new data:

```
procedure TDMod.UpDate2(Customer: TCustomer; Insert: Boolean);
const
  InsertString = 'Insert into "customer.db" ' +
    ' (CustNo, Company, Addr1, City, State, Zip) ' +
    ' Values(%s, "%s", "%s", "%s", "%s", "%s")';

  UpdateString = 'update Customer ' +
    ' set Company="%s", Addr1="%s", City="%s", State="%s", Zip="%s" ' +
    ' where CustNo = %s';

var
  S: string;
begin
  UpdateQuery2.Close;
  UpdateQuery2.SQL.Clear;
  if Insert then
    S := Format(InsertString, [Customer.CustNo, Customer.Company,
      Customer.Address, Customer.City, Customer.State, Customer.Zip])
  else
    S := Format(UpdateString, [Customer.Company, Customer.Address,
      Customer.City, Customer.State, Customer.Zip, Customer.CustNo]);
  UpdateQuery2.SQL.SetText(PChar(S));
  UpdateQuery2.ExecSql;
end;
```

The preceding is just standard TQuery code of the type that should be easy for anyone who understands the Delphi database tools to grasp. I declare two SQL statements: one for updating data and one for inserting data. I then format the statements with data supplied by the user and call ExecSQL to execute the statement.

When the client program wants to update a particular record, it calls this function from the DCOM object implementation:

```
function TDataCOM.UpdateRecord(Data: OleVariant): WordBool;
var
  P: Pointer;
  C: TCustomer;
begin
  C := Form1.VariantToCustomer(Data);
  Form1.UpdateCustomer(C);
end;
```

The code that translates a Variant into a TCustomer record looks like this:

```
function TForm1.VariantToCustomer(V: OleVariant): TCustomer;
var
  P: Pointer;
```

```
begin
  P := VarArrayLock(V);
  Move(P^, Result, SizeOf(TCustomer));
  VarArrayUnlock(V);
end;
```

This code really just creates a utility function that first locks the array, then accesses the data, and finally unlocks the array.

After the `Variant` is translated into a Customer record, I then ask the main form to call the `Update2` method described earlier in this section. I ask the main form to call the method rather than call it directly simply so that I keep one interface to my underlying code, thereby making program maintenance simpler.

You will probably want to study a few other parts of the `DataCOMServer` program on your own, but overall it is not a complex piece of work. One of the great advantages of DCOM and OLE automation is that both technologies are easy to use.

The `DataCOMClient` for Remote Datasets

The `DataCOMClient` application, found on the CD-ROM that accompanies this book, shows how to access a remote dataset from a client application. A simple menu allows you to retrieve a dataset from either a local OLE automation server or from a remote DCOM automation server. In both cases, the server is the `ServerData` application explained in the preceding section of this chapter. You won't be able to connect to the server either remotely or locally unless the server is registered. To register the server application on the server, copy the server application to the server and run it once.

After the user connects to the data, it is displayed in the main form of the program, as shown in Figure 20.6. He or she can then edit the data in a custom form, as shown in Figure 20.7.

The code for the `DataCOMClient` program is shown in Listing 20.12 and Listing 20.13. `DataComClient` is an OLE client that retrieves a database table from a server via OLE automation. I do not show the `Globals` unit here because it was included in the listings for the `ServerData` program.

FIGURE 20.6

Viewing the data retrieved over the network from a remote server.

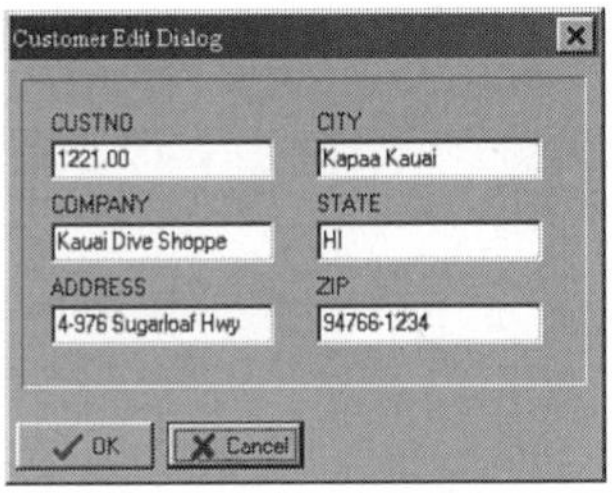

FIGURE 20.7

Editing a row of data before sending it back to the server.

LISTING 20.12   THE MAIN FORM OF THE DataCOMClient APPLICATION

```
//////////////////////////////////////
// Purpose: Light Weight Data Connection Client
// Project: DataCOMClient.dpr
// Copyright (c) 1998 by Charlie Calvert
//
unit MainClient;

interface

uses
  Windows, Messages, SysUtils,
  Classes, Graphics, Controls,
  Forms, Dialogs, StdCtrls,
  Grids, Menus, Globals,
```

continues

LISTING 20.12 CONTINUED

```
  DataCOMServer_TLB;

type
  TForm1 = class(TForm)
    Grid: TStringGrid;
    MainMenu1: TMainMenu;
    File1: TMenuItem;
    MakeConnection1: TMenuItem;
    Options1: TMenuItem;
    Edit1: TMenuItem;
    N1: TMenuItem;
    Exit1: TMenuItem;
    UpdateData1: TMenuItem;
    MakeConnectionLocal1: TMenuItem;
    procedure bMakeConnectionClick(Sender: TObject);
    procedure Edit1Click(Sender: TObject);
    procedure UpdateData1Click(Sender: TObject);
    procedure Exit1Click(Sender: TObject);
  private
    FCustomers: TCustomerRecords;
    FDataCom: IDataCom;
    procedure CreateConnection(IsRemote: Boolean);
    procedure FillGrid;
    procedure GetandDisplayData;
    function VariantToData(V: OleVariant): TCustomerRecords;
  end;

var
  Form1: TForm1;

implementation

uses
  CodeBox, DataEd1;

{$R *.DFM}

procedure TForm1.CreateConnection(IsRemote: Boolean);
var
  S: string;
begin
  Screen.Cursor := crHourGlass;
  try
    if IsRemote then begin
      S := '';
      if InputQuery('Server Name', 'Enter Server Name', S) then
        FDataCom := CoDataCOM.CreateRemote(S)
    end else
      FDataCom := CoDataCOM.Create;
```

```
  finally
    Screen.Cursor := crDefault;
  end;
end;

procedure TForm1.Exit1Click(Sender: TObject);
begin
  Close;
end;

procedure TForm1.FillGrid;
var
  i: Integer;
begin
  Grid.RowCount := FCustomers.Count;
  for i := 0 to FCustomers.Count do begin
    Grid.Cells[0, i] := FCustomers.CustAry[i].CustNo;
    Grid.Cells[1, i] := FCustomers.CustAry[i].Company;
    Grid.Cells[2, i] := FCustomers.CustAry[i].Address;
    Grid.Cells[3, i] := FCustomers.CustAry[i].City;
    Grid.Cells[4, i] := FCustomers.CustAry[i].State;
    Grid.Cells[5, i] := FCustomers.CustAry[i].Zip;
  end;
end;

procedure TForm1.GetandDisplayData;
var
  V: Variant;
begin
  if FDataCom <> nil then begin
    V := FDataCom.GetData;
    FCustomers := VariantToData(V);
  end;
end;

procedure TForm1.bMakeConnectionClick(Sender: TObject);
begin
  CreateConnection(TMenuItem(Sender).Tag = 0);
  GetAndDisplayData;
  FillGrid;
end;

procedure TForm1.Edit1Click(Sender: TObject);
var
  V: Variant;
begin
  if DataEdit.EditCustomer(FCustomers.CustAry[Grid.Selection.Top]) =
  ➥mrOk then
  begin
    FillGrid;
```

continues

20

DCOM

LISTING 20.12 CONTINUED

```
    V := DataEdit.GetCustomerAsVariant;
    FDataCom.UpDateRecord(V);
  end;
end;

procedure TForm1.UpdateData1Click(Sender: TObject);
begin
  GetAndDisplayData;
end;

function TForm1.VariantToData(V: OleVariant): TCustomerRecords;
var
  P: Pointer;
begin
  P := VarArrayLock(V);
  Move(P^, Result, SizeOf(TCustomerRecords));
  VarArrayUnlock(V);
end;

end.
```

LISTING 20.13 THE DataEd1 MODULE PROVIDES A FORM FOR EDITING AN INDIVIDUAL RECORD

```
unit DataEd1;

interface

uses
  Windows, Messages, SysUtils,
  Classes, Graphics, Controls,
  Forms, Dialogs, StdCtrls,
  Globals, ExtCtrls, Buttons;

// The Globals unit is in the Server directory

type
  TDataEdit = class(TForm)
    ECustNo: TEdit;
    ECompany: TEdit;
    EAddress: TEdit;
    ECity: TEdit;
    EState: TEdit;
    EZip: TEdit;
    Label1: TLabel;
    Label2: TLabel;
    Label3: TLabel;
    Label4: TLabel;
    Label5: TLabel;
```

```
    Label6: TLabel;
    BitBtn1: TBitBtn;
    BitBtn2: TBitBtn;
    Bevel1: TBevel;
    procedure BitBtn1Click(Sender: TObject);
  private
    FCustomer: TCustomer;
    procedure FillCustomer;
    procedure GetCustomer;
  public
    function EditCustomer(var ACustomer: TCustomer): Integer;
    function GetCustomerAsVariant: Variant;
  end;

var
  DataEdit: TDataEdit;

implementation

{$R *.DFM}

function TDataEdit.GetCustomerAsVariant: Variant;
var
  V: Variant;
  P: Pointer;
begin
  GetCustomer;
  V := VarArrayCreate([0, SizeOf(TCustomer)] , varByte);
  P := VarArrayLock(V);
  Move(FCustomer, P^, SizeOf(TCustomer));
  VarArrayUnlock(V);
  Result := V;
end;

procedure TDataEdit.GetCustomer;
begin
  with FCustomer do begin
    CustNo := ECustNo.Text;
    Company := ECompany.Text;
    Address := EAddress.Text;
    City := ECity.Text;
    State := EState.Text;
    Zip := EZip.Text;
  end;
end;


procedure TDataEdit.FillCustomer;
begin
  with FCustomer do begin
```

continues

LISTING 20.13   CONTINUED

```
      ECustNo.Text := CustNo;
      ECompany.Text := Company;
      EAddress.Text := Address;
      ECity.Text := City;
      EState.Text := State;
      EZip.Text := Zip;
   end;
end;

function TDataEdit.EditCustomer(var ACustomer: TCustomer): Integer;
begin
  FCustomer := ACustomer;
  FillCustomer;
  Result := ShowModal;
  if Result = mrOk then
    ACustomer := FCustomer;
end;

procedure TDataEdit.BitBtn1Click(Sender: TObject);
begin
  GetCustomer;
end;

end.
```

When you run this program, it provides a menu giving you the option of connecting to the server either locally or remotely. After you connect, a dataset is displayed in a TStringGrid rather than a TDBGrid because I'm just getting rows of data without any available database tools. If I were using MIDAS, I could use a real grid. Even without MIDAS, I could construct a TClientDataSet that would hold the data, fill it manually, and then let the user use a TDBGrid. However, this last option would include tools from the Client/Server version of Delphi, and the whole point of this exercise is not to use those tools.

The program allows you to pop up a dialog that would edit a single record. You can then send your edits back to the server and update a record. I do not include a method for inserting a record, though the infrastructure is available on the server side for supporting this kind of functionality.

Understanding the `DataCOMClient`

The DataCOMClient program starts by retrieving the server either locally or remotely:

```
procedure TForm1.CreateConnection(IsRemote: Boolean);
var
  S: string;
begin
```

```
  Screen.Cursor := crHourGlass;
  try
    if IsRemote then begin
      S := '';
      if InputQuery('Server Name', 'Enter Server Name', S) then
        FDataCom := CoDataCOM.CreateRemote(S)
    end else
      FDataCom := CoDataCOM.Create;
  finally
    Screen.Cursor := crDefault;
  end;
end;
```

All the code shown here was described in some depth earlier in the chapter. Notice that I use the proxy classes from the XXX_TLB file so that I don't have to call CoCreateInstance or CoCreateInstanceEx directly.

After you have hold of the server, you can ask it for a copy of the dataset from the Customer table and then display the data to the user:

```
procedure TForm1.GetandDisplayData;
var
  V: Variant;
begin
  if FDataCom <> nil then begin
    V := FDataCom.GetData;
    FCustomers := VariantToData(V);
    FillGrid;
  end;
end;

function TForm1.VariantToData(V: OleVariant): TCustomerRecords;
var
  P: Pointer;
begin
  P := VarArrayLock(V);
  Move(P^, Result, SizeOf(TCustomerRecords));
  VarArrayUnlock(V);
end;
```

This code calls the GetData function of the DataCOMServer program. It then translates the Variant retrieved from the server into a manageable block of data by calling the utility routine VariantToData. VariantToData locks down the Variant array returned by the server and extracts the custom record from it. This operation is the reverse of the operation performed in the server, where you saw how to pack the custom data into a Variant array.

The FillGrid method simply displays the data in a string grid:

```
procedure TForm1.FillGrid;
var
```

```
    i: Integer;
begin
  Grid.RowCount := FCustomers.Count;
  for i := 0 to FCustomers.Count do begin
    Grid.Cells[0, i] := FCustomers.CustAry[i].CustNo;
    Grid.Cells[1, i] := FCustomers.CustAry[i].Company;
    Grid.Cells[2, i] := FCustomers.CustAry[i].Address;
    Grid.Cells[3, i] := FCustomers.CustAry[i].City;
    Grid.Cells[4, i] := FCustomers.CustAry[i].State;
    Grid.Cells[5, i] := FCustomers.CustAry[i].Zip;
  end;
end;
```

The `Cells` property of the `TStringGrid` object allows you to access the array of data underlying the grid.

Editing a Row of Data

Now that the viewer can see the remote dataset, the only thing left to do is give him or her a chance to edit it:

```
procedure TForm1.Edit1Click(Sender: TObject);
var
  V: Variant;
  Customer: TCustomer;
begin
  Customer := FCustomers.CustAry[Grid.Selection.Top];
  if DataEdit.EditCustomer(Customer) = mrOk then begin
    FCustomers.CustAry[Grid.Selection.Top] := Customer;
    FillGrid;
    V := DataEdit.GetCustomerAsVariant;
    FDataCom.UpDateRecord(V);
  end;
end;
```

The following line of code retrieves the currently selected row from the string grid:

```
Customer := FCustomers.CustAry[Grid.Selection.Top];
```

The key point to grasp here is that `Grid->Selection.Top` designates the currently selected row in the grid.

NOTE

You could actually save two lines of code here by passing in `FCustomers.CustAry[Grid.Selection.Top]` directly to `DataEdit.EditCustomer`. Then you could cut both the first line of the procedure, and the first line of the

You could actually save two lines of code here by passing in
`FCustomers.CustAry[Grid.Selection.Top]` directly to `DataEdit.EditCustomer`.
Then you could cut both the first line of the procedure, and the first line of the
`if` statement. However, the resulting line of code is quite long. In fact, a line
that long is both hard to read and almost impossible to format neatly in a book
of this type. As a result, I took my usual route, which is to write somewhat verbose code that is easy to understand and maintain.

Inside the `TEditData` form, only one routine is of any real interest. This routine is called
`GetCustomerAsVariant`:

```
function TDataEdit.GetCustomerAsVariant: Variant;
var
  V: Variant;
  P: Pointer;
begin
  GetCustomer;
  V := VarArrayCreate([0, SizeOf(TCustomer)] , varByte);
  P := VarArrayLock(V);
  Move(FCustomer, P^, SizeOf(TCustomer));
  VarArrayUnlock(V);
  Result := V;
end;

procedure TDataEdit.GetCustomer;
begin
  with FCustomer do begin
    CustNo := ECustNo.Text;
    Company := ECompany.Text;
    Address := EAddress.Text;
    City := ECity.Text;
    State := EState.Text;
    Zip := EZip.Text;
  end;
end;
```

This code uses the `GetCustomer` function to retrieve the newly edited data from the
`TEditData` form. It then moves the data into a `Variant` array by first locking the array
down and then moving some bytes around via a call to `Move`. The `GetCustomer` method is
used to retrieve the data from the visual controls in the `TEditForm`.

Remote datasets are one of the more powerful aspects of DCOM, though I'm sure you
can imagine many other ways to use this technology.

Program Data and Automation Data

In this section, I want to talk briefly about the difference between data declared in the body of a server program and data declared as a private field of an automation object. The behavior described here concerns the default settings for an automation object, where you select Multiple Instance for instancing and Apartment for the threading model.

In this example, you will see that the data declared in the main form or in global variables will be shared between clients. Data that is declared as a field of the automation object, on the other hand, will be unique to each client. If you take the default settings in the Automation Wizard, each client gets its own instance of the automation object, but they all share the same instance of the server.

By default, when you create a Delphi automation object, one instance of your program will be run on the server. Each time a new client connects to the server, a new instance of the automation object or objects in your server will be created. This means that each client will have access to its own private data inside the automation object. However, the data declared in the nonautomation objects in your program will be shared among the multiple clients.

Consider the MultiUser program found on the CD-ROM that accompanies this book. The source for the server half of this program is shown in Listing 20.14 and Listing 20.15. This DCOM example features a client program called MultiUserClient and a server program called MultiUserServer.

LISTING 20.14 THE MultiUserServer PROGRAM'S AUTOMATION OBJECT

```
unit MainIMPL;

interface

uses
  ComObj, ActiveX, MultiUserServer_TLB;

type
  TMultiUser = class(TAutoObject, IMultiUser)
  private
    FYValue: Integer;
  protected
    function Get_XValue: Integer; safecall;
    procedure Set_XValue(Value: Integer); safecall;
```

```
    function Get_YValue: Integer; safecall;
    procedure Set_YValue(Value: Integer); safecall;
  end;

implementation

uses
  ComServ, MainServer;

function TMultiUser.Get_XValue: Integer;
begin
  Result := Form1.XValue;
end;

procedure TMultiUser.Set_XValue(Value: Integer);
begin
  Form1.XValue := Value;
end;

function TMultiUser.Get_YValue: Integer;
begin
  Result := FYValue;
end;

procedure TMultiUser.Set_YValue(Value: Integer);
begin
  FYValue := Value;
end;

initialization
  TAutoObjectFactory.Create(ComServer, TMultiUser, Class_MultiUser,
    ciMultiInstance, tmApartment);
end.
```

LISTING 20.15   THE MAIN FORM OF THE MultiUser PROGRAM

```
unit MainServer;

interface

uses
  Windows, Messages, SysUtils,
  Classes, Graphics, Controls,
  Forms, Dialogs, jpeg, ExtCtrls;

type
  TForm1 = class(TForm)
    Image1: TImage;
  private
```

continues

20

DCOM

LISTING 20.15 CONTINUED

```
    FXValue: Integer;
    procedure SetXValue(const Value: Integer);
  public
    property XValue: Integer read FXValue write SetXValue;
  end;

var
  Form1: TForm1;

implementation

{$R *.DFM}

{ TForm1 }

procedure TForm1.SetXValue(const Value: Integer);
begin
  FXValue := Value;
end;

end.
```

Note that this program has two pieces of private data: one called FXValue, which belongs to the main form; and one called FYValue, which is a field of the automation object.

In the Type Library Editor for this program, I declared an interface with two properties called XValue and YValue:

```
IMultiUser = interface(IDispatch)
  ['{74504123-2B8F-11D2-9CE8-006008928EEF}']
  function Get_XValue: Integer; safecall;
  procedure Set_XValue(Value: Integer); safecall;
  function Get_YValue: Integer; safecall;
  procedure Set_YValue(Value: Integer); safecall;
  property XValue: Integer read Get_XValue write Set_XValue;
  property YValue: Integer read Get_YValue write Set_YValue;
end;
```

This is the standard way to treat a property in OLE automation. In short, the concept of a true property is not understood by OLE, so you always have to write getters and setters, even if you only want direct access to an underlying data store.

The declaration for the implementation of the IDL code looks like this:

```
TMultiUser = class(TAutoObject, IMultiUser)
private
  FYValue: Integer;
protected
  function Get_XValue: Integer; safecall;
```

```
  procedure Set_XValue(Value: Integer); safecall;
  function Get_YValue: Integer; safecall;
  procedure Set_YValue(Value: Integer); safecall;
end;
```

Here, however, getters and setters would have been necessary in any case because the data the program wants to access resides not inside the automation object, but inside the main form of the server:

```
function TMultiUser.Get_XValue: Integer;
begin
  Result := Form1.XValue;
end;

procedure TMultiUser.Set_XValue(Value: Integer);
begin
  Form1.XValue := Value;
end;
```

In this code, you can see that the get and set methods access the XValue property from Form1.

The YValues, on the other hand, are just fields of the automation object:

```
function TMultiUser.Get_YValue: Integer;
begin
  Result := FYValue;
end;

procedure TMultiUser.Set_YValue(Value: Integer);
begin
  FYValue := Value;
end;
```

The client program that accesses this server has four edit controls and six buttons, as shown in Figure 20.8. The listing for the main form of the client program is shown in Listing 20.16.

FIGURE 20.8

The main form for the MultiUserClient *application.*

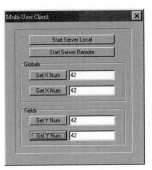

LISTING 20.16   THE MAIN FORM OF THE MultiUserClient PROGRAM

```pascal
unit MainClient;

interface

uses
  Windows, Messages, SysUtils,
  Classes, Graphics, Controls,
  Forms, Dialogs, StdCtrls,
  ExtCtrls, MultiUserServer_TLB;

type
  TForm2 = class(TForm)
    Bevel1: TBevel;
    StartServer: TButton;
    GetXNumBtn: TButton;
    SetXNumBtn: TButton;
    SetXNumEdit: TEdit;
    StartServerRemoteBtn: TButton;
    GetYNumEdit: TEdit;
    GetYNumBtn: TButton;
    SetYNumBtn: TButton;
    SetYNumEdit: TEdit;
    GroupBox1: TGroupBox;
    GroupBox2: TGroupBox;
    GetXNumEdit: TEdit;
    procedure StartServerClick(Sender: TObject);
    procedure StartServerRemoteBtnClick(Sender: TObject);
    procedure SetXNumBtnClick(Sender: TObject);
    procedure GetXNumBtnClick(Sender: TObject);
    procedure SetYNumBtnClick(Sender: TObject);
    procedure GetYNumBtnClick(Sender: TObject);
  private
    FMultiUser: IMultiUser;
  end;

var
  Form2: TForm2;

implementation

{$R *.DFM}

procedure TForm2.StartServerClick(Sender: TObject);
begin
  FMultiUser := CoMultiUser.Create;
end;


procedure TForm2.StartServerRemoteBtnClick(Sender: TObject);
var
```

```
    MachineName: string;
begin
    MachineName := '';
    if InputQuery('Machine Name', 'Machine Name', MachineName) then
        FMultiUser := CoMultiUser.CreateRemote(MachineName);
end;

procedure TForm2.SetXNumBtnClick(Sender: TObject);
begin
    if FMultiUser <> nil then
        FMultiUser.Set_XValue(StrToInt(SetXNumEdit.Text));
end;

procedure TForm2.GetXNumBtnClick(Sender: TObject);
begin
    if FMultiUser <> nil then
        GetXNumEdit.Text := IntToStr(FMultiUser.Get_XValue);
end;

procedure TForm2.SetYNumBtnClick(Sender: TObject);
begin
    if FMultiUser <> nil then
        FMultiUser.Set_YValue(StrToInt(SetYNumEdit.Text));
end;

procedure TForm2.GetYNumBtnClick(Sender: TObject);
begin
    if FMultiUser <> nil then
        GetYNumEdit.Text := IntToStr(FMultiUser.Get_YValue);
end;

end.
```

This program lets you set the global data in the server's main form and the local data declared as a field of the server's automation object. If you start multiple clients, you will see that each has its own copy of the automation object's data, but they all share the data declared in the server's main form. To see this, you should start up multiple clients. It is fine if all the clients are running on the same machine, or you can spread them out across the network, if you desire.

This program initializes the server either remotely or locally using the same techniques covered earlier in this chapter. After the server is running, it calls the get_XValue and set_XValue methods to get and set the underlying data store in the main form of the server program. If you connect to this server from two different instances of the client program located on two different machines, they will be able to pass integer values back and forth. In other words, if client A changes the FXPos value to 25, then client B will be able to read that same value back. This would not be the case if I had declared FXPos as a field of the automation object itself.

All this information may sound rather unexciting until you consider some of the possibilities. In particular, you could use this mechanism to share data when two remote users were collaborating on the same document. Gamers could use this mechanism to allow two remote users to participate in a chess or checkers match.

Testing the Remote Debugging System

If you are on an NT machine, you can debug both the client and server parts of a client/server application at the same time. That is, you can run both from inside the IDE and step through the code of both applications.

The client server version of Delphi lets you debug applications remotely. You might want to use this feature when a program runs okay on your development machine but does not run correctly on a second machine. It is also a way to test out client/server programs and to debug DirectX exclusive mode applications.

The purpose of this brief section is to describe how to debug an application remotely. To get started, put the client/server version of the Delphi CD in the drive and install remote debugging, if you have not done so already. On the first version of Delphi 4, before any patches or fixes were released, installing remote debugging makes it impossible for you to run MTS servers, so don't install this feature of you are running Delphi 4 and MTS is important to you.

Here is how to get started with remote debugging. On the remote machine, go to the `c:\program files\common files\borland shared\debugging` directory and type the following:

```
borrdbg -listen
```

This line starts the Borland Remote Debugger on the remote machine. On an NT machine, you can just run this executable as a service that you set from the Services applet in the Control Panel.

On the client machine, create a new application, put a single button on it, and write the following code in response to a click on the button:

```
procedure TForm1.Button1Click(Sender: TObject);
begin
  Caption := 'Foo';
end;
```

Select Project, Options and turn to the Linker page. Check Include Remote Debug Symbols. Then create a file called `Project1.rsm`.

Turn to the Directories Conditional page and set the output directory to some location you have mapped to on the remote machine. For instance, set it to `c:\temp`. Obviously, you can get the application you want to debug onto the remote machine in many other ways, but this method will do for testing purposes. Click OK to close the dialog.

Choose Run, Parameters. Turn to the Remote page in the Run Parameters dialog and type in the local path for the remote location of your executable. For instance, if you are going to place the application on the C: drive off the remote machine, type in the following:

```
C:\temp\project1.exe
```

Notice that I have included the full path on the remote machine, as well as the executable name that you are going to run. If you are mapped to the C: drive on the remote machine, do not type in the drive letter you have mapped to. For instance, if the C: drive of the remote machine is mapped to your N: drive, do not type the following:

```
N:\temp\project1.exe;
```

Type the name of the drive on the remote machine, not the logical drive, but the actual drive on the remote machine, as shown in the first of these two examples. Type the IP address or the name of your remote server in the Remote Host field. While you are in the Run Parameters dialog, make sure the Debug Project on Remote Machine option is checked. Click OK to close the Run Parameters dialog.

At this stage, you are ready to run. Set a breakpoint on the sole line of code in your program and run the application. The program should start visibly on the remote machine. Click the button on the form of the program on the remote machine. You should be taken back to the breakpoint you set in your source code on the local machine. You can now step through your code as if you were on your local machine.

Summary

In this chapter, you learned how to use Delphi to build applications that take advantage of the Distributed Component Object Model. You have seen that combining Delphi, DCOM, and OLE automation provides a simple method for allowing one application to control or use another application that resides on a second machine.

People who are interested in this field should look at Borland's Entera and OLE Enterprise products, as well as the Borland CORBA technology.

Because DCOM is so simple to use, distributing the workload of a particular application across multiple machines is now easy. My guess is that distributing computing will prove to be one of the most important fields of computer science over the next 5 to 10 years.

MIDAS

CHAPTER 21

In this chapter, you will learn about multitier database computing as implemented in a Delphi-hosted technology called MIDAS. Multitier database computing allows you to partition applications so you can access data on a second machine without having a full set of database tools on your local machine. It also allows you to centralize business rules and processes and distribute the processing load throughout the network.

The difference between this chapter and the preceding chapter, "DCOM," is that this chapter focuses on database computing, whereas the preceding chapter focused on distributed objects. One example in that chapter worked with databases, but it merely showed one custom and rather limited way to marshal data between machines without using MIDAS. This chapter uses MIDAS in all its examples, which means it features a more general-purpose and robust technology. It also means that you must have a copy of the Client/Server version of Delphi to run the programs in this chapter. The examples in the preceding chapter, however, did not require the Client/Server version of the product.

This chapter is divided into three parts:

- An introduction to multitier database computing
- An overview of Borland's MIDAS Technology
- A detailed look at creating MIDAS servers and clients

Throughout this chapter, I will use the terms *multitier computing*, *distributed datasets*, *remote datasets*, and *MIDAS* as approximate synonyms. In the next section of the chapter, you'll find some comments on terminology that should help you to understand the significance of these words.

An Overview of Multitier Computing

In this section, I make a few broad statements about multitier database computing. My goal is to give a general definition of the technology, particularly for the sake of users who are new to the subject. In later portions of the chapter, the discussion will be increasingly technical and increasingly specific.

Borland supports a three-tier technology, which in its classic form consists of the following:

- A database server on one machine
- An application server on a second machine
- A thin client on a third machine

The server would be a tool such as InterBase, Oracle, Sybase, MS SQL server, and so on. The application server and the thin client would be built in Delphi. The application server would contain the business rules and the tools for manipulating the data. The client would do nothing more than present the data to the user for viewing and editing.

In most scenarios, the database access software (for example, BDE, SQL*NET, and so on) would run on the same machine as the application server. Remember that this is simply the classic case, and many other configurations are possible.

N-tier computing refers to the fact that all these tiers can be spread out across multiple machines. For instance, you might have the employee server on one machine and the payroll server on another machine. One of these application servers might access Oracle data from machine C, and the other server might access InterBase data from machine D. Hence, you have not three tiers, but n-tiers.

> **NOTE**
>
> The term *n-tier* could be considered a bit misleading, at least from some perspectives. No matter how you break up your database servers, application servers, and clients, you still end up with three tiers of computing. Just because you have the middle tier spread out over 10 machines doesn't really change the fact that all 10 machines are involved in middle-tier computing.

The Delphi team refers to their specific tools for implementing this technology as distributed datasets or MIDAS. Delphi implements a multitier technology via a set of components, and our documents refer to the technology supported by these components as both distributed datasets. *MIDAS* is the term the marketing team uses to refer to this same technology.

If the definition of distributed technology given here seems a bit abstract to you, then it might help to consider the fact that the Web is a classic distributed technology. In particular, a person working on the Web can use a browser to view a dataset on a remote machine without having any database tools on the client. Quite frequently the database server does not run on the same machine as the Web server. As a result, you once again end up with three tiers: the browser on the client, the Web server on the middle tier, and the database server on the third tier. The same basic format is found on Borland's multitier implementation of distributed datasets.

Unlike MIDAS, browsers are limited in terms of functionality and performance. For instance, on the Web it is difficult to enforces constraints; to program a browser to perform a join; to create a fancy, modern, high-performance interface; or to set up tables in a one-to-many relationship. These chores are simple to execute inside a Delphi multitier application. Delphi's high-performance compiled applications are much faster and much more responsive than HTML-based applications. (However, you can put MIDAS in an ActiveForm and show that over the Web if your clients support ActiveX—that is, if your clients are using Internet Explorer.)

What Is MIDAS?

MIDAS is based on technology that allows you to package datasets in a Variant and send them across the network as parameters to remote method calls. It includes technology for converting a dataset into a Variant on the server side, and then unbundling the dataset on the client and displaying it to the user in a grid via the aid of the TClientDataSet component.

Seen from a slightly different angle, MIDAS is a technology for moving a dataset from a TTable or TQuery object on a server to a TClientDataSet object on a client. TClientDataSet looks, acts, and feels exactly like a TTable or TQuery component, except that it doesn't have to be attached to the BDE. In this particular case, the TClientDataSet gets its data from unpacking the variant that it retrieves from the server.

MIDAS allows you to use all the standard Delphi components including database tools in your client-side applications, but the client side does not have to include the Borland Database Engine, ODBC, or any client database libraries (for example, Oracle SQL*NET, Sybase CT-Lib, and so on). Somewhere on the network, the BDE or a similar engine needs to exist, but you don't need to have it on the client side. In short, you now need only one set of server-side database tools, whereas before you needed database tools on each client machine. A small (about 211KB) file called DBCLIENT.DLL is needed on the client side, but that is very little when compared with the many megabytes of files required by the BDE or other database middle-ware.

> **NOTE**
>
> Perhaps I should make a few brief comments about the word behind the technology. Midas was a mythical king of Greece who received from Dionysus a gift enabling him to turn all he touched into gold. After a period in which all his food and key members of his family were turned into gold, Midas grew weary of the gift and was released from it by washing his hands in a river. The sands of that river were then turned into golden-colored sand, a fact to which contemporary visitors of Greece can still attest today.

The two different layers of the MIDAS technology are as follows:

- The components found on the Component Palette and built in the VCL.
- The protocol used to send messages over the Internet. This layer might be DCOM, OLEnterprise, CORBA, or just plain old TCP/IP.

The built-in Delphi components enable you to easily connect two machines and pass datasets back and forth between them. In the simplest scenarios, they make it possible for you to build middle-tier and client applications with just a few clicks of the mouse.

Goals of Distributed Computing

One of the big goals of distributed computing is to create servers that contain all the rules and logic for accessing data. In a typical example, you might have one or more large NT servers hosting a series of MIDAS application servers built in Delphi. These servers can serve up data to its clients. All the logic and intelligence will be in the server, and the client will just be a thin shell that enables the user to view and edit the data.

You can create a whole complex of servers working together to represent complex entities such as a company or department. One server might represent the payroll department, another the human resources department, and a third might keep track of inventory. Or you could even break up the model into more fine-tuned entities, such as one server that represents an employee object, one that represents a widget, and a third that represents the company calendar.

As you can tell from the examples listed in the preceding two paragraphs, a clear parallel exists between distributed computing and OOP. Just as each entity in a program should have its own object, each entity, or perhaps each related group of entities, should have its own MIDAS application server.

This approach to distributed technology turns a network into a resource full of intelligent objects that can represent the entire structure of your company. The idea is to keep the clients simple and to put the intelligence in the middle tier. Over time the middle tier should become so intelligent that it appears to represent its own powerful force in the computing world. To a large degree, the Web has already achieved this goal. Furthermore, the claim of one bold company that the "network is the computer" very closely reflects the idea behind distributed computing.

Distributed datasets are one means of cutting down on network traffic. After you download data from the server, you can manipulate it on the client side, without initiating any more network traffic until you are ready to update the server. This means you can edit, insert, and delete multiple records without causing network traffic. When you're ready to update the server, you can send multiple data packets over the network at one specific, prechosen time.

Access to database constraints are another important aspect of the MIDAS technology. When you download data from the server, you can simultaneously download a set of constraints that will be automatically enforced. The constraints can help programmers ensure that the user enters only valid data. When you are reconnected to the network, your data can then be updated without mishap.

If perchance an error does occur while you are updating the dataset, then built-in mechanisms can aid the programmer in reporting and handling the error. For instance, if a second user has updated a record that you are trying to update, then that fact can be surfaced, and the user can be given a choice of options on how to proceed. A prebuilt form that ships in the Delphi Object Repository makes it simple to implement error handling in your application.

Yet another important feature of Borland's multitier computing includes distributing the load borne by a database over multiple servers, as well as providing fail over capabilities in case of an error. This subject will be explored in more depth in the next section and also in the technical sections found in the latter half of the chapter.

An Overview of the Briefcase Model

Using what is called the *briefcase model*, you can disconnect the client from the network and still access the data. Here's how it works:

- Save a remote dataset to disk, shut down your machine, and disconnect from the network. You can then boot up again and edit your data without connecting to the network.

- When you get back to the network, you can reconnect and update the database. A mechanism is provided for being notified about database errors and resolving any conflicts that might occur. For instance, if two people edited the same record, then you will be notified of the fact and given options to resolve the problem. All this occurs without the presence of large database tools on the client machine.

The point is that you don't have to actually be able to reach the server at all times to be able to work with your data. This capability is ideal for laptop users or for sites where you want to keep database traffic to a minimum.

Terminology

I want to spend a few paragraphs on terminology because the technology is new and is being interpreted in various ways by different companies. This chapter is about something called, at various times,

- Distributed computing
- Client/server computing
- Multitier computing
- n-tiered computing
- Remote datasets
- Distributed datasets

A host of other terms are also used, many of which are often cited out of context or in a very loosely defined manner. In general, I find this field of computing to be overrun with marketing propaganda. To get anything done, you have to understand the technology itself. You should work hard to avoid being sucked in by a lot of fancy word slingers who wouldn't know a curly brace from a `begin..end` pair, a `LongInt` from a `LongWord`, an integer from an interface, a `not` from a `null`, a variable from a reference, a buffer from a debugger, a substring from a subtype, a callback from a rollback, or a module from a mutex.

Finding a Broker

Delphi and MIDAS provide access to several different brokers. You can access world-class brokers like those you find in CORBA and Entera and smaller, more modest brokers such as Delphi's `TSimpleObjectBroker` and `OLEnterprise`. In between, you will find MTS, which is a growing technology with a future that is not yet clearly defined.

`OLEnterprise` provides an alternative to DCOM, which can, under some circumstances, simplify the task of connecting two machines and particularly of connecting two Windows 95/98 machines. `OLEnterprise` comes from Borland's purchase of the Open Environment Corporation. The purchase of OEC also gave Borland access to an Object Broker that allows you to randomly distribute the load of a task across several servers. In particular, you can load your server tools on several machines; then the broker will choose one of these machines each time you make a connection. For example, if you had 100 clients and three servers, the Object Broker would randomly divide the load across the three servers so that each had (approximately) 33 clients.

The broker also provides support for those occasions when a server is forced to shut down unexpectedly. By writing a few lines of code, you can provide fail over services that would switch clients of a downed server over to a running server. Furthermore, the broker would never attempt to connect a new client to a server that had gone down but would instead automatically connect the client to one of the servers that is still running. I include a sample 20-line procedure later in this chapter that demonstrates how to implement this fail over process in the section "Using OLEnterprise."

If you don't want to use OLEnterprise, fail over and load distribution are also provided by the TSimpleObjectBroker component. This component will serve up a computer name from a list of computer names, and then you can ask that computer for the interface you desire. In Delphi 4, TSimpleObjectBroker does not know anything about interfaces. It will only serve up a list of computer names, but it will give you the list in random order, thereby providing you with load balancing and support for fail over. Over time, the TSimpleObjectBroker technology may be improved and expanded, so if you are reading this book some months or years after Delphi 4 shipped, you might want to look for updates that expand the object's functionality.

Neither OLEnterprise nor the TSimpleObjectBroker provide the same level of service that you would get from a CORBA or Entera broker. Both CORBA and Entera are designed to provide true load balancing and fail over, and they are sophisticated enough to keep a mission-critical application server running 24 hours a day, seven days a week.

MTS provides a level of support somewhere between that provided by OLEnterprise and that provided by a technology such as CORBA. You can use MIDAS with either CORBA or MTS. MIDAS is somewhat harder to use on MTS, however, because MTS prefers that its objects not maintain state. For more information, read Chapter 23, "MTS," and Chapter 24, "CORBA."

Technology Details: Using Distributed Datasets

It is now time to start analyzing the technology involved in Delphi's Distributed datasets. In other words, the chapter now switches from theory to practice. This section gives an overview of the components involved in this technology, and the next section begins a detailed examination of the components.

Four key Delphi tools make Distributed datasets possible. The first two appear on the server side:

- *Remote data modules* are just like standard data modules, except that they help you broadcast data not to your current application, but to locations on the network. In particular, they turn a simple data module into a COM object, thereby allowing you to access the data module from a remote server via DCOM.

- The TProvider component resides on remote data modules just as a TTable object can reside on a standard data module. The difference is that a TProvider broadcasts a table across the network. Provider objects are also included in the TTable and TQuery objects as properties. However, if you access them as standalone components, you will have more flexibility and power. In particular, you hook up a TProvider component to a TTable or TQuery so that other programs on the network can access the data from the TTable or TQuery via DCOM. The job of the remote data module is to give clients access to the specific providers available on a server. The client first connects to the remote data module and then queries the remote data module for a list of available providers on its server.

On the client side, you use two components to access the data supplied by the server:

- The TRemoteServer component gives the client the ability to connect to the server. More specifically, it connects to the COM interface supported by the remote data module. Despite the implication inherent in its name, TRemoteServers exist on the client side, not on the server side. TRemoteServer is the component that knows how to browse the Registry in search of available servers. After the server is found, the TRemoteServer will connect to it.

- The TClientDataSet component hooks up to the TRemoteServer component and then attaches to a specific provider on the server. They give the data sources on the client application something to plug into when they want to connect to a remote dataset. In short, the TClientDataSet plays the same role as a TQuery or TTable, except that it serves up data from a remote site. Imagine the traditional TDatabase, TTable, TDataSource, TDBGrid configuration seen in many standard Delphi applications. In a remote dataset, you make a slight change to these configurations by using TRemoteServer, TClientDataSet, TDataSource, and TDBGrid. In this new scenario, TRemoteServer plays a role roughly parallel to TDatabase, and TClientDataSet plays a role fairly similar to that traditionally played by TTable or TQuery. I don't mean to imply a one-to-one correspondence between TDatabase and TRemoteServer, but a rough similarity can be seen between the roles played by the two components.

The diagram shown in Figure 21.1 depicts the architecture of a remote dataset application. On the top of half of the picture is the server side of the equation, which consists of a remote data module, three tables, and three providers. On the client side, you find a TRemoteServer and three TClientDatasets. Attached to the client dataset, you could have a series of data sources and visual controls. Notice that you need one provider and one client dataset for each table you want to broadcast. You could have varying numbers of tables, as well as many other objects, forms, and so on, on each side of the equation. My goal here is to focus on only the core elements in a proposed three-table scenario that must be present to make the concept of remote datasets work.

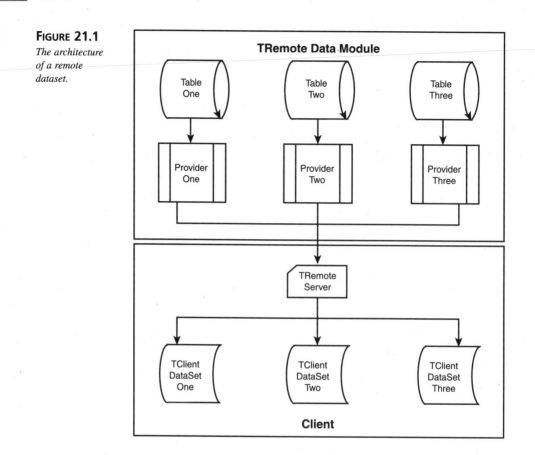

FIGURE 21.1

The architecture of a remote dataset.

Building a Simple MIDAS Application

In this section, I will describe one possible technique for building a server for a remote dataset. Here is a quick overview of the steps involved:

1. Start a new application, hook it up to some data as you would in any other Delphi application, and save it to disk.

2. Choose File, New to create a remote data module.

3. Place one or more TTable and TProvider components on the remote data module.

4. Hook up the TProvider to the TTable or TQuery object.

5. Right-click on the TProvider to create interface methods for accessing the provider on a remote machine.

6. Save your work and run the server once to register it.

On the disk that comes with this book you will find a sample program called SimpleMidas. It represents the simplest possible MIDAS application that you can build. You can see the key files in the client and server for this application in Listings 21.1 through 21.3.

LISTING 21.1 THE `MainImpl.pas` FILE CONTAINS THE IMPLEMENTATION OF THE SimpleMidas SERVER

```pascal
unit MainIMPL;

interface

uses
  Windows, Messages, SysUtils,
  Classes, Graphics, Controls,
  Forms, Dialogs, ComServ,
  ComObj, VCLCom, StdVcl,
  BdeProv, DataBkr, DBClient,
  SimpleMidasServer_TLB, Provider, Db,
  DBTables;

type
  TSimpleMidas = class(TRemoteDataModule, ISimpleMidas)
    CountryTable: TTable;
    CountryProvider: TProvider;
  private
    { Private declarations }
  public
    { Public declarations }
  protected
    function Get_CountryProvider: IProvider; safecall;
  end;

var
  SimpleMidas: TSimpleMidas;

implementation

{$R *.DFM}

function TSimpleMidas.Get_CountryProvider: IProvider;
begin
  Result := CountryProvider.Provider;
end;

initialization
  TComponentFactory.Create(ComServer, TSimpleMidas,
    Class_SimpleMidas, ciMultiInstance, tmApartment);
end.
```

LISTING 21.2   THE LIBRARY FILE FOR THE SimpleMidas SERVER

```
unit SimpleMidasServer_TLB;

//****************************************************************** //
// WARNING                                                          //
// -------                                                          //
// The types declared in this file were generated from data read    //
// from a Type Library. If this type library is explicitly or       //
// indirectly (via another type library referring to this type      //
// library) reimported, or the 'Refresh' command of the Type Library //
// Editor activated while editing the Type Library, the contents of //
// this file will be regenerated and all                            //
// manual modifications will be lost.                               //
//****************************************************************** //

// PASTLWTR : $Revision:   1.11.1.63  $
// File generated on 7/27/98 5:54:21 PM from Type Library
// described below.

//****************************************************************** //
// Type Lib: D:\SrcPas\Unleash4\Chap21\SimpleMidas\Server\
// SimpleMidasServer.tlb
// IID\LCID: {CD905942-257C-11D2-95FB-0060979302AC}\0
// Helpfile:
// HelpString: SimpleMidasServer Library
// Version:   1.0
//****************************************************************** //

interface

uses Windows, ActiveX, Classes, Graphics, OleCtrls, StdVCL;

//****************************************************************** //
// GUIDS declared in the TypeLibrary. Following prefixes are used:  //
//    Type Libraries     : LIBID_xxxx                               //
//    CoClasses          : CLASS_xxxx                               //
//    DISPInterfaces      : DIID_xxxx                               //
//    Non-DISP interfaces: IID_xxxx                                //
//****************************************************************** //
const
  LIBID_SimpleMidasServer: TGUID =
  ➥'{CD905942-257C-11D2-95FB-0060979302AC}';
  IID_ISimpleMidas: TGUID = '{CD905943-257C-11D2-95FB-0060979302AC}';
  CLASS_SimpleMidas: TGUID = '{CD905945-257C-11D2-95FB-0060979302AC}';
type

//****************************************************************** //
// Forward declaration of interfaces defined in Type Library        //
//****************************************************************** //
```

```
  ISimpleMidas = interface;
  ISimpleMidasDisp = dispinterface;

//****************************************************************** //
// Declaration of CoClasses defined in Type Library                //
// (NOTE: Here we map each CoClass to its Default Interface)        //
//****************************************************************** //
  SimpleMidas = ISimpleMidas;


//****************************************************************** //
// Interface: ISimpleMidas
// Flags:     (4416) Dual OleAutomation Dispatchable
// GUID:      {CD905943-257C-11D2-95FB-0060979302AC}
//****************************************************************** //
  ISimpleMidas = interface(IDataBroker)
    ['{CD905943-257C-11D2-95FB-0060979302AC}']
    function Get_CountryProvider: IProvider; safecall;
    property CountryProvider: IProvider read Get_CountryProvider;
  end;

//****************************************************************** //
// DispIntf:  ISimpleMidasDisp
// Flags:     (4416) Dual OleAutomation Dispatchable
// GUID:      {CD905943-257C-11D2-95FB-0060979302AC}
//****************************************************************** //
  ISimpleMidasDisp = dispinterface
    ['{CD905943-257C-11D2-95FB-0060979302AC}']
    property CountryProvider: IProvider readonly dispid 1;
    function GetProviderNames: OleVariant; dispid 22929905;
  end;

  CoSimpleMidas = class
    class function Create: ISimpleMidas;
    class function CreateRemote(const MachineName: string): ISimpleMidas;
  end;

implementation

uses ComObj;

class function CoSimpleMidas.Create: ISimpleMidas;
begin
  Result := CreateComObject(CLASS_SimpleMidas) as ISimpleMidas;
end;

class function CoSimpleMidas.CreateRemote(
  const MachineName: string): ISimpleMidas;
```

continues

LISTING 21.2 CONTINUED

```
begin
  Result := CreateRemoteComObject(MachineName,
    CLASS_SimpleMidas) as ISimpleMidas;
end;

end.
```

LISTING 21.3 THE SOURCE FOR THE MAIN FORM OF THE SimpleMidasClient
APPLICATION

```
unit MainClient;

interface

uses
  Windows, Messages, SysUtils,
  Classes, Graphics, Controls,
  Forms, Dialogs, Db,
  DBClient, MConnect, Grids,
  DBGrids, Menus;

type
  TForm2 = class(TForm)
    DCOMConnection1: TDCOMConnection;
    ClientDataSet1: TClientDataSet;
    DataSource1: TDataSource;
    DBGrid1: TDBGrid;
    MainMenu1: TMainMenu;
    Connect1: TMenuItem;
    procedure Connect1Click(Sender: TObject);
  private
    { Private declarations }
  public
    { Public declarations }
  end;

var
  Form2: TForm2;

implementation

{$R *.DFM}

procedure TForm2.Connect1Click(Sender: TObject);
begin
```

```
    DComConnection1.Connected := True;
    ClientDataSet1.Active := True;
end;

end.
```

This application and client pair display the Country table of the `DBDEMOS` database. The client side of the equation has a simple grid on it displaying the contents of the Country table, as shown in Figure 21.2. The server side has no interface, so I simply put a picture of some gargoyles on it, as shown in Figure 21.3.

Name	Capital	Continent	Area
Argentina	Buenos Aires	South America	27
Bolivia	La Paz	South America	10
Brazil	Brasilia	South America	851
Canada	Ottawa	North America	99
Chile	Santiago	South America	7
Colombia	Bagota	South America	11
Cuba	Havana	North America	1
Ecuador	Quito	South America	4
El Salvador	San Salvador	North America	
Guyana	Georgetown	South America	2
Jamaica	Kingston	North America	
Mexico	Mexico City	North America	19
Nicaragua	Managua	North America	1
Paraguay	Asuncion	South America	4
Peru	Lima	South America	12
United States of America	Washington	North America	93

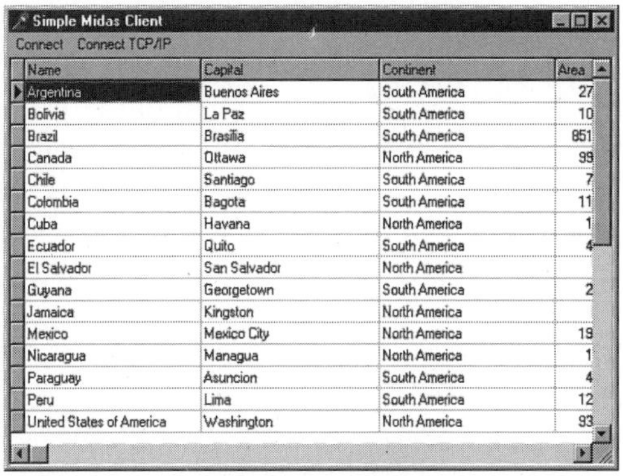

FIGURE 21.2
The main form of the `SimpleMidasClient` *displays the Country table in a standard Delphi grid.*

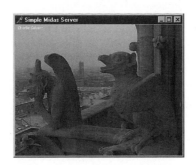

FIGURE 21.3
The main form of the `SimpleMidasServer` *has no interface to speak of, so I display a picture on its surface.*

Creating the `SimpleMidasServer`

To get started re-creating the `SimpleMidasServer`, you should start a Delphi application and save it to disk. When I made the program, I created a single directory called `SimpleMidas` and beneath it two directories called `Server` and `Client`. I saved the main form of the server as `MainServer.pas` and the project file itself as `SimpleMidasServer.dpr`.

> **NOTE**
>
> You will find me uncharacteristically dogmatic about the names I suggest you give the components and examples shown in this chapter. Of course, you are free to name your controls whatever you want, and ultimately I naturally expect and want you to give them your own names. The somewhat claustrophobic dogmatism that I exhibit in this chapter occurs because the names you give to various controls will come into play several times in ways that are not immediately evident at first.
>
> For instance, when you are creating the client/server pairs for the examples in this chapter, you will probably end up opening the Project Manager and displaying both the client and the server at the same time in a single group. If you call the main form of each program `Main.pas`, then you will have created two legal programs, but you will end up with two files called `Main.pas` open in the IDE. Having two such files is not an error, but it can waste your time, as you may find yourself pressing Ctrl+Tab to the wrong page on an annoyingly frequent basis. As a result, I suggest naming the server's main form `MainServer` and the client's main form `MainClient`. If you follow this convention, you will always know which form is which.
>
> Another example occurs later in the chapter when you drop down a control called `TProvider`. I will again ask you to give this control a specific name. The reason for using this naming convention is that you will be able to access this name from the client program. If you do not give the control a reasonable name, then you might not know what you are looking at when you are in your client program.
>
> In short, I believe that naming conventions are very important in this type of program. As a result, I get a bit dogmatic about the names I suggest. If you can stand a bit of overly confining rigidity for a short while, then after you grasp the reasoning behind my suggested names, you can develop your own conventions—or not—depending on your own inclinations.

Choose File, New, MultiTier and elect to create a new Remote Data Module. Set the `ClassName` field to `SimpleMidas` and leave everything else at its default value. By accepting the default threading and instance model, you will automatically create a server that has the correct threading model to handle multiple clients at the same time. Click OK and save your work as `MainIMPL.pas`.

Drop a `TTable` object on the remote data module and rename it `CountryTable`. Hook it up to the Country table from the DBDEMOS database. Drop down a `TProvider` component and rename it `CountryProvider`. Attach its `DataSet` field to the `TTable` object. Then right-click on it and choose Export Country Provider from Data Module from the menu. Save your work and run the application once to register it.

That is all you need to do to create a MIDAS server. If you get good at it, you should be able to finish all these steps in well under five minutes. That's not instantaneous, but it is an improvement of the time required by most other distributed database development platforms in the same way that taking a jet airplane from Washington, D.C., to San Francisco is an improvement over walking. Of course, you would learn a lot if you walked from the Washington monument to the Golden Gate, but perhaps this is not entirely the right time in your life to undertake such an adventure.

Understanding the Server

As simple as it is to build the server, you still need to understand a bit more of what goes on beneath the covers. You don't need detailed knowledge, but a few things should be laid out as clearly as possible.

The following is the main class in your implementation unit:

```
TSimpleMidas = class(TRemoteDataModule, ISimpleMidas)
  CountryTable: TTable;
  CountryProvider: TProvider;
protected
  function Get_CountryProvider: IProvider; safecall;
end;
```

Class declarations of this type provide an implementation for a COM object. The COM interface in question is called ISimpleMidas. You should note that ISimpleMidas is a dual-interfaced COM object, which means that it supports both IDispatch and ISimpleMidas. It can be accessed from other applications via OLE automation and from remote machines via distributed COM. ISimpleMidas has an accompanying type library, declared in a separate unit, and shown in Listing 21.2. (If you are having trouble understanding terms such as *COM object* or *type library*, you can go back and read Chapters 13, "Interfaces and the Basics of COM," and 14, "TComObject, TTypedComObject, and Type Libraries.")

Even if it didn't have any methods, you could access the TSimpleMidas object from a second application or second machine. Under such circumstances, you could do nothing more than launch the server. It would have no functionality.

To make the server useful, you have to provide a mechanism that allows the client to get at the TProvider object you dropped on the remote data module. More particularly, you need to access the IProvider interface supported by the TProvider component. To give

clients access to a provider, you need to add properties to the `ISimpleMidas` COM
object. This process is simple, but you can do it in several different simple ways. As a
result, I will treat all the options in the following section.

Exporting the `IProvider` Interface

You can choose from four ways to add a property to a Remote Data Module that will
automatically export the provider interface:

- As you have seen, you can right-click on a `TProvider` object and select Export
  XXX from Data Module, where *XXX* is the name of your `TProvider` component.
  The code produced by this action is explained later. If you right-click on the
  provider component and don't see this option, then that means it has already been
  selected. In other words, the option is removed from the menu after you select it
  once.

- You also have the option to export the provider interface directly from a `TTable` or
  `TQuery` object placed on a remote data module. Each `TTable` or `TQuery` object has
  a provider interface built into it. Most programmers will probably use this
  `IProvider` interface rather than the one from the `TProvider` object. I like to use a
  separate `TProvider` object because it makes my program easier to understand and
  provides me with a more flexible structure. In particular, I could point the standalone `TProvider` component to a different table and yield different results. You
  should also note the events associated with the `TProvider` component. These
  events are not available if you access this interface directly from a `TTable` or
  `TQuery`. Regardless of my preferences, your code will work perfectly well if you
  never drop a `TProvider` component on a remote data module but instead use the
  `IProvider` interface on the `TTable` or `TQuery` object.

- Another alternative is to select Edit, Add to Interface from the Delphi menu. You
  can then create a property called `CountryProvider` that returns an `IProvider` interface, as shown in Figure 21.4. In short, you can use this tool to add a property to
  the COM object that is being created behind the scenes. I describe this technique in
  more depth later in this same section of the chapter.

FIGURE 21.4

*Adding an inter-
face to a COM
object by choosing
Edit, Add to
Interface.*

- If you want to get even more technical, you can perform this same act using the Type Library Editor, which you can reach from the View menu.

Of these methods, a right-click action on the `TProvider`, `TQuery`, or `TTable` object is the simplest to perform, so they are the default techniques you should employ. As you know, I prefer to use a `TProvider` component, but in simple programs like this, my preference is merely a matter of taste.

If you select Edit, Add to Interface, a small dialog like the one shown in Figure 21.4 appears. Fill in the Declaration field with this line:

```
property CountryProvider: IProvider;
```

This line adds a property called `CountryProvider` to the `ISimpleMidas` COM object. The purpose of this property is to give remote clients access to the `CustomerProvider` object. The same ends will be achieved if you simply right-click on the object and select the appropriate menu item.

Whatever technique you choose, you should end up with a method that looks like this:

```
function TSimpleMidas.Get_CountryProvider: IProvider;
begin
  Result := CountryProvider.Provider;
end;
```

The declaration, `begin..end` pair, and single assignment statement for this method are created automatically by the IDE. If you used the Type Library Editor or chose Edit, Add to Interface to create the method, you would need to write the singe line of code that returns the `IProvider` interface from the `CountryProvider` object. This task is taken care of for you automatically if you just right-click on the component and select Export *XXX* from Data Module from the menu.

When you're using type libraries directly to create this method, you will notice that along with these `Get` methods, a `Set` method is also produced for the property. You can leave it blank or use the Type Library Editor to remove it. In other words, having an empty method in your `TCustOrdersRemoteData` object that looks like this is not an error:

```
function TCustOrdersRemoteData.Set_OrdersDataSet: IProvider;
begin

end;
```

Preparing the Server for the Client Program

If you now save your work and run the program once to register it with the system, then you will create a remote data server. You now have the choice of accessing the server locally or placing this object on a remote NT server, as described later in the chapter.

The following is a summary of the steps outlined in the sections on building a server:

1. Create a standard Delphi application.
2. Add a remote data module and drop down a TTable and a TProvider object on it.
3. Use the DataSet property of the TProvider to connect to the TTable object.
4. Right-click on the TProvider to create a method that retrieves the appropriate provider interface.
5. Compile the application and run it once on the client. You can now test your application. If you want to move the server to a remote machine, run it once on the client and once on the remote machine.

As you can see, building an application server in Delphi is simple. I have gone into such detail when explaining the process so that you can become familiar with the theory behind the process, thereby understanding not only how to build the server, but why it is architected in this particular manner.

Creating a Simple MIDAS Client

Creating MIDAS client that will talk to the SimpleMidasServer is extremely simple. At this stage, you should not be trying to run the client and the server on separate machines. Instead, get everything up and running on one machine, and then later you can distribute the application on the network.

This brief tutorial shows how to create the client:

1. Create a new application and save it into the Client directory right next to your Server directory. Save the main form as MainClient.pas and save the server as SimpleMidasClient.pas.
2. Drop down a TDCOMConnnection component from the Midas page and set its ServerName property to the Prog ID SimpleMidasServer.SimpleMidas. You should be able to pick this Prog ID from a drop-down list in the TDCOMConnection editor. If you can't find the server in this list, then the server is not properly registered on your system. All you need to do to register the server is run it once. Assuming everything is set up correctly, you should now be able to automatically launch the server by setting the DComConnection1.Connected property to True. You don't need to start the server first, as setting Connected to True should launch the server and make it visible on your screen.
3. Drop down a TClientDataSet component from the Midas page and set its RemoteServer property to TDCOMConnection1 and its ProviderName property to CountryProvider. Again, you should be able to pick CountryProvider from a drop-down list. If you can't, then either your server is not set up correctly, or else

you do not have the TDCOMConnection properly attached to your server. Common problems at this stage occur because you might not have properly hooked up the TProvider component to the TTable component or because you have not properly exported the Get_CountryProvider method from the server. In particular, check your type library in the server and make sure it lists the CountryProvider property as ISimpleMidas. If all is set up correctly, you should be able to set the ClientDataSet.Active property to True and connect to the data on your server.

4. At this stage, you can simply drop down a TDataSource, connect it to the TClientDataSet, and then add a grid and view your data.

As a final step, I like to turn the TClientDataSet.Active property to False and do the same with the Connected property to the TDComconnection. Now drop down a menu, add a menu item called Connected, and associate the following method with its OnClick event:

```
procedure TForm2.Connect1Click(Sender: TObject);
begin
  DComConnection1.Connected := True;
  ClientDataSet1.Active := True;
end;
```

This method is helpful because you don't want to close the client project when it is still hooked up to the server. If you leave it connected, then you can have trouble if you come back some months later and load the client application into the IDE when the server is not registered. In particular, the client will try to connect to the server, fail to do so, and leave the whole IDE seemingly locked up during the several minutes that it takes for the operation to time out.

> **NOTE**
>
> Let me take a moment to discuss the whole process of clients timing out when they can't talk to their server. If you try to talk to DCOM server but can't reach it, the system will not immediately give up the search. Instead, it can keep trying for a set period of time that rarely exceeds two minutes. During those two minutes, however, the application will be busy and will appear to be locked up. If the application is loaded into the IDE, then all of Delphi will appear to be locked up. You can have this problem when you do nothing more than attempt to set the Connected property of the TDCOMConnection component to True.

Before closing this section, I would like to add that you can perform the same operation shown in this section with either the TDCOMConnection, the TMidasConnection, or the

TRemoteServer. For all intents and purposes, these three components perform the same tasks.

Understanding the Simple MIDAS Client

Building a MIDAS client is clearly very simple. However, you should consider several points so that you can better understand not only what to do, but why you are doing it.

First, you need to be sure you understand how the client is connecting to the server. In this case, you are using the TDCOMConnection component. Because both the server and the client are on the same machine, you are really just using simple automation to attach the server and client. So in this one case, it's really a TCOMConnection component rather than a TDCOMConnection component.

When you set TDCOMConnection.Connected to True, you are causing CoCreateInstance to be called somewhere in the bowels of VCL. In other words, you are using the same technology that has been outlined in previous chapters that discussed COM, DCOM, or OLE automation.

MIDAS happens to work just as well if you are using other technologies such as OLEnterprise, TCP/IP, or even CORBA. This flexibility comes about because the core of the technology is the ability to wrap a dataset in an OleVariant (or a CORBA Any). The transport that is used to talk across the network is not really very important.

Having said this, nevertheless I have to point out that the MIDAS technology is based on the COM programming model. When MIDAS uses TCP/IP, it goes to considerable lengths to make TCP/IP look and feel like COM. In fact, even a TCP/IP-based version of IDispatch is built into the TCP/IP code that MIDAS uses. Even CORBA programs in Delphi 4 are forced to go through a COM layer before information is sent to or from a server.

The actual technology used to marshal the data back and forth across the network is encapsulated in a class called TDataPacketWriter found in the Provider.pas unit. This object has methods called PutField, PutArrayField, PutBlobField, AddColumn, and so on, all of which are clearly designed to allow you to wrap a standard dataset in a Variant.

On the other end, the TClientDataSet is smart enough to unpack this data and to make it available to the standard methods of a TDataSource component. In particular, you can set the TClientDataSet.Data property equal to a variant that contains a dataset, and the TClientDataSet will automatically unpack it and make it available to a TDataSource. You will have several chances to see this being done in Chapter 23.

Accessing the Server Remotely

At this stage, you should have a pretty good feel for how the `SimpleMidasServer` and its client work. The final stage is to make the connection not just locally, but also remotely.

The details of setting up DCOM were covered in Chapter 20, "DCOM." In that chapter, you learned that it is best to set up the server half of the DCOM program on a machine that's running as a Windows NT domain server. In particular, you don't want to run the server on a Windows 95 or Windows 98 machine, and it is best if the server machine is a domain server and the client machines are all part of this domain or on good terms with it. If you don't have an NT domain server available, then you probably should set up your client and server machine to have the same logon and the same password, at least during the initial stages of testing. Windows 98 ships with DCOM as part of the system, whereas Windows 95 machines need to have DCOM added to the system. You can download the DLLs necessary to implement DCOM on a Windows 95 machine from the Microsoft Web site.

You must have the server registered on both the client and the server machine. The client program could still locate and launch the server if you failed to register it, but COM could not marshal data back and forth if the type library for the server is not registered on the client machine. You can do so by running the server once on both machines, or just run it once on the server and then register the TLB file on the client using `TRegSvr.exe`. In this case, the TLB file is called `SimpleMidasServer.tlb`. This file was generated automatically when you created the server.

When you access this server remotely from a client machine, you need to install the single Delphi client executable on the client side only. No database tools are needed, other than the 211KB `DBClient.dll` file. On the server side, you should include `STDVCL40.DLL`. It will be installed automatically if Delphi is on the server.

Assuming you have everything set up correctly, then all you have to do to connect the client to the server is fill in the `ComputerName` property of the `TDCOMConnection` component. Letting the user fill in this property at runtime is often simplest:

```
procedure TForm2.Connect1Click(Sender: TObject);
var
  S: string;
begin
  S := '';
  if InputQuery('Enter Machine Name', 'Machine Name', S) then begin
    DComConnection1.ComputerName := S;
    DComConnection1.Connected := True;
    ClientDataSet1.Active := True;
  end;
end;
```

When the dialog pops up asking for the name of the machine that hosts the server, you can type in either a human-readable machine name or an IP address. You can find the name of your Windows 95 or 98 machine by choosing Start, Settings, Control Panel, Network, Identification from the Explorer menu.

If you don't want to prompt the user for the name of the server machine, then you can hard-code the information into the client using the `ComputerName` property in the Object Inspector. Or you could store the information in the Registry or tuck it away in an INI file. Whatever technique you use, DCOM will be able to take your machine name or IP address and use it to connect you to the server. After the connection is made, data can be marshaled over the network and displayed for the user.

> **NOTE**
>
> If you want, you can use `DComCfg.exe` to point DCOM to the remote machine when running your server, as explained in Chapter 20, or you can use `OLEnterprise` to do the same thing. In short, you have lots of different options, and the techniques I mention here are only suggestions.

Using Sockets Rather Than DCOM

If you don't have an NT domain server available on your network, then you should probably not try to use DCOM at all and instead should use TCP/IP. A socket connection will work even if no NT server is in the equation, and it is usually much easier to set up than a DCOM connection. However, security is much more difficult to enforce on a socket connection.

You can easily convert the `SimpleMidasClient` into a TCP/IP program. You don't need to make any changes to your server to make it work. Of course, your code will not be any good to you if you do not have TCP/IP set up correctly, as described in Chapter 19, "WinINet and FTP."

To get started building your sockets-based MIDAS program, run the `ScktSrvr.exe` program found in the `Delphi4/Bin` directory on the server machine. This program must be running on the server, or this system will not work.

Drop down a `TSocketConnection` component from the Midas page of the Component Palette on the main form of the client program. Set its `Address` property to the IP address of the machine where the server resides. It can be a remote machine or your current machine. Fill in the `ServerName` property, just as you did in the DCOM example. You should now be able to test your connection by setting the `Connected` property to `True`. As I explained earlier, you should not leave the `Connected` property set to `True`.

Assuming you have dropped down a `TSocketConnection` component on the form and set its `ServerName` property correctly, then you can simply add the following method to your `SimpleMidasClient` program to convert it into a single server that supports both DCOM and sockets.

```
procedure TForm2.ConnectTCPIP1Click(Sender: TObject);
var
  S: string;
begin
  S := '';
  if InputQuery('Enter Machine Name (or IP Address)',
    'Machine Name', S) then begin
    SocketConnection1.Address := S;
    ClientDataSet1.RemoteServer := SocketConnection1;
    ClientDataSet1.Active := True;
  end;
end;
```

This method should be called in response to a click on a menu item or button. In particular, you might add a second menu item that reads Connect TCP/IP to your program. When the user clicks on that button, he or she is prompted for the IP address of the machine where the server resides. Assuming your system is set up correctly, you can also pass in the human-readable equivalent of that IP address.

The code sets the `SocketConnection1.Address` property to the address supplied by the user. It then changes the `ClientDataSet1.RemoteServer` property so that it points not at the `TDCOMConnection` component, but at that `TSocketConnection` component. Finally, it sets the `Active` property of the `TClientDataSet` to `True`. Setting the `Active` property to `True` will automatically cause the `TSocketConnection.Connected` property to be set to `True`.

At this stage, you should be fully connected to your server and viewing your data. This approach will work equally well whether the server is on the same machine or on a remote machine. Furthermore, you don't need an NT Domain server or even an NT Server, though I recommend that you use one.

Finally, I should add that I do not think the `TSocketConnection` component plays second fiddle to the `TDCOMConnection` component. If security is not a big issue to you, then sockets can be an excellent solution and one that will prove to be quite robust. The `TSocketConnection` component even has threading support built into it.

> ### NOTE
>
> Aficionados of COM and sockets will be interested to see that the `TSocketConnection` component implements a pseudo `IDispatch` interface for use with sockets. This interface will let you use TCP/IP to call the methods of an object across the network. Because I have to set some limits on the material I cover in this chapter, I will not dwell on this subject here. However, later in this chapter, I'll cover the `AppServer` field of the `IProvider` interface, and that section should give you strong clues as to how to proceed. The portion of the chapter in question is called "Using the `AppServer` Variable of `TDCOMConnection`." Everything I say in that section also applies to the `TSocketConnection` component.

Building a One-to-Many Application

I will now show how to build a program featuring a master/detail relationship using MIDAS. The client portion of this program is shown in Figure 21.5. The main reason I am showing you this program is to drive home the point that you can do all the same things in a MIDAS application that you can do in a standard Delphi database application. All the same controls still work, and by and large, the same rules still apply. In the course of exploring this subject, I also bring out a number of other interesting aspects of MIDAS programming.

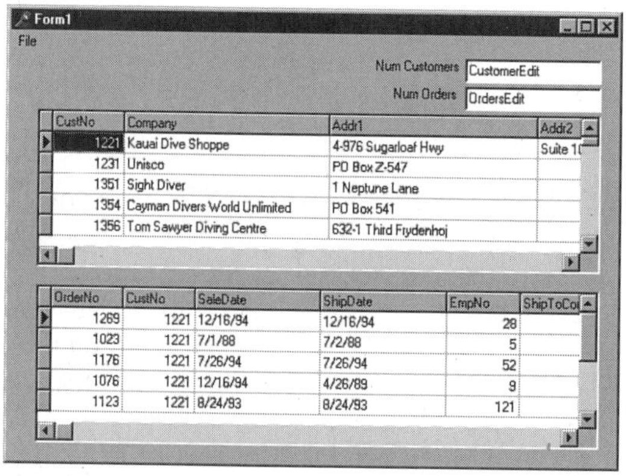

FIGURE 21.5

The interface for a simple client MIDAS application showing a one-to-many relationship between the Customers and Orders table from the DBDEMOS database.

Creating the One-to-Many Server

To get started building the server, create a new directory called `CustOrders`, and beneath it, create two directories called `Client` and `Server`. Construct a standard Delphi application and save it to disk in the Server directory. You can now choose File, New to create a remote data module. You will be prompted to supply a class name. I recommend giving this remote data module a descriptive name such as CustOrdersRemoteData. Remember that the remote data module is just like a standard data module, except that it has a COM interface on it. Accept the defaults for all other options.

Drop two TTable objects on the remote date module and connect one to the Customer and the other to the Orders table from the DBDEMOS alias. Create sensible names for the components you use. For instance, I call the table that points to the Customer table CustomerTable. The detail table is called OrdersTable.

In this example, do not create the one-to-many on the server; instead, you will do so on the client. In the NestedDataSet example, discussed later in this chapter, I take the opposite tack. In the section of this chapter called "Server-Side Logic Versus Client-Side Logic," I will explain the relative merits of each approach.

Continue your construction of the program by dropping down two TProvider controls from the Midas page of the Component Palette on the CustOrdersRemoteData module. Name the provider that is hooked up to the Customer table the CustomerProvider and the other control the OrdersProvider.

Right-click on both the CustomerProvider and the OrdersProvider and export them from the data module. When you are done, you should end up with two methods that look like this:

```
function TCustOrdersRemoteData.Get_CustomerProvider: IProvider;
begin
  Result := CustomerProvider.Provider;
end;

function TCustOrdersRemoteData.Get_OrdersProvider: IProvider;
begin
  Result := OrdersProvider.Provider;
end;
```

If you want, you can add a picture or some text to the main form of the application. At this point, you can save your work and run the application once to register it.

The act of running the server places an entry in the Windows Registry. To see the entry, run the Windows utility RegEdit.exe from the Run menu item on the Start menu. Open HKEY_CLASSES_ROOT and search for the name of the executable that contains the server. For instance, the key to search for in this case is called CustOrdersServer.CustOrdersRemoteData, which is also known as the Prog ID for the server. The first half of this key is from the executable name of the server, and the second half is from the name you gave to the remote data module, which is also, by default, the name of the exported COM interface.

When you find the entry for this Prog ID in the Registry, you will see that a Class ID is associated with it. Move up the Registry a short ways from the CustOrdersServer entry until you find the section called Class ID. Open this key and browse for the Class ID of your component. It should have a LocalServer32 key that points to CustOrdersServer.exe, and it should have another key called the Borland DataBroker. The Delphi IDE references this second key when it is deciding which servers should be shown in the drop-down list for the DCOMConnection.ServerName property on your client.

Building a Remote Data Client Application

Now that you have the server set up, the next thing to do is set up the client. In this example, I will assume you are running both the server and the client on the same machine. After the design phase is over, you can move the server to a remote machine, as discussed earlier in the chapter.

Here is quick overview of the steps involved in creating the client:

1. Drop down a TDCOMConnection and use its ServerName property to connect it to the CustOrdersServer. The Prog ID for this server should be listed in a drop-down combo box in the editor for the ServerName property. You should now be able to set the Connected property to True. If you cannot perform this last step, make sure you have run the server once on your current machine so that it is properly registered.

2. Drop down a TClientDataSet control and set its RemoteServer property to the TDCOMConnection component you just wired up. Set the ProviderName property to the name of the CustomerProvider from the server. The provider name should be listed in a drop-down combo. After you have everything set up properly, rename the control to CustomerClientDataSet. Drop down a second TClientDataSet and wire it up to the OrdersProvider on the server. Rename this second client dataset OrdersClientDataSet. Set the Active property to True for both client datasets. If you are having trouble completing these steps, refer to the notes on this subject in the previous example in this chapter.

3. Hook up database controls to the TClientDataSet just as you would if you were using a TTable or TQuery. That is, you should drop down two TDataSources and two TDBGrids and hook one pair up to the Customer table and the other to the Orders table.

4. Arrange the two `TClientDataSets` in a one-to-many relationship. To do so, connect the `MasterSource` property of the `OrdersClientDataSet` to the data source for the `CustomerClientDataSet`. Click on the `MasterFields` property of the `OrdersDataSet` and set up a relationship between the tables based on the `CustNo` key, as shown in Figure 21.6.

FIGURE 21.6

Establishing a one-to-many relationship in the `MasterFields` *property of the* `OrdersClientData-Set` *component.*

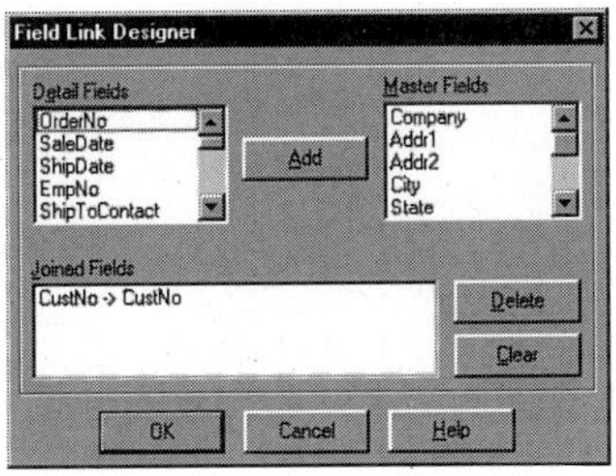

5. Now run your application. The code for the main form of the client is shown in Listing 21.4.

LISTING 21.4 THE CODE FOR THE MAIN FORM OF THE `CustOrdersClient` PROGRAM

```
unit MainClient;

interface

uses
  Windows, Messages, SysUtils,
  Classes, Graphics, Controls,
  Forms, Dialogs, DBClient,
  Db, Grids, DBGrids,
  Menus, StdCtrls, MConnect;

type
  TForm1 = class(TForm)
    CustomerClientDataSet: TClientDataSet;
    OrdersClientDataSet: TClientDataSet;
    CustomerSource: TDataSource;
    OrdersSource: TDataSource;
    DBGrid1: TDBGrid;
    DBGrid2: TDBGrid;
    MainMenu1: TMainMenu;
    File1: TMenuItem;
    OpenDataSets1: TMenuItem;
    BriefcaseSave1: TMenuItem;
    BriefcaseLoad1: TMenuItem;
    N1: TMenuItem;
```

continues

LISTING 21.4   CONTINUED

```pascal
    Exit1: TMenuItem;
    OrdersEdit: TEdit;
    CustomerEdit: TEdit;
    Label1: TLabel;
    Label2: TLabel;
    N2: TMenuItem;
    RefreshServer1: TMenuItem;
    N3: TMenuItem;
    DCOMConnection1: TDCOMConnection;
    Connect1: TMenuItem;
    procedure ApplyUpdates(Sender: TObject);
    procedure OpenDataSets1Click(Sender: TObject);
    procedure Exit1Click(Sender: TObject);
    procedure BriefcaseSave1Click(Sender: TObject);
    procedure BriefcaseLoad1Click(Sender: TObject);
    procedure RefreshServer1Click(Sender: TObject);
    procedure CustomerClientDataSetReconcileError
➥(DataSet: TClientDataSet;
      E: EReconcileError; UpdateKind: TUpdateKind;
      var Action: TReconcileAction);
    procedure Connect1Click(Sender: TObject);
  private
    { Private declarations }
  public
    { Public declarations }
  end;

var
  Form1: TForm1;

implementation

uses ReconcileErrorDialog2;

{$R *.DFM}

const
  CustomerFile = 'Customer.cds'; // CDS stands for ClientDataSet
  OrdersFile = 'Orders.cds';

procedure TForm1.ApplyUpdates(Sender: TObject);
begin
  CustomerClientDataSet.ApplyUpdates(-1);
end;

procedure TForm1.BriefcaseLoad1Click(Sender: TObject);
begin
  CustomerClientDataSet.LoadFromFile(CustomerFile);
  OrdersClientDataSet.LoadFromFile(OrdersFile);
```

```
end;

procedure TForm1.BriefcaseSave1Click(Sender: TObject);
begin
  CustomerClientDataSet.SaveToFile(CustomerFile);
  OrdersClientDataSet.SaveToFile(OrdersFile);
end;

procedure TForm1.Connect1Click(Sender: TObject);
begin
  DCOMConnection1.Connected := True;
  CustomerClientDataSet.Active := True;
  OrdersClientDataSet.Active := True;
end;

procedure TForm1.CustomerClientDataSetReconcileError(
  DataSet: TClientDataSet; E: EReconcileError; UpdateKind: TUpdateKind;
  var Action: TReconcileAction);
begin
  HandleReconcileError(DataSet, UpdateKind, E);
end;

procedure TForm1.Exit1Click(Sender: TObject);
begin
  Close;
end;

{------------------------------------------------------------------
  This record provides an alternative means of connecting to the server.
  Call it in lieu of calling Connect1Click.

  I include this code primarily to show you some of the fancy things
  you can do with the IProvider interface, as explained in the
  section of the Midas chapter called "PacketRecords." Code like this
  is not necessary to make the program work, I'm just throwing it
  in as a bonus.
------------------------------------------------------------------}
procedure TForm1.OpenDataSets1Click(Sender: TObject);
var
  V: OleVariant;
  RecsOut: Integer;
begin
  V := CustomerClientDataSet.Provider.GetRecords(-1, RecsOut);
  CustomerEdit.Text := IntToStr(RecsOut);
  CustomerClientDataSet.AppendData(V, True);
  V := OrdersClientDataSet.Provider.GetRecords(-1, RecsOut);
  OrdersEdit.Text := IntToStr(RecsOut);
  OrdersClientDataSet.AppendData(V, True);
end;
```

continues

LISTING 21.4   CONTINUED

```
procedure TForm1.RefreshServer1Click(Sender: TObject);
begin
  if CustomerClientDataSet.ApplyUpdates(-1) = 0 then
    CustomerClientDataSet.Refresh;
  if OrdersClientDataSet.ApplyUpdates(-1) = 0 then
    OrdersClientDataSet.Refresh;
end;

end.
```

Perhaps the most interesting aspect of the CustOrders sample program is its capability to use the MasterSource and MasterFields property of the TClientDataSet control to establish a one-to-many relationship. The point is that Delphi enables you to enforce rules and use visual controls in distributed programs much as you would in a local database program. This kind of power and flexibility lies very much at the heart of what's best in the MIDAS technology.

Updating and Refreshing Data

In this section, I briefly cover the simple subject of updating the server after you have edited records on the client. To the degree that it was possible, the Delphi team tried to make this process entirely transparent to you. However, you need to learn a few simple rules.

If you have edited one or more records and want to make the changes permanent, then you should call ApplyUpdates:

```
CustomerClientDataSet.ApplyUpdates(-1);
```

This method takes a single parameter called MaxErrors. Passing -1 to this method means that you want the update process to stop when an error occurs. If this happens, then no changes will occur to the server-side version of the data. The client-side log where Delphi tracks the changes you made to the dataset will also remain unchanged. You will be informed that the error occurred and told of its exact nature.

If you set MaxErrors to a positive number, then the update process will continue until it encounters the number of errors you specified in this parameter. If that happens, then no changes occur to either the server-side data or your change log. If fewer than MaxErrors occur, then all the successfully changed records are updated and removed from the change log. ApplyUpdates returns the number of errors it encountered.

To understand what is happening here, you have to understand that Delphi caches all the changes you make to a dataset. In other words, it keeps both the original record and the updated record. When you call ApplyUpdates, errors can be reported, and you will have the chance to revert to the original record or to attempt to push your changes through. Error handling is explained in the section "Error Handling."

If you have successfully updated the server, then you will probably also want to refresh your dataset with any changes made by other users. To do so, call `Refresh`. The following typical example shows how the whole process might look in action:

```
if CustomerClientDataSet.ApplyUpdates(-1) = 0 then
   CustomerClientDataSet.Refresh;
if OrdersClientDataSet.ApplyUpdates(-1) = 0 then
   OrdersClientDataSet.Refresh;
```

A quick glance at this code shows that it may be a bit difficult to understand, but it certainly is easy to implement.

The Briefcase Model

In this section, I'm going to talk about the briefcase model, which is one of the more interesting and useful aspects of this technology. It is particularly valuable for users who have laptops, but on other occasions, you might want to use it in standard MIDAS applications.

As described earlier, the briefcase model allows you to load or save the contents of a client dataset to disk. It depends on two methods of `TClientDataSet` called `LoadFromFile` and `SaveToFile`:

```
CustomerClientDataSet.SaveToFile('Customer.cds');
CustomerClientDataSet.LoadFromFile('Customer.cds');
```

Clearly, these simple methods take nothing more than the name of the file where the dataset will be stored. By convention, this file has a `.cds` extension, where CDS stands for client dataset. After you have created one of these files, any `TClientDataSet` object can read its contents.

In some applications, if you want to save two tables linked in a master detail relationship, you should save and read them both to separate files:

```
const
   CustomerFile = 'Customer.cds'; // CDS stands for ClientDataSet
   OrdersFile = 'Orders.cds';

procedure TForm1.BriefcaseLoad1Click(Sender: TObject);
begin
   CustomerClientDataSet.LoadFromFile(CustomerFile);
   OrdersClientDataSet.LoadFromFile(OrdersFile);
end;

procedure TForm1.BriefcaseSave1Click(Sender: TObject);
begin
```

```
CustomerClientDataSet.SaveToFile(CustomerFile);
OrdersClientDataSet.SaveToFile(OrdersFile);
end;
```

Saving the two files separately like this would not be necessary if you were working with nested datasets. A nested dataset would automatically be saved when you saved its parent.

After you have executed the Save portion of this equation, you can disconnect from the server and yet still access the data by simply calling the Load method. For instance, if you are using a laptop, you can connect once to your server and then save the information you retrieve to disk. Now you can shut down your laptop and take it home with you. At home or on the road, you can boot it up again and edit your database to your heart's content. When you get back to the shop and reconnect to the server, you can update the files by calling ApplyUpdates. Errors and conflicts are handled for you automatically, as explained in the section called "Error Handling."

Clearly, the act of saving and reading files from disk is trivial in the extreme. However, you need to take some additional points into consideration to use the briefcase model properly. Most of these points will be covered in the next section on PacketRecords.

NOTE

The briefcase model can even be applied to applications that do not use MIDAS. If you drop a TTable and TClientDataSet on a form, you can, while still in Design mode, connect the TClientDataSet directly to the TTable and then save the resulting dataset to disk. To do so, just hook the TTable object to a table using the BDE; then right-click on the TClientDataSet to draw the data from the TTable and save it to disk.

After you save the table to disk, you can delete the TTable object from your form, and move your program on to a machine that does not contain the BDE. Now just call ClientDataSet1.LoadFromFile to load the data from disk. This free technology does not cost you the usual fees associated with MIDAS. In my opinion, it is one of the more outstanding features of the Delphi database technology. Read the section "Required DLLs" later in this chapter so that you will know the small support files needed on your new, BDE free, machine.

PacketRecords

The important PacketRecords property of TClientDataSet is one you need spend some time contemplating. In the next few paragraphs, I will discuss it from several angles. In particular, I will make several references to its importance when using the briefcase model.

To make the briefcase model work correctly, you sometimes need to make sure the files on the server are not arranged in a one-to-many relationship and that you have set the `PacketRecords` property on both the `ClientDataSets` to -1. Setting `PacketRecords` to 0 brings down the metadata, setting it to -1 brings down all the data, and setting it to some positive number *n* brings down *n* records per request.

If you have already gotten the metadata for a dataset, then setting `PacketRecords` to -1 or to some positive number other than zero will retrieve only data. However, if you have not gotten the metadata, then setting `PacketRecords` to -1 or to some positive number other than zero will retrieve both the metadata and the records.

NOTE

When using distributed datasets, you don't want to bring down the whole of a large dataset onto the client. This is simply not the right model for this kind of computing. At most, you would probably want to bring down a few thousand records at one time, and I heartily recommend working with even smaller datasets. For some programmers, using small datasets may appear to be a severe limitation, but the user really does not want to see 10,000 or 20,000 records at one time. Find ways to filter your data with queries, or else set `PacketRecords` to some small number so you get a reasonable number of records for the user to peruse. Delphi automatically maintains state for you, so subsequent requests will get the next *n* number of records that you request rather than bring down the same *n* records you retrieved the first time. In saying this, I'm not implying that Delphi or your network can't bring down huge datasets at one time, only that you will be straining the patience of both Delphi and your network, potentially inciting their ire.

By the way, I use `TTable` objects in this chapter mostly because I want to create the simplest possible examples. In most cases, I assume programmers working in corporate settings will need to use queries to manipulate their data. That, however, is another subject altogether, and in this chapter, I am focusing on MIDAS.

If you want to use the briefcase model, then you usually should bring down the whole dataset, which means you want to set `PacketRecords` to -1. (Of course, a query on a server could already filter a large portion of a table for you, but you would still want to set `PacketRecords` to -1 to retrieve all the records from the query.)

If you just want to establish a one-to-many relationship and don't care about the brief-case model, then you will probably want to set `PacketRecords` to zero on the detail table and to `-1` on the master table. These settings retrieve all the records from the master table but only the metadata for the detail table. Then internally, Delphi will call `TClientDataSet.AppendData` to bring down just those detail records that are needed when you're viewing one particular master record. This capability is great for many situations, but it is probably not what you want if you are using the briefcase model. Instead, when using the briefcase model, you will usually set `PacketRecords` to `-1`, and the master detail will still be done, but the whole detail dataset will be available on the server at all times. Having the whole dataset available is obviously impractical when you're working with very large datasets.

Because this issue is so important, I am going to show you how to write some code that allows you to fine-tune this process. The following code represents a nonsensical case in which you first retrieve the metadata and then retrieve the records. I say this example is nonsensical because the metadata will be retrieved automatically the first time you access the data. However, assuming you had some reason to get the metadata first and then get all the records, you could write code that looks like this:

```
with ClientDataSet1 do begin
  Close;
  PacketRecords := 0;
  Open;
  PacketRecords := -1;
  GetNextPacket;
end;
```

Or, if you wanted to be very fancy, you can study this code from Delphi guru Josh Dahlby:

```
var
  RecsOut: Integer;
  V: OleVariant;
begin
  CustomerClientDataSet.Close;
  V := CustomerClientDataSet.Provider.GetMetaData;
  CustomerClientDataSet.AppendData(V, False)
  V := CustomerClientDataSet.Provider.GetRecords(-1,RecsOut);
  CustomerClientDataSet.AppendData(V, True);
end;
```

In this case, you first close the client dataset and then use the `GetMetaData` function to retrieve the metadata inside an `OleVariant`. At this time, you can pass the result of this function directly to `AppendData`, which will add the records you just retrieved to any that might currently be in the dataset.

AppendData takes two parameters. The first is the data retrieved from the server; the second is whether you hit EOF when retrieving the data. Remember that you don't have to use either GetRecords or AppendData; you should normally use GetNextPacket. Furthermore, the simplest way to perform this operation is simply to call Open or to set Active to True. I've shown you GetNextPacket and AppendData simply so you can have more control over the process if you happen to need it. Remember that you have the TPacketWriter code in Provider.pas if you want to create your own packets.

This method provides an alternative way to connect to the data on your server:

```
procedure TForm1.OpenDataSets1Click(Sender: TObject);
var
  V: OleVariant;
  RecsOut: Integer;
begin
  V := CustomerClientDataSet.Provider.GetRecords(-1, RecsOut);
  CustomerEdit.Text := IntToStr(RecsOut);
  CustomerClientDataSet.AppendData(V, True);
  V := OrdersClientDataSet.Provider.GetRecords(-1, RecsOut);
  OrdersEdit.Text := IntToStr(RecsOut);
  OrdersClientDataSet.AppendData(V, True);
end;
```

I've designed this method to report the number of rows in the Customer and Orders table. There is no need to retrieve this information, I'm just showing you that you can get at it if you are interested in seeing it.

A related subject that I will not cover in depth is this chapter is constraints. Just as you can automatically download the metadata for your application, so can you also download the constraints. To do so, set the Constraints field of the IProvider interface to True. When you do, the constraints set up on your server will automatically be enforced on your client.

Error Handling

When you're working with remote datasets, errors will occur on some occasions. For instance, if two users are accessing a table at the same time, they may both want to change the same record. In this case, the person who first performed the update would succeed in changing the record, and the second person would get an error.

Errors are passed back to a TClientDataSet and can be handled by responding to the OnReconcileErrorEvent. A detailed explanation of responding to errors would take up almost as many pages as I've written so far, so I will consider that topic beyond the scope of this chapter. However, I can cover a simple solution to this whole problem in just a few paragraphs.

The trick to handling errors returned from an Application Server is to use a form stored in the Delphi Object Repository. To find the form in question, select File, New, turn to the Dialogs page, and opt to Copy the Reconcile Error Dialog. Save the dialog in the same directory as your current project and remove it from the files that are automatically created at startup. To do so, choose Project, Options, Forms from the Delphi menu.

Add the Reconcile Error dialog to the uses list of the appropriate form in your project. In many cases, it will be the main form for your project. Now add the following in response to an OnReconcileError event:

```
procedure TForm1.CustomerClientDataSetReconcileError(
  DataSet: TClientDataSet; E: EReconcileError; UpdateKind: TUpdateKind;
  var Action: TReconcileAction);
begin
  Action := HandleReconcileError(DataSet, UpdateKind, E);
end;
```

This one-line function will launch the dialog you found in the Object Repository and enable the user to handle any errors, as shown in Figure 21.7.

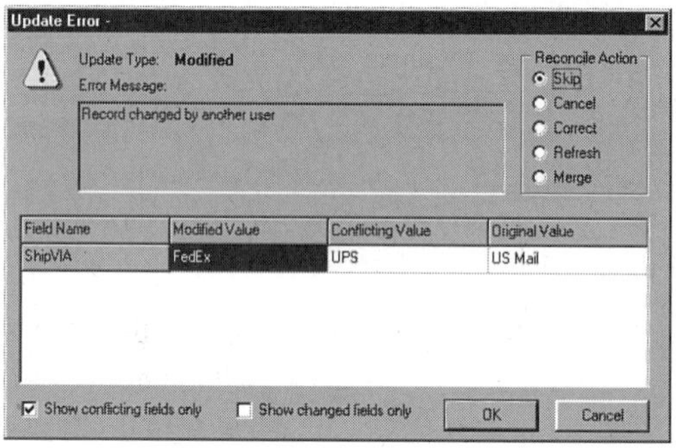

FIGURE 21.7

The ReconcileError *dialog from the Delphi Object Repository as it appears at run-time.*

The grid in the center of the form tells the name of the field on which the error occurred. The Modified Value is the value the client application wanted to insert into the record. The Conflicting Value is the value the "other guy" who beat you to the update inserted into the record. The Original Value is the value the record had before either update was made. As you can see, the user has the option to Skip, Cancel, Correct, Refresh, or Merge the data.

You can make all these changes and access all these options by writing your own code. However, it probably makes more sense just to use this dialog or to use the dialog as the basis for your own code.

Server-Side Logic Versus Client-Side Logic

You naturally have a choice as to how much logic you put on the middle tier—that is, the server—part of your applications. For instance, you decide whether to arrange the tables in a one-to-many on the server.

Under certain circumstances, if you arrange the tables this way, when you query the server from the client, you will get from the detail table only the records that are currently visible on the server. This result may, in fact, be exactly what you want, particularly if the detail table is large.

However, if both the master and detail tables are small, then you may prefer to access all records from both tables. In the NestedDataSet example on this book's CD, you will find a sample program that creates the one-to-many logic on the server side but brings the whole dataset over at once. In addition, the program allows you to work with nested datasets, where the detail table is literally embedded in one of the fields of the master table.

To create this program, start as you normally would, creating a directory called NestedDataSet and putting Client and Server directories beneath. Start your server application and save it as NestedServer.dpr. Add a remote data module to this program and save it as MainIMPL.pas. Call the interface for the data module INestedData or some other name of your choosing.

Drop down two tables on the remote data module and hook them up to the Customer and the Orders table. Drop down a TDataSource and hook it up to the Customer table. Create a one-to-many between the Customer and Orders table, with the Customer table being the master, using the same techniques described in the CustOrdersClient program.

At this stage, instead of dropping down two TProvider components, one for each table, you need only drop down one TProvider. When you query this object from the client, it will automatically contain both the complete Customer table and the Orders table nested inside it, as shown in Figure 21.8.

On the client side, the TDBGrid object you connected to the TClientDataSet will automatically have a new field appended to the end of each record. This field will, by default, be called (DataSet). To see the field, you will have to scroll all the way over to the far right of the DBGrid object.

If you click once on the DataSet field, you will see that it has an ellipses button on its far right. If you click on this button, a second dataset will appear showing the detail records for the currently selected record in the Customer table. Alternatively, you can just double-click on the `DataSet` field, and the detail grid will pop up automatically.

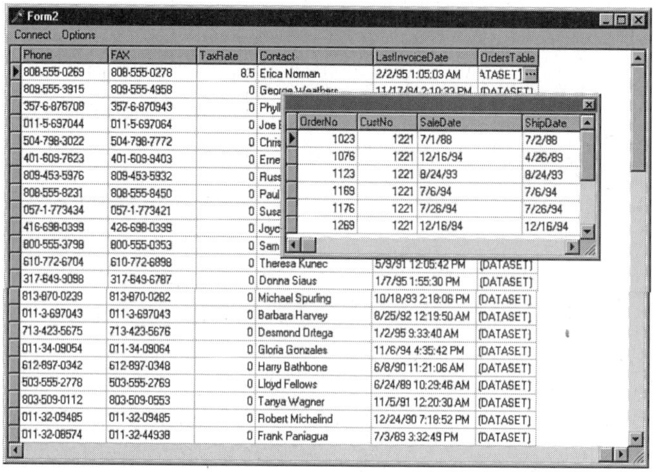

FIGURE 21.8

Here you can see the DataSet *field of the Customer table and the floating grid object that appears when you double-click on the* DataSet *field.*

As you can probably imagine, you don't need to do any special work on the client side to make all this happen. All you need to do is create a standard Delphi MIDAS client, dropping down a `TDCOMConnection`, `TClientDataSet` connection, a `TDataSource`, and `TDBGrid`. Hook them up following the same pattern laid out in the two previous programs from this chapter, and voila, you have a nested dataset with the logic all done on the server side.

Using the `AppServer` Variable of `TDCOMConnection`

The `NestedDataSet` example also contains logic to call custom methods on the server. If you have read the previous chapters that cover COM and DCOM, then you should intuit that calling methods this way is possible. After all, the `TRemoteDataModule` object is just a standard COM implementation supporting a standard COM interface. Obviously, there is no reason why you cannot add your own custom methods to this interface.

To get started, focus your server application and bring up the Type Library Editor. Click on the Add Method icon along the top of the Type Library Editor. If you do not see this icon, right-click on the Type Library Editor and select the Toolbar option. Name the method that you create `GetName`. Then turn to the Parameters page and specify that the method should return a `WideString`. Save your work and fill in the method you have created as follows:

```
function TNestedData.GetName: WideString;
begin
  Result := 'TNestedData';
end;
```

At this stage, your work on the server is finished, and you can compile and save your program. If you are unsure about some of the COM and type library-oriented steps that I have outlined in the preceding few paragraphs, then you can read about these matters in more depth by referring to Chapters 13 and 14.

On the client side of the equation, Delphi has made things very easy for you. In particular, the AppServer field of the TDCOMConnection object is a variant that contains an instance of the IDispatch wrapper for your server-side interface:

```
ShowMessage(DCOMConnection1.AppServer.GetName);
```

AppServer is a variant containing an instance of IDispatch, and you can use it to access the INestedData interface from your server. You can simply call the methods of the INestedData interface off this variable, letting the Delphi IDispatch mechanism take care of the details for you.

If you want, you can also retrieve an instance of the interface for your object:

```
uses
  NestedServer_TLB;

procedure TForm2.GetName1Click(Sender: TObject);
var
  F: INestedData;
begin
  F := IDispatch(DCOMConnection1.AppServer) as INestedData;
  ShowMessage(F.GetName);
end;
```

To make this procedure work, you need to add the NestedServer_TLB file to your uses clause. This file was automatically generated when you created your server. To reach it from the client program, you should choose Project, Options and add ..\Server to the Search Path in the Directory/Conditionals dialog.

The code shown here appeases the whims of the compiler by explicitly typecasting the AppServer variable as an instance of IDispatch:

```
F := IDispatch(DCOMConnection1.AppServer) as INestedData;
```

If you don't add this line, Delphi will complain that a simple OleVariant does not necessarily support an interface.

The only subject I did not cover in this chapter that might be relevant to you is COM callbacks, a subject that was covered in Chapter 20. The last two sections of this chapter cover first the very important subject of required DLLs for MIDAS applications and then a few words on OLEnterprise, a subject of interest to only a limited number of readers.

Required DLLs

When you are installing your MIDAS applications, several files are needed on both sides. Server-side files include the following:

- A complete installation of the BDE
- DBCLIENT.DLL
- IDPROV40.DLL
- STDVCL40.DLL

DBCLIENT and IDPROV40 are included only in the Client/Server version of Delphi. To get them on your system, you need to answer yes to the license agreement screen in the installation.

DBCLIENT and STDVCL40 need to be registered— that is, entered in the Registry. You can register them by using REGSVR32.EXE from Microsoft or the TRegServ Delphi program from the Bin directory.

DBCLIENT.DLL is the only DLL needed on the client. STDVCL40.DLL is not required, but you almost certainly will need it. It is the type library for IProvider and IDataBroker, and because all MIDAS applications use IProvider, you had better include it. DBCLIENT needs to be registered on the client. If it is on the path, then it will be registered automatically when your application loads.

Using OLEnterprise

OLEnterprise is an alternative to DCOM. If you use OLEnterprise, then you do not need to have DCOM on your system. Though I personally do not believe OLEnterprise is the future of distributed computing here on planet Earth, nevertheless, it has several advantages over DCOM, such as the following:

- It will allow you to make connections between two Windows 95 machines, even if no NT server is available. Connections without an NT server are all but impossible under DCOM, as explained in Chapter 20. Connections between two Windows 95 machines even when a server is present are either impossible or extremely problematic under DCOM. You can reliably connect from a Windows 95/98 machine to an NT machine with DCOM, but not vice versa, nor can you reliably connect between two Windows 95/98 machines.

- OLEnterprise has an Object Broker that will allow you to distribute the load of connections over multiple machines. In particular, each time a new user signs on to a database, he or she can be randomly routed to an available server, thereby distributing the load over multiple servers. The act of replicating the data between servers is, quite naturally, not supported by OLEnterprise but is instead the responsibility of the server itself.

- OLEnterprise has fail over capability, which is available if you write a few lines of code.

This fail over example was provided by the good graces of the indefatigable Mike Destein:

```
procedure TForm1.Button2Click(Sender: TObject);
begin
 try
  ClientDataset1.ApplyUpdates(-1);
 except
  on eOle : EOleException do begin
    Case eOle.Errorcode of
      -2147023169 : // I dont know the const name
        begin
          // Handle RPC failure by resetting server
          RemoteServer1.Connected := False;
          RemoteServer1.connected := TRUE;
          ClientDataset1.ApplyUpdates(-1);
        end;
      else showMessage(intToStr(eOle.errorCode));
    end;
  end;
 end;
end;
```

Some users have reported having trouble using this code with some versions of OLEnterprise.

Installing and Understanding OLEnterprise

When you're installing OLEnterprise on a Windows 95/98 machine, do not install into the default directory; instead, install off your root and try to avoid long filenames in the directory path. Any problems with OLEnterprise and long filenames on Windows 95 machines will be corrected in future releases of the product.

The four key pieces in the OLEnterprise toolset are as follows:

- The Object Broker, called Broker.exe. It should be run on the server machine before loading the Object Factory. If you start it with a -D option, it will spew out debug information that can help you understand your program and help you confirm that connections are occurring in the correct order and at the correct time.

- The OLEnterprise Configuration utility, called `OLECFG.exe`. This utility is used to specify whether you are using an Object Broker and what machine the Object Broker is running on. Remember that the broker's job is to distribute connections randomly; as such, it is not needed in order to make the connection. It is a helpful utility, but not a necessity. Therefore, the configuration gives you the option of turning it off. You should run the configuration utility on both the client and the server.

- The Object Factory, called `ObjFact.exe`. This utility is the core of the system, and you must run it on the server, or `OLEnterprise` will not work. However, you do not need to have this utility running on the client to make a connection.

- The Object Explorer, called `OLEntExp.exe`. This program plays a similar role to `DCOMCFG.exe`. It allows you to browse the objects available on your system, to export objects from a server, and to import objects from a remote system. You should remember that the Explorer uses the Registry as the main repository of information about the objects on a system. If you have run a server once on a machine, the Explorer will find the object in the Registry, and you can then use the menu to export or import the object. If you are on a client machine and are using the Explorer to search for programs on remote machines, then you must be sure that you have used the OLEnterprise Configuration utility to specify where the Object Broker you are currently using is running. If you launch the Explorer, and it takes a very long time to come up, or it appears to hang at times, then it is likely that the machine is searching for the Broker but cannot find it. The program can take several minutes before it allows the search to time out and return control to the user. The same thing will happen if you click on the Object Broker option in the program's left panel. One click, and a search for the Broker will begin. If the Broker is not found, use the configuration utility to specify its location, or else go to the remote machine and make sure the Broker is running. If you start the Broker with the `-D` option, then you should see output from it when you start an Object Factory on the same machine or when you try to connect to it from a remote machine.

When using the Explorer, you need to learn how to import and export objects. This intuitive process is accomplished by manipulating the menus or by right-clicking on items in the main panels of the application. You should probably spend some time using the default sample programs shipping with the product to make sure you understand importing and exporting objects. In particular, go to `etc\samples\auto\memoedit` to find a good prebuilt sample program.

`OLEnterprise` was an extremely valuable tool before Windows supported DCOM. At this time, I would still regard it as a useful tool, but I have to confess that it is not a particular favorite of mine.

Summary

In this chapter, you looked at Borland's multitier technology. In particular, you saw how to create servers and clients and how to use DCOM and OLEnterprise to connect to a remote server.

This technology is important for several reasons:

- It provides a means of creating thin clients that make few demands on the client system.

- It simplifies—in fact, nearly eliminates—the need to configure the client machine.

- It allows you to partition applications in logical compartments. If you wish, each of these compartments can be run on a separate machine, thereby distributing the load of the application.

- It provides a means for distributing a load over several server machines or for routing the load to a specific machine with the power to handle heavy demands. The previous bullet point covered breaking up the application into the server, application server, and client, whereas this bullet point covers the advantages of using multiple servers in conjunction with the Object Broker.

- It provides a robust architecture for handling and reporting errors, particularly in a multiuser environment. It also allows you to automatically download metadata and constraints onto your thin client, thereby enabling you to build robust applications with sophisticated interfaces and feedback for the user.

- It allows you to use a briefcase technology that stores files locally and then allows you to reload them when it is time to update the server. This capability is ideal for laptop users who spend a lot of time on the road.

For many users, this technology is so compelling that it entirely replaces the standard client/server database architectures. These users are attracted to the ability to partition the applications into logical pieces, even if the entire application is being run on a single machine. However, the biggest benefits achieved by this architecture become apparent when you bring multiple machines, and even multiple servers, into play.

Personally, I have no question but that distributed computing is going to become one of the most important fields in all of computer science. The materials shown in this chapter should get you started using some of the more sophisticated aspects of this technology. There will come a time when nearly every computer in the world will be continually connected to nearly every other computer, and when that occurs, distributed computing will become one of the most essential fields of study in computer programming.

ActiveForms

CHAPTER 22

In this chapter, you will learn how to create ActiveForms that can be displayed in a Web browser. You will also see how to convert a Delphi form into a component that can be displayed on any Windows-based machine equipped with Internet Explorer or any other ActiveX-aware HTML browser. For good measure, at least one of the forms shown in this chapter will contain the thin client portion of a multitier application.

Introduction to ActiveForms

One of Delphi's most powerful features is the capability to wrap an entire form inside an ActiveX control and publish it on the Web or insert it into another application such as VB or Word. You should read the following sections on ActiveForms even if you think you understand this technology from experience with Delphi 3. In particular, you will find changes to the issues involved in deploying ActiveForms.

You can do several different things with an ActiveForm. For instance, you can deploy it in another ActiveX-aware program such as Visual Basic, Word, or Excel. For most users, this technology is easy to use, but I will step you through the process of using an ActiveForm inside Word. People interested in this subject should read the bits on the Internet Explorer anyway, as you will find important points about distributing ActiveForms that you need to understand.

You can also deploy ActiveForms in Internet Explorer. This process is a bit tricky at times, so I will cover it in some depth. This technology is particularly important, however, because it can be an excellent way to create a distributed application.

In theory, you should be able to put an ActiveForm in any tool that can act as a container. However, you should be aware that the ActiveX technology is not well documented, and as a result many containers, even some from Microsoft, do not properly implement aspects of the specification. As a result, problems can occur. However, you should have no trouble running Delphi ActiveForms in VB, Word, Excel, or Internet Explorer.

The old joke about this technology involves the confusion fulminated in shops where management makes some brain-dead declaration such as "We support only Microsoft standards, so all applications must be built in VB." The solution to this form of madness is to build forms in Delphi and then just drop them into VB applications as ActiveX controls. That way, management personnel get their VB app, and you get to write your application in Delphi. And maybe someday, if people get really insistent on asking why your applications are so much faster and robust than the other apps turned out in the shop, you can tell them what you are really doing. Be careful, though. Anyone irrational enough to insist that you use VB is, by definition, capable of doing almost anything.

Before going on, I should mention that Microsoft distributes a free Web server called the Personal Web Server. This great tool allows you to test your ActiveForms inside Internet

Explorer. The Personal Web Server probably could not stand the strain of thousands of simultaneous users, but it is ideal for testing your controls or for using with small networks that have only a few users. It ships with FrontPage, some versions of Internet Explorer, and other Microsoft products such as the MSDN, and is usually available for free download from www.microsoft.com.

Building an ActiveForm

You can get started building an ActiveForm in two ways. One is to build the program from scratch; the other is to borrow an existing form from another application. I will start by building an ActiveForm from scratch. The program I will build is called EasyActiveForm, and you can find the source on the CD that accompanies this book. In the section called "Using Templates with ActiveForms," I will describe how to reuse a form from another application in an ActiveForm.

To build a form from scratch, choose File, New, ActiveX, Active Form. Then you will be prompted for a name for your project. You can use the default name if you want or choose a new name. You need to fill out three edit controls at this point, but usually you can get away with just changing the first one, called New ActiveX Name. If you change the New ActiveX Name, the names in the other fields change automatically. Name your project EasyActiveForm.

When you click OK in the Active Form Wizard, you will probably be told that you cannot add an ActiveX control to the current project because it is not an ActiveX library. (Of course, you won't get this message if you have already started an ActiveX library.) If you get the message, just click on OK to start a DLL that can host an ActiveX control.

You will probably want to select Project, Options, Packages and make sure the option labeled Build with Runtime Packages is turned off; it should be turned off by default. The issue here is that runtime packages will have to be included with your OCX if you elect to use them in your project. Distributing these packages with your project should not be difficult, as Delphi can handle that chore automatically. Nonetheless, you don't want to worry about that kind of thing when you are first starting out. So make sure the Runtime Packages option is turned off.

For this first form, keeping everything as simple as possible would be best. As a result, just drop down a single button on the form, and associate it with the following function:

```
procedure TEasyActiveForm.Button1Click(Sender: TObject);
begin
  ShowMessage('Hello from Delphi');
end;
```

Now save your project to disk. At this stage, you have completed the construction of your ActiveForm.

Deploying an ActiveForm for Use in Internet Explorer

The next step is to deploy your ActiveForm. In this case, the goal is to have it appear inside Internet Explorer, so you will not be able to proceed unless you have IE 3.X or higher.

If you are deploying onto the Web, start by choosing Web Deployment Options from the Project menu. A dialog like the one shown in Figure 22.1 will pop up. Before this dialog appears, your project must be compiled and linked, so you may experience a short delay while your files are processed.

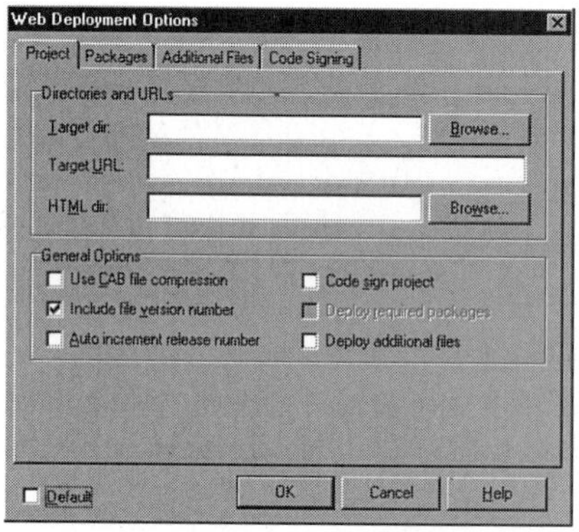

FIGURE 22.1

The Web Deployment Options dialog as it appears when you first open it.

Setting Options for an ActiveForm

At the top of the Deployment Options dialog are three controls:

- Target Dir
- Target URL
- HTML Dir

In the Target Dir field, you list where you want to deploy your OCX and any related binary files. These files can be distributed to anyone who attaches to your machine over the Web. If you have a Web server available, you typically should deploy these files in your wwwroot directory or in some directory beneath this location. For instance, you might place them in c:\webshare\wwwroot, c:\inetpub\wwwroot, or c:\inetpub\wwwroot\MyActiveForms.

The Target URL you specify is used by the HTML and/or INF file that launches your OCX. The string you enter in this field should point to the directory where your OCX is located when it is ready to be deployed. Usually, you should specify this directory as a URL. For instance, you might write `http://ccalvertpc3/MyActiveForms`.

This subject is complicated enough that I want to explain it in more depth. Furthermore, this explanation will be enhanced by numerous examples later in the chapter.

By default, Delphi will create sample HTML and INF files for your project. The HTML file can be loaded into a browser and used to launch your OCX. If your project deploys multiple files, the HTML file will reference a second file with an `.inf` extension. The INF file will contain the URL where your OCX resides, and any helper files needed by your project such as packages or the runtime library. If your project doesn't use packages or the runtime library, no INF file will be created. In short, the Target URL either points directly to your OCX or directly to an INF file that, in turn, points to your OCX, as well as any packages or related files you might be using.

If you are deploying your control on a Web server located on a machine called `ccalvertpc3`, and you deploy your OCX in the `wwwroot` directory, then you should type `http://ccalvertpc3` as the Target URL. This URL points, by default, to the `wwwroot` directory on your server machine. If you do not have a Web server available while you are testing, then simply hard-code in the name of the directory that you specified in the Target Dir, such as `c:\webshare\wwwroot\`. Of course, if you don't have a server, you can access the object only from the same machine or from a machine that has a mapped drive to your server.

HTML Dir indicates where the sample HTML and INF files that Delphi generates will be placed. Typically, this location is the same directory you specified in the Target Dir.

When you are done filling out these fields, make sure the Auto Increment Release Number check box is checked. Now close the Web Deployment Options dialog, and choose Web Deploy from the Project menu. Your project will be copied automatically into the directories you specified in the Web Deployment Options dialog.

> **NOTE**
>
> This last step is not nearly so simple if you are using packages. In that case, you will need to go through several more steps on several different dialogs before you're done. The steps aren't hard to complete, but they can test your patience. The "Working with CAB Files and Packages" section of this chapter explains these steps.

Connecting to an ActiveForm

At this point, you are ready to connect from another machine, download the OCX onto that second machine, and view it in a browser. To understand how this procedure works, consider the HTML generated by Delphi:

```
<HR><center><P>
<OBJECT
  classid="clsid:98BFA852-9D8A-11D1-BDFF-0060979302AC"
  codebase="http://ccalvertpc3/activestuff/
  ➥EasyFormProj1.ocx#version=1,0,0,0"
  width=696
  height=480
  align=center
  hspace=0
  vspace=0
>
</OBJECT>
</HTML>
```

The CLSID shown here specifies the GUID associated with your object. The line labeled codebase points to the place on your system where the OCX resides. You specified a portion of the contents of this line in the Target URL field of the Web Deployment Options dialog. If you are running on a single machine that does not feature a Web server, then this should be a DOS path rather than a URL. For instance, it might read as follows:

```
c:\webshare\wwwroot\activestuff\easyformproj1.ocx#version=1,0,0,0
```

In this example, I have actually deployed my ActiveX control in a directory called ActiveStuff beneath wwwroot. This is just a matter of housekeeping, however, and you can feel free to put your OCX in wwwroot or in some other location if you prefer. However, you almost certainly will not be able to run the version on the CD that accompanies this book unless you first change this line. Now, you can bring up a browser on your own machine or on a remote machine, and point it to the place where your HTML file is stored:

```
http://ccalvertpc3/activestuff/EasyFormProj1.htm
```

Of course, the specific place where your file is stored may differ depending on the machine you are using and the way you have set up your paths.

The ActiveX should now appear in your browser. If it does not, consider the following checklist:

- Are you using IE 3.X or higher? If not, then ActiveX controls may not be supported on your browser.

- If you are using IE 3.X, choose View, Options in the IE menu system and turn to the Security page. Choose Safety Level and set it to Medium. If you are using IE 4 or 4.1, then set it to Low. In general, you should give yourself as much security as possible, while still being able to use the ActiveX control.

- Make sure that you turned off the Runtime Packages option when you built your control.

When you are launching the control in the browser, you will probably see some security dialogs that ask questions about code signing. Just click yes to all their questions so that you can download your OCX. If you want to get involved in code-signing your OCXs, then go to `www.microsoft.com` and check out the articles on Authenticode and Security.

Understanding the OCCACHE

After you deploy an OCX, you will almost certainly see some changes that you want to make to it. This process would seem simple, but Bill G. decided it wouldn't be any fun if your life were quite that easy.

On Windows 95 or Windows 98, after an OCX is loaded into memory, the only way you can be sure it is unloaded is to reboot Windows. In other words, when you try to redeploy the OCX, you may keep getting the same OCX in your client app because the old DLL may not have been unloaded from memory. Although Windows officially lets go of a DLL when finished with it, Windows does not provide a practical way to definitively unload a DLL from memory. (Some people use DLL unloaders in these cases, and I have heard others perform a LoadLibrary once on the recalcitrant DLL, then two FreeLibraries.)

Furthermore, the OCXs that you download onto a machine are often stored in a directory called OCCACHE, which is just below the Windows or Winnt directory on Windows 95 and Windows NT 4 machines. (Windows 98 and those 95 machines with IE4 installed have a similar directory called Downloaded Files or Downloaded Program Files.) Sometimes you will find further directories called conflict.1, conflict.2, and so on beneath the OCCACHE directory.

If you are developing a program and want to be sure that you are starting with a clean client machine, you should be sure to not only reboot the system, but also to delete suspect files from all cache directories. Furthermore, you may find that other files are installed in the Windows\System or Winnt\System32 directories, as explained in the section called "Working with CAB Files and Packages." If necessary, you may have to hunt these files out, then unregister and delete them before you create a truly clean machine to run tests on. In particular, packages usually get installed in these directories.

I can't emphasize enough the extreme importance of testing your OCXs on clean machines before you attempt to distribute them to an unsuspecting public. A failed distribution of an OCX is extremely easy to perform.

Consider what happens if your code uses packages that were installed by default on your test machine, but that will not be available on prospective customers' machines. For instance, some poor ActiveX vendor somewhere in the world is undoubtedly distributing sample versions of his wares that do not install properly because of a missing DLL or package. As a result, everyone who tries this hapless vendor's code finds that it doesn't work and immediately abandons that product and searches out some other tool that will do the job correctly. Don't let this scenario happen to you. Understand what files are distributed with your OCX, and test to be sure they are distributed correctly.

If at all possible, try installing your OCX on a completely clean machine that has nothing on it but a copy of Windows. It is what software developers call a "Test Bed Box." Neglecting to take this step is the rough equivalent of taking off in a jet airplane without checking to make sure someone closed the door. You might be okay, but the odds are you are going to have trouble.

Working with CAB Files and Packages

A CAB file is a kind of compressed file that Windows understands and automatically decompresses. Delphi will automatically package your OCX and any additional files in CAB files if you check the Use CAB File Compression option in the Web Deployment Options dialog. CAB files transfer to a client machine faster than normal files because they are compressed.

On the CD that accompanies this book, you can find a second ActiveForm example in the `SimpleActiveForm` directory. In that example, I use packages and CAB files. Using both packages and CAB files may sound like a bit much, but it is almost certainly the way you will want to distribute the actual OCXs that you create. The reason this method is preferred is that it keeps the size of your OCXs to a minimum. It makes sense particularly if you are distributing multiple OCXs to the same system or set of systems.

> **NOTE**
>
> Packages save memory because they place commonly used code in a special DLL called a *package*. For instance, the database tools take up somewhere between
>
> *continues*

100 and 200KB in even a very simple database program. If you don't use packages, and you deploy six database apps, you will have that 200KB repeated in each executable. If you use packages and deploy six database apps, you will have to deploy the database code only once. During the deployment of six database apps, putting the database code in a package may save you approximately 1MB of disk space.

In this example, you will create an OCX called `SimpleFormProj1.ocx`. Fill out the ActiveX Wizard appropriately so that you get this filename for your control. This time, be sure that your project will use packages. This setting is not the default, so make sure this is indeed the setting for your code by choosing Project, Options, Packages.

Now add a `TImage` control from the Additional page of the Component Palette and a `TToolbar` control and `TImageList` control from the Win32 page of the Component Palette to the main form of your project. Double-click on the `ImageList` control to pop up its property page and browse to the `Program Files\Common Files\Inprise Shared\Images\Buttons` directory to add a few buttons to this control. Pick whichever ones strike your fancy. Now link the toolbar to the `TImageList` control via the `ToolBar.ImageList` property. Add a few buttons to the toolbar and hook them up to the proper offsets of some images in the image list. Finally, browse on your hard drive and insert an image into the `TImage` control on the form. Some pictures in the `Images\Splash` directory were created when you installed Delphi. When you are done, you might have a form that looks something like the image in Figure 22.2.

FIGURE 22.2

The form for the `SimpleFormProj1` *OCX control.*

In the Web Deployment Options dialog, check Use CAB File Compression. Then choose Project, Options, Packages, and make sure Build with Runtime Packages is turned on. Don't just assume these options are on. Check explicitly to see that they are on.

> **NOTE**
>
> When you are working in the Web Deployment Options dialog, you might notice that a Default check box appears at the bottom of a number of these pages. If you check this option, the current choices in your dialog, including the paths and directories, will be copied to the Registry and reused automatically the next time you open the project. This feature can be a big help if you are always deploying controls to the same directories with the same options.

At this point, you are finally ready to close the Web Deployment Options dialog and deploy your application. This process should take several minutes, as a CAB file needs to be created before it can be copied to your wwwroot directory or some other directory of your choosing.

Note that in the Web Deployment Options dialog you had the option of placing all your files in one big CAB file or of working with a set of distinct CAB files. In my case, I choose to put each control or package in a separate CAB file, mostly because doing so simulates a fairly complex installation that really puts the system through its paces.

You can now move to your client machine, type in the URL where you stored the HTML file generated by Delphi, and sit back and watch while each CAB file is copied over and automatically installed. For instance, you might type the following:

```
http://ccalvertpc3/activestuff/SimpleFormProj1.html
```

When you are finished, the OCX and INF files should be in the OCCACHE directory, and the package files with .bpl extensions should be in the System or System32 directory of your client machine. This is assuming you are working with Windows 95 or Windows NT 4. I do not know where these files will be put on Windows NT 5, though it would be reasonable to assume that at least the System and System32 directories will remain constant. On Windows 98, you might check the c:\Windows\Downloaded Program Files directory for the OCX and INF files. If that fails, open RegEdit and look up downloaded controls in the Registry. You will also find a program called SimpleActiveForm2 on the CD that accompanies this book. This program is similar to the SimpleFormProj1 program, but instead of using CAB files, I deploy the OCX and related packages separately. Deploying this way can be tricky because you have to be sure the package or packages you use get deployed to the right place. To get started, repeat all the steps for building the SimpleFormProj1 program, but turn off CAB files and turn on the option labeled Deploy Required Packages. Now turn to the Packages page, and make sure all packages are being deployed to the correct location. (In this program, you should need only

VCL40.BPL, but in other programs, you might need many more packages.) Don't just assume the packages will go to the right place; click on each one in the list box, and make sure it is going where you want it to go. In particular, make sure the package is deployed to the right directory, and has the same URL as you specified in the Target URL entry on the first page of the Web Deployment Options dialog.

My advice to you when you're working with this dialog is to be paranoid. Assume that it is trying to trick you and that you have to be very careful. In particular, click on each file you are going to deploy, and make sure its settings are correct. Don't just click on the top file; click on each one in turn. (In this case, you have only one, but in other cases, you will have to set the path and target URL multiple times, one for each file.)

Here is a little lecture I give myself when working with this technology: "Charlie, if you are having trouble getting a control to appear, don't panic! Remember, the OCX technology itself is solid. You don't have to worry about whether the control is built correctly. The likely problem is that you are not deploying the proper set of packages or additional files that your OCX is dependent on. This is happening because you aren't specifying the correct deployment directory or URL, not because Delphi is too dumb to know which files need to be deployed.

"Now," I tell myself, "go open the INF file for your control, and see whether everything you would expect to find is in there. Are the proper CAB or DLL files available in the wwwroot or related directories? Did they all get copied over to the client as expected? Can you find them on the client? This isn't black magic. The controls have to be somewhere on the client machine's hard drive. If they aren't there, then they probably aren't being copied over properly. Just think for a little bit, there has to be a reasonable explanation!"

If you have never used this technology before, you may find this lecture a bit absurd. However, IE's complete lack of error messages can be a bit disconcerting, and if something goes wrong, you need to have some way of focusing your mind on the likely causes of the problem.

NOTE

I assume IE emits no error messages because it doesn't want a user to be troubled with these messages when loading a Web page. Broken links aren't the user's fault, so perhaps it is logical that he or she shouldn't be bothered with error messages if problems occur.

Understanding INF Files

In Listing 22.1, you can see the INF file for the SimpleFormProj. Get used to reading these INF files. They are the road map to distributing an ActiveX control.

LISTING 22.1   THE INF FILE FOR THE SimpleFormProj SAMPLE PROGRAM

```
;Delphi-generated INF file for SimpleFormProj1.ocx
[Add.Code]
SimpleFormProj1.ocx=SimpleFormProj1.ocx

VCL40.bpl=VCL40.bpl

[SimpleFormProj1.ocx]
file=http://ccalvertpc3/activeStuff/SimpleFormProj1.cab
clsid={0483D605-9D6D-11D1-BDFF-0060979302AC}
RegisterServer=yes
FileVersion=1,0,4,0

[VCL40.bpl]
file=http://ccalvertpc3/activeStuff/VCL40.cab
FileVersion=4,0,3,58
DestDir=11
```

Check each of the CAB files listed in this INF source. Note the URL associated with the control. The client machine is going to use this URL when it tries to load the CAB file in question. If the URL doesn't make sense to you, then it won't make sense to the client machine. If you are having troubles, take a look at these URLs and make sure they say something sensible. If you are unsure of which controls go in which package, choose Component, Install Packages and browse through the available packages. If you click on the Components button when any one package is selected, you can see the controls found in that package.

> **NOTE**
>
> The DestDir specifies the System or System32 directory.

Here are some other entries that might show up in a database application distributed over the Web:

```
[ibsmp35.bpl]file=http://ccalvertpc3/activeStuff/ibevnt40.cab
DestDir=11

[vcldb40.bpl]
file=http://ccalvertpc3/activeStuff/vcldb40.cab
```

```
FileVersion=4,0,3,58
DestDir=11
```

Get to know these different packages so you can understand which ones you need in a particular project.

Overall, the Web deployment options for a form are not particularly difficult. However, they can be a bit tricky if you don't understand the issues involved. Take the time to make sure you understand the issues addressed in this section. If you know how to deploy your ActiveX control correctly, that knowledge will almost certainly save you time and heartache later in the development process.

Licensing Issues

You can build ActiveX controls that work only at design time, only at runtime, or that work in either situation. If you are distributing a control with one of your applications, you probably want it to work only at runtime so that it aids your application but can't be used by other developers. Conversely, if you want to sell a component to someone, you might like to give that person a sample control that he or she can use at design time but that can't be used at runtime. Or, conversely, perhaps you want to release your control for everyone's use, in which case you don't need a license.

IE gets the runtime licensing information for licensed components using LPK files. They are built with a utility named `LPKTOOL.EXE`, which resides on the server. IE knows about it via the `LPKPath PARAM` tag. Here's an example:

```
<OBJECT
    CLASSID="clsid:5220cb21-c88d-11cf-b347-00aa00a28331">
    <PARAM NAME="LPKPath" VALUE="MyCompnt.LPK">
</OBJECT>
```

The following URL is a good introduction to LPK files:

```
http://premium.microsoft.com/msdn/library/devprods/vb/vb50docs/
f1/d5/s1afa3.htm
```

Links on the Internet can change over time. If this one fails, you might try searching for the subject on `http://users.microsoft.com/msdn`.

Running an ActiveForm in Word

If you want to show your form in VB or some other standard application such as Word, all you have to do is compile and link it, and then make sure it is registered. In other words, you don't have to deploy the form to be able to use it in VB or Word, though you can do so if you want.

Registering Applications

You can register an application or DLL from inside the Delphi Type Library Editor. At the top of the editor is a small icon like the one associated with the standard Windows application called RegEdit. This icon is located second from the right. Click it to register your form. Your form can also be registered automatically when you deploy it.

You can also register your DLL with either the standard Microsoft application called RegSvr32.exe or with an Inprise application called TRegSvr.exe. To register an OCX named Sam.ocx, you would type Regsvr32 Sam.ocx or TRegSvr Sam.ocx. For additional help running either application, just type its name at the command prompt with no parameters.

Running Forms in Microsoft Word

To run the EasyActiveForm OCX in Word, you first need to learn a few basic facts about how Word Basic is put together. In this example, I will talk about Word 97.

Word comes with a fairly complete version of Visual Basic built into it. You can reach this application by selecting Tools, Macro, Visual Basic Editor from the Word menu.

Using the Visual Basic Editor

You don't start new projects in the Visual Basic Editor the same way you would start a new project in Delphi or the standard version of Visual Basic. Instead, you get a new embedded "project" for each new document you start in Word.

If you open Word and then create a single document, or just work with the default document, the Visual Basic Editor will normally have two projects open inside it. The first project, usually called Normal, is associated with your current template. The second project, usually called Document1 by default, is associated with your current default document. If you open or create additional documents, projects will also be associated with each of these documents.

To see a project in Visual Basic, go to the View menu and choose Project Explorer. Now you should be able to see a list of the currently open projects, as shown in Figure 22.3.

Adding Controls to a Document

Right-click on the project associated with your document, and you will be given the choice to insert a User Form or a Module. In this case, you might choose to insert a User Form, which brings up a form similar to one you would see in Delphi. Associated with the form is a Toolbox with several basic controls on it. Right-click on a blank area in this Toolbox, and you will get an option to pop up the Additional controls dialog box.

FIGURE 22.3

The Word Visual Basic Editor with the Project Explorer open on its left side.

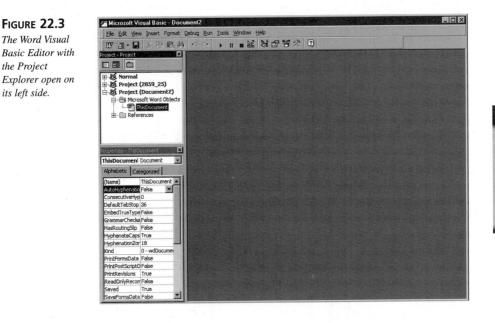

The Additional Controls dialog lists all the currently registered ActiveX controls on your system. Scroll around a bit, and you should be able to find and select the `EasyActiveForm` control, as shown in Figure 22.4.

FIGURE 22.4

Selecting the EasyActiveForm control from the Additional Controls dialog.

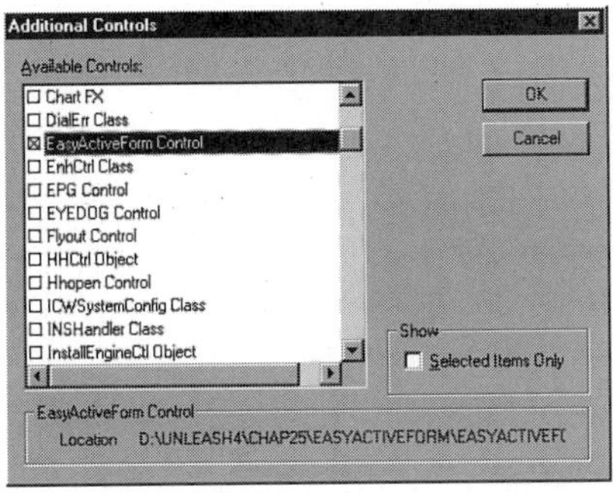

After you select the `EasyActiveForm` control, it will appear as an icon in the Toolbox associated with your form. Select this icon and then paste the form onto the main form of your Visual Basic application, as shown in Figure 22.5.

FIGURE 22.5

A Delphi form in the company of a Visual Basic form.

After pasting in your form, you can save your work and return to Word. Now go to the Word menu and select View, Toolbars, Control Toolbox. Doing so brings up a dialog or floating toolbar similar to the Toolbox you saw in Word Visual Basic. Select a button from the Toolbox, and drop it onto a form. Double-click on the button, and create a routine associated with it that looks something like the following:

```
Private Sub CommandButton1_Click()
   UserForm1.Show
End Sub
```

This code will bring up the contents of UserForm1. Assuming that UserForm1 contains your ActiveX control, this is the key to displaying a sophisticated Delphi control right in the midst of a Word document via the good graces of a lowly Visual Basic form. If you have trouble getting this project together, you will find a sample Word document in the directory called EasyActiveForm on the CD that accompanies this book. The document is called ShowEasyForm.doc, and it contains the code necessary to bring up the EasyActiveForm OCX as long as the OCX is available and registered on your system.

I suppose I ought to confess the truth here and admit that I really like this technology. Being able to embed Delphi forms in the midst of a Word document is great. In fact, if we can ever get past the roadblocks that prevent making easy sales from the Web, I wouldn't mind releasing books directly in Word documents that you can interact with in a manner similar to the one discussed in this section.

Using Templates with ActiveForms

Sometimes you might want to create an ActiveForm from an existing application. Delphi makes this process simple. The key to grabbing a form from a second application is to save it as an Active Template. In particular, if you bring up the form in the IDE, you can use the mouse to select all the components on the form. Now go to the Component menu and choose Create Component Template. A new template will be saved replete with all the controls and their associated code from your form.

At this point, you can go to the menu and choose File, New, ActiveX, Active Form. The environment will probably prompt you to create a new library, and you should say yes. Now go to the Templates page on the Component Palette, and select the new template you just finished making. Drop it on the ActiveForm. You can now save your project and compile it. That's all there is to building an ActiveForm that encapsulates an existing form in one of your projects.

At this point, you've learned all about creating ActiveX controls for distribution over the Web or in Word, VB, or some other third-party tool. By this time, you should understand most of the issues involved and should feel comfortable creating ActiveForms.

The only subject not covered in depth was code-signing your forms. To do that, you should go to the Microsoft Web site, and read up on the subject. The point here is that Inprise is not authorized to create valid code-signing documents for you. As a result, you should use the system that Microsoft has set up for this process. My understanding is that Microsoft will point you to a third-party vendor (`www.verisign.com`) that will arrange to code-sign your controls. That's how the security system works for ActiveX controls.

In the following section, you will see how to combine the ActiveForm technology with the MIDAS Sockets technology. This can give you the ability to create some sexy code that takes browsers into a new and fairly powerful realm.

Sockets and ActiveForms

In this section, I will give you a brief overview of sockets and show another way that you can use ActiveForms. The program I will show in this section will combine Inprise's MIDAS technology with Microsoft's ActiveForm technology to create a Web-based distributed application running inside a true Delphi binary. This technology will work using IE 3.X or IE 4.X only. It will not work with Netscape's technology unless you are using some form of plug-in that supports ActiveX controls. (For example, you can try ScriptActive from NCompass, `www.ncompasslabs.com`. Check the CD that accompanies this book because it might contain a trial copy.)

I will take a standard sockets-based MIDAS application and place it on an ActiveForm. The Windows user who connects to your server can then download this form and attach to a database on your system using the MIDAS Sockets technology. No database tools are needed on the client side.

Some of the technologies shown in this section, such as MIDAS, are covered elsewhere in this book. As a result, I will give only a brief overview and then move quickly to show how this technology works in the current context.

A Brief Overview of Sockets

Windows sockets provide connections based on the TCP/IP protocol. They also allow *connections that use the Xerox Network System (XNS), Digital's DECnet protocol, or* Novell's IPX/SPX family.

Sockets give you some of the power of DCOM without loading you down with concerns regarding connectivity, security, and Windows NT domains. The disadvantage of sockets is that they lack the backing of a full object-oriented scheme such as you find in COM.

Technically, sockets are very easy to use. Two sets of controls wrap this technology. One is the MIDAS controls on the database part of the Component Palette, and the other is the TServerSocket and TClientSocket controls from the Internet page. Both sets of controls are easy to use. The only slightly tricky catch is that you have to remember to first load the ScktSrvr.exe program found in the Delphi\Bin directory. However, new to Delphi 4 is also ScktSrvc.exe, which is a service that can be run under Windows NT to alleviate the necessity of having to remember to run ScktSrvr.exe. So keep this information in mind if you are developing under NT. Almost all the troubles I've ever had with sockets boiled down to my foolishly forgetting to load ScktSrvr.exe.

For many developers, the easy-to-use and flexible socket technology will be the ideal solution when building distributed applications. Because it is built on TCP/IP, this technology should be especially appealing to people who want to work across very large distances using the Internet.

Building the MIDAS ActiveForm with Sockets Support

Most distributed architectures are actually easy to build. Developing the infrastructure for a distributed application might be difficult, but that's not the responsibility of most programmers. Most developers simply use the infrastructure; they don't have to create it.

The average developer is going to build applications on top of TCP/IP, ActiveX, CORBA, RMI, or DCOM. Most developers aren't responsible for creating a distributed architecture any more than they are responsible for writing an operating system, compiler, or Web server. Sure, everyone knows that writing a compiler is a tricky job. But it isn't, or at least shouldn't be, difficult to use one. The same is true of building MIDAS-based ActiveForms. Some tricky technology is involved, but most programmers are just using the technology; they aren't actually developing it.

To build this distributed ActiveForm application, you have to start by creating an application server. This server will be a typical MIDAS application that exports a simple database containing pictures and text. The tables for the database are in a folder called `Data` on the CD that accompanies this book. The code for the examples in this section are found in the `ActiveSocketForm` directory. (The subdirectories beneath the `ActiveSocketForm` directory are called `SunsetServer` and `SunsetClient`. `SunsetServer` contains an application called `ActiveSocketForm`, while `SunsetClient` contains an application called `SunsetActiveFormProj1`.)

The actual database contains some pictures of a sunset that I took recently, along with some poems that William Shakespeare wrote some four or five hundred years ago. (If you want, you can consider both of these art forms as existing on the same level, and executed with the same degree of expertise. This will make me feel good, but I'm afraid it wouldn't bode well for your future as an art critic!) You should copy this data off the CD and create a Standard Paradox Alias called `SunsetData` that points to it, or you can just use the `D4Unleashed` alias, which you probably created while reading an earlier part of this book.

Start a new application, and turn it into a distributed database application by choosing File, New, Remote Data Module from the Delphi menu. This option takes a standard data module and wraps it inside a COM object. This COM object will be used to export an object called a `Provider`. `Provider`s are so called because they "provide" information about your data set to remote clients. In other words, the `Provider` object is the DCOM automation object that lets the client app talk to the server. What they talk about is the contents of a data set. That is, they talk about the pictures and poems in the `Sunset` database. More explicitly, the `Provider` marshals the data from the `Sunset` database between the client and the server.

When you are creating the remote data module, you will be prompted for a name. In this sample project, I called my remote data module `SocketObject`.

You should now save all your work into a unique directory. Your application server will reside in this directory, so put some thought into where you put it. Windows can always find the directory because a reference to it will be stored in the Registry. But you want the directory to be someplace on your hard drive that makes sense to you. I named the module where the data will reside `SocketFormIMPL.pas`, the main form `Main.pas`, and the project source `ActiveSocketForm.dpr`.

The next stage in developing the project involves dropping a `TTable` object on the remote data module and hooking it up to the Sunset table. You don't need to bother to activate the table, as that will be done automatically when a client connects to your server.

Drop a `TProvider` component from the MIDAS page of the Component Palette on the same form as the `TTable` object. Use the Object Inspector to hook up the `Tprovider.DataSet` property to the `TTable` object. Right-click on the `TProvider`, and choose `Export Provider1` from `DataModule`. This action produces the following lines of code:

```
function TSocketObject.Get_Provider1: IProvider;
begin
  Result := Provider1.Provider;
end;
```

The client will call this method when it wants to retrieve the `Provider` object. The `Provider` object is the one that knows how to marshal data back and forth between the client and the server. If you want, you can add something to the main form to make it recognizable when you see it again. I have added another piece of disparate art, this time in the form of a picture I took during a blurry, vaguely remembered vacation in the Loire valley.

At this point, you have finished creating your application server. Run it once to register it; then sit back and admire your work.

When all is said and done, nothing could be much simpler than this task. As I said earlier, building a distributed application is not a particularly difficult endeavor. If you have questions about this process, go to Chapter 21, "MIDAS," and read what I have to say there about creating automation objects.

Creating the MIDAS-Based ActiveForm

Now you will create an ActiveForm that will serve as the client for the server you created in the preceding section. You can then embed this form in a Web page and display your data across a network using a true, distributed architecture. In other words, you will be able to have one database, residing on one machine, and have your clients reside on any Windows machine that is running Internet Explorer 3 or 4.X.

All ActiveForms must appear in a DLL. As result, when you first choose File, New, ActiveX, Active Form, you will be prompted to create a new ActiveX library unless you already have one started. You will also be asked to provide the name of the ActiveX control you are creating. In the sample program shown in this section of the chapter, I call the program the `SocketForm`. This example is available in the directory called

ActiveSocketForm on the CD that accompanies this book. The actual OCX that lives in this directory is called the SunsetActiveFormProj1.

On the form that you created, you should create a standard MIDAS client. Start by dropping down a TSocketConnection component on the form. Now might be a good time to go to the Delphi\Bin directory and make sure that the ScktSrvr.exe application is running on your server machine. You won't be able to connect to your client unless the socket server application is running. Remember, IE won't give you any error messages if the connection fails. If you forgot to launch ScktSrvr.exe, nobody's going to be helpful enough as to actually tell you what you did wrong.

Click on the Address property of the TSocketConnection, and enter the name of the machine where you created your application server or its IP address. In most standard development situations, it will be the same machine on which you are building your client. Typically, you create the server and client on one machine, test them, and then move one or the other to a remote machine. (If you move the server, you need to change the name or number you put in the Address property.)

Drop down the ServerName property of the TSocketConnection, and you should now be able to pick the name of your application server from a drop-down list. If something goes wrong, the two most obvious problems would be that you didn't run your server and so it is not registered, or else you forgot to run the ScktSrvr.exe application.

Drop down a TClientDataSet, and hook its RemoteServer property to the TSocketConnection component. Drop down the ProviderName property of the TClientDataSet, and choose the provider you created, which is probably Provider1. If this field is blank, then the most likely problem is that you are no longer connected to the server. Alternatively, you may have forgotten to right-click on the Provider component back on the server so that you could choose the menu option that would write the code for exporting your provider. (In the bad old days of Delphi 3, the type library would occasionally forget to properly save itself, thereby forcing you to export the provider object a second time. This bug, however, is now fixed.)

After you connect the TClientDataSet to the Provider, you are home free. Now you can set the Active property of the control to True. The application server should now load into memory.

Drop down a TDataSource, and connect it to the TClientDataSet. Add a TDBImage and TDBMemo control to your form, and hook them up to the Picture and Description fields. You should now be able to see one of the pictures of the California sunset and some labyrinthine words from the holy blissful bard.

Your ActiveForm is complete at this point. The only change you might want to make to it involves giving the user the option to connect to the data after the form has loaded. This option is helpful because it separates the act of loading the form from the act of connecting to the database. As you know, the form will rely on several different packages. Just getting them loaded properly is enough for one operation. So it's best if you let that task stand on its own, and then check to make sure you can come up with a connection.

Troubleshooting the Form

You should note that the only things likely to go wrong when loading the form are that

- You somehow forgot to send one of the needed packages with the form. In this case, I am not using packages, so this should not be a problem.

- Perhaps you are experiencing some kind of versioning mismatch with one of the supporting files.

On the database side, the following errors might occur:

- You forgot to start the `ScktSrvr.exe` file on the server. I dwell on this possibility so frequently in the vague hope that multiple reminders will spare you the suffering of spending hours tracking down a bug that turns out to be nothing more than a simple failure to load `ScktSrvr.exe`. In particular, note that if you reboot your server frequently, you might want to put `ScktSrvr.exe` in the Start Up folder.

- You forgot to point the client to the right machine specified in the `Address` property.

Neither problem should be hard to solve. However, it helps if you know which problem you are wrestling with at the time it arises. If the form doesn't load, then it's a DLL or package problem. If the form loads okay, but you can't connect, then it's a `SckSrvr.exe` problem or perhaps a simple problem with an alias.

Testing the Form

To let the user connect to the database at runtime, first be sure that both the `Active` property of the `TClientDataSet` and the `Connected` property of the `TMidasConnection` component are set to `False`. Drop down a button on the form, and label it `Connect`. Associate the following method with the button:

```
procedure TSunsetFormX.Button1Click(Sender: TObject);
begin
    ClientDataSet1.Active := True;
end;
```

This code will set both the `TMidasConnection.Connected` and the
`TClientDataSet.Active` property to `True`. When you are done with your form, it might
look something like the image shown in Figure 22.6.

FIGURE 22.6

*The ActiveForm
for the*
`SunsetActiveForm`
`Proj1` *sample
program.*

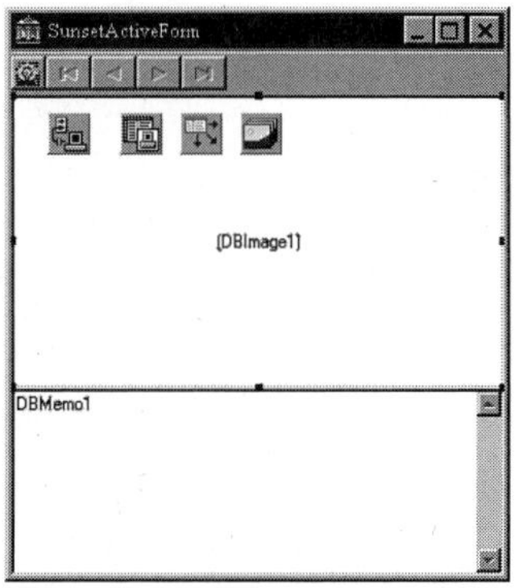

When working with this application, you should note that I have designed it so that all
the poems and pictures come down the wire at once when you connect to the database.
This design will work with a relatively small chunk of data like the one shown here,
especially if you are on a local network. However, if you move on to a 28.8Kbps modem
connection, or if you let the database grow much larger, you will have performance problems. The solution might be to eliminate the pictures or to use SQL to request one row of
data at a time.

If you need to pass a SQL statement back to the server, you can do so in a number of
ways. One of the simplest would be to add new methods to the object that exports your
provider interface. You could then call that method as needed to send data back to the
server.

I should perhaps expend a few more words talking about deploying your form on the
Web. I spent considerable time on this subject earlier in this discussion on ActiveForms.
As a result, I won't go into much depth.

The choices you make when distributing the ActiveForm are yours, but you probably
want to build with packages. Next, you will probably want to wrap all the pieces of the
application in CAB files and then deploy them to your `wwwroot` directory or some other
place where the controls can be available to users.

Now you can go to a client machine and access the OCX. For maximum effect, you
should go to a machine that doesn't have Delphi on it and that doesn't have any database
tools on it. When you attach to the URL where you stored your controls, the ActiveForm

will be downloaded, and the user can access the database running on your server. This is a classic thin client application. The great advantage here is that the code executing inside the Web browser is built entirely in Delphi and has very high performance characteristics that are atypical of the slow Java or HTML bound Web-based world. Of course, unlike Java, this is the only Windows solution. However, it is indeed a very powerful solution, and one that works on the platform supported by 90 percent of the computers in the world.

Summary

In this chapter, you learned about ActiveForms. You also saw how to move a multitiered database into the Web Browser arena, using an ActiveX form and the MIDAS Sockets technology.

If you are interested in this field, you should look at Inprise's Entera and OLE Enterprise products, as well as the CORBA technology discussed in this book. You should also consider the native Java technology called RMI.

In this chapter, you were exposed to the building blocks of multitiered database projects. The DirectX material found elsewhere in this book is arguably more fun, but probably no other material in this book is as important nor as innately interesting as what you saw in this chapter. We are entering the age when PCs are at last moving onto a great global network. This chapter introduced you to the information needed to program for the Internet.

MTS

23

The Microsoft Transaction Server (MTS) is a tool that helps you manage distributed applications that are shared by many clients. It does two things for you:

- MTS handles resources when clients access servers. It makes sure that the least number of clients need to be loaded into memory, and that database and other connections are shared between clients.

- MTS handles multipart transactions and automatically rolls back all the parts if one section fails. If you have a single client that accesses four different servers, conducting a part of a transaction on each server, then if any one part fails, the entire transaction will be automatically rolled back.

In this chapter, I will show you how to build simple MTS clients and servers, then simple MTS database clients and servers, and then more complex database servers that handle transactions spread out across three or more application servers.

I will also show how to use OLE automation to automatically configure MTS without ever opening any Microsoft tools. In particular, I will show how to programmatically create MTS packages and to register your server in those packages.

What Is MTS?

MTS is a tool for distributed database programming. In particular, it helps you create powerful, simple application servers.

In particular, MTS will remove your server from memory whenever you are not actively using it. This means that the NT Server will be able to handle more clients because fewer COM servers are in memory at any one time. The point is that the only servers actually in memory at any one time are those actively being used at a particular moment. If you have 100 clients connected to servers, but only 10 of them are active at any one time, then only 10 servers will be in memory at any one time. If your server can handle 100 COM servers at a time without bogging down from lack of RAM, then with MTS, your server can handle 1,000 clients; without MTS, it can handle only 100 clients. (I just pulled these artificial numbers from the top of my head. I'm not trying to write an ad for MTS here; I'm just trying to make it clear to you what MTS is all about.)

When you are not using a server, MTS unloads it from memory. When you call one of its methods again, MTS automatically loads your server. Unless you take specific actions to make it do so, MTS will not maintain the state of your object. For instance, if you initialize a property of your object to True and then go away for a bit, MTS will unload your object. When you next call your object, MTS will reload it into memory. In the process, your constructors will be called, and your properties will be set to their default values. This is what is meant by saying that an MTS server does not *maintain state*.

Of course, if you need to, you can maintain state in MTS. Furthermore, you can ask MTS not to unload your server until you are through using it. Of course, if you never let MTS unload your server, then you don't have much reason to use MTS.

Another thing that MTS does for you is pool your database connections. If 100 clients are talking to InterBase servers, then you would normally need to have 100 active database connections on your server. All these connections take up a sizable number of resources. MTS will allow you to pool your database connections. You can therefore let go of a database connection whenever you want, and MTS will ensure that it remains active. If another server needs a database connection, then MTS will "lend" your connection to that server. When the server is through, it disconnects, allowing the connection to go back into the pool. Now if you need the connection, you can get it again from MTS. This kind of system vastly improves the performance of a server.

For pooling to work, you must make sure that the MTS Pooling switch in the Init page of the BDE Administrator (which you access by choosing Configuration, System, Init) is set to True. As I will explain in some depth later in the chapter in the section "Working with MTS Transactions," this setting must also be turned on if you want to support MTS transactions.

> **NOTE**
>
> For MTS pooling to work, you have to continually connect and disconnect from your database. For instance, you no longer just set Table1.Active to True. You should first set Database1.Connected to True and then set your table to active. When you are done, disconnect from both your table and your database. If you don't, other servers you may have written can't use your connection. This action would normally take a lot of time, but because MTS has pooled your connection, the overhead of connecting to a database is considerably less than it would be under other circumstances. Furthermore, your server will be faster and more responsive in general if it is not supporting too many database connections at one time.

In my mind, application servers should mirror real-world objects. To make this work properly, you need to have independent servers representing each of the objects in your organization. For instance, you might have an employee server, a payroll server, a tech support server, and so on. If you are running a widget and gadget factory, then you need two servers, one for representing your widget factory and one for representing your gadget factory. You can easily imagine how you might create other servers representing the trucks that transport the gadgets and widgets, and others representing the payroll units in the factory, and so on.

The point is that you want to sort your objects through a fairly fine sieve. You don't want one big complex object representing the whole ball of wax. That kind of programming is too complex for most people to understand, debug, and maintain. Instead, you want, small, simple, specialized objects that each perform a few discreet tasks.

A business is not one big object. Instead, it is made up of smaller objects called employees, offices, desks, and so on. The closer we can come to representing these real-world objects with discreet computerized entities, the closer we can come to creating powerful, robust programs that represent the real world. Failing to recognize the objects in your programs is a serious mistake. If you create monolithic entities, then OOP will never work for you.

Given this scenario, the role of MTS is to manage the resources used by multiple clients accessing these servers at the same time, and to ensure that you can get multiple application servers to work together fairly seamlessly. In particular, if you need to ask the Widget machine to build a widget and load it onto a truck and debit some account, then you need to talk to several different servers. If one part of these transactions fails, then you want to make sure all the related transactions are rolled back. In particular, if the account doesn't contain enough money to complete the transaction, then you want to make sure that the widget is placed back in the warehouse and is not shown as having been sold. When MTS finds that the sale of the widget failed for whatever reason, it is capable of rolling back the other transactions in the deal, restoring things to the state they were in before the transaction began. This is true even if multiple types of database servers are involved in the transaction.

You could, of course, write the code for rolling back a complex, multiserver transaction yourself. But doing so would be an error-prone, complex operation. Having MTS handle this chore for you allows you to concentrate on the core tasks in your operation. MTS makes this whole business of creating complex distributed architectures a relatively simple task that any competent programmer can perform.

MTS performs for free the same services that extremely expensive pieces of software perform for huge corporations. When I say "extremely expensive," I am talking about systems that always cost at least $30,000 to $40,000, and that usually run into hundreds of thousands of dollars. MTS may not be as powerful, and particularly not as heterogeneous as many of these systems, but it is still a remarkable tool that provides all the services many companies will ever need. It's a little like owning your own small private jet, which you can fly for free. It's not quite as good as having Air Force One at your command, but then again, most people don't need Air Force One. In fact, most companies need only a small private jet and would consider a 747 overkill and a waste of resources.

How Do I Install MTS?

MTS comes in several different forms, but at the time of this writing, the most common is to download it from the Microsoft Web site as part of the NT 4 Option Pack. This option pack adds several new features to NT 4, including MTS. Later, of course, MTS will be folded into the operating system. For instance, it will ship as part of NT 5. Therefore, if you have NT 5, then you probably need do nothing to get hold of MTS; it's built into the operating system.

To install the NT 4 Option Pack, you need to upgrade to Internet Explorer 4.X or higher. In other words, you can't install the option pack if you don't first install IE 4.X. If this is too galling a pill for you to swallow, then you might try to find a separate version of MTS that comes without the NT 4 Option Pack. In my case, however, I just went ahead and upgraded to the next version of IE, and then performed the default installation of the option pack. I would advise not choosing all the tools in the option pack, as they take up over 100MB of RAM at runtime. Just stick with the default installation.

After you install MTS, you should find new menu items that let you reach the MTS Explorer. Make sure you can access this tool, as it is very valuable, and will be important to you while working with the material in this chapter.

By default, the MTS Explorer is housed inside the Microsoft Management Console (MMC). The MMC is another new tool that ships with the NT 4 Option Pack. The Management Console is a tool that will house various configuration utilities, such as the MTS Explorer. I imagine that in the future the various databases that exist, such as Oracle, InterBase, or MSSQL Server, will all house their configuration utilities inside the Microsoft Management Console. When you add a new utility to the Management Console, it is called a snap-in. Snap-ins are not germane to this chapter, and in fact, I will not discuss them further in this book.

> **NOTE**
>
> Installing MTS should be a very simple process, but if you are having trouble with it, contact the people at Microsoft, as they are the product's developers.

Creating a Simple MTS Server

To create a simple MTS server that has no database code in it, chose File, New, Multitier, MTS Object from the Delphi menu. You will be prompted to enter a class name. You can call your object anything you like, but to follow along with my example, call your class

23

MTS

MTSTestObject5. Choose Apartment for the threading model, choose Does Not Support Transactions, and elect not to generate any event support code, as shown in Figure 23.1.

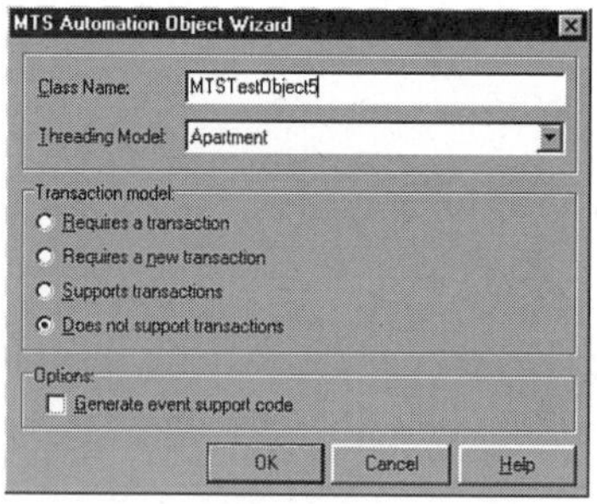

FIGURE 23.1

Defining an MTS object.

If you click on the OK button, the code for your server will be automatically generated. The Type Library Editor should show up on top, and you can begin entering the methods for your object.

> **NOTE**
>
> If you ever need to change the transaction support for one of your objects, you can do so in the Type Library Editor. Click on the CoClass for your object, and turn to the Transaction page. There you will be able to choose whether your object requires a transaction, supports a transaction, and so on.

Before entering any methods, you might want to save your project. At this point, your project will consist of two main files, which you can save to disk by choosing File, Save All:

- Unit1.pas—The place where your implementation is stored. Save this file as MTSObjectIMPL.pas. At times, I will refer to this file generically as the IMPL file.

- Project1.dpr—The project source for your application. Save this file as MTSTest5.dpr.

After saving these files, you will find the project also contains files called MTSTest5_TLB.pas and MTSTest5.tlb. The latter file is the type library for your project, and the former file is the Pascal implementation of the code in that type library.

Go back to the Type Library Editor, which you can reach by choosing View, Type Library. Highlight the interface for your object, which should be called

IMTSTestObject5. Click the icon for creating a new method, and call it GetName. Switch to the Parameters or Text page and enter a parameter that looks like this as IDL:

```
HRESULT _stdcall GetName([out] BSTR * Name );
```

The same method looks like this in the Text page if you have Pascal syntax turned on:

```
function GetName: WideString [dispid $00000001]; safecall;
```

> **NOTE**
>
> The Text page in the Type Library Editor is configurable. It can be made to show code in either IDL or in Pascal. To change back and forth between the two options, choose Tools, Environment Options, Type Library from the Delphi menu. There you will be able to set the language to either Pascal or IDL.
>
> If you choose Pascal, the output will look like this:
>
> ```
> function GetName: WideString [dispid $00000001]; safecall;
> ```
>
> If you choose IDL, the output will look like this:
>
> ```
> [id(0x00000001)] HRESULT _stdcall GetName([out, retval] BSTR * Value );
> ```
>
> You should understand that these two statements are simply two different ways of saying the same thing. One makes the statement in Pascal; the second, in IDL.
>
> As I explained in Chapter 13, "Interfaces and the Basics of COM," SafeCall is a convention that ensures you are creating a method that returns an HRESULT. Furthermore, the body of the method will be wrapped in a try..except block, and any errors that occur in the method will be propagated back to the client. You need do nothing to make these things happen; it all goes on behind the scenes.

If you are filling out the method dynamically, the Type Library Editor should look as it does in Figure 23.2. Click the Refresh button, and the code for your new method will be generated automatically.

Fill out the implementation for your method as follows:

```
procedure TMTSTestObject.GetName(out Name: WideString);
begin
  Name := 'TMTSTestObject';
end;
```

At this stage, you have finished creating your server. This simple server knows how to do nothing more than say its name.

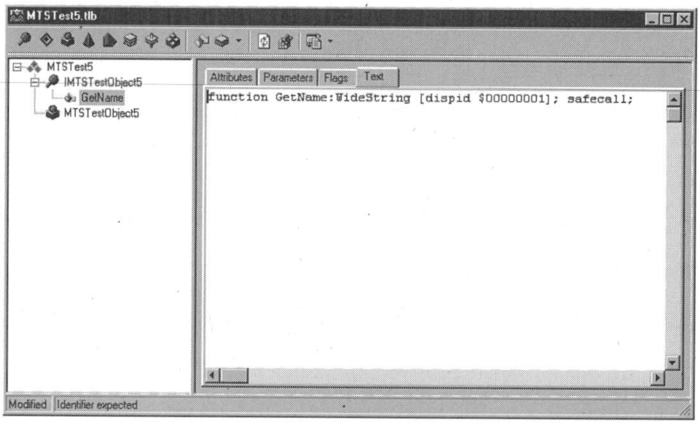

FIGURE 23.2

The Type Library Editor while creating the GetName *method.*

Remember, you usually should not have to type the header for this procedure. The header and begin..end pair should be generated for you automatically as a result of the code you wrote in the Type Library Editor. All you need to do is fill in the single line of code that returns the name of the object.

> **NOTE**
>
> Under some circumstances, the Type Library Editor might become confused and might not fill in the methods in your IMPL file automatically. If this happens, go ahead and write the code yourself. As long as the Type Library Editor and your XXX_TLB file are correct, you are not in an error state and can safely write the implementation yourself.
>
> For instance, when I am working with two interfaces in one CoClass, and both of those interfaces have the same name, the Type Library Editor will not correctly fill in the name of the second of the two methods that have the same name. To correct the problem, create your own method resolution call, as described in Chapter 15, "Creating COM Automation Servers and Clients."

At this stage, you have created a valid MTS server. You have now completely defined your simple MTS server. Go ahead and make sure you have saved your work, and then choose Build from the menu to be sure it is completely up-to-date.

Listings 23.1 through 23.3 show the code for a simple MTS server. This code should be generated for you when you follow the steps outlined in the preceding paragraphs.

LISTING 23.1   THE MAIN MODULE FOR A SIMPLE MTS SERVER

```
/////////////////////////////////////
//    File: MTSObjectIMPL.pas
// Project: MTSTest5
// Copyright (c) 1998 by Charlie Calvert
//
unit MTSObjectIMPL;

interface

uses
  ActiveX, MtsObj, Mtx,
  ComObj, MTSTest5_TLB;

type
  TMTSTestObject5 = class(TMtsAutoObject, IMTSTestObject5)
  protected
    function GetName: WideString; safecall;
  end;

implementation

uses ComServ;

function TMTSTestObject5.GetName: WideString;
begin
  Result := 'TMTSTestObject5';
end;

initialization
  TAutoObjectFactory.Create(
    ComServer,
    TMTSTestObject5,         // The object I want to create
    Class_MTSTestObject5,    // The GUID of the object I want to create
    ciMultiInstance,         // Instancing
    tmApartment              // Threading model
  );
end.
```

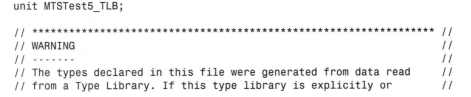

LISTING 23.2   THE TYPE LIBRARY FOR A SIMPLE MTS SERVER

```
unit MTSTest5_TLB;

// ***************************************************************** //
// WARNING                                                          //
// -------                                                          //
// The types declared in this file were generated from data read    //
// from a Type Library. If this type library is explicitly or        //
```

continues

LISTING 23.2   CONTINUED

```
// indirectly (via another type library referring to this type      //
// library) reimported, or the 'Refresh' command of the Type Library //
// Editor activated while editing the Type Library, the contents of  //
// this file will be regenerated and all                            //
// manual modifications will be lost.                               //
// ****************************************************************** //


// PASTLWTR : $Revision:   1.11.1.63  $
// File generated on 6/23/98 7:35:21 PM from Type Library
// described below.


// ****************************************************************** //
// Type Lib: D:\SrcPas\Unleash4\Chap23\MTSTest1\Server\MTSTest5.tlb
// IID\LCID: {DC62D910-0B0B-11D2-AED2-0060979302AC}\0
// Helpfile:
// HelpString: Project1 Library
// Version:    1.0
// ****************************************************************** //

interface

uses Windows, ActiveX, Classes, Graphics, OleCtrls, StdVCL;

// ****************************************************************** //
// GUIDS declared in the TypeLibrary. Following prefixes are used:   //
//   Type Libraries     : LIBID_xxxx                                //
//   CoClasses          : CLASS_xxxx                                //
//   DISPInterfaces     : DIID_xxxx                                 //
//   Non-DISP interfaces: IID_xxxx                                  //
// ****************************************************************** //
const
  LIBID_MTSTest5: TGUID = '{DC62D910-0B0B-11D2-AED2-0060979302AC}';
  IID_IMTSTestObject5: TGUID = '{DC62D911-0B0B-11D2-AED2-0060979302AC}';
  CLASS_MTSTestObject5: TGUID = '{DC62D913-0B0B-11D2-AED2-0060979302AC}';
type

// ****************************************************************** //
// Forward declaration of interfaces defined in Type Library        //
// ****************************************************************** //
  IMTSTestObject5 = interface;
  IMTSTestObject5Disp = dispinterface;

// ****************************************************************** //
// Declaration of CoClasses defined in Type Library                 //
// (NOTE: Here we map each CoClass to its Default Interface)         //
// ****************************************************************** //
```

```
  MTSTestObject5 = IMTSTestObject5;


// ****************************************************************** //
// Interface: IMTSTestObject5
// Flags:     (4416) Dual OleAutomation Dispatchable
// GUID:      {DC62D911-0B0B-11D2-AED2-0060979302AC}
// ****************************************************************** //
  IMTSTestObject5 = interface(IDispatch)
    ['{DC62D911-0B0B-11D2-AED2-0060979302AC}']
    function GetName: WideString; safecall;
  end;


// ****************************************************************** //
// DispIntf:  IMTSTestObject5Disp
// Flags:     (4416) Dual OleAutomation Dispatchable
// GUID:      {DC62D911-0B0B-11D2-AED2-0060979302AC}
// ****************************************************************** //
  IMTSTestObject5Disp = dispinterface
    ['{DC62D911-0B0B-11D2-AED2-0060979302AC}']
    function GetName: WideString; dispid 1;
  end;

  CoMTSTestObject5 = class
    class function Create: IMTSTestObject5;
    class function CreateRemote
    ➥(const MachineName: string): IMTSTestObject5;
  end;

implementation

uses ComObj;

class function CoMTSTestObject5.Create: IMTSTestObject5;
begin
  Result := CreateComObject(CLASS_MTSTestObject5) as IMTSTestObject5;
end;

class function CoMTSTestObject5.CreateRemote(const MachineName: string):
  IMTSTestObject5;
begin
  Result :=
    CreateRemoteComObject(MachineName,CLASS_MTSTestObject5)
    ➥as IMTSTestObject5;
end;

end.
```

23

MTS

LISTING 23.3   THE IDL FOR A SIMPLE MTS SERVER

```
[
  uuid(DC62D910-0B0B-11D2-AED2-0060979302AC),
  version(1.0),
  helpstring("Project1 Library")
]
library MTSTest5
{

  importlib("STDOLE2.TLB");
  importlib("STDVCL40.DLL");

  [
    uuid(DC62D911-0B0B-11D2-AED2-0060979302AC),
    version(1.0),
    helpstring("Dispatch interface for MTSTestObject5 Object"),
    dual,
    oleautomation
  ]
  interface IMTSTestObject5: IDispatch
  {
    [id(0x00000001)]
    HRESULT _stdcall GetName([out, retval] BSTR * Value );
  };

  [
    uuid(DC62D913-0B0B-11D2-AED2-0060979302AC),
    version(1.0),
    helpstring("MTSTestObject5 Object"),
    custom(17093CC6-9BD2-11CF-AA4F-304BF89C0001, 0)
  ]
  coclass MTSTestObject5
  {
    [default] interface IMTSTestObject5;
  };

};
```

For now, you don't have to do much with this code other than compile it and make sure that it is properly registered. To register your DLL as a COM object, rather than as an MTS COM object, you can click the Register icon at the far right of the icons at the top of the Type Library Editor, or you can go to the DOS prompt and enter

```
regsvr32 MTSTest5.dll
```

or

```
tregsvr MTSTest5.dll
```

All these actions perform the same service for you. `regsvr32.exe` comes with the operating system, and `tregsvr.exe` comes with Delphi.

Later in this chapter, I will show you how to test your object inside MTS. When you do that, you can skip registering the object from Delphi or the command line, as MTS will automatically register your object for you. However, I am going to ask you to put off using MTS just long enough to test the object once outside MTS. If you break things up into two steps, then you can first test the validity of your code and then test to be sure MTS is working correctly. Later on, you won't need to take these two steps, as you will already know whether MTS is set up correctly. But for now, I think it is best to do things in two steps, just so you can be sure you are proceeding correctly. To test your code, you need to create a client application.

Creating a Simple MTS Client

The code in Listing 23.4 shows how to create a simple MTS client. This code is identical to the code you would create for an ActiveX automation client. In fact, one of the main goals of MTS is to allow you to create clients that do not have to perform any special actions to access an MTS server. In other words, the code you write for an automation client should be identical to the code you write for an MTS client.

LISTING 23.4 THE MAIN FORM FOR A SIMPLE MTS CLIENT

```
//////////////////////////////////////
// Purpose: Test MTS Server
// Project: MTSTestClient5.dpr
// Copyright (c) 1998 by Charlie Calvert
//
unit MainClient;

{-------------------------------------------------
  This program is designed to test the simple MTS server called
  MTSTest5.dll. It will call that server's sole method locally,
  or from a remote location.
-------------------------------------------------}

interface

uses
  Windows, Messages, SysUtils,
  Classes, Graphics, Controls,
  Forms, Dialogs, StdCtrls;

type
  TForm1 = class(TForm)
```

continues

LISTING 23.4 CONTINUED

```delphi
    LocalBtn: TButton;
    RemoteBtn: TButton;
    LocalAPIBtn: TButton;
    procedure LocalBtnClick(Sender: TObject);
    procedure RemoteBtnClick(Sender: TObject);
    procedure LocalAPIBtnClick(Sender: TObject);
  end;

var
  Form1: TForm1;

implementation

uses
  MTSTest5_TLB, ActiveX, ComObj;

{$R *.DFM}

procedure TForm1.LocalBtnClick(Sender: TObject);
var
  F: IMTSTestObject5;
begin
  F := CoMTSTestObject5.Create;
  ShowMessage(F.GetName);
end;

procedure TForm1.LocalAPIBtnClick(Sender: TObject);
const
  CLSCTX = CLSCTX_INPROC_SERVER or CLSCTX_LOCAL_SERVER;
var
  Unknown: IUnknown;
  F: IMTSTestObject5;
  hr: HResult;
begin
  hr := CoCreateInstance
  ➥(Class_MTSTestObject5, nil, CLSCTX, IUnknown, Unknown);
  if SUCCEEDED(hr) then begin
    Unknown.QueryInterface(IMTSTestObject5, F);
    ShowMessage(F.GetName);
  end else
    OleCheck(hr);
end;

procedure TForm1.RemoteBtnClick(Sender: TObject);
var
  F: IMTSTestObject5;
  S: string;
```

```
begin
  S := '';
  if InputQuery('Machine Name or IP Address', 'Remote Machine: ', S)
➥then begin
    F := CoMTSTestObject5.CreateRemote(S);
    ShowMessage(F.GetName);
  end;
end;

end.
```

This program has three methods called LocalBtnClick, LocalAPIBtnClick, and RemoteBtnClick, each of which will talk to an instance of your server and call its GetName method. Obviously, you use the first two methods to retrieve a local instance of the object, and you use the second method to retrieve an instance of the object that is located on a second machine.

To test your project, run the client on the same machine as the server, and click the Get Local Object button. The server should be loaded into memory behind the scenes, and your client should pop up a message box showing the name of the server, using the string retrieved from the server.

Calling the Object Locally

You can call the object fairly easily from a local machine. In fact, the method that will launch the object is automatically generated for you by Delphi and is located in the XXX_TLB file.

This declaration of the method will launch your object:

```
class function CoMTSTestObject5.Create: IMTSTestObject5;
begin
  Result := CreateComObject(CLASS_MTSTestObject5) as IMTSTestObject5;
end;
```

Behind the scenes, this object does little more than call CoCreateInstance. If you have the source to Delphi, and you want to see the implementation of CreateComObject, hold down the Control key and move your cursor over the word CreateComObject till it is highlighted in blue, as if it were a hyperlink; now left-click. COMOBJ.PAS should be brought up automatically for you in the IDE, and you should be taken immediately to the implementation of CreateComObject.

You can create this method to call CoMTSTestObject5.Create:

```
procedure TForm1.LocalBtnClick(Sender: TObject);
var
```

23

MTS

```
  F: IMTSTestObject5;
begin
  F := CoMTSTestObject5.Create;
  ShowMessage(F.GetName);
end;
```

As you can see, this method does nothing more than call the method designed to create an instance of your object, and then shows the result of a simple method call to the user.

Here is another version of the same method, but this time I'm going to have the Windows API do all the work:

```
procedure TForm1.LocalAPIBtnClick(Sender: TObject);
const
  CLSCTX = CLSCTX_INPROC_SERVER or CLSCTX_LOCAL_SERVER;
var
  Unknown: IUnknown;
  F: IMTSTestObject5;
  hr: HResult;
begin
  hr := CoCreateInstance
  ➥(Class_MTSTestObject5, nil, CLSCTX, IUnknown, Unknown);
  if SUCCEEDED(hr) then begin
    Unknown.QueryInterface(IMTSTestObject5, F);
    ShowMessage(F.GetName);
  end else
    OleCheck(hr);
end;
```

This method calls CoCreateInstance directly, rather than asking the VCL to call it for us. As a result, it will execute somewhat more quickly than the first version of this method, which makes two method calls before reaching CoCreateInstance.

> **NOTE**
>
> For what it is worth, I don't think you should let the overhead of those two function calls bother you. LocalBtnClick is so much easier to write and maintain than LocalAPIBtnClick that I think its virtues are inherently obvious. Furthermore, calling an object via MTS is an innately lengthy process that takes a noticeable period of time, whereas no one is going to be able to physically notice the overhead of two function calls. Nevertheless, if you are interested in saving clock cycles, then this is one way to do it. However, optimizing this one method does not really save the user any time, while there may be a loop in some other part of your program that may benefit the user if it is optimized.

After calling CoCreateInstance, you can check the outcome of the call by using the SUCCEEDED macro. If the macro returns True, then you can call QueryInterface to retrieve the object you want to access. Once you have the object, you can call the GetName method off it.

Now that you have seen how to call the object locally, the next step is to test your object inside MTS and then to test it remotely. To do these things, you need to register your object with MTS, as described in the next section.

Registering an Object with MTS

Registering an object with MTS is extremely easy. To get started, copy the MTSTest5.DLL you created to a directory on your server. Bring up the Transaction Server Explorer. On my system, I can find this program by choosing Start, Programs, Windows NT 4 Options Pack, Microsoft Transaction Server, Transaction Server Explorer.

In the Explorer, choose Console Root, Computers, My Computer, Packages Installed in the tree view control on the left of the program. Right-click on Packages Installed, and create a new package by choosing Create an Empty Package. Call your package D4Unleashed, or name it after yourself by giving it a name like Charlie's Package.

Open the tree view node for your package. Find the Components node, and right-click on it to create a new component. Select Install New Component, and browse for the DLL you created. When you select it, your package will be automatically registered on the server. To make sure it is registered properly, open the tree view nodes for your component in the Transaction Server Explorer and see whether you can find the methods for your server. These methods should include the standard IDispatch routines such as Invoke and GetIDsOfNames. Among these standard methods should also be the routines you have created explicitly, which in this case is the single method called GetName.

Now that the object is registered, you can run the client and call your server. When you do so, everything will operate exactly as it did when you accessed the server as a standard COM object. In fact, at first blush, you cannot tell that anything has changed.

There is, in fact, a way to note that your object is now part of MTS and not part of standard COM. To see what I mean, you need to open the MTS Explorer, expand the D4Unleashed node, and click on the Component's node so that it is highlighted.

Now run the client program, click on one of the local buttons, and turn back to the MTS Explorer. The black and green icon with the cross on it should now be animated, as if it were a bowling ball spinning in place. This shows that your object is currently activated.

The animation often takes a second or two to begin, and will not occur unless your object is currently in memory; therefore, you should not click on the OK button in your client program until you are tired of watching the icon dance. If you design a method that immediately lets go of your object, then you will not see the icon spin. For this reason, I call ShowMessage because it keeps the object in scope, and therefore active, until you click the OK button.

Calling the Object Remotely

Running the program remotely from a second computer is similar to running the program from the local computer, and virtually identical to running the program as a remote automation server. You should therefore consider referencing Chapter 15 if you are having trouble getting the server up and running remotely. In particular, note that running the server on an NT domain name server is probably best, and the client machine should be part of the domain.

Here is the method for calling the object remotely:

```
procedure TForm1.RemoteBtnClick(Sender: TObject);
var
  F: IMTSTestObject5;
  S: string;
begin
  S := '';
  if InputQuery('Machine Name or IP Address', 'Remote Machine: ', S)
  ➡then begin
    F := CoMTSTestObject5.CreateRemote(S);
    ShowMessage(F.GetName);
  end;
end;
```

This method will not work correctly unless you have registered the server on both the remote and the local machine. On the server, register the object or its TLB file with MTS. On the client, just run the server once to register the object. The server does not need to be present on the client; it just needs to be registered on the client. Our servers will auto-register themselves when you run them. Just run the server once on the client machine, and then delete it. Alternatively, just map a drive from the client machine to the server, and then run the server once from the client machine across this mapped drive. Or, if you desire, you can just copy the TLB file to the client and register that with TRegsvr.exe.

> **NOTE**
>
> You have to register your server on the client because you are calling its methods off an interface. When you use an interface, you have to register the object, or COM won't know how to marshal your data. If you really, really, don't want to have to register the server on the client, then you can call all your methods dynamically, off a `Variant` or dispinterface. The point is that you don't have to register an object if you are only calling the methods of `IDispatch`, but you do have to register it if you are calling the methods of your own custom interface. As you know, you can call your own custom methods off `IDispatch`, but calling them that way takes longer than if you call them off an interface. Furthermore, you get compile-time type checking when you use custom interfaces rather than `IDispatch`. See Chapter 13, Chapter 14, "TComObject, TTypedComObject, and Type Libraries, and Chapter 15 for more information on interfaces, `Variant`s, and `IDispatch`.

When calling the `RemoteBtnClick` method, you have to specify the name of the machine on which the server is running. For instance, you could write `CreateRemote('EastFarthing')`, if that were the name of your server. You can change the parameter to whatever name you like. A raw IP address, passed as a string, will also work: `CreateRemote('111.111.11.11')`. Or if you'd like, you can prompt the user for the name or IP address of the server, as I have done in the `RemoteBtnClick` method.

That's all there is to creating an MTS client and server. If you already understand how to build automation clients and servers, then you should find this process very simple indeed. Remember, one of the goals of MTS programming is to make the creation of clients entirely transparent; you don't have to do anything special on the client to allow it to access an MTS object as compared to a simple COM or DCOM object.

Of course, for many programmers, the next step is going to be accessing a database via MTS. I will describe that process in the next section and then proceed to a third section where I will describe how to start, commit, and roll back transactions.

> **NOTE**
>
> Note that MTS is still valuable to you even if you do not use databases. For instance, if you have many clients accessing standard COM objects like the one you have just created, the MTS will automatically take the servers out of memory when they are not being used. This will leave more room for other servers,
>
> *continues*

23

MTS

> thereby increasing the number of clients you can service. Clearly, this kind of feature benefits both database servers and standard nondatabase DCOM servers.

Creating a Simple MTS Database Server

Moving from generating a simple MTS server to generating an MTS database server is a fairly simple step. The main thing you have to do differently is create an MTS data module rather than a simple MTS object.

Before going any further, I'm going to show you the code for the TMTSDataServer example found on the CD that accompanies this book and displayed here in Listings 23.5 through 23.7. After you have had a look at the code, I will explain how it works.

LISTING 23.5   THE MAIN MODULE IN A SIMPLE MTS DATABASE SERVER

```
/////////////////////////////////////
// Purpose: Simple MTS Data Server
// Project: MTSDataServer.dpr
// Copyright (c) 1998 by Charlie Calvert
//
unit MainServerIMPL;

interface

uses
  Windows, Messages, SysUtils,
  Classes, Graphics, Controls,
  Forms, Dialogs, ComServ,
  ComObj, VCLCom, StdVcl,
  BdeProv, BdeMts, DataBkr,
  DBClient, MtsRdm, Mtx,
  MTSDataTestServer_TLB, Provider, Db, DBTables;

type
  TMTSDataTest = class(TMtsDataModule, IMTSDataTest)
    BioLifeTable: TTable;
    BioLifeProvider: TProvider;
  protected
    function GetData: OleVariant; safecall;
    function GetRecords(RecordCount: Integer; out RecsOut: Integer):
      OleVariant; safecall;
```

```pascal
    function ApplyUpdates(Delta: OleVariant; MaxErrors: Integer;
      out ErrorCount: Integer): OleVariant; safecall;
  end;

var
  MTSDataTest: TMTSDataTest;

implementation

{$R *.DFM}

function TMTSDataTest.GetData: OleVariant;
begin
  try
    Result := BioLifeProvider.Data;
    SetComplete;
  except
    SetAbort;
  end;
end;

function TMTSDataTest.GetRecords(RecordCount: Integer;
  out RecsOut: Integer): OleVariant;
begin
  try
    Result := BioLifeProvider.GetRecords(RecordCount, RecsOut);
    SetComplete;
  except
    SetAbort;
  end;
end;

function TMTSDataTest.ApplyUpdates(Delta: OleVariant; MaxErrors: Integer;
  out ErrorCount: Integer): OleVariant;
begin
  BioLifeProvider.ApplyUpdates(Delta, MaxErrors, ErrorCount);
end;

initialization
  TComponentFactory.Create(ComServer, TMTSDataTest,
    Class_MTSDataTest, ciMultiInstance, tmApartment);
end.
```

LISTING 23.6   THE TYPE LIBRARY FOR A SIMPLE MTS DATABASE SERVER

```pascal
unit MTSDataTestServer_TLB;

// ***************************************************************** //
// WARNING                                                          //
```

continues

LISTING 23.6   CONTINUED

```
// -------                                                            //
// The types declared in this file were generated from data read     //
// from a Type Library. If this type library is explicitly or        //
// indirectly (via another type library referring to this type       //
// library) re-imported, or the 'Refresh' command of the Type        //
// Library Editor activated while editing the Type Library, the      //
// contents of this file will be regenerated and all                 //
// manual modifications will be lost.                                 //
// ***************************************************************    //

// PASTLWTR : $Revision:   1.11.1.63  $
// File generated on 7/3/98 12:50:24 PM from Type Library
// described below.


// ***************************************************************    //
// Type Lib: D:\SrcPas\Unleash4\Chap23\MTSDataTest1\Server\
// MTSDataTestServer.tlb
// IID\LCID: {A2BC0DA0-106F-11D2-AEFC-0060979302AC}\0
// Helpfile:
// HelpString: Project1 Library
// Version:    1.0
// ***************************************************************    //

interface

uses Windows, ActiveX, Classes, Graphics, OleCtrls, StdVCL;


// ***************************************************************    //
// GUIDS declared in the TypeLibrary. Following prefixes are used:    //
//   Type Libraries     : LIBID_xxxx                                  //
//   CoClasses          : CLASS_xxxx                                  //
//   DISPInterfaces      : DIID_xxxx                                  //
//   Non-DISP interfaces: IID_xxxx                                    //
// ***************************************************************    //
const
  LIBID_MTSDataTestServer: TGUID =
➥'{A2BC0DA0-106F-11D2-AEFC-0060979302AC}';
  IID_IMTSDataTest: TGUID = '{A2BC0DA1-106F-11D2-AEFC-0060979302AC}';
  CLASS_MTSDataTest: TGUID = '{A2BC0DA3-106F-11D2-AEFC-0060979302AC}';
type

// ***************************************************************    //
// Forward declaration of interfaces defined in Type Library         //
// ***************************************************************    //
  IMTSDataTest = interface;
  IMTSDataTestDisp = dispinterface;
```

```
// **************************************************************** //
// Declaration of CoClasses defined in Type Library               //
// (NOTE: Here we map each CoClass to its Default Interface)       //
// **************************************************************** //
  MTSDataTest = IMTSDataTest;


// **************************************************************** //
// Interface: IMTSDataTest
// Flags:     (4416) Dual OleAutomation Dispatchable
// GUID:      {A2BC0DA1-106F-11D2-AEFC-0060979302AC}
// **************************************************************** //
  IMTSDataTest = interface(IDataBroker)
    ['{A2BC0DA1-106F-11D2-AEFC-0060979302AC}']
    function GetData: OleVariant; safecall;
    function GetRecords(RecordCount: Integer;
      out RecsOut: Integer): OleVariant; safecall;
    function ApplyUpdates(Delta: OleVariant; MaxErrors: Integer;
      out ErrorCount: Integer): OleVariant; safecall;
  end;

// **************************************************************** //
// DispIntf:  IMTSDataTestDisp
// Flags:     (4416) Dual OleAutomation Dispatchable
// GUID:      {A2BC0DA1-106F-11D2-AEFC-0060979302AC}
// **************************************************************** //
  IMTSDataTestDisp = dispinterface
    ['{A2BC0DA1-106F-11D2-AEFC-0060979302AC}']
    function GetData: OleVariant; dispid 1;
    function GetRecords(RecordCount: Integer;
      out RecsOut: Integer): OleVariant; dispid 2;
    function ApplyUpdates(Delta: OleVariant; MaxErrors: Integer;
      out ErrorCount: Integer): OleVariant; dispid 3;
    function GetProviderNames: OleVariant; dispid 22929905;
  end;

  CoMTSDataTest = class
    class function Create: IMTSDataTest;
    class function CreateRemote(const MachineName: string): IMTSDataTest;
  end;

implementation

uses ComObj;

class function CoMTSDataTest.Create: IMTSDataTest;
begin
  Result := CreateComObject(CLASS_MTSDataTest) as IMTSDataTest;
end;
```

continues

23

MTS

LISTING 23.6   CONTINUED

```
class function CoMTSDataTest.CreateRemote(
  const MachineName: string): IMTSDataTest;
begin
  Result := CreateRemoteComObject(MachineName,
    CLASS_MTSDataTest) as IMTSDataTest;
end;

end.
```

LISTING 23.7   THE IDL DESCRIBING THE TYPE LIBRARY FOR A SIMPLE MTS DATABASE
SERVER

```
[
  uuid(A2BC0DA0-106F-11D2-AEFC-0060979302AC),
  version(1.0),
  helpstring("Project1 Library")
]
library MTSDataTestServer
{

  importlib("STDVCL40.DLL");
  importlib("STDOLE2.TLB");

  [
    uuid(A2BC0DA1-106F-11D2-AEFC-0060979302AC),
    version(1.0),
    helpstring("Dispatch interface for MTSDataTest Object"),
    dual,
    oleautomation
  ]
  interface IMTSDataTest: IDataBroker
  {
    [id(0x00000001)]
    HRESULT _stdcall GetData([out, retval] VARIANT * Value );
    [id(0x00000002)]
    HRESULT _stdcall GetRecords([in] long RecordCount,
      [out] long * RecsOut, [out, retval] VARIANT * Value );
    [id(0x00000003)]
    HRESULT _stdcall ApplyUpdates([in] VARIANT Delta,
    ➥[in] long MaxErrors,
      [out] long * ErrorCount, [out, retval] VARIANT * Value );
  };

  [
    uuid(A2BC0DA3-106F-11D2-AEFC-0060979302AC),
    version(1.0),
    helpstring("MTSDataTest Object"),
```

```
    custom(17093CC5-9BD2-11CF-AA4F-304BF89C0001, 0)
  ]
  coclass MTSDataTest
  {
    [default] interface IMTSDataTest;
  };

};
```

To get started, create a new project, or at least close all existing projects; then select File, New, Multitier, MTS Data Module from the Delphi menu. Give your object a name, such as MTSDataTest. Be sure to specify that your object supports transactions. Click OK to generate the MTS data module. Save Unit1 as MainServerIMPL.pas, and save the project as MTSDataTestServer.dpr.

At this point, you might intuitively jump to the conclusion that you can now create an application exactly as you would when building a standard Midas program. However, this is not the case. With MTS, you cannot export a PROVIDER object from your server to the client because an MTS application should not have to maintain state.

Providers have to maintain state for a number of reasons, but one of the most obvious has to do with keeping your place in a dataset. If you ask for a set of five records and then ask later for a second set of five records, you expect to be given the next five records in the dataset. If MTS has removed your server from memory, then obviously it will not be able to know which record you are on, and will simply return the first five records to you a second time. As a result, you simply cannot use the Provider object in the way you would in a standard Midas application.

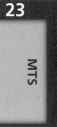

In an MTS application, you should drop a TTable or TQuery object on your data module and connect it to a dataset of some kind, just as you would in a normal single-tier application. Connect your table or query to the DBDemos database and to the BioLife table. Rename your table or query to BioLifeTable or BioLifeQuery.

Then drop a TProvider component on the data module, and connect its DataSet field to the TTable or TQuery you dropped on the form. Rename the TProvider component to TBioLifeProvider.

In a Midas application, you would then right-click on the TProvider to automatically export it from the server. In this case, you should not do that. Instead, open the Type Library Editor, and create a routine called GetData that returns an OleVariant. Delphi packages its remote data in Variant arrays, so that is why you choose OleVariant as the return type for your method. In other words, this method is going to return a dataset wrapped inside a Variant.

> **NOTE**
>
> Delphi will automatically wrap your dataset in a Variant. Or, if you prefer, you can create your own data packages using the TDataPacketWriter class found in the public section of Provider.pas. This class was not public in Delphi 3, and its presence as a public class in Delphi 4 is one of the more important new features in the product.
>
> I should emphasize, however, that in most cases you get at one of these data packets by simply referencing the GetData method of a Provider object. Most developers will not need to create their own data packets, but being able to do so can be a big deal in certain circumstances.

You can retrieve data from an MTS server like this:

```
function TMTSDataTest.GetData: OleVariant;
begin
  try
    Result := BioLifeProvider.Data;
    SetComplete;
  except
    SetAbort;
  end;
end;
```

The most important line of code here is the one that sets the Result of the function equal to the Data property of the BioLifeProvider.

Calling SetComplete tells MTS that you have finished your part in a transaction. Calling SetAbort tells MTS that you were not able to complete the transaction and that it should be rolled back.

Each transaction that you create will be part of its own action. If you call one application server, then everything that takes place from the beginning of that call to the end of that call will be part of one transaction. If all the routines called during this action return SetComplete, then the transaction will be committed automatically by MTS. If one of the routines called during this action calls SetAbort, then everything will be rolled back by MTS. The transaction begins the moment you make the call from the client, and it ends when the call from the server returns to the client. When you're calling the methods in the server that I am currently showing you, only one method is involved. You could, however, create a server in which one method called many other methods, each of which would have the option of calling SetAbort or SetComplete.

> **NOTE**
>
> If you want to call another server from inside the first server, or if you want to extend the life of a transaction, then you need to create your own Transaction Context. I will explain how to do so in the last section of the chapter, when I discuss the Rocket program.

SetAbort and SetComplete are available to you inside your IMPL file because they are methods of TMTSDataModule:

```
TMTSDataTest = class(TMtsDataModule, IMTSDataTest)
  BioLifeTable: TTable;
  BioLifeProvider: TProvider;
protected
  function GetData: OleVariant; safecall;
  function GetRecords(RecordCount: Integer; out RecsOut: Integer):
    OleVariant; safecall;
  function ApplyUpdates(Delta: OleVariant; MaxErrors: Integer;
    out ErrorCount: Integer): OleVariant; safecall;
end;
```

As you can see, TMTSDataTest descends from the VCL class called TMTSDataModule, and it implements the interface you created in the Type Library Editor.

Hold down the Ctrl key and move the mouse cursor over the word TMTSDataModule in the first line of code shown here. The word TMTSDataModule should turn blue and become underlined, as if it were a hyperlink. Now left-click on it, and if you have the source to the VCL, you will be taken to the source for this object. You will see this declaration:

```
TMtsDataModule = class(TRemoteDataModule, IObjectControl)
  private
    FOnActivate: TNotifyEvent;
    FOnDeActivate: TNotifyEvent;
    FObjectContext: IObjectContext;
  protected
    { IObjectControl }
    procedure Activate; safecall;
    procedure Deactivate; stdcall;
    function CanBePooled: Bool; stdcall;
    property ObjectContext: IObjectContext read FObjectContext;
  public
    procedure SetComplete;
    procedure SetAbort;
    procedure EnableCommit;
    procedure DisableCommit;
```

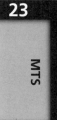

23

MTS

```
    function IsInTransaction: Bool;
    function IsSecurityEnabled: Bool;
    function IsCallerInRole(const Role: WideString): Bool;
  published
    property OnActivate: TNotifyEvent read FOnActivate write FOnActivate;
    property OnDeactivate: TNotifyEvent read FOnDeactivate write
    ➥FOnDeactivate;
  end;
```

The most important part of this object is the `FObjectContext` field. It contains an implementation of the `IObjectContext` interface on the MTS server. In other words, `IObjectContext` is an interface exported by MTS to your application. It allows you to tell MTS how it should handle transactions.

The methods in the `TMTSDataModule`, such as `SetComplete` and `SetAbort`, are just wrappers around the `TObjectContext`:

```
procedure TMtsDataModule.SetComplete;
begin
  if Assigned(FObjectContext) then FObjectContext.SetComplete;
end;
```

Or, if you want, you can call the `ObjectContext` property of the `TMTSDataModule` and get hold of the actual `ObjectContext` for your transaction. As you will see later in the chapter, you can create your own `ObjectContext`, with a scope and duration that you can control, by calling `CreateTransactionContextEx`. However, in most cases, you can just use the global instance of the object provided to you by Delphi.

So now you know how to call `SetComplete` and `SetAbort`. As a result, you know how to control the course of the transactions handled by your server.

The other methods on your server are fairly straightforward. You need to create the `GetRecords` method, for instance, so your client can specify how many records to see at a time:

```
function TMTSDataTest.GetRecords(RecordCount: Integer;
  out RecsOut: Integer): OleVariant;
begin
  try
    Result := BioLifeProvider.GetRecords(RecordCount, RecsOut);
    SetComplete;
  except
    SetAbort;
  end;
end;
```

This method allows you to state the number of records you want to see. It returns the actual count of records that it is returning, and it packages the records themselves in a `Variant`.

The `ApplyUpdates` method allows you to pass a dataset back to the server from the client so that you can update the database:

```
function TMTSDataTest.ApplyUpdates(Delta: OleVariant; MaxErrors: Integer;
  out ErrorCount: Integer): OleVariant;
begin
  BioLifeProvider.ApplyUpdates(Delta, MaxErrors, ErrorCount);
end;
```

I will explain more about how this method works when looking at the client application.

Before you create the client, however, you should start the MTS Explorer and register your object in the `D4Unleashed` package, or in some other package you have created. To do so, just follow the same steps you used when registering the simple `MTSTest5.dll`. After you register the object, click on the Components node of the MTS Explorer for your package, and select View properties from the MTS toolbar. You should now be able to see the Prog ID, Transaction, and DLL fields for your object. Make sure Transaction is set to `Required`. If it is not, you can change this field from inside the MTS Explorer by examining the properties for your object. (Actually, it doesn't matter whether this particular example supports transactions, but I want to show you how this process works. In the next two sample programs found in this chapter, I will dig a bit further into the mechanisms behind transactions and show you exactly how to control them.)

Creating a Simple MTS Database Client

The client application is not difficult to write. However, those of you who are familiar with standard Midas applications will have to pick up on the variations necessary to create a multitier client that does not maintain state.

To create this application, start a new project, and drop a `TDCOMConnection` and `TClientDataSet` on the main form. Name the `TDCOMConnection` object `TMTSDataConnection`, and name the `TClientDataSet` object `MTSDataSet`. Drop down the `ServerName` field of the object, and connect it to your server. If you followed my suggestions, the Prog ID for your server should be something like `MTSDataTestServer.MTSDataTest`. After you have selected your server, you can set the `Connected` property for the `TDCOMConnection` object to `True`. You should test this setting once to make sure it is working, but do not leave it set to `True`. Leaving `Connected` set to `True` can cause problems if you try to open your project inside Delphi when your server is not currently registered or available.

> **NOTE**
>
> The `ServerName` property knows which servers are available because it looks up this information in the Registry. Each Midas server on the system has the `Borland DataBroker` key in the Registry, so it can identify itself to the `ServerName` property of the `TDCOMConnection` object. To look up this key for yourself, first find the Prog ID in the `HKEY_CLASSES_ROOT` section of the `RegEdit.exe` program that ships with Windows. Find the CLSID of your object by looking at the entry found under your `Prog_ID`. Now find the `CLSID` section of the `HKEY_CLASSES_ROOT` section of the Registry and look for your CLSID. The listing for your CLSID should include the key `Borland DataBroker`.

You should now connect the `RemoteServer` field of your `TClientDataSet` to your `TDCOMConnection` component. Midas developers should beware at this point because you should not try to fill in the `ProviderName` field. Filling in the `ProviderName` property assumes that your server is exporting a provider. In this case, you are not exporting a provider because you do not want to have to maintain state.

In Listing 23.8, you will find the source for the `MTSDataClient` application found on the CD that comes with this book. This example shows how to connect to your server, retrieve data from your server, and update the server. Take a look at the source, and then I will explain its key methods.

LISTING 23.8 THE CLIENT PROGRAM FOR A SIMPLE MTS DATABASE CLIENT

```
/////////////////////////////////////////
// Purpose: Client program for MTSDataTest
// Project: MTSDataClient.dpr
// Copyright (c) 1998 by Charlie Calvert
//
unit Main;

{--------------------------------------------------------------
  This is a client program that talks to the MTSDataTestServer.

  It shows how to get data, how to get a specific number of records,
  and how to update data when using a stateless provider.

  The program also shows how to initialize data controls such as
  a TDBImage or TDBMemo in an MTS application. I also threw in
  splitters just for the good measure.
--------------------------------------------------------------}
interface
```

```
uses
  Windows, Messages, SysUtils,
  Classes, Graphics, Controls,
  Forms, Dialogs, StdCtrls,
  Db, DBClient, MConnect,
  Grids, DBGrids, Menus,
  MTSDataTestServer_TLB, ExtCtrls, DBCtrls;

type
  TForm1 = class(TForm)
    MTSDataSet: TClientDataSet;
    DBGrid1: TDBGrid;
    MTSDataSource: TDataSource;
    MTSDataConnection: TDCOMConnection;
    MainMenu1: TMainMenu;
    File1: TMenuItem;
    Connect1: TMenuItem;
    N1: TMenuItem;
    Exit1: TMenuItem;
    Options1: TMenuItem;
    GetData1: TMenuItem;
    GetRecords1: TMenuItem;
    ApplyUpdates1: TMenuItem;
    Panel1: TPanel;
    DBImage1: TDBImage;
    DBMemo1: TDBMemo;
    Splitter1: TSplitter;
    Splitter2: TSplitter;
    procedure ApplyUpdates1Click(Sender: TObject);
    procedure Connect1Click(Sender: TObject);
    procedure Exit1Click(Sender: TObject);
    procedure GetData1Click(Sender: TObject);
    procedure GetRecordsClick(Sender: TObject);
  private
    FMTSDataServer: IMTSDataTest;
    procedure AssignBlobs;
  public
    { Public declarations }
  end;

var
  Form1: TForm1;

implementation

{$R *.DFM}

procedure TForm1.ApplyUpdates1Click(Sender: TObject);
var
```

continues

23

MTS

LISTING 23.8   CONTINUED

```
  ErrorCount: Integer;
begin
  FMTSDataServer.ApplyUpdates(MTSDataSet.Delta, 2, ErrorCount);
end;

procedure TForm1.AssignBlobs;
begin
  DBMemo1.DataField := 'Notes';
  DBImage1.DataField := 'Graphic';
end;

{-- Connect1Click ------------------------------------------------------
    Make a live connection to the server, and return a pointer to the
    IMTSDataTest interface. The AppServer variable is a Variant that
    contains an IDispatch pointer, here I use the VCL as operator to
    call QueryInterface on that instance of IDispatch.
  ---------------------------------------------------------------------}
procedure TForm1.Connect1Click(Sender: TObject);
begin
  MTSDataConnection.Connected := True;
  FMTSDataServer := IDispatch(MTSDataConnection.AppServer)
  ➥as IMTSDataTest;
  if ((FMTSDataServer <> nil) and (Sender <> nil)) then
    ShowMessage
    ➥('Connection Successful. Use option menu to retrieve data');
end;

procedure TForm1.Exit1Click(Sender: TObject);
begin
  Close;
end;

procedure TForm1.GetData1Click(Sender: TObject);
begin
  if not MTSDataConnection.Connected then
    Connect1Click(nil);
  MTSDataSet.Data := FMTSDataServer.GetData;
  AssignBlobs;
end;

procedure TForm1.GetRecordsClick(Sender: TObject);
const
  Title = 'Record Count (Zero for metadata)';
  Prompt = 'Number of Records';
var
  RecsOut: Integer;
  S: string;
begin
```

```
  if not MTSDataConnection.Connected then
    Connect1Click(nil);

  S := '';
  if InputQuery(Title, Prompt, S) then begin
    MTSDataSet.Data := FMTSDataServer.GetRecords(StrToInt(S), RecsOut);
    AssignBlobs;
  end;

end;

end.
```

When you run this program, you can use the menu to view data from your server or to update the server with new data. On the surface, this program looks a lot like a standard Midas application, but you will see some subtle differences.

The most important method in the client is the one that connects to the server:

```
procedure TForm1.Connect1Click(Sender: TObject);
begin
  MTSDataConnection.Connected := True;
  FMTSDataServer := IDispatch(MTSDataConnection.AppServer)
➥as IMTSDataTest;
  if ((FMTSDataServer <> nil) and (Sender <> nil)) then
    ShowMessage
➥('Connection Successful. Use option menu to retrieve data');
end;
```

This method first sets the TDCOMConnection object's Connected property to True. The next step is to retrieve the MTSDataTest object from your server. It happens that Delphi already has a copy of your object available for your use in the AppServer field of the TDCOMConnection object. If you want, you can directly call the methods of your object off the AppServer field, which is of type Variant:

```
MTSDataConnection.AppServer.GetData;
MTSDataConnection.AppServer.GetRecords(5, RecsOut);
```

This approach is a perfectly reasonable way to proceed. However, you might want to work not with a Variant, but with a pointer to the actual interface on your object. To get the interface from the Variant, just use the as operator:

```
var
  FMTSDataServer: IMTSDataTest;
...
FMTSDataServer := IDispatch(MTSDataConnection.AppServer) as IMTSDataTest;
```

23

MTS

After you get the interface, your calls to your server will execute more quickly, and you will be able to get compile-time type checking and Code Insight support on your methods. However, this means that you will have to register your server or its type library on the client machine before you can use the client. This process was explained earlier in this chapter. If you don't want to register the server on the client, then just call your methods off the AppServer variable. As I stated earlier, remote MTS methods are so slow that the user is unlikely to notice the difference in most cases. However, sometimes, particularly inside loops, you need to get every bit of speed possible. As a result, I have shown you how to get the interface if you decide you need it. In my opinion, as long as you don't have any big reason not to get the interface, then you might as well go ahead and get it, thereby accruing the benefits inherent therein.

After you are connected to the server, then you can retrieve the data from your server:

```
procedure TForm1.GetData1Click(Sender: TObject);
begin
  if not MTSDataConnection.Connected then
    Connect1Click(nil);
  MTSDataSet.Data := FMTSDataServer.GetData;
  AssignBlobs;
end;
```

I don't really have much to say about this simple method, so I'll simply add that you would normally retrieve the data as part of the same method you use when connecting to your server. However, in this case, I have split up the two functions, as I want to give you the choice of using a second method that I provide for retrieving data from your server:

```
procedure TForm1.GetRecordsClick(Sender: TObject);
const
  Title = 'Record Count (Zero for metadata)';
  Prompt = 'Number of Records';
var
  RecsOut: Integer;
  S: string;
begin
  if not MTSDataConnection.Connected then
    Connect1Click(nil);

  S := '';
  if InputQuery(Title, Prompt, S) then begin
    MTSDataSet.Data := FMTSDataServer.GetRecords(StrToInt(S), RecsOut);
    AssignBlobs;
  end;

end;
```

This method first checks to make sure you are connected to your server. It then asks the user how many records he or she wants to see. With this data in hand, the method can call the GetRecords method on your server and retrieve the data for the user's perusal.

When you want to update the server, call ApplyUpdates:

```
procedure TForm1.ApplyUpdates1Click(Sender: TObject);
var
  ErrorCount: Integer;
begin
  FMTSDataServer.ApplyUpdates(MTSDataSet.Delta, 2, ErrorCount);
end;
```

Notice that I pass in the Delta field of the TClientDataSet object. This field contains all the records that you have updated since the last time you called ApplyUpdates. The second parameter says how many errors you will allow before aborting the update. The ErrorCount variable tells you the number of errors that occurred. I don't use it here, but the ApplyUpdates function returns a Variant containing any errors that occurred when updating your dataset. You should see Chapter 21, "MIDAS," for more information on handling errors on a provider interface.

Working with MTS Transactions

In this section, you will get a look at working with transactions and MTS. In particular, I will create a simple server and client pair that will show you how to create transactions, roll them back, or commit them. The program is designed to let you experiment with the technology. Later in the chapter, I will show you a complete program that will allow you to use transactions in a more real-world setting. The program used in this section is found in the Chap23\PDXRockets\GadgetMTS directory on the CD. This same program will be used later in the chapter as part of the multiserver Rockets example.

To get started, you should be sure you have MTS set up properly. After you install Delphi, your copy of MTS should contain a package called BDE-MTS. In the MTS Explorer, select this package, open it, and highlight the Components folder. Choose View, Transactions, and you should be able to see the PROG_ID, Transaction, and DLL properties for the BDEMTSDispenser, as shown in Figure 23.3. Check this listing and make sure that transactions are supported and that the DLL path points to a valid instance of DISP.DLL.

23

MTS

FIGURE 23.3

MTS displaying the BDEMTSDispenser.

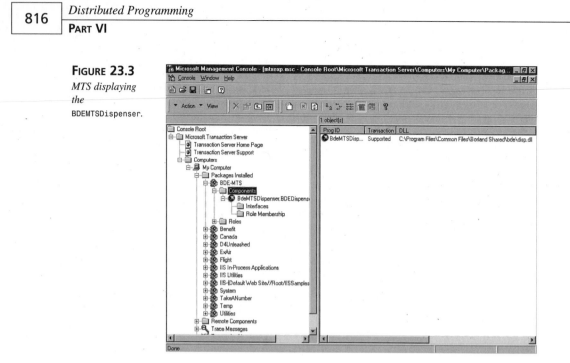

After you have checked to be sure that the BDEMTSDispenser is properly installed, open the BDE Administrator from the Start menu or from inside the SQL Explorer. Make sure that MTS Pooling is turned on. You can do so by turning to the Configuration page, and selecting System, Init. This same key is in the Registry at the following address:

```
'\SOFTWARE\BORLAND\DATABASE ENGINE\SETTINGS\SYSTEM\INIT';
```

The following method, from the MTSPooling demo that ships with Delphi, will allow you to toggle the setting:

```
procedure TForm1.MTSPoolingClick(Sender: TObject);
const
  MTSRegistryKey : PChar =
    '\SOFTWARE\BORLAND\DATABASE ENGINE\SETTINGS\SYSTEM\INIT';
var
  reg : TRegistry;
begin
  // Set the registry value to whatever the flag is
  reg := TRegistry.Create;
  reg.RootKey := HKEY_LOCAL_MACHINE;
  if ( reg.OpenKey( MTSRegistryKey, False) ) then
  begin
    if MTSPooling.Checked then
      reg.WriteString('MTS POOLING', 'TRUE')
    else
      reg.WriteString('MTS POOLING', 'FALSE');
```

```
    reg.CloseKey;
  end;
  reg.Destroy;
end;
```

If MTS Pooling is turned on, then transactions and pooling of database connections will
be available. If MTS Pooling is turned off, then you will have no support for
transactions.

Now create a simple server that will allow you to test MTS transactions. To do so,
choose File, New, Multi-Tier, and choose MTS Data Module. Give your module a name,
and accept all the defaults.

Drop down a TDatabase object on the MTS data module, and connect it to the
D4Unleashed alias, discussed in the readme on the CD for this book. (Or, if you want,
just connect to the DBDemos alias, and use the Country table. The data you use here is not
important.) Drop down a TTable object, connect it to this alias, and hook it up to the
RocketGadget.db table from the CD that accompanies this book (or connect it to the
Country table). Drop down a TProvider component, hook it up to the table, and export it
from the data module by creating a method called GetGadgets in the type library:

```
function TPDXGadgetObject.GetGadgets: OleVariant;
begin
  Result := GadgetProvider.Data;
end;
```

Remember, you don't directly export a Provider object from an MTS server because
you must have stateless code. So, instead of exporting the provider, just export the data
from the provider, as shown in the GetGadgets method.

Also, you must use a TDatabase object, or this program will not work. If you don't have
MTS Pooling turned on, and if you don't use a TDatabase object, then you will get no
joy from this process. If you need help setting things up, look at the example in the
PDXRockets\GadgetMTS directory on the CD that accompanies this book.

In the type library for this server, you will need to create a number of different methods,
as shown in Figure 23.4. These methods should look as follows when declared in your
program:

```
function GetGadgets: OleVariant; safecall;
function GetName: WideString; safecall;
procedure AddStandardGadget; safecall;
procedure DeleteStandardGadget; safecall;
procedure CallAbort; safecall;
procedure CallComplete; safecall;
```

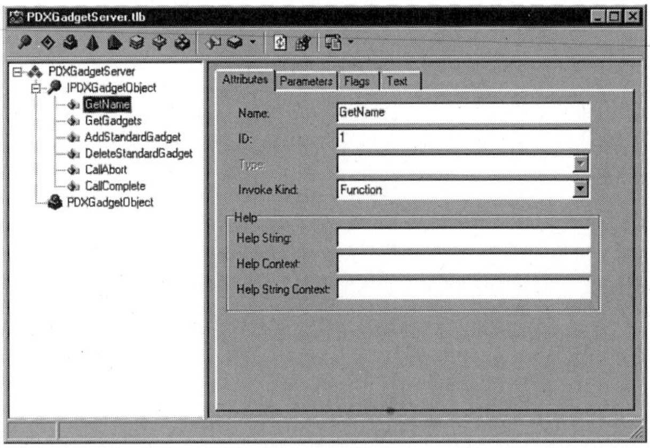

FIGURE 23.4

The type library as it appears when creating the PDXGadgetServer.

You are now ready to create the server. When you are done, your code should look like the sample shown in Listing 23.9.

LISTING 23.9   THE CODE FOR THE PDXGadgetServer IMPLEMENTATION

```
//////////////////////////////////////
//    File: MainServerIMPL.pas
// Project: PDXGadgetServer
// Copyright (c) 1998 by Charlie Calvert
//
unit MainServerIMPL;

interface

uses
  Windows, Messages, SysUtils,
  Classes, Graphics, Controls,
  Forms, Dialogs, ComServ,
  ComObj, VCLCom, StdVcl,
  BdeProv, BdeMts, DataBkr,
  DBClient, MtsRdm, Mtx,
  PDXGadgetServer_TLB, Provider, Db,
  DBTables;

type
  TPDXGadgetObject = class(TMtsDataModule, IPDXGadgetObject)
    GadgetTable: TTable;
    GadgetProvider: TProvider;
    Database1: TDatabase;
    procedure PDXGadgetObjectCreate(Sender: TObject);
  private
    { Private declarations }
  public
```

```
      { Public declarations }
    protected
      function GetGadgets: OleVariant; safecall;
      function GetName: WideString; safecall;
      procedure AddStandardGadget; safecall;
      procedure DeleteStandardGadget; safecall;
      procedure CallAbort; safecall;
      procedure CallComplete; safecall;
    end;

const
  AFileName = 'c:\mtsGadgetPDX.txt';

var
  DebugFile: TextFile;
  PDXGadgetObject: TPDXGadgetObject;

implementation

{$R *.DFM}

procedure AddInfo(S: string);
begin
  AssignFile(DebugFile, AFileName);
  Append(DebugFile);
  WriteLn(DebugFile, S + ': ' + DateTimeToStr(Now));
  CloseFile(DebugFile);
end;

procedure InTransaction(ObjectContext: IObjectContext);
begin
  if ObjectContext.IsInTransaction then
    AddInfo('In Transaction: ' + DateTimeToStr(Now))
  else
    AddInfo('Not In Transaction: ' + DateTimeToStr(Now))
end;

function TPDXGadgetObject.GetGadgets: OleVariant;
begin
  Result := GadgetProvider.Data;
end;

function TPDXGadgetObject.GetName: WideString;
begin
  Result := 'TPDXGadgetObject';
end;

procedure TPDXGadgetObject.AddStandardGadget;
begin
```

23

MTS

continues

LISTING 23.9 CONTINUED

```
    AddInfo('AddStandardGadget called');
    InTransaction(ObjectContext);
    try
      GadgetTable.Open;
      GadgetTable.Append;
      GadgetTable.FieldByName('Name').Value := 'Gadget';
      GadgetTable.FieldByName('Description').Value := 'A Big Gadget';
      GadgetTable.Post;
      GadgetTable.Close;
      AddInfo('Set complete called');
    except
      SetAbort;
      AddInfo('Set abort called');
    end;
end;

procedure TPDXGadgetObject.DeleteStandardGadget;
begin
  AddInfo('DeleteStandardGadget called');
  InTransaction(ObjectContext);
  try
    GadgetTable.Open;
    GadgetTable.Delete;
    GadgetTable.Close;
  except
    SetAbort;
    AddInfo('SetAbort called');
    raise;
  end;
end;

procedure TPDXGadgetObject.CallAbort;
begin
  SetAbort;
end;

procedure TPDXGadgetObject.CallComplete;
begin
  SetComplete;
end;

procedure TPDXGadgetObject.PDXGadgetObjectCreate(Sender: TObject);
begin
  AddInfo('    -    ');
  AddInfo('----------------');
  AddInfo('OnCreate called');
end;

initialization
```

```
AssignFile(DebugFile, AFileName);
  try
    Append(DebugFile);
  except
    ReWrite(DebugFile);
  end;
  WriteLn(DebugFile);
  WriteLn(DebugFile, '--------------------');
  WriteLn(DebugFile, 'GadgetMTS Initialization called: ' +
  ➥DateTimeToStr(Now));
  CloseFile(DebugFile);
  TComponentFactory.Create(ComServer, TPDXGadgetObject,
    Class_PDXGadgetObject, ciMultiInstance, tmApartment);
end.
```

To use this program, you should first compile it. Then open the MTS Transaction Explorer, and create or use the package called D4Unleashed. Now install your new component into the package.

Note that the GetGadgets method on this server does not call SetComplete. The Rockets program wants this method to call SetComplete, so that call may be part of the example on the disk. If it is, comment out the call to SetComplete in the GetGadgets method while using this example. Then later in the chapter, uncomment the call so the Rocket program will run smoothly. Or conversely, define GetGadgets to take a Boolean parameter specifying whether to call SetComplete.

After you have installed the server, you should take a moment to make sure you understand how it works. To understand this program, you must recall that SetComplete is the method you call to cause a transaction to be committed, whereas SetAbort is the method you call to roll back a transaction. Notice that in the normal course of operation, neither SetComplete nor SetAbort will be called unless you explicitly call it from the client program. In particular, look at the following method:

```
procedure TPDXGadgetObject.DeleteStandardGadget;
begin
  AddInfo('DeleteStandardGadget called');
  InTransaction(ObjectContext);
  try
    GadgetTable.Open;
    GadgetTable.Delete;
    GadgetTable.Close;
  except
    SetAbort;
    AddInfo('SetAbort called');
    raise;
  end;
end;
```

This method will delete the first record from a dataset. Unless something goes wrong, neither `SetAbort` nor `SetComplete` will be called by this method.

Now notice the following two routines, both of which are exported from the server:

```
procedure TPDXGadgetObject.CallAbort;
begin
  SetAbort;
end;

procedure TPDXGadgetObject.CallComplete;
begin
  SetComplete;
end;
```

You can call either of these methods to commit or roll back a transaction. You would not normally proceed this way in a standard MTS application. However, having this kind of control over the server can be very useful when you are first learning about MTS. In particular, you will be able to either commit or roll back each move you take, thereby allowing yourself to try various combinations of actions, and testing the results of each combination.

Listing 23.10 shows the client program that allows you to work with the server.

LISTING 23.10   THE CLIENT PROGRAM FOR THE PDXGadgetServer

```
//////////////////////////////////////
//    File: MainClient.pas
// Project: GadgetClient
// Copyright (c) 1998 by Charlie Calvert
//
unit MainClient;

interface

uses
  Windows, Messages, SysUtils,
  Classes, Graphics, Controls,
  Forms, Dialogs, DBClient,
  MConnect, ExtCtrls, Grids,
  DBGrids, Db, Menus;

type
  TForm1 = class(TForm)
    Panel1: TPanel;
    ClientDataSet1: TClientDataSet;
    DataSource1: TDataSource;
    DBGrid1: TDBGrid;
    MainMenu1: TMainMenu;
```

```
    Connect1: TMenuItem;
    Options1: TMenuItem;
    AddGadget1: TMenuItem;
    DeleteGadget1: TMenuItem;
    N1: TMenuItem;
    TestRollback1: TMenuItem;
    Abort1: TMenuItem;
    Complete1: TMenuItem;
    DCOMConnection1: TDCOMConnection;
    procedure Connect1Click(Sender: TObject);
    procedure AddGadget1Click(Sender: TObject);
    procedure DeleteGadget1Click(Sender: TObject);
    procedure TestRollback1Click(Sender: TObject);
    procedure Abort1Click(Sender: TObject);
    procedure Complete1Click(Sender: TObject);
  private
    { Private declarations }
  public
    { Public declarations }
  end;

var
  Form1: TForm1;

implementation

{$R *.DFM}

procedure TForm1.Connect1Click(Sender: TObject);
begin
  DCOMConnection1.Connected := True;
  ClientDataSet1.Data := DCOMConnection1.AppServer.GetGadgets;
end;

procedure TForm1.AddGadget1Click(Sender: TObject);
begin
  DCOMConnection1.AppServer.AddStandardGadget;
  ClientDataSet1.Data := DCOMConnection1.AppServer.GetGadgets;
end;

procedure TForm1.DeleteGadget1Click(Sender: TObject);
begin
  DCOMConnection1.AppServer.DeleteStandardGadget;
  ClientDataSet1.Data := DCOMConnection1.AppServer.GetGadgets;
end;

procedure TForm1.TestRollback1Click(Sender: TObject);
begin
  DCOMConnection1.AppServer.AddStandardGadget;
  DCOMConnection1.AppServer.AddStandardGadget;
```

continues

LISTING 23.10 CONTINUED

```
  DCOMConnection1.AppServer.AddStandardGadget;
  DCOMConnection1.AppServer.CallAbort;
  ClientDataSet1.Data := DCOMConnection1.AppServer.GetGadgets;
end;

procedure TForm1.Abort1Click(Sender: TObject);
begin
  DCOMConnection1.AppServer.CallAbort;
end;

procedure TForm1.Complete1Click(Sender: TObject);
begin
  DCOMConnection1.AppServer.CallComplete;
end;

end.
```

This client program allows you to connect to the PDXGadgetServer. You can then add or edit records, for example. After you have taken a certain number of actions, you can call either SetAbort or SetComplete to commit or roll back the transactions:

```
procedure TForm1.Abort1Click(Sender: TObject);
begin
  DCOMConnection1.AppServer.CallAbort;
end;

procedure TForm1.Complete1Click(Sender: TObject);
begin
  DCOMConnection1.AppServer.CallComplete;
end;
```

Notice in particular that you use the Variant AppServer property of the DCOMConnection1 component to dynamically access the methods of your server. In particular, the method called Abort1Click calls the CallAbort method on your Delphi MTS server.

To get started using the program, first click the Connect button so you can see the table. You should be able to see a few rows of data or, if the table is empty, at least the names of the fields in the table. Now use the Options button to add a few records to your table. Then choose Options, Abort to abort your action. To see the results of your work, click the Connect button again. The records you added should now be removed from the table.

Conversely, you can try deleting some records from the table and then clicking Abort and Connect to see the results of your actions. Or, if you wish, you can add records and then call Complete to make your changes permanent.

At this stage, you should be getting a feeling for how this process works. However, you should study one last element so that you can fine-tune your understanding. In the MTS Explorer is an option called Transaction Statistics way down at the bottom of the tree you find when you click on the My Computer icon. Double-clicking on the Transaction Statistics node brings up a dialog like the one shown in Figure 23.5.

The Transaction Statistics allow you to see the exact state your transactions are in at any one time. For instance, if you have clicked the Connect button at the top of the client program, you will notice that the Transaction Statistics dialog shows you as being in the middle of a transaction. Of course, you have nothing to roll back or commit at this time; nonetheless, you have connected to the server and are considered to be in the middle of a transaction until you either call SetComplete, SetAbort, or close your connection to the server.

At this point, you can call Complete to finish your transaction. By doing so, you tell MTS that it can unload your server from memory if it so desires. To track this process more completely, I have laced the server program with calls to a text file placed in the root of your C: drive. Make a few runs on the server; then check this file. It will tell you each time your server was loaded and unloaded. It does so by recording calls to your project's OnCreate event:

```
procedure TPDXGadgetObject.PDXGadgetObjectCreate(Sender: TObject);
begin
  AddInfo('    -    ');
  AddInfo('----------------');
  AddInfo('OnCreate called');
end;
```

Each time `PDXGadgetObjectCreate` gets called, the `AddInfo` method places a note in a text file:

```
const
  AFileName = 'c:\mtsGadgetPDX.txt';

var
  DebugFile: TextFile;

procedure AddInfo(S: string);
begin
  AssignFile(DebugFile, AFileName);
  Append(DebugFile);
  WriteLn(DebugFile, S + ': ' + DateTimeToStr(Now));
  CloseFile(DebugFile);
end;
```

The point here is for you to study both the Transaction Statistics dialog and your text-based log file so that you can understand exactly when you are in the middle of a transaction, when your server is loaded into memory, and any other details you might want to know about your server. MTS transactions are not innately difficult to grasp, but understanding how they work takes some time. Use this program to see exactly when you are in the middle of a transaction, what happens when you end a transaction, and when MTS loads and unloads your file.

For instance, delete a few records, and then look at the Transaction Statistics dialog. Note that you are in the middle of a transaction. Now call `SetComplete`. Go back and look at the Transaction Statistics dialog. The results will not show up right away, but within two or three seconds, you should note that the current transaction is complete. Now do something else to start a new transaction—call `SetAbort`—and go back to check the Transaction Statistics dialog. When you are done, look at the text file called `PDXGadgetMTS.txt` in the root of your C: drive. This file should record everything that happened to your server, including the times it was taken out of memory and re-created by MTS.

In the next section, you will see a more complex server that uses InterBase tables and three servers. In that program, you will see how to roll back transactions that are spread out across multiple servers.

Building an MTS Example That Spans Multiple Servers

By this time, you know most of the key facts you need to understand about MTS. The one remaining key piece of information is how to start your own transaction context and control its life span. With this information, you can start one transaction that spans multiple servers and takes multiple calls to execute.

Mastering this subject would seem to be difficult. In fact, it turns out to be very simple. In the next few paragraphs, I will show you how it works. Then I will wrap up the chapter, and you can begin creating your own MTS servers and clients.

The key to building an MTS example that spans multiple servers is the CreateTransactionEx function. Consider the following method:

```
procedure TPDXRocketMTS.CreateStandardRocket;
var
  Transaction: ITransactionContextEx;
begin
  Transaction := CreateTransactionContextEx;
  OleCheck(Transaction.CreateInstance(CLASS_PDXGadgetObject,
    IPDXGadgetObject, FGadgetObject));
  OleCheck(Transaction.CreateInstance(CLASS_PDXWidgetMTS,
    IPDXWidgetMTS, FWidgetObject));
  try
    DeleteGadget;
    DeleteWidget;
    RocketTable.Open;
    RocketTable.Append;
    RocketTable.FieldByName('Name').Value := 'Standard Rocket';
    RocketTable.FieldByName('Type').Value := 1;
    RocketTable.Post;
    RocketTable.Close;
    Transaction.Commit;
  except
    Transaction.Abort;
    raise;
  end;
end;
```

This code shows how to create a single transaction that spans three different servers. To understand this method, you first have to remember that it is taking place within a server. In other words, a client program calls this method to begin the transaction. The first server is the current one, the one from which the method is being called. The other two servers are called GadgetObject and WidgetObject. All three servers work together to create a single transaction in which a widget and a gadget are combined to create a rocket.

The code shown here first calls CreateTranscationContextEx to create a transaction context. This context will control all the other transactions that occur. In some senses, this process is a bit like calling StartTransaction. The method returns an instance of ITransactionContextEx. This interface has three methods called CreateInstance, Commit, and Abort. I will describe all three of these methods over the next few paragraphs.

The next two lines of code create instances of the GadgetObject and the WidgetObject:

```
OleCheck(Transaction.CreateInstance(CLASS_PDXGadgetObject,
   IPDXGadgetObject, FGadgetObject));
OleCheck(Transaction.CreateInstance(CLASS_PDXWidgetMTS,
   IPDXWidgetMTS, FWidgetObject));
```

You call these lines of code in lieu of using a TDCOMConnection object. In a typical Midas or MTS program, you would first drop a TDCOMConnection object on your form and then hook it up to the servers. In this case, you don't use the TDCOMConnection at all, and instead call the CreateInstance method of the ITransactionContextEx interface. CreateInstance takes three parameters:

- The Class ID of your object. It is declared in the XXX_TLB file for your object.
- The interface, or type, of your object. Again, it is declared in the XXX_TLB file for your object.
- A pointer to your object. It is returned by the routine. You call CreateInstance so that it will initialize and return this pointer to you.

The next step is to call the methods on the Gadget and Widget servers:

```
procedure TPDXRocketMTS.DeleteGadget;
begin
   FGadgetObject.DeleteStandardGadget;
end;

procedure TPDXRocketMTS.DeleteWidget;
begin
   FWidgetObject.DeleteStandardWidget;
end;
```

Here I call two methods off the objects returned to me by TransactionContextEx.CreateInstance. If both of these methods succeed, then my transaction is complete, and I can call the Commit method of ITransactionContextEx:

```
Transaction.Commit;
```

However, either no gadgets or no widgets may be available. In such a case, you would want to abort the transaction:

```
Transaction.Abort;
```

If you abort the transaction, then all your work will be rolled back. In other words, if you successfully delete a gadget and then find that you can't delete a widget, calling `Transaction.Abort` will automatically roll back the deletion of your gadget.

The code in the Gadget and Widget servers is very simple. For instance, the `DeleteStandardGadget` method looks like this:

```
procedure TPDXGadgetObject.DeleteStandardGadget;
begin
  try
    GadgetTable.Open;
    GadgetTable.Delete;
    GadgetTable.Close;
  except
    SetAbort;
    raise;
  end;
end;
```

The really important line of code here is the one that raises an exception. Delphi will automatically propagate this back to the `CreateStandardRocket` method in the Rocket server, thereby causing the `Transaction.Abort` method to be called:

```
try
  DeleteGadget;
  DeleteWidget;
  ... // Code ommitted here
  Transaction.Commit;
except
  Transaction.Abort;
  raise;
end;
```

In other words, if neither the Gadget nor Widget server raise an exception, then `Transaction.Commit` gets called, and if either one raises an exception, then `Transaction.Abort` gets called.

The following are the two most important facts about this example:

- It shows how to allow one single transaction to span multiple servers.
- It would still work even if the Gadget server used an InterBase database, the Widget server used MS SQL server, and the Rocket server used Paradox tables. In other words, the code supports heterogeneous databases.

The Code for the Rocket Program

The complete code for the Rocket is quite long, and much of it is redundant and not particularly interesting. As a result, I will show you only the main form for the client program in Listing 23.11. The data module for the client is shown in Listing 23.12. Listings 23.13 through 23.15 show the IMPL files for the three servers in the program.

LISTING 23.11 THE MAIN FORM FOR THE CLIENT PROGRAM IN THE ROCKET EXAMPLE

```
//////////////////////////////////////
// Purpose: Call the three servers in this multitier application
// Project: Rockets.dpr
// Copyright (c) 1998 by Charlie Calvert
//
unit Main;

interface

uses
  Windows, Messages, SysUtils,
  Classes, Graphics, Controls,
  Forms, Dialogs, StdCtrls,
  Gauges, ComCtrls, ExtCtrls,
  Menus, BDEMTS;

type
  TStrAry = array[1..3] of string;

const
  GadgetStr: TStrAry = (
    'Preparing Gadget 1', 'Preparing Gadget 2', 'Preparing Gadget 3');

  WidgetStr: TStrAry = (
    'Preparing Widget 1', 'Preparing Widget 2', 'Preparing Widget 3');

type
  TDataProc = procedure of object;

  TForm1 = class(TForm)
    Timer1: TTimer;
    Timer2: TTimer;
    Timer3: TTimer;
    MainMenu1: TMainMenu;
    File1: TMenuItem;
    RocketInfo1: TMenuItem;
    N1: TMenuItem;
    Exit1: TMenuItem;
    Help1: TMenuItem;
    About1: TMenuItem;
    Options1: TMenuItem;
    MakeWidget1: TMenuItem;
    MakeGadget1: TMenuItem;
    Panel3: TPanel;
    Panel1: TPanel;
```

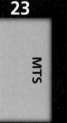

```
      Gauge1: TGauge;
      Gauge2: TGauge;
      Gauge3: TGauge;
      Label1: TLabel;
      Panel4: TPanel;
      Label2: TLabel;
      Panel2: TPanel;
      Gauge4: TGauge;
      Gauge5: TGauge;
      Gauge6: TGauge;
      BuildRocket1: TMenuItem;
      Edit1: TEdit;
      N2: TMenuItem;
      Context1: TMenuItem;
      procedure Timer1Timer(Sender: TObject);
      procedure FormCreate(Sender: TObject);
      procedure RocketInfo1Click(Sender: TObject);
      procedure About1Click(Sender: TObject);
      procedure MakeWidget1Click(Sender: TObject);
      procedure MakeGadget1Click(Sender: TObject);
      procedure Exit1Click(Sender: TObject);
      procedure BuildRocket1Click(Sender: TObject);
      procedure Context1Click(Sender: TObject);
    private
      Gauges: array[1..3] of TGauge;
      Timers: array[1..3] of TTimer;
      FLabel: TLabel;
      FInfoStr: TStrAry;
      FDataProc: TDataProc;
      procedure GadgetsSetup;
      procedure WidgetsSetup;
    public
    end;

var
  Form1: TForm1;

implementation

uses
  RocketInfo1, AboutBox1, DMod1,
  MTX;

{$R *.DFM}

procedure TForm1.FormCreate(Sender: TObject);
begin
  GadgetsSetup;
end;
```

continues

LISTING 23.11 CONTINUED

```
procedure TForm1.Timer1Timer(Sender: TObject);
var
  Gauge: TGauge;
  Index: Integer;
begin
  Index := TTimer(Sender).Tag;
  Gauge := Gauges[Index];
  Gauge.AddProgress(10);
  FLabel.Caption := FInfoStr[Index];
  if Gauge.Progress = Gauge.MaxValue then begin
    Timers[Index].Enabled := False;
    Inc(Index);
    if Index < 4 then
      Timers[Index].Enabled := True
    else begin
      MessageBeep(0);
      FDataProc;
    end;
  end;
end;


procedure TForm1.RocketInfo1Click(Sender: TObject);
begin
  RocketInfo.Show;
end;

procedure TForm1.About1Click(Sender: TObject);
begin
  AboutBox.ShowModal;
end;

procedure TForm1.MakeWidget1Click(Sender: TObject);
begin
  WidgetsSetup;
  Timer1.Enabled := True;
end;

procedure TForm1.MakeGadget1Click(Sender: TObject);
begin
  GadgetsSetup;
  Timer1.Enabled := True;
end;

procedure TForm1.GadgetsSetup;
var
  i: Integer;
begin
  FLabel := Label2;
```

```
    FDataProc := DMod.AddGadget;
    for i := 1 to 3 do begin
      Gauges[i] := TGauge(FindComponent('Gauge' + IntToStr(i + 3)));
      Gauges[i].Progress := 0;
      Timers[i] := TTimer(FindComponent('Timer' + IntToStr(i)));
      FInfoStr[i] := GadgetStr[i];
    end;
    Application.ProcessMessages;
  end;

procedure TForm1.WidgetsSetup;
var
  i: Integer;
begin
  FDataProc := DMod.AddWidget;
  FLabel := Label1;
  for i := 1 to 3 do begin
    Gauges[i] := TGauge(FindComponent('Gauge' + IntToStr(i)));
    Gauges[i].Progress := 0;
    Timers[i] := TTimer(FindComponent('Timer' + IntToStr(i)));
    FInfoStr[i] := WidgetStr[i];
  end;
end;

procedure TForm1.Exit1Click(Sender: TObject);
begin
  Close;
end;

procedure TForm1.BuildRocket1Click(Sender: TObject);
begin
  try
    Screen.Cursor := crHourGlass;
    Edit1.Text := 'Building Rocket';
    Edit1.Color := clYellow;
    Edit1.UpDate;
    try
      DMod.BuildRocket;
      Edit1.Color := clWhite;
      Edit1.Text := 'Rocket built';
    except
      Edit1.Text := 'Rocket build failed';
    end;
  finally
    Screen.Cursor := crDefault;
  end;
end;

procedure TForm1.Context1Click(Sender: TObject);
var
```

continues

LISTING 23.11 CONTINUED

```
  Context: IUnknown;
begin
  Context := GetObjectContext;
  if Context = nil then
    ShowMessage('No Context')
  else
    ShowMessage('Got Context');

end;

end.
```

LISTING 23.12 THE DATA MODULE FOR THE ROCKETS CLIENT PROGRAM

```
////////////////////////////////////
// Purpose: Handle the datamodule for the Rockets program
// Project: Rockets.dpr
// Copyright (c) 1998 by Charlie Calvert
//
unit DMod1;

interface

uses
  Windows, Messages, SysUtils,
  Classes, Graphics, Controls,
  Forms, Dialogs, DBClient,
  MConnect, MidasCon, Db;

type
  TDMod = class(TDataModule)
    RocketDataSet: TClientDataSet;
    RocketSource: TDataSource;
    WidgetConnection: TMidasConnection;
    WidgetDataSet: TClientDataSet;
    WidgetSource: TDataSource;
    GadgetConnection: TDCOMConnection;
    GadgetDataSet: TClientDataSet;
    GadgetSource: TDataSource;
    RocketConnection: TDCOMConnection;
    procedure DModCreate(Sender: TObject);
  private
    { Private declarations }
  public
    { Public declarations }
    procedure AddGadget;
```

```
    procedure AddWidget;
    procedure BuildRocket;
  end;

var
  DMod: TDMod;

implementation

{$R *.DFM}

procedure TDMod.DModCreate(Sender: TObject);
begin
  try
    RocketConnection.Connected := True;
    WidgetConnection.Connected := True;
    GadgetConnection.Connected := True;
    RocketDataSet.Data := RocketConnection.AppServer.GetRockets;
    WidgetDataSet.Data := WidgetConnection.AppServer.GetWidgets;
    GadgetDataSet.Data := GadgetConnection.AppServer.GetGadgets(True);
  except
    on E:Exception do begin
      ShowMessage(E.ClassName + ' : ' + E.message);
      raise;
    end;
  end;

end;

procedure TDMod.AddGadget;
begin
  GadgetConnection.Connected := True;
  GadgetConnection.AppServer.AddStandardGadget;
  GadgetConnection.Connected := False;
end;

procedure TDMod.AddWidget;
begin
  WidgetConnection.Connected := True;
  WidgetConnection.AppServer.AddStandardWidget;
  WidgetConnection.Connected := False;
end;

procedure TDMod.BuildRocket;
begin
  RocketConnection.AppServer.CreateStandardRocket;
end;

end.
```

23

MTS

LISTING 23.13 THE IMPLEMENTATION FOR THE GADGET SERVER INCLUDES CODE THAT WRITES OUTPUT TO A DEBUG TEXT FILE

```
////////////////////////////////////////
//    File: MainServerIMPL.pas
// Project: PDXGadgetServer
// Copyright (c) 1998 by Charlie Calvert
//
unit MainServerIMPL;

interface

uses
  Windows, Messages, SysUtils,
  Classes, Graphics, Controls,
  Forms, Dialogs, ComServ,
  ComObj, VCLCom, StdVcl,
  BdeProv, BdeMts, DataBkr,
  DBClient, MtsRdm, Mtx,
  PDXGadgetServer_TLB, Provider, Db,
  DBTables;

type
  TPDXGadgetObject = class(TMtsDataModule, IPDXGadgetObject)
    GadgetTable: TTable;
    GadgetProvider: TProvider;
    Database1: TDatabase;
    procedure PDXGadgetObjectCreate(Sender: TObject);
  private
    { Private declarations }
  public
    { Public declarations }
  protected
    function GetGadgets(CallSetComplete: WordBool): OleVariant; safecall;
    function GetName: WideString; safecall;
    procedure AddStandardGadget; safecall;
    procedure DeleteStandardGadget; safecall;
    procedure CallAbort; safecall;
    procedure CallComplete; safecall;
  end;

const
  AFileName = 'c:\mtsGadgetPDX.txt';

var
  DebugFile: TextFile;
  PDXGadgetObject: TPDXGadgetObject;

implementation
```

```
{$R *.DFM}

procedure AddInfo(S: string);
begin
  AssignFile(DebugFile, AFileName);
  Append(DebugFile);
  WriteLn(DebugFile, S + ': ' + DateTimeToStr(Now));
  CloseFile(DebugFile);
end;

procedure InTransaction(ObjectContext: IObjectContext);
begin
  if ObjectContext = nil then
    AddInfo('ObjectContext = nil, MTS not running?')
  else if ObjectContext.IsInTransaction then
    AddInfo('In Transaction: ' + DateTimeToStr(Now))
  else
    AddInfo('Not In Transaction: ' + DateTimeToStr(Now))
end;

function TPDXGadgetObject.GetGadgets
➥(CallSetComplete: WordBool): OleVariant;
begin
  Result := GadgetProvider.Data;
  if CallSetComplete then
    SetComplete;    // Don't call when using the GadgetClient
end;

function TPDXGadgetObject.GetName: WideString;
begin
  Result := 'TPDXGadgetObject';
end;

procedure TPDXGadgetObject.AddStandardGadget;
begin
  AddInfo('AddStandardGadget called');
  InTransaction(ObjectContext);
  try
    GadgetTable.Open;
    GadgetTable.Append;
    GadgetTable.FieldByName('Name').Value := 'Gadget';
    GadgetTable.FieldByName('Description').Value := 'A Big Gadget';
    GadgetTable.Post;
    GadgetTable.Close;
  except
    SetAbort;
    AddInfo('Set abort called');
  end;
end;
```

continues

LISTING 23.13 CONTINUED

```pascal
procedure TPDXGadgetObject.DeleteStandardGadget;
begin
  AddInfo('DeleteStandardGadget called');
  InTransaction(ObjectContext);
  try
    GadgetTable.Open;
    GadgetTable.Delete;
    GadgetTable.Close;
  except
    SetAbort;
    AddInfo('SetAbort called');
    raise;
  end;
end;

procedure TPDXGadgetObject.CallAbort;
begin
  SetAbort;
end;

procedure TPDXGadgetObject.CallComplete;
begin
  SetComplete;
end;

procedure TPDXGadgetObject.PDXGadgetObjectCreate(Sender: TObject);
begin
  AddInfo('   -    ');
  AddInfo('----------------');
  AddInfo('OnCreate called');
end;

initialization
AssignFile(DebugFile, AFileName);
  try
    Append(DebugFile);
  except
    ReWrite(DebugFile);
  end;
  WriteLn(DebugFile);
  WriteLn(DebugFile, '--------------------');
  WriteLn(DebugFile, 'GadgetMTS Initialization called: ' +
➥DateTimeToStr(Now));
  CloseFile(DebugFile);
  TComponentFactory.Create(ComServer, TPDXGadgetObject,
    Class_PDXGadgetObject, ciMultiInstance, tmApartment);
end.
```

LISTING 23.14   THE IMPLEMENTATION FOR THE WIDGET SERVER

```
/////////////////////////////////////
// Purpose: A Widget Server
// Project: PDXWidgetServer.dpr
// Copyright (c) 1998 by Charlie Calvert
//
unit MainServerIMPL;

interface

uses
  Windows, Messages, SysUtils,
  Classes, Graphics, Controls,
  Forms, Dialogs, ComServ,
  ComObj, VCLCom, StdVcl,
  BdeProv, BdeMts, DataBkr,
  DBClient, MtsRdm, Mtx,
  PDXWidgetServer_TLB, Provider, Db,
  DBTables;

type
  TPDXWidgetMTS = class(TMtsDataModule, IPDXWidgetMTS)
    WidgetDatabase: TDatabase;
    WidgetTable: TTable;
    WidgetProvider: TProvider;
  protected
    function GetWidgets: OleVariant; safecall;
    procedure AddStandardWidget; safecall;
    procedure DeleteStandardWidget; safecall;
  end;

var
  PDXWidgetMTS: TPDXWidgetMTS;

implementation

{$R *.DFM}

function TPDXWidgetMTS.GetWidgets: OleVariant;
begin
  Result := WidgetProvider.Data;
  SetComplete;
end;

procedure TPDXWidgetMTS.AddStandardWidget;
begin
  try
    WidgetTable.Open;
    WidgetTable.Append;
```

23

MTS

continues

LISTING 23.14 CONTINUED

```
    WidgetTable.FieldByName('Name').Value := 'Widget';
    WidgetTable.FieldByName('Description').Value := 'A Big Widget';
    WidgetTable.Post;
    WidgetTable.Close;
  except
    SetAbort;
    raise;
  end;
end;

procedure TPDXWidgetMTS.DeleteStandardWidget;
begin
  try
    WidgetTable.Open;
    WidgetTable.Delete;
    WidgetTable.Close;
  except
    SetAbort;
    raise;
  end;
end;

initialization
  TComponentFactory.Create(ComServer, TPDXWidgetMTS,
    Class_PDXWidgetMTS, ciMultiInstance, tmApartment);
end.
```

LISTING 23.15 THE MTSROCKET SERVER IS THE SERVER THAT CONTROLS THE WIDGET AND GADGET SERVER

```
///////////////////////////////////////
// Purpose: A Rocket Server
// Project: MainServerIMPL
// Copyright (c) 1998 by Charlie Calvert
//
unit MainServerIMPL;

{-------------------------------------------------------------------
  Use the D4Unleashed alias, which should point at the main directory
  where you are storing the paradox tables that come with D4 Unleashed.
  The table you want to use is called Rocket.db. Remember, you must
  use a TDatabase or the transactions will not roll back properly.

  When working with the project manager, you sometimes want the client
  to build second, so that you can Build All, and end up with the active
  application being the client. That way you can just click the green
  button and run the client after the build. To change which application
  gets built first, and which gets built second, right-click on the
  project manager, directly on top of one of your projects.
-------------------------------------------------------------------}
```

```
interface

uses
  Windows, Messages, SysUtils,
  Classes, Graphics, Controls,
  Forms, Dialogs, ComServ,
  ComObj, VCLCom, StdVcl,
  BdeProv, BdeMts, DataBkr,
  DBClient, MtsRdm, Mtx,
  PDXRocketServer_TLB, Provider, Db,
  DBTables, MConnect,
  PDXGadgetServer_TLB, PDXWidgetServer_TLB;


type
  TPDXRocketMTS = class(TMtsDataModule, IPDXRocketMTS)
    RocketDatabase: TDatabase;
    RocketTable: TTable;
    RocketProvider: TProvider;
  private
    FGadgetObject: IPDXGadgetObject;
    FWidgetObject: IPDXWidgetMTS;
    procedure DeleteGadget;
    procedure DeleteWidget;
  protected
    function GetRockets: OleVariant; safecall;
    procedure CreateStandardRocket; safecall;
    procedure DeleteStandardRocket; safecall;
  end;

var
  PDXRocketMTS: TPDXRocketMTS;

implementation

{$R *.DFM}

function TPDXRocketMTS.GetRockets: OleVariant;
begin
  Result := RocketProvider.Data;
  SetComplete;
end;

procedure TPDXRocketMTS.CreateStandardRocket;
var
  Transaction: ITransactionContextEx;
begin
  Transaction := CreateTransactionContextEx;
  OleCheck(Transaction.CreateInstance(CLASS_PDXGadgetObject,
```

continues

LISTING 23.15   CONTINUED

```pascal
    IPDXGadgetObject, FGadgetObject));
  OleCheck(Transaction.CreateInstance(CLASS_PDXWidgetMTS,
    IPDXWidgetMTS, FWidgetObject));
  try
    DeleteGadget;
    DeleteWidget;
    RocketTable.Open;
    RocketTable.Append;
    RocketTable.FieldByName('Name').Value := 'Standard Rocket';
    RocketTable.FieldByName('Type').Value := 1;
    RocketTable.Post;
    RocketTable.Close;
    Transaction.Commit;
  except
    Transaction.Abort;
    raise;
  end;
  // Do I need to free the transaction or WidgetObject and GadgetObject?
end;

procedure TPDXRocketMTS.DeleteGadget;
begin
  FGadgetObject.DeleteStandardGadget;
end;

procedure TPDXRocketMTS.DeleteWidget;
begin
  FWidgetObject.DeleteStandardWidget;
end;

procedure TPDXRocketMTS.DeleteStandardRocket;
begin
  try
    RocketTable.Open;
    RocketTable.Delete;
    RocketTable.Close;
    SetComplete;
  except
    SetAbort;
  end;
end;

initialization
  TComponentFactory.Create(
    ComServer,            // Controls your server
    TPDXRocketMTS,        // Object you want to create
    Class_PDXRocketMTS,   // GUID of object you create
```

```
    ciMultiInstance,      // Instancing
    tmApartment           // Threading
  );
end.
```

When you run this program, you will have the option of viewing the data in the Rocket, Gadget, and Widget tables. These Paradox tables are found in the standard Data directory on CD that accompanies this book. You should copy the tables onto your hard drive before you attempt to use them.

Each of the servers uses an MTS data module. On the data module, you should drop down a TDataBase object and a TTable object. Connect the database to the D4Unleashed alias that points to the Data directory you copied from the CD that comes with this book. You will need to place a TProvider object on these data modules and then create methods for each of the providers so that you can access the tables' data in a stateless manner, as described earlier in this chapter.

Notice the code I have written to connect to these servers from the client:

```
procedure TDMod.DModCreate(Sender: TObject);
begin
  try
    RocketConnection.Connected := True;
    WidgetConnection.Connected := True;
    GadgetConnection.Connected := True;
    RocketDataSet.Data := RocketConnection.AppServer.GetRockets;
    WidgetDataSet.Data := WidgetConnection.AppServer.GetWidgets;
    GadgetDataSet.Data := GadgetConnection.AppServer.GetGadgets;
  except
    on E:Exception do begin
      ShowMessage(E.ClassName + ' : ' + E.message);
      raise;
    end;
  end;
end;
```

This code first connects to the server and then retrieves data from the server so it can be viewed by the user. To actually view the data, choose the View Data option from the program's menu. Choosing this option brings up a modeless dialog that you can keep on the desktop during the whole run of the application. Notice that you have to manually update these tables to see the results of your work in the program.

The program itself is quite simple. It gives you the option of building a new widget, building a new gadget, or building a rocket. Each time you build a rocket, you will use up one widget and one gadget.

To see the program in action, you should first turn off exception handling in the IDE by selecting Tools, Debugger Options, and turning off Integrated Debugging. Now run the application, and view the data. Make sure that at least one widget and one gadget appear in the database. If you need to create some, use the program's menu to build the widgets. You can tell this activity is very complicated because lots of stuff is going on in the program's interface whenever you create a widget or a gadget.

Now create a rocket. Use the menu to view the data, and notice that one gadget and one widget were removed from the database. Furthermore, one rocket was also added to the database.

A more interesting example occurs when you have either a few gadgets and no widgets, or a few widgets and no gadgets. Now attempt to build a rocket. You will notice that an error occurs. When you look in the database, you will see that no widgets or gadgets were deleted from the database. Of course, in some situations a gadget is deleted from the database, and yet a rocket is not successfully built because no widgets are available. In this case, `Transaction.Abort` must be called to roll back the transaction on the `Gadget` table.

Take some time to have fun with the Rocket server example. This key program really shows what you can do with MTS and databases.

Summary

In this chapter, you have looked at building standard MTS objects and database objects. You learned about how MTS manages resources, pools database connections, and handles transactions. A considerable portion of the chapter was dedicated to exploring the subject of stateless database objects.

There is only one important missing piece. It turns out that Microsoft uses OLE automation to allow you to manipulate MTS even from a remote location. In other words, you can call several interfaces on the MTS server to find about the available packages, create new packages, and create new servers. Because of space considerations, I won't discuss doing that in this book. Instead, I will refer you to the `MTSMonitor` application on the CD that accompanies this book. That application shows how you can get started automating MTS so that you can automatically install your own packages and servers.

CORBA

CHAPTER 24

This chapter is about using CORBA in Delphi 4 Client/Server. In particular, you will see

- How to use the basic tools of CORBA such as the ORB, the BOA, and the Smart Agent
- How to create a simple CORBA server and client
- How to create a simple CORBA database object
- How to call a CORBA object using dynamic invocation
- How to use the Interface Repository

The struggle to get all programs on all systems talking to each other, regardless of which language they are written in, is one of the grandest quests yet undertaken by programmers. Certainly, DCOM shares in this quest, but for now it is more limited than CORBA because it lacks CORBA's cross-platform agenda. Of course, DCOM has the advantage of riding the crest of Windows development, and it does not come with a forbidding price tag that limits a technology's usefulness. But still, it is CORBA that has the grandest agenda, and everyone who works with this technology should feel something of the excitement inherent in the endeavor.

Understanding CORBA

Delphi Client/Server does not provide a complete CORBA solution. In particular, it has no `IDL2PAS` file that will convert a CORBA interface into a Delphi object. Delphi Client/Server makes it easy for you to create CORBA objects and to connect to them using dynamic invocation. Dynamic invocation is a technology I will discuss in some depth later in this chapter. The Delphi Client/Server Type Library Editor uses COM IDL rather than CORBA IDL; as a result, it will not fully support all possible CORBA interfaces. Nevertheless, you should still be able to connect to those interfaces using dynamic invocation. Delphi Client/Server also has no code to make it easy for you to access many of the CORBA services such as the naming service or event service.

What Delphi Client/Server does offer is a very easy-to-use interface to CORBA programming. Components and wizards are available to allow you to create and access CORBA objects from Delphi with very little effort on your part. The objects you access can be written in any CORBA-compliant language, and the objects you create can be accessed using traditional CORBA programming techniques from any other CORBA-aware language such as Java or C++.

In the next few pages, I will explain what CORBA is and how it works. After this brief introduction to the subject, I will show you several hands-on examples. In particular, the next few introductory sections will cover the following topics:

- What is CORBA?
- What is an ORB?
- What is the Smart Agent?
- What is the BOA?
- What are proxies, stubs, and skeletons?

What Is CORBA?

This chapter is designed to get you up to speed with CORBA and Delphi 4 Client Server. If you are using the Enterprise version of Delphi 4, then you should go to http://www.inprise.com, http://users.aol.com/charliecal, and http://www.inprise.com/techvoyage, and look for additional information specific to Delphi Enterprise. Another important CORBA link is http://www.acl.lanl.gov/CORBA/, where you can find many articles on CORBA development. A key book on this subject is *Client Server Programming with Java and CORBA*, by Robert Orfali and Dan Harkey. It is sometimes also called the "Martian book" because of the pictures of Martians used throughout the text.

CORBA is an acronym standing for the Common Object Request Broker Architecture. If the acronym had been chosen more for its usefulness rather than its marketing value, it might have been called OMDC, or the Object Model for Distributed Computing.

CORBA was created by the OMG, or Object Management Group. Their Web site is http://www.omg.org, and anyone interested in this technology should visit that URL regularly. The OMG has many contributing members, and many of them are large companies such as Microsoft, Netscape, Sun Microsystems, Oracle, Novell, Micro Focus, Lockheed Martin, IBM, Inprise, Informix, Iona, Hewlett-Packard, Computer Associates, Anderson Consulting, Fujitsu, Platinum, Rational Software, Rogue Wave, Sybase, and Xerox. Many others also are auditing or influencing the process.

24

CORBA

NOTE

The OMG uses a lot of jargon, most of which can be ignored. For instance, I found prose on the OMG site that talks about "system aspects that are not part of an object's interface." What are "system aspects"? Could the author possibly mean, "operating system-specific features?" Did he really mean something as simple as "anything else but the object's interface"? It's impossible to know.

continues

Another catchy phrase used quite often is "transparently invoke." Just what does it mean to "transparently invoke" something? What the heck is a "single implementation language-independent specification?" How do you "model a legacy component"? I'm not saying that I can't occasionally guess what these people must be trying to say, but only that I am baffled by their reluctance to say it in plain English. And I'm sure that if the AMA did a study on this use of language, they could prove that even relatively coherent phrases such as the following are carcinogenic: "[An] ORB provides interoperability between applications on different machines in heterogeneous distributed environments and seamlessly interconnects multiple object systems."

My point here is not that the OMG's mission is not a good one; in fact, it is excellent. But for some reason, the promoters of CORBA tend to be even more egregiously in violation of the basic rules of common sense than are their counterparts from such highly suspect organizations as Microsoft or JavaSoft.

To my mind, the primary goal of the OMG is to create an OOP-based, cross-platform, distributed architecture that can host a large number of servers and clients and that scales well, even under extremely heavy pressure. In particular, the developers of CORBA design their specification to support millions of servers and tens of thousands of simultaneous users. CORBA has an extremely robust architecture that meets the needs of large corporations.

The OMG drew up the specification for CORBA. Companies such as Visigenic and IONA actually implement the specification. As you might know, Visigenic was acquired by Inprise during the spring of 1998, which means that Inprise is now in control of a commonly used implementation of CORBA.

Throughout this chapter, I will always be talking about the Inprise/Visigenic version of CORBA unless I specifically say otherwise. The name for Inprise's implementation of CORBA is the VisiBroker.

Not all the things I say apply to CORBA as a whole, as you can take certain shortcuts when using the Visigenic ORB that are not specifically mentioned in the CORBA specification. These shortcuts make your life easier, and they are built on top of a fully correct implementation of the OMG 2.1 standard for CORBA. In other words, the presence of these extensions does not imply that the Visigenic ORB is not fully compliant with the CORBA 2.1 standard.

Comparing DCOM and CORBA

If you come from Windows, you might be wondering what the difference is between CORBA and DCOM. In many ways, the technologies parallel each other, and indeed they perform very similar tasks.

Both COM and CORBA provide a means of creating distributed, object-oriented architectures. In other words, they both provide means of calling an object residing in a binary executable on another machine.

Both COM and CORBA have various utilities that support them, such as MTS, ITS, brokers, registries, and so on. And yet, each architecture has specific advantages.

COM, being a Microsoft and Windows-based technology, has the advantage of being integrated into 90 percent of the desktop machines in the world. It is free and has excellent support from a wide range of vendors.

CORBA is probably somewhat better at this time at providing true 24-hour-a-day, seven-day-a-week support. For instance, it probably has better support for fail over and load distribution than COM does, though this balance of power is changing even as I write. For instance, Delphi now provides the `TSimpleObjectBroker` component to provide load balancing and fail over for DCOM objects. Certainly, CORBA has much better support for a wide range of operating systems than does COM.

Finally, both architectures are similar in the fanaticism of their adherents. I've heard people from both sides of this ongoing battle claim that they have complete dominance of the distributed architecture playing field. The truth of the matter is that this is very much an ongoing battle. COM is widespread, but CORBA has important friends in big companies such as Sun, Netscape, and IBM.

The truth is that no one knows who is going to win this battle, just as people once didn't know if OS2 or Windows was going to win, or if Apple or Microsoft was going to win. In this unfolding story, the only serious mistake you can make is taking at face value the occasionally absurd claims and accusations made by both sides of this argument. For instance, COM programmers sometimes claim that COM works well on a range of operating systems or will soon work well on a range of operating systems. Such statements should be taken with a grain of salt. Likewise, I find suspect CORBA adherents' claims of "transparent" interoperability between different ORBs and sometimes even different operating systems. CORBA's pretty good, but not quite that good.

The only way to know which side is really going to win is to wait and watch, always taking into account the possibility that both technologies will exist into the indefinite future.

24

CORBA

What Is an ORB?

An ORB, or Object Request Broker, is often spoken of as merely the generic name for the set of services used to connect a client and a server and to pass method calls and information back and forth between a client and a server. As such, it is not so much a specific entity as it is a concept.

However, the ORB has to be implemented somewhere. In Windows, it is made manifest by a series of DLLs designed to help you link objects across the network or across process boundaries. These DLLs have names like ORB_R.DLL, and they are installed by default in the C:\Program Files\Borland\VisiBroker\Bin directory. Because the ORB is implemented in DLLs, they reside in process with your server and client implementations. Because you do not have to call across process boundaries to access their methods, in-process DLLs are fast.

These DLLs total several megabytes in size, and they need to be installed on all client and server machines that use CORBA. You are unlikely to ever have occasion to call specific functions in these DLLs, but you will be using them continually without ever directly referencing them. In other words, you call routines or objects that reside inside these DLLs, but you do not need to know what functions or methods reside in which DLLs, or even that the functions or methods are in fact stored in DLLs. The VCL takes care of those kinds of details for you.

You need to understand that the ORB DLLs are merely artifacts of Visigenic's implementation of the CORBA standard. The standard itself does not say anything about these DLLs, but Visigenic created them to implement the requirements laid down in the specification. In other words, the DLLs were one logical and robust way to create an implementation of the specification.

By now, you probably sense the extreme importance placed on the specification developed by the OMG. This specification is the CORBA standard, and if CORBA is not centered on standards, then it has almost no meaning. The whole point of CORBA is that it is a cross-platform standard for building distributed object architectures. If the standard is violated, then the various pieces might not work together, and then the whole system is useless.

To sum up, from the Delphi programmer's point of view, an ORB is a set of DLLs residing in the VBroker\Bin directory. However, you should remember that this is just one possible way to implement a set of functionality described by the OMG in their specification. More important than the specific implementation are the things that an ORB does for a programmer. These things are perhaps best understood by looking at the Smart Agent.

What Is the Smart Agent?

The Smart Agent is a directory service that helps your client automatically locate a server. When you start a client, it will automatically ask the Smart Agent to look up your server in its directory. It does so and helps the two applications to establish a relationship. (Needless to say, you can expect the relationship to be warm and fuzzy and very tasteful!)

Starting the Smart Agent

Like the ORB DLLs, the Smart Agent is not part of the CORBA specification. It is merely a means of obtaining an end. However, it is one of the most important parts of the VisiBroker.

If you are on an NT system, then the Smart Agent is a service that you can access by starting the control panel, loading the Services applet, and then scrolling down toward the bottom of the list until you find the Visigenic services. If you are using Delphi 4, you should visit this location and make sure that the VisiBroker is started. In most situations, you should also set the service to start automatically. Note that you cannot assume that Delphi did these things during your installation.

If you are on Windows 95/98, then there is no concept of a service, and the Smart Agent cannot be started automatically. Instead, you should run `OSAgent.exe`, which is located in the `VisiBroker\Bin` directory. (OSAgent is also the name of the file that is run as a service on an NT box.)

> **NOTE**
>
> Whether you are running on Windows 95 or Windows NT, you must make sure the Smart Agent is running. If it is not, you will not be able to do any CORBA programming with the VisiBroker ORB.

24

CORBA

You don't need to run the Smart Agent on every machine, but one version of the Smart Agent should be running on each local area network that supports CORBA. During development, it is simplest just to run the Smart Agent on your current machine and to save till later the task of deciding how to set up your local area network.

Understanding the Smart Agent

The purpose of the Smart Agent is to help clients connect to servers, and to perform other important tasks such as load balancing and restarting crashed objects. When a client is launched, it uses the ORB to talk to the Smart Agent, and the Smart Agent connects the client program to a server. In other words, the Smart Agent contains directory services that track the location of objects and connect clients to them.

> **NOTE**
>
> As far as the Smart Agent is concerned, all objects that it knows about are already running. It doesn't know how to start a service automatically. There is, however, a second service, called the OAD, that will fool the Smart Agent into thinking that a service is running. Then, when the Smart Agent is asked for an object, it relays the request to the OAD, and the OAD starts the object.
>
> This system is quite different from the one used by COM and DCOM. DCOM clients can never access their server unless the server is actually registered in the Registry. If it is registered, then it can be started automatically. CORBA servers, on the other hand, can be accessed without being officially registered. However, they must already be running, or this process won't work. If you want a CORBA object to behave like a DCOM object, then you have to first learn about the OAD. The OAD will not be discussed in this book.

A client or server program does not need to know where its copy of the Smart Agent is located. The moment the ORB is loaded into memory by a client or server, it will send out broadcast messages searching for the Smart Agent. Once it finds the agent, it will communicate with it using UDP.

Be sure to note that the ORB finds a Smart Agent automatically, without having to be told its location. This point is important because it allows the client to be set up without any configuration other than installing the ORB DLLs. In particular, the files ORB_R.dll and CW3240MT.DLL should both be on the path. ORB_R.dll is a threaded version of ORB.dll.

Normally, you will want to start multiple Smart Agents on a single local area network. That way, if one of the smart agents goes down, others can step in to take its place. The details of ensuring that all Smart Agents know about all the objects on the system are taken care of for you automatically, without any intervention on your part. In other words, you just start the Smart Agent, and it will automatically discover all the servers running on your LAN.

You can have more than one domain of servers on a single LAN, and obviously you can get Smart Agents on different LANs to talk to one another. In particular, you do so by working with the agentaddr file kept in a directory specified by the VBROKER_ADM environment variable. For more information on this topic, see the VisiBroker Programmers Guide (`vbcpgmr.pdf`), available on the VisiBroker Web site at `http://www.inprise.com`.

You can ensure that a particular server will not go down by starting more than one instance of the server on a LAN. Then if one instance goes down, the Smart Agent will automatically connect the client to the second instance of the object. This failover technology works best if your object is stateless, but reconnecting to an object that maintains state is possible if you perform extra work. Again, you should read the VisiBroker Programmer's guide for more details.

The Smart Agent is actually an extension of the Basic Object Adaptor (BOA) standard. This standard will be discussed in the next section of this chapter. You should note, however, that in many cases a close relationship exists between the BOA and the Smart Agent. The BOA is part of the CORBA standard, whereas the Smart Agent is a VisiBroker-specific extension to the standard designed to make your life easier. (In the future, something called the POA will replace the BOA. I'll discuss the POA briefly later in this chapter.)

In Delphi, the ORB is encapsulated inside a VCL class and is available to you automatically as a global variable declared in `CorbaObj.pas`. You can find the `CorbaObj` unit in the `source\rtl\corba` directory on versions of Delphi that come with the VCL source.

The following is the declaration of the ORB object:

```
TORB = class
private
  ORB: IORB;
public
  class procedure Initialize; overload;
  class procedure Initialize(const CommandLine: TCommandLine); overload;
  function StringToObject(const ObjectString: string): IObject;
  function ObjectToString(const Obj: IObject): string;
  procedure Shutdown;
  function Bind(const RepositoryID: string; const ObjectName:
    string = ''; const HostName: string = ''): IObject; overload;
  function Bind(const InterfaceID: TGUID; const ObjectName: string = '';
    const HostName: string = ''): IObject; overload;
end;
```

I will describe what you can do with this object later in the chapter.

What Is the BOA?

The Basic Object Adaptor, or BOA, allows a server to register itself. When a server is launched, among the first things it does is to initialize the ORB, and the second thing it does is get a copy of the BOA from the ORB. The CORBA 2 specifies that all ORBs should support a BOA. (As I mentioned earlier, the OMG does not say that all ORBs should support a Smart Agent. The Smart Agent is something like a super BOA, designed to make it easy for you to connect with servers, to perform load balancing, and automatically support fail over.)

> **NOTE**
>
> Even standard Delphi MIDAS applications now support load balancing and fail over via the `TSimpleObjectBroker` component.

The client never has anything to do with the BOA, and indeed the client does not need to know that the BOA even exists. Only the server deals with the BOA, and most, but by no means all, of the BOA's activities occur automatically without intervention from the server.

I'm going to write some pseudocode that shows what happens when a server registers itself at load time:

```
Orb := Orb.Create(Params);
BOA := Orb.InitializeBOA;
MyCorbaObject := TMyCorbaObject.Create;
BOA.ObjectIsReady(MyCorbaObject);
BOA.ImplementationIsReady;
```

Before going any further, let me emphasize that you will not find code like this anyplace in the VCL source nor will you find any such thing as a method called `InitializeBOA`, `ObjectIsReady`, or `ImplementationIsReady`. However, similar methods are being called behind the scenes, and similar code is called in standard Java or C++ programs. Nevertheless, this example is pseudocode, and it is designed only to give you some sense of what happens behind the scenes when you launch a server.

The key points to note when you're studying this pseudocode are that the BOA is retrieved from the ORB and that CORBA makes a distinction between registering an object (`ObjectIsReady`) and announcing that a server is usable (`ImplementationIsReady`). In particular, an individual server might call `ObjectIsReady` many times, one for each of its objects. It would then call `ImplementationIsReady` once to announce that it has initialized all its objects and is ready to go. (I use the term `ImplementationIsReady` because it closely follows the language used by CORBA venders. If I were using my own terms, I would say `ServerIsReady`.)

Behind the scenes, Delphi calls `ObjectIsReady` and `ImplemenationIsReady` to register objects with the Smart Agent. In other words, when a server is launched, these calls are made, and the end result is that the Smart Agent knows about your object. (In the case of the VisiBroker, the Smart Agent implements the BOA for you automatically. So in a sense the Smart Agent is the BOA, except that it is really a kind of super BOA because it does more than the BOA specification ever declares to be necessary.)

> **NOTE**
>
> Having said all this, I have to confess that I still find the BOA to be a somewhat nebulous entity whose precise lineaments appear to be lost in the thick, swirling fog that lingers around the Smart Agent's actual implementation. Perhaps this is due to some shortcoming on my part, but I think it may be also due to the fact that the OMG did not properly define the BOA when the specification was first drawn up. As a result, each vendor had to come up with its own solution to certain poorly defined aspects of the specification.
>
> In the future, the BOA will probably be replaced with the POA, or Portable Object Adaptor. The POA, which is a more completely fleshed-out specification, should prove to be easier to understand. However, at this stage a huge amount of code is already implemented on top of the BOA, so the change to the POA will probably not occur overnight. (I assume it is called the Portable Object Adaptor because it is meant to be portable between vender implementations.)

What Are Proxies, Stubs, and Skeletons?

In a distributed application, the client cannot talk directly to a server, and a server cannot talk directly to a client. Instead, function calls and their parameters have to be marshaled across the network from one application to the other. As programmers, we don't usually care how this marshaling takes place any more than we care exactly how a compiler turns our Pascal code into machine code. I'm not saying that it might not be helpful to have an intimate knowledge of such matters, but it is not something most programmers concern themselves with on a day-to-day basis.

It is clear that information about function calls and their parameters flows back and forth between the client and the server over some unspecified protocol such as TCP/IP, or in the case of CORBA, over a TCP/IP derivative called IIOP. To make this architecture work, a proxy must be established on both the client and the server side.

The proxy on the client side is called a *stub*, and the proxy on the server side is called a *skeleton*. Together, this pair of conspirators trick the client into believing that it is talking directly to the server. In other words, the client has a bunch of "faked up" methods that make it think that it is talking directly to the server as if it were just another object inside the client application. On the server side, a second proxy is established to relay the client's calls directly to real methods in the server. A schematic overview of the Smart Agent and the rest of the CORBA architecture is shown in Figure 24.1.

FIGURE 24.1

A CORBA client and server use proxies to talk to the ORB, BOA, and Smart Agent.

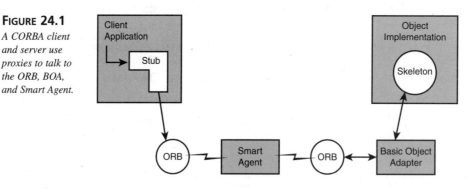

Consider the following pseudocode representing a proxy stub method for the client:

```
function TMyRemoteStub.Square(I: Integer): Integer;
begin
  MarshalDataToServer('Square', I);  // Call the real square method
  Result := UnMarshalDataFromServer;
      // Get the result back from the server
end;
```

If a method like this existed on a client, then the client could call this function as if it were a real routine that actually returned the square of an integer. However, when the function is called, what actually happens is that a pseudo function called MarshalDataToServer is called. MarshalDataToServer is designed to be able to invoke a remote call across a network and to marshal parameters over the network to the remote routine. In other words, MarshalDataToServer knows all about IIOP and the ORB, and it can use that technology to make remote procedure calls.

After the call to the server is completed, the method can then ask for the return value to the remote procedure call. This return value is then passed on to the user as the result of the `TMyRemoteStub.Square` method call.

As far as the client application is concerned, it just made a simple call into a local method called `Square`. Underneath the covers, something much more complicated occurred. The client didn't have to know about any of those details because the proxy stub method surreptitiously took care of all the hard work. These types of methods are generically known as proxies, and they are known inside CORBA as stubs on the client and skeletons on the server.

On the opposite side of the equation, the server has its own set of proxy methods called a skeleton. Pseudocode for a typical skeleton looks like this:

```
procedure TMySkeleton.Square;
var
  I: Integer;
begin
  UnMarshalDataFromClient(I);    // Get the parameter from the client
  I := TMyObject.Square(I);      // Call the real square method
  SendDataBackToClientStack(I);  // Send the result back to the client
end;
```

This method will be called automatically when word is sent over the network to the server that the client has called the `Square` method. The exact method used to invoke the `Square` method is again not relevant to this discussion any more than the exact method Windows uses to write a message box to the screen is not relevant to most discussions of Windows API programming. Clearly, the client passed a string to the server saying that it wanted to call the `Square` method, and somehow the server resolved that string into a real call to the `TMyObject.Square` method. The details are not important, nor are they necessarily made known to the programmer.

After `TMySkeleton.Square` is invoked, the first task is to marshal the data across from the client. Again, a custom method is called to perform this low-level task. Then the real `Square` method on the server is invoked, and the result is returned in a local variable called `I`. Finally, the result of the function call is sent back to the client, where it waits in a queue for the client stub function to retrieve it.

The programmer doesn't have to write the stub and skeleton methods that marshal functions and parameters back and forth between the client and the server. Instead, this process is taken care of automatically by Delphi. As you will see later in the chapter, the actual stub and skeleton objects are placed in the files created by the Type Library Editor with a naming convention that follows the `XXX_TLB.pas` format. You don't ever actually have to look at these methods, but I think you will find it helpful if I point them out to

24

CORBA

you so that you understand exactly what is happening. If you look at the actual methods, you will see that they are similar to the pseudocode I have written here but not identical. A more in-depth discussion of stubs and skeletons occurs later in this chapter in the sections "Understanding the Stub" and "Understanding the Skeleton."

Understanding Delphi and CORBA

By this time, you should have a fairly good understanding of how CORBA works and what kinds of things you can do with it. As you have seen, it does more or less the same things that DCOM does, except that it will work cross platform. To wind up this overview of CORBA, I'm going to spend a few more paragraphs discussing the limitations of the Delphi Client/Server implementation of CORBA.

The basic operation of a CORBA client is very simple, but underneath the hood something fairly complex is going on. In particular, at the time Delphi Client/Server was created, no tight binding existed between the Pascal language and CORBA. Other languages, such as C++ and Java, could easily call and create CORBA servers because the VisiBroker had already laid the groundwork. In the future, the same should be true of Object Pascal. But at the time I am writing, there is no easy way for a Pascal programmer to call or create CORBA servers using standard CORBA techniques such as calling IDL2JAVA or IDL2CPP. In other words, no IDL2DELPHI utility is available.

Delphi Client/Server provides a solution to this problem. Many of the details of how this solution works are wrapped up in ORBPAS.DLL, which ships with each copy of Delphi Client/Server. The source for this DLL is unfortunately not available, and as a result, the actual details of how Delphi allows you to call and create CORBA servers are shrouded in mystery.

Programmers naturally don't like black boxes, but I should point out that distributed architectures always include black boxes. The actual way that functions get called and parameters get marshaled is never explained in CORBA, DCOM, Entera, or in any other distributed architecture that I have used. So Delphi has its own black box, but nothing is really unusual about that.

A perhaps more serious issue in Delphi Client/Server is the fact that you use COM IDL to define the interface for your object. This means that certain types commonly used in CORBA IDL cannot be properly defined in Delphi because of limitations in the structure of COM IDL. Furthermore, you cannot easily convert standard CORBA IDL into Object Pascal. As a result, using static binding is difficult when you're connecting a Delphi client to a CORBA server written in some other language. The solution to this problem is to use dynamic binding; that technique will, in fact, be discussed in this chapter and illustrated with a sample program.

Overall, there is no denying that you are limited in what you can do with Delphi Client/Server and CORBA. However, the technology does make it very easy for you to create CORBA servers. Furthermore, you can use dynamic binding to talk to CORBA objects that are made by other compilers and that might be running on other, non-Windows–based platforms. You will see how to do so in the next chapter. Finally, I should point out that CORBA programming in Delphi is much easier than traditional CORBA programming in Java or in C++. Delphi Client/Server makes CORBA programming easy, and that is no mean accomplishment.

Two Important CORBA Repositories

In this brief section, I will quickly introduce you to the concept of an Interface and Implementation Repository. These important services are provided by CORBA. Delphi should automatically register your objects with both the Interface and Implementation Repositories, and though the code for doing so is found at the bottom of the XXX_TLB file, the process does not work correctly in the very first version of Delphi 4. However, you can still use these services with just a little work, and automatic registration with these services should be part of Delphi 4.1 and higher.

What Is the Interface Repository?

The Interface Repository is a place where you can store the details about your objects, such as their methods and the parameters passed to them. This repository serves three purposes:

- It provides a place where users can look up relatively detailed information about the objects available on the network or on their own system.
- It provides a mechanism that allows CORBA to perform type checking on method calls.
- It also allows you to make dynamic calls to an object at runtime rather than forcing you to statically prepare the call at compile time. In other words, it lets you do the equivalent in CORBA to calling a COM object off a Variant.

You can see the Interface Repository GUI in Figure 24.2.

24

CORBA

FIGURE 24.2

The Interface Repository showing the interface to a simple CORBA object.

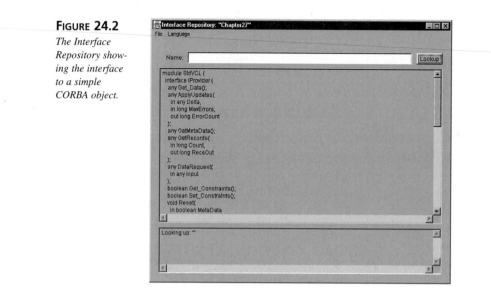

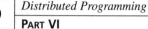

As I will explain in more depth later in the chapter, you can start the Interface Repository by typing `irep.exe MyRepository` at the command line, where `MyRepository` is a randomly chosen name that distinguishes one instance of the repository from another. After loading the repository, you can use a utility called `IDL2IR.exe` to load IDL files into the repository, or else you can use the IREP GUI. These IDL files contain the definitions of the interfaces that are stored in the repository. I will explain this topic in more depth later in the chapter.

What Is the Implementation Repository?

The Implementation Repository is used to store information about servers so that a server can be automatically started by the Smart Agent. In particular, the Implementation Repository contains information on the name of servers and on the path to the directory where their executables can be found.

When a CORBA service called the OAD, or Object Activation Daemon, needs to start a server, OAD can locate the server by looking it up in the Implementation Repository and then executing the file listed there. When you register a DCOM server, you are asking the Windows Repository to play more or less the same role that the Implementation Repository plays in CORBA development. In other words, the Implementation Repository is just a place to store the path and executable name for a server, along with some other related information. The Smart Agent asks the OAD to start the server if the server is not running and if it is registered in the Implementation Repository. The OAD can also be used to restart a server that has crashed.

By default, you can find the actual files used to define the implementation repository in the VBroker\Adm directory or in a subdirectory immediately beneath it. You can use an environment variable to point to the VBroker\Adm directory. I will not be discussing the OAD in depth in this chapter.

Simple CORBA Objects

It is now time to dig into the code for creating a CORBA application. Delphi Client/Server makes this process very simple. In fact, distinguishing between creating a standard Delphi COM object or MIDAS application and creating a Delphi\CORBA application is difficult.

The similarity between Delphi MIDAS and CORBA applications gives you the advantage of being able to write one set of code that works in either environment. However, you should not be mislead into thinking that these two technologies are, in fact, truly similar. As you have seen from the discussion in the opening portions of this chapter, CORBA is a very different animal from DCOM, and those differences become more apparent, rather than less apparent, the deeper you go into the subject.

However, you can automatically convert an OLE automation server into a CORBA server by right-clicking on the code for your server. An item called Expose as CORBA Object will appear in the local menu. Choosing this option will automatically make it possible for you to call your COM object from CORBA.

> **NOTE**
>
> If you are using Windows 98 or 95, you should add the OSAgent to the Tools menu in Delphi. Select Tools, Configure Tools and add the OSAgent to your Delphi Tools menu. By default, you will find the OSAgent in the c:\Program Files\Borland\VBroker directory.

Finally, let me just add one general programming tip that you can use whenever you are using Delphi Client/Server to program CORBA. The heart of the Delphi Client/Server implementation of Delphi is in CorbaObj.pas and OrbPas.pas. The following are global CORBA objects from the CorbaObj unit:

```
var
  CorbaSkeletonManager: TCorbaSkeletonManager;
  CorbaStubManager: TCorbaStubManager;
  CorbaInterfaceIDManager: TCorbaInterfaceIDManager;
  ORB: TORB;
  BOA: TBOA;
```

24

CORBA

You should take time to examine these units and to be at least vaguely aware of how they are structured.

The Server

It's now time to see exactly how to create a simple CORBA application that contains no database tools. As I said earlier, this process is similar to building a standard MIDAS application or, in this case, a simple OLE Automation server. However, you will find some differences in the way you handle the two technologies, so you should read over the next few paragraphs fairly carefully.

Complete the following steps to create a CORBA server:

1. Create a standard application and save it into its own directory. I like to create one directory named after the server application I want to create, and beneath that directory I create two additional subdirectories, one named `Client` and the second named `Server`. Needless to say, I usually put the client application in the `Client` directory and server application in the `Server` directory.

2. Choose File, New, turn to the multitier page, and select CORBA Object. On the surface, this act is very similar to choosing Automation Object from the ActiveX page, but as I've already explained, the underlying technologies are quite different. When you are prompted for a name for your object, you should call it `CorbaTestObject`. Leave all other settings on their defaults.

3. Open the Type Library Editor and create a method called `GetName` as part of `ICorbaTestObject`. Be careful not to add it to the root (Project Name) where the editor will not allow a method to be added (because it doesn't make sense to do so).

4. The return type for the method should be `WideString`. You set this value on the Parameters page, near the top. The COM IDL for the method should look like this: `HRESULT _stdcall GetName([out, retval] BSTR * Name )`, whereas the Delphi declaration looks like this: `function GetName: WideString [dispid $00000001]; safecall;`. The method will automatically be declared `safecall`, but that fact might not be evident in the Type Library Editor.

5. Click the Refresh button to generate the code for your method. Fill in the implementation for the method so that it returns a string containing the name of your object.

6. Save your work. Then run the application once. At this stage, the application must be running ahead of time, or your client won't be able to access it.

If you are working in Windows NT, you will be able to run both the client and server application from the Delphi IDE. If you are working in Windows 98 or 95, you will have to run the server from the Windows Explorer and the client from inside the IDE, or vice versa.

When you try to run the server, if you get an error stating that ORBPAS.DLL can't be found, then you probably don't have the Delphi Bin directory on your path. You could move ORBPAS.DLL into the Windows\System directory, but doing so can be dangerous, as it won't be automatically deleted or replaced when you update Delphi to a new version.

In Listings 24.1 through 24.4, you will find the code for the Simple CORBA server object you created in the six steps listed previously. You can find this program in the CorbaTest1 directory on the CD that comes with this book. The main form for the server is saved under the name Main.pas, the implementation is called CorbaTestImpl.pas, and the server is called CorbaTestServer1.dpr.

LISTING 24.1 THE MAIN FORM FOR A SIMPLE CORBA OBJECT SERVER

```
/////////////////////////////////////////
// Purpose: TestImpl.pas is the main file for the project
// Project: CorbaTestServer1.dpr
// Copyright (c) 1998 by Charlie Calvert
//
unit Main;

{------------------------------------------------------------------
  Each time a new instance of the server object is created or destroyed,
  it calls the main form and shows the user the number of clients
  currently connected.
------------------------------------------------------------------}
interface

uses
  Windows, Messages, SysUtils,
  Classes, Graphics, Controls,
  Forms, Dialogs, jpeg,
  ExtCtrls;

type
  TForm1 = class(TForm)
    Image1: TImage;
    Panel1: TPanel;
  private
    FClientCount: Integer;
  public
    procedure ChangeCount(Increment: Boolean);
  end;
```

continues

LISTING 24.1   CONTINUED

```
var
  Form1: TForm1;

implementation

{$R *.DFM}

{ TForm1 }

procedure TForm1.ChangeCount(Increment: Boolean);
begin
  if Increment then
    Inc(FClientCount)
  else
    Dec(FClientCount);
  Panel1.Caption := 'Client Count: ' + IntToStr(FClientCount);
end;

end.
```

LISTING 24.2   THE IMPLEMENTATION FOR A CORBA OBJECT

```
////////////////////////////////////////
// Purpose: Show simple CORBA server.
// Project: CorbaTestServer.dpr
// Copyright (c) 1998 by Charlie Calvert
//
unit CorbaTestIMPL;

{------------------------------------------------------------------------
  This simple CORBA server will track the number of clients that it has.
  Other than that, it's just meant to be a minimal example to show how
  to create a CORBA server.

  It has a dog-oriented theme because the main form has a picture of a
  dog on it.
------------------------------------------------------------------------}

interface

uses
  Windows, Messages, SysUtils,
  Classes, Graphics, Controls,
  ComObj, StdVcl, CorbaObj,
  CorbaTestServer1_TLB;
```

```pascal
type
  TCorbaTestObject = class(TCorbaImplementation, ICorbaTestObject)
  protected
    function GetName: WideString; safecall;
    function Bark: WideString; safecall;
  public
    constructor Create(Controller: IObject; AFactory: TCorbaFactory);
    override; destructor Destroy; override;
  end;

implementation

uses
  Main, CorbInit;

constructor TCorbaTestObject.Create(Controller: IObject;
  AFactory: TCorbaFactory);
begin
  inherited Create(Controller, AFactory);
  Form1.ChangeCount(True);
end;

destructor TCorbaTestObject.Destroy;
begin
  Form1.ChangeCount(False);
  inherited Destroy;
end;

function TCorbaTestObject.GetName: WideString;
begin
  Result := 'TCorbaTestObject: ' + DateTimeToStr(Now);
end;

function TCorbaTestObject.Bark: WideString;
begin
  Result := 'Bow wow!';
end;

initialization
  TCorbaObjectFactory.Create(
    'CorbaTestObjectFactory',                      // Factory Name
    'CorbaTestObject',                             // Interface Name
    'IDL:CorbaTestServer1/CorbaTestObjectFactory:1.0', // Repository ID
    ICorbaTestObject,                              // Interface
    TCorbaTestObject,                              // Implementation
    iMultiInstance,                                // Instancing
    tmSingleThread);                               // Threading
end.
```

LISTING 24.3   THE IDL FOR A SIMPLE CORBA OBJECT

```
module CorbaTestServer1
{

  interface ICorbaTestObject
  {
    wstring GetName();
    wstring Bark();
  };

  interface CorbaTestObjectFactory
  {
    ICorbaTestObject CreateInstance(in string InstanceName);
  };

};
```

LISTING 24.4   THE OBJECT PASCAL TYPE LIBRARY

```
unit CorbaTestServer1_TLB;

// ******************************************************************* //
// WARNING                                                            //
// -------                                                            //
// The types declared in this file were generated from data read      //
// from a Type Library. If this type library is explicitly or         //
// indirectly (via another type library referring to this type        //
// library) reimported, or the 'Refresh' command of the Type Library //
// Editor activated while editing the Type Library, the contents of   //
// this file will be regenerated and all                              //
// manual modifications will be lost.                                 //
// ******************************************************************* //

// PASTLWTR : $Revision:   1.11.1.63  $
// File generated on 6/22/98 4:08:48 PM from Type Library
// described below.

// ******************************************************************* //
// Type Lib: C:\SrcPas\Unleash4\Chap24\CorbaTest1\Server\
// CorbaTestServer1.tlb
// IID\LCID: {8459BCC0-09E5-11D2-BDFF-0080C743528B}\0
// Helpfile:
// HelpString: CorbaTestServer1 Library
// Version:    1.0
// ******************************************************************* //

interface
```

```
uses Windows, ActiveX, Classes, Graphics, OleCtrls, StdVCL,
  SysUtils, CORBAObj, OrbPas, CorbaStd;

// ***************************************************************** //
// GUIDS declared in the TypeLibrary. Following prefixes are used:  //
//    Type Libraries     : LIBID_xxxx                              //
//    CoClasses          : CLASS_xxxx                              //
//    DISPInterfaces     : DIID_xxxx                               //
//    Non-DISP interfaces: IID_xxxx                                //
// ***************************************************************** //
const
  LIBID_CorbaTestServer1: TGUID =
  ➡'{8459BCC0-09E5-11D2-BDFF-0080C743528B}';
  IID_ICorbaTestObject: TGUID =
  ➡'{8459BCC1-09E5-11D2-BDFF-0080C743528B}';
  CLASS_CorbaTestObject: TGUID =
  ➡'{8459BCC3-09E5-11D2-BDFF-0080C743528B}';
type

// ***************************************************************** //
// Forward declaration of interfaces defined in Type Library       //
// ***************************************************************** //
  ICorbaTestObject = interface;
  ICorbaTestObjectDisp = dispinterface;

// ***************************************************************** //
// Declaration of CoClasses defined in Type Library                //
// (NOTE: Here we map each CoClass to its Default Interface)        //
// ***************************************************************** //
  CorbaTestObject = ICorbaTestObject;


// ***************************************************************** //
// Interface: ICorbaTestObject
// Flags:      (4416) Dual OleAutomation Dispatchable
// GUID:       {8459BCC1-09E5-11D2-BDFF-0080C743528B}
// ***************************************************************** //
  ICorbaTestObject = interface(IDispatch)
    ['{8459BCC1-09E5-11D2-BDFF-0080C743528B}']
    function GetName: WideString; safecall;
    function Bark: WideString; safecall;
  end;

// ***************************************************************** //
// DispIntf:  ICorbaTestObjectDisp
// Flags:      (4416) Dual OleAutomation Dispatchable
// GUID:       {8459BCC1-09E5-11D2-BDFF-0080C743528B}
// ***************************************************************** //
```

continues

LISTING 24.4 CONTINUED

```pascal
  ICorbaTestObjectDisp = dispinterface
    ['{8459BCC1-09E5-11D2-BDFF-0080C743528B}']
    function GetName: WideString; dispid 1;
    function Bark: WideString; dispid 2;
  end;

  TCorbaTestObjectStub = class(TCorbaDispatchStub, ICorbaTestObject)
  public
    function GetName: WideString; safecall;
    function Bark: WideString; safecall;
  end;

  TCorbaTestObjectSkeleton = class(TCorbaSkeleton)
  private
    FIntf: ICorbaTestObject;
  public
    constructor Create(const InstanceName: string;
      const Impl: IUnknown); override;
    procedure GetImplementation(out Impl: IUnknown); override; stdcall;
  published
    procedure GetName(const InBuf: IMarshalInBuffer; Cookie: Pointer);
    procedure Bark(const InBuf: IMarshalInBuffer; Cookie: Pointer);
  end;

  CoCorbaTestObject = class
    class function Create: ICorbaTestObject;
    class function CreateRemote(const MachineName: string):
      ICorbaTestObject;
  end;

  TCorbaTestObjectCorbaFactory = class
    class function CreateInstance(const InstanceName: string):
      ICorbaTestObject;
  end;

implementation

uses ComObj;

{ TCorbaTestObjectStub }

function TCorbaTestObjectStub.GetName: WideString;
var
  OutBuf: IMarshalOutBuffer;
  InBuf: IMarshalInBuffer;
begin
  FStub.CreateRequest('GetName', True, OutBuf);
  FStub.Invoke(OutBuf, InBuf);
  Result := UnmarshalWideText(InBuf);
```

```
end;

function TCorbaTestObjectStub.Bark: WideString;
var
  OutBuf: IMarshalOutBuffer;
  InBuf: IMarshalInBuffer;
begin
  FStub.CreateRequest('Bark', True, OutBuf);
  FStub.Invoke(OutBuf, InBuf);
  Result := UnmarshalWideText(InBuf);
end;

{ TCorbaTestObjectSkeleton }

constructor TCorbaTestObjectSkeleton.Create(const InstanceName: string;
  const Impl: IUnknown);
begin
  inherited;
  inherited InitSkeleton('CorbaTestObject', InstanceName,
    'IDL:CorbaTestServer1/ICorbaTestObject:1.0',
    tmMultiThreaded, True);
  FIntf := Impl as ICorbaTestObject;
end;

procedure TCorbaTestObjectSkeleton.GetImplementation(out Impl: IUnknown);
begin
  Impl := FIntf;
end;

procedure TCorbaTestObjectSkeleton.GetName(const InBuf: IMarshalInBuffer;
  Cookie: Pointer);
var
  OutBuf: IMarshalOutBuffer;
  Retval: WideString;
begin
  Retval := FIntf.GetName;
  FSkeleton.GetReplyBuffer(Cookie, OutBuf);
  OutBuf.PutWideText(PWideChar(Pointer(Retval)));
end;

procedure TCorbaTestObjectSkeleton.Bark(const InBuf: IMarshalInBuffer;
  Cookie: Pointer);
var
  OutBuf: IMarshalOutBuffer;
  Retval: WideString;
begin
  Retval := FIntf.Bark;
  FSkeleton.GetReplyBuffer(Cookie, OutBuf);
  OutBuf.PutWideText(PWideChar(Pointer(Retval)));
end;
```

24

CORBA

continues

LISTING 24.4   CONTINUED

```
class function CoCorbaTestObject.Create: ICorbaTestObject;
begin
  Result := CreateComObject(CLASS_CorbaTestObject) as ICorbaTestObject;
end;

class function CoCorbaTestObject.CreateRemote(
  const MachineName: string): ICorbaTestObject;
begin
  Result := CreateRemoteComObject(MachineName,
    CLASS_CorbaTestObject) as ICorbaTestObject;
end;

class function TCorbaTestObjectCorbaFactory.CreateInstance(
  const InstanceName: string): ICorbaTestObject;
begin
  Result := CorbaFactoryCreateStub(
    'IDL:CorbaTestServer1/CorbaTestObjectFactory:1.0',
    'CorbaTestObject',
    InstanceName, '',
    ICorbaTestObject) as ICorbaTestObject;
end;

initialization
  CorbaStubManager.RegisterStub(ICorbaTestObject, TCorbaTestObjectStub);
  CorbaInterfaceIDManager.RegisterInterface(ICorbaTestObject,
    'IDL:CorbaTestServer1/ICorbaTestObject:1.0');
  CorbaSkeletonManager.RegisterSkeleton(ICorbaTestObject,
    TCorbaTestObjectSkeleton);
end.
```

To run this program, you must first start OSAgent.exe on Windows 95/98 or start the Smart Agent service on Windows NT. After doing that, you should be able to successfully compile and run the program.

This server has no interface to speak of. I put a picture of a dog on the front of its form, but that is only a conceit and adds no functionality to the program. For all intents and purposes, the server is useless without a client. Therefore, before I discuss this application in any depth, I think it will be helpful if you first build a client application.

The Client

It is now time to see how to create a client application that can access the CORBA server. This chore is not particularly difficult. In fact, it adheres very closely to the patterns established in OLE automation programming.

Complete the following steps to build your client:

1. Start a regular application.

2. Add the XXX_TLB.pas file created by the server to your main form's uses clause. Then add CorbInit to your uses clause. In this case, the XXX_TLB file is called CorbaTestServer1_TLB.pas. This file is auto-generated for you when you build the server.

3. Create a button response method.

4. Get the CreateInstance call from the XXX_TLB.pas file and copy it into your button response method, removing extraneous bits and saving the type it returns.

5. Declare a local variable named FCorbaTest of the type the object returns—in this case, ICorbaTestObject. Set it equal to the function you copied from the TLB. Pass any string of your choice to CreateInstance:

   ```
   FCorbaTest :=
   TCorbaTestObjectCorbaFactory.CreateInstance('CorbaTest');
   ```

6. Write code to call methods off the object instance returned from the function you copied from the TLB.

7. Make sure that the Smart Agent is started and then launch your server and client application. Call into the methods defined on your server. (Remember, unless you are using OAD, you must explicitly start your server. It won't start automatically.)

In Listing 24.5, you will find the source to a simple CORBA client application. Take a look at the code and then read on to learn some of the details of how this application is put together.

> **NOTE**
>
> In the version of this project found on the CD that accompanies this book, I use the TGradient object on the main form of the client. Like the picture on the server, this object adds no real-world functionality to the client. It's just there for aesthetic reasons, and pretty dubious ones at that. If you want to use it, just load the Unleash package in the Units directory that comes on the CD that accompanies this book. (The package comes precompiled and takes about 3 seconds to load when you choose Component, Add Package from the Delphi menu.) If you don't want to use it, just ignore the error you get when you load the project. The program works fine without it.

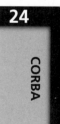

LISTING 24.5 THE MAIN FORM FOR A SIMPLE CORBA CLIENT

```
///////////////////////////////////////
// Purpose: Client to the CorbaTestServer1 server
// Project: CorbaTestClient.dpr
// Copyright (c) 1998 by Charlie Calvert
//
unit MainClient;

interface

{
  This example uses the Gradient component, found in the
  Unleash Package from the units directory. Install the
  package, then load this program. (If you don't
  want to see the Gradient, the program's not going to
  run any different without it. So just load the program
  and ignore the error you get about the gradient
  component not being found.)
}

uses
  Windows, Messages, SysUtils,
  Classes, Graphics, Controls,
  Forms, Dialogs, StdCtrls,
  Gradient, Buttons, CorbaTestServer1_TLB;

type
  TForm1 = class(TForm)
    Button1: TBitBtn;
    Gradient1: TGradient;
    Edit1: TEdit;
    BarkBtn: TBitBtn;
    procedure Button1Click(Sender: TObject);
    procedure BarkBtnClick(Sender: TObject);
  private
    FCorbaTest: ICorbaTestObject;
    procedure InitializeTest;
  end;

var
  Form1: TForm1;

implementation

uses
  CorbInit;

{$R *.DFM}
```

```
procedure TForm1.InitializeTest;
begin
  if FCorbaTest = nil then
    FCorbaTest :=
    ➡TCorbaTestObjectCorbaFactory.CreateInstance('CorbaTest');
end;

procedure TForm1.Button1Click(Sender: TObject);
begin
  if FCorbaTest = nil then
    InitializeTest;
  Edit1.Text := FCorbaTest.GetName;
end;

procedure TForm1.BarkBtnClick(Sender: TObject);
begin
  if FCorbaTest = nil then
    InitializeTest;
  Edit1.Text := FCorbaTest.Bark;
end;

end.
```

To run this extremely simple program, first compile and launch the server. Then compile and launch the client, and click one of the buttons on the main form of the client. A message will be retrieved from the server and shown in an edit control, as depicted in Figure 24.3.

FIGURE 24.3

The CorbaTest1 *client and server programs in action.*

If you are using Windows NT, you can run both the server and the client from inside the IDE. To do so, choose Project, Build All. Then select View, Project Manager, focus the server application, and run it. Now use the Project Manager to focus the client application and run it. The key to this whole process is making sure that both applications are fully built before you run either of them. Building the applications first is necessary because building or making a Delphi project is impossible while one or more applications are being run from the IDE.

Understanding the Client

The client application consists of a simple form. After launching the application, you can click on a button on the form. If the server is already running, and if the Smart Agent is running, then the button click will connect you with the server and allow you to call the GetName method. The value returned from the GetName method is shown in a message box.

CAUTION

The classic place to make an error with these applications is to forget to add CorbInit to your uses clause. Your client will still compile fine without CorbInit, but it will not run correctly.

The relevant code in the very short CorbInit unit looks like this:

```
var
  SaveInitProc: Pointer = nil;

procedure InitCorba;
begin
  CorbaInitialize;
  if SaveInitProc <> nil then TProcedure(SaveInitProc);
end;

initialization
  if not IsLibrary then
  begin
    SaveInitProc := InitProc;
    InitProc := @InitCorba;
  end;

end.
```

This code does nothing more than call CorbaInitialize through a fairly roundabout method. To understand how this method works, you need to remember the code in the project source for all Delphi applications:

```
begin
  Application.Initialize;
  Application.CreateForm(TForm1, Form1);
  Application.Run;
end.
```

The call to Application.Initialize looks like this:

```
procedure TApplication.Initialize;
begin
  if InitProc <> nil then TProcedure(InitProc);
end;
```

As you can see, this code usually does nothing more than check to see whether InitProc is set to nil. If it is not set to nil, then the routine pointed to by InitProc is called. In the case of CorbInit, that routine simply calls

> CorbaInitialize. After making the call, the VCL checks to see whether InitProc is set to nil, and if not, it simply calls the next initialization procedure in the chain.

As simple as the client may be, you still need to consider two tricky parts of it. The first is remembering to add CorbInit to your uses clause, and the second is writing the following lines of code:

```
FCorbaTest: ICorbaTestObject;
   ...
procedure TForm1.InitializeTest;
begin
  if FCorbaTest = nil then
    FCorbaTest :=
    ➥TCorbaTestObjectCorbaFactory.CreateInstance('CorbaTest');
end;
```

This code will differ slightly from client to client, but the basic pattern will be followed over and over again. The parameter that you pass into CreateInstance is optional and can contain any value you desire. It is simply your chance to name the instance of the object that you are about to create. (Due to bugs in some versions of the VisiBroker, it is probably best that you pass something in this string, though what you pass is entirely optional.)

The call to TCorbaTestObjectCorbaFactory comes from the Pascal code in the TLB file:

```
class function TCorbaTestObjectCorbaFactory.CreateInstance(
  const InstanceName: string): ICorbaTestObject;
begin
  Result := CorbaFactoryCreateStub(
    'IDL:CorbaTestServer1/CorbaTestObjectFactory:1.0', // RepositoryID
    'CorbaTestObject',                                 // FactoryID
    InstanceName,                                      // InstanceName
    '',                                                // HostName
    ICorbaTestObject                                   // GUID
  ) as ICorbaTestObject;
end;
```

This code is auto-generated by the compiler. Its purpose is to bind you to an instance of your server. Note that this is a class function, which means you can call it without first creating an instance of the TCorbaTestObjectFactory object.

This code is mostly tied to the Delphi Client/Server-specific implementation of CORBA. It is neither important nor particularly helpful for you to struggle with the details of what

24

CORBA

is going on in the `CorbaFactoryCreateStub` method. The only relevant point is that it returns a pointer to the client's interface to the object. To learn more, you would need to have access to the code in `ORBPAS.DLL`, and because we can't see that code, there is no real point in digging into this subject in too much depth. The method is a black box, and you can just call it via the `CreateInstance` wrapper whenever you need to bind to the server.

> **NOTE**
>
> Once again, I don't see any point in getting too concerned about the presence of a black box in this portion of Delphi. The code that marshals function calls and parameters between a client and server is a black box in DCOM, in standard CORBA, and nearly everywhere else it appears. Most Windows API calls are black boxes. They are simply places where programmers run across black boxes, and Delphi's hidden methods here are not at all unusual, nor is this is a peculiar place to find them.

One significant part of the code shown here is the bit that specifies the Factory Repository ID: `IDL:CorbaTestServer1/CorbaTestObjectFactory:1.0`. This string uniquely identifies the object that creates an instance of the `ICorbaTestServer` interface. You should be careful not to confuse the Factory Repository ID with the Interface Repository ID: `'IDL:CorbaTestServer1/ICorbaTestObject:1.0'`. If you want to create an instance of the object, then use the Factory Repository ID, not the Interface Repository ID.

After you have called `CorbaFactoryCreateStub`, what you get back is an instance of the CORBA factory. The factory is not the same thing as your object. It is merely a tool designed to allow you to access the interface of your object. It's the black box that Delphi uses to pull the interface out of the dark depths of the CORBIC mystery!

To retrieve your interface from the factory, Delphi uses the as operator. The result of this simple operation is the fruit of your endeavor, the interface itself. After you have an instance of the CORBA object, you are then free to call its methods. For instance, you could write either of the following two lines:

```
Edit1.Text := FCorbaTest.GetName;
Edit1.Text := FCorbaTest.Bark;
```

Remember that even simple examples such as this capture the very essence of this technology. The whole point here is to make function calls between methods on separate machines. This technology makes porous the barrier that separates one machine from another, one binary entity from another. The goal is to achieve a technology that flows back and forth across the network, that connects the machines on the Internet, and the people who run them, each to each.

If you want to run this program so that it works across the network, just keep the OSAgent and server running somewhere on the LAN and copy your client out to another machine that has an ORB installed on it. Now run the client. It will find the server automatically and connect to it. I have better luck running the server on NT than I do running the server on 95 or 98. The client can be on either a 95/98 machine or on an NT machine.

Understanding the CORBA Stub

Perhaps taking a moment to consider the proxies that play such a key role in binding a client to its server is worthwhile. Though this code is also generated for you automatically by Delphi, taking a few moments to penetrate its mysteries is still worthwhile.

The following is an actual client stub method from the `CorbaTestServer1_TLB` file rather than the pseudocode I showed you earlier:

```
function TCorbaTestObjectStub.GetName: WideString;
var
  OutBuf: IMarshalOutBuffer;
  InBuf: IMarshalInBuffer;
begin
  FStub.CreateRequest('GetName', True, OutBuf);
  FStub.Invoke(OutBuf, InBuf);
  Result := UnmarshalWideText(InBuf);
end;
```

As you recall, this is a really "faked up" method designed to fool the client into thinking it is talking directly to the server, as if the server were merely another object inside the client.

The `FStub` data member referenced here is from the `CorbaObj` unit, where it is declared to be of type `IStub`. Again, understanding how `IStub` works is not really important. The only important point is that it will resolve the calls you make to the server. It is part of the black box that lies at the heart of this technology.

The `FStub.CreateRequest` method binds the name of the function you wish to call in a variable of type `IMarshalOutBuffer`, which can be sent across the Internet. After the package is constructed, you call `Invoke` to send the message to the server and to retrieve a response from that same server. The `InBuf` variable, of type `IMarshalInBuffer`, contains the response, and you can call `UnmarshalWideText` to taste the fruits of your labors.

24

CORBA

As you can see, the calls inside the client stub are not difficult to understand. This elegant system was designed to speed your messages back and forth across the network. You could create your own stubs if you wanted, but letting Delphi do the job for you is much simpler.

Understanding the CORBA Skeleton

The skeleton is no more complicated than the stub. Remember that its purpose is simply to receive the message sent by the stub's call to Invoke. After it receives the message, it calls the real GetName method and then bundles up the result and whisks it back to the client:

```
procedure TCorbaTestSkeleton.GetName(const InBuf: IMarshalInBuffer;
  Cookie: Pointer);
var
  OutBuf: IMarshalOutBuffer;
  Retval: WideString;
begin
  Retval := FIntf.GetName;
  FSkeleton.GetReplyBuffer(Cookie, OutBuf);
  OutBuf.PutWideText(PWideChar(Pointer(Retval)));
end;
```

The first step is to call GetName off the internal FIntf variable set up automatically by Delphi. FIntf is merely a variable pointing to the real interface of your object. Because you are now inside the server itself, this is a real pointer to the actual object you created, and this call executes your code and returns the value you assign to the function result.

The next step is to bundle up the function result and send it back to the client. You do so through calls to GetReplyBuffer and PutWideText. The first creates an object that is immediately put to work sending the result to the client.

Understanding the IDL Interface to the Server

In the preceding few pages, you had a chance to see how to construct a simple CORBA client and server pair. I hope that you have sensed that this simple and elegant process makes a complicated task easy.

The real power of CORBA, however, comes not from creating Delphi clients and servers, but from creating servers in one language or platform and calling them from another language or platform. All this is possible because of the IDL code that serves as a bridge between one application and the next.

You can generate two types of IDL for the interface to your server. One type of IDL is COM-based; the second is CORBA-based. To generate either type, go into the Type Library Editor and choose the icon on the far right of the toolbar at the top of the editor. (If you don't see any toolbar at all, right-click on the editor and select the Toolbar option.)

Here is the Microsoft version of the IDL used to define the interface from the CorbaTest program:

```
interface ICorbaTestObject:.IDispatch
{
  [id(0x00000001)]
  HRESULT _stdcall GetName([out, retval] BSTR * Value );
  [id(0x00000002)]
  HRESULT _stdcall Bark([out, retval] BSTR * Value );
};
```

This interface descends from IDispatch, which is a COM interface. The interface contains two new methods: one called GetName and the other called Bark. The first method has a DispID of 1. This DispID is used by COM to uniquely identify the method within the scope of the object. No other method in the object can have the same DispID. Using the IDispatch.Invoke interface, you can call this method using this DispID.

The method returns an HRESULT, is declared to support the STDCALL calling convention, and returns a pointer to a BASIC string, which in Object Pascal is known as a WideString.

The most obvious fact about this interface is that it is entirely concerned with COM-related issues rather than CORBA issues. IDispatch is a COM interface, not a CORBA interface; HRESULT is a COM error value, not a CORBA value; and BSTR is a COM type, not a CORBA type. In short, Delphi Client/Server uses COM services to aid in the creation of CORBA servers.

The close relationship between COM and CORBA in Delphi Client/Server is in part the result of expediency: Borland wanted to use existing tools to good advantage. However, this cross-pollination of technologies allows you to develop a single application that can be used as either a COM server or a CORBA server. To do so, first create a COM server, right-click on the source code of a COM server, and then choose Expose as CORBA Object from the local menu. Or, conversely, simply access a CORBA server as a COM server.

Of course, you can also access a Delphi server from another language, such as Java or C++. To do so, you should work with the CORBA version of the IDL from your type library, as explained in the next chapter. Here, for instance, is the CORBA IDL describing the interface to your object:

```
interface ICorbaTestObject
{
  wstring GetName();
  wstring Bark();
};
```

This code is admirably clean and succinct. It looks vaguely C++ like, but remember that it is meant to be language neutral. In other words, Inprise tools can convert an interface like this into C++ objects or Java objects. Over time, you will also have tools for converting an interface like this in Object Pascal.

> **NOTE**
>
> You can create a CORBA IDL file from the command line like this:
>
> `TLibImp -p- -c- -j+ MyTypeLib.tlb` produces the IDL file.
>
> At minimum, the following files need to be on your path when you are using the VisiBroker: `orb_r.dll`, `cw3240mt.dll`, and the DLLs in the Delphi's `Bin` directory. There is no advantage to running the utility from the command line rather than using the Type Library Editor, but I include this information in case you want to create batch files that automatically process your code.

Simple CORBA Dynamic Project

The next thing to explore is how to call a CORBA server using dynamic invocation. This technology closely parallels calling a COM server off a Variant. In particular, CORBA has a type called `Any`, which plays roughly the same role in CORBA that a Variant plays in COM. In other words, this CORBA technology is like the COM technology I showed you in Chapter 16, "Using Delphi to Automate Word and Excel."

Dynamic invocation is important in Delphi Client/Server because no `IDL2PAS.exe` utility is available with the product. Because you cannot automatically create a Delphi client for a C++ or Java server, then the simplest approach is to connect directly to a server and start calling its methods dynamically. If you call them correctly, then you will have success at runtime. If you make a mistake, then at runtime CORBA will tell you that you have a parameter mismatch or that you tried to call a method that does not exist. Under such circumstances, checking your calls at compile time is impossible.

To make a dynamic call, you have to load the IDL for your server into an Interface Repository. You can start the Interface Repository by typing `irep MyName` at the command prompt, where `irep` is the name of a utility, and `MyName` is the name you give to a particular instance of the Interface Repository.

After you start the Interface Repository, you can use its menu to browse across your hard drive and locate an IDL file. When you choose the file, the repository reads it in and keeps a record of its contents. The ORB can then check this record when you make a dynamic call. You must load the IDL for your server in the Interface Repository, or your dynamic call will not succeed. It is not optional.

The Interface Repository can also serve as a single place where you can reference the objects available on your system. If you load two or more objects into the repository, then you can save them to disk by using the program's interface. The next time you load the Interface Repository, you can then read these two interfaces back in with a single gesture, by simply loading the file you saved to disk.

After you have the Interface Repository set up, you can call the methods on your server with a few simple lines of code. Here, for example, you can see how to call a Delphi server:

```
procedure TForm2.DynamicBtnClick(Sender: TObject);
var
  DynamicFactory: TAny;
  DynamicObject: TAny;
begin
  DynamicFactory :=
  ➥Orb.Bind('IDL:DynamicServer/DynamicObjectFactory:1.0');
  DynamicObject := DynamicFactory.CreateInstance('DynamicObject');
  ShowMessage(DynamicObject.Get_Description);
end;
```

The first method binds you to the server. You do not need to do anything to prepare the Orb variable other than include CorbObj in your uses clause. This call will not succeed if you do not pass in the correct Repository ID. You can usually retrieve the Repository ID from the server code or reassemble it from the bits and pieces in the Interface Repository. Later in this chapter, I will tell you how you can find the Repository ID for an application using something called the VisiBroker Manager.

In Delphi 4, you can tell that your Bind call succeeded by checking to see the value of the TAny variable it returns. A TAny in Delphi is defined as a Variant, and it allows you to work with the CORBA Any type. Your call succeeded if the TAny variable called DynamicFactory is set equal to Unknown. If it is set equal to Unassigned, then the call failed. (I'm not sure the significance of these return values are stated so explicitly anywhere in the documentation, but they are the values I always get upon either success or failure.)

If you were working with a standard CORBA object, you would be free to make calls directly off the return value of Orb.Bind, as shown in the next chapter. However, when calling a Delphi server, you need to first retrieve a factory and then call CreateInstance

24

CORBA

on that factory. The return value of the call to CreateInstance can be used to invoke methods on your server.

As you can see, dynamic invocation is easy to use. It can help to make CORBA programming in Delphi a relatively simple and enjoyable process.

Listings 24.6 through 24.8 show how to create a simple Delphi server and client, where the client uses both static and dynamic binding to call the server. In the next chapter and in the last program in this chapter, you will see that this technology plays a key role in Delphi Client/Server.

LISTING 24.6   THE IMPLEMENTATION FOR THE SERVER

```
/////////////////////////////////////
// Purpose: Corba Server
// Project: DynamicServer
// Copyright (c) 1998 by Charlie Calvert
//
unit DynamicObjectIMPL;

interface

uses
  Windows, Messages, SysUtils,
  Classes, Graphics, Controls,
  ComObj, StdVcl, CorbaObj,
  DynamicServer_TLB;

type

  TDynamicObject = class(TCorbaImplementation, IDynamicObject)
  private
    { Private declarations }
  public
    { Public declarations }
  protected
    function Get_Description: WideString; safecall;
    function GetName: WideString; safecall;
  end;

implementation

uses CorbInit;

function TDynamicObject.Get_Description: WideString;
begin
  Result := 'I took this picture in Prague, in the spring of 1998. ' +
    'I was there doing Delphi training, and also spent some time with ' +
    'Richard Kubat, the head of Borland Inprise in Prague. He showed ' +
```

```
      'me a castle outside of town, took me to see jazz, talked ' +
      'politics, told me about gypsies, and exhibited excellent taste ' +
      'in music, which included an admirable interest in Pat Metheny ' +
      'and the redoubtable Frank Zappa.';
end;

function TDynamicObject.GetName: WideString;
begin
  Result := 'TDynamicObject';
end;

initialization
  TCorbaObjectFactory.Create('DynamicObjectFactory', 'DynamicObject',
    'IDL:DynamicServer/DynamicObjectFactory:1.0', IDynamicObject,
    TDynamicObject, iMultiInstance, tmSingleThread);
end.
```

LISTING 24.7 THE TYPE LIBRARY FOR THE DynamicServer

```
unit DynamicServer_TLB;

// ****************************************************************** //
// WARNING                                                           //
// -------                                                           //
// The types declared in this file were generated from data read     //
// from a Type Library. If this type library is explicitly or        //
// indirectly (via another type library referring to this type       //
// library) reimported, or the 'Refresh' command of the Type Library //
// Editor activated while editing the Type Library, the contents of  //
// this file will be regenerated and all                             //
// manual modifications will be lost.                                //
// ****************************************************************** //

// PASTLWTR : $Revision:    1.11.1.63  $
// File generated on 7/4/98 11:57:45 PM from Type Library
// described below.

// ****************************************************************** //
// Type Lib: D:\SrcPas\Unleash4\Chap24\DynamicCorba\Server\
// DynamicServer.tlb
// IID\LCID: {C8C76AA5-1396-11D2-9CE8-006008928EEF}\0
// Helpfile:
// HelpString: DynamicServer Library
// Version:    1.0
// ****************************************************************** //

interface

uses
```

24

CORBA

continues

LISTING 24.7   CONTINUED

```pascal
Windows, ActiveX, Classes,
Graphics, OleCtrls, StdVCL,
SysUtils, CORBAObj, OrbPas,
CorbaStd;

// ******************************************************************* //
// GUIDS declared in the TypeLibrary. Following prefixes are used:   //
//   Type Libraries     : LIBID_xxxx                                 //
//   CoClasses          : CLASS_xxxx                                 //
//   DISPInterfaces     : DIID_xxxx                                  //
//   Non-DISP interfaces: IID_xxxx                                   //
// ******************************************************************* //
const
  LIBID_DynamicServer: TGUID = '{C8C76AA5-1396-11D2-9CE8-006008928EEF}';
  IID_IDynamicObject: TGUID = '{C8C76AA6-1396-11D2-9CE8-006008928EEF}';
  CLASS_DynamicObject: TGUID = '{C8C76AA8-1396-11D2-9CE8-006008928EEF}';
type

// ******************************************************************* //
// Forward declaration of interfaces defined in Type Library         //
// ******************************************************************* //
  IDynamicObject = interface;
  IDynamicObjectDisp = dispinterface;

// ******************************************************************* //
// Declaration of CoClasses defined in Type Library                  //
// (NOTE: Here we map each CoClass to its Default Interface)          //
// ******************************************************************* //
  DynamicObject = IDynamicObject;


// ******************************************************************* //
// Interface: IDynamicObject                                         //
// Flags:     (4416) Dual OleAutomation Dispatchable                 //
// GUID:      {C8C76AA6-1396-11D2-9CE8-006008928EEF}                 //
// ******************************************************************* //
  IDynamicObject = interface(IDispatch)
    ['{C8C76AA6-1396-11D2-9CE8-006008928EEF}']
    function GetName: WideString; safecall;
    function Get_Description: WideString; safecall;
    property Description: WideString read Get_Description;
  end;

// ******************************************************************* //
// DispIntf:  IDynamicObjectDisp                                     //
// Flags:     (4416) Dual OleAutomation Dispatchable                 //
// GUID:      {C8C76AA6-1396-11D2-9CE8-006008928EEF}                 //
// ******************************************************************* //
  IDynamicObjectDisp = dispinterface
```

```
      ['{C8C76AA6-1396-11D2-9CE8-006008928EEF}']
      function GetName: WideString; dispid 1;
      property Description: WideString readonly dispid 2;
  end;

  TDynamicObjectStub = class(TCorbaDispatchStub, IDynamicObject)
  public
      function GetName: WideString; safecall;
      function Get_Description: WideString; safecall;
  end;

  TDynamicObjectSkeleton = class(TCorbaSkeleton)
  private
      FIntf: IDynamicObject;
  public
      constructor Create(const InstanceName: string;
        const Impl: IUnknown); override;
      procedure GetImplementation(out Impl: IUnknown); override; stdcall;
  published
      procedure GetName(const InBuf: IMarshalInBuffer; Cookie: Pointer);
      procedure Get_Description(const InBuf: IMarshalInBuffer;
      ➥Cookie: Pointer);
  end;

  CoDynamicObject = class
      class function Create: IDynamicObject;
      class function CreateRemote(const MachineName: string):
      ➥IDynamicObject;
  end;

  TDynamicObjectCorbaFactory = class
      class function CreateInstance(const InstanceName: string):
      ➥IDynamicObject;
  end;

implementation

uses ComObj;

{ TDynamicObjectStub }

function TDynamicObjectStub.GetName: WideString;
var
  OutBuf: IMarshalOutBuffer;
  InBuf: IMarshalInBuffer;
begin
  FStub.CreateRequest('GetName', True, OutBuf);
  FStub.Invoke(OutBuf, InBuf);
  Result := UnmarshalWideText(InBuf);
end;
```

continues

LISTING 24.7   CONTINUED

```
function TDynamicObjectStub.Get_Description: WideString;
var
  OutBuf: IMarshalOutBuffer;
  InBuf: IMarshalInBuffer;
begin
  FStub.CreateRequest('Get_Description', True, OutBuf);
  FStub.Invoke(OutBuf, InBuf);
  Result := UnmarshalWideText(InBuf);
end;


{ TDynamicObjectSkeleton }

constructor TDynamicObjectSkeleton.Create(const InstanceName: string;
  const Impl: IUnknown);
begin
  inherited;
  inherited InitSkeleton('DynamicObject', InstanceName,
    'IDL:DynamicServer/IDynamicObject:1.0',
tmMultiThreaded, True);
  FIntf := Impl as IDynamicObject;
end;

procedure TDynamicObjectSkeleton.GetImplementation(out Impl: IUnknown);
begin
  Impl := FIntf;
end;

procedure TDynamicObjectSkeleton.GetName(const InBuf: IMarshalInBuffer;
  Cookie: Pointer);
var
  OutBuf: IMarshalOutBuffer;
  Retval: WideString;
begin
  Retval := FIntf.GetName;
  FSkeleton.GetReplyBuffer(Cookie, OutBuf);
  OutBuf.PutWideText(PWideChar(Pointer(Retval)));
end;

procedure TDynamicObjectSkeleton.Get_Description(const InBuf:
  IMarshalInBuffer; Cookie: Pointer);
var
  OutBuf: IMarshalOutBuffer;
  Retval: WideString;
begin
  Retval := FIntf.Get_Description;
  FSkeleton.GetReplyBuffer(Cookie, OutBuf);
  OutBuf.PutWideText(PWideChar(Pointer(Retval)));
end;
```

```
class function CoDynamicObject.Create: IDynamicObject;
begin
  Result := CreateComObject(CLASS_DynamicObject) as IDynamicObject;
end;

class function CoDynamicObject.CreateRemote(
  const MachineName: string): IDynamicObject;
begin
  Result := CreateRemoteComObject(MachineName,
    CLASS_DynamicObject) as IDynamicObject;
end;

class function TDynamicObjectCorbaFactory.CreateInstance(
  const InstanceName: string): IDynamicObject;
begin
  Result :=
    CorbaFactoryCreateStub('IDL:DynamicServer/DynamicObjectFactory:1.0',
      'DynamicObject', InstanceName, '', IDynamicObject)
      as IDynamicObject;
end;

initialization
  CorbaStubManager.RegisterStub(IDynamicObject, TDynamicObjectStub);
  CorbaInterfaceIDManager.RegisterInterface(IDynamicObject,
    'IDL:DynamicServer/IDynamicObject:1.0');
  CorbaSkeletonManager.RegisterSkeleton(IDynamicObject,
    TDynamicObjectSkeleton);
end.
```

LISTING 24.8   THE CLIENT SHOWING HOW TO DYNAMICALLY CALL A CORBA OBJECT USING THE TAny TYPE

```
/////////////////////////////////////
// Purpose: Client showing dynamic corba invocation
// Project: DynamicClient
// Copyright (c) 1998 by Charlie Calvert
//
unit MainClient;

interface

uses
  Windows, Messages, SysUtils,
  Classes, Graphics, Controls,
  Forms, Dialogs, StdCtrls;

type
```

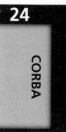

continues

LISTING 24.8   CONTINUED

```delphi
  TForm2 = class(TForm)
    StaticBtn: TButton;
    DynamicBtn: TButton;
    procedure DynamicBtnClick(Sender: TObject);
    procedure StaticBtnClick(Sender: TObject);
  private
    { Private declarations }
  public
    { Public declarations }
  end;

var
  Form2: TForm2;

implementation

uses
  DynamicServer_TLB, CorbaObj;

{$R *.DFM}

procedure TForm2.DynamicBtnClick(Sender: TObject);
var
  DynamicFactory: TAny;
  DynamicObject: TAny;
begin
  DynamicFactory :=
  ➥Orb.Bind('IDL:DynamicServer/DynamicObjectFactory:1.0');
  DynamicObject := DynamicFactory.CreateInstance('DynamicObject');
  ShowMessage(DynamicObject.Get_Description);
end;

procedure TForm2.StaticBtnClick(Sender: TObject);
var
  F: IDynamicObject;
begin
  F := TDynamicObjectCorbaFactory.CreateInstance('Random String');
  ShowMessage(F.Description);
end;

end.
```

As usual, you should first check to make sure the OSAgent is running as a program or service; then go ahead and launch the server. When you run the client, you should be able to call either of the program's two methods.

By now, you should be able to quickly find the Repository ID by looking at the `CreateInstance` method in the `XXX_TLB` file:

```
class function TDynamicObjectCorbaFactory.CreateInstance(
  const InstanceName: string): IDynamicObject;
begin
  Result :=
    CorbaFactoryCreateStub('IDL:DynamicServer/DynamicObjectFactory:1.0',
      'DynamicObject', InstanceName, '', IDynamicObject)
      as IDynamicObject;
end;
```

Notice that both of the methods hosted by the server are declared as `safecall`:

```
function Get_Description: WideString; safecall;
function GetName: WideString; safecall;
```

As you may recall, `safecall` ensures that the body of the methods will automatically be wrapped in a `try except` block, and that they will propagate exceptions back to the client. You don't have to do anything to get your methods declared as `safecall` because the Type Library Editor always prepares your methods in this fashion.

The main point here is that dynamic invocation is very simple. You can use this powerful technique to quickly and easily start accessing a wide range of CORBA servers. To make it work, all you need is the IDL from the server and the ability to mentally translate simple IDL into Object Pascal so that you can craft methods that will successfully call your server.

> **NOTE**
>
> The first version of Delphi Client/Server cannot call server properties. If you see IDL that uses attributes rather than simple methods, then Delphi cannot call the properties associated with the attributes. This problem should appear only in Delphi 4 and should be fixed in Delphi 4.01 or later.

24

CORBA

Simple CORBA Database Objects

It is time now to turn the focus away from a simple CORBA server and look instead at CORBA database applications. Constructing this type of application is a similar process to creating a MIDAS program, but you need to consider a few differences, particularly beneath the covers.

Creating a CORBA Database Server

To create a CORBA database server, you should complete the following steps:

1. Start a new application.

2. Select File, New to bring up the Object Repository and elect to create a new CORBA Data Module from the Multitier page.

3. Give your data module a name, set its Instancing to Instance-per-client, and set its Threading model to Single-threaded.

4. Drop down a `TTable` object and a `TProvider` object on the CORBA data module. (You can use the `Provider` interface that is part of the `TTable` object if you want. A main advantage of `TProvider` is that it gives you some extra events to help fine-tune the behavior of your program.)

5. Connect the `TTable` object to a table such as the Country table from the `DBDEMOS` alias.

6. Connect the provider to the table. Then right-click on the provider and export from the server.

7. Save your work and run the application once to make sure it is working correctly.

That's all there is to creating a CORBA data server. As you can see, this process is nearly identical to creating a standard MIDAS application.

> **NOTE**
>
> When working with this project, I saved the main form of the server as `MainServer.pas`, the implementation of the server I called `MainServerIMPL`, and the project itself I called `CorbaDataTestServer2`. The client's main form I saved as `MainClient.pas`, and the client project I saved as `CorbaDataTestClient.dpr`.

In Listings 24.9 through 24.12, you will find the code for a simple CORBA data server. This application follows the seven steps laid out previously in this section, but I have also added to the server's interface a single method that exports the name of the server from the application. This extra method serves no particular purpose other than to show you how to start adding additional methods to the interfaces to your database applications. This program is found in the `Chap24/CorbaDataTest1` directory on the CD.

LISTING 24.9   THE DATA MODULE FOR A SIMPLE CORBA DATABASE SERVER

```
unit MainServerIMPL;

interface

uses
  Windows, Messages, SysUtils,
  Classes, Graphics, Controls,
  Forms, Dialogs, ComObj,
  VCLCom, StdVcl, BdeProv,
  DataBkr, CorbaRdm, CorbaObj,
  CorbaDataTestServer2_TLB, Provider, Db,
  DBTables;

type

  TCorbaDataObject2 = class(TCorbaDataModule, ICorbaDataObject2)
    Table1: TTable;
    Provider1: TProvider;
  protected
    function Get_Provider1: IProvider; safecall;
    function GetName: WideString; safecall;
  end;

var
  CorbaDataObject2: TCorbaDataObject2;

implementation

{$R *.DFM}

uses CorbInit, CorbaVcl;

function TCorbaDataObject2.Get_Provider1: IProvider;
begin
  Result := Provider1.Provider;
end;

function TCorbaDataObject2.GetName: WideString;
begin
  Result := 'TCorbaDataObject2';
end;

initialization
  TCorbaVclComponentFactory.Create('CorbaDataObject2Factory',
    'CorbaDataObject2',
    'IDL:CorbaDataTestServer2/CorbaDataObject2Factory:1.0',
    ICorbaDataObject2,
```

24

CORBA

continues

LISTING 24.9   CONTINUED

```
    TCorbaDataObject2,
    iMultiInstance,
    tmSingleThread);
end.
```

LISTING 24.10   THE TypeLibrary WRAPPER FOR A SIMPLE CORBA DATABASE
APPLICATION

```
unit CorbaDataTestServer2_TLB;

// ****************************************************************** //
// WARNING                                                           //
// -------                                                           //
// The types declared in this file were generated from data read    //
// from a Type Library. If this type library is explicitly or        //
// indirectly (via another type library referring to this type       //
// library) reimported, or the 'Refresh' command of the Type Library //
// Editor activated while editing the Type Library, the contents of  //
// this file will be regenerated and all                             //
// manual modifications will be lost.                                //
// ****************************************************************** //

// PASTLWTR : $Revision:   1.11.1.63  $
// File generated on 7/9/98 12:07:56 PM from Type Library
// described below.

// ****************************************************************** //
// Type Lib:
//   D:\SrcPas\Unleash4\Chap24\CorbaDataTest2\Server\
// CorbaDataTestServer2.tlb
// IID\LCID: {118A3F20-1724-11D2-9CE8-006008928EEF}\0
// Helpfile:
// HelpString: CorbaDataTestServer2 Library
// Version:    1.0
// ****************************************************************** //

interface

uses
  Windows, ActiveX, Classes,
  Graphics, OleCtrls, StdVCL,
  SysUtils, CORBAObj, OrbPas,
  CorbaStd;

// ****************************************************************** //
// GUIDS declared in the TypeLibrary. Following prefixes are used:   //
//   Type Libraries     : LIBID_xxxx                                 //
```

```
//   CoClasses          : CLASS_xxxx                                 //
//   DISPInterfaces     : DIID_xxxx                                  //
//   Non-DISP interfaces: IID_xxxx                                   //
// ********************************************************** //
const
  LIBID_CorbaDataTestServer2: TGUID =
  ➥'{118A3F20-1724-11D2-9CE8-006008928EEF}';
  IID_ICorbaDataObject2: TGUID =
  ➥'{118A3F21-1724-11D2-9CE8-006008928EEF}';
  CLASS_CorbaDataObject2: TGUID =
  ➥'{118A3F23-1724-11D2-9CE8-006008928EEF}';
type

// ********************************************************** //
// Forward declaration of interfaces defined in Type Library     //
// ********************************************************** //
  ICorbaDataObject2 = interface;
  ICorbaDataObject2Disp = dispinterface;

// ********************************************************** //
// Declaration of CoClasses defined in Type Library              //
// (NOTE: Here we map each CoClass to its Default Interface)      //
// ********************************************************** //
  CorbaDataObject2 = ICorbaDataObject2;


// ********************************************************** //
// Interface: ICorbaDataObject2
// Flags:     (4416) Dual OleAutomation Dispatchable
// GUID:      {118A3F21-1724-11D2-9CE8-006008928EEF}
// ********************************************************** //
  ICorbaDataObject2 = interface(IDataBroker)
    ['{118A3F21-1724-11D2-9CE8-006008928EEF}']
    function Get_Provider1: IProvider; safecall;
    function GetName: WideString; safecall;
    property Provider1: IProvider read Get_Provider1;
  end;

// ********************************************************** //
// DispIntf:  ICorbaDataObject2Disp
// Flags:     (4416) Dual OleAutomation Dispatchable
// GUID:      {118A3F21-1724-11D2-9CE8-006008928EEF}
// ********************************************************** //
  ICorbaDataObject2Disp = dispinterface
    ['{118A3F21-1724-11D2-9CE8-006008928EEF}']
    property Provider1: IProvider readonly dispid 1;
    function GetName: WideString; dispid 2;
    function GetProviderNames: OleVariant; dispid 22929905;
  end;
```

continues

24

CORBA

LISTING 24.10 CONTINUED

```pascal
TCorbaDataObject2Stub = class(TDataBrokerStub, ICorbaDataObject2)
public
  function Get_Provider1: IProvider; safecall;
  function GetName: WideString; safecall;
end;

TCorbaDataObject2Skeleton = class(TDataBrokerSkeleton)
private
  FIntf: ICorbaDataObject2;
public
  constructor Create(const InstanceName: string; const Impl:
    IUnknown); override;
  procedure GetImplementation(out Impl: IUnknown); override; stdcall;
published
  procedure Get_Provider1(const InBuf: IMarshalInBuffer; Cookie:
    Pointer);
  procedure GetName(const InBuf: IMarshalInBuffer; Cookie: Pointer);
end;

CoCorbaDataObject2 = class
  class function Create: ICorbaDataObject2;
  class function CreateRemote(const MachineName: string):
    ICorbaDataObject2;
end;

TCorbaDataObject2CorbaFactory = class
  class function CreateInstance(const InstanceName: string):
    ICorbaDataObject2;
end;

implementation

uses ComObj;

{ TCorbaDataObject2Stub }

function TCorbaDataObject2Stub.Get_Provider1: IProvider;
var
  OutBuf: IMarshalOutBuffer;
  InBuf: IMarshalInBuffer;
begin
  FStub.CreateRequest('Get_Provider1', True, OutBuf);
  FStub.Invoke(OutBuf, InBuf);
  Result := UnmarshalObject(InBuf, IProvider) as IProvider;
end;

function TCorbaDataObject2Stub.GetName: WideString;
var
```

```
    OutBuf: IMarshalOutBuffer;
    InBuf: IMarshalInBuffer;
  begin
    FStub.CreateRequest('GetName', True, OutBuf);
    FStub.Invoke(OutBuf, InBuf);
    Result := UnmarshalWideText(InBuf);
  end;


{ TCorbaDataObject2Skeleton }

constructor TCorbaDataObject2Skeleton.Create(const InstanceName: string;
  const Impl: IUnknown);
begin
  inherited;
  inherited InitSkeleton('CorbaDataObject2', InstanceName,
    'IDL:CorbaDataTestServer2/ICorbaDataObject2:1.0',
    tmMultiThreaded, True);
  FIntf := Impl as ICorbaDataObject2;
end;

procedure TCorbaDataObject2Skeleton.GetImplementation
➥(out Impl: IUnknown);
begin
  Impl := FIntf;
end;

procedure TCorbaDataObject2Skeleton.Get_Provider1(
  const InBuf: IMarshalInBuffer; Cookie: Pointer);
var
  OutBuf: IMarshalOutBuffer;
  Retval: IProvider;
begin
  Retval := FIntf.Get_Provider1;
  FSkeleton.GetReplyBuffer(Cookie, OutBuf);
  MarshalObject(OutBuf, IProvider, Retval);
end;

procedure TCorbaDataObject2Skeleton.GetName
➥(const InBuf: IMarshalInBuffer;
  Cookie: Pointer);
var
  OutBuf: IMarshalOutBuffer;
  Retval: WideString;
begin
  Retval := FIntf.GetName;
  FSkeleton.GetReplyBuffer(Cookie, OutBuf);
  OutBuf.PutWideText(PWideChar(Pointer(Retval)));
end;
```

continues

LISTING 24.10   CONTINUED

```
class function CoCorbaDataObject2.Create: ICorbaDataObject2;
begin
  Result := CreateComObject(CLASS_CorbaDataObject2) as ICorbaDataObject2;
end;

class function CoCorbaDataObject2.CreateRemote
  (const MachineName: string): ICorbaDataObject2;
begin
  Result := CreateRemoteComObject(MachineName, CLASS_CorbaDataObject2)
    as ICorbaDataObject2;
end;

class function TCorbaDataObject2CorbaFactory.CreateInstance(
  const InstanceName: string): ICorbaDataObject2;
begin
  Result := CorbaFactoryCreateStub(
    'IDL:CorbaDataTestServer2/CorbaDataObject2Factory:1.0',
    'CorbaDataObject2',
    InstanceName, '',
    ICorbaDataObject2) as ICorbaDataObject2;
end;

initialization
  CorbaStubManager.RegisterStub(ICorbaDataObject2,
    TCorbaDataObject2Stub);
  CorbaInterfaceIDManager.RegisterInterface(ICorbaDataObject2,
    'IDL:CorbaDataTestServer2/ICorbaDataObject2:1.0');
  CorbaSkeletonManager.RegisterSkeleton(ICorbaDataObject2,
    TCorbaDataObject2Skeleton);
end.
```

LISTING 24.11   THE IDL FOR A SIMPLE CORBA SERVER

```
#include "StdVCL.idl"

module CorbaDataTestServer2
{

  interface ICorbaDataObject2: StdVCL:IDataBroker
  {
    StdVCL:IProvider Get_Provider1();
    wstring GetName();
  };

  interface CorbaDataObject2Factory
  {
```

```
      ICorbaDataObject2 CreateInstance(in string InstanceName);
    };

};
```

___

LISTING 24.12 THE MAIN FORM OF THE CLIENT PROGRAM THAT TALKS TO THE
CorbaDataTest1 SERVER
___

```
//////////////////////////////////////
// Purpose: Connect to CorbaDataTest2 Server
// Project: CorbaDataTestClient2
// Copyright (c) 1998 by Charlie Calvert
//
unit MainClient;

{---------------------------------------------------------------
  When running this program, first be sure the OSAgent is started
  and your server is running. It is best not to connect to a
  server at design time, because if you leave connected set to true
  you can have trouble loading the client in the IDE if the server
  is not running.

  To call the GetName method, you must use Dynamic invocation. To
  get this work, feed Both.idl into irep, using a command line like
  this: irep MyName Both.idl, where MyName is a string of your choosing
  that names the repository.
-----------------------------------------------------------------}

interface

uses
  Windows, Messages, SysUtils,
  Classes, Graphics, Controls,
  Forms, Dialogs, DBClient,
  CorbaCon, Db, Menus,
  Grids, DBGrids;

type
  TForm2 = class(TForm)
    CorbaConnection1: TCorbaConnection;
    ClientDataSet1: TClientDataSet;
    DataSource1: TDataSource;
    DBGrid1: TDBGrid;
    MainMenu1: TMainMenu;
    File1: TMenuItem;
    Connect1: TMenuItem;
    GetName1: TMenuItem;
    N1: TMenuItem;
    Exit1: TMenuItem;
```

24

CORBA

continues

LISTING 24.12   CONTINUED

```
    procedure Connect1Click(Sender: TObject);
    procedure GetName1Click(Sender: TObject);
    procedure Exit1Click(Sender: TObject);
  end;

var
  Form2: TForm2;

implementation

{$R *.DFM}

procedure TForm2.Connect1Click(Sender: TObject);
begin
  CorbaConnection1.Connected := True;
  ClientDataSet1.Active := True;
  // Caption := CorbaConnection1.AppServer.GetName;
end;

{ GetName1Click ---------------------------------------------------------
  This method uses dynamic invocation. It will not work unless your
  interface is registred in the Interface Repository (IREP).
  --------------------------------------------------------------------}
procedure TForm2.GetName1Click(Sender: TObject);
begin
  if CorbaConnection1.Connected then
    ShowMessage(CorbaConnection1.AppServer.GetName);
end;

procedure TForm2.Exit1Click(Sender: TObject);
begin
  Close;
end;

end.
```

The server does nothing of interest when run on its own. A database server of this type is valuable only when called from an application. So running the server standalone is a rather unfulfilling undertaking that yields little more than an empty window. To use the program, first make sure the OSAgent is running, then load the server, then load IREP as described next, and then load the client. I will describe how to create the client in the next section of this chapter. Both the client and server are pictured in Figure 24.4.

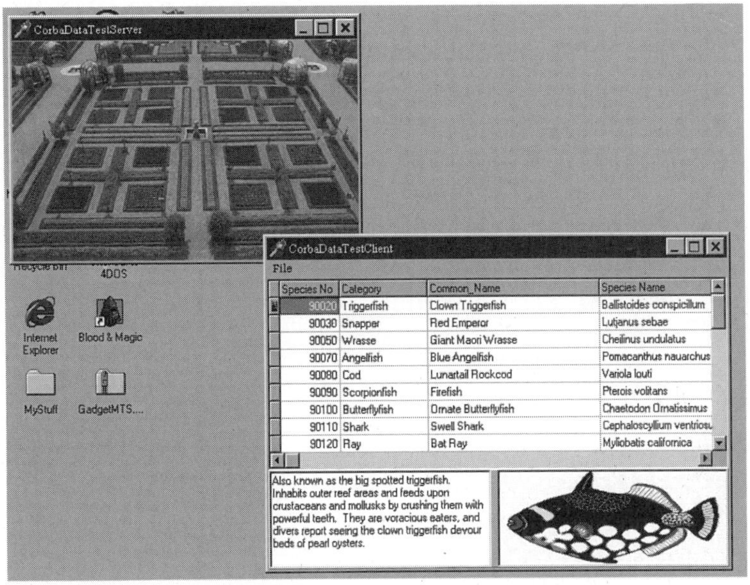

FIGURE 24.4

The client and server for the CORBA database application.

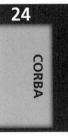

After the client is running, you are at last able to call the server from the client's menu. Doing so fills up the grid with data and sets the caption of the client equal to a value sent from the server.

> **NOTE**
>
> By default, I comment out the line in the `Connect1Click` method that calls the `GetName` method of the server. I do so because `GetName` can only be called using dynamic invocation, and it is possible to connect successfully to the server, retrieve the data, and still not have the dynamic invocation business set up properly. To test whether dynamic invocation is working, use the `GetName` option from the menu. If it is working properly, then you can close the client and restore the line in the `Connect1Click` method.

You have already heard how to create the server, and because it is so similar to a standard MIDAS application, I will only touch on it further for a few brief moments. The most important lines in the server are the ones that export the provider interface:

```
function TD4CorbaObject.Get_Provider1: IProvider;
begin
  Result := Provider1.Provider;
end;
```

24

CORBA

This code will be called by the client when it needs to establish a database connection with the server. The method returns an instance of the TProvider object. The client and server can use this object to communicate. In particular, this object has methods for retrieving a dataset and other methods for updating the server after the user has made changes to the dataset. I will not, however, go into any more depth on this topic at this time, as the workings of the TProvider component are discussed in Chapter 21, "MIDAS."

Creating the Client

When you create the client application, first be sure the OSAgent is started and your server is running. Then drop down a TCORBAServerConnection component. Fill in its Repository ID property with the following line retrieved from the CreateInstance method in the XXX_TLB file:

```
IDL:CorbaDataTestServer2/CorbaDataObject2Factory:1.0
```

Do not confuse this Repository ID with the Repository ID that appears in the initialization section of the XXX_TLB file. You want the factory ID, not the object ID.

It is best not to connect to a server at design time for more than a few moments; if you leave the client connected, you can have trouble loading the client in the IDE if the server is not running. For instance, if you have the client selected as the default project in the IDE and then crash the IDE, when you try to restart the IDE, you will suffer long delays while the IDE tries to load a client that is trying to connect to a server that may not be in memory. CORBA programs can sometimes take a few seconds or a few minutes to time out when they fail to connect. In the meantime, your system may appear to be hung. To avoid that kind of frustration, you should write code that will connect you to your server at runtime. As a result, you will always be able to load the client program into the IDE without mishap.

To call the GetName method, you must use dynamic invocation. To get started, select the Type Library Editor and export the CORBA IDL using the icon on the far right of the toolbar. This action should produce a file called CorbaDataTest2.idl. Feed CorbaDataTestServer2.idl into irep, using a command line like this:

```
irep MyName CorbaDataTestServer2.idl.
```

Here MyName is a string of your choosing that names the repository. Be sure the file called stdvcl.idl is in the current directory. You can find stdvcl.idl in the Delphi4\imports\idl directory from the standard installation of Delphi 4.

If you want, you can start IREP by simply typing the following command:

```
irep CharlieIR.
```

Now you have a version of IREP running. You can now load IDL into it by typing the following line at the command prompt:

```
idl2ir -ir CharlieIR CorbaDataTestServer2.idl
```

You can also try to load the IDL using the menu of the IREP GUI, but this approach does not always work for me. So I suggest using IDL2IR. Both IREP and IDL2IR are VisiBroker tools from the `Borland\VBroker\Bin` directory.

To test to make sure that the IR is set up correctly, load a utility such as the VisiBroker Manager, or type `OSFind` at the command prompt, or click the Lookup button in IREP GUI itself. Of these three methods, the last is probably the easiest to use in most cases.

At this stage, you should have everything set up correctly. You can now call the `GetName` method of the server of the `AppServer` variable of the `CorbaConnection` component. The `AppServer` variable is of type `TAny`, which in Delphi Client/Server 4 resolves to type Variant. In other words, you are just performing a standard dynamic invocation of the type shown in the section called "Simple CORBA Dynamic Project."

TIP

When loading the IDL into IREP, you may find it awkward to use the IDL directly as it is exported from the Type Library Editor. If you want a second technique, you can combine the IDL from the Delphi IDE with the IDL from `stdvcl.idl`, which is kept in the `Delphi4\Imports\IDL` directory. The end result looks like this:

```
module CorbaDataTestServer2
{
  interface IProvider
  {
    any Get_Data();
    any ApplyUpdates(in any Delta, in long MaxErrors, out long
ErrorCount);
    any GetMetaData();
    any GetRecords(in long Count, out long RecsOut);
    any DataRequest(in any Input);
    boolean Get_Constraints();
    boolean Set_Constraints();
    void Reset(in boolean MetaData);
    void SetParams(in any Values);
  };

  interface IStrings
  {
```

continues

24

CORBA

```
     any Get_ControlDefault(in long Index);
     any Set_ControlDefault(in long Index);
     long Count();
     any Get_Item(in long Index);
     any Set_Item(in long Index);
     void Remove(in long Index);
     void Clear();
     long Add(in any Item);
     Object NewEnum();
   };

   interface IDataBroker
   {
     any GetProviderNames();
   };

   interface ICorbaDataObject2: IDataBroker
   {
     IProvider Get_Provider1();
     wstring GetName();
   };

   interface CorbaDataObject2Factory
   {
     ICorbaDataObject2 CreateInstance(in string InstanceName);
   };

};
```

The first three interfaces are all from StdVcl, and the last two interfaces are from the current project. When they are combined like this into a single file, IREP can read all the interfaces with no compilation errors. This technique makes the IDL usable from the IREP GUI, though the other technique works fine from the command line using IDL2IR.

As you can see, CORBA database connectivity in Delphi 4 is a lot like MIDAS. The big differences come when you try to perform dynamic invocation and when you examine the contents of the XXX_TLB files that are generated. Of course, the act of connecting to the server is a bit different because, with CORBA, you have to fill out the Repository ID by hand rather than select it from a drop-down list. However, that is a small price to pay considering the power and ease of use inherent in the MIDAS technology upon which the Delphi CORBA database connectivity is based.

Working with the VisiBroker Manager and `OSFind`

Two tools can help you when working with CORBA programming. One is a VisiBroker add-on called the VisiBroker Manager. A trial version of this tool can be downloaded from the Inprise Web site. The second is a command-line utility called `OSFind`.

The VisiBroker Manager is called `VBM.exe`. Before you run it, you must first make sure the OSAgent is running, and you must load the Location Server, which is a separate executable that comes with the VisiBroker Manager.

The VisiBroker Manager uses a tabbed notebook metaphor. On the first page is a list of services and servers running on the current LAN. You can use this list to find the correct Repository ID of a server. You can also see what other servers might be running on your system or on your LAN, as shown in Figure 24.5.

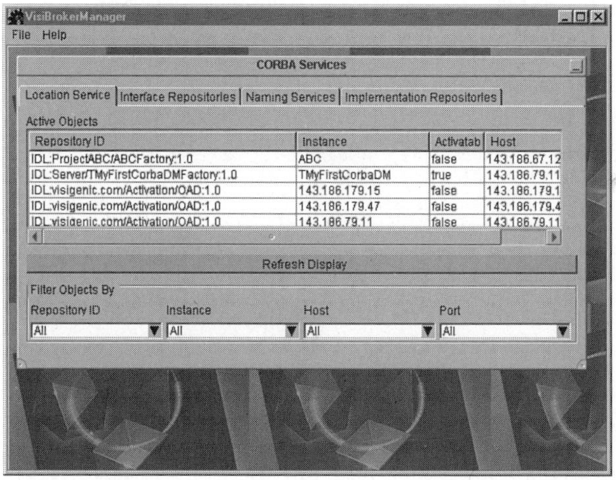

FIGURE 24.5

Browsing CORBA objects in the VisiBroker Manager.

The second page of the VisiBroker Manager lets you explore any Interface Repositories that might be loaded. You can drill down in this dialog, seeing the individual methods in an interface and even checking the parameters passed to them. I use this tool primarily to be sure the IR contains the correct values for my current server. In other words, it helps me debug my CORBA servers.

You can explore the other pages in the VisiBroker Manager at your own leisure. The most important of these helps you work with the OAD, which is a service for starting servers automatically. I will not be covering the OAD in this book.

If you don't want to use the VisiBroker Manager, you have a good built-in alternative in the command-line–based OSFind utility. To use this program, just go to a command window and type OSFIND. The following is standard output from an OSFind session:

```
osfind: Found one agent at port 14000
HOST: ccalvertpc7

osfind: There are no OADs running on in your domain.

osfind: There are no Object Implementations registered with OADs.

osfind: Following are the list of Implementations started manually.
HOST: CCALVERTPC7

REPOSITORY ID: IDL:visigenic.com/tools/ir/RepositoryManager:1.0
OBJECT NAME: Charlie

REPOSITORY ID: IDL:CorbaDataTestServer2/CorbaDataObject2Factory:1.0
OBJECT NAME: CorbaDataObject2

REPOSITORY ID: IDL:visigenic.com/irtx/Repository:1.0
OBJECT NAME: Charlie
```

The output shown here says the Smart Agent is running at port 14000 on ccalvertpc7. No OADs or Object Implementations are available. An Interface Repository named Charlie and one object named CorbaDataObject2 are loaded.

Summary

In this chapter, you looked at CORBA programming with Delphi. You saw how to create simple CORBA servers, how to create simple CORBA database servers, and how to handle dynamic invocation. Other subjects covered in this chapter included IDL, the VisiBroker Manager, the Interface Repository, and OSFind.

In the next chapter, you will see how to call Delphi CORBA applications from C++ and Java and how to call C++ and Java CORBA servers from Delphi. By the time you are through, you will have had a fairly in-depth introduction to the basics of CORBA programming.

CHAPTER 25

Delphi, Java, and C++

In this chapter, you will learn how to use CORBA to share objects among Delphi, JBuilder, and C++Builder. The chapter takes you through several different examples, allowing you to create servers in Delphi, JBuilder, and C++Builder and clients in Delphi, JBuilder, and C++Builder.

One of the most important topics covered in this chapter is dynamic invocation, which is the primary means Delphi has of accessing a CORBA server not built in Delphi. Dynamic invocation was discussed in depth in the preceding chapter, but here you will get a chance to see it in action in a setting similar to the one you are likely to experience in your own programs. The examples I show here are simpler than the ones you are likely to encounter in your work. They focus, however, on the interaction between Delphi and other languages such as C++ and Java. This kind of multilanguage interaction is exactly what many CORBA programmers are likely to encounter.

The code that I show you in this chapter is designed to run with GUI programs produced by C++Builder and JBuilder. As such, they have C++Builder- and JBuilder-specific features in them and are not necessarily portable across a wide variety of platforms. (The Java code will port, of course, but you would need to bring your JBCL packages with you.) Furthermore, my client programs buck the trend of CORBA examples, which are usually command line based. My desire here is to show you how to create programs that users would actually understand and would feel comfortable using.

When you're reading this chapter, I'm going to assume you have an understanding of JBuilder 2 and C++Builder 3. If you need more information on JBuilder, I recommend *Sams Teach Yourself Borland JBuilder in 21 Days*, by Donald Doherty and Michelle Manning (Sams Publishing) or *JBuilder Essentials*, by Carey Jensen (Osborne/McGraw Hill). If you need information on C++Builder, I recommend *Sams Teach Yourself C++Builder in 21 Days*, by Kent Reisdorph, also published by Sams Publishing. If you have no interest in either of these environments, then the code I am writing is still Java and C++ source, so I'm sure you can adopt it to work in your tool of choice. I'm going to confine all my examples to Windows applications, but there is no reason why the same type of code shouldn't work from a UNIX box or on any OS that supports CORBA and Java.

Using CORBA with Delphi and Java

In this section, I'm going to show you two sets of client/server programs that link Delphi and Java using CORBA. As I'm sure you can guess, one pair of programs will be a Java client talking to a Delphi server, and the other will be a Delphi client talking to a Java server.

Creating a Java Client for Your Delphi Server

The first example I want to show you calls a Delphi server from a Java client. The server in this case is the one found in the `CorbaTest1/Server` directory from the preceding chapter. To get started creating this example, you need to export the interface to your Delphi object as CORBA IDL. You do so from the toolbar at the top of the Delphi Type Library Editor, as explained in the preceding chapter.

After you have created the IDL, you can bring up JBuilder and start a new project. Don't add a program to it; just start the project. Now add the CORBA IDL into your JBuilder project. Right-click on the IDL file inside JBuilder and choose Make. When you do so, a set of classes designed to help you access your object is automatically generated. In particular, you will find a set of files generated in a directory called `..\myclasses\Generated Source`. The files in this directory are read only, and they do not ship on the CD that accompanies this book. This means that even if you are just running the example that ships with the CD, then you still have to right-click on the IDL file and generate these files by running Make.

> **NOTE**
>
> When you right-click on the IDL and choose Make, JBuilder will go out and run `IDL2Java.exe`. This file comes with the VisiBroker, but not necessarily with the Delphi version of the VisiBroker. You can run `IDL2Java` yourself from the command line, and the same files referenced in the preceding paragraph will be generated for you automatically. In other words, you don't have to have JBuilder to do this exercise. You just need VisiBroker and a valid Java compiler.
>
> I find the files that are generated to be extremely hard to read because of the way the code is formatted. One thing you can do to help is to turn off the option that generates comments. To turn off comments, right-click on the IDL file and choose IDL Properties from the menu. The code generated inside the IDE when you run `IDL2Java` is read only. As a result, you cannot reformat it.

Listings 25.1 through 25.4 contain the source for some of the key files in this project. I do not include all the source files in these listings, but you can find them on the CD that accompanies this book in the `JavaClient` directory, or else you can auto-generate them.

LISTING 25.1 THE SOURCE FOR THE MAIN FRAME FROM THE JAVA PROGRAM THAT CALLS YOUR DELPHI SERVER

```java
package CorbaTestJava;

// See CorbaTestJava.html for a description of the project.

import java.awt.*;
import java.awt.event.*;
import borland.jbcl.control.*;
import borland.jbcl.layout.*;

public class Frame1 extends DecoratedFrame
{
  //Construct the frame
  BorderLayout borderLayout1 = new BorderLayout();
  XYLayout xYLayout2 = new XYLayout();
  BevelPanel bevelPanel1 = new BevelPanel();
  ButtonControl buttonControl1 = new ButtonControl();
  TextFieldControl textFieldControl1 = new TextFieldControl();

  public Frame1()
  {
    try
    {
      jbInit();
    }
    catch (Exception e)
    {
      e.printStackTrace();
    }
  }
//Component initialization

  private void jbInit() throws Exception
  {
    this.setLayout(borderLayout1);
    this.setSize(new Dimension(400, 300));
    this.setTitle("Frame Title");
    buttonControl1.setLabel("buttonControl1");
    buttonControl1.addActionListener(new java.awt.event.ActionListener()
    {
      public void actionPerformed(ActionEvent e)
      {
        buttonControl1_actionPerformed(e);
      }
    });
    textFieldControl1.setText("textFieldControl1");
    bevelPanel1.setLayout(xYLayout2);
    this.add(bevelPanel1, BorderLayout.CENTER);
    bevelPanel1.add(buttonControl1,
    ➡new XYConstraints(117, 125, 152, 76));
```

```
  bevelPanel1.add(textFieldControl1,
  ➡new XYConstraints(84, 32, 209, 26));
  }

/*********************************************************************
 *  Attach to the orb.
 *  Get a copy of the factory.
 *  Call CreateInstance on the Factory to get your object.
 *  Call the methods of your object.
 *********************************************************************/
  void buttonControl1_actionPerformed(ActionEvent e)
  {
    String[] args = {};

    org.omg.CORBA.ORB orb = org.omg.CORBA.ORB.init(args,null);

    CorbaTestServer1.CorbaTestObjectFactory Factory =
      CorbaTestServer1.CorbaTestObjectFactoryHelper.bind(orb,
        "CorbaTestObject");

    CorbaTestServer1.ICorbaTestObject TestObject =
      Factory.CreateInstance("CorbaTestObject");

    String AName = TestObject.GetName();

    textFieldControl1.setText(AName);
  }
}
```

LISTING 25.2 THE SOURCE TO THE AUTOMATICALLY GENERATED JAVA DEFINITION FOR YOUR INTERFACE: CorbaTestObject.java

```
package CorbaTestServer1;

public interface ICorbaTestObject extends org.omg.CORBA.Object
{
  public java.lang.String GetName();
  public java.lang.String Bark();
}
```

LISTING 25.3 THE SOURCE TO THE DEFINITION FOR THE OBJECT FACTORY: CorbaTestObjectFactory.java

```
package CorbaTestServer1;

public interface CorbaTestObjectFactory extends org.omg.CORBA.Object
```

continues

LISTING 25.3 CONTINUED

```
{
  public CorbaTestServer1.ICorbaTestObject CreateInstance(
    java.lang.String InstanceName
  );
}
```

LISTING 25.4 THE SOURCE TO THE AUTOMATICALLY GENERATED JAVA DEFINITION FOR THE FACTORY HELPER CLASS

```
package CorbaTestServer1;

abstract public class CorbaTestObjectFactoryHelper
{
  public static CorbaTestServer1.CorbaTestObjectFactory
    narrow(org.omg.CORBA.Object object)
  {
    return narrow(object, false);
  }

  private static CorbaTestServer1.CorbaTestObjectFactory
    narrow(org.omg.CORBA.Object object, boolean is_a)
  {
    if(object == null)
    {
      return null;
    }

    if(object instanceof CorbaTestServer1.CorbaTestObjectFactory)
    {
      return (CorbaTestServer1.CorbaTestObjectFactory) object;
    }

    if(is_a || object._is_a(id()))
    {
      CorbaTestServer1._st_CorbaTestObjectFactory result =
        (CorbaTestServer1._st_CorbaTestObjectFactory)new
          CorbaTestServer1._st_CorbaTestObjectFactory();
      ((org.omg.CORBA.portable.ObjectImpl) result)._set_delegate
        (((org.omg.CORBA.portable.ObjectImpl) object)._get_delegate());
      ((org.omg.CORBA.portable.ObjectImpl) result._this())._set_delegate
        (((org.omg.CORBA.portable.ObjectImpl) object)._get_delegate());
      return (CorbaTestServer1.CorbaTestObjectFactory) result._this();
    }

    return null;
  }
```

```
public static CorbaTestServer1.CorbaTestObjectFactory
  bind(org.omg.CORBA.ORB orb)
{
  return bind(orb, null, null, null);
}

public static CorbaTestServer1.CorbaTestObjectFactory
  bind(org.omg.CORBA.ORB orb, java.lang.String name)
{
  return bind(orb, name, null, null);
}

public static CorbaTestServer1.CorbaTestObjectFactory
  bind(org.omg.CORBA.ORB orb, java.lang.String name,
    java.lang.String host, org.omg.CORBA.BindOptions options)
{
  return narrow(orb.bind(id(), name, host, options), true);
}

private static org.omg.CORBA.ORB _orb()
{
  return org.omg.CORBA.ORB.init();
}

public static CorbaTestServer1.CorbaTestObjectFactory
  read(org.omg.CORBA.portable.InputStream _input)
{
  return CorbaTestServer1.CorbaTestObjectFactoryHelper.narrow(
    _input.read_Object(), true);
}

public static void write(org.omg.CORBA.portable.OutputStream _output,
  CorbaTestServer1.CorbaTestObjectFactory value)
{
  _output.write_Object(value);
}

public static void insert(org.omg.CORBA.Any any,
  CorbaTestServer1.CorbaTestObjectFactory value)
{
  org.omg.CORBA.portable.OutputStream output =
  ➥any.create_output_stream();
  write(output, value);
  any.read_value(output.create_input_stream(), type());
}

public static CorbaTestServer1.CorbaTestObjectFactory
  extract(org.omg.CORBA.Any any)
```

continues

LISTING 25.4   CONTINUED

```
  {
    if(!any.type().equal(type()))
    {
      throw new org.omg.CORBA.BAD_TYPECODE();
    }
    return read(any.create_input_stream());
  }

  private static org.omg.CORBA.TypeCode _type;

  public static org.omg.CORBA.TypeCode type()
  {
    if(_type == null)
    {
      _type = _orb().create_interface_tc(id(), "CorbaTestObjectFactory");
    }
    return _type;
  }

  public static java.lang.String id()
  {
    return "IDL:CorbaTestServer1/CorbaTestObjectFactory:1.0";
  }
}
```

Before you run this program, you should make sure that you have launched your Delphi server. If you are running on Windows NT, make sure that the Smart Agent service is running. If you are running on Windows 95/98, make sure that OSAGENT.exe is running.

Run the Java client application and click the button on the form. The server will be contacted, and a string will be returned from it and displayed in the client's text control, as shown in Figure 25.1.

FIGURE 25.1

The Java client application retrieves a string from the barking Delphi dog server.

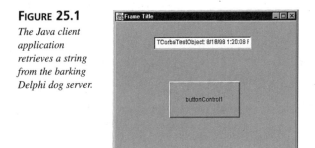

You don't need to understand all the code I have shown here, though much of it is very simple. For instance, Listings 25.2 and 25.3 are the auto-generated interfaces to the `CorbaTestObject` and `CorbaTestObjectFactory`. Here, for instance, is the `CorbaTestObject` interface:

```
package CorbaTestServer1;

public interface ICorbaTestObject extends org.omg.CORBA.Object
{
  public java.lang.String GetName();
  public java.lang.String Bark();
}
```

The first line states that this is a package. A package is the Java equivalent of a unit. The next line declares the interface for the object, just like an interface declaration in Delphi. The last two lines declare the methods supported by the interface, along with their function return types. In this case, both methods return a string.

Here is the declaration for the `CorbaTestObjectFactory`:

```
package CorbaTestServer1;

public interface CorbaTestObjectFactory extends org.omg.CORBA.Object
{
  public CorbaTestServer1.ICorbaTestObject CreateInstance(
    java.lang.String InstanceName);
}
```

Again, this object is declared in a package. The `CorbaTestObjectFactory` supports one method that takes a string as a parameter. This declaration is very straightforward, but I find it interesting to see how easily Delphi code can be translated into Java with the aid of an IDL file working as an intermediary. In fact, I'm showing you these files primarily so you can see that `IDL2Java` can translate your Object Pascal classes into valid Java classes. Because this translation would not be possible without the IDL, the code shown here should help drive home the key role that IDL plays in this technology.

Implementing the Java Client

After you have generated the Java helper classes produced by `IDL2Java`, the next step is to create a client program that can converse with your server. To do so, choose File, New from the JBuilder menu and create a new application. Drop a button and a `textFieldControl` control on your new frame, and associate the following code with the button click:

```
void buttonControl1_actionPerformed(ActionEvent e)
{
  String[] args = {};
```

```
org.omg.CORBA.ORB orb = org.omg.CORBA.ORB.init(args,null);

CorbaTestServer1.CorbaTestObjectFactory Factory =
  CorbaTestServer1.CorbaTestObjectFactoryHelper.bind(orb,
    "CorbaTestObject");

CorbaTestServer1.ICorbaTestObject TestObject =
  Factory.CreateInstance("CorbaTestObject");

String AName = TestObject.GetName();
textFieldControl1.setText(AName);
}
```

This code first ensures that the ORB DLLs are loaded into memory. Then it creates an instance of the Factory object by calling a method in the `CorbaTestObjectFactoryHelper.java` file. `CorbaTestObjectFractoryHelper.java` was auto-generated for you when you right-clicked on the IDL file and chose Make, or when you ran `IDL2Java` from the command line.

After you have an instance of the Factory, then you can call its `CreateInstance` method to get an instance of the `ICorbaTestObject` interface. At this stage, you are all set up and can begin calling Delphi methods to your heart's content from inside a Java program.

The code on the button response method calls the `bind` method in the auto-generated `CorbaTestObjectFactoryHelper`. The relevant code in that auto-generated file looks like this:

```
public static CorbaTestServer1.CorbaTestObjectFactory
  bind(org.omg.CORBA.ORB orb, java.lang.String name)
{
  return bind(orb, name, null, null);
}
```

This example is one of several overloaded `bind` methods, each distinguished by the parameters it takes. For instance, this one takes two parameters and sets the remaining parameters of the real `bind` method to `null`. The other versions of the `bind` method take more or fewer parameters and set some corresponding number of the parameters to `null`.

When you call `bind`, the code you use looks like this:

```
org.omg.CORBA.ORB orb = org.omg.CORBA.ORB.init(args,null);

CorbaTestObjectFactory Factory =
  CorbaTestObjectFactoryHelper.bind(orb, "CorbaTestObject");
```

The first line initializes the ORB, and the second line passes in the ORB to the `bind` method. You also pass in the name of the object you want to connect to. You can find this name in the `XXX_TLB` file generated for you by Delphi, in the second parameter passed to `CorbaFactoryCreateStub`:

```
class function TCorbaTestObjectCorbaFactory.CreateInstance(
  const InstanceName: string): ICorbaTestObject;
begin
  Result :=
    CorbaFactoryCreateStub(
      'IDL:CorbaTestServer1/CorbaTestObjectFactory:1.0',
      'CorbaTestObject',
      InstanceName,
      '',
      ICorbaTestObject) as ICorbaTestObject;
end;
```

After you've written the few lines I've discussed here, you can run the Smart Agent, start the Delphi server, and call it with this Delphi program. This system will work equally well whether all the programs are on one machine or whether they are spread out across a LAN.

> **NOTE**
>
> Consult the VisiBroker documentation when your CORBA objects are on different domains (subnets) because they won't work out of the box in that state. They will need some additional configuration. You may want to test that configuration with some of the sample CORBA objects supplied with the product before attempting to work with programs you develop yourself.
>
> If you are very new to working with networks, then don't let this note confuse you. For instance, if you are working on a simple Windows network at home, then you can ignore everything in this note. It applies only to people who have complex network setups.

When all is said and done, writing this code is quite simple, though I do find the numerous files produced by IDL2Java to be a bit confusing. However, the level of complexity is relatively mild, and you should soon be able to start cranking out programs of this type in fairly short order.

Calling a Java Server from Delphi

The technique involved in calling a Java server is very similar to what you saw in the last section when working with a Delphi server. However, when you work with Java to create the server, you probably won't have a factory class. As a result, on the Delphi client, you have to take only the one step of binding to the server.

The Java sample server used in this section is found in the Chap27/JavaServer directory. Beneath that directory you will find a directory called DelphiClient; it holds the client program that calls the Java server.

This is a Delphi book, but I am going to talk briefly about building a server in Java. The code for the key modules in the Java server appears in Listings 25.5 through 25.7. Listing 25.8 shows the Delphi client that talks to the server.

LISTING 25.5 THE IDL THAT DEFINES THE INTERFACE FOR THE OBJECT SUPPORTED BY THE JAVA SERVER

```
module DelphiCORBA
{
  interface DelphiServer
  {
    wstring GetName();
  };
};
```

LISTING 25.6 THE CODE FOR THE INTERFACE OF THE OBJECT IN THE JAVA SERVER

```
package JavaServerForDelphi;

public class DelphiServer extends DelphiCORBA._DelphiServerImplBase
{
  String FName;  public DelphiServer(java.lang.String name)
  {
    super(name);
    FName = name;
  }

  public DelphiServer()
  {
    super();
    FName = "DelphiServer calling from Java";
  }

  public java.lang.String GetName()
  {
    return FName;
  }
}
```

LISTING 25.7 THE CODE THAT BINDS THE JAVA SERVER TO THE ORB

```
package JavaServerForDelphi;

import java.util.*;
```

```java
public class JavaDelphiServer
{
  public static void main(String[] args)
  {
    try {
      org.omg.CORBA.ORB orb = org.omg.CORBA.ORB.init();
      org.omg.CORBA.BOA boa = orb.BOA_init();
      DelphiCORBA.DelphiServer implObject =
      ➥new DelphiServer("DelphiServer");
      boa.obj_is_ready(implObject);
      System.out.println(implObject+ " is ready.");
      boa.impl_is_ready();
    }
    catch (Exception e) {
      e.printStackTrace();
    }
  }
}
```

LISTING 25.8 THE DELPHI CLIENT THAT CALLS THE SERVER

```delphi
unit MainClient;

interface

uses
  Windows, Messages, SysUtils,
  Classes, Graphics, Controls,
  Forms, Dialogs, StdCtrls;

type
  TForm1 = class(TForm)
    JavaServerBtn: TButton;
    Edit1: TEdit;
    procedure JavaServerBtnClick(Sender: TObject);
  end;

var
  Form1: TForm1;

implementation

uses
  CorbaObj, CorbInit;

{$R *.DFM}

procedure TForm1.JavaServerBtnClick(Sender: TObject);
var
```

25

DELPHI, JAVA,
AND C++

continues

LISTING 25.8   CONTINUED

```
 DynamicFactory: TAny;
begin
 DynamicFactory := Orb.Bind('IDL:DelphiCORBA/DelphiServer:1.0');
 Edit1.Text := DynamicFactory.GetName;
end;

end.
```

The Java server shows up in a simple command-line window. It contains nothing more to see than a few simple lines of text, as shown in Figure 25.2. To access the server, you use a very simple Delphi client, as shown in Figure 25.3.

FIGURE 25.2

The Java server appears in a text window.

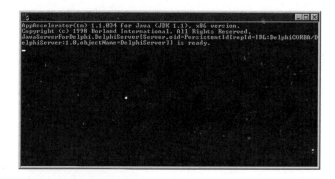

FIGURE 25.3

The Delphi client has a button and edit control. The program retrieves a string from the server.

Before the Delphi client will work using dynamic binding, you have to set up the Interface Repository. You must do so because CORBA cannot dynamically invoke a method unless it knows the parameters to pass to the method. The only way that CORBA can learn the parameters is if you put them in the Interface Repository. To do so, go to the command prompt and type the following line:

```
irep MyStuff JavaServerForDelphi.idl
```

This code starts the VisiBroker `irep` utility. It gives the session of `irep` that you are creating the name `MyStuff` and passes in the name of the IDL file for your project.

On the `irep` GUI is a button called Lookup. If all goes well, you should be able to click this button to see a version of the IDL for the Java server. This procedure was explained in more depth in the preceding chapter.

The IDL for the server describes a single simple interface with a method called `GetName` in it:

```
module DelphiCORBA
{
  interface DelphiServer
  {
    wstring GetName();
  };
};
```

This time you have to write the IDL by hand, as there is no Type Library Editor on the JBuilder side of the equation. For that matter, I'm not sure you can find any other Type Library Editors anywhere in the industry. Delphi's IDL tool is unique and extremely useful.

You could enter IDL this simple in the Delphi Type Library Editor so that you could see how to perform static binding to the Java server. However, I am not going to do that here because most servers will be more complicated than this and, therefore, more likely candidates for dynamic binding than for static binding. To put the matter slightly differently, the developers of Delphi 4 Client/Server expect you to bind to your servers using dynamic invocation. At the time of this writing, this approach is the recommended way to proceed when working with Delphi 4.

You should do the same thing with this IDL file that you did with the Delphi-generated IDL in the previous example. That is, add it to a new JBuilder project, right-click on it, and choose Make to auto-generate a number of Java source files.

One of the files you create will be a sample implementation of your server called `_example_DelphiServer.java`. If this file is not created automatically, right-click on the IDL file inside JBuilder, choose IDL Properties from the menu, and make sure the Generate sample implementation option is checked.

The `_example_DelphiServer` file is read only, so you can't edit it. Instead, copy it to the Clipboard and then create a new file called `DelphiServer.java` based on this example. The file you want to create is shown in Listing 25.6. Notice in particular that I have changed the name of the class that was auto-generated and that I wrote a few lines of code to properly implement my methods.

25

DELPHI, JAVA, AND C++

> **NOTE**
>
> I have heard some users say that they like to generate the sample files, copy them to a separate directory, and then regenerate the IDL without the examples. These users told me that this helped them avoid naming conflicts and made it easier to cut and paste without the need to modify names.
>
> The main point here is not which specific technique you use, but only that you understand what needs to be done and that you find some way to do it.

`DelphiServer.java` has two key methods in it. The first is the constructor, which assigns a string to an internal datastore:

```
public DelphiServer()
{
  super();
  FName = "DelphiServer calling from Java";
}
```

The second method is the implementation of the `GetName` routine:

```
public java.lang.String GetName()
{
  return FName;
}
```

As you can see, this method does nothing more than return the string you initialized in the constructor.

After you have declared the implementation for your server object, JBuilder will automatically wrap it in a server object for you. To accomplish this goal, choose File, New, VisiBroker, Corba Server from the JBuilder menu. A dialog, as shown in Figure 25.4, will appear with a default name for your server. I ended up saving this file, shown in Listing 25.7, under the name `JavaDelphiServer.java`.

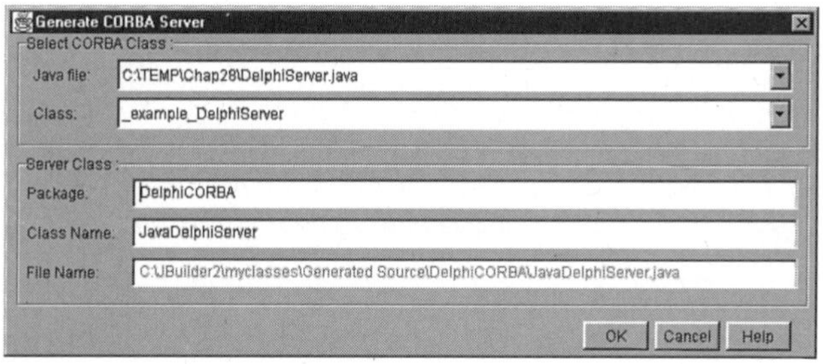

FIGURE 25.4

The dialog JBuilder shows the user when it is about to auto-generate the code for a CORBA server.

The code in `JavaDelphiServer.java` is designed to register the server with the ORB when the server gets loaded into memory. This code accomplishes the task:

```
org.omg.CORBA.ORB orb = org.omg.CORBA.ORB.init();
org.omg.CORBA.BOA boa = orb.BOA_init();
DelphiCORBA.DelphiServer implObject = new DelphiServer("DelphiServer");
boa.obj_is_ready(implObject);
System.out.println(implObject+ " is ready.");
boa.impl_is_ready();
```

The first line of code initializes the ORB. The second retrieves an instance of the BOA from the ORB. The third line creates an instance of the server. The fourth line tells the ORB that the interface supported by the `DelphiServer` object is ready to use. The final line in the program starts a loop that keeps repeating until your server is taken out of memory.

At this stage, the server is built, and you can simply launch it from the JBuilder IDE. It creates a text window stating that the server is ready. Then the VisiBroker loop kicks in, and the server just sits there waiting for a client to call on it.

On the client side, writing a simple Delphi method that will call the server is extremely easy:

```
procedure TForm1.JavaServerBtnClick(Sender: TObject);
var
  DynamicObject: TAny;
 begin
  DynamicObject := Orb.Bind('IDL:DelphiCORBA/DelphiServer:1.0');
  Edit1.Text := DynamicObject.GetName;
end;
```

This code declares a variable called `DynamicObject` as a `TAny`. In Delphi Client/Server, a `TAny` is just a `Variant`. As a result, it supports late binding, just as a `Variant` does in COM. A single line of code will bind you to the object you created. The string you pass in to the `bind` method is found in the auto-generated `DelphiServerHelper.java` file from your JBuilder project.

After you have an instance of your object, you can simply call the `GetName` method directly off it. As you can see, Delphi translates the string into something that you can use in an Object Pascal program. Remember that none of this will work unless you have the Smart Agent running and unless you have properly set up the Interface Repository.

In the next section, I will show you the same type of code, but this time I'll be working with C++Builder.

Calling a Delphi CORBA Server from C++Builder

The process you go through when calling a Delphi CORBA server from C++ is very similar to the one you go through when calling the server from Java. In particular, you run IDL2CPP on the IDL from the Delphi server and then create a program that calls the bind method from that server. IDL2CPP does not come with Delphi, but if you have the C++ version of the CORBA ORB, then you will have a copy of the file.

> **NOTE**
>
> If you are working with C++Builder 3 and VisiBroker 3.2, you might get a series of access violations and the message Object Not Found when you first run your C++ client or server. You can ignore these messages. In fact, you can hush them up by choosing Tools, Environment Options, Debugger, Exceptions, Handled By, User Program from the Delphi menu. This problem occurred with the first release of this technology, and it has most likely been cleaned up by the time you read this chapter.
>
> You may also want to turn off the Dynamic RTL in the C++Builder, Project, Options, Linker page.

The C++ example shown here is again running against the Delphi CorbaTestObject program created in the preceding chapter, and found in the CorbaTest1/Server directory. This means you should use the IDL from that project when you are running IDL2CPP:

```
module CorbaTestServer1
{

  interface ICorbaTestObject
  {
    wstring GetName();
    wstring Bark();
  };

  interface CorbaTestObjectFactory
  {
    ICorbaTestObject CreateInstance(in string InstanceName);
  };

};
```

As I pointed out earlier in the chapter, the IDL you use to make this program work is generated automatically in the Delphi Type Library Editor if you click on the icon at the far right of the toolbar. If you don't see the toolbar, right-click on the Type Library Editor and select the option to make the toolbar visible. You can then convert that IDL to C++ code by running IDL2CPP and passing in the IDL as the program's sole parameter.

When you run IDL2CPP, four files will be generated. Two are the header and implementation for a CORBA server based on the IDL you supply. These two files have names that end in _s. The other two files are the header and implementation for a CORBA client based on the IDL you supply. These latter two files have names that end in _c. In this particular case, they will be named CorbaTestServer1_c.cc and CorbaTestServer1_c.hh.

As you have seen, these lengthy, difficult-to-read source files have funny extensions such as .hh and .cc rather than .h and .cpp. I simply rename the files to give them normal extensions and then do what I can to format them in a manner that I find semi-readable.

Despite the formidable initial appearance of these files, working with them is not difficult. As you will see over the next few pages, you have to write only a few lines of very simple code to create a C++Builder client. Most of the code in the auto-generated files can be ignored, and indeed, most of it is generated out of a desire to provide you with all the possible services you could need from the client or server. Most of these services can be ignored in a simple program, but knowing they are available is nice.

Listings 25.9 through 25.11 are designed to give you some sense of the code involved in creating your BCB project. I have included all the important code that you must create inside BCB. However, due to space limitations, I have included only the header from the client program from the four files that are auto-generated when you run IDL2CPP. Take a look at the code, and then I will explain why it takes this shape and how you can use it.

Listing 25.9 The Header the C++Builder Program That Calls the CORBA Server

```
//////////////////////////////////////////
//          File: Main.h
// Description: BCBCorbaTest.dpr
// Copyright 1998 by Charlie Calvert
//
#ifndef MainH
#define MainH
#include <Classes.hpp>
#include <Controls.hpp>
#include <StdCtrls.hpp>
#include <Forms.hpp>

class TForm1 : public TForm
```

continues

LISTING 25.9   CONTINUED

```
{
__published:
    TEdit *Edit1;
    TButton *CallCorbaBtn;
    void __fastcall CallCorbaBtnClick(TObject *Sender);
private:
public:
    __fastcall TForm1(TComponent* Owner);
};

extern PACKAGE TForm1 *Form1;

#endif
```

LISTING 25.10   THE MAIN FORM FOR THE C++ PROGRAM THAT CALLS THE DELPHI
CORBA SERVER

```
//////////////////////////////////////////
//          File: Main.cpp
// Description: BCBCorbaTest main form
// Copyright 1998 by Charlie Calvert
//
#include <vcl.h>
#pragma hdrstop
#include "Main.h"
#include "CorbaTestServer1_C.hh"
#pragma package(smart_init)
#pragma resource "*.dfm"

TForm1 *Form1;

//-------------------------------------------------------------------------
// Constructor
//-------------------------------------------------------------------------
__fastcall TForm1::TForm1(TComponent* Owner)
    : TForm(Owner)
{
}

char * const * argV;
int argC;

//-------------------------------------------------------------------------
// Button2Click
//-------------------------------------------------------------------------
void __fastcall TForm1::CallCorbaBtnClick(TObject *Sender)
{
```

```
    CorbaTestObjectFactory_ptr Foo;

    CORBA::ORB_var orb = CORBA::ORB_init(argC, argV);
    Foo = CorbaTestObjectFactory::_bind("CorbaTestObject");
    ICorbaTestObject* Goo = Foo->CreateInstance("CorbaTest");
    Edit1->Text = Goo->GetName();
}
```

LISTING 25.11 THE HEADER FOR THE CLIENT CODE THAT IS AUTO-GENERATED WHEN YOU RUN IDL2CPP: CorbaTestServer1_c.h

```
#ifndef _CorbaTestServer1_c_hh
#define _CorbaTestServer1_c_hh

/***********************************************************************
 *                                                                     *
 *                        -- DO NOT MODIFY --                          *
 * This file is automatically generated by the VisiBroker IDL compiler.*
 * Generated code conforms to OMG's IDL-to-C++ 1.1 mapping as specified*
 * in OMG Document Number: 96-01-13                                    *
 *                                                                     *
 * VisiBroker is copyrighted by Visigenic Software, Inc.               *
 ***********************************************************************/

#include "corba.h"

class CorbaTestServer1
{
public:

#ifndef _CorbaTestServer1_ICorbaTestObject_var_
#define _CorbaTestServer1_ICorbaTestObject_var_

  class ICorbaTestObject;
  typedef ICorbaTestObject* ICorbaTestObject_ptr;
  typedef ICorbaTestObject_ptr ICorbaTestObjectRef;

  friend VISistream& operator>>(VISistream&, ICorbaTestObject_ptr&);
  friend VISostream& operator<<(VISostream&, const ICorbaTestObject_ptr);

  class ICorbaTestObject_out;

  class ICorbaTestObject_var: public CORBA::_var
  {
    friend class ICorbaTestObject_out;

  private:
    ICorbaTestObject_ptr _ptr;
```

continues

LISTING 25.11 CONTINUED

```cpp
public:
  void operator=(const ICorbaTestObject_var& _v)
  {
    if ( _ptr ) _release(_ptr);
    if ( _v._ptr )
      _ptr = _duplicate(_v._ptr);
    else
      _ptr = (ICorbaTestObject_ptr)NULL;
  }

  static ICorbaTestObject_ptr _duplicate(ICorbaTestObject_ptr);
  static void _release(ICorbaTestObject_ptr);

  ICorbaTestObject_var();
  ICorbaTestObject_var(ICorbaTestObject_ptr);
  ICorbaTestObject_var(const ICorbaTestObject_var&);
  ~ICorbaTestObject_var();
  ICorbaTestObject_var& operator=(ICorbaTestObject_ptr);
  operator ICorbaTestObject_ptr() const { return _ptr; }
  ICorbaTestObject_ptr operator->() const { return _ptr; }
  ICorbaTestObject_ptr in() const { return _ptr; }
  ICorbaTestObject_ptr& inout() { return _ptr; }
  ICorbaTestObject_ptr& out();
  ICorbaTestObject_ptr _retn() {
    ICorbaTestObject_ptr _tmp_ptr;
    _tmp_ptr = _ptr;
    _ptr = (CorbaTestServer1::ICorbaTestObject_ptr)NULL;
    return _tmp_ptr;
  }
  friend VISistream& operator>>(VISistream&, ICorbaTestObject_var&);
  friend VISostream& operator<<
  ➥(VISostream&, const ICorbaTestObject_var&);
  friend Istream& operator>>(Istream&, ICorbaTestObject_var&);
  friend Ostream& operator<<(Ostream&, const ICorbaTestObject_var&);
  friend VISostream& operator<<
  ➥(VISostream&, const ICorbaTestObject_var&);
};

class ICorbaTestObject_out {
private:
  ICorbaTestObject_ptr & _ptr;
  static ICorbaTestObject* _nil() { return (ICorbaTestObject*)NULL; }
  void operator=(const ICorbaTestObject_out&);
  void operator=(const ICorbaTestObject_var&);

public:
  ICorbaTestObject_out(const ICorbaTestObject_out& _o) :
  ➥_ptr(_o._ptr) {}
  ICorbaTestObject_out(ICorbaTestObject_ptr & _p) : _ptr(_p) {
```

```
     _ptr = _nil();
  }
  ICorbaTestObject_out(ICorbaTestObject_var& _v) : _ptr(_v._ptr) {
      ICorbaTestObject_var::_release(_ptr); _ptr = _nil();
  }
  ~ICorbaTestObject_out() {}
  ICorbaTestObject_out& operator=(ICorbaTestObject_ptr _p) {
      _ptr = _p; return *this;
  }
  operator ICorbaTestObject_ptr& () { return _ptr; }
  ICorbaTestObject_ptr& ptr() { return _ptr; }
  ICorbaTestObject_ptr operator->() { return _ptr; }
};


#endif

  class ICorbaTestObject : public virtual CORBA_Object
  {
  private:
    static const CORBA::TypeInfo _class_info;
    ICorbaTestObject(const ICorbaTestObject&){ _root = this; }
    void operator=(const ICorbaTestObject&){}

  protected:
    ICorbaTestObject_ptr _root;
    void set_root(ICorbaTestObject_ptr root)
    {
      _root = root;
    }

  public:

    static  const CORBA::TypeInfo *_desc();
    virtual const CORBA::TypeInfo *_type_info() const;
    virtual void *_safe_narrow(const CORBA::TypeInfo& ) const;
    static CORBA::Object *_factory();

    ICorbaTestObject_ptr _this();
  protected:

    ICorbaTestObject(const char *obj_name = NULL):
    ➥CORBA_Object(obj_name, 1)
    {
      _root = this;
    }
  public:
    virtual ~ICorbaTestObject() {}
```

continues

LISTING 25.11 CONTINUED

```
    static ICorbaTestObject_ptr _duplicate(ICorbaTestObject_ptr _obj)
    {
      if ( _obj ) _obj->_ref();
      return _obj;
    }
    static ICorbaTestObject_ptr _nil()
    ➥{ return (ICorbaTestObject_ptr)NULL; }
    static ICorbaTestObject_ptr _narrow(CORBA::Object *_obj);
    static ICorbaTestObject_ptr _clone(ICorbaTestObject_ptr _obj)
    {
      CORBA::Object_var _obj_var(__clone(_obj));
#if defined(_HPCC_BUG)
      return _narrow(_obj_var.operator CORBA::Object_ptr());
#else
      return _narrow(_obj_var);
#endif

    }

    static ICorbaTestObject_ptr _bind(
        const char *_object_name = NULL,
        const char *_host_name = NULL,
        const CORBA::BindOptions* _opt = NULL,
        CORBA::ORB_ptr _orb = NULL);

    virtual CORBA::WChar* GetName();

    virtual CORBA::WChar* Bark();

    friend VISistream& operator>>
      (VISistream& _strm, ICorbaTestObject_ptr& _obj);
    friend VISostream& operator<<(VISostream&
      _strm, const ICorbaTestObject_ptr _obj);
    friend Ostream& operator<<(Ostream& _strm,
      const ICorbaTestObject_ptr _obj)
    {
      _strm << (CORBA::Object_ptr)_obj;
      return _strm;
    }

    friend Istream& operator>>
    ➥(Istream& _strm, ICorbaTestObject_ptr& _obj)
    {
      VISistream _istrm(_strm);
      _istrm >> _obj;
      return _strm;
    }

};
```

```
#ifndef _CorbaTestServer1_CorbaTestObjectFactory_var_
#define _CorbaTestServer1_CorbaTestObjectFactory_var_

  class CorbaTestObjectFactory;
  typedef CorbaTestObjectFactory* CorbaTestObjectFactory_ptr;
  typedef CorbaTestObjectFactory_ptr CorbaTestObjectFactoryRef;

  friend VISistream& operator>>
  ➥(VISistream&, CorbaTestObjectFactory_ptr&);
  friend VISostream& operator<<(VISostream&,
    const CorbaTestObjectFactory_ptr);

  class CorbaTestObjectFactory_out;

  class CorbaTestObjectFactory_var: public CORBA::_var
  {
    friend class CorbaTestObjectFactory_out;

  private:
    CorbaTestObjectFactory_ptr _ptr;

  public:
    void operator=(const CorbaTestObjectFactory_var&_v)
    {
      if ( _ptr ) _release(_ptr);
      if ( _v._ptr )
        _ptr = _duplicate(_v._ptr);
      else
        _ptr = (CorbaTestObjectFactory_ptr)NULL;
    }

    static CorbaTestObjectFactory_ptr _duplicate
    ➥(CorbaTestObjectFactory_ptr);
    static void _release(CorbaTestObjectFactory_ptr);

    CorbaTestObjectFactory_var();
    CorbaTestObjectFactory_var(CorbaTestObjectFactory_ptr);
    CorbaTestObjectFactory_var(const CorbaTestObjectFactory_var&);
    ~CorbaTestObjectFactory_var();
    CorbaTestObjectFactory_var& operator=(CorbaTestObjectFactory_ptr);
    operator CorbaTestObjectFactory_ptr() const { return _ptr; }
    CorbaTestObjectFactory_ptr operator->() const { return _ptr; }
    CorbaTestObjectFactory_ptr in() const { return _ptr; }
    CorbaTestObjectFactory_ptr& inout() { return _ptr; }
    CorbaTestObjectFactory_ptr& out();
    CorbaTestObjectFactory_ptr _retn()
    {
```

25

DELPHI, JAVA,
AND C++

continues

LISTING 25.11 CONTINUED

```
      CorbaTestObjectFactory_ptr _tmp_ptr;
      _tmp_ptr = _ptr;
      _ptr = (CorbaTestServer1::CorbaTestObjectFactory_ptr)NULL;
      return _tmp_ptr;
    }
  friend VISistream& operator>>
  ➡(VISistream&, CorbaTestObjectFactory_var&);
  friend VISostream& operator<<(VISostream&,
    const CorbaTestObjectFactory_var&);
  friend Istream& operator>>(Istream&, CorbaTestObjectFactory_var&);
  friend Ostream& operator<<
  ➡(Ostream&, const CorbaTestObjectFactory_var&);
  friend VISostream& operator<<(VISostream&,
    const CorbaTestObjectFactory_var&);
};


class CorbaTestObjectFactory_out
{
private:
  CorbaTestObjectFactory_ptr & _ptr;
  static CorbaTestObjectFactory* _nil()
  {
    return (CorbaTestObjectFactory*)NULL;
  }
  void operator=(const CorbaTestObjectFactory_out&);
  void operator=(const CorbaTestObjectFactory_var&);

public:
  CorbaTestObjectFactory_out(const CorbaTestObjectFactory_out& _o):
    _ptr(_o._ptr) {}
  CorbaTestObjectFactory_out(CorbaTestObjectFactory_ptr & _p) :
  ➡_ptr(_p)
  {
    _ptr = _nil();
  }
  CorbaTestObjectFactory_out(CorbaTestObjectFactory_var& _v) :
  ➡_ptr(_v._ptr)
  {
      CorbaTestObjectFactory_var::_release(_ptr); _ptr = _nil();
  }
  ~CorbaTestObjectFactory_out() {}
  CorbaTestObjectFactory_out& operator=(CorbaTestObjectFactory_ptr _p)
  {
      _ptr = _p; return *this;
  }
  operator CorbaTestObjectFactory_ptr& () { return _ptr; }
  CorbaTestObjectFactory_ptr& ptr() { return _ptr; }
  CorbaTestObjectFactory_ptr operator->() { return _ptr; }
```

```
    };


#endif
    class CorbaTestObjectFactory : public virtual CORBA_Object
    {
    private:
      static const CORBA::TypeInfo _class_info;
      CorbaTestObjectFactory(const CorbaTestObjectFactory&)
      {
        _root = this;
      }
      void operator=(const CorbaTestObjectFactory&){}

    protected:
      CorbaTestObjectFactory_ptr _root;
      void set_root(CorbaTestObjectFactory_ptr root)
      {
        _root = root;
      }

    public:

      static  const CORBA::TypeInfo *_desc();
      virtual const CORBA::TypeInfo *_type_info() const;
      virtual void *_safe_narrow(const CORBA::TypeInfo& ) const;
      static CORBA::Object *_factory();

      CorbaTestObjectFactory_ptr _this();
    protected:

      CorbaTestObjectFactory(const char *obj_name = NULL):
        CORBA_Object(obj_name, 1)
      {
        _root = this;
      }
    public:
      virtual ~CorbaTestObjectFactory() {}

      static CorbaTestObjectFactory_ptr
        _duplicate(CorbaTestObjectFactory_ptr _obj)
      {
        if ( _obj ) _obj->_ref();
        return _obj;
      }
      static CorbaTestObjectFactory_ptr _nil()
      {
        return (CorbaTestObjectFactory_ptr)NULL;
      }
```

25

DELPHI, JAVA, AND C++

continues

LISTING 25.11 CONTINUED

```
    static CorbaTestObjectFactory_ptr _narrow(CORBA::Object *_obj);
    static CorbaTestObjectFactory_ptr _clone
    ➥(CorbaTestObjectFactory_ptr _obj)
    {
        CORBA::Object_var _obj_var(__clone(_obj));
#if defined(_HPCC_BUG)
        return _narrow(_obj_var.operator CORBA::Object_ptr());
#else
        return _narrow(_obj_var);

#endif
    }
    static CorbaTestObjectFactory_ptr _bind(
        const char *_object_name = NULL,
        const char *_host_name = NULL,
        const CORBA::BindOptions* _opt = NULL,
        CORBA::ORB_ptr _orb = NULL);

    virtual ICorbaTestObject_ptr CreateInstance(
        const char* _InstanceName
        );

    friend VISistream& operator>>(VISistream& _strm,
      CorbaTestObjectFactory_ptr& _obj);
    friend VISostream& operator<<(VISostream& _strm,
      const CorbaTestObjectFactory_ptr _obj);
    friend Ostream& operator<<(Ostream& _strm,
      const CorbaTestObjectFactory_ptr _obj)
    {
      _strm << (CORBA::Object_ptr)_obj;
      return _strm;
    }

    friend Istream& operator>>(Istream& _strm,
      CorbaTestObjectFactory_ptr& _obj)
    {
      VISistream _istrm(_strm);
      _istrm >> _obj;
      return _strm;
    }
  };
};

#endif
```

The BCBCorbaTest program has a simple form with one button and one edit control on it, as shown in Figure 25.5. When you click the button, a string is retrieved from the server and displayed in the edit control. The program will not work unless you run the server first and unless you have the OSAgent loaded as a service on NT or as a program on Windows 95/98.

FIGURE 25.5

The BCBCorbaTest *program is shown here after connecting to the Delphi barking dog server, which appears in the background.*

The auto-generated files are quite lengthy, as you can see from glancing through Listing 25.11. However, you need only concentrate on two objects in this file: the first called ICorbaTestObject and the second CorbaTestObjectFactory. If you look carefully, you will see that ICorbaTestObject has two methods called Bark and GetName that give you access to the Delphi implementation of these methods on your server. In other words, they are stub methods that let you call into the server.

CorbaTestObjectFactory also has two important methods. One is called _bind, and the other is called CreateInstance. The first call binds you to the server, and the second is the stub for the Delphi CreateInstance method.

To start creating your client, begin a standard C++Builder application and add a button and an edit control to your form. Rename the button to CallCorbaBtn and create a handler for button click methods.

The code that you write to connect to the server is fairly straightforward:

```
void __fastcall TForm1::CallCorbaBtnClick(TObject *Sender)
{
    CorbaTestObjectFactory_ptr Foo;

    CORBA::ORB_var orb = CORBA::ORB_init(argC, argV);
    Foo = CorbaTestObjectFactory::_bind("CorbaTestObject");
    ICorbaTestObject* Goo = Foo->CreateInstance("CorbaTest");
    Edit1->Text = Goo->GetName();
}
```

You first declare a variable of type CorbaTestObjectFactory_ptr. It will be a pointer to the factory object used by Delphi. The next step is to initialize the ORB. You never actually do anything with the variable you get back, but you must initialize the ORB, or your program won't work. In this case, I don't pass anything in the `argC` and `argV` variables. I simply declare them globally in my program and then never use them:

```
char * const * argV;
int argC;
```

After you have the ORB running, you call `CorbaTestObjectFactory::_bind` to connect to an instance of your object. The `CorbaTestObjectFactory` is auto-generated for you when you run `IDL2CPP`. You pass the name of your object to the `bind` method. As you recall, you can find the name of your object by checking the second parameter to the `CorbaFactoryCreateStub` stub call in the `XXX_TLB` file for your Delphi object.

The factory is just a means enabling you to access the interface to your object. As a rule, CORBA objects don't have a factory like this, but Delphi objects do. As a result, you must call the `CreateInstance` method of the factory, passing in some random string as a parameter to retrieve an instance of your object. After you have the instance, you are at last ready to call the methods of your server.

I'm not going to spend any more time discussing this program, as it is really quite simple. Don't be intimidated by the reams of code auto-generated by `IDL2CPP`. It should be apparent to you, however, that the C++ interface into CORBA is quite rich and has considerable depth. This book, however, is not the place to explore this subject. If you are eager for more information on this subject, one good place to start would be the Visigenic section of the Inprise Web site.

Building a CORBA Server in C++ and Calling It from Delphi

To build a CORBA server in C++, you once again start with an IDL file and run it against `IDL2CPP`. The IDL file I have created for this example, shown in Listing 25.12, is again extremely minimal.

After running `IDL2CPP`, you are again going to get two pairs of files: one set for the client and the other set for the server. The client files will have _c appended to their names, and the two server files will have _s appended to their names. Both sets will have `.hh` and `.cc` extensions, which you can rename if you want. I describe this process in more depth shortly after the listings for the program.

The sample program is kept in the `BCBCorbaServer` directory, and the Delphi client is kept in a directory beneath it called `DelphiClient`. The source code for the server header file generated by `IDL2CPP` is shown in Listing 25.13, and the code for the main form of the BCB server is shown in Listing 25.14. The source for the Delphi client program is shown in Listing 25.15.

LISTING 25.12 THE IDL FOR THE BCB SERVER

```
module BCBCorbaServer
{
  interface BCBCorbaObject
  {
    wstring GetName();
  };
};
```

LISTING 25.13 THE AUTO-GENERATED FILE CREATED BY RUNNING IDL2CPP

```
#ifndef _BCBCorbaServer_s_hh
#define _BCBCorbaServer_s_hh

/**************************************************************************
 *                                                                       *
 *                        -- DO NOT MODIFY --                            *
 * This file is automatically generated by the VisiBroker IDL compiler. *
 * Generated code conforms to OMG's IDL-to-C++ 1.1 mapping as specified *
 * in OMG Document Number: 96-01-13                                     *
 *                                                                       *
 * VisiBroker is copyrighted by Visigenic Software, Inc.                *
 **************************************************************************/

#include "BCBCorbaServer_c.h"


class _sk_BCBCorbaServer
{
public:

  class _sk_BCBCorbaObject : public  BCBCorbaServer::BCBCorbaObject
  {
  protected:

    _sk_BCBCorbaObject(const char *_obj_name = (const char *)NULL);
    _sk_BCBCorbaObject(
        const char *_service_name,
        const CORBA::ReferenceData& _data);
    virtual ~_sk_BCBCorbaObject() {}

  public:
    static const CORBA::TypeInfo _skel_info;

    // No op function to force base skeletons to be linked in
    static void ___noop();
    // The following operations need to be implemented
```

continues

LISTING 25.13   CONTINUED

```cpp
    virtual CORBA::WChar* GetName() = 0;

    // Skeleton Operations implemented automatically

    static void _GetName(
        void *_obj,
        CORBA::MarshalInBuffer &_istrm,
        CORBA::Principal_ptr _principal,
        const char *_oper,
        void *_priv_data);

  };

};

template <class T>
class BCBCorbaServer_tie_BCBCorbaObject :
  public BCBCorbaServer::BCBCorbaObject
{
private:
  CORBA::Boolean _rel_flag;
  T& _ref;

public:
  BCBCorbaServer_tie_BCBCorbaObject(
      T& _t,
      const char *_obj_name=(char*)NULL,
      CORBA::Boolean _r_f=0)
    :_ref(_t) {
    _rel_flag = _r_f;
    _object_name(_obj_name);
    _usesWChar();
  }

  BCBCorbaServer_tie_BCBCorbaObject(
      T& _t,
      const char *_serv_name,
      const CORBA::ReferenceData& _id,
      CORBA::Boolean _r_f=0)
    :_ref(_t) {
    _rel_flag = _r_f;
    _service(_serv_name, _id);
    _usesWChar();
  }

  ~BCBCorbaServer_tie_BCBCorbaObject() { if (_rel_flag) delete &_ref; }

  CORBA::Boolean rel_flag() { return _rel_flag; }
  void rel_flag(CORBA::Boolean _r_f) { _rel_flag = _r_f; }
```

```
  CORBA::WChar* GetName()
  {
    return _ref.GetName();
  }

};


#endif
```

LISTING 25.14 THE MAIN FORM FOR THE BCB SERVER

```cpp
/////////////////////////////////////////
//          File: BCBCorbaServer1.cpp
// Description: Example CORBA Server written in BCB
// Copyright (c) 1998 by Charlie Calvert
//
#pragma hdrstop
#include <vcl.h>
#include <condefs.h>
#include "BCBCorbaServer_s.h"

//-------------------------------------------------------------
USEUNIT("BCBCorbaServer_s.cpp");
USEUNIT("BCBCorbaServer_c.cpp");
USELIB("C:\Program Files\Borland\vbroker\lib\orb_r.lib");
//-------------------------------------------------------------
class BCBCorbaIMPL: public _sk_BCBCorbaObject
{
public:
  BCBCorbaIMPL(const char *object_name=NULL) :
    _sk_BCBCorbaObject(object_name)
  {
  }

  virtual CORBA::WChar* GetName()
  {
    return WideString("BCBCorbaIMPL");
  }
};

#pragma argsused
int main(int argc, char **argv)
{
  try
  {
    // Initialize the ORB and BOA
    CORBA::ORB_var orb = CORBA::ORB_init(argc, argv);
    CORBA::BOA_var boa = orb->BOA_init(argc, argv);
```

continues

LISTING 25.14 CONTINUED

```cpp
    // Create a new account object.
    BCBCorbaIMPL BCBServer("SomeString");

    // Export the newly created object.
    boa->obj_is_ready(&BCBServer);
    cout << "BCBCorbaIMPL object is ready." << endl;

    // Wait for incoming requests
    boa->impl_is_ready();

  }
  catch(const CORBA::Exception& Foo)
  {
    cerr << Foo << endl;
    return(1);
  }
  return(0);
}
```

LISTING 25.15 THE MAIN FORM FOR THE DELPHI CLIENT PROGRAM

```pascal
unit MainClient;

interface

uses
  Windows, Messages, SysUtils,
  Classes, Graphics, Controls,
  Forms, Dialogs, StdCtrls;

type
  TForm1 = class(TForm)
    Edit1: TEdit;
    Button1: TButton;
    procedure Button1Click(Sender: TObject);
  end;

var
  Form1: TForm1;

implementation

uses
  CorbaObj, CorbInit;

{$R *.DFM}

procedure TForm1.Button1Click(Sender: TObject);
```

```
var
  DynamicFactory: TAny;
begin
  DynamicFactory := Orb.Bind('IDL:BCBCorbaServer/BCBCorbaObject:1.0');
  Edit1.Text := DynamicFactory.GetName;
end;

end.
```

Like the Java server you saw earlier, this program does nothing more than open a console window and display a string stating that the server is ready. On the client side, you see a standard Delphi form with an edit control and a button on it. If you click the button, a string is retrieved from the server and displayed in the edit control, as shown in Figure 25.6.

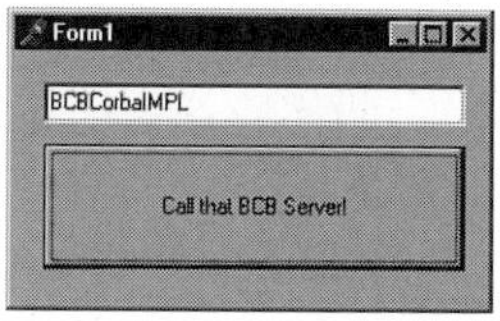

FIGURE 25.6

The BCBCorbaServer *and the Delphi client program are shown as they appear at run-time.*

When creating this program, you need to access Corba.h, declared in the Visigenic\Include directory that comes with the C++ version of the VisiBroker. You also need to link in orb_r.lib, which comes from the lib directory that ships with the C++ version of the VisiBroker. In my program, I have hard-coded the paths to both of these files. Because there is no standard place to install these files, you will almost certainly have to change the paths I use so that they match your system. To do so, you should open the BCB Project Manager and delete my orb_r.lib from the project; then browse across your hard drive to find your copy of this file. You will also need to choose Project, Options and then set the Include path on the Directories/Conditionals page. The Include path should point to the place where corba.h is stored.

After you run the server, you need to set up the Interface Repository. To do so, go to the command prompt and type the following line:

```
irep MyStuff BCBCorbaServer.idl
```

This code starts the VisiBroker irep utility. It gives the session of irep that you are creating the name MyStuff. It then loads the IDL you created into irep by passing in the name of your IDL file. On the irep GUI is a button called Lookup. If all goes well, you should be able to click this button to see a version of the IDL for the BCB server.

As I explained earlier, you need to call irep because CORBA cannot make a dynamic call to an object unless you tell it the parameters of the method. You tell CORBA the parameters of the method by placing the IDL for your object in the Interface Repository. If irep is already started when you launch your server, you can load a new IDL file into it by typing the following line:

```
idl2ir -ir MyStuff BCBCorbaServer.idl
```

Understanding the `BCBCorbaServer`

The key to the server half of this program is the _sk_BCBCorbaObject class that is auto-generated when you run IDL2CPP. This code is the skeleton half of the program; it is the server-side stub code. It is needed to marshal the calls back and forth from the client:

```
class _sk_BCBCorbaObject : public BCBCorbaServer::BCBCorbaObject
{
protected:

  _sk_BCBCorbaObject(const char *_obj_name = (const char *)NULL);
  _sk_BCBCorbaObject(
      const char *_service_name,
      const CORBA::ReferenceData& _data);
  virtual ~_sk_BCBCorbaObject() {}

public:
  static const CORBA::TypeInfo _skel_info;

  // No op function to force base skeletons to be linked in
  static void ___noop();
  // The following operations need to be implemented

  virtual CORBA::WChar* GetName() = 0;

  // Skeleton Operations implemented automatically

  static void _GetName(
      void *_obj,
      CORBA::MarshalInBuffer &_istrm,
      CORBA::Principal_ptr _principal,
      const char *_oper,
      void *_priv_data);
};
```

In this code, the GetName method is declared as virtual abstract:

```
virtual CORBA::WChar* GetName() = 0;
```

Below this declaration is a declaration for the _GetName method, which is the stub method that will call the real instance of GetName. What I am showing you here is the object as it is declared in the header. The actual implementation for the `_GetName` stub method looks like this:

```
void _sk_BCBCorbaServer::_sk_BCBCorbaObject::_GetName(
    void *_obj,
    CORBA::MarshalInBuffer &_istrm,
    CORBA::Principal_ptr _principal,
    const char *_oper,
    void *_priv_data)
{
  VISistream& _vistrm = _istrm;
  BCBCorbaServer::BCBCorbaObject *_impl =
  ➡(BCBCorbaServer::BCBCorbaObject *)_obj;

  CORBA_WString_var _ret = _impl->GetName();

  VISostream& _ostrm = *(VISostream *)
    (CORBA::MarshalOutBuffer*)_impl->_prepare_reply(_priv_data);
  _ostrm << _ret;
}
```

Here you can see the rather mystifying code that calls the real implementation of the `GetName` method off the `_impl` object. In other words, it is not the real implementation of `GetName`; this is the stub code that ends up calling it. If you find this code confusing, you might want to run the server out of the BCB IDE and put a breakpoint on the call to `_impl->GetName`. Now launch the Delphi client, and you will find that it calls this BCB method and that you can step into your real implementation of the `GetName` method in the BCB IDE. I will discuss that implementation in just one moment.

After calling the real `GetName` method, the code then calls `_prepare_reply` and the overloaded `<<` operator to marshal the result back to the client. Note that this code will not work unless you link in the auto-generated code for the client because that is the place where `BCBCorbaObject` is declared. In short, before you can create the server, you must link in all four files auto-generated by `IDL2CPP`.

After the BCB programmer has linked in the auto-generated code, all he or she has to do is create a descendant of `_sk_BCBCorbaServer` and implement the actual `GetName` method:

```
virtual CORBA::WChar* GetName()
{
  return WideString("BCBCorbaIMPL");
}
```

This code will get called from the stub method described earlier in this section. As I stated previously, you can easily step through this code in the debugger if you want to see how it works at runtime.

As you have seen, putting this CORBA server together is fairly simple. The main difficulty is in seeing what you are expected to do and in understanding the logic found in the auto-generated code.

Here is the sole method in the Delphi client:

```
procedure TForm1.Button1Click(Sender: TObject);
var
  DynamicFactory: TAny;
begin
  DynamicFactory := Orb.Bind('IDL:BCBCorbaServer/BCBCorbaObject:1.0');
  Edit1.Text := DynamicFactory.GetName;
end;
```

You have seen this code several times before in this chapter and the previous chapter. It first binds the Delphi client to ORB, thereby establishing a link with the server. The code then calls the GetName method on the server and displays the result to the user in an edit control. Once again, this code will not work properly unless you

- Have the OSAgent running either as a program or as an NT service
- Have first launched the server BCBCorbaServer
- Have first loaded the IDL for the server into the Interface Repository

Summary

In this chapter, you learned how to get Delphi, C++Builder, and Java all working together by creating a series of CORBA servers and clients. You can write the same type of code shown in all the Delphi client programs to talk to C++ or Java servers running on UNIX, the MAC, or on any other operating system that supports CORBA.

The code in this chapter focused on using dynamic invocation to call the Delphi and Java servers. This approach is necessary because Delphi Client/Server version 4 does not include a copy of IDL2PAS. If an IDL2PAS utility is created at some point in the future, it will be relatively simple to statically link to servers, regardless of their language or platform.

In this chapter and the preceding chapter, you looked at Delphi's support for CORBA. At this time, CORBA is the only major cross-platform solution for creating distributed objects. CORBA is, however, in direct competition with DCOM, which is the tool of choice when creating distributed objects on the Windows platform. Watching what happens over the next few years will be interesting as these two technologies struggle for dominance in a marketplace hungry for cross-platform distributed programming solutions.

Game Programming

IN THIS PART

CHAPTER 26

VCL Graphics Classes

by Jeff Cottingham

IN THIS CHAPTER

Many programmers find graphics development to be the most enjoyable type of programming. In fact, I like to say that we are all just frustrated artists at heart. Developing graphics is your chance to exercise your artistic skills inside your own programs and also to have some fun.

Graphics give an application the capability to draw itself on the screen. They can also be used to make an application stand out. For example, if an application takes a long time to initially load, having a splash screen to look at is much nicer than just the Windows desktop.

When I buy a new programming book, the first section I turn to is the one covering graphics. I want to see whether it has any new methods, tips, or tricks that I haven't seen before. In this chapter, which covers Visual Component Library (VCL) graphics classes, I'm going to focus on the following:

- The GDI
- TCanvas
- Brushes
- Pens
- Fonts
- Palettes
- Bitmaps
- Metafiles

By the time you are done with this chapter, you should know how to draw directly on the surface of a form or other component. This knowledge will allow you to create flexible, interesting applications. It will also lay the foundation for more advanced work in graphics. On the CD that accompanies this book, I have also included several additional sections that cover other graphics topics of interest.

The Windows GDI and the VCL TCanvas

In the next few sections of the chapter, I will introduce you to graphics programming using Delphi. In particular, I will focus on the technology used to draw to the screen in Windows. Windows presents this technology to you in a system called the Graphics Device Interface, or GDI. It is presented to you by the VCL in an object called TCanvas and in all the supporting classes of TCanvas. TCanvas wraps the GDI and makes it much easier to use.

Understanding GDI

The GDI is the key to standard graphics programming in Windows. Like any artist, you need to have something to draw, scribble, or paint on. In straight WinAPI programming, this surface is the window itself. You access the surface of that window through the GDI. Remember that everything you need to draw on this window must be accessed through a Device Context.

The GDI function group contains all the necessary functions to allow you to draw on the surface of a window. These functions allow you to draw text, shapes, and bitmaps to the screen. They provide complete control over fonts, colors, line thickness, shading, scaling, orientation, and many other related matters. However, you must do several things before you start drawing.

First, you must get the Device Context, or DC, of the window, do your painting or drawing, and then release the Device Context. This last step is very important because if you don't release the DC, at the very least, you would have a resource leak in your program. At the very worst, you could experience what we at Inprise like to call "the blue screen of death," or in layman's terms, a system crash.

The simple procedure that follows shows how to use the GDI to change a pixel at screen coordinate 10,10 to pure red:

```
Var
    FDC: HDC;
begin
    fDC := GetDC(fHandle);
    SetPixel(fDC, 10,10,RGB(255,0,0));
    ReleaseDC(fHandle, fDC);
end;
```

The first call in this three-step process is GetDC, which returns a Device Context. This function takes one parameter, which is the handle of the window on which you want to draw. Now you are ready to write to the screen. Every time you draw to the screen you must use the Device Context. In particular, you pass the DC as the first parameter of SetPixel. The final call releases the Device Context. If you omit this call, you will have the problems I discussed earlier that can lead to the dreaded blue screen of death.

Most GDI functions take a Device Context in the first parameter. That's the signature of a GDI function.

The VCL Makes Graphics Programming Easy

The VCL provides you with the TCanvas object, which is a wrapper around the GDI. The TCanvas object handles all the DC and resource management for you behind the scenes.

At the same time, it does not make the DC inaccessible. If you need to get at the Device Context, it is always available through the Handle property of the TCanvas object. This property is, in reality, just the handle to the Device Context of the object's canvas. You access it as shown in the following line of code:

```
MyCanvas.Handle
```

A VCL example of the same code snippet in the previous section would be as follows:

```
Canvas.Pixels[10, 10] := clRed;
```

In this code, you are accessing the Canvas property of the main form. In particular, you are accessing the Pixels property of the TCanvas object. Later in the chapter, I will explain the Pixels property in depth, but for now, you can see that it provides an easy way to draw to the screen without your having to worry about Device Contexts.

To you, the programmer, this makes one less thing you have to worry about. It lets you concentrate on the task at hand. Also, using the VCL classes, the amount of code you have to write is diminished. Three lines of code were boiled down to one. This difference might not seem like much, but as your application grows, you will appreciate the terseness of the VCL.

You don't need to understand the underlying workings of the Windows GDI to use the VCL classes. Nevertheless, it is to your advantage to get a good understanding of what is going on behind the scenes.

Working with TCanvas

The TCanvas object is a standard property of classes such as TForm, TGraphicControl, and their descendants. It provides a surface to paint and render objects and controls on.

Because you must first learn to walk before you can run, this chapter focuses on the basics of the TCanvas class. The TCanvas object uses aggregation to encompass a number of graphics-related VCL classes. It gives you access to them through the following properties:

- Brush
- CopyMode
- Font
- Pen
- PenPos
- Pixels
- ClipRect

This list is not exhaustive, but these properties of TCanvas will be covered in this chapter. The code for VCL graphics classes can be found in Graphic.pas. You will be exploring most of these classes in the upcoming chapter.

Here are some guidelines to keep in mind when you first start working with the TCanvas object:

> If you are working inside a form on the form's canvas, you don't need to qualify each reference to the Form's TCanvas object. In other words, you can write the following:

```
Canvas.Rectangle(10, 10, 10, 10);  // This works.
```

> You do not have to qualify the Canvas object by specifying its owner:

```
Form1.Canvas.Rectangle(10, 10, 10, 10); // This works, but is
// unnecessary
```

> If you are using a specific control, such as an Image component, you don't need to declare the control:

```
Image1.Canvas.Pen.Width := 5;
```

> You cannot access a property of the Canvas object directly from a control:

```
Image1.Pen.Width := 5;
```

All the code that follows uses the form's canvas unless otherwise noted.

Exploring and Using Brushes

In the next few sections, you will get a look at the TBrush object. In particular, I will show you four of its most important methods or properties:

- Color
- Style
- Assign
- Bitmap

A brush, or a VCL TBrush object, is a graphics tool that an application uses to paint the interior of polygons, ellipses, or the background of a window or windowed control. Figure 26.1 shows a form that has its Canvas's brush color set to white. You will notice that the entire background of the form is white, and not the default color clBtnFace. To achieve this effect, I simply set the color of the form in the Object Inspector to clWhite. This setting, in effect, changes the Form's brush color to white and paints the background white instead of gray.

FIGURE 26.1

FIGURE 26.1

An example of setting the form's brush to paint the background of the form to white.

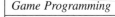

The `TBrush.Color` Property Explored

When using a canvas or objects and shapes on a canvas, you need to specify what color to use to paint or "fill" the canvas or shape. You do so with a brush, or more specifically with a `TBrush` object. You don't need to create a brush, as the VCL has already created one for you to use. The default color of the brush is white and is defined as `clWhite` unless otherwise specified in the `Color` property of the object. For example, a form usually has `clBtnFace` as its default color. A more in-depth discussion of colors and palettes follows later in this chapter. So for now, I will just use some of the predefined Windows colors.

So, how do you go about setting the brush's color to one of your own choosing? This process is very simple and is done through the brush's `Color` property, as shown:

```
Canvas.Brush.Color := clRed;
```

Here is a partial list of predefined colors that you can use: `clBlack`, `clMaroon`, `clGreen`, `clOlive`, `clNavy`, `clPurple`, `clTeal`, `clGray`, `clSilver`, `clRed`, `clLime`, `clBlue`, `clFuchsia`, `clAqua`, and `clWhite`.

The `TBrush.Style` Property Explored

The next property of `TBrush` I need to discuss is its `Style`. The `Style` is what pattern the brush uses when it paints. Table 26.1 shows the predefined patterns that are available to you and can be assigned to the `Canvas`'s brush.

TABLE 26.1   `TBrush` STYLE TYPES

Value	Description
bsSolid	A solid color
bsCross	Intersecting vertical and horizontal lines

Value	Description
bsClear	Transparent
bsDiagCross	Intersecting diagonal lines in both directions
bsBDiagonal	Backward diagonal lines
bsHorizontal	Horizontal lines
bsFDiagonal	Forward
bsVertical	Vertical lines

You set the pattern or style of the brush as shown:

```
Canvas.Brush.Style := bsCross;
```

In Figures 26.2 and 26.3, you can see examples of two of the different types of pattern brushes that are available.

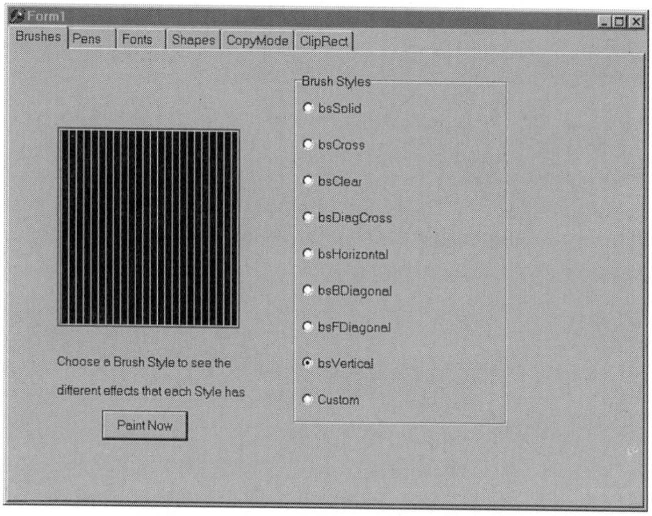

FIGURE 26.2

An example of using the pattern brush style bsVertical *to paint the background of an* Image *component.*

In addition to these predefined patterns, you can also create your own custom patterns stored in bitmap format or use preexisting bitmaps. These custom bitmaps are loaded through the Bitmap property of the brush. Keep in mind that the bitmap that the brush uses is an image that is eight pixels by eight pixels. If the image is larger than this, only the top-left eight-by-eight region is used. Another thing to remember is that if you do use a custom pattern, it will override whatever style you have set. So, after you're done with the custom pattern, you have to do your own cleanup because the brush will not do it for you.

FIGURE 26.3

*An example of
using the pattern
brush style*
bsBDiagonal *to
paint the back-
ground of an*
Image *component.*

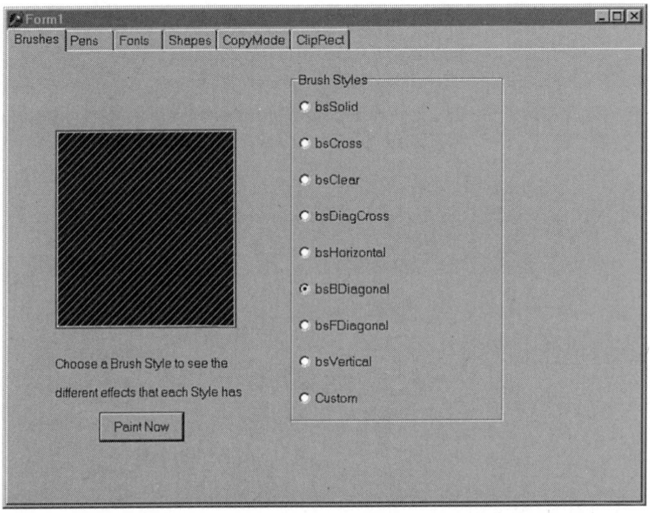

> **NOTE**
>
> Windows bitmaps are simply a binary representation of a graphical image and
> have an extension of .bmp.

The following code snippets show you how to set the brush to a bitmap. The first thing
you have to do is declare a variable of type TBitmap:

```
var
 MyCustomBrush: TBitmap;
```

Next, you need to create an instance of this type, load a bitmap into the instance, and
then make the assignment to the Brush object:

```
MyCustomBrush := TBitmap.Create;
MyCustomBrush.LoadFromFile('MyPattern.bmp');
Canvas.Brush.Bitmap := MyCustomBrush;
```

Always remember to reset this property to NIL and free the bitmap when you are done
with it:

```
Canvas.Brush.Bitmap := NIL;
MyCustomBrush.Free;
```

Figure 26.4 shows an example of an image component with the preceding code in effect.

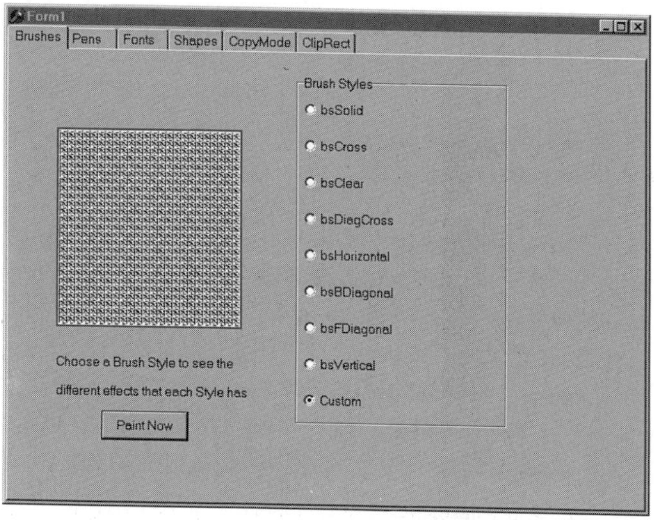

FIGURE 26.4

A custom or bitmapped brush used to paint the background of the Image *component.*

The TBrush.Assign Method Explored

The last thing I need to talk about before moving on is the brush's Assign method. This rather handy feature allows you to copy one brush's contents to another TBrush instance. You can create several custom brushes and work with them at the same time simply by switching brushes. The following example copies the current brush into myBrush. In the following example, it is understood that myBrush was declared in the var section.

```
myBrush := TBrush.Create;
myBrush.Assign(Image1.Canvas.Brush);
```

Now myBrush has all the attributes of the current brush.

Exploring and Using Pens

The TPen object specifies the kind of pen the canvas uses for drawing lines and outlining shapes. The pen has several properties and methods in common with the brush. Both the Color and Style properties and the Assign method function the same way for both the pen and the brush. In the next few sections, I will discuss the properties that are different, which are the following:

- Style
- Width
- Mode

The `TPen.Style` Property Explored

The one of the differences between a pen and a brush is that the pen has different style types. Table 26.2 shows the different pen styles that the pen can assume.

TABLE 26.2 PEN STYLE TYPES

Pen Style	Description
psSolid	A solid line
psDash	A dashed line
psDot	A dotted line
psDashDot	A line consisting of dashes and dots
psDashDotDot	A line consisting of one dash and two dots
psClear	A transparent line
psInsideFrame	A solid line, but one that can use a dithered color if the width is greater than one pixel

The pen styles shown in Table 26.2, with the exception of psSolid, have an effect only when the pen's Width property is set to one pixel. If the width is greater than one, this property is ignored.

The `TPen.Width` Property Explored

The Width property allows you to change the width, in pixels, of a Pen object at runtime. Here's how:

```
Canvas.Pen.Width := 5;
```

This example sets the form's pen width to five pixels. So now every time you draw a line on the form's canvas, the pen width will be five pixels wide.

The `TPen.Mode` Property Explored

The Mode property dictates how the color of the pen interacts with the color of the Canvas. Three factors are taken into consideration when a line is drawn on the canvas:

- The pen color
- The destination color
- The pen mode

The pen mode is known as an ROP (Raster Operation). Table 26.3 describes the different available pen modes. The "Boolean Operation" column uses bitwise operator syntax to show how the pen and surface colors are combined.

TABLE 26.3   Pen Modes, Where (P) Is the Pen Color and (D) Is the Destination on the Canvas

TPenMode	Description	Boolean Operation
pmBlack	Always black	0
pmWhite	Always white	1
pmNop	Unchanged	D
pmNot	Inverse of canvas background color	notD
pmCopy	Pen color specified in Color property	P
pmNotCopy	Inverse of pen color	notP
pmMergePenNot	Combination of pen color and inverse of canvas background	notP or D
pmMaskPenNot	Combination of colors common to both pen and inverse of canvas background	P or notD
pmMergeNotPen	Combination of canvas background color and inverse of pen color	notP or D
pmMaskNotPen	Combination of colors common to both canvas background and inverse of pen	notP and D
pmMerge	Combination of pen color and canvas background color	P or D
pmNotMerge	Inverse of pmMerge: combination of pen color and canvasbackground color	not(P or D)
pmMask	Combination of colors common to both pen and canvas background	P and D
pmNotMask	Inverse of pmMask: combination of colors common toboth pen and canvas background	not(P and D)
pmXor	Combination of colors in either pen or canvasbackground, but not both	P xor D_
pmNotXor	Inverse of pmXor: combination of colors in eitherpen or canvas background, but not both	not(P xor D)

The following code, which demonstrates pmMergePenNot, is in effect for Figure 26.5:

```
Canvas.Pen.Mode := pmMergePenNot;
Canvas.Pen.Color := clRed;
Canvas.Pen.Width := 5;
```

FIGURE 26.5

An example of pen mode pmMergePenNot *with a pen color of* clRed.

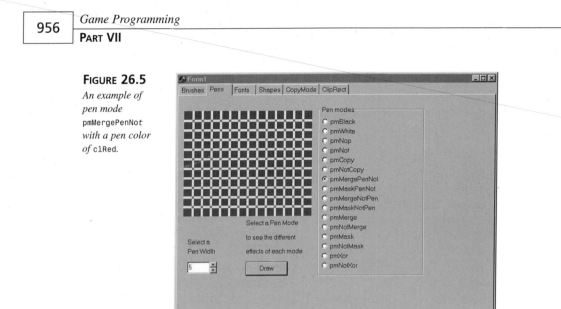

As you can see, where the lines intersect, the result is the pen drawing the inverse of the merging operation with the pen and the surface color. Remember, once you draw something, it then becomes part of the drawing surface. This means that where the lines intersect, you have a red pen color on a red surface and the result of red merging or "anding" with red is red. Now you take the inverse of this merge, and you see the result as shown at the intersection point. If you run the BrushMain program, you can see the different effects that the different modes have. You might also try setting the pen's color to different colors and observing the effects also.

> **NOTE**
>
> The easiest way that I know to learn the effects of the pen mode is to just use them. You can also use a calculator in binary mode to calculate the results that you want and pick the mode that applies.

Exploring and Using Fonts

Just like pens and brushes, fonts are just another type of drawing you can do on the canvas. Fonts are the way you present text on the screen. Fonts are represented in the VCL via the TFont object and are surfaced for your use through the Font property. The font properties that are available for you to use are the following:

- Height
- Size
- Name
- Style

I will discuss the most used font properties and methods in the upcoming sections. Because I have already covered the Color property in the preceding sections, I will start with the Height property.

The `TFont.Height` Property Explored

The Height of a font is simply the height of the font without the internal leading that appears at the top of the font. The Height of a font is measured in pixels. Delphi determines the value of the Height property using this formula:

```
Font.Height := -Font.Size * Font.PixelsPerInch div 72
```

Therefore, whenever you enter a positive value for the Height property, the font's Size property value changes to a negative number. Conversely, if you enter a positive value for the Size property, the font's Height property changes to a negative number. A positive Height includes the internal leading, and negative excludes it.

The `TFont.Size` Property Explored

Because the Size property is relational with the Height, I should talk about it next. The Size property should be something that you are familiar with if you have ever used a word processor. A font's size is just its point size. An example would be 10-point Arial, where 10 is the font's Size property. Delphi calculates size using this formula:

```
Font.Size := -Font.Height * 72 div Font.PixelsPerInch
```

Therefore, whenever you enter a point size in the Size property, you'll notice the Height property changes to a negative value. Conversely, if you enter a positive Height value, the Size property value changes to a negative value. Figure 26.6 breaks down just how a font is put together in Windows.

FIGURE 26.6
Just what makes up a font.

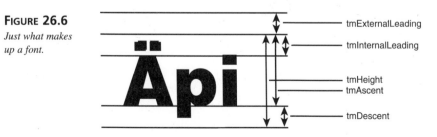

The `TFont.Name` Property Explored

The `Name` property defines the font that is to be used, such as Arial, Times New Roman, and even Wingdings. You can use any preexisting installed font on the system, or you can even create your own custom font. I have found many interesting fonts on the Internet; my favorite one is an Elven font created from the writings of J. R. R. Tolkien. The `Name` property takes an `AnsiString`. In Delphi, you can set the `Name` property by doing this:

```
Canvas.Font.Name := 'Arial';
```

The `TFont.Style` Property Explored

To conclude the discussion of the `TFont` object, you need to visit the `Style` property. Unlike the `Style` property of pens and brushes, which are enumerated data types, the `Style` property of the `TFont` object is a set. By having this property as a set, you can have one or more in effect at any given time. You access this property through the `TFontStyles` data type. You can use these predefined styles:

- `fsBold`
- `fsItalic`
- `fsUnderline`
- `fsStrikeOut`

The following example shows how to set two styles concurrently:

```
var
Fstyle: TFontStyles;

Fstyle := Fstyle + [fsBold,fsUnderline];
Canvas.Font.Style := Fstyle;
```

If you do not understand what a set is, you can find a good explanation in the Delphi online help files, or you can view the source. An important thing to remember is that Search, Find in Files is your best friend when coding. My favorite saying is "Use the Source, Luke. Use the Source."

Exploring and Using `TCanvas.PenPos`

The `PenPos` property is a very simple property. `PenPos` is just a placeholder for the current position of the active pen on the canvas or drawing surface. The pen position is stored in a point structure and can be accessed by the following means:

```
Canvas.PenPos.x;
Canvas.PenPos.y;
```

You can read the current pen position, as shown in the following code:

```
my.x := Canvas.PenPos.x;
my.y := Canvas.PenPos.y;
```

This is the starting point of a line drawn by the LineTo method. You can also write to PenPos, as shown in the following code:

```
Canvas.PenPos.x := my.x;
Canvas.PenPos.y := my.y;
```

Setting the PenPos property is equivalent to calling the MoveTo method. Like I said, PenPos is a very simple property.

Exploring and Using TCanvas.ClipRect

The ClipRect property defines a specific rectangular region that you want to draw in. If you specify a clipping rectangle, no drawing is done outside this region even if the image or shape is larger than the ClipRect. An example would be to define a rectangular region on a canvas that is smaller than the canvas itself and try to draw a larger shape on the canvas that intersects the clipping rectangle. In Figure 26.7, notice that only the portion of the shape that falls within the clipping rectangle is drawn; everything else outside this ClipRect is not drawn.

FIGURE 26.7

An example of creating different clipping regions on the canvas.

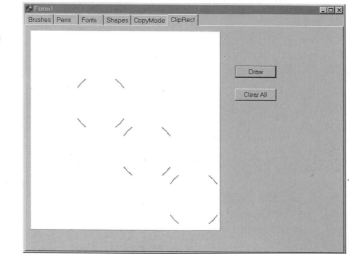

Exploring and Using TCanvas.CopyMode

The CopyMode property is similar to the pen's Mode property. This property determines how an image is copied from one canvas to another. Set CopyMode to affect the way graphical images are drawn onto the canvas. You use the CopyMode when copying an image from another canvas using the CopyRect method. You can create many different effects by using the CopyMode property, including special effects such as merging images and making parts of a bitmap transparent by combining multiple images with different CopyModes. To see the effects of CopyMode, run the MainBrush program, which you can find in the Chapter 26\BrushMain directory on the accompanying CD, and choose the Copy Mode tab. Play with this program to see what it is all about is worthwhile. Table 26.4 shows the different modes that are available.

TABLE 26.4   CopyModeS

CopyMode	Description
cmBlackness	Fills the destination rectangle on the canvas with black.
cmDstInvert	Inverts the image on the canvas and ignores the source.
cmMergeCopy	Combines the image on the canvas and the source bitmap by using the Boolean AND operator.
cmMergePaint	Combines the inverted source bitmap with the image on the canvas by using the Boolean OR operator.
cmNotSrcCopy	Copies the inverted source bitmap to the canvas.
cmNotSrcErase	Combines the image on the canvas and the source bitmap by using the Boolean OR operator, and inverts the result.
cmPatCopy	Copies the source pattern to the canvas.
cmPatInvert	Combines the source pattern with the image on the canvas using the Boolean XOR operator.
cmPatPaint	Combines the inverted source bitmap with the source pattern by using the Boolean OR operator. Combines the result of this operation with the image on the canvas by using the Boolean OR operator.
cmSrcAnd	Combines the image on the canvas and source bitmap by using the Boolean AND operator.
cmSrcCopy	Copies the source bitmap to the canvas.
cmSrcErase	Inverts the image on the canvas and combines the result with the source bitmap by using the Boolean AND operator.

CopyMode	Description
cmSrcInvert	Combines the image on the canvas and the source bitmap by using the Boolean XOR operator.
cmSrcPaint	Combines the image on the canvas and the source bitmap by using the Boolean OR operator.
cmWhiteness	Fills the destination rectangle on the canvas with white.

Exploring and Using
TCanvas.Pixels

To conclude the discussion of the TCanvas properties, I will finish with the Pixels property. The Pixels property allows you either to read the color of the pixel at a specified location inside a clipping rectangle or to change the color of that pixel. You will be using examples of both in the code examples both in this and the following chapter. You set the pixel at the clipping rectangle coordinate 10,10 to the color red like this:

```
Canvas.Pixels[10][10] := clRed;
```

Exploring and Understanding the
TCanvas Methods

An in-depth discussion of the methods of TCanvas is really not necessary as they are better understood when they are put to use. Table 26.5 provides a short description of each method. The sample programs in this chapter and in the Paint program that is included on the CD that accompanies this book show how to implement and use some of these drawing functions.

TABLE 26.5 THE TCanvas METHODS

Method	Description	Function Call
Arc	Renders an arc	Arc(X1,Y1,X2,Y2,X3,Y3,X4,Y4)
Chord	Renders an arc with a line that joins the endpoints of the arc	Chord(X1,Y1,X2,Y2,X3,Y3,X4,Y4)
CopyRect	Transfers part of the image on another canvas to the image of the TCanvas object	CopyRect(Dest,Canvas, Source)

continues

TABLE 26.5   CONTINUED

Method	Description	Function Call
Draw	Draws a graphical image on the canvas	`Draw(X,Y,Graphic)`
Ellipse	Renders an ellipse	`Ellipse(X1,Y1,X2,Y2)`
FillRect	Fills a rectangle	`FillRect(Rect)`
FloodFill FillStyle)	Fills an enclosed area	`FloodFill(X,Y,Color,`
FrameRect	Draws a border around a rectangle	`FrameRect(Rect)`
LineTo	Renders a line	`LineTo(x,y)`
MoveTo	Renders a line	`MoveTo(x,y)`
Pie	Renders a pie-shaped area	`Pie(X1,Y1,X2,Y2,X3,Y3,X4,Y4)`
Polygon TPoints)	Renders a many-sided shape	`Polygon(Points:array of`
PolyLine TPoints)	Connects a series of points on a canvas	`Polyline(Points:array of`
Rectangle	Renders a rectangle	`Rectangle(X1,Y1,X2,Y2)`
RoundRect	Renders a rectangle with rounded image to the size corners	`RoundRect(X1,Y1, X2,Y2,X3,Y3)`
StretchDraw	Fits the graphical of the canvas	`StretchDraw(Rect, Graphic)`
TextHeight	Determines the height a string will occupy in the image	`TextHeight(constText:String)`
TextOut	Writes a string on to the canvas	`TextOut(X,Y,Text)`
TextRect	Writes a string within a limite drectangular region	`TextRect(Rect, X,Y,Text)`
TextWidth	Determines the length a string will occupy in theimage	`TextWidth(Text)`

MainBrush Sample Code

So far you haven't really seen much code, but that situation is about to change. You needed to get a good understanding of the tools you will be using before you started using them. Now I will show just how these tools do the things you want them to do by putting them to practice. So, let's not waste any more time. Listing 26.1 shows the source code for the BrushMain program. Take a moment to familiarize yourself with the code because I will be dissecting and discussing the major functions of this program.

LISTING 26.1   BrushMain.pas

```pascal
unit BrushMain;

interface

uses
  Windows, Messages, SysUtils, Classes, Graphics, Controls, Forms,
  Dialogs, Buttons, ExtCtrls, StdCtrls, ComCtrls;

type
  TForm1 = class(TForm)
    PageControl1: TPageControl;
    TabSheet1: TTabSheet;
    Image1: TImage;
    Label1: TLabel;
    Label2: TLabel;
    RadioGroup1: TRadioGroup;
    Button2: TButton;
    TabSheet2: TTabSheet;
    Image2: TImage;
    Label3: TLabel;
    Label4: TLabel;
    Label5: TLabel;
    Label6: TLabel;
    Label7: TLabel;
    RadioGroup2: TRadioGroup;
    UpDown1: TUpDown;
    Edit1: TEdit;
    Button1: TButton;
    TabSheet3: TTabSheet;
    Image3: TImage;
    Label8: TLabel;
    Label9: TLabel;
    Image4: TImage;
    Label10: TLabel;
    Label11: TLabel;
    GroupBox1: TGroupBox;
    CheckBox1: TCheckBox;
    CheckBox2: TCheckBox;
    CheckBox3: TCheckBox;
    CheckBox4: TCheckBox;
    Edit2: TEdit;
    CheckBox5: TCheckBox;
    TabSheet4: TTabSheet;
    Label12: TLabel;
    Label13: TLabel;
    Panel1: TPanel;
    Image5: TImage;
    Panel2: TPanel;
```

continues

LISTING 26.1   CONTINUED

```
  SpeedButton1: TSpeedButton;
  SpeedButton2: TSpeedButton;
  SpeedButton3: TSpeedButton;
  SpeedButton4: TSpeedButton;
  SpeedButton5: TSpeedButton;
  TabSheet5: TTabSheet;
  Panel3: TPanel;
  Image6: TImage;
  RadioGroup3: TRadioGroup;
  Panel4: TPanel;
  Image7: TImage;
  BitBtn1: TBitBtn;
  BitBtn2: TBitBtn;
  BitBtn3: TBitBtn;
  TabSheet6: TTabSheet;
  Panel5: TPanel;
  Image8: TImage;
  Button3: TButton;
  Button4: TButton;
  procedure RadioGroup1Click(Sender: TObject);
  procedure RadioGroup2Click(Sender: TObject);
  procedure Button1Click(Sender: TObject);
  procedure Button2Click(Sender: TObject);
  procedure FormShow(Sender: TObject);
  procedure Edit2Change(Sender: TObject);
  procedure CheckBox1Click(Sender: TObject);
  procedure FormCreate(Sender: TObject);
  procedure Image5MouseDown(Sender: TObject; Button: TMouseButton;
    Shift: TShiftState; X, Y: Integer);
  procedure Image5MouseUp(Sender: TObject; Button: TMouseButton;
    Shift: TShiftState; X, Y: Integer);
  procedure Image5MouseMove(Sender: TObject; Shift: TShiftState; X,
    Y: Integer);
  procedure SpeedButton2Click(Sender: TObject);
  procedure SpeedButton4Click(Sender: TObject);
  procedure SpeedButton1Click(Sender: TObject);
  procedure SpeedButton3Click(Sender: TObject);
  procedure RadioGroup3Click(Sender: TObject);
  procedure BitBtn1Click(Sender: TObject);
  procedure BitBtn2Click(Sender: TObject);
  procedure BitBtn3Click(Sender: TObject);
  procedure Button3Click(Sender: TObject);
  procedure Button4Click(Sender: TObject);
private
  procedure DrawShape(w,x,y,z: integer);
  procedure Render(x,y: integer);
public
  { Public declarations }
end;
```

```
type
  TEnum = (dsLine,dsRectangle,dsEllipse);

var
  Form1: TForm1;
  Check,Rendering,CanRender: boolean;
  myBrushStyle: TBrushStyle;
  myMode: TPenMode;
  oldstyle: TFontStyles;
  mystyle: TFontStyles;
  TFontHeight: integer;
  Point1,Point2: TPoint;
  dsCurrentShape: TEnum;
  TCopyMode: Longint;

implementation

{$R *.DFM}

procedure TForm1.RadioGroup1Click(Sender: TObject);
begin
      case RadioGroup1.ItemIndex of
            8 : Check := true;
            7 : myBrushStyle := bsVertical;
            6 : myBrushStyle := bsFDiagonal;
            5 : myBrushStyle := bsBDiagonal;
            4 : myBrushStyle := bsHorizontal;
            3 : myBrushStyle := bsDiagCross;
            2 : myBrushStyle := bsClear;
            1 : myBrushStyle := bsCross;
            0 : myBrushStyle := bsSolid;
         end;

end;

procedure TForm1.RadioGroup2Click(Sender: TObject);
begin
    case RadioGroup2.ItemIndex of
        15 : myMode := pmNotXor;
        14 : myMode := pmXor;
        13 : myMode := pmNotMask;
        12 : myMode := pmMask;
        11 : myMode := pmNotMerge;
        10 : myMode := pmMerge;
         9 : myMode := pmMaskNotPen;
         8 : myMode := pmMergeNotPen;
         7 : myMode := pmMaskPenNot;
         6 : myMode := pmMergePenNot;
         5 : myMode := pmNotCopy;
```

continues

LISTING 26.1   CONTINUED

```pascal
        4 : myMode := pmCopy;
        3 : myMode := pmNot;
        2 : myMode := pmNop;
        1 : myMode := pmWhite;
        0 : myMode := pmBlack;
    end;
end;

procedure TForm1.Button1Click(Sender: TObject);
var
    y: integer;
    x: integer;
    i: integer;
begin
    y := 20;
    x := 20;
    Image2.Canvas.Pen.Mode := myMode;
    Image2.Canvas.Pen.Width := StrToInt(Edit1.Text);

    for i := 0 to 9 do begin
        Image2.Canvas.MoveTo(0,y);
        Image2.Canvas.LineTo(Image2.Width,y);
        inc(y,20);
    end;

    for i := 0 to 12 do begin
        Image2.Canvas.MoveTo(x,0);
        Image2.Canvas.LineTo(x,Image2.Height);
        inc(x,20);
    end;
end;

procedure TForm1.Button2Click(Sender: TObject);
var
    CustomBrush: TBitmap;
begin
    if Check then
    begin
        CustomBrush := TBitmap.Create;
        try
          CustomBrush.LoadFromFile('Custom.bmp');
          Image1.Canvas.Brush.Bitmap := CustomBrush;
          Image1.Canvas.FillRect(Rect(3,3,Image1.Width - 3,
          ➥Image1.Height - 3));
        finally
          Image1.Canvas.Brush.Bitmap := NIL;
          CustomBrush.Free;
        end;
        Check := false;
```

```
      end
      else
      begin
         Image1.Canvas.Brush.Style := myBrushStyle;
         Image1.Canvas.FillRect(Rect(3,3,Image1.Width - 3,
         ➥Image1.Height - 3));
      end;
end;

procedure TForm1.FormShow(Sender: TObject);
begin
   Image1.Canvas.Rectangle(0,0,Image1.Width,Image1.Height);
   Image2.Canvas.FillRect(Image2.Canvas.ClipRect);
   Image3.Canvas.FillRect(Image3.Canvas.ClipRect);
   Image4.Canvas.FillRect(Image4.Canvas.ClipRect);
   Image5.Canvas.FillRect(Image5.Canvas.ClipRect);
   Image6.Canvas.FillRect(Image6.Canvas.ClipRect);
   Image7.Canvas.FillRect(Image7.Canvas.ClipRect);
   Image8.Canvas.FillRect(Image8.Canvas.ClipRect);
end;

procedure TForm1.Edit2Change(Sender: TObject);
begin
   myStyle := oldStyle;

   Image3.Canvas.Font.Style := myStyle;

   if CheckBox1.Checked then
   begin
      myStyle := myStyle + [fsBold];
      Image3.Canvas.Font.Style := myStyle;
   end;
   if CheckBox2.Checked then
   begin
      myStyle := myStyle + [fsItalic];
      Image3.Canvas.Font.Style := myStyle;
   end;
   if CheckBox3.Checked then
   begin
      myStyle := myStyle + [fsUnderline];
      Image3.Canvas.Font.Style := myStyle;
   end;
   if CheckBox4.Checked then
   begin
      myStyle := myStyle + [fsStrikeOut];
      Image3.Canvas.Font.Style := myStyle;
   end;
   if CheckBox5.Checked then
```

continues

LISTING 26.1   CONTINUED

```pascal
begin
    Image3.Canvas.Font.Height := TFontHeight - 10;
end
else
begin
    Image3.Canvas.Font.Height := TFontHeight;
    Image3.Canvas.Font.Size := 20;
end;

    Image3.Canvas.FillRect(Image3.ClientRect);
    Image3.Canvas.TextOut(10,20,Edit2.Text);

    Image4.Canvas.FillRect(Image4.ClientRect);
    Image4.Canvas.TextOut(10,20,Edit2.Text);
end;

procedure TForm1.CheckBox1Click(Sender: TObject);
begin
    Edit2.SetFocus;
    Edit2.SelStart := Edit2.SelLength;
end;

procedure TForm1.FormCreate(Sender: TObject);
begin
    Image1.Canvas.Pen.Width := 3;
    Image1.Canvas.Pen.Color := clRed;

    Image2.Canvas.Brush.Style := bsSolid;
    Image2.Canvas.Brush.Color := clBlue;
    Image2.Canvas.Pen.Color := clRed;

    Image3.Canvas.Font.Size := 20;
    TFontHeight := Image3.Canvas.Font.Height;
    oldStyle := Image3.Canvas.Font.Style;

    Image4.Canvas.Font.Size := 20;
end;

procedure TForm1.Image5MouseDown(Sender: TObject; Button: TMouseButton;
  Shift: TShiftState; X, Y: Integer);
begin
    Point1.x := X;
    Point1.y := Y;
    Point2.x := X;
    Point2.y := Y;
    Rendering := true;
end;

procedure TForm1.Image5MouseUp(Sender: TObject; Button: TMouseButton;
```

```
      Shift: TShiftState; X, Y: Integer);
begin
   Rendering := false;
   Image5.Canvas.Pen.Style := psSolid;
   Image5.Canvas.Pen.Mode := pmCopy;
   if CanRender and not Rendering then DrawShape(Point1.x,Point1.y,X,Y);
   if SpeedButton5.Down then
   begin
      Image5.Canvas.Brush.Color := clRed;
      Image5.Canvas.FloodFill(X,Y,clBlack,fsBorder);
      Image5.Canvas.Brush.Color := clWhite;
   end;
end;

procedure TForm1.DrawShape(w,x,y,z: integer);
begin
   case dsCurrentShape of
      dsEllipse : Image5.Canvas.Ellipse(w,x,y,z);
      dsRectangle : Image5.Canvas.Rectangle(w,x,y,z);
      dsLine :
      begin
         Image5.Canvas.MoveTo(w,x);
         Image5.Canvas.LineTo(y,z);
      end;
   end;
end;

procedure TForm1.Render(x,y: integer);
begin
   if CanRender and Rendering and not SpeedButton4.Down then
   begin
      Image5.Canvas.Brush.Style := bsClear;
      Image5.Canvas.Pen.Mode := pmNotXor;
      Image5.Canvas.Pen.Style := psDot;
      DrawShape(Point1.x,Point1.y,Point2.x,Point2.y);
      Point2.x := x;
      Point2.y := y;
      DrawShape(Point1.x,Point1.y,Point2.x,Point2.y);
   end
   else
   begin
      Rendering := false;
   end;
end;

procedure TForm1.Image5MouseMove(Sender: TObject; Shift: TShiftState; X,
   Y: Integer);
begin
   if CanRender then Render(X,Y);
end;
```

continues

LISTING 26.1   CONTINUED

```
procedure TForm1.SpeedButton2Click(Sender: TObject);
begin
   CanRender := true;
   dsCurrentShape := dsEllipse;
end;

procedure TForm1.SpeedButton4Click(Sender: TObject);
begin
   CanRender := false;
   Rendering := false;
   Image5.Canvas.Brush.Style := bsSolid;
   Image5.Canvas.FillRect(Image5.ClientRect);
end;

procedure TForm1.SpeedButton1Click(Sender: TObject);
begin
   CanRender := true;
   dsCurrentShape := dsLine;
end;

procedure TForm1.SpeedButton3Click(Sender: TObject);
begin
   if(Sender as TSpeedButton).Down then CanRender := true;
   if(Sender as TSpeedButton).Name = 'SpeedButton1' then
      dsCurrentShape := dsLine
   else if(Sender as TSpeedButton).Name = 'SpeedButton2' then
      dsCurrentShape := dsEllipse
   else if (Sender as TSpeedButton).Name = 'SpeedButton3' then
      dsCurrentShape := dsRectangle;
end;

procedure TForm1.RadioGroup3Click(Sender: TObject);
begin
  case RadioGroup3.ItemIndex of
      14 : TCopyMode := cmWhiteness;
      13 : TCopyMode := cmSrcPaint;
      12 : TCopyMode := cmSrcInvert;
      11 : TCopyMode := cmSrcErase;
      10 : TCopyMode := cmSrcCopy;
       9 : TCopyMode := cmSrcAnd;
       8 : TCopyMode := cmPatPaint;
       7 : TCopyMode := cmPatInvert;
       6 : TCopyMode := cmPatCopy;
       5 : TCopyMode := cmNotSrcErase;
       4 : TCopyMode := cmNotSrcCopy;
       3 : TCopyMode := cmMergePaint;
       2 : TCopyMode := cmMergeCopy;
       1 : TCopyMode := cmDstInvert;
       0 : TCopyMode := cmBlackness;
```

```
      end;
end;

procedure TForm1.BitBtn1Click(Sender: TObject);
begin
    Image6.Canvas.Brush.Color := clWhite;
    Image6.Canvas.Brush.Style := bsSolid;
    Image6.Canvas.FillRect(Image6.Canvas.ClipRect);
    Image6.Canvas.Brush.Color := clGreen;
    Image6.Canvas.Rectangle(25,25,140,140);
end;

procedure TForm1.BitBtn2Click(Sender: TObject);
begin
    Image7.Canvas.Brush.Color := clWhite;
    Image7.Canvas.Brush.Style := bsSolid;
    Image7.Canvas.FillRect(Image7.Canvas.ClipRect);
    Image7.Canvas.Brush.Color := clBlue;
    Image7.Canvas.Rectangle(60,60,190,190);
end;

procedure TForm1.BitBtn3Click(Sender: TObject);
begin
    Image7.Canvas.CopyMode := TCopyMode;
    Image7.Canvas.CopyRect(Image7.Canvas.ClipRect,Image6.Canvas,
                           Image6.Canvas.ClipRect);
end;

procedure TForm1.Button3Click(Sender: TObject);

var
    myRgn: HRGN;
begin
    MyRgn := CreateRectRgn(100,100,200,200);
    SelectClipRgn(Image8.Canvas.Handle,MyRgn);
    Ellipse(Image8.Canvas.Handle,90,90,210,210);
    Image8.Invalidate;
    SelectClipRgn(Image8.Canvas.Handle,0);
    DeleteObject(MyRgn);

    MyRgn := CreateRectRgn(200,200,300,300);
    SelectClipRgn(Image8.Canvas.Handle,MyRgn);
    Ellipse(Image8.Canvas.Handle,190,190,310,310);
    Image8.Invalidate;
    SelectClipRgn(Image8.Canvas.Handle,0);
    DeleteObject(MyRgn);

    MyRgn := CreateRectRgn(300,300,400,400);
    SelectClipRgn(Image8.Canvas.Handle,MyRgn);
```

continues

LISTING 26.1   CONTINUED

```
    Ellipse(Image8.Canvas.Handle,290,290,410,410);
    Image8.Invalidate;
    SelectClipRgn(Image8.Canvas.Handle,0);
    DeleteObject(MyRgn);
end;

procedure TForm1.Button4Click(Sender: TObject);
begin
    Image8.Canvas.FillRect(Image8.Canvas.ClipRect);
end;

end.
```

If you run the BrushMain program, you can see that you have the beginnings of a fairly simple Paint program. So let's get started looking at Listing 26.1 piece by piece.

The OnCreate Event

Begin by looking at BrushMain's OnCreate event:

```
procedure TForm1.FormCreate(Sender: TObject);
begin
    Image1.Canvas.Pen.Width := 3;
    Image1.Canvas.Pen.Color := clRed;

    Image2.Canvas.Brush.Style := bsSolid;
    Image2.Canvas.Brush.Color := clBlue;
    Image2.Canvas.Pen.Color := clRed;

    Image3.Canvas.Font.Size := 20;
    TFontHeight := Image3.Canvas.Font.Height;
    oldStyle := Image3.Canvas.Font.Style;

    Image4.Canvas.Font.Size := 20;
end;
```

As you can see, I am assigning various values to the Pen, Font, and Brush objects that I am going to use when the form first paints itself. They can always be changed later at runtime, as you will see later in this chapter. You don't need to do this if you are just going to use the default values that are set when each object is created. I am also saving the current values of Image1's Font, Height, and Style properties so that I can use them later to restore the default values after I change them and want to change them back. The defaults will be used later in this program, and this saves you time and effort restoring them.

> **TIP**
>
> I find it is easier to group relevant lines of code together and separate them by a space. Grouping makes the code a lot more readable, but it is based on my own coding style and is a matter of personal preference.

The FormShow Method

Now that I have set the values that I want, I need to address any drawing that I want done when the form first shows itself. I do so in the form's FormShow method:

```
procedure TForm1.FormShow(Sender: TObject);
begin
    Image1.Canvas.Rectangle(0,0,Image1.Width,Image1.Height);
    Image2.Canvas.FillRect(Image2.Canvas.ClipRect);
    Image3.Canvas.FillRect(Image3.Canvas.ClipRect);
    Image4.Canvas.FillRect(Image4.Canvas.ClipRect);
    Image5.Canvas.FillRect(Image5.Canvas.ClipRect);
    Image6.Canvas.FillRect(Image6.Canvas.ClipRect);
    Image7.Canvas.FillRect(Image7.Canvas.ClipRect);
    Image8.Canvas.FillRect(Image8.Canvas.ClipRect);
end;
```

Because all the images' canvases have not been drawn on, I need to initialize them so the Canvas's brush paints them white when the form is shown. You will notice that for Image1 I am using the rectangle function. The result is the three-pixel wide red border drawn around the rectangle. This was just done for demonstration purposes so you could see how the canvas uses the pen to draw the borders of the shapes. As for the rest of the images, I am just filling the ClipRect, which at this point is the largest rectangle that can be drawn on the canvas. You will see later in the code how to adjust the ClipRect to fit your needs if you have to adjust it.

Now look at the code that demonstrates setting the Brush styles:

```
procedure TForm1.RadioGroup1Click(Sender: TObject);
begin
    case RadioGroup1.ItemIndex of
        8 : Check := true;
        7 : myBrushStyle := bsVertical;
        6 : myBrushStyle := bsFDiagonal;
        5 : myBrushStyle := bsBDiagonal;
        4 : myBrushStyle := bsHorizontal;
        3 : myBrushStyle := bsDiagCross;
        2 : myBrushStyle := bsClear;
```

```
      1 : myBrushStyle := bsCross;
      0 : myBrushStyle := bsSolid;
   end;

end;
```

All I am doing in this procedure is setting a brush style into the variable myBrushStyle for use in the next procedure, which follows:

```
procedure TForm1.Button2Click(Sender: TObject);
var
   CustomBrush: TBitmap;
begin
   if Check then
   begin
      CustomBrush := TBitmap.Create;
      try
        CustomBrush.LoadFromFile('Custom.bmp');
        Image1.Canvas.Brush.Bitmap := CustomBrush;
        Image1.Canvas.FillRect(Rect(3,3,Image1.Width - 3,
        ➥Image1.Height - 3));
      finally
        Image1.Canvas.Brush.Bitmap := NIL;
        CustomBrush.Free;
      end;
      Check := false;
   end
   else
   begin
      Image1.Canvas.Brush.Style := myBrushStyle;
      Image1.Canvas.FillRect(Rect(3,3,Image1.Width - 3,
      ➥Image1.Height - 3));
   end;
end;
```

This procedure sets the brush's style on the brush's TabSheet. In this procedure, I am using either one of the stock brush styles or a custom bitmap for the brush. I wrap the code for using the custom brush in a try..finally block. I use this block so the application will not cause an access violation if the LoadFromFile function call fails. I simply catch the exception and handle it. If you want to, you can put a MessageBox in the finally block to let the user know if the application could not load the bitmap. In your own code, you should combine the preceding two procedures into one. I coded them this way for demonstration purposes only. If you combine these two procedures into one, you can eliminate the two global variables Check and myBrushStyle and make them local to the procedure. This is good coding style; you should use global variables only when really necessary. As I said earlier in the chapter, you need to set the brush's bitmap property to NIL when you are done with it.

Setting the Pen Mode

Now look at the code for the Pen's TabSheet:

```
procedure TForm1.RadioGroup2Click(Sender: TObject);
begin
    case RadioGroup2.ItemIndex of
        15 : myMode := pmNotXor;
        14 : myMode := pmXor;
        13 : myMode := pmNotMask;
        12 : myMode := pmMask;
        11 : myMode := pmNotMerge;
        10 : myMode := pmMerge;
         9 : myMode := pmMaskNotPen;
         8 : myMode := pmMergeNotPen;
         7 : myMode := pmMaskPenNot;
         6 : myMode := pmMergePenNot;
         5 : myMode := pmNotCopy;
         4 : myMode := pmCopy;
         3 : myMode := pmNot;
         2 : myMode := pmNop;
         1 : myMode := pmWhite;
         0 : myMode := pmBlack;
    end;
end;
```

This procedure is the same as the brush's style except that I am setting the pen mode in the myMode variable for use in the next procedure:

```
procedure TForm1.Button1Click(Sender: TObject);
var
    y: integer;
    x: integer;
    i: integer;
begin
    y := 20;
    x := 20;
    Image2.Canvas.Pen.Mode := myMode;
    Image2.Canvas.Pen.Width := StrToInt(Edit1.Text);

    for i := 0 to 9 do begin
        Image2.Canvas.MoveTo(0,y);
        Image2.Canvas.LineTo(Image2.Width,y);
        inc(y,20);
    end;

    for i := 0 to 12 do begin
        Image2.Canvas.MoveTo(x,0);
        Image2.Canvas.LineTo(x,Image2.Height);
        inc(x,20);
    end;
end;
```

As with the brush's `TabSheet`, in your own code, you should combine these procedures into one procedure. The preceding code allows the user of this application to set the width of the pen through the spin edit control. I just set the range that he or she can use in the properties of this control. You can see how this was done if you use the Object Inspector to look at its properties. I also used this procedure to introduce you to the `MoveTo` and `LineTo` methods. The first `for` loop draws the horizontal lines, and the next `for` loop draws the vertical lines.

Working with Fonts

Now look at the code for the font's `TabSheet`. Here, you will see the use of the different font properties and methods:

```
procedure TForm1.Edit2Change(Sender: TObject);
begin
   myStyle := oldStyle;

   Image3.Canvas.Font.Style := myStyle;

   if CheckBox1.Checked then
   begin
      myStyle := myStyle + [fsBold];
      Image3.Canvas.Font.Style := myStyle;
   end;
   if CheckBox2.Checked then
   begin
      myStyle := myStyle + [fsItalic];
      Image3.Canvas.Font.Style := myStyle;
   end;
   if CheckBox3.Checked then
   begin
      myStyle := myStyle + [fsUnderline];
      Image3.Canvas.Font.Style := myStyle;
   end;
   if CheckBox4.Checked then
   begin
      myStyle := myStyle + [fsStrikeOut];
      Image3.Canvas.Font.Style := myStyle;
   end;
   if CheckBox5.Checked then
   begin
      Image3.Canvas.Font.Height := TFontHeight - 10;
   end
   else
   begin
      Image3.Canvas.Font.Height := TFontHeight;
      Image3.Canvas.Font.Size := 20;
   end;
```

```
    Image3.Canvas.FillRect(Image3.ClientRect);
    Image3.Canvas.TextOut(10,20,Edit2.Text);

    Image4.Canvas.FillRect(Image4.ClientRect);
    Image4.Canvas.TextOut(10,20,Edit2.Text);
end;
```

This procedure is interesting in that it covers a lot of ground and demonstrates many things that I have previously discussed in concept. The first line of code simply clears all styles that have been previously set in the `myStyle` variable and returns the style to the default values, which I saved in the `OnCreate` event. Next, I assign this variable to the canvas's `Font.Style` property. The next four `if` statements load a style if the check box is checked. I do this with the `[ ]` operator. Remember, with font styles, you are dealing with a set, as I discussed earlier. In the next `if` statement, I am simply playing around with the size and height properties to show you how this works. The last four lines are kind of interesting. What I am doing here is allowing any changes made to the style to show up as the user types in characters in the edit box, making the changes in real-time. The `FillRect` call repaints the image box, and `TextOut` puts the new string on the image's canvas with all the changes in effect.

Drawing Shapes on the Canvas

Now look at the shape's `TabSheet`. A lot is going on in this section, so I will spend a fair amount of time here. The first procedure I would like to discuss is `DrawShape`:

```
procedure TForm1.DrawShape(w,x,y,z: integer);
begin
    case dsCurrentShape of
        dsEllipse : Image5.Canvas.Ellipse(w,x,y,z);
        dsRectangle : Image5.Canvas.Rectangle(w,x,y,z);
        dsLine :
        begin
            Image5.Canvas.MoveTo(w,x);
            Image5.Canvas.LineTo(y,z);
        end;
    end;
end;
```

The whole purpose of `DrawShape` is to just draw the shape that the user has selected on the canvas via the `dsCurrentShape` variable. I will also need it to do my cleanup, as you will see when you look at the `Render` function. But before I describe that process, look at several functions that determine when you should be drawing and when you should not. The following methods decide what to draw:

```
procedure TForm1.SpeedButton1Click(Sender: TObject);
begin
```

```
    CanRender := true;
    dsCurrentShape := dsLine;
end;
```

The preceding method just sets two variables. `CanRender` is a Boolean flag that I set to `True` when a valid shape has been chosen to draw. `dsCurrentShape` is just a placeholder for the shape the user has selected and that I am going to draw. Each shape has its own `Click` method. However, you can combine all the methods into one common method, as shown here:

```
procedure TForm1.SpeedButton3Click(Sender: TObject);
begin
    if(Sender as TSpeedButton).Down then CanRender := true;
    if(Sender as TSpeedButton).Name = 'SpeedButton1' then
        dsCurrentShape := dsLine
    else if(Sender as TSpeedButton).Name = 'SpeedButton2' then
        dsCurrentShape := dsEllipse
    else if (Sender as TSpeedButton).Name = 'SpeedButton3' then
        dsCurrentShape := dsRectangle;
end;
```

Either way is valid coding; however, if you have a lot of different shape values that `dsCurrentShape` can assume, writing a method for each is better. This approach is better because you will encounter a performance hit due to the fact that each value must be evaluated until a match is encountered.

After the user has chosen a valid shape, I must draw it where he or she wants it to be drawn. I will use the `MouseDown` event to set some further values that I need:

```
procedure TForm1.Image5MouseDown(Sender: TObject; Button: TMouseButton;
    Shift: TShiftState; X, Y: Integer);
begin
    Point1.x := X;
    Point1.y := Y;
    Point2.x := X;
    Point2.y := Y;
    Rendering := true;
end;
```

Here, I have two point structures and a Boolean. The `Point1` variable is used to memorize the starting or anchor point of the shape I am going to draw. `Point2` is a placeholder for the current mouse position. `Rendering` is used to let the application know that I can start drawing. As the user starts to move the mouse, I must start drawing, so I will use the `MouseMove` event as follows:

```
procedure TForm1.Image5MouseMove(Sender: TObject; Shift: TShiftState; X,
    Y: Integer);
begin
    if CanRender then Render(X,Y);
end;
```

If a valid shape is chosen, I call the Render function and pass the current mouse position:

```
procedure TForm1.Render(x,y: integer);
begin
  if CanRender and Rendering and not SpeedButton4.Down then
  begin
      Image5.Canvas.Brush.Style := bsClear;
      Image5.Canvas.Pen.Mode := pmNotXor;
      Image5.Canvas.Pen.Style := psDot;
      DrawShape(Point1.x,Point1.y,Point2.x,Point2.y);
      Point2.x := x;
      Point2.y := y;
      DrawShape(Point1.x,Point1.y,Point2.x,Point2.y);
  end
  else
  begin
      Rendering := false;
  end;
end;
```

The first thing I do here is to check to see whether I can draw. CanRender and Rendering work in tandem to determine when I can do something and when I cannot. Without this check, I could be drawing when the user doesn't want to, which might really annoy the user and cause him or her not to use my program again. Next, I set the brush style to bsClear so I do not erase the background; then I set the pen mode to pmNotXor. The Render method demonstrates what is known as *rubber banding*. Notice that DrawShape is called twice. The first call will erase the old image because of the pen mode pmNotXor at the previous location. I then assign the new cursor position to Point2 and call Render again to draw the shape using the current coordinates. This cycle goes on erasing and redrawing until the user lets go of the mouse button.

```
procedure TForm1.Image5MouseUp(Sender: TObject; Button: TMouseButton;
  Shift: TShiftState; X, Y: Integer);
begin
   Rendering := false;
   Image5.Canvas.Pen.Style := psSolid;
   Image5.Canvas.Pen.Mode := pmCopy;
   if CanRender and not Rendering then DrawShape(Point1.x,Point1.y,X,Y);
   if SpeedButton5.Down then
   begin
      Image5.Canvas.Brush.Color := clRed;
      Image5.Canvas.FloodFill(X,Y,clBlack,fsBorder);
      Image5.Canvas.Brush.Color := clWhite;
   end;
end;
```

In the preceding, I draw the final shape. I set Rendering to False so that I won't do any inadvertent drawing, reset the pen to draw the final shape, and draw it at the current position by calling DrawShape one last time. I also check to see whether the user wants to fill a selected area by using `SpeedButton5.Down`, and if this is true, I fill it, in this particular case, with the red brush. I reset the brush color, and I am done.

Using CopyModes

Heading for the home stretch, we come to the `CopyMode TabSheet`. It is so similar to the pen's and brush's sheets that I don't need to discuss all the methods here. The only method that I need to discuss is the following:

```
procedure TForm1.BitBtn3Click(Sender: TObject);
begin
    Image7.Canvas.CopyMode := TCopyMode;
    Image7.Canvas.CopyRect(Image7.Canvas.ClipRect,Image6.Canvas,
                            Image6.Canvas.ClipRect);
end;
```

Here, I am just setting the `CopyMode` to the one that the user has chosen and then copying the rectangle on `Image6`'s canvas to `Image7`'s canvas using this mode.

Modifying the ClipRect

Last is the `ClipRect TabSheet`. It is also very interesting because I need to combine Win32 API calls with VCL code:

```
procedure TForm1.Button3Click(Sender: TObject);

var
    myRgn: HRGN;
begin
    MyRgn := CreateRectRgn(100,100,200,200);
    SelectClipRgn(Image8.Canvas.Handle,MyRgn);
    Ellipse(Image8.Canvas.Handle,90,90,210,210);
    Image8.Invalidate;
    SelectClipRgn(Image8.Canvas.Handle,0);
    DeleteObject(MyRgn);

    MyRgn := CreateRectRgn(200,200,300,300);
    SelectClipRgn(Image8.Canvas.Handle,MyRgn);
    Ellipse(Image8.Canvas.Handle,190,190,310,310);
    Image8.Invalidate;
    SelectClipRgn(Image8.Canvas.Handle,0);
    DeleteObject(MyRgn);

    MyRgn := CreateRectRgn(300,300,400,400);
    SelectClipRgn(Image8.Canvas.Handle,MyRgn);
    Ellipse(Image8.Canvas.Handle,290,290,410,410);
    Image8.Invalidate;
    SelectClipRgn(Image8.Canvas.Handle,0);
    DeleteObject(MyRgn);
end;
```

In this procedure, I am changing the clipping region from the VCL default rectangle that is the whole canvas to one of my own definition. Because the `ClipRect` property is read only, I can't set it directly. I must do some behind-the-scenes work and then let the VCL do its work. First, I need to define a region. I do so with the API call `CreateRectRgn` and pass it the region I want to create. In the fist case, I am creating a 100×100 pixel square region anchored at `100,100` on the canvas. Next, I select this region as the clipping `Rect` by using `SelectClipRgn`. This function takes two parameters: a DC, which in this case is `Image8.Canvas.Handle`, and the region I want to select. Next, I draw my ellipse immediately followed by a call to the `Invalidate` method. This method causes a `WM_PAINT` message to be dispatched, and the VCL reads the `ClipRect`, which is now the region that I defined, and does the drawing accordingly. A second call to `SelectClipRgn` that passes `0` as the second parameter reselects the original clipping region I had prior to my redefining it. Last, I need to do my own cleanup, so I have to make the call to `DeleteObject` to release the region. So there you have a good example of how to mix VCL code with straight Windows API code.

Finally, you can see that the `ClipRect` has indeed been reset to the default value:

```
procedure TForm1.Button4Click(Sender: TObject);
begin
    Image8.Canvas.FillRect(Image8.Canvas.ClipRect);
end;
```

This function call repaints the whole canvas, so the `ClipRect` is back to normal.

A Line by Any Other Name

Up until now, I have used the pen to draw lines. The only property that you could manipulate that would affect how that line was drawn on the canvas was the `Width` property. You could altar how wide the line was drawn but little else. Granted, if the width was one pixel, you could draw dots and dashes also. What if you want to have a custom line, for example, a line that looks as if it were drawn by a calligraphy pen. The fact is, you can draw just about any type of line that you want. The only catch is that it will not be a line at all. About now, some of you might be wondering what I am talking about, drawing a line that is not a line, indeed. But you can create such a line by drawing a series of shapes that are connected so that they appear to be a line. To draw a line that appears and acts like one drawn by a calligraphy pen is really quite simple. You use the canvas method `Polygon` to draw what are called parallelograms. Figure 26.8 demonstrates what a "line" like this would look like.

Remember that a shape method, when called, draws the outline of the shape with the current pen, and then that shape is filled with the current brush. So, if you set both the pen and brush to the same color, you get what appears to be your custom "line," as shown in Figure 26.9.

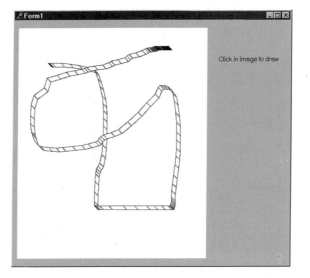

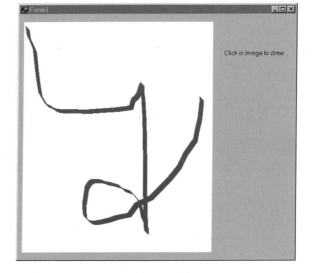

The `PatternMain` program shown in Listing 26.2 will draw calligraphy pen-type lines.

LISTING 26.2   PatternMain.pas

```
//////////////////////////////////////////////////////////////////
//  PatternMain.pas                                              //
//  Project: Pattern                                             //
//  Copyright (c) 1998 by Jeff Cottingham                        //
//////////////////////////////////////////////////////////////////

unit Patternmain;

interface

uses
  Windows, Messages, SysUtils, Classes, Graphics, Controls, Forms,
  Dialogs, StdCtrls, ExtCtrls;

type
  TForm1 = class(TForm)
    Image1: TImage;
    Label1: TLabel;
    procedure Image1MouseDown(Sender: TObject; Button: TMouseButton;
      Shift: TShiftState; X, Y: Integer);
    procedure Image1MouseMove(Sender: TObject; Shift: TShiftState; X,
      Y: Integer);
    procedure Image1MouseUp(Sender: TObject; Button: TMouseButton;
      Shift: TShiftState; X, Y: Integer);
    procedure FormCreate(Sender: TObject);
  private
    { Private declarations }
  public
    { Public declarations }
  end;

var
  Form1: TForm1;
  FRendering: boolean;
  org,next1: TPoint;

implementation

{$R *.DFM}

procedure TForm1.Image1MouseDown(Sender: TObject; Button: TMouseButton;
  Shift: TShiftState; X, Y: Integer);
begin
  FRendering := true;
  org := Point(X,Y);
  next1 := Point(X,Y);
end;

procedure TForm1.Image1MouseMove(Sender: TObject; Shift: TShiftState; X,
  Y: Integer);
```

continues

LISTING 26.2   CONTINUED

```
var
    points: array[1..4] of TPOINT;
begin
    if FRendering then
        begin
        next1 := Point(X,Y);
        points[1] := org;
        points[2] := next1;
        points[3] := Point(next1.x + 8,next1.y + 8);
        points[4] := Point(org.x + 8,org.y + 8);
        Image1.Canvas.Polygon(points);
        org := Point(X ,Y );
    end;
end;

procedure TForm1.Image1MouseUp(Sender: TObject; Button: TMouseButton;
  Shift: TShiftState; X, Y: Integer);
begin
    FRendering := false;
end;

procedure TForm1.FormCreate(Sender: TObject);
begin
    Image1.Canvas.Brush.Color := clRed;
    Image1.Canvas.Pen.Color := clRed;
end;

end.
```

In the `FormCreate` method, I assign the same color to the pen and brush. In the `MouseDown` method, I get the points at which to begin drawing. The real work is done with the `MouseMove` method:

```
procedure TForm1.Image1MouseMove(Sender: TObject; Shift: TShiftState; X,
  Y: Integer);
var
    points: array[1..4] of TPOINT;
begin
    if FRendering then
        begin
        next1 := Point(X,Y);
        points[1] := org;
        points[2] := next1;
        points[3] := Point(next1.x + 8,next1.y + 8);
        points[4] := Point(org.x + 8,org.y + 8);
        Image1.Canvas.Polygon(points);
        org := Point(X ,Y );
    end;
end;
```

In this method, while the mouse is moving and the rendering flag is true, I am drawing a polygon using the ending points of the last polygon as the starting points of the next one.

By using your imagination, you can now draw any style of line that you want to by simply using different shapes, combinations of shapes, pen and brush colors, and pen width. You can even use bitmap brushes to fill the shapes. To put this information into perspective, you should now see that anything is possible.

Looking Deeper into the VCL

In the next section, I will drill down a little bit further into the VCL and look at some of the basics that all graphical programming is built upon.

From there, I will move on to discuss some of the higher-level VCL graphical container classes. Finally, I will show you some sample code on how to manipulate bitmaps.

An In-Depth Look at `TColor`

The `TColor` type is one of the most basic VCL types. Most of the upper-level classes are built on this fundamental type.

In Windows programming, colors are defined as RGB values. This means that you have three base colors—red, green, and blue—each having a value from 0 to 255. These values make up all the different colors that you see on your screen. The following is how `TColor` is declared in the VCL source:

```
type TColor = -$7FFFFFFF-1..$7FFFFFFF;
```

This declaration tells you that the value stored in `TColor` is a hex value. The low three bytes represent RGB color intensities for blue, green, and red, respectively.

The value `00FF0000` represents full-intensity, pure blue; `0000FF00` is pure green; and `000000FF` is pure red. `00000000` is black, and `00FFFFFF` is white.

If the highest-order byte is zero (`00`), the color obtained is the closest matching color in the system palette. If the highest-order byte is one (`01`), the color obtained is the closest matching color in the currently realized palette. If the highest-order byte is two (`02`), the value is matched with the nearest color in the logical palette of the current device context.

`Graphics.pas` contains definitions of useful constants for `TColor`. For example, some of the definitions include `clBlue`, `clGreen`, and `clRed`. These constants map either directly to the closest matching color in the system palette (for example, `clBlue` maps to blue) or to the corresponding system screen element color defined in the Appearance section of the Windows Control Panel Icon Display. For example, `clBtnFace` maps to the system color for button faces. If you do not know what a palette is, I'll discuss them shortly.

You can make an assignment to any object that has a color property by using the hexadecimal value of a color, as shown here:

```
Form1.Color := $00C700  // a shade of green
```

Or you can make a direct assignment into the `Color` property of an object in the Object Inspector, as shown in Figure 26.10.

FIGURE 26.10

Making a direct color assignment in the Object Inspector.

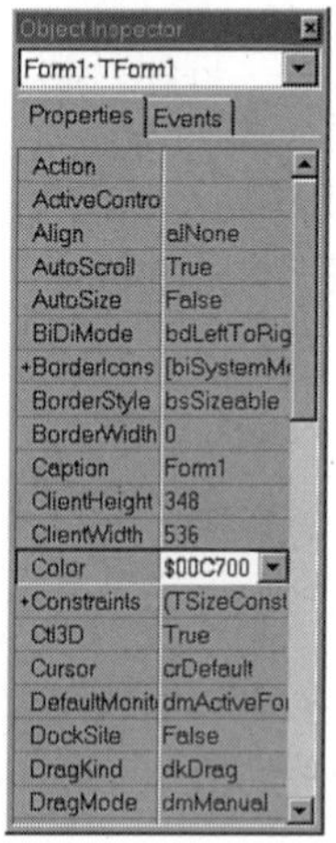

The constants that map to the closest matching system colors are `clAqua`, `clBlack`, `clBlue`, `clDkGray`, `clFuchsia`, `clGray`, `clGreen`, `clLime`, `clLtGray`, `clMaroon`, `clNavy`, `clOlive`, `clPurple`, `clRed`, `clSilver`, `clTeal`, `clWhite`, and `clYellow`.

The constants that map to the system screen element colors are `clActiveBorder`, `clActiveCaption`, `clAppWorkSpace`, `clBackground`, `clBtnFace`, `clBtnHighlight`, `clBtnShadow`, `clBtnText`, `clCaptionText`, `clGrayText`, `clHighlight`, `clHighlightText`, `clInactiveBorder`, `clInactiveCaption`, `clInactiveCaptionText`, `clMenu`, `clMenuText`, `clScrollBar`, `clWindow`, `clWindowFrame`, and `clWindowText`. If you search in the Delphi help file for `TColor`, you will find a full explanation of these color constants and how they relate to real-world colors.

The Colors Sample Project

When I first started programming for the Windows OS using straight WinAPI, one of the first programs that I wrote to start understanding how Windows graphics worked was this Colors sample project. At that time, the program took about five pages of code and a whole lot longer to write than this example did. Here, I am doing the same thing in the eight lines of code that I have to write. The shortness of this code says a lot about the power and eloquence of the VCL and Delphi. Listing 26.3 illustrates how to manipulate colors in a program.

LISTING 26.3 THE ColorMain.pas FILE

```pascal
///////////////////////////////////////////////////////////////////
//  ColorMain.pas                                                  //
//  Project: Colors                                                //
//  Copyright (c) 1998 by Jeff Cottingham                          //
///////////////////////////////////////////////////////////////////

unit Colormain;

interface

uses
  Windows, Messages, SysUtils, Classes, Graphics, Controls, Forms,
  Dialogs, StdCtrls, ExtCtrls, ComCtrls;

type
  TForm1 = class(TForm)
    Label1: TLabel;
    Label2: TLabel;
    Label3: TLabel;
    Label4: TLabel;
    Label5: TLabel;
    Label6: TLabel;
    Label7: TLabel;
    TrackBar1: TTrackBar;
    TrackBar2: TTrackBar;
    TrackBar3: TTrackBar;
    Panel1: TPanel;
    PaintBox1: TPaintBox;
    Edit1: TEdit;
    Edit2: TEdit;
    Edit3: TEdit;
    Edit4: TEdit;
    procedure TrackBar1Change(Sender: TObject);
    procedure PaintBox1Paint(Sender: TObject);
  private
    { Private declarations }
  public
    { Public declarations }
  end;

var
```

continues

LISTING 26.3   CONTINUED

```
  Form1: TForm1;

implementation

{$R *.DFM}

procedure TForm1.TrackBar1Change(Sender: TObject);
begin
   PaintBox1.Canvas.Brush.Color := RGB(TrackBar1.Position,
                                       TrackBar2.Position,
                                       TrackBar3.Position);
   Edit1.Text := IntToStr(TrackBar1.Position);
   Edit2.Text := IntToStr(TrackBar2.Position);
   Edit3.Text := IntToStr(TrackBar3.Position);
   Edit4.Text := IntToHex(PaintBox1.Canvas.Brush.Color,8);

   PaintBox1.Canvas.FillRect(PaintBox1.ClientRect);
end;

procedure TForm1.PaintBox1Paint(Sender: TObject);
begin
   PaintBox1.Color := RGB(TrackBar1.Position,
                          TrackBar2.Position,
                          TrackBar3.Position);
   PaintBox1.Canvas.FillRect(PaintBox1.Canvas.ClipRect);
end;

end.
```

The OnChange Event Handler

ColorMain has only two methods: an OnChange event handler for the TrackBar and a
Paint event handler for the PaintBox. I will discuss only the OnChange event handler
here and will reserve the discussion of the OnPaint event handler for later in the chapter
when I talk about the PaintBox component.

```
procedure TForm1.TrackBar1Change(Sender: TObject);
begin
   PaintBox1.Canvas.Brush.Color := RGB(TrackBar1.Position,
                                       TrackBar2.Position,
                                       TrackBar3.Position);
   Edit1.Text := IntToStr(TrackBar1.Position);
   Edit2.Text := IntToStr(TrackBar2.Position);
   Edit3.Text := IntToStr(TrackBar3.Position);
   Edit4.Text := IntToHex(PaintBox1.Canvas.Brush.Color,8);

   PaintBox1.Canvas.FillRect(PaintBox1.ClientRect);
end;
```

Although `TrackBar1Change` is a very simple method, a lot is going on here. On the surface, all I am doing is using the value of each `TrackBar`'s current position to set the red, green, and blue values of the color I want. I can do a direct read of this value because I gave the `Trackbar` a range from 0 to 255. I then complete the following steps:

1. Use the `RGB()` Windows API macro, which takes the three values of the `Trackbars` and converts them to a `COLORREF` data type.

2. Display the values and fill the `PaintBox` with the new color whenever a change occurs in any of the three values using the `FillRect` method of the `PaintBox`'s canvas.

When your computer has its display mode set to anything greater than 256 colors, everything looks normal and great. Figure 26.11 shows how a pure color looks in 24-bit color. But if you are running in 256-color mode, you might get a screen that looks like the one in Figure 26.12.

FIGURE 26.11

A view of a pure color.

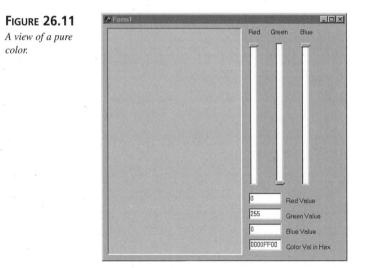

Today, as computers become more and more powerful, having differing color modes is not a factor because most new computers can display true color, but it is still worth discussion. What you see in Figure 26.12 is an effect called *dithering*. In 256-color mode, only 236 colors are available to use at any given time; Windows uses the other 20 colors for itself. So the question is, "What about all the other colors that we might want to use, the rest of the rainbow, so to speak?" Windows uses dithering to display these colors. What is really happening is that Windows is creating a custom brush that is composed of a pixel pattern that combines pixels of different pure colors to "fool" your eyes into seeing the color that you are requesting. In 256-color mode, Windows can display about

262,144 different dithered colors. If you play with the Colors program in 256-color mode, you will see what I am talking about.

FIGURE 26.12

A view of a dithered color in 256-color mode.

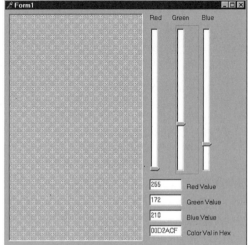

Palettes

Now I will break away from colors and give a brief overview of palettes. In 16- or 256-color mode, which are the only modes that support palettes, a palette is just a collection of colors stored in a Windows LOGPALETTE structure. Palettes are used by controls and graphical images to store information about the specific colors that they will need when they are drawn on the screen. Windows refers to this process as *realizing palettes*. Realizing palettes is the process of ensuring that the topmost window uses its full palette and that windows in the background use as much of their palettes as possible and then map any other colors to the closest available colors in the "real" palette. As windows move in front of one another, the Windows OS continually realizes the palettes. The VCL provides no specific support for creating or maintaining palettes, other than in bitmaps.

If you want to explore how to work with palettes in Windows, you might want to start by looking at the Palette functions in the Win32 API. In the following paragraphs, I'll list some of the various functions that you may find useful if you do want to work with palettes. You can find the explanations of these functions in the MS Help Win32 API help files.

The following are the color structures used by Windows:

```
COLORREF
LOGPALETTE
PALETTEENTRY
```

The following functions are used with color structures and are also used to manipulate palettes:

AnimatePalette	RealizePalette
CreateHalftonePalette	ResizePalette
CreatePalette	SelectPalette
GetColorAdjustment	SetColorAdjustment
GetNearestColor	SetPaletteEntries
GetNearestPalette	SetSystemPaletteUse
IndexGetPaletteEntries	UnrealizeObject
GetSystemPaletteEntries	UpdateColors
GetSystemPaletteUse	

An In-Depth Look at Image File Formats in Windows

Earlier in the chapter, I gave a very short and sweet definition of a bitmap. It was sufficient to allow you to do what you needed. It is now time to revisit bitmaps and other Windows image file formats to gain a greater understanding of the files that you will be working with.

Exploring Bitmaps and Dibs

You already know that a bitmap is just a binary representation of an image, but what does this really mean? A bitmap consists of two distinct parts. The first part is a BITMAPINFO structure describing the dimensions of the bitmap and color palette that Windows will use when the image is displayed. If this structure does not contain any color palette information, Windows will use the system palette when it is displayed. You refer to this type of bitmap as a device-dependent bitmap, or BMP. If it does contain color palette information, you refer to it as a device-independent bitmap, or DIB. The second part of the file contains the array of bytes defining the pixels of the bitmap. After the image is stored in memory, however, there is no difference between the two. A BMP image might vary slightly when displayed on machines that have different video hardware installed, whereas a DIB will always look the same because it contains its own palette information. Both types of bitmaps are identified by the .bmp file extension.

Exploring Icons

Icons are *Windows resources* and usually have a file extension of .ico. Like any other Windows resource, they can also be stored in a resource file that an application uses. Icons typically come in two sizes, large and small. Windows uses a large icon to represent the application on the desktop. This type of icon's size is 32×32 pixels. A small icon is displayed in the upper-left corner of a window. This type of icon's size is 16×16 pixels. Figure 26.13 shows an icon during the design or drawing phase. When you create an icon using the Image Editor that ships with Delphi, a second image or mask is also created for you. Figure 26.14 shows the icon and the mask. This mask causes a certain color in the icon to be transparent. Almost always, you use the mask if you do not want the background of the icon to be displayed. If your application uses a large number of icons, you should use an ImageList component to manage these icons for you. Icons are represented in Delphi as TIcon objects.

FIGURE 26.13

Designing an icon in the Image Editor.

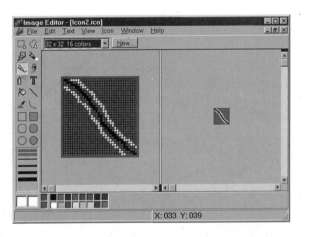

FIGURE 26.14

An icon and its mask in the Image Editor.

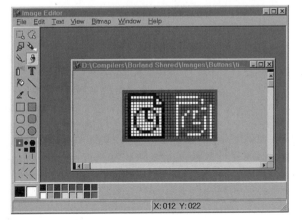

Exploring Metafiles

Metafiles are different from other image formats in that they are not graphical images at all, but a series of GDI functions that represent how an image is drawn. If you have ever written a keystroke macro, you already have a basic understanding of how a metafile works. You basically "record" a drawing routine and then "play" it to display the image. The following sample code is a text representation of how a metafile might look:

```
Rectangle(hdcmeta,0,0,100,100);
Rectangle(hdcmeta,20,20,120,120);
Rectangle(hdcmeta,40,40,140,140);
```

This example will draw three overlapping rectangles when "played" onto an `Image` canvas. Figure 26.15 displays a metafile after it has been "played" to the screen.

FIGURE 26.15

A displayed metafile.

Using this type of image format poses both advantages and disadvantages. One of the major advantages is the size of the file. Because a metafile does not have to store information about each pixel to be drawn, only how to draw the overall image, the actual file size can be dramatically reduced. The other advantage of using metafiles is the ability to precisely edit the contents of the picture. You get this advantage because metafiles are just a series of shapes that can be edited separately through the shape's function call. The major disadvantage is that because a metafile is just a series of function calls, you cannot store a scanned image in this format simply or easily.

Metafiles come in two flavors: 16-bit .wmf (Windows Metafile) files and 32-bit .emf (Enhanced Metafile) files. The EMF files are far more powerful than the WMF files. The code shown in Listing 26.4 makes use of this type of graphic file.

LISTING 26.4   THE MetaMain.pas FILE

```
////////////////////////////////////////////////////////////////////
//  MetaMain.pas                                                    //
//  Project: Metafile                                               //
//  Copyright (c) 1998 by Jeff Cottingham                           //
////////////////////////////////////////////////////////////////////

unit Metamain;

interface

uses
  Windows, Messages, SysUtils, Classes, Graphics, Controls, Forms,
  Dialogs, StdCtrls, ExtCtrls;

type
  TForm1 = class(TForm)
    Image1: TImage;
    Button1: TButton;
    Button2: TButton;
    Button3: TButton;
    Button4: TButton;
    Button5: TButton;
    procedure Button1Click(Sender: TObject);
    procedure Button2Click(Sender: TObject);
    procedure Button3Click(Sender: TObject);
    procedure FormCreate(Sender: TObject);
    procedure Button5Click(Sender: TObject);
    procedure Button4Click(Sender: TObject);
    procedure FormClose(Sender: TObject; var Action: TCloseAction);
  private
    { Private declarations }
  public
    { Public declarations }
  end;

var
  Form1: TForm1;
  pMetafile: TMetafile;
  pCanvas: TMetafileCanvas;

implementation

{$R *.DFM}
```

```
procedure TForm1.Button1Click(Sender: TObject);
begin
  try
     pMetafile.LoadFromFile('enhanced.emf');
     Image1.Canvas.Draw(0,0,pMetafile);
  except
     Application.MessageBox('Could not load Metafile', NIL, MB_OK);
  end;
end;

procedure TForm1.Button2Click(Sender: TObject);
begin
  try
     pCanvas := TMetafileCanvas.Create(pMetafile, 0);
     pCanvas.Draw(0,0,pMetafile);
     pCanvas.Brush.Color := clYellow;
     pCanvas.Ellipse(100,100,200,200);
  finally
     pCanvas.Free;
     pCanvas := NIL;
  end;
  Image1.Canvas.Draw(0,0,pMetafile);
end;

procedure TForm1.Button3Click(Sender: TObject);
begin
  pMetafile.SaveToFile('modified.emf');
end;

procedure TForm1.FormCreate(Sender: TObject);
begin
  pMetafile := TMetafile.Create;
end;

procedure TForm1.Button5Click(Sender: TObject);
begin
  Image1.Canvas.Brush.Color := clWhite;
  Image1.Canvas.FillRect(Image1.Canvas.ClipRect);
end;

procedure TForm1.Button4Click(Sender: TObject);
begin
  try
     pMetafile.LoadFromFile('modified.emf');
     Image1.Canvas.Draw(0,0,pMetafile);

  except
     Application.MessageBox('Could not load Metafile', NIL, MB_OK);
  end;
end;
```

continues

LISTING 26.4 CONTINUED

```
procedure TForm1.FormClose(Sender: TObject; var Action: TCloseAction);
begin
   pMetafile.Free;
   if pCanvas <> NIL then
      pCanvas.Free;
end;

end.
```

Examine the important parts of the code in Listing 26.4. The first method you need to look at is the FormCreate method:

```
procedure TForm1.FormCreate(Sender: TObject);
begin
   pMetafile := TMetafile.Create;
end;
```

Here, I am simply creating a new metafile object for my use.

Next, you need to look at Button1Click:

```
procedure TForm1.Button1Click(Sender: TObject);
begin
  try
     pMetafile.LoadFromFile('enhanced.emf');
     Image1.Canvas.Draw(0,0,pMetafile);
  except
     Application.MessageBox('Could not load Metafile', NIL, MB_OK);
  end;
end;
```

Here, I am loading a preexisting metafile from a file and playing it onto the canvas of Image1. I also could have loaded it directly into the Picture property and let the VCL do all the drawing.

```
Image1.Picture.LoadFromFile('enhanced.emf');
```

This method will not let you do any further drawing on it, however. So, if you just want to display a metafile, this method is the proper way to do it.

Next, you come to the meat of the program:

```
procedure TForm1.Button2Click(Sender: TObject);
begin
   try
      pCanvas := TMetafileCanvas.Create(pMetafile, 0);
      pCanvas.Draw(0,0,pMetafile);
      pCanvas.Brush.Color := clYellow;
      pCanvas.Ellipse(100,100,200,200);
   finally
```

```
      pCanvas.Free;
      pCanvas := NIL;
   end;
   Image1.Canvas.Draw(0,0,pMetafile);
end;
```

Here, I am creating a `MetafileCanvas`. Each `MetafileCanvas` is associated with a particular metafile. The next step is important but a little confusing. Before you can record or modify a metafile, you need to create a `MetafileCanvas`. After you have done so, you are free to modify it. Here, the confusing part comes in; you must first delete the `MetafileCanvas` before you can play it. You can think in terms of using a tape recorder: You must record something before you can play it. When you delete the `MetafileCanvas`, this action is the same as pushing the Stop recording button and then hitting the Rewind button. After you do so, you are ready to play what you recorded. The other functions are fairly self-explanatory, so I don't need to expound on them.

Exploring `TPaintBox` and `TImage`

Although you have used both the `TPaintBox` and `TImage` components, I have yet to talk about them, so it is about time I did. They may seem like they are interchangeable and have the same properties, but they have some major but subtle differences that are worth talking about. You can use either control to add custom images to a form. I will first talk about `TPaintBox` and then finish with `TImage`.

`TPaintBox` requires you to draw directly on a canvas. Because no mechanism is in place for a `PaintBox` to remember what was drawn on the canvas at any given time, you must do all the redrawing yourself when its canvas is invalidated. An example would be when another window passes in front of your window. If you do not override the `OnPaint` event handler, nothing will get redrawn, which basically is very bad. Figure 26.16 shows what happens if you do not override the `OnPaint` method of the `Colors` program from earlier in the chapter.

The following code is from the `Colors` example:

```
procedure TForm1.PaintBox1Paint(Sender: TObject);
begin
   PaintBox1.Color := RGB(TrackBar1.Position,
                          TrackBar2.Position,
                          TrackBar3.Position);
   PaintBox1.Canvas.FillRect(PaintBox1.Canvas.ClipRect);
end;
```

FIGURE 26.16

The paint method is not overridden, and the form is not repainted properly.

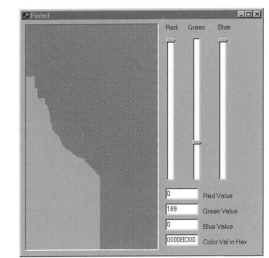

With this code in place, I am overriding the OnPaint method, and my program properly repaints itself when the need arises. As you might have guessed by now, sometimes using this control would make your task completely impossible. When this is the case, you have the TImage component to fall back on. TImage displays an image that is stored in a bitmap, icon, or metafile. It also maintains an in-memory internal bitmap that you can use to draw on. Thus, when its canvas is invalidated, it has the mechanism to know and remember how to repaint itself. When it needs to repaint itself, it simply copies the current state of this bitmap onto the canvas. TImage does not have an OnPaint method, as it handles all the repainting internally; so you do not even have to concern yourselves with it.

A Bit More About Bitmaps

Before I start this section, I need to say a few words about graphics programming in general. Most of the time in graphics programming, you are concerned with speed and how fast you can get your drawing algorithm to draw. Sometimes, this means rolling some of your code out to assembly so that you control how it behaves and not the compiler. Other times, this means simply thinking about what you want to do and doing it in the most efficient way possible. None of the code in this section has been optimized for speed; it is just there to give you a starting place to write truly fast code using the VCL. I will touch on some areas to make the code faster when the need arises. Whole books are written on the art of code optimization if you want to explore this part of programming.

So far, you have learned how to load a bitmap, display it, and draw on its canvas. What if you want to manipulate the image itself directly or copy it to another bitmap in an altered state and display the altered image. A good example would be to display the image upside down. You could use the `Pixels` property to copy the color of a pixel on the first bitmap one by one to the location you choose on the second bitmap. This process would be very inefficient and would also be obnoxiously slow. Luckily, Delphi gives you a property of `TBitmap` to make your job easier, not to mention faster. This property is the `ScanLine` property. `ScanLine` allows you to get an entire row of pixels at once that can be addressed like an array. What this means to you is that instead of having to do a read for each pixel in the bitmap, you can do a read for each line instead. Reading this way will speed up your routine immensely. In this section, you are going to look at an example of how to use this property. In the example, you see five simple manipulation algorithms using two bitmaps.

A Moving Display

The `Manipulation` program, shown in Listing 26.5, combines two bitmaps to make a third image that is then displayed. So again take a look at the following code before I examine how it works. Also hazard a guess at what it does before I tell you.

LISTING 26.5   THE `Bitmanip.pas` FILE

```
//////////////////////////////////////////////////////////////////////
//  Bitmanip.pas           .                                        //
//  Project: Manipulation                                           //
//  Copyright (c) 1998 by Jeff Cottingham                           //
//////////////////////////////////////////////////////////////////////

unit Main;

interface

uses
  Windows, Messages, SysUtils,
  Classes, Graphics, Controls,
  Forms, Dialogs, Menus, ExtCtrls;

type
  TForm1 = class(TForm)
    MainMenu1: TMainMenu;
    File1: TMenuItem;
    Exit1: TMenuItem;
    Effect1: TMenuItem;
    SlideFromLeft1: TMenuItem;
    SlideFromRight1: TMenuItem;
```

continues

LISTING 26.5   CONTINUED

```pascal
    ShutterHorizontal1: TMenuItem;
    ShutterVertical1: TMenuItem;
    Image1: TImage;
    procedure FormCreate(Sender: TObject);
    procedure SlideFromLeft1Click(Sender: TObject);
    procedure SlideFromRight1Click(Sender: TObject);
    procedure ShutterHorizontal1Click(Sender: TObject);
    procedure ShutterVertical1Click(Sender: TObject);
    procedure Unroll1Click(Sender: TObject);
    procedure FormCLose(Sender: TObject; var Action: TCloseAction);
  private
    Bitmap1, Bitmap2, Bitmap3: TBitmap;
    Image1Loaded, Image2Loaded: Boolean;
    { Private declarations }
  public
    { Public declarations }
  end;

var
  Form1: TForm1;

implementation


{$R *.DFM}

procedure TForm1.FormCreate(Sender: TObject);
begin
    bitmap1 := Graphics.TBitmap.Create;
    bitmap2 := Graphics.TBitmap.Create;
    bitmap3 := Graphics.TBitmap.Create;
    bitmap1.PixelFormat := pf8bit;
    bitmap2.PixelFormat := pf8bit;
    bitmap3.PixelFormat := pf8bit;

    try
       bitmap1.LoadFromFile('factory.bmp');
       bitmap2.LoadFromFile('handshak.bmp');
       Image1Loaded := true;
       Image2Loaded := true;
       bitmap3.Palette := bitmap1.Palette;
       bitmap3.Height := bitmap1.Height;
       bitmap3.Width := bitmap1.Width;
    except
       Image1Loaded := false;
       Image2Loaded := false;
    end;
end;
```

```
procedure TForm1.SlideFromLeft1Click(Sender: TObject);
var
  Current: PByteArray;
  Next: PByteArray;
  ToDisplay: PByteArray;
  i, y, j, z: Integer;
begin
    if not (Image1Loaded) then
      ShowMessage('Bitmap1 not loaded');
    if not (Image2Loaded) then
      ShowMessage('Bitmap2 not loaded');
    if((Image1Loaded) and (Image2Loaded)) then begin
      for i := 0 to bitmap1.Width - 1 do begin
          for y := 0 to bitmap1.Height -1 do begin
              Current := bitmap1.ScanLine[y];
              Next := bitmap2.ScanLine[y];
              ToDisplay := bitmap3.ScanLine[y];
              for z := 0 to i - 1 do
                  ToDisplay[z] := Next[z];
              for j := i to bitmap1.Width - 1 do
                  ToDisplay[j] := Current[j];
          end;;
          Image1.Canvas.Draw(0,0,bitmap3);
          Application.ProcessMessages();
        end;
    end;

end;

procedure TForm1.SlideFromRight1Click(Sender: TObject);
var
  Current: PByteArray;
  Next: PByteArray;
  ToDisplay: PByteArray;
  i, y, j, z: Integer;
begin
    if not (Image1Loaded) then
      ShowMessage('Bitmap1 not loaded');
    if not (Image2Loaded) then
      ShowMessage('Bitmap2 not loaded');
    if ((Image1Loaded) and (Image2Loaded)) then begin
      for i := 0 to bitmap1.Width - 1 do begin
          for y := 0 to bitmap1.Height - 1 do begin
              Current := bitmap1.ScanLine[y];
              Next := bitmap2.ScanLine[y];
              ToDisplay := bitmap3.ScanLine[y];
              for z := 0 to bitmap1.Width - i do
                ToDisplay[z] := Current[z];
              for j := bitmap1.Width - i to bitmap1.Width -1 do
```

continues

LISTING 26.5   CONTINUED

```
                ToDisplay[j] := Next[j];
          end;;
          Image1.Canvas.Draw(0,0,bitmap3);
          Application.ProcessMessages();
        end;;
    end;;
end;

procedure TForm1.ShutterHorizontal1Click(Sender: TObject);
var
 Next: PByteArray;
 ToDisplay: PByteArray;
 i, x, FY: Integer;
begin
 FY := 0;
 if not (Image1Loaded) then
   ShowMessage('Bitmap1 not loaded');
 if not (Image2Loaded) then
   ShowMessage('Bitmap2 not loaded');
   if((Image1Loaded) and (Image2Loaded)) then begin
      bitmap3.Canvas.CopyRect(Rect(0,0,bitmap3.Width,bitmap3.Height),
        bitmap1.Canvas,Rect(0,0,bitmap1.Width, bitmap1.Height));
      for i := 0 to 29 do begin
         while FY < bitmap1.Height do begin
            Next := bitmap2.ScanLine[FY + i];
            ToDisplay := bitmap3.ScanLine[Fy + i];
            for x := 0 to bitmap3.Width - 1 do
               ToDisplay[x] := Next[x];
            FY := FY + 30;
         end;
         Image1.Canvas.Draw(0,0,bitmap3);
         Application.ProcessMessages();
         Sleep(40);
         FY := 0;
      end;
    end;
end;

procedure TForm1.ShutterVertical1Click(Sender: TObject);
var
 Next: PByteArray;
 ToDisplay: PByteArray;
 i, y, FX: Integer;
begin
 if not (Image1Loaded) then
   ShowMessage('Bitmap1 not loaded');
 if not (Image2Loaded) then
   ShowMessage('Bitmap2 not loaded');

   if((Image1Loaded) and (Image2Loaded)) then begin
```

```
    bitmap3.Canvas.CopyRect(Rect(0,0,bitmap3.Width,bitmap3.Height),
                        bitmap1.Canvas,Rect(0,0,bitmap1.Width,
                        bitmap1.Height));
  FX := 0;
  for i := 0 to 29 do begin
    for y := 0 to bitmap1.Height -1 do begin
      ToDisplay := bitmap3.ScanLine[y];
      while FX < bitmap3.Width - 1 do begin
        Next := bitmap2.ScanLine[y];
        ToDisplay[FX + i] := Next[FX + i];
        FX := FX + 30;
      end;
      FX := 0;
    end;
    Image1.Canvas.Draw(0,0,bitmap3);
    Application.ProcessMessages();
    Sleep(40);
  end;
  end;
end;


procedure TForm1.Unroll1Click(Sender: TObject);
var
 Next: PByteArray;
 ToDisplay: PByteArray;
 i, j,  y: Integer;
begin
 if not (Image1Loaded) then
   ShowMessage('Bitmap1 not loaded');
 if not (Image2Loaded) then
   ShowMessage('Bitmap2 not loaded');

  if((Image1Loaded) and (Image2Loaded)) then begin
    bitmap3.Canvas.CopyRect(Rect(0,0,bitmap3.Width,bitmap3.Height),
                        bitmap1.Canvas,Rect(0,0,bitmap1.Width,
                        bitmap1.Height));
    for i := 0 to bitmap1.Width do begin
      for y := 0 to bitmap1.Height - 1 do begin
        Next := bitmap2.ScanLine[y];
        ToDisplay := bitmap3.ScanLine[y];
        if(i < bitmap1.Width - 15) then begin
          for j := 1 to 14 do
            if((y = 0) or (y = bitmap1.Height - 1)) then
              ToDisplay[i+j] := clBlack
            else
              ToDisplay[i+j] := Next[i+10-j];
        end;
        ToDisplay[i] := Next[i];
```

continues

LISTING 26.5   CONTINUED

```
            end;
            Sleep(10);
            Image1.Canvas.Draw(0,0,bitmap3);
            Application.ProcessMessages();
        end;;
    end;;
end;
procedure TForm1.FormClose(Sender: TObject; var Action: TCloseAction);
begin
    bitmap1.Free;
    bitmap2.Free;
    bitmap3.Free;
end;

end.
```

Did you hazard a guess as to what Listing 26.5 does? Well, if you thought that one image slides on top of the other, among other things, you would be right. Take a closer look at what is going on. In the `FormCreate` method, I am using three bitmaps instead of two. Look at what happens when I load the first image:

```
procedure TForm1.FormCreate(Sender: TObject);
begin
    bitmap1 := Graphics.TBitmap.Create;
    bitmap2 := Graphics.TBitmap.Create;
    bitmap3 := Graphics.TBitmap.Create;
    bitmap1.PixelFormat := pf8bit;
    bitmap2.PixelFormat := pf8bit;
    bitmap3.PixelFormat := pf8bit;

    try
        bitmap1.LoadFromFile('factory.bmp');
        bitmap2.LoadFromFile('handshak.bmp');
        Image1Loaded := true;
        Image2Loaded := true;
        bitmap3.Palette := bitmap1.Palette;
        bitmap3.Height := bitmap1.Height;
        bitmap3.Width := bitmap1.Width;
    except
        Image1Loaded := false;
        Image2Loaded := false;
    end;
end;
```

I could not assign the `bitmap3` size or palette until I loaded the first bitmap. I need to know the properties of the first bitmap so that I can assign them to the third one, my work area. I am also setting a Boolean flag `ImageLoaded`. This flag is used in later functions.

Next, look at the methods that do all the work. Because the algorithm is basically the same for SlideLeft and SlideRight, you need to examine only one to understand how the other works:

```
procedure TForm1.SlideFromLeft1Click(Sender: TObject);
var
  Current: PByteArray;
  Next: PByteArray;
  ToDisplay: PByteArray;
  i, y, j, z: Integer;
begin
  if not (Image1Loaded) then
    ShowMessage('Bitmap1 not loaded');
  if not (Image2Loaded) then
    ShowMessage('Bitmap2 not loaded');
  if((Image1Loaded) and (Image2Loaded)) then begin
    for i := 0 to bitmap1.Width - 1 do begin
      for y := 0 to bitmap1.Height -1 do begin
        Current := bitmap1.ScanLine[y];
        Next := bitmap2.ScanLine[y];
        ToDisplay := bitmap3.ScanLine[y];
        for z := 0 to i - 1 do
          ToDisplay[z] := Next[z];
        for j := i to bitmap1.Width - 1 do
          ToDisplay[j] := Current[j];
      end;
      Image1.Canvas.Draw(0,0,bitmap3);
      Application.ProcessMessages();
    end;
  end;
end;
```

First, I check to see if I have valid bitmaps loaded into the two source bitmaps. If I have two valid images, I do the slide. The slide is done with my loop logic, which is how the loops are constructed. The outer loop is the most interesting, so I will examine it first. This loop controls the actual drawing of the changed image on the screen:

```
Image1.Canvas.Draw(0,0,bitmap3);
Application.ProcessMessages;
```

The first line just draws the image. The second lets the application actually draw it on the screen. You must give the application the time to draw the bitmap to the screen, and you do so with ProcessMessages. If you didn't realize it, the outer loop is going to send 240 separate paint messages, one for each time through the loop. Sending this many paint messages will make for very smooth drawing but is very slow. To speed up this portion of the loop, you might want to do the draw only every second or third pixel. The overall effect will hardly be noticeable to the eye, but the slide will be a lot faster. The two inner loops are also interesting:

```
for z := 0 to i - 1 do
   ToDisplay[z] := Next[z];
for j := i to bitmap1.Width - 1 do
   ToDisplay[j] := Current[j];
```

Here, I am copying only the part of each bitmap that I want to be displayed to the work area. At this place, you could speed things up dramatically. If you do not want to preserve the original image, you could draw the second image onto the first and gain a great deal of speed.

The other effects are just different variations on the preceding algorithm. Let me just add an interesting side note: I wrote this code while I was working in a demo booth at SDWest98 (Software Developer Conference West) this year. Until I had the loop logic dialed in, every time I ran the application, it would cause an access violation. I had this problem in front of everybody, so do not get discouraged if you get a few violations while coding, because as an old support engineer used to say, "If it doesn't break every so often while you are writing it, you're not doing anything worthwhile anyway."

Summary

In this chapter I have covered the center point of VCL Graphics programming and the tools that it uses. This center point is the TCanvas object. I have also covered most of the basic building blocks that you need to get started. I suggest that you take the time to play with the different pen modes, brush styles and copy modes to fully understand what effects each one has. You also saw how to create your own custom line with a little imagination. You also learned one of the most basic of the VCL graphics types, TColor. You then worked through palettes and on into the different windows graphical file formats. You took a brief stop to see how metafiles work. You then took a good look at the components that are used to display these files, TImage and TPaintBox. Finally, you saw how to manipulate bitmaps and display them on the screen. You should now have a very good understanding of basic graphics programming using the VCL. I also suggest you take a look at the additional supplements that are included on the CD.

DirectDraw

This chapter is about DirectDraw programming. This technology is designed to allow you to create high-performance graphics applications. DirectDraw is a COM interface that gives you direct access to the hardware on Windows 95/98 or Windows NT machines. Using it, you can create applications that run as fast as DOS applications that have complete control over the hardware on a machine.

By the time you complete this chapter, you will understand how to do the following:

- Initialize DirectDraw
- Run DirectDraw in Exclusive mode
- Run DirectDraw in Windowed mode
- Animate objects using DirectDraw
- Manipulate palettes using DirectDraw

This subject is moderately demanding, but with a little bit of work, you should have no trouble mastering this material.

Understanding DirectDraw

The next few sections of the chapter describe DirectDraw programming. In particular, they cover the following topics:

- What is DirectDraw?
- How do I initialize DirectDraw?
- What is a `DirectDrawSurface`?

DirectDraw is part of a complex set of tools called DirectX, which consists of several different technologies such as DirectDraw, Direct3D, DirectSound, DirectPlay, DirectInput, and DirectSetup. Each of these technologies focuses on a different type of multimedia or gaming technology, such as sound, 3D graphics, network play, hardware devices such as mice or force feedback, and so on. This chapter, however, will zero in exclusively on DirectDraw—a subject that is easily big enough to fill up this chapter and several more. However, I know this topic pretty well by this time, and I can get you up and running in short order, and I can leave you with plenty of other resources that you can follow up on for further study.

DirectDraw programs require that you have the DirectDraw runtime DLLs on your system. The runtime files, which are just a set of DLLs, are available from Microsoft's Web site, though many machines have them installed already, as they ship with a wide variety of products, including games, Windows 98, and the future operating system Windows NT 5. If you are using NT 4, you should upgrade to at least Service Pack 3 so that you can have access to DirectDraw 3, which is part of that Service Pack. (NT 5, beta 2 [current as I write this text], supports DirectX 6.) Don't try to install the DirectDraw runtime on a Windows NT system; instead, get the latest Service Pack. The runtime installation is meant only for Windows 95 or 98. One way to tell whether you have DirectDraw on your system is to look in the `Windows/System` directory or `Winnt/System32` directory for the files `DDRAW.DLL` and `DSOUND.DLL`. If you have those files, then DirectDraw is installed on your system.

If at all possible, you should try to acquire the DirectDraw SDK from Microsoft. This SDK can usually be downloaded from Microsoft's Web site, but beware, as it is at least 30MB in size. If you install the SDK, it creates a directory called `DXSDK` on your hard drive. Beneath this directory is the `SDK` directory, which contains various documents, sample files in C/C++, and help files. You may also be able to obtain the SDK directly from Microsoft. In particular, it may be shipped as part of the MSDN. The book *Inside DirectX*, from Microsoft Press, also contains the DirectX SDK.

For best results, you should have at least 2MB of memory on your video card. For additional information beyond that supplied in this chapter, go to the DirectDraw area on Microsoft's Web site at `http://www.microsoft.com/directx/default.asp`, or visit my Web site at `http://users.aol.com/charliecal`, where you will find links to various DirectX programmer's sites.

What Is DirectDraw?

DirectDraw is an interface that gives you access to the video hardware on your system. Having immediate access to hardware allows you to create fast, colorful displays that catch the users' eyes and hold their attention. It can also allow you to create advanced games with the most extreme cutting-edge performance characteristics.

As I stated earlier in the book, programs are fast enough when they don't force the users to wait for something to happen. Most of the time, the standard Windows GDI will allow you to create programs that run fast enough to satisfy most users. This is true even of the interface for many traditional, animated games.

Many programmers have failed to notice that as computers improved, so have the performance of standard graphics routines. Contemplate the evolution from 486s, to Pentium 90s and 120s, then on to 150s and 166s, and on yet further to 200s and 266s, and now finally to the world of 333 and 450MHz machines. A lot has changed during this evolutionary process, and of course, by the time you read this, even faster processors will come out that will dwarf the performance of the fastest machines I mention here. The video cards we now use are highly optimized for standard Windows video routines. As a result, the standard Windows GDI has become an increasingly viable tool for creating animations. I will prove this point in the last chapter of this book, when I show you code that performs well in both DirectDraw and in Windows GDI versions.

Nevertheless, sometimes you want to extract the last bits of performance out of your machine. To do so, you should use DirectDraw.

In standard Windows programming, every time you write to the screen, you must do so without directly accessing the hardware. Instead, you request that a set of drivers built by third parties perform the actions you want to carry out. This process is a bit like asking a robot to perform actions for you. The robot is very efficient and very reliable, but it is not much help when certain kinds of speed and dexterity are required. Think, for instance, of the robots in *Star Wars*. They did certain things very well, but it is hard to imagine them performing magic tricks as well as a sleight of hand artist. Traditional Windows video drivers have the same characteristics: They give you remarkable device independence, but you usually lose speed in the process.

Windows forces you to access video memory through a set of drivers for two reasons:

- The drivers are designed so that you can issue one set of commands that will work equally well on a wide range of hardware. For instance, under Windows GDI, you don't have to create new versions of your program when a new video card comes out.

- Windows is a protected mode operating system that protects you and other users of the system from careless programmers who can accidentally crash the system by making mistakes when writing directly to hardware. When programmers write directly to a hardware device, they can easily make a mistake that crashes the whole system. To prevent a situation like this from happening, the Windows GDI will not let you write directly to hardware devices such as video cards. These restrictions make the system safer, but graphics programmers are therefore prevented from directly manipulating the memory they most want to access.

The main purpose of DirectDraw is to allow you to write directly to video memory if you want. It will also allow you to easily manipulate offscreen buffers that can be quickly flipped on to visible video memory. This way, you can create smooth animations through a technique called double buffering, which I will explain later in this chapter.

DirectDraw is also designed to automatically give you access to the latest features of video cards, even if you are not aware that those features exist. In other words, the DirectX team is working full time to give you access to the latest features. In particular, the team builds those features into DirectX, so you get access to them without having to even be conscious of their existence. For instance, if a new video card supports manipulating rectangles in an extremely optimized way, or stretching a graphic in a fast, powerful manner, DirectDraw will automatically take advantage of that capability when you draw rectangles to the screen. A specific example was the MMX technology that Intel introduced awhile back. Even if you wrote your DirectX game before MMX was created, you will get access to MMX functionality automatically because the latest DirectDraw drivers take advantage of it.

Another feature of DirectDraw is that it can allow you to set the screen resolution and bit depth of your program. In other words, you can take over the whole screen, switch to 300×200 mode, and set the bit depth to 256 colors if you so like. Likewise, you can switch to very high resolutions and get whatever color depth you want. The decision is up to you.

To a large degree, DirectDraw removes the shackles that inhibit fast video output in Windows. However, DirectDraw still does everything it can to ensure that you will not accidentally crash Windows. For instance, it provides you with a preallocated pointer that gives you direct access to video memory. This capability is different from allowing you to write to a specific video address. In particular, it ensures the buffer you are writing to is valid video memory, and it will swap you out into main memory automatically if you need more room for your images, text, or animations.

You need to understand that DirectDraw is not the API you should use to create 3D graphics. The technology is sufficiently powerful to allow you to create powerful, high-performance 3D games on the order of Doom or Quake, but the amount of work involved would be prohibitive. If you want to create 3D games, then use Direct3D, which is described in the next chapter. Direct3D provides the primitives you need to quickly create 3D games or graphics.

A Few Thoughts on Double Buffering

Before I get into much depth regarding the way this code works, I need to spend a few minutes talking about double buffering. The idea behind this technology is to emulate as closely as possible the frame-based techniques used in celluloid-based movies. Double buffering simply shows the users a series of still pictures at a rate sufficiently hurried as to give the illusion of fluid motion or animation.

In particular, what you do is compose a frame offscreen and then flip it in front of the viewers. While the viewers are absorbing this information, you compose another scene and then flip it to the screen. For instance, you might start out with the first frame showing a ball at the far left of the screen; then, to create the illusion of movement, you can move the ball from left to right a few pixels each frame. With each slight change of position, you flip a new picture in front of the users. You are showing a series of static pictures of a ball, but the users perceive this as animated motion.

The average movie flips the screen at a rate of approximately 25 frames per second. These kinds of rates are so rapid that the human eye never detects the presence of individual frames but instead sees a convincing illusion of true motion. If you move a ball across the screen at rates close to 25 frames per second, then the users will think they are seeing not a series of still pictures of a ball, but an actual movie of a ball moving through space. Depending on the quality of your code, DirectX is capable of performing at rates much higher than 25 frames per second.

> **TIP**
>
> I should perhaps mention that when I first started creating animations, I got it into my head that it was foolish to compose an entire buffer and flip it to the screen. This seemed like a wasteful operation to me, and I was determined to make all my changes directly on the screen, so as to not needlessly consume resources.
>
> It turned out that my approach was entirely wrong headed, particularly when I tried to create relatively sophisticated effects. Over time, I found that it was very hard to hide from a user the changes you make directly on the screen. The act of blotting out one portion of the screen and then painting something in near to it created very messy artifacts that were easy to see, even when done as efficiently as possible. This kind of slight of hand should almost always be done on a back buffer, out of sight of the user. Then when you flip the picture to the screen, the user sees only a fully composed image.
>
> Everyone knows that John Carmack's Quake is used as a bench mark to measure the capability of a video card to perform page flipping, which is just another term for double buffering. If this technology is good enough for John Carmack, then it is very likely that it is good enough for you.
>
> If you are still unconvinced, recall what I said earlier about the DirectDraw subsystem guaranteeing that page flips will occur in sync with a screen refresh. I've never met anyone who could see a 72MHz screen refresh actually taking place. If a picture is refreshed at that rate, the user will not be able to consciously detect the instant when you blit an image to the screen.
>
> I greatly fear that no matter what I say, some readers will be determined to try to make changes to the area of the screen the user is actually looking at. Although there are a few occasions when this is appropriate, the vast majority of the time you want to compose your images offscreen and then flip them in front of the user. So if you really want to try doing things that way, go ahead, and if you get frustrated, come back and try double buffering. You'll be amazed at how quickly it solves seemingly intractable problems.

DirectDraw allows you to create a back buffer, draw to it, and then flip it to the visible area in your video memory. Assuming that you are in Exclusive mode and have enough video memory to keep both your primary surface and back surface in video RAM, then the flip operation is not a copy procedure. Instead, the flip operation simply changes the address of the block of memory referenced by the visible area of your video card's memory. In other words, when you perform page flips, only four bytes of memory need to change; everything else can stay where it is. The only thing that changes is the four bytes of memory that point to the currently active video page. Therefore, the operation is very fast; furthermore, it is guaranteed to happen in sync with the refresh operations on your monitor. As a result, you can use DirectDraw to perform very smooth animations.

Hardware Versus Emulation

DirectDraw and other DirectX technologies do the best they can to provide you with a sophisticated set of video routines. For instance, the 3D routines attempt to use the hardware to perform super-fast operations. However, many video cards or other hardware devices do not provide all the functionality you might desire. In these cases, DirectX will attempt to emulate the missing functionality in software.

The whole question of which kinds of functionality are provided in software and which are provided in hardware is an extremely technical subject, well beyond the scope of this book. However, you can keep tabs on the status of DirectDraw on your particular system by running the DirectX Viewer that comes with the Microsoft SDK. This viewer exercises a series of DirectX capability routines that report on the status of various types of multimedia hardware on a particular system. You can also query these subsystems yourself at runtime, but that is a subject which I touch on only tangentially in this book.

For now, all you really need to know is that some DirectX functionality is executed in hardware, and other parts are emulated. The emulated functions are, perhaps somewhat whimsically, handled by the HEL, or Hardware Emulation Layer. The nonemulated parts of your program are handled by a second subsystem with yet another rather whimsical name, the HAL, or Hardware Abstraction Layer. Either the HEL or the HAL handle all your DirectDraw operations. These drivers make DirectDraw possible.

> **NOTE**
>
> You can initialize DirectDraw to use either the HEL or the HAL exclusively. However, this is a rather advanced feature, and one that you are unlikely to need to call on in the course of even rather rigorous performance tests.

A Simple DirectDraw Program

Now that you have some idea what DirectDraw is all about, the next step is to start learning how it all works. DirectDraw is not a simple API, but neither is it enormously complex. One of the difficulties of the technology is that a lot of the most complex code needs to be mastered up front, before you can start programming. Even relatively difficult tasks are much easier to master if you can get up and running quickly, and then master the details one step at a time. Unfortunately, in this case, a considerable amount of complexity must be mastered up front, and then you can get a chance to play with the technology.

In such situations, people want to have complex technology wrapped up in components that help to simplify the programmer's task. I will, in fact, show you such a technology later in the book, and I will also point you to other third parties who provide this kind of technology for Delphi programmers. However, I strongly suggest that you understand the basics of DirectDraw programming before using such a library.

To get you started with DirectDraw, I have created the `DirectDraw1` program, which allows you to see all the basic functionality needed in a DirectDraw program. Listing 27.1 shows the source code for this program.

LISTING 27.1 THE `DirectDraw1` PROGRAM

```
unit Main;

interface

uses
  Windows, Messages, SysUtils,
  Classes, Graphics, Controls,
  Forms, Dialogs, ExtCtrls,
  DirectX;

type
  TForm1 = class(TForm)
    Timer1: TTimer;
    procedure FormCreate(Sender: TObject);
    procedure FormDestroy(Sender: TObject);
    procedure FormKeyDown(Sender: TObject; var Key: Word;
      Shift: TShiftState);
    procedure FormPaint(Sender: TObject);
    procedure Timer1Timer(Sender: TObject);
  private
    FDirectDraw: IDirectDraw;              // DirectDraw object
    FPrimarySurface: IDirectDrawSurface; // DirectDraw primary surface
    FBackSurface: IDirectDrawSurface;    // DirectDraw back surface
    FActive: Boolean;                     // is application active?
    FPhase: Byte;
    FFrontMsg: string;
    FBackMsg: string;
    procedure Start;
    { Private declarations }
```

```
  public
    { Public declarations }
  end;

const
  AFileName = 'c:\debug.txt';

var
  Form1: TForm1;
  DebugFile: TextFile;
implementation

{$R *.DFM}

procedure TForm1.FormCreate(Sender: TObject);
begin
  Width := 640;
  Height := 480;
  FDirectDraw := nil;
  FPhase := 0;
  FActive := False;
  FFrontMsg := 'Front buffer (F12 or Esc to quit)';
  FBackMsg := 'Back buffer (F12 or Esc to quit)';
end;

procedure TForm1.FormDestroy(Sender: TObject);
begin
  if(FDirectDraw <> nil) then begin
    FDirectDraw.FlipToGDISurface;
    FDirectDraw.SetCooperativeLevel(Handle, DDSCL_NORMAL);
    if FBackSurface <> nil then
      FBackSurface := nil;
    if FPrimarySurface <> nil then
      FPrimarySurface := nil;
    FDirectDraw := nil;
  end;
end;

procedure TForm1.Start;
var
  hr: HRESULT;
  SurfaceDesc: TDDSURFACEDESC ;
  DDSCaps: TDDSCAPS;
  DC: HDC;
begin
  hr := DirectDrawCreate(nil, FDirectDraw, nil);
  if(hr = DD_OK) then begin
    // Get exclusive mode
    hr := FDirectDraw.SetCooperativeLevel(Handle, // DDSCL_NORMAL);
      DDSCL_EXCLUSIVE or DDSCL_FULLSCREEN);
    if(hr = DD_OK) then begin
```

continues

LISTING 27.1   CONTINUED

```
      hr := FDirectDraw.SetDisplayMode(640, 480, 8);
      if(hr = DD_OK) then begin
        // Create the primary surface with 1 back buffer
        SurfaceDesc.dwSize := sizeof(SurfaceDesc);
        SurfaceDesc.dwFlags := DDSD_CAPS or DDSD_BACKBUFFERCOUNT;
        SurfaceDesc.ddsCaps.dwCaps := DDSCAPS_PRIMARYSURFACE or
                              DDSCAPS_FLIP or
                              DDSCAPS_COMPLEX;
        SurfaceDesc.dwBackBufferCount := 1;
        hr := FDirectDraw.CreateSurface(SurfaceDesc,
        ➥FPrimarySurface, nil);
        if(hr = DD_OK) then begin
          // Get a pointer to the back buffer
          ddscaps.dwCaps := DDSCAPS_BACKBUFFER;
          hr := FPrimarySurface.GetAttachedSurface(ddscaps,
                                              FBackSurface);

          if(hr = DD_OK) then begin
            // draw some text.
            if (FPrimarySurface.GetDC(DC) = DD_OK) then begin
              SetBkColor(DC, RGB(0, 0, 255));
              SetTextColor(DC, RGB(255, 255, 0));
              TextOut(DC, 0, 0, PChar(FFrontMsg), Length(FFrontMsg));
              FPrimarySurface.ReleaseDC(DC);
            end;

            if (FBackSurface.GetDC(DC) = DD_OK) then begin
                SetBkColor(DC, RGB(0, 0, 255));
                SetTextColor(DC, RGB(255, 255, 0));
                TextOut(DC, 0, 0, PChar(FBackMsg), Length(FBackMsg));
                FBackSurface.ReleaseDC(DC);
            end;

            // Create a timer to flip the pages
             FActive := True;
            Timer1.Enabled := True;
            Exit;
          end;
        end;
      end;
    end;
  end;
  MessageBox(Handle, PChar(Format('Direct Draw Init Failed %x', )),
    'ERROR', MB_OK);
  Close();
end;

procedure TForm1.FormKeyDown(Sender: TObject; var Key: Word;
  Shift: TShiftState);
begin
  case Key of
```

```
    VK_F3: Start();
    VK_ESCAPE, VK_F12: begin
      Timer1.Enabled := False;
      Close;
    end;
  end;
end;

procedure TForm1.FormPaint(Sender: TObject);
const
  Msg = 'Page Flipping Test: Press F3 to start, F12 or Esc to exit';
var
  rc: TRect;
  size: TSize;
  DC: HDC;
begin
  if not(FActive) then begin
    DC := GetDC(Handle);
    rc := GetClientRect;
    WriteLn(DebugFile, 'Left: ', rc.Left,
                       ' Top: ', rc.Top,
                       ' Right: ', rc.right,
                       ' Bottom: ', rc.Bottom);
    GetTextExtentPoint(DC, Msg, Length(Msg), size);
    SetBkColor(DC, RGB(0, 0, 0));
    SetTextColor(DC, RGB(255, 255, 0));
    TextOut(DC, (rc.right - size.cx) div 2,
      (rc.bottom - size.cy) div 2, PChar(Msg), Length(Msg)-1);
    ReleaseDC(Handle, DC);
  end;
end;

procedure TForm1.Timer1Timer(Sender: TObject);
var
  DC: HDC;
  hr: HResult;
begin
  if (FBackSurface.GetDC(DC) = DD_OK) then begin
    if FPhase <> 0 then begin
      SetBkColor(DC, RGB(0, 0, 255));
      SetTextColor(DC, RGB(255, 255, 0));
      TextOut(DC, 0, 0, PChar(FFrontMsg), Length(FFrontMsg));
      Fphase := 0;
    end else begin
      SetBkColor(DC, RGB(0, 0, 255));
      SetTextColor(DC, RGB(0, 255, 255));
      TextOut(DC, 0, 0, PChar(FBackMsg), Length(FBackMsg));
      FPhase := 1;
    end;
    FBackSurface.ReleaseDC(DC);
  end;
```

continues

LISTING 27.1   CONTINUED

```
  while (True) do begin
    hr := FPrimarySurface.Flip(nil, 0);

    if (hr = DD_OK) then
      break;

    if(hr = DDERR_SURFACELOST) then begin
      hr := FPrimarySurface.Restore();
      if(hr <> DD_OK) then
        break;
    end;

    if(hr <> DDERR_WASSTILLDRAWING) then
      break;
  end;
end;

initialization
  AssignFile(DebugFile, AFileName);
  ReWrite(DebugFile);
finalization
  CloseFile(DebugFile);
end.
```

The code shown here is the simplest possible DirectDraw program. It is modeled closely after the DDX1 C++ example that ships with the Microsoft's DirectDraw SDK. I've simply taken that program and rewritten it to compile under a form-based environment. In particular, the code uses a TTimer object rather than calling SetTimer, and it responds to events such as OnKeyDown rather than directly handling WM_KEYDOWN messages. The conversion to a form-based paradigm makes the code easier to read but doesn't change its underlying structure.

The code in this project has six methods:

- OnCreate—Performs trivial initialization of variables.
- OnDestroy—Destroys the DirectDraw surfaces created in the Start method.
- Start—Calls DirectDrawCreate, which initializes DirectDraw and returns a pointer to a DirectDraw object. Calls SetCooperativeLevel to switch into Exclusive mode. Calls SetDisplayMode to switch to 640×480 8-bit resolution. Calls CreateSurface to create a primary surface. Calls GetAttachedSurface to get a pointer to the back surface. Paints the front and back surface to black, and paints text to each so you can recognize them when they are flipped to the screen. Enables the timer.

- `FormKeyDown`—Responds to key presses designating the user's desire to switch into Exclusive mode and begin the demo. Responds to the F12 or Esc keys by shutting down the application.

- `FormPaint`—Paints some simple instructions for the user in the middle of the screen. This method is not called while the program is in Exclusive mode. In other words, it tells the user how to activate DirectX and begin the demo proper.

- `Timer1Timer`—Flips between the primary and back surfaces. This is the key method in this demo, as it shows how to swap two different surfaces, which is what you want to do in an animated graphics program. This method is somewhat misleading, though, because most of the time you will want to swap at the fastest rate possible rather than wait for the timer to call your program and ask you to swap. For instance, a smooth animation should have a frame rate of at least 25 frames per second, a rate that is not practical to achieve using a timer. Later, I will show you how to set this rate, but for now I want you to be conscious of each page flipping, so I slow things down to the point where you can see it happen.

A few of the steps outlined here require more detailed examination. In particular, I want to describe the code that initializes DirectDraw, the code that flips between the front and back surface, and the code that deallocates memory for the object.

Initializing DirectDraw

To create a DirectDraw object, you should call `DirectDrawCreate`:

```
hr := DirectDrawCreate(nil, FDirectDraw, nil);
```

This function is part of the Windows DirectDraw API. To include it in your project, add the DirectX unit to your uses clause.

> **NOTE**
>
> The `DirectX.pas` file included with this book was not created by Borland. Instead, it is the work of third-party developers who are freely giving their time to the Delphi community. I did not find the file they produced to be perfect, so I made several small changes to it. You should feel free to do the same, if you so desire. However, overall, I consider the work done to create this file to be of excellent quality, and we are all in the debt of the people who did this work for us. The current version of this file that I have supports DirectX 5.

27

DIRECTDRAW

DirectDrawCreate is declared like this:

```
function DirectDrawCreate(lpGUID: PGUID; out lplpDD: IDirectDraw;
  pUnkOuter: IUnknown): HRESULT; stdcall;
```

In almost all cases, you can set the first and third parameters to nil. In fact, I have never seen a case in which anyone has done otherwise. In the second parameter, you should pass in the variable that will be assigned a pointer of type DirectDraw.

NOTE

Some of the identifiers in the DirectX file are given absurd names such as lplpDD. This parameter name was created by Microsoft, and the creators of the DirectX Pascal file are simply engaging in the admirable endeavor of copying it verbatim.

lplpDD is an abbreviation for a long pointer to a long pointer to a DirectDraw object. In Object Pascal, all objects are pointers; there is no need for one of the two lps because it is assumed.

The second pointer is taken care of by the fact that this is an out parameter, which effectively hides one level of indirection from the programmer by automatically passing in a parameter by reference. In other words, writing out MyVariable in Object Pascal is the same thing as writing &MyVariable in C.

At this stage, you have seen that the elegantly constructed Object Pascal language makes it unnecessary to make a big deal out of the fact that you are working with a pointer to a pointer. This leaves you with the abbreviation DD, which stands for DirectDraw. To my mind, abbreviations of this sort are confusing, without being the least bit useful. (Modern compilers don't duplicate variable names in an application's code, but instead use tokens.) As a result, I would declare the function as follows:

```
function DirectDrawCreate(GUID: PGUID; out DirectDraw: IDirectDraw;
  OuterUnknown: IUnknown): HRESULT; stdcall;
```

It is not wrong to use the first translation of the code, and it has the advantage of closely following Microsoft's original, if somewhat misguided, efforts. If you look at the source to similar files translated at Borland, you will find that some follow my preferences, while others follow the straight and narrow path laid down by the busy worker bees from the great hive in Redmond.

Here is the rundown on the parameters you can pass to DirectDrawCreate:

- The first parameter to DirectDraw should be nil unless you want to force DirectDraw to always use hardware-specific code (the HAL) or to always use emulation (the HEL). Pass in DDCREATE_HARDWAREONLY to use hardware only, and pass in `DDCREATE_EMULATIONONLY` if you want to always use the HEL regardless of the capabilities of your current system. If you choose the first option, any calls that cannot be executed in hardware will fail with a return value of `DDERR_UNSUPPORTED`.

- The second parameter you pass in will return a fully initialized instance of the `IDirectDraw` object. I will discuss this object in more depth later in this chapter in the section "Getting into Exclusive Mode and Changing Screen Resolution."

- The final parameter is currently unsupported but may be used in the future to support COM aggregation. For now, Microsoft regards it as an error to pass in anything but `nil` in this parameter.

If `DirectDrawCreate` fails, it will return one of the following self-explanatory values:

```
DDERR_DIRECTDRAWALREADYCREATED
DDERR_GENERIC
DDERR_INVALIDDIRECTDRAWGUID
DDERR_INVALIDPARAMS
DDERR_NODIRECTDRAWHW
DDERR_OUTOFMEMORY
```

The only identifier requiring explanation here is `DDERR_NODIRECTDRAWHR`, which means you have attempted to create a hardware-only instance of DirectDraw on a system that has no DirectDraw hardware.

By now, you know more about `DirectDrawCreate` than you probably ever wanted to know or imagined necessary. Nevertheless, I'm not quite done with this little fellow, because it happens that using it in a component that runs on NT will cause Delphi to have trouble loading packages. As even the Microsoft DirectX team will admit, this difficulty is due to some peculiarities in the way the `DirectDrawCreate` function is designed and has nothing to do with Delphi packages.

Fortunately, you can use a simple workaround for those cases when you don't want to call `DirectDrawCreate` directly:

```
var
  FDirectDraw: IDirectDraw;
begin
  Hr = CoCreateInstance(CLSID_DirectDraw,
    nil, CLSCTX_ALL, IID_IDirectDraw, FDirectDraw);
  FDirectDraw.Initialize(nil);
end;
```

These two calls use standard COM calls to create the DirectDraw object. The first is a call to `CoCreateInstance`, which is the standard COM routine for creating a COM object. The second call ensures that DirectDraw is properly initialized. You do not need to call `Initialize` if you use `DirectDrawCreate`.

27

DIRECTDRAW

Deallocating Interfaces

As a rule, an interface will be deallocated automatically by Delphi without your having to do anything. However, you can explicitly deallocate memory in two ways:

```
if DirectDrawSurface <> nil then begin
  Result := DirectDrawSurface._Release;
  DirectDrawSurface := nil;
end;

if DirectDrawSuface <> nil then
  DirectDrawSurface := nil;
```

The second of these two techniques is obviously simpler, but you will find that I am sometimes partial to the first because it explicitly shows what is happening. In other words, COM programmers know that Release needs to be called, and they might be confused by its absence. The first example makes utterly clear what is happening.

The Delphi developers argue that you should never have to do anything to release a COM object because the compiler will perform that operation for you automatically the moment your object goes out of scope. However, I find that I frequently want to free a COM object before it has gone out of scope, so you will see this code in my program quite frequently.

> **NOTE**
>
> The _Release method will return an Integer value stating the number of counts against a particular object. For instance, if you have allocated memory for an interface twice, the first time you call _Release, the method will return 1, and if you call it a second time, it will return 0. This knowledge can sometimes help you debug an application.

Getting into Exclusive Mode and Changing Screen Resolution

After you initialize an instance of DirectDraw, the next step is to set the cooperative level:

```
hr := FDirectDraw.SetCooperativeLevel(Handle,
  DDSCL_EXCLUSIVE or DDSCL_FULLSCREEN);
```

The code shown here sets the CooperativeLevel to full-screen Exclusive mode. As a result, your program will take up the whole screen, and no other windows will be allowed to overlap it unless you explicitly flip away from your program by pressing Ctrl+Alt+Tab. You can also initialize the cooperative level to DDSCL_NORMAL, which is a Windowed mode. For now, I'm going to ignore that setting, as it is, in some ways, considerably more complicated than Exclusive mode.

You have the choice of setting the resolution and bit depth of your program if you are in Exclusive mode. You can proceed as follows:

```
hr := FDirectDraw.SetDisplayMode(640, 480, 8);
```

This code sets the screen resolution to 640×480 and gives you a bit depth of 8, which means you can show a maximum of 256 colors.

Until quite recently, picking a resolution and bit depth any greater than this was fruitless. About 300KB is required to hold a single copy of a 640×480 screen, which means you need at least 600KB to hold one screen and back buffer. That was about the max you could expect to get from most systems, so trying a higher resolution was fruitless. Now some video cards will, in fact, give decent performance if you go to a higher resolution, but it is still not something you can count on. As a result, I usually stick with this relatively simple resolution, though it does mean that I have to learn to cope with palettes.

What Is a DirectDraw Surface?

After you set the cooperative level and screen resolution, the next step is to get the two surfaces that you will flip between. In other words, you have to create a pointer to the video memory that the user looks at and to a back buffer that you can use for double buffering, or for page flipping. You can proceed like this:

```
var
  hr: HRESULT;
  SurfaceDesc: TDDSURFACEDESC ;
  DDSCaps: TDDSCAPS;
begin
  ...
  SurfaceDesc.dwSize := sizeof(SurfaceDesc);
  SurfaceDesc.dwFlags := DDSD_CAPS or DDSD_BACKBUFFERCOUNT;
  SurfaceDesc.ddsCaps.dwCaps :=
    DDSCAPS_PRIMARYSURFACE or DDSCAPS_FLIP or DDSCAPS_COMPLEX;
  SurfaceDesc.dwBackBufferCount := 1;
  hr := FDirectDraw.CreateSurface(SurfaceDesc, FPrimarySurface, nil);
  ddscaps.dwCaps := DDSCAPS_BACKBUFFER;
  hr := FPrimarySurface.GetAttachedSurface(ddscaps, FBackSurface);
```

This admittedly rather convoluted chunk of code creates both your primary surface and the back surface. The primary surface is what the user sees, and the back surface is what will be flipped onto the primary surface when you call the DirectDraw Flip function to implement double buffering.

Here is the DDSCaps structure:

```
TDDSCaps = record
  dwCaps: DWORD;           // capabilities of surface wanted
end;
```

This record may appear fairly simple at first glance, but a little exploration will prove that it is indeed quite complex. In fact, both the DDSCaps and the SurfaceDesc records are almost hopelessly complex structures that handle a painfully large number of constants. Rather than drive both you and me mad trying to describe them, I will tell you that you simply have to get the DirectX SDK to look up these parameters in the online help. For instance, the sole field of the DDSCaps structure, called dwCaps, takes 30 possible constants, many of which are quite complicated to explain. Here, however, is a list of a few of the most important ones:

```
DDSCAPS_3D                  = $00000001;
DDSCAPS_ALPHA               = $00000002;
DDSCAPS_BACKBUFFER          = $00000004;
DDSCAPS_COMPLEX             = $00000008;
DDSCAPS_FLIP                = $00000010;
DDSCAPS_FRONTBUFFER         = $00000020;
DDSCAPS_OFFSCREENPLAIN      = $00000040;
DDSCAPS_OVERLAY             = $00000080;
DDSCAPS_PALETTE             = $00000100;
DDSCAPS_PRIMARYSURFACE      = $00000200;
DDSCAPS_PRIMARYSURFACELEFT  = $00000400;
DDSCAPS_SYSTEMMEMORY        = $00000800;
DDSCAPS_TEXTURE             = $00001000;
DDSCAPS_3DDEVICE            = $00002000;
DDSCAPS_VIDEOMEMORY         = $00004000;
DDSCAPS_VISIBLE             = $00008000;
DDSCAPS_WRITEONLY           = $00010000;
DDSCAPS_ZBUFFER             = $00020000;
DDSCAPS_OWNDC               = $00040000;
DDSCAPS_LIVEVIDEO           = $00080000;
DDSCAPS_HWCODEC             = $00100000;
DDSCAPS_MODEX               = $00200000;
DDSCAPS_MIPMAP              = $00400000;
DDSCAPS_ALLOCONLOAD         = $04000000;
```

Here is the TDDSurfaceDesc record:

```
TDDSurfaceDesc = record
  dwSize: DWORD;                    // size of the DDSURFACEDESC
                                    // structure
  dwFlags: DWORD;                   // determines what fields are valid
  dwHeight: DWORD;                  // height of surface to be created
  dwWidth: DWORD;                   // width of input surface
  lPitch: Longint;                  // distance to start of next line
  dwBackBufferCount: DWORD;         // number of back buffers requested
  case Integer of
```

```
0: (
    dwMipMapCount: DWORD;           // number of mip-map levels requested
    dwAlphaBitDepth: DWORD;         // depth of alpha buffer requested
    dwReserved: DWORD;              // reserved
    lpSurface: Pointer;             // pointer to the associated
                                    // surface memory
    ddckCKDestOverlay: TDDColorKey; // color key for destination
                                    // overlay use
    ddckCKDestBlt: TDDColorKey;     // color key for destination
                                    // blt use
    ddckCKSrcOverlay: TDDColorKey;  // color key for source
                                    // overlay use
    ddckCKSrcBlt: TDDColorKey;      // color key for source blt use
    ddpfPixelFormat: DDPIXELFORMAT; // pixel format description
                                    // of the surface
    DDSCaps: TDDSCaps;              // direct draw surface
                                    // capabilities
    );
1: (dwZBufferBitDepth: DWORD;      // depth of Z buffer requested
    );
2: (dwRefreshRate: DWORD;          // refresh rate
    );
end;
```

The complexity of this record is enough to make a grown man cry; or at any rate, it is enough to drive an author to utter distraction. Rather than take you through this monstrosity field by field, I will instead point out that this record can be used to retrieve the size, height, width, pixel depth, and a pointer to the actual bytes that describe a surface. One of the more tricky fields here is called Pitch, which describes the distance to the start of the next line of a surface. This is not necessarily the width of your surface, so you need to make a special call to retrieve the real width. Pay close attention to the pitch when you are directly manipulating the bytes (or bits) of a DirectDraw surface.

After you create the primary surface, you can easily get to the premade back surface that you use for page flipping:

```
ddscaps.dwCaps := DDSCAPS_BACKBUFFER;
hr := FPrimarySurface.GetAttachedSurface(ddscaps, FBackSurface);
```

This simple code retrieves the back surface. I always maintain a pointer to the back surface so I can access it when I need it.

In Chapter 28, "More DirectX Technologies," I will show that you often should create a third surface or even multiple additional surfaces. When I work with DirectDraw, I use the DirectDraw CreateSurface routine to create a third surface that I call the WorkSurface. I then paint my images onto this surface, blit it to the back surface, and then flip the back surface so that the user can see it. I have come to doubt the usefulness of my WorkSurface object, but you will definitely want to work with more than just the back surface sometimes. This topic will come up again later in this chapter.

Writing Text to the Screen

Now that you have the primary surface and the back surface, you can draw something to the back surface and show it to the user by performing a page flip. Here is how to get started:

```
if (FBackSurface.GetDC(DC) = DD_OK) then begin
  SetBkColor(DC, RGB(0, 0, 255));
  SetTextColor(DC, RGB(255, 255, 0));
  TextOut(DC, 0, 0, PChar(FFrontMsg), Length(FFrontMsg));
  FPrimarySurface.ReleaseDC(DC);
end;
```

In this code, I call the GetDC method of the back surface to retrieve a device context. Then I blit some text to the back buffer, using standard Windows calls. I should point out that most of the time you are actually working with bitmaps rather than standard GDI calls like those shown here. Custom DirectDraw functions are available for working with bitmaps, but the technology also supports standard GDI code as shown here.

You might find yourself wondering why I make GDI calls here after going to such lengths to explain that GDI is inherently inferior to DirectDraw when it comes to performance. Well, it is true that the GDI is slower, and the calls shown here, in fact, take a ridiculously long time to execute. On the other hand, one of the goals of DirectDraw is to allow you to use existing Windows technology if you want. In this case, I do, in fact, want to use that existing technology, and DirectDraw will let me do so, even if some of the DirectX developers wince to see me do it. Later in the book, I will show you how to use a Delphi TCanvas object in conjunction with a DirectDraw surface.

Flipping Surfaces

So now, at long last, you are ready to show the user something. The following code will let the user see what you have been up to:

```
while (True) do begin
  hr := FPrimarySurface.Flip(nil, 0);

  if (hr = DD_OK) then
    break;

  if(hr = DDERR_SURFACELOST) then begin
    hr := FPrimarySurface.Restore();
    if(hr <> DD_OK) then
      break;
  end;

  if(hr <> DDERR_WASSTILLDRAWING) then
    break;
end;
```

The key line of code here is the call to `Flip`. This method will swap the primary buffer and the back buffer so that the primary buffer becomes the back buffer and the back buffer becomes the primary buffer. (Remember that you got the back buffer from the primary buffer by calling `GetAttachedSurface`. The two surfaces are linked in the mind of DirectDraw, so this kind of thing comes to you for free.)

If all goes well, you can immediately break out of the `while` statement that encapsulates the call to `Flip`. However, the call sometimes fails, usually for one of two reasons:

- The surface was lost. This failure occurs when you press Alt+Tab to move away from a DirectDraw application and then press Alt+Tab to move back. When you press Alt+Tab to move back, the surface you were working with needs to be restored before it can be used. The following code performs that function:

```
if(hr = DDERR_SURFACELOST) then begin
  hr := FPrimarySurface.Restore();
  if(hr <> DD_OK) then
    break;
end;
```

- The previous flip operation has not yet completed, or you are still busy drawing something to the back surface. In that case, you need to cycle through the `while` loop one or more times, waiting for the surfaces to become free so they can be flipped. The extremely simple code for handling this situation is shown at the end of the `while` loop.

That's all there is to page flipping, or double buffering, as I often call it. This relatively simple process of swapping the primary and back buffers is probably the single most important piece of technology in the entire DirectX API. This is what makes DirectX so fast, and this is the technology you need to master if you want to get good at this stuff.

> **NOTE**
>
> You can call `Flip` only when you are in full-screen Exclusive mode. You can't use this technology when you are in Windowed mode. However, I'm not saying that DirectDraw can be of no significant help to you in Windowed mode. The concept of surfaces is still available to you in Windowed mode, which means you have an offscreen buffer you can write to. Furthermore, DirectDraw provides functions that allow you to speedily blit one surface onto another. As a result, you can quickly blit your secondary surface onto the primary surface, thereby showing it to the user. This technology is not as good as true flipping, but it is sufficient to handle most situations.

27

DIRECTDRAW

Deallocating Memory

This code cleans up the surfaces when you are ready to exit the program:

```
Procedure TForm1.FormDestroy(Sender: TObject);
begin
  if(FDirectDraw <> nil) then begin
    FDirectDraw.FlipToGDISurface;
    FDirectDraw.SetCooperativeLevel(Handle, DDSCL_NORMAL);
    if FBackSurface <> nil then
      FBackSurface := nil;
    if FPrimarySurface <> nil then
      FPrimarySurface := nil;
    FDirectDraw := nil;
  end;
end;
```

The first significant step in this method is to call `FlipToGDISurface`. You need to make this call if you want to show a dialog or other standard Windows window to the user. I then get out of Exclusive mode, which ensures that standard windowing behavior will be available on the desktop. Finally, I call `Release` on my surfaces by setting them equal to `nil`.

All this work might seem a bit like overkill to some users. The reason I am being so cautious before deallocating my surfaces is simply that raising an exception while you are in Exclusive mode is not a good idea. If an exception is raised, then a dialog will be popped up and shown to the user. But if you are in Exclusive mode, then you completely own the desktop, which means that Windows will not be able to pop up a dialog where the user can see it. Unfortunately, behind the scenes, Windows will pop up the dialog. You won't be able to see it and therefore won't know where to click to shut it down. Furthermore, if Delphi tries to take you to the line of code where the exception occurred, Delphi also won't be able to show you what it is doing. The end result is a situation in which your machine appears to be locked up, even though you really are probably doing little more than handling a simple exception.

These kinds of problems do have solutions. They involve catching exceptions before they are shown to the user and then flipping to the GDI surface so that you can inform the user about what has happened.

> **NOTE**
>
> If you are in Exclusive mode and want to raise an exception, you should first make a call to DirectDraw.FlipToGDISurface. In fact, you can make this call whenever you want to show a message box or Delphi form to the user.
>
> The following two methods (from the SimpleHermes2 program found in the Chap28 directory on the CD that accompanies this book) shows one generic solution to handling exceptions:
>
> ```
> procedure TForm1.FormCreate(Sender: TObject);
> begin
>   Width := 640;
>   Height := 480;
>   Application.OnException := FormException;
> end;
>
> procedure TForm1.FormException(Sender: TObject; E: Exception);
> begin
>   if Hermes1.ScreenMode in [sm640X480X16, sm640X480X8] then begin
>     Hermes1.DirectDraw.FlipToGDISurface;
>     ShowMessage(E.Message);
>   end;
> end;
> ```
>
> This code ensures that all the exceptions you don't explicitly handle will be passed on to a method called FormException. This method first calls FlipToGDISurface and then calls ShowMessage. If you do explicitly handle an exception someplace else in your code, you should call FlipToGDISurface before showing your message. After calling FlipToGDISurface, until you restore the DirectDraw surface, you can show a Delphi form or a MessageBox. Then the next time you call DirectDraw.Flip in your code, you will need to restore the DirectDraw surface. The code I'm showing you usually does that automatically.

Smooth Animation

On the CD that accompanies this book, you will find several more examples of relatively simple DirectDraw programs. Most of them come with explanations of what is happening in the code. You should run these programs and study them to learn how they work. In particular, take a look at the DirectDraw3 program, which animates a series of color shapes, as shown in Figure 27.1.

FIGURE 27.1

The DirectDraw3 program shows that you can smoothly animate multiple shapes in Delphi DirectDraw application.

To create smooth animation, you need to respond to the OnIdle event of the Application object. This event can be initialized in your program's constructor:

```
Application.OnIdle := IdleEvent;
```

The actual OnIdleEvent looks like this:

```
procedure TForm1.IdleEvent(Sender: TObject; var Done: Boolean);
var
  hr: HResult;
begin
  Done := False;

  if not FActive then Exit;

  PerformAction;

  while (True) do begin
    hr := FPrimarySurface.Flip(nil, 0);
    if (hr = DD_OK) then
      break;

    if(hr = DDERR_SURFACELOST) then begin
      hr := FPrimarySurface.Restore();
      if(hr <> DD_OK) then
        break;
    end;
```

```
    if(hr <> DDERR_WASSTILLDRAWING) then
      break;
  end;
end;
```

This code sets the `Done` variable passed to the `IdleEvent` to `False`. This means that you want Delphi to call the `IdleEvent` again as soon as possible. The next time your application is idle, the `OnIdle` event will be called.

As you can see, the main code in the `IdleEvent` does little more than prepare the back surface by calling `PerformAction` and then flip the back and primary surfaces. The whole point here is that the `OnIdle` method will be called at every possible opportunity, and that when it is called, you will prepare the back buffer and then perform a page flip. As a result, you get the fastest possible frame rate and therefore the smoothest possible animation.

Listing 27.2 shows the complete code for the `DirectDraw3` program. You should study this code to get some sense of how the flow of events is channeled in a DirectDraw program that has some small degree of complexity in it.

LISTING 27.2 THE `DirectDraw3` PROGRAM AUTOMATES SEVERAL SMOOTHLY SCROLLING SHAPES

```
unit Main;

interface

uses
  Windows, Messages, SysUtils,
  Classes, Graphics, Controls,
  Forms, Dialogs, ExtCtrls,
  DirectX;

const
  WM_RUNAPP = WM_USER;
  CIRCLETYPE = 0;
  RECTTYPE = 1;


type
  TDrawShape = class(TObject)
  private
    FX: Integer;
    FY: Integer;
    FX1: Integer;
    FY1: Integer;
    FMoveValX: Integer;
    FMoveValY: Integer;
```

continues

LISTING 27.2   CONTINUED

```pascal
    FShapeType: Integer;
    FPrevRect, FPrevRect2: TRect;
    FColor: TColor;
    function GetRect: TRect;
    procedure SetRect(R: TRect);
  public
    constructor Create(ValX, ValY, X, Y, AType: Integer;
      AColor: TColor);
    constructor CreateTwo(ValX: Integer; ValY: Integer);
    procedure Move;
    procedure Draw(var DC: HDC);
    property ShapeRect: TRect read GetRect write SetRect;
    property ShapeType: Integer read FShapeType write FShapeType;
    property Color: TColor read FColor write FColor;
  end;

  TForm1 = class(TForm)
    procedure FormCreate(Sender: TObject);
    procedure FormDestroy(Sender: TObject);
    procedure FormKeyDown(Sender: TObject; var Key: Word;
      Shift: TShiftState);
    procedure FormPaint(Sender: TObject);
  private
    FDirectDraw: IDirectDraw;                // DirectDraw object
    FPrimarySurface: IDirectDrawSurface; // DirectDraw primary surface
    FBackSurface: IDirectDrawSurface;    // DirectDraw back surface
    FActive: Boolean;                    // is application active?
    FPhase: Byte;
    FFrontMsg: string;
    FBackMsg: string;
    FValueAdd: Integer;
    FShapeRect: TRect;
    FShapeList: TList;
    procedure DrawShape(var DC: HDC);
    procedure IdleEvent(Sender: TObject; var Done: Boolean);
    procedure PaintSurfaces;
    procedure Start;
    procedure BuildList;
    procedure PerformAction;
  public
    { Public declarations }
  end;

const
  AFileName = 'c:\debug.txt';

var
  Form1: TForm1;
  DebugFile: TextFile;
implementation
```

```
{$R *.DFM}

//-----------------------------------------------------------------
// --- TDrawShape --------------------------------------------------
//-----------------------------------------------------------------

constructor TDrawShape.Create(ValX, ValY, X, Y, AType: Integer;
  AColor: TColor);
begin
  FMoveValX := ValX;
  FMoveValY := ValY;
  ShapeRect := Rect(X, Y, X+25, Y+25);
  ShapeType := AType;
  Color := AColor;
end;

constructor TDrawShape.CreateTwo(ValX: Integer; ValY: Integer);
begin
  FMoveValX := ValX;
  FMoveValY := ValY;
end;

function TDrawShape.GetRect: TRect;
begin
  Result := Rect(FX,FY,FX1,FY1);
end;

procedure TDrawShape.SetRect(R: TRECT);
begin
  FX := R.left;
  FY := R.top;
  FX1 := R.right;
  FY1 := R.bottom;
end;

procedure TDrawShape.Move;
begin
  FPrevRect2 := Rect(FPrevRect.left, FPrevRect.top, FPrevRect.right,
    FPrevRect.bottom);
  FPrevRect := Rect(FX, FY, FX1, FY1);
  FX := FX + FMoveValX;
  FY := FY + FMoveValY;
  FX1 := FX1 + FMoveValX;
  FY1 := FY1 + FMoveValY;
  if (FX1 > 637) then
    FMoveValX := -2;
  if (FX < 3) then
    FMoveValX := 2;
  if (FY1 > 477) then
    FMoveValY := - 2;
  if (FY < 3) then
```

continues

27

LISTING 27.2   CONTINUED

```pascal
    FMoveValY := 2;
end;

/////////////////////////////////////////
// Draw
/////////////////////////////////////////
procedure TDrawShape.Draw(var DC: HDC);
var
  Brush, OldBrush: HBrush;
begin
  Brush := CreateSolidBrush(RGB(0, 0, 0));
  OldBrush := SelectObject(DC, Brush);
  if (FShapeType =CIRCLETYPE) then
    Ellipse(DC, FPrevRect2.left-1, FPrevRect2.top-1, FPrevRect2.right+1,
      FPrevRect2.bottom+1)
  else if (FShapeType = RECTTYPE) then
    Rectangle(DC, FPrevRect2.left-1, FPrevRect2.top-1,
      FPrevRect2.right+1, FPrevRect2.bottom+1);

  SelectObject(DC, OldBrush);
  DeleteObject(Brush);

  Move;

  Brush := CreateSolidBrush(FColor);
  OldBrush := SelectObject(DC, Brush);

  if (FShapeType = CIRCLETYPE) then
    Ellipse(DC, FX, FY, FX1, FY1)
  else if (FShapeType = RECTTYPE) then
    Rectangle(DC, FX, FY, FX1, FY1);

  SelectObject(DC, OldBrush);
  DeleteObject(Brush);

  WriteLn(DebugFile, 'Draw');
end;

//----------------------------------------------------------------------
// --- TForm1 ----------------------------------------------------------
//----------------------------------------------------------------------


procedure TForm1.FormCreate(Sender: TObject);
begin
  Width := 640;
  Height := 480;
  FDirectDraw := nil;
  FPhase := 0;
  FActive := False;
```

```
    FFrontMsg := 'Front buffer (F12 or Esc to quit)';
    FBackMsg := 'Back buffer (F12 or Esc to quit)';
    FShapeRect := Rect(25, 25, 50, 50);
    Application.OnIdle := IdleEvent;
    FValueAdd := 2;
    BuildList;
end;

procedure TForm1.BuildList;
begin
  FShapeList := TList.Create;

  FShapeList.Add(TDrawShape.Create(-2, 2, 175, 175, CIRCLETYPE, clLime));
  FShapeList.Add(TDrawShape.Create(2, 2, 125, 125, RECTTYPE, clBlue));
  FShapeList.Add(TDrawShape.Create(2, -2, 200, 200, RECTTYPE, clYellow));
  FShapeList.Add(TDrawShape.Create(2, -2, 75, 75, CIRCLETYPE, clRed));
  FShapeList.Add(TDrawShape.Create(-2, 2, 325, 350, RECTTYPE, clPurple));
  FShapeList.Add(TDrawShape.Create
➥(-2, -2, 275, 250, CIRCLETYPE, clFuchsia));
  FShapeList.Add(TDrawShape.Create(-2, 2, 125, 325, CIRCLETYPE, clTeal));
  FShapeList.Add(TDrawShape.Create(2, 2, 350, 175, RECTTYPE, clNavy));
  FShapeList.Add(TDrawShape.Create
➥(2, -2, 150, 250, CIRCLETYPE, clOlive));
  FShapeList.Add(TDrawShape.Create
➥(-2, 2, 225, 25, CIRCLETYPE, clSilver));
end;

procedure TForm1.IdleEvent(Sender: TObject; var Done: Boolean);
var
  hr: HResult;
begin
  Done := False;

  if not FActive then Exit;

  PerformAction;

  while (True) do begin
    hr := FPrimarySurface.Flip(nil, 0);
    if (hr = DD_OK) then
      break;

    if(hr = DDERR_SURFACELOST) then begin
      hr := FPrimarySurface.Restore();
      if(hr <> DD_OK) then
        break;
    end;

    if(hr <> DDERR_WASSTILLDRAWING) then
      break;
  end;
```

continues

LISTING 27.2   CONTINUED

```pascal
end;

procedure TForm1.FormDestroy(Sender: TObject);
var
  Shape: TDrawShape;
  i: Integer;
begin
  if FShapeList <> nil then begin
    for i := 0 to FShapeList.Count - 1 do begin
      Shape := TDrawShape(FShapeList.Items[i]);
      Shape.Free;
    end;
    FShapeList.Free;
  end;

  if(FDirectDraw <> nil) then begin
    FDirectDraw.FlipToGDISurface;
    FDirectDraw.SetCooperativeLevel(Handle, DDSCL_NORMAL);
    if FBackSurface <> nil then
      FBackSurface := nil;
    if FPrimarySurface <> nil then
      FPrimarySurface := nil;
    FDirectDraw := nil;
  end;
end;

procedure TForm1.Start;
var
  hr: HRESULT;
  SurfaceDesc: TDDSURFACEDESC ;
  DDSCaps: TDDSCAPS;
begin
  hr := DirectDrawCreate(nil, FDirectDraw, nil);
  if(hr = DD_OK) then begin
    // Get exclusive mode
    hr := FDirectDraw.SetCooperativeLevel(Handle, // DDSCL_NORMAL);
      DDSCL_EXCLUSIVE or DDSCL_FULLSCREEN);
    if(hr = DD_OK) then begin
      hr := FDirectDraw.SetDisplayMode(640, 480, 8);
      if(hr = DD_OK) then begin
        // Create the primary surface with 1 back buffer
        SurfaceDesc.dwSize := sizeof(SurfaceDesc);
        SurfaceDesc.dwFlags := DDSD_CAPS or DDSD_BACKBUFFERCOUNT;
        SurfaceDesc.ddsCaps.dwCaps := DDSCAPS_PRIMARYSURFACE or
                          DDSCAPS_FLIP or
                          DDSCAPS_COMPLEX;
        SurfaceDesc.dwBackBufferCount := 1;
        hr := FDirectDraw.CreateSurface
        ➥(SurfaceDesc, FPrimarySurface, nil);
        if(hr = DD_OK) then begin
```

```pascal
          // Get a pointer to the back buffer
          ddscaps.dwCaps := DDSCAPS_BACKBUFFER;
          hr := FPrimarySurface.GetAttachedSurface
          ➥(ddscaps, FBackSurface);
          if(hr = DD_OK) then begin
            PaintSurfaces;
            Exit;
          end;
        end;
      end;
    end;
  end;
  MessageBox(Handle, PChar(Format('Direct Draw Init Failed %x', )),
    'ERROR', MB_OK);
  Close();
end;

procedure TForm1.FormKeyDown(Sender: TObject; var Key: Word;
  Shift: TShiftState);
begin
  case Key of
    VK_F3: begin
      FActive := True;
      Start();
    end;

    VK_ESCAPE, VK_F12: begin
      FActive := False;
      Close;
    end;
  end;
end;

procedure TForm1.FormPaint(Sender: TObject);
const
  Msg = 'Page Flipping Test: Press F3 to start, F12 or Esc to exit';
var
  rc: TRect;
  size: TSize;
  DC: HDC;
begin
  if not(FActive) then begin
    DC := GetDC(Handle);
    rc := GetClientRect;
    GetTextExtentPoint(DC, Msg, Length(Msg), size);
    SetBkColor(DC, RGB(0, 0, 0));
    SetTextColor(DC, RGB(255, 255, 0));
    TextOut(DC, (rc.right - size.cx) div 2,
      (rc.bottom - size.cy) div 2, PChar(Msg), Length(Msg)-1);
    ReleaseDC(Handle, DC);
  end;
```

27

DIRECTDRAW

continues

LISTING 27.2   CONTINUED

```
end;

procedure TForm1.PerformAction;
var
  DC: HDC;
begin
  // Don't step through code that has lock on it!
  // Getting a DC may put a lock on video memory.
  if FBackSurface.GetDC(DC) = DD_OK then begin
    DrawShape(DC);
    FBackSurface.ReleaseDC(DC);
  end;
end;

procedure TForm1.DrawShape(var DC: HDC);
var
  Shape: TDrawShape;
  i: Integer;
begin
  WriteLn(DebugFile, 'Count: ', FShapeList.Count);
  for i := 0 to FShapeList.Count - 1 do begin
    Shape := TDrawShape(FShapeList.Items[i]);
    Shape.Draw(DC);
  end;
end;

procedure TForm1.PaintSurfaces;
var
  DC: HDC;
  Brush, OldBrush: HBrush;
begin
  if (FPrimarySurface.GetDC(DC) = DD_OK) then begin
    SetBkColor(DC, RGB(0, 0, 255));
    SetTextColor(DC, RGB(255, 255, 0));
    TextOut(DC, 0, 0, PChar(FFrontMsg), Length(FFrontMsg));
    FPrimarySurface.ReleaseDC(DC);
  end;

  if (FBackSurface.GetDC(DC) = DD_OK) then begin
    Brush := CreateSolidBrush(RGB(0, 0, 0));
    OldBrush := SelectObject(DC, Brush);
    SetBkColor(DC, RGB(0, 0, 0));
    SetTextColor(DC, RGB(255, 255, 0));
    TextOut(DC, 0, 0, PChar(FBackMsg), Length(FBackMsg));
    Rectangle(DC, 0, 0, 640, 480);
    SelectObject(DC, OldBrush);
    DeleteObject(Brush);
    FBackSurface.ReleaseDC(DC);
  end;
end;
```

```
initialization
  AssignFile(DebugFile, AFileName);
  ReWrite(DebugFile);
finalization
  CloseFile(DebugFile);
end.
```

When you run this program, a series of colored shapes appear on the screen. As you watch, they smoothly scroll back and forth.

The following code updates the back surface of the application whenever the IdleEvent is called:

```
procedure TForm1.PerformAction;
var
  DC: HDC;
begin
  // Don't step through code that has lock on it!
  // Getting a DC may put a lock on video memory.
  if FBackSurface.GetDC(DC) = DD_OK then begin
    DrawShape(DC);
    FBackSurface.ReleaseDC(DC);
  end;
end;

procedure TForm1.DrawShape(var DC: HDC);
var
  Shape: TDrawShape;
  i: Integer;
begin
  WriteLn(DebugFile, 'Count: ', FShapeList.Count);
  for i := 0 to FShapeList.Count - 1 do begin
    Shape := TDrawShape(FShapeList.Items[i]);
    Shape.Draw(DC);
  end;
end;
```

Notice that the first method shown here warns you not to step through code that has a DC in it taken from a DirectDrawSurface. If you do attempt to step through this code, you will almost certainly lock up the system about as hard and as finally as you could ever imagine.

The DrawShape method works with a list containing a series of colored shapes. You can retrieve these shapes from the program and then use simple polymorphism to paint them to the screen. Really, this process is very simple. The only hard part is initializing DirectDraw and understanding how to flip back and forth between surfaces. After you master these technologies, you can do quite a bit in DirectDraw without exerting any undo effort.

27

DIRECTDRAW

DirectDraw is not entirely simple. However, the amount of complexity you find here is manageable. Furthermore, most of the code you have seen is boilerplate. You can write it once and then use it over and over again. However, you need to understand it if you are going to work with DirectDraw.

Working with Bitmaps

Before closing this chapter, I want to show you how to work with bitmaps in a DirectDraw application. The program shown in Listing 27.3 and Figure 27.2 is the simplest I could devise that would still allow you to see how to use a bitmap in a DirectDraw program.

FIGURE 27.2

Blitting a picture to the screen using DirectDraw.

The DirectDrawPicture2 program, shown in Figure 27.3, is a more interesting example of what you can do with bitmaps in DirectDraw. However, the core issue you need to master is that of simply loading a bitmap into a DirectDraw program and then showing it to the user. The DirectDrawPicture1 program is designed to show you that process in the clearest and most uncluttered way possible.

FIGURE 27.3

The DirectDraw-
Picture2 *program
shows how to
work with sprites
and how to create
transparent areas.*

LISTING 27.3　THE DirectDrawPicture1 PROGRAM SHOWS HOW TO WORK WITH
BITMAPS

```
unit Main;

interface

uses
  Windows, Messages, SysUtils,
  Classes, Graphics, Controls,
  Forms, Dialogs, ExtCtrls,
  DirectX;

const
  TIMER_ID = 1;
  TIMER_RATE = 500;
  Background = 'BACK';

type
  TForm1 = class(TForm)
    Timer1: TTimer;
    procedure FormCreate(Sender: TObject);
    procedure FormDestroy(Sender: TObject);
    procedure FormKeyDown(Sender: TObject; var Key: Word;
      Shift: TShiftState);
    procedure FormPaint(Sender: TObject);
    procedure Timer1Timer(Sender: TObject);
```

continues

LISTING 27.3 CONTINUED

```pascal
  private
    FDirectDraw: IDirectDraw;                    // DirectDraw object
    FPrimarySurface: IDirectDrawSurface;         // DirectDraw primary
                                                 // surface
    FBackSurface: IDirectDrawSurface;            // DirectDraw back surface
    FDirectDrawPalette: IDIRECTDRAWPALETTE;      // DirectDraw palette
    FActive: Boolean;                            // is application active?
    FPhase: Byte;
    FFrontMsg: string;
    FBackMsg: string;
    procedure Start;
    procedure PaintSurfaces;
    procedure GetPicture;
    { Private declarations }
  public
    { Public declarations }
  end;

const
  AFileName = 'c:\debug.txt';

var
  Form1: TForm1;
  DebugFile: TextFile;
implementation

uses
  DDUtils1;

{$R *.DFM}
{$R COAST.RES}

procedure TForm1.FormCreate(Sender: TObject);
begin
  Width := 640;
  Height := 480;
  FDirectDraw := nil;
  FPhase := 0;
  FActive := False;
  FFrontMsg := 'Front buffer (F12 or Esc to quit)';
  FBackMsg := 'Back buffer (F12 or Esc to quit)';
end;

procedure TForm1.FormDestroy(Sender: TObject);
begin
  if(FDirectDraw <> nil) then begin
    FDirectDraw.FlipToGDISurface;
    FDirectDraw.SetCooperativeLevel(Handle, DDSCL_NORMAL);
    if FDirectDrawPalette <> nil then
```

```
      FDirectDrawPalette := nil;
    if FBackSurface <> nil then
      FBackSurface := nil;
    if FPrimarySurface <> nil then
      FPrimarySurface := nil;
    FDirectDraw := nil;
  end;
end;

procedure TForm1.GetPicture;
var
  hr: HResult;
begin
  FDirectDrawPalette := DDLoadPalette(FDirectDraw, Background);
  if FDirectDrawPalette <> nil then begin
    hr := FPrimarySurface.SetPalette(FDirectDrawPalette);
    if hr = DD_OK then begin
      DDReLoadBitmap(FBackSurface, Background);
    end;
  end;
end;

procedure TForm1.Start;
var
  hr: HRESULT;
  SurfaceDesc: TDDSURFACEDESC ;
  DDSCaps: TDDSCAPS;
begin
  hr := DirectDrawCreate(nil, FDirectDraw, nil);
  if(hr = DD_OK) then begin
    // Get exclusive mode
    hr := FDirectDraw.SetCooperativeLevel(Handle, // DDSCL_NORMAL);
      DDSCL_EXCLUSIVE or DDSCL_FULLSCREEN);
    if(hr = DD_OK) then begin
      hr := FDirectDraw.SetDisplayMode(640, 480, 8);
      if(hr = DD_OK) then begin
        // Create the primary surface with 1 back buffer
        SurfaceDesc.dwSize := sizeof(SurfaceDesc);
        SurfaceDesc.dwFlags := DDSD_CAPS or DDSD_BACKBUFFERCOUNT;
        SurfaceDesc.ddsCaps.dwCaps := DDSCAPS_PRIMARYSURFACE or
                            DDSCAPS_FLIP or
                            DDSCAPS_COMPLEX;
        SurfaceDesc.dwBackBufferCount := 1;
        hr := FDirectDraw.CreateSurface
        ➥(SurfaceDesc, FPrimarySurface, nil);
        if(hr = DD_OK) then begin
          ddscaps.dwCaps := DDSCAPS_BACKBUFFER;
          hr := FPrimarySurface.GetAttachedSurface
          ➥(ddscaps, FBackSurface);
          if(hr = DD_OK) then begin
            PaintSurfaces;
```

continues

LISTING 27.3 CONTINUED

```
                GetPicture;
                Timer1.Enabled := True;
                FActive := True;
                Exit;
              end;
            end;
          end;
        end;
      end;
    MessageBox(Handle, PChar(Format('Direct Draw Init Failed %x', )),
      'ERROR', MB_OK);
    Close();
end;

procedure TForm1.FormKeyDown(Sender: TObject; var Key: Word;
  Shift: TShiftState);
begin
  case Key of
    VK_F3: Start();
    VK_ESCAPE, VK_F12: begin
      Timer1.Enabled := False;
      Close;
    end;
  end;
end;

procedure TForm1.FormPaint(Sender: TObject);
const
  Msg = 'Page Flipping Test: Press F3 to start, F12 or Esc to exit';
var
  rc: TRect;
  size: TSize;
  DC: HDC;
begin
  if not(FActive) then begin
    DC := GetDC(Handle);
    rc := GetClientRect;
    GetTextExtentPoint(DC, Msg, Length(Msg), size);
    SetBkColor(DC, RGB(0, 0, 0));
    SetTextColor(DC, RGB(255, 255, 0));
    TextOut(DC, (rc.right - size.cx) div 2,
      (rc.bottom - size.cy) div 2, PChar(Msg), Length(Msg)-1);
    ReleaseDC(Handle, DC);
  end;
end;

procedure TForm1.Timer1Timer(Sender: TObject);
var
  DC: HDC;
  hr: HResult;
```

```
begin
  GetPicture;

  if (FBackSurface.GetDC(DC) = DD_OK) then begin
    if FPhase <> 0 then begin
      SetBkColor(DC, RGB(0, 0, 255));
      SetTextColor(DC, RGB(255, 255, 0));
      TextOut(DC, 0, 0, PChar(FFrontMsg), Length(FFrontMsg));
      Fphase := 0;
    end else begin
      SetBkColor(DC, RGB(0, 0, 255));
      SetTextColor(DC, RGB(0, 255, 255));
      TextOut(DC, 0, 0, PChar(FBackMsg), Length(FBackMsg));
      FPhase := 1;
    end;
    FBackSurface.ReleaseDC(DC);
  end;

  while (True) do begin
    hr := FPrimarySurface.Flip(nil, 0);

    if (hr = DD_OK) then
      break;

    if(hr = DDERR_SURFACELOST) then begin
      hr := FPrimarySurface.Restore();
      if(hr <> DD_OK) then
        break;
    end;

    if(hr <> DDERR_WASSTILLDRAWING) then
      break;
  end;
end;

procedure TForm1.PaintSurfaces;
var
  DC: HDC;
begin
  if (FPrimarySurface.GetDC(DC) = DD_OK) then begin
    SetBkColor(DC, RGB(0, 0, 255));
    SetTextColor(DC, RGB(255, 255, 0));
    TextOut(DC, 0, 0, PChar(FFrontMsg), Length(FFrontMsg));
    FPrimarySurface.ReleaseDC(DC);
  end;

  if (FBackSurface.GetDC(DC) = DD_OK) then begin
    SetBkColor(DC, RGB(0, 0, 255));
    SetTextColor(DC, RGB(255, 255, 0));
    TextOut(DC, 0, 0, PChar(FBackMsg), Length(FBackMsg));
    FBackSurface.ReleaseDC(DC);
```

27

DIRECTDRAW

continues

LISTING 27.3   CONTINUED

```
    end;
end;

initialization
  AssignFile(DebugFile, AFileName);
  ReWrite(DebugFile);
finalization
  CloseFile(DebugFile);
end.
```

This program shows a picture of the Santa Cruz coastline. The code that gets the picture and displays it to the user is both very simple and quite complex, depending on how carefully you look at it:

```
procedure TForm1.GetPicture;
var
  hr: HResult;
begin
  FDirectDrawPalette := DDLoadPalette(FDirectDraw, Background);
  if FDirectDrawPalette <> nil then begin
    hr := FPrimarySurface.SetPalette(FDirectDrawPalette);
    if hr = DD_OK then begin
      DDReLoadBitmap(FBackSurface, Background);
    end;
  end;
end;
```

This code works with the Background variable, which can be used to reference a bitmap stored in a resource linked in with the program's executable. In other words, the executable has a bitmap bound into it, and I can access that bitmap just be passing Windows the name of the resource I want to use. The Background variable is a string listing the name of that resource.

The core routines here are called DDLoadPalette and DDReLoadBitmap. The first of these routines opens a bitmap and discovers its palette. After you have a handle to the palette, you can use the SetPalette routine to inform DirectDraw of the palette you want to use.

The next step is to load the bitmap you want to use and to blit it into the back surface. I end up calling this method right before I call Flip. Therefore, it will first be loaded into the original back surface and then loaded into the original primary surface. As a result, it is part of both surfaces and is shown continuously to the user.

DDLoadPalette and DDReloadBitmap are utility routines that ship with the DirectX SDK. A friend of mine named Mike Scott originally translated these routines into Pascal. You can examine the routines if you want, but they consist primarily of low-level code that need not claim your attention unless you have some particular reason to be interested in it.

Game Resources

Game programming is more complicated than most standard Windows programming tasks for many reasons. The root of this complexity is the need to use special graphics tools such as DirectX. Many first-time game programmers underestimate the complexity of creating art.

Many books are available on game programming and on producing art for games. Two that I have found useful are

- *Tricks of the Game Programming Gurus.* LaMothe, Ratcliff, et al., Sams Publishing
- *The Ultimate Game Developers Sourcebook.* Ben Sawyer, Coriolis Group Books.

You will also need a paint program. I find that the inexpensive shareware program called Paint Shop Pro (www.jasc.com) meets most of my needs, although many other powerful programs such as Fractal Paint (www.fractal.com) are available. Here's the contact information for Paint Shop Pro:

JASC, Inc.

P.O. Box 44997

Eden Prairie, MN 55344

930-9171

www.jasc.com

Other key paint programs that I use often include TrueSpace (www.caligari.com) and VistaPro (www.romt.com) from Virtual Reality Laboratories in San Luis Obispo. TrueSpace allows you to create three-dimensional objects, and VistaPro allows you to create landscapes. The background scenes that show rolling hills, mountains, and trees in the figures for this chapter were created in VistaPro (Virtual Reality Laboratories in San Luis Obisbo, CA, 805-545-8515, email: VRLI@aol.com, WWW: http://www.romt.com).

You might find additional game components, links, or code available at these sites:

- www.spinlogic.com/GameDev/
- www.geocities.com/SiliconValley/Way/3390/
- users.aol.com/charliecal/

27

DIRECTDRAW

- `http://www.microsoft.com/directx/default.asp`

Many other Web sites are of interest to game developers, but you can find links to most of them from the sites listed here. On CompuServe, type `GO GAMEDEV` to find the game developers' forum.

As I stated previously, game programming is an extremely complex undertaking. The biggest mistake you can make is to try to create your own tools from scratch. Use the tools included in this book to get some sense of what you can gain from a graphics engine and a set of gaming tools. Then go out and search the Web and your local bookstores for ready-made graphics and game engines. Build your games using these tools; don't try to create your own tools from scratch unless you're sure, double-sure, and then triple-sure you know what you're doing and why.

If you have never built a game before, then don't even consider building one from scratch. Build your first game with someone else's engine. Then, after you understand something about the tools that are available, you might finally be in a position to consider creating some of your own tools. Even then, however, I still recommend using someone else's tools rather than trying to create your own. The *Ultimate Game Developers Sourcebook*, mentioned previously, offers a great deal of information on finding third-party game engines.

Summary

In this chapter, you had a look at DirectDraw technology. In particular, you saw how to

- Initialize DirectDraw
- Flip between surfaces
- Use DirectDraw and the GDI at the same time
- Load and blit bitmaps to the screen

You have considerably more to learn about DirectDraw. However, by now, you should have the basics under your belt. You will have the opportunity to study this subject in more depth while reading the next chapter.

More DirectX Technologies

CHAPTER

28

This chapter contains samples of DirectSound and Direct3D code. It also features a reasonably enjoyable game called `DelphiMan`, which is very loosely based on the old Pacman arcade game. `DelphiMan` takes advantage of both DirectDraw and DirectSound technologies.

The DirectSound and `DelphiMan` parts of the chapter use a set of components called Mercury that allow you to manipulate DirectSound and DirectDraw with relative ease. They are not professional-level components, but if you are willing to baby them some, they will allow you to create games in a fairly short period of time. I do not have an OOP-based encapsulation of Direct3D.

Any one of the subjects covered in this chapter could easily fill several hundred pages of text. Unfortunately, I do not have the room available to explore these subjects in such depth. As a result, you will find that the material presented here is a bit cursory in nature, and I have not included full listings for the projects in this chapter. However, I will tell you enough to get you up and running using the code that I provide, and the full source is available on the CD.

DirectSound

DirectSound has two primary benefits:

- It allows you to play a sound at a particular instant. Consider the case in which you are creating a game and need to play a sound the moment two sprites come in contact. It won't do if the sound is played a few seconds after the user sees the sprites collide. The collision and the sound must occur at the same instant. DirectSound is designed to allow you to play a sound the instant you request that the sound be played.

- DirectSound allows you to play two or more sounds at the same time.

The DirectSound technology that I will show you comes in a component called `TZounds`. `TZounds` relies on a binary file called `SoundLib.dll`, which must be on your path, or else the component will not work. The source for `SoundLib` is provided on the CD that accompanies this book, but it is written in C++ and can be compiled with C++Builder 3. The code kept in the DLL is boilerplate code meant for reading and writing WAV files from disk. I simply did not have the heart for translating these algorithms from C++ to Object Pascal, so I just popped them into a DLL where they could be called from Delphi. The important code for the `TZounds` component is in Object Pascal; the stuff in the DLL is just grunt code that reads WAV files.

> **NOTE**
>
> I will endeavor to ensure that SoundLib is built when the CD that accompanies this book ships. However, don't despair if by some chance you cannot find the DLL on the CD, and you don't have a copy of C++Builder. First check to see whether a copy of the compiled DLL is on my Web site at http://users.aol.com/charliecal. If it is not there, write me, and I will upload it to the site.

I will not show you the code from SoundLib, as it is supremely uninteresting. However, the class declaration for the TZounds component is shown in Listing 28.1, and the small Pascal file used as an interface into SoundLib.dll is shown in Listing 28.2. The entire component is available on the CD, but I have not included it all here because of space restrictions. Much of the code that I do not include in the listings is found in the analysis of the object that follows these listings.

LISTING 28.1   THE TZounds COMPONENT ALLOWS YOU TO USE DIRECTSOUND IN YOUR PROGRAMS

```
unit Zounds;

interface

uses
  Windows, Classes, MMSystem,
  DsgnIntF, DirectX;

const
  MAXSOUNDBUFFERS = 2;

type
  TBufferInfo = record
    DirectSoundBuffer: IDirectSoundBuffer;
    WaveFormatInfo: PWaveFormatEx;
    Data: PBYTE;
  end;

  TZounds = class(TComponent)
  private
    FDirectSound: IDirectSound;
    FBufferInfo: array[0..MAXSOUNDBUFFERS] of TBufferInfo;
    function AppCreateBasicBuffer(lpDirectSound: IDIRECTSOUND;
```

continues

LISTING 28.1   CONTINUED

```
    var ADirectSoundBuffer: IDIRECTSOUNDBUFFER ; FileSize: Integer;
    WaveFormatInfo: PWaveFormatEx): Boolean;
  function AppWriteDataToBuffer(ADirectSoundBuffer:
    IDirectSoundBuffer; dwOffset: DWord; var lpbSoundData: PByte;
    dwSoundBytes: DWord): Boolean;
  procedure LoadWaveFile(pszFileName: PChar; var cbSize: UINT;
    var pcSamples: DWord; var ppwfxInfo: PWaveFormatEx;
    var ppbData: PByte);
  procedure CloseWaveFile(var phmmio: HMMIO; var ppwfxSrc:
    PWAVEFORMATEX);
  function IsValidWave(pszFileName: PChar): Boolean;
  procedure CleanBufferInfo(Buffer: Integer);
  procedure CleanBuffers;
protected
public
  constructor Create(AOwner: TComponent); override;
  procedure CreateObject;
  destructor Destroy; override;
  function EnumerateDrivers(List: TStrings): Boolean;
  procedure OpenFile(S: PChar; Buffer: Integer);
  procedure Play(Buffer: Integer; Loop: Boolean);
  function GetVolume(Buffer: Integer): Integer;
  function GetFrequency(Buffer: Integer): Integer;
end;


/////////////////////////////////////////
// TSceneEditor //////////////////////////
/////////////////////////////////////////
  TZoundsEditor = class(TComponentEditor)
  public
    procedure Edit; override;
  end;

procedure Register;

implementation

// The implementation of this object is found on the CD that comes
// with this book. I have not included it here in order to save space.

procedure Register;
begin
  RegisterComponents('Unleash', [TZounds]);
end;

end.
```

LISTING 28.2 THE WaveDLL.dll FILE PROVIDES AN INTERFACE INTO A C++ DLL THAT READS AND WRITES INFORMATION FROM WAV FILES

```
unit WaveDLL;

interface

uses
  Windows, MMSystem;

const
  SoundLib = 'SoundLib.dll';

function WaveOpenFile(FileName: PChar; var MMIO: HMMIO;
  var WAVEFORMATEX: PWaveFormatEx; var MMCkInfo: TMMCKINFO):
    Integer; stdcall;
function WaveStartDataRead(var MMIO: HMMIO; var CKINFO: MMCKINFO;
  var CKINFO2: MMCKINFO): Integer; stdcall;
function WaveReadFile(MMIO: HMMIO; cbRead: UINT; Dest: PBYTE;
  var CheckInfo: MMCKINFO; var ActualRead: UINT): Integer; stdcall;
function WaveCloseReadFile(var MMIO: HMMIO;
  var WaveFormat: PWAVEFORMATEX): Integer; stdcall;

implementation

function WaveOpenFile; external SoundLib name 'WaveOpenFile';
function WaveStartDataRead; external SoundLib name 'WaveStartDataRead';
function WaveReadFile; external SoundLib name 'WaveReadFile';
function WaveCloseReadFile; external SoundLib name 'WaveCloseReadFile';

end.
```

28

MORE DIRECTX TECHNOLOGIES

The TZounds component allows you to work with two WAV files at the same time. DirectSound will allow you to work with many more files, but I have only taken the component to this stage at the current time. The DirectSoundTest example, found on the CD that comes with this book and shown in Figure 28.1, provides a simple method for using the component in a nonvisual context:

```
procedure TForm1.Button1Click(Sender: TObject);
var
  Z: TZounds;
begin
  if Z = nil then
    Z := TZounds.Create(Self);
  Z.EnumerateDrivers(ListBox1.Items);
  if OpenDialog1.Execute then begin
    Z.OpenFile(PChar(OpenDialog1.FileName), 1);
    Z.Play(1, False);
  end;
end;
```

Figure 28.1

The
DirectSoundTest
*plays a WAV file
and shows the
available drivers
on the system.*

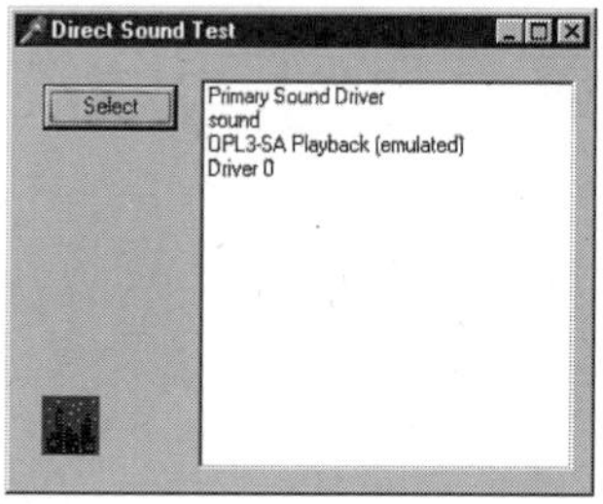

The Button1Click method first creates an instance of the object and then shows the available drivers on the system to the user. You need not iterate through the drivers, but the option is there if you want it. Finally, the code calls the OpenFile method and the Play method. All four calls—to Create, Enumerate Drivers, OpenFile, and PlayFile—will be discussed over the course of the next few pages of this chapter.

Initializing DirectSound

In this section, I discuss the code necessary to initialize an instance of the DirectSound object.

The field of the TZounds component called FDirectSound is of type IDirectSound. This interface plays the same role in DirectSound that the IDirectDraw interface does in DirectDraw. TZounds initializes its instance of IDirectSound in the CreateObject method, called when the user first opens a file:

```
procedure TZounds.CreateObject;
var
  HR: HResult;
  Handle: Hwnd;
begin
  if (FDirectSound <> nil) then Exit;

  hr := DirectSoundCreate(nil, FDirectSound, nil);
  if (hr <> 0) then
    raise Exception.Create('DirectSoundCreate failed');

  Handle := (Owner as TForm).Handle;
  hr := FDirectSound.SetCooperativeLevel(Handle, DSSCL_PRIORITY);
  if (hr <> 0) then
    raise Exception.Create('SetCooperativeLevel failed');
end;
```

This code exits immediately if the DirectSound object is already initialized. If not, DirectSoundCreate is called:

```
function DirectSoundCreate(
```

```
    lpGUID: PGUID;            // Pass in nil for default driver
    out lpDS: IDirectSound;   // Returns your DirectSound object
    pUnkOuter: IUnknown)      // Not currently used, must be nil.
  : HRESULT; stdcall;
```

The first parameter of `DirectSoundCreate` can be one of the GUIDs returned when you enumerate the available drivers on the system, as described later in this section. If you just want the default driver, pass in `nil`. The second parameter is the object you are endeavoring to create, and the last parameter must always be `nil`.

After you have created the `DirectSoundObject`, you should call `SetCooperativeLevel`:

```
function SetCooperativeLevel(
  hwnd: HWND;            // Handle of the Window for the application
  dwLevel: DWORD):  // EXCLUSIVE, NORMAL, PRIORITY or WRITEPRIMARY
HRESULT; stdcall;
```

The first parameter of this function is the handle of the main window for your application. The second parameter can take one of the following flags:

- `DSSCL_EXCLUSIVE`—If you use this flag, when your application has the focus, it owns the sound card.

- `DSSCL_NORMAL`—Your application will share the sound card with other applications if you use this flag. This choice is probably the best for most applications, and my component would be better if it gave the user the option of using this flag.

- `DSSCL_PRIORITY`—This flag allows you to call `SetFormat` and `Compact`.

- `DSSCL_WRITEPRIMARY`—This flag, which sets the highest priority, gives you access to primary sound buffers, which are the buffers the user is currently hearing.

Enumerating the Sound Drivers

You can use this method to enumerate the sound drivers on the system:

```
function TZounds.EnumerateDrivers(List: TStrings): Boolean;
begin
  if (DirectSoundEnumerate(DSEnumProc, List) <> DS_OK) then begin
    ShowMessage('No Enumeration');
    Result := False;
    Exit;
  end;
  Result := True;
end;
```

This method sets up a standard Windows callback, where the procedure that is called looks like this:

```
function DSEnumProc(lpGuid: PGUID; lpstrDescription: LPCSTR;
```

28

MORE DIRECTX
TECHNOLOGIES

```
    lpstrModule: LPCSTR; lpContext: Pointer): BOOL; stdcall;
var
  List: TStrings;
begin
  List := TStrings(lpContext);
  if lpstrDescription <> nil then
    List.Add(lpstrDescription);
  if lpstrModule <> nil then
    List.Add(lpstrModule);
  Result := True;
end;
```

When you call `DirectSoundEnumerate`, you are telling Windows that you want to be told about the drivers on the system. Windows does so by calling a function repeatedly, once for each driver on the system. The parameters passed to this function describe each driver in turn. The function that is called must have a particular signature that is predetermined by the engineers who developed Windows. In this case, the signature looks like this:

```
function(
  lpGuid: PGUID;              // Guid that can be passed to
                             // DirectSoundCreate
  lpstrDescription: LPCSTR;  // Description of driver
  lpstrModule: LPCSTR;       // Virtual device driver file
  lpContext: Pointer)        // User defined data.
: BOOL; stdcall;
```

The first parameter can be passed to `DirectSoundCreate` if you want to use a particular driver. The second parameter describes the driver, and the third lists the VXD where the driver is implemented. For instance, my AWE32 card is using `SB16.VXD`.

The last parameter is a pointer to any kind of user-defined data you might want to set up. You can define this data when you first call `DirectSoundEnumerate`. In my case, I pass in the strings from a list box:

```
function TZounds.EnumerateDrivers(List: TStrings): Boolean;
begin
  if (DirectSoundEnumerate(DSEnumProc, List) <> DS_OK) then begin
  ... // Code omitted here
end;
```

This `TStrings` object is then passed to the Windows callback, and I can use it as I see fit:

```
function DSEnumProc(lpGuid: PGUID; lpstrDescription: LPCSTR;
    lpstrModule: LPCSTR; lpContext: Pointer): BOOL; stdcall;
var
  List: TStrings;
begin
  List := TStrings(lpContext);
  if lpstrDescription <> nil then
```

```
    List.Add(lpstrDescription);
  // Code omitted here
end;
```

Here, you can see that I typecast the user-defined data as a `TStrings` object, which action will in this case prove to be valid. I then add data to the list box back in the main form of the application.

In your own programs, you will probably want to handle this situation somewhat differently. My point is not that you should follow this specific example, but only that you be aware that the parameter is available if you need it.

Working with a `DirectSoundBuffer`

Besides the `IDirectSound` object itself, perhaps the single most important part of the DirectSound code is the `IDirectSoundBuffer` interface. `IDirectSoundBuffer` is a DirectX interface designed to encapsulate and manipulate a WAV file. For instance, after you have initialized an instance of this interface, you can call its `Play` method to play a WAV file:

```
DirectSoundBuffer.Play(0,0,Flags);
```

I will discuss the `Play` method in more depth later in the chapter. All I'm doing here is giving you some sense of the importance of this interface.

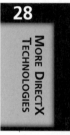

When you first create the `TZounds` component, the following code is called:

```
constructor TZounds.Create(AOwner: TComponent);
var
  i: Integer;
begin
  inherited Create(AOwner);
  FDirectSound := nil;
  for i := 0 to MAXSOUNDBUFFERS do
    FBufferInfo[i].DirectSoundBuffer := nil;
end;
```

Note that I set each instance of the `DirectSoundBuffer` to `nil`, which is my way of telling the component that the buffer is currently uninitialized. The `Create` method works with a custom array of records of type `TBufferInfo`:

```
TBufferInfo = record
  DirectSoundBuffer: IDirectSoundBuffer;
  WaveFormatInfo: PWaveFormatEx;
  Data: PBYTE;
end;
```

The other fields of the TBufferInfo record are used to initialize the DirectSoundBuffer. This method actually initializes the buffer:

```
function TZounds.AppCreateBasicBuffer(lpDirectSound: IDIRECTSOUND;
  var ADirectSoundBuffer: IDIRECTSOUNDBUFFER; FileSize: Integer;
  WaveFormatInfo: PWaveFormatEx): Boolean;
var
  BufferDesc: TDSBUFFERDESC ;
  hr: HRESULT;

begin
  // Set up DSBUFFERDESC structure.
  FillChar(BufferDesc, sizeof(TDSBUFFERDESC), #0); // Zero it out.
  BufferDesc.dwSize := sizeof(TDSBUFFERDESC);

  // Need default controls (pan, volume, frequency).
  BufferDesc.dwFlags := DSBCAPS_CTRLDEFAULT or DSBCAPS_STATIC or
    DSBCAPS_GETCURRENTPOSITION2;

  // 3-second buffer.
  BufferDesc.dwBufferBytes := FileSize;
  BufferDesc.lpwfxFormat := WaveFormatInfo;

  // Create buffer.
  hr := lpDirectSound.CreateSoundBuffer
  ➥(BufferDesc, ADirectSoundBuffer, nil);
  if(DS_OK = hr) then
  begin  // Succeeded. Valid interface is in *DSBuffer.
    Result := TRUE;
    Exit;
  end else begin  // Failed.
    ADirectSoundBuffer := nil;
    Result := FALSE;
    Exit;
  end;
end;
```

You can call the method this way:

```
AppCreateBasicBuffer(FDirectSound,
  FBufferInfo[Buffer].DirectSoundBuffer,
  Size, FBufferInfo[Buffer].WaveFormatInfo)
```

As you can see, the call into the object uses the field of the FBufferInfo structure. By the time you make this call, the FBufferInfo.WaveFormatInfo structure is filled out in another procedure that gets the information it needs from reading in the WAV file itself.

The AppCreateBasicBuffer method fills out a DirectSound buffer description record and then passes it to the CreateSoundBuffer method of the IDirectSound interface. The result is a valid instance of an IDirectSoundBuffer interface that is specifically designed to handle a particular WAV file.

Opening a WAV File

The OpenFile method of the TZounds component looks like this:

```
procedure TZounds.OpenFile(S: PChar; Buffer: Integer);
var
  Size: UINT;
  Samples: DWORD;
begin
  Dec(Buffer);

  if ((Buffer >= MAXSOUNDBUFFERS) or (Buffer < 0)) then
    raise Exception.Create('OpenFile: Buffer number error!');

  if (FDirectSound = nil) then
    CreateObject();

  if (FBufferInfo[Buffer].DirectSoundBuffer <> nil) then
    CleanBufferInfo(Buffer);

  if not(IsValidWave(S)) then begin
    ShowMessage('Wave File Invalid');
    Exit;
  end;

  LoadWaveFile(PChar(S), Size, Samples,
    FBufferInfo[Buffer].WaveFormatInfo,
    FBufferInfo[Buffer].Data);

  if(AppCreateBasicBuffer(FDirectSound,
    FBufferInfo[Buffer].DirectSoundBuffer,
    Size, FBufferInfo[Buffer].WaveFormatInfo)) then
      AppWriteDataToBuffer(FBufferInfo[Buffer].DirectSoundBuffer, 0,
        FBufferInfo[Buffer].Data, Size);
end;
```

28

MORE DIRECTX
TECHNOLOGIES

This function takes two parameters. The first is the name of the WAV that you want to play, and the second is the buffer number you want to assign to the file. This buffer number is stored in an internal variable kept by the TZounds component. As I mentioned earlier, this version of the component supports only two buffers, so the only valid values to pass in this parameter are 1 or 2.

NOTE

I have never made any attempt to increase the number of buffers that this component will handle. When I wrote the component, I tried to set things up so that the program could handle a variable number of buffers. So in theory, you

continues

> can simply increase the MAXSOUNDBUFFERS constant declared at the top of the program if you want to work with more than two sound files at a time. However, I have never tested that feature, so you are on your own if you try it.

The code in the open file procedure first decrements the buffer count the user passed to the procedure. This operation is necessary because I want the user to work with a one-based set of numbers, but the internal data of the component is zero-based. After decrementing the count, I check that the number passed in is within a valid range. If the DirectSoundObject is not yet initialized, I then initialize it as explained earlier in this chapter. If this is not the first time the buffer has been used, I then dispose of all the old data in the current BufferInfo record:

```
procedure TZounds.CleanBufferInfo(Buffer: Integer);
var
  AResult: Cardinal;
begin
  if (FBufferInfo[Buffer].DirectSoundBuffer <> nil) then begin
    FBufferInfo[Buffer].DirectSoundBuffer := nil;
  end;

  if (FBufferInfo[Buffer].WaveFormatInfo <> nil) then begin
    GlobalUnlock(LongWord(FBufferInfo[Buffer].WaveFormatInfo));
    AResult := GlobalFree(LongWord(FBufferInfo[Buffer].WaveFormatInfo));
    if AResult <> 0 then
      raise Exception.Create('CleanBufferInfo Error');
    FBufferInfo[Buffer].WaveFormatInfo := nil;
  end;

  if (FBufferInfo[Buffer].Data <> nil) then begin
    GlobalUnlock(LongWord(FBufferInfo[Buffer].Data));
    AResult := GlobalFree(LongWord(FBufferInfo[Buffer].Data));
    if AResult <> 0 then
      raise Exception.Create('CleanBufferInfo Error');
    FBufferInfo[Buffer].Data := nil;
  end;
end;
```

I'm showing you this code because all the memory deallocations in it are nonstandard. To free the DirectSoundBuffer, which is a COM object, you just set it to nil. This approach is the equivalent of calling _Release on the object and then setting it to nil. Calling _Release on the object is okay but unnecessary, but if you do, you must set it to nil. Otherwise, Delphi will try to call _Release a second time, thereby generating an access violation. The point here is that Delphi will automatically dispose COM objects for you, so if you want to take over the task, you must set the variable to nil so that Delphi will know you have already completed the task.

The other portions of the `TBufferInfo` record were allocated either in the `SoundLib.lib` or in other portions of the component by calling `GlobalAlloc`. This means you need to call `GlobalFree` when you deallocate them. If the result of this operation is 0, then you know it was successful; otherwise, the system could not deallocate the memory.

Now that you see how to clean up the `TBufferInfo` record, I need to turn my attention back to the `OpenFile` method, which is still not quite fully explained. The next step in the `OpenFile` method's long journey is to check whether the file you want to open is valid:

```
function TZounds.IsValidWave(pszFileName: PChar): Boolean;
var
  mmio: HMMIO;
  mmck: MMCKINFO;
  pwfx: PWaveFormatEx;
begin
  Result := False;
  pwfx := nil;
  mmio := 0;

  WaveOpenFile(pszFileName, mmio, pwfx, mmck);

  if (pwfx <> nil) and (pwfx.wFormatTag = WAVE_FORMAT_PCM) then
    Result := True;

  CloseWaveFile(mmio, pwfx);
end;
```

`WaveOpenFile` is in `SoundLib.dll`, but you don't need to understand how it works. It just opens a WAV file and returns a description of some of its features. After you have the file open, you get back a variable of type `TWaveFormatEx`, which contains a field called `wFormatTag`. This field must be set to `WAVE_FORMAT_PCM`, or else the other methods used by the `TZounds` component will not work correctly. Most, but by no means all, WAV files use this format.

> **NOTE**
>
> Because the routines shown here work with most, but not all, WAV files, you should not use this code for creating a generic WAV player. However, it should work fine for most games and custom applications; in those situations, you can control which WAV files are being played.
>
> If you are desperate to use a WAV file that is not handled by these routines, then you might want to try converting the file into a standard format. For instance, I have used the WaveStudio utility that comes with my AWE64 card to
>
> *continues*

> convert between a nonstandard and a standard WAV format. Most other sound cards have similar utilities, and various utilities of this type are available on the Internet.

The last lines of the OpenFile routine call LoadWaveFile and AppCreateBasicBuffer. The first routine loads a WAV file, and the second creates an IDirectSoundBuffer that wraps the file, as shown earlier in this chapter.

Playing a Sound File

After you finally have a DirectSoundBuffer initialized, using it is extremely easy:

```
procedure TZounds.Play(Buffer: Integer; Loop: Boolean);
var
  Flags: Integer;
  hr: HResult;
  S: string;
begin
  Flags := 0;

  Dec(Buffer);
  if (Loop) then
    Flags := DSBPLAY_LOOPING;

  if (FBufferInfo[Buffer].DirectSoundBuffer <> nil) then begin
    hr := FBufferInfo[Buffer].DirectSoundBuffer.Play(0,0,Flags);
    if hr <> DS_OK then begin
      case hr of
        DSERR_BUFFERLOST: S := 'Buffer Lost';
        DSERR_INVALIDCALL: S := 'Invalid Call';
        DSERR_INVALIDPARAM: S := 'Invalid Param';
        DSERR_PRIOLEVELNEEDED: S := 'PriorLevel';
        else
          S := 'Unknown';
      end;
      raise Exception.Create(S);
    end;
  end;
end;
```

This routine takes the number of the buffer you want to play in its first parameter. This number was assigned to the buffer when you called OpenFile. The second parameter specifies whether you want to play the file once or whether you want to have the buffer played in a loop. If a loop is requested, then the third parameter to the DirectSoundBuffer's Play method should be set to DSBPLAY_LOOPING:

```
DirectSoundBuffer.Play(0,0, DSBPLAY_LOOPING);
```

DSBPLAY_LOOPING is the only valid flag for the Play method. If you don't want the buffer to loop, then pass in 0. The first two parameters are reserved and must be set to 0.

As you can see, I also test for the most likely errors that can occur when the Play method is called. If a problem occurs, I raise an exception. You might want to tweak this code in your own programs, particularly if you are concerned about exceptions happening when you are in DirectDraw exclusive mode.

Playing Large Files

The TZounds component reads in an entire WAV file at a time. Playing entire files works fine for short sound effects in a game. However, if you want to work with very large files, then you don't want to read them in all in at once. Instead, you would create a buffer, one end of which is continually being played by DirectSound, and the second end of which you are continually feeding from an open file stream. Nothing inherent in the routines I have provided would keep you from mplaying files this way, but you would need to tweak my code in several different places to implement it.

Playing Two WAV Files at Once

On the CD that accompanies this book is a program called DirectSoundTwo that uses the TZounds component. The program allows you to fill both buffers of the component and to play them back at the same time. To help emphasize the fact that both files are being played at once, I loop the first file you elect to play and then let you select a menu item to play the second file.

The following code loads the files the user selects:

```
procedure TForm1.Buffer11Click(Sender: TObject);
begin
  if OpenDialog1.Execute then
    Zounds1.OpenFile(PChar(OpenDialog1.FileName), 1);
end;

procedure TForm1.Buffer21Click(Sender: TObject);
begin
  if OpenDialog1.Execute then
    Zounds1.OpenFile(PChar(OpenDialog1.FileName), 2);
end;
```

Notice that I pass the first filename to buffer 1 of the TZounds component and the second filename to buffer 2.

The following code plays the files:

```
procedure TForm1.PlayBufferOne1Click(Sender: TObject);
begin
```

```
    Zounds1.Play(1, True);
end;

procedure TForm1.PlayBufferTwo1Click(Sender: TObject);
begin
    Zounds1.Play(2, False);
end;
```

Notice that the first routine loops through the first buffer, whereas the second routine plays the second buffer only once. This way, you can keep a continuously playing file in the background and then play the second buffer on top of it. If you happen to have the sounds from the Windows Jungle sound scheme on your system, I find it is fun to work them when testing this program. For instance, you can pass in the sound of a frog croaking in the first buffer so that it is repeated continuously in the background as if you were near a pond on a summer's evening. Then, on top of this sound, you can have lions roar, or monkeys howl, or any other sound that might create a nice effect calculated to favorably impress your neighbors.

This introduction to DirectSound has not been particularly in depth, but it should have given you enough information to begin using the technology in your own programs. Certainly, the TZounds component is easy to use, and you should feel free to drop it into your own programs whenever you need it.

Creating a DirectX Game

In this section, I show how to build a simple arcade game using a set of DirectX components. The components I have created are stored in a package called MercDX40, which is shown in Listing 28.3.

LISTING 28.3   THE PACKAGE FOR A SET OF DIRECTX COMPONENTS

```
package MercDX40;

{$R *.RES}
{$R 'Mercury1.dcr'}
{$ALIGN ON}
{$ASSERTIONS ON}
{$BOOLEVAL OFF}
{$DEBUGINFO ON}
{$EXTENDEDSYNTAX ON}
{$IMPORTEDDATA ON}
{$IOCHECKS ON}
{$LOCALSYMBOLS ON}
{$LONGSTRINGS ON}
{$OPENSTRINGS ON}
```

```
{$OPTIMIZATION ON}
{$OVERFLOWCHECKS OFF}
{$RANGECHECKS OFF}
{$REFERENCEINFO ON}
{$SAFEDIVIDE OFF}
{$STACKFRAMES OFF}
{$TYPEDADDRESS OFF}
{$VARSTRINGCHECKS ON}
{$WRITEABLECONST ON}
{$MINENUMSIZE 1}
{$IMAGEBASE $00400000}
{$DESCRIPTION 'THermes and Mercury DirectX'}
{$IMPLICITBUILD OFF}
{$DEFINE USEDIRECTX}
{$DEFINE NOPALETTE}

requires
  VCL40;

contains
  Mercury1 in 'Mercury1.pas',
  Creatures1 in 'Creatures1.pas',
  HermesDirect1 in 'HermesDirect1.pas',
  HermesBase in 'HermesBase.pas',
  DDUtils1 in 'DDUtils1.pas',
  Errors in 'Errors.pas',
  Zounds in 'Zounds.pas',
  WaveDLL in 'WaveDLL.pas';

end.
```

For various reasons, none of which are relevant to the current discussion, this code must be compiled with both USEDIRECTX defined and NOPALETTE defined. You can see that I hard-code these DEFINEs into the last two compiler directives, right before the requires clause. If you do not define the first of these values, the code will link in other files and will not use DirectX at all. Instead, all the code will use GDI routines. If you do not define the NOPALETTE option, you can be in trouble unless you stay in 8-bit 256-color mode.

Here is a description of the files used in this package:

> You already know about Zounds.pas and WaveDLL.pas.
>
> Errors.pas allows you to convert some of the DirectDraw errors from HRESULTs into strings so that you can give meaningful messages when exceptions occur.
>
> HermesBase.pas contains the mostly abstract class definitions for the set of routines that are used both by the DirectX components used in this book and a set of parallel GDI components that are not discussed in this book.

`HermesDirect1.pas` contains all the DirectX-specific code for implementing these components.

`Creatures1.pas` provides a lot of custom code that I use in another, much more complicated game that is not included in this book. This custom code is needed by the `THermesTiler` and `THermesChart` components, neither of which is discussed in this book. These components are designed to support scrolling tiled backgrounds.

`Mercury1.pas` can be compiled to use either the GDI code or the DirectX code. This unit must have `USEDIRECTX` defined, or the code used in this book won't work correctly.

When you compile this package and install it, you end up with five key components:

- `THermes`—This component is a wrapper around the `IDirectDraw` object. It allows you to go into windowed or exclusive mode and to choose from a few simple resolutions. A `THermes` object is useless unless you attach its `Scene` property to either a `TScene` or `TSpriteScene` object. In a sense, the relationship between the `THermes` component and the `TScene` component is roughly similar to the relationship between a `TTable` component and `TDataSource` component. In particular, the `THermes` component needs to be linked to a `TScene` component before it can be used to display graphics to the user.

- `TScene`—This object automatically creates a primary surface, back surface, and work surface. You can add a bitmap to the work surface and display it to the user, or you can simply blank the surface and draw on it. You should always add at least one small bitmap to the `TScene` object, even if you don't want to display it. Don't ever use a bitmap that is larger than the resolution that you choose. For instance, if you go into 640×480 exclusive mode, then don't try to display a picture larger than 640×480. You can load pictures into this control either directly from disk or by first placing them inside a resource file that is part of a DLL.

- `TSpriteScene` and `TSprite`—Use these objects if you want to have a background picture and then one or more sprites that you display on top of it. These controls, rather than `TScene`, are the ones I use in the `DelphiMan` game that will be developed in this chapter.

- `TZounds`—This DirectSound component is explored in the first section of this chapter.

I am not going to spend much time discussing these components, as they are really nothing more than wrappers around the functionality described in the preceding chapter. In other words, they are designed to automatically call `DirectDrawCreate` (or `CoCreateInstance`), `SetCooperativeLevel`, `SetDisplayMode`, and to create the surfaces you need. I have tested these components extensively under Windows 95/98 and under Windows NT 4.

The only tricky parts involved in using the objects can be covered by the following bullet points:

- Be sure to use the Object Inspector to assign the Scene property of the THermes object to a TScene or TSpriteScene object. As I mentioned earlier, this process is a bit like connecting a TTable object and a TDataSource object.

- Set the ShowBitmap and BlankScene properties of the TScene and TSpriteScene objects to their appropriate values. If you are in 256-color mode, you can define a transparent color for a sprite by selecting its palette offset with the TransparentColor property of TSprite.

- Setting up the Sprite objects takes a single line per object. These simple lines of code assign a sprite to a TSpriteScene object just as you must assign a TScene object to a THermes object. The following code sets up seven Sprite objects that are owned by a single TSpriteScene object:

```
procedure TForm1.SpriteScene1SetupSurfaces(Sender: TObject);
begin
  SpriteScene1.AddSprite(DotSprite);
  SpriteScene1.AddSprite(BlankSprite);
  SpriteScene1.AddSprite(VertSprite);
  SpriteScene1.AddSprite(ManSprite);
  SpriteScene1.AddSprite(BadSprite1);
  SpriteScene1.AddSprite(BadSprite2);
  SpriteScene1.AddSprite(BadSprite3);
end;
```

- When you are ready to run the components you have set up, call the Run method:

```
Hermes1.Run(Handle);
```

On the CD that comes with this book, you will find three programs called SimpleHermesSprite, SimpleHermes1, and SimpleHermesDraw. These programs are designed to show the minimal settings for using these components in their various modes. For instance, SimpleHermes1 shows the simplest possible program that uses THermes and TScene to display a bitmap. SimpleHermesSprite shows the simplest possible program that displays a background bitmap with one sprite on it. SimpleHermesDraw loads a tiny bitmap that is never displayed and then draws animated pictures on the surfaces provided by these components. (My code simply won't work correctly without a bitmap because several of my methods assume that there is one. The component would be better if I didn't make this assumption. You will find that there is custom code in the components that create DirectDraw surfaces that don't rely on bitmaps, but I have not yet incorporated that code into all the necessary routines.)

Because of space considerations, I will not discuss these programs in depth. They are available for you to study so that you can learn the basics of how to use my components. The DelphiMan program provides a more in-depth look at how to work with these components.

28

MORE DIRECTX
TECHNOLOGIES

Creating the `DelphiMan` Program

`DelphiMan` uses the `THermes`, `TSpriteScene`, `Tsprite`, and `TZounds` components to create a Pacman-like game, as shown in Figure 28.2. The game allows you to move through a succession of four different mazes, each one more complex than the one that precedes it. To move from one maze to the next, you must make the character eat all the dots in the "halls" of the maze.

FIGURE 28.2

The DelphiMan *game allows you to run around a maze eating dots while being chased by brightly colored, highly voracious beasts of prey.*

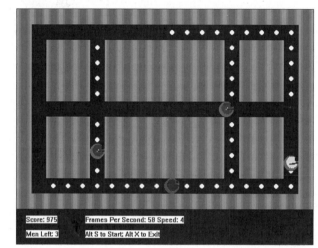

While you run down the dark corridors of the maze, you are pursued by vicious, brightly colored beasts. The beasts do not explicitly follow you but instead pursue entirely random patterns that are likely to put them in your way. If you get eaten by the beasts four times, then you lose the game. If you make it past all the beasts and eat all the dots in all four mazes, then you win the game.

The game can be played in exclusive mode, as shown in Figure 28.2, or in Windowed mode, as shown in Figure 28.3. When you first start the game, you are presented with a simple dialog that lets you choose the mode you want. The dialog is shown in Figure 28.4.

When you run `DelphiMan`, a small display at the bottom of the screen shows how many frames are being displayed per second. On my 266 machine with an NVIDIA card, this number is usually around 59 or 60 in exclusive mode. On my old 133 with the 512K video card, the game runs about 35 frames per second in exclusive mode and about 22 frames per second in windowed mode. Going much slower than 22 frames per second would probably take most of the fun out of the game. To help compensate for slower machines, I give you an option to run the game in fast mode, which means that the sprites move four pixels rather than two each time the surfaces are flipped.

FIGURE 28.3

The DelphiMan *program running in Windowed mode, displaying the last and most complicated maze.*

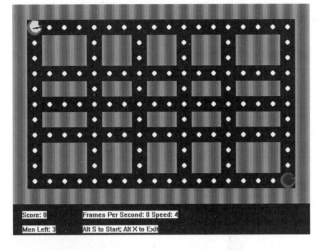

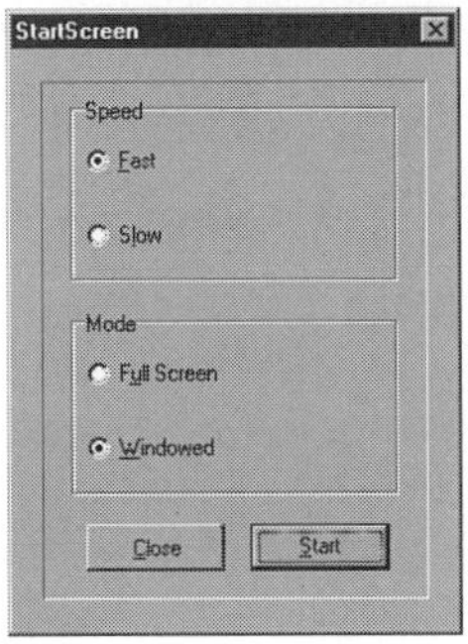

FIGURE 28.4

The dialog you see when the program first starts allows you to customize the appearance of the game.

28

MORE DIRECTX
TECHNOLOGIES

This game is designed to run in 640×480 mode. If you run in Windowed mode, you must use that size, and if you are in exclusive mode, you should also select that size, or else the game won't look quite right. The components I have created support either 16-bit or 8-bit color, but the bitmaps in the shipping version of the game are designed for a 256-color 8-bit palette.

Even without including the source for the THermes, TSpriteScene, and TScene components, the listings for this game are quite long and would take up over 15 pages. As a result, I have cut them down to the bare minimum, showing only the class declarations from most of the units. Portions of the main form for the program are shown in Listing 28.4. Listings 28.5 through 28.7 show abbreviated versions of the other supporting units. You can find the full code for the program on the CD that accompanies this book.

LISTING 28.4   THE MAIN FORM FOR THE DelphiMan PROGRAM

```pascal
unit Main;

{------------------------------------------------------------------
  This program uses MercDX40.bpl. This package must be installed
  or the program won't work. Before compiling, select Project |
  Options | Directories/Conditionals and declare the following
  two conditional defines: USEDIRECTX;NOPALETTE. After defining
  them, do a build.

  The main form of this program is caleld StartScreen. This is the
  form that implements the game itself, but the first thing the
  user will see is TStartScreen. TStartScreen creates an instance
  of this form when it is time to run the game.
------------------------------------------------------------------}
interface

uses
  Windows, Messages, SysUtils,
  Classes, Graphics, Controls,
  Forms, Dialogs, Mercury1,
  DirectX3, HermesBase, HermesDirect1,
  Robots1, GameScore1, Zounds,
  Grid1;

const
  MaxBadMen = 3;
  WM_STARTALL = WM_USER;

type
  TForm1 = class(TForm)
    Hermes1: THermes;
    SpriteScene1: TSpriteScene;
    DotSprite: TSprite;
    VertSprite: TSprite;
    ManSprite: TSprite;
    BadSprite1: TSprite;
    BadSprite2: TSprite;
    BlankSprite: TSprite;
    Zounds1: TZounds;
    BadSprite3: TSprite;
    procedure FormCreate(Sender: TObject);
    procedure FormKeyDown(Sender: TObject; var Key: Word;
      Shift: TShiftState);
    procedure FormShow(Sender: TObject);
    procedure SpriteScene1SetupSurfaces(Sender: TObject);
    procedure SpriteScene1DrawScene(Sender: TObject);
    procedure FormDestroy(Sender: TObject);
    procedure FormClose(Sender: TObject; var Action: TCloseAction);
  private
```

```
    FBadMen: array[0..MaxBadMen - 1] of TBadMan;
    FFrameRate: LongWord;
    FFrameCount: LongWord;
    FFrameCount0: LongWord;
    FFrameTime: LongWord;
    FFrameTime0: LongWord;
    FGameScore: TGameScore;
    FMainMan: TMainMan;
    procedure BlankDot;
    procedure CheckError(hr: HResult);
    procedure CheckGameStatus;
    function Collision: Boolean;
    procedure DrawBadGuy(Value: Integer);
    procedure DrawMan;
    procedure DrawStats;
    procedure GameOver;
    function HasWon: Boolean;
    procedure IdleProc(Sender: TObject; var Done: Boolean);
    procedure Move;
    procedure ResetAll;
    procedure SetupBadMen;
    procedure DrawBackGround;
    procedure CheckFrameCount;
    procedure WMStartAll(var Msg: TMessage); message WM_STARTALL;
  public
    property GameScore: TGameScore read FGameScore write FGameScore;
  end;

var
  Form1: TForm1;

implementation

// The implementation for this unit is found on the CD that
// accompanies this book.

end.
```

28

MORE DIRECTX
TECHNOLOGIES

LISTING 28.5 THE Robots1 MODULE HANDLES THE LOGIC FOR THE CHARACTERS THAT MOVE IN THE MAZE

```
unit Robots1;

interface

uses
  HermesDirect1, DirectX3, GameScore1,
  Grid1;
```

continues

LISTING 28.5 CONTINUED

```pascal
  TDirection = (tdNone, tdRight, tdLeft, tdUp, tdDown);

  TRobot = class
  private
    FXPos: Integer;
    FYPos: Integer;
    FGridX: Integer;
    FGridY: Integer;
    FDirection: TDirection;
    FRequestDir: TDirection;
    FSprite: TSprite;
    procedure CheckRequest(Board: TBoard);
    procedure SetDirection(const Value: TDirection);
    procedure SetGridX(const Value: Integer);
    procedure SetGridY(const Value: Integer);
    procedure SetRequestDir(const Value: TDirection);
    procedure SetXPos(const Value: Integer);
    procedure SetYPos(const Value: Integer);
  public
    constructor Create; virtual;
    destructor Destroy; override;
    procedure Draw(Hermes1: THermes; Sprite: TSprite);
    procedure Move(GameScore: TGameScore); virtual;
    property Direction: TDirection read FDirection write SetDirection;
    property GridX: Integer read FGridX write SetGridX;
    property GridY: Integer read FGridY write SetGridY;
    property RequestDir: TDirection read FRequestDir write SetRequestDir;
    property Sprite: TSprite read FSprite write FSprite;
    property XPos: Integer read FXPos write SetXPos;
    Property YPos: Integer read FYPos write SetYPos;
  end;

  TBadMan = class(TRobot)
  public
    procedure Move(GameScore: TGameScore); override;
  end;

  TMainMan = class(TRobot)
  private
  public
    constructor Create; override;
    procedure Home;
    procedure Move(GameScore: TGameScore); override;
  end;

implementation

// The body of the implementation for this unit is available on the
// CD that accompanies this book.
end.
```

LISTING 28.6   THE GRID UNIT HANDLES THE VARIOUS MAZES DISPLAYED BY THE GAME

```
unit Grid1;

interface

const
  DibSize = 32;
  MaxLevels = 4;
  MaxY = 12;
  MaxX = 19;
  svBlank = 2;
  svDot = 0;
  svVert = 1;

type
  TGrid = array[0..MaxY, 0..MaxX] of Integer;

type
  TBoard = class
  private
    FCurLevel: Integer;
    FData: array[0..MaxLevels - 1] of TGrid;
    FLevel: Integer;
    FNumLevels: Integer;
  public
    constructor Create; virtual;
    procedure SetDataXY(X, Y, Value: Integer);
    function GetDataXY(X, Y: Integer): Integer;
    function GotoNextLevel: Boolean;
    property Level: Integer read FLevel;
  end;


implementation

// The implementation for this object is found on the CD
// that accompanies this book.
end.
```

LISTING 28.7   THE GameScore1 UNIT

```
unit GameScore1;

interface

uses
  Grid1;
```

continues

LISTING 28.7   CONTINUED

```
type
  TGameStatus = (gsPaused, gsStopped, gsRunning,
    gsGameOverWon, gsGameOverLost, gsLevelOver);

  TGameScore = class
  private
    FBoard: TBoard;
    FMenLeft: Integer;
    FPoints: LongWord;
    FStatus: TGameStatus;
    FSpeed: Integer;
    procedure SetMenLeft(const Value: Integer);
    procedure SetPoints(const Value: LongWord);
    procedure SetStatus(const Value: TGameStatus);
    procedure SetBoard(const Value: TBoard);
  public
    constructor Create; virtual;
    destructor Destroy; override;
    procedure Faster;
    procedure Slower;
    property Board: TBoard read FBoard write SetBoard;
    property MenLeft: Integer read FMenLeft write SetMenLeft;
    property Points: LongWord read FPoints write SetPoints;
    property Speed: Integer read FSpeed;
    property Status: TGameStatus read FStatus write SetStatus;
  end;

implementation

{ TGameScore }

// The implementation for this unit is available on the CD that
// accompanies this book.

end.
```

As I explained in Chapter 1, "Program Design Basics," the key to writing a robust OOP-based program is discovering the objects of which it consists. The objects I found in the DelphiMan program look like this:

- TForm1—This is the main form that controls all the core objects in the program.

- TRobot, TBadMan, and TMainMan—These characters run through the maze. TRobot defines the default behavior for a character, and TBadMan is a descendant of TRobot that defines additional behavior for the vicious creatures that inhabit the maze. TMainMan is another descendant of TRobot; it is the sprite the user controls while playing the game.

- TBoard—This board object is used to draw and define the maze through which the characters in the program run.
- TGameScore—This simple object owns the TBoard object and also tracks basic facts about the game such as the score, the speed the characters move, and the number of bad guys on the board.

Each of these objects was quite easy to create. Building the maze that the characters run in was simple, as was building each of the characters and keeping track of the score. The only slightly tricky part was teaching the bad guys to roam about in a truly random fashion, but even that was not particularly difficult.

However, if you take all these different factors and put them together inside the context of a single program, then the sheer number of details begins to add up. This is the problem I discussed in the first chapter of the book. Each step in creating a computer program is usually very simple. What's difficult is managing the sheer volume of individual steps.

In this case, I managed complexity by creating simple objects, each entirely discrete, each with its own manageable problem domain. At the top level, I could then call on these objects to perform their assigned task. For instance, when it comes time to move the characters on the board, I just call this simple method:

```
procedure TForm1.Move;
var
  i :Integer;
begin
  FMainMan.Move(FGameScore);
  for i := 0 to MaxBadMen - 1 do
    FBadMen[i].Move(FGameScore);
end;
```

All the logic for moving the characters is buried in the TMainMan and TBadMan objects. Taken individually on a character-by-character basis, this logic is pretty simple. But if I had tried to include it in the main form of the program, it would have soon become unmanageable. Here, I avoid that quagmire by simply delegating the logic to a secondary object.

Likewise, when it comes time to actually draw the new state of the board, I write the following code:

```
procedure TForm1.DrawBackground;
var
  Sprites: TSpriteAry;
begin
  Sprites[svDot] := DotSprite;
  Sprites[svVert] := VertSprite;
```

28

MORE DIRECTX
TECHNOLOGIES

```
    Sprites[svBlank] := BlankSprite;

  FGameScore.Board.Draw(Hermes1, Sprites);
end;

procedure TForm1.DrawBadGuy(Value: Integer);
begin
  FBadMen[Value].Draw(Hermes1, FBadMen[Value].Sprite);
end;

procedure TForm1.DrawMan;
begin
  FMainMan.Draw(Hermes1, ManSprite);
end;
```

Except for a little setup in the DrawBackground method, the act of drawing a character to the screen consists of nothing more than calling its Draw methods. When I call the Draw methods, I pass in entire objects as parameters. This approach could be a way to get myself in trouble, particularly if I started letting these objects access one another's private data. However, I don't do that, but instead carefully force each object to access other objects through a defined interface.

The act of sharing data between two components creates two components that are bound together in an unnatural way. To understand how I use data hiding to avoid cross linking objects, you might want to consider the way the TBoard object from the Grid1 unit is defined. Each individual maze is defined as a two-dimensional array of Integers:

```
type
  TGrid = array[0..MaxY, 0..MaxX] of Integer;

const
  Data1: TGrid =
    ((1, 1, 1, 1, 1, 1, 1, 1, 1, 1, 1, 1, 1, 1, 1, 1, 1, 1, 1, 1),
     (1, 0, 0, 0, 0, 0, 0, 0, 0, 0, 0, 0, 0, 0, 0, 0, 0, 0, 0, 1),
     (1, 0, 1, 1, 1, 0, 1, 1, 1, 1, 1, 1, 1, 1, 0, 1, 1, 1, 0, 1),
     (1, 0, 1, 1, 1, 0, 1, 1, 1, 1, 1, 1, 1, 1, 0, 1, 1, 1, 0, 1),
     (1, 0, 1, 1, 1, 0, 1, 1, 1, 1, 1, 1, 1, 1, 0, 1, 1, 1, 0, 1),
     (1, 0, 1, 1, 1, 0, 1, 1, 1, 1, 1, 1, 1, 1, 0, 1, 1, 1, 0, 1),
     (1, 0, 0, 0, 0, 0, 0, 0, 0, 0, 0, 0, 0, 0, 0, 0, 0, 0, 0, 1),
     (1, 0, 1, 1, 1, 0, 1, 1, 1, 1, 1, 1, 1, 1, 0, 1, 1, 1, 0, 1),
     (1, 0, 1, 1, 1, 0, 1, 1, 1, 1, 1, 1, 1, 1, 0, 1, 1, 1, 0, 1),
     (1, 0, 1, 1, 1, 0, 1, 1, 1, 1, 1, 1, 1, 1, 0, 1, 1, 1, 0, 1),
     (1, 0, 1, 1, 1, 0, 1, 1, 1, 1, 1, 1, 1, 1, 0, 1, 1, 1, 0, 1),
     (1, 0, 0, 0, 0, 0, 0, 0, 0, 0, 0, 0, 0, 0, 0, 0, 0, 0, 0, 1),
     (1, 1, 1, 1, 1, 1, 1, 1, 1, 1, 1, 1, 1, 1, 1, 1, 1, 1, 1, 1));
```

Every time I list the number 1, then I want to draw a wall in the maze, and when I list the number 0, then I am defining part of the hallway of the maze. The TBoard object has an array of TGrid objects in it:

```
FData: array[0..MaxLevels - 1] of TGrid;
```

At this point, the rubber meets the road. A TGrid array is easy to work with, and just giving other objects direct access to this array of data is supremely tempting:

```
property Data: TData read GetData write SetData;
```

In this case, the GetData and SetData methods would give you direct access to the currently selected maze in the FData array.

The problem with using this approach is that it gives other objects direct access to the underlying data structures upon which the mazes are built. If you do so, a number of things can start going wrong:

- You are locked into this one data format. If you ever wanted to change the format, you would have to rewrite not only this object, but any object that was using its data.

- The other objects would have to deal with the quirks of the way this data is stored, which could lead to errors. For instance, the TGrid object stores points in Y-X order rather than X-Y order: MyMazePoint := Gird[Y, X]. Here, the rows are stored before the columns, which is the opposite order from which PC programmers generally work. As a result, you can accidentally write MyMazePoint := Grid[X, Y] easily, thereby introducing a bug.

- After you give a second object a piece of data, the object might start doing things with the data that are not properly part of its domain. For instance, if a secondary object wanted to zero out the dots in a grid, it might be tempted to perform that task itself because it already has direct access to the grid. Really, a task like that should be taken care of by the TBoard object itself via a method with a name like TBoard.ClearDots. By not sharing data with other objects, you can help to remind the other objects not to overstep their bounds, and in the process, you remind yourself to add methods such as ClearDots to the proper object.

Instead of giving other objects direct access to the underlying grid, I provide a set of access methods:

```
procedure SetDataXY(X, Y, Value: Integer);
function GetDataXY(X, Y: Integer): Integer;
```

28

MORE DIRECTX
TECHNOLOGIES

If another object wants to know what's going on at a particular point in the grid, it can use these methods. Notice that the parameters to the methods are declared in X-Y order, so they follow the conventions of traditional PC programming.

This technique is slower from a performance perspective than giving other objects direct access to internal data. If I had completed the project and decided that performance was a problem, then I might have revisited this issue. But after all, this program runs at 59 frames per second on my mid-range 266 MHz computer with a 4MB video card. Running 59 frames a second is pretty darn fast, so I don't really feel that I have a performance problem. You also need to consider that 8 and 12MB video cards are becoming standard, and 500 and even 1000 MHz machines are just around the corner. Furthermore, I have a funny feeling that even if I did allow these objects to share data, this sharing would probably not affect the frame rate at all, and I am almost certain that it would not raise the rate more than one or two frames per second. In other words, I doubt that this part of the program is a good candidate for optimizations because these optimizations are unlikely to significantly improve overall performance.

> **NOTE**
>
> One extremely interesting footnote to this matter is the fact that on my STB NVIDIA card, my program runs much faster in windowed mode than it does in exclusive mode. I am seeing rates of 131 frames per second when I go into windowed mode on this machine, which is so blindingly fast that I'm a little embarrassed and somewhat confused by it. On all other machines on which I have run this program, exclusive mode is nearly twice as fast as windowed mode. On this one machine, though, I see things go the opposite way, which is a somewhat mind-boggling fact that I'm not sure I can fully explain.
>
> Running 131 frames per second is too fast for this program, and I really need to add logic to it that will slow it down on these fast machines.

Notes on Implementing the `DelphiMan` Program

By this time, you should understand the main objects from which the `DelphiMan` program is made. I will now add a short overview of the structure of the program so that you can easily begin working with it and find out the details of its construction.

The program starts by creating the main objects needed during a run of the game:

```
procedure TForm1.FormCreate(Sender: TObject);
begin
  FMainMan := TMainMan.Create;
```

```
  FGameScore := TGameScore.Create;
  SetupBadMen;

  ClientHeight := 480;
  ClientWidth := 640;
  Application.OnIdle := IdleProc;
  Zounds1.OpenFile('Temp1.wav', 1);
end;
```

Here, I create the MainMan object and call SetupBadMen to create the three vicious characters that roam the maze:

```
procedure TForm1.SetupBadMen;
var
  i: Integer;
begin
  for i := 0 to MaxBadMen - 1 do begin
    FBadMen[i] := TBadMan.Create;
    FBadMen[i].GridX := 18;
    FBadMen[i].GridY := 11;
    FBadMen[i].XPos := FBadMen[i].GridX * DibSize;
    FBadMen[i].YPos := FBadMen[i].GridY * DibSize;
    FBadMen[i].RequestDir := tdUp;
    FBadMen[i].Sprite :=
    ➥TSprite(FindComponent('BadSprite' + IntToStr(i + 1)));
  end;
end;
```

This code simply defines the startup position for each for the bad guys, tells them the direction they should move when the games starts, and assigns them a TSprite object.

The FormCreate method also creates an instance of the TGameScore object, which in turn instantiates an instance of the TBoard object. The code also ensures that the main form is 640×480 in size, has an active OnIdle event, and that the TZounds component has a sound it can play when the main man eats a dot.

When the OnShow message is sent to the game form, the following code is executed:

```
procedure TForm1.FormShow(Sender: TObject);
begin
  Hermes1.Run(Handle);
  PostMessage(Handle, WM_STARTALL, 0, 0);
end;
```

This code first initializes the mercury components by calling Run. The Run method ensures that DirectDrawCreate (CoCreateInstance, in this case) is called, that the DirectDraw surfaces are set up properly, and that the video screen is set to the right mode.

After setting up the components, I post a WM_STARTALL message to the main form. WM_STARTALL is custom message designed for use in this one program:

```
const
  WM_STARTALL = WM_USER;
```

The response handler for the message looks like this:

```
procedure TForm1.WMStartAll(var Msg: TMessage);
begin
  DrawBackground;
  Hermes1.Flip;
  Hermes1.Active := False;
end;
```

WMStartAll is called after the form has been shown to the user. If I called it during the OnShow event, then the form would not have been drawn to the screen, and DirectX might not handle the drawing correctly in windowed mode. The job of the WMStartAll method is to simply paint the maze to the screen and then set the Hermes1 component in the inactive state so that no animation will occur before the user is ready to begin the game.

When the user is ready to start playing, he or she presses Alt+S, which is handled by the FormKeyDown method:

```
procedure TForm1.FormKeyDown(Sender: TObject; var Key: Word;
  Shift: TShiftState);
begin
  if (Key = VK_ESCAPE) then begin
    Close;
    Exit;
  end;

  if (ssAlt in Shift) then
    case Char(Key) of
      'X': begin
        Close;
        Exit;
      end;
      'S': begin
        FGameScore.Status := gsRunning;
        Hermes1.Active := True;
      end;
    end;
  case Key of
    VK_LEFT: FMainMan.RequestDir := tdLeft;
    VK_RIGHT: FMainMan.RequestDir := tdRight;
    VK_DOWN: FMainMan.RequestDir := tdDown;
    VK_UP: FMainMan.RequestDir := tdUp;
  end;
end;
```

FormKeyDown closes the game form if the user chooses VK_ESCAPE or press Alt+X. It also tells the main man if the user wants to move in a new direction. But the most important role it has is to set Hermes1.Active to True if the user is ready to play.

If Active is True, then the IdleProc can be used as an engine to drive the program's animation:

```
procedure TForm1.IdleProc(Sender: TObject; var Done: Boolean);
begin
  Done := False;
  if Hermes1.Active then begin
    Move;
    Hermes1.Flip;
    CheckGameStatus;
    CheckFrameCount;
  end;
end;
```

The idle loop sets the Done parameter to False, which ensures that Delphi will call the method again the moment it is free to do so. The code then calls the Move method, which calculates the next position for the bad guys and the main man. I then flip the surfaces, which draws the characters to the screen.

Each time Hermes1.Flip is called, an event called THermes.OnDrawScreen gets called:

```
procedure TForm1.SpriteScene1DrawScene(Sender: TObject);
var
  i: Integer;
begin
  if Hermes1.DrawState = tsDrawAll then
    DrawBackground;
  DrawMan;
  for i := 0 to MaxBadMen - 1 do
    DrawBadGuy(i);
  DrawStats;
end;
```

This event is set up to give the developer a chance to do any custom drawing to the screen just before the surfaces are flipped. Here, for instance, is the code that ends up drawing the bad guy or main man sprite to the screen:

```
procedure TRobot.Draw(Hermes1: THermes; Sprite: TSprite);
var
  hr: HResult;
begin
  hr := Hermes1.DDBackSurface.BltFast(XPos, YPos,
    TDirectDrawSurface(Sprite.Surface).DDSurface, Sprite.SpriteBounds,
    DDBLTFAST_WAIT or DDBLTFAST_SRCCOLORKEY);
```

28

MORE DIRECTX
TECHNOLOGIES

```
   if (not Succeeded(hr)) and (hr <> DDERR_SURFACELOST) then begin
     Hermes1.ErrorEvent(GetOleError(hr));
     Hermes1.Active := False;
   end;
end;
```

BltFast is a method of the IDirectDrawSurface object that paints a bitmap on a surface
with the fastest methods available on any particular system. Notice that I perform the bit
blit from the Sprite surface object to the BackSurface object. After this method executes,
then THermes calls IDirectDraw.Flip, which flips the back surface and the primary surface, showing the user the new state of affairs.

Controlling the Robots

The characters that move in the maze always have momentum that carries them in a particular direction. The momentum is implemented using the same techniques shown for
animating the objects in the preceding chapter.

Each time one of the bad guys reaches a turning point in the maze, it has a fifty-fifty
chance of taking the turn or of continuing on in the same direction. I use the random
function to calculate the odds of one of the bad guys making a turn in a new direction.

The user controls the main man. As you saw in the FormKeyDown method, the main man
has a RequestDir property, which stores the direction the user wants the main man to
move. Whenever the main man reaches a turning point in the maze, it checks the
RequestDir property, and if it specifies a direction to take, then the main man heads off
in that new direction. For instance, if the user wants to turn to the right, the following
code is executed:

```
case RequestDir of
  tdRight:
    if (YPos mod DibSize = 0) and
      (Board.GetDataXY(GridX + 1, GridY) in [svDot,svBlank]) then
      Direction := tdRight;

  // Code for turning in other directions omitted...
end;
```

If you can evenly divide (using the modulus operator) the current Y position by the size
of the character's bitmap, then that means the character might be lined up along one of
the empty hallways in the maze. To confirm this fact, I check the current tile in the maze
that is immediately to the character's right. If it is a Dot or a Blank, then the character is
free to turn to the right, and I set the character's new direction to tdRight. If it is not a
Dot or a Blank, then the position next to the main character is either a bad guy or a wall
of the maze. In either case, he can't turn and will continue on in the current direction. Of

course, if the character next to him is a bad guy, then he is probably about to be eaten, but I don't try to confirm that logic in this method but instead let a different custom routine handle that situation.

Considerably more code is used to control the movements of the characters. However, most of it is similar to what I have shown you here, so I do not bother to discuss it in this text, though you may want to pursue the subject with the aid of the debugger.

Summarizing the `DelphiMan` Program

In the preceding few pages, I showed you how to put together a game using Delphi and DirectX. If you are interested in this technology, I'm sure you will want to dig into this code a little more deeply than I have in this book. However, you now have the outline of how to proceed and an example of how to start creating your own interactive games.

A Brief Look at Direct3D

On the CD that accompanies this book, you will find two programs called `Direct3DView` and `Room3D` that show how to use the Direct3D API in a Delphi program. Unfortunately, this subject is much too complicated to explain in the space remaining in this chapter. I will, however, give a brief overview of the subject so that you will have a place to start when you begin examining the programs on your own.

The `Direct3DView` program is part of a Direct3D program written by the highly talented John Thomas for my *C++Builder 3 Unleashed* book. When the program starts, you are given the chance of selecting a file with an `.x` extension. X files are a Microsoft format for describing three-dimensional objects. For instance, if you want to draw a cube to the screen, you can define it as a series of points and lines in space. The points define the four corners of the cube, and the lines define the edges of the cube. You can also store color and shading information in an X file. I have included a few X files on the CD that accompanies this book, and you can get many more from the Microsoft DirectX Web site or from the Microsoft DirectX Development Kit. Microsoft offers utilities that convert 3DS files from 3D Studio format to X files.

After you have loaded a mesh from an X file, the next step is to select a texture that will be painted on the mesh. When you are playing Wolfenstein, Doom, or Quake, you will notice that the walls and buildings you see are not just simple line drawings; they appear to be made of brick, stone, wood, or some other real-world substance. These bricks or other materials are actually just bitmaps painted on top of the points and lines that form the framework for a scene. These bitmaps are called *textures*, and they are a key ingredient in most of the 3D code you see in contemporary games.

When the `Direct3DView` program loads, it gives you a chance to select not only a mesh, but also a texture that can be painted on top of the mesh. Combining these two objects allows you to view a rotatable 3D object like the one shown in Figure 28.5.

FIGURE 28.5

The `Direct3DView` *program allows you to manipulate 3D objects such as this spaceship.*

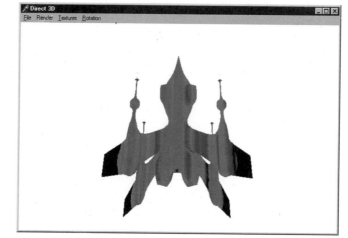

Key 3D Technologies

Direct3D programmers have a choice between two different technologies: Immediate mode and Retained mode. Immediate mode is very low level and difficult to use. It is also very fast. Retained mode is based on a series of relatively high-level functions for manipulating 3D objects. The code used in the `Direct3DView` and `Room3D` programs is all Retained mode code. One of the great benefits of using Retained mode is that it lets you work directly with X files rather than having to individually define all the nodes and polygons in your objects. A third, non-DirectX technology is called OpenGL. It is similar to Direct3D Immediate mode, but it is not covered at all in this book.

When working with Direct3D, you need a way to describe 3D spaces. The keystone for describing a 3D space is the origin. The *origin* is the base point from which all other points in the scene are defined. Usually, the origin is defined as resting at point `0, 0, 0`.

Three-dimensional space has three axes: X, Y, and Z. A *point* is an infinitely small area in space described by three values, one for each axis. A *vector* is a line between two points. *Planes* are flat surfaces that extend infinitely in two directions. A *vertex* is a point used to describe the corners of a face. In Direct3D, a *face* is a triangular area on a plane.

You can describe 3D shapes with a mesh, usually built in a third-party tool and stored in an X file. A mesh is made up of a series of faces. *Normals* are vectors used to describe the colors of the faces in a mesh. You control a mesh with the `IDirect3DRMMesh` or `IDirect3DRMMeshBuilder` interfaces. The `IDirect3DRMMeshBuilder` interface is easier to use, but it is slower. (3DRM stands for 3D Retained Mode.)

The act of moving a 3D object through space in Direct3D is called a *translation*. If you change the size of a 3D object, then you are *scaling* it. To turn an object in Direct3D, you rotate it. You can move objects in several ways in a Direct3D program, but you often use the `IDirect3DRMMeshBuilder` or `IDirect3DRMMeshBuilderFrame` interfaces.

Textures and materials are bitmaps painted on a mesh. Textures are what Wolfenstein, Doom, and Quake are all about. You can scale, wrap, and animate textures by using the `IDirect3DRMTexture` and the `IDirect3DRmTextureWrap` interfaces.

A material controls whether an object is shiny, dull, or appears to emit light. Use the `IDirect3DRMMaterial` interface to control this feature.

Lights in Direct3D can be colored, or they can be just plain white ramp lights. Ambient lights illuminate an entire scene, whereas a point light emanates in all directions from one location. Directional lights come from one direction but have no particular origin. Spot lights produce light in the shape of cone. You can manipulate lights in Direct3D with the `Direct3DRMLight` interface, which is created by the `CreateLight` and `CreateLightRGB` functions. You can use the `AddLight` method of the `IDirect3DRMFrame` interface to attach lights to a frame.

Z Buffering is a technique to make sure time is not wasted drawing surfaces that are never shown to the user. Rendering is performed in front to back order, so hidden surfaces are never drawn. A program running in 800×600 16-bit mode requires a megabyte of memory to render a single frame.

You can render a scene in several different ways. WireFrame mode draws only the edges of a face. Unlit scenes render quickly, but objects appear flat and lifeless. Flat mode renders a mesh with each face completely flat. It uses face normals. Gouraud shading uses vertex normals, and light intensities are averaged over the face to create realistic effects. Phong shading uses vertex normals and calculates light intensities over the face to create very smooth, pleasing shapes that look like real-world objects.

Animating an object in Direct3D is fairly easy. Motion attributes will allow you to translate, rotate, or scale an object. Key-framing technologies allow you to declare the starting and ending points of a path. The computer then moves the object from point A to B over a vector or spline path. You can do so by using the `IDirect3DRMAnimation` interface.

This brief overview of Direct3D should give you a starting point when you begin digging into the sample programs on the CD. A considerable amount of additional information is

28

MORE DIRECTX TECHNOLOGIES

available in the Microsoft DirectX SDK or in John Thomas's chapters from my book *C++Builder 3 Unleashed.*

> **NOTE**
>
> Before I call any Direct3D methods, I pass a constant to the Delphi Set8087CW method:
>
> ```
> const
>   MCW_EM = DWord($133f);
> begin
>   Set8087CW(MCW_EM);
>   // Code omitted here
> end;
> ```
>
> This code disables all floating-point exceptions, which makes the Borland compiler compatible with Microsoft's floating-point routines. Additional information is available on the Intel Web site, where you can see how to handle floating-point code.

Summary

Material covered in this chapter includes a discussion of DirectSound, an overview of a set of components that can be used to help you add RAD technology to your game development, and a brief look at Direct3D. Perhaps the most interesting portions of the chapter shows how to put together a Pacman-like game in which a good guy runs through a perilous maze while being pursued by fiendish monsters.

Some day I would like to write an entire book on game and multimedia development. *Delphi 4 Unleashed*, however, wasn't the place to go into these subjects in depth. Instead, I showed you a few simple DirectX technologies that you can use in your own programs. This code should be enough to show you how to get started using the powerful DirectX code bases in your own programs.

You should be aware that I have only touched the surface of DirectX technologies. The new DirectMusic code in DirectX 6 provides a rich playing field for professional musicians who want to work with Windows. DirectInput helps you work with mice and joysticks. Other important DirectX topics include network support, DirectAnimation, and DirectMovie.

Delphi is a great platform for game development, and I hope the last two chapters have provided you with enough information to get started using DirectX to create games of simulations. Of course, I also hope that you have had some fun playing with this great technology, and that it is has perhaps given you a little spark of enthusiasm that will help you derive more pleasure from your career or hobby as a programmer.

Finally, I want to close this chapter and the book with a prediction that this DirectX code will prove to be much more important in the computer world than some might suspect. Over the next few years, we are going to get machines that will run Windows the same way our current machines run DOS. In other words, they will whiz through standard Windows code in no time, leaving developers free to start adding new features to those programs. My bet is that sound, 3D graphics and real-world simulations will take up a lot of those free clock cycles.

When people decide to start building programs that simulate real-world scenes, then DirectDraw, DirectSound, and Direct3D are likely to start playing very important roles in standard programming technology. After all, why provide a database that lets you look up volumes in a library if you can create an actual library simulation that lets you browse the shelves of a set of virtual stacks? Why have people learn how to use a database when you can create a 3D simulation that looks and feels like a real filing cabinet or that lets you walk down the corridors of a real building? These possibilities sound like science fiction to us now, but 20 years ago—even 10 years ago—almost everything I covered in this book would have sounded like science fiction.

INDEX

X - Z

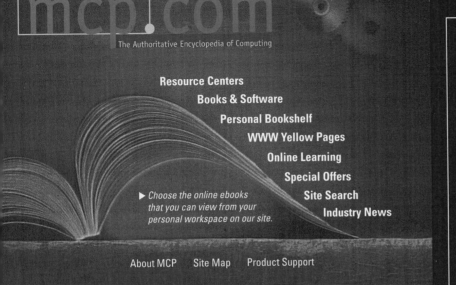

Sams Teach Yourself JBuilder 2 in 21 Days

—Don Doherty

Sams Teach Yourself JBuilder 2 in 21 Days is in the format of the other bestselling *Sams Teach Yourself* books. This book presents information on JBuilder 2 and teaches you how to use it to develop. JBuilder 2 is Borland International's updated graphical development environment that uses the Java programming language and is compatible with Sun's JDK 1.2. Because JBuilder's programming language is Java, this book also teaches you how to program with Java within the JBuilder development environment, touching on Java fundamentals and the object-oriented approach. It doesn't assume that you already know Java.

JBuilder has built an excellent reputation in the Java development market in the tradition of Delphi and C++Builder. With its updated capabilities and release timed with Sun's JDK 1.2, it should gain even more ground in version 2.

Price: $39.99 USA/$57.95 CAN   *Beginning–Intermediate*

ISBN: 0-672-31318-9   *700 pages*

Delphi 4 Developer's Guide

—Xavier Pacheco, Steve Teixeira, et al.

Delphi 4 Developer's Guide is an advanced-level reference showing developers what they need to know most about Delphi 4. The authors deal with developers every day and offer sound skills, advice, and technical knowledge on the most advanced features of Delphi 4. The covered topics include advanced-level components such as embedded links, special features and DLLs, creating your own Visual Component Libraries, advanced OOP, and Object Pascal. The authors discuss issues about application design and framework concepts for client/server, enterprise, and desktop-level database applications, along with Delphi's Multitier Distributed Applications Services Suite (MIDAS) and how it works with Delphi.

This is the most advanced developers' technical reference on Delphi 4. Xavier Pacheco and Steve Teixeira are the award-winning authors of *Delphi 2 Developer's Guide* and are key members of Borland's Delphi development team. This book contains the latest information on the best ways to build efficient, usable applications with Delphi 4, including Borland's new enterprise features, cross-component compatibility, and Internet-enabling capabilities.

Price: $59.99 USA/$85.95 CAN   *Advanced*

ISBN: 0-672-31284-0   *1,200 pages*

Sams Teach Yourself Borland C++Builder 3 in 21 Days

—Kent Reisdorph

The drag-and-drop power of Borland C++Builder 3 is yours to command with *Sams Teach Yourself Borland C++Builder 3 in 21 Days*. In no time, you'll be able to rapidly build programs from reusable ActiveX controls, Java Beans, and Delphi components. Using the methods taught in this book, you can increase your productivity and leverage your knowledge of C++ 3 and Delphi to develop mainstream applications. The proven, step-by-step techniques of the *Sams Teach Yourself* series show you how to accomplish specific tasks with this powerful new programming interface. This is a key revision to an already-successful Borland Press book, with 30 percent new and updated content by a well-known author in the Borland development community.

Stop programming C++ the old-fashioned way and start tapping into the visual programming power of Borland C++Builder 3! It has a large potential customer base, and most developers are predicted to upgrade within 6 months of the product release.

Price: $39.99 USA/$57.95 CAN

ISBN: 0-672-31266-2

Beginning–Intermediate

832 pages

Charlie Calvert's C++Builder 3 Unleashed

—Charlie Calvert

Charlie Calvert's C++Builder 3 Unleashed teaches you how to use object-oriented programming to maximize your code reusability, develop Web applications by incorporating ActiveX and Internet functions into your programs, employ property editors to check your documents, and create updated, dynamic links between documents with OLE. You will also learn about implementing the new multimedia features to program 2D and 3D graphics, writing multimedia instructions for Windows with DirectX, connecting to your corporate data with scalable database tools, and developing C++ programs visually with drag-and-drop methods. Finally, this book covers how to Internet-enable client/server applications for your entire network.

Price: $59.99 USA/$85.95 CAN

ISBN: 0-672-31265-4

Intermediate–Advanced

1,200 pages

What's on the CD-ROM

The companion CD-ROM contains Chapters 3–5 and 8–9 of the book, all the authors' source code, samples from the book, and some third-party software products.

Windows NT 3.5.1 Installation Instructions

1. Insert the CD-ROM disc into your CD-ROM drive.

2. From File Manager or Program Manager, choose Run from the File menu.

3. Type `<drive>\START.EXE` and press Enter, where `<drive>` corresponds to the drive letter of your CD-ROM. For example, if your CD-ROM is drive D:, type `D:\START.EXE` and press Enter.

4. Follow the onscreen instructions to finish the installation.

Windows 95, Windows 98, and Windows NT 4 Installation Instructions

1. Insert the CD-ROM disc into your CD-ROM drive.

2. From the desktop, double-click the My Computer icon.

3. Double-click the icon representing your CD-ROM drive.

4. Double-click the icon titled `START.EXE` to run the installation program.

5. Follow the onscreen instructions to finish the installation.

> **NOTE**
>
> If Windows 95, Windows 98, or Windows NT 4 is installed on your computer and you have the AutoPlay feature enabled, the `START.EXE` program starts automatically whenever you insert the disc into your CD-ROM drive.